Copyright 2009
Reformed Church
Publications
P.O Box 171
Zeeland, MI 49464
www.reformedchurch
publications.org

Mr. RICHARD BAXTER,

From an Original Painting in the British Museum.

Published by R. Edwards, Crane Court, Fleet Street, London 1810.

A PARAPHRASE ON THE NEW TESTAMENT,

WITH NOTES,

Doctrinal and Practical.

FITTED TO THE USE OF RELIGIOUS FAMILIES,

IN THEIR

DAILY READING OF THE SCRIPTURES.

WITH

AN ADVERTISEMENT OF DIFFICULTIES

IN

THE REVELATIONS.

BY THE LATE
REV. MR. RICHARD BAXTER.

TO WHICH IS ADDED,

Mr. Baxter's Account of his Notes

ON SOME PARTICULAR TEXTS, FOR WHICH HE WAS IMPRISONED.

A NEW EDITION, REVISED AND CORRECTED.

Choose you this day whom you will serve: But as for me and my house, we will serve the Lord.
Josh. xxiv. 15.

AN ACCOUNT OF THE REASON AND USE
OF THIS
PARAPHRASE.

READER,

THIS Paraphrase, written for my own use, being published for yours, in order to that end I owe you this account of it. A friend long urging me to write a paraphrase on the epistle to the Romans, as being hard to be understood; when I had done that, I found so much profit by that attempt, that it drew me to go on till I had finished what I offer you. It was like almost all my other public works, done by the unexpected conduct of God's urgent providence, not only without, but contrary to my former purposes. God hath blessed his church with many men's excellent commentaries on the Scriptures; and I never thought myself fit to do it better than they have done: but that is best for some persons and uses which is not best to others. I long wished that some abler hand would furnish vulgar families with such a brief exposition, as might be fitted to the use of their daily course in reading the Scriptures and instructing their households. I found that many who have done it better than I can do, are too large and costly for this use: some (like Deodate) very sound, are unsatisfactorily brief; some have parcelled their annotations into so numerous shreds, that readers (especially in a family course) will not stay to search and set them together, to make up the sense. I like Dr. Hammond's order best:—But, 1. I differ from him in so much of the matter; 2. and took his style to be too lax: 3. and his criticisms not useful to the vulgar: 4. And his volume too big and costly: and therefore I chose more plainly, and yet more briefly and practically, by the way of paraphrase, to suit it to my intended end.

But I must give the readers notice, 1. That where I seem, but in few words to vary from the text, those words answer the large criticisms of divers expositors, as the learned may find by searching them and the Greek text; though I must not stay to give the reason of them as I go on. 2. That though I have studied plainness, yet brevity is unavoidably obscure to unexercised persons, who, as learners, cannot understand things without many words. 3. That where the evangelists oft repeat the same things, to avoid tediousness, I repeat not the whole exposition; and yet thought not meet wholly to pass it by. 4. That where the text is plain of itself, instead of an exposition, I fill up the space by doctrinal, or practical observations, seeing practice is the end of all, and to learners, this part is of great necessity. 5. That where great doctrinal controversies depend on the exposition of any text, I have handled those more largely than the rest, and I hope with pacificatory and satisfactory evidence.

My great desire and care is, that I may hereby promote Christian piety in families. To which special end I also wrote my Poor Man's Family Book, and The Catechising of Householders. And had I not done it in many books so oft already, I should here set myself with greater earnestness to urge and entreat all Christian parents, to the more faithful practice of family religion, especially in the wise and diligent instruction and education of their children. Sure no good Christians should come behind the

Jews, who had far less light and help than we have, who yet are twice commanded by God, Deut. vi. 4—9. Yet how many thousand families called Christians, account this much Puritanism, and needless preciseness; as if the Scripture (even the gospel of salvation) were only for the use of priests; yea, some that disown the Papists' restraint of the laity unlicensed, from reading it translated in a known tongue, do worse than Popishly refrain themselves. And those that in baptism vowed to bring up their children as Christians in the knowledge of the gospel of Christ, perfidiously break that solemn vow, as they hypocritically made it; and by ungodly negligence betray to Satan the souls of their children (and themselves) which they devoted to God.

Reader, I beg of you as from Christ, for his sake, for your soul's sake, for your children's sake, for the sake of the church and kingdom, that you will conscientiously and seriously set up family religion, calling upon God, singing his praises, and instructing your children and servants in the scripture and catechism, and in a wise and diligent education of youth. Hear me, as if I begged it of you, with tears on my knees. Alas, what doth the world suffer by the neglect of this! It is out of ungodly families that the world hath ungodly rulers, ungodly ministers, and a swarm of serpentine enemies of holiness and peace, and their own salvation. What country groaneth not under the confusions, miseries, and horrid wickedness, which are all the fruits of family neglects, and the careless and ill education of youth? It is a work of great skill and constant care to instruct and educate your children, and to keep them from tempting company and snares. To cry out of dumb or unfaithful ministers, while you are worse at home yourselves, is but self-condemnation: are ministers more obliged to care for your childrens' souls, by nature, or by vow and covenant, than you are? Can they do that for whole parishes, which you will not do for one household, or your own children? The first charge and part is yours: if families treacherously neglect their part, and then look that all should be done at the church, you may as wisely send boys to the universities, before they are taught to read or write in lower schools. If there be any hope of the amendment of a wicked, miserable, and distracted world, it must be mostly done by family-religion, and the Christian education of youth. Godliness is profitable to all things; but the curse of God is in the house of the wicked, and the ungodly betrayers of souls, of themselves, children, and servants, will very quickly be summoned to a terrible account: especially those that should as rulers be exemplary to the vulgar, and are ashamed to own serious family-religion, as if all beyond some formal hypocrisy and lip-labour, were a dishonour to their houses, or a needless thing.

These helps which I offer them that need it, is, that when they read the New Testament daily in their houses, they may (not read all the paraphrase to their families, but) such particulars of exposition and doctrinal notes, as they find most suitable to their case.

And I think it will not be unuseful to the younger and weaker sort of ministers, and the poor ones, that cannot buy large commentaries. And if rich men will give their tenants and neighbours such books as are suitable to the instruction of families, and the people will diligently use them, it may do much to keep up saving knowledge and practice, where the public ministry faileth most. The God of mercy teach foolish men to have mercy on their families and themselves.

THE
NEW TESTAMENT

OF

OUR LORD AND SAVIOUR JESUS CHRIST.

Though it be not known when, or by whom, all the Books of the New Testament, were gathered and made up into one, nor when, or by whom, this title was set before them: and though for a time some churches received not the epistle to the *Hebrews*, nor that of *James*, the *second* of *Peter*, the *second* and *third* of *John*, that of *Jude*, or the *Revelations;* yet it hath nevertheless satisfactory evidence of its truth, for this uncertainty and delay.

I. For, as long as we know it is all the *word of the Spirit of God*, it satisfieth our faith, whether all be bound up in one book or many. And *John* the apostle living long after all the rest, it is more than probable that none were received in his time, but by his approbation and consent; and even in the days of the apostles they gave testimony to the writings of one another; so *Peter* doth of *Paul's*, and *Jude* transcribeth much of 2 *Peter* 2. (telling us, that even inspired apostles disdained not to use and repeat each others writings; without any guilt of vain repetition or being plagiaries.)

II. And that the few books doubted of by some, were commonly afterwards received, tends more to the confirming than the shaking of our belief of their authority; certainty after doubt, is the most confirmed certainty. It must needs be some time before all the churches, to whom the several epistles were written, could produce and communicate them by convincing proof to all the rest. And yet we must know, that the epistles to particular churches were sent to them as to members of the church universal, and they were obliged to communicate them to others: so that we must not take them as private letters.

III. Whoever first gave this title to the whole book, *(The New Testament,* or *Covenant,* &c.) it is of no great moment to know: it was *(The New Testament)* before it was so entitled as one volume; but the church hath by continual owning this title, shewed that they have received all these books as God's Word and the whole New Testament, and that no more are to be received as such.

The Greek word (of which Grotius in his preface hath spoken at large) signifieth indeed, God's *statute law concerning man's duty and salvation,* or God's *constituted and proposed terms of life.* And though it more strictly signifies usually a mutual covenant; this doth but imply the consent of man to the law or terms of God. It is the same thing that is called a law and a covenant in several respects: as God enacts it, and promulgated it, before man's consent, it is a law, and a conditional deed of gift and testament; and an offered covenant in several respects. When man consents, it is a law accepted, a gift and testament accepted, and a *mutual actual covenant:* the law hath its introductory history and doctrine, its precepts, prohibitions, promises, and threats; and the covenant hath the same parts only denominated from mutual consent. But because there are laws of more or less rigour, and of various tenors; it is the *law of Faith or Grace* which is the covenant, testament, and gospel, which is now before us denominated from the *donative* and *promissory* parts, though precept and threatening be included.

IV. It is of great importance that we err not by giving too little or too much to the sacred scriptures, from both which extremes many dangerous errors flow. 1. On the left hand, those err that deny it to be God's word, of infallible truth, intelligible, and *perfect* as to its *proper use*, without human supplements, written or oral, doctrinal or canon laws: and those that deny it to have infallible ascertaining evidences of its truth. These befriend infidelity, heresies, profaneness, church tyranny, (leaving it to clergymen to make us a new faith, new sacraments, and a new religion, at their pleasure; and to persecute good men, that dare not renounce the scripture-sufficiency and Christ's perfection) by obeying their dictates and canons as co-ordinate with Christ, if not co-equal: these make church concord utterly impossible, while they deny the sufficiency, not only of the essentials, but of all the Bible, to be the terms of concord, without their supplements, or additions; as if Christ, who is the author and finisher of our faith, and the maker of his own church, had not so much as told us what a Church or a Christian is, or whom we must take for such into our love and communion, nor fixed the necessary terms of union; but left them to none knoweth whom, even fallible men, liable to error and tyranny, that can but get uppermost, and say then that they are the true church, and the masters that must be obeyed, while they are themselves of as many minds, as they are of different countries, interests, and degrees of knowledge and sincerity.

2. On the other side, those who overdo, in ascribing to the scripture, who say that God had no church, or the church no infallible rule of faith and life, before the writing of it: and who say that men converted by the creed, catechisms, preaching, or tradition, without knowing the scripture, can have no saving faith; and that think none can be saved that doubt of any canonical books, text, or matter, whether it be God's word; or that say, scripture is so perfect, that there is no human imperfection of the penmen found in phrase, word, or method, find that God could not have made it better, or that every book may be known to be canonical, and every reading to be right, when copies vary, without historical tradition, by its own evident light, and that we have no more cause to doubt of any word or matter, than of the truth of the gospel; and that reason is of small use either for the proof or exposition of the scripture, but the most illiterate, if he found a Bible that he had never heard of, may by its own light know its truth and sense, as well as studious learned men, and that no other books need to be read; and that the scripture is a sufficent teacher of physic, logic, grammar, &c. and that nothing is to be used or done in the *external forms, modes*, and *accidents* of God's *worship*, but what is particularly commanded in scripture; and that it telleth every man whether he be sincere and justified or not, and not only telleth him how to know it by inward evidence; with many other such mistakes, proceeding from mistaking the use of the scripture, by which its perfection must be measured. Which all tend to confusion, and at last to infidelity, or doubting of the whole, when these errors are discerned.

V. And though all the scripture be of equal truth, as it is God's Word, yet many untruths are in it as uttered by men and devils; which God truly recordeth. And all parts are not of equal necessity or weight: and, as many err by casting off the Old Testament, so others err by equalling it to us with the New: it is God's Word, left to acquaint us what was heretofore, and to shew us how Christ was prophesied of and expected, and how the church was governed in the darker and more servile state and times. But we have great cause to take heed of over-valuing its use to us; lest we contradict Paul, that saith, that even that which was written in stone is done away, and the law changed with the priesthood, and the old and faulty covenant for a better; of which see the first nine chapters to the *Hebrews*, &c. Judaizers are they that most of *Paul's* epistles are written against; and as *John Baptist* was greater than the prophets, so the least in the kingdom of God is greater than he. Even the holy patriarchs, and *David*, had a far more obscure revelation of Christ, and grace, and the love of God, and the glory to come, than we have: and accordingly we should have much more faith, holiness, and comfort, than they. It is dangerous making the best of them our examples in points of faith or duty, wherein they came far short of Gospel light and grace. God doth not now bear with polygamy as he did then, nor with such divorces; nor doth the Gospel countenance such streams of blood as the *Israelites* ordinarily shed, nor such lies as *David* was oft guilty of; nor such a strange life as *Solomon* lived: I mean, that such faults will not now consist with true grace under our fuller light and mercy, as would do then to men in a darker infant age; and therefore let us take heed of presuming on their example: Christ and his apostles are far fitter for our imitation. *David* fills most of his psalms with such complaints of his enemies, and curses against them, as shew a far deeper sense of the sufferings of the flesh, and the concerns of this life, than *Peter* and *Paul* shewed, who suffered far more, and for a holier cause, and rejoiced in tribulation; and then is suitable either to the precepts or examples of Christ. All was not well said and done by good men which is recited in the New Testament, much less in the Old.

So far are they mistaken that say, the Jews and Gentiles were bound to believe the apostles in no more than they proved out of the Scripture, that most of the creed was to be believed by other evidences, and Christ and his apostles gave us so full proof of the truth of the Gospel, as that their attestation of the Old Testament is to us a more convincing proof of its Divine authority, than any others.

Therefore Christians must read and honour the Old Testament, and study it, but the New far more; to which it is that the heart and life must be conformed. There heavenly glory shineth far more clearly, and the wonders of Divine Love are more abundantly manifested; and far greater power of the Spirit is given, to make all effectual in faith, hope, and patience, humility, obedience, and love, which now are become the very nature of a true believer.

VI. How the infallible truth of the Gospel is proved by the sole witness of the Holy Ghost, I have opened so largely in many books, that I must not here repeat it: that is, 1. By the old testimonies of prophecies, types, sacrifices. 2. By the inherent and concomitant testimonies, even God's image of divine wisdom, love, and power, on Christ and the Gospel. 3. The manifold testimonies in and by the apostles, their miraculous works and holy doctrine, &c. 4. The testimony of the spirit in the Christians of those times, who received the Holy Ghost by the imposition of the apostles' hands, for the like gifts and miracles. 5. The continued evidence of the Spirit's sanctification in all true believers in all generations, &c.

But it must be known that Christ's resurrection and miracles, and most of the apostles, sealed the Gospel as preached, before it was written. And that the necessary sum of the Gospel so sealed, was in narrow room, even the Sacramental Covenant with its explications, and the history of Christ therein supposed. And that the sincere belief and practice of so much will certainly be saving: but yet the usefulness of the whole Scripture, as containing the complete Revelation of God's will recorded for all succeeding ages, is an unspeakable mercy to the church: so weak is man's memory; so bad a great part of the world, and the Clergy, as well as others, so inclinable to errors and sects, and to force even God's word to seem to justify their errors and sins; and of so many cross interests and minds are men, so very false the worst, and so untrusty even the better sort, and so liable all worldly things to degenerate and change, that he is utterly blinded herein, who thinks that oral tradition would have safely delivered down the whole mind of God unchangeably, and with certainty. And yet to his praise we must acknowledge, that, 1. The essentials of religion have by themselves been delivered us in baptism, and many ways (oft named) with infallible certainty. 2. And so hath the Bible itself, even by such historical tradition which hath an evidence truly called physical; in that it ariseth not only from free contingent, but from necessary causes, even the consent of men of contrary interests, in acts which are truly necessary; and because there are not in nature causes that could produce a falsification (as is elsewhere opened.)

As for them that are so far from taking the New Testament to have the nature of a law, that they say, *Christ hath no law*, or hath made none, they thereby make him to be no king, and have no sovereign governing power (of which legislation is the chief part:) and so far are they from the truth, as that there is no divine law but *Christ's* in force, for all power in heaven and earth is given now to him, and all things delivered into his hand, and the Father (without him) judgeth no man, but hath committed all judgment to the Son, who for this end died, rose and revived, that he might be Lord of the dead and living, and Head over all things to his church, *Matt.* xxviii. 19. *John* xiii. 1, 2, 3—17. *2 John*, v. 22. *Rom.* xiv. 10. *Eph.* i. 22, 23. So that the law of nature continued is now *Christ's* law, to which he hath added his supernatural institutions, and repealed all the law of *Moses*, as such, having made the natural parts his own.

VII. As to the method of the New Testament, it is perfect as to its intended use: 1. The method of the *doctrine* is exact, though as wrapped up in all the words and circumstances, the unskilful discern it not; but in the baptismal covenant, creeds, Lord's prayer and decalogue, it is easily discerned. 2. And as to the order of the *books and words*, it was meet that it should begin with the history of *Christ's* life, death, resurrection, and ascension; and then give us a taste of the history of the apostles, and last of all give us the applicatory part, first to establish the understanding in the truth against errors, and then to direct and quicken us to holiness of life, and to comfort, and patience in sufferings, and a joyful expectation of the glorious reward. For if the history had not gone first, which gives us both the matter and the miraculous reasons and grounds of our belief, the application would have been built upon an insufficient foundation.

VIII. It is the Gospel that is God's most wonderful declaration of his love to mankind; the *world sheweth* his greatness, but it was his *goodness and love* which sin, guilt, and fear, had made hardest to our belief, which God hath glorified in the face of *Christ:* it is *Christ* that is the believer's daily and delightful study; the best sort of learning and wisdom, which giveth quietness, and hope, and comfort to the soul, when all other studies, except in pure subservience to this, are but trifling, diverting, delusory, and vain. To study *Christ* in his nature, person, offices, doctrines, examples, miracles, sufferings, and death, resurrection, and ascension; sending down the spirit of miracles and holiness, reigning and interceding in heaven, coming to judgment and glorified with his church for ever; this, this is the high and noble, the sanctifying and comfortable study, daily to behold the face of God's love in this glass of our redemption, till confirmed faith raise joyful hope, and turn our very nature into holy love to God and man, and stablish us in obedience and patience against all temptations, sufferings and fear of death, and make us long to be with *Christ,* and love his appearing, and cry, Come Lord Jesus: this is the true life of *Christian* faith.

Readers, Pray earnestly and daily to God, to give you that same Spirit which indited the Scripture, to qualify you to read and hear it, with understanding, belief, hope, love, and resolved obedience: and make it the law and rule of your hearts and lives.

And if any fanatics tell you, that because the spirit is greater than the letter, we must try the scriptures by the spirit, and not the spirit by the scriptures; tell them in these few plain words, that the question is not rightly put: but whether they or we have the spirit in the same measure, and to the same uses, as the apostles and prophets had. And whether we must not rather try the spirit and words of men now, by the spirit and words of the apostles, than theirs by ours. The spirit was given by *Christ* to his apostles, to lead them into all truth, and bring all his doctrine and commands to remembrance, to teach them to all nations, recording them to be our continued instruction, law, and rules. But the spirit is not given to the Quakers to these ends, nor in this measure. And it is given now to the faithful, not to reveal to them a new law, and gospel, but to cause them to understand, believe, love, and obey, that already revealed.

THE GOSPEL

ACCORDING TO

ST. MATTHEW.

That is, the History of Christ's Birth, Life, Death, Resurrection, Ascension, Doctrine, Covenant, Example, and Mission of his Apostles to preach Salvation through Him to the world. Written by St. Matthew, a converted publican, one of the twelve Apostles, as tradition saith, eight years after Christ's ascension; whether in Greek or in Hebrew, is uncertain.

CHAP. I.

THE book of the generation of Jesus Christ,ᵃ the son of David, the son of Abraham.

1. I begin this history of Christ with the genealogy or catalogue of his ancestors, according to the line of Joseph, his reputed legal father after the flesh, so far as to evince that he was the son of David and Abraham, the rightful king of the Jews, and the promised seed by their own acknowledgment.

2. Abraham begat Isaac, and Isaac begat Jacob, and Jacob begat Judas and his brethren. 3. And Judas begat Phares and Zara of Thamar, and Phares begat Esrom, and Esrom begat Aram, and Aram begat Aminadab, and Aminadab begat Naasson, and Naasson begat Salmon, 5. and Salmon begat Booz of Rachab, and Booz begat Obed of Ruth, and Obed begat Jesse, 6. and Jesse begat David the king, and David the king begat Solomon, of her *that had been* the wife of Urias, 7. and Solomon begat Roboam, and Roboam begat Abia, and Abia begat Asa, 8. and Asa begat Josaphat, and Josaphat begat Joram, and Joram begat Ozias.

ᵇ. Ahaziah, Joash, and Amazia, are here passed by, perhaps as being, by the mother of Ahazia, of

Omri's cursed line, or for other unknown cause: Note, That the lawful succession, much more the grand-child or distant issue, is with the Hebrews called the son or begotten, though not immediately.

9. And Ozias begat Joatham, and Joatham begat Achaz, and Achaz begat Ezekias, 10. and Ezekias begat Manasses, and Manasses begat Amon, and Amon begat Josias, 11. and Josias begat Jechonias and his brethren, about the time they were carried away to Babylon.

9. They were oft carried away: But this was a little before the most notable captivity.

12. And after they were brought to Babylon, Jechonias begat Salathiel, and Salathiel begat Zorobabel, 13. and Zorobabel begat Abiud, and Abiud begat Eliakim, and Eliakim begat Azor.

12. One old copy hath before [Josias begat Jakim, and Jakim begat Jechonias.] Dr. Hammond saith, in a very ancient Hebrew copy of this gospel, this verse runs [and Eliakim begat Abner, and Abner begat Azor:] by either of which the number of fourteen generations is kept entire.

14. And Azor begat Sadoc, and Sadoc begat Achim, and Achim begat Eliud, 15. and Eliud begat Eleazar, and Eleazar begat Matthan, and Matthan begat Jacob, 16. and

Jacob begat Joseph, the husband of Mary, of whom was born Jesus who is called Christ. 17. So all the generations from Abraham to David *are* fourteen generations, and from David until the carrying away into Babylon, *are* fourteen generations, and from the carrying away into Babylon, unto Christ, *are* fourteen generations.

17. I reduce them to fourteen in the recitation, for memory-sake and other reasons: This sufficeth to my intended end.

18. Now the birth of Jesus Christ was on this wise: When as his mother Mary was espoused to Joseph, before they came together, she was found with child of the Holy Ghost.

18. Note, The Holy Ghost did miraculously cause her conception, without a human father.

19. Then Joseph her husband, being a just man, and not willing to make her a public example, was minded to put her away privily.

19. Joseph being a good man, averse to hurtfulness, thought rather to hide all by putting her privily away, than to expose her to the shame and punishment due by the law, to such as he thought her to be.

20. But while he thought on these things, behold, the angel of the Lord appeared unto him in a dream, saying, Joseph thou son of David, fear not to take unto thee Mary thy wife, for that which is conceived in her, is of the Holy Ghost. 21. And she shall bring forth a Son, and thou shalt call his name Jesus, for he shall save his people from their sins.

21, 22. Note, It was a dream that had its convincing evidence; for ordinary dreams give no such certainty. 2. The name Jesus, a Saviour, signifieth his office, which is to *save his people from their sins,* and from deserved punishment.

22. Now all this was done, that it might be fulfilled which was spoken of the Lord by the prophet, saying, 23. Behold, a Virgin shall be with child, and shall bring forth a Son, and they shall call his name Emmanuel, which being interpreted is, God with us.

22, 23. In all this, the prophecy of Isa. vii. 14. to Ahaz, in how short time God would then deliver them, was fulfilled in a farther sense intended by the Holy Ghost than that nearest foretold event: Note, God with us, is God taking our nature, appearing to us, and reconciling and bringing us to himself.

24. Then Joseph being raised from sleep, did as the angel of the Lord had bidden him, and took unto him his wife: 25. And knew her not, till she had brought forth her first-born son, and he called his name Jesus.

24, 25. Note, Though these words are no full proof that Mary had any other children after, yet at least they make it utterly uncertain; and as it is no article of faith as to the moment of it, so neither as to the certainty: Yet the papal sect have pretended tradition for it, that Mary lived and died a Virgin, as of so much weight as to hereticate the deniers of it: And so they make all the scripture insufficient, not only as to matters of order, discipline, and worship, but also as to the articles of faith: that they may, on pretence of faith, and orthodoxy, destroy Christian unity and love, and exercise domination by excommunicating and damning men, on pretended tradition or authority, at their pleasure.

CHAP. II.

NOW when Jesus was born in Bethlehem of Judea, in the days of Herod the king, behold there came wise men from the East to Jerusalem: 2. saying, Where is he that is born King of the Jews, for we have seen his Star in the East, and are come to worship him.

1, 2. Some time after Christ's birth, Astronomers of great note came from the east-country *(Chaldea* or *Arabia)* saying, we have seen an extraordinary star, which signifieth the birth of the King of the Jews, the Messiah whom they expected, and are come to do our homage and honour to him.

3. When Herod the king had heard *these things* he was troubled, and all Jerusalem with him. 4. And when he had gathered all the chief Priests and Scribes of the people together, he demanded of them, where Christ should be born.

3, 4. Note, 1. When Christ cometh to save men, it casts the world into disturbance. 2. The first that was troubled, and rose up against Christ, was the king, because his cross interest was the greatest. 3. All Jerusalem is troubled with the king.

5. And they said unto him, In

Bethlehem of Judea, for thus it is written by the prophet: 6. And thou Bethlehem *in* the land of Juda, art not the least among the princes of Juda; for out of thee shall come a Governor, that shall rule my people Israel.

5, 6. Note, Bethlehem was the city of David's birth and of Christ's: the prophecy is in Mic. v. 2. a clear prophecy of Christ, but thou *Bethlehem-Ephrata* though thou be little among the thousands of Judah, (thousands had their proper rulers) *yet out of thee shall he come forth unto me, that is to be ruler in Israel,* whose goings forth *have been* from of old, from the days of eternity.

7. Then Herod, when he had privily called the wise men, inquired of them diligently what time the star appeared. 8. And he sent them to Bethlehem, and said, Go, and search diligently for the young child, and when ye have found *him*, bring me word again, that I may come and worship him also.

7, 8. Note, His malice contrived to have made use of the wise men to further his cruelty, cloaking it with hypocrisy.

9. When they had heard the king they departed, and lo! the star which they saw in the East, went before them till it came and stood over where the young child was.

9. Note, How this differed from other stars, and how it moved and directed them, is not to be clearly apprehended by us at this distance of time and place, who saw it not.

10. When they saw the star they rejoiced with exceeding great joy.

10. They greatly rejoiced that God thus renewed their direction. Note, Some ancient fathers thought this star was an angel: he maketh his angels spirits, and his ministers a flame of fire.

11. And when they were come into the house, they saw the young child with Mary his mother, and fell down and worshipped him; and when they had opened their treasures, they presented unto him gifts, gold, and frankincense, and myrrh. 12. And being warned of God in a dream, that they should not return to Herod, they departed into their own country another way.

11, 12. They did their homage as sent by God: and then God defeated the malice of Herod.

13. And when they were departed, behold, the angel of the Lord appeareth to Joseph in a dream, saying, Arise, and take the young child, and his mother, and flee into Egypt, and be thou there until I bring thee word: for Herod will seek the young child to destroy him. 14. When he arose, he took the young child and his mother by night, and departed into Egypt.

13, 14. Note, God could have cut off Herod, or secured Christ by other ways or miracles. But to shew that he will not make miracles ordinary, but work by usual means, Christ must fly into Egypt, a land of heathen enemies, to be saved from the king and people of Israel; such flight was not unlawful.

15. And was there until the death of Herod, that it might be fulfilled which was spoken of the Lord by the prophet, saying, Out of Egypt have I called my Son.

15. Note, Whether the prophet Hos. xi. 1, understood this of any more than Israel's first deliverance from Egypt or no, yet the Holy Ghost looked further and meant more, even the case of Christ.

16. Then Herod, when he saw that he was mocked of the wise men, was exceeding wroth, and sent forth, and slew all the children that were in Bethlehem, and in all the coasts thereof, from two years old and under, according to the time which he had diligently inquired of the wise men.

16. Note, Interest and malignity conjoined, made this king stick at no inhuman bloody cruelty: innocency was no defence against him.

17. Then was fulfilled that which was spoken by Jeremy the prophet, saying, 18. In Ramah was there a voice heard, lamentation, and weeping, and great mourning, Rachel weeping *for* her children, and would not be comforted, because they are not.

17, 18. Though it was another case that the prophet meant, God's Spirit might look to this: or the words may signify, *This case was much like to that* mentioned, Jer. xxxi. 15. and so speak by an allusion.

19. But when Herod was dead, behold, an angel of the Lord appeareth in a dream to Joseph in Egypt, 20. saying, Arise, and take the young child, and his mother, and go into the land of Israel: for they are dead which sought the young child's life. 21. And he arose and took the young child, and his mother, and came into the land of Israel. 22. But when he heard that Archelaus did reign in Judea, in the room of his father Herod, he was afraid to go thither: notwithstanding, being warned of God in a dream, he turned aside into the parts of Galilee. 23. And he came and dwelt in a city called Nazareth, that it might be fulfilled which was spoken by the prophets, He shall be called a Nazarene.

19, &c. Note, 1. Still Christ is preserved by avoiding men's rage. 2. The Jews called Christ a Nazarite, from that place of his dwelling; but he was truly *Netzer* the branch, and a Nazarene devoted to absolute purity, of whom Samson's order was a type, described also Numb. vi. Lam. iv. 7. Amos ii. 11, 12. This seemeth the sense by allusion.

CHAP. III.

IN those days came John the Baptist, preaching in the Wilderness of Judea, 2. And saying, Repent ye, for the kingdom of heaven is at hand.

1, 2. In those days, John as a prophet inspired by God, baptized, upon preaching in the wilderness of Judea, that the kingdom of the Messiah, long looked for, was now just at hand: and therefore they should, by true repentance, be prepared for its entertainment.
Note, 1. It is called the kingdom of heaven, because it is a theocracy, a special government of God by a Saviour sent from heaven to lead men to heaven: as distinct from the profane kingdoms of the world, who look but to human power and laws, and bodily prosperity. 2. That of Mal. iii. 7. iv. 2, 3. was here fulfilled. The Jews longed for Christ's coming, supposing it would have exalted their nation in temporal prosperity; but could not endure him, when he was for humility, spirituality, and a heavenly kingdom.
3. Though repentance be always a duty, it is specially necessary to our special and great mercies, and our assurance of pardon by a Saviour. A purified mind and life are suitable to the consolation of Christ, and the indwelling of the comforting Spirit.

3. For this is he that was spoken of by the prophet Esaias, saying, The voice of one crying in the wilderness, Prepare ye the way of the Lord, make his paths straight.

3. It was John that Isaiah prophecied of, and foretold what his preaching should be. Though it be grace that prepareth for further grace, man's duty must be used thereunto; and the exalting work of grace presupposeth the humbling work of repentance as a necessary preparation.

4. And the same John had his raiment of camel's hair, and a leathern girdle about his loins, and his meat was locusts and wild honey.

4. He was clothed with hair cloth, bound to him with a leather-girdle, and fed on what the wilderness afforded, which was locusts, (which some think was an herb so called, but most, a sort of flies like great grasshoppers, that devour all green things,) and wild honey.
Note. Though the friars and hermits, by superstitiously over-valuing such austerities, have tempted others to despise them, yet God approved of John's signification of his contempt of the world and fleshly pleasures by such abasing of the flesh. And other men's superstition of hypocrisy, will not excuse men's superfluity, or accuse mortification.

5. Then went out to him Jerusalem, and all Judea, and all the region round about Jordan. 6. And were baptized of him in Jordan, confessing their sins.

5. So glad were the people to hear that the kingdom of the Messiah was at hand, that they all flocked to him to be baptized, professing repentance, that they might be prepared for the kingdom.
Note, 1. We grant that baptism then was by washing the whole body: and did not the differences of our cold country as to that hot one, teach us to remember, (*I will have mercy and not sacrifice*) it should be so here. 2. Though many say John's baptism and Christ's were all one, it is easy to prove, that if any were now baptized with John's baptism, he ought to be baptized again, in the name of the Father, Son, and Holy Ghost, on the profession of many articles of the creed, which John required not.

7. But when he saw many of the Pharisees and Sadducees come to his baptism, he said unto them, O generation of vipers, who hath warned you to flee from the wrath to come? 8. Bring forth therefore fruits meet for repentance.

7. Knowing what these Pharisees and Sadducees were, he said, O generation of vipers, Are you

aware indeed that wrath is coming upon you? And do you think that the Messiah will indulge your sin, and come to promote your carnal interest: If you profess repentance, and would have part in the kingdom of the Messiah, resolve against your sins, and live in that righteousness and holiness, which is the fruit of true repentance

9. And think not to say within yourselves, We have Abraham to our Father: For I say unto you, That God is able of these stones to raise up children unto Abraham.

9. Think not that the Messiah will advance you, for being the carnal seed of Abraham, if you have not the faith and holiness of Abraham: If you be wicked unbelievers, God will cast you off, though Abraham was your father; and can of the Gentiles (or the very stones) raise up such as shall be blest with Abraham's believing seed.

10. And now also the axe is laid unto the root of the trees: therefore every tree which bringeth not forth good fruit, is hewn down, and cast into the fire.

10. The Messiah cometh with salvation to some, and judgment to others: He layeth the axe to the root, to cut down all of you that bring not forth the fruit of true faith and repentance, and will cast such into the fire of temporal and eternal punishment.

11. I indeed baptize you with water unto repentance: But he that cometh after me, is mightier than I, whose shoes I am not worthy to bear: he shall baptize you with the Holy Ghost and *with* fire.

11. I do but baptize you preparatorily with water to repentance: But he that is coming after me, is mightier than I, whose shoes I am not worthy to bear: he shall baptize not only with water, but with the pouring out of his Spirit on believers, and with that fiery trial, which shall refine the gold, the faithful, but separate the dross, and destroy the rebellious unbelievers.

12. Whose fan *is* in his hand, and he will throughly purge his floor, and gather his wheat into the garner: but he will burn up the chaff with unquenchable fire.

12. He will winnow and throughly separate the wheat from the chaff, the faithful from the rebellious, and will gather the faithful into his heavenly kingdom, and into his church in order hereto, but he will burn the unbelievers and unpersuadable as chaff, and that with destruction here, and unquenchable fire hereafter.

13. Then cometh Jesus from Galilee to Jordan unto John, to be baptized of him, 14. But John forbade him, saying, I have need to be baptized of thee, and comest thou to me?

13, 14. Note, Christ was not baptized to the same ends as other men. He had no sins to repent of, nor saviour to receive, but, as the general, will wear the same colours with his soldiers. Christ received baptism for the ends he was capable, as to profess that the kingdom of God was at hand.

15. And Jesus answering, said unto him, Suffer *it to be so* now; for thus it becometh us to fulfil all righteousness. Then he suffered him.

15. I must fulfil the law of Moses, and thy prophetic mission, and be thus entered on my proper work.

16. And Jesus when he was baptized, went up straightway out of the water: and lo, the heavens were opened unto him, and he saw the Spirit of God descending like a Dove, and lighting upon him.

16. As Jesus went up out of the water, John saw the heavens open to Christ, and the Spirit of God, in some resemblance, of a dove, (or as a dove doth light on any place,) descending on him, (it is like in a lucid appearance) and resting on him.

17. And lo, a voice from Heaven, saying, This is my beloved Son, in whom I am well pleased.

17. And with the apparition came a voice from heaven, saying, This is, &c. This is my beloved Son the *Messiah*, sent from heaven as the Mediator to reveal my will, and to fulfil it, and by his perfect righteousness and sacrifice to reconcile the world to me, and be the propitiation for their sins.

CHAP. IV.

THEN was Jesus led up of the Spirit into the wilderness, to be tempted of the Devil.

Note, 1. That though Christ was God, his human nature was actuated by the Holy Ghost, to whom in scripture is ascribed divine perfection of operation on creatures. 2. Man was overcome by the temptation of Satan, and so sin and death, and all evil, did invade mankind; therefore our Redeemer must deliver us from sin and Satan, and misery, by conquering the tempter in his way of temptation, by which he conquered: to give us also notice, that the warfare preparatory to our future state, is managed by overcoming temptations, or being overcome by them. And therefore the study of temptations and the resistance is a great part of the Christian life. 3. Christ cast not himself on temptations, but was led to it by the Spirit. 4. To be tempted is no sin.

2. And when he had fasted forty days, and forty nights, he was afterward an hungred.

Note, 1. In this Moses was a type of Christ. 2. Fasting and trial by temptation were great preparatives to Christ's exercise of his prophetic office: and his ministers should not be strangers to it; the sensual are never true to Christ. To serve the flesh by the ministry, by seeking preferment, honour, and fleshly ease, and fulness, more than men's salvation, is to serve the devil, as conquered by his temptations. 3. Hunger and bodily sufferings give Satan advantage for many temptations, though not so dangerously as prosperity and fleshly pleasures do.

3. And when the tempter came to him, he said, If thou be the Son of God, command that these stones be made bread.

3. The Son of God can do what he will, feed thyself now by miracle.
Note, 1. Whether the devil thought by this to tempt him to doubt, whether he were the Son of God, or only as supposing it to draw him to sin, by obeying him, is uncertain. 2. Satan cannot tempt us when he will, but when God permitteth him 3. His design was to obscure Christ's godhead and glory.

4. But he answered and said, It is written, Man shall not live by bread alone, but by every word that proceedeth out of the mouth of God.

4. Note, 1. Christ himself was not above making use of God's written word.
2. It is by this word that the tempter must be confuted and overcome. 3. It is by God's will that our food doth nourish us, and his will and love is more necessary to us than our food.

5. Then the devil taketh him up into the holy city, and setteth him on a pinnacle of the temple, 6. And saith unto him, If thou be the Son of God, cast thyself down: for it is written, He shall give his angels charge concerning thee, and in their hands they shall bear thee up, lest at any time thou dash thy foot against a stone.

5, 6. Then the devil, permitted by God, carried the body of Christ through the air, and set him on the battlements, or some high place on the Temple, and said, Cast thyself down, &c.
Note, 1. God may give Satan power even to carry our bodies about, and yet not overcome our souls. 2. The devil would tempt us to think, that we may do any thing that hath no danger to us, though it be out of the way of our obedience. 3. He that will have God's protection must keep in the way of his duty to God, and not presume that God shall save him out of his way in our own.

7. Jesus said unto him, It is written again, Thou shalt not tempt the Lord thy God.

7. Note, 1. Though the devil use scripture for temptation, this is no dishonour to scripture, but we must confute misapplication of scripture, by scripture rightly expounded and applied. Papists and all heretics, and the devil himself, may use scripture, (and therefore all must not be believed that use it:) But that is an honour to it, signifying that it is God's word, or else it would not serve the hypocrite's turn. As all contenders pretend to reason, and yet reason must decide their controversies.
2. Tempting God is distrusting his ordinary care, and providence, and prescribing to him our own ways.

8. Again the devil taketh him up into an exceeding high mountain, and sheweth him all the kingdoms of the world, and the glory of them: 9. And saith unto him, All these things will I give thee, if thou wilt fall down and worship me.

8, 9. Note, 1. Satan took advantage of Christ's voluntary poverty and fasting, to tempt his flesh to the desire of earthly prosperity and dominion. 2. By [all kingdoms] is meant, many that were within prospect. 3. How far God hath given the power of earthly kingdoms and glory to the devil, is not fully certain. But we see he hath given him power to tempt men by them, and, it is like, much to dispose of them as far as those temptations prevail. That he useth almost all the empires of the world against Christ and holiness, by malignity and worldly interests, to keep up ignorance and ungodliness, is notorious by sad experience. 4. The devil thinketh not kingdoms and glory too great price to win and undo souls. 5. Christ himself was tempted to the most odious sin, even to worship the devil. Therefore mere temptation, even to blasphemy, should not discourage melancholy persons, who hate and resist it.

10. Then saith Jesus unto him, Get thee hence, Satan: for it is written, Thou shalt worship the Lord thy God, and him only shalt thou serve.

10. 1. Note, When it cometh to blasphemous and atheistical temptations, Satan should be driven away, and no longer disputed with and endured : 2. Yet even then scripture must be given for confuting his blasphemies. 3. Whether Satan do all this in pride, as desiring to be worshipped, or in hatred to God and souls, is doubtful; but it is like to be from all these. 4. [Only] excludeth other Gods, and all competitors and opposites, but not parents, masters, princes, as subordinate to God.

11. Then the devil leaveth him. And behold, angels came and ministered unto him.

11. Note, 1. Satan can stay no longer than God will. 2. Angels are God's servants for Christ and his church. 3. As Christ had the ministry of angels, we need it much more.

12. Now when Jesus heard that John was cast into prison, he departed into Galilee.

12. Note, Christ avoided persecution till his hour was come. And so may we.

13. And leaving Nazareth, he came and dwelt in Capernaum, which is upon the sea coast, in the borders of Zabulon and Nephthalim: 14. That it might be fulfilled which was spoken by Esaias the prophet, saying, 15. The land of Zabulon, and the land of Nephthalim, *by* the way of the sea beyond Jordan, Galilee of the Gentiles: 16. The people which sat in darkness saw great light, and to them which sat in the region and shadow of death, light is sprung up.

15. &c Of which I may use the words of Isa. ix. though then spoken to another purpose, as now fulfilled literally as they seem to sound, and as perhaps the Holy Ghost might farther mean them, &c.

17. From that time Jesus began to preach, and to say, Repent, for the kingdom of heaven is at hand.

17. From that time Jesus exercised his prophetic office, preaching to them, 1. That the time of the kingdom of the Messiah was now at hand: and 2. therefore that they should repent, that they might be fit subjects for his kingdom, and might believe and receive remission of sins.

18. And Jesus walking by the sea of Galilee, saw two brethren, Simon called Peter, and Andrew his brother, casting a net into the sea; (for they were fishers.) 19. And he saith unto them, Follow me, and I will make you fishers of men. 20. And they straightway left *their* nets, and followed him.

18, 19, 20. It being part of Christ's office to appoint teachers under him, as he walked by the lake of Genesareth he saw Simon and Andrew, &c. And he called them to be teachers, to save souls; and that so powerfully, as prevailed with them to leave all, and follow him.

21. And going on from thence he saw other two brethren, James *the* *son* of Zebedee, and John his brother, in a ship with Zebedee their father, mending their nets: and he called them. 22. And they immediately left the ship and their father, and followed him.

21, 22. Note, His call no doubt did reach the heart: what persuasives he before used is not mentioned.

23. And Jesus went about all Galilee, teaching in their synagogues, and preaching the gospel of the kingdom, and healing all manner of sickness, and all manner of disease, among the people.

23. And from that time he went about in that country of Galilee, teaching and preaching the joyful tidings that the Messiah's kingdom was at hand, and that his miracles might confirm his doctrine, he miraculously healed all manner of diseases where he came.

24. And his fame went throughout all Syria; and they brought unto him all sick people, that were taken with divers diseases and torments, and those which were possessed with devils, and those which were lunatic, and those that had the palsy, and he healed them. 25. And there followed him great multitudes of people from Galilee, and *from* Decapolis, and *from* Jerusalem, and *from* Judea, and *from* beyond Jordan.

24, 25. Note, 1. Christ began his great prophetic and miraculous works among the poorest contemned part, and not in Jerusalem among the greatest. 2. The multitude of the miraculous cures, and that of old diseases, such as palsies and leprosies, &c. left no place for suspicion of deceit.

CHAP. V.

AND seeing the multitudes, he went up into a mountain, and when he was set, his disciples came unto him. 2. And he opened his mouth and taught them, saying,

1. And seeing the multitudes that followed him as admirers and learners, (not yet made full baptised Christians) he went for convenience of hearing, into a mountain, and there being set, he taught them as followeth.

Note, Phrases follow the custom of countries, And so [*he opened his mouth*] by that custom as no such absurd phrase, as it would be now.

3. Blessed *are* the poor in spirit: for theirs is the kingdom of heaven.

3. Blessed are ye my true disciples, though you be poor in the world, if you have spirits suited to your poverty, for you shall have the kingdom of heaven for riches.

Note, [*Poor in spirit*] signifieth a mind that is above the love of worldly riches, and the sins that riches use to breed and feed, (that is, Sodom's sins, *pride, fulness,* and idleness, and unmercifulness to the poor ;),and such as are contented with food and raiment, having mortified the lusts of the flesh, which thirsts after worldly plenty and delight.

4. Blessed *are* they that mourn: for they shall be comforted.

4. Though you are under sorrows now, you are blessed, if you are godly, and have godly sorrow, for your comfort will be time enough and full enough hereafter.

Note, There are many sorts of sinful sorrows which have none of this promise; such as are the common fruits of over-loving some creature, and distrusting God. But it is holy mourning that is here meant, that is, for our own or other men's sins, and God's dishonour, and displeasure, and our want of more grace, and for the miseries of the wicked, and suffering world.

5. Blessed *are* the meek: for they shall inherit the earth.

5. Though lowly meekness and quiet patience seem a depressed miserable state with men, indeed those that are such are the most happy sort of men even in this world, and their way is the most probable for escaping of outward suffering: while the contrary minded vex themselves with their own impatience and pride, and provoke others to hurt them, and suffer much because they cannot suffer a little: and raising seditions and wars, do ruin themselves by revenge and ruining others, and perish by the sword to which they trust.

6. Blessed *are* they that hunger and thirst after righteousness: for they shall be filled.

6. Blessed are you, though now you hunger for want of bread, if you hunger and thirst after righteousness of heart and life towards God and man, as those that would wish to be perfect in holiness, and doing good to all; and that not with a sluggish wish, but a desire that useth effectual endeavour: For you shall have full satisfaction of all such desires, and more than you can desire now, when the full are sent empty away.

7. Blessed *are* the merciful: for they shall obtain mercy.

7. Though God's grace and mercy be free, yet men must be fit receivers and not reject it: And it is the merciful that are thus blessed, as qualified for saving mercy from God: while the cruel, and oppressors, and persecutors, and unmerciful, reject mercy by their forfeiture and incapacity, and undo themselves by hurting others.

8. Blessed *are* the pure in heart: for they shall see God.

8. God will not bless impure, unholy souls with the light of his countenance and the comfort of his love; nor dwell with the filthy workers of iniquity: without holiness none shall see God. But you whose hearts, his grace hath purified from the filth of fleshly worldly lusts, and the love of sin, are a blessed people, for grace hath fitted you for begun communion with God here, and you shall see him in heavenly glory hereafter. He hath not purified your hearts in vain.

9. Blessed *are* the peace-makers: for they shall be called the children of God.

9. Though peace-makers use to be hated by both extremes and sides of the contentious, whom they would reconcile, yet they are blessed that do it sincerely from the predominant love of God, and man, and peace; for as children are like the father, so are they to the God of love and peace, who hath reconciled his enemies to him by Christ.

10. Blessed *are* they which are persecuted for righteousness sake: for theirs is the kingdom of heaven.

10 Though men think them miserable that are oppressed and ruined in the world; they are blessed, if they are persecuted for righteousness sake: For it is God's cause, who will reward them with the kingdom of heaven, and never let any be a loser by his obedience to him.

11. Blessed *are* ye when men shall revile you, and persecute *you,* and shall say all manner of evil against you falsely for my sake.

11. Think not that I am come to advance you to worldly honour; but look to be reviled and persecuted, not only by heathens, but by Jews, and to have all manner of evil charged on you, and reported of you falsely, for my sake, because you believe me and obey me: But in all this you are blessed, while your false accusers and persecutors are miserable.

12. Rejoice and be exceeding glad: for great *is* your reward in heaven: for so persecuted they the prophets which were before you.

12. Though such usage would break the hearts of worldly men and hypocrites, do not you only bear it patiently, but joyfully, with exceeding gladness; because your reward in heaven will be so much the surer and greater: for you do but follow the prophets that are gone this way to heaven before you, whom the carnal church persecuted and murdered, though their posterity honour their names when they are dead, but go on and imitate them in hating and persecuting the living.

13. Ye are the salt of the earth: but if the salt have lost its savour,

wherewith shall it be salted? It is thenceforth good for nothing, but to be cast out, and to be trodden under foot of men.

13. The world is putrified with the corruption of all sin; and you that follow me must be as salt to it, to recover it from this corruption. But if you prove filthy, and corrupt yourselves, what or who shall be salt to you for your recovery: Corrupt professors of Christianity are more miserable, hopeless, and forlorn, than heathens.

14. Ye are the light of the world. A city that is set on a hill cannot be hid. 15. Neither do men light a candle, and put it under a bushel, but on a candlestick, and it giveth a light unto all that are in the house.

14, 15. God hath honoured you to be lights to a dark world: It is not therefore an obscure and hidden sort of goodness that beseemeth you. You are called out to be conspicuous in the world, like a city on a hill that cannot be hid; by your difference from them in doctrine and life: Men do not light a candle to hide it, but to set it up to be a light to the house; and so doth God call you to be open lights in doctrine and life.

16. Let your light so shine before men, that they may see your good works, and glorify your Father which is in heaven.

16. Note, That 1. the good works of Christians are the due appointed means to win others to the glorifying of God: and they that do not this, are guilty of perfidiousness to God and man, as dumb ministers are by omitting their work. 2. Therefore our good works must not be so few and small as to be undiscernable: They must not be done in hypocrisy to be seen of men for our praise; but they must shine forth in sincerity to God's praise. 3. By good works is meant holiness to God, sobriety to ourselves, and justice and works of love to others.

17. Think not that I am come to destroy the law or the prophets: I am not come to destroy but to fulfil.

17. Take me not for an enemy to the law and the prophets, as if I came to blame and destroy them. As to the ceremonial part, it was but a typifying prediction of me, and is to be fulfilled in me: and it is the honour of types and prophecies to be fulfilled. And as to the natural part I own and establish it, and am so far from evacuating it, that I teach the fullest keeping of it.

18. For verily I say unto you, Till heaven and earth pass, one jot, or one tittle, shall in no wise pass from the law, till all be fulfilled.

18. I tell you, the law is so true, as being God's own word, that one letter or tittle of it shall not be frustrated, or fail of its performance to the end of the world, but shall be all fulfilled.

19. Whosoever, therefore, shall break one of these least commandments, and shall teach men so, he shall be called the least in the kingdom of heaven: but whosoever shall do and teach *them*, the same shall be called great in the kingdom of heaven.

19. If any shall presume to break the least of these commands, because it is a little one, and teach men so to do, he shall be vilified as he vilified God's law, and not thought fit for a place in the kingdom of the Messiah: but he shall be there greatest, that is most exact in doing and teaching all the law of God.

Note, Are not those preachers and prelates then the *least* and basest, that preach and tread down Christian love of all that dissent from any of their presumptions; and so preach down not the least but the great command!

20. For I say unto you, That except your righteousness shall exceed *the righteousness* of the Scribes and Pharisees, ye shall in no case enter into the kingdom of heaven.

20. So far am I from preaching looseness, or favouring sin, that I tell you, though the scribes and pharisees pretend to the strictest keeping of the law; if you keep it not better than they do, and be not a better and a more righteous sort of men, you shall in no case enter into the kingdom of heaven.

Note, That besides Christ's righteousness, there is necessary to all (at age) that will be saved, a righteousness consisting in more careful exact obedience to God, than any formal hypocrites hath. And this God's Spirit worketh them unto.

21. Ye have heard, that it was said by them of old time, Thou shalt not kill, and whosoever shall kill shall be in danger of the judgment. 22. But I say unto you, That whosoever is angry with his brother without a cause, shall be in danger of the judgment: and whosoever shall say to his brother, Raca, shall be in danger of the council: But whosoever shall say, *Thou fool,* shall be in danger of hell-fire.

21. Moses's law was, that murder shall be punished with death (by the lesser *Sanhedrim*). And the carnal Jews have taken this to be all that the sixth commandment condemned. But God's law is perfect, however carnal men misunderstand it. And I tell you, That 1. whoever lets out this

passion of hurtful and uncharitable anger, against any man, without or beyond just cause, doth in some degree break the sixth commandment, and therefore deserveth answerable punishment. And, 2. whoever shall causelessly scorn or revile his brother, breaketh the commandment yet more, and deserveth greater punishment. But whosoever shall utterly despise him causelessly, with an uncharitable conclusion that he is a fool, or a wicked man, or a schismatic, or an heretic, when it is not so, shall have yet far greater punishment, even hell-fire, answering that in the valley of Hinnom.

23. Therefore, if thou bring thy gift to the altar, and there rememberest that thy brother hath ought against thee; 24. Leave there thy gift before the altar, and go thy way, first be reconciled to thy brother, and then come and offer thy gift.

23. Therefore, see that you prefer not sacrifice before love and mercy, but if thou bring thy gift to the altar, and be just ready to offer it, and rememberest that thou hast wronged thy brother, or given him occasion of uncharitable thoughts of thee: lay more upon love than on thine offering. Leave it there, and go presently and make restitution, confession, or whatever is necessary to reconciliation, and then come and offer thy gift.

Note, 1. O Christians, lay this deeply to heart, that your Saviour was so great a teacher of love, that he preferreth it before all things, even acts of outward worship, and will take him for no Christian that is not so minded. 2. O what a dreadful aggravation of wickedness is it to turn the very sacraments themselves into snares of wrath and cruelty, and to curse and damn, and tear from the church, all that dare not subscribe and swear to all the inventions of popes and councils: And for the preachers of love and peace, to say more than [*thou fool ;*] even to silence, and ruin, or burn all as heretics or schismatics, that dare not justify all this!

25. Agree with thine adversary quickly, whiles thou art in the way with him: lest at any time the adversary deliver thee to the judge, and the judge deliver thee to the officer, and thou be cast into prison. 26. Verily I say unto thee, Thou shalt by no means come out thence, till thou hast paid the uttermost farthing.

25, 26. If thou hast wronged any man, delay not reparation of his wrong, and reconciliation: lest he extort his reparation from thee by law, and put thee to extremity, when thou mightest have compounded, or appeased him by submission. And so obey God in thy duty of love, and restitution and submission to men, lest he enter into judgment with thee, and make thy utmost punishment answer the debt.

27. Ye have heard that it was said by them of old time, Thou shalt not commit adultery. 28. But I say unto you, That whosoever looketh on a woman to lust after her, hath committed adultery with her already in his heart.

27. So Moses said in the seventh commandment, Thou shalt not commit adultery: And the carnal Jews looked but little deeper: But I tell you that whoever casteth on a woman a wanton eye, stirring up lust, and unlawful carnal imaginations and pleasure, or useth his other senses to stir up such lusts, as do: le the mind, or tend towards fornication, he hath in his heart broken the seventh commandment in some degree.

29. And if thy right eye offend thee, pluck it out, and cast it from thee: for it is profitable for thee that one of thy members should perish, and not that thy whole body should be cast into hell. 30. And if thy right hand offend thee, cut it off, and cast it from thee: for it is profitable for thee that one of thy members should perish, and not that thy whole body should be cast into hell.

29, 30. It may be some will say, *My eye is so inclinable to enticing looks, and my hand to some forbidden touches or acts, that they offend when I know they should not,* and if it go no further, I hope it is safe: But I tell you, this so poor an excuse, that if you had not the command of eye and hand, and had no other way to avoid the sin, it were less hurt to you to pluck out that eye, and cut off that hand, than to sin and be damned with it. Not that I bid you do so, for you have power otherwise to avoid the sin; but if ye had not, it were your wisest way, much more to deny your eye or hand all forbidden pleasure.

31. It hath been said, Whosoever shall put away his wife, let him give her a writing of divorcement. 32. But I say unto you, That whosoever shall put away his wife, saving for the cause of fornication, causeth her to commit adultery; and whosoever shall marry her that is divorced, committeth adultery.

31, 32. Moses bade you give your wife a bill of divorcement, if you put her way: And so you have been taught that this is lawful; But I say to you, that you must not put away a wife, save for fornication; and if you do, you are guilty of making her commit adultery, and he will live in adultery that shall marry her.

Note, That Christ here supposeth such other causes as nature itself alloweth: As if husband or wife should resolvedly seek the others death, or be infected with a mortal contagious disease, self-preservation alloweth avoidance till the danger is over. And if any other cause make their cohabitation utterly inconsistent with safety, or the ends of marriage, they may by consent live asunder while that cause continueth.

33. Again, ye have heard that it hath been said by them of old time, Thou shalt not forswear thyself, but shalt perform unto the Lord thine oaths. 34. But I say unto you, Swear not at all; neither by heaven, for it is God's throne: 35. Nor by the earth, for it is his footstool: neither by Jerusalem, for it is the city of the great King: 36. Neither shalt thou swear by thy head, because thou canst not make one hair white or black. 37. But let your communication be, Yea, yea; Nay, nay; for whatsoever *is* more than these cometh of evil.

33, &c. You have been told that perjury is a heinous sin, and oaths must be kept: This is past doubt; but I tell you more; that you must not needlessly swear at all, or make any oaths a part of your discourse: Think not that it is a small matter to swear by creatures, while you profane not the name of God: for all that you can swear by, is related to God, and his law is broken by it: If it be by heaven, it is his throne; if by the earth, it is his footstool; if by Jerusalem, it is his holy city; if by the head, it is his work, of which thou makest not so much as the colour of one hair. Therefore, content yourselves in your discourse with a sober *yea* or *nay:* for your oaths and needless vehement protestations, are but the expressions of passion, or some other vice, and are stirred up by Satan.

Note, That the common definition (that an oath is always to appeal to another as a knower and avenger of falsehood) is not good: It is the pawning of the verity or honour of one thing known, to verify another unknown: As to say, This is as true as that the heaven is over me: Or if this be not true, the earth is not under my feet; it is as true as that I have a head; or, as that there is a God, who knoweth all things, &c. Though it is true that swearing by God, includeth an appeal to him.

38. Ye have heard that it hath been said, An eye for an eye, and a tooth for a tooth. 39. But I say unto you, that ye resist not evil: but whosoever shall smite thee on thy right cheek, turn to him the other also. 40. And if any man will sue thee at the law, and take away thy coat, let him have thy cloak also. 41. And whosoever shall compel thee to go a mile, go with him twain.

38, &c. You have heard that injuries must be repaid but with equal hurt: an eye for an eye: It is true that magistrates having the charge of the *common welfare,* and the execution of God's laws, they must punish injuries, and not suffer all men to do as much mischief as they will: But you that are private persons must prefer *LOVE* and *patience* before reparation of your losses, preservation of your rights, or personal revenge: And therefore when it is not the public good that requireth it, but your own right, resist not injuries, by any means which violate *love* or *patience*. If, when you are stricken you strike again, you do but stir up the person to more wrath, to hurt you more, when as *love* and *patience* may make him ashamed that he hath wronged you; Revenge will but enrage him, and suffer more when *love* and *patience* may win him. Yea, if he abuse the law to injure you, prefer not the righting of yourselves before the winning of him by *love:* And patience may cost you less than a law-suit, or revenge. If he injuriously force you to any service, bear that and more, rather than by striving to violate charity.

Note, That the rule here intended by Christ is, That we prefer the winning of a man's soul by love, and the exercise of *patience* before our *right,* and that we bear tolerable wrongs rather than alienate men by exasperation, and increase our own sufferings by revenge; usually the patient suffer least, and win enemies most. But 1.- this extendeth not to magistrates strengthening sin by impunity. 2. Nor to private men pardoning sins against God, which is not in our power. 3. Nor to neglect the safety of the *commonwealth* by favouring evil. 4. Nor by forbearing the necessary defence of our own or others lives or welfare against insufferable assaults: nor may we give away that which is due to wives and children, or the poor, which is not in our power.

42. Give to him that asketh thee: and from him that would borrow of thee, turn not thou away.

42. Note, The sense is, Be not unwilling to give wherever thou oughtest, but as willing to give as men are to ask, and *asking* is one part of thy direction to whom to give. But this excludeth not the use of prudent reason in our giving. 1. We must not give that to one person, which we should rather give to others; not to the unworthy or unfit, because they ask, when we should seek after the more needy and worthy that ask not: nor must we give that to one that is due to many; nor give to a lesser good, when by it we may do a greater; nor give that which is not in our power. As to the question, How much we must give? 1. A thousand come far short, for one that charitably gives too much. 2. Every man should study to do God the greatest service he can with his estate, and prudently discern the way. 3. The necessities of others must be preferred, before our pleasure and unnecessaries.

43. Ye have heard that it hath been said, Thou shalt love thy neighbour, and hate thine enemy: 44. But I say unto you, Love your enemies, bless them that curse you, do good to them that hate you, and pray for them which despitefully use you and persecute you: 45. That ye may be the children of your Father which is in heaven: for he maketh his sun to rise on the evil, and on the good, and sendeth rain on the just, and on the unjust.

43, 44. God did let out the Israelites to execute so great slaughters on their heathen enemies, that occasioned many of old to restrain love to too narrow an object, and to incline to hatred and hurtfulness to enemies, too much: But I tell you that you must love all your enemies according to the degree of amiableness in them; that is, All men as men: All sober moral men as such; All visible members of the church as such; and all notably sincere, eminent, excellent, and useful Christians as such: and let not enmity to you suspend this love; (though you be not bound to love all alike, nor to trust any mortal man too far.) And it is not enough that you do your enemies no hurt; nor will their hating, cursing, or spiteful usage and persecution of you, excuse you from your duty: but notwithstanding all this, you must love them that hate you, and pray for them that despitefully use you and persecute you, speak well of them, and bless them that speak ill of you and curse you; for you are not God's children if you be not like him, and imitate him, who maintaineth the life, health, and natural comforts of the just and the unjust.

Note, O how little conscience do most Christians, even the religious, make of this command of Christ! How freely do they speak evil of their enemies, and think themselves excused by saying, *It is as they are Christ's enemies and not ours!* Hate the sin, and dislike the sinner as such; so you will but love all that is lovely in him, and remember, that it is love that must overcome evil, and make bad men lovely.

46. For if you love them which love you, what reward have ye? do not even the publicans the same? 47. And if ye salute your brethren only, what do you more *than others?* do not even the publicans so? 48. Be ye therefore perfect, even as your Father which is in heaven is perfect.

46, 47, 48. If you look for any reward from God, it must be for obeying and serving him. But to love men for loving you, is but to serve yourselves and your self-love, and then you must reward yourselves. What bad man will not love men for loving him? And if as Jews ye be kind to Jews, or praise, honour, and love those of your own sect or party, or opinion, what bad men or heathens do not the like? All, out of self-esteem, love and honour their party, and those of their own opinion. But if you will approve yourselves the children of God, and have his reward, love men for his sake, even all men impartially, whether they be for you or against you, so far as any thing of God is in them, whether it be nature or grace, common grace or special; yea, for their capacity of being good and doing good hereafter. The most full universal love is that perfection in which you must be like to God. Judge of yourselves by it; and reckon that ye have no more goodness than you have love.

CHAP. VI.

TAKE heed that ye do not your alms before men, to be seen of them: otherwise ye have no reward of your Father which is in heaven.

1. Be careful to avoid hypocrisy, and a proud desire of praise in your works of charity: You may do it when men see you: but not to be seen: If you take men's esteem and praise for your reward, you forfeit and lose God's heavenly reward.

2. Therefore, when thou dost *thine* alms, do not sound a trumpet before thee, as the hypocrites do in the synagogues, and in the streets, that they may have glory of men. Verily I say unto you, They have their reward.

2. Make not ostentation of your charity, as hypocrites: They shall have no better reward than the vain-glory which they chuse: (Alas, what a pitiful reward!)

3. But when thou dost alms, let not thy left hand know what thy right hand doth. 4. That thine alms may be in secret: And thy Father which seeth in secret, himself shall reward thee openly.

3, 4. But though your good works must shine before men to God's glory, yet, be so carefully afraid of all affectation of vain-glory to yourselves, as purposely to conceal all, when nothing but your own praise requireth openness, yea, do not note it too much in yourselves, to puff you up; and then as your hearts and lives are all known to God, he will openly reward them to the full.

5. And when thou prayest, thou shalt not be as the hypocrites *are:* for they love to pray standing in the synagogues, and in the corners of the streets, that they may be seen of

men: Verily I say unto you, They have their reward.

5. So let not your prayer be like the hypocrites, all done in public, as on a stage, to be seen of men: I tell ye, men's praise is all the reward they shall have.

Note, Not but that public church-prayer, and family prayer, are as great duties as secret prayer: but they must not be done for to be thought religious, nor secret prayer made open or neglected. 2. Standing is a lawful praying posture in itself: But where kneeling signifieth more reverence, it must be preferred in humbling duties.

6. But when thou prayest, enter into thy closet, and when thou hast shut thy door, pray to thy Father which is in secret; and thy Father which seeth in secret shall reward thee openly.

6. But do thou pray secretly where only God is witness of thy prayers, (and therefore approve to him thy secret desires and heart, as well as thy words) and believe that God will openly reward thee.

Note, 1. Both public and secret prayer are our duty. 2. Praying only before men is gross hypocrisy: but all secret prayer will not prove sincerity. 3. They that say, We must not serve God for reward, oppose Christ, and scripture, and all religion. It is not a reward in *commutative justice*, as if we profited God; but in *fatherly love* and justice, as pleasing God through Christ, as fathers reward good children, and not bad ones.

7. But when ye pray, use not vain repetitions, as the heathen do: for they think they shall be heard for their much speaking. 8. Be not ye therefore like unto them; for your Father knoweth what things ye have need of, before ye ask him.

7. When you pray, do not so repeat over the same words, or lengthen your prayers with unmeet repetitions, as the heathens do, that think canting over certain words, or spinning out prayers to such a length, is acceptable to God; or as if God were moved by terms or length. For God is your father, and knows what you need before you speak, and pitieth you according to your needs: and your prayers are not to move and change him, but by exercising your own desires, and faith, and repentance, and thankfulness, to make you fit to receive his further gifts.

9. After this manner, therefore, pray ye:

9. I will give a perfect directory for the matter and order of your desires and prayers, and in words fit for your use, when you pray but summarily.

9, 10, &c. Our Father which art in heaven, hallowed be thy name. Thy kingdom come. Thy will be done on earth as *it is* in heaven. Give us this day our daily bread. And forgive us our debts, as we forgive our debtors. And lead us not into temptation, but deliver us from evil: For thine is the kingdom, and the power and the glory, for ever. Amen.

9, &c. We come not to thee as our unreconciled avenging judge, but as to our merciful Father reconciled to us by Christ; the only God, whose glory is eminently in heaven, infinite in perfection of being, and of power, knowledge, and goodness, our absolute Owner, our supreme Ruler, and our most loving Father by creation, redemption, and regeneration, whose we are, and whom we must serve, and whom we must love and trust; we are sinful, needy, miserable, and unworthy in ourselves, but thy children by Christ our Intercessor, who is worthy; whose hearts are by desire towards thee as our God, and to the good of others as our brethren, as well as by necessity to our own felicity; We know, that as all things are of thee, and through thee, and to thee; so thou art our ultimate end: and therefore, we first humbly beg that thy great, wise, and good, and holy name may be known, and shine forth, and be glorified, and holily regarded upon earth, and not blasphemed or be unknown and disregarded by atheists, infidels, or wicked hypocrites: nor the honour of men be set up against thee: but that the nations of the earth, and all societies, and ourselves, may be wholly devoted and live to thy glory.

And our next petition is, that the world, or its societies, or our own and our brethren's souls, may not be given up to the wicked tyrannical kingdom of Satan, or men that are his ministers, and governed by him, nor to the wars, blood, and cruelty of such: but that thy divine government, even the kingdom of the Messiah, may come on earth in that fulness as may destroy the kingdom of Satan: that faith, love, and righteousness, may be the constitution of societies and souls; and the reign of grace may prepare us for glory: which we specially pray for.

And our third petition is, that in this thy kingdom, societies and souls, our own and others, may in disposition be conformed to thy governing will, and in practice obey it, and in faith, hope, and love, with joyful trust expect the promised reward, and patiently submit to thy fatherly corrections and disposals. And that in all these aforesaid three requests, this earth that is grown so near to hell, may be made more like to them in heaven, who know, love, and obey, and glorify thee, with perfection, unity, and full delight.

And because thou hast made our natures such as cannot but love ourselves, and hast bound us to seek our own and others welfare, and grace presupposeth *nature*, and our *being* is necessary first to our *well-being*: Therefore our fourth petition is, that thou wilt support our natures, and maintain them by necessary food and sustenance, and make us content with thy allowance, and save us from covetousness and over-much love to worldly fulness, prosperity, and wealth, and cause us to subserve thy providence by our wise and diligent labours, and not to forfeit thy maintenance by our self-confidence, idleness, or vicious sensuality, nor turn our strength to serve our sinful lust.

And knowing that holiness and justice require the punishment of sin, we next beseech thee to look on us in Christ, whom thy love and mercy sent into the world to be a sacrifice and propitiation for sin: whose perfect righteousness and sacrifice have merited that pardon and grace, which he hath given in his covenant, and proclaimed and offered to us all in the gospel; Forgive all the sins of our former life, and the remaining corruption of our hearts, and the daily faults that we are guilty of in our state of imperfection. And knowing that thou forgivest none but penitent believers, and biddest us to love and forgive others as ever we would be forgiven, we confess and lament our manifold sins of corrupt nature and practice, of ignorance, and of knowledge, of negligence, rashness, and presumptuous wilfulness. The remembrance of them is our grief and shame, we loathe ourselves for them, and earnestly beg to be healed of them: We cast ourselves by believing trust (though, alas! too weak) on Jesus our Saviour, his merits and intercession, and thy love, and mercy, and promises in him, desiring henceforth to be ruled by him, and sanctified by his Spirit and grace. And we unfeignedly love and forgive all those that have wronged us: we beseech thee, therefore, charge not our sins upon us, but acquit us from the everlasting punishment, and all vindictive penalties in this life on soul or body: and grant the same to all our brethren for whom we pray.

And because, if thou keep us not, we shall run on in guilt by new temptations, lose all that thou hast given us: We lastly beseech thee, to save us from all dangerous temptations, either by Satan's inward suggestions, or outward snares, by our own ill inclinations, or worldly allurements, or by such sufferings as may be too strong for our faith, hope, and patience, or would suppress our holy love, and thankfulness, and joyful praise, and save us from Satan, from ourselves, our enemies, and our friends, that would tempt us to any evil, and from the sin, and misery, and thy deserved judgments, of which we are in danger. And fortify us with thy confirming, comforting Spirit.

And we beg all these mercies of thee to this end, that we may employ them with all thy saints, in joyful praises of thy kingdom and government in heaven and earth, and in holy admiration of thy power, and all thy perfections, and in glorifying thy infinite goodness and blessedness, with the glorified society for evermore. These are the desires of our souls, and the requests of our lips, which we humbly and earnestly, in faith and hope, do present to thee our heavenly Father, by the motion of thy Spirit, through Jesus Christ, our Intercessor, Lord, and Saviour, Amen.

Note, Reader, So perfect is the method of the Lord's prayer, that I had thought to have anatomized it, and set it before thee in a scheme. But I now write for the less learned that cannot well comprehend accurateness: They that can, may find it done already in my *Latin method of Theology*: and the lower sort may find such a brief and plain exposition as such are capable of, in my *Family Catechism*: And in both, the controversies hereabout resolved.

14. For if ye forgive men their trespasses, your heavenly Father will also forgive you. 15. But if ye forgive not men their trespasses, neither will your Father forgive your trespasses.

14. Lest you should think that no qualification for pardon and other gifts are necessary in you, I again repeat what selfish nature is loathe to observe, that though God be your heavenly Father, yet your love and forgiveness of your brother is so necessary to his forgiving you, that without it, you shall not be forgiven: for if you have not this in sincerity, you are not God's children, and he is called *your heavenly father* but as offering you his grace. But if you have sincere love, with notable defects in your forgiving others, God will correct you as children, and will not forgive you some sharp chastisements: but make you know, that you must love others, if you will have the comfort of his love.

16. Moreover, when ye fast, be not as the hypocrites, of a sad countenance, for they disfigure their faces, that they may appear unto men to fast. Verily I say unto you, They have their reward.

16. Do not, for to be thought godly, seem to be more humbled than you are; nor shew that outwardly, which should be a concealed, secret fast: such hypocrites shall have no better reward, than the esteem and praise of men, which they thus seek.

17. But thou, when thou fastest, anoint thine head, and wash thy face: 18. That thou appear not unto men to fast, but unto thy Father which is in secret: and thy Father which seeth in secret, shall reward thee openly.

17, 18. But look thou for thine approbation and reward from God, and hide from the notice of the world thy private humiliations, (though public humiliations of churches and nations, and for open wrongs, must be publicly shewn) and God will openly reward thee.

19. Lay not up for yourselves treasures upon earth, where moth and rust doth corrupt, and where thieves break through and steal.

19. Note. 1. By *treasure* is meant that which a man *most loveth* and *trusteth* to for his supply and

comfort, and practically placeth his chief welfare in.
2. By *laying up*, is meant, over-valuing, eagerly desiring, and seeking, and caring for. That which rust, moths, and thieves can soon bereave you of, is unfit to be your beloved, trusted treasure.

20. But lay up for yourselves treasures in heaven, where neither moth nor rust doth corrupt, and where thieves do not break through nor steal.

20. But by faith, place your happiness in heaven, and on that, lay out your care, and love, and labour; and so use your wealth as God has promised to reward in heaven. For that treasure is incorruptible, inviolable, and everlasting.

Note, That though it be our God and Saviour that layeth up our treasure in heaven, and saveth us freely by grace, yet it is we that are commanded to lay it up, and save ourselves subordinately, by faith, hope, love, and labour, which qualify us as fit receivers of it.

21. For where your treasure is, there will your heart be also.

21. And by this you may know, whether you truly place your treasure in heaven or on earth, (not by your speculative opinion of words; for what hypocrite will not say, that heaven is better than earth!) But by the bent of your hearts. Your love, care, trust, and hope, will be where your treasure is. That which you 1. highliest value practically, 2. and most desire and chuse, 3. and labour for, though with the greatest care and cost, that is it that is indeed your treasure.

22. The light of the body is the eye; if, therefore, thine eye be single, thy whole body shall be full of light. 23. But if thine eye be evil, thy whole body shall be full of darkness. If, therefore, the light that is in thee be darkness, how great is that darkness?

22, 23. As the eye seeth not for itself alone, but for the whole body to guide its action; so thy understanding, or practical judgment is that superior visive faculty that must guide all thy love, and choice, and life. If, therefore, thy judgment be sound, and thou knowest the difference between laying up a treasure in heaven and on earth, it will rightly guide all the actions of thy heart and life, but if thy judgment be blinded in this great affair, it will misguide thy love, thy choice, and all the tenor of thy life. If thy judgment then be blind, which must guide thee, what a miserable erroneous wretch wilt thou be; and how dismal will that error prove.

24. No man can serve two masters: for either he will hate the one, and love the other; or else he will hold to the one, and despise the other. Ye cannot serve God and mammon.

24. And take heed of the self-deceit of hypocrites, who flatter themselves with the hope of having a treasure both on earth and in heaven; resolving to keep and prefer this world while they can keep it, and hope that heaven will be a reserve when they can keep the world no longer; and so they will be as religious as will stand with their fleshly, worldly interest. But I tell you, No man can serve two such contrary masters; he will love one better than the other, or obey and serve one to the neglect and injury of the other. You cannot love and serve God as God, and yet love and seek worldly wealth and prosperity, as your most beloved, trusted treasure. God will not stoop to the world; therefore, the world must in your esteem and choice, stoop to God, and be used for him.

25. Therefore, I say unto you, Take no thought for your life, what ye shall eat, or what ye shall drink; nor yet for your body, what ye shall put on: is not the life more than meat, and the body than raiment?

25. Therefore, take this as my special warning, *Wholly trust God for life, and all the concerns of life*, and shew not your selfishness and worldly love, by being distrustfully anxious, or solicitous for meat, and drink, and clothes. If you know not which way to get them, God knows which way to give them. *Your lives and bodies* are his gift, and in his power; and did he give you these, and cannot you trust him for food and clothing?

26. Behold the fowls of the air, for they sow not, neither do they reap, nor gather into barns; yet your heavenly Father feedeth them. Are ye not much better than they?

26. You see that God feedeth the many sort of fowls, that make no store-houses or provision for time to come: and God that made you better than they, will not neglect you.

27. Which of you, by taking thought, can add one cubit unto his stature?

27. Study your duty, and use just means while you trust on God. But your self-troubling, distrustful care, and thoughtfulness, is but unprofitable self-vexation. All your care cannot make you any taller of stature, nor keep your bodies from decay or death.

28. And why take ye thought for raiment? Consider the lilies of the field how they grow; they toil not, neither do they spin. 29. And yet I say unto you, That even Solomon

in all his glory, was not arrayed like one of these. 30. Wherefore, if God so clothe the grass of the field, which to-day is, and to-morrow is cast into the oven, *shall he* not much more *clothe* you, O ye of little faith?

28, 29, 30. And why do you distrustfully care for clothing? You see the lilies of the field that neither sow nor spin, have yet a more beautiful flower than Solomon's most splendid ornaments could match. And doth God so clothe these and other plants with beauty and sweetness, and are you so distrustful and weak in faith, as to fear he will neglect you?

Note, That Christ here neither blameth *sowing, spinning*, or other meet labour, nor would have it done imprudently and carelessly; much less doth he approve of an idle, slothful life, on pretence of trusting God. Six days must we labour, and not eat the bread of idleness. Paul saith, He that will not work, (when he can) let him not eat. Idleness corrupteth body and soul. Such care as we must take to feed and clothe the poor, such, at least, we may take for ourselves.

31. Therefore, take no thought, saying, What shall we eat? or what shall we drink? or wherewithal shall we be clothed?

31. Therefore, when you have done your duty, trust God, and do not with murmuring, or self-troubling, distrustfully say, Whence shall I have food and raiment?

32. (For after all these things do the Gentiles seek) for your heavenly Father knoweth that ye have need of all these things.

32. This is the practice of the heathens, who fear and compliment their idol-gods, but cannot trust them for what they want, but by self-trusting, and self-seeking, are drowned in worldly love and care. But your heavenly Father is far better acquainted with all your wants than you are, and doth not disregard them.

33. But seek ye first the kingdom of God, and his righteousness, and all these things shall be added unto you.

33. But I make this promise which you may boldly trust; see that you *seek first God's kingdom of* grace and glory, and that *righteousness*, *(relative, habitual,* and *actual,)* to which, through Christ, he hath promised acceptance and salvation; seek these, I say, before all worldly prosperity and fleshly interest, with your chief and predominant *esteem*, *choice*, and *endeavour;* and then all bodily things shall be given in as additions to the greater blessings, so far as God seeth them fit for you, and you for them, (for godliness hath the promise of this life, and of that to come.)

34. Take, therefore, no thought for the morrow: for the morrow shall take thought for the things of itself: sufficient unto the day is the evil thereof.

34. Therefore (beg of God your daily bread in faith, and in the use of honest labour but) take no distrustful, troubling, careful thoughts, for the time to come; it will be time enough to-morrow to take notice of to-morrow's wants, and to do to-morrow's work. Every day hath its own duty and difficulty, and sufferings must be expected. Do not anticipate them, and take to-day the trouble on yourself by care and fear, which belongs to the time to come. The burden and troubling part by such sufferings as you must expect, will come time enough, and a day's sense of the suffering, is enough for one day's evil or burden. Preparatory notice of death and suffering is useful. But should we foreknow all the particular sufferings that are to come on us, it would but overwhelm us, by an untimely suffering every day by fear and care of all that which we should suffer but by little tolerable parcels while every day hath its own proportion.

CHAP. VII.

JUDGE not, that ye be not judged. 2. For with what judgment ye judge, ye shall be judged: and with what measure ye mete, it shall be measured to you again.

1, 2. Make not yourselves judges of other men and their actions without a just call, and be not censorious meddlers, nor bold severe condemners of others without proof, and beyond cause. For otherwise, you must look for severe judgment from God, and to be repaid by man, and used as you used others.

3. And why beholdest thou the mote that is in thy brother's eye, but considerest not the beam that is in thine own eye? 4. Or how wilt thou say to thy brother, Let me pull out the mote out of thine eye; and behold, a beam is in thine own eye?

3, 4. So censorious are hypocrites, of others, that the mote of a small infirmity or dissent is seen in their eyes, as if it were some intolerable thing, which they must pluck out, (as the Pharisees censured Christ and his disciples for not observing their ceremonies and traditions.) But if thou know thyself, mayest thou not find worse than this in thyself? (Hath a Pharisee nothing worse than non-conformity to his ceremonies and traditions?) How canst thou think his mote of ceremonial, or small difference intolerable, while thou easily bearest thy own formality, magisterial pride, and worldly mind, and other great and deadly sins?

5. Thou hypocrite, first cast out the beam out of thine own eye; and then shalt thou see clearly to cast out the mote out of thy brother's eye?

5. Thou hypocrite, first see that thou have no greater fault thyself; cast away the beam of pride, worldliness, formality, malignity, and fleshly vice, out of thyself, and then thou wilt be more capable to judge of thy brother's failings, and fitter to reprove him.

6. Give not that which is holy unto the dogs, neither cast ye your pearls before swine, lest they trample them under their feet, and turn again and rend you.

6. And as it is not every one that is fit to reprove, so it is not every one that is fit to be reproved. Though to seek men's salvation by teaching and reproof, be a work of great moment, when it is used in season, to them that are capable of it; yet, take this rule: pretend not duty to teach and reprove when it is clearly like to do more hurt than good. Some men are hardened scorners, and some senseless neglecters, and some hateful persecutors. To such as those, holy counsel, doctrine, and reproof, is but like casting sacramental, or consecrated bread to the dogs, or pearls before swine. To be thus wise, and righteous overmuch, is but the way to perish and be rent, or at least made a scorn to beastly men. It is no duty where it is no means to good, yea, to greater good than hurt.

Note, Yet if a slothful hypocrite shall rashly censure others to be dogs and swine, and desperate, to excuse himself from duty and trouble, this is but a doubling of his sin.

7. Ask, and it shall be given you: seek, and ye shall find: knock, and it shall be opened unto you. 8. For every one that asketh, receiveth: and he that seeketh, findeth: and to him that knocketh, it shall be opened.

7. And to obtain grace and mercy to yourselves, true prayer is God's appointed means. Ask of God and he will give it you, seek diligently, and you shall find, &c For every one that asketh in sincerity, and seeketh with diligence and constancy, shall obtain.

Note. That is, if he pray to God, believing his power and goodness, in the name of Christ, and trusting in his merits and intercession, and this first and chiefly for God's glory, and for things spiritual and everlasting, and for earthly things as means to these, and if he be earnest, diligent, and constant in such askings, seekings, and knocking, he shall certainly have grace and glory, and all outward things so far as they are fit for him, and he for them.

9. Or what man is there of you, whom if his son ask bread, will he give him a stone? 10. Or if he ask a fish, will he give him a serpent? 11. If ye then being evil, know how to give good gifts unto your children, how much more shall your Father which is in heaven, give good things to them that ask him!

9, 10, 11. Do not distrust God's goodness and willingness to do good; all the love that is good in you, is but a spark from the God of infinite goodness. Therefore, if you would not give a stone to your children that ask bread of you, nor a serpent to that child that asketh a fish; and if you, that are so bad men, will give good things, and not evil to your children, O how much more abundantly should you believe your heavenly Father ready and willing to do good to his children, who ask it of him, being fitted to receive it.

12. Therefore all things whatsoever ye would that men should do to you, do ye even so to them; for this is the law and the prophets.

12. And as you may gather by your own love to your children what love God hath to you; so if you would have God over-rule the hearts and actions of men to love you and do you good, see that you first love them, and do them good, and that is the most probable way to obtain it. It is desirable that all men do use you with justice and charity: Do you therefore be sure so to use all men: (Not that a man who hurteth himself, or would have another hurt him by temptation or sin, may therefore hurt another. But) be more forward to do good, than to expect it from others; and put yourself in their case, and to do to them, whatever (prudently and justly) you would have them do to you, supposing their case and yours were exchanged.

13. Enter ye in at the strait gate; for wide is the gate, and broad is the way that leadeth to destruction, and many there be which go in thereat; 14. Because strait is the gate, and narrow is the way which leadeth unto life, and few there be that find it.

13, 14. And let not the straitness of the gate and way of life discourage you. The gate is wide, and the way is broad that leadeth to destruction: it is easy to please the flesh, and to neglect a holy life, and great is the multitude that go this way; but do not you follow the multitude in sin unto damnation. The entrance into a life of faith and holiness is strait, and the way is narrow, requiring self-denial, mortification, holy diligence, and patient suffering; and it is but few that find this way, and the life to which it leads. But life eternal cannot be too dearly obtained: therefore let no difficulties stop you or turn you off.

Note 1. It is because of our corrupt averseness (such as sick men have to a feast) and the restraints and sufferings of the flesh, that godliness or faith is called difficult or strait. But in itself, and to a sound understanding and will, it is the only pleasant life. To believe God's love, and our everlasting glory, must needs be sweeter than to live in guilt and terror, and in despair of any future happiness. 2. The gate, is the entrance by conversion into a life of faith and holiness as the way, and the devil, the world, and the flesh, will strive hard against both; but grace will conquer, and make all a delight. 3. Fewer turned Christians then, than did after Christ's ascension. But if most on earth perish, how little is the earth, to the vast and glorious regions of the blessed.

15. Beware of false prophets, which come to you in sheep's clothing, but inwardly they are ravening wolves. 16. Ye shall know them by their fruits. Do men gather grapes of thorns, or figs of thistles?

15, 16. And you must expect the temptation, of teachers falsely pretending divine inspiration and authority, they will come to you with enticing pretences, as speaking for God, for truth, for godliness, for your salvation, for order, peace, &c. but *mischief and hurtfulness is in their heart and design:* And if you think their pretences too hard for you to confute, look to the tendency and effects. Thorns and thistles prick and hurt, and grapes and figs are sweet and nourishing; if their *counsel* and their *practice* be *hurtful and destroying,* they are *wolves,* and not of God. Their bloody jaws and teeth will bewray them though in sheep's clothing. If they would draw you to wickedness, or turn you from a sober, just, and holy life, or if instead of *love,* and *peace,* and *doing good,* they are for hatred, contention, cruelty, oppression, unjust silencing, excommunicating, and persecuting, by these fruits you may know them.

Note, Though every cruel wicked man is not a false teacher, nor every man is not to be believed in *all his doctrines* who is *loving and godly;* Yet, 1. That doctrine that tendeth to do more hurt than good is naught. 2. And usually, God teacheth the meek, and loving, and holy persons all necessary truth, and forsaketh most, the understanding of the wicked, proud, and worldly, and though not mere ornamental accomplishment, yet the saving gifts of the Spirit go together: that is, illumination, and holy love, and obedience, and peace. And who can be confident that God's Spirit teacheth those men the truth above others, whom he never taught the known necessary duties of love, peace, justice, holiness, and temperance. When their lives tell us that they serve the devil, it is hard to believe that they are inspired of God as extraordinary men, though they may preach the truth for reputation and advantage.

17. Even so every good tree bringeth forth good fruit; but a corrupt tree bringeth forth evil fruit. 18. A good tree cannot bring forth evil fruit: neither can a corrupt tree bring forth good fruit. 19. Every tree that bringeth not forth good fruit, is hewn down and cast into the fire. 20. Wherefore by their fruits ye shall know them.

17—20. As the man is, so will he do. Therefore, by the badness of their fruit you may know that they speak not from the Spirit of God.

Note, 1. That Christ giveth us not this rule to know ordinary priests and preachers' doctrine by; for when rulers and countries own sound doctrine, wicked worldly men will own it for preferment and worldly ends. But it is to try *prophets* by, who pretend to the Spirit's inspiration: He that is not ruled by the Spirit is not like to be inspired by the Spirit. 2. And though this hold true as to all wickedness, yet the fruit that Christ specially meaneth is *hurtfulness;* as the names of wolves, thorns, and thistles, shew. 3. If a good man speak or do ill, it is because he is not perfectly good, but partly bad. For instance, the papal church pretendeth to the infallible guidance of the Spirit when pope and councils agree, which is, *to prophetical inspiration* beyond the *mere improvement of their own knowledge.* How shall we know whether their pretence be true? 1. We find that they cherish ignorance, by forbidding the reading the scripture in a known tongue without a licence, and praying in a tongue not understood. 2. We find that they divide the Christian world by laying its unity and peace on impossible terms, even a multitude of their own canons. 3. We find they are adversaries to catholic love, by damning all the Christian world save their own sect, and keeping up their church and religion by bloody doctrines, inquisitions, and massacres. 4. And that it is a worldly interest that is thus managed, these being all wolfish, thorny, hurtful fruits, disprove their pretence to the Spirit's infallibility. But it being their interest to be for the deity, christianity, and immortality of souls, in that they may own the truth. And if the reformed churches have had some errors, it is because they are but of imperfect knowledge and reformation.

21. Not every one that saith unto me, Lord, Lord, shall enter into the kingdom of heaven; but he that doeth the will of my Father which is in heaven.

21. It is not verbal professions, and pretending to the Spirit, or to be orthodox, or to be better than others, nor is it formal worshipping God as the hypocrites do, nor honouring him with the lips and knees alone, that will save any one, but it is only the holy obedient believer that shall be saved.

22. Many will say to me in that day, Lord, Lord, have we not prophesied in thy name? and in thy name have cast out devils? and in thy name done many wonderful works? 23. And then will I pro-

fess unto them, I never knew you; depart from me ye that work iniquity.

22, 23 Many will then plead not only that they were bishops or preachers in the church, but even that they prophesied, and wrought miracles in my name, to whom I will say, Depart from me all you that lived wickedly, whatever you said or did in my name, I never owned you, nor will I save you

24. Therefore, whosoever heareth these sayings of mine, and doeth them, I will liken him unto a wise man which built his house upon a rock: 25. And the rain descended, and the floods came, and the winds blew, and beat upon that house, and it fell not; for it was founded upon a rock.

24, 25. He that heareth, believeth, and obeyeth that which I have now taught you, is like a wise man, &c.
Note. The obedient believer is the only wise man, that buildeth the hopes of his salvation on a sure foundation.

26. And every one that heareth these sayings of mine, and doeth them not, shall be likened unto a foolish man which built his house upon the sand. 27. And the rain descended, and the floods came, and the winds blew, and beat upon that house; and it fell, and great was the fall of it.

26, 27. Note 1. Ungodly men, that hear Christ's gospel and obey it not, are fools, and build their hopes of salvation as on the sands. 2. All men's religion and hopes shall be tried, as a house by storms, whether it be well-founded and built or not. 3. Grievous will be the overthrow of the religious hopes of all hypocrites and ungodly livers.

28. And it came to pass, when Jesus had ended these sayings, the people were astonished at his doctrine. 29. For he taught them as one having authority, and not as the scribes.

28, 29. The hearers admired his doctrine, for he spoke not as the scribes and ordinary teachers, but as by prophetic authority, and the majestic power of the Spirit.

CHAP. VIII.

WHEN he was come down from the mountain, great multitudes followed him. 2. And behold, there came a leper and worshipped him, saying, Lord, if thou wilt, thou canst make me clean.

1, 2. Note, 1. A leprosy is so long and so visible a disease, as that there could be no fraud in the cure. 2. The belief of Christ's power shewed that he believed him to be sent of God; and therefore was an acceptable faith, though he doubted of Christ's will.

3. And Jesus put forth *his* hand, and touched him, saying, I will, be thou clean. And immediately his leprosy was cleansed.

3. Note, Christ shewed both *power* and *will* to cure him miraculously that believed his power.

4. And Jesus saith unto him, See thou tell no man, but go thy way, shew thyself to the priest, and offer the gift that Moses commanded, for a testimony unto them.

4. Do not thyself divulge this cure, but go shew the priest that thou art cleansed, and let him inquire if he will how it was done: perform thou thy offering according to the law, and let it stand as a testimony of me, whether they will use it or not.
Note, 1. Christ would have his miracles divulged but by degrees, and so himself made known; not all at first, but in due season, when it would do more good than hurt. Not to encourage men against him before the time: but when his greatest work is all done, might, set together, make a complete evidence.
2. Though the high-priest was no due successor of Aaron's line, but yearly brought in by heathen powers to him that purchased the place, and the office much corrupted, yet Christ bids the leper do his duty according to the law, to such as had possession.

5. And when Jesus was entered into Capernaum, there came unto him a centurion, beseeching him, 6. And saying, Lord, my servant lieth at home sick of the palsy, grievously tormented. 7. And Jesus saith unto him, I will come and heal him.

5, 6, 7. Note, This captain (of an hundred soldiers) shewed his faith by asking, and Christ promised a cure.

8. The centurion answered and said, Lord, I am not worthy that thou shouldst come under my roof: but speak the word only, and my servant shall be healed. 9. For I am a man under authority, having

soldiers under me; and I say to this *man*, Go, and he goeth; and to another, Come, and he cometh. And to my servant, Do this, and he doeth it.

8, 9. The captain said, &c. And if my soldiers and servants obey my words, 'It is easy with thee to command deliverance.

10. When Jesus heard it, he marvelled, and said to them that followed, Verily, I say unto you, I have not found so great faith, no, not in Israel.

10. At this Christ expressed admiration by the way of praise, saying, *I have not found so great faith* in any Israelites that waited for the Messiah, as in this Roman captain.

11. And I say unto you, that many shall come from the east and west, and shall sit down with Abraham, and Isaac, and Jacob, in the kingdom of heaven: 12. But the children of the kingdom shall be cast out into outer darkness; there shall be weeping and gnashing of teeth.

11, 12. I tell you that many of the Gentiles shall be converted, and from east and west shall be gathered into the church, and into the heavenly kingdom to Abraham, Isaac, and Jacob, whose faithful (though not natural) children they are reputed; when the Jews that are the natural seed, and thought that the promise had been only theirs, shall be cast out from heavenly felicity into outer darkness, and utmost misery; there shall be crying, and weeping, and gnashing of teeth, (as men do with cold, or with rage.)

13. And Jesus said unto the centurion, Go thy way, and as thou hast believed, so be it done unto thee. And his servant was healed in the self-same hour.

13. And Jesus gave him presently the reward of his faith, promising and performing the cure of his servant.

14. And when Jesus was come into Peter's house, he saw his wife's mother laid, and sick of a fever. 15. And he touched her hand, and the fever left her: and she arose and ministered unto them.

14. Note. The speed of the cure; she presently went about her business, and served them.

16. When the even was come, they brought unto him many that were possessed with devils; and he cast out the spirits with his word, and healed all that were sick:

16. Note, 1. The scripture doth not separate diseases and devils so much as they that think there is no devil in a disease that hath natural causes. For devils are often God's executioners, even when there are natural causes of the disease, and do add many extraordinary symptoms by their own operation. 2. Christ healed bodies to win souls, by such gifts as all are capable of valuing, and to shew his mercy to body and soul.

17. That it might be fulfilled which was spoken by Esaias the prophet, saying, Himself took our infirmities, and bare *our* sicknesses.

17. And as in Isa. liii. he is said to *take our infirmities* by suffering for our sins, the words may also be verified in another sense, even of his *compassion* and his *cure of men's diseases*.

18. Now when Jesus saw great multitudes about him, he gave commandment to depart unto the other side. 19. And a certain scribe came and said unto him, Master, I will follow thee whithersoever thou goest. 20. And Jesus saith unto him, The foxes have holes, and the birds of the air *have* nests; but the Son of Man hath not where to lay *his* head.

18, 19. 20. Note, That when Christ saw a man desirous to follow him, either for worldly ends, or with a mind not loosed from worldly interest, he trieth him, and turneth him off by undeceiving him.

21. And another of his disciples said unto him, Lord, suffer me first to go and bury my father. 22. But Jesus said unto him, Follow me, and let the dead bury their dead.

21, 22. Another whom Christ saw better resolved and qualified, he would not permit so much as to go home and bury his father, but using a proverbial speech saith, *Let the dead bury their dead;* that is, If thou be devoted to me, follow me, and my service, for this is now thy greatest business, to which burying thy father must not be preferred. Others that are not engaged as thou art, may bury thy father. If they would not, it were better he were unburied than thou, shouldst desert or neglect me and my service.

23. And when he was entered into a ship, his disciples followed him, 24. And behold, there arose a great tempest in the sea, insomuch

that the ship was covered with the waves; but he was asleep. 25. And his disciples came to him, and awoke him, saying, Lord, save us; we perish.

23, 24, 25. Note, The ship is safe where Christ is, though he seem asleep. 2. Yet dangers cast weak believers into fear.

26. And he saith unto them, Why are ye fearful, O ye of little faith? Then he arose and rebuked the winds, and the sea, and there was a great calm.

26. Great fears are the ordinary effects of sinful distrust, and the symptoms of but little faith. 2. Get Christ on our side, and he can command all the world to be for us, or not to hurt us.

27. But the men marvelled, saying, What manner of man is this, that even the winds and the sea obey him?

27. Note, 1. Christ's works proved that he was a Saviour fully to be trusted. 2. Do but obey Christ, and he will make all creatures obey him for your good and safety.

28. And when he was come to the other side into the country of the Gergesenes, there met him two possessed with devils, coming out of the tombs, exceeding fierce, so that no man might pass by that way.

28. That is, two that were mad and possessed, and acted by devils in their madness.

29. And behold, they cried out, saying, What have we to do with thee, Jesus, thou Son of God? art thou come hither to torment us before the time?

29. And the devils in them by the men's voice cried out, saying, Meddle not with us, Jesus, thou Son of God. Increase not our torments before the appointed time of their increase.

30. And there was a good way off from them, an herd of many swine, feeding. 31. So the devils besought him, saying, If thou cast us out, suffer us to go away into the herd of swine.

30, 31. And (many Gentiles dwelling there who kept swine, and perhaps some Jews, to sell, though they eat not swine's flesh) there was a great herd of swine; and the devils being a base sort of spirits, and bent to all mischief, craved leave, if they must be cast out, to go into the swine, partly to mischief them, and partly to discontent their owners.

32. And he said unto them, Go. And when they were come out, they went into the herd of swine; and behold, the whole herd of swine ran violently down a steep place into the sea, and perished in the waters.

32. That is, They were mad, and in madness ran into the sea and were drowned.

33. And they that kept them fled, and went their ways into the city, and told every thing, and what was befallen to the possessed of the devils. 34. And behold, the whole city came out to meet Jesus; and when they saw him, they besought him that he would depart out of their coasts.

33, 34. When they heard all this, the whole city was moved with a desire to see so strange a man. But the loss of their swine made them intreat him to be gone and leave their coasts.

CHAP. IX.

AND he entered into a ship, and passed over, and came into his own city. 2. And behold, they brought to him a man sick of the palsy, lying on a bed: and Jesus seeing their faith, said unto the sick of the palsy, Son, be of good cheer, thy sins be forgiven thee.

1, 2. That is, This disease which is the punishment of thy sin is remitted, and thou shalt be healed.

3. And behold, certain of the scribes said within themselves, This man blasphemeth. 4. And Jesus knowing their thoughts, said, Wherefore think ye evil in your hearts? 5. For whether is easier to say, Thy sins be forgiven thee? or to say, Arise and walk?

3, 4, 5. That is, What is forgiving the sin, but forgiving the punishment of it? And is one any harder than the other when it is the same thing.

6. But that ye may know that the Son of Man hath power on earth to forgive sins, (then saith he to the sick of the palsy) Arise, take

up thy bed, and go unto thine house. 7. And he arose and departed to his house.

6, 7. But your own senses shall tell you that I can forgive sin, that is, the punishment of sin on earth—Arise, &c so he was healed before them, and took up his bed and went home,

8. But when the multitude saw *it*, they marvelled, and glorified God which had given such power unto men.

8. It made them wonder and glorify God, that had sent a man with so great power into the world.

9. And as Jesus passed forth from thence, he saw a man named Matthew, sitting at the receipt of custom; and he saith unto him, Follow me. And he arose, and followed him.

9. Matthew that wrote this, a toll-gatherer: and at Christ's call, he immediately left all and followed him.

10. And it came to pass, as Jesus sat at meat in the house, behold, many publicans and sinners came and sat down with him and his disciples. 11. And when the Pharisees saw *it*, they said unto his disciples, Why eateth your master with publicans and sinners?

10, 11. Note, The Pharisees pretended greater strictness than Christ, in flying from other men as sinners. But they were not so strict in reforming themselves, nor zealous of love, and doing good.

12. But when Jesus heard *that*, he said unto them, They that be whole need not a physician, but they that are sick.

12. My work is to save souls; and who but sinners have need of a Saviour.

13. But go ye and learn what that meaneth, I will have mercy and not sacrifice: for I am not come to call the righteous, but sinners to repentance.

13. O ye that take on you to be the teachers of the ignorant, what great need have you to be taught, and to study what that saying meaneth, *I will have mercy and not sacrifice.* Mercy is a far greater and more pleasing work than sacrifice, ceremonies, or outward rites. And the greatest good is still to be preferred. Note, O how little do the Roman persecuting clergy regard this.

14. Then came to him the disciples of John, saying, Why do we and the Pharisees fast oft, but thy disciples fast not?

14. We and the Pharisees are stricter than thy disciples; we fast oft, and ye do not.

15. And Jesus said unto them, Can the children of the bridechamber mourn, as long as the bridegroom is with them? but the days will come when the bridegroom shall be taken from them, and then shall they fast.

15. The Messiah is the messenger of the greatest joy. It is a most joyful marriage-feast that I call them to; and that is not the season of fasting and mourning. But when I am taken from them, then fasting and patience in a malicious world will be more seasonable.

16. No man putteth a piece of new cloth unto an old garment; for that which is put in to fill it up, taketh from the garment, and the rent is made worse. 17. Neither do men put new wine into old bottles; else the bottles break, and the wine runneth out, and the bottles perish: but they put new wine into new bottles, and both are preserved.

16, 17. As a piece of new cloth put on a breach in an old worn garment, will but make it wider; and new wine put into old bottles will but break them and be spilt: s , if young disciples should be put upon religious exercises unsuitable to their condition, and unseasonable, it would do them hurt. And that which would hurt them by reason of their incapacity, is not to be put upon them.

Note, What their bottles were then made of that would not hold new wine when they were old, is uncertain. But it is likely they were made of the skins of goats or such creatures.

18. While he spake these things unto them, behold, there came a certain ruler and worshipped him, saying, My daughter is even now dead; but come and lay thy hand upon her, and she shall live.

18. A ruler of one of their lesser judicatures or consistories came, &c.

Note, This man did believe the power of Christ, because he had experience of his success; but whether he believed him to be the Christ is uncertain. But it was notable faith, to believe that he could raise the dead.

19. And Jesus arose and followed him, and *so did* his disciples.

CHAP. IX. ST. MATTHEW. 23

19. They were all desirous to go and see whether he could raise the dead.

20. (And behold, a woman which was diseased with an issue of blood twelve years, came behind *him,* and touched the hem of his garment. 21. For she said within herself, If I may but touch his garment, I shall be whole. 22. But Jesus turned him about, and when he saw her, he said, Daughter, be of good comfort; thy faith hath made thee whole. And the woman was made whole from that hour.)

20, 21, 22. Note, A belief of Christ's power was necessary to their receiving the effects of his power, as a belief of his love and good will is needful to our receiving the special fruits of his love; and the belief of his wisdom and authority is needful to our obeying him, and receiving his rewards.

23. And when Jesus came into the ruler's house, and saw the minstrels and the people making a noise, 24. He said unto them, Give place; for the maid is not dead, but sleepeth. And they laughed him to scorn.

23, 24. When he saw the music and stir that was made according to the custom about the dead, he said, Give place; for the death of the maid shall be but as a sleep, from which I will presently awake her, but they derided him, seeing that she was dead indeed.

25. But when the people were put forth, he went in, and took her by the hand, and the maid arose. 26. And the fame hereof went abroad into all that land.

25. Qu. Where was the soul of this maid (and Lazarus) after death? Answ. When God will tell us we shall know.

27. And when Jesus departed thence, two blind men followed him, crying, and saying, Thou Son of David, have mercy on us. 28. And when he was come into the house, the blind men came to him: And Jesus saith unto them, Believe ye that I am able to do this? they said unto him, Yea, Lord. 29. Then touched he their eyes, saying, According to your faith be it unto you. 30. And their eyes were opened.

27, &c. Note, These believed Christ to be the Messiah, though it is like they knew little of the nature of his office. Their faith was their capacity of a cure.

And Jesus straightly charged them saying, See that no man know *it.* 31. But they, when they were departed, spread abroad his fame in all that country.

30, 31. Note, Christ's command of silence was partly to give us an example of avoiding ostentation and hypocrisy, and to be content with the approbation of God alone.

32. As they went out, behold, they brought to him a dumb man possessed with a devil. 33. And when the devil was cast out, the dumb spake; and the multitudes marvelled, saying, It was never so seen in Israel.

32, 33. Note, His dumbness was caused by the devil's possession. And it is like he was mad also.

34. But the Pharisees said, He casteth out the devils through the prince of the devils.

34. Note, This was the blaspheming of the Holy Ghost; what can convince men who, when they see all this done, will say, The devil doth it? As if power, and love, and government were the devil's work. 2. This verse is out of some copies, but the same is in Matt. xii. The devils, it seems, have one monarch.

35. And Jesus went about all the cities and villages teaching in their synagogues, and preaching the gospel of the kingdom, and healing every sickness, and every disease among the people.

35. Note, 1. The gospel of the kingdom is the glad news that the kingdom of the Messiah was at hand, and what it was. 2. Had he separated from the synagogue manner of worship, they had not permitted him ordinarily to preach among them. 3. Christ that taught us to know false prophets by their hurtful fruits, (their malice, cruelty, persecuting, and hurtful doctrines) doth accordingly justify his own mission and doctrine, by *speaking* and *doing good,* all that he did being for men's own benefit; healing and saving souls and bodies. And the world will judge of men's pretences by their fruits, when persecutors have done their worst.

36. But when he saw the multitudes, he was moved with compassion on them, because they fainted and were scattered abroad, as sheep having no shepherd. 37. Then

saith he unto his disciples, The harvest truly *is* plenteous, but the labourers *are* few. 38. Pray ye therefore, the Lord of the harvest, that he will send forth labourers into his harvest.

36. Note, Christ's example teacheth preachers to compassionate a willing multitude when they want sufficient teachers; and to pray God to send forth more labourers, when there are too few; and not to give over labouring for them themselves, without being utterly disabled, though men forbid them. Some parishes in London have about 70,000 souls, some 60,000, some 30,000, and all the city and country and much more have but one bishop, (or pastor as some speak.) And the curates or preachers cannot be heard by above 3000 at once, or thereabouts.

CHAP. X.

AND when he had called unto him his twelve disciples, he gave them power *against* unclean spirits, to cast them out, and to heal all manner of sickness, and all manner of diseases.

1. And as he bid them pray for more labourers, accordingly he chose twelve, and gave them power to preach and to work miracles, and do good against devils and diseases, to confirm their words.

2. Now the names of the twelve apostles are these, The first, Simon, who is called Peter, and Andrew his brother, James *the son* of Zebedee, and John his brother. 3. Philip, and Bartholomew, Thomas, and Matthew the publican, James *the son* of Alpheus, and Lebbeus, whose surname was Thaddeus. 4. Simon the Canaanite, and Judas Iscariot, who also betrayed him. 5. These twelve Jesus sent forth, and commanded them, saying, Go not into the way of the Gentiles, and into *any* city of the Samaritans enter ye not. 6. But go, rather to the lost sheep of the house of Israel.

2, &c. Note, 1. Peter had a priority, though no government over the rest. 2. Lebbeus is Judas that wrote the epistle extant. 3. Simon is not called a Canaanite, as to nation, but his name signifieth, the Zealot, Luke xv. Acts i. 13. 4. Christ chose the twelve in respect to the twelve tribes of Israel, to whose service they were first confined. But when the Jews rejected him, and the Gentiles were to be called, he added Paul, to shew that he confined not the gospel to the Jews, but the church now must be catholic.

5. By the Samaritans is meant those that were not of Abraham's seed, but were sent thither at the translation in king Hosea's time. And by the Israelites is meant all Abraham's seed that were chiefly in Judea, but scattered also where the twelve tribes had lived.

7. And as ye go, preach, saying, The kingdom of heaven is at hand.

7. As ye go, Proclaim to them, that the kingdom of the Messiah whom God promised to send from heaven is now at hand. You may see the Christ so long expected.

8. Heal the sick, cleanse the lepers, raise the dead, cast out devils: freely ye have received, freely give.

8. I give you power to heal, &c. Doing good is your work. Do it freely, as freely I give it you.

9. Provide neither gold, nor silver, nor brass in your purses: 10. Nor scrip for your journey, neither two coats, neither shoes, nor yet staves; (for the workman is worthy of his meat.)

9. You go not on your own work but mine. Provide neither money, nor victuals for your journey, nor clothing as for long time to come, nor a defensive weapon or staff; but look for your maintenance for your work.

11. And into whatsoever city or town ye shall enter, inquire who in it is worthy, and there abide till ye go thence. 12. And when ye come into an house, salute it. 13. And if the house be worthy, let your peace come upon it; but if it be not worthy, let your peace return to you.

11, &c. Inquire who is a godly person, willingest to entertain the gospel. And when you come to any house say, Peace be to this house; that is, *God's blessing be here.* And if the persons be godly, and *truly qualified* for his blessing, it shall come upon them, else not, but you shall be clear. Note, 1. There is a worthiness consistent with free grace. 2. And a worthiness before their receiving of the gospel. This had two degrees, 1. The highest degree was true faith and godliness suited to that knowledge that the faithful had before Christ's incarnation: who were in a state of salvation, but yet had not the knowledge of the gospel, (fully so called) and that Jesus was the Christ. Such was Zachary and Elisabeth, and Nathanael, and the centurion, Acts x. &c. 2. And those that had but preparatory grace, or a teachable, tractable, willing disposition, were more worthy (or less unworthy) than the refractory.

2. Ministers being not heart-searchers, must

pronounce God's blessing on men on uncertainties and mere probability of the event. 3. This benediction hath ever a condition implied, if the person be worthy or capable of it. 4. If that person be unworthy and unblest, the minister is blameless, if he went according to probable profession: the fault was his own. 5. No ministerial blessing, (baptizing, the Lord's supper, absolution, &c.) will save an unworthy person, that is, one not qualified for salvation according to God's promise.

14. And whosoever shall not receive you, nor hear your words; when ye depart out of that house, or city, shake off the dust of your feet.

14. And seeing you come not for any gain of your own, but to bring them the joyful tidings of salvation, so heinous is the sin of unthankful, churlish refusal, that you shall shake off the dust of your feet, as signifying the labour you used in vain for their salvation, as a witness against them in time to come.

15. Verily I say unto you, It shall be more tolerable for the land of Sodom and Gomorrha, in the day of judgment, than for that city.

15. Note, 1. There are different degrees of punishment hereafter; some are more tolerable than others. 2. Sodom's punishment shall be less than the refusers of the gospel, because they sinned against less means, light, and mercies. False Christians then will have a heavy doom.

16. Behold, I send you forth as sheep in the midst of wolves; be ye therefore wise as serpents, and harmless as doves.

16. It is not a life of ease and worldly preferment, or man-pleasing that I send you on; but as sheep in the midst of many wolves; such enmity against the gospel and godliness is in the corrupt nature and interest of man, and specially of the obdurate, that instead of thankfully entertaining you and your message, they will tear and devour you, if God do not restrain them. Therefore be wise to carry yourselves inoffensively and cautiously, preserving yourselves by lawful means; but be ye harmless and innocent, that they may have no just accusation against you; and use no unlawful means. Sheep and doves are no good fighters against wolves and hawks.

17. But beware of men, for they will deliver you up to the councils, and they will scourge you in their synagogues. **18.** And ye shall be brought before governors and kings for my sake, for a testimony against them and the Gentiles.

17, 18. But keep out of their hands, (as I do) by just means. For the Jews will deliver you up to their councils of priests and elders, and they will scourge you as malefactors in their synagogues; and if they can make your crimes seem capital, they will deliver you up to the Roman power; that both Jews and Gentiles while you are accused, may hear from you what the gospel is, and be unexcusable in their sin.

19. But when they deliver you up, take no thought how or what ye shall speak, for it shall be given you in that same hour what ye shall speak. **20.** For it is not ye that speak, but the Spirit of your Father which speaketh in you.

19, 20. And let not your own slowness of speech put you on anxiety, (as it did Moses and Isaiah) for God's Spirit in you, will help you and teach you what and how to speak in season.

21. And the brother shall deliver up the brother to death, and the father the child: and the children shall rise up against *their* parents, and cause them to be put to death. **22.** And ye shall be hated of all men for my name's sake:

21, 22. So great is the enmity of the flesh against the spirit, and against faith and holiness, that it will overcome even natural affection of brethren and parents, and children, so that they shall bring their nearest relations to martyrdom and other sufferings. And the world will hate you for my sake.

But he that endureth to the end, shall be saved.

22. But he that overcometh all these trials, and holds out in faith and patience to the end, shall be saved.

23. But when they persecute you in this city, flee ye into another: for verily I say unto you, ye shall not have gone over the cities of Israel, till the Son of Man be come.

23. But it is your duty so far to preserve yourselves for further service, as to flee from persecutors, to go preach elsewhere, (so it be not when you have any greater obligation to the contrary than your lives be worth.) And I tell you, you shall not have gone over all the cities in Israel in the performance of this work that I lay upon you, till they shall see the Messiah in his own person, openly owning his office, and preaching to them, as such, himself.

Note. This hard text is variously expounded. 1. Some say, that the Romans' destruction of Jerusalem is Christ's coming here meant. 2. Others say, that it is his coming by Constantine's conversion to set up christianity in power and honour, and that the meaning is, that the cities of Judea shall not be all converted till then. 3. Others say, it is Christ's coming to judgment, or, say others, to call the Jews at his personal reign, till when they will not be generally converted. 4. It seems to me more probable that it is his own open declaring himself to be the Christ, and that his kingdom is come. For 1. He yet preached but much like John, that the kingdom of God (the Messiah) is at hand. 2. And he did not yet bring his own disciples to confess it, it being after extorted from Peter, Matt. xvi. and he highly praised for confessing him. 3. And he forbade Peter, and those he healed, and the very devils to confess him. 4. So that properly, his kingdom began at his exaltation, even his resurrection, ascension, and sending down the Spirit. 5. There is another exposition of some that think he meant, Though I send you from me now, let not my absence discourage you; I will be with you again, before you have gone over all the cities: As if he spake of their return to him at their next meeting.

24. The disciple is not above *his* master, nor the servant above his lord. 25. It is enough for the disciple that he be as his master, and the servant as his lord: if they have called the master of the house Beelzebub, how much more *shall they call* them of his household?

24, 25. You are not greater or better than I; it is enough if you be used but as I am. If they say that I work by Beelzebub, what words, or false accusations are so bad which you may not expect that are my followers.

26. Fear them not therefore: for there is nothing covered that shall not be revealed, and hid, that shall not be known.

26. Therefore, fear not their false accusations, or their threats, for there is nothing now covered with false, pretences, reasonings, or slanders, which shall not be uncovered, and truly opened: and not any thing hidden by fraud or force, which shall not be made known.

27. What I tell you in darkness, *that* speak ye in light: and what ye hear in the ear, *that* preach ye upon the house tops.

27. What I speak to you alone, or in parables, that publish fearlessly to all the world.

28. And fear not them which kill the body, but are not able to kill the soul: but rather fear him which is able to destroy both soul and body in hell.

28. Your bodies are mortal, and must die, and God may suffer men to kill them. But fear not men that can do no more, nor can kill or undo the soul that is immortal. But fear God and offend not him, who can destroy both body and soul in hell.

29. Are not two sparrows sold for a farthing? and one of them shall not fall on the ground without your Father. 30. But the very hairs of your head are all numbered.

29, 30. If God's providence dispose of the least motions and events of the least of his creatures, such as a poor sparrow is, will he not take care of you that are his children. Yea, he regardeth every hair of your heads, how much more your lives and souls.

31. Fear ye not, therefore, ye are of more value than many sparrows.

31. Trust God and fear not men. For he that made you better than sparrows, will regard you accordingly.

32. Whosoever, therefore, shall confess me before men, him will I confess also before my Father which is in heaven. 33. But whosoever shall deny me before men, him will I also deny before my Father which is in heaven.

32, 33. Note, 1. By confessing Christ is meant, open owning him as our Lord and Saviour, whatever we suffer by it. 2. To be owned by God through Christ our advocate, is the great interest that we should first secure.

34. Think not that I am come to send peace on earth: I came not to send peace, but a sword. 35. For I am come to set a man at variance against his father, and the daughter against her mother, and the daughter-in-law against her mother-in-law. 36. And a man's foes *shall be* they of his own household.

34, 35, 36. Think not that the coming of the Messiah is to settle Israel in power, and bring all nations to subjection or peaceable confederacy with them, and to set my disciples in a state of prosperity: you must expect the contrary, that by owning me and my doctrine, your very friends and kindred will turn your enemies, parents and children will hate and persecute you, and out of your own houses will arise your most dangerous enemies.

37. He that loveth father or mother more than me, is not worthy of me: and he that loveth son or daughter more than me, is not worthy of me.

37. And let not this turn you off. For if you love father or mother, son or daughter, more than me, and would forsake me rather than be forsaken or persecuted by them, you are not capable of being my true disciples such as I will save.

38. And he that taketh not his cross and followeth after me, is not worthy of me.

38. And he that, if he be put to it, will not follow me under the cross, and suffer a shameful death rather than deny me, or forsake faith and godliness, is not a true Christian, nor qualified for salvation; nor will I own him in the day of judgment.

39. He that findeth his life shall lose it: and he that loseth his life for my sake shall find it.

39. He that will save his life by denying me, or by any sin, shall lose it, for he shall lose everlasting life, and shall die as well as others, and perhaps as soon. And he that is put to death for faith and righteousness, hath not lost his life, when as death is but a passage to life everlasting.

40. He that receiveth you, receiveth me; and he that receiveth me, receiveth him that sent me.

40. And seeing you are my messengers, and your commission shall be sealed by the convincing evidence of the miraculous and sanctifying operations of the Holy Ghost, I will own you in all that you say, do, or suffer according to your commission, and will reward them that receive you and your words, as if they received me myself, (for I am not to stay on earth to do all my work myself, but will do it by my ministers.) And he that receiveth me shall be accepted by my Father, as if he had received him.

Note. As this is a most strong and comfortable obligation to the receiving of Christ's true ministers, so it is a dreadful profaneness to hear a proud, domineering enemy of godliness, that hath got by force into the title of the ministry, and labours to make true godliness odious, and persecuteth the most faithful, to plead this text, as if he that heard and received their malignant scorns of piety, did hear and receive Jesus Christ.

41. He that receiveth a prophet in the name of a prophet, shall receive a prophet's reward; and he that receiveth a righteous man, in the name of a righteous man, shall receive a righteous man's reward.

41. Note, 1. This tells us that God rewardeth not men according to their gifts, but according to the will and heart. And it is a great comfort to every ungifted and poor inferior Christian, that they may have the reward of preachers, if they do but receive them, and further their works as they are able; yea, if they do but love them, and would receive them if they could, God taketh it as done.

2. But by the same reward is meant the same in kind but not in degree.

3. And by a righteous man, is meant an eminent godly man, and that he that loveth such and entertaineth them, shall be numbered with the truly righteous. But it meaneth not that every wicked liver shall speed as the righteous, if he will but receive such, though be amend not himself. But he that loveth a good man because he is such, and sheweth by receiving him, though to his cost and danger, that his love is sincere, shall be numbered with such himself.

42. And whosoever shall give to drink unto one of these little ones, a cup of cold water only, in the name of a disciple, verily, I say unto you, he shall in no wise lose his reward.

42. He that loveth a Christian as such, more than his riches, and would give him more if he had it, if he give but a cup of cold water, to the poorest, weakest Christian, because he is a Christian, shall not lose the reward that I here promise.

Note, 1. What a safe way of usury hath Christ taught all believers? He is an unbeliever who thinks he shall be a loser by any obedience to Christ.

2. It is not the rich only that shall have the reward of charity, but the poor also that do their best, and would give if they were able.

3. It is not only charity to preachers and rare persons, but to the least Christians that Christ will reward.

4. Therefore it is not only slandering, reviling, and persecuting the eminent servants of Christ, but even the little ones, and weak Christians, that Christ will condemn. And it will be a miserable pretence, to say they were erroneous, or faulty, (perhaps for dissenting from the dictates of usurpers) as if any men were free from all error.

CHAP. XI.

AND it came to pass, when Jesus had made an end of commanding his twelve disciples, he departed thence to teach and to preach in their cities.

1. Having given his twelve disciples their instructions, he went about also to preach himself.

2. Now when John had heard in the prison the works of Christ, he sent two of his disciples, 3. And said unto him, Art thou he that should come, or do we look for another?

2, 3. Note, It is doubtful whether (John being in prison and not seeing Jesus) the meaning be, Art thou the same Jesus that I baptized, &c. Or, (as is more likely) that he sent his disciples that they might be convinced by more than John's testimony.

4. Jesus answered and said unto them, Go and shew John again those things which ye do hear and

see: 5. The blind receive their sight, and the lame walk, the lepers are cleansed, and the deaf hear, the dead are raised up, and the poor have the gospel preached to them. 6. And blessed is he whosoever shall not be offended in me.

4, 5, 6. It is not my bare word, but my works that shall answer you; it is by the fruit that the tree must be known. The miraculous works of divine power are done, and the works of love to men's bodies, and the gospel of salvation is preached for their souls. And these being God's works, are God's testimony what I am. And yet the meanness of my appearance, and my contempt and suffering from men, will be to many a stumbling-block, and make the work of believing difficult, and blessed are they that believe notwithstanding all these difficulties.

7. And as they departed, Jesus began to say unto the multitudes concerning John, What went ye out into the wilderness to see? A reed shaken with the wind? 8. But what went ye out for to see? A man clothed in soft raiment? behold, they that wear soft clothing are in king's houses. 9. But what went ye out for to see? A prophet? yea, I say unto you, and more than a prophet.

7, 8, 9. Jesus took this occasion to describe John to the people, saying, What went you to John in the wilderness to see? not a toy like a shaken reed? Nor yet a pompous gallant in gay clothes? such be not in wildernesses, but in kings' houses: you will say, A prophet? Yes, and greater than any foregoing prophets. A nearer messenger of the kingdom of God.

10. For this is he of whom it is written, Behold, I send my messenger before thy face, which shall prepare thy way before thee.

10. For this is the harbinger of the Messiah, promised by other prophets.

11. Verily I say unto you, among them that are born of women, there hath not risen a greater than John the Baptist: notwithstanding, the least in the kingdom of heaven is greater than he.

11. There hath not been a greater than John before him, as being nearest the kingdom of the Messiah. But yet, the least of my ministers in this my kingdom, is greater than he, and shall have more eminent gifts of the Spirit, as well as a more excellent office and work; so far shall my kingdom, begun after my ascension, excel all ages that were before it.

12. And from the days of John the Baptist until now, the kingdom of heaven suffereth violence, and the violent take it by force.

12. And as the people crowded to John in the wilderness, and now as you see flock after me, so since John began to preach, I may say, that these multitudes of inferior people, crowd as it were into the kingdom of heaven, and will not lose it, while it is neglected by the higher sort.

13. For all the prophets, and the law prophesied until John. 14. And if ye will receive *it*, this is Elias which was for to come. 15. He that hath ears to hear, let him hear.

13, 14, 15. The law and the prophets till John indeed foretold the Messiah; but not so determinately and nearly as John did. And if you can receive it, I tell you, John is that Elias that Malachi foretold should go before to prepare the way to Christ. The belief of this is of great moment to your faith.

16. But whereunto shall I liken this generation? It is like unto children sitting in the markets, and calling unto their fellows, 17. And saying, We have piped unto you, and ye have not danced: we have mourned unto you, and ye have not lamented.

16, 17. But the unbelievers of this generation, do as children in their games, complain of one another; you will neither dance when we pipe, nor lament when we mourn to you; you are cross to us whatever game we play.

18. For John came neither eating or drinking, and they say, He hath a devil. 19. The Son of Man came eating and drinking, and they say, Behold a man gluttonous, and a wine bibber, a friend of publicans and sinners: but wisdom is justified of her children.

18, 19. John lived austerely on locusts and wild honey, and they took him for a possessed madman. And of me that exercise no such unusual austerity of diet, but mere temperance, they say, I am a gluttonous man, and a lover of wine. No innocency will suffice to escape the false censures of malignants. But the sons of wisdom will justify it.

20. Then began he to upbraid

the cities wherein most of his mighty works were done, because they repented not. 21. Woe unto thee Chorazin, woe unto thee Bethsaida; for if the mighty works which were done in you, had been done in Tyre and Sidon, they would have repented long ago in sackcloth and ashes. 22. But I say unto you, It shall be more tolerable for Tyre and Sidon at the day of judgment, than for you.

20, 21, 22. Note. 1. Christ's own preaching and miracles had so little success, as that he is put to upbraid the places where he had wrought them, for their impenitence. Therefore the best preachers may be put to the like. 2. The punishment of such as are unconverted under the most convincing preaching, will be most intolerable. 3. Though it be God's grace which converteth souls, yet he usually so proportioneth it to the means he useth, that the same means ordinarily would convert some, which converts not others.

23. And thou Capernaum which art exalted unto heaven, shall be brought down to hell: for if the mighty works, which have been done in thee, had been done in Sodom, it would have remained until this day. 24. But I say unto you, that it shall be more tolerable for the land of Sodom, in the day of judgment than for thee.

23, 24. Thou Capernaum, where I have dwelt, hast by my presence, preaching, and works been honoured with the heavenly gifts; but for impenitence shalt be destroyed. If Sodom had seen and heard what thou hast, their repentance would have prevented their destruction. But their doom at the day of judgment shall be more tolerable than thine.

25. At that time Jesus answered and said, I thank thee, O Father, Lord of heaven and earth, because thou hast hid these things from the wise and prudent, and hast revealed them unto babes. 26. Even so, Father, for so it seemed good in thy sight.

25, 26. Then Jesus said to God his Father, I thank thee, O Father, who being Lord of heaven and earth, hath the absolute right to dispose of all, that thou hast chosen the despised unlearned sort of men to make known effectually the gospel of salvation to, rather than the men of reputation for learning and wisdom in the world, and hast left proud, self-conceited men in their ignorance,

whilst thou hast taught the humble and meek. This pleaseth me, as being the choice and good pleasure of thy wisdom.

27. All things are delivered unto me of my Father: and no man knoweth the Son but the Father: neither knoweth any man the Father save the Son, and he to whomsoever the Son will reveal *him*.

27. All things are delivered by the Father to me, upon my right of redemption, in order to the ends of my saving office; so that I am (under the divine nature) even in my humanity, made the universal *owner, ruler,* and *benefactor.* And as none can comprehend the mystery of my person, office, and works, save the Father that sent me, so none can savingly know God the Father, but the Son, and he to whom the Son will make him known, by the gospel and the illumination of the Spirit.

28. Come unto me all ye that labour and are heavy-laden, and I will give you rest. 29. Take my yoke upon you, and learn of me, for I am meek and lowly in heart; and ye shall find rest unto your souls. 30. For my yoke is easy, and my burden is light.

28, 29, 30. Come to me all ye that are under the slavery of sin and Satan, and under God's displeasure by your guilt, and under the burdensome ceremonies and cursing law, and the Pharisees' tutorage, and under the toil of a poor afflicted condition in the world; and I will give you deliverance and rest. Take on you the yoke of my government and covenant, and learn of me as your teacher by my doctrine and example; for I am meek and lowly, and my doctrines are not suited to the pomp and grandeur of this world, nor to the interest and mind of the proud and covetous, but to men of a low and humble quality; and in this you shall find rest to your tired, troubled, fearful souls. For my service and law is gracious, and easy, fitted to the relief of the guilty and distressed, and all that I lay on you by my word and works is light, in comparison of the heavy burdens that you undergo.

CHAP. XII.

AT that time Jesus went on the sabbath-day through the corn, and his disciples were an hungred, and began to pluck the ears of corn, and to eat.

Note. Both the labour, and the early eating seem here meant, but specially the first.

2. But when the Pharisees saw *it*, they said unto him, Behold, thy

disciples do that which is not lawful to do upon the sabbath-day.

2. Art thou a good teacher who sufferest thy disciples to break God's law?

Note, That the Pharisees controversy against Christ was, that he was not religious, and strict enough in keeping God's law; so that pretended strictness is no proof that men are in the right.

3. But he said unto them, Have ye not read what David did when he was an hungred, and they that were with him. 4. How he entered into the house of God, and did eat the shew-bread, which was not lawful for him to eat, neither for them which were with him, but only for the priests? 5. Or, have ye not read in the law, how that on the sabbath-days the priests in the temple profane the sabbath, and are blameless?

3, 4, 5. Your strictness and your accusation of my disciples, are but from your ignorance of the scripture. Have ye not read that hunger justified David and his company for eating the consecrated bread, which else none but the priests might lawfully eat. And that the priests in the temple labour on the sabbath, and break the outward rest of the day, which would be profanation, did not the temple service justify it.

6. But I say unto you, that in this place is *one* greater than the temple.

6. But if the temple service can justify labour, I am greater than the temple, and my service and authority can justify it.

7. But if ye had known what this meaneth, I will have mercy, and not sacrifice, ye would not have condemned the guiltless.

7. If instead of ignorant preciseness for ceremonies, you had but learnt the true meaning of God, in his preferring mercy before sacrifice, you would not have thought that ceremonies and externals are commanded men for their hurt, and must be observed against mercy to ourselves or others. God's commands are all for man's good; and he maketh not externals and ceremonies for a snare to hurt men. You would not have censured the guiltless as sinners, had you understood this.

Note, This (twice repeated) most openly condemneth the papal church-government.

8. For the Son of Man is Lord even of the sabbath-day.

8. And as Moses's law was but to lead men to Christ, in whom it is fulfilled; so it cannot bind any against him and his authority and saving work; for which work's sake, all things are delivered into his hands; even the law and sabbath, of which he is Lord.

9. And when he was departed thence, he went into their synagogue. 10. And behold, there was a man which had *his* hand withered; and they asked him, saying, Is it lawful to heal on the sabbath-days? that they might accuse him.

9, 10. Note, That the ceremonial outward strictness of hypocrites, is used to ensnare and hurt those that are not of their mind.

11. And he said unto them, What man shall there be among you, that shall have one sheep, and if it fall into a pit on the sabbath-day, will he not lay hold on it, and lift *it* out?

11. Will you not draw a sheep out of a pit on the sabbath-day, if you have but one.

12. How much then is a man better than a sheep? wherefore it is lawful to do well on the sabbath-days.

12. It is lawful to prefer and do a greater duty before a less.

13. Then saith he to the man, Stretch forth thine hand; and he stretched *it* forth; and *it* was restored whole, like as the other. 14. Then the Pharisees went out, and held a council against him, how they might destroy him.

13, 14. Note, That it is part of the religion of hypocrites, to destroy men for doing the greatest good, against their laws.

15. But when Jesus knew *it*, he withdrew himself from thence, and great multitudes followed him, and he healed them all. 16. And charged them that they should not make him known.

15, 16. Note, 1. It is a duty to avoid the hands of murderers and persecutors, unless when our sufferings are like to do more good than our lives. 2. Christ forbid them making him known, partly to avoid the envy and rage of persecutors, and partly because the time was not yet come, till all his works set together with his resurrection and Spirit, should make up a full proof.

17. That it might be fulfilled which was spoken by Esaias the prophet, saying, 18. Behold my servant whom I have chosen, my

beloved in whom my soul is well-pleased: I will put my Spirit upon him, and he shall shew judgment to the Gentiles. 19. He shall not strive nor cry, neither shall any man hear his voice in the streets. 20. A bruised reed shall he not break, and smoking flax shall he not quench, till he send forth judgment unto victory. 21. And in his name shall the Gentiles trust.

17, &c. In all this he fulfilled what was prophesied by Isaiah, Behold, &c. Him whom I have selected for this work of salvation, in whom I am well pleased, as fulfilling all my will. 'He shall have the fulness of the Spirit, and he shall teach the nations the way of truth and righteousness. He shall not subdue men by tumults, violence, or wars, but as the Prince of peace and grace, he shall deal gently with the weak, and cherish the least degree of goodness, and pardon the faults of the penitent, and not use severity of justice, till he have gathered his church out of the world, and overcome and judged his final enemies. And it is he in whom all nations shall be blessed.

22. Then was brought unto him one possessed with a devil, blind and dumb, and he healed him, insomuch that the blind and dumb both spake and saw. 23. And all the people were amazed, and said, Is not this the Son of David?

22, 23. This people were so astonished to see his works, that they said, Sure this is the Messiah, the Son of David.

24. But when the Pharisees heard it, they said, This *fellow* doth not cast out devils, but by Beelzebub the prince of the devils. 25. And Jesus knew their thoughts, and said unto them, Every kingdom divided against itself, is brought to desolation: and every city or house divided against itself, shall not stand. 26. And if Satan cast out Satan, he is divided against himself; how then shall his kingdom stand.

24, &c. The Pharisees could not deny the matter of fact, it being notorious, and therefore they had no shift left for their unbelief, but saying, that, *All such works are not of God*. The prince *of devils, to deceive the people, giveth him power to cast out devils, and do his miracles*. But Christ said, If the devil have a kingdom, he hath wit to preserve it. Is it the devil's work to do good to men's souls and bodies? If holy doctrine, and casting out devils, and healing the diseased, be against Satan, and his kingdom, then he is against himself, if he be the author of it. Kingdom, city, or house will not stand if it be divided and fight against itself.

27. And if I by Beelzebub cast out devils, by whom do your children cast *them* out? therefore they shall be your judges. 28. But if I cast out devils by the Spirit of God, then the kingdom of God is come unto you.

27, 28. And if you think me a conjurer, and confederate with Satan, what say you of your own countrymen my disciples, who cast them out by the power they receive from me? Are they all conjurers too. Therefore they shall be witness against your unbelief and blasphemy. But if all this be certainly done by me, by no less power than the Spirit of God, you should see that this is God's attestation to me, and that his kingdom is come, in which the Messiah is to conquer Satan, and destroy his works.

29. Or else, how can one enter into a strong man's house, and spoil his goods, except he first bind the strong man? and then he will spoil his house.

29. How could I cast out Satan from his possession and destroy his works, if I did not overcome him.

30. He that is not with me, is against me: and he that gathereth not with me, scattereth abroad.

30. So far am I from working by the devil, that I take him for my enemy that doth not serve me in my opposition to his kingdom, and will judge him as one that is for Satan.

Note, In war men used to say of their own soldiers, [*He that is not for us, is against us*, and to be counted an enemy;] But of the *countrymen* and the enemies quarters, [*He that is not against us is for us*;] that is, If he do us no harm he doth us good, and let us use him kindly. So Christ saith of *profest Christians*; if they be not effectually for me, I will judge them as treacherous and against me, and shall not save them. But of those *without the church*, he saith, He that is not against us is for us; that is, though he be not himself in a state of salvation as true Christians are, yet it is commendable to do us no harm, and the church is assisted by such fair and moderate unbelievers.

31. Wherefore I say unto you, All manner of sin and blasphemy shall be forgiven unto men: but the blasphemy *against* the Holy Ghost shall not be forgiven unto men. 32. And whosoever speaketh a word against the Son of Man, it

shall be forgiven him: but whosoever speaketh against the Holy Ghost, it shall not be forgiven him, neither in this world, neither in the *world* to come.

31, 32. All other sin and blasphemy against me, as I appear in my human nature, hath some excuse, and may be cured, and so be pardoned; but seeing the great works of the Holy Ghost done by me, and to be done by my disciples, in miracles and sanctification, are the greatest evidences that God will give the world to convince them of the truth of my gospel; he that is convinced of the fact that all these miracles and this holiness is wrought, and will yet deny it to be God's attestation, and blasphemously stand to it, that it is the work of the devil, this man rejecteth the greatest evidence, and shall have no greater, and so his infidelity is incurable, and aggravated with blasphemy and obstinacy, and will never be repented of, nor forgiven.

Note, This blaspheming the Holy Ghost, 1. Is the sin of none but resolved infidels. 2. And such of them only as are convinced of the great works of the Holy Ghost, miraculous and others. 3. And yet rather than they will believe in Christ, by this divine testimony, will believe and say, that it is by the devil and conjuration that all this is done.

See my treatise of the blasphemy of the Holy Ghost, in my book called, *The Unreasonableness of Infidelity.*

33. Either make the tree good, and his fruit good; or else make the tree corrupt, and his fruit corrupt; for the tree is known by *his* fruit.

33. Judge of the tree by the fruit: of the power which I work by, by the works. If it be no good work to heal the sick, and blind, and lame, and cast out devils, and preach repentance and forgiveness of sin, to convert and save souls, then God is not the author of them. If they be bad works, they have a bad cause; if they be good works, they have a good author: either say plainly (you that ascribe them to the devil) that the works are good, and the devil is good; or else that the devil is bad, and the works are bad; or if you confess the works to be good, confess that they are done by the Spirit of God.

34. O generation of vipers, how can ye, being evil, speak good things? for out of the abundance of the heart the mouth speaketh.

34. I need go no further for an instance than yourselves; were you not a generation of vipers, the serpent's seed, ye would not blaspheme the Holy Ghost and his works: for your mouths speak out of the evil of which your heart is full. As you are, so you speak; you are so bad, that you cannot speak well. And if I worked by the devil, my works would be bad as the devil is.

35. A good man out of the good treasure of the heart, bringeth forth good things: and an evil man out of the evil treasure bringeth forth evil things.

35. Good men are such, first at the heart, where goodness is a settled habit and nature, and out of this treasure they bring forth good words and deeds. And a bad man, being such at heart, doth speak and do accordingly.

Note, Though hypocrites may have words and deeds much better than their hearts, that is, but in some by-instances, and not in the tenor of their lives. Fictions are narrow and soon overcome.

36. But I say unto you, That every idle word that men shall speak, they shall give account thereof in the day of judgment.

36. And think not lightly of your belying and blaspheming the Holy Ghost; for I tell you, that for every lie you shall give account in the day of judgment, and be condemned, if you be not proved penitent believers.

Note. In the Hebrews' use, ' idle' and ' vain.' were taken for deceitful, false, or lying.

37. For by thy words thou shalt be justified, and by thy words thou shalt be condemned.

37. For (though thou must be made and accounted by God, a just man, by thy inward change, and forgiveness, in order before thy words or works, yet) supposing, that thou survive, God who hath made a law for thy words (and works) will judge thee by that law, as justified and rewardable, or as unjust and punishable in the day of judgment. Christ hath not made us lawless, nor made us a law (of grace) in vain. No man shall be saved that is not justifiable against the accusation, that *he lived and died an impenitent ungodly man*, any more than if he had died an infidel.

38. Then certain of the Scribes, and of the Pharisees answered, saying, Master, we would see a sign from thee.

38. We would see some certain sign from heaven, that indeed God doth own thee and thy word.

39. But he answered and said to them, An evil and adulterous generation seeketh after a sign, and there shall no sign be given to it, but the sign of the prophet Jonas. 40. For as Jonas was three days and three nights in the whale's belly: so shall the Son of Man be three days and three nights in the heart of the earth.

39, 40. A false-hearted people that will not be

convinced by miracles, but ascribe them to the devil, yet would have a sign from heaven of their own chusing. But God will not gratify their insolent demand; they shall have no sign but that of Jonas, who was a type of me, lying in the whale's belly three days and nights (as I shall, part of three days).

41. The men of Nineveh shall rise in judgment with this generation, and shall condemn it, because they repented at the preaching of Jonas, and behold, a greater than Jonas *is* here. 42. The queen of the south shall rise up in judgment with this generation, and shall condemn it, for she came from the uttermost parts of the earth to hear the wisdom of Solomon, and behold, a greater than Solomon *is* here.

41, 42. Nineveh repented at a far less warning and convincing means, than the miracles and words of the Messiah sent from heaven. And the queen of the south came from a far land to hear the wisdom of Solomon; but these men despise a far greater than Solomon; these therefore shall condemn them.

43. When the unclean spirit is gone out of a man, he walketh through dry places, seeking rest, and findeth none. 44. Then he saith, I will return into my house from whence I came out, and when he is come, he findeth *it* empty, swept, and garnished. 45. Then goeth he, and taketh with himself seven other spirits more wicked than himself, and they enter in and dwell there; and the last state of that man is worse than the first. Even so shall it be also unto this wicked generation.

45, &c. The case of this wicked generation is like that of a man that had the devil cast out of him, but being unthankful, and continuing in his sin, the devil (by God's permission) possesseth him again, and bringeth with him seven worse spirits, and so his end is worse than he was before he was delivered. So I have preached the gospel, and cast out devils in this land; but being rejected by the obstinate unbelievers, the devil will get a worse possession of them than that from which I did eject him, and they shall be cut off for their unbelief.

46. While he yet talked to the people, behold, his mother and his brethren stood without, desiring to speak with him. 47. Then one

said unto him, Behold, thy mother and thy brethren stand without desiring to speak with thee. 48. But he answered and said unto him that told him, Who is my mother? and who are my brethren?

46, &c. Dost thou know who they be that I esteem as my mother and brethren?

49. And he stretched forth his hand towards his disciples, and said, Behold my mother, and my brethren. 50. For whosoever shall do the will of my Father which is in heaven, the same is my brother, and sister, and mother.

49, 50. Note, 1. Christ spake not this to teach men to dishonour parents, or to lay by natural affection; but to let all know, that regeneration puts men into a more honourable, beloved, and happy relation to him, than natural generation or kindred; 2. Which is exceeding comfort for every true Christian, 3. And direction to us how to love such. 4. And a terrible prognostic of the misery of those that hate and persecute them.

CHAP. XIII.

THE same day went Jesus out of the house, and sat by the sea side. 2. And great multitudes were gathered together unto him, *so* that he went into a ship, and sat, and the whole multitude stood on the shore. 3. And he spake many things unto them in parables, saying, Behold, a sower went forth to sow.

1, 2, 3. Note, Christ thought a ship, or a house, or a mountain, no unmeet place to preach in, and yet avoided not the temple or synagogues. 2. They that will have the word with God's blessing, must follow after it. 3. Similitudes were suitable to such learners. 4. Preaching is like sowing seed.

4. And when he sowed, some *seeds* fell by the way-side, and the fowls came and devoured them up. 5. Some fell upon stony places, where they had not much earth; and forthwith they sprung up, because they had no deepness of earth; 6. And when the sun was up, they were scorched; and because they had not root, they withered away. 7. And some fell among thorns; and the thorns sprung up and chok-

ed them. 8. But other fell into good ground, and brought forth fruit, some an hundred fold, some sixty fold, some thirty fold. 9. who hath ears to hear, let him hear.

4, &c. Note, The first sort was not earthed. The second sort had little earth and rooting. The third sort had earth and root, but among thorns, which had greater possession, and choked it. Of so great weight is it to understand this difference of hearers, that it is as much as our ears and understandings are worth.

10. And the disciples came and said unto him, Why speakest thou unto them in parables? 11. He answered and said unto them, Because it is given unto you to know the mysteries of the kingdom of heaven, but to them it is not given.

10, 11. Because though God hath given you some knowledge already of the mysteries of the kingdom of the Messiah, these men are ignorant like children, and must be taught by familiar similitudes accordingly, being yet incapable of other manner of teaching.

12. For whosoever hath, to him shall be given, and he shall have more abundance: but whosoever hath not, from him shall be taken away, even that he hath.

12. For here it is true, that *to him that hath shall be given, &c.* He that hath already the understanding of the rudiments and fundamentals, is thereby capable of receiving and understanding more: one truth openeth the way unto another. But they that have no considerable knowledge, are hardly taught it, and if it be by their wilful neglect or contempt, are like by their guilt and folly to lose all the profitable use even of their reason.

13. Therefore speak I to them in parables: because, they seeing, see not: and hearing, they hear not, neither do they understand. 14. And in them is fulfilled the prophecy of Esaias, which saith, By hearing ye shall hear, and shall not understand: and seeing, ye shall see, and shall not perceive. 15. For this people's heart is waxed gross, and their ears are dull of hearing, and their eyes they have closed, lest at any time they should see with *their* eyes, and hear with *their* ears, and should understand with *their* heart: and should be converted, and I should heal them.

13, &c. I speak to them in similitudes, as children must be first taught to spell, because, though they have understanding, eyes, and ears, they are so ignorant, that they understand not even what eyes, and ears, and reason tell them. As the prophet Isaiah saith, &c. This people by wilful neglect of knowledge are such, as will not understand even what they hear and see; for their hearts are stupified, and their understanding so dull, and they have so sinfully shut their own eyes, for want of care and love to truth, that thus they keep out the knowledge of the gospel, and shut out my offered grace, which else would convince and convert them, and they would be healed.

Note, 1. That the way of *parables* is not mentioned as an obscure way to hide the truth: but as a low familiar way, as ignorant carnal men are capable of. 2. The prophecy, nor Christ, means not that it is God's intent to hide the truth lest it convert men, but that this is the effect and event of their own wilful neglect, whereby their conversion is as effectually hindered, as if they did it purposely, lest they should be converted.

16. But blessed *are* your eyes, for they see; and your ears for they hear. 17. For verily, I say unto you, that many prophets and righteous men have desired to see those things which ye see, and have not seen *them:* and to hear those things which ye hear, and have not heard *them.*

16, 17. How great is God's mercy to you, that hath given you both teaching and understanding, by which you are made capable of more. I tell you, prophets and righteous men of old, did desire to see and hear what you do, but it was not granted them, but reserved for you.

18. Hear ye, therefore, the parable of the sower. 19. When any one heareth the word of the kingdom, and understandeth *it* not, then cometh the wicked one, and catcheth away that which was sown in his heart: this is he which received seed by the ways-side.

18, 19. Note, 1. By not understanding is meant also, Not considering it to take it in. 2. It is said to be *sown in his heart,* only because it was by the sower so intended, but not as there received.

20. But he that received the seed into stony places, the same is he that heareth the word, and anon with joy receiveth it: 21. Yet hath he not root in himself, but dureth

for a while: for when tribulation or persecution ariseth because of the word, by and by he is offended.

20, 21. Note, That the reason why such fall away, was the want of rooting of the word, is plain. But whether such should be saved if they had died before they fell away, is a controversy too long to be here handled, and not so needful as some think.

22. He also that received seed among the thorns, is he that heareth the word: and the care of this world, and the deceitfulness of riches choke the word, and he becometh unfruitful.

22. That is, He loveth the wealth and prosperity of this world more than the word, and so that which he most loveth doth prevail against the other, and he liveth more to the world than unto God; and for the world will forsake his duty, and Christ himself in strong temptations.

23. But he that received seed into the good ground, is he that beareth the word, and understandeth it, which also beareth fruit, and bringth forth some an hundred fold, some sixty, some thirty.

23. Note, Qu. What is it that makes the ground called good, before the receiving of the word? Answ. 1. There was a certain degree of faith which was a state of salvation before Christ was personally known or preached as incarnate: These persons that had this, were good ground, ready to hear the gospel when it was preached: Those that truly repented according to John's preaching, were prepared to receive Christ. 2. And those that faithfully obey that light of truth already revealed to them, desiring more, are better prepared for more, than other men.

24. Another parable put he forth unto them, saying, The kingdom of heaven is likened unto a man which sowed good seed in his field: 25. But while men slept, his enemy came and sowed tares among the wheat, and went his way.

24, 25. Another similitude he used, to shew how the church will be corrupted with heresies and vices.

26. But when the blade was sprung up, and brought forth fruit, then appeared the tares also.

26. Note, Heresies and church-corruptions appear not at first; but when time and temptation ripen them.

27. So the servants of the householder came, and said unto him, Sir, didst not thou sow good seed in thy field? from whence then hath it tares?

27. Note, Seeing God and his word are good, it puzzleth men to think, how the church and world come to be so bad.

28. He said unto them, an enemy hath done this. The servants said unto him, Wilt thou then that we go and gather them up? 29. But he said, Nay, lest while ye gather up the tares, ye root up also the wheat with them.

28, 29. Note, 1. Satan is the sower of heresy and vice (whoever be his ministers.) 2. Ministers and others are more inclined to vindictive severity oft than Christ is. 3. God forbeareth the hypocrites and wicked (not through indifference but) lest the godly suffer by their destruction. 4. Christ oft denieth the revengeful and severe desires of his servants.

30. Let both grow together until the harvest, and in the time of harvest I will say to the reapers, Gather ye together first the tares, and bind them in bundles to burn them: but gather the wheat into my barn.

30. Note, 1. God's delay to execute his judgment on the wicked, is no sign of their safety; their misery will surely come at last. 2. We must not misinterpret God's patience with the ungodly.

31. Another parable put he forth unto them, saying, The kingdom of heaven is like to a grain of mustard seed, which a man took and sowed in his field. 32. Which indeed is the least of all seeds: but when it is grown, it is the greatest among herbs, and becometh a tree: so that the birds of the air come and lodge in the branches thereof.

31. As a grain of mustard-seed is one of the smallest sort of seeds, and yet becometh a plant like a tree, &c. so the kingdom of the Messiah beginneth in a few poor men, but shall become a kingdom that shall flourish in the world, so that worldly men shall obtrude into it for worldly ends, and desire the protection of Christian governors.
Note, That the mustard-plant was much greater in Judea than it is with us.

33. Another parable spake he unto them, The kingdom of heaven

is like unto leaven, which a woman took and hid in three measures of meal, till the whole was leavened.

33. As a little leaven doth leaven a great quantity of meal: so the gospel shall convert a few at first, where it comes, and afterward, by the help of those few, whole towns and countries shall turn Christians, and own the truth.

34. All these things spake Jesus unto the multitude in parables, and without a parable spake he not unto them: 35. That it might be fulfilled which was spoken by the prophet, saying, I will open my mouth in parables, I will utter things which have been kept secret from the foundation of the world.

34, 35. Thus Jesus taught them only by similitudes, as it is written, &c. I will utter great and excellent mysteries, which former ages have not known, and that by the way of familiar similitudes.

36. Then Jesus sent the multitude away, and went into the house: and his disciples came unto him, saying, Declare unto us the parable of the tares of the field.

36. Note. It is the part of learners, to ask their teachers help, to understand that which they understand not.

37. He answered and said unto them, He that soweth the good seed, is the Son of Man: 38. The field is the world: the good seed are the children of the kingdom: but the tares are the children of the wicked one: 39. The enemy that sowed them, is the devil: the harvest is the end of the world: and the reapers are the angels.

37, &c. It is Christ that soweth the good seed, by preaching the gospel and planting the churches by himself and his servants. The world is the first object of the gospel preached, and out of which believers are gathered: The good seed, (as sown, is the gospel, but) as springing up in fruit are the faithful, who are properly the members of the church of Christ: The tares, (as sown, are evil doctrines and temptations, but) as sprung up in fruit, are the children of the devil, who is the father of wickedness: The enemy of God, and goodness, and man, that sowed them, by himself and his servants, signifieth the devil: the time of harvest, is the end of this world, even the day of judgment: The reapers, or executioners are the angels.

40. As therefore the tares are gathered and burnt in the fire, so shall it be in the end of this world. 41. The Son of Man shall send forth his angels, and they shall gather out of his kingdom all things that offend, and them which do iniquity: 42. And shall cast them into a furnace of fire; there shall be wailing and gnashing of teeth.

40, &c. So in the end of this world: Christ shall send forth his angels as his executing ministers; and they shall gather out of the world (which he is over) and specially out of the visible church, all rebellious, unholy, wicked, scandalous, carnal men, and shall cast them into hell, which is likened to a lake of fire; where they shall live in torment, and a self-afflicting conscience.

43. Then shall the righteous shine forth as the sun, in the kingdom of their Father. Who hath ears to hear, let him hear.

43. Then shall the righteous, who are now obscured by infirmities and malignant slanders, and are oppressed in the world, shine forth in glory in the kingdom of love, even of God as their father in Christ, as the sun shineth in the heavens in resplendent glory. As ever you will use your ears or understandings, believe and foresee this glorious blessed day to believers.

44. Again, the kingdom of heaven is like unto treasure hid in a field: the which, when a man hath found, he hideth, and for joy thereof goeth and selleth all that he hath, and buyeth that field.

44. The way of salvation by Christ, sheweth men the certain hopes of so inestimable a treasure in the life to come, as maketh the faithful choose it for their best, and part with all their pleasure, profit, and honour of the world to obtain it.

45. Again, the kingdom of heaven is like unto a merchant-man, seeking goodly pearls: 46. Who, when he had found one pearl of great price, he went and sold all that he had, and bought it.

45, 46. Note, He that findeth not by faith, enough in the love of God and heavenly glory, and in Christ the way thereto, to make him consent sincerely and practically, to sell or part with all the world rather than lose it, is not capable of a just title to it, nor shall obtain it.

47. Again, the kingdom of heaven is like unto a net that was cast into the sea, and gathered of every kind. 48. Which, when it was full, they drew to shore, and sat down,

and gathered the good into vessels, but cast the bad away.

47, 48. The church is gathered, as men by casting a net into the sea gather fishes, good and bad. And at the day of judgment, Christ will take the good to heaven, and cast away the bad to hell.

Note, 1. It is not to be wondered at, that the visible church hath good and bad. 2. Yet this is not the design of the gospel, which is fitted to make all men good, but by the intrusion of hypocrites. Nor is it an excuse for the neglect of discipline, and the just discrimination of the good and bad.

49. So shall it be at the end of the world: the angels shall come forth, and sever the wicked from amongst the just. 50. And shall cast them into the furnace of fire; there shall be wailing and gnashing of teeth.

49, 50. These plain and dreadful words, more need belief and deep consideration, than exposition.

51. Jesus saith unto them, Have ye understood all these things? They say unto him, Yea, Lord. 52. Then said he unto them, Therefore every scribe which is instructed unto the kingdom of heaven, is like unto a man that is an householder, which bringeth forth out of his treasure, things new and old.

51, 52. All that are furnished with holy knowledge, and are fitted to teach others, must have an habitual treasure of it in their minds, from whence they may be able to open the truth, exhort, reprove, and confute all the erroneous, on all just occasions: as a housekeeper is stocked for the provision of his family.

53. And it came to pass, that when Jesus had finished these parables, he departed thence. 54. And when he was come into his own country, he taught them in their synagogue, insomuch, that they were astonished, and said, Whence hath this man this wisdom, and these mighty works? 55. Is not this the carpenter's son? is not his mother called Mary? and his brethren James, and Joses, and Simon, and Judas? 56. And his sisters, are they not all with us? whence then hath this man all these things?

53, &c. Note, 1. Familiarity breeds contempt. It is no impediment to our faith, that we saw not Christ's person, parentage, and education. 2. Carnal men are not satisfied by the evidence of divine attestation, unless they can give a reason of it, and overcome the difficulty and scandal of objections. 3. It is uncertain whether Mary had other children after Jesus, or these were his brethren, or only his kindred.

57. And they were offended in him. But Jesus said unto them, A prophet is not without honour, save in his own country, and in his own house. 58. And he did not many mighty works there, because of their unbelief.

57, 58. Unbelief made men uncapable receivers of those miracles which else Christ would have wrought.

CHAP. XIV.

AT that time, Herod the tetrarch heard of the fame of Jesus, 2. And said to his servants, This is John the Baptist, he is risen from the dead, and therefore mighty works do shew forth themselves in him.

1, 2. Note, That Herod did believe the immortality of the soul; else he could not have believed John's resurrection.

3. For Herod had laid hold on John, and bound him, and put *him* in prison for Herodias' sake, his brother Philip's wife. 4. For John said unto him, It is not lawful for thee to have her. 5. And when he would have put him to death, he feared the multitude, because they counted him a prophet.

3, 4, 5. Note, 1. Faithful prophets did tell kings of their sin. 2. But such as Herod cannot bear reproof. 3. The persecution of faithful teachers is usually for telling great men of their sins. 4. The multitude then did so much reverence prophets, that they were a terror and restraint to persecuting rulers.

6. But when Herod's birth-day was kept, the daughter of Herodias danced before them, and pleased Herod. 7. Whereupon he promised with an oath, to give her whatsoever she should ask. 8. And she being before instructed of her mother, said, Give me here John Baptist's head in a charger.

6, 7, 8. Note, Great men's feasts and frolics, are

ST. MATTHEW.   CHAP. XIV.

a usual season of great sin, and carnal pleasures are their snares. 2. Rash oaths are the fruit of vice, and the seed of more. 3. Voluptuous wantons are oft the most cruel and bloody persecutors. 4. The devil seldom wanteth suggestors of cruelty.

9. And the king was sorry: nevertheless for the oath's sake, and them which sat with him at meat, he commanded *it* to be given *her*.

9. Note, 1. Wicked men oft sin with troubled conscience: but yet will do it for their base ends. 2. Hypocrites that dare murder the just, yet may make the conscience of a wicked oath their pretence. (How conscionably then should bad oaths be avoided, and good ones kept!) 3. The reputation of men in bad company, is a usual snare of iniquity.

10. And he sent and beheaded John in prison. 11. And his head was brought in a charger, and given to the damsel: and she brought *it* to her mother. 12. And his disciples came, and took up the body and buried it, and went and told Jesus.

10, 11, 12. Note, The blood of saints is vile and cheap to tyrants, that can sell them to a whore or wanton; but they shall pay dear for it at the last. 2. So great a prophet as John must be a martyr, that he may be like to Christ. 3. It is as true martyrdom to suffer for duty as for faith. 4. The blood of saints is part of the sport and pleasure of lascivious wicked women.

13. When Jesus heard of *it*, he departed thence by ship into a desert place apart: and when the people had heard *thereof*, they followed him on foot out of the cities

13. Note, 1. The Lord of life, that came in flesh to save the world, was fain to fly for his life into a wilderness from the face of men, yea, of the eminent members of the Jewish church. 2. It is not cowardice, or unlawful to fly from persecutors, till we have some special call to suffer.

14. And Jesus went forth, and saw a great multitude, and was moved with compassion towards them, and he healed their sick.

14. Note, Those that follow Christ and seek to him, are liker to find his compassion, than those that drive him away.

15. And when it was evening, his disciples came to him, saying, This is a desert place, and the time is now past: send the multitude away, that they may go into the villages, and buy themselves victuals. 16. But Jesus said unto them, They need not depart, give ye them to eat. 17. And they say unto him, We have here but five loaves, and two fishes. 18. He said, Bring them hither to me. 19. And he commanded the multitude to sit down on the grass, and took the five loaves, and the two fishes, and looking up to heaven, he blessed, and brake, and gave the loaves to his disciples, and the disciples to the multitude.

15, &c. Note, 1. Christ fed the body to win the soul, and so must we. 2 Nothing is too little which God will bless. 3. Though God be every where, yet Christ directeth us in prayer to him, to look up to heaven; for there is the glory in which he will appear to glorify his people. 4. If the Son of God must look up to heaven, and bless his food, surely we must not take it like brutes, without craving God's blessing on it.

20. And they did all eat, and were filled: and they took up of the fragments that remained, twelve baskets full. 21. And they that had eaten were about five thousand men, beside women and children:

20, 21. Note, 1. This miracle was done before five thousand witnesses and more, that there might be no suspicion of deceit, or misreport. 2. He that was Lord of all, and could feed by miracle, yet would not have the fragments lost.

22. And straightway Jesus constrained his disciples to get into a ship, and to go before him unto the other side, while he sent the multitudes away. 23. And when he had sent the multitudes away, he went up into a mountain apart, to pray: and when the evening was come, he was there alone.

22, 23. Note, Christ used to pray alone, because his case so differed from all men's in the world, (having no sin, &c.) that the same prayers would not suit the case of others, which were fit for him.

24. But the ship was now in the midst of the sea, tossed with waves: for the wind was contrary. 25. And in the fourth watch of the night, Jesus went unto them walking on the sea.

CHAP. XV. ST. MATTHEW. 39

24, 25. Note, 1. Christ permits dangers to us, that he may the more notably deliver us. 2. The waters can bear him, when he will walk on them. All elements are at his service.

26. And when the disciples saw him walking on the sea, they were troubled, saying, It is a spirit: and they cried out for fear.

26. Note, Nature maketh man afraid of apparitions of spirits, because unknown and unusual.

27. But straightway Jesus spake unto them, saying, Be of good cheer, It is I, be not afraid.

27. Note, Christ's true disciples should be so far from being afraid of him, as hurtful to them, that they should make him their comfort and courage against the fears of men and devils.

28. And Peter answered him, and said, Lord, if it be thou, bid me come unto thee on the water.

28. Note, This shewed much faith in Peter. Yet none must tempt God, nor go unbidden into danger.

29. And he said, Come. And when Peter was come down out of the ship, he walked on the water to go to Jesus. 30. But when he saw the wind boisterous, he was afraid: and beginning to sink, he cried, saying, Lord, save me. 31. And immediately Jesus stretched forth *his* hand, and caught him, and said unto him, O thou of little faith, wherefore didst thou doubt?

29, &c. Note, 1. Even strong faith hath its weakness, and is liable to fears. 2. Our weak faith causing great fear, would expose us to sinking, did not Christ lay hold on us.

32. And when they were come into the ship, the wind ceased. 33. Then they that were in the ship, came and worshipped him, saying, Of a truth thou art the Son of God.

32, 33. Note, Renewed great convictions renew and increase the exercise of faith, and praise to Christ.

34. And when they were gone over, they came into the land of Genesaret. 35. And when the men of that place had knowledge of him, they sent out into all that country round about, and brought unto him all that were diseased, 36. And besought him, that they might only touch the hem of his garment, and as many as touched, were made perfectly whole.

34, &c. Note, What great cause have we to trust a Saviour so able and willing to save body and soul, and to believe his word!

CHAP. XV.

THEN came to Jesus, Scribes and Pharisees, which were of Jerusalem, saying, 2. Why do thy disciples transgress the tradition of the elders? for they wash not their hands when they eat bread.

1, 2. Note, Poor souls that know not God, do take up with ceremonies of their own and their forefathers' making, and put the name of religion on these to cheat themselves, when such things are not so much as an image of true religion. O what base thoughts have these men of God, who think he is pleased or displeased with men, as they keep or neglect such trifles.

3. But he answered, and said unto them, Why do you also transgress the commandment of God by your tradition?

3. Note, The rebels that break God's laws by their laws, yet charge God's servants with sin, for not keeping their laws and traditions against God's laws: they think God's laws too many and too strict, and yet make more of their own, and are precise for keeping them.

4. For God commanded, saying, Honour thy father and mother: and he that curseth father or mother, let him die the death. 5. But ye say, Whosoever shall say to *his* father or *his* mother, *It is* a gift by whatsoever thou mightest be profited by me, 6. And honour not his father or his mother, *he shall be free.* Thus have ye made the commandment of God of none effect by your tradition.

4, 5, 6. God's command to honour parents binds you to relieve them, if they be in want: and duty to parents is so great, that contempt of them deserves death. But ye have like hypocrites got a trick to pretend to devote your estates to God, that you may defeat your parents, and so quite frustrate God's commandment.

7. Ye hypocrites, well did Esaias prophesy of you, saying, 8. This people draweth nigh unto me with

their mouth, and honoureth me with their lips: but their heart is far from me. 9. But in vain they do worship me, teaching for doctrines the commandments of men.

7, 8, 9. Note, 1. It is the part of hypocrites to pretend religion for lip labour, and traditions and ceremonies of their own, and think God is honoured and pleased with the injunctions and canons of men, while they break God's commands (and hate and persecute those that keep them.) 2. This human religion of hypocrites is vain, (and worse than vain:) It is lost labour, and sinful profanation.

10. And he called the multitude, and said unto them, Hear and understand. 11. Not that which goeth into the mouth defileth a man; but that which cometh out of the mouth, this defileth a man.

10, 11. It is not the quality or uncleanness of your food, that is sin and foul defilement; but it is sinful words (and deeds) the product of sinful hearts, that God will charge on you as your uncleanness.

12. Then came his disciples, and said unto him, Knowest thou that the Pharisees were offended after they heard this saying?

12. Note, Erroneous men and hypocrites are offended at the clearest truth, which crosseth their odd opinions and way.

13. But he answered and said, Every plant which my heavenly Father hath not planted, shall be rooted up. 14. Let them alone: they be blind leaders of the blind. And if the blind lead the blind, both shall fall into the ditch.

13, 14. Their opinions and traditions, and their sect in making a religion of these, are not of God, but of their own invention, and therefore God will root them up. God will not bless human religions. Let them alone awhile; their judgment is near. They and their disciples, as blind leaders and followers, will fall into the ditch of temporal and eternal perdition.

15. Then answered Peter and said unto him, Declare unto us this parable. 16. And Jesus said, Are ye also yet without understanding? 17. Do not ye yet understand, that whatsoever entereth in at the mouth goeth into the belly, and is cast out into the draught. 18. But those things which proceed out of the mouth, cometh forth from the heart, and they defile the man.

15, &c. Meat that passeth through a man cannot defile his soul: but it is the product of a sinful heart that defiles it.

19. For out of the heart proceed evil thoughts, murders, adulteries, fornications, thefts, false witness, blasphemies. 20. These are the things which defile a man: but to eat with unwashen hands, defileth not a man.

19, 20. It is out of a sinful heart that all sins proceed, as evil thoughts and designs, &c.
Note, The heart itself is not here excluded from guilt, but included as the defiled and defiling cause of all actual sin.

21. Then Jesus went thence, and departed into the coasts of Tyre and Sidon. 22. And behold, a woman of Canaan came out of the same coasts, and cried unto him, saying, Have mercy on me, O Lord, thou Son of David, my daughter is grievously vexed with a devil.

21, 22. Then he went to the borders of Israel near the heathen country, and a heathen Canaanitish, or Syrophoenician woman hearing of his fame, went to him, and begged of him to heal her daughter vexed with a devil.

23. But he answered her not a word. And his disciples came, and besought him, saying, Send her away, for she crieth after us. 24. But he answered and said, I am not sent, but unto the lost sheep of the house of Israel.

23, 24. Dismiss her, that she trouble us not. He said, My personal ministry is to be to the straying Jews, and not to the heathens.

25. Then came she, and worshipped him, saying, Lord, help me. 26. But he answered and said, It is not meet to take the children's bread, and to cast it to the dogs. 27. And she said, Truth, Lord: yet the dogs eat of the crumbs which fall from their master's table.

25, &c. To give that which it designed for Israel to heathens, is but like casting the children's bread to dogs. She said, It is true, Lord: and I confess myself to be but as one of the dogs, and claim not the children's portion; but if I have a dogs, the crumbs that fall, they will have never the less.

28. Then Jesus answered and said unto her, O woman, great *is* thy faith: be it unto thee even as thou wilt. And her daughter was made whole from that very hour.

28. Note. Great faith maketh men capable of great mercies, even of having what they justly desire.

29. And Jesus departed from thence, and came nigh unto the sea of Galilee, and went up into a mountain, and sat down there. 30. And great multitudes came unto him, having with them those that were lame, blind, dumb, maimed, and many others, and cast them down at Jesus' feet, and he healed them:

29, 30. Note, How earnestly will men seek for bodily health, who are senseless of their souls' concerns. If Christ's ministers could give all men health and wealth, what abundance of followers would they have, and who would for this, imprison, persecute, or silence them?

31. Insomuch, that the multitude wondered when they saw the dumb to speak, the maimed to be whole, the lame to walk, and the blind to see: and they glorified the God of Israel.

31. Note, Great and sensible miracles and benefits force men to acknowledge the hand of God, and to praise him.

32. Then Jesus called his disciples unto him, and said, I have compassion on the multitude, because they continue with me now three days, and have nothing to eat: and I will not send them away fasting, lest they faint in the way. 33. And his disciples say unto him, Whence should we have so much bread in the wilderness, as to fill so great a multitude? 34. And Jesus saith unto them, How many loaves have ye? and they said, seven, and a few little fishes. 35. And he commanded the multitude to sit down on the ground. 36. And he took the seven loaves and the fishes, and gave thanks, and brake them, and gave to his disciples, and the disciples to the multitude. 37. And they did all eat, and were filled; and they took up of the broken meat that was left, seven baskets full. 38. And they that did eat, were four thousand men, beside women and children. 39. And he sent away the multitude, and took ship, and came into the coasts of Magdala.

32, &c. This was the second miracle of compassionate feeding the hungry. Is not Christ in heaven as merciful and sufficient for soul and body, as he was on earth?

CHAP. XVI.

THE Pharisees also with the Sadducees, came, and tempting, desired him that he would shew them a sign from heaven.

1. Not believing the reports of all his miracles, they desired that they themselves might see some sign from heaven, which might certainly prove that God had sent him: thinking that he could not do it.

2. He answered and said unto them, When it is evening ye say, *It will be* fair weather; for the sky is red. 3. And in the morning, *It will be* foul weather to day, for the sky is red and louring. O *ye* hypocrites, ye can discern the face of the sky, but can ye not *discern* the signs of the times?

2, 3. You can conjecture what weather will be by the sky. And is it to you so hard a matter to know by my doctrine and all the miracles and good works that I have done, that I am sent of God, that you must prescribe what signs God shall shew you from heaven, before you will believe.

4. A wicked and adulterous generation seeketh after a sign, and there shall no sign be given unto it, but the sign of the prophet Jonas; and he left them, and departed.

4. When your own wickedness hindereth your belief, you call for a sign from heaven to convince you. But I again tell you, you shall have no sign but that of the prophet Jonah. He that is filthy, let him be filthy still.

5. And when his disciples were come to the other side, they had for-

gotten to take bread. 6. Then Jesus said unto them, Take heed, and beware of the leaven of the Pharisees, and of the Sadducees.

5, 6. Note, Christ doth not bid them to avoid all converse with these men, or not to hear them read the law of Moses, but to take heed of receiving any of their false doctrine.

7. And they reasoned among themselves, saying, *It is* because we have taken no bread, 8. *Which* when Jesus perceived, he said unto them, O ye of little faith, why reason ye among yourselves, because ye have brought no bread: 9. Do ye not yet understand, neither remember the five loaves of the five thousand, and how many baskets ye took up? 10. Neither the seven loaves of the four thousand, and how many baskets ye took up? 11. How is it that ye do not understand, that I speak it not to you concerning bread, that ye should beware of the leaven of the Pharisees, and Sadducees? 12. Then understood they how that he bade them not beware of the leaven of bread, but of the doctrine of the Pharisees, and of the Sadducees.

7, &c. We are dull of understanding till Christ instruct us, and apt to put a carnal sense upon his words.

13. When Jesus came into the coasts of Cesarea Philippi, he asked his disciples, saying, Whom do men say, that I, the Son of man, am?

13. Note, Christ would not so much as urge his own disciples to confess him to be the Christ, till his works were a cogent testimony; that their faith might not be precarious, nor by bare command, but by convincing evidence.

14. And they said, Some *say that thou* art John the Baptist, some Elias, and others Jeremias, or one of the prophets.

14. Note, 1. Men were convinced that he was of God, (that is, the multitude, but not the rulers.) But they thought he was not the Messiah, but some great prophet's soul in a new body. 2. By this it is evident, that the multitude then believed the immortality of the soul: else they could not think that those souls came into other bodies.

15. He saith unto them, But whom say ye that I am? 16. And Simon Peter answered and said, Thou art Christ, the son of the living God.

15,16. Note, 1. It was meet, that those that were to preach Christ to others, should be brought to an open confession of him themselves. 2. It is like the rest believed as Peter, though he only spake.

17. And Jesus answered and said unto him, Blessed art thou Simon Bar-jona: for flesh and blood hath not revealed *it* unto thee, but my Father which *is* in heaven.

17. It is a point of so great importance to sanctification, justification, and salvation, verily to believe me to be the Christ and Saviour, that this faith is the evidence and means of thy blessedness. It is not mere man that hath revealed this, so as to make thee a true believer, but my heavenly Father, by my works and word, and by his grace.

18. And I say also unto thee, that thou art Peter, and upon this rock I will build my church: and the gates of hell shall not prevail against it.

18. And as thou hast confessed me to be Christ, I will say to thy comfort, that as thy name signifieth a rock or stone, so by thee (and thy brethren) I will build my Church on this Rock, against which all the powers of hell, the devil, and wicked men shall not prevail.

Note, 1. It is a great controversy whether by [*this* Rock] be meant, 1. Christ himself, 2. or the faith and confession of Christ, 3. Or Peter himself. But no doctrinal controversy dependeth on it: For all three are certain truths. 1. No doubt but primarily Christ is the Rock on which the church is built. 2. And no doubt but *faith* and *confession* being the condition of our part in Christ, the church is so far built thereon. 3. And no doubt but the Apostles are called foundation-stones on which the church is built, and therefore Peter, whose name importeth it, and was a chief speaker among them, as the foreman of a jury. 4. Though the powers of hell may seem to prevail, as they did over Christ, while he was on the cross, they are then next an overthrow themselves.

19. And I will give unto thee the keys of the kingdom of heaven: and whatsoever thou shalt bind on earth, shall be bound in heaven; and whatsoever thou shalt loose on earth, shall be loosed in heaven.

19. And hereafter I will make thee a ruling steward over my church, as it is God's kingdom on earth, preparatory to the heavenly kingdom of glory: and the due administration of thy office by these keys of power, shall be the ordinary

way to heaven, and a forerunner of the final justification of the faithful, and of the final condemnation of the impenitent and ungodly, whom by my doctrine and the due application of it, thou bindest over to my judgment.

Note, As Peter was the foreman or speaker in their common confession, so by Peter the promise is made to them all. And to them all Christ after gave this power. But he never made Peter governor of the rest of the apostles, much less the Pope.

20. Then charged he his disciples that they should tell no man that he was Jesus the Christ.

20. Note, Because this honour was reserved chiefly, 1. To the time of the accomplishment of all the evidences by his resurrection and ascension, and giving of the Holy Ghost. 2. And to the work of the Spirit then on the apostles, by which they were suddenly advanced to a fitness for this work, above what they attained by Christ's personal teaching them on earth.

21. From that time forth began Jesus to shew unto his disciples, how that he must go unto Jerusalem, and suffer many things of the elders, and chief priests, and scribes, and be killed, and be raised again the third day.

21. Note, 1. This Christ did, 1. To make them know that he knew things to come. 2. And to make them know that it was not to reign as an earthly king that he was sent. 3. And to prepare them to bear his sufferings, and not to expect fleshly prosperity by him. 4. It was the poor that followed Christ, and the rulers and teachers that crucified him.

22. Then Peter took him, and began to rebuke him, saying, be it far from thee, Lord: this shall not be unto thee.

22. Peter contradicted him, saying, God forbid; Lord favour thyself, and expose not thyself to this.

Note, 1. The flesh is ready to suggest fleshly counsel, and to oppose all that tends to suffering. 2. We have need to be fortified against temptations of loving friends as well as enemies.

23. But he turned and said unto Peter, Get thee behind me Satan, thou art an offence unto me; for thou savourest not the things that be of God, but those that be of men.

23. He looked at him with displeasure, and said to Peter, I say to thee as I said to the devil when he tempted me, Get thee behind me, for thou dost the work of Satan the adversary, in tempting me for self-preservation, to violate my Father's command, and my undertaking, and to forsake the work of man's redemption and salvation. As thy counsel savoureth not the things that be of God, (his will, work, and glory,) but the things that be of men, (the love of the body and this present life,) so it signifieth what is in thy heart: (take heed lest this carnality prevail.)

Note, 1. All things must displease us that displease God, and are against his interest, and the good of man.

2. Even the best men and nearest friends may by temptation and error, be made Satan's instruments to do his work in some particulars of great moment.

3. Good men do the devil's work oft times when they know it not, but verily think it is all for Christ.

4. No love or respect to men's nearness or goodness, must draw us to flatter them in sin, or to speak lightly of it; we must not mince it or extenuate it, because good men commit it; we must lay it home on them, that would by justifying it, make it pass for duty. Lest the name of good men should serve Satan more effectually than men of known wickedness can do.

5. It is no railing on just occasions to tell tempting friends, and godly men or ministers, that they are doing the devil's work, and are instead of devils to the tempted.

6. To hinder us in God's work and men's salvation, is to be Satans to us. O how many Satans then are called Reverend Fathers, who silence, and persecute men for God's work, as the whole course of the papal discipline and worship manifesteth.

7. It is carnal savouring worldly and fleshly interest too much, and the things of God, the soul, and heaven too little, which is the common cause of the sinful counsels, and course, even of sacred men.

24. Then said Jesus unto his disciples, if any man will come after me, let him deny himself, and take up his cross, and follow me. 25. For whosoever will save his life shall lose it: and whosoever will lose his life for my sake, shall find it.

24. Christ took this occasion to preach self-denial to his disciples, saying, Let him that will be my disciple and follow me, and expect salvation by me, resolve to deny his carnal self, and self-interest, and resign himself to me, as being not his own, but mine: Not *making* the cross, but patiently taking and bearing it when it is laid upon him, and follow me by sufferings unto glory. For this is the method determined by God, that whoever resolveth to save his life, and not be undone in the world to avoid sin, this man shall finally lose his life, and life eternal. And whoever will lose his life, rather than by sin to forsake me and his duty, shall find that life with felicity in heaven, which he lost on earth.

Note, Christ's peremptory terms of salvation, are to prefer it and Him before our lives.

26. For what is a man profited, if he shall gain the whole world, and lose his own soul? or what shall a man give in exchange for his soul?

26. Will it not be an ill bargain to gain all the world for a short time to the flesh, and lose one's own soul and its happiness for ever? And what will compensate the loss of the soul? For what price would you sell its happiness.

Note, 1. Man hath a soul that liveth when he leaveth this world. 2. It were a mad bargain to sell a man's soul for all that this world can afford. O how many do that daily in deed, which they durst not do by an express bargain with the devil.

27. For the Son of Man shall come in the glory of his Father, with his angels: and then he shall reward every man according to his works.

27. Believe it, I shall come at last in judgment, in divine glory, attended by angels, and then I will reward those that were faithful to me, or perfidious, and all men according to their works: therefore whatever you suffer now, prepare for the judgment of that day.

28. Verily, I say unto you, There be some standing here, which shall not taste of death, till they see the Son of Man coming in his kingdom.

28. And I tell you, lest you think this my coming in glory to judgment incredible, that some here shall live to see a visible representation of that my glorious appearing.

Note, That this is meant of his transfiguration, the addition of it in the several evangelists sheweth. Nor is Dr. H.'s reason against it from the former verse of any force, it being not the same coming that is here spoken of, but its representation.

CHAP. XVII.

AND after six days, Jesus taketh Peter, James, and John his brother, and bringeth them up into a high mountain apart, 2. And was transfigured before them, and his face did shine as the sun, and his raiment was white as the light.

1, 2. And as Christ had promised them a glimpse of his kingly glory, so within six days he performed it, to Peter, James, and John, whom he selected for peculiar favours. In a high mountain he was transfigured into a glorious appearance, his face shining like the sun, and his raiment like light.

Note, Christ would have this help of sense to confirm their faith. Of this transfiguration, I have written at large in a book, called, *My Dying Thoughts*.

3. And behold, there appeared unto them Moses and Elias talking with him.

3. Note, 1. Moses whose body was buried, and Elias, whose body was but changed, appeared alike. 2. The chief legislator and chief prophet appeared, to shew that the law and the prophets did but lead to Christ. 3. Did not the departed saints live after death, they could not appear in glory. 4. They talked with Christ of his sufferings at Jerusalem. 5. Either Christ told the three disciples who they were, or their own appearance shewed it. 6. How much better company is above than here.

4. Then answered Peter, and said unto Jesus, Lord, it is good for us to be here: if thou wilt, let us make here three tabernacles; one for thee, and one for Moses, and one for Elias.

4. Note, 1. We are apt to desire more of heaven on earth than God will allow, (but not so apt to desire to go by death to that glory where it is:) Fain we would have it come down to us. 2. A glimpse of glory is enough to wrap a soul into ecstasy. 3. We know not what we say when we talk of felicity in tabernacles on earth. 4. A glimpse of glory will make us out of love with worldly company and vanity. How loath then would the souls in heaven be to come down.

5. While he yet spake, behold, a bright cloud overshadowed them: and behold, a voice out of the cloud, which said, This is my beloved Son in whom I am well pleased; hear ye him.

5. Note, 1. Heavenly inhabitants must not stay on earth; nor heavenly visions and raptures be here long or frequent. 2. God again owned his Son by a voice from heaven as perfectly righteous and as pleasing him by man's redemption, and reconciling us to him, and teaching the doctrine which is pleasing to him.

6. And when the disciples heard it, they fell on their face, and were sore afraid.

6. Note, The voice of God even when he speaketh mercy, is enough to humble and prostrate man.

7. And Jesus came and touched them, and said, Arise, and be not afraid.

7. Note, It is Christ that must raise our troubled and humbled souls from our dejectedness and fear.

8. And when they had lift up their eyes, they saw no man, save Jesus only.

8. Note, Christ will stay with us, when Moses and Elias will not; nor are earthly comforts durable.

9. And as they came down from

CHAP. XVII.   ST. MATTHEW.   45

the mountain, Jesus charged them, saying, Tell the vision to no man, until the Son of Man be risen again from the dead.

9. The reason is before mentioned: After the resurrection was the fittest season.

10. And his disciples asked him, saying, Why then say the scribes, that Elias must first come?

10. Why say the Jewish doctors that Elias must come before the Messiah; if this was he that we saw.

11. And Jesus answered and said unto them, Elias truly shall first come, and restore all things: 12. But I say unto you, that Elias is come already, and they knew him not, but have done unto him whatsoever they listed: likewise shall also the Son of Man suffer of them. 13. Then the disciples understood that he spake unto them of John the Baptist.

11, &c. It is true that is said out of Mal. that Elias must come, but it was John that was meant under the name of Elias, whom they knew not, but killed him while they looked for him, and so they will do by me.

14. And when they were come to the multitude, there came to him a *certain* man kneeling down to him, and saying, 15. Lord, have mercy on my son, for he is lunatic, and sore vexed: for oft-times he falleth into the fire, and oft into the water. 16. And I brought him to thy disciples, and they could not cure him.

14. Note, By [lunatic] is meant one that had the epilepsy, or some such disease upon the change of the moon. A real disease, of which yet the devil was the executioner, and further joined with it extraordinarily.

17. Then Jesus answered and said, O faithless and perverse generation, how long shall I be with you? how long shall I suffer you? bring him hither to me.

17. It is long of your own unbelief and perverseness, that they could not cure him: how long shall I work miracles among you before you will believe? will you drive me from among you by your unbelief, to go to others?

Note, This seemeth plainly spoken to the man of himself and such others, and not as some say, to the disciples.

18. And Jesus rebuked the devil, and he departed out of him: and the child was cured from that very hour. 19. Then came the disciples to Jesus apart, and said, Why could not we cast him out? 20. And Jesus said unto them, Because of your unbelief:

18, &c. Your unbelief as well as the man's, was that which hindered you; you are all therein to be blamed.

20. For verily I say unto you, If ye have faith as a grain of mustard-seed, ye shall say unto this mountain, Remove hence to yonder place, and it shall remove; and nothing shall be impossible unto you.

20. For if you have the least true belief and trust in my power and will for the working of any such miracle, as I commission you to work, if it were as hard as the removing of a mountain, it should not be too hard for you.

Note, It is not faith, but presumption which hath no promise of success, if they or any are confident of working any miracle which Christ never commissioned or called them to work, or promised his blessing to.

21. Howbeit this kind goeth not out, but by prayer and fasting.

21. But by faith, I mean not confident presumption, that God will do it in your own way: But for such as this, God will be sought by fasting and fervent prayer, in which way you may expect success, if the person also be capable that seeketh help.

22. And while they abode in Galilee, Jesus said unto them, The Son of Man shall be betrayed into the hands of men: 23. And they shall kill him, and the third day he shall be raised again: and they were exceeding sorry.

22, 23. Again, Christ foretels them of his death and resurrection, to instruct and prepare them for it: which they were grieved at.

24. And when they were come to Capernaum, they that received tribute-*money,* came to Peter, and said, Doth not your master pay tribute? 25. He saith, Yes. And when he was come into the house, Jesus prevented him, saying, What thinkest thou, Simon? of whom do the kings of the earth take custom or tribute? of their own children, or of stran-

gers? 26. Peter said unto him, Of strangers. Jesus saith unto him, Then are the children free.

24, 25, 26. Note, They had two sorts of tribute, but that here meant it is the likest was poll-money, imposed by Augustus first: And by [*children*] is not meant *free subjects;* for such did pay; but their own families. And then it is hard to know what Christ's answer meant, unless it were as many say, *Then this tribute belongs of right to the house of David, and I being of it am free.* Or else, [if king's own families be not taxed, I that am the Son of the universal King, from whom is all power, and whose subjects they are, am rightfully freer than their children.] This seemeth to me to be the sense. But he questioneth not but tribute is due to kings and other powers.

27. Notwithstanding, lest we should offend them, go thou to the sea, and cast a hook, and take up the fish that first cometh up; and when thou hast opened his mouth, thou shalt find a piece of money: that take, and give unto them for me and thee.

27. But we must deny our own right to avoid offence; go therefore, and cast a hook, and I will bring a fish to thy hand with half-a-crown (a stater) in his mouth; which is the poll-money for two persons: pay them that for thee and me.
Note, 1. This shewed the great power of Christ.
2. But why did he pay for Peter, and not the rest? Answ. Peter had a house in Capernaum where they were, and was there to pay his poll-money, Matt. v. 8, 14.
If it be, as others think, the tax to the sanctuary that is here meant, it will make no doctrinal alteration. The sense then will be, [a tax due to God, is rather due *to* me, than *from* me, that am the Son of God.]

CHAP. XVIII.

AT the same time came the disciples unto Jesus, saying, Who is the greatest in the kingdom of heaven?

1. Ambition stirred in them, to debate who should be greatest in Christ's church or kingdom, next himself.

2. And Jesus called a little child unto him, and set him in the midst of them, 3. And said, Verily, I say unto you, Except ye be converted, and become as little children, ye shall not enter into the kingdom of heaven.

2, 3. Christ set a child before them as a visible answer, and said, Except true conversion give you a new and humble mind, and take you off from ambitious over-valuing earthly pomp and power, that as teachable and obedient disciples to me, you may be drawn to set more by heavenly things, you cannot be capable of entering into the heavenly kingdom, much less of being greatest there: nor are you fit for a place in the church on earth (much less of power) without covenanting this.

4. Whosoever, therefore, shall humble himself as this little child, the same is greatest in the kingdom of heaven.

4. Though worldly men will think otherwise, I tell you that the humblest Christian is the best, and the best is indeed the greatest, as being dearest unto God, and he is fittest also for church power.

5. And whoso shall receive one such little child in my name, receiveth me.

5. And he that receiveth or sheweth kindness to any such humble godly Christian, I will take and reward it as done to me.
Note, How do the papal clergy read this, that hate, revile, silence, and ruin or burn such. But they cheat their souls by saying, that such are but heretics and schismatics, and deny them to be Christ's, and then they think they are disobliged, and may use them as they first judge and call them.

6. But whoso shall offend one of these little ones which believe in me, it were better for him that a millstone were hanged about his neck, and *that* he were drowned in the depth of the sea.

6. But whoever he be that shall gall, discourage, or by threatening, derision, or persecution seek to drive the least from faith and holy living, it were less hurt to that man, (how big soever he now look and talk) that he were drowned in the sea, with a millstone about his neck; for God will take vengeance on him.

7. Woe unto the world because of offences: for it must needs be that offences come: but woe to that man by whom the offence cometh.

7. Woe to the world by reason of the scandals, oppositions, and impediments to faith, holiness, and salvation, which men will lay before each other, some by error, some by crimes, and some by persecution: such scandals, and hindrances, and temptations there will be: God will permit them for trial, and men will commit them. But the sin is great, and it will be woe to the guilty, especially the malignant persecutors and seducers.

8. Wherefore if thy hand or thy foot offend thee, cut them off, and

cast *them* from thee: it is better for thee to enter into life halt or maimed, rather than having two hands or two feet, to be cast into everlasting fire. 9. And if thine eye offend thee, pluck it out, and cast *it* from thee: it is better for thee to enter into life with one eye, rather than having two eyes to be cast into hell fire.

8, 9. Let nothing seem too dear to thee to secure thy salvation against such scandals, and hindrances, and temptations. If it be friend or interest as dear to thee as thy hand, or foot, or eye, it is a smaller loss to cast it away here, and be saved hereafter, than to keep it here, and be damned hereafter to endless misery. If thou hadst no other way to avoid sin but dismembering thy body, it would be a duty, and no loss to do it.

Note, 1. Christ had said this before, Matt. v. 30. It is no fault to say the same thing often. 2. If it be so dangerous to be tempted by others, it is worse to be our own tempters.

10. Take heed that ye despise not one of these little ones, for I say unto you, that in heaven their angels do always behold the face of my Father which is in heaven.

10. Note, O what men are they that read and preach this, and yet not only despise them, but first ignorantly or maliciously slander them, and then by this justify their railing, persecuting and destroying them. 2. What a comfort is it to the least true Christian, that they have their angels that have charge of them, who always see God's face in glory: And shall not we then see it?

11. For the Son of Man is come to save that which was lost.

11. And I that came into the world to save sinners, will require it at your hands, if you wrong or persecute them, or hinder them from the way of their salvation.

12. How think ye? if a man have an hundred sheep, and one of them be gone astray, doth he not leave the ninety and nine, and goeth into the mountains, and seeketh that which is gone astray? 13. And if so be that he find it, verily I say unto you, he rejoiceth more of that sheep, than of the ninety and nine which went not astray.

12, 13. Christ likeneth himself to men that have by unexpected success in recovering the lost, a more sensible joy than for the rest, though not a higher esteem. And if he so much rejoice in them, how will he take it of those that hate, persecute or tempt them.

14. Even so it is not the will of your Father which is in heaven, that one of these little ones should perish.

14. God loveth them better than you love sheep; therefore he will save them, and judge all those that would affright, or drive away from their duty, the meanest person.

15. Moreover, if thy brother shall trespass against thee, go and tell him his fault between thee and him alone: if he shall hear thee, thou hast gained thy brother. 16. But if he will not hear *thee, then* take with thee one or two more, that in the mouth of two or three witnesses every word may be established. 17. And if he shall neglect to hear them, tell it unto the church: but if he neglect to hear the church, let him be unto thee as an heathen man, and a publican.

15, &c. And according to this compassionate tenderness of God, and your Saviour, must be your dealing with one another; not to favour sin in any, but to seek by love to save the sinner: Therefore, if any one that thou hast brotherly communion with, do trespass against thee, by injury, or by scandalous crimes within thy notice, go and tell him his fault privately in brotherly love and tenderness, yet shewing him the evil of his sin that he may repent: If he hear thee so as to repent and amend, thou hast won him from the danger of his guilt, which may be a comfort to thee; But if he defend his sin, or will not repent and amend, cease not thy love or labour, but take with thee one or two meet persons, that two or three witnesses may the more awe him, or credibly convict him. And if he neglect to hear them, (having exercised due patience for the trial, and fit means to convince him,) then make it publie by telling the church, in whose communion he liveth: either by opening it in the congregation, that the church guides may reprove him and exhort him to repent, and pray for his repentance; or when that is not convenient, tell it to the guides of the church, that they may make it public, and do their office. And if he neglect to hear this publie exhortation, have no more communion or familiarity with him than with a heathen or publican, but so carry it, that he and others may see that thou esteemest him not as one of the Christian society whom Christ will own.

Note, This text which is Christ's law of church-discipline, is perverted divers ways, by several sorts of mistakers. Some feign that it speaketh not of sins against God, but of injuries against men: and that by the Church is meant the civil judicature that then was, (inferior or superior sanhedrim.) But, 1. it is evident that it is to Christians or disciples that Christ giveth this law, others received no law from him. And it was how to deal with a brother in order to repentance and salvation, as the foregoing verses shew. 2. Christ knew that the sanhedrim were his deadly enemies, and foretold that they would condemn him; and therefore never made a law to his disciples to use them as their ordinary judicature. 3. He knew that they would hate and persecute his disciples, and therefore never sent them to them for right. 4. He came to abrogate Moses's law, and overthrow their Mosaic policy; and therefore did not establish it by this law. 5. He could never mean that Christians must take him for a heathen, that heard not the Jews' council, when he foretold them how that council would scourge them in their synagogues, and cast out their names, and say all manner of evil of them falsely.

Nor did Christ set up a Christian judicature of magistrates, having the power of the sword instead of the Jewish. For, 1. Christ himself refused to use such a power on earth. 2. He forbade it his disciples that strove for it. 3. The text speaketh of no forcing power, but persuasive, and of no penalty but alienation and disowning. 4. The apostles did never set up any such coactive civil judicature, nor the church after them for 300 years and much more: which they would have done had Christ commanded it. 5. But they did set up such ecclesiastic judicatures wherever they gathered churches, which was their actual visible exposition of this law of Christ. 6. It is not restitution or recovery of lands, goods, or rights that is here mentioned as the end, but the *winning* of a brother by repentance. 7. And what is more noted by Christ as an offence or trespass against us, than scandal, and dishonouring the Christian name and society, and grieving good men by sinning against God. I think these evidences prove past doubt, that it is the discipline of Christian churches Christ here institutes by a standing law, for which he gave the power of the keys.

2. The church is told and heard when the rulers are told and heard, either before the whole congregation, or that they may publish it. The whole congregation is not to speak and be heard, nor necessarily to be told by the offended himself. But as the city is said to *receive* and to *execute* any order from the king when the magistrates do their part in it, and the people theirs, so it is with the church.

3. But how the telling of one lay-chancellor or civilian, and hearing or not hearing him, and being excommunicate by him concerns this law, I know not, no, nor telling or not hearing one single person that judgeth alone over many hundred churches at a distance, and without their notice.

4. This discipline is of great moment, for the honour of Christ and his church, that it be not as impure as the infidel world, nor a swine-sty instead of a society of saints: And that it may be known that Christ 'came not as deceivers do, to get himself a number of followers as bad as other men, but to sanctify a peculiar people to God, zealous of good works, and forsaking the world, the flesh, and the devil; and to keep Christians from the snare and shame of infectious and wicked associates: and to keep sin under open disgrace.

5. Yet if pastors neglect this holy discipline, the sin is theirs: It doth not necessitate the innocent to forsake the church, unless their doctrine or practice amount to a profest rejection of some essentials of Christianity, or else they force men to sin or own their sin. But they that can chuse better without more hurt than benefit, should prefer it before undisciplined churches.

18. Verily I say unto you, Whatsoever ye shall bind on earth, shall be bound in heaven: and whatsoever ye shall loose on earth, shall be loosed in heaven.

18. I tell you that my church on earth is the seminary or suburbs of my church in heaven, and those that you as my ministers absolve according to my word, they being not deceitful, but true professors of faith and repentance, they shall be absolved in heaven. And those that you bind over as impenitent to my judgment, being such indeed, shall be condemned and shut out of heaven: and I will own and confirm your judgment of men by the power I give you, if you do it according to my word. Note, God giveth pastors power to condemn and cast out none from heaven, nor to save any, but only such as condemn and cast out themselves, or such as save themselves by faith, more than the church can do.

19. Again, I say unto you, that if two of you shall agree on earth, as touching any thing that they shall ask, it shall be done for them of my Father which is in heaven.

19. And I tell you, that I may encourage you to concord, that if two of you (much more, if all, or many) shall agree in your prayers, discipline, or appeal to God, he will accept your endeavours, and they shall not be in vain, but blessed.

20. For where two or three are gathered together in my name, there am I in the midst of them.

20. For as I am with every single Christian, so I will more eminently bless with the fruits of my presence, the assemblies of the faithful, be they never so small.

Note, It is an hatred to Christ's presence and name, that Satan persecuteth such meetings.

21. Then came Peter to him, and said, Lord, how oft shall my brother sin against me, and I forgive him? till seven times?

21. Peter said unto him, What if my brother do often sin to my injury or scandal, and be often thus admonished, how oft must I forgive him? seven times seems much.

22. Jesus saith unto him, I say not unto thee, Until seven times: but until seventy times seven.

22. It is not the number of times, but his true repentance that is to be here regarded. Note, There are some sins that oft committing, will prove that the repentance is not true. He that should daily or

weekly beat you, steal, murther, fornicate, and as oft say, *I repent*, is not to believed, but forfeiteth his credit. But he that is but oft 'angry, or defective in the degrees of sincere duty, may be believed, if he oft profess repentance.

23. Therefore is the kingdom of heaven likened unto a certain king, which would take account of his servants. 24. And when he had begun to reckon, one was brought unto him which owed him ten thousand talents. 25. But forasmuch as he had not to pay, his lord commanded him to be sold, and his wife and children, and all that he had, and payment to be made.

23, &c. And that you may know on what terms you must look for mercy and forgiveness yourselves, I will liken God's government to a king that would call his servants to account, and demand his due, and make his debtors know what he might expect of them in justice.

26. The servant therefore, fell down and worshipped him, saying, Lord, have patience with me, and I will pay thee all.

26. The servant unable to pay, appealed from justice, and begged mercy, promising to pay when he should be able.

27. Then the lord of that servant was moved with compassion, and loosed him, and forgave him the debt.

27. As he appealed to mercy, he found mercy, and his lord forgave him, and set him free.

28. But the same servant went out, and found one of his fellowservants, which owed him an hundred pence: and he laid hands on him, and took *him* by the throat, saying, Pay me that thou owest. 29. And his fellow-servant fell down at his feet, and besought him, saying, Have patience with me, and I will pay thee all. 30. And he would not: but went and cast him into prison, till he should pay the debt.

28, &c. He that had received so much mercy, used his fellow-servant with unmerciful rigour, exacting all his due.

31. So when his fellow-servants saw what was done, they were very sorry, and came and told unto their
2.

lord all that was done. 32. Then his lord, after that he had called him, said unto him, O thou wicked servant, I forgave thee all that debt because thou desiredst me: 33. Shouldest not thou also have had compassion on thy fellow-servant, even as I had pity on thee?

31, &c. I forgave thee a great debt, and shouldest not thou forgive a little one? If mercy was so necessary to thee, why didst not thou shew mercy to thy fellow-servant as I did to thee?

34. And his lord was wroth, and delivered him to the tormentors, till he should pay all that was due unto him. 35. So likewise shall my heavenly Father do also unto you, if ye from your hearts forgive not every one his brother their trespasses.

34, 35. Note, Here it is doubted, 1. How God is said to forgive unmerciful men, 2. And to demand the debt which he had forgiven, and to unpardon it again. Answ. God hath divers degrees of forgiveness. 1. To give the world a pardon of all sin, on condition of thankful acceptance, is a great degree of forgiveness, though it be no actual discharge till accepted. 2. To suspend the execution of punishment (with such an offer) and to give him time, ease, and mercy, who deserved to be all that time in hell, is a degree of actual forgiveness: for to forgive the sin, is to forgive the punishment; and bad men have much punishment here forgiven them, which they deserved. And both these may be reversed by men's unbelief and sin.
3. Whether the sins of infants pardoned in baptism, may return in guilt by covenant-breaking; or any other that have not confirming grace, but such as Adam and the angels had and lost, is a controversy that is yet undecided among Christians.
4. But were perseverance never so sure eventually, yet in the tenor of the covenant, pardon and salvation are given on condition. And God may well say, If you perform not the condition, you "shall yet perish. That by this warning they may be moved to perform it. And should pardoned sin be unpardoned again, it would be no change in God, nor in his word, but in man. He that saith, The faithful shall be accepted, and the unfaithful perish, changeth not if any should perish by unbelief; God and his word are still the same. And forgiving others, is part of the condition of our continued forgiveness.

CHAP. XIX.

AND it came to pass, that when Jesus had finished these sayings, he departed from Galilee, and came into the coasts of Judea beyond Jordan: 2. And great multitudes fol-
E

lowed him, and he healed them there. 3. The Pharisees also came unto him, tempting him, and saying unto him, Is it lawful for a man to put away his wife for every cause?

1, &c. When Christ had thus long preached in his own country where he dwelt, far off from Jerusalem, he drew nearer it into Judea, and there also multitudes flocked after him; and the Pharisees attempted by questions to ensnare him, &c.

4. And he answered and said unto them, Have ye not read, that he which made *them* at the beginning, made them male and female, 5. And said, For this cause shall a man leave father and mother, and shall cleave to his wife: and they twain shall be one flesh. 6. Wherefore they are no more twain, but one flesh. What therefore, God hath joined together, let not man put asunder.

4, &c. Look to the original, and you shall find that God made them one male and one female, and by the law of conjugality, united them for procreation and converse as into one; the relative union being likened to a natural union of the parts of one body: and that so nearly, that on this account, father and mother were to be left for a closer union with a wife. Therefore do not you separate that which God hath so nearly united.

7. They say unto him, Why did Moses then command to give a writing of divorcement, and to put her away?

7. They thought to take advantage by this against him, as contradicting Moses's law, and said, &c.

8. He saith unto them, Moses because of the hardness of your hearts, suffered you to put away your wives: but from the beginning t was not so.

8. You mistake a permission for a command: your athers were an ignorant, dull, unruly sort of people, and Moses was put to make but such laws as they could bear. Therefore he permitted putting away, but only commanded that they should not do it without a bill of divorcement.

9. And I say unto you, Whosoever shall put away his wife, except *it be* for fornication, and shall marry another, committeth adultery: and whoso marrieth her which is put away, doth commit adultery.

9. Note, 1. The fornication must be proved, and not only suspected. 2. It must be fornication since marriage. 3. A man is not *commanded* for this to put her away, and not forgive it, if there be reason for it, but only *permitted*. 4. In commonwealths the magistrate must be judge, for public safety. 5. The woman is not so fitly said to *put away her husband;* but by the magistrate may have the same remedy of a divorce when she doth desire it.

10. His disciples say unto him, If the case of the man be so with *his* wife, it is not good to marry.

10. Then the danger and misery of unsuitable marriage is so great, that it is better never to marry.

11. But he said unto them, All men cannot receive this saying, save *they* to whom it is given.

11. He said, Men must not avoid a lesser evil by a greater: some men's temperament, and some men's condition in the world, make marriage necessary to them. All have not the gift of chastity.

12. For there are some eunuchs which were so born from *their* mother's womb: and there are some eunuchs, which were made eunuchs of men; and there be eunuchs, which have made themselves eunuchs for the kingdom of heaven's sake. He that is able to receive *it*, let him receive *it*.

12. There are some unfit for congress with women who were born so. And some are made so by men. by castration. And some have made themselves such, that they might the better avoid all venereous temptations. He that is able to live in a continent single life, without greater hurt, let him do it; but all cannot.

13. Then were there brought unto him little children, that he should put *his* hands on them, and pray: and the disciples rebuked them. 14. But Jesus said, Suffer little children, and forbid them not, to come unto me, for of such is the kingdom of heaven.

13, 14. Some brought their children to him that he would lay his hands on them and bless them according to their infant capacity: and the disciples chid them away, thinking such company below him. But Jesus said, Hinder them not, and forbid not little children to come or be brought to me: for I tell you, that it is not the self-conceitedly wise, but those that are as ready to learn and be ruled as such children are, that yet set not their wit and will against instruction, but are as it were, beginning the world, that will make up the Christian church.

15. And he laid *his* hands on them, and departed thence.

15. Qu. But why did he not baptize them? Answ. He baptized few of the aged yet that believed, and that baptism which he used, was but little differing from John's, till after his resurrection the Christian baptism was not fully instituted, as the entrance into his gospel-church.

16. And behold, one came and said unto him, Good master, what good thing shall I do that I may have eternal life?

16. Note, 1. It was then taken for granted, except by the Sadducees, that an eternal life of happiness was to be attained. 2. And that well-doing on man's part, was the way to attain it.

17. And he said unto him, Why callest thou me good? *there is* none good but one, *that is* God: but if thou wilt enter into life, keep the commandments.

17. Thou knowest not how great a word thou speakest of me, when thou callest me *good: Goodness* is *God's* name and *attribute:* There is none *essentially, absolutely,* and *most perfectly good but God.* But if thou wilt enter into life, keep God's commandments.

18. He saith unto him, Which? Jesus said, Thou shalt do no murder, Thou shalt not commit adultery, Thou shalt not steal, Thou shalt not bear false witness. 19. Honour thy father and *thy* mother, and, Thou shalt love thy neighbour as thyself.

18, 19. Note, Christ knew the order of the commandments; but named the fifth and the tenth by themselves, as being of special note: the fifth for government itself, and the ninth, the summary of the second table. For, Thou shalt love thy neighbour as thyself, is that which is meant by, *Thou shalt not covet thy neighbour's, &c,* that is, not by *self-love want love to him,* and draw from him to thyself, or oppose his good.

20. The young man saith unto him, All these things have I kept from my youth up: what lack I yet?

20. Note, No doubt but he had broken these commands, especially the last; but he judged by his freedom from the gross acts of sin.

21. Jesus said unto him, If thou wilt be perfect, go *and* sell that thou hast, and give to the poor, and thou shalt have treasure in heaven: and come *and* follow me.

21. Jesus said, the state of Christianity, or qualification for salvation is this, resolvedly and practically, to prefer heaven, before all the prosperity of this world, so as to part with all for heaven, when thou art called to it: Therefore I will now try thee, whether thou canst do this: Go sell all, and give to the poor, and follow me, and take the hopes of a treasure in heaven, instead of all.

22. But when the young man heard that saying, he went away sorrowful: for he had great possessions.

22. But this seemed so hard a motion to him, that he would not consent, but went away sorrowful; for he was very rich.

23. Then said Jesus unto his disciples, Verily I say unto you, that a rich man shall hardly enter into the kingdom of heaven. 24. And again I say unto you, It is easier for a camel to go through the eye of a needle, than for a rich man to enter into the kingdom of God.

23, 24. The difficulty of a rich man's being a sound Christian and saved is great, that I may express it by the common proverb, of a camel's going through a needle's eye.

25. When his disciples heard *it*, they were exceedingly amazed, saying, Who then can be saved? 26. But Jesus beheld them, and said unto them, With men this is impossible, but with God all things are possible.

25, 26. This amazing the disciples, he said, So naturally and strongly do men love this world, and its prosperity, and so hardly do they believe, and love the unseen heavenly felicity, that it is impossible for mere fleshly man, to make so great a change upon the heart; but the grace of Almighty God can, and will do it.

27. Then answered Peter, and said unto him, Behold we have forsaken all, and followed thee; what shall we have therefore?

27. Peter said, We have consented to thy terms, and forsaken all, and followed thee: What shall be our reward?

28. And Jesus said unto them, Verily I say unto you, that ye which have followed me in the regeneration, when the Son of Man shall sit

52 ST. MATTHEW. CHAP. XX.

in the throne of his glory, ye also shall sit upon twelve thrones, judging the twelve tribes of Israel.

28. Fear not being losers by forsaking all: You that have sincerely forsaken all for me, shall in my kingdom and future state, have ruling power, dignity and honour.

Note, It is doubted by expositors, Whether this speaks only of their chief power on earth in the Catholic church, and unswerable glory in heaven: Or of any peculiar reign over the tribes of Israel, in heaven, or on earth, after the resurrection. The general sense is sure, though what more there is be doubtful.

29. And every one that hath forsaken houses, or brethren, or sisters, or father, or mother, or wife, or children, or lands for my name's sake, shall receive an hundred-fold, and shall inherit everlasting life:

29. And it is not you only, but all others that lose and forsake any thing here, for my name's sake, in the hope of the kingdom of heaven, shall be so great gainers by it, that they shall have in this life a hundred-fold better in value than they lost, and in the world to come everlasting life. The worst condition of the faithful, is an hundred times better than others.

30. But many *that are* first, shall be last; and the last *shall be* first.

30. But as to the degree of glory, I must tell you, it will not be given according to the priority of age, or conversion, but according to the preparations of grace. And many that are now called, and have less holiness, will have less glory, than many that will be more eminent saints many ages hence.

CHAP. XX.

FOR the kingdom of heaven is like unto a man that is an householder, which went out early in the morning to hire labourers into his vineyard. 2. And when he had agreed with the labourers for a penny a day, he sent them into his vineyard.

1, 2. Note, The parable is to shew, That God will not give men more glory than others, because they were the first Christians; but, because his grace hath made them the best, though in time after others.

3. And he went out about the third hour, and saw others standing idle in the market-place, 4. And said unto them, Go ye also into the vineyard, and whatsoever is right I will give you. And they went their way.

5. Again he went out about the sixth and ninth hour, and did likewise. 6. And about the eleventh hour he went out, and found others standing idle, and said unto them, Why stand ye here all the day idle? 7. They say unto him, Because no man hath hired us. He saith unto them, Go ye also into the vineyard, and whatsoever is right, *that* shall ye receive.

3, &c. The hours were about nine o'clock, and at twelve, and at three, and at five. God is not for idleness; but hath work for all times and ages.

8. So when even was come, the lord of the vineyard saith unto his steward, Call the labourers, and give them *their* hire, beginning from the last unto the first.

8. Note, God's reward is in the evening of our days, and the evening of the world; when work is done.

9. And when they came that *were hired* about the eleventh hour, they received every man a penny. 10. But when the first came, they supposed that they should have received more, and they likewise received every man a penny. 11. And when they had received *it*, they murmured against the good man of the house, 12. Saying, These last have wrought but one hour, and thou hast made them equal unto us, which have borne the burden and heat of the day.

9—12. He made no difference in their wages for the *time* of their work: But he will make difference for the *work itself*: They that are called, near the end of the world, shall have as much as those that heard Christ preach: And those that are converted in their age, if they be more holy than those that began in youth, will be more happy. 8. This parable meaneth not that our reward is *wages for the value of our work*, as beneficial to God, in commutative justice; but only speaketh of the proportion. 3. Nor doth it imply, That any in heaven will murmur at other men's salvation, but that the Jewish disciples were yet inclined to grudge, that the Gentiles were equalled with them. And it is to cure such envy now.

13. But he answered one of them and said, Friend, I do thee no wrong; didst not thou agree with me for a penny? 14. Take *that* thine *is*, and go thy way: I will give unto

this last, even as unto thee. 15. Is it not lawful for me to do what I will with mine own? is thine eye evil because I am good?

13–15. I break no covenant with thee: Thou art not meet to give me laws of equity: Liberality to another is no wrong to thee. Am I not the rightful disposer of my own? Must I give none more than the value of their work deserveth? All shall have equity, but all shall not have equal bounty. Thou shouldest be glad of thy brother's receivings.

16. So the last shall be first, and the first last: for many be called, but few chosen.

16. So the last called in time, may be made the chief in dignity; and the first called in time, may be in grace and glory among the lowest. Yes, of many that come into the church at the first calling (as the Jewish disciples,) few may prove sincere and be saved.

17. And Jesus going up to Jerusalem, took the twelve disciples apart in the way, and said unto them, 18. Behold, we go up to Jerusalem, and the Son of Man shall be betrayed unto the chief priests, and unto the scribes, and they shall condemn him to death, 19. And shall deliver him to the Gentiles to mock, and to scourge, and to crucify *him*: and the third day he shall rise again.

17, 18, 19. He foretold them, that at Jerusalem he should suffer, be crucified, and rise again, &c.

Note, This frequent prediction was a full proof of Christ's truth, and voluntary suffering.

20. Then came to him the mother of Zebedee's children, with her sons, worshipping *him*, and desiring a certain thing of him. 21. And he said unto her, What wilt thou? She saith unto him, Grant that these my two sons may sit, the one on thy right hand, and the other on the left, in thy kingdom.

22, 21. Note, Ambition is even in Christ's disciples, till special grace humble them; seeking preferment and honour in the church, is a vice that Christ giveth us this warning to avoid. Carnality is apt to corrupt the minds even of eminent ministers, and disciples.

22. But Jesus answered and said, Ye know not what ye ask. Are ye able to drink of the cup that I shall drink of, and to be baptized with the baptism that I am baptized with? They say unto him, we are able.

22. You think to find worldly honour and dignity in my kingdom, but you are mistaken; it is suffering for me, that you must expect: Can you drink of this bitter cup, as I must do, and be baptized in blood, as I must be? And they over-confidently answered, We are able: Not knowing their trial, or their weakness.

23. And he saith unto them, Ye shall drink indeed of my cup, and be baptized with the baptism that I am baptized with: but to sit on my right hand, and on my left, is not mine to give, but *it shall be given to them* for whom it is prepared of my Father.

23. Ye shall indeed suffer more than now ye think of (James was quickly martyred;) But to be next me in my kingdom, is not to be given by me upon such petitioning, but only to those for whom my Father hath prepared it; and who shall be fittest for it?

24. And when the ten heard *it*, they were moved with indignation against the two brethren.

24. Note, 1. As some are prone to ambition, so others to envy them, and be too much offended. 2. This ambitious part of Christ's ministers here, began discontent that tended to schism, had not Christ soon rebuked it. 3. Christ's own twelve apostles had their own mutual distastes.

25. But Jesus called them unto him, and said, Ye know that the princes of the Gentiles exercise dominion over them, and they that are great, exercise authority upon them. 26. But it shall not be so among you; but whosoever will be great among you, let him be your minister. 27. And whosoever will be chief among you, let him be your servant.

25, 26, 27. Christ rebuketh these ambitious desires of superiority among them, and saith, The civil government by the sword, which the Gentiles exercise, is as lords by force and fear; and the great in strength command the rest to do their wills. But in my church as such, among you my disciples it shall not be so: But (though you must be subject to the coercive government of magistrates, yet) your own proper government and preeminence shall be, by serviceable humility and love, over volunteers: Church-greatness shall consist, in being most greatly serviceable to the conversion and edification of souls, and in most humble condescension to that end: And he shall be accounted the chief pastor and Christian, who is most humbly serviceable to all. And the proud, and domineering, and unserviceable, shall be the lowest and basest.

28. Even as the Son of Man came not to be ministered unto, but to minister, and to give his life a ransom for many.

28. As I myself came not to live in state, with great attendance of servants, but to serve men for their good; not to receive by their service to me, but to save them by my service for them, and giving my life a ransom for many.

29. And as they departed from Jericho, a great multitude followed him. 30. And behold, two blind men sitting by the way side, when they heard that Jesus passed by, cried out, saying, Have mercy on us, O Lord, thou Son of David. 31. And the multitude rebuked them, because they should hold their peace: but they cried the more, saying, Have mercy on us, O Lord, thou Son of David.

29, 30, 31. The blind hearing by fame, that he healed all, cried to him for mercy, believing that he could heal them.

32. And Jesus stood still, and called them, and said, What will ye that I shall do unto you?

32. Note, Believers may have what they will of Christ, which is meet for them, and they for it.

33. They say unto him, Lord, that our eyes may be opened. 34. So Jesus had compassion on them, and touched their eyes: and immediately their eyes received sight, and they followed him.

33, 34. Note, 1. Bodily calamities are easily felt, and bodily welfare is easily desired. 2. And though Christ most value those who prefer spiritual mercies, yet he hath compassion also on men's bodies, as serviceable to their souls, and to his glory.

CHAP. XXI.

AND when they drew nigh unto Jerusalem, and were come to Bethphage, unto the mount of Olives, then sent Jesus two disciples, 2. Saying unto them, Go into the village over against you, and straightway ye shall find an ass tied, and a colt with her: loose *them*, and bring *them* unto me. 3. And if any man say ought unto you, ye shall say, The Lord hath need of them; and straightway he will send them. 4. All this was done, that it might be fulfilled which was spoken by the prophet, saying, 5. Tell ye the daughter of Sion, Behold thy king cometh unto thee, meek, and sitting upon an ass, and a colt, the foal of an ass.

1, &c. Note, Christ's way of travel was as poor men's, on foot: And it was the rich sort of persons that rode on asses, (they being there bigger than ours,) and only men of great state or war that rode on horses: And Christ knowing that the people would at his entrance into Jerusalem, applaud him with *Hosannah*, as the *Messiah*, and king of the Jews, resolved to own their testimony so far, as to ride in some state. 2. Though both the ass and colt be loosed, and brought; it was the colt only that Christ rode on.

6. And the disciples went, and did as Jesus commanded them, 7. And brought the ass, and the colt, and put on them their clothes, and they set *him* thereon. 8. And a very great multitude spread their garments in the way; others cut down branches from the trees, and strewed *them* in the way. 9. And the multitudes that went before, and that followed, cried, saying, Hosannah to the Son of David: Blessed is he that cometh in the name of the Lord, Hosannah in the highest.

6—9. Note, This was the common people's proclaiming him king, and the Messiah: spreading garments and boughs being their solemnization and *Hosannah* their acclamation; (a word which signifieth [*Save now*] and was used with that sort of pomp.) [*Blessed is he that cometh in the name of the Lord*] signified *Blessed* be the Messiah and king whom we have long looked for, and God hath now sent. [To which in Luke is added], *Peace in heaven, and glory in the highest:* That is, Let the heavenly prosperity and glory come down upon this kingdom, and his kingdom tend to heavenly peace or prosperity, and glory to God, and Man with God.

10. And when he was come into Jerusalem, all the city was moved, saying, Who is this? 11. And the multitude said, This is Jesus, the prophet of Nazareth of Galilee.

CHAP. XXI. ST. MATTHEW. 55

10, 11. The citizens all came to see who it was, that came in so applauded: And the people that accompanied him in, told them, It is Jesus, the famous prophet whose miracles you have heard of.

12. And Jesus went into the temple of God, and cast out all them that sold and bought in the temple, and overthrew the tables of the money-changers, and the seats of them that sold doves, 13. And said unto them, It is written, My house shall be called the house of prayer, but ye have made it a den of thieves.

12, 13. In this state he went on to the temple, and as one in power, he cast out them that had turned the temple into a *market-place*, to furnish men with sacrifices; and overthrew the tables of them that like goldsmiths or bankers exchanged money for advantage; Alleging, Isa. lvi. 7. *My house*, &c. Ye have made a *market-place* of it; where the covetous defraud men for gain.

14. And the blind and the lame came to him in the temple, and he healed them.

14. He wrought out his miracles openly in the Temple, as he had done in the country.

15. And when the chief priests and scribes saw the wonderful things that he did, and the children crying in the temple, and saying, Hosannah to the Son of David; they were sore displeased, 16. And said unto him, Hearest thou what these say?

15, 16. The rulers that knew they were under the Roman power, and saw that Jesus was not like to deliver them from it, were greatly displeased when they heard the inferior multitude, and youths crying him up as the King, and Messiah, and said, *Hearest thou what these say of thee: wilt thou suffer them to raise a sedition for thee, and expose us all to the Romans' wrath.*

16. And Jesus saith unto them, Yea; have ye never read, Out of the mouth of babes and sucklings thou hast perfected praise?

16. Yea, as it is written, Psa. viii. 2. &c. Note, The Septuagint, which Matthew useth differs from the Hebrew; but not in sense.

17. And he left them, and went out of the city into Bethany, and he lodged there. 18. Now in the morning as he returned into the city, he hungered. 19. And when he saw a fig-tree in the way, he came to it, and found nothing thereon, but leaves only, and said unto it, let no fruit grow on thee henceforward for ever. And presently the fig-tree withered away. 20. And when the disciples saw it, they marvelled, saying, How soon is the fig-tree withered away?

17—20. Note, It began then to die: but it was the next day that the disciples saw it and wondered.

21. Jesus answered and said unto them, Verily I say unto you, If ye have faith, and doubt not, ye shall not only do this *which is done* to the fig-tree, but also if ye shall say unto this mountain, Be thou removed, and be thou cast into the sea; it shall be done. 22. And all things whatsoever ye shall ask in prayer, believing ye shall receive.

21, 22. Nothing shall be too hard, which God hath promised, and ye by faith and prayer are fit to receive.

23. And when he was come into the temple, the chief priests and the elders of the people came unto him as he was teaching, and said, by what authority doest thou these things? and who gave thee this authority?

23. The chief priests and elders examined him, to shew his authority.

24. And Jesus answered and said unto them, I also will ask you one thing, which if ye tell me, I in likewise will tell you by what authority I do these things. 25. The baptism of John, whence was it? from heaven, or of men? And they reasoned with themselves, saying, If we shall say, From heaven; he will say unto us, Why did ye not then believe him? 26. But if we shall say, Of men; we fear the people; for all hold John as a prophet.

24, 25, 26. They perceived the advantage Christ would have by their answer: Either John's testimony, or the power of the multitude, who reverenced prophets sent from God, and would have stoned them. *Luke* xx. 6.

27. And they answered Jesus, and said, We cannot tell. And he said unto them, Neither tell I you by what authority I do these things.

27. If you will not answer my question, neither will I answer yours.

28. But what think you? A certain man had two sons, and he came to the first, and said, Son, go work to-day in my vineyard; 29. He answered and said, I will not: but afterward he repented, and went. 30. And he came to the second, and said likewise. And he answered and said, I *go*, sir; and went not. 31. Whether of them twain did the will of his father?

28. &c. That you may see that your highest profession of holiness and knowledge, while you disobey God, doth leave you worse than the Publicans, and vulgar whom you vilify; I will tell you a parable, &c.

31. They say unto him, The first. Jesus saith unto them, Verily I say unto you, that the publicans and the harlots go into the kingdom of God before you. 32. For John came unto you in the way of righteousness, and ye believed him not: but the publicans and the harlots believed him. And ye when ye had seen *it*, repented not afterward, that ye might believe him.

31. These despised sinners believed John, and repented; which you with all your knowledge did not, nor yet do; and so are further from the kingdom of God, than they; having no obedient religion, but words and ceremonies.

33. Hear another parable: There was a certain householder which planted a vineyard, and hedged it round about, and digged a winepress in it, and built a tower, and let it out to husbandmen, and went into a far country.

33. Note, God did what was necessary to have made the Jews a happy church, as to means prepared: By digging a wine-press is meant, hollowing a trough to bruise the grapes in, and building a tower, is a setting up, or building a lodge or dwelling for the workmen.

34. And when the time of the fruit drew near, he sent his servants to the husbandmen, that they might receive the fruits of it.

34. God required the fruit of all his teachings, and mercies to the Jews.

35. And the husbandmen took his servants, and beat one, and killed another, and stoned another. 36. Again, he sent other servants, more than the first: and they did unto them likewise.

35, 36. They persecuted and murdered the prophets, age after age, and yet seemed to honour prophets.

37. But last of all, he sent unto them his son, saying, They will reverence my son.

37. Note, This doth not mean that God thought so, and was mistaken; but speaking after the manner of men, tells them, what he might require in reason of them.

38. But when the husbandmen saw the son, they said among themselves, This is the heir, come, let us kill him, and let us seize on his inheritance. 39. And they caught *him*, and cast him out of the vineyard, and slew *him*.

38, 39. Note, This meaneth not, that the Jews reckon him to be the Son of God, but might and should have known it.

40. When the Lord therefore of the vineyard cometh, what will he do unto those husbandmen? 41. They say unto him, He will miserably destroy those wicked men, and will let out *his* vineyard unto other husbandmen, which shall render him the fruits in their seasons.

40, 41. Thus God will destroy the murderous Jews, and call the Gentiles.

Note, Luke reciteth these words as Christ's, and tells us, That the grandees said, God forbid. It is likely they consented to it, till they heard it applied to themselves; and then said, God forbid.

42. Jesus saith unto them, Did ye never read in the scriptures, The stone which the builders rejected, the same is become the head of the corner: this is the Lord's doing, and it is marvellous in our eyes?

42. Note, Though this was spoken Ps. cxviii. immediately of David, it ultimately meant Christ, who should be the foundation and head of the church, when the Jews had crucified him.

43. Therefore say I unto you, The kingdom of God shall be taken from you, and given to a nation bringing forth the fruits thereof.

43. I tell you this doleful truth, You that boasted of your peculiarity and hopes of the kingdom of the *Messiah*, shall be deprived of it for your sin; and it shall be given to the Gentiles who will better entertain it, and obey it, and be thankful for it.

44. And whosoever shall fall on this stone, shall be broken: but on whomsoever it shall fall, it will grind him to powder.

44. Bare unbelief of such as stumble at the cross, or turn away from Christ, through offence and temptation, will undo all that continue in it: But to those that prove malignant enemies, and fight against Christ, he will be as a stone, too heavy for him that taketh it up to cast away, which will fall upon them, to their greater destruction.

45. And when the chief priests and Pharisees had heard his parables, they perceived that he spake of them. 46. But when they sought to lay hands on him, they feared the multitude, because they took him for a prophet.

45, 46. Note, 1. Personal close reproofs, and denunciation of God's judgments enrageth hardened sinners. 2. The Jews that applauded Christ, thought it no sedition to defend a prophet against their high-priest and rulers, who for fear of them, durst not openly take Christ.

CHAP. XXII.

AND Jesus answered, and spake unto them again by parables, and said, 2. The kingdom of heaven is like unto a certain king which made a marriage for his son, 3. And sent forth his servants to call them that were bidden to the wedding, and they would not come.

1, 2, 3. The calling of men into the church, is like a king's inviting guests to his son's marriage feast, that would not come.

4. Again, he sent forth other servants, saying, Tell them which are bidden, Behold I have prepared my dinner: my oxen and *my* fatlings *are* killed, and all things *are* ready: come unto the marriage.

4. Christ's ministers are oft to invite men, and importune them to come in; and to tell them that Christ and his merits are sufficient for them, and all is ready and done on his part, preparatory to their belief, reception, and consent: they shall not perish for want of a sufficient sacrifice.

5. But they made light of *it*, and went their ways, one to his farm; another to his merchandize: 6. And the remnant took his servants, and entreated *them* spitefully, and slew *them*.

5, 6. Note, As did the Jews, so do many others make *light of Christ*, and all his offers of grace and glory, and mind more their farms and merchandise, their worldly interest and prosperity. And others more wicked than they, do persecute those that would convert and save them. O odious unthankfulness, thus to requite the greatest offers of Christ and his servants!

7. But when the king heard *thereof*, he was wroth: and he sent forth his armies, and destroyed those murderers, and burnt up their city.

7. Note, So did God send the Romans to destroy the Jews and burn Jerusalem; and hath often plagued persecutors; and the day of revenge will come.

8. Then saith he to his servants, The wedding is ready, but they which were bidden were not worthy. 9. Go ye therefore into the high-ways, and as many as ye shall find, bid to the marriage.

8, 9. All was ready on Christ's part, but the Jews unworthily rejected him. Go call all the Gentiles that will come.

10. So those servants went out into the *high*-ways, and gathered together all as many as they found, both bad and good: and the wedding was furnished with guests.

10. So the gospel was preached to the Gentiles of all sorts, and high and low came into the church.

11. And when the king came in to see the guests, he saw there a man which had not on a wedding garment: 12. And he saith unto him, Friend, how camest thou in hither, not having a wedding garment? And he was speechless.

11, 12. Note, Among the Jews, the marriages of rich men were solemnized with extraordinary pomp and feasting; and by the *wedding* or *festival garment*, is meant, true faith and repentance. Note, 1. Though all must be called into the church, it is meant that they come as Christians indeed, with true faith and repentance, and dishonour not the church by worldly common hearts and lives. 2. God will find out every hypocrite in the church. 3. None will be more unexcusable and speechless in judgment, than ungodly hypocrites called Christians, that live wickedly. 4. It is not the minister that called such, nor the company that joined with them, that are blamed.

13. Then said the king to the servants, Bind him hand and foot, and take him away, and cast *him* into outer darkness: there shall be weeping and gnashing of teeth.

13. Note, As it is a double sin to be ungodly after baptism, and in the church, dishonouring the Christian name, so such shall have greater punishment than ignorant infidels.

14. For many are called, but few *are* chosen.

14. For those that are baptized and called Christians are many, but those that have true faith and repentance, and godliness, and shall be saved, are few.

15. Then went the Pharisees, and took counsel how they might entangle him in *his* talk.

15. The malicious Pharisees consulted how to get some words from him, for which they might accuse him.

16. And they sent out unto him their disciples with the Herodians, saying, Master, we know that thou art true, and teachest the way of God in truth, neither carest thou for any man: for thou regardest not the person of men. 17. Tell us therefore, what thinkest thou? Is it lawful to give tribute unto Cæsar, or not?

16, 17. There were then two parties among the Jews: The king Herod's party who were for giving tribute to the Romans, and the Pharisees' party that were against the right of it. And they sought to ensnare Christ, saying, It is the part of a prophet not to fear man how great soever, but plainly to speak the truth; and we know thou art such an one: Therefore tell us, &c.

Note, That the Jews fell under the Roman power, by division, two brethren striving for the principality. And one of them got the better by the Romans' help, consenting to be tributary under them. And his party (which ruled) were for this tribute. But the party of the other brother who was overcome, took them but for usurpers, and such were the lower sort, and many Pharisees. So that they thought to draw Christ, either to fall under the Roman severity, or to lose the populacy, by his answer. (A way of ensnaring not yet ended.)

18. But Jesus perceived their wickedness, and said, Why tempt ye me, ye hypocrites? 19. Shew me the tribute-money. And they brought unto him a penny. 20. And he saith unto them, Whose *is* this image and superscription? 21. They say unto him, Cesar's. Then saith he unto them, Render therefore, unto Cesar, the things which are Cesar's: and unto God, the things that are God's.

18, &c. He knowing their wicked ensnaring design, said, ye hypocrites, Why come you to ensnare me, on pretence of being resolved by me?

Note, That they are three distinct questions, 1. Whether it be lawful to pay tribute to Cæsar, as being an owning of his power? 2. Whether it be a duty? and, 3. Whether Cæsar had true right to demand it? And Christ was desired to answer the first: And he had taught his disciples how lawful it was for peace to give away their right: much more now doth he intimate this to be lawful for public peace and safety: 2. And the second question is by intimation resolved in the first: For if it be lawful, public peace will make it a duty: But he answered so cautiously, as not to resolve the third question, Whether Cæsar had right, or were an usurper, and so avoided their snare. Some think that Hircanus's dedication to the Romans gave them right, and others think he represented not the nation. And some think that many years possession gave him right, and others say that mere possession without right groweth not to right by time. And some think that the Jews so long using Cæsar's coin and officers, signifieth consent, and gave him right. And others say, That this alone signified but submission or non-resistance, through disability and not subjection or consent to government. If Cæsar were an usurper, paying tribute owned not his right any more than contribution to conquering soldiers; A man may buy his life or peace of a robber. But Christ seemeth to answer but to the question asked him, and not to meddle with any more.

Obj. The tax intended in the question, was that which Cæsar alienated from the temple, and therefore the meaning was, (Is it not sacrilege to pay that to Cæsar that should be paid to God.) Answ. And Christ's answer is perfectly suited to such a question: as if he had said, (without determining Cæsar's right to govern them.) You need not ask whether you shall pay it to God or to Cæsar: you may do both, if you are able: Pay Cæsar that which is Cæsar's and give God nevertheless his due.

22. When they heard *these words*,

CHAP. XXII.   ST. MATTHEW.

they marvelled, and left him, and went their way.

22. When they saw they could not ensnare him, they went away confounded and disappointed.

23. The same day came to him the Sadducees, which say that there is no resurrection, and asked him, 24. Saying, Master, Moses said, If a man die, having no children, his brother shall marry his wife, and raise up seed unto his brother. 25. Now there were with us seven brethren, and the first when he had married a wife, deceased, and having no issue, left his wife unto his brother. 26. Likewise the second also, and the third, unto the seventh. 27. And last of all the woman died also. 28. Therefore in the resurrection, whose wife shall she be of the seven? for they all had her.

23, &c. These Sadducees were heretics that believeth no life after this, nor angels, nor spirits, and yet professed to believe the five books of Moses, and so pretended Moses's words to countenance their foolish error.

29. Jesus answered and said unto them, Ye do err, not knowing the scriptures, nor the power of God. 30. For in the resurrection they neither marry, nor are given in marriage; but are as the angels of God in heaven.

29, 30. You err through the ignorance of your gross and carnal minds, and carnally misunderstand the scriptures, and the nature and power of God, and so of spiritual things. In the life after this, they have not flesh and blood that lusteth and generateth as here; but they are spiritual substances like the angels in heaven that generate not.

31. But as touching the resurrection of the dead, have ye not read that which was spoken unto you by God, saying, 32. I am the God of Abraham, and the God of Isaac, and the God of Jacob? God is not the God of the dead, but of the living.

31, 32. That there is a life after this, is proved by God's words: I am the God, &c. That God is their God, implieth that they are his people, and therefore live: For to be their God, is to be their ruler, and their benefactor, and felicity; a relation which the dead are not capable of. And it is not said, I was their God, but I am their God. And if Abraham, &c. be alive, so are the souls of other men; and as they die not with the body, but live with spirits, so they are capable of a spiritual body which God will give them.

Note. It is well noted by Dr. Hammond, that as the Sadducees denied not only the rising of the body, but the immortality of the soul, and all our life after this, so it was this future life which they here meant, and Christ doth prove out of the books which they received: And that the Greek word signifieth not only the resurrection of the body, but our living after this life, when the body is dead. And if the soul were not immortal, there could be no resurrection of the same man: Another soul would be another man imbodied: And God doth not make new souls to be rewarded or punished for that which they never did.

33. And when the multitude heard *this*, they were astonished at his doctrine.

34. But when the Pharisees had heard that he had put the Sadducees to silence, they were gathered together. 35. Then one of them *which was* a lawyer, asked *him* a question, tempting him, and saying, 36. Master, which *is* the great commandment in the law?

33, &c. To try whether they could oppose him, or ensnare him in his answer, one asked this question.

37. Jesus said unto him, Thou shalt love the Lord thy God with all thy heart, and with all thy soul, and with all thy mind. 38. This is the first and great commandment. 39. And the second *is* like unto it, Thou shalt love thy neighbour as thyself.

37, &c. Note, 1. Heart, soul, and mind, seem to mean but wholly with all thy power; though we may distinguish them, as meaning the faculties vital, sensitive, and intellectual must be devoted to God: Or as some say, The will, affections, and understanding. 2. Christ tells us of a great difference between God's commands: These two are great above the rest.

40. On these two commandments hang all the law and the prophets.

40. These two are the very sum and end of all that is said in the law and by the prophets. Love comprehends all.

41. While the Pharisees were gathered together, Jesus asked them, 42. Saying, What think ye of Christ? whose son is he? They say unto

him, *The son* of David. 43. He saith unto them, How then doth David in spirit call him Lord, saying, 44. The LORD said unto my Lord, Sit thou on my right hand, till I make thy enemies thy footstool? 45. If David then call him Lord, how is he his son? 46. And no man was able to answer him a word, neither durst any man (from that day forth) ask him any more questions.

41, &c. Note, They knew not that Christ must be the Son of God. They ceased their tempting questions when they found themselves but silenced.

CHAP. XXIII.

THEN spake Jesus to the multitude, and to his disciples, 2. Saying, The scribes and the Pharisees sit in Moses's seat. 3. All, therefore, whatsoever they bid you observe, *that* observe and do; but do not ye after their works: for they say, and do not.

1, 2, 3. The Scribes and Pharisees when they read and expound Moses's law, do a work appointed of God: therefore (though you must beware of the leaven of their corrupt exposition, yet) hear the law which they read, and do all which they command you out of the law: But imitate not their sinful practice; for they live not according to Moses's law which they deliver.

4. For they bind heavy burdens, and grievous to be borne, and lay *them* on men's shoulders, but they themselves will not move them with one of their fingers.

4. It is easy to preach strictly, but not to live so; They preach the rigour of the law, but keep it not.

5. But all their works they do, for to be seen of men: they make broad their phylacteries, and enlarge the borders of their garments, 6. And love the uppermost rooms at feasts, and the chief seats in the synagogues, 7. And greetings in the markets, and to be called of men, Rabbi, Rabbi.

5, 6, 7. They place their religion in outward ceremonies and actions of the body, which man can see: They write out the law in rolls, and wear them like a chain; and make broad the borders of their garments, as Numb. xv. 38. Deut. xxii. 12. And affect pre-eminence, great names, and applause.

8. But be not ye called Rabbi: for one is your master, *even* Christ, and all ye are brethren.

8. Do not you affect these titles of reverence, such as Doctor, or any that giveth too much to man.

9. And call no man your father upon the earth: for one is your Father which is in heaven.

9. And call none in excess of reverence, the father of your religion: for God only is such a father.

10. Neither be ye called masters; for one is your master, *even* Christ.

10. And affect not the title of masters in religion; for you are all scholars to your master Christ.

11. But he that is greatest among you, shall be your servant. 12. And whosoever shall exalt himself, shall be abased: and he that shall humble himself, shall be exalted.

11, 12. Church greatness and dignity consisteth in being most greatly serviceable: But if you affect domination and preferment, you shall be abased: and he that humbleth himself shall be accounted the chief by God, and used accordingly.

13. But woe unto you scribes and Pharisees, hypocrites; for ye shut up the kingdom of heaven against men: for ye neither go in yourselves, neither suffer ye them that are entering, to go in.

13. You keep men from believing that they might be saved, pretending to be masters and teachers of the law, you pervert it, and harden yourselves in unbelief, and are against others preaching the gospel and believing it.

14. Woe unto you scribes and Pharisees, hypocrites; for ye devour widows' houses, and for a pretence make long prayer: therefore ye shall receive the greater damnation.

14. You are unmerciful, covetous, and oppressors, and think your long prayers will salve all with God, and men, and conscience.

Qu. Were they extemporary prayers, or long liturgies and forms? Answ. If the former, the Pharisees had more of the gift of utterance than Christ's disciples then. But no doubt but they were long liturgies or forms; for else they were

CHAP. XXIII.   ST. MATTHEW.

not suitable to the times or the character of the Pharisees, who were church-rulers, and all for tradition, and ceremony and outside: And yet Christ blameth not the *forms*, or the length, but their hypocrisy, and oppressing cruelty. Only good is fit to cover evil.

15. Woe unto you scribes and Pharisees, hypocrites; for ye compass sea and land to make one proselyte: and when he is made, ye make him twofold more the child of hell than yourselves.

15. Ye are very diligent to convert men to your religion, and make them more guilty and more fierce against Christians, than yourselves.

16. Woe unto you, ye blind guides, which say, Whosoever shall swear by the temple, it is nothing: but whosoever shall swear by the gold of the temple, he is a debtor.

16. By a foolish distinction you feign a man not bound to keep his oath, nor guilty if he break it, who sweareth by the temple; and yet say he is bound that sweareth by the gold of the temple, as more holy.

17. Ye fools and blind: for whether is greater, the gold, or the temple that sanctifieth the gold?

17. Is not the temple consecrated to God before its gold, which is but an accident to the temple?

18. And whosoever shall swear by the altar, it is nothing: but whosoever sweareth by the gift that is upon it, he is guilty. 19. Ye fools and blind: for whether *is* greater, the gift, or the altar that sanctifieth the gift?

18, 19. Is not the altar consecrated before the gift, on which the gift must be offered if consecrated?

Qu. *Doth not Christ here cross his own law, by calling them fools and blind?* Ans. No: It is railing and reproach by venting hurtful passion which he forbids. But for a friend or a preacher to convince men of the folly of sinning, and reprove it, is a duty.

20. Whoso therefore shall swear by the altar, sweareth by it, and by all things thereon. 21. And whoso shall swear by the temple, sweareth by it, and by him that dwelleth therein. 22. And he that shall swear by heaven, sweareth by the throne of God, and by him that sitteth thereon.

20, &c. The altar is to be taken as relating to the offering, and the temple and heaven as relating to God, in the sense of the oath.

23. Woe unto you, scribes and Pharisees, hypocrites; for ye pay tithe of mint, and anise, and cummin, and have omitted the weightier matters of the law, judgment, mercy, and faith: these ought ye to have done, and not to leave the other undone.

23. What hypocrisy is it to be precise in tything and trifling small things, and withal to neglect the great duties of the law, just judging, mercy, and faithful dealing! These are the things which you should have first done, with greatest zeal and care, and the small things to come in their proper place.

24. Ye blind guides, which strain at a gnat, and swallow a camel.

24. Note, They may be sharply reproved as blind guides, who place their religion in ceremonies and small things, while they omit justice, mercy, fidelity, and such great duties.

25. Woe unto you scribes and Pharisees, hypocrites; for ye make clean the outside of the cup, and of the platter, but within, they are full of extortion and excess.

25. You wash the outside of your cups and platters; but what contain they within but the drink and the meat which you have got by extortion, and use to intemperance and excess.

26. Thou blind Pharisee, cleanse first that *which is* within the cup and platter, that the outside of them may be clean also.

26. See that thy dish and cup contain not the fruit of extortion, nor the food of fleshly lust: and do thus by thy heart also, as well as by thy cup and dish.

27. Woe unto you scribes and Pharisees, hypocrites; for ye are like unto whited sepulchres, which indeed appear beautiful outward, but are within full of dead men's bones, and of all uncleanness. 28 Even so ye also outwardly appear righteous unto men, but within ye are full of hypocrisy and iniquity.

27, 28. So ye are adorned with your outward ceremonies, and legal and traditional observances, but within are hypocrites and wicked,

27. Woe unto you scribes and Pharisees, hypocrites; because ye build the tombs of the prophets, and garnish the sepulchres of the righteous, 30. And say, If we had been in the days of our fathers, we would not have been partakers with them in the blood of the prophets. 31. Wherefore ye be witnesses unto yourselves, that ye are the children of them which killed the prophets. 32. Fill ye up then, the measure of your fathers.

29, &c. As hypocrites ye honour by your ceremonies and words the memory of the prophets and righteous men, whom your fathers murdered: and you say, you would not have done it; and yet you do the same, and worse. You confess, that you are the offspring of those murderers and therefore liable to be plagued for your forefather's sins if you repent not: No wonder if you imitate them, and fill up the measure till you be ripe for vengeance.

33. Ye serpents, ye generation of vipers, how can ye escape the damnation of hell?

33. How can ye escape damnation, who are the seed of such Serpents and Vipers, of the same nature, and go on in the same way of sin?

34. Wherefore behold, I send unto you prophets, and wise men, and scribes; and *some* of them ye shall kill and crucify, and *some* of them shall ye scourge in your synagogues, and persecute *them* from city to city: 35. That upon you may come all the righteous blood shed upon the earth, from the blood of righteous Abel, unto the blood of Zacharias, son of Barachias, whom ye slew between the temple and the altar. 36. Verily I say unto you, All these things shall come upon this generation.

34, &c. I foretel you now what will befal you: I will send unto you yet greater prophets, &c. And thus you will use them. And so when you have filled up the measure of your national sin, the destruction deserved by your ancestors, but suspended by the patience and long-suffering of God, shall be suspended no longer, but shall fall on this forsaken generation, and God will remember all at once, in the day that he dreadfully destroyeth you.

Note, 1. Whether this Zacharias was the son of Jehojada, in Joash's days: and the name of Barachias, slept into the text by some scribe's conjecture out of the description of the Prophet Zachary: or whether it were any other, is of no great moment.

2. The sins of their ancestors are said to be punished on that generation. 1. Because it being a national punishment, which was procured by national sins, many ages. 2. Because children derive nature and guilt in part from parents' sin, and not from Adam's only, as the whole history of Scripture sheweth. 3. Because they sinned as their ancestors did.

The sin here described, is much like theirs now, who canonise the saints whom their ancestors persecuted and murdered, and kept holidays for them, and visit their shrines, and carry their relics, and account their names the honour of their church; and at the same time hate, persecute, silence, and murder those that imitate them.

37. O Jerusalem, Jerusalem, thou that killest the prophets, and stonest them which are sent unto thee, how often would I have gathered thy children together, even as a hen gathereth her chickens under *her* wings, and ye would not!

37. How oft have I offered by my messengers and attempted to gather thee into a state of greatest favour and safety, with tenderest love; but you would not consent.

Note, 1. Christ would have taken the whole city and nation into his church, had they not refused: And therefore infants as they were before. 2. If the Jews had all believed in Christ, he would not have continued the law of Moses, and that policy, which did but lead to him, nor have forsaken the rest of the world, to make them only his church; but would have made them a part of the Catholic church.

38. Behold, your house is left unto you desolate. 39. For I say unto you, Ye shall not see me henceforth, till ye shall say, Blessed *is* he that cometh in the name of the Lord.

38, 39. Your temple and city are near to certain desolation. When you have executed your fury on me, I will leave you to the fury of destroyers, and you shall see me no more till conviction constrain you to desire me, as your Saviour.

Note, That the country of Judea where the remnant of the Jews, after the destruction of Jerusalem, abode, were converted to Christ, as other countries were, in the days of Constantine, and after; and a patriarch settled at Jerusalem: and a Bishop at Cesarea, and many Bishops and churches among them, though some remained obstinate.

CHAP. XXIV.

AND Jesus went out, and departed from the temple; and his disciples came to *him* for to shew him the buildings of the temple. 2. And Jesus said unto them, See ye not all these things? Verily I say unto you, There shall not be left here one stone upon another, that shall not be thrown down.

1, 2. All this shall be cast down for the sin of this people.

3. And as he sat upon the mount of Olives, the disciples came unto him privately, saying, Tell us when shall these things be? and what *shall be* the sign of thy coming, and of the end of the world?

3. They desired him, who had so oft told them, that he must be crucified, and rise again, and yet come again, to tell them the meaning, and signs of this his coming, which they did not well understand. Some expositors of this hard chapter think, That the question meaneth no more, than [what shall be the signs of thy coming to destroy Jerusalem; and of the end of their policy:] Others think, That they expected that Christ should presently come and reign at Jerusalem and set up a kingdom so excellent, as should be the beginning of a new age, or world: as Noah's after the deluge, when all the world of wicked men should submit to him or be destroyed. Others say, That these questions are put of different things and times, and accordingly answered: 1. When the temple should be destroyed? 2. When Christ should set up his kingdom? 3. When the world should end? The two first undoubtedly they meant; but by his coming, I do not think they meant, either his sending the Roman army, nor his coming at the day of the resurrection and judgment: but his coming to a visible monarch, and declaring himself king, and reigning accordingly. And 3. By the end of the world, whether they meant the utter desolation at last, or the end of the unreformed age or world, which his kingdom should overthrow, I am not certain. And though Christ do not presently blame their mis-expectations, his answers approve them not, but tend to rectify them.

4. And Jesus answered and said unto them, Take heed that no man deceive you. 5. For many shall come in my name, saying, I am Christ: and shall deceive many.

4, 5. It is true that this temple shall be destroyed, and my kingdom shall be set up, and the world of enemies be subdued, (and that of nature be dissolved). But for your question of the time, let me first admonish you to be fortified by patience and faith, against many deceivers that will for trial be permitted to pretend, that not I, but they are the true Messiah: (such were Simon Disitheus, Theudas,) and look for a visible monarch.

6. And ye shall hear of wars, and rumours of wars: see that ye be not troubled: for all *these things* must come to pass, but the end is not yet.

6. There will be fearful commotions, risings, and wars, before these things come to pass; let not that disturb you.

7. For nation shall rise against nation, and kingdom against kingdom: and there shall be famines, and pestilences, and earthquakes in divers places. 8. All these *are* the beginning of sorrows.

7, 8. Wars by sedition among yourselves, and wars of other nations, with other plagues and commotions, and signs, shall be but forerunners of that sorrowful time.

9. Then shall they deliver you up to be afflicted, and shall kill you: and ye shall be hated of all nations for my name's sake.

9. And before that day foreknow what shall befal yourselves: Persecution, murder, and common hatred, for my name's sake.

10. And then shall many be offended, and shall betray one another, and shall hate one another.

10. And the temptations of those days shall prevail against many that professed faith, and shall pervert them, and draw them to betray, and hate my true disciples, and shew their unfaithfulness.

11. And many false prophets shall rise, and shall deceive many.

11. And many that make themselves the masters of sects and heresies, shall pretend inspiration and revelation for lies, and pernicious doctrines; and many shall be deceived and follow them.

12. And because iniquity shall abound, the love of many shall wax cold.

12. And iniquity shall so far abound, both in the world assaulting the church, and in the declining of church members (by worldliness, fleshliness, pride, and heresy) that the first fervours of Christian love shall be abated.

13. But he that shall endure unto the end, the same shall be saved.

13. But he that overcometh these temptations, and keepeth his integrity, and persevereth in his fidelity, shall attain the end of his faith, and be saved.

14. And this gospel of the kingdom shall be preached in all the world for a witness unto all nations, and then shall the end come.

14. And the Jews driving you away by persecution, you shall preach the gospel to the *heathen* nations, who, by receiving it, shall condemn the Jews: And then shall come the desolation of their state, and the ending of their law and policy.

15. When ye therefore shall see the abomination of desolation, spoken of by Daniel the prophet, stand in the holy place, (whoso readeth let him understand), 16. Then let them which be in Judea, flee into the mountains. 17. Let him which is on the house-top, not come down to take any thing out of his house: 18. Neither let him which is in the field return back to take his clothes.

15—18. When ye see the desolating *heathen* army come to use their force and violence, against the sacred place of the Jews, answering that which Daniel saith of others, then stay not but be gone, and be glad if by flight you can save your lives, but stay not to save your goods or clothes.

19. And woe unto them that are with child, and to them that give suck in those days.

19. And those that are made slow by impediments of children, &c. are like to lose their lives.

20. But pray ye that your flight be not in the winter, neither on the sabbath-day:

20. It will increase the calamity of your flight, if it should fall out in the winter, when the weather will delay you; or on a sabbath-day, when the Jews scruple journeying; or a sabbath year, when the land untilled beareth not fruit.

21. For then shall be great tribulation, such as was not since the beginning of the world to this time, no, nor ever shall be. 22. And except those days should be shortened, there should no flesh be saved: but for the elect's sake, those days shall be shortened.

21, 22. Note, This was most dreadfully fulfilled, as Josephus, who was then among them, hath fully written, 1,100,000 killed, and 97,000 captives.

22. If these slaughters, by the Romans should continue long, no Jews would be left alive. But God will so far preserve the believers, that their armies shall stay but a little while.

23. Then if any man shall say unto you, Lo, here is Christ, or there: believe it not. 24. For there shall arise false Christs, and false prophets, and shall shew great signs and wonders, insomuch that (if it *were* possible) they shall deceive the very elect. 25. Behold, I have told you before.

23, 24, 25. In this desolation it will add to their misery, that false Christs and prophets shall arise, and promise to deliver them, and lead them further into snares: And they shall do such signs and wonders, as, if God did not preserve them, would deceive the very chosen of God, the true believers. But whatsoever fame you hear of such, believe it not: I have fore-warned you.

26. Wherefore, if they shall say unto you, Behold, he is in the desert, go not forth: behold, *he is* in the secret chambers, believe it not.

26. Go not after any such deceiver whatever they say he is, though he promise deliverance.

27. For as the lightning cometh out of the east, and shineth even unto the west: so also shall the coming of the Son of Man be.

27. For as you must look for no other Saviour; so my coming will not be such an appearance in flesh, but by heavenly light shining forth from the east unto the western parts of the world, by my word and spirit, turning men from darkness to light; in preparation to my coming to judgment, in which I will suddenly appear from heaven in glory to all the world, as lightning doth in a moment in the skies.

Note, Some expositors rather think, it speaketh of his sudden destroying Jerusalem.

28. For wheresoever the carcase is, there will the eagles be gathered together.

28. And as for these forlorn Jews whose deserved destruction is decreed of God; they are as a carcase to the eagles: the Roman messengers of God's wrath will find them out.

Note, Others expound it [where the gospel is preached, thither will the people flock.]

29. Immediately after the tribulation of those days, shall the sun be darkened, and the moon shall not give her light, and the stars shall fall from heaven, and the powers of the heavens shall be shaken.

CHAP. XXIV.   ST. MATTHEW.   65

29. Note, Some expound this metaphorically, of the overthrow of all the Jewish state, power, policy. Others, of the Roman wars and concussions. Others, properly, of dreadful prodigies that shall appear before Christ's coming to judgment, Joel ii. 31, and iii. 15.

30. And then shall appear the sign of the Son of Man in heaven: and then shall all the tribes of the earth mourn, and they shall see the Son of Man coming in the clouds of heaven, with power and great glory.

30. As some, [Then the Jews shall be convinced that their destruction was Christ's revenge for his death, and rejection.: and all the tribes of their land shall mourn, as if they had seen Christ coming himself against them in the clouds, with power and glory.] As others, [The sign of the cross shall appear to Constantine in the sky; and all the *heathen* nations shall mourn, and be cast down; and they shall see Christ setting up his kingdom, by imperial arms, with power and glory.] As others, [Then shall Christ suddenly appear from heaven, to judge the world, and come in the clouds, with power and glory, to the grief and terror of all the wicked.] Supposing that Christ passed from the destruction of Jerusalem, to speak of his last coming.

31. And he shall send his angels with a great sound of a trumpet, and they shall gather together his elect from the four winds, from one end of heaven to the other.

31. As some, [He shall gather the believers in all Judea whom he saved from this destruction.] As others, [He shall send forth his apostles with the gospel, as a trumpet, to call his chosen out of the world, into his church.] As others, [By Constantine and Christian powers, he shall through all the empire set Christians in honour and power over the *heathens*.] As others, literally, [He shall at his appearing, and judgment, send his angels, and gather all his elect to himself.

32. Now learn a parable of the fig-tree: when his branch is yet tender, and putteth forth leaves, ye know that summer *is* nigh; 33. So likewise ye, when ye shall see all these things, know that -it is near, even at the doors.

32, 33. By the similitude of the fig-tree, I tell you, that there must be time for these changes; but when ye see the beginning of these signs, know that the accomplishment is not far off.

34. Verily I say unto you, This generation shall not pass, till all these things be fulfilled. 35. Heaven and earth shall pass away, but my words shall not pass away.

34 35. As some, [Some yet alive, shall see all fulfilled that I have hitherto spoken; that is, Only of the destruction of Jerusalem.] As others, [That part that I have spoken of the destruction of Jerusalem, some alive shall see.] (For it was but thirty-eight years after.) As others, [Some yet alive shall see the beginning of the performance of all that I have said, and the rest will follow; and a thousand years with the Lord, is but as one day.] When heaven and earth passeth away, you shall see, that my word is all fulfilled: They shall see the Catholic church.

36. But of that day and hour knoweth no man, no, not the angels of heaven, but my Father only.

36. The day and hour of the Jews' destruction, say some, Of the end of the world, say others; none knows but God.

Note, 1. Whence the ancient doctors gathered, that Christ had a two-fold knowledge, (will and operation.) One human and imperfect, the other divine and perfect. 2. Angels may increase in knowledge.

37. But as the days of Noe *were*, so shall also the coming of the Son of Man be. 38. For as in the days that were before the flood, they were eating and drinking, marrying, and giving in marriage, until the day that Noe entered into the ark. 39. And knew not until the flood came, and took them all away; so shall also the coming of the Son of Man be.

37, 38, 39. As in the days of Noe they would not believe their danger, till it surprised them, but lived sumptuously in their fleshly pleasure, and worldly business: so will it be with sinners at my coming; (Both at the destruction of Jerusalem, and at the day of judgment.)

40. Then shall two be in the field, the one shall be taken, and the other left. 41. Two *women shall be* grinding at the mill, the one shall be taken, and the other left.

40, 41. [Then I will manifest my distinguished providence: One, that is, a believer shall be taken to me, and be saved, and the other left to delusion, and destruction in unbelief.]

Note, The difficulty of most of these foregoing texts, forbids me to be peremptory in determining, whether they speak only of the destruction of Jerusalem, as in Mark, the question seemeth to intimate. (Or also of the end of the world, as some words in the answer seem to intimate.) And I incline to think, that as the types and prophesies of the Old Testament, spake proximately of the *things* and *persons* typified, but remotely and chiefly thereby of Christ, and things typified: so these texts speak, first, of the destruction of Jerusalem, and next of the calling of the Gentiles,

2.   F

and Catholic church, but thereby finally and chiefly of the end of the world: As if Christ said, As it will be here now, so it will be then, parabolically.

42. Watch, therefore, for ye know not what hour your Lord doth come.

42. This therefore is the necessary wisdom of all, to be as men on their watch, never asleep, or mindless; but always ready, as expecting the coming of your Lord: And then, though you understand not all circumstances beforehand, you shall be safe.

43. But know this, that if the good man of the house had known in what watch the thief would come, he would have watched, and would not have suffered his house to be broken up. 44. Therefore, be ye also ready; for in such an hour as you think not, the Son of Man cometh.

43, 44. Seeing men will watch against a thief, if they knew when he would come, watch you for the preventing of surprise, because you know not, but it may presently be the time: and it must be a continual readiness that must be your safety: not only as to the destruction of Jerusalem, but as to every man's particular judgment: (For Christ spake for the use of us all to the end, and not only for the few Jews that heard him.)

45. Who then is a faithful and wise servant, whom his Lord hath made ruler over his household, to give them meat in due season? 46. Blessed is that servant, whom his Lord when he cometh shall find so doing.

45, 46. And those that are faithful and wise teachers and rulers of his church, to give them meet and seasonable instruction, as food for their souls, shall be found at their Lord's coming, blessed persons, and shall be abundantly gainers by their labours and their sufferings.

47. Verily I say unto you, that he shall make him ruler over all his goods.

47. I tell you such ministers, (how poor or despised soever now by the world,) shall be advanced to a far greater dignity than their present pastoral office, even to a participation under Christ of the universal government.

48. But and if that evil servant shall say in his heart, My Lord delayeth his coming. 49. And shall begin to smite *his* fellow-servants, and to eat and drink with the drunken:

48, 49. But if any assume the sacred ministry, and shall say in his heart, it is long since Christ promised to come, and now his coming is either uncertain, or will not be in haste; and thereupon shall indulge his fleshly lusts, and shall turn a malignant abuser of his fellow-servants, and persecute, silence, and oppress them, and give himself up to the pleasure of his appetite, in feasting and drunkenness;

50. The Lord of that servant shall come in a day when he looketh not for him, and in an hour that he is not aware of: 51. And shall cut him asunder, and appoint *him* his portion with the hypocrites: there shall be weeping and gnashing of teeth.

50. The lord of that servant will surprise him in his sin and security, when he least suspecteth it; and will execute that vengeance on him, which is due to such as aggravate their wickedness, by hypocrisy; and make him feel that as it is odious, so it is dreadful to profane holy things, and to fight against holiness in the name of Christ, and at once, to be a minister, a worldling, a sensualist, and a persecutor.

ANNOTATION.

It is of great moment, for the understanding of this chapter, and much of Christ's gospel, to know the true meaning of Christ's *kingdom*, and his *coming*. Though oft he spake directly of his last coming to judgment; yet ordinarily this seemeth his meaning. His kingdom is that reign in heaven and earth at once, which he was to exercise as the Messiah, or God incarnate, having redeemed lost man. The little poor nation of Israelites were his *peculiar people before:* Upon his ascension, the Gentile world was to be called, and a Catholic church gathered over the earth, in a more excellent covenant of peculiarity; and this Catholic church, is the kingdom of the Messiah: His coming, is not his sending his enemies to destroy Jerusalem; nor yet his visible appearance in person, (till judgment) but his setting up this his kingdom: his coming to reign, that is, to erect this Catholic church: This is plainly expounded in Luke xvii. 20, 21, 23. The Pharisees demanded, when the kingdom of God should come? He told them, The kingdom of God cometh not with observation or outward shew, (by personal visible appearance of the king, in pomp and splendour, with a court, as monarchs rule) nor shall they say, Lo here or Lo there; (no head, king, or court shall be visible:) for behold, the kingdom of God is in you, (or among you:) It is a spiritual reign in souls, and in the church; of which you have already some beginnings. 24. For as the lightning that lighteneth out of one part under the heaven, shineth to the other part under heaven; so shall also the Son of Man be in his day: but first he must suffer and be rejected of this generation, &c. that is, when he hath suffered, and been rejected, he will rise, ascend, and from heaven send his spirit and word to enlighten the world from east to west, and call a Catholic church amongst the Gentiles, and this is his kingdom and reign; and this generation shall not pass, till this Catholic church be gathered, though not perfected. What else can be meant by Christ's many parables, that the kingdom of God is like a grain of mustard-seed. A little leaven hid in meal. A field sown, that after had tares. A net cast into the sea, &c. When the Catholic church was made, Christ's kingdom came; and when his kingdom came, he came as king to govern it, by his spirit, word, and ministers, Matt. xxi. 43. The kingdom of God, (that is, the church state of peculiarity) shall be taken from you, and given to a nation (the Gentile world) bringing forth the fruit thereof: But the perfection of the kingdom will be at last. And as to the time of his appearing for judgment, it must specially be observed, that he tells them, That it was not known either to angels, or to himself. And if Christ knew it not, (as man) how presumptuous are they that foretel it. And whereas they say, It was but the day and the hour, and not the year, that he knew not? I answer, That by day and hour is meant in general, the time. And if Christ knew it not, no wonder if he foretold it not to his disciples, but told them to this effect, It shall be uncertain to you, that you may be always ready: Therefore, though it be false that Grotius saith, That Paul thought, that the coming of Christ would be in his days; It is true, That Paul knew not but that it might be in his days. They might know indeed, that it would not be till certain signs foretold, came to pass; but after that, they were still to expect it as uncertain.

CHAP. XXV.

THEN shall the kingdom of heaven be likened unto ten virgins, which took their lamps, and went forth to meet the bridegroom. 2. And five of them were wise, and five *were* foolish.

1. When Christ cometh to judgment, either on the Jews as aforesaid, or on any with death; or on all, at the last day, the administration of his kingly government, towards the ready, and unready may be illustrated by this similitude, of ten virgins, &c.

Note, The custom of the Jews was, to make very pompous feasts, at weddings, and many virgins used to go to the bride's house, and thence with hand-lamps to go, and attend her to the wedding.

3. They that were foolish, took their lamps, and took no oil with them. 4. But the wise took oil in their vessels with their lamps.

3, 4. The foolish made no preparation but for the present; but the wise provided for the time to come, supposing there might be some delay.

Note, The parable is, to stir up all to preparation for death and judgment; and all the trials that are to come: and to prove it damning foolishness, after all warnings to delay, and be unprepared.

5. While the bridegroom tarried, they all slumbered and slept.

5. Note, The lamp, and the vessel of oil signify, preparation by sudden act, and preparation by a stated habit: Wise and foolish, good and bad, may slee, upon delay; and keep not up still the same lively activity: But the godly have still the holy nature and habits.

6. And at midnight there was a cry made, Behold, the bridegroom cometh, go ye out to meet him.

6. And when they are deepest in security, or forgetfulness, and minding worldly things, they suddenly hear that Christ by death or judgment is coming; He is just at hand: There is no more delay, you must presently come away to judgment, and to be saved, if you are his.

7. Then all those virgins arose, and trimmed their lamps.

7. When the midnight cry cometh, and there is no longer stay, all men, good and bad, wise and foolish, will be awakened, to attempt some sudden preparation: The worst almost under the sentence of death will think, what now must I do to be saved? Self-love and fear, will make them cry for mercy, with some kind of repentance though they be unconverted.

8. And the foolish said unto the wise, Give us of your oil, for our lamps are gone out.

8. The unprepared unholy souls, when death and judgment comes, would fain then be found in the state of holy believers, and would die the death of the righteous, and wish for their preparations.

9. But the wise answered, saying, *Not so*; lest there be not enough for us and you: but go ye rather to them that sell, and buy for yourselves.

9. These wishes then are vain: One man cannot be saved by another man's righteousness. It must be your own, or it will not save you. Go, therefore, and make your own preparation.

10. And while they went to buy, the bridegroom came, and they that were ready, went in with him to the marriage; and the door was shut.

10. Death and judgment will not stay for the unready: They that then are found unsanctified

only under fears and wishes to be saved, will be shut out, when holy prepared souls are let in.

11. Afterward came also the other virgins, saying, Lord, Lord, open to us.

11. Self-love and fear, will make the unholy cry in vain too late for mercy.

12. But he answered and said, Verily I say unto you, I know you not.

12. But he will not own, or open to such seekers, but reject them. Note, Not that true conversion and holiness is ever too late. But those fears and cries for mercy, which in time might have been good preparations for a true change, may be all lost, and come short of it at the last extremity.

13. Watch, therefore, for ye know neither the day, nor the hour wherein the Son of Man cometh.

13. God hath purposely concealed the time of Christ's coming from the knowledge of all men, that all might be obliged to be in constant, watchful readiness: yea, it is said, That Christ himself knew it not as man. They that say, The year may be known, though not the day, or hour, distort the text which meaneth by *day* and *hour*, the *time:* as if he had said, You are not sure (save by the signs forementioned not fulfilled) but it may be the next day, or hour: so that the apostles themselves were uncertain, though they rebuked them that pretended to know, that it was at hand, before Jerusalem was destroyed. From their days till now, God hath kept the church uncertain, but that it might quickly come. So that Grotius is mistaken that thinks Paul believed it would be in his days; as if he had by a false motive drawn men to godliness: But Paul knew not how soon it might have come. Ignorance of it is needful; but error is hurtful: (of which before.)

14. For *the kingdom of heaven is* as a man travelling into a far country, who called his own servants, and delivered unto them his goods:
15. And unto one he gave five talents, to another two, and to another one, to every man according to his several ability, and straightway took his journey.

14, 15. Christ passing into the heavens, committeth to his servants the word, means, and mercies of his grace, that they may improve them till he come by death and judgment to call them to account; not giving the same degree of means and mercy to all, but to some more, and to some less.

16. Then he that had received the five talents, went and traded with the same, and made *them* other five talents. 17. And likewise he that had received two, he also gained other two.

16, 17. They that had the greater means and helps improved them, to their own increase of grace, and the good of others, and the service and honour of their Lord.

18. But he that had received one, went and digged in the earth, and hid his lord's money.

18 Note, Though the least helps should be answerably improved, yet the less (such as those have, who have little more than the light of nature) excite not men so powerfully to an improvement.

19. After a long time, the Lord of those servants cometh, and reckoneth with them.

19. Note, Christ here intimateth that his coming to reckon with them would not be hasty.

20. And so he that had received five talents, came and brought other five talents, saying, Lord, thou deliveredst unto me five talents: behold I have gained besides them five talents more.

20. I have used them to the increase of thy grace in me, and to the good of men, and to thy glory.

21. His lord said unto him, Well done, thou good and faithful servant: thou hast been faithful over a few things, I will make thee ruler over many things: enter thou into the joy of thy lord.

21. His Lord who freely gave him his talents to use, yet rewarded his faithful usage of them, and praised his fidelity, saying, I will give thee great things, because thou hast well and faithfully used the smaller mercies of this life which I gave thee.

22. He also that had received two talents, came and said, Lord, thou deliveredst unto me two talents: behold, I have gained two other talents besides them. 23. His lord said unto him, Well done, good and faithful servant; thou hast been faithful over a few things, I will make thee ruler over many things: enter thou into the joy of thy lord.

22, 23. Note, 1. The reward of glory given for our diligent improvement of the mercies of this life, is consistent with the freeness of the gift. 2. God himself will praise the fidelity of his servants as worthy of praise. 3. Great rewards will crown the faithful for little things here sincerely done.

4. It is our Lord's own joy that the faithful shall enter and partake of.

24. Then he which had received the one talent, came and said, Lord, I knew thee that thou art an hard man, reaping where thou hast not sown, and gathering where thou hast not strawed: 25. And I was afraid, and went and hid thy talent in the earth: lo, there thou hast, *that is* thine.

24, 25. The fear of thy severity made me think it safest to keep thy money merely from being lost.

Note. Hard thoughts of God make men backward to his service, which is a work of love: and sinful fear is an enemy to holy diligence and fruitfulness.

26. His lord answered and said unto him, Thou wicked and slothful servant, thou knewest that I reap where I sowed not, and gather where I have not strawed: 27. Thou oughtest, therefore, to have put my money to the exchangers, and then at my coming I should have received mine own with usury.

26, 27. Note, 1. God will take a slothful servant for a wicked servant; unprofitableness and omission of duty, is damnable unfaithfulness in us that are but stewards and servants. To do no harm is a praise fit for a stone and not a man. 2. To confess God's holy government, and yet to be unholy, is to be self-condemning.

Qu. Doth this text justify usury? Answ. It speaketh of that sort of increase made by exchange and trading, without reproof, and with seeming approbation. Gain by trading and merchandise is one sort of usury: all usury is unlawful which is against *justice* or *charity*. And all other is lawful; and some that is a work of charity is to some a duty.

28. Take, therefore, the talent from him, and give it unto him which hath ten talents. 29. For unto every one that hath shall be given, and he shall have abundance: but from him that hath not, shall be taken away, even that which he hath.

28, 29. He shall be deprived of the mercies of this life, who improved them not for a better life, when he that so improved them shall have an abundant reward, the mercies of this life, and that to come.

30. And cast ye the unprofitable servant into outer darkness: there shall be weeping and gnashing of teeth.

30, Note, 1. Omission and unprofitableness is a damning sin. 2. Hell is called *fire* for pain, and *darkness* for uncomfortableness.

31. When the Son of Man shall come in his glory, and all the holy angels with him, then shall he sit upon the throne of his glory. 32. And before him shall be gathered all nations; and he shall separate them one from another, as a shepherd divideth his sheep from the goats: 33. And he shall set the sheep on his right hand, but the goats on the left.

31, &c. The coming of Christ shall be in glory, with all his holy angels, who served him here for the good of his elect; and as judge he shall sit on his throne of glory; and all persons and nations shall be called by him to judgment, and he shall separate them as sheep and goats, &c.

34. Then shall the King say unto them on his right hand, Come ye blessed of my Father, inherit the kingdom prepared for you from the foundation of the world.

34. Then Christ shall pronounce this sentence on the faithful, *Come, &c.* Note, O comfortable words, [*Come*,] Whither? To Christ, to God, to heaven! [*ye blessed of my Father,*] sure such shall be blessed indeed, [*inherit*] not only *use* [*the kingdom,*] in participation with the king of glory, [*prepared for you*] by eternal love, and degree.

35. For I was an hungered, and ye gave me meat: I was thirsty, and ye gave me drink: I was a stranger, and ye took me in: 36. Naked, and ye clothed me: I was sick, and ye visited me: I was in prison, and ye came unto me.

35, 36. Note, 1. These works are noted as the effects of faith and love, without which they would have been but *dead works*. 2. The casual [*for*] signifieth not any merit by commutative justice, as giving God any benefit: But their *moral qualification* and fitness to receive the kingdom freely given, but on such conditions, that we signify our thankful acceptance by true devotedness to Christ. And thus all are judged (that is, finally justified or condemned) according to their works, as judged by the law of grace and faith, and not by Moses's law, or that of innocency. 3. Love to Christ is not sincere, if it will not cause us to prefer his interest in his poor saints, (much more in the whole church) before our ease, wealth, and safety.

37. Then shall the righteous answer him, saying, Lord, when saw we thee an hungered, and fed *thee?* or thirsty, and gave *thee* drink? 38. When saw we thee a stranger, and took *thee* in? or naked, and clothed *thee?* 39. Or when saw we thee sick, or in prison, and came unto thee?

37, &c. Christ doth more interest himself in his servants' love and good works, than they thought or can easily believe, and valueth these more than we do ourselves.

40. And the King shall answer, and say unto them, Verily I say unto you, Inasmuch as ye have done *it* unto one of the least of these my brethren, ye have done *it* unto me.

40. Note, 1. Those poor and weak Christians which the proud despise and scorn, Christ calleth his brethren: 2. And he taketh that as done to him that is done to them for his sake.

41. Then shall he say also unto them on the left hand, Depart from me, ye cursed, into everlasting fire, prepared for the devil and his angels.

41. Note, Every word unspeakably terrible. The cursed state is to depart from Christ into everlasting fire with devils, who were first adjudged to it, and drew the wicked to be their companions in torments by following them in sin. Wicked men are so like devils that they must dwell with them for ever in misery.

42. For I was an hungered, and ye gave me no meat? I was thirsty, and ye gave me no drink: 43. I was a stranger, and ye took me not in: naked, and ye clothed me not: sick, and in prison, and ye visited me not.

42, 43. Note, That it is not only hating, hurting, persecuting, scorning, or oppressing, that men are damned for to hell fire with devils, but also not loving, relieving, and helping Christ's servants: for he trusted them with his gifts for that use and trial. If these must be in hell with devils, where will oppressors, persecutors, and murderers be?

44. Then shall they also answer him, saying, Lord, when saw we thee an hungered, or athirst, or a stranger, or naked, or sick, or in prison, and did not minister unto thee?

44. Note, Wicked men know not the greatness of their own sin, nor how much that is against Christ which is against his servants.

45. Then shall he answer them, saying, Verily, I say unto you, In as much as ye did *it* not to one of the least of these, ye did *it* not to me.

45. Note, The wicked shall suffer, not only for hurting, but for not helping the faithful, as if it had been Christ himself that they neglected. O what a motive is this to charity!
Qu. Will it not be endless thus to convince and judge all the world? Ans. No: though this be spoken after the manner of men, God can at once open every man's case to his own conscience, and judge all the world in a moment, as the sun doth at once enlighten all the eyes on earth.

46. And these shall go away into everlasting punishment: but the righteous into life eternal.

46. The execution shall presently follow the sentence. All that shewed not their faith in Christ, and love to him, by loving his servants above their worldly wealth and pleasure, shall go to everlasting punishment with devils that deceived them: And the faithful that loved Christ, and his interest and servants above their fleshly interests, shall go into endless life and blessedness. But this doth not extend to condemn infants or poor unable persons for not doing what they could not; nor to deprive them of a reward that had a will to do more than they were able.

CHAP. XXVI.

AND it came to pass, when Jesus had finished all these sayings, he said unto his disciples, 2. Ye know that after two days is *the feast of* the passover, and the Son of Man is betrayed to be crucified.

1, 2. Note, Christ went not ignorantly or constrained to his death, but willing and foreknowing it.

3. Then assembled together the chief priests, and the scribes, and the elders of the people, unto the palace of the high-priest, who was called Caiaphas, 4. And consulted that they might take Jesus by subtilty, and kill *him.* 5. But they said, Not on the feast *day,* lest there be an uproar among the people.

3, &c. Note, 1. The chief men, priests and rulers were the chief murderers. 2. It is a wonder that the people were not destroyed as seditious rebels, rather than feared by such rulers; when they would have resisted or stoned them that had assaulted Christ or a prophet.

6. Now when Jesus was in Bethany, in the house of Simon the leper, 7. There came unto him a woman having an alabaster-box of very precious ointment, and poured *it* on his head, as he sat at *meat.* 8. But when his disciples saw *it*, they had indignation, saying, To what purpose is this waste? 9. For this ointment might have been sold for much, and given to the poor.

6, &c. 1. It being usual at great feasts in the country to anoint, she signified by this her great love and honour to Christ. 2. Judas was the chief murmurer, but perhaps some others might object.

10. When Jesus understood *it*, he said unto them, why trouble ye the woman? for she hath wrought a good work upon me. 11. For ye have the poor always with you, but me ye have not always. 12. For in that she hath poured this ointment on my body, she did *it* for my burial.

10, &c. Note, Though works of charity to the poor are highly esteemed by Christ, and preferred before many rites and smaller matters, yet some works of piety must be preferred before them. And that duty may in its season be greater, which is not so at another time.

13. Verily I say unto you, Wheresoever this gospel shall be preached in the whole world, *there* shall also this that this woman hath done, be told for a memorial of her.

13. Note, 1. How highly Christ valueth the true love and costly piety of the meanest! 2. Christ knew and decreed that the gospel or history of his life, death, and burial, and resurrection, should be preached throughout the world, yea, and written too. The words in Matt. xxiv. [*Let him that readeth understand*] seem to be Christ's own words, and to imply that all those his words should be written: at least we may well answer them that ask, Where did Christ command them to write the scripture? that 1. His spirit in them commanded it. 2. *Writing is but the most public sort of preaching:*

14. Then one of the twelve, called Judas Iscariot, went unto the chief priests, 15. And said *unto them*, What will ye give me, and I will deliver him unto you? And they covenanted with him for thirty pieces of silver. 16. And from that time he sought opportunity to betray him.

14, 15, 16. Note, Christ knowingly permitted an hypocrite in the apostleship, and to betray him, to foretel us that covetous, false-hearted hypocrites will be in the visible church; and will betray it. 2. Covetous love of money is the root of treachery in hypocrite ministers and others. 3. Judas's sin was not by sudden passion, but deliberate, contrived, and contracted (for three pounds, fifteen shillings.)

17. Now the first *day* of the *feast of* unleavened bread, the disciples came to Jesus, saying unto him, Where wilt thou that we prepare for thee to eat the passover?

17. On the fifth day of the week called now Thursday at eventide, &c.

18. And he said, Go into the city to such a man, and say unto him, The master saith, My time is at hand, I will keep the passover at thy house with my disciples.

18. Note, As to the great controversies here, whether Christ and the Jews did eat the passover the same day, and whether Christ did eat the *paschal lamb,*or only the *unleavened bread* and *bitter herbs;* which was the beginning of the passover, being to have eaten the lamb at the next evening, if he had not been sacrificed himself: I leave the discussion of them to commentators, who handle them at large, not troubling ordinary readers with them.

19. And the disciples did as Jesus had appointed them, and they made ready the passover. 20. Now when the even was come, he sat down with the twelve. 21. And as they did eat, he said, Verily, I say unto you, that one of you shall betray me. 22. And they were exceeding sorrowful, and began every one of them to say unto him, Lord, is it I? 23. And he answered and said, He that dippeth his hand with me in the dish, the same shall betray me.

19, &c. Note, 1. Christ being under the law, was to keep the law of the passover. 2. The innocent disciples were troubled both at the tidings of the thing, and that they should be under suspicion.

24. The Son of Man goeth as it is written of him: but woe unto that man by whom the Son of Man is betrayed; it had been good for that man, if he had not been born.

ST. MATTHEW. CHAP. XXVI

24. Note, God's decree to bring good out of men's evil, extenuateth not men's sin or punishment; the escaping of a greater evil, is here called [good] not in itself, but to that man.

25. Then Judas which betrayed him, answered and said, Master, is it I? He said unto him, Thou hast said.

25. Note, Judas was before resolved and hardened; so that this notice did not stop him from the sin.

26. And as they were eating, Jesus took bread, and blessed *it*, and brake it, and gave *it* to the disciples, and said, Take, eat; this is my body.

26. Note, 1. This bread was unleavened and part of the passover. 2. The blessing it, was the separating it to this holy use, and praying God to bless it, and pronouncing it blest. 3. The breaking it, signified, the breaking of Christ's body, represented hereby as the sacrifice for sin. 4. The giving it, signifieth the giving himself to believing receivers; with and for their spiritual and everlasting life. For the sacrament as administered hath these three parts, 1. The consecration, 2. The commemoration, or representation, 3. The communication. 5. [*This is my body*] meaneth, [This is my sacrificed body representative.] When it is consecrated it is not to be called [bread,] that is, mere bread, for it hath now another form, and *forma denominat ;* But it is only a relative form; If you ask what matter it hath, It is bread still: If you ask what form, it is Christ's sacramental body. As if you ask of the king's coin, what is it, it is in general, money, particularly this or that piece of money: The answer is not, it is silver or gold, for that speaketh not the form: But if you ask what metal it is made of, it is silver or gold, so is it here.

6. It is not Christ's body as glorified in heaven that is represented in the sacrament, but as crucified flesh. The second council at Nice, with the foregoing general council at Constantinople, agree, that Christ's body in heaven is not flesh, (though they differ about images.) Flesh and blood enter not there, but spiritual bodies; it is not flesh, if it consist not of fibrous coagulated blood and chyme made of food; which is not there.

7. But it is the true body of Christ that was first offered to God in sacrifice, and as such given to believing receivers, so far as to be theirs in relation of mystical union, and the meritorious cause of their pardon, grace, and glory.

8. What a novel monster the fiction of transubstantiation is, I have fully opened in a little treatise called " Full and Easy Satisfaction what is the True Religion." The circumstances of Christ's action are occasional, and no laws for us: As are 1. Giving it at a passover; 2. At the end of a meal; 3. At supper, or at night; 4. In an inn, or guest-chamber; 5. To none but his family; 6. To none but men; 7. To none but ministers; 8. In an upper room; 9. Lying along in each others' bosoms; 10. But once in his life; 11. Giving it to all at once, and not one by one, (though that seem of more importance than the rest.) 12. Delivering the bread before he gave thanks over the cup, and not over both at once; (though no doubt these may safely be imitated.)

9. Whether Judas was present or not, is uncertain, (and of no doctrinal moment) if he were, and Christ also washed his feet with the rest, it shewed his obdurateness, that could go presently forth to betray him. Doubtless if wicked hypocrites intrude, the sin and punishment is only their own, so be it we sin not by neglecting discipline; for the keys are given to the pastors to keep out men proved incapable by impenitence.

27. And he took the cup, and gave thanks, and gave *it* to them, saying, Drink ye all of it. 28. For this is my blood of the New Testament, which is shed for many for the remission of sins.

27, 28. Note, Giving to one by one, is not necessary. 2. The evangelists speak not all the same words in reciting Christ's administration. Matthew hath no more but [*this is my body*] nor Mark neither; leaving out [*which is given for you*] as Luke hath it, or [*which is broken for you*] as Paul hath it [*do this in remembrance of me.*] And of the cup, there are different words of Matthew, Mark, Luke, and Paul; and Mark mentioneth their drinking it before Christ's words [*this is my blood of the New Testament, &c.*] But what is not spoken by one, is by another, and the sense is the same; and it tells us, that if such a difference be in our administration, it nullifieth not the sacrament.

28. This wine is representatively or sacramentally my blood shed, (not as that of the paschal lamb, for Jews only to seal that old covenant of their peculiarity, but) for the Gentiles also, or the world, to purchase and seal the universal covenant of grace, which giveth free pardon and life to all true believing acceptors.

29. But I say unto you, I will not drink henceforth of this fruit of the vine, until that day when I drink it new with you in my Father's kingdom.

29. Two difficulties here arise, 1. Did not Christ drink with them after his resurrection? Answ. 1. Some say, he drank no wine, but water which was their ordinary drink. 2. Others answer, The kingdom of his Father began at his resurrection. 3. Others say it meaneth, [Shortly I shall leave you, and drink no more with you.] 4. Others probably think he meant, [I shall no more keep a passover or sacrament with you.]

2, The other difficulty is, How he will drink of it in the kingdom of his Father. 1. Some say, Literally after the resurrection on earth. 2. Some say, That a thousand years before the end of the world; all things shall be restored to the primitive paradise state, and Christ reigning on earth, shall drink of the fruit of the vine new, or renewed. 3. Others say, This will be after the resurrection in the new earth. 4. But the usual sad safest exposition is, that the metaphor signifieth only mutual joy in heaven.

30. And when they had sung an hymn, they went out into the mount of Olives.

30. Note, Whether this hymn was that used by the Jews, (which were all the cxiii. to the cxviii. Psalms,) or one made for that use by Christ is uncertain: But they all joined, and tell us, how suitable thanksgiving, and singing psalms or hymns at sacraments and feasts is.

31. Then saith Jesus unto them, All ye shall be offended because of me this night: for it is written, I will smite the shepherd, and the sheep of the flock shall be scattered abroad.

31. You will all be troubled at my apprehension, and be affrighted away from me; as it is written, &c.

32. But after I am risen again, I will go before you into Galilee.

32. Note, Christ oft foretelling his resurrection, proveth his truth, why he would not appear in Jerusalem, and to all, but in Galilee, and to few; he gave us not the reason of it: But he foreknew the Jews' rejection, and would not force belief in them by sight.

33. Peter answered and said unto him, Though all men shall be offended because of thee, *yet* will I never be offended.

33. Nothing shall affright me from thee. Note, His resolution was good, but his self-confidence was bad.

34. Jesus said unto him, Verily I say unto thee, that this night before the cock crow, thou shalt deny me thrice.

34. Before the time called cock's crowing be past. &c. Note, Christ knoweth before, what man's free-will will do.

35. Peter said unto him, Though I should die with thee, yet will I not deny thee. Likewise also said all the disciples.

35. Note, When men are resolved, they are oft too insensible of their weakness and mutability.

36. Then cometh Jesus with them unto a place called Gethsemane, and saith unto the disciples, Sit ye here, while I go and pray yonder.

37. And he took with him Peter, and the two sons of Zebedee, and began to be sorrowful, and very heavy.

36, 37. Qu. Why did not Christ use to pray with his disciples, but by himself? Answ. 1. We know not whether he used it or not. 2. He sung a hymn with them at the passover. But his case so differed from all other men's, that (except in thanksgivings, and generals) the same prayer would not suit him and them.

38. Then saith he unto them, My soul is exceeding sorrowful, even unto death: tarry ye here, and watch with me.

38. Note, Christ took our nature though not our sin: And nature is averse to death, and sensible of its hurt: And the sense of God's enmity to sin, (though not to him) was the chief part of his suffering.

39. And he went a little further, and fell on his face, and prayed, saying, O my Father, if it be possible, let this cup pass from me: nevertheless not as I will, but as thou wilt.

39. Note, 1. Prostration was a humbling posture; but this example binds us not to the same gesture.
2. The first act of man's will is simple complacence in good, and averseness to evil, as such: According to this, as Christ was a man, he was averse to death and suffering, as man is, (else it would be no penalty.) And this is it that he expresseth, first, in his prayer. But the second act of man's will is, about ends and means that stand in competition, and is called choosing, or refusing: when two things inconsistent stand in competition, the better is to be chosen: And according to this Christ formeth the second part of his prayer, [*Not as I will,*] q. d. Thou hast given me a nature, which doth, and must desire good, and not evil, which desireth that I may not suffer. But it is thy will, and my consent to suffer; Therefore thy will, and not my simple volition be done.

40. And he cometh unto the disciples and findeth them asleep, and saith unto Peter, what, could ye not watch with me one hour? 41. Watch and pray that ye enter not into temptation, the spirit indeed *is* willing, but the flesh *is* weak.

40, 41. Note, Christ was to have no support from man in his sufferings. 2. Sleeping, when we should watch and pray is a fault, but such a one as may stand with grace. 3. Watching and praying is God's means appointed to save men from, and in temptation. 4. The spirit of the faithful is willing to do more good than they are able. 5. The flesh in faithful men, may prevail against the spirit in sins of natural infirmity, for a time, though not in gross sins, in the design and bent of heart and life. 6. Christ tenderly excuseth his servants' infirmities.

42. He went away again the second time, and prayed, saying, O my Father, if this cup may not pass away from me, except I drink it, thy will be done.

42. I resign my will to submit to thine, and I desire to fulfil it, for which I came in flesh.

43. And he came and found them asleep again: for their eyes were heavy: 44. And he left them, and went away again, and prayed the third time, saying the same words.

43, 44. Oft speaking the same things in prayer, is meet for them that have the same causes and wants.

45. Then cometh he to his disciples, and saith unto them, Sleep on now, and take your rest; behold, the hour is at hand, and the Son of Man is betrayed into the hands of sinners. 46. Rise, let us be going; behold, he is at hand that doth betray me. 47. And while he yet spake, lo, Judas, one of the twelve came, and with him a great multitude, with swords and staves, from the chief priests and elders of the people.

45, 46, 47. Note, To be hunted to death by the chief priests and rulers, to have a multitude ready to serve them in it with armed violence, to be betrayed by one of his disciples, and forsaken by the rest, was the case of Christ's suffering, in which we must be prepared to follow him.

48. Now he that betrayed him, gave them a sign, saying, Whomsoever I shall kiss, the same is he, hold him fast. 49. And forthwith he came to Jesus, and said, Hail, master? and kissed him. 50. And Jesus said unto him, Friend, wherefore art thou come? Then came they and laid hands on Jesus, and took him.

48, &c. Note, 1. Hypocrites's cruelty is exercised under the name of friendship. How many thousand persecute Christ, in his cause, and servants on pretence of faith, religion, order, and enmity to sin. 2. It is a pitiful sight to see poor ignorant people, in obedience to rulers, persecuting Christ to their own destruction? As if it were he and his servants that were their dangerous enemies.

51. And behold one of them which were with Jesus, stretched out his hand, and drew his sword, and struck a servant of the high-priest's, and smote off his ear.

51. Natural inclination to defence, and love to Christ, overcame Peter's consideration and patience.

52. Then saith Jesus unto him, Put up again thy sword into his place: for all they that take the sword, shall perish with the sword.

52. Put up thy sword, and let us patiently submit to violence : For as none must use the sword, without just warrant and authority; so usually they that fight for themselves, are destroyed, and suffer more than they that patiently endure violence and injustice,

Note, Christ doth not in these words make all self-defence, or war unlawful, but he doth more than forbid unwarrantable fighting; meaning, that not only unlawful resistance of power, and revenge, but even wars and fighting against injuries and enemies usually hasten death, and increase men's sufferings. And therefore they should forethink, whether war, or patience, be like to do more hurt.

53. Thinkest thou that I cannot now pray to my Father, and he shall presently give me more than twelve legions of angels?

53. Note, 1. Angels are ready to serve Christ at his desire. 2. It should stop our impatient thoughts of rash and unlawful self-defence, to think, that God can otherwise deliver us.

54. But how then shall the scriptures be fulfilled, that thus it must be?

54 Note, We must not strive against events, which we foreknow will come to pass.

55. In that same hour said Jesus to the multitudes, Are ye come out as against a thief with swords and staves for to take me? I sat daily with you teaching in the temple, and ye laid no hold on me.

55. Why did you not take me in the temple, but thus in the night like a thief.

56. But all this was done, that the scriptures of the prophets might be fulfilled. Then all the disciples forsook him, and fled.

56. All this was foretold in scripture. They let his disciples go, and they fled away in fear.

57. And they that had laid hold

on Jesus, led *him* away to Caiaphas, the high-priest, where the scribes and the elders were assembled. 58. But Peter followed him afar off unto the high-priest's palace, and went in, and sat with the servants to see the end.

57, 58. They brought him to their arch-priest, as glorying in their success: And Peter went in where the servants sat.

59. Now the chief priests and elders, and all the council, sought false witness against Jesus to put him to death, 60. But found none: yea, though many false witnesses came, yet found they none. At the last came two false witnesses, 61. And said, This *fellow* said, I am able to destroy the temple of God, and to build it in three days.

59, &c. Note, 1. As hypocrites in religion, are worse than Pagans, in that they farther their wickedness on God and religion, so hypocrites, judges, and lawyers, are herein worse than lawless murderers, that they abuse and disgrace law, and government by using them to injustice, and bloodshed. 2. No man is so good or innocent, that false witness may not condemn.

62. And the high-priest arose, and said unto him, Answerest thou nothing? what *is it which* these witness against thee? 63. But Jesus held his peace.

62, 63. Note, Christ was silent, to shew, 1. That he was not over solicitous for his life. 2. When malignant false judges are resolved what to do against innocency and right, it is oft in vain to talk it out with them. And they watched for words of his own to accuse him of.

And the high-priest answered and said unto him, I adjure thee by the living God that thou tell us, whether thou be the Christ, the Son of God.

63. Note, 1. Once for all, take notice that [answering] was then among the Jews a common phrase for [speaking in course] though no question was asked. 2. It was the malignant policy of that arch-priest, to make Christ his own accuser, and witness, when they could get no other: For they knew that he that bound his disciples to confess him, would not refuse to confess himself, when adjured by God: though he was silent as to his defence against personal accusations. And so it is with Christ's enemies to this day, who put Christians, that dare neither lie, nor conceal necessary truth upon self-accusation. As they could find nothing against Daniel, except about the law of his God, which he durst not break to save his life; so do the devil's officers take advantage of good men's consciences, to destroy them.

64. Jesus saith unto him, Thou hast said: nevertheless I say unto you, Hereafter shall ye see the Son of Man sitting on the right hand of power, and coming in the clouds of heaven.

64. I am he, and though I stand here to be judged by you, your eyes shall see me coming in glory, and in power, to judge you, and all the world: (or as some say, To destroy you by the Romans.)

65. Then the high-priest rent his clothes, saying, He hath spoken blasphemy; what further need have we of witnesses? behold, now ye have heard his blasphemy. 66. What think ye? They answered and said, He is guilty of death.

65, 66. Then the high-priest had that which he desired, and by rending his clothes, showed his abhorrence of the supposed sin of Christ, and demanded the sentence of the court against him, as a blasphemer. And they voted him for it guilty of death.

Note, 1. How foolish a thing is it to think, that any law, or any mans's innocency, or goodness, will preserve justice or piety, while bad men are judges. Can any law be better than God's? Or any person better than Christ? The devil's judges possessing the place that God instituted to defend truth and equity, will condemn God himself manifest in flesh, by his own law, as sinning against himself. And they are since the same.

2. The very murderers of Christ, would seem greater enemies to blasphemy, and more zealous for God's honour, than God himself: So little are false men to be believed.

67. Then did they spit in his face, and buffeted him, and others smote *him* with the palms of their hands, 68. Saying, Prophesy unto us, thou Christ, who is he that smote thee?

67, 68. Note, It was God in the flesh that submitted to all this scorn and abuse for our sin. 1. O then, what doth sin deserve? 2. And why should we look for better, and be over-tender of our flesh or reputation.

69. Now Peter sat without in the palace; and a damsel came unto him, saying, Thou also wast with Jesus of Galilee. 70. But he denied before them all, saying, I know not what thou sayest. 71. And when he was gone out into the porch,

another *maid* saw him, and said unto them that were there, This *fellow* was also with Jesus of Nazareth. 72. And again he denied with an oath, I do not know the man.

69, &c. Note, 1. A man that is forwardest in professing courage, and in drawing the sword, and laying about him, is in greater danger basely cowarded by silly wenches. So uncertain a thing is man. 2. Distrustful fear, and love of life, may draw men into multiplied heinous sin.

73. And after a while came unto him they that stood by, and said to Peter, Surely thou also art *one* of them, for thy speech bewrayeth thee. 74. Then began he to curse and to swear, *saying*, I know not the man. And immediately the cock crew.

73. Matthew mentioneth but one cock-crowing; It being the middle or second that is meant. 2. To ask, what had become of Peter, if he had died in this sin, and how far he did fall from grace, is not so profitable, as to consider our own frailty and danger, and how to escape the like.

75. And Peter remembered the words of Jesus, which said unto him, Before the cock crow thou shalt deny me thrice. And he went out, and wept bitterly.

75. Note, Christ looked on Peter (as John saith) and this began to melt him into repentance, with the hearing of the second cock: Yet, though he wept he did not return, and openly confess Christ, as he did after. Doubtless the disciples had far more grace, and were less liable to fall after the Holy Ghost came down on them at Pentecost, than before.

CHAP. XXVII.

WHEN the morning was come, all the chief priests and elders of the people, took counsel against Jesus to put him to death.

1. Note, The Romans had taken from the Jews the power of putting men to death: Therefore they consulted how to get the Roman government to do it: Priests and rulers, all conspire it.

2. And when they had bound him, they led *him* away, and delivered him to Pontius Pilate the governor.

2. When they had judged him to deserve death after their law, they bring him bound to Pilate the Roman governor, to have him condemned, and crucify him.

3. Then Judas which had betrayed him, when he saw that he was condemned, repented himself, and brought again the thirty pieces of silver to the chief priests and elders, 4. Saying, I have sinned, in that I have betrayed the innocent blood. And they said, What *is that* to us? see thou to *that*.

3, 4. Note, 1. It is uncertain whether Judas was before emboldened to betray him for gain, by thinking that he would deliver himself by a miracle; or whether he was made senseless by the devil, till now that God awakened his conscience. 2. O how differently doth sin appear in the hour of flattering temptation, and when conscience is thoroughly awakened! It seems not then the same thing, because conscience is not in the same case. 3. We see here, what cold comfort companions in sin will give a man in misery or despair? *See thou to that*, is all that can be got then from them that tempted and hired him to sin. 4. O the stupidity of seared sleepy consciences! that these arch-priests and rulers should not be touched with Judas's terror and repentance, but say, *What is that to us*, when it was they that hired him to sin, and sinned still.

5. And he cast down the pieces of silver in the temple, and departed, and went and hanged himself.

5. Note, 1. Sinners' gain will at last be like a hot iron, too hot to hold: Despair shall force restitution, when true repentance will not do it. This will be all the comfort of unlawful gain at last. 2. That Judas strangled himself, and that he fell headlong, and his bowels burst out, are both certain: But how he was strangled, whether by mere terror, or by a cord, and how he burst, whether by mere suffocation, or by the fall, and how he fell, whether by precipitation, or by breaking of the cord, &c. are things uncertain.

6. And the chief priests took the silver pieces, and said, It is not lawful for to put them into the treasury, because it is the price of blood.

6. Note, Thus arch-hypocrites make conscience of ceremony, and make no conscience of perjury, persecution, and murdering the innocent. Blood they thirst for and own; and they will give money to procure it; but the price of blood must not be consecrated.

7. And they took counsel, and bought with them the potter's field, to bury strangers in.

7. Note, This was supposed to be a pious use: so holy and charitable would they be!

8. Wherefore that field was called the field of blood unto this day. 9. (Then was fulfilled that which

was spoken by Jeremy the prophet, saying, And they took the thirty pieces of silver, the price of him that was valued, whom they of the children of Israel did value: 10. And gave them for the potter's field, as the Lord appointed me.)

9, &c. Note, How punctually was this foretold? But by whom is a doubt still. The text here saith by Jeremy: the words are found only in Zachary, ch. xi. 12. Some think that Zachary did but recite them from some tradition from Jeremy: Others think that Matthew forgot their names: Others, that the scribes since have mistaken: But Mr. Mede thinks, that this and the rest of Zachary to the end, are truly part of Jeremy's book, misjoined with Zachary by old mistake.

11. And Jesus stood before the governor; and the governor asked him, saying, Art thou the king of the Jews? And Jesus said unto him, Thou sayest.

11. Note, It is like Pilate asked in derision, but Christ affirmed it in earnest, that he was their king by right.

12. And when he was accused of the chief priests and elders, he answered nothing. 13. Then saith Pilate unto him, Hearest thou not how many things they witness against thee? 14. And he answered him to never a word, insomuch, that the governor marvelled greatly.

12, &c. Note, Christ knew the time to speak, and the time to be silent, when speaking would do no good.

15. Now at *that* feast the governor was wont to release unto the people a prisoner, whom they would. 16. And they had then a notable prisoner, called, Barabbas. 17. Therefore, when they were gathered together, Pilate said unto them, Whom will ye that I release unto you? Barabbas, or Jesus, which is called Christ? 18. For he knew that for envy they had delivered him.

15, &c. He knew that it was the doing of the priests and rulers to prosecute him, and thought that possibly the people might be for his life, rather than for such a one as Barabbas.

19. When he was set down on the judgment-seat, his wife sent unto him, saying, Have thou nothing to do with that just man: for I have suffered many things this day in a dream, because of him.

19. Women and dreams may be better monitors to some rulers, than arch-priests, their wit, and interest.

20. But the chief priests and elders persuaded the multitude that they should ask Barabbas, and destroy Jesus.

20. Note, It is the priests and rulers that stir up the malignity of the rabble to do mischief.

21. The governor answered and said unto them, Whether of the twain will ye that I release unto you? They said, Barabbas.

21. Note, The people were of two parties; one part were for Christ, and that so many, that the priests for fear of them durst not take him openly: But the other party were the malignant rabble, who were ready to call for innocent blood, if priests and elders did but set them on.

22. Pilate saith unto them, What shall I do then with Jesus, which is called Christ? They all say unto him, Let him be crucified.

22. Note, Nothing is so bad that ignorant wicked men may not do; nor any so good that they may not murder.

23. And the governor said, Why, what evil hath he done? But they cried out the more, saying, Let him be crucified.

23. Note, It is in vain to call for reason or justice to an ignorant malignant rabble. A heathen ruler was less unjust, than the priests, and their blind followers.

24. When Pilate saw that he could prevail nothing, but that rather a tumult was made, he took water, and washed his hands before the multitude, saying, I am innocent of the blood of this just person: see ye *to it*.

24. Note, Just judges will not do unjustly for the sake of any: But this hypocrite thought the rabble, and the priests' importunity would excuse him: And the guilt was only theirs.

25. Then answered all the people, and said, His blood *be* on us, and on our children.

25. Note, And so it hath been to this day with a most dreadful vengeance; they being killed with a most horrid slaughter, their city and tem-

ple burnt, and the unbelieving offspring being vagabonds over the earth, abhorred by all nations where they come. O dreadful curse! What need any other than themselves to make ignorant wicked people miserable: They are the most direful enemies, yea, devils, and a hell unto themselves.

26. Then released he Barabbas unto them: and when he had scourged Jesus, he delivered him to be crucified.

26. Note, He was scourged after he was sentenced to death: Yet John mentioneth it before.

27. Then the soldiers of the governor took Jesus into the common hall, and gathered unto him the whole band *of soldiers*. 28. And they stripped him, and put on him a scarlet robe. 29. And when they had platted a crown of thorns, they put *it* upon his head, and a reed in his right hand: and they bowed the knee before him, and mocked him, saying, Hail, king of the Jews. 30. And they spit upon him, and took the reed, and smote him on the head.

27, &c. Note, It was God in flesh that was thus made as a fool, the common sport and scorn for our sins: And shall we think to be saved in a life of fleshly pleasure, without partaking of the cross? No wonder if the cross was a stumbling block to the Jews, and foolishness to the Gentiles; to trust life and soul on one that was thus used: till the Holy Ghost by miracle and power conquered unbelief.

31. And after that they had mocked him, they took the robe off from him, and put his own raiment on him, and led him away to crucify him.

31. When they had done with derision they proceed to his execution. All this he suffered for us.

32. And as they came out, they found a man of Cyrene, Simon by name: him they compelled to bear his cross.

32. Note, He that was compelled was innocent, but they that compelled him were the murderers.

33. And when they were come unto a place called Golgotha, that is to say, a place of a scull. 34. They gave him vinegar to drink, mingled with gall: and when he had tasted *thereof*, he would not drink.

33. Note, This called gall, and by Mark, myrrh, is supposed to be a drink that was poisonous, commonly given to malefactors to hasten death for their ease: which Christ refused.

35. And they crucified him, and parted his garments, casting lots: that it might be fulfilled which was spoken by the prophet, They parted my garments among them, and for my vesture did they cast lots.

35. They divided his other garments, and cast lots for his seamless coat.

36. And sitting down, they watched him there: 37. And set up over his head his accusation written, THIS IS JESUS THE KING OF THE JEWS.

36, 37. So it was pretended treason or usurpation that he died for by the Romans, and blasphemy by the Jews: To bear the imputation of such wickedness was not the least of Christ's sufferings.

38. Then were there two thieves crucified with him: one on the right hand, and another on the left.

38. Note, Thus was he numbered with the transgressors, to expiate transgressions.

39. And they that passed by, reviled him, wagging their heads. 40. And saying, Thou that destroyest the temple, and buildest *it* in three days, save thyself; if thou be the Son of God, come down from the cross. 41. Likewise also the chief priests mocking him, with the scribes and elders, said, 42. He saved others, himself he cannot save: if he be the king of Israel, let him now come down from the cross, and we will believe him. 43. He trusted in God; let him deliver him now, if he will have him: for he said, I am the Son of God.

39, &c. Note, Had they known him, and foreknown what would follow, this scorn had been forborne. 2. They make his own words the matter of their accusation, by perverting them. A way still used by such men. 3. They turn his profession of himself into scorn, little knowing that this derided King would judge them and all the world. 4. They turn his saving of others into his derision: Neither the goodness nor the great-

ness of his miraculous works will restrain them. 5. They turn his very relation to God, and trust in him, to his scorn. 6. Infidels will prescribe Christ the terms on which they will believe in him, or else they will not believe: But the faithful take God's terms and cogent evidences, and presume not to prescribe terms unto him.

44. The thieves also which were crucified with him, cast the same in his teeth.

44. Note, 1. All conspire to reproach the Son of God. 2. When we are in suffering all sorts take liberty to load him that is cast down: As in wars all talk against them that are conquered. 3. The thieves here are said to do that, which only one of them did, (a usual phrase).

45. Now from the sixth hour there was darkness over all the land unto the ninth hour.

45. Note, It was extraordinary darkness; but not so great as to hinder converse: therefore it did not convince them. 2. The sun must not shine on that odious fact, which yet the hardened agents glory in, and in darkness go on in the works of darkness.

46. And about the ninth hour, Jesus cried with a loud voice, saying, *Eli, Eli, lama sabachthani?* that is to say, *My God, My God, why hast thou forsaken me?*

46. Note, He either spoke in the Syriac tongue, Psal. xxii. 1. (which was a prophecy of him) or as some think the express Hebrew words, though now variously written.

2. By God's forsaking him, is not meant any abatement of divine love: but that God both exposed him to this death by wicked men, and withdrew from his human nature the sense of his complacence, and let out upon his soul a deep afflicting sense of his displeasure against man for sin, which was his penalty, as he was our surety, and suffered in our stead as a sacrifice for our sin. 3. Christ was thus far forsaken for us, that we might never be quite forsaken.

47. Some of them that stood there, when they heard that, said, This man calleth for Elias.

47. Note, It is uncertain whether they speak this in ignorance of the language, whether Hebrew (which the Jews had forgotten) or Syriac (which the Roman soldiers might not understand:) Or, (which is more probable) in mere profane scorn.

48. And straightway one of them ran, and took a spunge, and filled *it* with vinegar, and put *it* on a reed, and gave him to drink. 49. The rest said, Let be, let us see whether Elias will come to save him.

48, 49. Note, In mere scorn.

50. Jesus, when he had cried again with a loud voice, yielded up the ghost.

50. Note, Luke tells us his last words, [*Father, into thy hand I commend my spirit.*]

51. And behold, the vail of the temple was rent in twain, from the top to the bottom; and the earth did quake, and the rocks rent, 52. And the graves were opened, and many bodies of saints which slept, arose, 53. And came out of the graves after his resurrection, and went into the holy city, and appeared unto many.

51, &c. Note, By the vail some think is meant a curtain hung; others say, The stone wall that was built between the inner sanctuary and the outer; This renting signified the ending of the Jewish law and sanctuary, and the opening to us an access to God by Christ. The earthquake and the rending of the rocks, and opening of the graves went sometime before his resurrection: But the rising and appearing of them was after. It is not the souls of saints that slept, but those bodies that rose. All this convinced not the hardened Jews.

54. Now when the centurion, and they that were with him watching Jesus, saw the earthquake, and those things that were done, they feared greatly, saying, Truly this was the Son of God.

54. Note, The heathen soldiers were not so obdurate as the hypocrite priests and rulers and their followers.

55. And many women were there (beholding afar off) which followed Jesus from Galilee, ministering unto him. 56. Among which was Mary Magdalene, and Mary the mother of James and Joses, and the mother of Zebedee's children.

55, 56. Note. These women stuck closer to Christ than his twelve chief disciples did.

57. When the even was come, there came a rich man of Arimathea, named Joseph, who also himself was Jesus' disciple: 58. He went to Pilate, and begged the body of Jesus: then Pilate commanded the body to be delivered.

57, 58. Note, Christ's death ended not Joseph's love. 2. Pilate was less malignant than the Jews.

59. And when Joseph had taken the body, he wrapped it in a clean linen cloth, 60. And laid it in his own new tomb which he had hewed out in the rock: and he rolled a great stone to the door of the sepulchre, and departed.

59, 60. Note, Well might he lend him a grave who would save him from the grave by a resurrection.

61. And there was Mary Magdalene, and the other Mary, sitting over against the sepulchre.

61. Note, To follow him in love as far as they were able.

62. Now the next day that followed the day of the preparation, the chief priests and Pharisees came together unto Pilate, 63. Saying, Sir, we remember that that deceiver said, while he was yet alive, After three days I will rise again. 64. Command, therefore, that the sepulchre be made sure until the third day, lest his disciples come by night, and steal him away, and say unto the people, He is risen from the dead: so the last error shall be worse than the first. 65. Pilate said unto them, Ye have a watch, go your way, make *it* as sure as you can. 66. So they went and made the sepulchre sure, sealing the stone, and setting a watch.

62, &c. Note, God permitted and over-ruled their malignant suspicion, to prevent all such calumnies and objections against our faith, ever after.

CHAP. XXVIII.

IN the end of the sabbath, as it began to dawn towards the first *day* of the week, came Mary Magdalene, and the other Mary, to see the sepulchre.

1. Note, They came in love with spices to have embalmed his body.

2. And behold, there was a great earthquake; for the angel of the Lord descended from heaven, and came and rolled back the stone from the door, and sat upon it. 3. His countenance was like lightning, and his raiment white as snow. 4. And for fear of him the keepers did shake, and became as dead men.

2, &c. Note, 1. Well might Abraham say, If one rose from the dead they will not be persuaded, when all this would not convince men. 2. If an angel be so dreadful, what will God be to the wicked?

5. And an angel answered and said unto the women, Fear not ye: For I know that ye seek Jesus which was crucified. 6. He is not here: for he is risen, as he said: come, see the place where the Lord lay. 7. And go quickly, and tell his disciples that he is risen from the dead; and behold, he goeth before you into Galilee, there shall ye see him, lo, I have told you.

5. Note, Angels were the preachers of Christ's birth to shepherds, and they are the first preachers of his resurrection to women.

8. And they departed quickly from the sepulchre, with fear and great joy, and did run to bring his disciples word.

8. Note, Women must be the first preachers of Christ's resurrection to his apostles.

9. And as they went to tell his disciples, behold, Jesus met them, saying, All hail. And they came and held him by the feet, and worshipped him.

9. Note, It was poor women that had been sinners, that Christ honoured with his first appearance.

10. Then said Jesus unto them, Be not afraid; go tell my brethren, that they go into Galilee, and there shall they see me.

10. Note, 1. He would not shew himself so openly to the malicious forsaken people at Jerusalem. 2. His disciples and kinsmen are called his brethren. 3. No one evangelist mentioneth the whole of this history; but what one omitteth, another hath (of which after.)

11. Now when they were going, behold, some of the watch came into the city, and shewed unto the

CHAP. XXVIII. ST. MATTHEW. 81

chief priests all the things that were done. 12. And when they were assembled with the elders, and had taken counsel, they gave large money unto the soldiers, 13. Saying, Say ye, His disciples came by night, and stole him away while we slept. 14. And if this come to the governor's ear, we will persuade him, and secure you.

11. Note, What will convince hardened, forsaken men?

15. So they took the money, and did as they were taught: and this saying is commonly reported among the Jews until this day.

15. Note, 1. Lying is the devil's great means against faith; and the love of money is the means that subserveth it. 2. They that will not believe the truth, easily believe deceiving lies.

16. Then the eleven disciples went away into Galilee, into a mountain, where Jesus had appointed them. 17. And when they saw him, they worshipped him: but some doubted.

17. Note, Though the evangelists say no more of Christ's meeting them on this mountain, and what he there said to them; and Luke and John say nothing of it, and there seem a strange difference in their narratives of Christ's appearances, it is but one saying what another had omitted; and no one of them saying all (of which after on John xx, and xxi.)

18. And Jesus came, and spake unto them, saying, All power is given unto me in heaven and in earth. 19. Go ye therefore and teach all nations, baptizing them in the name of the Father, and of the Son, and of the Holy Ghost:

18. After these and other appearings to them, Jesus said, As I have died to redeem the world, in order to the ends of my undertaking, the Father hath given me an universal propriety and governing power by the right of redemption, as chief administrator under him in heaven and earth. So that henceforth all the concerns of men in this world and the other, are at my disposal; and all men under my government by right and obligation. By which authority I now commission you, to go abroad in the world, and make all nations (to the uttermost of your power) my disciples; taking them into my church by solemn covenant, celebrated by baptizing them into the name of the Father, Son, and Holy Ghost.

Note, 1. Christ's right of dominion and empire 2.

is founded in the Father's covenant with him as redeemer. 2. And being universal Lord, redemption is so far universal, as to prove these and other common effects, Rom. xiv. 9. To this end Christ died, rose, and revived, that he might be Lord both of the dead and of the living.

2. The word translated teach, signifieth [disciple to me] or [make nations my disciples.]

3. All Christians should endeavour to make christianity the national religion, that the kingdoms of the world may become the kingdoms of the Lord, and of his Christ; that is, that they be [Christian kingdoms] and not only Christians gathered out of kingdoms.

4. This maketh not all to be Christians, who are in those kingdoms, but only such as are discipled.

5. Infants being parts of all kingdoms, this text commandeth to disciple and baptize them, they are made disciples, by being justly dedicated to Christ, by those that have true power to dispose of them, to learn of him, and obey him as they grow up and are capable. As Christ was relatively, head of the church in his infancy, when his human nature was not capable of the actual administration; so are infants capable of being disciples by covenant dedication, (by those that have the disposal of them for their good, and can covenant for them with men) and by relation and obligation. God had never a church on earth, of which infants were not infant members, since there were infants into the world.

6. To be baptized into the name of the Father, Son, and Holy Ghost; is no less than by solemn covenant to give up one's self to God the Father, as our Father reconciled by Christ: our chief owner and ruler, and, our chief benefactor, even as our God; and to Christ as our saviour, and the Holy Ghost as our sanctifier. And merely to consent to learn of Christ makes one a baptizable disciple.

7. Baptism is christening, and is the badge of those that must love and take each other for Christians; and the terms of church unity, till it be nullified by verbal or actual apostacy.

And it is church tyranny and schism, to make canons which shall exclude those from the church of Christ, whom he taketh in by baptism; before they impenitently nullify that covenant in whole or in some essential part, viz. by proved denying essentials of faith, or forsaking some essential part of obedience.

8. Baptism making us Christians, is our state of regeneration by which we may know our right to justification and salvation; that is, he that consenteth heartily and unfeignedly to the baptismal covenant, is regenerate and justified, and shall be saved. And he that doth consent but with the mouth and outward sign, or leaveth out some essential part in his heart-consent, is regenerate only sacramentally, and a visible member of the church, but is not justified, nor shall be saved.

20. Teaching them to observe all things whatsoever I have commanded you: and lo, I am with you always, even unto the end of the world. Amen.

20. And when you have baptized them, and so united them to me and my universal church;

G

(upon their understanding professed faith and repentance, and dedication of their seed to me,) then congregate them in order under faithful pastors. And as you as general teachers to all the churches, must deliver to them all the commands which I have committed to your trust (by word and writing;) so these pastors must further instruct them that they may grow up in knowledge of all these my commands: And in the performance of this charge, I shall by the help of my spirit, and protection, be present with you and such pastors in their course, to the end of this world, (or age,) till I shall come in glory to the final judgment. Though you see me not, I shall be as really assisting to you, and regardful of you, even in your labours and sufferings, as if you saw me.

Note, 1. This general command of teaching all nations Christ's commands, includeth writing the scriptures, without which they could not teach posterity in all nations his commands.

2. It maketh them his intrusted apostles, from whose fidelity we may believingly receive his commands: And therefore implieth the promise of his spirit to make them true and credible reporters.

3. It implieth that his commands are the universal laws for his Catholic church. And no man or men have authority to make laws for the universal church on earth but he; and to undertake it, is to undertake the prerogative of Christ, and to be Vice-Christ by usurpation: be it Pope or councils.

4. Yet the precept of observing his commands, forbids not the observing of the commands of any lawful limited local rulers under him, not crossing his commands: parents, masters, pastors, princes, must be obeyed in their provinces and places, even about God's worship. If men make subordinate laws, according to God's general laws of love, concord, edification, order, they must be obeyed, (as e. g. what translations of Scripture to use, what psalms, metres, tunes, gestures, time, place, and abundance such like.)

THE GOSPEL

ACCORDING TO

ST. MARK.

NOTE, 1. *That this is the same* Mark *against whom, as not fit to be taken with them,* St. Paul *sharply contended with* Barnabas, *even to parting asunder. But it was not as charging him with any crime, but as unfit to be taken with them in so long and hard a work, which he before deserted.* 2. *It is said by some to be a tradition, that* Mark *wrote this from the mouth of* Peter; *but that is uncertain.* 3. *It is questioned, seeing it is only the eleven apostles to whom Christ promised the eminent help of the spirit to bring all his doctrine to their remembrance, and lead them to all truth; how can we be sure that* Mark *and* Luke *who were no Apostles, and had not this promise, did never mistake in their writing the Gospel?* Answ. *Though Christ promised not infallibility to all preachers then, he promised and gave the eminent miraculous gifts of the spirit to others, as well as to the Apostles, as appeared in* Stephen, Philip, *and others. And this spirit was to fit them for the work to which they were called, which his miracles by them attested.* 2. *And the Apostles that then lived, approved these writings of* Mark *and* Luke, *and so did the churches where the gifts of the spirit did then most abound; who also delivered them down to us.*

Whether this Mark was bishop of Alexandria, or only a transient evangelist there a while, is an historical controversy of no great moment. When Antioch had at once so many great Apostles, Prophets, and Teachers, and no one of them then a bishop to rule the rest as their pastor, we may well conjecture, that the case of Alexandria did not much differ from that of Antioch and Jerusalem, (where neither James nor any one was governor of the Apostles.
The reader must not expect that I repeat at large the pharaphrases or notes which are written on Matthew, when the same History and words are by Mark repeated.

CHAP. I.

THE beginning of the gospel of Jesus Christ, the Son of God. 2. As it is written in the prophets, Behold, I send my messenger before thy face, which shall prepare the way before thee. 3. The voice of one crying in the wilderness, Prepare ye the way of the Lord, make his paths straight.

1. &c. The public entrance of Christ on his ministry, and preaching the glad tidings of salvation, was by the preparation of John's ministry preaching repentance, to fit men for the kingdom of the Messiah at hand; which the prophets had foretold.

Note, Whether by the prophets be here meant Esay and Malachi; or only Esay, is a controversy of small moment.

4. John did baptize in the wilderness, and preach the baptism of repentance for the remission of sins.

4. John told the Jews, that the Messiah was now come, and brought pardon and salvation to all that received him, and therefore persuaded them all to repent, that they might be pardoned, and it members of his kingdom; and baptized those that professed this.

5. And there went out unto him all the land of Judea, and they of Jerusalem, and were all baptized of him in the river of Jordan, confessing their sins.

5. The generality of the people (longing for the promised Messiah,) were glad of this news that he was come, and thronged to John, confessing their sins, and professing repentance, and were baptized by him.

6. And John was clothed with camel's hair, and with a girdle of a skin about his loins: and he did eat locusts and wild honey:

6. Note, This kind of eremitical life, and abstinence, is over-valued by them, who place merit or perfection in it, and is unjustly vilified by some, who know not of how great use it is to some persons to withdraw from worldly vanities and temptations.

7. And preached, saying, There cometh one mightier than I after me, the latchet of whose shoes I am not worthy to stoop down and unloose.

7. Note, Christ and his servants are patterns of humility: But Satan and his servants are known by pride.

8. I indeed have baptized you with water: but he shall baptize you with the Holy Ghost.

8. My baptism doth but prepare you, but his shall pour out the Spirit on the baptized.

9. And it came to pass in those days, that Jesus came from Nazareth of Galilee, and was baptized of John in Jordan.

9. Note, Qu. Did Christ profess repentance for the remission of sins? If not, how was he capable of John's baptism? Answ. He was not baptized to the same uses, as other men, but as owning John's baptism, and the coming of the kingdom of God. As a general will wear the same colours with his soldiers, though theirs signify subjection to him.

10. And straightway coming up out of the water, he saw the heavens opened, and the spirit like a dove descending upon him.

10. See on Matt. iii.

11. And there came a voice from heaven, *saying,* Thou art my beloved Son, in whom I am well pleased.

11. Note, God from heaven preached the gospel at Christ's baptism.

12. And immediately the spirit driveth him into the wilderness. 13. And he was there in the wilderness forty days tempted of Satan, and was with the wild beasts, and the angels ministered unto him.

12, 13. Note, 1. To conquer temptations, is to conquer Satan. 2. Angels brought him meat at the end of the forty days.

14. Now after that John was put in prison, Jesus came into Galilee, preaching the gospel of the kingdom of God,

14. That the kingdom of God was coming.

15. And saying, the time is fulfilled, and the kingdom of God is at hand: repent ye and believe the gospel.

15. The promised time of the Messiah's appearing is come: Repent, and believe the glad tidings.

16. Now as he walked by the sea of Galilee, he saw Simon, and Andrew his brother, casting a net into the sea; for they were fishers. 17. And Jesus said unto them, Come ye after me, and I will make you to become fishers of men. 18. And staightway they forsook their nets, and followed him.

16, &c. See on John i. 40. & Matt. iv. 18.

19. And when he had gone a little further thence, he saw James *the son* of Zebedee, and John his brother, who also were in the ship mending their nets. 20. And straightway he called them: and they left their father Zebedee in the ship with the hired servants, and went after him.

19, 20. Note, He spake to their hearts.

21. And they went into Capernaum, and straightway on the sabbath-day he entered into the synagogue, and taught. 22. And they were astonished at his doctrine: for he taught them as one that had authority, and not as the scribes.

21, 22. He spake as authorized by God to speak in his name, and not as an ordinary expositor of the law.

23. And there was in their synagogue a man with an unclean spirit, And he cried out, 24. Saying, Let us alone, what have we to do with thee, thou Jesus of Nazareth? art thou come to destroy us? I know thee who thou art, the holy one of God. 25. And Jesus rebuked him, saying, Hold thy peace, and come out of him. 26. And when the unclean spirit had torn him, and cried with a loud voice, he came out of him. 27. And they were all amazed, insomuch that they questioned among themselves, saying, What thing is this? what new doctrine *is* this? for with authority commandeth he even the unclean spirits, and they do obey him.

23, &c. Note, 1. By an unclean spirit, he meant the devil as such. 2. Forced obedience is common to devils; Willing and loving obedience belongeth to children.

28. And immediately his fame spread abroad throughout all the region round about Galilee. 29. And forthwith when they were come out of the synagogue, they entered into the house of Simon and Andrew with James and John.

29. Note, Christ's chief apostles dwelt in Capernaum.

30. But Simon's wife's mother lay sick of a fever, and anon they tell him of her. 31. And he came and took her by the hand, and lift her up; and immediately the fever left her, and she ministered unto them.

30, 31. She was presently so cured, that she served them.

32. And at even, when the sun did set, they brought unto him all that were diseased, and them that were possessed with devils. 33. And all the city was gathered together at the door. 34. And he healed many that were sick of divers diseases, and cast out many devils, and suffered not the devils to speak because they knew him.

&c. He needed not the devil's testimony.

35. And in the morning, rising up a great while before day, he went out, and departed into a solitary place, and there prayed.

35. Note, Have not we sinners more need to break our sleep for secret prayer? He prayed not with his disciples, because the same confessions and prayers were not fit for him and them.

36. And Simon, and they that were with him, followed after him. 37. And when they had found him, they said unto him, All men seek for thee. 38. And he said unto them, Let us go into the next towns, that I may preach there also; for therefore came I forth.

36, 37, 38. I must preach in more places than one.

39. And he preached in their synagogues throughout all Galilee, and cast out devils. 40. And there came a leper to him, beseeching him, and kneeling down to him, and saying unto him, If thou wilt, thou canst make me clean. 41. And Jesus moved with compassion, put forth *his* hand, and touched him, and saith unto him, I will, be thou clean. 42. And as soon as he had spoken, immediately the leprosy departed from him, and he was cleansed.

39, 40. Believing his power he found that he was willing.

43. And he straitly charged him, and forthwith sent him away; 44. And saith unto him, See thou say nothing to any man: but go thy way, shew thyself to the priest, and offer for thy cleansing those things which Moses commanded, for a testimony unto them.

43. Note, Christ required the legal duties to the unlawfully-called, and bad priests.

45. But he went out, and began to publish *it* much, and to blaze abroad the matter, insomuch that Jesus could no more openly enter into the city, but was without in desert places: and they came to him from every quarter.

45. Publication raised envy, and caused Christ to withdraw into the wilderness: what wonder if our hearers' indiscretion hurt us?

CHAP. II.

AND again he entered into Capernaum, after *some* days, and it was noised that he was in the house. 2. And straightway many were gathered together, insomuch that there was no room to receive *them*, no not so much as about the door: and he preached the word unto them.

1, 2. He preached to them that were within the house, and without the door, not fearing the reproach of a conventicle.

3. And they come unto him, bringing one sick of the palsy, which was born of four. 4. And when they could not come nigh unto him for press, they uncovered the roof where he was: and when they had broken *it* up, they let down the bed wherein the sick of the palsy lay. 5. When Jesus saw their faith, he said unto the sick of the palsy, Son, thy sins be forgiven thee.

5. The sin for which thou art thus afflicted, is forgiven thee.

6. But there were certain of the scribes sitting there, and reasoning in their hearts, 7. Why doth this man thus speak blasphemies? who can forgive sins but God only?

7. None, but God, can forgive any wrong done to God. But 1. Christ was God. 2. A minister of God may declare God's forgiveness.

8. And immediately, when Jesus perceived in his spirit that they so reasoned with themselves, he said unto them, Why reason ye these things in your hearts? 9. Whether is it easier to say to the sick of the palsy, Thy sins be forgiven thee: or to say, Arise, and take up thy bed and walk? 10. But that ye may know that the Son of Man hath power on earth to forgive sins: (he saith to the sick of the palsy,) 11. I say unto thee, Arise, and take up thy bed, and go thy way into thine

house. 12. And immediately he arose, took up the bed, and went forth before them all, insomuch that they were all amazed, and glorified God, saying, We never saw it on this fashion.

8, &c. Is it not all one to forgive the sin, and to forgive the punishment. We never saw such works before.

13. And he went forth again by the sea-side, and all the multitude resorted unto him, and he taught them.

13. Note, In field-meetings, house-meetings, mountain-meetings, ship-meetings, synagogue-meetings, and temple-meetings, he taught the people, and preached the gospel.

14. And as he passed by, he saw Levi *the son* of Alpheus sitting at the receipt of custom, and said unto him, Follow me. And he arose and followed him.

14. Note, He called 'Publicans.

15. And it came to pass, that as Jesus sat at meat in his house, many publicans and sinners sat also together with Jesus and his disciples: for there were many, and they followed him. 16. And when the scribes and Pharisees saw him eat with publicans and sinners, they said unto his disciples, How is it that he eateth and drinketh with publicans and sinners?

17. When Jesus heard *it*, he saith unto them, They that are whole have no need of the physician, but they that are sick: I came not to call the righteous, but sinners to repentance.

15, &c. Note, 1. The hypocrite Pharisees will be more strict and holy than Christ, if separating from others, and aggravating other men's sins, and justifying themselves be holiness. 2. I came to be a Saviour to sinners, by calling them to repentance, that they may be converted and forgiven. If you are no sinners, I am no saviour for you.

18. And the disciples of John, and of the Pharisees used to fast; and they come and say unto him, Why do the disciples of John, and of the Pharisees fast, but thy disciples fast not? 19. And Jesus said unto them, Can the children of the bride-chamber fast while the bridegroom is with them? as long as they have the bridegroom with them, they cannot fast. 20. But the days will come, when the bridegroom shall be taken away from them, and then shall they fast in those days.

18. Why do you think you merit by your fasting? Which is to be used only in its season. You use not to fast, but feast at your marriages; my presence is more joyful to them, than a marriage-feast; when I am ascended, and they are exposed to the scorn and persecution of men, they shall fast. Humiliation will be more suitable to their outward state, though they inwardly rejoice.

21. No man also seweth a piece of new cloth on an old garment: else the new piece that filled it up taketh away from the old, and the rent is made worse. 22. And no man putteth new wine into old bottles, else the new wine doth burst the bottles, and the wine is spilled, and the bottles will be marred: but new wine must be put into new bottles.

21, 22. They are not yet fit for austerities.

23. And it came to pass that he went, through the corn-fields on the sabbath-day, and his disciples began as they went, to pluck the ears of corn. 24. And the Pharisees said unto him, Behold, why do they on the sabbath-day that which is not lawful?

23, 24. Ceremonious hypocrites will be still stricter than Christ in the ceremonious part, while they violate morals.

25. And he said unto them, Have ye never read what David did, when he had need, and was an hungered, he, and they that were with him? 26. How he went into the house of God in the days of Abiathar the high priest, and did eat the shew-bread, which is not lawful to eat, but for the priests, and gave also to them which were with him?

25, &c. Do you not know that precepts of rites and ceremonies, give place to necessity, and pre cepts of charity, and self-preservation? And that David's instance proveth this, in the days of Abiathar, a little before he was high-priest, even in his father Abimilech's priesthood, he and his company did eat the hallowed bread, which without necessity had not been lawful.

27. And he said unto them, The sabbath was made for man, and not man for the sabbath: 28. Therefore the Son of Man is Lord also of the sabbath.

27, 28. The sabbath is appointed to be a means of the good of man, and not man a means of it: And no means is to be used against its end, but for it; even the good of man. And therefore I that come to settle the laws of grace, as conducing to the recovery and good of man, have power of dispensation or alteration of the sabbath, as shall tend to the end of man's good and salvation.

CHAP. III.

AND he entered again into the synagogue, and there was a man there which had a withered hand. 2. And they watched him, whether he would heal him on the sabbath-day, that they might accuse him.

1, 2. Note, Malignity is not to be restrained by miracles.

3. And he saith unto the man which had the withered hand, Stand forth. 4. And he saith unto them, Is it lawful to do good on the sabbath-days, or to do evil? to save life, or to kill? but they held their peace,

3, 4. Do you, ceremonious murderers, that lay wait for my life now, keep the sabbath? And do I break it by saving men's lives?

5. And when he had looked round about on them with anger, being grieved for the hardness of their hearts, he saith unto the man, Stretch forth thine hand. And he stretched it out: and his hand was restored whole as the other.

5. Note, 1. Anger and grief for men's sin, were justified by Christ's example. 2. A hard heart can sin against miracles and mercy.

6. And the Pharisees went forth, and straightway took counsel with the Herodians against him, how they might destroy him.

6. Note, It is folly to doubt whether there be devils, while devils incarnate dwell among us; what else but devils sure, could make ceremonious hypocrites, consult with politic royalists to destroy the Son of God, for saving men's health and lives by miracle? Quer. Whether if this withered hand had been their own, they would have plotted to kill him, that would have cured them by a miracle as a sabbath-breaker? And whether their successors would silence and imprison godly ministers, if they could cure them of all their sicknesses, and help them to preferment, and give them money to feed their lusts?

7. But Jesus withdrew himself with his disciples to the sea: and a great multitude from Galilee followed him, and from Judea,

7. Note, They that will drive away mercy from them, shall be without it; and speed as they choose, and those that follow after Christ and mercy sincerely, shall have their desires.

8. And from Jerusalem, and from Idumea, and from beyond Jordan, and they about Tyre and Sidon, a great multitude, when they had heard what great things he did, came unto him. 9. And he spake to his disciples, that a small ship should wait on him, because of the multitude, lest they should throng him. 10. For he had healed many, insomuch that they pressed upon him for to touch him, as many as had plagues.

9, 10. Were men but as regardful of their souls as of their bodies, how universally and joyfully would Christianity and godliness be received!

11. And unclean spirits, when they saw him, fell down before him, and cried, saying, Thou art the Son of God. 12. And he straightly charged them, that they should not make him known.

11, 12. Note, he would not have the devil preach the gospel, lest it should bring it under suspicion.

13. And he goeth up into a mountain, and calleth unto him whom he would: and they came unto him. 14. And he ordered twelve, that they should be with him, and that he might send them forth to preach.

13, 14. Note, Apostles were witnesses and preachers, but not lords, nor silencers, nor persecutors.

15. And to have power to heal sicknesses, and to cast out devils.

15. Note, But not to do mischief, and promote the devil's kingdom, by fighting against love and godliness.

16. And Simon he surnamed Peter. 17. And James *the son* of Zebedee, and John the brother of James (and he surnamed them Boanerges, which is the sons of thunder.) 18. And Andrew, and Philip, and Bartholomew, and Matthew, and Thomas, and James *the son* of Alpheus, and Thaddeus, and Simon the Canaanite, 19. And Judas Iscariot, which also betrayed him: and they went into an house.

16, &c. Note, He suited the number to the twelve tribes, till the church was to be made Catholic, and then he encreased the number.

20. And the multitude cometh together again, so that they could not so much as eat bread. 21. And when his friends heard *of it*, they went out to lay hold on him; for they said, He is beside himself.

20, 21. His kindred thought that all this ado, did signify some ectasy, and would have got him home. But one very old Greek copy (Besa's) readeth it thus [When the scribes and the rest heard of it, they came to apprehend him, for they said, that he made men mad.]

22. And the scribes which came down from Jerusalem, said, He hath Beelzebub, and by the prince of the devils casteth he out devils.

22. They denied not the matter of fact of his miracles, but said that he did it by the prince of the devils.

23. And he called them unto him, and said unto them in parables, How can Satan cast out Satan. 24. And if a kingdom be divided against itself, that kingdom cannot stand. 25. And if a house be divided against itself, that house cannot stand. 26. And if Satan rise up against himself, and be divided, he cannot stand, but hath an end. 27. No man can enter into a strong man's house, and spoil his goods, except he will first bind the strong man, and then he will spoil his house.

27, &c. It is not by the devil's own consent that he is cast out, but by overcoming him.

28. Verily I say unto you, All sins shall be forgiven unto the sons of men, and blasphemies wherewith soever they shall blaspheme: 29. But he that shall blaspheme against the Holy Ghost, hath never forgiveness, but is in danger of eternal damnation: 30. Because they said He hath an unclean spirit.

28, &c. All other sin and blasphemy is curable and pardonable: But if men will take all the miracles, gifts, and graces of the Holy Ghost, by which I and my servants prove me to be sent from God, to be all done by the devil to deceive them: there is no greater evidence of God's attestation left to convince them; and therefore their blasphemous unbelief is incurable and unpardonable.

31 There came then his brethren and his mother, and standing without, sent unto him, calling him. 32. And the multitude sat about him, and they said unto him, Behold thy mother and thy brethren without seek for thee. 33. And he answered them, saying, Who is my mother, or my brethren? 34. And he looked round about on them which sat about him, and said, Behold my mother and my brethren. 35. For whosoever shall do the will of God, the same is my brother, and my sister, and mother.

31, &c. If you would know me, you must look beyond my fleshly kindred and relations: As I am of an higher offspring, so I have higher works to do, than to please natural kindred. (I draw you not from due regard to your natural kindred: God commandeth you to honour parents.) But spiritual relations to me as such, are more amiable and happy than mere natural relations as such. It is a more amiable thing to be a lover of God, and to obey him, than to be my mother, sister, or brother: If they had no better, they would perish for ever. But all that love God and obey him, shall be saved. (This is great comfort to every true Christian, that they are dearer to Christ, than mother, brother, or sister, as such would have been, had they been holy.)

CHAP. IV.

AND he began again to teach by the sea-side: and there was gathered unto him a great multitude, so that he entered into a ship, and sat in the sea, and the whole multitude was by the sea, on the land. 2. And he taught them many things by parables, and said unto them in his doctrine, 3. Hearken, Behold, there went out a sower to sow: 4. And it came to pass as he sowed, some fell by the way-side, and the fowls of the air came and devoured it up. 5. And some fell on stony ground, where it had not much earth, and immediately it sprang up, because it had no depth of earth. 6. But when the sun was up, it was scorched, and because it had no root, it withered away. 7. And some fell among thorns, and the thorns grew up, and choaked it, and it yielded no fruit. 8. And other fell on good ground, and did yield fruit that sprang up and increased, and brought forth some thirty, and some sixty, and some an hundred. 9. And he said unto them, He that hath ears to hear, let him hear.

See paraphrase on Matt. xiii.

10. And when he was alone, they that were about him with the twelve, asked of him the parable.

10. He is said to be alone, when the multitude were gone.

11. And he said unto them, unto you it is given to know the mystery of the kingdom of God: but unto them that are without, all *these* things are done in parables: 12. That seeing they may see, and not perceive, and hearing they may hear, and not understand: lest at any time they should be converted, and *their* sins should be forgiven them.

See Matt. xiii. 12, 13. God hath vouchsafed you greater help and light than to those without, that are not my disciples: Parables are fitted to their ignorant state, who wilfully neglect instruction, and are never the better for what they hear, so that it doth not convert and heal them. Did they enquire and diligently search for truth, it should be more fully opened to them.

13. And he said unto them, Know ye not this parable? and how then will you know all parables?

13. If ye understand not this plain similitude, how will ye understand many more which you must hear.

14. The sower soweth the word. 15. And these are they by the wayside, where the word is sown, but when they have heard, Satan cometh immediately, and taketh away the word that was sown in their hearts. 16. And these are they likewise which are sown on stony ground, who when they have heard the word, immediately receive it with gladness: 17. And have no root in themselves, and so endure but for a time: afterward when affliction or persecution ariseth for the word's sake, immediately they are offended. 18. And these are they which are sown among thorns: such as hear the word. 19. And the cares of this world, and the deceitfulness of riches, and the lusts of other things entering in, choak the word, and it becometh unfruitful.

See Matt. xiii. The several writers of Christ's words give us the same in sense, though there be some small difference in the words.

20. And these are they which are sown on good ground, such as hear the word, and receive *it*, and bring forth fruit, some thirty-fold, some sixty, and some an hundred.

20. Note, All sound Christians are not equally fruitful. 2. The quality of the hearts of the hearers, causeth the differing success of the same doctrine or sermons on different persons.

21. And he said unto them, Is a candle brought to be put under a bushel, or under a bed? and not to be set on a candlestick?

21. God doth not give you more light than others, to hide it, but to use it for the good of many.

22. For there is nothing hid which shall not be manifested: neither was any thing kept secret, but that it should come abroad.

22. Light is for the manifesting of all things, and it will manifest all things, how dark or secret soever they seem.

23. If any man have ears to hear, let him hear.

23. Let him that hath ears and understanding see that he hear God's word regardfully, with all the serious attention of his heart: for it is of great concernment to his soul.

24. And he said unto them, Take heed what you hear: with what measure ye mete, it shall be measured to you: and unto you that hear shall more be given. 25. For he that hath, to him shall be given: and he that hath not, from him shall be taken even that which he hath.

24, 25. See that you set your hearts to the word you hear: For as you use God's words, he will use you: Learn faithfully, and you shall be taught more: but if you stifle or neglect the truth, your knowledge will be as none, or worse than none to you, and God may forsake your understandings.

26. And he said, So is the kingdom of God, as if a man should cast seed into the ground, 27. And should sleep, and rise night and day, and the seed should spring and grow up, he knoweth not how.

26, 27. Note, Man soweth, but God blesseth it; and we see it not grow, but see that it hath grown. Who then shall exact of another an account, just when or how he was converted?

28. For the earth bringeth forth fruit of herself; first the blade, then the ear, after that the full corn in the ear. 29. But when the fruit is brought forth, immediately he putteth in the sickle, because the harvest is come.

28. Do your part in sowing, and God will prosper it: And though you see not present fruit, it will ripen and shew itself at last, and be rewarded and fully blest.

30. And he said, Whereunto shall we liken the kingdom of God? or with what comparison shall we compare it? ·31. *It is* like a grain of mustard-seed, which when it is sown in the earth, is less than all the seeds that be in the earth. 32. But when it is sown, it groweth up, and becometh greater than all herbs, and shooteth out great branches, so that the fowls of the air may lodge under the shadow of it.

30, &c. You all look for the kingdom of the Messiah, but you mistake in expecting a sudden visible pompous appearance of it: It is the Catholic church for which now I am sowing the seed of the gospel, and seemeth like a grain of mustard-seed, a small inconsiderable thing, one of the most contemptible societies on earth: But God will prosper this seed so, that my church shall become so conspicuous and eminent, that princes, and nations, and worldly men, shall be glad for their interest, to have the name of Christians, and to be under the protection of the Christian powers.

33. And with many such parables spake he the word unto them, as they were able to hear *it*. 34. But without a parable spake he not unto them: and when they were alone, he expounded all things to his disciples.

33, 34. He spake to them according to their low capacities, as to children, by familiar comparisons, further teaching the sense of all to those that as scholars came to learn of him.

35. And the same day when the even was come, he saith unto them, Let us pass over unto the other side. 36. And when they had sent away the multitude, they took him even as he was in the ship, and there were also with him other little ships. 37. And there arose a great storm of wind, and the waves beat into the ship, so that it was now full. 38. And he was in the hinder part of the ship, asleep on a pillow: and they awake him, and say unto him, Master, carest thou not that we perish?

35, &c. Note, God raiseth dangers to shew us our weakness and his power in our deliverance. 2. They are safe who are in the same ship with Christ. 3. Yet Christ seemeth for a time to neglect us in our dangers, as if he cared not what became of us.

39. And he arose and rebuked the wind, and said unto the sea, Peace, be still: and the wind ceased, and there was a great calm. 40. And he said unto them, Why are ye so fearful? how is it that ye have no faith? 41. And they feared exceedingly, and said one to another, What manner of man is this, that even the wind and the sea obey him?

39, &c. Note, All things obey Christ save ye

lantary sinners. **2.** It is but a word of his, that is needful to allay all our dangers. **3.** Too much fear sheweth too little faith. Trusting Christ is the cure of such fear. **4.** How greatly should he be reverenced and obeyed by man, whom wind and seas, and all creatures must obey.

CHAP. V.

AND they came over unto the other side of the sea, into the country of the Gadarenes. 2. And when he was come out of the ship, immediately there met him out of the tombs, a man with an unclean spirit, 3. Who had *his* dwelling among the tombs, and no man could bind him, no not with chains: 4. Because that he had been often bound with fetters and chains, and the chains had been plucked asunder by him, and the fetters broken in pieces: neither could any man tame him. 5. And always night and day he was in the mountains, and in the tombs, crying, and cutting himself with stones.

Matt. viii. 28. Tells us, that they were two; which Mark denieth not, though he mentioneth but one.

6. But when he saw Jesus afar off, he ran and worshipped him,

6. Devil's worship is but a constrained confession of Christ's power over them.

7. And cried with a loud voice, and said, What have I to do with thee, Jesus, thou Son of the most high God? I adjure thee by God, that thou torment me not.

7. Note, It is no wonder if malicious hypocrites abuse the name of God by excommunications and reproaching of his truest servants, when the devil durst use God's name to adjure Christ himself.

8. (For he said unto him, Come out of the man thou unclean spirit):

8. Note, It appeareth that devils are not always just in the same condition, but when they are restrained from going about to do mischief, it is to them an imprisonment and torment; as it is to a wolf to be tied up from killing sheep.

9. And he asked him, What *is* thy name? And he answered, saying, My name *is* legion: for we are many.

9. Note, Spirits lose not their individuation by falling into one common soul. 2. Seeing the greatest multiplicity is among the least of beings (there are more boughs and sprigs than trunks of trees, more flies than men, &c.) It seems that the very nature of devils is debased with their quality; and they are not now of so light a spiritual nature as they were before their fall, if there were so great a number to afflict one man.

10. And he besought him much, that he would not send them away out of the country. 11. Now there was there nigh unto the mountains, a great herd of swine feeding. 12. And all the devils besought him, saying, Send us into the swine, that we may enter into them. 13. And forthwith Jesus gave them leave. And the unclean spirits went out, and entered into the swine, and the herd ran violently down a steep place into the sea, (they were about two thousand) and were choaked in the sea.

10, &c. Let us play a small game rather than none: It will somewhat abate our pain, to do some mischief though a less and not to be imprisoned in the deep: Note, The reason why devils hurt us no more, is because God will not give them leave.

14. And they that fed the swine fled, and told *it* in the city, and in the country. And they went out to see what it was that was done. 15. And they come to Jesus, and see him that was possessed with the devil, and had the legion, sitting, and clothed, and in his right mind, and they were afraid. 16. And they that saw *it*, told them how it befel to him that was possessed with the devil, and also concerning the swine. 17. And they began to pray him to depart out of their coasts.

14, &c. Note, When they were healed by Christ they followed him: But when they lost their swine by him, they would be rid of him.

18. And when he was come into the ship, he that had been possessed with the devil, prayed him that he might be with him. 19. Howbeit, Jesus suffered him not, but saith unto him, Go home to thy friends, and tell them how great things the

Lord hath done for thee, and hath had compassion on thee. 20. And he departed, and began to publish in Decapolis, how great things Jesus had done for him: and all men did marvel.

<small>19, &c. Note, All must honour God in their places; but not all in one place and station.</small>

21. And when Jesus was passed over again by ship unto the other side, much people gathered unto him, and he was nigh unto the sea. 22. And behold, there cometh one of the rulers of the synagogue, Jairus by name, and when he saw him, he fell at his feet. 23. And besought him greatly, saying, my little daughter lieth at the point of death, *I pray thee* come and lay thy hands on her, that she may be healed, and she shall live. 24. And *Jesus* went with him, and much people followed him, and thronged him.

<small>21. Note, Each synagogue had more than one ruler. 2. It was then a great mercy to be afflicted: For such came to Christ for help; while others maligned him.</small>

25. And a certain woman which had an issue of blood twelve years, 26. And had suffered many things of many physicians, and had spent all that she had, and was nothing bettered, but rather grew worse, 27. When she had heard of Jesus, came in the press behind, and touched his garment. 28. For she said, If I may touch but his clothes, I shall be whole. 29. And straightway the fountain of her blood was dried up: and she felt in her body that she was healed of that plague.

<small>25, &c. Note, Her strong faith prepared her a speedy cure.</small>

30. And Jesus immediately knowing in himself, that virtue had gone out of him, turned him about in the press, and said, Who touched my clothes? 31. And his disciples said unto him, Thou seest the multitude thronging thee, and sayest thou, Who touched me? 32. And he looked round about to see her that had done this thing. 33. But the woman fearing and trembling, knowing what was done in her, came and fell down before him, and told him all the truth. 34. And he said unto her, Daughter, thy faith hath made thee whole; go in peace, and be whole of thy plague.

<small>30, &c. Note, Many touched his clothes that were never the better: So many use his name. when they that use it in faith, are healed. 2. She feared Christ was angry with her, when he healed her.</small>

35. While he yet spake, there came from the ruler of the synagogue's *house, certain* which said, Thy daughter is dead, why troublest thou the master any further? 36. As soon as Jesus heard the word that was spoken, he saith unto the ruler of the synagogue, Be not afraid, only believe.

<small>35, &c. Take heed, lest distrust deprive thee of thy desire.</small>

37. And he suffered no man to follow him, save Peter, and James, and John the brother of James. 38. And he cometh to the house of the ruler of the synagogue, and seeth the tumult, and them that wept and wailed greatly. 39. And when he was come in, he saith unto them, Why make ye this ado, and weep? the damsel is not dead, but sleepeth. 40. And they laughed him to scorn: but when he had put them all out, he taketh the father and the mother of the damsel, and them that were with him, and entereth in where the damsel was lying. 41. And he took the damsel by the hand, and said unto her, Talitha cumi, which is, being interpreted, Damsel (I say unto thee) arise. 42. And straightway the damsel arose, and walked; for she was *of the age* of twelve years: and they were astonished with a great astonishment. 43. And he charged them

straightly, that no man should know it: and commanded that something should be given her to eat.

1, &c. Note, It was needful that he, on whom all must trust for life everlasting, should shew, that he hath the power of life and death: Yet would he not have it divulged, to avoid untimely persecution.

CHAP. VI.

AND he went out from thence, and came into his own country, and his disciples followed him. 2. And when the sabbath-day was come, he began to teach in the synagogue: and many hearing *him*, were astonished, saying, From whence hath this man these things? and what wisdom *is* this which is given unto him, that even such mighty works are wrought by his hands? 3. Is not this the carpenter, the son of Mary, the brother of James and Joses, and of Juda, and Simon? and are not his sisters here with us? And they were offended at him.

2. Because they knew his visible original, and education, and kindred to be like that of other of their neighbours, they were, by this, made backward to believe him to be the Son of God.

4. But Jesus said unto them, A prophet is not without honour, but in his own country, and among his own kin, and in his own house.

4. It is usual for prophets to be least set by at home, where men that see their natural original, yet see not the Spirit of God in them, nor know his operations.

5. And he could there do no mighty work, save that he laid his hands upon a few sick folk, and healed *them*. 6. And he marvelled because of their unbelief. And he went round about the villages, teaching.

5. It was not for want of power in Christ; but because they were incapable receivers. Thus sin goes on from bad to worse: Unbelief deprived them of the miracles, that should have cured it.

7. And he calleth unto him the twelve, and began to send them forth by two and two, and gave them power *over* unclean spirits.

7. He assigned not to any one, a singular province; but sent them by two's, of which no one was ruler of another.

8. And commanded them that they should take nothing for *their* journey, save a staff only: no scrip, no bread, no money in *their* purse: 9. But *be* shod with sandals: and not put on two coats. 10. And he said unto them, In what place soever ye enter into an house, there abide till ye depart from that place.

8, &c. Note, This is no binding example to all preachers.

11. And whosoever shall not receive you, nor hear you, when he depart thence, shake off the dust under your feet, for a testimony against them. Verily I say unto you, it shall be more tolerable for Sodom and Gomorrha in the day of judgment, than for that city.

11. Note, Rejecting the greatest mercy, and gospel-light, deserveth the greatest punishment in hell: What then will become of persecutors!

12. And they went out, and preached that men should repent.

12. Note, Repentance is as real a part of the gospel, as faith: And repenting of unbelief, as it signifieth conversion, is faith itself. Alas, that so reasonable a duty as repenting, should be so hardly obtained!

13. And they cast out many devils, and anointed with oil many that were sick, and healed *them*.

13. And when the miraculous power ceaseth, the ceremony of anointing ceaseth.

14. And king Herod heard *of him*, (for his name was spread abroad) and he said, That John the Baptist was risen from the dead, and therefore mighty works do shew forth themselves in him.

14. Note, Herod believed the immortality of the soul; else he could not have believed the resurrection.

15. Others said, That it is Elias. And others said, That it is a prophet, or as one of the prophets. 16. But when Herod heard *thereof*,

he said, It is John whom I beheaded, he is risen from the dead.

15, 16. His conscience put him in fear of John.

17. For Herod himself had sent forth and laid hold upon John, and bound him in prison for Herodias' sake, his brother Philip's wife; for he had married her.

17. Note, He could bear the guilt, but not the reproof; But God will make the proudest bear more.

18. For John had said unto Herod, It is not lawful for thee to have thy brother's wife.

18. Note, He that hath a call to tell kings of their sin, must do it faithfully.

19. Therefore Herodias had a quarrel against him, and would have killed him, but she could not.

19. Note, See the bloody mind of a wicked queen! The cause of John's death, is but his telling a sinner of his sin.

20. For Herod feared John, knowing that he was a just man, and an holy, and observed him, and when he heard him, he did many things, and heard him gladly.

20. His conscience telling him, that John was a just and holy man, made him reverence him; and do many things which John preached to him; and hear him with some pleasure: But could not make him leave his darling sin.

21. And when a convenient day was come, that Herod on his birthday made a supper to his lords, high captains, and chief estates of Galilee: 22. And when the daughter of the said Herodias came in, and danced, and pleased Herod, and them that sat with him, the king said unto the damsel, Ask of me whatsoever thou wilt, and I will give *it* thee. 23. And he sware unto her, Whatsoever thou shalt ask of me, I will give *it* thee, unto the half of my kingdom.

21, &c. Note, 1. Yet will such wretches lose the kingdom of heaven, rather than let go a base lust for God. So much more liberal are they to their flesh and fellow-sinners!

24. And she went forth, and said unto her mother, What shall I ask? And she said, The head of John the Baptist. 25. And she came in straightway with haste unto the king, and asked, saying, I will that thou give me by and by in a charger, the head of John the Baptist.

24, 25. Note, Blood and revenge is by lustful woman preferred before half a kingdom. Such are the enemies of holy men.

26. And the king was exceeding sorry, *yet* for his oath's sake, and for their sakes which sat with him, he would not reject her.

26. All unwillingness and sorrow for sin is not true repentance; but that, which is more effectual against sin, than the temptation is for it.

27. And immediately the king sent an executioner, and commanded his head to be brought: and he went and beheaded him in the prison. 28. And brought his head in a charger, and gave it to the damsel: and the damsel gave it to her mother.

27, 28. This wicked, bloody king wanted not an executioner to do his will, in the most heinous sin.

29. And when his disciples heard *of it*, they came and took up his corps, and laid it in a tomb. 30. And the apostles gathered themselves together unto Jesus, and told him all things, both what they had done, and what they had taught.

29, 30. Of their doctrines and miracles.

31. And he said unto them, Come ye yourselves apart into a desert place, and rest a while; for there were many coming and going, and they had no leisure so much as to eat. 32. And they departed into a desert place by ship privately. 33. And the people saw them departing, and many knew him, and ran afoot thither out of all cities, and outwent them, and came together unto him.

33. Note, Fervent desire is very diligent and laborious.

34. And Jesus when he came out, saw much people, and was moved with compassion toward them, because they were as sheep not having

a shepherd: and he began to teach them many things. 35. And when the day was now far spent, his disciples came unto him, and said, This is a desert place, and now the time is far passed: 36. Send them away, that they may go into the country round about, and into the villages, and buy themselves bread: for they have nothing to eat. 37. He answered and said unto them, Give ye them to eat. And they say unto him, Shall we go and buy two hundred pennyworth of bread, and give them to eat?

34. *Their penny was seven-pence halfpenny. Beza reckoneth the two hundred pence, to thirty-five pound frank of tours.*

Note, The luxurious bellies of this land would have taken bread but for a dry feast, though they had the fishes also.

38. He saith unto them, How many loaves have ye? go and see. And when they knew, they say, Five, and two fishes. 39. And he commanded them to make all sit down by companies upon the green grass. 40. And they sat down in ranks by hundreds and by fifties. 41. And when he had taken the five loaves, and the two fishes, he looked up to heaven, and blessed, and brake the loaves, and gave *them* to his disciples to set before them; and the two fishes divided he among them all. 42. And they did all eat, and were filled. 43. And they took up twelve baskets full of the fragments, and of the fishes. 44. And they that did eat of the loaves, were about five thousand men.

38. *&c. Note, 1. This miracle had witnesses enough. 2. Though God do not now feed his servants by miracle, he doth perform his promise, and provide for them nevertheless; and is no less to be trusted. 3. Even miraculous food is to be sanctified by heavenly benediction.*

45. And straightway he constrained his disciples to get into the ship, and to go to the other side before unto Bethsaida, while he sent away the people. 46. And when he had sent them away, he departed into a mountain to pray. 47. And when even was come, the ship was in the midst of the sea, and he alone on the land. 48. And he saw them toiling in rowing: (for the wind was contrary unto them) and about the fourth watch of the night he cometh unto them, walking upon the sea, and would have passed by them. 49. But when they saw him walking upon the sea, they supposed it had been a spirit, and cried out. 50. For they all saw him, and were troubled. And immediately he talked with them, and saith unto them, Be of good cheer, it is I, be not afraid. 51. And he went up unto them into the ship, and the wind ceased: and they were sore amazed in themselves beyond measure, and wondered.

45, &c. *Note, 1. If Christ must pray so much what need have we! 2. If Christ say, [It is I, be not afraid,] this should quiet timorous souls. 3. Even the appearance of Christ himself in a strange way, may amaze the faithful.*

52. For they considered not *the miracle* of the loaves, for their heart was hardened.

52. *Had they duly considered the miracle of feeding, no further miracle would have seemed so strange to them. Note; They that have not hearts hardened as the wicked, may be hardened as to some particular thing.*

53. And when they had passed over, they came into the land of Gennesaret, and drew to the shore. 54. And when they were come out of the ship, straightway they knew him, 55. And ran through that whole region round about, and began to carry about in beds those that were sick, where they heard he was. 56. And whithersoever he entered, into villages, or cities, or country, they laid the sick in the streets, and besought him that they might touch, if it were but the border of his garment: and as many as touched him, were made whole.

53. *Note, O that we were as earnest followers of Christ for salvation, as they were for the good of their bodies! And that we could as boldly be-*

lieve and trust him for our souls, as common experience of success caused them to do for their bodily health.

CHAP. VII.

THEN came together unto him the Pharisees, and certain of the scribes, which came from Jerusalem. 2. And when they saw some of his disciples eat bread with defiled, that is to say, with unwashen hands, they found fault. 3. For the Pharisees, and all the Jews, except they wash *their* hands oft, eat not, holding the tradition of the elders. 4. And *when they come* from the market, except they wash, they eat not. And many other things there be, which they have received to hold, as the washing of cups, and pots, brazen vessels, and of tables.

1, &c. If these hypocrites had not ceremony and tradition, and obedience to their councils to make religion of, how could they quiet their consciences in their worldly wicked lives? And what pretence could they have had to persecute Christ and his apostles, had not disobedience to their masterships, and councils, and traditions in ceremony, served their malignity for a pretence? The devil will be religious to destroy religion.

5. Then the Pharisees and scribes asked him, Why walk not thy disciples according to the tradition of the elders, but eat bread with unwashen hands?

5. Why observe you not the canons.

6. He answered and said unto them, Well hath Esaias prophesied of you hypocrites, as it is written, This people honoureth me with *their* lips, but their heart is far from me. 7. Howbeit, in vain do they worship me, teaching for doctrines the commandments of men.

6, &c. Well doth Esay describe you hypocrites, This people, &c. give me an outside ceremonious worship, but their hearts are void of true holiness, religion, and spiritual worship. But all their hypocritical worship of me is in vain, while they make doctrines and laws of religion of the injunctions of men, and the traditions or canons of their councils or elders.

8. For laying aside the commandment of God, ye hold the tradition of men, as the washing of pots and cups: and many other such like things ye do.

8. God commands one to preach and obey his word, and to live in love, and shew mercy, &c. These you lay aside, and hinder the preaching of his word, and persecute his servants, and then you are zealous for your ceremonies. Note, It is not washing for cleanliness, but for ceremony that Christ speaketh against.

9. And he said unto them, Full well ye reject the commandment of God, that ye may keep your own tradition.

9. You think it very well done, to set against godliness and God's own laws: or make nothing of them, that you may keep your own presumptuous canons or traditions. Note, By [Full well] is meant [Full ill.] Christ sheweth us that all use of ironies or derisions is not unlawful.

10. For Moses said, Honour thy father and thy mother: and, Whoso curseth father or mother, let him die the death.

10. Whoso revileth.

11. But ye say, If a man shall say to his father or mother, *It is* Corban, that is to say, a gift, by whatsoever thou mightest be profited by me; *he shall be free.*

11. If he say, It is devoted to God. Note, God accepteth not any thing vowed to him for worship, which he before bound us by his command to employ another way.

12. And ye suffer him no more to do ought for his father or his mother: 13. Making the word of God of none effect through your tradition, which ye have delivered: and many such like things do ye.

13. Note, They thought that their canons could loose men from God's commands. As if a canon should forbid men to give to the poor, or to preach the gospel, or worship God, who are bound to it by God's law.

14. And when he had called all the people unto him, he said unto them, Hearken unto me every one of you, and understand. 15. There is nothing from without a man that entering into him can defile him: but the things which come out of him, those are they that defile the

man. 16. If any man have ears to hear, let him hear.

16, &c. Note, He speaketh of defiling by guilt.

17. And when he was entered into the house from the people, his disciples asked him concerning the parable. 18. And he saith unto them, Are ye so without understanding also? Do ye not perceive, that whatsoever thing from without entereth into the man, it cannot defile him. 19. Because it entereth not into his heart, but into the belly, and goeth out into the draught, purging all meats?

17, &c. Meat maketh not a sinful heart or will, as such.

20. And he said, That which cometh out of the man, that defileth the man. 21. For from within, out of the heart of men, proceed evil thoughts, adulteries, fornications, murders, 22. Thefts, covetousness, wickedness, deceit, lasciviousness, an evil eye, blasphemy, pride, foolishness: 23. All these evil things come from within, and defile the man.

23. These make him a sinner and guilty. And so do gluttony and drunkenness, but not as meat and drink, but as sinful excess.

24. And from thence he arose, and went into the borders of Tyre and Sidon, and entered into an house, and would have no man know it; but he could not be hid. 25. For a certain woman, whose young daughter had an unclean spirit, heard of him, and came and fell at his feet: 26. (The woman was a Greek, a Syrophenician by nation) and she besought him that he would cast forth the devil out of her daughter. 27. But Jesus said unto her, Let the children first be filled: for it is not meet to take the children's bread, and to cast it unto the dogs.

26. Note, Phenice and Canaan were one place. 27. I am sent first to the Israelites, God's peculiar people, with whom you Canaanites go for dogs, and must not have their part.

28. And she answered and said unto him, Yes Lord: yet the dogs under the table eat of the children's crumbs. 29. And he said unto her, For this saying, go thy way, the devil is gone out of thy daughter. 30. And when she was come to her house, she found the devil gone out, and her daughter laid upon the bed.

28, &c. Note, Not for the wittiness of her saying, but for her faith and importunity. They that will take no denial of Christ, shall have no denial.

31. And again departing from the coasts of Tyre and Sidon, he came unto the sea of Galilee through the midst of the coasts of Decapolis. 32. And they bring unto him one that was deaf, and had an impediment in his speech: and they beseech him to put his hand upon him. 33. And he took him aside from the multitude, and put his fingers into his ears, and he spit and touched his tongue, 34. And looking up to heaven, he sighed, and saith unto him, Ephphatha, that is, Be opened. 35. And straightway his ears were opened, and the string of his tongue was loosed, and he spake plain. 36. And he charged them that they should tell no man: but the more, he charged them, so much the more a great deal they published it, 37. And were beyond measure astonished, saying, He hath done all things well: he maketh both the deaf to hear, and the dumb to speak.

33. Christ looking up to heaven and sighing, implieth some more than ordinary difficulty in the cure. Bodily mercies are magnified by all.

CHAP. VIII.

IN those days the multitude being very great, and having nothing to eat, Jesus called his disciples unto him, and saith unto them, 2. I have compassion on the multitude, because they have now been with me three days, and have nothing to eat: 3. And if I send them away fasting to their own houses, they will faint by the way: for divers of them came from far.

2. Christ's compassion is our great consolation and ground of trust.

4. And his disciples answered him, From whence can a man satisfy these men with bread here in the wilderness? 5. And he asked them, How many loaves have ye? And they said, Seven. 6. And he commanded the people to sit down on the ground: and he took the seven loaves, and gave thanks, and brake, and gave to his disciples to set before *them:* and they did set *them* before the people. 7. And they had a few small fishes: and he blessed, and commanded to set them also before *them.* 8. So they did eat, and were filled: and they took up of the broken meat that was left, seven baskets, 9. And they that had eaten were about four thousand: and he sent them away.

Note, It is like their loaves then were but like our cakes, by the custom of breaking them.

10. And straightway he entered into a ship with his disciples, and came into the parts of Dalmanutha. 11. And the Pharisees came forth, and began to question with him, seeking of him a sign from heaven, tempting him.

10, 11. They would try whether he were the Son of God, by a sign from heaven of their own choosing.

12. And he sighed deeply in his spirit, and saith, Why doth this generation seek after a sign? verily, I say unto you, There shall no sign be given to this generation.

12. He deeply groaned in grief for their obdurateness, and said, Have not this kind of men had signs enough to convince them? Must they further choose what miracles they shall have? Verily no such desire of these perverse men, shall be satisfied (the miracle of my resurrection they shall have.)

13. And he left them, and entering into the ship again, departed to the other side. 14. Now *the disciples* had forgotten to take bread, neither had they in the ship with them more than one loaf. 15. And he charged them, saying, Take heed, beware of the leaven of the Pharisees, and *of* the leaven of Herod.

15. The dangerous enemies of the gospel are the ceremonious Pharisees, and king Herod a jealous Roman governor. Take special heed that neither the Pharisees seduce you by their deceits, nor the king and his officers affright you from the faith by their cruelty

16. And they reasoned among themselves, saying, *It is* because we have no bread. 17. And when Jesus knew *it*, he saith unto them, Why reason ye, because ye have no bread? perceive ye not yet, neither understand? have ye your heart yet hardened? 18. Having eyes, see ye not? and having ears, hear ye not? and do ye not remember? 19. When I brake the five loaves among five thousand, how many baskets full of fragments took ye up? They say unto him, Twelve. 20. And when the seven among four thousand, how many baskets full of fragments took ye up? And they said, Seven. 21. And he said unto them, How is it that ye do not understand?

18. Note, It is a great sin to have a power of understanding and considering, and not to use it. 2. And a great sin quickly to forget miracles, or marvellous providences, and to fall into new distrustful reasonings in our next wants.

22. And he cometh to Bethsaida, and they bring a blind man unto him, and besought him to touch him. 23. And he took the blind man by the hand, and led him out of the town; and when he had spit on his eyes, and put his hands upon him, he asked him if he saw ought? 24. And he looked up, and said, I see men as trees, walking.

24, &c. I discern not men from trees by their shape; but suppose them men, because they walk.

25. After that, he put *his* hands again upon his eyes, and made him

look up: and he was restored, and saw every man clearly. 26. And he sent him away to his house, saying, Neither go into the town, nor tell *it* to any in the town.

25, 26. To avoid ostentation and envy.

27. And Jesus went out, and his disciples into the towns of Cesarea Philippi: and by the way he asked his disciples, saying unto them, Whom do men say that I am?

27. Not but that he knew: but his question was to occasion their confession.

28. And they answered, John the Baptist: but some *say*, Elias; and others, One of the prophets. 29. And he saith unto them, But whom say ye that I am? And Peter answereth and saith him, Thou art the Christ. 30. And he charged them that they should tell no man of him.

29. Men were to discern who he was by his works: And he would not have it commonly proclaimed, till his resurrection and spirit had completed those works and evidences by which it was to be proved.

31. And he began to teach them, that the Son of Man must suffer many things, and be rejected of the elders and of the chief priests, and scribes, and be killed, and after three days rise again. 32. And he spake that saying openly. And Peter took him, and began to rebuke him. 33. But when he had turned about, and looked on his disciples, he rebuked Peter, saying, Get thee behind me, Satan: for thou savourest not the things that be of God, but the things that be of men.

Note, 1. Christ made them know that he designed not a worldly kingdom, when he tells them of his death and resurrection. 2. Peter in his fleshly wisdom thought Christ was not so wise as he. No wonder if novices now think themselves wiser than their wisest teachers: And especially, if such are censured as imprudent for not avoiding suffering. 3. Even a Peter by such carnal wisdom may so far serve Satan, as to deserve so sharp a rebuke as to be called a Satan. 4. Savouring the things of men and flesh, more than of God, is the great sin that we are all in danger of, and deserveth sharp rebuke.

34. And when he had called the people unto him, with his disciples also, he said unto them, Whosoever will come after me, let him deny himself, and take up his cross, and follow me. 35. For whosoever will save his life, shall lose it; but whosoever shall lose his life for my sake and the gospel's, the same shall save it.

34. The case of Peter occasioned Christ to call off his disciples from worldly expectations, and to tell them what they must trust to; and that they are no disciples for him, if they cannot trust him with their lives; and if they believe not that they shall gain more by him than their lives are worth. Note, To deny a man's self, is to forsake his life rather than forsake Christ. As to deny Christ, was to forsake him to save life or any thing else. He that will save his life by denying Christ, shall lose it and his salvation: And he that denieth his life for Christ and the hope of salvation, shall save it for ever.

36. For what shall it profit a man, if he shall gain the whole world, and lose his own soul? 37. Or what shall a man give in exchange for his soul?

36. How poor a price is all the profit and pleasure of this life, to hire a man by sin to lose his salvation! or what can make up that man's loss? Note, And will pride, revenge, gluttony, drunkenness, or fornication then make him a saver, that loseth his soul by them? or will preferment, lordship, and pomp, and power recompense him?

38. Whosoever therefore shall be ashamed of me, and of my words, in this adulterous and sinful generation, of him also shall the Son of Man be ashamed when he cometh in the glory of his Father, with the holy angels.

38. If men be so far ashamed of a crucified, a scorned, a persecuted Christ, as to deny him, to escape shame or suffering: a glorified Christ in judgment before angels and men, will disown them, and say, I know you not. It is not a popedom, or a cardinalship, nor a lordship, that nominal Christians are ashamed of; but it is poor persecuted Christianity.

CHAP. IX.

AND he said unto them, Verily I say unto you, that there be some of them that stand here, which shall not taste of death, till they have seen the kingdom of God come with power.

1. Till they see a glimpse of that glorious or powerful appearance of the King of the church, in which he shall come at last.

2. And after six days Jesus taketh with him Peter, and James, and John, and leadeth them up into an high mountain apart by themselves: and he was transfigured before them. 3. And his raiment became shining, exceeding white as snow; so as no fuller on earth can white them. 4. And there appeared unto them Elias, with Moses: and they were talking with Jesus. 5. And Peter answered and said to Jesus, Master, it is good for us to be here: and let us make three tabernacles; one for thee, and one for Moses, and one for Elias. 6. For he wist not what to say, for they were sore afraid.

2. This was the performance of the foregoing promise.
See on Matt. xvii.
Note, For glorified saints from heaven to wait on Christ in his own splendour, was a glimpse resembling his last coming. 2. If the sight of Christ, Moses, and Elias, in glorious splendour made the three apostles, through the strangeness of it, *sore afraid:* no wonder, if even the thought of what we shall see after death, possess us with dread, though it be our hope and joy.

7. And there was a cloud that overshadowed them; and a voice came out of the cloud, saying, This is my beloved Son: hear him.

7. Hear and obey him as the chief messenger of my will, of whom I give you this testimony from heaven.

8. And suddenly when they had looked round about, they saw no man any more, save Jesus only with themselves. 9. And as they came down from the mountain, he charged them that they should tell no man what things they had seen, till the Son of Man were risen from the dead. 10. And they kept that saying with themselves, questioning one with another what the rising from the dead should mean.

10, &c. Though he had oft told them of his resurrection, they understood him not.

11. And they asked him, saying, Why say the scribes that Elias must first come? 12. And he answered and told them, Elias verily cometh first, and restoreth all things, and how it is written of the Son of man, that he must suffer many things, and be set at nought. 13. But I say unto you, that Elias is indeed come, and they have done unto him whatsoever they listed, as it is written of him.

11, &c. John Baptist was Elias; (not the soul of Elias reincorporate, but he that was meant in Malachi:) And they have used him as they will do me; as Elias was persecuted by Ahab.

14. And when he came to *his* disciples, he saw a great multitude about them, and the scribes questioning with them. 15. And straightway all the people, when they beheld him, were greatly amazed, and running to him, saluted him. 16. And he asked the scribes, What question ye with them? 17. And one of the multitude answered and said, Master, I have brought unto thee my son, which hath a dumb spirit: 18. And wheresoever he taketh him, he teareth him; and he foameth, and gnasheth with his teeth, and pineth away: and I spake to thy disciples, that they should cast him out, and they could not.

14, &c. See on Matt. xvii. 14. Note, The disciples yet had not the full power, that they had after Christ's resurrection.

19. He answered him, and saith, O faithless generation, how long shall I be with you? how long shall I suffer you? bring him unto me.

19. The want of faith in you, did more to your frustration, than the want of power in my disciples.

20. And they brought him unto him: and when he saw him straightway the spirit tare him, and he fell on the ground, and wallowed, foaming.

20. Here is the perfect description of an epilepsy: And the folly of atheists tells them, That natural diseases are not to be imputed to devils:

That is, Because an axe or a halter kills a man; therefore the law, the judges, or the executioner are no causes of it.

21. And he asked his father, How long is it ago since this came unto him? And he said, Of a child. 22. And oft-times it hath cast him into the fire, and into the water to destroy him: but if thou canst do any thing, have compassion on us, and help us.

21. Note, It appeareth this man's faith was weak, in saying, [*If thou canst do any thing;*] Yet be had some hope.

23. Jesus said unto him, If thou canst believe, all things *are* possible to him that believeth.

23 If thy faith make thee a capable receiver, thou shalt find that I want not power.

24. And sraightway the father of the child cried out, and said with tears, Lord, I believe; help thou mine unbelief.

24. He was afraid of losing the cure of his child for want of faith, and yet his faith was weak and wavering, and therefore he said, If I had no belief in thee, I had not come to thee, but I am weak and timorous, and therefore pray thee to strengthen my faith, and make up in thy mercy what is wanting in my belief. This is (alas!) the case of most Christians.

25. When Jesus saw that the people came running together, he rebuked the foul spirit, saying unto him. Thou dumb and deaf spirit, I charge thee, Come out of him, and enter no more into him. 26. And *the spirit* cried, and rent him sore, and came out of him; and he was as one dead, insomuch that many said, He is dead.

25, 26. Note, Christ's cures seem sometimes to the flesh, to put men into a worse condition than they were before.

27. But Jesus took him by the hand, and lifted him up, and he arose, 28. And when he was come into the house, his disciples asked him privately, Why could not we cast him out? 29. And he said unto them, This kind can come forth by nothing, but by prayer and fasting.

27, &c. Note, 1. Even miraculous cures may require the use of means; and those means may serve for one, that will not for another. 2. A double qualification may be necessary, one in the minister, and another in the patient.

30. And they departed thence, and passed through Galilee; and he would not that any man should know *it*. 31. For he taught his disciples, and said unto them, The Son of Man is delivered into the hands of men, and they shall kill him, and after that he is killed he shall rise the third day. 32. But they understood not that saying, and were afraid to ask him.

30, &c. Note, Christ saw it necessary often to foretel his sufferings, and resurrection; which is a great argument for our faith.

33. And he came to Capernaum, and being in the house, he asked them, What was it that ye disputed among yourselves by the way? 34. But they held their peace: for by the way they had disputed among themselves, who *should be* the greatest. 35. And he sat down and called the twelve, and saith unto them, If any man desire to be first, the same shall be last of all, and servant of all.

33, 34, &c. Note, They were ashamed to own their ambition.
The pre-eminence among my ministers, consisteth in being the most humble, and the most serviceable.

36. And he took a child and set him in the midst of them: and when he had taken him in his arms, he said unto them, 37. Whosoever shall receive one of such children in my name, receiveth me: and whosoever shall receive me, receiveth not me, but him that sent me.

36, 37. Humble and harmless Christians are so dear to me, that whosoever in love and mercy receiveth and sheweth kindness to one of these, I will take it, as if he did it to myself; and my Father will take that which is done in love and obedience to me, to be done as to himself. If you will be great in my kingdom, and dear to me, be humble and harmless.

38. And John answered him, saying, Master, we saw one casting out

devils in thy name, and he followed not us; and forbad him, because he followed not us.

38. Note, Had John been now as full of love, as he was afterwards, he would not have forbidden this man to do good.

39. But Jesus said, Forbid him not: for there is no man which shall do a miracle in my name, that can lightly speak evil of me. 40. For he that is not against us, is on our part.

39. Note, Men that preach in Christ's name therefore, are not to be silenced, though faulty; if they do more good than harm. Dreadful then is the case of them, that silence Christ's faithful ministers.
40. In point of service to the church, He that is not against us, is some way for it; as soldiers say of countrymen that are not against them. But as to their own salvation, He that is not for Christ above all the world, is against him, and no sincere Christian; As captains say to their listed soldiers, Fight, or be cashiered.

41. For whosoever shall give you a cup of water to drink, in my name, because ye belong to Christ, verily I say unto you, he shall not lose his reward.

41. He that doth the least good to a Christian, from a true love to Christ, would do more were it in his power: And he that doth good but from common principles, though he be not saved, shall have some reward, and shall be no loser, but a gainer, by all the good that he doth.

42. And whosoever shall offend one of *these* little ones that believe in me, it is better for him that a millstone were hanged about his neck, and he were cast into the sea.

42. Note, O then what will become of tempters, persecutors, and malignant enemies! By [offending] is meant, [hindering from faith and a holy life.] And by [better] is meant, [it is a smaller hurt.]

43. And if thy hand offend thee, cut it off: it is better for thee to enter into life maimed, than having two hands, to go into hell, into the fire that never shall be quenched: 44. Where their worm dieth not, and the fire is not quenched. 45. And if thy foot offend thee, cut it off: it is better for thee to enter halt into life, than having two feet to be cast into hell, into the fire that never shall be quenched: 46. Where their worm dieth not, and the fire is not quenched. 47. And if thine eye offend thee, pluck it out: it is better for thee to enter into the kingdom of God with one eye, than having two eyes to be cast into hell fire: 48. Where their worm dieth not, and the fire is not quenched.

43, &c. So great is the difference between the welfare of this flesh, and the life to come, that you cannot get to heaven, and escape hell-fire at too dear a rate: If a hand, or foot, or eye, were so strong a hindrance, as that you had no other way to avoid sin and hell, it is a far less evil to lose such a member, than to lie in hell. Note, The meaning is not, that any man is in such a case, that he hath no better way to avoid sin and hell: But if he had no better, he should choose this: Nor doth it mean, that maimed persons are maimed in heaven: but if it were so, it were a less evil.

49. For every one shall be salted with fire, and every sacrifice shall be salted with salt. 50. Salt *is* good: but if the salt have lost his saltness, wherewith will ye season it? Have salt in yourselves, and have peace one with another.

49. And be sure, that the fire of affliction shall be as salt to you all, that now are thinking of pre-eminence: and those of you that are sound, it shall make fitter to be pure sacrifices to God. 50. And you that are preachers, and professors of Christianity, being thus salted, yourselves must be the salt of the earth, to season others, by holy doctrine and practice. But if you should lose sound doctrine and Christianity, what then shall season you? Keep up sound truth (that seasoneth, though it cause some smart) in yourselves, and instead of seeking superiority, live in peace and meekness with one another.

CHAP. X.

AND he arose from thence, and cometh into the coasts of Judea, by the farther side of Jordan: and the people resort unto him again; and as he was wont, he taught them again. 2. And the Pharisees came to him, and asked him, Is it lawful for a man to put away his wife? tempting him. 3. And he answered and said unto them, What did Moses command you? 4. And they said, Moses suffered to write a bill of divorcement, and to put her away.

1. Note, These hypocrites seemed by putting cases of conscience, to be afraid of sinning.

5. And Jesus answered and said unto them, For the hardness of your heart, he wrote you this precept. 6. But from the beginning of the creation, God made them male and female. 7. For this cause shall a man leave his father and mother, and cleave to his wife: 8. And they twain shall be one flesh: so then they are no more twain, but one flesh. 9. What therefore God hath joined together, let not man put asunder.

5. This law was good in itself, because it was fitted to your condition: But it was the badness and hardness of your hearts, that made such a toleration needful to you to keep you from worse: so it was not a full approbation of the thing: For the perfect law of innocency so united man and wife, that no man should separate them, for his own pleasure without God's licence.

10. And in the house his disciples asked him again of the same matter. 11. And he saith unto them, Whosoever shall put away his wife, and marry another, committeth adultery against her. 12. And if a woman shall put away her husband, and be married to another, she committeth adultery.

10, &c. Note, Though Mark mentions not the exception of the case of adultery, mentioned by other evangelists, it is implied.

1. Ques. Doth adultery dissolve marriage? Answ. It giveth cause of a dissolution, by divorce, or desertion: But in some cases, it is lawful for the injured person to forgive the wrong, and continue in the relation, without being married over again.

2. Quest. May the woman put away her husband for adultery? Answ. They that deny it, because only the man hath governing power, say nothing: For the man doth it not as governor, but as an injured contractor, seeketh it as justice from the magistrate; or writeth himself, if permitted by the magistrate; or if unjustly forbidden. And the woman may be an injured contractor, as well as the man, and may seek to the magistrate for a divorce; and in some cases, if denied by the magistrate, may right herself by desertion. But whether that desertion be called, A putting away, is but a controversy about the name, and not the thing. In what cases it is lawful to marry again, is a different controversy.

13. And they brought young children to him, that he should touch them; and his disciples rebuked those that brought them. 14. But when Jesus saw it, he was much displeased, and said unto them, Suffer the little children to come unto me, and forbid them not: for of such is the kingdom of God.

13, 14. Note, Though they brought them not to be baptized, (Christian baptism not being fully instituted till after Christ's resurrection,) yet they are offered to Christ for his acceptance and benediction. 2. He gave them such acceptance and blessing, and declared them to be such, as the kingdom (or church) of God consisteth of. He could not mean only [of adult persons that are like these infants in the kingdom of God:] else he might have taken up a lamb or a dove, and blessed them, and said [of such harmless creatures is the kingdom of God.] But he must mean [of them and such as them,] or of such both in age, and also in humble teachable receptivity, is the kingdom of God: Else there would be no reason to bless them. Which can be nothing lower than acceptance as visible infant-church-members.

2. He that in all ages from the beginning took infants to be infant-members of his church, and came not to destroy, but to enlarge mercies to the faithful and their seed, and saith, They are holy: and was much displeased with his erroneous apostles for forbidding them to be brought to his benediction; sure will not be well pleased with those that now forbid them to be dedicated in the baptismal covenant to him. But yet, if any man will say, I deny not the interest of the infants of the faithful in the church and covenant, but only think that baptism was appointed only for the solemn reception of the adult, and so will be baptized at age, after (or without) infant baptism, merely to satisfy conscience, and then live in love and peace with those of another mind, I should gladly live in love and peace with such.

15. Verily I say unto you, Whosoever shall not receive the kingdom of God as a little child, he shall not enter therein. 16. And he took them up in his arms, put his hands upon them, and blessed them.

Note, 1. These words plainly intimate that he received them as capable of the kingdom of God, that is, the church on earth and in heaven. Christ doth not thus bless unbelievers and their seed, but those that, 1 Cor. vii. 14. are called holy.

17. And when he was gone forth into the way, there came one running, and kneeled to him, and asked him, Good Master, what shall I do that I may inherit eternal life?

17. Note, It hence appeareth, that the Jews (except the Sadducees) then believed an everlasting

life. 2. And that we should do whatever God would have us to do to attain it.

18. And Jesus said unto him, Why callest thou me good? *there is none good, but one, that is* God.

18. Good indeed in the prime sense is a high title, none being more proper to God himself, and none perfectly and primarily and essentially good but God: It is a greater matter to be good than thou deemest.

19. Thou knowest the commandments, Do not commit adultery, Do not kill, Do not steal, Do not bear false witness, Defraud not, Honour thy father and mother.

19. Note, Defraud not, is the sense of the tenth commandment, that is, love thy neighbour as thyself, so as not to desire from him any thing to his hurt? Qu. 1. Why doth Christ mention none of the commandments of the first table? Answ. The man is supposed to confess God, and consequently his duty to him, and to mean in his question. What good works must I do towards others? Qu. 2. Why doth not Christ recite the commandments in their true order? Answ. When the matter alone is intended, the order is not necessary. 2. The evangelists recite not all Christ's words in the same order that he spake them, as is evident in the difference of their recitals. These very words are otherwise recited by Matt. xix. 18, 19. [Thou shalt do no murder] is first, and, Thou shalt love thy neighbour as thyself, is last, and instead of [*Defraud not.*]

20. And he answered and said unto him, Master, all these have I observed from my youth.

20. Note, He meant that he had not directly in the outward act broken any of these; not knowing how far the law reacheth.

21. Then Jesus beholding him, loved him, and said unto him, One thing thou lackest: go thy way, sell whatsoever thou hast, and give to the poor; and thou shalt have treasure in heaven; and come, take up the cross, and follow me.

21. Jesus beheld him with kindness, approving in him what was good, and said, So far thou hast done well: But there is more than this necessary to obtain everlasting life, even to prefer it before all the wealth and pleasure of this world, and life itself: and to try thee herein: Go, and sell all and give to the poor, and take heaven for thy treasure instead of all, and follow me in self-denial unto suffering. Note, Not that all are bound to sell all; but all are bound so to prefer heaven, as will make them forsake all that stands against it.

22. And he was sad at that saying, and went away grieved: for he had great possessions.

22. Carnal men may be sorry that they cannot bring God down to their terms: Good and bad would be as well as they can both here and hereafter: but when they see they cannot have both earth and heaven; the faithful choose heaven (though sensible of earthly sufferings,) and the worldly choose the world; and most to keep off sorrow and despair, do force on themselves a hope that they shall have both, and that God will save them on their own terms.

23. And Jesus looked round about, and saith unto his disciples, How hardly shall they that have riches enter into the kingdom of God!

23. How hard is it to persuade rich men to love heaven better than earth, and to yield to the conditions of salvation.

24. And the disciples were astonished at his words. But Jesus answereth again, and saith unto them, Children, how hard is it for them that trust in riches to enter into the kingdom of God! 25. It is easier for a camel to go through the eye of a needle, than for a rich man to enter into the kingdom of God.

24. So bad is the heart of man, that it is exceeding hard to have riches, and not to place men's trust in them: and such as do so, cannot be true Christians, and be saved.

Note, To trust in riches is to take them for our best, and to take and expect more comfort from them, than from Christ and heaven.

26. And they were astonished out of measure, saying among themselves, Who then can be saved? 27. And Jesus looking upon them, saith, With men *it is* impossible, but not with God: for with God all things are possible.

27. Note, Sure the inordinate desire to be rich must needs signify unbelief: Can men seek that which they believe maketh their salvation almost impossible? The same, I say, of murmuring poverty.

28. Then Peter began to say unto him, Lo, we have left all, and have followed thee. 29. And Jesus answered and said, Verily I say unto you, There is no man that hath left house, or brethren, or sisters, or

father, or mother, or wife, or children, or lands, for my sake and the gospel's, 30. But he shall receive an hundred-fold now in this time, houses, and brethren, and sisters, and mothers, and children, and lands, with persecutions, and in the world to come eternal life. 31. But many *that are* first, shall be last: and the last, first.

29, &c. Note, To forsake them for Christ, is rather to displease them or part with them, than with Christ and our duty: when they stand in competition, as comforts, or in opposition, as adversaries: it is not to forsake them in passion, or for want of due love to them; nor to go into a monastery, or as rebellious prodigals, or on any unjust cause.
2. A hundred fold in this life, is in value; God will here do better for them, in things of greater worth. And all Christians shall be endeared to them in love and communion.

32. And they were in the way going up to Jerusalem: and Jesus went before them, and they were amazed, and as they followed, they were afraid. And he took again the twelve, and began to tell them what things should happen unto him, 33. *Saying*, Behold, we go up to Jerusalem, and the Son of Man shall be delivered unto the chief priests, and unto the scribes: and they shall condemn him to death, and shall deliver him to the Gentiles. 34. And they shall mock him, and shall scourge him, and shall spit upon him, and shall kill him: and the third day he shall rise again.

32. When they were before put in fear of going to Jerusalem, he told them again plainly what and how he must suffer, and rise again. Note, Of all prophecies, this is the most confirming.

35. And James and John the sons of Zebedee come unto him, saying, Master, we would that thou shouldest do for us whatsoever we shall desire. 36. And he said unto them, What would ye that I should do for you? 37. They said unto him, Grant unto us that we may sit, one on thy right hand, and the other on thy left hand, in thy glory.

35, &c. They came with their mother. Note, Though this might shew a strong belief of his resurrection and kingdom, if it were spoken as here placed, next his telling them of his death and resurrection: yet afterward this faith seemeth to be almost forgotten: and they were far from perfect, while they were so selfish, ambitious, and presumptuous in their request.

38. But Jesus said unto them, Ye know not what ye ask: can ye drink of the cup that I drink of? and be baptized with the baptism that I am baptized with?

38. It is meeter for you to consider whether you can suffer with and for me.

39. And they said unto him, We can. And Jesus said unto them, Ye shall indeed drink of the cup that I drink of; and with the baptism that I am baptized withal, shall ye be baptized: 40. But to sit on my right hand, and on my left hand, is not mine to give, but *it shall be given* to them for whom it is prepared.

39. Note, Their purpose was good, but not their self-confidence. 40. It is to be given by way of reward to the most excellent and meet, according to my Father's decree, and not by me now by way of partial favour, as courtiers obtain of princes.

41. And when the ten heard *it*, they began to be much displeased with James and John.

41. Note, Christ's own followers and apostles had their great displeasures and indignation at each other: No wonder then if such arise in the church now. 2. It was then the aspiring ambition of two that would have been above the rest, that caused this breach and indignation: No wonder if the same cause have the same effects, and worse, when it is in worse men, and in very many.

42. But Jesus called them to him, and saith unto them, Ye know that they which are accounted to rule over the Gentiles, exercise lordship over them; and their great ones exercise authority upon them. 43. But so shall it not be among you: but whosoever will be great among you, shall be your minister: 44. And whosoever of you will be the chiefest, shall be servant of all.

42, &c. Jesus purposely thus decided the controversy: You are not called to an empire or dominion. The rulers of the nations exercise lordship and command on them. But your preeminence shall be moral, and he that is the worthiest in humility, and serviceableness to the rest, and in that light and love that fits them for it, shall have the chief authority with you: For his wisdom, and service, reason, and love, shall most prevail with Christians for respect in church affairs.

45. For even the Son of Man came not to be ministered unto, but to minister, and to give his life a ransom for many.

45. Why should you set up a higher dominion over one another, than I have exercised over you? Have not I been more a servant to you in teaching and guiding you, than you have been to me, by any service you have done me: Have not I stooped to you all, and will do even to death.

46. And they came to Jericho: and as he went out of Jericho with his disciples, and a great number of people, blind Bartimeus, the son of Timeus, sat by the highway-side, begging. 47. And when he heard that it was Jesus of Nazareth, he began to cry out, and say, Jesus, thou son of David have mercy on me. 48. And many charged him that he should hold his peace: but he cried the more a great deal, Thou son of David, have mercy on me. 49. And Jesus stood still, and commanded him to be called: and they call the blind man, saying unto him, Be of good comfort, rise: he calleth thee. 50. And he casting away his garment, arose, and came to Jesus. 51. And Jesus answered and said unto him, What wilt thou that I should do unto thee? The blind man said unto him, Lord, that I might receive my sight. 52. And Jesus said unto him, Go thy way; thy faith hath made thee whole. And immediately he received his sight, and followed Jesus in the way.

46, &c. See on Matt. xx. 30. Note, 1. It is great comfort to be called to Christ. 2. Christ maketh whole efficiently; but faith, by moral receptive qualification of a free gift.

CHAP. XI.

AND when they came nigh to Jerusalem, unto Bethphage, and Bethany, at the mount of Olives, he sendeth forth two of his disciples, 2. And saith unto them, Go your way into the village over against you; and as soon as ye be entered into it, ye shall find a colt tied, whereon never man sat; loose him, and bring him. 3. And if any man say unto you, Why do ye this? say ye that the Lord hath need of him; and straightway he will send him hither. 4. And they went their way, and found the colt tied by the door without, in a place where two ways met: and they loose him. 5. And certain of them that stood there said unto them, What do ye loosing the colt? 6. And they said unto them even as Jesus had commanded: and they let them go.

1. Note, Christ knew things distant, and what men would say and do. Though man's acts be free, God accomplisheth his will, by man's freest acts. 2. It was an ass with her colt; though Mark names but the colt.

7. And they brought the colt to Jesus, and cast their garments on him; and he sat upon him. 8. And many spread their garments in the way: and others cut down branches off the trees, and strawed them in the way. 9. And they that went before, and they that followed, cried, saying, Hosannah, blessed is he that cometh in the name of the Lord. 10. Blessed be the kingdom of our father David, that cometh in the name of the Lord; Hosannah in the highest.

7. We receive with all joyful applause the Messiah that is come from God; Blessed be he and blessed be his kingdom: Let the heavens applaud and bless it.

11. And Jesus entered into Jerusalem, and into the temple; and when he had looked round about upon all things, and now the eventide was come, he went out unto Bethany with the twelve. 12. And on the morrow when they were come from Bethany, he was hungry, 13. And seeing a fig-tree afar off, having leaves, he came, if haply he

might find any thing thereon: and when he came to it, he found nothing but leaves; for the time of figs was not yet.

11, &c. Note, It is not likely that Christ was ignorant, that figs hit not that year; and that this tree was fruitless: But by this miracle he shewed the destruction of fruitless Jews and hypocrites. 3. It is most likely he lay out of door at Bethany, as he used to do by night in the garden where he was taken, because he would not burden poor men's houses with all his followers: Else sure he would not have come away hungry.

14. And Jesus answered and said unto it, No man eat fruit of thee hereafter for ever. And his disciples heard it.

14. Note. 1. This phrase of answering to a fig-tree, must be expounded by the use of the word in those times, when [to answer] signified but [to say.] 2. The curse hurteth not the tree, but to instruct men.

15. And they come to Jerusalem: and Jesus went into the temple, and began to cast out them that sold and bought in the temple, and overthrew the tables of the money-changers, and the seats of them that sold doves; 16. And would not suffer that any man should carry any vessel through the temple.

15. Note, He shewed that he had the authority of a king, though he would not set up a temporal kingdom. 16. Christ now seemed to be more ceremonious than the Pharisees: But he was made under the law, and would not abrogate one tittle till all were fulfilled by him; He was to keep it, to save men from it. 3. He yet teacheth us to reverence the place of solemn worship, for the worship sake.

17. And he taught, saying unto them, Is it not written, My house shall be called of all nations the house of prayer? but ye have made it a den of thieves.

17. The temple was dedicated for holy worship for Jews and proselytes of all nations; but these aye merchandise here, and rob men by deceit.

Ques. May places new be temples dedicated to holy worship? Answ. No doubt of it, but that the reverence of God's name and worship not only alloweth, but requireth us when we can, to separate comely places to holy worship, from common use; And why they may not be called temples, I know not.

18. And the scribes and chief priests heard it, and sought how they might destroy him: for they feared him, because all the people was astonished at his doctrine.

18. Though one would think Christ's zeal for the temple should have pleased them that cried it up as their glory, and accused Christ, and Stephen, and Paul for dishonouring it; yet because Christ did it as he did, by the people's countenance, they feared the wrath of the Romans, lest they would take it for sedition, and so they should suffer by it.

19. And when even was come, he went out of the city.

19. Lest they should surprise him in the night, as they did at last.

20. And in the morning, as they passed by, they saw the fig-tree dried up from the roots. 21. And Peter calling to remembrance, saith unto him, Master, behold, the fig-tree which thou cursedst, is withered away. 22. And Jesus answering, saith unto them, Have faith in God. 23. For verily I say unto you, that whosoever shall say unto this mountain, Be thou removed, and be thou cast into the sea, and shall not doubt in his heart, but shall believe in those things which he saith shall come to pass, he shall have whatsoever he saith. 24. Therefore I say unto you, What things soever ye desire when ye pray, believe that ye receive *them*, and ye shall have *them*.

23. No difficulty shall hinder you from obtaining what God hath promised, and is fit to be done, if you firmly trust his love and promise.

25. And when ye stand praying, forgive, if ye have ought against any: that your father also which is in heaven may forgive you your trespasses.

25. And forgiving and charity is necessary to success as well as believing: Believing supposeth other requisites.

26. But if you do not forgive, neither will your Father which is in heaven forgive your trespasses.

26. Note, This sheweth that the promise of granting believers' prayers, meaneth *cæteris paribus*, other requisites being answerable.

27. And they come again to Jeru-

salem: and as he was walking in the temple, there come to him the chief priests, and the scribes, and the elders, 28. And say unto him, By what authority doest thou these things? and who gave thee this authority to do these things?

27. Note, They judged truly that they were not to be done without authority: But knew not that his authority was from God.

29. And Jesus answered and said unto them, I will also ask of you one question, and answer me, and I will tell you by what authority I do these things. 30. The baptism of John, was it from heaven, or of men? answer me.

30. Note, Had they confessed John to be of God, he would have produced his testimony: Had they denied it, they had gainsayed themselves, and the people's voice: For the generality of them were baptized by John, in hope that their Messiah and his kingdom, and their deliverance were at hand.

31. And they reasoned with themselves, saying, If we shall say, From heaven, he will say, Why then did ye not believe him? 32. But if we shall say, Of men, they feared the people: for all men counted John, that he was a prophet indeed. 33. And they answered and said unto Jesus, We cannot tell. And Jesus answering, saith unto them, Neither do I tell you by what authority, I do these things.

31. Note, It was well that they considered what might be said against them, which now most Christians do not in their disputes. 2. These persecutors and the Romans had some charity and consideration, in that they were restrained by the fear of the people, and did not accuse and fine them as for routs, riots, and seditions. 3. They that deny necessary premises are not to be disputed with.

CHAP. XII.

AND he began to speak unto them by parables. A *certain* man planted a vineyard, and set an hedge about it, and digged *a place for* the wine-fat, and built a tower, and let it out to husbandmen, and went into a far country. 2. And at the season he sent to the husbandmen a servant, that he might receive from the husbandmen of the fruit of the vineyard. 3. And they caught *him*, and beat him, and sent *him* away empty. 4. And again he sent unto them another servant; and at him they cast stones, and wounded *him* in the head, and sent *him* away shamefully handled. 5. And again he sent another; and him they killed: and many others, beating some, and killing some.

1. See on Matt. xxi. Note, who did this? Answ. The only national church on earth. 2. Did they cease upon this warning of Christ? Answ. No, but do worse. 3. Why did they do it? Answ. Through folly and wickedness. 4. The things that have been, are: This is no strange thing yet on earth.

6. Having yet therefore one son, his well-beloved, he sent him also last unto them, saying, They will reverence my son. 7. But those husbandmen said amongst themselves, This is the heir; come, let us kill him, and the inheritance shall be ours. 8. And they took him, and killed *him*, and cast *him* out of the vineyard.

8. Note, No wonder that no innocency, or worth can preserve his ministers from their rage, and from being cast out of the vineyard.

9. What shall therefore the Lord of the vineyard do? he will come and destroy the husbandmen, and will give the vineyard unto others.

9. He will destroy these Jews, and call the Gentiles to become his church.

10. And have ye not read this scripture? The stone which the builders rejected is become the head of the corner. 11. This was the Lord's doing, and it is marvellous in our eyes.

10. Psal. cxviii. Isa. xxviii. 16.

12. And they sought to lay hold on him, but feared the people; for they knew that he had spoken the parable against them: and they left him, and went their way.

12. *Note, That which is spoken against bad men enrageth them, be it never so true and necessary.*

13. And they send unto him certain of the Pharisees, and of the Herodians, to catch him in *his* words. 14. And when they were come, they say unto him, Master, we know that thou art true, and carest for no man: for thou regardest not the person of men, but teachest the way of God in truth: Is it lawful to give tribute to Cæsar, or not?

13. They send those that thought Cæsar an usurper, or at least had no right to that sort of tribute, alienated from the sanctuary, and the Herodians that were for Cæsar's right. Note, They give Christ a flattering character to ensnare him.

15. Shall we give, or shall we not give? But he knowing their hypocrisy, said unto them, Why tempt ye me? bring me a penny, that I may see *it*. 16. And they brought *it*: and he saith unto them, Whose *is* this image and superscription? And they said unto him, Cæsar's. 17. And Jesus answering, said unto them, Render to Cæsar the things that are Cæsar's, and to God the things that are God's. And they marvelled at him.

15. See on Matt. xxi. Note, We are not bound to answer directly to all such ensnaring questions, nor to satisfy the tempters.

18. Then come unto him the Sadducees, which say there is no resurrection; and they asked him, saying, 19. Master, Moses wrote unto us, If a man's brother die, and leave his wife behind him, and leave no children, that his brother should take his wife, and raise up seed unto his brother. 20. Now there were seven brethren: and the first took a wife, and dying left no seed. 21. And the second took her, and died, neither left he any seed: and the third likewise. 22. And the seven had her, and left no seed: last of all the woman died also. 23. In the resurrection therefore, when they shall rise, whose wife shall she be of them? for the seven had her to wife.

23. Erroneous men, from one false supposition, infer many that are worse.

24. And Jesus answering, said unto them, Do ye not therefore err, because ye know not the scriptures, neither the power of God? 25. For when they shall rise from the dead, they neither marry, nor are given in marriage: but are as the angels which are in heaven.

24. Carnal men think carnally of things heavenly: Spiritual glorified bodies are like angels, and as they die not, so they generate not any more than they; (nor eat and drink as here.)

26. And as touching the dead, that they rise: have ye not read in the book of Moses, how in the bush God spake unto him, saying, I am the God of Abraham, and the God of Isaac, and the God of Jacob? 27. He is not the God of the dead, but the God of the living: ye therefore do greatly err.

See on Matt. xxii.

28. And one of the scribes came, and having heard them reasoning together, and perceiving that he had answered them well, asked him, Which is the first commandment of all? 29. And Jesus answered him, The first of all the commandments *is*, Hear, O Israel, the Lord our God is one Lord; 30. And thou shalt love the Lord thy God with all thy heart, and with all thy soul, and with all thy mind, and with all thy strength: this is the first commandment. 31. And the second *is* like, *namely* this, Thou shalt love thy neighbour as thyself: there is none other commandment greater than these.

Note, Love is the most full and final act of the soul. It is the total inclination, and adherence of the will to God as God, the infinite good, and to man, for his sake, as far as his conformity to God hath made him amiable. It fervently riseth towards God here by desire and seeking; and fully delighteth in him hereafter.

32. And the scribe said unto him, Well Master, thou hast said the truth: for there is one God, and there is none other but he. 33. And to love him with all the heart, and with all the understanding, and with all the soul, and with all the strength, and to love *his* neighbour as himself, is more than all whole burnt-offerings and sacrifices. 34. And when Jesus saw that he answered discreetly, he said unto him, Thou art not far from the kingdom of God. And no man after that durst ask him any question.

34. Note, If the confession of these two great commands, was a matter so greatly esteemed both of Christ, and by this scribe; how greatly do they differ from Christ, who, besides the profession of the whole baptismal faith and covenant, require abundance of unnecessary or uncertain things to church communion and concord, if not to salvation?

35. And Jesus answered and said, while he taught in the temple, How say the scribes that Christ is the son of David? 36. For David himself said by the Holy Ghost, The LORD said to my Lord, Sit thou on my right hand, till I make thine enemies thy footstool. 37. David therefore himself calleth him Lord; and whence is he *then* his son?

37. He is the Lord in his divine nature, and his son in his human nature.

37. And the common people heard him gladly. 38. And he said unto them in his doctrine, Beware of the scribes, which love to go in long clothing, and *love* salutations in the market-places, 39. And the chief seats in the synagogues, and the uppermost rooms at feasts: 40. Which devour widows' houses, and for a pretence make long prayers: these shall receive greater damnation.

37. Let not these proud hypocrites deceive you, who by their long liturgies, and ceremonies, and claim of superiority, do but cloak their worldliness, pride and oppression, and are religious to their greater damnation.

41. And Jesus sat over against the treasury, and beheld how the people cast money into the treasury: and many that were rich cast in much. 42. And there came a certain poor widow, and she threw in two mites, which make a farthing. 43. And he called unto him his disciples, and saith unto them, Verily I say unto you, that this poor widow hath cast more in, than all they which have, cast into the treasury. 44. For all *they* did cast in of their abundance: but she of her want did cast in all that she had, *even* all her living.

41. It is no more of self-denying piety, to serve God so liberally of that which the flesh can spare, and which costeth the flesh no denial of its desires, but to serve it with the first, and God with its leaving. 2. God accepteth a willing mind, where wealth and power is wanting.

CHAP. XIII.

AND as he went out of the temple, one of his disciples saith unto him, Master, see what manner of stones, and what buildings *are* here. 2. And Jesus answering said unto him, Seest thou these great buildings? there shall not be left one stone upon another, that shall not be thrown down. 3. And as he sat upon the mount of Olives, over against the temple, Peter, and James, and John, and Andrew, asked him privately, 4. Tell us, when shall these things be? and what *shall be* the sign when all these things shall be fulfilled?

See in Matt. xxiv. Note, Nature would foreknow even the evil to come.

5. And Jesus answering them, began to say, Take heed lest any man deceive you. 6. For many shall come in my name, saying, I am *Christ:* and shall deceive many.

6. Many shall pretend that they are sent to restore the Jewish kingdom, and draw in people to their destruction.

7. And when ye shall hear of wars and rumours of wars, be ye

not troubled: for *such things* must needs be; but the end *shall* not be yet. 8. For nation shall rise against nation, and kingdom against kingdom: and there shall be earthquakes in *divers* places, and there shall be famines, and troubles: these *are* the beginnings of sorrow.

8. Many commotions must go before the destruction.

9. But take heed to yourselves: for they shall deliver you up to councils; and in the synagogues ye shall be beaten, and ye shall be brought before rulers and kings for my sake, for a testimony against them.

9. I allow you by lawful means to keep yourselves out of their hands; but I foretel you that their councils will condemn you, and in their synagogues they will scourge you like malefactors, and cast you out, and you shall be brought before such as Herod, Agrippa, and the Roman procurators, to answer for being Christians. That your testimony may evince against them, that they heard the gospel, and did not obey it.

10. And the gospel must first be published among all nations.

10. Before their destruction, the gospel must be spread and published abroad, both to Jews and Gentiles.

11. But when they shall lead you, and deliver you up, take no thought beforehand what ye shall speak, neither do ye premeditate; but whatsoever shall be given you in that hour, that speak ye: for it is not ye that speak, but the Holy Ghost.

11. Though you may be discouraged for want of matter, boldness, or utterance, let not this trouble you; for I promise you the present help of my spirit.

12. Now the brother shall betray the brother to death, and the father the son: and children shall rise up against *their* parents, and shall cause them to be put to death. 13. And ye shall be hated of all men for my name's sake: but he that shall endure unto the end, the same shall be saved.

12, 13. Your kindred themselves shall be your enemies, and shall not spare your very lives: And the vulgar of all sorts shall be seduced to take you for the plagues of the world, and commonly mention you as a hateful sort of men; But bear all this patiently: Trust God, and hold out to the end, and you shall be saved from all this and more.

14. But when ye shall see the abomination of desolation, spoken of by Daniel the prophet, standing where it ought not, (let him that readeth, understand) then let them that be in Judea flee to the mountains: 15. And let him that is on the house-top not go down into the house, neither enter therein, to take any thing out of his house. 16. And let him that is in the field, not turn back again for to take up his garment.

14. But when ye shall see the Roman ensigns set up against Jerusalem, like Antiochus's desolating abomination, mentioned by Daniel (expect not that I should speak more plainly to you, to enrage the Roman power,) then speedily be gone, and shift for yourselves, and be glad though you lose your goods, if you save your lives.

17. But woe to them that are with child, and to them that give suck in those days. 18. And pray ye that your flight be not in the winter. 19. For in those days shall be affliction, such as was not from the beginning of the creation which God created, unto this time, neither shall be.

17. It will be an increase of misery to all that are hindered in the flight: For the affliction of those days will be unparalleled.

20. And except that the Lord had shortened those days, no flesh should be saved: but for the elect's sake, whom he hath chosen, he hath shortened the days.

20. Those calamities shall not destroy all; but God hath some chosen ones whom he will preserve.

21. And then if any man shall say to you, Lo, here *is* Christ, or lo, *he is* there: believe *him* not. 22. For false Christs and false prophets shall rise, and shall shew signs and wonders, to seduce, if *it were* possible, even the elect. 23. But take ye heed: behold, I have foretold you all things.

21. The miserable Jews will follow divers that will pretend that they are sent to be their Saviours: but I warn you, Trust none such.

24. But in those days, after that tribulation, the sun shall be darkened, and the moon shall not give her light: 25. And the stars of heaven shall fall, and the powers that are in heaven shall be shaken. 26. And then shall they see the Son of Man coming in the clouds with great power and glory.

See Matt. xxiv. 29, 30.

27. And then shall he send his angels, and shall gather together his elect from the four winds, from the uttermost part of the earth, to the uttermost part of heaven.

See Matt. xxiv. 31.

28. Now learn a parable of the fig-tree: when her branch is yet tender, and putteth forth leaves, ye know that summer is near: 29. So ye in like manner, when ye shall see these things come to pass, know that it is nigh, *even* at the doors. 30. Verily I say unto you, that this generation shall not pass, till all these things be done. 31. Heaven and earth shall pass away: but my words shall not pass away.

29, 30. Expect the destruction of Jerusalem, when ye see these signs: And doubt not my word: Some now alive shall live to see it. (It was not forty years.)

32. But of that day and *that* hour knoweth no man, no not the angels which are in heaven, neither the Son, but the Father.

32. But these things not coming discernibly, as effects of natural causes, neither angels, nor Christ as man can foretel just the day and hour, because they depend on the mere will of God.

33. Take ye heed, watch and pray: for ye know not when the time is.

33 It is kept unknown to you, that you may watch and pray, and be still prepared.

34. *For the Son of Man is* as a man taking a far journey, who left his house, and gave authority to his servants, and to every man his work, and commanded the porter to watch. 35. Watch ye therefore, (for ye know not when the master of the house cometh, at even, or at midnight, or at the cock-crowing, or in the morning.) 36. Lest coming suddenly, he find you sleeping. 37. And what I say unto you, I say unto all, Watch.

34. So long shall Christ be out of sight, that he will seem to men as one in a far country: But see that you do the work he set you, and watch for his coming in a wakeful prepared state continually. This is my charge to you and to all.

Note, It occasioneth great perplexity to the readers here and Matt. xxiv. that the destruction of Jerusalem, and the final coming of Christ, seem to be set so near together, as if the latter were to come soon after the former. Ver. xxiv. [In those days] or [Immediately:] which causeth them to expound the latter part allegorically, as meaning only the great commotions in Judea: Which seemeth a very hard exposition of Christ's coming with his angels visibly in the clouds, and gathering his elect from the four ends of heaven, &c. The apparition to Constantine, and the powerful deliverance of the Christians from heathen rage is less harsh than this. But 1. Things of greatest distance may be quickly set together in writing; and the questions may occasion the conjunction. 2. Christ spake for all ages as well as for them. 3. A thousand years with the Lord is as one day. 4. And it is undeniable that the writers gave us not just all the words that Christ spake. For 1. He spoke in Chaldee, and they translated them into Greek. 2. In this and other instances, their words oft differ among themselves. 3. They profess to omit much that Christ said. 4. They place his words oft in divers orders. Therefore we must not gather any thing from a word, or from the omission of a clause, which contradicteth the scope of the text, and the certain truth.

CHAP. XIV.

AFTER two days was *the feast of* the passover, and of unleavened bread; and the chief priests and the scribes sought how they might take him by craft, and put him to death. 2. But they said, not on the feast-day, lest there be an uproar of the people.

2. They feared the people's rescuing him.

3. And being in Bethany, in the house of Simon the leper, as he sat at meat, there came a woman, having an alabaster-box of ointment of spikenard, very precious; and she

brake the box, and poured it on his head.

3. Note, This Simon, it is most like, having been cured by him of a leprosy, shewed his thankfulness in entertaining him. 2. Bethany like the villages near London, contained a large circuit of ground, it being usual for citizens to set their country-houses, and for such grounds to be so populous. 3. It was a cruise of precious spike-oil, shaken and poured out.

4. And there were some that had indignation within themselves, and said, Why was this waste of the ointment made? 5. For it might have been sold for more than three hundred pence, and have been given to the poor. And they murmured against her.

4. Note, Whether it was any beside Judas is doubtful. Man's wit is apt to be censorious against good works: on pretence of some good which they more value. 2. Three hundred pence of theirs, is, as Budeus and Beza calculate, fifty two French crowns and a half. A crown is six shillings and eight pence, our noble.

6. And Jesus said, Let her alone, why trouble ye her? she hath wrought a good work on me. 7. For ye have the poor with you always, and whensoever ye will, ye may do them good: but me ye have not always.

6. Note, That is not best at one time, that is best at another; but every thing in its season.

8. She hath done what she could: she is come aforehand to anoint my body to the burying. 9. Verily I say unto you, Wheresoever this gospel shall be preached throughout the whole world, *this* also that she hath done, shall be spoken of for a memorial of her.

9. Note, The greatest honouring of Christ tendeth to our own greatest honour, (though despised at present by the profane.)

10. And Judas Iscariot, one of the twelve, went unto the chief priests, to betray him unto them.

10. Note, The devil draweth sinners to be the seekers of their own temptation, sin and misery.

11. And when they heard *it*, they were glad, and promised to give him money. And he sought how he might conveniently betray him.

11. Note, 1. The wicked are glad to be assisted in sin. 2. Money is the bait of wickedness and blood. 3. When the heart once consenteth to sin, men study how to accomplish it.

12. And the first day of unleavened bread, when they killed the passover, his disciples said unto him, Where wilt thou that we go and prepare, that thou mayest eat the passover? 13. And he sendeth forth two of his disciples, and saith unto them, Go ye into the city, and there shall meet you a man bearing a pitcher of water: follow him. 14. And wheresoever he shall go in, say ye to the good man of the house, The Master saith, Where is the guest-chamber, where I shall eat the passover with my disciples? 15. And he will shew you a large upper room furnished and prepared: there make ready for us. 16. And his disciples went forth, and came into the city, and found as he had said unto them: and they made ready the passover:

16. Note, Carist knew what was future and unseen, even voluntary acts.

17. And in the evening he cometh with the twelve. 18. And as they sat and did eat, Jesus said, Verily I say unto you, One of you which eateth with me, shall betray me. 19. And they began to be sorrowful, and to say unto him one by one, Is it I? and another, *said*, Is it I? 20. And he answered and said unto them, *It is* one of the twelve, that dippeth with me in the dish.

19. Note, They feared themselves and his suspicion, and were troubled at the prognostic. 2. Christ's giving Judas the sop, is here past by.

21. The Son of Man indeed goeth, as it is written of him: but woe to that man by whom the Son of Man is betrayed: good were it for that man if he had never been born.

21. Note, 1. God's foreknowledge or decrees excuse not man's sin. 2. By [Good] is meant [A less evil.]

22. And as they did eat, Jesus took bread, and blessed, and brake it, and gave to them, and said, Take, eat: this is my body.

22. Note, Here it is called at once bread, and his body: bread naturally, and his body sacramentally, that is representatively, and significantly: For [It] is the relative, and [bread] is the antecedent: What did Christ take? Bread: What did he bless? [It:] What did he break? [It.] What is [It] but that before-named bread? Yet by so doing he made it his body. How? As the king maketh a piece of wax to become his great seal, by which he conveyeth land, liberty, and life: or a piece of silver to be money.

23. And he took the cup, and when he had given thanks, he gave it to them: and they all drank of it. 24. And he said unto them, This is my blood of the new testament, which is shed for many.

23. By the cup is meant the wine.
Note, It is strange that men, who find that Christ throughout the gospel still taught by parables or similitudes, (saying, This is such a thing, and That is such a thing, as *the seed is the word*, *the field is the world, the reapers are the angels*, &c.) should force themselves to believe that there is no similitude used here. The Lord deliver his church from those who burn men that believe not that bread is not bread, but made Christ himself; while themselves believe not that Christ himself is Christ indeed, but are infidels.

25. Verily I say unto you, I will drink no more of the fruit of the vine, until that day that I drink it new in the kingdom of God. 26. And when they had sung an hymn, they went out into the mount of Olives.

25. See Matt. xxiv. It is more than probable that this hymn was a form.

27. And Jesus saith unto them, All ye shall be offended because of me this night: for it is written, I will smite the shepherd, and the sheep shall be scattered.

27. Your faith shall stagger, and you shall forsake me, and fly in fear.

28. But after that I am risen, I will go before you into Galilee.

28. See John xxi. 1, 2, 3.

29. But Peter said unto him, Although all shall be offended, yet will not I. 30. And Jesus saith unto him, Verily I say unto thee, that this day, *even* in this night before the cock crow twice, thou shalt deny me thrice.

30. Note, This is not contrary to other evangelists, that say [Before the cock crow.] For 1. They mean [before cock's crowing time be past, or before the second cock's crowing.] 2. The writers speak the sense of Christ's words, and not always the precise words themselves.

31. But he spake the more vehemently, If I should die with thee, I will not deny thee in any wise. Likewise also said they all.

31. Note, If the apostles so little know themselves, what wonder if most Christians know not how bad they are?

32. And they came to a place which was named Gethsemane: and he saith to his disciples, Sit ye here while I shall pray. 33. And he taketh with him Peter, and James, and John, and began to be sore amazed, and to be very heavy: 34. And saith unto them, My soul is exceeding sorrowful unto death: tarry ye here, and watch. 35. And he went forward a little, and fell on the ground, and prayed, that if it were possible the hour might pass from him. 36. And he said, Abba, Father, all things *are* possible unto thee, take away this cup from me: nevertheless, not what I will, but what thou wilt.

34. Note, It is an error that Christ's Godhead was instead of a human soul: For his soul was sorrowful and suffered, but so could not his godhead. 2. His nature in the first instant had a sinless averseness to suffering as such, but his reason and will submit to it in the second instant, because it is according to God's will, for greater benefit.

37. And he cometh and findeth them sleeping, and saith unto Peter, Simon, sleepest thou? couldest not thou watch one hour? 38. Watch ye, and pray, lest ye enter into temptation: the spirit truly *is* ready, but the flesh *is* weak.

37. Hast thou strength to die with me, who cannot watch one hour with me? Watching and praying is the means to avoid temptation, and consequently sinning and suffering for sin. The

mind and will, sanctified by God's Spirit, is inclined to duty, but it hath not an absolute despotical power over the fleshly weakness and backwardness, but a political only.

39. And again he went away and prayed, and spake the same words. 40. And when he returned, he found them asleep again (for their eyes were heavy) neither wist they what to answer him. 41. And he cometh the third time, and saith unto them, Sleep on now, and take your rest: it is enough, the hour is come; behold, the Son of Man is betrayed into the hands of sinners.

40. They were ashamed 41. Now I have no more use for your watching with me: Take your own course, or rest: My apprehenders are at hand.

42. Rise up, let us go: lo he that betrayeth me is at hand. 43. And immediately, while he yet spake, cometh Judas, one of the twelve, and with him a great multitude with swords and staves, from the chief priests, and the scribes, and the elders. 44. And he that betrayed him, had given them a token, saying, Whomsoever I shall kiss, the same is he; take him, and lead *him* away safely. 45. And as soon as he was come, he goeth straightway to him, and saith, Master, master; and kissed him.

44. Note, Thus Satan's servants that wear Christ's livery, both priests and magistrates, betray Christ, by his own titles, and by pretence of love and honour.

46. And they laid their hands on him, and took him. 47. And one of them that stood by, drew a sword, and smote a servant of the high priest, and cut off his ear.

47. Note, Had but one Peter done this rash unwarrantable act against Papists, when they are killing true Christians, as butchers do sheep, they would publish to the world, that the whole party are seditious rebels: yea, if any do but speak against their murderers. I mean they have done thus.

48. And Jesus answered and said unto them, Are ye come out as against a thief, with swords and *with* staves, to take me? 49. I was daily with you in the temple, teaching, and ye took me not: but the scriptures must be fulfilled.

49. The scripture foretold all this usage.

50. And they all forsook him and fled. 51. And there followed him a certain young man, having a linen cloth cast about his naked body; and the young men laid hold on him. 52. And he left the linen cloth, and fled from them naked.

50. All the disciples locally forsook him to save themselves, though not so as totally to desert him with their heart. 51. Being in the night, some young man, either undressed, or raised out of bed, was come thither.

53. And they led Jesus away to the high priest: and with him were assembled all the chief priests, and the elders, and the scribes.

53. They led Christ as prisoner to those that sent them to take him, which was the Jews' church representative, or council.

54. And Peter followed him afar off, even into the palace of the high priest: and he sat with the servants, and warmed himself at the fire. 55. And the chief priests, and all the council sought for witness against Jesus to put him to death; and found none. 56. For many bare false witness against him, but their witness agreed not together.

55. They first resolve on his death, and afterwards search for some pretended cause: But their suborned witness spake not crime enough for death.

57. And there arose certain, and bare false witness against him, saying, 58. We heard him say, I will destroy this temple that is made with hands, and within three days I will build another made without hands. 59. But neither so did their witness agree together.

58. Note, We have men seemingly wise now, that would say, Why did Christ speak so unadvisedly as to give occasion to such accusers? But what can be spoken so well, from whence such men will not take occasion of calumny?

60. And the high priest stood up in the midst, and asked Jesus, saying, Answerest thou nothing? what

is it which these witness against thee?

60. Note, The arch-priest who was relatively and by profession the holiest man of that nation, and of the whole world, was the arch-enemy and persecutor of Christ, and the greatest plague of his whole country.

61. But he held his peace, and answered nothing. Again the high priest asked him, and said unto him, Art thou the Christ, the Son of the Blessed? 62. And Jesus said, I am: and ye shall see the Son of Man sitting on the right hand of power, and coming in the clouds of heaven.

61. When the subtle priest could prove nothing against him, he craftily puts a question to him (equal to an *ex officio* oath) which he knew he would answer, that he might out of his own words accuse him.

63. Then the high priest rent his clothes, and saith, What need we any further witnesses? 64. Ye have heard the blasphemy: what think ye? And they all condemned him to be guilty of death.

63. Note. He had been better had he rent his heart for his wickedness: Here is diabolism itself clothed with the highest pretence of holy zeal, by the holy prelate, and his confederates. No wonder if the whole convocation condemn Christ, when such an high-priest leads them.

65. And some began to spit on him, and to cover his face, and to buffet him, and to say unto him, Prophesy: and the servants did strike him with the palms of their hands.

65. Note, This the Son of God endured for our sins: And doth it beseem us to be tender of suffering abuse.

66. And as Peter was beneath in the palace, there cometh one of the maids of the high priest. 67. And when she saw Peter warming himself, she looked upon him, and said, And thou also wast with Jesus of Nazareth. 68. But he denied, saying, I know not, neither understand I what thou sayest. And he went out into the porch; and the cock crew.

66. Note, it is dangerous among persecutors to be a friend to Christ. 2. Wonderful that the first cock did not waken Peter's conscience, having been so warned! But what will we not do, if God leave us to ourselves.

69. And a maid saw him again, and began to say to them that stood by, This is *one* of them. 70. And he denied it again. And a little after, they that stood by said again to Peter, Surely thou art *one* of them: for thou art a Galilean, and thy speech agreeth *thereto*. 71. But he began to curse and to swear, *saying*, I know not this man of whom ye speak. 72. And the second time the cock crew.

70. Note, No man is long safe in the mouth of great temptation, if extraordinary mercy save him not.

72. And Peter called to mind the word that Jesus said unto him, Before the cock crow twice, thou shalt deny me thrice. And when he thought thereon, he wept.

72. Note, Before the love of life, and fear of death, prevailed (in act.) But now the love of Christ beginneth to prevail again, and grieve, and shame him for his sin.

CHAP. XV.

AND straightway in the morning the chief priests held a consultation with the elders and scribes, and the whole council, and bound Jesus, and carried *him* away, and delivered *him* to Pilate.

1. To be put to death.

2. And Pilate asked him, Art thou the king of the Jews? And he answering said unto him, Thou sayest it.

2. I am.

3. And the chief priests accused him of many things: but he answered nothing. 4. And Pilate asked him again, saying, Answerest thou nothing? behold, how many things they witness against thee. 5. But Jesus yet answered nothing; so that Pilate marvelled.

CHAP. XV. ST. MARK. 117

5. He would not strive against calumniators, nor against the death which he came to undergo.

6. Now at that feast he released unto them one prisoner, whomsoever they desired. 7. And there was *one* named Barabbas, which lay bound with them that had made insurrection with him, who had committed murder in the insurrection. 8. And the multitude crying aloud, began to desire *him to do* as he had ever done unto them. 9. But Pilate answered them, saying, Will ye that I release unto you the king of the Jews? 10. (For he knew that the chief priests had delivered him for envy).

9. Note, He called him their king in scorn.

11. But the chief priests moved the people, that he should rather release Barabbas unto them. 12. And Pilate answered, and said again unto them, What will ye then that I shall do *unto him* whom ye call the king of the Jews? 13. And they cried out again, Crucify him.

12. Note, The people are but the mouth of the priests.

14. Then Pilate said unto them, Why, what evil hath he done? And they cried out the more exceedingly, Crucify him. 15. And *so* Pilate willing to content the people, released Barabbas unto them, and delivered Jesus, when he had scourged *him*, to be crucified.

14. Pilate to please the people, and they to please the priests, all please the devils, displease God, and undo themselves. And yet by all this God is saving the world.

16. And the soldiers led him away into the hall called Pretorium; and they call together the whole band. 17. And they clothed him with purple, and platted a crown of thorns, and put it about his *head*, 18. And began to salute him, Hail King of the Jews. 19. And they smote him on the head with a reed, and did spit upon him, and bowing *their* knees, worshipped him. 20. And when they had mocked him, they took off the purple from him, and put his own clothes on him, and led him out to crucify him.

16. As the priests are the chief contrivers of the murder, the soldiers are fittest for execution; such usually being hardened by blood and wickedness into a destroying inclination, the great executioners of the devil, for the ruin of the world. Alas, mad sinners, little know you whom you scorn, and how your sport will end at last! Reader, see here what sin is: and what thou and I have deserved, that needeth such a sacrifice.

21. And they compel one Simon a Cyrenian, who passed by, coming out of the country, the father of Alexander and Rufus, to bear his cross. 22. And they bring him unto the place Golgotha, which is, being interpreted, the place of a scull. 23. And they gave him to drink, wine mingled with myrrh: but he received *it* not. 24. And when they had crucified him, they parted his garments, casting lots upon them, what every man should take. 25. And it was the third hour, and they crucified him. 26. And the superscription of his accusation was written over, THE KING OF THE JEWS.

See on Matt. xxvii.
24. See on John xix. 24.
26. Meaning that they put him to death, for proclaiming his kingdom, though it was a spiritual one.

27. And with him they crucify two thieves; the one on his right hand, and the other on his left. 28. And the scripture was fulfilled, which saith, And he was numbered with the transgressors.

27. Note, Men imputed sin itself to him: God only reputed him a sacrifice for our sins.

29. And they that passed by, railed on him, wagging their heads, and saying, Ah thou that destroyest the temple, and buildest *it* in three days, 30. Save thyself, and come down from the cross. 31. Likewise also the chief priests mocking, said among themselves, with the scribes, He saved others, himself he cannot save. 32. Let Christ the king of Israel descend now from the

cross, that we may see, and believe. And they that were crucified with him, reviled him.

29. Note, All this tells us what sin is; And when his servants follow him in sufferings, priests, soldiers, and rabble will insult with scorns.

33. And when the sixth hour was come, there was darkness over the whole land, until the ninth hour. 34. And at the ninth hour Jesus cried with a loud voice, saying, Eloi, Eloi, lama sabachthani? which is, being intepreted, My God, my God, why hast thou forsaken me?

33. Note, Christ was forsaken so far as to be left to the power of Satan's servants and deprived of life, and to have the sense of God's justice against man's sin: And this to shew that we deserved to be forsaken, and to keep us from being utterly forsaken. But God's love and esteem of him was not abated, but his suffering was meritorious.

35. And some of them that stood by, when they heard it, said, Behold, he calleth Elias. 36. And one ran and filled a spunge full of vinegar, and put it on a reed, and gave him to drink, saying, Let alone; let us see whether Elias will come to take him down.

36. In scorn they still insult.

37. And Jesus cried with a loud voice, and gave up the ghost.

37. Saying, Father into thy hand I commend my spirit.

38. And the vail of the temple was rent in twain, from the top to the bottom. 39. And when the centurion which stood over against him, saw that he so cried out, and gave up the ghost, he said, Truly this man was the Son of God.

39. That he died not as other men in that case do.

40. There were also women looking on afar off: among whom was Mary Magdalene, and Mary the mother of James the less, and of Joses, and Salome; 41. Who also when he was in Galilee, followed him, and ministered unto him; and many other women which came up with him unto Jerusalem. 42. And now when the even was come, (because it was the preparation, that is, the day before the sabbath):

40. Note, It is likely that it is James that is called the brother of Christ, that is, he that is called James the less: for Joses and James are called brethren, as here, so Matt. xiii. 55. But whether littleness of stature or dignity be meant it is uncertain.

43. Joseph of Arimathea, an honourable counsellor, which also waited for the kingdom of God, came, and went in boldly unto Pilate, and craved the body of Jesus. 44. And Pilate marvelled if he were already dead: and calling unto him the centurion, he asked him whether he had been any while dead. 45. And when he knew it of the centurion, he gave the body to Joseph.

45. Note, He feared lest he should seem dead and be taken down alive, till inquiry resolved the doubt.

46. And he brought fine linen, and took him down, and wrapped him in the linen, and laid him in a sepulchre which was hewn out of a rock, and rolled a stone unto the door of the sepulchre. 47. And Mary Magdalene, and Mary the mother of Joses, beheld where he was laid.

46. Note, Joseph shewed great boldness and faith, in owning Christ so openly when he was dead: and so did Nicodemus who joined with him. 2. As Ahab's court had one Obadiah, so even the Jewish rulers had a Joseph, and a Nicodemus: And there were saints in Nero's house. 3. Christ's being buried in fine linen, maketh it not our duty nor a sin to be buried in wollen: yea, though it had been the greatest enemy of Christ that in opposition to him had made the new law which doth command it.

The grave was also sealed and watched.

Christ's burial hath in some sort sanctified the grave to true believers. We may boldly there lay down these bodies, as still in his power and care that was buried for us.

CHAP. XVI.

AND when the sabbath was past, Mary Magdalene, and Mary the mother of James, and Salome, had bought sweet spices, that they might come and anoint him. 2. And very early in the morning, the first *day* of the week, they came unto the sepulchre at the rising of the sun. 3. And they said among themselves, Who shall roll us away the stone from the door of the sepulchre ? 4. (And when they looked, they saw that the stone was rolled away) for it was very great.

4. The angel had before done it, and frighted away the soldiers.

5. And entering into the sepulchre, they saw a young man sitting on the right side, clothed in a long white garment ; and they were affrighted. 6. And he saith unto them, Be not affrighted: ye seek Jesus of Nazareth, which was crucified: he is risen, he is not here: behold the place where they laid him.

See on John xx. The reconciling of the seeming difference of the evangelists, about the apparitions.

7. But go your way, tell his disciples and Peter, that he goeth before you into Galilee: there shall ye see him, as he said unto you.

See John xxi. 1, 2.

8. And they went out quickly, and fled from the sepulchre; for they trembled, and were amazed: neither said they any thing to any man; for they were afraid.

8. Fear made them silent.

9. Now when *Jesus* was risen early the first *day* of the week, he appeared first to Mary Magdalene, out of whom he had cast seven devils.

9. The rest were near her.

10. *And* she went and told them that had been with him, as they mourned and wept.

10. She was the first messenger of joy, to the mourning weeping disciples.

11. And they, when they had heard that he was alive, and had been seen of her, believed not.

11. Note, Christ's disciples found a great difficulty to believe his resurrection: and he took them not at the worst.

12. After that, he appeared in another form unto two of them, as they walked, and went into the country. 13. And they went and told *it* unto the residue: neither believed they them.

14. Afterward he appeared unto the eleven as they sat at meat, and upbraided them with their unbelief, and hardness of heart, because they believed not them which had seen him after he was risen.

12. Mark doth but give us a brief touch of some of Christ's appearances and leaves much recorded by others. Note, Unbelief and hardness of heart, are radical sins in us, and of difficult cure. Note, Christ findeth so much of these in us, as to upbraid us with them, as our fault and shame ; and directing us what to blame and resist in ourselves.

15. And he said unto them, Go ye into all the world, and preach the gospel to every creature. 16. He that believeth and is baptized, shall be saved ; but he that believeth not, shall be damned.

15. To all men as far as ye are able. 16. He that upon your preaching believeth the gospel, and sincerely giveth up himself in the baptismal covenant to God the Father, the Son, and the Holy Ghost, by a practical and obedient trust, and dedication, shall be forgiven and be saved from sin, from the curse of the law, from Satan, and from hell. But those to whom you preach, who will not believe, and take me for their Saviour, and God for their God, shall be condemned to hell as refusers of salvation.

17. And these signs shall follow them that believe; In my name shall they cast out devils, they shall speak with new tongues, 18. They shall take up serpents, and if they drink any deadly thing, it shall not hurt them ; they shall lay hands on the sick, and they shall recover.

17. And because it cannot be expected that all people believe things so strange and unlikely to nature, upon your affirmation, I will by sending down the Holy Ghost, attest your word by these miraculous signs: They that believe, and specially you my apostles, shall in my name cast out devils from the possessed, and make them obey me and confess me: You shall speak in various languages which you never learnt. Poison shall not hurt you, either serpents outwardly, or taken inwardly: And you shall pray and lay your hands on the sick in my name,

and they shall recover. Note, 1. That not every one shall have all these gifts, but some one, and some another, not that you shall use them, when and how you will, but as pleaseth the Holy Ghost that giveth them.

19. So then after the Lord had spoken unto them, he was received up into heaven, and sat on the right hand of God.

19. Note, His ascension they beheld, and his glorification they believed, by the Spirit's revelation.

20. And they went forth, and preached every where, the Lord working with them, and confirming the word with signs following. Amen.

20. And accordingly they began in Judah, and thence went abroad through the Gentile world, every where preaching the gospel of Christ, (his person, life, doctrine, sufferings, resurrection, ascension, kingdom, judgment, glory, and blessing to his church.) The Lord by his grace, making their teaching successful, and assisting, and confirming it by the promised miracles.

THE GOSPEL

ACCORDING TO

ST. LUKE.

CHAP. I.

FORASMUCH as many have taken in hand to set forth in order a declaration of those things which are most surely believed among us, 2. Even as they delivered them unto us, which from the beginning were eye-witnesses, and ministers of the word:

1. Divers having published the declaration or history in order, of those matters of fact and doctrine, which have been done, and are fully believed among us Christians. 2. Even as those men did faithfully deliver them to us, who from the beginning were eye-witnesses of the works of Jesus, and ministers who attended him, and have preached his word.

3. It seemed good to me also, having had perfect understanding of all things from the very first, to write unto thee in order, most excellent Theophilus,

3. I also thought good to write the same history in order to thee, most excellent Theophilus, both to confirm what is by others written, and to add, especially in the beginning of the history, what in others is omitted; having myself, by very diligent search, got very full notice of these matters, from the very first, which others mention not.

4. That thou mightest know the certainty of those things wherein thou hast been instructed.

4. That I may contribute my endeavour to increase thy knowledge, and confirm thy belief of those things concerning Jesus Christ, which thou hast already learned among us.

5. THERE was in the days of Herod the king of Judea, a certain priest named Zachariah, of the course of Abia: and his wife *was* of the daughters of Aaron, and her name *was* Elisabeth.

5. Note, The families of the priests officiated in their courses, and Abia's course was the eighth of old, 1 Chron. xxiv. 10. After it was the twelfth,

CHAP. I. ST. LUKE. 121

Nehem. xii. 1. And after that the eleventh, Nehem. xii. 17.

6. And they were both righteous before God, walking in all the commandments and ordinances of the Lord blameless.

6. They were both sincere godly persons, living in true obedience to all the commandments and ordinances of God, according to the law and light which they were under, without the blot of any gross or scandalous sin.

7. And they had no child, because that Elisabeth was barren, and they both were *now* well stricken in years. 8. And it came to pass, that while he executed the priest's office before God in the order of his course, 9. According to the custom of the priest's office, his lot was to burn incense when he went into the temple of the Lord. 10. And the whole multitude of the people were praying without, at the time of incense.

7—10. Note, The priest went into the sanctuary to offer, and the people that while prayed without the sanctuary, not without the temple. In imitation of which our temples usually are built in three parts. The chancel for the clergy, the body of the church for the laity, and all below the font for the catechumens, and suspended, who are no communicants; (as the outward court was for Gentiles.)

11. And there appeared unto him an angel of the Lord, standing on the right side of the altar of incense. 12. And when Zacharias saw *him*, he was troubled, and fear fell upon him. 13. But the angel said unto him, Fear not, Zacharias: for thy prayer is heard, and thy wife Elisabeth shall bear thee a son, and thou shalt call his name John. 14. And thou shalt have joy and gladness, and many shall rejoice at his birth.

11—14. He was born to an austere life, and to martyrdom, yet his birth was joyful, though to such a painful life and death, for the church's service.

15. For he shall be great in the sight of the Lord, and shall drink neither wine nor strong drink; and he shall be filled with the Holy Ghost, even from his mother's womb.

15. Note, 1. The best men and most useful are greatest in God's sight. 2. Extraordinary denying the flesh agreeth well with the extraordinary gift of the Spirit. 3. Infants may have the Holy Ghost, before it appeareth.

16. And many of the children of Israel shall he turn to the Lord their God.

16. Note, To turn many by repentance to God was the effect of the Holy Ghost, and of John's extraordinary worth and work.

17. And he shall go before him in the spirit and power of Elias, to turn the hearts of the fathers to the children, and the disobedient to the wisdom of the just, to make ready a people prepared for the Lord.

17. He shall be possessed with such fulness of spirit and power, to prepare the way for Christ, as Elias had, as is prophesied in Mal. iv. 6. Note, By turning the hearts of the fathers to the children, some think is meant [turning the tyrannical oppression of rulers, to fatherly love and lenity to inferiors.] But Dr. H. more probably translateth it (with the children;) That is, he shall turn fathers and children, old and young. Others say it is but to turn men's minds to the love of one another, and those that disobey God, to the true wisdom of just men, who obey and trust him.

18. And Zacharias said unto the angel, whereby shall I know this? for I am an old man, and my wife well stricken in years. 19. And the angel answering, said unto him, I am Gabriel, that stand in the presence of God: and am sent to speak unto thee, and to shew thee these glad tidings. 20. And behold, thou shalt be dumb, and not able to speak, until the day that these things shall be performed, because thou believest not my words, which shall be fulfilled in their season.

18, 19, 20. I am one of the many angels that stand before God, and am sent to tell thee this; and to reprove thy unbelief; And to convince thee for a sign, thou shalt be dumb, &c.

21. And the people waited for Zacharias, and marvelled that he tarried so long in the temple. 22. And when he came out, he could not speak unto them: and they perceived that he had seen a vision in

the temple: for he beckened unto them, and remained speechless.

21, 22. Sanctuary. 22. Some revelation.

23. And it came to pass, that as soon as the days of his ministration were accomplished, he departed to his own house.

23. That ceremonious service might be done by a dumb man; but so cannot the gospel ministration.

24. And after those days his wife Elisabeth conceived, and hid herself five months, saying, 25. Thus hath the Lord dealt with me, in the days wherein he looked on me, to take away my reproach among men.

24, 25. She retired from people's observation and discourse, saying, the Lord hath shewed me mercy in taking away my reproach.

26. And in the sixth month the angel Gabriel was sent from God, unto a city of Galilee, named Nazareth, 27. To a virgin espoused to a man whose name was Joseph, of the house of David; and the virgin's name was Mary.

26, 27. Not married, but betrothed.

28. And the angel came in unto her, and said, Hail thou that art highly favoured, the Lord is with thee: blessed art thou among women.

28. Rejoice, for thou art highly favoured of the Lord, who maketh thee blessed above all women.

29. And when she saw him, she was troubled at his saying, and cast in her mind what manner of salutation this should be. 30. And the angel said unto her, Fear not, Mary: for thou hast found favour with God. 31. And behold, thou shalt conceive in thy womb, and bring forth a son, and shalt call his name Jesus. 32. He shall be great, and shall be called the Son of the Highest; and the Lord God shall give unto him the throne of his father David.

29—32. She understood it not. This glorious kingdom meant in the promise to David's seed, of which his kingdom was but a type.

33. And he shall reign over the house of Jacob for ever, and of his kingdom there shall be no end.

33. His kingdom over the faithful Israel of God, begun in grace, shall be everlasting in glory.

34. Then said Mary unto the angel, How shall this be, seeing I know not a man? 35. And the angel answered and said unto her, The Holy Ghost shall come upon thee, and the power of the Highest shall overshadow thee: therefore also that holy thing which shall be born of thee, shall be called the Son of God.

34, 35 This shall be done without man, by the Holy Ghost, and the overshadowing power of God, and therefore he shall be properly called *the Son of God.*

Note, 1. Though this gave us the most known reason, why Christ is called the Son of God in scripture, it is not said to be the only reason, excluding his eternal generation. 2. Yet Christ oft calleth himself, the Son of Man, which signifieth no more, but that he was truly a man, and born of a woman.

36. And behold, thy cousin Elisabeth, she hath also conceived a son in her old age: and this is the sixth month with her, who was called barren. 37. For with God nothing shall be impossible.

36, 37. Note, 1. Though Elisabeth was of the tribe of Aaron, and Mary of the tribe of Judah, they were a-kin by Elisabeth's mother marrying a Levite.

2. Nothing should seem difficult to faith, when it is known to be God's will and word.

38. And Mary said, Behold the handmaid of the Lord, be it unto me according to thy word.

38. Amen! Let thy word come to pass: (They are the expression of Mary's faith and hope.)

38. And the angel departed from her. 39. And Mary arose in those days, and went into the hill country with haste, into a city of Juda. 40. And entered into the house of Zacharias, and saluted Elisabeth.

38, 39, 40. The angel's words made her go see how it was with Elisabeth.

41. And it came to pass, that when Elisabeth heard the salutation of Mary, the babe leaped in her

womb: and Elisabeth was filled with the Holy Ghost. 42. And she spake out with a loud voice, and said, Blessed *art* thou among women, and blessed *is* the fruit of thy womb. 43. And whence *is* this to me, that the mother of my Lord should come to me? 44. For lo, as soon as the voice of thy salutation sounded in mine ears, the babe leaped in my womb for joy. 45. And blessed *is* she that believed: for there shall be a performance of those things which were told her from the Lord.

41—45. *The Holy Ghost filled her to speak out these words prophetically, &c.*

46. And Mary said, My soul doth magnify the Lord, 47. And my spirit hath rejoiced in God my Saviour, 48. For he hath regarded the low estate of his handmaiden: for behold, from henceforth all generations shall call me blessed.

46, 47, 48. *Mary also filled with the Spirit, speaks these words of praise to God; My soul, &c. 48. He hath raised me highest who was one of the lowest.*

49. For he that is mighty hath done to me great things, and holy *is* his name. 50. And his mercy *is* on them that fear him, from generation to generation.

49, 50. *Mercy to all that fear God and their posterity, is the great name or notification of the most holy God to man.*

51. He hath shewed strength with his arm, he hath scattered the proud, in the imagination of their hearts. 52. He hath put down the mighty from *their* seats, and exalted them of low degree. 53. He hath filled the hungry with good things, and the rich he hath sent empty away.

51, 52, 53. *He hath shewed that it is he that is Almighty, by scattering the proud in their own vain imaginations; And by casting down the high, and exalting the low; and by satisfying the needy, and bringing the prosperous to distress.*

54. He hath holpen his servant Israel in remembrance of *his* mercy,

55. As he spake to our fathers, to Abraham and to his seed for ever.

54, 55. *The promises, which he made to Abraham and his seed, he is now performing in their proper sense, for the saving of all the believing seed: The mercy which promised it, is now performing it.*

56. And Mary abode with her about three months, and returned to her own house.

56. *Note, It was many months between Mary's espousal to Joseph, and their marriage.*

57. Now Elisabeth's full time came, that she should be delivered: and she brought forth a son. 58. And her neighbours, and her cousins heard how the Lord had shewed great mercy upon her; and they rejoiced with her.

57, 58. *In giving a son to one so old.*

59. And it came to pass, that on the eighth day they came to circumcise the child; and they called him Zacharias, after the name of his father. 60. And his mother answered and said, Not *so:* but he shall be called John. 61. And they said unto her, There is none of thy kindred that is called by this name. 62. And they made signs to his father, how he would have him called. 63. And he asked for a writing-table, and wrote, saying, His name is John. And they marvelled all.

59—62. *Note, They would have the name keep the memorial of ancestors. 63. By signs.*

64. And his mouth was opened immediately, and his tongue *loosed*, and he spake, and praised God. 65. And fear came on all that dwelt round about them: and all these sayings were noised abroad throughout all the hill-country of Judea. 66. And all they that had heard *them*, laid *them* up in their hearts, saying, What manner of child shall this be? And the hand of the Lord was with him.

64, 65, 66. *It raised in all the country great expectations, what this child would prove: And God did extraordinarily bless him.*

67. And his father Zacharias was filled with the Holy Ghost, and prophesied, saying, 68. Blessed be the Lord God of Israel, for he hath visited and redeemed his people, 69. And hath raised up an horn of salvation for us, in the house of his servant David; 70. As he spake by the mouth of his holy prophets, which have been since the world began; 71. That we should be saved from our enemies, and from the hand of all that hate us.

67—71. Spake by inspiration. Note, Christ was prophesied of from the beginning of the world, after Adam's fall: Note, Though God's Spirit in him understood just what manner of Saviour Christ would be, and what sort of deliverance from enemies he would bring (by the destruction of the Jews, and calling the Gentiles;) we know not that Zachary, Elisabeth, and Mary understood this while they thus prophesied.

72. To perform the mercy *promised* to our fathers, and to remember his holy covenant: 73. The oath which he sware to our father Abraham, 74. That he would grant unto us, that we being delivered out of the hands of our enemies, might serve him without fear, 75. In holiness and righteousness before him, all the days of our life.

72—75. That the Messiah delivering us from all our enemies, spiritual and corporal, we may serve him in safety, not terrified by them.
Note, Holiness and righteousness are the sum of God's acceptable service.
Note, The chief benefit of deliverance from cruel enemies, is, that we freely and peaceably serve God.

76. And thou child shalt be called the prophet of the Highest: for thou shalt go before the face of the Lord, to prepare his ways; 77. To give knowledge of salvation unto his people, by the remission of their sins.

76, 77. Thou shalt be a prophet of God, to go before Christ, to prepare men to receive him, by calling men to repentance, proclaiming that a Saviour is come to save his people, by pardoning their sins.

78. Through the tender mercy of our God; whereby the dayspring from on high hath visited us, 79. To give light to them that sit in darkness, and in the shadow of death, to guide our feet into the way of peace.

78, 79. The tender mercy of God, having given us from heaven, the Sun of heavenly light to visit us. 79. Even to them that lived in the darkness of sin and misery, and to guide us into the way of life and happiness.

80. And the child grew, and waxed strong in spirit, and was in the deserts till the day of his shewing unto Israel.

80. And John, with his increase of age and strength, shewed great strength of the Spirit of God in him, and he dwelt in the wilderness, (or, say some, in the hill country of Judea,) bred up in a life of holiness and mortification,) till the time that he set upon his public ministry, of preaching the kingdom of the Messiah, and repentance, and baptizing.

CHAP. II.

AND it came to pass in those days, that there went out a decree from Cæsar Augustus, that all the world should be taxed. 2. (And this taxing was first made when Cyrenius was governor of Syria.) 3. And all went to be taxed, every one into his own city.

1, 2, 3. Augustus decreed that all the empire, called the Roman world, should be enrolled in their several families and cities: That he might know the state of his empire, and how to tax them.

4. And Joseph also went up from Galilee, out of the city of Nazareth, into Judea, unto the city of David, which is called Bethlehem, (because he was of the house and lineage of David.) 5. To be taxed with Mary his espoused wife, being great with child.

4, 5. She was now married, though called espoused.

6. And so it was, that while they were there, the days were accomplished that she should be delivered. 7. And she brought forth her first-born son, and wrapped him in swaddling clothes, and laid

CHAP. II.   ST. LUKE.   125

him in a manger, because there was no room for them in the inn.

6, 7. Note, It should be rather [in the stables] than [in the manger,] Had Joseph been a rich man, it is likely he would have found better room.

8. And there were in the same country shepherds abiding in the field, keeping watch over their flock by night.

8. Some one part of the night, and some another, by turns (as is most likely.)

9. And lo, the angel of the Lord came upon them, and the glory of the Lord shone round about them; and they were sore afraid. • 10. And the angel said unto them, Fear not: for behold, I bring you good tidings of great joy, which shall be to all people. 11. For unto you is born this day, in the city of David, a Saviour, which is Christ the Lord. 12. And this *shall be* a sign unto you; Ye shall find the babe wrapped in swaddling clothes, lying in a manger.

9, 10 Glory is light, Christ's birth is cause of universal joy. 12. Stable.

13. And suddenly there was with the angel a multitude of the heavenly host praising God, and saying, 14. Glory to God in the highest, and on earth peace, good will towards men.

13, 14. Note, Angels are the heavenly host. Note, God's praise and glory is the end of all his works. Note, Angels rejoiced at Christ's birth, and for man's redemption.

14. In Christ the Redeemer God will be glorified in heaven, peace will be made on earth, by this great Reconciler, and God's love or benevolence will be towards men.

Or,[Glory be to God in the heavens through the Redeemer, and reconciliation, or peace, on earth to men that are the objects of God's good will.]

Qu. Is it necessary or lawful to keep a day as holy in remembrance of Christ's birth ? Answ. 1. If any should appoint a weekly day for it, it would be an usurping of the same power that hath already separated a weekly day for it, it would be an usurping of the same power that hath already separated a weekly day for commemorating the work of redemption, though specially for Christ's resurrection: And it would seem an accusing Christ's law of insufficiency. 2. And if any should make a yearly day's observation necessary to the universal church, 1. They would usurp a power, not given to any, (to make laws for all the church.)

2. And they would accuse Christ's law as imperfect.

But if particular Christians, churches, or countries, voluntarily agree to celebrate yearly the memorial of Christ's birth, it is but what almost all the churches on earth do, and have done at least 1300 years. And it is lawful to keep a yearly day of remembrance for any great deliverance, or mercy to the church, even in an apostle. But if any Christian think that it is an unlawful addition to the institution of the Lord's day, which God set apart for our commemorating the whole work of redemption, such should not be forced to keep it against their consciences; but must avoid affronting them that do.

15. And it came to pass, as the angels were gone away from them into heaven, the shepherds said one to another, Let us now go even unto Bethlehem, and see this thing which is come to pass, which the Lord hath made known unto us. 16. And they came with haste, and found Mary and Joseph, and the babe lying in a manger. 17. And when they had seen *it*, they made known abroad the saying which was told them concerning this child. 18. And all they that heard *it*, wondered at those things which were told them by the shepherds. 19. But Mary kept all these things, and pondered *them* in her heart. 20. And the shepherds returned, glorifying and praising God for all the things that they had heard and seen, as it was told unto them.

15—18. In a stable. 19. Regarded them, as tending to what was promised her. 20. Angels are not first sent to princes, but to poor shepherds, who must preach Christ.

21. And when eight days were accomplished for the circumcising of the child, his name was called JESUS, which was so named of the angel before he was conceived in the womb.

21. Jesus is [a Saviour.] He was circumcised, as bound to keep the law of Moses, not as a seal of pardon of sin to him.

22. And when the days of her purification, according to the law of Moses, were accomplished, they brought him to Jerusalem, to present *him* to the Lord.

22. To the priest, as in Numb. iii. 12, 46.

23. (As it is written in the law of the Lord, Every male that openeth the womb shall be called holy to the Lord), 24. And to offer a sacrifice according to that which is said in the law of the Lord, A pair of turtle doves, or two young pigeons.

23, 24. See Levit. xii. 6, 8.

25. And behold, there was a man in Jerusalem, whose name *was* Simeon; and the same man *was* just and devout, waiting for the consolation of Israel: and the Holy Ghost was upon him. 26. And it was revealed unto him by the Holy Ghost, that he should not see death, before he had seen the Lord's Christ.

25. Note, The Messiah was much expected at that time.
Note, They are just and devout men, that God specially favoureth by extraordinary gifts of his Spirit.

27. And he came by the spirit into the temple: and when the parents brought in the child Jesus, to do for him after the custom of the law, 28. Then took he him up in his arms, and blessed God, and said, 29. Lord, now lettest thou thy servant depart in peace, according to thy word. 30. For mine eyes have seen thy salvation: 31. Which thou hast prepared before the face of all people: 32. A light to lighten the Gentiles, and the glory of thy people Israel.

27—32. Praised God, saying, Now thou hast performed thy word, by letting me live to see Christ, let me die in peace as soon as it pleaseth thee: For I have seen the Saviour, whom thou hast appointed to be a light to the Gentile world, to lead them into the way of faith and righteousness to thee, and to be the honour of the Jews, of whom he is born after the flesh; but the special glory of all that by faith receive him.

33. And Joseph and his mother marvelled at those things which were spoken of him. 34. And Simeon blessed them, and said unto Mary his mother, Behold, this *child* is set for the fall and rising again of many in Israel; and for a sign which shall be spoken against:

33, 34. He shall prove eventually, a stumbling block, on which many Israelites shall fall to their destruction, and the chief corner-stone, on which believers shall be built up to salvation; and the talk and obloquy of men.

35. (Yea, a sword shall pierce through thy own soul also) that the thoughts of many hearts may be revealed.

35. Yea thou also shalt bear a deep part in sufferings by grief of heart; and men, in these trials, shall shew what they are, even the different state of their secret thoughts.

36. And there was one Anna a prophetess, the daughter of Phanuel, of the tribe of Aser; she was of a great age, and had lived with an husband seven years from her virginity: 37. And she *was* a widow of about fourscore and four years: which departed not from the temple, but served *God* with fastings and prayers night and day.

36, 37. She kept close to the temple-worship, and was constant in the duties of fasting, mortification, and prayer.
Note, It is not proved that she deserted all outward calling or labour in the world, on pretence of religion, while she was able for it: And if it be done but when age or sickness disableth one, it is lawful and well.
Note, Some think fasting unfit for age and weakness: But digestion being then weakest, and most dying by that suffocation of crudities, and not by mere defect of nutrimental matter, moderate fasting may be fit for the aged, as well as for the young.
Note, She was not of the sick mind of the profane nominal Christians, that cannot abide long prayers, and religious strictness.

38. And she coming in that instant, gave thanks likewise unto the Lord, and spake of him to all them that looked for redemption in Jerusalem.

38. She was inspired then to come in, and to prophesy of Christ, and declare him to the people, that looked for the Messiah.

39. And when they had performed all things according to the law of the Lord, they returned into Galilee, to their own city Nazareth. 40. And the child grew and

waxed strong in spirit, filled with wisdom; and the grace of God was upon him.

39, 40. Qu. What increase of spiritual strength was Christ capable of, and what greater fulness of wisdom and grace? Answ. His divine nature was capable of no increase: But the human was capable, 1. Of increase of bodily stature and strength. 2. Of seeing more objects, than he saw at first. 3. Of actual knowing them by that sight. 4. Of improving them to holy uses as known, which he did not in infancy. 5. Of doing many good works, which he could not do in infancy. 6. And of the increase of such habits, by all these acts as are acquired by them. As Adam when new created had perfect faculties; but not perfect knowledge of all the creatures before he saw them, nor the fullest improvement of them, nor the perfect habit of such use, as it is distinct from the faculties' perfection.

41. Now his parents went to Jerusalem every year at the feast of the passover. 42. And when he was twelve years old, they went up to Jerusalem, after the custom of the feast. 43. And when they had fulfilled the days, as they returned, the child Jesus tarried behind in Jerusalem; and Joseph and his mother knew not *of it*. 44. But they supposing him to have been in the company, went a day's journey; and they sought him among *their* kinsfolk and acquaintance.

41—44. Note, It may seem an unnatural neglect of a child : But they had found him so manlike in all other matters, that they trusted him by himself.

45. And when they found him not, they turned back again to Jerusalem, seeking him. 46. And it came to pass, that after three days, they found him in the temple, sitting in the midst of the doctors, both hearing them, and asking them questions.

45, 46. Note, Christ himself disdained not to hear the Jewish doctors, and to ask them questions.

47. And all that heard him were astonished at his understanding and answers. 48. And when they saw him, they were amazed: and his mother said unto him, Son, why hast thou thus dealt with us? behold, thy father and I have sought thee sorrowing.

47, 48. Note, If Christ's holy mother blamed him, as dealing ill with his parents, by mistake, for want of true knowledge of the inside of the case, what wonder if the best persons do, by the like ignorance of the case, by mistake, blame and censure one another, and misreport accordingly?

49. And he said unto them, How is it that ye sought me ? wist ye not that I must be about my Father's business ? 50. And they understood not the saying which he spake unto them.

49, 50. Where should I be but in my Father's house, about his work? Your ignorance maketh you blame me.

51. And he went down with them, and came to Nazareth, and was subject unto them : but his mother kept all these sayings in her heart.

51. Note, Christ, who submitted in his humanity, to a state of infancy, (sanctifying that state, and shewing, that as an infant was yet in title, king and head of the church; so infants may be members of him, and it) did also in his childhood subject himself to his supposed father, and to his mother, reverencing them, and obeying them, both as part of his meritorious humiliation, and to sanctify a state of subjection, and become a pattern thereof to us all: And it will greatly condemn proud, rebellious children, and youth, who will not obey the just government of parents, (but their fleshly appetites and lusts) when the Son of God incarnate, condescended to subjection.

Mary's laying up all these sayings, was the working of her faith and hope, perceiving that God was going on to fulfil the promises made to her.

52. And Jesus increased in wisdom and stature, and in favour with God and man.

52. His human nature increased, as in stature, so in actual human knowledge, and its habits, knowing more than he knew in infancy as man : And God, that by way of approbation and complacence, loveth all things, so far as they are lovely, so approved and loved his humanity more, as it grew more in act and habit toward perfection.

CHAP. III.

NOW in the fifteenth year of the reign of Tiberius Cæsar, Pontius Pilate being governor of Judea, and Herod being tetrarch of Galilee, and his brother Philip tetrarch of Iturea, and of the region of Trachonitis, and Lysanias the tetrarch of Abilene, 2. Annas and Caiaphas being the high priests, the word of God came unto John the son of Zacharias in the wilderness.

1, 2. Note, A tetrarch is the governor of the fourth part of a province, or large country. Whether Annas and Caiaphas were both high priests (by corruption) at once, or exercised it by turns; or being yearly chosen, one had it in one part of the year, and the other succeeded him; or whether Annas is so called for his power with, or over the high priest by affinity and interest, or whether Annas though so called, had another sort of government distinct from the priesthood, expositors are not agreed. But it is certain, that the high priesthood was greatly corrupted, and usually bought of the Romans.

3. And he came into all the country about Jordan, preaching the baptism of repentance for the remission of sins;

3. Preaching pardon to all true penitents, and telling them that public deliverance from their national calamity was at hand to be offered them, if they would prepare for it by repentance.

4. As it is written in the book of the words of Esaias the prophet, saying, The voice of one crying in the wilderness, Prepare ye the way of the Lord, make his paths straight. 5. Every valley shall be filled, and every mountain and hill shall be brought low; and the crooked shall be made straight, and the rough ways shall be made smooth; 6. And all flesh shall see the salvation of God.

4, 5, 6. Prepare yourselves for the kingdom of God, in which he will raise the humble and the oppressed, and take down the proud and the oppressors, and will bring in justice and reformation into an unrighteous, wicked world; and the Saviour of the world shall appear, and his salvation be proclaimed and wrought throughout the earth.

7. Then said he to the multitude that came forth to be baptized of him, O generation of vipers, who hath warned you to flee from the wrath to come? 8. Bring forth therefore fruits worthy of repentance, and begin not to say within yourselves, We have Abraham to our father: for I say unto you, that God is able of these stones to raise up children unto Abraham.

7, 8. Do you think to escape the wrath that is coming on you by an hypocritical repentance, and the ceremony of baptism? Shew that you truly repent by your reformed lives, and presume not on your being Abraham's seed: For God that can make men of stones, can of the Gentiles raise a seed of believers to Abraham.

9. And now also the ax is laid unto the root of the trees: every tree therefore which bringeth not forth good fruit, is hewn down and cast into the fire.

9. God is entering into judgment with you, and will cut down wicked and fruitless hypocrites for the fire.

10. And the people asked him, saying, What shall we do then? 11. He answereth and saith unto them, He that hath two coats, let him impart to him that hath none; and he that hath meat, let him do likewise.

10, 11. Love others as yourselves, and see them not suffer in want, while you have supply for them, and can spare it from your plenty: Prefer their necessity before your fulness or superfluity.

12. Then came also publicans to be baptized, and said unto him, Master, what shall we do? 13. And he said unto them, Exact no more than that which is appointed you.

12, 13. Excise, or tax-gatherers.

14. And the soldiers likewise demanded of him, saying, And what shall we do? And he said unto them Do violence to no man, neither accuse *any* falsely, and be content with your wages.

14. Live not as soldiers use to do, by violence to the poor people that cannot resist them, and by false accusing, and robbing, and plundering.

Note, He meaneth not that it is enough to salvation, to amend the crimes of their lives, without a renewed, holy heart; but that this also must be done.

15. And as the people were in expectation, and all men mused in their hearts of John, whether he were the Christ or not; 16. John answered, saying unto them all, I indeed baptize you with water; but

CHAP. III. ST. LUKE. 129

one mightier than I cometh, the latchet of whose shoes I am not worthy to unloose: he shall baptize you with the Holy Ghost, and with fire.

15, 16. See on Matt. iii. Note, The great and peculiar work and notification of Christ, was his sending the Holy Ghost on his disciples.

17. Whose fan *is* in his hand, and he will throughly purge his floor, and will gather the wheat into his garner; but the chaff he will burn with fire unquenchable. 18. And many other things in *his* exhortation preached he unto the people.

17, 18. Who will winnow you throughly, and will gather and save all true believers, and burn the unbelievers in fire unquenchable.
Note, Christ, that is a Saviour, is the severe destroyer of his obstinate enemies.

19. But Herod the tetrarch, being reproved by him, for Herodias his brother Philip's wife, and for all the evils which Herod had done, 20. Added yet this above all, that he shut up John in prison.

19, 20. Note, John would not forbear the faithful discharge of his office in reproving a wicked king to save his liberty or life. 2. To imprison and persecute his reprover, was wicked in Herod above all his former wickedness.

21. Now when all the people were baptized, it came to pass, that Jesus also being baptized and praying, the heaven was opened: 22. And the Holy Ghost descended in a bodily shape like a dove upon him, and a voice came from heaven, which said, Thou art my beloved Son, in thee I am well pleased.

21, 22. Note, Baptism, with his own prayer, were the means thus miraculously approved by God, in which he will bear witness to his Son from Heaven.
Note, The descent of the Holy Ghost, on Christ, with God's vocal testimony, was a fit investiture of him in the office, of the Captain of our Salvation, who was to mark out his soldiers with the same gift of the Holy Ghost and his adopting word.

23. And Jesus himself began to be about thirty years of age, being (as was supposed) the son of Joseph, which was *the son* of Heli,
2.

24. Which was *the son* of Matthat, which was *the son* of Levi, which was *the son* of Melchi, which was *the son* of Janna, which was *the son* of Joseph. 25. Which was *the son* of Mattathias, which was *the son* of Amos, which was *the son* of Naum, which was *the son* of Esli, which was *the son* of Nagge, 26. Which was *the son* of Maath, which was *the son* of Mattathias, which was *the son* of Semei, which was *the son* of Joseph, which was *the son* of Judah, 27. Which was *the son* of Joanna, which was *the son* of Rhesa, which was *the son* of Zorobabel, which was *the son* of Salathiel, which was *the son* of Neri, 28. Which was *the son* of Melchi, which was *the son* of Addi, which was *the son* of Cosam, which was *the son* of Elmodam, which was *the son* of Er, 29. Which was *the son* of Jose, which was *the son* of Eliezer, which was *the son* of Jorim, which was *the son* of Matthat, which was *the son* of Levi, 30. Which was *the son* of Simeon, which was *the son* of Juda, which was *the son* of Joseph, which was *the son* of Jonan, which was *the son* of Eliakim, 31. Which was *the son* of Melea, which was *the son* of Menan, which was *the son* of Mattatha, which was *the son* of Nathan, which was *the son* of David, 32. Which was *the son* of Jesse, which was *the son* of Obed, which was *the son* of Booz, which was *the son* of Salmon, which was *the son* of Naasson, 33. Which was *the son* of Aminadab, which was *the son* of Aram, which was *the son* of Esrom, which was *the son* of Phares, which was *the son* of Juda, 34. Which was *the son* of Jacob, which was *the son* of Isaac, which was *the son* of Abraham, which was *the son* of Thara, which was *the son* of Nachor, 35. Which was *the son* of Saruch, which was *the son* of Ragau, which was *the son* of Phalec, which was *the son* of
K

130   ST. LUKE.   CHAP. IV.

Heber, which was *the son* of Sala, 36. Which was *the son* of Cainan, which was *the son* of Arphaxad, which was *the son* of Sem, which was *the son* of Noe, which was *the son* of Lamech, 37. Which was *the son* of Mathusala, which was *the son* of Enoch, which was *the son* of Jared, which was *the son* of Maleleel, which was *the son* of Cainan, 38. Which was *the son* of Enos, which was *the son* of Seth, which was *the son* of Adam, which was *the son* of God.

23—38. He entered on his public office about thirty; And now young novices run into the ministry. Luke reciteth the pedigree of Joseph; and Matthew of Mary. Qu. Whence had Luke that part of the pedigree that is not written in the scripture before? Answ. By other history and tradition, with the help of God's spirit.

The genealogical controversies I pass by.

CHAP. IV.

AND Jesus being full of the Holy Ghost, returned from Jordan, and was led by the spirit into the wilderness, 2. Being forty days tempted of the devil; and in those days he did eat nothing: and when they were ended, he afterwards hungered. 3. And the devil said unto him, If thou be the Son of God, command this stone that it may be made bread. 4. And Jesus answered him, saying, It is written, That man shall not live by bread alone, but by every word of God. 5. And the devil taking him up into an high mountain, shewed unto him all the kingdoms of the world in a moment of time. 6. And the devil said unto him, All this power will I give thee, and the glory of them; for that is delivered unto me, and to whomsoever I will, I give it. 7. If thou, therefore wilt worship me, all shall be thine. 8. And Jesus answered and said unto him, Get thee behind me, Satan: for it is written, Thou shalt worship the Lord thy God, and him only shalt thou serve.

1—8. See on Matt. iv. strongly inspired by the Holy Ghost, was led by him, &c.

6. Though Satan lied in part, yet he hath great power over the kingdoms and glory of the world, partly as a tempter, and partly as God's executioner, but all under God's absolute will: The success sheweth that too many receive them from him, that they may serve him by them, as enemies to the church of Christ.

Note, Blasphemous temptations must be answered with rejecting hatred.

9. And he brought him to Jerusalem, and set him on a pinnacle of the temple, and said unto him, If thou be the Son of God, cast thyself down from hence. 10. For it is written, He shall give his angels charge over thee, to keep thee. 11. And in *their* hands they shall bear thee up, lest at any time thou dash thy foot against a stone. 12. And Jesus answering, said unto him, It is said, Thou shalt not tempt the Lord thy God.

9—12. Note, Satan useth to tempt by perverted scripture, yet it is by right expounded scripture, that he must be repelled.

Qu. How did the writers know these secret things? Answ. Christ told them to his disciples (though that be not written).

13. And when the devil had ended all the temptation, he departed from him for a season.

13. Luke reciteth them not in the same order with Matthew, but the same things.

Note, Christ's victory over the tempter was part of his saving work, and to prepare for our victory.

14. And Jesus returned in the power of the spirit into Galilee: and there went out a fame of him through all the region round about.

14. Note, Though the constitution of Christ's person was by the divine nature of the second in the trinity, yet the scripture usually ascribeth his works to the operation of the Holy Ghost in him.

15. And he taught in their synagogues, being glorified of all. 16. And he came to Nazareth, where he had been brought up: and, as his custom was, he went into the synagogue on the sabbath-day, and stood up for to read.

15, 16. Note, Christ separated not from the Jews' corrupt church.

17. And there was delivered unto

him the book of the prophet Esaias; and when he had opened the book, he found the place where it was written, 18. The Spirit of the Lord *is* upon me, because he hath anointed me to preach the gospel to the poor, he hath sent me to heal the broken-hearted, to preach deliverance to the captives, and recovering of sight to the blind, to set at liberty them that are bruised, 19. To preach the acceptable year of the Lord.

17, 18, 19. Note, He chose a text that described his own office, and applied it.

20. And he closed the book, and he gave *it* again to the minister, and sat down: and the eyes of all them that were in the synagogue were fastened upon him. 21. And he began to say unto them, This day is this scripture fulfilled in your ears.

20, 21. Note, This Instance proveth it not necessary to sit in preaching: but lawful, where custom or circumstances forbid it not.

22. And all bare him witness, and wondered at the gracious words which proceeded out of his mouth. And they said, Is not this Joseph's son?

22. They applauded his preaching, but undervalued him for being known to be their neighbour's son.

23. And he said unto them, Ye will surely say unto me this proverb, Physician, heal thyself: whatsoever we have heard done in Capernaum, do also here in thy country.

23. As a physician must first heal himself, so do thou do thy miracles here among thy kindred and neighbours.

24. And he said, Verily, I say unto you, No prophet is accepted in his own country.

24. God can cause him to be accepted; but as he worketh ordinarily by means: familiarity breeds contempt.

25. But I tell you of a truth, Many widows were in Israel in the days of Elias, when the heaven was shut up three years and six months, when great famine was throughout all the land: 26. But unto none of them was Elias sent, save unto Sarepta, *a city* of Sidon, unto a woman that was a widow. 27. And many lepers were in Israel in the time of Eliseus the prophet: and none of them was cleansed, saving Naaman the Syrian.

25, 26, 27. Prophets cure not all that are diseased: You shall not see miracles, nor be saved, for being my neighbours, if you be not believers: And familiarity and prejudice maketh fewer of you believe, than of others.

28. And all they in the synagogue, when they heard these things, were filled with wrath, 29. And rose up, and thrust him out of the city, and led him unto the brow of the hill (whereon their city was built) that they might cast him down headlong.

28, 29. Note, They that applauded his preaching, when the application grated on them, would have killed him; even the Nazarite neighbours that hated him not heretofore.

30. But he passing through the midst of them, went his way: 31. And came down to Capernaum, a city of Galilee, and taught them on the sabbath-days. 32. And they were astonished at his doctrine: for his word was with power.

30, 31, 32. By miracle, unhurt.

33. And in the synagogue there was a man which had a spirit of an unclean devil, and cried out with a loud voice, 34. Saying, Let us alone; what have we to do with thee, thou Jesus of Nazareth? art thou come to destroy us? I know thee who thou art; the holy one of God.

33, 34. Christ's power over devils forced this confession.

35. And Jesus rebuked him, saying, Hold thy peace, and come out of him. And when the devil had thrown him in the midst, he came out of him, and hurt him not. 36.

And they were all amazed, and spake among themselves, saying, What a word *is* this? for with authority and power he commandeth the unclean spirits, and they come out. 37. And the fame of him went out into every place of the country round about.

35, 36, 37. *Christ specially cured the diseases, that the devils caused, to shew that he came to conquer Satan, and save men from his power.*

38. And he arose out of the synagogue, and entered into Simon's house: and Simon's wife's mother was taken with a great fever; and they besought him for her. 39. And he stood over her, and rebuked the fever, and it left her. And immediately she arose and ministered unto them.

38, 39. *Note, We have still the same physician.*

40. Now when the sun was setting, all they that had any sick with divers diseases, brought them unto him: and he laid his hands on every one of them, and healed them. 41. And devils also came out of many, crying out, and saying, Thou art Christ the Son of God. And he rebuking them, suffered them not to speak: for they knew that he was Christ.

40, 41. *Experience made them believe that he could heal them*

42. And when it was day, he departed, and went into a desert place: and the people sought him, and came unto him, and stayed him, that he should not depart from them. 43. And he said unto them, I must preach the kingdom of God to other cities also: for therefore am I sent. 44. And he preached in the synagogues of Galilee.

42, 43. *Note, Preaching the gospel was his great business, to the belief of which, his miracles were but means subservient.*

CHAP. V.

AND it came to pass, that as the people pressed upon him to hear the word of God, he stood by the lake of Gennesareth, 2. And saw two ships standing by the lake: but the fishermen were gone out of them, and were washing *their* nets. 3. And he entered into one of the ships which was Simon's, and prayed him that he would thrust out a little from the land: and he sat down, and taught the people out of the ship.

1, 2, 3. *That he might not be crowded.*

4. Now when he had left speaking, he said unto Simon, Launch out into the deep, and let down your nets for a draught. 5. And Simon answering said unto him, Master, we have toiled all the night, and have taken nothing: nevertheless at thy word I will let down the net. 6. And when they had this done, they enclosed a great multitude of fishes; and their net brake. 7. And they beckoned unto *their* partners which were in the other ship, that they should come and help them. And they came and filled both the ships, so that they began to sink.

4—7. *Note, The sea, and earth, and all therein are at Christ's command.*

8. When Simon Peter saw *it*, he fell down at Jesus' knees, saying, Depart from me, for I am a sinful man, O Lord. 9. For he was astonished, and all that were with him, at the draught of the fishes which they had taken: 10. And so *was* also James and John the sons of Zebedee, which were partners with Simon. And Jesus said unto Simon, Fear not; from henceforth thou shalt catch men.

8, 9, 10. *Note, The miracle and danger made him afraid.*

11. And when they had brought their ships to land, they forsook all, and followed him.

11. *Note, It was not only by his bare command [Follow me,] but by this miracle that they were moved.*

12. And it came to pass, when

he was in a certain city, behold, a man full of leprosy: who seeing Jesus, fell on *his* face, and besought him, saying, Lord, if thou wilt, thou canst make me clean. 13. And he put forth *his* hand, and touched him, saying, I will; be thou clean. And immediately the leprosy departed from him. 14. And he charged him to tell no man: but go and shew thyself to the priest, and offer for thy cleansing, according as Moses commanded, for a testimony unto them.

12, 13, 14. Note, A miracle that the priests themselves were to have notice of. See Matt. viii.

15. But so much the more went there a fame abroad of him: and great multitudes came together to hear, and to be healed by him of their infirmities. 16. And he withdrew himself into the wilderness, and prayed. 17. And it came to pass on a certain day, as he was teaching, that there were Pharisees and doctors of the law sitting by, which were come out of every town of Galilee, and Judea, and Jerusalem: and the power of the Lord was *present* to heal them. 18. And behold, men brought in a bed a man which was taken with the palsy: and they sought means to bring him in, and to lay *him* before him. 19. And when they could not find by what way they might bring him in, because of the multitude, they went upon the house top, and let him down through the tiling with *his* couch, into the midst before Jesus.

15—19. Note, O that we were all as diligent and believing for the healing of our souls!

20. And when he saw their faith, he said unto him, Man, thy sins are forgiven thee. 21. And the scribes and the Pharisees began to reason, saying, Who is this which speaketh blasphemies? Who can forgive sins, but God alone? 22. But when Jesus perceived their thoughts, he answering said unto them, What reason ye in your hearts? 23. Whether is easier to say, Thy sins be forgiven thee, or to say, Rise up and walk?

20—23. To forgive the punishment, is to forgive the sin; which you shall see I have power to do.

24. But that ye may know that the Son of Man hath power upon earth to forgive sins, (he said unto the sick of the palsy) I say unto thee, Arise, and take up thy couch, and go into thine house. 25. And immediately he rose up before them, and took up that whereon he lay, and departed to his own house, glorifying God. 26. And they were all amazed, and they glorified God, and were filled with fear, saying, We have seen strange things to-day.

24, 25, 26. The glory of all great things is due only to God, whoever is the agent.

27. And after these things he went forth, and saw a publican named Levi, sitting at the receipt of custom: and he said unto him, Follow me. 28. And he left all, rose up, and followed him.

27, 28. Levi is Matthew.

29. And Levi made him a great feast in his own house: and there was a great company of publicans, and of others that sat down with them. 30. But their scribes and Pharisees murmured against his disciples, saying, Why do ye eat and drink with publicans and sinners? 31. And Jesus answering, said unto them, They that are whole need not a physician: but they that are sick.

29, 30, 31. Note, It is none of the meaning of God's law, to be against charity, or man's good, but to keep us from encouraging evil.

32. I came not to call the righteous, but sinners to repentance.

32. They are sinners that need me for a Saviour, and the unconverted that need conversion.

33. And they said unto him,

Why do the disciples of John fast often, and make prayers, and likewise *the disciples* of the Pharisees; but thine eat and drink?

33. The disciples of John, and the Pharisees, used more strictness in tasks of fasting, and making prayers, and in bodily austerities, than Christ's disciples did.

34. And he said unto them, Can ye make the children of the bride-chamber fast, while the bridegroom is with them? 35. But the days will come, when the bridegroom shall be taken away from them, and then shall they fast in those days.

34, 35. Then shall they have days of sadness.

36. And he spake also a parable unto them, No man putteth a piece of a new garment upon an old: if otherwise, then both the new maketh a rent, and the piece that was *taken* out of the new, agreeth not with the old. 37. And no man putteth new wine into old bottles; else the new wine will burst the bottles, and be spilled, and the bottles shall perish. 38. But new wine must be put into new bottles; and both are preserved.

36, 37, 38. Doctrines and precepts must be suited to men's capacity. See Matt. ix.

39. No man also having drunk old *wine*, straightway desireth new: for he saith, The old is better.

39. They that have been used to a free life, will not suddenly like austerities.

CHAP. VI.

AND it came to pass on the second sabbath after the first, that he went through the corn-fields, and his disciples plucked the ears of corn, and did eat, rubbing *them* in *their* hands. 2. And certain of the Pharisees said unto them, Why do ye that which is not lawful to do on the sabbath-days?

1, 2. The reason of the name of the second sabbath, after the first, is doubtful to us that live at this distance. Many conjectures there be. Some,

that it is the last day of unleavened bread; others, that it is the day of Pentecost, &c.

3. And Jesus answering them, said, Have ye not read so much as this, what David did, when himself was an hungered, and they which were with him: 4. How he went into the house of God, and did take and eat the shew-bread, and gave also to them that were with him, which is not lawful to eat, but for the priests alone?

3, 4. Hypocrites will be stricter than Christ, but it is when they err, or are strict in evil, or in shadows against the greater things.

5. And he said unto them, That the Son of Man is Lord also of the sabbath.

5. I have power to use all ceremonies to the ends of redemption, for the good of man.

6. And it came to pass also, on another sabbath, that he entered into the synagogue and taught: and there was a man whose right hand was withered. 7. And the scribes and Pharisees watched him, whether he would heal on the sabbath-day: that they might find an accusation against him. 8. But he knew their thoughts, and said to the man which had the withered hand, Rise up, and stand forth in the midst. And he arose, and stood forth. 9. Then said Jesus unto them, I will ask you one thing, Is it lawful on the sabbath-days to do good, or to do evil? to save life, or to destroy *it*?

6—9. See Matt. xii. What better work for the Sabbath-day, than to save life. And he that will not do that, when he may, is guilty of murder.

10. And looking round about upon them all, he said unto the man, Stretch forth thy hand. And he did so: and his hand was restored whole as the other. 11. And they were filled with madness; and communed one with another what they might do to Jesus.

10, 11. Note, Nothing so enrageth the devil and his servants, as doing the greatest good: This is to them the greatest crime.

Chap. vi. ST. LUKE. 135

12. And it came to pass in those days, that he went out into a mountain to pray, and continued all night in prayer to God.

12. Note. What need then have we to pray!

13. And when it was day, he called unto him his disciples: and of them he chose twelve, whom also he named Apostles:

13. Note. His prayer seemeth to be in order to the choice of his apostles, that is, deputed commissionated messengers, next under him, to gather and guide his church.

14. Simon (whom he also named Peter) and Andrew his brother, James and John, Philip and Bartholomew, 15. Matthew and Thomas, James *the son* of Alpheus, and Simon called Zelotes, 15. And Judas *the brother* of James, and Judas Iscariot, which also was the traitor. 17. And he came down with them, and stood in the plain, and the company of his disciples, and a great multitude of people out of all Judea and Jerusalem, and from the sea-coast of Tyre and Sidon, which came to hear him, and to be healed of their diseases: 18. And they that were vexed with unclean spirits; and they were healed. 19. And the whole multitude sought to touch him: for there went virtue out of him, and healed them all.

14—19. O the wonderful mercy of our Saviour to bodies and souls!

20. And he lifted up his eyes on his disciples, and said, Blessed *be* ye, poor: for yours is the kingdom of God.

20. Ye my disciples, though poor in the world. Note, Matthew more fully repeateth this sermon than Luke.

21. Blessed *are* ye that hunger now: for ye shall be filled. Blessed *are* ye that weep now: for ye shall laugh.

21. See Matt. v.

22. Blessed are ye when men shall hate you, and when they shall separate you *from their company*, and shall reproach *you*, and cast out your name as evil, for the Son of man's sake.

22. Blessed are ye though you now hunger, weep, are hated, &c. because it is for righteousness sake.

23. Rejoice ye in that day, and leap for joy: for behold, your reward *is* great in heaven: for in the like manner did their fathers unto the prophets.

23. Note. But we must see that the cause be good, and that our hearts be found with God in the main, and in all other cases.

24. But woe unto you that are rich: for ye have received your consolation. 25. Woe unto you that are full: for ye shall hunger. Woe unto you that laugh now: for ye shall mourn and weep. 26. Woe unto you when all men shall speak well of you: for so did their fathers to the false prophets.

24, 25, 26. Woe to you ungodly unbelievers, though you be now rich, and full, and merry, and well-spoken of: (Not because you are rich and full, &c.) But though you are so, because you have no better: For man's welfare is to be judged of, by what he shall have hereafter, and not by what he hath here.

Note. Luke omitteth divers of the beatitudes, but reciteth the woes which Matthew omitteth; Whether this sermon was twice spoken by Christ, (or which is likelier) but once, is uncertain.

27. But I say unto you which hear, Love your enemies, do good to them which hate you: 28. Bless them that curse you, and pray for them which despitefully use you. 29. And unto him that smiteth thee on the *one* cheek, offer also the other: and him that taketh away thy cloak, forbid not *to take thy* coat also. 30. Give to every man that asketh of thee; and of him that taketh away thy goods, ask *them* not again.

27—30. See on Matt. v. Prefer charity and peace before thy right; and right not thyself to thy neighbour's greater hurt.

31. And as ye would that men should do to you, do ye also to them likewise.

31. Love your neighbours as yourselves, and make not too great a difference between their interest and your own: For justice will not be maintained without love.

32. For if ye love them which love you, what thank have ye? for sinners also love those that love them. 33. And if ye do good to them which do good to you, what thank have ye? for sinners also do even the same. 34. And if ye lend to them of whom ye hope to receive, what thank have ye? for sinners also lend to sinners, to receive as much again.

32, 33, 34. All this is but the exercise of self-love, and is not so much as virtue; much less that charity, in which you must excel all wicked men.

35. But love ye your enemies, and do good, and lend, hoping for nothing again: and your reward shall be great, and ye shall be the children of the highest: for he is kind unto the unthankful, and *to* the evil. 36. Be ye therefore merciful, as your Father also is merciful.

35, 36. Let your love and good works be in imitation of God your Father, taking his approbation for your full reward.

37. Judge not, and ye shall not be judged: condemn not, and ye shall not be condemned: forgive, and ye shall be forgiven: 38. Give, and it shall be given unto you: good measure, pressed down, and shaken together, and running over, shall men give into your bosom. For with the same measure that ye mete withal, it shall be measured to you again.

37, 38. God's rewards are sure and full.

Note, The word [men] v. 38. is not in the text; but [They shall give,] signifieth, [It shall be given,] as Luke xvi. 9. [They shall receive you into everlasting habitations] is, [That ye may be received:] And angels are liker to be the instruments than men, from whom we cannot expect to be measured to, as we measure to them. Yet the promise may extend to this, that when God seeth it good, he will make men, yea, enemies, the instruments of his reward.

39. And he spake a parable unto them; can the blind lead the blind? shall they not both fall into the ditch?

39. He that will be a teacher of others, must himself first understand what he teacheth. Teaching ignorance is the calamity of the church, the deceiver of souls, and the condemnation of teachers.

40. The disciple is not above his master: but every one that is perfect shall be as his master.

40. You must look to speed no better than I that am your master, but it will be your perfection to imitate me; learn of me, and suffer with me, and you shall be blessed with me.

But some expound it, [you cannot expect that the disciples of ignorant teachers should attain to any higher perfection than their masters] which they gather from the context: But Luke useth oft to conjoin various sayings and subjects. See Matt. x. 24.

41. And why beholdest thou the mote that is in thy brother's eye, but perceivest not the beam that is in thine own eye? 42. Either how canst thou say to thy brother, Brother, let me pull out the mote that is in thine eye, when thou thyself beholdest not the beam that is in thine own eye? Thou hypocrite, cast out first the beam out of thine own eye, and then shalt thou see clearly to pull out the mote that is in thy brother's eye.

41, 42. It is of great necessity for teachers and reprovers, to know themselves, and be free from scandals, and the crimes which they reprove; and not as Pharisees, to be loose in morals, and cruel to others, while they are zealous for their ceremonies; else their hypocrisy will aggravate their iniquity.

43. For a good tree bringeth not forth corrupt fruit: neither doth a corrupt tree bring forth good fruit. 44. For every tree is known by his own fruit: for of thorns men do not gather figs, nor of a bramble bush gather they grapes.

43, 44. If thou be a bad man thyself, and guilty of worse than thou preachest against, who will believe thee, or expect good fruit from so bad a man?

Note, But Matthew otherwise connecteth these sayings.

45. A good man out of the good treasure of his heart, bringeth forth that which is good: and an evil

man out of the evil treasure of his heart, bringeth forth that which is evil: for of the abundance of the heart his mouth speaketh.

_{45. As the man is, so usually will his words and actions be; (for hypocritical force is usually short lived.)}

46. And why call ye me Lord, Lord, and do not the things which I say?

_{46. All the good words and praises of God and religion, from disobedient men, do but aggravate their sin.}

47. Whosoever cometh to me, and heareth my sayings, and doeth them, I will shew you to whom he is like. 48. He is like a man which built an house, and digged deep, and laid the foundation on a rock: and when the flood arose, the stream beat vehemently upon that house, and could not shake it: for it was founded upon a rock.

_{47, 48. As a building on a rock will stand in storms, so he that obeyed my word, will stand in trial. Qu. How is our obedience made the rock that we build on? Is not Christ the rock? Answ. Similitudes must not be stretched beyond their intent. It is only the stability of the obedient that is meant.}

49. But he that heareth and doeth not, is like a man that without a foundation built an house upon the earth, against which the stream did beat vehemently, and immediately it fell, and the ruin of that house was great.

_{49. Hypocritical, disobedient hearers, and professors, have no firm foundation and stability, trusting to a barren opinion instead of the true faith, and so fall by woeful ruin in their trials.}

CHAP. VII.

NOW when he had ended all his sayings in the audience of the people, he entered into Capernaum. 2. And a certain centurion's servant, who was dear unto him, was sick, and ready to die. 3. And when he heard of Jesus, he sent unto him the elders of the Jews, beseeching him that he would come and heal his servant. 4. And when they came to Jesus, they besought him instantly, saying, That he was worthy for whom he should do this. 5. For he loveth our nation, and he hath built us a synagogue.

_{1—5. See Matt. viii. 9.}

6. Then Jesus went with them. And when he was now not far from the house, the centurion sent friends to him, saying unto him, Lord, trouble not thyself, for I am not worthy that thou shouldest enter under my roof. 7. Wherefore neither thought I myself worthy to come unto thee: but say in a word, and my servant shall be healed. 8. For I also am a man set under authority, having under me soldiers, and I say unto one, Go, and he goeth: and to another, Come, and he cometh: and to my servant, Do this, and he doeth it.

_{6, 7, 8. Note, The devotion of this man in building a synagogue, and his great humility, shew that he was better prepared for faith than many others.}

9. When Jesus heard these things he marvelled at him, and turned him about, and said unto the people that followed him, I say unto you, I have not found so great faith, no, not in Israel.

<sub>9. As man, he marvelled, as God, he foreknew it.
Note, Whether he took Christ for his Saviour, is uncertain; but the hearing of his works had caused him strongly to believe his power to heal.</sub>

10. And they that were sent, returning to the house, found the servant whole that had been sick. 11. And it came to pass the day after, that he went into a city called Nain; and many of his disciples went with him, and much people. 12. Now when he came nigh to the gate of the city, behold, there was a dead man carried out, the only son of his mother, and she was a widow: and much people of the city was with her. 13. And when the Lord saw her, he had compassion on her, and said unto her, Weep

not. 14. And he came and touched the bier, (and they that bare him stood still) and he said, Young man, I say unto thee, Arise. 15. And he that was dead sat up, and began to speak: and he delivered him to his mother. 16. And there came a fear on all: and they glorified God, saying, That a great prophet is risen up among us; and, That God hath visited his people.

10—16. Note, This Saviour hath still the same love and pity, though he use not miracles so much. He is still lord of life and death.

17. And this rumour of him went forth throughout all Judea, and throughout all the rigion round about. 18. And the disciples of John shewed him of all these things 19. And John calling unto him two of his disciples, sent *them* unto Jesus, saying, Art thou he that should come, or look we for another?

17, 18, 19. Note, It is likely John did it to convince his disciples.

20. When the men were come unto him, they said, John Baptist hath sent us unto thee, saying, Art thou he that should come, or look we for another?

20. See Matt. xi.

21. And in that same hour he cured many of *their* infirmities, and plagues, and of evil spirits, and unto many that were blind he gave sight. 22. Then Jesus answering, said unto them, Go your way, and tell John what things ye have seen and heard, how that the blind see, the lame walk, the lepers are cleansed, the deaf hear, the dead are raised, to the poor the gospel is preached. 23. And blessed is he whosoever shall not be offended in me.

21, 22, 23. Tell John what is done, and let him judge by the works. But men's great danger is, of being scandalised at my visible meanness, and my sufferings.

24. And when the messengers of John were departed, he began to speak unto the people concerning John, What went ye out into the wilderness for to see? A reed shaken with the wind? 25. But what went ye out for to see? A man clothed in soft raiment? Behold, they which are gorgeously apparelled, and live delicately, are in kings' courts. 26. But what went ye out for to see? A prophet? Yea, I say unto you, and much more than a prophet. 27. This is he of whom it is written, Behold, I send my messenger before thy face, which shall prepare thy way before thee. 28. For I say unto you, Among those that are born of women, there is not a greater prophet than John Baptist: but he that is least in the kingdom of God, is greater than he.

24—28. The least true believer in my church hath a more honourable state and work, see Matt. xi.

29. And all the people that heard *him*, and the publicans justified God, being baptized with the baptism of John.

29. All the people that heard Christ speak so highly of John, were pleased at it, and justified God that sent him; for they had been baptised by him. Or, as others expound it, [all the people that heard John; and the publicans received his message from God, &c.]

30. But the Pharisees and lawyers rejected the counsel of God against themselves, being not baptized of him.

30. [Rejected God's message sent by John] or [rejected Christ's testimony of John.]

31. And the Lord said, Whereunto then shall I liken the men of this generation? and to what are they like? 32. They are like unto children sitting in the market-place, and calling one to another, and saying, We have piped unto you, and ye have not danced: we have mourned to you, and ye have not wept. 33. For John the Baptist came neither eating bread, nor drinking wine; and ye say, He hath a devil.

31, 32, 33. See Matt. xi. 33. That he is distracted.

34. The son of man is come eating and drinking; and ye say, Behold, a gluttonous man, and a wine-bibber, a friend of publicans and sinners. 35. But wisdom is justified of all her children.

34, 35. Neither his austerity, nor my free conversation, do escape your censure. But the wise will justify wisdom.

36. And one of the Pharisees desired him that he would eat with him. And he went into the Pharisee's house, and sat down to meat. 37. And behold, a woman in the city, which was a sinner, when she knew that Jesus sat at meat in the Pharisee's house, brought an alabaster-box of ointment,

38. And stood at his feet behind him weeping, and began to wash his feet with tears: and did wipe *them* with the hairs of her head, and kissed his feet, and anointed *them* with the ointment.

36, 37, 38. A woman who had been of a bad life.

39. Now when the Pharisee which had bidden him, saw *it*, he spake within himself, saying, This man, if he were a prophet, would have known who and what manner of woman *this is* that toucheth him: for she is a sinner.

39. Christ and the Pharisees agreed that sin is hateful.

40. And Jesus answering, said unto him, Simon, I have somewhat to say unto thee. And he saith, Master, say on. 41. There was a certain creditor which had two debtors: the one oweth five hundred pence, and the other fifty. 42. And when they had nothing to pay, he frankly forgave them both. Tell me therefore, which of them will love him most? 43. Simon answered and said, I suppose that he to whom he forgave most. And he said unto him, Thou hast rightly judged.

40—43. Note, When God forgiveth great sins, it is that we may love him much.

44. And he turned to the woman, and said unto Simon, Seest thou this woman? I entered into thine house, thou gavest me no water for my feet: but she hath washed my feet with tears, and wiped *them* with the hairs of her head. 45. Thou gavest me no kiss: but this woman, since the time I came in, hath not ceased to kiss my feet. 46. Mine head with oil thou didst not anoint: but this woman hath anointed my feet with ointment.

44, 45, 46. She hath shewed more love than thou.

47. Wherefore I say unto thee, Her sins, which are many, are forgiven; for she loved much; but to whom little is forgiven, the same loveth little. 48. And he said unto her, Thy sins are forgiven.

47. Her great love sheweth that her great sins are forgiven, for it is her grateful return: But they that think they need but little pardon, will return but little thankfulness for it.
48. Note, No doubt they were truly repented of, hated, and forsaken.

49. And they that sat at meat with him, began to say within themselves, Who is this that forgiveth sins also? 50. And he said to the woman, Thy faith hath saved thee; go in peace.

49. Note, None can forgive sins against God but God, and man after (not before him) by declaring and delivering God's pardon.
50. God pardoneth and saveth all true believers; and thou hast shewed that thou art a believer. Though God freely give pardon and salvation, thy faith maketh thee a qualified receiver, and so saveth thee.

CHAP. VIII.

AND it came to pass afterward, that he went throughout every city and village preaching, and shewing the glad tidings of the kingdom of God: and the twelve *were* with him; 2. And certain women which had been healed of evil spirits and infirmities, Mary called Magdalene, out of whom went seven devils; 3. And Joanna the wife of Chuza Herod's steward, and Susanna, and many others, which ministered unto him of their substance.

1, 2, 3. In the thankful sense of their deliverance attended him, and contributed to his maintenance.
Note. Christ that was Lord of all, and gave others life and salvation, disdained not to live on others gifts and contribution.

4. And when much people were gathered together, and were come to him out of every city, he spake by a parable: 5. A sower went out to sow his seed: and as he sowed, some fell by the way-side, and it was trodden down, and the fowls of the air devoured it. 6. And some fell upon a rock, and as soon as it was sprung up it withered away, because it lacked moisture. 7. And some fell among thorns, and the thorns sprang up with it, and choaked it. 8. And other fell on good ground, and sprang up, and bare fruit an hundred-fold. And when he had said these things, he cried, He that hath ears to hear, let him hear.

4—8. See the exposition on Matt. xiii.
Note, It is the difference of the receivers, and reception, which is the notable cause of different successes of the same word; yet supposing God's election.

9. And his disciples asked him, saying, What might this parable be? 10. And he said, Unto you it is given to know the mysteries of the kingdom of God: but to others in parables: that seeing they might not see, and hearing they might not understand.

9, 10. Note. The reception of one truth prepareth for more, and the rejection of God's calls prepareth men to be forsaken.

11. Now the parable is this: The seed is the word of God. 12. Those by the way-side, are they that hear; then cometh the devil, and taketh away the word out of their hearts, lest they should believe and be saved. 13. They on the rock, *are* they, which when they hear, receive the word with joy; and these have no root, which for a while believe, and in time of temptation fall away. 14. And that which fell among thorns, are they, which when they have heard, go forth, and are choaked with cares, and riches, and pleasures of *this* life, and bring no fruit to perfection.

11—14. Note, Hopeful and fair beginnings, in very many, fall short of salvation.

15. But that on the good ground, are they which in an honest and good heart, having heard the word, keep it, and bring forth fruit with patience.

15. Who receive the gospel so, as to renew them, their hearts before prepared, being by it sanctified; and persevere to maturity.

16. No man when he hath lighted a candle, covereth it with a vessel, or putteth *it* under a bed: but setteth it on a candlestick, that they which enter in may see the light.

16. Light is not to be hid, nor God's gifts and man's knowledge, being given not only for themselves, but for the good of all about them.
Note, 1. Woe then to unjust silencers of God's faithful ministers! And 2. To idle, treacherous, unfaithful pastors.
Note, These passages are otherwise connected in Matthew.

17. For nothing is secret, that shall not be made manifest: neither any thing hid, that shall not be known, and come abroad.

17. Note, Oh then how vain is the hiding endeavour of the hypocrite! And how little should we trust to lies, or to the secresy of our sins!
Note, The connection of these sentences is not too much to be minded.

18. Take heed therefore how ye hear: for whosoever hath, to him shall be given; and whosoever hath not, from him shall be taken even that which he seemeth to have.

18. The thankful receiving of what is given you, and the well using of what you have, is the way to have more given you: But the rejection or abuse of it, forfeiteth what you have.

Note, When Luke collecteth several passages, spoken on several occasions, like Solomon's proverbs; to feign an Analysis, and thence put the sense on them, is to make the sense, and not to expound it.

19. Then came to him his mother and his brethren, and could not come at him for the press. 20. And it was told him *by certain*, which said, Thy mother and thy brethren stand without, desiring to see thee. 21. And he answered and said unto them, My mother and my brethren are these which hear the word of God, and do it.

19, 20, 21 Note. He knew that their acquaintance with his parents, kindred and education, was the hindrance of their faith; and therefore he lets them know that he had a higher original and kindred, and valued spiritual before carnal relations.

22. Now it came to pass on a certain day, that he went into a ship with his disciples: and he said unto them, Let us go over unto the other side of the lake. And they launched forth. 23. But as they sailed, he fell asleep: and there came down a storm of wind on the lake, and they were filled *with water*, and were in jeopardy. 24. And they came to him, and awoke him, saying, Master, master, we perish. Then he arose, and rebuked the wind, and the raging of the water: and they ceased, and there was a calm.

22, 23, 24. Note, And cannot be with a word rebuke all popular and tyrannical rage against his church?

25. And he said unto them, Where is your faith? And they being afraid, wondered, saying one to another, What manner of man is this? for he commandeth even the winds and water, and they obey him.

25. Note, And shall not we obey him?

26. And they arrived at the country of the Gadarenes, which is over against Galilee. 27. And when he went forth to land, there met him out of the city, a certain man which had devils long time, and ware no clothes, neither abode in *any* house, but in the tombs. 28. When he saw Jesus, he cried out and fell down before him, and with a loud voice said, What have I to do with thee, Jesus, thou Son of God most high? I beseech thee torment me not. 29. (For he had commanded the unclean spirit to come out of the man. For oftentimes it had caught him: and he was kept bound with chains, and in fetters; and he brake the bands, and was driven of the devil into the wilderness.) 30. And Jesus asked him, saying, What is thy name? And he said, Legion: because many devils were entered into him. 31. And they besought him that he would not command them to go out into the deep.

26...31. See on Matt. viii. and Mark v. 8, 9. The bottomless pit. Note, The devils are not yet confined to hell, nor in the utmost misery.

32. And there was there an herd of many swine feeding on the mountain: and they besought him that he would suffer them to enter into them. And he suffered them. 33. Then went the devils out of the man, and entered into the swine: and the herd ran violently down a steep place into the lake, and were choaked. 34. When they that fed them saw what was done, they fled, and went and told *it* in the city and in the country. 35. Then they went out to see what was done; and came to Jesus, and found the man out of whom the devils were departed, sitting at the feet of Jesus, clothed, and in his right mind: and they were afraid. 36. They also which saw *it*, told them by what means he that was possessed of the devils, was healed.

32...36. Note, 1. One man is of more worth, than multitudes of swine; (though swinish sinners vilify themselves.) 2. What would not devils do against us, if God should permit them?

37. Then the whole multitude of the country of the Gadarenes

round about, besought him to depart from them; for they were taken with great fear: and he went up into the ship, and returned back again. 38. Now the man out of whom the devils were departed, besought him that he might be with him: but Jesus sent him away, saying, 39. Return to thine own house, and shew how great things God hath done unto thee. And he went his way, and published throughout the whole city, how great things Jesus hath done unto him.

37, 38, 39. Note, All men's service of God is not in one way; some may do most good at home, and in a private state of life, and some more publicly.

40. And it came to pass, that when Jesus was returned, the people *gladly* received him: for they were all waiting for him. 41. And behold, there came a man named Jairus, and he was a ruler of the synagogue: and he fell down at Jesus feet, and besought him that he would come into his house: 42. For he had one only daughter, about twelve years of age, and she lay a dying. (But as he went, the people thronged him.)

40, 41, 42. Bodily gifts are gladly received, and earnestly sought.

43. And a woman having an issue of blood twelve years, which had spent all her living upon physicians, neither could be healed of any, 44. Came behind him, and touched the border of his garment: and immediately her issue of blood stanched. 45. And Jesus said, Who touched me? When all denied, Peter, and they that were with him, said, Master, the multitude throng thee, and press *thee*, and sayest thou, Who touched me? 46. And Jesus said, Somebody hath touched me: for I perceive that virtue is gone out of me.

43—46. Note, Peter carped at Christ's words, because he knew not the reason of them.

47. And when the woman saw that she was not hid, she came trembling, and falling down before him, she declared unto him before all the people, for what cause she had touched him, and how she was healed immediately.

47. She was afraid lest he would be angry with her, for stealing a cure without his consent.

48. And he said unto her, Daughter be of good comfort: thy faith hath made thee whole; go in peace.

48. Note, Faith healeth not efficiently, but as the necessary moral qualification of the receiver of a free gift.

49. While he yet spake, there cometh one from the ruler of the synagogue's *house*, saying to him, Thy daughter is dead; trouble not the Master. 50. But when Jesus heard *it*, he answered him, saying, Fear not: believe only, and she shall be made whole. 51. And when he came into the house, he suffered no man to go in, save Peter, and James, and John, and the father and the mother of the maiden. 52. And all wept, and bewailed her: but he said, Weep not: she is not dead, but sleepeth.

49—52. Permitting it to come to extremity magnified the miracle.

53. And they laughed him to scorn, knowing that she was dead.

53. She was dead by the cessation of natural life and motion, and not dead by a remote departure of the soul; it being detained to restore the suspended life: And so both Christ and they said true.

54. And he put them all out, and took her by the hand, and called, saying, Maid, arise. 55. And her spirit came again, and she arose straightway; and he commanded to give her meat. 56. And her parents were astonished: but he charged them that they should tell no man what was done.

54, 55, 56. See on Mark v.

CHAP. IX.

THEN he called his twelve disciples together, and gave them power and authority over all devils, and to cure diseases. 2. And he sent them to preach the kingdom of God, and to heal the sick.

1, 2. To save bodies and souls.

3. And he said unto them, Take nothing for your journey, neither staves, nor scrip, neither bread, neither money; neither have two coats apiece. 4. And whatsoever house ye enter into, there abide, and thence depart. 5. And whosoever will not receive you, when ye go out of that city, shake off the very dust from your feet for a testimony against them.

3, 4, 5. See on Matt. x. 10, 11. To witness, that it is not long of your unwillingness, but their own, that they are forsaken and perish.

6. And they departed and went through the towns preaching the gospel, and healing every where. 7. Now Herod the tetrarch heard of all that was done by him: and he was perplexed, because that it was said of some, that John was risen from the dead. 8. And of some, that Elias had appeared: and of others, that one of the old prophets was risen again. 9. And Herod said, John have I beheaded: but who is this of whom I hear such things? And he desired to see him.

6—9. Note, Christ, that was familiar with the poor, would not gratify the desire of a king, a persecutor, that desired to see him.

10. And the apostles when they were returned, told him all that they had done. And he took them, and went aside privately into a desert place, belonging to the city called Bethsaida.

10. Note, Had we the history of all the apostles' miracles before, and after Christ's resurrection, how large would it be!

11. And the people when they heard it, followed him: and he received them, and spake unto them of the kingdom of God, and healed them that had need of healing.

11. Note, Christ rejected none that followed after him, with desire and diligent seeking him.

12. And when the day began to wear away, then came the twelve and said unto him, Send the multitude away, that they may go into the towns and country round about, and lodge, and get victuals: for we are here in a desert place. 13. But he said unto them, Give ye them to eat. And they said, We have no more but five loaves and two fishes; except we should go and buy meat for all this people. 14. For they were about five thousand men. And he said to his disciples, Make them sit down by fifties in a company. 15. And they did so, and made them all sit down.

12—15. See Matt. viii. Then they obeyed, expecting some miracle.

16. Then he took the five loaves, and the two fishes, and looking up to heaven, he blessed them, and brake, and gave to the disciples to set before the multitude, 17. And they did eat, and were all filled: and there was taken up of fragments that remained to them, twelve baskets.

16, 17. See on Matt. xiv.

18. And it came to pass as he was alone praying, his disciples were with him: and he asked them, saying, Whom say the people that I am? 19. They answering, said, John the Baptist: but some *say* Elias: and others *say*, that one of the old prophets is risen again.

18, 19. Came to him. See Matt. xvi. 15, 20.

20. He said unto them, But whom say ye that I am? Peter answering, said, The Christ of God. 21. And he straightly charged them, and commanded *them* to tell no man that thing.

20, 21. Qu. What then was the gospel which

they were sent to preach, and which he preached? Answ. Much like John Baptist's preaching that the kingdom of God is come; and moreover, that Jesus did such and such miracles, as he told John's disciples; not directly saying, I am the Christ, but proposing those evidences from whence they were themselves to gather it: Because his resurrection, &c. was to make the evidence full, before the gospel was fully preached.

Qu. But what then was the baptism he used before his resurrection, if men were not to be told and to profess that he was the Christ? Answ. Just answerable to his preaching: and like John's baptism; but much different from the following baptism in the name of the Father, Son, and Holy Ghost. Men were to profess repentance and hope of salvation, by learning of Christ, and so listed themselves under him as his disciples; but not yet to profess that He was the Christ; which after was necessary.

22. Saying, The Son of Man must suffer many things, and be rejected of the elders, and chief priests, and scribes, and be slain, and be raised again the third day.

22. All this is part of the gospel which you must hereafter preach; and when this is done, it will be seasonable to preach it.

23. And he said to them all, If any man will come after me, let him deny himself, and take up his cross daily, and follow me. 24. For whosoever will save his life, shall lose it: but whosoever will lose his life for my sake, the same shall save it.

23, 24. Carnal self-love, and the love of worldly prosperity being man's lapsed sinful state: it is from these that I come to save men; and therefore will save none, but by saving them from these, and teaching them to deny their carnal selves, and worldly prosperity.

25. For what is a man advantaged, if he gain the whole world, and lose himself, or be cast away?

25. See on Matt. x. and Mark viii. Alas, then, for how little a part of this vain world do millions sell their souls!

26. For whosoever shall be ashamed of me and of my words, of him shall the Son of Man be ashamed, when he shall come in his own glory and in *his* Father's, and of the holy angels.

26. They that, to save their estates or lives, are ashamed now to own me and the gospel, I will reject them as ashamed to own them, or such as them, in the day of glory, and their extremity in judgment.

27. But I tell you of a truth, there be some standing here which shall not taste of death till they see the kingdom of God.

27. Note, All the three evangelists, prefixing this immediately before the history of Christ's transfiguration, do plainly tell us, that it was that glimpse of his glory which he meant.

28. And it came to pass about an eight days after these sayings, he took Peter, and John and James, and went up into a mountain to pray.

28. Matt. xvii. 1. Saith, after six days, not reckoning the two parts of the foregoing and the last day.

29. And as he prayed, the fashion of his countenance was altered, and his raiment *was* white and glistering. 30. And behold, there talked with him two men, which were Moses and Elias. 31. Who appeared in glory, and spake of his decease which he should accomplish at Jerusalem. 32. But Peter, and they that were with him, were heavy with sleep: and when they were awake, they saw his glory, and the two men that stood with him. 33. And it came to pass, as they departed from him, Peter said unto Jesus, Master, it is good for us to be here; and let us make three tabernacles, one for thee, and one for Moses, and one for Elias: not knowing what he said. 34. While he thus spake, there came a cloud and overshadowed them: and they feared as they entered into the cloud. 35. And there came a voice out of the cloud, saying, This is my beloved Son, hear him.

29—35. See on Matt. xvii. I have largely opened all this in my book called, " My Dying Thoughts." Note, If this glimpse of glory was so sweet, why do we fear to pass hence into the blessed vision and fruition!

36. And when the voice was past, Jesus was found alone, and they kept *it* close, and told no man in those days any of those things which they had seen.

36. For Christ so commanded.

37. And it came to pass, that on the next day, when they were come down from the hill, much people met him. 38. And behold, a man of the company cried out, saying, Master, I beseech thee, look upon my son, for he is mine only child: 39. And lo, a spirit taketh him, and he suddenly crieth out, and it teareth him that he foameth again, and bruising him, hardly departeth from him. 40. And I besought thy disciples to cast him out, and they could not. 41. And Jesus answering, said, O faithless and perverse generation, how long shall I be with you, and suffer you? Bring thy son hither. 42. And as he was yet a coming, the devil threw him down, and tare *him;* and Jesus rebuked the unclean spirit, and healed the child, and delivered him again to his father.

37—42. See on Matt. xvii. 15, 16. Since I have myself known one yet living, that had an old and violent epilepsy, once, twice, or thrice a day, perfectly cured, (near thirty years ago, and so continueth,) after other great means used, merely by fasting, and earnest prayer, suddenly in the midst of prayer the second day; I do the easier believe that the devil and a natural disease, of which he is the executioner, may consist together.

43. And they were all amazed at the mighty power of God: But while they wondered every one at all things which Jesus did, he said unto his disciples, 44. Let these sayings sink down into your ears: for the Son of Man shall be delivered into the hands of men.

43, 44. Let not my glory and power put you in vain expectations of earthly dominion. Observe, and forget not that I tell you again and again, that I must suffer, (and rise again.)

45. But they understood not this saying, and it was hid from them, that they perceived it not: and they feared to ask him of that saying.

45. Note, Even the apostles understood not that Christ must be crucified and rise again, though he often told it them, and charged them that it might sink down into their ears. Therefore the belief of it was not then necessary to salvation, as it is now.

2.

46. Then there arose a reasoning among them, which of them should be greatest.

46. Note, Alas, that pride and ambition should begin so near to Christ, and foretel the calamity of the church!

47. And Jesus perceiving the thought of their heart, took a child, and set him by him, 48. And said unto them, Whosoever shall receive this child in my name, receiveth me: and whosoever shall receive me, receiveth him that sent me: for he that is least among you all, the same shall be great.

47, 48. Humility must be your greatness.

49. And John answered and said, Master, we saw one casting out devils in thy name: and we forbad him, because he followeth not with us. 50. And Jesus said unto him, Forbid *him* not: for he that is not against us, is for us.

49, 50. See on Matt. xii. 30.

51. And it came to pass, when the time was come that he should be received up, he stedfastly set his face to go to Jerusalem.

51. The time of his approaching crucifixion, and his ascension to heaven.

52. And sent messengers before his face: and they went, and entered into a village of the Samaritans to make ready for him. 53. And they did not receive him, because his face was as though he would go to Jerusalem.

52, 53. Note, For the Jews and the Samaritans disowned each other, upon their controversies about worship.

54. And when his disciples, James and John saw this, they said, Lord, wilt thou that we command fire to come down from heaven and consume them, even as Elias did? 55. But he turned and rebuked them, and said, Ye know not what manner of spirit ye are of. 56. For the Son of Man is not come to destroy men's lives, but to save *them.* And they went to another village.

L

54, 55, 56. That which you take for the spirit of Elias, and zeal for me against sin, is a selfish, uncharitable revengeful spirit, and not that which I will give you, which is a spirit of love and gentleness: You know not your own hearts, but take that for good in you, which is evil; and you know not me as you should do: I come to save, and not to destroy men.

This is the third sin against charity, recorded of John, who was after the great preacher of love.

57. And it came to pass that as they went in the way, a certain man said unto him, Lord, I will follow thee whithersoever thou goest. 58. And Jesus said unto him, Foxes have holes, and the birds of the air *have* nests, but the Son of Man hath not where to lay *his* head.

57, 58. I have no entertainment for any, but self-denying persons, that can forsake all for me.

59. And he said unto another, Follow me: But he said, Lord, suffer me first to go and bury my father. 60. Jesus said unto him, Let the dead bury their dead; but go thou and preach the kingdom of God.

59, 60. The work of my gospel, and God's kingdom, must be preferred before the burying of a father.

Note, Christ fitted his answer to the disposition of those he spake to. He knew that this man was fitter to be put on, and the former to be stopt.

61. And another also said, Lord, I will follow thee, but let me first go bid them farewel which are at home at my house. 62. And Jesus said unto him, No man having put his hand to the plough, and looking back, is fit for the kingdom of God.

61, 62. If thou wilt be my minister, thou must be like a man ploughing, who looketh still before him on the furrow, and not behind him: The kingdom of God must be first sought, and all things that would hinder the true service of it, must be put behind, and denied, and forsaken: (Not that it dissolveth relative duties, but puts all behind the works and interest of God, and forsaketh that which is against it.)

CHAP. X.

AFTER these things, the Lord appointed other seventy also, and sent them two and two before his face into every city, and place, whither he himself would come. 2. Therefore said he unto them, The harvest truly *is* great, but the labourers *are* few: pray ye therefore the Lord of the harvest, that he would send forth labourers into his harvest.

1, 2. As he had chosen twelve, with respect to the twelve tribes: so he chose seventy, according to the number of the great council, it is like 70 being put for 72, as an ancient copy hath it. By which it appeareth he settled a disparity in his ministers.

2. Note, Priests now are many, but labourers few; What men are they that hate and silence the faithfullest labourers, suspecting that they are not for their interest?

3. Go your ways: behold I send you forth as lambs among wolves. 4. Carry neither purse, nor scrip, nor shoes: and salute no man by the way.

3, 4. I send you on such work, in which you shall suffer from wicked men, as I must do. Let not the care of provision, nor any matters of inferior concern, as human respects are, stop you in your work and undertaken ministry, (not that all civility is forbidden.)

5. And into whatsoever house ye enter, first say, Peace *be* to this house. 6. And if the son of peace be there, your peace shall rest upon it: if not, it shall turn to you again.

5, 6. For the necessary capacity of the receiver is implied, as a condition of the effect. The same benediction is effectual to a capable receiver, and uneffectual to another, (as is also the sacrament.)

7. And in the same house remain, eating and drinking such things as they give: for the labourer is worthy of his hire. Go not from house to house. 8. And into whatsoever city ye enter, and they receive you, eat such things as are set before you.

7, 8. Maintenance is your due for your work.

9. And heal the sick that are therein, and say unto them, The kingdom of God is come nigh unto you.

9. This was the gospel that they were to preach.

10. But into whatsoever city ye enter, and they receive you not, go

your ways out into the streets of the same, and say, 11. Even the very dust of your city which cleaveth on us, we do wipe off against you: notwithstanding, be ye sure of this, that the kingdom of God is come nigh unto you.

10, 11. See Matt. x. 14.

12. But I say unto you, that it shall be more tolerable in that day for Sodom, than for that city.

12. At the judgment. There will be some punished in hell more tolerably than others.

13. Woe unto thee Chorazin, woe unto thee Bethsaida: for if the mighty works had been done in Tyre and Sidon, which have been done in you, they had a great while ago repented, sitting in sackcloth and ashes.

13. The same means, which prevaileth not with some, would have converted others that now perish.

14. But it shall be more tolerable for Tyre and Sidon at the judgment, than for you. 15. And thou Capernaum, which art exalted to heaven, shalt be thrust down to hell.

14, 15. The loss of the greatest means and mercy, prepareth for the heaviest judgment.

16. He that heareth you, heareth me: and he that despiseth you, despiseth me: and he that despiseth me, despiseth him that sent me.

16. So far as you do my works, I will take what is done to you as done to myself.

17. And the seventy returned again with joy, saying, Lord, even the devils are subject unto us through thy name. 18. And he said unto them, I beheld Satan as lightning, fall from heaven.

17, 18. Satan shall be cast down from much of his tyranny over mankind, by me and my gospel.

19. Behold, I give unto you power to tread on serpents and scorpions, and over all the power of the enemy; and nothing shall by any means hurt you.

19. Note, The kingdom of Christ is set up against the devil and his kingdom, and not against kings as such.

2. It seems serpents are used as Satan's instruments to hurt man.

20. Notwithstanding in this rejoice not, that the spirits are subject unto you: but rather rejoice, because your names are written in heaven.

20. Even wicked men may cast out devils, but it is greater matter of joy to be saints that shall be saved.

21. In that hour Jesus rejoiced in spirit, and said, I thank thee, O Father, Lord of heaven and earth, that thou hast hid these things from the wise and prudent, and hast revealed them unto babes: even so, Father, for so it seemed good in thy sight.

21. That thou hast revealed the heavenly wisdom to those that are despised, as unlearned in the world, rather than to men counted wise and learned for their human wit and knowledge. See Matt. xi. 15.

22. All things are delivered to me of my Father: and no man knoweth who the Son is, but the Father; and who the Father is, but the Son, and he to whom the Son will reveal *him*.

22. Christ is made the Lord of all; and he is perfectly known by none but God: And there is no true knowledge of God the Father, but by the teaching of Christ.

23. And he turned him unto *his* disciples, and said privately, Blessed *are* the eyes which see the things that ye see.

23. See Matt. xiii. 17.

24. For I tell you, that many prophets and kings have desired to see those things which ye see, and have not seen *them;* and to hear those things which ye hear, and have not heard *them.*

24. Such as David, Solomon, Isaiah, &c.

25. And behold, a certain lawyer stood up, and tempted him, saying, Master, what shall I do to inherit eternal life?

25. To try his skill.

26. He said unto him, What is written in the law? how readest thou?

26. Note. They err who say, that the law of Moses prescribed not the means to eternal life.

27. And he answering, said, Thou shalt love the Lord thy God with all thy heart, and with all thy soul, and with all thy strength, and with all thy mind; and thy neighbour as thyself. 28. And he said unto him, Thou hast answered right: this do, and thou shalt live.

27, 28. Note, This is not the same history that is mentioned, Matt. xix. 16. there is much of the same, and yet much difference: There Christ repeateth the commands particularly, but here the lawyer repeateth them summarily. So Mark x. 17. agreeth with Matthew. But that in Luke xviii. 18. is the same with this, and a distinct history.

Note, Whoever loveth God sincerely, and his neighbour as himself, shall be saved. But this will never be done without regenerating grace.

29. But he willing to justify himself, said unto Jesus, And who is my neighbour?

Note, This overwillingness to justify ourselves, is one of the deepest rooted, and commonest vices in corrupted nature.

30. And Jesus answering, said, A certain man went down from Jerusalem to Jericho, and fell among thieves, which stripped him of his raiment, and wounded *him*, and departed, leaving *him* half dead. 31. And by chance there came down a certain priest that way; and when he saw him, he passed by on the other side. 32. And likewise a Levite, when he was at the place came and looked on *him*, and passed by on the other side. 33. But a certain Samaritan, as he journeyed, came where he was: and when he saw him, he had compassion *on him*, 34. And went to him, and bound up his wounds, pouring in oil and wine, and set him on his own beast, and brought him to an inn, and took care of him. 35. And on the morrow when he departed, he took out two-pence, and gave *them* to the host, and said unto him, Take care of him; and whatsoever thou spendest more, when I come again, I will repay thee.

30, 31, &c. The priest and the Levite, who should be the most holy and charitable, past by him without helping him; but a Samaritan, one contemned by them as a heretic, or profane rustic, took him up, and helped him.

Note, They abuse the text that say, by the Samaritan, is meant Christ, and by two-pence, the two Testaments, &c.

36. Which now of these three, thinkest thou, was neighbour unto him that fell among thieves?

36. Which of them took the man for his neighbour, and dealt as a neighbour with him.

37. And he said, He that shewed mercy on him. Then said Jesus unto him, Go, and do thou likewise.

37. So do thou, and though he be a Samaritan, a schismatic, a heretic, use him with such charity as thy neighbour.

Note, Do they so, that ruin, hunt, and destroy such, and better men?

38. Now it came to pass, as they went, that he entered into a certain village: and a certain woman named Martha, received him into her house. 39. And she had a sister called Mary, which also sat at Jesus' feet, and heard his word.

38, 39. Martha was the house-keeper, or owner.

40. But Martha was cumbered about much serving, and came to him, and said, Lord, dost thou not care that my sister hath left me to serve alone, bid her therefore that she help me.

40. The followers of Christ to be provided for, were many, and the work seemed necessary.

41. And Jesus answered, and said unto her, Martha, Martha, thou art careful, and troubled about many things: 42. But one thing is needful, and Mary hath chosen that good part, which shall not be taken away from her.

41, 42. Thou troublest thyself more than needs, and unseasonably, about many things of less necessity. But to learn the way of salvation, and so to be blessed in the kingdom of God, is the one thing of absolute necessity. This Mary hath preferred; and so shouldst thou, and have left serving to the second place: and none shall deprive her of that better portion which she hath chosen.

Note, 1. Christ doth not blame Martha for her care and work, but for not preferring better; nor speaks this so much to blame her, as to commend Mary, and to teach us all what to prefer.

2. One thing only (in a comprehensive sense, as containing salvation, and its necessary means) is of such absolute necessity to man, that all things else should be put behind it.

3. Preferring things less necessary, though good, and troubling ourselves about need-nots, is a common fault, even of religious persons.

4. That is a fault out of its due time and place, which is a great duty in its season.

5. They that prefer and chuse the best, shall have the best, whoever is against it.

6. Even godly persons and near, are apt upon cross interests and opinions, to censure and accuse each other upon mistake, when the fault is in the accuser, and that to Christ.

7. But Christ will justify the right.

CHAP. XI.

AND it came to pass, that as he was praying in a certain place, when he ceased, one of his disciples said unto him, Lord, teach us to pray, as John also taught his disciples.

1. It seems they had till now been too little and unskilful in prayer.

2. And he said unto them, When ye pray, say, Our Father which art in heaven, Hallowed be thy name. Thy kingdom come. Thy will be done, as in heaven so in earth. 3. Give us day by day our daily bread. 4. And forgive us our sins; for we also forgive every one that is indebted to us. And lead us not into temptation, but deliver us from evil.

2, 3, 4. See the exposition of the Lord's prayer on Matt. vi. 9.

Note, It is evident that Christ gave them this prayer to be used both as a directory for matter and method, and as a meet form of words, when they pray comprehensively and summarily. though not tying them always to use these very words, nor to go through the whole method, when occasion confines them to some one branch, or requires them to insist most on it; much less obliging or allowing them to use no other: And so the apostles, and all the churches understood it.

The small difference in words between Matthew and Luke, are not material; save that Luke omitteth the doxology in the end.

By [Debt] verse 4, is meant chiefly wrong or sin: For so the Syriac signifieth, in which Christ spake: Though also our obligation to keep the law of innocency on pain of death, or for justification, is a debt which God remitteth by the law of faith and grace, and accepteth on our part faith and sincere obedience, for the merit of Christ, who fulfilled that perfect law.

5. And he said unto them, Which of you shall have a friend, and shall go unto him at midnight, and say unto him, Friend, lend me three loaves: 6. For a friend of mine in his journey is come to me, and I have nothing to set before him: 7. And he from within shall answer and say, Trouble me not: the door is now shut, and my children are with me in bed; I cannot rise and give thee. 8. I say unto you, Though he will not rise and give him, because he is his friend: yet because of his importunity, he will rise and give him as many as he needeth.

5, 6, &c. Though God be not as man; that giveth to the importunate to be eased of them, yet importunity also prevaileth with him as it fits the receiver for his gifts.

9. And I say unto you, Ask and it shall be given you: seek, and ye shall find: knock, and it shall be opened unto you. 10. For every one that asketh, receiveth: and he that seeketh, findeth: and to him that knocketh, it shall be opened.

9, 10. He that will spare for no labour, and take no denial, shall have no denial finally: He that easily giveth over his suit, and will not be at pains and patience, forfeiteth mercy by contempt.

11. If a son shall ask bread of any of you that is a father, will he give him a stone? or if *he ask* a fish, will he for a fish give him a serpent? 12. Or if he shall ask an egg, will he offer him a scorpion? 13. If ye then, being evil, know how to give good gifts unto your children: how much more shall *your* heavenly Father give the holy Spirit to them that ask him?

11, 12, 13. Note, God's goodness is a great ground of hope that he will grant our prayers; that is, as far as he hath promised; 1. Grace and glory certainly to all penitent believers. 2. And the things of this life on these three conditions; 1. If they are such as are fit for the person. 2. And he be fit for them. 3. And it be fit to subserve God's higher ends, his glory, and the public good, and do not cross them.

So much of his spirit as is necessary to salvation, he will give to all true believers: And the additional degrees and gifts, he giveth on the terms aforesaid.

14. And he was casting out a devil, and it was dumb. And it came to pass, when the devil was gone out, the dumb spake: and the people wondered. 15. But some of them said, He casteth out devils through Beelzebub, the chief of the devils.

14, 15. See Matt. xii. They were so convinced of the fact of his miracles, that they had no plea for their unbelief left them, but to say, he did them by conjuration, which is the blaspheming of the Holy Ghost.

16. And others tempting *him*, sought of him a sign from heaven. 17. But he knowing their thoughts, said unto them, Every kingdom divided against itself, is brought to desolation: and a house *divided* against a house, falleth. 18. If Satan also be divided against himself, how shall his kingdom stand? because ye say, that I cast out devils through Beelzebub. 19. And if I by Beelzebub cast out devils, by whom do your sons cast them out? therefore shall they be your judges.

16, 17, &c. Note, When Satan laboureth to divide the church of Christ, it is that he may destroy it: And should we do worse against Christ's kingdom, than Satan will do by his own?

20. But if I with the finger of God cast out devils, no doubt the kingdom of God is come upon you.

20. It is the approving work of God, to set up his kingdom against the devil's.

21. When a strong man armed keepeth his palace his goods are in peace. 22. But when a stronger than he shall come upon him, and overcome him, he taketh from him all his armour wherein he trusted, and divideth his spoils.

21, 22. If I did not conquer Satan, I could not cast him out of his possession of bodies and souls.

23. He that is not with me, is against me: and he that gathereth not with me, scattereth.

23. See Matt. xii. 30.

24. When the unclean spirit is gone out of a man, he walketh through dry places, seeking rest: and finding none, he saith, I will return unto my house whence I came out. 25. And when he cometh, he findeth *it* swept and garnished. 26. Then goeth he, and taketh to him seven other spirits more wicked than himself, and they enter in, and dwell there: and the last state of that man is worse than the first.

24, 25, &c. But let him that is delivered from Satan's possession of body or soul, take heed that he return not: For when Satan is cast out, he trieth by his temptations to get possession of some others: And when he hath assaulted many, and is resisted and frustrate by the grace of God, he resolveth again to try his assaults, on him that was delivered; and finding him careless, unwatchful, and ready to receive his temptations, he suggested worse things to him than those that be had renounced, and bringeth in on fair pretences seven-fold worse vices than he had before: And the end of that man is worse than was his first captivity to Satan.

Note, It is some kind of rest to devils to deceive and destroy souls; as it is to a malicious man to do mischief by revenge. Devils are not yet at their most easeless state. See Matt. xii. 48.

27. And it came to pass, as he spake these things, a certain woman of the company lifted up her voice, and said unto him, Blessed *is* the womb that bare thee, and the paps which thou hast sucked. 28. But he said, Yea, rather blessed *are* they that hear the word of God, and keep it.

27, 28. Note, Carnal persons most regard carnal relations. 2. Christ accounts them that hear and keep God's word, as more amiable and blessed, than it would be to have been his own mother: And we must judge as he doth: Though when God maketh the provision for our families, our duty must obey him as his stewards in our distributions; yet grace is more amiable than natural relations.

29. And when the people were gathered thick together, he began to say, This is an evil generation: they seek a sign, and there shall no sign be given it, but the sign of Jo-

was the prophet. 30. For as Jonas was a sign unto the Ninevites, so shall also the Son of Man be to this generation.

29, 30. As Jonas after three days abode in the sea, was sent to preach; so after my three days in the grave, I will rise and call the world to repentance, by mine apostles and my spirit, and save them as Nineve was saved.

31. The queen of the south shall rise up in the judgment with the men of this generation, and condemn them: for she came from the utmost parts of the earth, to hear the wisdom of Solomon; and behold, a greater than Solomon *is* here.

31. It shall appear that the Jews are worse than her, and deserve destruction for being so much worse, and averse to faith.

32. The men of Nineve shall rise up in judgment with this generation, and shall condemn it: for they repented at the preaching of Jonas; and behold, a greater than Jonas *is* here.

32. See Matt. xii. 40.

33. No man when he hath lighted a candle, putteth *it* in a secret place, neither under a bushel: but on a candlestick, that they which come in may see the light.

33. God would not have us hide his truth, much less silence it by a diabolical persecution.

34. The light of the body is the eye: therefore when thine eye is single, thy whole body is also full of light: but when *thine eye* is evil, thy body also is full of darkness.

34. The light of man is his true understanding: As that is, so is the man a child of light, or of darkness.

35. Take heed therefore, that the light which is in thee be not darkness.

35. Take heed lest that understanding be ignorant, or erroneous.

36. If thy whole body therefore be full of light, having no part dark, the whole shall be full of light, as when the bright shining of a candle doth give thee light.

36. See Mark vi. 66.

37. And as he spake, a certain Pharisee besought him to dine with him: and he went in and sat down to meat. 38. And when the Pharisee saw *it*, he marvelled that he had not first washed before dinner.

37, 38. See Matt. vii. 3, and xv. 2.

39. And the Lord said unto him, Now do ye Pharisees make clean the outside of the cup and the platter: but your inward part is full of ravening and wickedness. 40. Ye fools, did not he that made that which is without, make that which is within also? 41. But rather give alms of such things as you have: and behold, all things are clean unto you.

39, 40, 41. True cleanness is to be acceptable to God: Be charitable and liberal, and your meat will be clean to you.

42. But woe unto you Pharisees: for ye tithe mint and rue, and all manner of herbs, and pass over judgment and the love of God: these ought ye to have done, and not to leave the other undone.

42. See Matt. xxiii. 23. The love of God, and justice with men, are far greater matters than religious rites and ceremonies, or church-orders. God's laws are some far greater than others, though none to be violated.

43. Woe unto you Pharisees: for ye love the uppermost seats in the synagogues, and greetings in the markets. 44. Woe unto you scribes and Pharisees, hypocrites: for ye are as graves which appear not, and the men that walk over *them*, are not aware *of them.*

43, 44. Note, Hypocrisy is pride covered with formal, ceremonious shews of religion, sometime unknown to the hypocrite himself.

45. Then answered one of the lawyers, and said unto him, Master, thus saying, thou reproachest us also. 46. And he said, Woe unto you also ye lawyers: for ye lade men with burdens grievous to be borne, and ye yourselves touch not

the burdens with one of your fingers.

45, 46. Note 1. Bad men can bear guilt, but no reproach for it. 2. Strict doctrine condemneth loose and guilty preachers.

47. Woe unto you ; for ye build the sepulchres of the prophets, and your fathers killed them. 48. Truly ye bear witness that ye allow the deeds of your fathers: for they indeed killed them, and ye build their sepulchres.

47, 48. See Matt. xxiii. 30. Hypocrites glory in the names and honour of dead martyrs and saints, and kill the living.

49. Therefore also said the wisdom of God, I will send them prophets and apostles, and *some* of them they shall slay and persecute: 50. That the blood of all the prophets which was shed from the foundation of the world, may be required of this generation.

49, 50. Your fore-fathers' sins, and yours shall be revenged on you shortly.

51. From the blood of Abel unto the blood of Zacharias, which perished between the altar and the temple: verily I say unto you, it shall be required of this generation. 52. Woe unto you lawyers; for ye have taken away the key of knowledge : ye entered not in yourselves, and them that were entering in, ye hindered.

51, 52. Note, The just description of a wicked clergy.

53. And as he said these things: unto them, the scribes and the Pharisees began to urge *him* vehemently, and to provoke him to speak of many things : 54. Laying wait for him, and seeking to catch something out of his mouth, that they might accuse him.

53, 54. Their wrath set their wits on work to ensnare him.

CHAP. XII.

IN the mean time, when they were gathered together an innumerable multitude of people, insomuch that they trode one upon another, he began to say unto his disciples first of all, Beware ye of the leaven of the Pharisees, which is hypocrisy.

1. Note, He dissuaded none from joining with them in any good, or hearing the law from them, but to avoid their hypocrisy, and ceremonious covers of iniquity, joined with malice against Christ.

2. For there is nothing covered, that shall not be revealed ; neither hid, that shall not be known. 3. Therefore whatsoever ye have spoken in darkness, shall be heard in the light: and that which ye have spoken in the ear in closets, shall be proclaimed upon the house-tops.

2, 3. Trust not to secresy and deceit; for all secret sins shall be opened at the last.

Note. O how many will that day shame ! It is our wisdom, by due confession, to take shame sooner to ourselves.

4. And I say unto you my friends, Be not afraid of them that kill the body, and after that have no more that they can do. 5. But I will forewarn you whom you shall fear. Fear him, which after he hath killed, hath power to cast into hell: yea, I say unto you, Fear him.

4, 5. I give it you as the most friendly counsel, Take heed of too much fear of man, lest it cause you to betray your souls : They can but kill the body : The soul overliveth it ; and man's welfare or misery is after death: persecutors or tyrants cannot reach or hurt you after death. But, as you love yourselves, fear God, whose justice will be executed on the ungodly after death, and when he hath taken away their souls, he will cast them into hell : Again, I say, be sure to fear him.

6. Are not five sparrows sold for two farthings, and not one of them is forgotten before God ? 7. But even the very hairs of your head are all numbered. Fear not therefore: ye are of more value than many sparrows.

6, 7. God's providence extendeth to a sparrow, and to the smallest creatures ; (for he is omnipotent, and all sufficient, and maintaineth all ;) and much more to you: There is not an hair of your heads not caused, not known, and not regarded by him : And doth he disregard your lives' welfare, whom he hath raised above the rank of brutes?

Note, God is as sufficient for every creature and event, as if he had but that one to mind.

8. Also I say unto you, Whoso-

ever shall confess me before men, him shall the Son of Man also confess before the angels of God.

8. Own me sincerely in the time of trial, and I will own you before angels, where are your greatest concerns.

9. But he that denieth me before men, shall be denied before the angels of God.

9. Without true repentance.

10. And whosoever shall speak a word against the Son of Man, it shall be forgiven him: but unto him that blasphemeth against the Holy Ghost, it shall not be forgiven.

10. To speak against me as a man, is pardonable: But when I shall send the Spirit of miracles and holiness to be my witness in the world, they that will not be convinced by this Spirit, but blasphemously say, It is the power and work of the devils, do sin against the last and great means of conviction, and being encured, are unpardonable.

11. And when they bring you unto the synagogues, and *unto* magistrates, and powers, take ye no thought how or what thing ye shall answer, or what ye sall say: 12. For the Holy Ghost shall teach you in the same hour, what ye ought to say.

11, 12. Let not the fear of your unready speech discourage you, but trust the Spirit of God to help you.

13. And one of the company said unto him, Master, speak to my brother, that he divide the inheritance with me. 14. And he said unto him, Man, who made me a judge, or a divider over you?

13, 14. Note, Whether the man would have had Christ taken on him an authoritative decision, or only a free arbitration, is uncertain; which ever it was, Christ refuseth it: A work of worldly rule he disclaimed: And he would not be so imprudent as to offend men by an arbitration without need.

15. And he said unto them, Take heed, and beware of covetousness: for a man's life consisteth not in the abundance of the things which he possesseth.

*15. Take heed of being too desirous of wealth or plenty: For neither life, nor the comfort of life, depends on plenty, but on the holy and obe-*dient use of what you have, and on the blessing and love of God.

16. And he spake a parable unto them, saying, The ground of a certain rich man brought forth plentifully. 17. And he thought within himself, saying, What shall I do, because I have no room where to bestow my fruits? 18. And he said, This will I do: I will pull down my barns, and build greater; and there will I bestow all my fruits and my goods. 19. And I will say to my soul, Soul, thou hast much goods laid up for many years; take thine ease, eat, drink, *and* be merry. 20. But God said unto him, Thou fool, this night thy soul shall be required of thee: then whose shall those things be which thou hast provided?

16, 17, &c. Note, The damning folly of wicked men, is, 1. In over-loving the pleasures of the flesh, to eat, and drink, and be merry, and live at ease. 2. To over-love riches and plenty, as provision for this fleshly pleasure. 3. To flatter themselves with the conceit of long life, and to forget the shortness of time, and their latter end. 4. To neglect a due dependance on God for all things. 5. To neglect the due care of the soul, and preparation for another world, and to set less by heaven than earth; such are the most miserable fools.

21. So *is* he that layeth up treasure for himself, and is not rich towards God.

21. Such is every one, whose chief care and labour is, to have plenteous provision for his own body, and is not rich in grace, nor useth his riches to please God in good works.

22. And he said unto his disciples, Therefore I say unto you, Take no thought for your life, what ye shall eat; neither for the body, what ye shall put on. 23. The life is more than meat, and the body *is more* than raiment.

22, 23. Note, Luke brings in things spoken at several times, on several occasions, for the matters' sake. See Matt. vi. Trust him for the less, who hath freely given you the greater.

24. Consider the ravens; for they neither sow nor reap: which neither have store-house nor barn; and God feedeth them: How much more are ye better than the fowls? 25

And which of you with taking thought can add to his stature one cubit? 26. If ye then be not able to do that thing which is least, why take ye thought for the rest? 27. Consider the lilies how they grow: They toil not, they spin not: and yet I say unto you, that Solomon in all his glory was not arrayed like one of these. 28. If then God so clothe the grass, which is to-day in the field, and to-morrow is cast into the oven: how much more *will he clothe* you, O ye of little faith?

24, 25, &c. Note, All this is against distrustful care and trouble, and not diligent labour in a calling, or prudent care to do our work, and avoid evil. See Matt. vi.

29. And seek not ye what ye shall eat, or what ye shall drink, neither be ye of doubtful mind. 30. For all these things do the nations of the world seek after: and your Father knoweth, that ye have need of these things.

29, 30. Be not anxious or troubled. Note, 1. The *faithful* must live quite above the life of worldlings. 2. It should quiet a child of God, that his Father knoweth all his wants.

31. But rather seek ye the kingdom of God, and all these things shall be added unto you.

31. Seek first, &c.

32. Fear not, little flock: for it is your Father's good pleasure to give you the kingdom.

32. Note, 1. Christ's flock was then little, and will be so comparatively on earth, but not in heaven. 2. They shall have a kingdom. 3. By the gift of God's good pleasure. 4. They that shall have the kingdom of heaven, should be above distrustful fear on earth.

33. Sell that ye have, and give alms: provide yourselves bags which wax not old, a treasure in the heavens that faileth not, where no thief approacheth, neither moth corrupteth.

33. See Matt. vi. 19, 20. The wisdom of faith is to do all we can in this world, in preparation for another, and at any rate, to make sure of salvation.

34. For where your treasure is, there will your heart be also.

34. Either by desire, if you are uncertain to obtain it, or by delight, if you have assurance or strong hope, or in full joy when you possess it.

Note, A man's treasure is that which he believeth will make him most happy, and loveth and seeketh it accordingly.

A dreadful word to worldly men, whose hearts are not on heaven.

35. Let your loins be girded about, and *your* lights burning; 36. And ye yourselves like unto men that wait for their Lord, when he will return from the wedding; that when he cometh and knocketh, they may open unto him immediately.

35, 36. Live in a constant prepared waiting for my coming, and your change; and let not your preparation be to make at last.

37. Blessed *are* those servants, whom the Lord when he cometh shall find watching: verily I say unto you, that he shall gird himself, and make them to sit down to meat, and will come forth and serve them.

37. Christ will do more for them, than if he were a servant to them.

38. And if he shall come in the second watch, or come in the third watch, and find *them* so, blessed are those servants.

See Matt. xxiv. 23.

39. And this know, that if the good man of the house had known what hour the thief would come, he would have watched, and not have suffered his house to be broken through. 40. Be ye therefore ready also: for the Son of Man cometh at an hour when ye think not.

39, 40. Every one would be awaked just at the time, if they foreknew the hour. But God will conceal it, that ye may be always ready.

41. Then Peter said unto him, Lord, speakest thou this parable unto us, or even to all? 42. And the Lord said, Who then is that faithful and wise steward, whom *his* lord shall make ruler over his household, to give *them their* portion of meat in due season? 43. Blessed *is* that servant, whom his lord when he cometh, shall find so doing. 44.

Of a truth I say unto you, that he will make him ruler over all that he hath.

41, 42, &c. I speak it to all so far as they are God's stewards of their several trusts: But especially to those who are ruling stewards over the churches, appointed to give the children their due food in season: All such shall be rewarded.

45. But and if that servant say in his heart, My lord delayeth his coming; and shall begin to beat the men servants, and maidens, and to eat and drink and to be drunken: 46. The lord of that servant will come in a day when he looketh not for him, and at an hour when he is not aware, and will cut him in sunder, and will appoint him his portion with the unbelievers.

45, 46. Note, This dreadful threatening is also a prophecy of a worldly persecuting sort, that should arise under pretence of ruling and feeding the household of Christ, both civil and ecclesiastical.

47. And that servant which knew his lord's will, and prepared not *himself*, neither did according to his will, shall be beaten with many *stripes*.

47. The sins against knowledge are greater far than those of ignorance.
Note, There are degrees of pain in hell.
Note, And wicked clergymen and teachers will have the greatest torment.

48. But he that knew not, and did commit things worthy of stripes, shall be beaten with few *stripes*. For unto whomsoever much is given, of him shall be much required: and to whom men have committed much, of him they will ask the more.

48. Some in hell have few stripes comparatively.
Note, Great gifts must be used with great diligence; and great power, and trust, and charges, are rather to be feared than ambitiously sought. Little do the great conquerors of the world, or those that strive for church preferment, believe and consider what duty, or deep damnation, they so much labour for.

49. I am come to send fire on earth, and what will I, if it be already kindled? 50. But I have a baptism to be baptized with, and how am I straitened till it be accomplished.

49, 50. I come to do that work that will set the world on fire, and occasion persecution: And it is already begun. And I am to lead the way in suffering, and to go through these flames myself: And I am as in pain till it be accomplished.

51. Suppose ye that I am come to give peace on earth? I tell you, Nay; but rather division. 52. For from henceforth there shall be five in one house divided, three against two, and two against three. 53. The father shall be divided against the son, and the son against the father: the mother against the daughter, and the daughter against the mother: the mother-in-law against her daughter-in-law, and the daughter-in-law against her mother-in-law.

51, 52, 53. Some think that the coming of the Messiah, will settle an universal peace; but they are mistaken: I come to conquer Satan's kingdom, and save souls from sin, which will not be without a conflict: I come to divide men from sin and Satan, who possessed them in peace; And the soldiers of Satan will pursue those that by grace escape; natural kindred will not reconcile them.

54. And he said also to the people, when ye see a cloud rise out of the west, straightway ye say, There cometh a shower; and so it is. 55. And when *ye see* the south wind blow, ye say, There will be heat; and it cometh to pass. 56. Ye hypocrites, ye can discern the face of the sky, and of the earth: but how is it, that ye do not discern this time?

54, 55, 56. You have by experience learned to foretel the weather by the winds; and why learn you not, by the signs in your own hearts and lives to foresee what is like to befal you; even the destruction that is at hand.

57. Yea, and why even of yourselves judge ye not what is right?

57. Yea, why do you not gather it from the nature of duty and sin, and of the justice of God.

58. When thou goest with thine adversary to the magistrate, *as thou art* in the way, give diligence that thou mayest be delivered from him; lest he hale thee to the judge; and the judge deliver thee to the officer, and the officer cast thee into prison.

59. I tell thee, thou shalt not depart thence, till thou hast paid the very last mite.

58, 59. Carry it towards God, as thou wouldest do to one that hath a just action against thee at law: Thou shouldest make thy peace with him by all means, before the magistrate take the cause in hand, and judge thee to prison, till thou hast paid all the debt, and deliver thee to the jailor to that end: So make thy peace with God by Christ, by timely and true repentance and faith, before judgment pass on thee the irrevocable sentence.

Note, 1. This was spoken by Christ on another accusation, and Luke sets various things together, like Solomon's proverbs; (unless it were spoken twice by Christ.)

Note, 2. Timely repentance must prevent too late wishes, and utter destruction.

Note, 3. They err, that hence gather that men in hell shall at last come out, by paying the very last mite. The sense of similitudes must not be extended beyond the designed end of him that speaketh, upon any pretence of the strict sense of the words.

CHAP. XIII.

THERE were present at that season, some that told him of the Galileans, whose blood Pilate had mingled with their sacrifices.

1. Some Pilate had killed for stirring up the people against the Roman government.

2. And Jesus answering, said unto them, Suppose ye that these Galileans were sinners above all the Galileans, because they suffered such things? 3. I tell you, Nay: but except ye repent, ye shall all likewise perish.

2, 3. Note, We must not judge them the greatest sinners that suffer most here: The judge on the bench may do more wrong than the thief whom he hangeth: And famous conquerors, than robbers. The day is coming that must set all right. These Jews after suffered much more.

4. Or those eighteen, upon whom the tower of Siloam fell, and slew them, think ye that they were sinners above all men that dwelt in Jerusalem? 5. I tell you, Nay: but except ye repent, ye shall all likewise perish.

4, 5. Note, Worse did befal the other Jews.

6. Ye spake also this parable: A certain man had a fig-tree planted in his vineyard, and he came and sought fruit thereon, and found none. 7. Then said he unto the dresser of his vineyard, Behold, these three years I come seeking fruit on this fig-tree, and find none: cut it down, why cumbereth it the ground? 8. And he answering, said unto him, Lord, let it alone this year also, till I shall dig about it, and dung *it*: 9. And if it bear fruit, *well:* and if not, *then* after that, thou shalt cut it down.

6, 7, &c. Christ had three years preached to the obstinate Jews.

10. And he was teaching in one of the synagogues on the sabbath: 11. And behold, there was a woman which had a spirit of infirmity eighteen years, and was bowed together, and could in no wise lift up *herself.*

10, 11. Satan was the executioner of her disease.

12. And when Jesus saw her, he called *her* to him, and said unto her, Woman thou art loosed from thine infirmity. 13. And he laid *his* hands on her: and immediately she was made straight, and glorified God.

12, 13. By divine power.

14. And the ruler of the synagogue answered with indignation, because that Jesus had healed on the sabbath-day, and said unto the people, There are six days in which men ought to work: in them therefore come, and be healed, and not on the sabbath-day.

15. The Lord then answered him, and said, Thou hypocrite, doth not each one of you on the sabbath loose his ox or *his* ass from the stall, and lead *him* away to watering? 16. And ought not this woman being a daughter of Abraham, whom Satan hath bound, lo these eighteen years, be loosed from this bond on the sabbath-day?

14, 15, 16. Note, It is the part of hypocrites to

set up ceremony and circumstances against moral duties, (or necessary good works) to body or soul.

17. And when he had said these things, all his adversaries were ashamed: and all the people rejoiced for all the glorious things that were done by him.

17. His reason and his miracle convinced the common people of the shameful error of that ceremonious rule.

18. Then said he, Unto what is the kingdom of God like? and whereunto shall I resemble it? 19. It is like a grain of mustard-seed, which a man took and cast into his garden, and it grew, and waxed a great tree: and the fowls of the air lodged in the branches of it. 20. And again he said, Whereunto shall I liken the kingdom of God? 21. It is like leaven, which a woman took and hid in three measures of meal, till the whole was leavened.

18, 19, &c. Note, Though Christ's flock was little at first, the kingdoms of the world were after to become his kingdom, and nations to be discipled and baptised.

22. And he went through the cities and villages, teaching and journeying towards Jerusalem. 23. Then said one unto him, Lord, are there few that be saved? And he said unto them, 24. Strive to enter in at the strait gate: for many I say unto you will seek to enter in, and shall not be able.

22, 23, 24. Instead of inquiring, How many? do thou labour to be one: And know, that the gate is strait: A life of faith and holiness must cost men sufferings in the flesh; therefore do not hastily wish and seek, but strive and spare no pains or cost: For many that seek erroneously, or slothfully, and, as hypocrites, give God but the second place, shall never be saved.

25. When once the master of the house is risen up, and hath shut to the door, and ye begin to stand without, and to knock at the door, saying, Lord, Lord, open unto us; and he shall answer, and say unto you, I know you not whence you are: 26. Then shall ye begin to say, We have eaten and drunk in thy presence, and thou hast taught in our streets. 27. But he shall say, I tell you, I know you not whence you are; depart from me all ye workers of iniquity.

25, 26, 27. All would be saved, and cry for mercy, when it is too late; therefore strive without delay: And then all pretences of familiarity with Christ, or clergy, or church-privileges, will save no unsanctified man.

28. There shall be weeping and gnashing of teeth, when ye shall see Abraham, and Isaac, and Jacob, and all the prophets in the kingdom of God, and you *yourselves* thrust out.

28. It will increase your torment, to see those that never saw and heard what you have done, to be in heaven, and you thrust out to hell for your unbelief and wickedness.

29. And they shall come from the east, and *from* the west, and from the north, and *from* the south, and shall sit down in the kingdom of God. 30. And behold, there are last which shall be first, and there are first which shall be last.

29, 30. The faithful shall be received from all parts of the earth: And some that shall be born and called long hence, shall be more excellent persons, and have a more glorious crown, than many that are called now; and when you Jews are rejected, who were a church before them.

31. The same day there came certain of the Pharisees, saying unto him, Get thee out, and depart hence: for Herod will kill thee. 32. And he said unto them, Go ye and tell that fox, Behold, I cast out devils, and I do cures to-day and to-morrow, and the third day I shall be perfected.

31, 32. Note, He likens Herod to a fox for subtilty and cruelty. This example of Christ will not justify any contumelious language against kings; though they, that are called to it, may plainly and humbly tell them of their sin and danger, regarding their due honour. And historians may truly describe them when they are dead.

33. Nevertheless, I must walk to-day and to-morrow, and the day following: for it cannot be that a prophet perish out of Jerusalem.

33. Whatever Herod do, I shall do my work, and finish it; and shall not suffer by Herod in Galilee, which is his jurisdiction, but at Jerusalem, the place of killing prophets.

34. O Jerusalem, Jerusalem, which

killest the prophets, and stonest them that are sent unto thee: how often would I have gathered thy children together, as a hen *doth gather* her brood under *her* wings, and ye would not?

34. O sinful, miserable Jerusalem! how oft would I have gathered thy whole city and nation (old and young) into my bosom of love, and my church, by making you my disciples: as tenderly as a hen doth gather and love her chickens; not casting out your children, but taking in your nation, as God did before: if you had not cut off yourselves by unbelief, and obstinate rejecting the grace offered to your nation?

35. Behold, your house is left unto you desolate: And verily I say unto you, ye shall not see me, until the time come when ye shall say, Blessed *is* he that cometh in the name of the Lord.

35. Your temple which you glory in, shall shortly be demolished, and your city destroyed: And I tell you, that you shall not rejoice in the salvation of the Messiah, for whom you wait; till you learn to honour me with Hosannas, and to welcome them that preach my gospel to you.

CHAP. XIV.

AND it came to pass, as he went into the house of one of the chief Pharisees to eat bread on the sabbath-day, that they watched him. 2. And behold, there was a certain man before him, which had the dropsy. 3. And Jesus answering spake unto the lawyers and Pharisees, saying, Is it lawful to heal on the sabbath-day? 4. And they held their peace. And he took *him,* and healed him, and let *him* go.

1, 2, &c. Note, Christ chose so usually to heal on the sabbath, that it seems he purposely chose that time, to shew them what work should be preferred. He would not forbear doing good, to avoid the offence of erroneous hypocrites.

5. And answered them, saying, which of you shall have an ass, or an ox fallen into a pit, and will not straightway pull him out on the sabbath-day? 6. And they could not answer him again to these things?

5, 6. They could not confute his plain reason; (But the wranglers of this age can answer any thing.)

7. And he put forth a parable to those which were bidden, when he marked how they chose out the chief rooms; saying unto them, 8. When thou art bidden of any man to a wedding, sit not down in the highest room: lest a more honourable man than thou be bidden of him. 9. And he that bade thee and him, come and say to thee, Give this man place; and thou begin with shame to take the lowest room. 10. But when thou art bidden, go and sit down in the lowest room: that when he that bade thee cometh, he may say unto thee, Friend, go up higher: then shalt thou have worship in the presence of them that sit at meat with thee.

7, 8, &c. Note, Christ disdained not to give rules of decency for civil conversation, when the virtue of humility, or the vice of pride are concerned therein.

11. For whosoever exalteth himself, shall be abased; and he that humbleth himself, shall be exalted.

11. God will exalt the humble, and abase the proud, and therefore we must humble ourselves.

12. Then said he also to him that bade him, When thou makest a dinner or a supper call not thy friends, nor thy brethren, neither thy kinsmen, nor *thy* rich neighbours; lest they also bid thee again, and a recompence be made thee. 13. But when thou makest a feast, call the poor, the maimed, the lame, the blind; 14. And thou shalt be blessed; for they cannot recompense thee: for thou shalt be recompensed at the resurrection of the just.

12, 13, &c. It is good in its season to make feasts of amity, and to rejoice with friends; but to avoid prodigality, let thy most usual feastings be feasts of charity; and in them it is the poor that thou must feast, and from God that thou must expect thy reward.

Note, Some hence infer, that there is no reward till the resurrection: But in scripture the resurrection is oft taken for the life after this, even before the resurrection of the body.

Note, Christ oft forbids things in absolute words, when he meaneth but comparatively: So here, feast not rich friends, that is, not so much as the poor.

15. And when one of them that

CHAP. XIV. ST. LUKE. 159

sat at meat with him, heard these things, he said unto him, Blessed *is* he that shall eat bread in the kingdom of God.

15. They will be happy, that shall live to see, and rejoice in the kingdom of the Messiah when he cometh.

16. Then said he unto him, A certain man made a great supper, and bade many : 17. And sent his servant at supper-time to say to them that were bidden, Come, for all things are now ready.

16, 17, &c. Note, God sent his Son And the gospel to Jews, and invited them into the kingdom of the Messiah: and bade his ministers tell them, that Christ was come, and all is ready on his part. He is a sufficient Saviour, and none shall perish for want of the performance of his part (antecedent.)

18. And they all with one *consent* began to make excuse. The first said unto him, I have bought a piece of ground, and I must needs go and see it: I pray thee have me excused. 19. And another said, I have bought five yoke of oxen, and I go to prove them: I pray thee have me excused. 20. And another said, I have married a wife, and therefore I cannot come.

18, 19, 20. All seemed to them sufficient reasons. And so you Jews, that wish for the kingdom of God, prefer your worldly interest; and for that, refuse it when it is come, (and so do all ungodly men indeed.)

21. So that servant came and shewed his lord these things. Then the master of the house being angry, said to his servant, Go out quickly into the streets and lanes of the city, and bring in hither the poor and the maimed, and the halt, and the blind. 22. And the servant said, Lord, it is done as thou hast commanded, and yet there is room.

21, 22. God was angry with the Jews, and sent his ministers to call the Gentiles, whom the Jews despised as profane.

23. And the Lord said unto the servant, Go out into the high-ways, and hedges, and compel them to come in, that my house may be filled.

23. Go to the most barbarous remote nations, and call them into the church, and be importunate with them, and take no denial, that my church may be Catholic and enlarged.

24. For I say unto you, that none of those men which were bidden, shall taste of my supper.

24. Those refusing Jews, that were first invited, shall not come into the church of Christ.

25. And there went great multitudes with him: and he turned and said unto them, 26. If any man come to me, and hate not his father, and mother, and wife, and children, and brethren, and sisters, yea, and his own life also, he cannot be my disciple.

25, 26. If he love them not less than my kingdom, and cannot for it forsake them: as men do a hated thing.

Note, This disobligeth none from natural affection and duty; but Christ must be preferred.

27. And whosoever doth not bear his cross, and come after me, cannot be my disciple.

27. He that cannot suffer for me, and for salvation, but sets more by his life, can be no true disciple of mine.

28. For which of you intending to build a tower, sitteth not down first, and counteth the cost, whether he have *sufficient* to finish *it*? 29. Lest haply after he hath laid the foundation, and is not able to finish *it*, all that behold *it*, begin to mock him, 30. Saying, This man began to build and was not able to finish. 31. Or what king going to make war against another king, sitteth not down first and consulteth whether he be able with ten thousand to meet him that cometh against him with twenty thousand? 32. Or else, while the other is yet a great way off, he sendeth an ambassage, and desireth conditions of peace.

28, 29, &c. All wise men will consider, what it will cost them to finish before they begin.

33. So likewise, Whosoever he be of you, that forsaketh not all that he hath, he cannot be my disciple.

33. If he prefer not the kingdom of heaven before all worldly interest, and forsake not all

comparatively in esteem and resolution now, and in act when he is called to it.

34. Salt *is* good: but if the salt have lost its savour, wherewith shall it be seasoned? 35. It is neither fit for the land, nor yet for the dunghill; *but* men cast it out. He that hath ears to hear, let him hear.

34, 35. Ye are the salt of this corrupted world: But if you, my disciples, especially preachers, should apostatize, you would be the vilest and most hopeless men on earth; despised, and cast out by God and man: Therefore count your cost, before you undertake the sacred ministry, or Christian profession.

CHAP. XV.

THEN drew near unto him all the publicans and sinners for to hear him. 2. And the Pharisees and scribes murmured, saying, This man receiveth sinners, and eateth with them. 3. And he spake this parable unto them, saying, 4. What man of you having an hundred sheep, if he lose one of them, doth not leave the ninety and nine in the wilderness, and go after that which is lost, until he find it? 5. And when he hath found *it*, he layeth *it* on his shoulders, rejoicing. 6. And when he cometh home, he calleth together *his* friends and neighbours, saying unto them, Rejoice with me, for I have found my sheep which was lost.

1, 2, &c. Should not I do more for a lost sinner than you would do for a lost sheep?

7. I say unto you, that likewise joy shall be in heaven over one sinner that repenteth more than over ninety and nine just persons, which need no repentance.

7. The heavenly society rejoice over one converted sinner, more than over many that need no conversion from a state of sin, (though they need daily sorrow for daily failings.)
Note, More joy signifieth not more love to that person: But Christ speaketh of the angels, after the manner of men, that are most affected with unexpected things, and after sorrow most rejoice.

8. Either what woman having ten pieces of silver, if she lose one piece, doth not light a candle, and sweep the house, and seek diligently till she find *it*? 9. And when she hath found *it*, she calleth *her* friends and *her* neighbours together, saying, Rejoice with me, for I have found the piece which I had lost. 10. Likewise I say unto you, There is joy in the presence of the angels of God, over one sinner that repenteth.

8, 9, 10. Note, 1. Oh what love do we owe to angels, who so much love us? Why do we not desire their company more, than that of this wicked world?
Angels' love is but a copy of God's love: And shall we distrust, fear, and fly from love itself? 2. Angels and good men rejoice at a sinner's conversion: Devils and wicked men are against it. How contrary are these; 3. Do angels rejoice at the conversion of a sinner? What joy should the converted themselves then have in it? 4 Unconverted sinners gratify devils, and deny angels the joy of love.

11. And he said, a certain man had two sons: 12. And the younger of them said to *his* father, Father, give me the portion of goods that falleth *to me*. And he divided unto them *his* living. 13. And not many days after, the younger son gathered all together, and took his journey into a far country, and there wasted his substance with riotous living.

11, 12, 13. Note, 1. Foolish sinners had rather have their concerns in their own hands, than in God's. Note, 2. When it is left to themselves, it is soon wasted. Note, 3. Riotous flesh-pleasing is the destructive sin. Note, 4. When sinners go from God their Father, they go to destruction.

14. And when he had spent all, there arose a mighty famine in that land; and he began to be in want. 15. And he went and joined himself to a citizen of that country; and he sent him into his fields to feed swine. 16. And he would fain have filled his belly with the husks that the swine did eat: and no man gave unto him.

14, 15, 16. He hired himself a servant to feed swine, to prevent famishing; and they would not let him fill his belly with the cods of the crab tree, which was the swine's meat.
Note, 1. Worldly treasure will soon be spent. Note, 2. Foolish sinners will submit to the basest servitude, and be attendants of swine, rather than

CHAP. XV.   ST. LUKE.   161

return to God. Note, 3. All worldly hopes and helps will fail ungodly prodigals at last.

17. And when he came to himself, he said, How many hired servants of my father's have bread enough and to spare, and I perish with hunger?

17. Note, 1. Prodigal sinners are beside themselves. 2. Conversion is a man's coming to himself, or his right wits. 3. It is consideration, specially of a man's own safety and interest, which bringeth a man to himself. 4. Utter distress and necessity is oft needful to drive home sinners unto God, when they see that there is no other way of hope. 5. And the consideration that the poorest Christian, is in a far better condition than the prodigal; They have all, and he hath nothing.

18. I will arise, and go to my father, and will say unto him, Father, I have sinned against heaven, and before thee, 19. And am no more worthy to be called thy son: make me as one of thy hired servants.

18, 19. Note, 1. Conversion beginneth in a purpose to return to God (though at first constrained by necessity.) 2. It worketh by a penitent confession of sin, and utter unworthiness. 3. It would be glad of the lowest place in God's church, and of the lowest terms of mercy.

20. And he arose, and came to his father. But when he was yet a great way off, his father saw him, and had compassion, and ran, and fell on his neck, and kissed him.

20. Note, 1. True purposes will appear in practice and performance: They stop not in sluggish wishes, but arise and go to God. 2. God is readier to meet and receive sinners than they are to return to him. 3. He surpriseth returning sinners with kindness, and embraces them who expected frowns and wrath, and useth them not after their desert. 4. Though necessity and self-love begin conversion, God's love meeteth such and perfecteth it. 5. God is reconcileable to the sinner, by his goodness though not to his sin.

21. And the son said unto him, Father, I have sinned against heaven, and in thy sight, and am no more worthy to be called thy son.

21. Note, Our own humble and penitent confessions, must go before God's forgiveness and entertainment.

22. But the father said to his servants, Bring forth the best robe, and put *it* on him, and put a ring on his hand, and shoes on *his* feet.

22. Note, God findeth sinners in shameful rags, and misery, but clotheth them as his children with righteousness and holiness.

23. And bring hither the fatted calf, and kill *it*; and let us eat and be merry.

23. Let us feast and rejoice for the return of a prodigal son.

24. For this my son was dead, and is alive again; he was lost, and is found. And they began to be merry.

*24. Note, The state of sin is a lost condition, and a converted sinner is found and recovered; it is a dead condition, and conversion is a reviving. It giveth the life of grace in order to the life of glory.
God speaketh of himself as rejoicing in a sinner's conversion. How little cause then have such to doubt whether God will receive them? Ques. How is God called a Father to wicked prodigals? Answ. As his nature is love itself, and as he made man's nature capable of happiness, and as he hath conditionally pardoned all through Christ.*

25. Now his elder son was in the field: and as he came and drew nigh to the house, he heard music and dancing. 26. And he called one of the servants, and asked what these things meant. 27. And he said unto him, Thy brother is come; and thy father hath killed the fatted calf, because he hath received him safe and sound.

25, 26, 27. Thy Father hath received him with joy.

28. And he was angry, and would not go in: therefore came his father out, and entreated him.

*28. He envied his brother's entertainment, and was offended with his father's love and mercy.
Note, 1. The elder brother is the Jew, (who not only in his unbelief despiseth the Gentiles, but) when converted to Christ, is hardly brought to communion with the Gentiles. And also all that have from their childhood served God, and are ready to grudge at the entertainment of wicked men converted. Note, 2. There is in the best of us, though we need God's mercy ourselves, a disposition to envy his grace to others. Note, 3. God is put to bear with the faults of his children, and in mercy to stoop to them in their envy and quarrelsomeness with others. Note, 4. There is a sinful esteem of their own goodness, that inclineth God's own servants even to withdraw and separate from his house, because he entertaineth returning prodigals. Thus God is put to bear with all.*

2.   M

29. And he answering said to his father, Lo, these many years do I serve thee, neither transgressed I at any time thy commandment, and yet thou never gavest me a kid, that I might make merry with my friends :

29. Note, We be apt to over-value our own service of God, and to under-value his mercy.

30. But as soon as this thy son was come, which hath devoured thy living with harlots, thou hast killed for him the fatted calf.

30. Note, 1. Even good men are apt to grudge at God's mercy to sinners, and would not have him so gracious to them as he is; and they are not so ready to forgive it, but upbraid others with sin, which God doth not upbraid them with, who hateth it more than we can do. 2. Were we in the hands of our best brethren, we should speed worse than in God's hands.

31. And he said unto him, Son, thou art ever with me, and all that I have is thine.

31. Note, 1. Obedient children are always with God, and in his favour. 2. What great happiness doth it signify to say, All that I have is thine? that is, all that thou art fit for, and that is fit for thee. 3. God giveth suddener joy oft-times to returning prodigals, than to his children that have been true to him from their youth. 4. Yet the constant safety, happiness, and peace, of those long obedient children, is a greater blessing and good, than those sudden joys of converted sinners.

32. It was meet that we should make merry, and be glad: for this thy brother was dead, and is alive again: and was lost, and is found.

32. Note, God is pleased to reason his froward children out of their envious, self-esteeming, censorious, separating, quarrelsome distempers, and not to let them go, and take them at the worst. He that will pardon the wicked life of a penitent prodigal, will not rigorously despise a froward wrangling child. And rulers and pastors, that learn of God, will do so too, and not as Satan's ministers, abhor the faithful, and aggravate their infirmities, and cast them out of the church, while they connive at the ungodly, and encourage them.

This parable is very instructive to bad and good, and very comfortable to the truly penitent and converted: And speaketh God's mercy to the Gentiles, against the froward, self-esteeming Christian Jews.

CHAP. XVI.

AND he said also unto his disciples, There was a certain rich man which had a steward : and the same was accused unto him that he had wasted his goods. 2. And he called him, and said unto him, How is it that I hear this of thee? give an account of thy stewardship: for thou mayest be no longer steward.

1, 2. Note, We are all God's stewards, our time and blessings are his goods, of which we must shortly give account, and shall here be no longer stewards.

3. Then the steward said within himself, what shall I do? for my lord taketh away from me the stewardship : I cannot dig, to beg I am ashamed.

3. Note, 1. Nature teacheth all men, in danger and misery to save themselves, and study which way they may escape, and be provided for. 2. There is somewhat for ourselves to do for our own welfare. 3. We must think first, what is not to be trusted to, and what way we must not take, before we think what way to trust and take to. I cannot dig, &c. We cannot save ourselves, and the world cannot save us, therefore to trust to those, we are sure will deceive us, that is not the way.

4. I am resolved what to do, that when I am put out of the stewardship, they may receive me into their houses.

4. I will make me friends that will receive me when I am cast off.

Note, 1. When we are sure no other way will save us, and have found the only way that will. self-love and reason should soon resolve us what to do, and what to trust to.

2. The way to be resolved on, is that which will help us, when all others fail.

5. So he called every one of his lord's debtors unto him, and said unto the first, How much owest thou unto my lord? 6. And he said, An hundred measures of oil. And he said unto him, Take thy bill, and sit down quickly, and write fifty. 7. Then said he to another, And how much owest thou? And he said, An hundred measures of wheat, And he said unto him, Take thy bill, and write fourscore.

5, 6, 7. Note, They were ready for their commodity to join in the fraud.

8. And the lord commended the unjust steward, because he had done wisely: for the children of this

world are in their generation wiser than the children of light.

8. Note, His lord that hated his falsehood, yet commended his wit. 2. O that we had as much wit and care, and diligence for our souls' everlasting welfare, as false worldly men have for this vain world!

9. And I say unto you, Make to yourselves friends of the mammon of unrighteousness: that when ye fail, they may receive you into everlasting habitations.

9. It is counsel of great importance to you, so to use your time and estates, which worldly men abuse to sin, that when you must shortly and certainly die, and leave all your wealth behind you, ye may be received into the everlasting heavenly mansions.

Note, 1. The wealth, that by the wicked is abused to damnation, may, by believers, be used to salvation. 2. All this world will fail and forsake us. 3. It is not those that we do good to, but yet it is God, for the good we do them, that will receive us into heaven. 4. This is a testimony of the soul's immortality, and of the life to come: When we leave this world, we are received into everlasting habitations.

10. He that is faithful in that which is least, is faithful also in much: and he that is unjust in the least, is unjust also in much.

10. God will much judge men according to their use of the little things of this world, and will judge them meet for the great things of glory that have used these well: But he will judge them unmeet for heavenly felicity, that could not use well the small things of this transitory life.

11. If therefore ye have not been faithful in the unrighteous mammon, who will commit to your trust the true *riches?*

11. Do you think God will judge you meet for heaven, that were false in your use of earthly things?

12. And if ye have not been faithful in that which is another man's, who shall give you that which is your own?

12. And if ye have proved false and untrusty in your stewardship, and use of God's entrusted mercies in this life of trial, where you had no assurance to stay an hour, do you think God will place such, as proprietors, in the everlasting kingdom.

13. No servant can serve two masters: for either he will hate the one, and love the other; or else he will hold to the one, and despise the other. Ye cannot serve God and mammon.

13. A divided heart between God and the world, is false to God and to itself: Ye cannot be true Christians and worldlings too.

14. And the Pharisees also who were covetous, heard all these things: and they derided him.

14. Note, The love of riches rises up against holy and mortifying doctrine, with hatred and scorn.

15. And he said unto them, Ye are they which justify yourselves before men; but God knoweth your hearts; for that which is highly esteemed amongst men, is abomination in the sight of God.

15. You applaud one another, and keep up a worldly reputation, but God seeth all the evil of your hearts: and he abhorreth the covetous, whom you bless, and all proud and prosperous worldlings, when they are highest in men's esteem.

16. The law and the prophets *were* until John: since that time the kingdom of God is preached, and every man presseth into it.

16. Till John's days, the law and the prophets, that darkly foretold the kingdom of God as afar off, were the chief teachers of the church: but since John's preaching that this kingdom is at hand, multitudes gladly receive that tidings, and crowd or press into it with earnestness.

17. And it is easier for heaven and earth to pass, than one tittle of the law to fail.

17. The law is God's true word, and shall never prove false: The natural moral part shall continue; the ceremonious part the types and prophecies, pass not away unfulfilled: They all pointed unto Christ, who fulfilleth them, though he abrogate them.

18. Whosoever putteth away his wife, and marrieth another, committeth adultery, and whosoever marrieth her that is put away from *her* husband, committeth adultery.

18. See Matt. v. 32.

19. There was a certain rich man which was clothed in purple, and fine linen, and fared sumptuously every day.

19. Note, This is the description of a sensualist that liveth after the flesh, To be clothed in purple and silk, and to have every day a costly table of delightful meat and drink. Sensual flesh-please ing is the common damning sin; and riches are the fuel of fleshly desires.

20. And there was a certain beggar named Lazarus, which was laid at his gate, full of sores. 21. And desiring to be fed with the crumbs which fell from the rich man's table: moreover the dogs came and licked his sores.

20, 21. Note, 1. It is like he had some relief there, else he would not have lain there. 2. The worst men are not usually most afflicted in this life. 3. Rich fleshly men make too great a difference between themselves and the poor, and think their superfluities, and sumptuous delicious fare, must be preferred before the necessities of their poor brethren. 4. Dogs help him, whom the rich sensualist would not help in any competent degree.

22. And it came to pass that the beggar died, and was carried by the angels into Abraham's bosom: the rich man also died and was buried.

22. Note, Though this be a parable, Christ would not by it insinuate false doctrine: Therefore it sheweth, that the soul doth not die with the body, but goeth to joy or misery. Abraham is there alive and Lazarus in his bosom; (before the final resurrection.) 2. Death quickly levelleth rich and poor; the voluptuous and the afflicted. 3. Angels that guard the just in life, refuse not at death to serve their souls as their convoy unto happiness. 4. To be buried in a grave, and rot to dust, is the best that the pampered flesh of the wicked can expect.

23. And in hell he lift up his eyes, being in torments, and seeth Abraham afar off, and Lazarus in his bosom.

23. Note, 1. Such notice as spirits have, is called seeing. 2. The souls of the wicked pass to hell torments. 3. Joyful felicity is called Abraham's bosom, to a Jew. Some think nations are joined in happiness or misery hereafter, as rewarded in the relations in which they did good or evil.

24. And he cried and said, Father Abraham, have mercy on me, and send Lazarus, that he may dip the tip of his finger in water and cool my tongue; for I am tormented in this flame.

24. Note, 1. The parable speaketh metaphorically, of souls, as if they had tongues, which signifieth no more than, they have a torment suitable to their kind. 2. Voluptuous rich men would shortly beg even for a very little, and that of those whom they here despised, if they could help them. 3. By flame is meant a means of torment.

25. But Abraham said, Son, remember that thou in thy life-time receivedst thy good things, and likewise Lazarus evil things: but now he is comforted, and thou art tormented.

25. Thou hadst that which thou didst choose: Thou didst prefer fleshly pleasure before the hopes of heaven, and thou hast had them. And Lazarus submitted to sufferings on earth for the hopes of heaven, which he preferred, and he hath now his choice.

Note, 1. God doth not damn any man for his being rich, but for being sensual, and preferring self pleasing before his salvation: Nor doth he save any for having suffered in this world, but for preferring God and heaven before prosperity and ease; and for suffering to attain salvation. 2. The next life will set all strait, and tell us who made the wisest choice, and were indeed the happy men.

26. And besides all this, between us and you there is a great gulf fixed: so that they which would pass from hence to you, cannot; neither can they pass to us, that *would come* from thence.

26. Heaven and hell may have some knowledge of each others' case, but no access for converse: Damnation is a remediless state: The damned may wish for ease and help, and mercy, but shall have none.

27. Then he said, I pray thee, therefore, father, that thou wouldst send him to my Father's house: 28. For I have five brethren; that he may testify unto them, lest they also come into this place of torment.

27. O send him to my brethren on earth, to tell them what I suffer; and why: that they may not come hither, who are yet recoverable, and in a state of hope, though my case be desperate.

Note, Whether the damned retain any love to, and care of their brethren on earth, or whether this be spoken only to explain their condition here, is uncertain.

29. Abraham saith unto him, They have Moses and the prophets; let them hear them.

29. The God of wisdom and power hath determined of the way and means of converting men, which is by his word and ministers, and not by messengers from the dead. If they will be saved, it must be by God's appointed means, and not any other.

30. And he said, Nay, father Abraham: but if one went unto them from the dead, they will repent.

CHAP. XVII. ST. LUKE. 165

30. Sure such an apparition would convince them, and affright them to repentance.

31. And he said unto him, If they hear not Moses and the prophets, neither will they be persuaded, though one rose from the dead.

31. (If it were so, God will not change his way of salvation to persuade wilful, sensual sinners.) But it is not so; for God's word and ministers are a more suitable means of converting sinners, than a man would be from the dead: God will bless his own means: And affrighting men will not renew their natures, and kindle in them a love to God and holiness. And how little should we know whether one from the dead were a devil, or credible messenger? and whether he said true or false? Should he dwell with us as long as ministers do, men would again despise and persecute him: Should he come but once, it would not equal the daily solicitations of God's ministers. Will one from the dead heal all diseases with a word, and raise the dead, and send down the Holy Ghost on all the faithful, and give such proof of his truth, as the prophets, and Christ, and the apostles have done? Will his words have more light and power, than God's word hath? Or would not your fleshly brethren accuse him of scandalising and slandering the soul of their noble deceased brother, for telling them he is in hell, and persecute him, if he were within their power.

Note, Christians, remember with thankfulness, that you have a far better means for your salvation, than one from the dead would be; and use it accordingly.

CHAP. XVII.

THEN said he unto the disciples, It is impossible but that offences will come: but woe *unto him* through whom they come. 2. It were better for him that a millstone were hanged about his neck, and he cast into the sea, than that he should offend one of these little ones.

1, 2. It is a thing that will certainly come to pass, and must be expected, that divers hindrances and oppositions will meet men to keep them from faith and holiness, and that by divers sorts of persons: But the sin of such hinderers is heinous, tending to oppose the gospel of salvation, and to damn souls; and woe to them that by their malignity do thus serve Satan against Christ. 2. They may blindly flatter themselves by malice, or false reasoning, or worldly interest; but their case is more miserable, than if they were drowned in the depth of the sea.

3. Take heed to yourselves: If thy brother trespass against thee, rebuke him; and if he repent, forgive him. 4. And if he trespass against thee seven times in a day, and seven times in a day turn again to thee, saying, I repent; thou shalt forgive him.

3, 4. Take heed that you hinder not any man in the matters of his salvation, by persuasion, example, or persecution: But if any man offend you by sin, or injury, reprove him; and if he repent, forgive him.

Note, 1. The meaning is not, that the mock-repentance of one that will seven times a day commit gross sins, or injury, and say, I repent, when it is notorious that he doth not, should be forgiven for an hypocritical word: But that true repentance should be accepted, how oft soever men offend.

Qu. Must we not forgive men, unless they confess and repent? Answ. There are several degrees of forgiveness: 1. We must so far forgive the impenitent, as to love them as men, and desire and endeavour their good, without revenge. 2. But we must forgive none but the penitent so far, as to take them into the special love, which belongeth to Christian friends. But then it supposeth that the fault be gross sin, and not an injury by tolerable error, which he is not convinced of, nor can be.

5. And the apostles said unto the Lord, Increase our faith.

5. Seeing it is by faith that we must do miracles, and must be saved, give us more faith.

6. And the Lord said, If ye had faith as a grain of mustard seed, ye might say unto this sycamine tree, Be thou plucked up by the root, and be thou planted in the sea; and it should obey you.

6. If your faith be true, though but small, no difficulty shall prevail against it, nor any miracle be too hard, when God by his Spirit shall move you to it, who will be the chooser of miracles.

7. But which of you having a servant ploughing, or feeding cattle, will say unto him by and by, when he is come from the field, Go, and sit down to meat? 8. And will not rather say unto him, Make ready wherewith I may sup, and gird thyself, and serve me till I have eaten and drunken; and afterward thou shalt eat and drink? 9. Doth he thank that servant because he did the things that were commanded him? I trow not. 10. So likewise ye, when ye shall have done all those things which are commanded you, say, We are unprofitable

servants: we have done that which was our duty to do.

7, 8, &c. But see that neither your faith nor miracles puff you up, or make you think too highly of yourselves: Nor must you desire it to make you conspicuous in the world, but for your master's service, which is your duty, and by which you must not think that you are profitable to him, but obedient to him for your own and other men's good. If you have servants yourselves, you will not let them prefer themselves and their own interest, before you and your commands: So you, when you have preached and cast out devils and done your best, think not that you have profited God, and thereby deserve to be dignified for the merit of your work; but say, we did but our duty, and the privilege and benefit is our own and others.

Note, 1. It is hard to analize Luke's words, because it is uncertain when he sets them together that were spoken together; and when he joineth words spoken on divers occasions.

2. When Christ judgeth the unprofitable servant to utter darkness, and yet here calleth all unprofitable; the sense is, that no man can add any thing to God, or profit him; nor is he a receiver, but a giver; no angel can merit of him in commutative justice. But we must be profitable to one another, and ourselves, by improving God's mercies: And Christ so loveth his own, as that he will reward this, as if it profited himself.

11. And it came to pass as he went to Jerusalem, that he passed through the midst of Samaria and Galilee. 12. And as he entered into a certain village, there met him ten men that were lepers, which stood afar off: 13. And they lifted up *their* voices, and said, Jesus Master, have mercy on us. 14. And when he saw *them,* he said unto them, Go shew yourselves unto the priests. And it came to pass, that as they went, they were cleansed.

11, 12, &c. Note, He intimated thereby a purpose to heal them: (And he bid them use the ill-called corrupt priests:) But whether he sent them to the priests as those that were to judge of leprosies before the cleansing, or to shew that they were cleansed, is doubtful; though the first seems to me most probable.

15. And one of them, when he saw that he was healed, turned back and with a loud voice glorified God. 16. And fell down on *his* face at his feet, giving him thanks: and he was a Samaritan.

15, 16. He judged it no breach of Christ's command to return first to him, and glorify God, and give him thanks.

17. And Jesus answering said, Were there not ten cleansed? but where *are* the nine? 18. There are not found that returned to give glory to God, save this stranger.

17, 18. This one man, accounted a heretic by the Jews, is the only man of ten that returneth to glorify God for his cure.

Note, Many receive mercies, but few glorify God with true thanksgiving.

19. And he said unto him, Arise, go thy way; thy faith hath made thee whole.

19. Note, This oft-used word of Christ, is against them, that say, that because it is Christ that healeth, or justifieth, it is not faith: As if the office of Christ, and of faith, might not concur hereunto.

20. And when he was demanded of the Pharisees, when the kingdom of God should come; he answered them, and said, The kingdom of God cometh not with observation. 21. Neither shall they say, Lo here, or lo there: for behold, the kingdom of God is within you.

20, 21. You know not what the kingdom of God is: It is not Christ's appearance in visible pomp, as earthly princes reign: It is a moral spiritual kingdom, opposite not to monarchs, but to the kingdom of Satan: As Satan reigneth not visibly by himself, but by corrupt princes and teachers, to do his works, and by his invisible suggestions and his baits, so the kingdom of God is to destroy Satan's kingdom, and to sanctify and save men, not by Christ's visible pompous reign, but by holy rulers and teachers, and by his word and Spirit, and promises and blessings to work on souls.

22. And he said unto the disciples, The days will come when ye shall desire to see one of the days of the Son of Man, and ye shall not see *it.*

22. Days of suffering are not far off, when you will wish for my presence to deliver you, (or, as some, when you shall wish for days, as easy and quiet as these are now,) or others think, though he spake to his disciples, it is the Pharisees or the Jewish nation that he spake to them of.

23. And they shall say to you, See here, or see there: go not after *them,* nor follow *them.* 24. For as the lightning that lightneth out of the one *part* under heaven, shineth unto the other *part* under heaven: so shall also the Son of man be in his day.

23, 24. Believe not them that tell you a deliverer or Christ is in such or such a place. For my kingdom shall not be managed by my personal appearance, but by the light of my word and Spirit, which shall shine from one part of the world to another, as lightning from heaven; [or, my last coming will be like lightning, sudden, and glorious to all men's sight.]

25. But first must he suffer many things, and be rejected of this generation. 26. And as it was in the days of Noe, so shall it be also in the days of the Son of Man. 27. They did eat, they drank, they married wives, they were given in marriage, until the day that Noe entered into the ark: and the flood came and destroyed them all.

25, 26, 27. See Matt. xxiv. Whether the day of Christ be the day of his just destruction of the Jews, or of his reign by the gospel, joined with the fall of them and other enemies, or his last coming, is doubted of by expositors.

28. Likewise also as it was in the days of Lot, they did eat, they drank, they bought, they sold, they planted, they builded: 29. But the same day that Lot went out of Sodom, it rained fire and brimstone from heaven, and destroyed them all: 30. Even thus shall it be in the day when the Son of Man is revealed.

28, 29, 30. Christ's coming, (whether to destroy his enemies, or to judge the world,) will be sudden, unexpected, and terrible.

31. In that day, he which shall be upon the house-top, and his stuff in the house, let him not come down to take it away: and he that is in the field, let him likewise not return back. 32. Remember Lot's wife.

31, 32. Let all go, and be glad to save your lives: Look not back with grief for your losses, lest you speed as Lot's wife did.

33. Whosoever shall seek to save his life, shall lose it; and whosoever shall lose his life, shall preserve it.

33. Self-saving, by forsaking the truth, will prove self-destroying, and venturing and losing life for me, shall prove the surest saving way.

34. I tell you, in that night there shall be two men in one bed: the one shall be taken, and the other shall be left. 35. Two women shall be grinding together; the one shall be taken, and the other left. 36. Two men shall be in the field; the one shall be taken, and the other left.

34, 35. I will carefully separate my own from the rest, and save them, when unbelievers perish, (whether at the end, or sooner.)

37. And they answered and said unto him, Where, Lord? And he said unto them, Wheresoever the body is, thither will the eagles be gathered together.

37. Where shall all these things be done? He said, where those designed to destruction are, thither God's justice will send his executioners. And where his chosen are, there shall be deliverance. See Matt. xxiv.

CHAP. XVIII.

AND he spake a parable unto them, *to this end*, that men ought always to pray, and not to faint;

1. To hold on in earnest importunity and hope, and not to grow cold, and slack, and heartless.

2. Saying, There was in a city a judge which feared not God, neither regarded man. 3. And there was a widow in that city, and she came unto him, saying, Avenge me of mine adversary.

2, 3. Note, Woe to the land that hath such judges. She said, Do me justice against mine adversary.

4. And he would not for a while: but afterward he said within himself, Though I fear not God, nor regard man; 5. Yet because this widow troubleth me, I will avenge her, lest by her continual coming she weary me.

4, 5. Note, Where there is no fear of God, yet avoiding clamour and shame for injustice, may make a judge do justice to the oppressed. But they that come to diabolical malignity, will delight to do mischief, and destroy the just, and will take their wickedness for their glory.

6. And the Lord said, Hear what the unjust judge saith. 7. And shall not God avenge his own elect, which cry day and night unto him,

though he bear long with them? 8. I tell you that he will avenge them speedily. Nevertheless, when the Son of Man cometh, shall he find faith on the earth?

6, 7, 8. Will importunity prevail with a wicked judge? and will not importunate prayer prevail with God to do justice for his chosen, praying people? I tell you, though the time seem long to you, he will make no delay to do them justice in due time.

Note, Importunity moved the man by wearying him; but it procureth mercy from God only, by making us fit receivers of it. Men will despond by impatience, before deliverance cometh.

9. And he spake this parable unto certain which trusted in themselves that they were righteous, and despised others:

9. He thought meet to rebuke those who thought too well of their own goodness, and were too censorious and contemptuous of those that seemed worse than they.

10. Two men went up into the temple to pray; the one a Pharisee, and the other a publican. 11. The Pharisee stood and prayed thus with himself, God, I thank thee, that I am not as other men *are*, extortioners, unjust, adulterers, or even as this publican. 12. I fast twice in the week, I give tithes of all that I possess.

10, 11, 12. The Pharisees' prayer was a boasting of his goodness, and not an humble bewailing of sins and wants. All this was praise-worthy in itself, but much more was necessary in him.

13. And the publican standing afar off, would not lift up so much as his eyes unto heaven, but smote upon his breast, saying, God be merciful to me a sinner.

13. His prayer was in the deep sense of his sin, a humble begging mercy of God; (not with a purpose to go on in sin, but with penitence and conversion, resolving of a new life.)

14. I tell you, this man went down to his house justified *rather* than the other: for every one that exalteth himself, shall be abased; and he that humbleth himself, shall be exalted.

14. God took this for a juster or better man, for his penitent confession than the Pharisee, for all that formal righteousness which he boasted of: For God will exalt the humble, and abase the proud.

(But this supposeth the publican's repentance to be a true conversion, and not mere conviction and confessing in fear.)

15. And they brought unto him also infants, that he should touch them: but when *his* disciples saw *it*, they rebuked them. 16. But Jesus called them unto him, and said, Suffer little children to come unto me, and forbid them not: for of such is the kingdom of God. 17. Verily I say unto you, Whosoever shall not receive the kingdom of God as a little child, shall in no wise enter therein.

15, 16, 17. See on Matt. x. 14. xix. 13, 14, 15.

18. And a certain ruler asked him, saying, Good Master, what shall I do to inherit eternal life? 19. And Jesus said unto him, Why callest thou me good? none *is* good save one, *that is* God. 20. Thou knowest the commandments, Do not commit adultery, Do not kill, Do not steal, Do not bear false witness, Honour thy father and thy mother. 21. And he said, All these have I kept from my youth up. 22. Now when Jesus heard these things, he said unto him, Yet lackest thou one thing: sell all that thou hast, and distribute unto the poor, and thou shalt have treasure in heaven: and come, follow me. 23. And when he heard this, he was very sorrowful: for he was very rich.

18, 19, &c. See Matt. xix. 20. and Mark x. 17.

Note, This renunciation of the world is not required by Christ, to a high degree of holiness only, but to the obtaining of eternal life.

Note, Multitudes of nominal Christians go not so far as this worldly Jew; in believing a life eternal, and in care to inherit it, and in doing so much for it, from his youth.

24. And when Jesus saw that he was very sorrowful, he said, How hardly shall they that have riches enter into the kingdom of God! 25. For it is easier for a camel to go through a needle's eye, than for a rich man to enter into the kingdom of God. 26. And they that

heard *it*, said, Who then can be saved?

24, 25, 26. See Matt. xix.
Note, To enter into the kingdom of God, and to be saved, was understood by the hearers to be all one.

27. And he said, the things which are impossible with men, are possible with God.

27. Note, Possibility, though with great difficulty, must make us true seekers, and then we may attain to certainty.

28. Then Peter said, Lo, we have left all, and followed thee. 29. And he said unto them, Verily I say unto you, there is no man that hath left house, or parents, or brethren, or wife, or children for the kingdom of God's sake. 30. Who shall not receive manifold more in this present time, and in the world to come life everlasting.

28, 29, 30. You shall be no losers by me.
Note, The blessings even of suffering Christians in this life, are better than all that they forsake for Christ.

31. Then he took unto him the twelve, and said unto them, Behold, we go up to Jerusalem, and all things that are written by the prophets concerning the Son of Man shall be accomplished. 32. For he shall be delivered unto the Gentiles, and shall be mocked and spitefully entreated, and spitted on: 33. And they shall scourge *him*, and put him to death: and the third day he shall rise again. 34. And they understood none of these things: and this saying was hid from them, neither knew they the things which were spoken.

31, 32, &c. Note, We must not wonder if many of our hearers then are dull of understanding.

35. And it came to pass, that as he was come nigh unto Jericho, a certain blind man sat by the wayside begging. 36. And hearing the multitude pass by, he asked what it meant. 37. And they told him, that Jesus of Nazareth passed by. 38. And he cried, saying, Jesus, thou son of David, have mercy on me. 39. And they which went before, rebuked him, that he should hold his peace: but he cried so much the more, Thou son of David, have mercy on me. 40. And Jesus stood and commanded him to be brought unto him: and when he was come near, he asked him, 41. Saying, What wilt thou that I shall do unto thee? And he said, Lord, that I may receive my sight. 42. And Jesus said unto him, Receive thy sight: thy faith hath saved thee. 43. And immediately he received his sight, and followed him, glorifying God: and all the people when they saw *it*, gave praise unto God.

35, 36, &c. See on Matt. xx. 18, 19, 20. Note, Faith fitteth us to receive mercy; and mercy teacheth us to glorify God.

CHAP. XIX.

AND *Jesus* entered, and passed through Jericho. 2. And behold, *there was* a man named Zaccheus, which was the chief among the publicans, and he was rich. 3. And he sought to see Jesus who he was, and could not for the press, because he was little of stature. 4. And he ran before, and climbed up into a sycamore-tree to see him; for he was to pass that way. 5. And when Jesus came to the place, he looked up and saw him, and said unto him, Zaccheus, make haste, and come down: for to-day I must abide at thy house.

1, 2, &c. Desire, and diligent seeking prepare us for Christ's acceptance and abode with us.

6. And he made haste, and came down, and received him joyfully.

6. Note, He hoped but for a sight of him, and obtained more. Mercy exceedeth the seekers' expectation.

7. And when they saw *it*, they all murmured, saying, that he was gone to be guest with a man that is a sinner.

7. *Note*, As if Christ were not holy and strict enough, because he went to sinners for their salvation.

8. And Zaccheus stood, and said unto the Lord, Behold, Lord, the half of my goods I give to the poor; and if I have taken any thing from any man by false accusation, I restore *him* four-fold.

8. *Note*, 1. This proceeding from faith in Christ, proved him a true convert. 2. False accusation was the publican's notable sin.

9. And Jesus said unto him, This day is salvation come to this house, forasmuch as he also is the son of Abraham.

9. *Note*, 1. Where true faith and conversion cometh, there salvation cometh. 2. All true believers are children of Abraham, that is, of the promise made to Abraham and his seed.

10. For the Son of Man is come to seek and to save that which was lost.

10. To this end came I into the world, to redeem, convert, and save lost sinners.

11. And as they heard these things, he added, and spake a parable, because he was nigh to Jerusalem, and because they thought that the kingdom of God should immediately appear.

11. To take them off such expectations.

12. He said therefore, A certain nobleman went into a far country, to receive for himself a kingdom, and to return.

12. Christ was to go from earth to heaven, to receive his own kingly glory, and to reign there over heaven and earth, and to return to judge men according to their works.

13. And he called his ten servants and delivered them ten pounds, and said unto them, occupy till I come.

13. He giveth men, that profess to be his servants, his gifts and mercies, and commands them to use them faithfully in his service, and do good in his church, and profit others, expecting his return.

14. But his citizens hated him, and sent a message after him, saying, We will not have this man to reign over us.

14. The Jews, to whom he first offered grace, rejected him and his government with scorn.

15. And it came to pass, that when he was returned, having received the kingdom, then he commanded those servants to be called unto him, to whom he had given the money, that he might know how much every man had gained by trading.

15. When he came to exercise judgment over his subjects and servants, he called first those that professed Christianity, to take an account how they had used the blessings of the gospel.

16. Then came the first, saying, Lord, thy pound hath gained ten pounds.

16. Thy grace and gifts have been improved to the profit of many, and to my own increase in holiness.

17. And he said unto him, Well, thou good servant: because thou hast been faithful in a very little, have thou authority over ten cities.

17. Thou shalt have a reward above others, according to thy service.

Note, 1. Christ will praise his faithful servants and their works. 2. He rewardeth them, because they have been faithful, as the moral qualification of the receivers; but not in commutative justice, nor in distributive governing justice, according to the law of innocency, or of Moses, but in distributive paternal justice, according to the law of grace and faith.

18. And the second came saying, Lord, thy pound hath gained five pounds. 19. And he said likewise to him, Be thou also over five cities.

18, 19. Their reward shall be answerable.

20. And another came, saying, Lord, behold, *here is* thy pound which I have kept laid up in a napkin: 21. For I feared thee, because thou art an austere man: thou takest up that thou layedst not down, and reapest where thou didst not sow.

20, 21. Here is thy own: I have wasted none of it: But thou art so severe that I durst not trade with it, lest I should lose it.

22. And he said unto him, Out of thine own mouth will I judge thee, thou wicked servant. Thou knewest that I was an austere man,

CHAP. XIX. ST. LUKE.

taking up that I laid not down, and reaping that I did not sow: 23. Wherefore then gavest not thou my money into the bank, that at my coming I might have required mine own with usury?

22, 23. Note, Wicked men are apt to excuse their sloth, and accuse God's strictness: But out of their own confessions and words shall hypocrites, that profess Christianity, be condemned.

Qu. What usury is it which Christ by this parable seemeth to countenance? Answ. Such as God had not forbidden: To us now all usury is sinful, that is against either justice or charity, or the public good, and no other: For Moses's political law bindeth not us.

24. And he said unto them that stood by, Take from him the pound: and give it to him that hath ten pounds. 25. (And they said unto him, Lord, he hath ten pounds). 26. For I say unto you, that unto every one which hath, shall be given: and from him that hath not, even that he hath shall be taken away from him.

24. Add it to his reward.

25, 26. He that hath gained by his faithful industry, shall be trusted and rewarded with more; and he that unfaithfully neglected to use the mercy trusted with him, shall be deprived of that mercy, gifts, time, &c. which he neglected.

27. But those mine enemies which would not that I should reign over them, bring hither, and slay *them* before me.

27. Those Jews that hated and rejected me, and all such rebellious infidels, shall be destroyed.

28. And when he had thus spoken, he went before, ascending up to Jerusalem. 29. And it came to pass, when he was come nigh to Bethphage and Bethany, at the mount called *the mount* of Olives, he sent two of his disciples, 30. Saying, Go ye into the village over against *you;* in the which at your entering ye shall find a colt tied, whereon yet never man sat: loose him, and bring *him* hither. 31. And if any man ask you, Why do ye loose *him?* thus shall ye say unto him, Because the Lord hath need of him. 32. And they that were sent, went their way, and found even as he had said unto them. 33. And as they were loosing the colt, the owners thereof said unto them, Why loose ye the colt? 34. And they said, The Lord hath need of him.

28, 29, &c. Note, Though Luke name only the colt, that denieth not the ass named by other writers.

See Matt. xxi. 1, 7, 8.

35. And they brought him to Jesus: and they cast their garments upon the colt, and they set Jesus thereon. 36. And as he went, they spread their clothes in the way. 37. And when he was come nigh, even now at the descent of the mount of Olives, the whole multitude of the disciples began to rejoice, and praise God with a loud voice, for all the mighty works that they had seen, 38. Saying, Blessed *be* the King that cometh in the name of the Lord: peace in heaven, and glory in the highest.

37. See on Matt. xxi. 9, 10, 11.

39. And some of the Pharisees from among the multitude said unto him, Master, rebuke thy disciples. 40. And he answered and said unto them, I tell you, that if these should hold their peace, the stones would immediately cry out.

39, 40. They do but what God doth cause them to do, and if they did not, God would have it done, though by miracle.

41. And when he was come near, he beheld the city, and wept over it, 42. Saying, If thou hadst known, even thou, at least in this thy day, the things *which belong* unto thy peace! but now they are hid from thine eyes.

41. O that thou hadst known the things that are necessary to thy own peace and safety, before the day of grace be past. But by thy wilful sin and blindness, they are unknown to thee.

Note, Christ as man, by weeping over self-destroying sinners, sheweth his love and pity, though not equal to that which he exerciseth on his elect whom he will save.

43. For the days shall come upon thee, that thine enemies shall cast

a trench about thee, and compass thee round, and keep thee in on every side. 44. And shall lay thee even with the ground, and thy children within thee: and they shall not leave in thee one stone upon another: because thou knewest not the time of thy visitation.

43, 44. All this was done about thirty-eight years after, by the dreadfullest siege for famine and murder, that any history recordeth.

45. And he went into the temple, and began to cast out them that sold therein, and them that bought, 46. Saying unto them, It is written, My house is the house of prayer: but ye have made it a den of thieves.

45, 46, See Matt. xxi. 12. Note, Christ shewed his authority by reforming; and his zeal even for the temple, while the law stood.

47. And he taught daily in the temple, But the chief priests and the scribes, and the chief of the people sought to destroy him.

47. The priests and rulers were they that were Christ's enemies and persecutors.

48. And could not find what they might do: for all the people were very attentive to hear him.

48. They durst not lay hands on him, because the multitude hearing and admiring him, were as his guard.

CHAP. XX.

AND it came to pass, that on one of those days, as he taught the people in the temple, and preached the gospel, the chief priests and the scribes came upon him, with the elders, 2. And spake unto him, saying, Tell us, by what authority doest thou these things? or who is he that gave thee this authority?

1, 2. Such things are not to be done without authority.

3. And he answered and said unto them, I will also ask you one thing; and answer me: 4. The baptism of John, was it from heaven, or of men? 5. And they reasoned with themselves, saying, If we shall say, From heaven; he will say, Why then believed ye him not? 6. But, and if we say, Of men; all the people will stone us: for they be persuaded that John was a prophet. 7. And they answered, that they could not tell whence *it was*. 8. And Jesus said unto them, Neither tell I you by what authority I do these things.

3, 4, &c. They ought to have known his authority by his miracles. See Matt. xxi.

9. Then began he to speak to the people this parable: A certain man planted a vineyard, and let it forth to husbandmen, and went into a far country for a long time. 10. And at the season, he sent a servant to the husbandmen, that they should give him of the fruit of the vineyard: but the husbandmen beat him, and sent *him* away empty. 11. And again he sent another servant, and they beat him also, and entreated *him* shamefully, and sent *him* away empty. 12. And again he sent the third; and they wounded him also, and cast *him* out. 13. Then said the lord of the vineyard, What shall I do? I will send my beloved son: it may be they will reverence *him* when they see him. 14. But when the husbandmen saw him, they reasoned among themselves, saying, This is the heir: come, let us kill him, that the inheritance may be ours. 15. So they cast him out of the vineyard, and killed *him*. What therefore shall the Lord of the vineyard do unto them? 16. He shall come and destroy these husbandmen, and shall give the vineyard to others. And when they heard *it*, they said, God forbid.

9, 10, &c. The vineyard is the land of Israel; the husbandmen are the Israelites; the owner is God; the messengers are the prophets; the son is Christ, &c. See Matt. xxi.

17. And he beheld them, and said, What is this then that is writ-

CHAP. XX.   ST. LUKE.   173

ten, The stone which the builders rejected, the same is become the head of the corner? 18. Whosoever shall fall upon that stone, shall be broken: but on whomsoever it shall fall, it will grind him to powder.

17, 18. Whoever sins against Christ by unbelief, will perish in his sin: But they that strive against him by malignity and opposition, will fall under his victorious judgment, which will make them the most miserable.

19. And the chief priests and the scribes the same hour sought to lay hands on him; and they feared the people: for they perceived that he had spoken this parable against them.

19. Note, That which is said against their sin, enrageth the impenitent, be it never so true and needful to their conviction.

20. And they watched *him*, and sent forth spies, which should feign themselves just men, that they might take hold of his words, that so they might deliver him unto the power and authority of the governor.

20. Blood-thirsty hypocrites would ensnare him to get some word for which they might accuse him, to the Roman governor, as treason against Cæsar.

Note, How like in all ages are the nature and ways of wicked men! Thus was Naboth used by Jezebel, &c.

21. And they asked him, saying, Master, we know that thou sayest and teachest rightly, neither acceptest thou the person *of any*, but teachest the way of God truly. 22. Is it lawful for us to give tribute unto Cæsar, or no? 23. But he perceived their craftiness, and said unto them, Why tempt ye me? 24. Shew me a penny: whose image and superscription hath it? They answered and said, Cæsar's. 25. And he said unto them, Render therefore unto Cæsar the things which be Cæsar's, and unto God the things which be God's. 26. And they could not take hold of his words before the people: and they marvelled at his answer, and held their peace.

21, 22, &c. Note, There is poison in the seeming kindness of cruel hypocrites; they flatter that they may hurt. Note, It is lawful to put off bloody ensnares with doubtful answers.

27. Then came to him certain of the Sadducees (which deny that there is any resurrection) and they asked him, 28. Saying, Master, Moses wrote unto us, If any man's brother die, having a wife, and he die without children, that his brother should take his wife, and raise up seed unto his brother. 29. There were therefore seven brethren: and the first took a wife, and died without children. 30. And the second took her to wife, and he died childless. 31. And the third took her; and in like manner the seven also. And they left no children, and died. 32. Last of all the woman died also. 33. Therefore in the resurrection, whose wife of them is she: for seven had her to wife.

27, 28, &c. Carnal men, from their own error, do foolishly cavil against the truth which they understand not.

34. And Jesus answering said unto them, The children of this world marry, and are given in marriage: 35. But they which shall be accounted worthy to obtain that world, and the resurrection from the dead, neither marry, nor are given in marriage. 36. Neither can they die any more; for they are equal unto the angels, and are the children of God, being the children of the resurrection.

34, 35, 36. Note, Worthiness of that world, is such a qualification as is required in God's promise. Note, The blessed shall be like the angels, and with them, and be immortal. Note, By the resurrection here is meant the next life, even to separated souls, and not only the resurrection of the body. O why do we not long for such a change!

37. Now that the dead are raised, even Moses shewed at the bush, when he calleth the Lord the God of Abraham, and the God of Isaac, and the God of Jacob. 38. For he is not a God of the dead, but of the living: for all live unto him.

37, 38. See Matt. xxii. He is the Lord and owner of the dead and living: But to be their God, signifieth more, even to be their governor and protector, and their end and portion, and their all.

39. Then certain of the scribes answering said, Master, thou hast well said. 40. And after that, they durst not ask him any question at all.

39, 40. They were out of hope of entrapping him by their questions.

41. And he said unto them, How say they that Christ is David's son? 42. And David himself saith in the book of Psalms, The LORD said unto my Lord, Sit thou on my right hand, 43. Till I make thine enemies thy footstool. 44. David therefore calleth him Lord, how is he then his son?

41, 43, &c. See Matt. xxii.

45. Then in the audience of all the people, he said unto his disciples, 46. Beware of the scribes, which desire to walk in long robes, and love greetings in the markets, and the highest seats in the synagogues, and the chief rooms at feasts; 47. Which devour widows houses, and for a shew make long prayers: the same shall receive greater damnation.

45, 46, 47. Note, The character of formal hypocrites, is to be worldly, cruel, unjust, proud, and to be devout in a ceremonious religion and lip labour, to quiet their conscience, and keep their reputation. Note, Though no doubt but some hypocrites can use long prayers ex tempore, it is most likely that that of the scribes and Pharisees was a form or liturgy.

CHAP. XXI.

AND he looked up, and saw the rich men casting their gifts into the treasury. 2. And he saw also a certain poor widow, casting in thither two mites. 3. And he said, Of a truth I say unto you, that this poor widow hath cast in more than they all. 4. For all these have of their abundance cast in unto the offerings of God: but she of her penury hath cast in all the living that she had.

1, 2, &c. See on Mark xii. 41, 42. God judges not of our service by the bulk.

5. And as some spake of the temple, how it was adorned with goodly stones, and gifts, he said, 6. As for these things which ye behold, the days will come, in the which there shall not be left one stone upon another, that shall not be thrown down.

5, 6. See Matt. xxiv.

7. And they asked him, saying, Master, but when shall these things be? and what sign *will there be* when these things shall come to pass.

7. Note, Corrupt nature is more desirous to know things to come, than to prepare for them by present duty.

8. And he said, Take heed that ye be not deceived: for many shall come in my name, saying, I am *Christ:* and the time draweth near: go ye not therefore after them.

8. Take you more care of yourselves, than to know the time; and be not deceived by false Christs, and false prophets.

9. But when ye shall hear of wars, and commotions, be not terrified: for these things must first come to pass, but the end *is* not by and by. 10. Then said he unto them, Nation shall rise against nation, and kingdom against kingdom: 11. And great earthquakes shall be in divers places, and famines and pestilences, and fearful sights, and great signs shall there be from heaven. 12. But before all these, they shall lay their hands on you, and persecute *you,* delivering *you* up to the synagogues, and into prisons, being brought before kings and rulers for my name's sake. 13. And it shall turn to you for a testimony.

9, 10, &c. See Matt. xxiv. Note, Christ did not draw in disciples with the hopes of prosperity. It shall be your witness or martyrdom, to divulge the gospel, and condemn unbelievers.

14. Settle *it* therefore in your hearts, not to meditate before what ye shall answer. 15. For I will give you a mouth and wisdom, which all your adversaries shall not be able to gainsay, nor resist.

14, 15. Note, It is Christ in heaven that giveth grace and gifts to his servants on earth by his Spirit.

16. And ye shall be betrayed both by parents, and brethren, and kinsfolks, and friends; and *some* of you shall they cause to be put to death. 17. And ye shall be hated of all men for my name's sake. 18. But there shall not an hair of your head perish.

16, 17, 18. Ye shall be no losers by all your sufferings; you shall be preserved till you are ripe for your full reward.

19. In your patience possess ye your souls.

19 While you keep your innocence and patience, you keep your souls from danger and loss.

20. And when ye shall see Jerusalem compassed with armies, then know that the desolation thereof is nigh. 21. Then let them which are in Judea, flee to the mountains; and let them which are in the midst of it, depart out; and let not them that are in the countries, enter thereinto. 22. For these be the days of vengeance, that all things which are written may be fulfilled.

20, 21, 22. Jerusalem's calamity shall be so great, that all that will be safe, must fly from it.

23. But woe unto them that are with child, and to them that give suck in those days: for there shall be great distress in the land, and wrath upon this people. 24. And they shall fall by the edge of the sword, and shall be led away captive into all nations: and Jerusalem shall be trodden down of the Gentiles, until the times of the Gentiles be fulfilled.

23, 24. Till heathens be turned Christians themselves, (in Constantine's days) and then Jerusalem shall be restored, and be the dwelling of Christians.

25. And there shall be signs in the sun, and in the moon, and in the stars; and upon the earth distress of nations, with perplexity, the sea and the waves roaring: 26. Men's hearts failing them for fear, and for looking after those things which are coming on the earth: for the powers of heaven shall be shaken. 27. And then shall they see the Son of Man coming in a cloud with power and great glory. 28. And when these things begin to come to pass, then look up, and lift up your heads; for your redemption draweth nigh.

25, 26, &c. See Matt. xxiv. Judgment, though slow, is sure and terrible.

29. And he spake to them a parable, Behold the fig-tree, and all the trees: 30. When they now shoot forth, ye say and know of your ownselves, that summer is now nigh at hand. 31. So likewise ye, when ye see these things come to pass, know ye that the kingdom of God is nigh at hand.

29, 30, 31. The kingdom of God is the reign of the Messiah, destroying Satan's kingdom, beginning indeed at his resurrection, but notable as Catholic, upon the great conversion of the Gentiles, specially when emperors owned Christ, the Jews being partly destroyed, and partly converted; and at last perfected in glory.

32. Verily I say unto you, This generation shall not pass away, till all be fulfilled. 33. Heaven and earth shall pass away; but my word shall not pass away.

32, 33. Till the Jews be destroyed, and the Gentiles begin to receive the gospel through the world.

34. And take heed to yourselves, lest at any time your hearts be overcharged with surfeiting and drunkenness, and cares of this life, and so that day come upon you unawares. 35. For as a snare shall it come on all them that dwell on the face of the whole earth.

34, 35. Either the ruin of the Jews shall suddenly come on all that land; or the day of judgment on all the world: And our duty is to be always ready; and therefore to avoid sensuality and worldliness, which is unreadiness.

36. Watch ye therefore, and pray always, that ye may be accounted worthy to escape all these things that shall come to pass, and to stand before the Son of Man.

36. A life of obedient watching against sin, waiting for judgment, and constant prayer, is our gospel-worthiness to escape God's judgments, and our preparation for a comfortable meeting our judge.

37. And in the day-time he was teaching in the temple, and at night he went out, and abode in the mount that is called the *mount* of Olives. 38. And all the people came early in the morning to him in the temple, for to hear him.

37, 38. Note, They could not silence him. 1. Because it was the Jews' law, that prophets and great teachers should speak freely. 2. And the Romans limited their power. 3. And they feared the multitude of his hearers.

CHAP. XXII.

NOW the feast of unleavened bread drew nigh, which is called the passover. 2. And the chief priests and scribes sought how they might kill him; for they feared the people.

1, 2. The feast of unleavened bread, was the day of the passover, and seven days after.

3. Then entered Satan into Judas surnamed Iscariot, being of the number of the twelve. 4. And he went his way, and communed with the chief priests and captains, how he might betray him unto them.

3, 4. Note, There is more of Satan in sin, than sinners think; He hath access as a tempter to the imagination, and when his temptation prevaileth, he gets greater possession of the heart.

5. And they were glad, and covenanted to give him money.

5. Note, 1. Wicked purposes or desires, use to meet with encouragement from wicked men. 2. It is a heinous crime, when men dare covenant to sin for gain.

6. And he promised, and sought opportunity to betray him unto them in the absence of the multitude.

6. To avoid tumult.

7. Then came the day of unleavened bread, when the passover must be killed. 8. And he sent Peter and John, saying, Go and prepare us the passover, that we may eat. 9. And they said unto him, Where wilt thou that we prepare? 10. And he said unto them, Behold, when ye are entered into the city, there shall a man meet you, bearing a pitcher of water; follow him into the house where he entereth in. 11. And ye shall say unto the good man of the house, The Master saith unto thee, Where is the guest-chamber, where I shall eat the passover with my disciples? 12. And he shall shew you a large upper room furnished: there make ready. 13. And they went and found as he had said unto them: and they made ready the passover.

7, 8, &c. Note, 1, Christ knew what would befal them out of sight. 2. Being made under the law, he would keep even that part that typified himself.

14. And when the hour was come, he sat down, and the twelve apostles with him. 15. And he said unto them, With desire I have desired to eat this passover with you before I suffer.

14. Note, Christ earnestly desired the fulfilling of his undertaken work, and holy communion with his servants.

16. For I say unto you, I will not any more eat thereof, until it be fulfilled in the kingdom of God. 17. And he took the cup, and gave thanks, and said, Take this, and divide *it* among yourselves. 18. For I say unto you, I will not drink of the fruit of the vine, until the kingdom of God shall come.

16, 17, 18. Till we meet in heaven; or till I celebrate that sacrament which is the Christian passover with you, in the holy assemblies, where I will be spiritually present.

Qu. How comes the cup twice mentioned? Answ. The first part was the passover. But Beza noteth, that the 18th and 19th verses are not in the Syrian translation, which is most ancient: And in his very old Greek copy now at Cambridge,

[This do in remembrance of me,] is left out of the 19th verse; and he conjectures some verses are transposed.

19. And he took bread, and gave thanks, and brake *it*, and gave unto them, saying, This *is* my body which is given for you: this do in remembrance of me. 20. Likewise also the cup after supper, saying, This cup *is* the new testament in my blood, which is shed for you.

19, 20. See Matt. xxvi. Note, Seeing the evangelists use not all the very same words, it seems not of absolute necessity to use just the same still: Yet all the substance must be retained; and it is safest repeating all set together which they recite; and as Paul most fully reciteth them.

21. But behold, the hand of him that betrayeth me, *is* with me on the table. 22. And truly the Son of Man goeth as it was determined: but woe unto that man by whom he is betrayed. 23. And they began to inquire among themselves, which of them it was that should do this thing.

21, 22, 23, Note, How hard was Judas's heart, that took not this warning.

24. And there was also a strife among them, which of them should be accounted the greatest.

24. Note, This strife was before, Matt. xx. But Luke keepeth not to the order of time.

25. And he said unto them, The kings of the Gentiles exercise lordship over them; and they that exercise authority upon them, are called benefactors. 26. But ye *shall* not *be* so: but he that is greatest among you, let him be as the younger; and he that is chief, as he that doth serve.

25, 26. (I am not for parity among all my disciples: You know I have chosen you only to be apostles: But though you be rulers over the churches, you must not be rulers of one another: And that sort of pre-eminence which you have, must not be like that of the princes of the world, who rule by the sword, or outward force, and in worldly pomp or state, constraining subjects to batter them with high titles, but it must be grounded in an excellency of grace and gifts, love, meekness, humility, being the most useful, and devoted to the good of all; as ruling only the voluntary, 2.

and therefore by the clearest reason, and greatest love, and most exemplary profitable lives: strive and spare not, for this pre-eminence and disparity.)

27. For whether *is* greater, he that sitteth at meat, or he that serveth? *is* not he that sitteth at meat? but I am among you as he that serveth.

27. Would you rule, as greater than I?, what hath my government of you been, but to do you good, by doctrine, love, and good example, without force?

28. Ye are they which have continued with me in my temptations. 29. And I appoint unto you a kingdom, as my Father hath appointed unto me:

28. As a reward for your faithful sticking to me in all my trials and sufferings, I appoint, &c.
Note, This promise is three ways expounded;
1. The aspiring clergy say it is, I make you apostles the chief rulers of my church, though in persecuting times, and your successors shall be patriarchs, metropolitans, archbishops, &c. and over-top emperors and kings.
2. Others say, that this lower world is but a shadow of the upper; and that the office of angels, and the titles in Daniel of [Michael your prince] and so of other angels, sheweth that there be kingdoms in the spiritual world above us, answerable to all the kingdoms on earth, and incomparably more; and that therefore Christ saith, *In my Father's house are many mansions:* And that there the twelve apostles have their kingdoms, (at least over the twelve tribes,) as being equal with the angels.
3. But most think that it is only an expression of the eminent glory of the apostles after the resurrection.
I see not but part of all three expositions may be included, that is, you shall be chief in my church on earth, and equal with angels after death, but specially after the day of judgment.

30. That ye may eat and drink at my table in my kingdom, and sit on thrones, judging the twelve tribes of Israel.

30. That ye may be feasted by me in heaven with spiritual everlasting joys, and may be superiors to the glorified Israelites, and in the mean time on earth may be the chiefest in my church.

31. And the Lord said, Simon, Simon, behold, Satan hath *desired to have* you, that he may sift *you* as wheat: 32. But I have prayed for thee, that thy faith fail not; and when thou art converted, strengthen thy brethren.

ST. LUKE. CHAP. XXII.

31, 32. Satan has got leave to try, and sift you all, and thee in special: But I have by prayer prevailed, that though thou sin in denying me, thou mayest not fall from sincere faith: And when by repentance thou art recovered from thy fall, strengthen thy brethren, who will forsake me also.

33. And he said unto him, Lord, I am ready to go with thee both into prison, and to death. 34. And he said, I tell thee, Peter, the cock shall not crow this day, before that thou shalt thrice deny that thou knowest me.

33. Note, Christ that knew Satan's request, and knew the event, knew Peter's weakness better than he himself did.

35. And he said unto them, When I sent you without purse, and scrip, and shoes, lacked ye any thing: And they said Nothing. 36. Then said he unto them, But now he that hath a purse, let him take *it*, and likewise *his* scrip: and he that hath no sword, let him sell his garment, and buy one. 37. For I say unto you, that this that is written, must yet be accomplished in me, And he was reckoned among the transgressors: for the things concerning me have an end.

35, 36, 37. When the people followed and applauded me for my cures and miracles, I knew that they would receive you, and provide for you for my sake: But now I am to be crucified and scorned as a transgressor, they will also cast you off: Therefore now look for hard usage, and moderately provide for yourselves.

38. And they said, Lord, behold, here *are* two swords. And he said unto them, It is enough.

38. I do not mean that you should now fight for me, but that you take care of your safety.

39. And he came out, and went, as he was wont, to the mount of Olives; and his disciples also followed him.

39. It seems he used there to lodge out of doors on the ground, and his disciples with him.

40. And when he was at the place, he said unto them, Pray, that ye enter not into temptation.

40. Prayer is the way both to escape temptation, and in it to overcome.

41. And he was withdrawn from them about a stone's cast, and kneeled down and prayed, 42. Saying, Father, if thou be willing, remove this cup from me: nevertheless, not my will, but thine be done.

41, 42. Note, For Christ, in the first act, by a simple nolition to be unwilling to suffer, was no sin, nor resisting God, but the property of human nature: But if he had been averse in the second comparative act, called nlection, when he knew it was God's will, this would have been evil.

43. And there appeared an angel unto him from heaven, strengthening him.

43. Note, Had Christ, as man, need of an angel's strengthening? What need then have we in the approach of death and great sufferings? And may we not also expect angel's help?

44. And being in an agony, he prayed more earnestly: and his sweat was as it were great drops of blood falling down to the ground.

44. Note, This was not from the fear of death, but the deep sense of God's wrath against sin, which he, as our sacrifice, was to bear in greater pain than mere dying, which his servants oft bear with peace.

45. And when he rose up from prayer, and was come to his disciples, he found them sleeping for sorrow. 46. And said unto them, Why sleep ye? rise and pray, lest ye enter into temptation.

45, 46. Note, We are apt to sleep when we have most need to watch and pray, and have need to be awakened.

47. And while he yet spake, behold a multitude, and he that was called Judas, one of the twelve, went before them, and drew near unto Jesus, to kiss him. 48. But Jesus said unto him, Judas, betrayest thou the Son of Man with a kiss

47, 48. Note, God permitted one so near Christ to betray him, to warn us how far to expect evil from our professed friends.

49. When they which were about him, saw what would follow, they said unto him, Lord, shall we smite with the sword? 50. And one of them smote the servant of the high priest, and cut off his right ear.

49, 50. Self-defence is natural, but God's la must rule it: They were the more put to fly, b cause they had resisted.

51. And Jesus answered and said, Suffer ye thus far. And he touched his ear and healed him.

51. Note, This miracle, wrought for one that came to destroy him, neither melted nor convinced hardened sinners.

52. Then Jesus said unto the chief priests, and captains of the temple, and the elders which were come to him, Be ye come out as against a thief, with swords and staves? 53. When I was daily with you in the temple, ye stretched forth no hands against me: but this is your hour, and the power of darkness.

52, 53. This is the time which God hath granted Satan to make use of you his instruments against me, and the prince of darkness will seem to conquer.

54. Then took they him, and led *him*, and brought him into the high priest's house. And Peter followed afar off. · 55. And when they had kindled a fire in the midst of the hall, and were set down together, Peter sat down among them. 56. But a certain maid beheld him as he sat by the fire, and earnestly looked upon him, and said, This man was also with him.

54, 55, 56. Note, When trial must come, instruments will not be wanting.

57. And he denied him, saying, Woman, I know him not.

57. Note, Had he not been conscious of smiting with the sword, he had not been in so much danger of fear.

58. And after a little while another saw him, and said, Thou art also of them. And Peter said, Man, I am not.

58. Note, It was a woman, here called man, only as one of mankind, not to distinguish the sex.

59. And about the space of one hour after, another confidently affirmed, saying, Of a truth this *fellow* also was with him; for he is a Galilean.

59. Note, To belong to Christ, and follow him, is crime enough, when enemies are judges.

60. And Peter said, Man, I know not what thou sayest. And immediately while he yet spake, the cock crew. 61. And the Lord turned, and looked upon Peter; and Peter remembered the word of the Lord, how he had said unto him, Before the cock crow, thou shalt deny me thrice. 62. And Peter went out, and wept bitterly.

60, 61, 62. Note, Christ's own danger did not make him forget a sinning disciple.

63. And the men that held Jesus, mocked him, and smote *him*. 64. And when they had blindfolded him, they struck him on the face, and asked him, saying, Prophesy, who is it that smote thee? 65. And many other things blasphemously spake they against him.

63, 64, 65. Note, What is it that the ignorant rabble will not say and do against the best of men, when men called sacred and great encourage them?

66. And as soon as it was day, the elders of the people, and the chief priests, and the scribes came together, and led him into their council, 67. Saying, Art thou the Christ? tell us. And he said unto them, If I tell you, you will not believe. 68. And if I also ask *you*, you will not answer me, nor let *me* go.

66, 67, 68. It is in vain to discourse with you; for you are resolved what to do with me, and trust to force, and not to truth.

69. Hereafter shall the Son of Man sit on the right hand of the power of God.

69. I shall shortly be advanced in heaven as man, to be Lord of all.

70. Then said they all, Art thou then the Son of God? And he said unto them, Ye say that I am. 71. And they said, What need we any further witness? for we ourselves have heard of his own mouth.

70, 71. Note, Though Christ answered not their other accusations, he would not to save his life, by silence seem to fear to own his nature, dignity, and office; else he that laid our salvation upon our open confessing him in the face of greatest danger, should have required more of us, than he would do himself. Paul saith, With the mouth con-

fession is made unto salvation; and giveth Timothy Christ's example, who *before* Pontius Pilate *witnessed a good confession*, Rom. x. 9, 10. 1 Tim. vi. 13.

CHAP. XXIII.

AND the whole multitude of them arose, and led him unto Pilate. 2. And they began to accuse him, saying, We found this *fellow* perverting the nation, and forbidding to give tribute to Cæsar, saying, that he himself is Christ a king.

1, 2. Note. The last clause, which was true, gave a colour to the former which was false: They thought that Pilate could not believe that he could claim a kingdom, and not be against Cæsar's reign. And to this day the devil's design is to make princes jealous that Christ's kingdom is against theirs, when they have all their true power from him. No way seemeth so effectual to the diabolists to get down Christ's kingdom, as to raise jealousy and enmity in kings against it.

3. And Pilate asked him, saying, Art thou the King of the Jews? And he answered him and said, Thou sayest *it*.

3. I am so; I will not deny my office and dignity, (But my kingdom is not of this world.)

4. Then said Pilate to the chief priests and *to* the people, I find no fault in this man.

4. Though he call himself a king, he raiseth no war or sedition against Cæsar, and so the law will not reach him.

5. And they were the more fierce, saying, He stirreth up the people, teaching throughout all Jewry, beginning from Galilee to this place.

5. His preaching is seditious, disaffecting the people to the government, and to the public peace.

6. When Pilate heard of Galilee, he asked whether the man were a Galilean. 7. And as soon as he knew that he belonged unto Herod's jurisdiction, he sent him to Herod, who himself was also at Jerusalem at that time. 8. And when Herod saw Jesus, he was exceeding glad: for he was desirous to see him of a long season, because he had heard many things of him; and he hoped to have seen some miracle done by him.

6, 7, 8. Note, When the King of glory, in the form of a servant, was thus tossed in triumph and scorn, from ruler to ruler, it was to shew what we deserved, and what we must expect.

9. Then he questioned with him in many words; but he answered him nothing.

9. Note, As he was not over solicitous to repel their accusations; so he would not accuse himself, nor give them matter against him out of his own mouth: He would not have taken an *ex officio* oath, to answer whatever question they should ask him, though they told him not what.

10. And the chief priests and scribes stood and vehemently accused him.

10. Note, Consecrated men are Satan's agents with the king against Christ.

11. And Herod with his men of war set him at nought, and mocked *him*, and arrayed him in a gorgeous robe, and sent him again to Pilate.

11 Note, The king and his soldiers thought they were far enough above a despised unarmed prisoner.

12. And the same day Pilate and Herod were made friends together; for before they were at enmity between themselves.

12. Note, They can agree in enmity and persecution of the just, who cannot agree about their worldly interest.

13. And Pilate when he had called together the chief priests, and the rulers, and the people, 14. Said unto them, Ye have brought this man unto me, as one that perverteth the people: and behold, I having examined *him* before you, have found no fault in this man touching those things whereof ye accuse him; 15. No nor yet Herod: for I sent you to him, and lo, nothing worthy of death is done unto him. 16. I will therefore chastise him and release *him*. 17. For of necessity he must release one unto them at the feast.

13, 14, &c. His accusation of sedition is not proved to me, nor to Herod: I will therefore scourge him, and so release him.

18. And they cried out all at once, saying, Away with this *man*, and release unto us Barabbas:

18. Note, A murderer, or the most debauched, seems better than Christ himself to malignant hypocrites.

19. (Who for a certain sedition made in the city, and for murder, was cast into prison). 20. Pilate therefore willing to release Jesus, spake again to them. 21. But they cried, saying, Crucify *him*, crucify him, 22. And he said unto them the third time, Why, what evil hath he done? I have found no cause of death in him, I will therefore chastise him, and let *him* go.

19, 20, &c. Note, The malignant Jews are worse than heathens in persecuting rage.

23. And they were instant with loud voices, requiring that he might be crucified: and the voices of them, and of the chief priests prevailed. 24. And Pilate gave sentence that it should be as they required.

23, 24. Note, Wicked men dare deny God's importunity and mercy, but cannot deny temptations from men's importunity, and worldly interest.

25. And he released unto them, him that for sedition and murder was cast into prison, whom they had desired; but he delivered Jesus to their will.

25. Note, 1. It is the greatest means of bad men's ruin, to let them have their wills. 2. God in flesh was not innocent enough in the eyes of wicked men, to escape condemnation.

26. And as they led him away, they laid hold upon one Simon a Cyrenian, coming out of the country, and on him they laid the cross, that he might bear *it* after Jesus. 27. And there followed him a great company of people, and of women, which also bewailed and lamented him. 28. But Jesus turning unto them, said, Daughters of Jerusalem, weep not for me, but weep for yourselves, and for your children. 29. For behold, the days are coming, in the which they shall say, Blessed *are* the barren, and the wombs that never bare, and the paps which never gave suck.

26, 27, &c. It is not my case that you have cause to lament, but your own and your children's, for the dreadful destruction that is coming.

30. Then shall they begin to say to the mountains, Fall on us; and to the hills, Cover us. 31. For if they do these things in a green tree, what shall be done in the dry?

30, 31. Dreadful will be the approaching vengeance: For if they thus use me for my good works, what shall they endure, who by their heinous sin are as wood dried for the fire.

32. And there were also two other malefactors led with him to be put to death. 33. And when they were come to the place which is called Calvary, there they crucified him, and the malefactors; one on the right hand, and the other on the left.

32, 33. Thus, for us, the Son of God was numbered with malefactors, by the most ignominious death.

34. Then said Jesus, Father, forgive them; for they know not what they do. And they parted his raiment, and cast lots.

34. Qu. Was this an absolute prayer of Christ? If so, were they not all forgiven, seeing he was always heard? And doth not he himself foretel their dreadful punishment? Answ. It is as if he had said [I am dying to purchase pardon of sin to all that repent and believe; I come not to destroy and condemn, but to save: It is therefore my part to desire their repentance and salvation: Take them not as unpardonable, for they do this in ignorance and unbelief: Tender them forgiveness, and give them yet time of repentance, and draw thine elect to effectual faith, and condemn none for killing me, that do not after my resurrection obstinately reject thy offered mercy to the last.] This also was the sense of Stephen's, *Lay not this sin to their charge.* But final unbelief, and rejecting grace, is the unpardonable sin, which retaineth all the rest.

35. And the people stood beholding: and the rulers also with them derided *him*, saying, He saved others; let him save himself, if he be Christ the chosen of God.

35. O unthankful men, to turn so many miracles of love and mercy into cruel insulting scorn! Reader, behold in these instances the nature of fallen man, and be humbled, and fear thyself.

36. And the soldiers also mocked him, coming to him, and offering him vinegar, 37. And saying, If thou be the king of the Jews, save thyself.

36, 37. Note, He came to save us, and not himself, till his resurrection; How glad would his enemies shortly be to be saved by him! And how will their tune be changed!

38. And a superscription also was written over him in letters of Greek, and Latin, and Hebrew, THIS IS THE KING OF THE JEWS.

38. Note, As the reason of his death, and scorn both of him, and all the Jewish nation.

39. And one of the malefactors, which were hanged, railed on him, saying, If thou be Christ, save thyself and us.

39. Note, The cross of Christ was the great scandal to all: They thought that he could not be the Christ, that did not save himself; because they knew not the use of his sacrifice for man's redemption. But it shews the power of sin, when even a malefactor crucified shall go out of the world in such reproach.

40. But the other answering, rebuked him, saying, Dost not thou fear God, seeing thou art in the same condemnation? 41. And we indeed justly; for we receive the due reward of our deeds: but this man hath done nothing amiss.

40, 41. Wilt thou die in sin? Are not we justly suffering for it, when he unjustly suffereth, being innocent?

42. And he said unto Jesus, Lord remember me when thou comest into thy kingdom.

42. Lord, I believe that thou art the true Messiah, and the promised king, remember me a sinner with pardoning mercy and acceptance, when thou reignest in thy glory.

43. And Jesus said unto him, Verily I say unto thee, To-day shalt thou be with me in paradise.

43. Trust my promise: Thou shalt this very day be with me in a celestial paradise of joy.
Note, 1. This example sheweth us what election freely doth in calling one, while another is past by.
2. Christ would give this present proof of the virtue of his sacrifice to call and justify sinners.
3. True conversion is never too late, to the obtaining of mercy and salvation.
4. True faith and repentance, how late soever, will have its fruits. This man was not saved without good works. 1. He confessed his sin. 2. He confessed the justness of his punishment. 3. He confessed Christ's kingdom. 4. He justified Christ's Innocency. 5. He reproved the reviler, and taught him to repent. 6. He prayed even to a crucified dying Christ. 7. He prayed not for present deliverance, but for a place in Christ's kingdom.
5. The departed souls of the faithful go presently to paradise.
6. This paradise is where Christ will be with us. Some heretics, by gross perversion, joun [This day] with [I say,] as if it had been only the day of Christ's speaking this, and not of the man's being in paradise: But it is by falsification, contrary to the pointing of all Greek copies: and one copy saith Beza, hath [That this day.]

44. And it was about the sixth hour, and there was darkness over all the earth, until the ninth hour.

44. Over all the land, from twelve o'clock till three, there was an unusual degree of darkness, whether by an eclipse, or extraordinary clouds, is uncertain: But it was not such darkness as is in the night.

45. And the sun was darkened, and the vail of the temple was rent in the midst.

45 Some take the veil to be a hanging, but it is liker to be a wall: For the temple was divided into three parts: 1. The outer court, where the Gentiles might come. 2. The sanctuary where the Jews came. 3. The inner sanctuary, or holiest, where only the high priest came once a year. If it was the wall that enclosed the holiest, then the rending signified the access we have now to God by Christ: If it was the second wall, it signified the removal of the Mosaical separation of Jews and Gentiles.

46. And when Jesus had cried with a loud voice, he said, Father, into thy hands I commend my spirit: and having said thus he gave up the ghost.

46. Note, The certain glory that Christ expected, was by the way of trusting his soul into his Father's hands: And what other way have we to die in hope and peace, but to commit our souls with trust to our Father and our Redeemer, and conjoin the dying words of Christ and Stephen!

47. Now when the centurion saw what was done, he glorified God, saying, Certainly this was a righteous man.

47. See Matt. xxvii. 54. Though Matthew recite his words thus, [Verily this was the Son of God.] Luke's words are not contrary, but we may conclude that the centurion spake both.

48. And all the people that came together to that sight, beholding the things which were done, smote their breasts and returned. 49. And all his acquaintance, and the women that followed him from Galilee, stood afar off beholding these things.

48, 49. Note, Soldiers and common people were not so hardened as the priests and rulers.

50. And behold, *there was* a man named Joseph, a counsellor, *and he was* a good man, and a just:

50. One of the council that governed.

51. (The same had not consented to the counsel and deed of them) *he was* of Arimathea, a city of the Jews (who also himself waited for the kingdom of God).

51. Who having looked for the coming of the Messiah, believed that Christ was he.

52. This man went unto Pilate and begged the body of Jesus.

52. Note, 1. He that concealed his faith before, shewed his love to Christ when he was dead. 2. The body of the Son of God was at the disposal and power of a heathen, even his who was Lord of all the world.

53. And he took it down, and wrapped it in linen, and laid it in a sepulchre that was hewn in stone, wherein never man before was laid.

53. Prepared for himself.

54. And that day was the preparation, and the sabbath drew on. 55. And the women also which came with him from Galilee, followed after, and beheld the sepulchre, and how his body was laid. 56. And they returned, and prepared spices and ointments; and rested the sabbath-day, according to the commandment.

54, 55, 56. According to Moses's law, which required ceremonial rest, it being not then abrogated.

CHAP. XXIV.

NOW upon the first *day* of the week, very early in the morning, they came unto the sepulchre, bringing the spices which they had prepared, and certain *others* with them.

1. Obj. Did not Nicodemus and Joseph wrap his body in spices at his burial? Answ. They laid it in haste in the dry aloes and myrrh, deferring the full embalming of it, with the added ointments, till after the sabbath.

2. And they found the stone rolled away from the sepulchre. 3. And they entered in, and found not the body of the Lord Jesus. 4. And it came to pass, as they were much perplexed thereabout, behold two men stood by them in shining garments. 5. And as they were afraid, and bowed down *their* faces to the earth, they said unto them, Why seek ye the living among the dead?

2, 3, &c. See the reconciliation of the seeming differences of the evangelists herein, on Matt. xxviii. and Mark xvi. and John xx.

6. He is not here, but is risen: remember how he spake unto you when he was yet in Galilee, 7. Saying, The Son of Man must be delivered into the hands of sinful men, and be crucified, and the third day rise again.

6, 7. Note, Luke saith more of this sermon of the angels to the women than the other evangelists did.

8. And they remembered his words, 9. And returned from the sepulchre, and told all these things unto the eleven, and to all the rest. 10. It was Mary Magdalene, and Joanna, and Mary *the mother* of James, and other *women that were* with them, which told these things unto the apostles. 11. And their words seemed to them as idle tales, and they believed them not.

8, 9, &c. Note, Here is much passed by which the other evangelists have: For no one of them pretended to write all that was done.

12. Then arose Peter, and ran unto the sepulchre, and stooping down, he beheld the linen clothes laid by themselves, and departed, wondering in himself at that which was come to pass.

12. See this more fully in John xx.

13. And behold, two of them went that same day to a village called Emmaus, which was from Jerusalem *about* threescore furlongs. 14. And they talked together of all these things which had happened,

15. And it came to pass that while they communed *together*, and reasoned, Jesus himself drew near, and went with them.

13, 14, 15. Christ came to them but as unknown.

16. But their eyes were holden, that they should not know him.

16. It is like the cause was partly in them, and partly in the change of the countenance of Christ.

17. And he said unto them, What manner of communications are these that ye have one to another, as ye walk, and are sad?

17. Note, He was not ignorant of their discourse, but asked them, that he might instruct them.

18. And the one of them, whose name was Cleopas, answering, said unto him, Art thou only a stranger in Jerusalem, and hast not known the things which are come to pass there in these days? 19. And he said unto them, What things? And they said unto him, Concerning Jesus of Nazareth, which was a prophet mighty in deed and word before God, and all the people:

18, 19. In miracles, and prophecy, and doctrine.

20. And how the chief priests and our rulers delivered him to be condemned to death, and have crucified him. 21. But we trusted that it had been he which should have redeemed Israel: and beside all this, to-day is the third day since these things were done.

20, 21. Note, They still believed that he was a prophet: for many prophets were murdered: But they now seemed to doubt, yea, almost to give up their belief that he was the Messiah.

22. Yea, and certain women also of our company made us astonished, which were early at the sepulchre: 23. And when they found not his body, they came, saying, that they had also seen a vision of angels, which said that he was alive. 24. And certain of them which were with us, went to the sepulchre, and found *it* even so as the women had said; but him they saw not.

22, 23, 24. And yet we know not what to think, but are under mere astonishment, and further expectation; for certain women, &c.

25. Then he said to them, O fools, and slow of heart to believe all that the prophets have spoken!

25. Were you not very ignorant men, and of dull hearts, you would not be so unacquainted with, and backward to believe, that which all the prophets did foretel.

26. Ought not Christ to have suffered these things, and to enter into his glory?

26. Have they not all foretold that Christ must thus suffer, and then enter into the heavenly glory, where is his throne, where he is to reign?

27. And beginning at Moses, and all the prophets, he expounded unto them in all the scriptures, the things concerning himself.

27. Note, Though it hath not pleased God to give us down this expository sermon of Christ, yet his Spirit, by his apostles hath given us enough for our use.

28. And they drew nigh unto the village, whither they went: and he made as though he would have gone further.

28. Note, Not by any false words, but by his carriage, concealing his purpose to stay with them.

29. But they constrained him, saying, Abide with us, for it is towards evening, and the day is far spent. And he went in to tarry with them.

29. Note, Importunity is the means to prevail for Christ's presence, even when he purposeth to stay.

30. And it came to pass as he sat at meat with them, he took bread, and blessed *it*, and brake, and gave to them.

30. Note, Not the sacrament, but as the master of the family was wont to do; save the peculiar holiness of his manner of doing it.

31. And their eyes were opened, and they knew him; and he vanished out of their sight.

31. It is like partly by God's change on them and partly by Christ's more discernible discovery they knew him.

Note, Though Christ rose in the same body, and was not yet fully glorified, it was greatly changed, so that he could appear and vanish when and where he pleased, and be known or unknown to beholders.

32. And they said one to another, Did not our heart burn within us, while he talked with us by the way, and while he opened to us the scriptures?

32. Note, They told each other how they felt their hearts affected while he preached to them.

33. And they rose up the same hour, and returned to Jerusalem, and found the eleven gathered together, and them that were with them, 34. Saying, The Lord is risen indeed, and hath appeared to Simon.

33, 34. As soon as they came in among them, the eleven first told these two, that the Lord was risen, &c.

35. And they told what things *were done* in the way, and how he was known of them in breaking of bread.

35. Then the two also told the eleven, and the company, what they had seen and heard in the way, &c.

36. And as they thus spake, Jesus himself stood in the midst of them, and saith unto them, peace *be* unto you.

36. Note, We need not feign that he opened the door, when he could appear and disappear, when and where he would: He did not lie hidden in some corner, when they saw him so seldom in forty days, but disappeared. Note, 2. Peace is the voice of a risen Saviour, who purchased it so dearly, and giveth it as the great peace-maker.

37. But they were terrified and affrighted, and supposed that they had seen a spirit.

37. If he had opened the door, and come in as other men, it is like they would not have taken him for a spirit.

38. And he said unto them, Why are ye troubled, and why do thoughts arise in your hearts? 39. Behold my hands and feet, that it is myself: handle me, and see, for a spirit hath not flesh and bones, as ye see me have. 40. And when he had thus spoken, he shewed them *his* hands and *his* feet.

38, 39, 40. Troubling thoughts are ready to surprise ignorant persons; but Christ to suppress them, appealed to their senses: For man is apt to believe what he seeth and feeleth, but is hardly brought to believe any thing above sense. Note, Spirits have not flesh and blood.

41. And while they yet believed not for joy, and wondered, he said unto them, Have ye here any meat?

41. Note, There was some belief called hope, or else they could not have had joy: But it is hard fully to believe great things which we desire, through the power of fear, lest it should not prove true.

42. And they gave him a piece of a broiled fish, and of an honey-comb. 43. And he took *it*, and did eat before them.

42, 43. Note They dieted skilfully: broiling and honey correct both the pituitous frigidity, and the corruptibility of fish.

2. Eating proved Christ to be no mere spirit. When angels did eat, they first took bodies, or else seemed to do what they did not: Therefore glorified bodies eat not, because they are spiritual, though not mere spirits, and have their sustenance without eating.

44. And he said unto them, These *are* the words which I spake unto you, while I was yet with you, that all things must be fulfilled which were written in the law of Moses, and *in* the prophets, and *in* the psalms concerning me.

44. Note, This testimony of Christ confirmeth the law of Moses, the prophets and the Psalms, to be the true word of God.

45. Then opened he their understanding, that they might understand the scriptures.

45. This was a greater effect of divine power, (to open men's understandings) than to appear without opening the door: The understanding of man is shut up against the understanding of things spiritual, till Christ open it. O pray for this opening.

46. And said unto them, Thus it is written, and thus it behoved Christ to suffer, and to rise from the dead the third day:

46. This should not seem new or strange to you, which the scriptures so fully foretold.

47. And that repentance and re-

mission of sins should be preached in his name, among all nations, beginning at Jerusalem. 48. And ye are witnesses of these things.

47, 48. I have by redemption purchased an act of grace and oblivion, a free universal pardon of sin to all that repent and will accept it, as my gift: This must be preached to all nations; and you must do it first by office, who are my witnesses of the matter of fact.

49. And behold, I send the promise of my Father upon you: but tarry ye in the city of Jerusalem, until ye be endued with power from on high.

49. And the great promise of the Holy Ghost, for miracles, tongues, and holiness, as my agent, seal and earnest, I will quickly pour out upon you. But wait together at Jerusalem, till it be done, and you be endued with the foresaid power from God.

50. And he led them out as far as to Bethany: and he lift up his hands, and blessed them. 51. And it came to pass, while he blessed them, he was parted from them, and carried up into heaven.

50, 51. Afterward, at the end of forty days, when he had oft appeared to them, and given them their commission to go and disciple all nations, baptizing them in the name of the Father, Son, and Holy Ghost, teaching them to observe all things that he had commanded them, promising to be with them to the end of the world, Matt. xxi. 19, 20. Mark xvi. 15, 16. See Acts i. 9.

Note, Christ, that parted from earth with a blessing, will bless his church here and for ever.

52. And they worshipped him, and returned to Jerusalem with great joy.

52. Note, Though their Lord was gone from them on earth, they were now assured that they had a King and Saviour in heaven, whence his influence would be most extensive and efficacious.

53. And were continually in the temple, praising and blessing God. Amen.

53. As they worshipped their glorified Redeemer, so they continued together assembled, in the temple, (not yet alienated from all Jewish worship,) praising and magnifying the name of God, who had bestowed a Saviour and his grace upon them, and had given the church so gracious and glorious a Saviour and head, and done such wonders to confirm their faith. Amen.

THE GOSPEL
ACCORDING TO
ST. JOHN.

CHAP. I.

IN the beginning was the Word, and the Word was with God, and the Word was God. 2. The same was in the beginning with God.

1, 2, The WORD (which hath been since incarnate) was in the beginning before the world was made; And this WORD was with God, yea, the WORD was God, Thus this same WORD was in the beginning of time, and causality with God, being God.

3. All things were made by him, and without him was not any thing made that was made.

3. He was a causal beginning to the whole creation; for all things were made by him: nothing was made without him by the Father, in creating or forming the world.

4. In him was life, and the life was the light of men.

4. Being GOD and one with the Father, he was especially LIFE, even in and with the Father, the infinite, eternal, self-living God; and so he was radically, and communicatively LIFE to the world; even intellectual life, by which he is the LIGHT of man, as intellectual, and as taught by revelation. Note, It is usual with the scripture and school divines to ascribe by some eminency of attribution, LIFE and POWER to the Father, LIGHT and WISDOM to the Son, and LOVE, JOY, and PERFECTIONS to the Holy Ghost: yet so that the same also are attributed to each person in common: And so the WORD is said here to have life as one with the Father, and yet eminently to be this LIFE, by the way of intellective LIGHT and illumination.

5. And the light shineth in darkness, and the darkness comprehendeth it not.

5. And this LIGHT shineth communicatively unto this darkened world, which receiving it but according to the mode and disposition of the receivers, through their wilful resistance, receiveth the illumination and teaching so defectively, as that most (in Judea and elsewhere) remain in darkness still.

6. There was a man sent from God, whose name *was* John. 7. The same came for a witness, to bear witness of the light, that all men through him might believe. 8. He was not that light, but *was sent* to bear witness of that light.

6, 7, 8. God sent John Baptist before us, as Elias, to preach repentance and faith in the Messiah, as ready to appear, and as a witness from God to prepare and call the Jews to receive him that was the true LIGHT of the world, (which himself was not.)

9. *That* was the true light, which lighteth every man that cometh into the world.

9. He is the true LIGHT, who giveth all the world that light which, they do enjoy: As the Lord and spring of nature, he giveth all men their intellectual natural light: And as the repriever and restorer of blinded intellect, he giveth all men that measure of moral and restored light and revelation which they have.

10. He was in the world, and the world was made by him, and the world knew him not.

10. He was in the world (in a more excellent manner than the soul is in the body,) for the world was made by him, and therefore maintained by him; and he at last appeared to the world incarnate, and yet the world knew him not in either of his appearances.

11. He came unto his own, and his own received him not.

11. He came in flesh to his people the Jews, and they not believing him, received him not.

12. But as many as received him, to them gave he power to become the sons of God, *even* to them that believe on his name:

12. But to as many as took him by unfeigned consent for their Lord and Saviour, even to them that believing him to be the Son of God, and true Messiah, did place all their trust in him for reconciliation with God, and for salvation; to all these he gave right to the state and dignity of adoption which he purchased, even to be the sons of God as united to him, and heirs of the heavenly glory.

13. Which were born, not of blood, nor of the will of the flesh, nor of the will of man, but of God.

13. Who (as children have a like nature communicated from the parents, so) have a nature holy and divine, by spiritual life, light, and love, inclined to do the will of God, and to desire things holy and heavenly: which nature is not produced of mere natural generation, nor of any mere human documents or laws, but is the effect of God's grace by his sanctifying Spirit.

14. And the word was made flesh, and dwelt among us (and we beheld his glory, the glory as of the only begotten of the Father) full of grace and truth.

14. And the Word that made the world, assumed human nature in which he dwelt, as a better tabernacle than that of shadows; and we saw his glory appearing in this tabernacle in his heavenly doctrine, life, miracles, and transfigurations, which shewed him to be the only begotten of the Father, glorious in the fulness of grace and truth, which the shadowy tabernacle and ceremonies did but prefigure.

15. John bare witness of him, and cried, saying, This was he of whom I spake, He that cometh after me, is preferred before me; for he was before me.

15. John pointed to him, saying, This is he; even the King of Israel: Though I am before him in time in my ministry, he is before me in dignity, and was before me in time also.

16. And of his fulness have all we received, and grace for grace.

16. And as he is full of wisdom and love, of grace and spiritual life, he as our head communicateth so much as is meet for us, and we receive greater measures than were given under the law; even measures answerable to his new appearance and covenant.

17. For the law was given by Moses, but grace and truth came by Jesus Christ.

17. For though Moses delivered legal precepts,

types, and ceremonies, it is by Jesus Christ that we have grace both for holiness and pardon, and by him are the real substances which those shadows typified. The measure of grace that the faithful had under the law, was through him, the promised Messiah, and the fuller measure under the gospel, is by his fuller access and communication to us, as the image on the wax answereth that on the signet.

18. No man hath seen God at any time; the only begotten Son, which is in the bosom of the Father, he hath declared *him*.

18. How little should we have known of God whom no man ever saw, if his Son that is in the bosom of the Father had not declared him and his will to man.

Note, I know not whether these words were the words of John the Baptist, or the apostles.

19. And this is the record of John, when the Jews sent priests and Levites from Jerusalem, to ask him, Who art thou? 20. And he confessed, and denied not; but confessed, I am not the Christ. 21. And they asked him, What then? Art thou Elias? And he saith I am not. Art thou that prophet? And he answered, No.

19. John constantly affirmed that he was not Christ, nor Elias personally, nor the prophet mentioned Deut. xviii. 15. Qu. Doth not Christ say, that John was Elias? Answ. Not the person of old Elias, but the person prophesied under that name.

22. Then said they unto him, Who art thou? that we may give an answer to them that sent us: what sayest thou of thyself?

22. Tell us then what thou art, that we may give an account why thou undertakest to prophesy and baptize.

23. He said, I *am* the voice of one crying in the wilderness, Make straight the way of the Lord, as said the prophet Esaias.

23. I am he that Isaiah prophesied of in these words, Isa. xl. 3.

24. And they which were sent, were of the Pharisees. 25. And they asked him, and said unto him, Why baptizest thou then, if thou be not that Christ, nor Elias, neither that prophet? 26. John answered them, saying, I baptize with water:

but there standeth one among you, whom ye know not; 27. He it is who coming after me is preferred before me, whose shoes' latchet I am not worthy to unloose.

24, &c. The Pharisees professed to reverence prophets, and therefore were inquisitive to know whether John was a prophet, or what he was, who presumed to baptize: But he told them that it was his office by baptizing with water, to prepare them to receive him that already was among them unknown, who will baptize with the Holy Ghost, to whom he was unworthy to do the office of the lowest servant.

28. These things were done in Bethabara beyond Jordan, where John was baptizing. 29. The next day John seeth Jesus coming unto him, and saith, Behold the Lamb of God, which taketh away the sin of the world.

28, 29. The next day after the Pharisees' questions, John seeing Christ, gave him personally this testimony: Behold this man is appointed to be sacrificed to God, as the lambs were under the law, to make expiation for the sins of the world, that all that believe on him may be pardoned.

30. This is he of whom I said, After me cometh a man which is preferred before me: for he was before me. 31. And I knew him not: but that he should be made manifest to Israel: therefore am I come baptizing with water.

30, 31. I knew that the Messiah was come, but I knew not that this was he, till God made it known to me, and I saw the Holy Ghost come on him afterward: But because he is come, I baptize men to prepare them to receive him.

32. And John bare record, saying, I saw the Spirit descending from heaven, like a dove, and it abode upon him. 33. And I knew him not: but he that sent me to baptize with water, the same said unto me, Upon whom thou shalt see the Spirit descending and remaining on him, the same is he which baptizeth with the Holy Ghost. 34. And I saw, and bare record that this *is* the Son of God.

32. Note, John's testimony was both by revelation and vision of the descent of the Spirit in some visible appearance. And whether John only heard the voice from heaven mentioned Matt. iii. 17. is uncertain.

35. Again the next day after, John stood, and two of his disciples: 36. And looking upon Jesus as he walked, he saith, Behold the Lamb of God. 37. And the two disciples heard him speak, and they followed Jesus.

37. Not followed him yet as his disciples, but as inquirers after him, in order to a closer following him.

38. Then Jesus turned, and saw them following, and saith unto them, What seek ye? They said unto him, Rabbi, (which is to say, being interpreted, Master) where dwellest thou? 39. He saith unto them, Come and see. They came and saw where he dwelt, and abode with him that day: for it was about the tenth hour. 40. One of the two which heard John *speak*, and followed him, was Andrew, Simon Peter's brother. 41. He first findeth his own brother Simon, and saith unto him, We have found the Messias, which is, being interpreted, the Christ. 42. And he brought him to Jesus. And when Jesus beheld him, he said, Thou art Simon the son of Jona: thou shalt be called Cephas, which is by interpretation, a stone.

38. Note, By all this it appeareth, that when Peter and Andrew were after called, and suddenly left all, and followed Christ, it was not without some previous notice of him, and preparation thereto.

43. The day following, Jesus would go forth into Galilee, and findeth Philip, and saith unto him, follow me. 44. Now Philip was of Bethsaida, the city of Andrew and Peter. 45. Philip findeth Nathanael, and saith unto him, We have found him of whom Moses in the law, and the prophets did write, Jesus of Nazareth, the son of Joseph.

45. The long expected Messias is now come, and we have found him, he is Jesus of Nazareth, &c.

46. And Nathanael said unto him, Can there any good thing come out of Nazareth? Philip saith unto him, Come and see.

46. Do the prophets tell us that the Messiah shall come out of Nazareth: Galilee produceth not prophets. Philip saith, Come and see him, and then judge.

47. Jesus saw Nathanael coming to him, and saith of him, Behold an Israelite indeed, in whom is no guile.

47. A sincere true-hearted man. Qu. Were any unbelievers such? Answ. He was not an unbeliever, though yet he knew not Christ: For he had that belief which men were saved by, before Christ's coming.

48. Nathanael saith unto him, Whence knowest thou me? Jesus answered and said unto him, Before that Philip called thee when thou wast under the fig-tree, I saw thee. 49. Nathanael answered and saith unto him, Rabbi, thou art the Son of God, thou art the king of Israel.

48. Note, He judged that none but God, or by God, could know what men said and did at such a distance. 2. It was well for Nathanael, that he came to see Christ; experience convinced him: And yet no doubt but God's special grace did it? For the Pharisees saw more, and yet believed not.

50. Jesus answered and said unto him, Because I said unto thee, I saw thee under the fig-tree, believest thou? thou shalt see greater things than these.

50. Doth this much convince thee? I will do greater things than this to convince the world.

51. And he saith unto him, Verily, verily I say unto you, Hereafter you shall see heaven open, and the angels of God ascending and descending upon the Son of Man.

51. You shall see heaven open, and the angels owning me and ministering unto me, especially at my ascension.

CHAP. II.

AND the third day there was a marriage in Cana of Galilee; and the mother of Jesus was there. 2. And both Jesus was called, and his disciples, to the marriage.

1, 2. Christ refused not that familiar converse, which marriage feasts are used to.

3. And when they wanted wine, the mother of Jesus saith unto him, They have no wine. 4. Jesus saith unto her, Woman, what have I to do with thee? mine hour is not yet come.

3, 4. These words are not a breach of the fifth commandment; but as much as to say [I am not to do miracles] by the direction of a mother's authority, or by man, but in the time and manner as by the divine wisdom shall be determined. And by this and other passages, Christ seems to foresee how papists would overvalue his mother.

5. His mother saith unto the servants, Whatsoever he saith unto you, do it.

5. Note. She believed his power, though he repressed her presumption.

6. And there were set there six water-pots of stone, after the manner of the purifying the Jews, containing two or three firkins a piece. 7. Jesus saith unto them, Fill the water-pots, and they filled them up to the brim. 8. And he saith unto them, Draw out now, and bear unto the governor of the feast. And they bear it.

6, &c. Note, It is conjectured to be about one thousand, eight hundred pounds or pints of wine that Christ made: which shewed that the guests were very many, or that he was at such festivals for freer drinking of wine than is fit among us; perhaps all their wine was small, and not all of them drunk: but this and the like occasioned the Pharisees' censure of him.

9. When the ruler of the feast had tasted the water that was made wine, and knew not whence it was, (but the servants which drew the water knew) the governor of the feast called the bridegroom, 10. And saith unto him, Every man at the beginning doth set forth good wine; and when men have well drunk, then that which is worse: *but* thou hast kept the good wine until now.

9. Marriages among the Jews were celebrated with great feasting, where moderate jocundity was thought seasonable. The reason Christ giveth for his disciples not fasting, was because the bridegroom was yet with them. When they had drunk to temperate hilarity, small wine was most suitable: The vulgar Latin is [when they are drunk] and, perhaps with drunkards that might be the custom, to bring smaller wine when they could not well distinguish them.

11. This beginning of miracles did Jesus in Cana of Galilee, and manifested forth his glory; and his disciples believed on him.

11. By this he shewed them his divine power, and convinced his disciples that he was the Messiah.

12. After this, he went down to Capernaum, he, and his mother, and his brethren, and his disciples, and they continued there not many days. 13. And the Jews passover was at hand, and Jesus went up to Jerusalem. 14. And found in the temple those that sold oxen, and sheep, and doves, and the changers of money, sitting: 15. And when he had made a scourge of small cords, he drove them all out of the temple, and the sheep, and the oxen; and poured out the changers money, and overthrew the tables; 16. And said unto them that sold doves, Take these things hence; make not my Father's house a house of merchandize.

12, &c. It seems probable, that Christ did thus cleanse the temple twice: and that this is not the same history with that, Matt. xxi. though indeed it is very like it.

17. And his disciples remembered that it was written, The zeal of thine house hath eaten me up.

17. They believed that his zeal for God's house, might warrant this action in the Messiah, as Ps. lxix. 9.

18. Then answered the Jews, and said unto him, What sign shewest thou unto us, seeing that thou doest these things?

18. These arbitrary actions require some extraordinary commission to warrant them: By what sign dost thou prove that thou hast such authority?

19. Jesus answered and said unto them, Destroy this temple, and in three days I will raise it up. 20. Then said the Jews, Forty and six years was this temple in building, and wilt thou rear it up in three days? 21. But he spake of the temple of his body.

19. Note, He told them enigmatically what should be after plainly expounded. Many prophecies written darkly, are not intended to be presently understood, but when they are fulfilled.

22. When therefore he was risen from the dead, his disciples remembered that he had said this unto them: and they believed the scripture, and the word which Jesus had said.

22. When this was performed by his resurrection, his disciples believed the prophecies of him, and his own words.

23. Now when he was in Jerusalem at the passover, in the feast-day, many believed in his name, when they saw the miracles which he did.

23. His miracles made many believe that he was the Christ, that yet were no thorough disciples.

24. But Jesus did not commit himself unto them, because he knew all men, 25. And needed not that any should testify of man: for he knew what was in man.

24, 25. But Christ that knew the hearts of men, and how many have but an unrooted, mutable, uneffectual belief, would not trust himself into their hands by familiarity.

CHAP. III.

THERE was a man of the Pharisees, named Nicodemus, a ruler of the Jews: 2. The same came to Jesus by night, and said unto him, Rabbi, we know that thou art a teacher come from God; for no man can do these miracles that thou doest, except God be with him.

1, 2. Being a ruler, he durst not be seen to come to Christ by day light, but came by night, and said, Rabbi, I am come to learn of thee: for I know thou art a teacher sent by God; for no man can do such miracles as thou doest, but by God's power; and God will not lend such power to any whom he doth not approve and justify.

3. Jesus answered and said unto him, Verily, verily I say unto thee, Except a man be born again, he cannot see the kingdom of God.

3. As I could not do the works of God by miracles and doctrine, unless God were with me, so neither can any man become a sound believer, and do the works of faith and be saved, as a true member of the kingdom of God, unless by God's Spirit he be begotten again, and have a new qualitative nature given him.

4. Nicodemus saith unto him, How can a man be born when he is old? can he enter the second time into his mother's womb, and be born?

4. Nicodemus grossly misunderstanding Christ saith, How can, &c.

5. Jesus answered, Verily verily I say unto thee, Except a man be born of water and *of* the Spirit, he cannot enter into the kingdom of God.

5. I tell thee most certainly, that unless a man have as it were, a new nature, and be made a new man, by being washed from his former sin and guilt, and sanctified by the renewing work of God's Spirit, he cannot enter into the kingdom of God.

Note, This is all signified and celebrated by baptism; but it is the washing, and sanctifying the soul only, that hath the promise of salvation; But the church on earth being as the porch, womb, or seminary to heaven, it is not another kind of faith, but that same which in the sincere is saving, which is required to be professed in baptism, for admittance into the visible church.

6. That which is born of the flesh, is flesh; and that which is born of the Spirit, is spirit.

6. Men generate men, but God maketh saints by a spiritual generation: Nature begets but nature, but God's Spirit giveth a holy and heavenly nature or inclination.

7. Marvel not that I said unto thee, Ye must be born again. 8. The wind bloweth where it listeth, and thou hearest the sound thereof, but canst not tell whence it cometh, and whither it goeth: so is every one that is born of the Spirit.

7, 8. Count not this an incredible thing. Thou hearest the sound of the wind, and knowest certainly by the effects, that such a thing as wind there is, and that it causeth those effects, which thy sense perceiveth; but thou knowest not fully, the nature of this wind, nor whence it cometh, nor whither it goeth, and so thou mayest know that God's Spirit doth this sanctifying work on souls, though thou canst not comprehend the nature of the Spirit, nor the way of its operation, nor why it worketh on one soul and not on another that seemeth equal to it.

9. Nicodemus answered and said unto him, How can these things be?

9. Note, The reason of man, not yet illuminated, is apt to be so confident in its ignorance, as

to take those spiritual things for incredible, which it comprehendeth not: It lifts up itself against Christ's teaching, with a *How can these things be?*

10. Jesus answered and said unto him, Art thou a master of Israel, and knowest not these things? 11. Verily, verily I say unto thee, We speak that we do know, and testify that we have seen; and ye receive not our witness.

10, 11. It is a shame for thee, that art a master of Israel, to be ignorant of these things (without which all thy knowledge is but shells and shadows:) I tell thee, we speak that which we certainly know, by intuition and experience on holy souls, and yet you carnal Jews believe us not, not knowing what your own shadows do import.

12. If I have told you earthly things, and ye believe not, how shall ye believe if I tell you of heavenly things?

12. When I tell you but what God doth here on earth on all that he will save, and illustrate it to you by a similitude which your senses do perceive, and it is a thing that your ceremonies signify, how shall you believe, if I tell you the unseen things of heaven, if you believe not things so evident, as these.

13. And no man hath ascended up to heaven, but he that came down from heaven, *even* the Son of Man which is in heaven.

13. And if you will not believe me, what satisfying notice can you have of the state of things in heaven: For no man hath ascended up into heaven, and can tell you by sure notice what is there, but I that came down from heaven, and so came down by assuming flesh, as that yet I am now in heaven in my Godhead.

14. And as Moses lifted up the serpent in the wilderness, even so must the Son of Man be lifted up: 15. That whosoever believeth in him should not perish, but have eternal life.

14, 15. And the way of salvation which God by me revealed to you, is this, that as Moses in the wilderness set up a brazen serpent, that all that were stung with serpents might be cured, if they did look up to this: So I must be lift up on the cross as a sacrifice for sin, that whoever truly believeth in me, and trusteth me as the Redeemer and Saviour, should not perish, but have everlasting life.

16. For God so loved the world, that he gave his only begotten Son, that whosoever believeth in him, should not perish, but have everlasting life.

16. For God, who is love itself, so far loved lapsed and lost mankind, as that he gave his only begotten Son to be incarnate, and to be their redeemer, by his meritorious life, and death, and resurrection, and to make them this promise, covenant, and offer, that whoever truly believeth in him, should have his sin forgiven; and should not perish, but have everlasting blessed life.

17. For God sent not his Son into the world to condemn the world: but that the world through him might be saved.

17. For if the world be condemned, they shall never have cause to lay the blame on Christ: For it was not to condemn them that God sent him into the world, but to be the saviour of the world; which his doctrine, life, and sufferings shew.

18. He that believeth on him, is not condemned: but he that believeth not, is condemned already, because he hath not believed in the name of the only begotten Son of God.

18. He that believeth on him, is thereupon by him delivered from the condemnation that he was under, and shall be saved; but he that believeth not, is not delivered from his guilt and condemnation, but is under the guilt of a severer punishment, the law of grace itself condemning him, because he hath rejected the Son of God, sent from heaven with his doctrine, his grace and offered mercy; so that both the law of nature and of grace condemn the neglecters of so great salvation.

19. And this is the condemnation, that light is come into the world, and men loved darkness rather than light, because their deeds were evil.

19. For the true cause of men's condemnation is (not that they have no Saviour or ransom, being left as devils to remediless despair, but) that a Saviour as light is come into the world, and men love darkness rather than light, and so reject him and his truth and grace, because they love and live in that sin which cannot endure the light.

20. For every one that doeth evil, hateth the light, neither cometh to the light, lest his deeds should be reproved.

20. For it is the part of light to detect and shame men's evil deeds: and therefore malefactors hate and avoid the light, lest it reprove them and condemn them.

21. But he that doeth truth, cometh to the light, that his deeds may

be made manifest, that they are wrought in God.

21. But light is the honour of well doing, which is not afraid to be known; and therefore he that doth that which is truly good, loveth the light, and cometh to it, that his deeds may appear to be as they are, the work commanded and approved by God: And therefore they will receive me that am the light of the world.

22. After these things came Jesus and his disciples into the land of Judea, and there he tarried with them, and baptized.

22. He by his disciples baptized those that believed and repented.

23. And John also was baptizing in Enon, near to Salim, because there was much water there: and they came, and were baptized. 24. For John was not yet cast into prison.

23, 24. John ceased not baptizing, even when Christ baptized, nor till he was imprisoned.

25. Then there arose a question between *some* of John's disciples and the Jews, about purifying.

25. Note, What the dispute was is uncertain.

26. And they came unto John, and said unto him, Rabbi, he that was with thee beyond Jordan, to whom thou bearest witness, behold, the same baptizeth, and all men come to him.

26. On this occasion they told John how the people flocked to the baptism of Christ.

27. John answered and said, A man can receive nothing, except it be given him from heaven. 28. Ye yourselves bear me witness, that I said, I am not the Christ, but that I am sent before him.

27. This doth but confirm what I said of him: His power is from heaven: I pretend to none such as his.

29. He that hath the bride, is the bridegroom: but the friend of the bridegroom, which standeth and heareth him, rejoiceth greatly because of the bridegroom's voice: this my joy is therefore fulfilled.

29. It is he that is the King and Saviour of the church: I am but his friend that rejoice in his kingdom and success.

30. He must increase, but I *must* decrease.

2.

30. His kingdom and glory must increase to perfection, but my preparatory ministry will soon end.

31. He that cometh from above, is above all: he that is of the earth, is earthly, and speaketh of the earth: he that cometh from heaven, is above all.

31. He came from heaven, and therefore is above us all: We that are but men, inhabitants of earth, (Though so far as God inspires us we speak his word) yet being of earthly mold, speak and do like ourselves, in a human earthly manner; But he that cometh from heaven doth excel us all.

32. And what he hath seen and heard, that he testifieth; and no man receiveth his testimony. 33. He that hath received his testimony, hath set to his seal, that God is true.

32. We tell you what God teacheth us in our several measures; but he telleth you that which he hath seen and heard in heaven: And ye the most reject his testimony; but they that truly receive it by faith, do in believing him, believe God himself, that cannot lie.

34. For he whom God hath sent, speaketh the words of God: for God giveth not the spirit by measure *unto him.*

34. He that is thus sent from heaven by God, speaketh God's own words fully and infallibly, as fully known to him, and is not like us and other prophets, that have but our limited measures of the spirit for some particular revelation and use.

35. The Father loveth the Son, and hath given all things into his hand.

35. The love of the Father to the Son is transcendant; and he hath delivered lapsed man, and all this world into his hand or power, as Redeemer, Lord, and administrator of all.

36. He that believeth on the Son hath everlasting life: and he that believeth not the Son, shall not see life; but the wrath of God abideth on him.

36. He that believeth Christ to be the Son of God and Saviour of the world, and with trust giveth up himself to be taught, ruled, and saved by him, hath a right to everlasting life by the covenant of grace, and the beginning of it, by the Holy Ghost in him, and shall shortly have the full possession. But he that by unbelief rejecteth Christ and his offered grace, shall not see this blessed life, but the wrath of God for his unpardoned sin and aggravated guilt, abideth on him.

O

CHAP. IV.

WHEN therefore the Lord knew how the Pharisees had heard that Jesus made and baptized more disciples than John, 2. (Though Jesus himself baptized not, but *his* disciples.) 3. He left Judea, and departed again into Galilee.

1. They knowing that, which he knew would exasperate them, to avoid persecution, he removed to Galilee, (till his time came.)

4. And he must needs go through Samaria. 5. Then cometh he to a city of Samaria, which is called Sychar, near to the parcel of ground that Jacob gave to his son Joseph. 6. Now Jacob's well was there. Jesus therefore being wearied with *his* journey, sat thus on the well; and it was about the sixth hour.

4, 5, 6. Note, Christ travelled all on foot, and had a body wearied with travel, the sixth hour was noon.

7. There cometh a woman of Samaria to draw water: Jesus saith unto her, Give me to drink. 8. For his disciples were gone away unto the city to buy meat. 9. Then saith the woman of Samaria unto him, How is it that thou being a Jew, askest drink of me, which am a woman of Samaria? for the Jews have no dealings with the Samaritans.

7, &c. Note, Christ was not so much for separation, as the other Jews.

10. Jesus answered and said unto her, If thou knewest the gift of God, and who it is that saith to thee, Give me to drink; thou wouldst have asked of him, and he would have given thee living water.

10. Note, It was usual to call a running spring living water, Christ meant more; but she understood him not.

11. The woman saith unto him, Sir, thou hast nothing to draw with, and the well is deep: from whence then hast thou that living water? 12. Art thou greater than our father Jacob, which gave us the well, and drank thereof himself, and his children, and his cattle?

11. Note, They made their honour of Jacob the pretence for not going to Jerusalem: he being before Solomon's temple.

13. Jesus answered and said unto her, Whosoever drinketh of this water shall thirst again: 14. But whosoever drinketh of the water that I shall give him, shall never thirst: but the water that I shall give him, shall be in him a well of water springing up into everlasting life.

13. That which I call water, is the spirit of grace, which will give men everlasting satisfaction and joy, and leave them no fleshly or unsatisfied desires.

15. The woman saith unto him, Sir, give me this water, that I thirst not, neither come hither to draw.

15. The ignorant mistaking God's grace to be what it is not, may ask it so for carnal ends.

16. Jesus saith unto her, Go, call thy husband, and come hither. 17. The woman answered and said, I have no husband. Jesus said unto her, Thou hast well said, I have no husband: 18. For thou hast had five husbands, and he whom thou now hast is not thy husband; in that saidst thou truly.

16. It was not delusory equivocation that Christ calls [well saying] but meant only that truth, not commonly known, it's like.

19. The woman saith unto him, Sir, I perceive that thou art a prophet. 20. Our fathers worshipped in this mountain; and ye say, that in Jerusalem is the place where men ought to worship.

19, 20. I perceive by thy knowing secrets, that thou art a prophet: Tell me then, whether you Jews, or we that follow our eldest fathers, be in the right about the place of worship. Note, This is the use of ignorant, carnal people, to start some controversy about circumstantials or ceremonies in religion, instead of great and needful things.

21. Jesus saith unto her, Woman, believe me, the hour cometh when ye shall neither in this mountain, nor yet at Jerusalem worship the Father.

21. Alas, poor woman, hast thou no greater matter than ceremony, even the place of worship to mind? Believe me, that time is at hand, when Jerusalem shall be destroyed, and you scattered and a better way of worship settled, so that you shall no more keep up your ceremonious worship, either at Shiloh or Jerusalem.

22. Ye worship ye know not what: we know what we worship: for salvation is of the Jews.

22. You worship ignorantly and corruptly, you know not what, ever since the captivity of the ten tribes; and you strive about the place and ceremonies, when you have more need to learn who he is that you must worship. It is of the tribe of Judah, that the Saviour cometh, who must teach you how to worship God; and in this the Jews do rightly, to believe and own none in worship but the true God.

23. But the hour cometh, and now is, when the true worshippers shall worship the Father in spirit and in truth: For the Father seeketh such to worship him.

23. The time is now at hand, yea come, when true worshippers shall not take up with shadows, nor worship God by Mosaical ceremonies, or Samaritan traditions, but with that spiritual worship which types and ceremonies did signify, even from the spirit of God within them as their principle, and according to the spiritual law or word, as their rule, and not with bodily exercise that profiteth nothing.

24. God *is* a spirit, and they that worship him, must worship *him* in spirit and in truth.

24. Acceptable worship must be suited to the God you worship; and therefore they that worship him must worship him spiritually, and not by Jewish ceremony, because he is a spirit. Note, Though [spirit] signify a nature more excellent than [body] yet that and all human words are too low to speak the essence of God, any otherwise than analogically or metaphorically; for God is above all our formal conceptions or expressions; but created spirits, being the highest created beings known to us, and our souls of that nature, they are the clearest glass in which we can know God; and though the word [spirit] first signify created spirit, it doth transcendantly, eminently, signify the Infinite Father of Spirits; and we can say nothing higher of God's essence, than that he is the infinite, perfect, transcendent Spirit; what our best conceptions of a spirit are, I have opened in Methodo Theologiæ, &c.

25. The woman saith unto him, I know that Messias cometh which is called Christ: when he is come, he will teach us all things.

25. Note, Even the Samaritans expected the Messiah: But with misconceivings of him.

26. Jesus saith unto her, I that speak unto thee am *he.*

26. Note, Why did Christ tell that to this woman, which he forbad others to tell abroad? Ans. He knew where and when it was seasonable, and would do more good than harm.

27. And upon this came his disciples, and marvelled that he talked with the woman: yet no man said, What seekest thou? or, Why talkest thou with her?

27. Though they presumed not to ask him why? yet they thought it strange that he should talk so long with one woman.

28. The woman then left her water-pot, and went her way into the city, and saith to the men, 29. Come, see a man which told me all things that ever I did: is not this the Christ?

28. Telling her secrets, persuaded her to believe him, saying I am he.

30. Then they went out of the city, and came unto him. 31. In the mean while his disciples prayed him, saying, Master, eat. 32. But he said unto them, I have meat to eat that ye know not of. 33. Therefore said the disciples one to another, Hath any man brought him *ought* to eat? 34. Jesus saith unto them, My meat is to do the will of him that sent me, and to finish his work.

30, &c. Note, The converting of one soul was more pleasing to Christ than his natural food; and so must it be to us. He that loveth God and Christ, and the Holy Ghost and the church; must rejoice when there is one more converted, to please and worship God, to honour Christ and his Spirit, to increase the church: He that loveth his country, must rejoice that one more is made a blessing to it, when the wicked are its enemies: He that loveth souls, will rejoice in that grace which is better to them than all riches: He that loveth God's word will rejoice in its success: He that loveth heaven will be glad that there is one more to possess it: He that loveth himself aright, will be glad that there is one more made like him, to love him, and pray for him. And he that hateth sin and Satan, will be glad that there is one less to serve him.

35. Say not ye, There are yet four months, and *then* cometh harvest? behold, I say unto you, Lift up your eyes, and look on the fields; for they are white already to harvest.

35. You rejoice that within four months it will be harvest: And shall not I rejoice to see the harvest of my husbandry even at hand, in the conversion of many souls to God?

36. And he that reapeth, receiveth wages, and gathereth fruit unto life eternal: that both he that soweth and he that reapeth, may rejoice together.

36. And as I sow the seed, so you that I shall send out as apostles shall see and reap more plenteous fruit hereafter, and shall for your labour under me, be well rewarded: that I that have sowed and you that reap may rejoice together in the success.

37. And herein is that saying true, One soweth, and another reapeth. 38. I sent you to reap that whereon ye bestowed no labour: other men laboured, and ye are entered into their labour.

38. The prophets and John and I after all, have sowed the seed and been at the costliest labour, and yet it is you that must see the success in gathering the universal church, when I that laboured and suffered am gone.

39. And many of the Samaritans of that city believed on him, for the saying of the woman, which testified, He told me all that ever I did.

39. Note, That to believe in Christ by the means of men's credible testimony of his words and miracles, is not (as many falsely say) to resolve our faith into the credit of man, and to make it a mere human faith. They that believe apostles who said they saw Christ's miracles, resurrection, and ascension, believe by a divine faith, on the same evidence that the apostles were convinced by, but not conveyed by the same mean: what they received by their eyes and ears immediately, we receive mediately by their report, living at a distance: So that their testimony is not believed instead of Christ's, nor instead of the evidence of his truth, but as the conveyance of this evidence instead of our mediate sight and hearing: so is it as to the tradition of the bible, baptism, creed, &c. That tradition doth but deliver to us the same word mediately which the first churches received immediately from the apostles. He that cannot read, may be saved by the believing the gospel translated and read, or reported by the preachers.

40. So when the Samaritans were come unto him, they besought him, that he would tarry with them: and he abode there two days. 41. And many more believed, because of his own word: 42. And said unto the woman, Now we believe, not because of thy saying: for we have heard him ourselves, and know that this is indeed the Christ, the Saviour of the world.

42. Not so much because of thy saying. Note, Yet this was the same sort of faith, though by the evidence divers ways conveyed.

43. Now after two days he departed thence, and went into Galilee: 44. For Jesus himself testified, that a prophet hath no honour in his own country.

43. He went into Galilee, not to Nazareth where he had lived, but to Cana: For he had testified that a prophet is despised in his own country; where they have seen his common parentage and education, but see not God's spirit in him: and familiarity breeds contempt.

45. Then when he was come into Galilee, the Galileans received him, having seen all the things that he did at Jerusalem at the feast: for they also went unto the feast.

45. His former and later miracles caused these Galileans to receive him.

46. So Jesus came again into Cana of Galilee, where he made the water wine. And there was a certain nobleman, whose son was sick at Capernaum. 47. When he heard that Jesus was come out of Judea into Galilee, he went unto him, and besought him that he would come down and heal his son: for he was at the point of death. 48. Then said Jesus unto him, Except ye see signs and wonders, ye will not believe. 49. The nobleman saith unto him, Sir, come down ere my child die. 50. Jesus saith unto him, Go thy way; thy son liveth. And the man believed the word that Jesus had spoken unto him, and he went his way. 51. And as he was now going down, his servants met him, and told him, saying, thy son liveth. 52. Then inquired he of them the hour when he began to amend: and they said unto him, Yesterday at the seventh hour the fever left him. 53. So the father knew that it was at the same hour, in the which Jesus said unto him, Thy son liveth; and

himself believed, and his whole house. 54. This *is* again the second miracle *that* Jesus did, when he was come out of Judea into Galilee.

46, &c. Note. 1. Outward necessities which nature is sensible of, drived many to seek to Christ. 2. Children speed the better for their parents' faith: And if in the body, why not in the soul. 3. When the rulers of families believe, they must endeavour the conversion of their whole families. And God oft blesseth such endeavours. 4. Bodily mercies tend to the good of souls, and should be so improved.

CHAP. V.

AFTER this there was a feast of the Jews, and Jesus went up to Jerusalem. 2. Now there is at Jerusalem, by the sheep-*market* a pool, which is called in the Hebrew tongue, Bethesda, having five porches. 3. In these lay a great multitude of impotent folk, of blind, halt, withered, waiting for the moving of the water. 4. For an angel went down at a certain season into the pool, and troubled the water: whosoever then first after the troubling of the water stepped in, was made whole of whatsoever disease he had.

Note, 1. Some few think that this was a pond that the blood of the sacrifices ran into, and was stirred by a messenger (not an angel) at the time of the passover when the blood was newly run into it, and so healed, not miraculously, but by the ordinary virtue of the new shed blood, and that it is not all diseases that are meant; and that it was not eight and thirty years that the man had waited in that hospital, but that he had so long been ill: So Dr. Hammond; others think it was the pond made by Hezekiah, and healed by unaccountable miracle.

5. And a certain man was there, which had an infirmity thirty and eight years.

5. How great a mercy is it to live eight and thirty years under God's wholesome discipline? How unexcusable was this man if he had been proud, or worldly, or careless of his everlasting state? O my God, I thank thee for the like discipline of eight and fifty years, how safe a life is this in comparison of full prosperity and pleasure?

6. When Jesus saw him lie, and knew that he had been now a long time *in that case*, he saith unto him,

wilt thou be made whole? 7. The impotent man answered him, Sir, I have no man, when the water is troubled, to put me into the pool: but while I am coming, another steppeth down before me. 8. Jesus saith unto him, Rise, take up thy bed, and walk.

6. *Note,* 1. When human help faileth, Christ sheweth his love, and power, and commandeth health at a word.

9. And immediately the man was made whole, and took up his bed, and walked: and on the same day was the sabbath.

9. The man shewed them all that he was cured: And Christ chose the sabbath for this good work.

10. The Jews therefore said unto him that was cured, It is the sabbath-day; it is not lawful for thee to carry *thy* bed.

10. The Jews were stricter than Christ for ceremony and rites: but looser for charity and pleaded that it was a breach of Moses' law to carry his couch.

11. He answered them, He that made me whole, the same said unto me, Take up thy bed and walk.

11. I know not whom I should obey; if not a man that can work so great a miracle.

12. Then asked they him, What man is that which said unto thee, Take up thy bed and walk?

12. Who is he that durst thus break the law?

13. And he that was healed wist not who it was: for Jesus had conveyed himself away, a multitude being in *that* place.

13. Christ did it not for human applause, and therefore was not known to be the man.

14. Afterward Jesus findeth him in the temple, and said unto him, Behold, thou art made whole: sin no more, lest a worse thing come unto thee.

14. It was for thy sin that thou wast corrected. Beware of sin, lest the next be worse.

15. The man departed, and told the Jews that it was Jesus which had made him whole.

15. He told them in the praise of Jesus that it was he that healed him.

16. And therefore did the Jews persecute Jesus, and sought to slay him, because he had done these things on the sabbath-day.

16. O the blindness and madness of malignants, that will seek to kill men for doing good and healing men.

17. But Jesus answered them, My Father worketh hitherto, and I work.

17. To save the afflicted, is a work beseeming my Father and Me, whom you oppose.

18. Therefore the Jews sought the more to kill him, because he not only had broken the sabbath, but said also, that God was his Father, making himself equal with God.

18. Note, Malignants' zeal fathereth even error and persecution on God.

19. Then answered Jesus, and said unto them, Verily, verily I say unto you, The Son can do nothing of himself, but what he seeth the Father do: for what things soever he doeth, these also doeth the Son likewise.

19. I tell you by condemning my works you condemn my Father's also: For I do nothing but what I know he doth and approveth, and he doth them in and by me, and I do nothing without him.

20. For the Father loveth the Son, and sheweth him all things that himself doeth: and he will shew him greater works than these, that ye may marvel.

20. For the Father's infinite love communicateth to the Son that wisdom and power by which he doth all that the Father doth: and by which you shall see greater things than these, and wonder.

21. For as the Father raiseth up the dead, and quickeneth *them:* even so the Son quickeneth whom he will.

21. As the Father is the Lord of life, and giveth and restoreth life at his pleasure; so also doth the Son.

22. For the Father judgeth no man: but hath committed all judgment unto the Son:

22. For the Father as mere creator according to the law of innocency judgeth no man: but hath given up the government of this world to the Son as Redeemer, to judge them as ransomed, according to that law and measure of grace which they are under.

23. That all men should honour the Son, even as they honour the Father. He that honoureth not the Son, honoureth not the Father which hath sent him.

23. And so it is by honouring the Son, that the Father will be honoured, and by dishonouring him, the Father is dishonoured.

24. Verily, verily I say unto you, He that heareth my word, and believeth on him that sent me, hath everlasting life, and shall not come into condemnation; but is passed from death unto life.

24. I tell you if you hear my word obediently, and shall believe on God the Father, as sending me on the office of a saviour, you shall have everlasting life by my merits and gift, and shall not be condemned.

25. Verily, verily I say unto you, the hour is coming, and now is, when the dead shall hear the voice of the Son of God: and they that hear shall live.

25. I tell you that the hour is coming, yea now is already come, in which it shall appear that the Son of God hath the power of life and death, natural, spiritual, and eternal; and that they that are dead in sin and unbelief, shall hear his gospel, and be regenerate and made alive to God, and that natural life shall be restored by him, to some bodies at his own resurrection, and to all at last, when he shall effectually call up all the dead to judgment.

26. For as the Father hath life in himself; so hath he given to the Son to have life in himself;

26. As the Father is essential, underived self-life, communicating life to creatures: so the Son, as God, and as redeemer, hath the power of giving life from himself to the redeemed.

27. And hath given him authority to execute judgment also, because he is the Son of Man.

27. And as redeemer, being the Son of God in his divine nature, and his human nature advanced into personal union with the divine, he hath authority given him to govern the world, and according to the law of grace to do justice for the faithful, and against the impenitent unbelievers.

28. Marvel not at this: for the hour is coming, in the which all

CHAP. V. ST. JOHN. 199

that are in the graves shall hear his voice, 29. And shall come forth, they that have done good unto the resurrection of life; and they that have done evil, unto the resurrection of damnation.

28, 29. Let not this seem incredible to you: For the hour is coming in which the bodies now turned to dust, shall by the soul's return be revived, and hear his voice that calls them up: and there shall be a resurrection of the just and unjust: they that have done good according to the tenor of that law of grace which they were under, shall come forth to a life of happiness, and they that have done evil, violating the conditions of life in that law, to the resurrection of damnation.

30. I can of mine own self do nothing: As I hear I judge: and my judgment is just; because I seek not mine own will, but the will of the Father, which hath sent me.

30. I am not to judge according to the weakness of humanity, as princes govern: I do nothing, but according to divine infallible decree and appointment, which I assuredly know: And my judgment is just, because I seek not my own human will, as my rule or end, but the will of my Father who sent me; that is my rule and end.

31. If I bear witness of myself, my witness is not true. 32. There is another that beareth witness of me, and I know that the witness which he witnesseth of me, is true.

31, 32. If I had no testimony but my own word, you were not to take it for credible truth: But there is another, who giveth you convincing evidences of his truth; even my Father by his voice from heaven, and by his Spirit and works.

33. Ye sent unto John, and he bare witness unto the truth. 34. But I receive not testimony from man: but these things I say, that ye might be saved.

33, 34. You sent to John, and he told you of me as the Messiah. I need not his or any man's testimony: But it nearly concerneth your own safety to believe him.

35. He was a burning and a shining light: and ye were willing for a season to rejoice in his light.

35. God set him up to be as a burning and shining light, to lead you out of darkness to the kingdom of the Messiah, which you expected: and a while you gladly heard that news, and were baptised by him: till you were told that I am he, and then you turned back.

36. But I have greater witness than *that* of John: for the works which the Father hath given me to finish, the same works that I do, bear witness of me, that the Father hath sent me.

36. Note, For these works could not be done but by God's power and will, who will not be the world's deceiver.

37. And the Father himself which hath sent me, hath borne witness of me. Ye have neither heard his voice at any time, nor seen his shape. 38. And ye have not his word abiding in you; for whom he hath sent, him ye believe not.

37, 38. By a voice from heaven God testified me to be his beloved Son: but indeed you were not the persons that heard it: For you never heard his voice, nor saw his appearance, nor understand or believe his word: else you would believe on me that am sent by him.

39. Search the scriptures, for in them ye think ye have eternal life; and they are they which testify of me.

39. You own the authority of Moses and the prophets, and look to have eternal life by keeping their word, search their writings, and you will find that they testify of me.

40. And ye will not come to me, that ye might have life.

40. And though they tell you that it is in and by me, that this life must be attained, ye will not believe in me and come to me that you may attain it.

41. I receive not honour from men. 42. But I know you, that ye have not the love of God in you.

41, 42. It is not the applause of men that I seek for; but your own salvation: but I know for all your boasting of being the peculiar people of God, you are indeed no true lovers and obeyers of God.

43. I am come in my Father's name, and ye receive me not: if another shall come in his own name, him ye will receive.

43. I come with testimony from heaven of the mission and approbation of my Father, and this prevaileth not against your prejudice to believe me. But when a deceiver shall come with ostentation without any evidence from God, and shall promise you a temporal kingdom, you will take him for the Messiah.

44. How can ye believe, which receive honour one of another, and

seek not the honour that *cometh* from God only?

44. How can you receive the Messiah sent from God, who do not seek and trust to God's approbation, and his way of saving you; but must have a worldly kingdom, and be saved and advanced after the manner of worldly men, and look for a saviour suited to such ends.

45. Do not think that I will accuse you to the Father; there is *one* that accuseth you, *even* Moses, in whom ye trust. 46. For had ye believed Moses, ye would have believed me: for he wrote of me, 47. But if ye believe not his writings, how shall ye believe my words?

45, 46, 47. I say not all this as if I came to be your accuser to my Father; even Moses in whom you trust will accuse you; had you understood and believed the prophecies and types of Moses, ye would have believed me: For it is me that they all speak of and point you to; But if you will not be convinced by his writings whom you glory in, no wonder if you reject my words.

CHAP. VI.

AFTER these things, Jesus went over the sea of Galilee, which is *the sea* of Tiberias. 2. And a great multitude followed him, because they saw his miracles which he did on them that were diseased.

1, 2. Note, The first motives that draw men toward Christ, are usually such as nature itself is somewhat capable to esteem and judge of, such as miracles are.

3. And Jesus went up into a mountain, and there he sat with his disciples. 4. And the passover, a feast of the Jews was nigh. 5. When Jesus then lift up *his* eyes, and saw a great company come unto him, he saith unto Philip, Whence shall we buy bread that these may eat? 6. (And this he said to prove him: for he himself knew what he would do).

3, &c. Note, Christ's relief of bodies, was in love to bodies and souls. 2. Christ's questions were to instruct the hearers and not himself.

7. Philip answered him, Two hundred penny-worth of bread is not sufficient for them, that every one of them may take a little.

7. Note, Philip's sense of the difficulty, was a preparation to the value of the miracle.

8. One of his disciples, Andrew, Simon Peter's brother, saith unto him, 9. There is a lad here, which hath five barley-loaves, and two small fishes: but what are they among so many?

8, 9. Note, It was not delicious fare, but barley bread and two fishes that Christ used a miracle about.

10. And Jesus said, Make the men sit down. Now there was much grass in the place. So the men sat down, in number about five thousand. 11. And Jesus took the loaves, and when he had given thanks, he distributed to the disciples, and the disciples to them that were set down; and likewise of the fishes, as much as they would.

10, 11. Note, If Christ would not distribute barley bread, and that miraculously till he had given thanks; (not deterred by the suspicions of a riot or conventicle) sure we should imitate him in our ordinary repast, and eat and drink to the glory of God, in a holy thankfulness for his liberality.

12. When they were filled, he said unto his disciples, Gather up the fragments that remain, that nothing be lost. 13. Therefore they gathered *them* together, and filled twelve baskets with the fragments of the five barley-loaves, which remained over and above unto them that had eaten.

12, 13. Note, To lose any of our useful food, is a sin against God: Where there is the greatest plenty, no fragments should be lost, while the poor do need it. How much less should we lose God's word or helps, or our time, or any such greater mercies?

14. Then those men, when they had seen the miracle that Jesus did, said, This is of a truth that prophet that should come into the world.

14. Note, A miracle done upon five thousand at once, made a common conviction of them that Christ was the Messiah, or a great prophet.

15. When Jesus therefore per-

ceived that they would come and take him by force, to make him a king, he departed again into a mountain himself alone.

15. When they would have made a captain and visible monarch of him, he shunned it and avoided them.

16. And when even was now come, his disciples went down unto the sea, 17. And entered into a ship, and went over the sea towards Capernaum: and it was now dark, and Jesus was not come to them. 18. And the sea arose by reason of a great wind that blew. 19. So when they had rowed about five and twenty, or thirty furlongs, they see Jesus walking on the sea, and drawing nigh unto the ship: and they were afraid. 20. But he saith unto them, It is I, be not afraid.

16, &c. Note, This miracle shewed Christ to be above nature.

21. Then they willingly received him into the ship: and immediately the ship was at the land whither they went.

21. Note, They might well be glad to receive him that could rule sea and land.

22. The day following, when the people which stood on the other side of the sea, saw that there was none other boat there, save that one whereinto his disciples were entered, and that Jesus went not with his disciples into the boat, but *that* his disciples were gone away alone: 23. (Howbeit there came other boats from Tiberias, nigh unto the place where they did eat bread, after that the Lord had given thanks). 24. When the people therefore saw that Jesus was not there, neither his disciples, they also took shipping, and came to Capernaum, seeking for Jesus.

22, 23, 24. How earnest did these persons seem in following Christ?

25. And when they had found him on the other side of the sea, they said unto him, Rabbi, when camest thou hither? 26. Jesus answered them, and said, Verily, verily I say unto you, Ye seek me, not because ye saw the miracles, but because ye did eat of the loaves, and were filled.

26. Note, It seems these were a very poor sort of people, that would follow Christ for barley bread.

27. Labour not for the meat which perisheth, but for that meat which endureth unto everlasting life, which the Son of Man shall give unto you: for him hath God the Father sealed.

27. Labour first and chiefly for the food which endureth to everlasting life; even the spirit of holiness renewing you by the gospel, and an union with me who am the bread of life, which I will give unto all true believers: to which use God hath sent and sealed me by fulness of the spirit and power; And trust God for bodily food while you labour for it, but in the second place. Note, The words have a comparative signification: Labour not, is labour less, or but subordinately.

28. Then said they unto him, What shall we do, that we may work the works of God?

28. What is that labour for the everlasting life which God requireth of us? What must we do for it?

29. Jesus answered and said unto them, This is the work of God, that ye believe on him whom he hath sent.

29. This is your first and great work which God requireth, that you believe on me whom God hath sent, and take me for your teacher and Saviour, that I may guide and sanctify you, and teach you your further duty, in order to fit you for everlasting life.

30. They said therefore unto him, What sign shewest thou then, that we may see, and believe thee? what dost thou work? 31. Our fathers did eat manna in the desert; as it is written, He gave them bread from heaven to eat.

30. If thou wouldest have us believe in thee, convince us yet by further miracles? Canst thou procure us bread from heaven as Moses did? Note, 1. Strange! that they should call for more miracles when they newly came from seeing one? 2. It was a feeding miracle that these expected; which might gratify their flesh as well as their faith.

32. Then Jesus said unto them,

Verily, verily I say unto you, Moses gave you not that bread from heaven; but my Father giveth you the true bread from heaven. 33. For the bread of God is he which cometh down from heaven, and giveth life unto the world.

32. It was not Moses that gave you the true bread from heaven: Manna and other types did but fore-signify me, who am the true bread which my Father giveth you from heaven, whence I come; called bread, because I give life to the world.

34. Then said they unto him, Lord, evermore give us this bread.

34. Note, Their carnal minds, had carnal desires, and understood Christ accordingly.

35. And Jesus said unto them, I am the bread of life: he that cometh to me, shall never hunger; and he that believeth on me, shall never thirst.

35. As your bodies live by food, so he that cometh to me by true faith, and is united to me, shall have by me true spiritual everlasting life, and shall have all his necessities of hunger and thirst satisfied.

36. But I said unto you, that ye also have seen me, and believe not.

36. But I know your hearts, that many of you that have seen my miracles, and thus crowd after me, for the strangeness and novelty, yet are no true believers.

37. All that the Father giveth me, shall come to me; and him that cometh to me, I will in no wise cast out.

37. All that the Father hath given to me, as fully resolved to save them, shall believe and take me for their Saviour: I come not into the world upon an uncertainty of success. I have undertaken the effectual saving of those that are given me by the Father to be certainly saved: All those will come to me, and I will refuse none that by obedient trust doth come to me.

38. For I came down from heaven, not to do my own will, but the will of him that sent me.

38. For I came not at random, or on any selfish temporal design, but to fulfil my Father's will, who will give the kingdom to his selected flocks.

Note, It is a troubling controversy, how Christ is said to come down from heaven: His human nature was never there, and his divine, removed not thence, and is every where. To pass by their opinion, who say it is a middle, super-angelical, first created nature, between the divine and human that came down: I answer, that the divine is said to come down, not by a substantial removal or change of place, but by a transcendant influx and operation, on the human nature of Christ: Men may talk in the dark how they please, but it is certain that that divine essence is every where, without inequality or existence; and is no more in Christ's human nature, as to essential presence, than he is every where: But as he is said to be in heaven, because there he operateth by glorious refulgency and love to the glorified, so he is more eminently and peculiarly united to the manhood of Christ, for and by a more eminent and peculiar operation on the human nature: As the sun is more in the eye than in the hand or foot, more in the plants that it quickeneth than in the stones; so is the godhead in the human nature of Christ. And so the godhead came down from heaven, as the sun doth when it shineth in at our windows, or on a burning glass, or rather as it animateth plants.

39. And this is the Father's will which hath sent me, that of all which he hath given me, I should lose nothing, but should raise it up again at the last day.

39. And it is the special commission which I have from my Father, that I should effectually save all these his chosen, and raise them up to life everlasting.

40. And this the will of him that sent me, that every one which seeth the Son, and believeth on him, may have everlasting life: and I will raise him up at the last day.

40. And it is my Father's will, that every one that by notice of the evidence of my truth, truly believeth on me, shall have everlasting life, to which (first here begun) I will raise him at the last.

41. The Jews then murmured at him, because he said, I am the bread which came down from heaven. 42. And they said, Is not this Jesus the son of Joseph, whose father and mother we know? how is it then that he saith, I came down from heaven?

41. Note, This difficulty staggered their faith, not knowing the mystery of Christ's person and incarnation.

43. Jesus therefore answered and said unto them, Murmur not among yourselves. 44. No man can come to me, except the Father which hath sent me, draw him: and I will raise him up at the last day.

43. The objections which you murmur on, do

indeed require divine grace to overcome them; and therefore none can sincerely believe and come to me as a Christian, except the Father who sent me to save men, convince and draw them to me to be saved, and all those I will raise to life everlasting.

45. It is written in the prophets, And they shall be all taught of God. Every man therefore that hath heard, and hath learned of the Father, cometh unto me.

45. As the prophets speak of a divine teaching, so those that are thus taught of God, are they that come to me.

46. Not that any man hath seen the Father, save he which is of God, he hath seen the Father.

46. Not by a teaching by seeing him: For it is I only that come from him, that have seen him.

47. Verily, verily, I say unto you, He that believeth on me hath everlasting life. 48. I am that bread of life. 49. Your fathers did eat manna in the wilderness, and are dead. 50. This is the bread which cometh down from heaven, that a man may eat thereof, and not die. 51. I am the living bread, which came down from heaven: if any man eat of this bread, he shall live for ever: and the bread that I will give, is my flesh, which I will give for the life of the world.

47. I tell you, he that believeth on me, hath that everlasting life, which manna gave not, for they are dead that did eat it: I am the bread that came indeed from heaven and give life, not temporary, but everlasting, not to a few, but to the world, or universal church: My sacrificed flesh shall purchase this.

52. The Jews therefore strove amongst themselves, saying, How can this man give us *his* flesh to eat? 53. Then Jesus said unto them, Verily, verily, I say unto you, except ye eat the flesh of the Son of Man, and drink his blood, ye have no life in you. 54. Whoso eateth my flesh, and drinketh my blood, hath eternal life, and I will raise him up at the last day. 55. For my flesh is meat indeed, and my blood is drink indeed.

52. This seemed to them a saying not to be digested, and Christ at that time would no further explain it to them, than by saying, I tell you, unless that you live by virtue of my flesh and blood received by faith, as food is by your mouth, ye have no spiritual saving life: It is all they, that thus by faith partake of my sacrificed flesh and blood, that have the title and beginning of eternal life, and I will at last raise them up to the full fruition of it: For my sacrificed flesh and blood are truly enlivening and saving.

56. He that eateth my flesh, and drinketh my blood, dwelleth in me, and I in him.

56. He that by true faith trusteth in my sacrificed flesh and blood, professeth thereby to be united to me, as digested food is to the body, whereby I also dwell in him, and I will give him the spirit of life, and he shall live by influence from me.

57. As the living Father hath sent me, and I live by the Father: so he that eateth me, even he shall live by me.

57. As the Father is essential self-life, and I live by communication from him: so he that is intimately united to me, and I to him, as food is to the body by digestion, by a covenanting lively faith, shall live by me a life of grace and glory.

58. This is that bread which came down from heaven: not as your fathers did eat manna, and are dead, he that eateth of this bread, shall live for ever.

58. I am the true bread from heaven, who give everlasting life, when your fathers who did eat manna died, and were not by that made immortal.

59. These things said he in the synagogue, as he taught in Capernaum.

59. Note, Remember, it was not those only that had followed him that he spake this to, and the following sharp passages; but to his auditors at Capernaum.

60. Many therefore of his disciples, when they had heard *this*, said, This is an hard saying, who can hear it?

60. Note. Christ would not forbear this mysterious doctrine, though the hearers could not digest it, but would make an ill use of it, to depart from him.

61. When Jesus knew in himself, that his diciples murmured at it, he said unto them, Doth this offend you? 62. *What* and if ye shall see

the Son of Man ascend up where he was before?

61. I will ere long ascend up visibly to heaven: And will not that prove that I came from heaven?

63. It is the spirit that quickeneth, the flesh profiteth nothing: the words that I speak unto you, *they* are spirit, and *they* are life.

63. And as to your offence at my words of the eating of my flesh, you know that flesh of itself would be a dead and senseless thing, were it not for the soul that is its life: And so it is not my mere dead flesh that I say shall give you life; but my flesh as it is in dignity the body of the Son of God, purchasing life for the world, and as it is accompanied with the operation of the Holy Ghost, which animateth them spiritually, who by faith are united to me: And thus not only my flesh, but the words that I speak to you, are by my Spirit made the means of communicating to you spirit and life.

64. But there are some of you that believe not. For Jesus knew from the beginning, who they were that believed not, and who should betray him.

64. But there are some of you that follow me, that are not true believers, and therefore have not this quickening spirit. For he knew their hearts, and knew who would after betray him.

Note. Though Christ knew Judas and other hypocrites, he did not expel them, but sent out Judas to preach with the rest, to tell us how the visible church will be constituted and must be ordered.

65. And he said, Therefore said I unto you, that no man can come unto me, except it were given unto him of my Father.

65. Note, That the word [can] speaketh not of physical power, but partly moral indisposition, and partly an hypothetical impossibility of event. 2. That though God's grace be the cause of faith, no man is deprived of that grace but by his own wilful sin, which maketh him inexcusable.

66. From that *time* many of his disciples went back, and walked no more with him.

66. By forsaking him, they shewed that they were never sound believers.

67. Then said Jesus unto the twelve, Will ye also go away? 68. Then Simon Peter answered him, Lord, to whom shall we go? thou hast the words of eternal life. 69. And we believe, and are sure that thou art that Christ the Son of the living God.

67. Note, 1. Christ puts none away, till they put away themselves. 2. He forceth none to stay. 3. It greatly fixeth a Christian's resolution to stick to Christ, to know there is none else to go to: as it resolveth us to look for happiness to God and heaven, because we are sure there is no other. 4. Sound faith may attain assurance that Christ is the Son of the living God: it hath always objective certainty, and a prevalent certainty, and a prevalent confidence, and may reach to a mental confirmed certainty.

70. Jesus answered them, Have not I chosen you twelve, and one of you is a devil? 71. He spake of Judas Iscariot, *the son* of Simon: for he it was that should betray him, being one of the twelve.

70, 71. Even of you twelve whom I have chosen out of all the rest to be next me, one is a devil, that is Judas.

Note, 1. Some men are so bad that they may be called Devils. Both as false calumniators, whence is the name Diabolus; and as they are the very agents of the Devil, and minded like him, and ruled by him, and do what he moveth them to do, in his three great works, lying, or (deceit,) hatred, or (malignity,) and hurtfulness and murder. 2. Such may be latent in the holiest society. 3. Which yet must not be denominated by such.

CHAP. VII.

AFTER these things, Jesus walked in Galilee: for he would not walk in Jewry, because the Jews sought to kill him.

Note, 1. Christ's own example tells us, That it is no sinful cowardice to avoid persecution, till our suffering or death be like to do more good than liberty, or life.

2. Now the Jews feast of tabernacles was at hand. 3. His brethren therefore said unto him, Depart hence, and go into Judea, that thy disciples also may see the works that thou doest. 4. For *there is* no man *that* doeth any thing in secret, and he himself seeketh to be known openly: If thou do these things, shew thyself to the world. 5. For neither did his brethren believe in him.

2, &c. Note, Christ's own kindred believed not on him a long time: And censured him for not appearing more publicly in the face of dangers and

CHAP. VII.   ST. JOHN.

rulers, if he were sent from God. Thus men will teach and reprove those of whom they should learn. Foolish men will seem wiser than Christ, and dislike his ways

6. Then Jesus said unto them, My time is not yet come: but your time is alway ready. 7. The world cannot hate you; but me it hateth, because I testify of it, that the works thereof are evil. 8. Go ye up unto this feast: I go not up yet unto this feast, for my time is not yet full come. 9. When he had said these words unto them, he abode *still* in Galilee. 10. But when his brethren were gone up, then went he also up unto the feast, not openly, but as it were in secret.

6, &c. Note, 1. Christ here also avoided persecution. 2. He trusted not his brethren with his purpose.

11. Then the Jews sought him at the feast, and said, Where is he? 12. And there was much murmuring among the people concerning him: for some said, He is a good man: others said, Nay; but he deceiveth the people. 13. Howbeit, no man spake openly of him, for fear of the Jews.

12, 13. The people divided in their judgments of him, did not openly speak their minds, for fear of the rulers that were most against him.

14. Now about the midst of the feast, Jesus went up into the temple, and taught. 15. And the Jews marvelled, saying, How knoweth this man letters, having never learned? 16. Jesus answered them, and said, My doctrine is not mine, but his that sent me. 17. If any man will do his will, he shall know of the doctrine, whether it be of God, or *whether* I speak of myself.

14. He that is sent of God, may know more than he hath learned of man: God tells me what to speak. And those that truly obey so much of the will of God as they know, are prepared to know more, and to discern my doctrine to be of God: but wilful sinners are not.

18. He that speaketh of himself, seeketh his own glory: but he that seeketh his glory that sent him, the same is true, and no unrighteousness is in him.

18. Did I seek vain-glory, or any private ends of my own, you might suppose that I spake my own words: but if I only seek the glory of God, and good of men, though to my own suffering, you have no cause to suspect me of deceit or any ill design.

19. Did not Moses give you the law, and *yet* none of you keepeth the law? Why go ye about to kill me?

19. But how unfit are you to discern what doctrine is of God, who keep not the law of Moses which you boast of. For that law forbiddeth murder, and yet you seek to murder me.

20. The people answered and said, Thou hast a devil: who goeth about to kill thee?

20. Note, They supposed him distracted. And the distracted were usually taken for demoniacs.

21. Jesus answered and said unto them, I have done one work, and ye all marvel. 22. Moses therefore gave unto you circumcision, (not because it is of Moses, but of the fathers) and ye on the sabbath-day circumcise a man. 23. If a man on the sabbath-day receive circumcision, that the law of Moses should not be broken; are ye angry at me, because I have made a man every whit whole on the sabbath-day.

21. Note, The history of his cure, and their plotting his death for it, is here past over and supposed: But Christ knew their malicious design.

24. Judge not according to the appearance, but judge righteous judgment.

24. Judge not by outward shows and worldly men's opinions, but according to the evidence of truth.

25. Then said some of them of Jerusalem, Is not this he whom they seek to kill? 26. But lo, he speaketh boldly, and they say nothing unto him: do the rulers know indeed that this is the very Christ?

25. Do they suffer him because they believe him to be Christ.

27. Howbeit, we know this man

whence he is: but when Christ cometh, no man knoweth whence he is.

27. Note, They knew his visible original, but they knew not his heavenly nature and glory.

28. Then cried Jesus in the temple as he taught, saying, Ye both know me, and ye know whence I am: and I am not come of myself, but he that sent me is true, whom ye know not. 29. But I know him, for I am from him, and he hath sent me.

28. Note, Ye know my visible original: But you know not my heavenly Father who sent me: But I know him, for I, &c.

30. Then they sought to take him: but no man laid hands on him, because his hour was not yet come. 31. And many of the people believed on him, and said, When Christ cometh, will he do more miracles than these which this *man* hath done?

30, 31. His miracles convinced some against all prejudices and objections.

32. The Pharisees heard that the people murmured such things concerning him: and the Pharisees, and the chief priests sent officers to take him. 33. Then said Jesus unto them, Yet a little while am I with you, and *then* I go unto him that sent me. 34. Ye shall seek me, and shall not find *me:* and where I am, *thither* ye cannot come.

32, &c. The Pharisees and priests thought persecuting necessary to keep people from believing on him: And Christ told them, It is but a little while, till I shall be out of the reach of your malice.

35. Then said the Jews among themselves, Whither will he go, that we shall not find him? will he go unto the dispersed among the Gentiles, and teach the Gentiles? 36. What *manner of* saying is this that he said, Ye shall seek me, and shall not find *me:* and where I am, *thither* ye cannot come?

35. Will he go to those Jews who are dispersed abroad the world, or what meaneth he?

37. In the last day, that great *day* of the feast, Jesus stood and cried, saying, If any man thirst, let him come unto me, and drink. 38. He that believeth on me, as the scripture hath said, out of his belly shall flow rivers of living water. 39. (But this spake he of the Spirit, which they that believe on him should receive: for the Holy Ghost was not yet *given,* because that Jesus was not yet glorified.

37. In the last and great day of that feast, Christ proclaimed the promised gift of the Spirit, under the name of rivers of living waters, to all that should truly believe on him: That is, when he was glorified: For till then the Holy Ghost for the operation of these eminent gifts was not given.

40. Many of the people therefore, when they heard this saying, said, Of a truth this is the prophet. 41. Others said, This is the Christ. But some said, Shall Christ come out of Galilee? 42. Hath not the scripture said, That Christ cometh of the seed of David, and out of the town of Bethlehem, where David was? 43. So there was a division among the people because of him.

40. His words and works inclined many to believe in him: but they could not answer objections from his original.

44. And some of them would have taken him; but no man laid hands on him.

44. Note, God hindereth bad men from doing what they would do, and they know not how he doth it.

45. Then came the officers to the chief priests and Pharisees; and they said unto them, Why have ye not brought him? 46. The officers answered, Never man spake like this man.

45, 46. God made Christ's words effectual at the present to convince and restrain them from violence.

47. Then answered them the Pharisees, Are ye also deceived? 48. Have any of the rulers, or of the Pharisees believed on him? 49.

But this people who knoweth not the law are cursed.

47, 48. Note, The vain respect to men of reputation and power, is a usual cause of unbelief and disobedience to God. 2. They rightly judged that ignorance is the cause of error and deceit; but they falsely thought their literal knowledge with prejudice and worldly minds, had been a safe state.

50. Nicodemus said unto them, (he that came to Jesus by night, being one of them,) 51. Doth our law judge any man before it hear him, and know what he doeth?

50, 51. Nicodemus bearing a good will to Christ, stopped them by a common rule of justice, that by the law no man should be condemned till he be heard speak for himself, and the case be well tried.

52. They answered and said unto him, Art thou also of Galilee? Search and look: for out of Galilee ariseth no prophet. 53. And every man went unto his own house.

52. Note, 1. They give him a scorn instead of a good answer. 2. And then how poor a reason satisfieth them against all the miracles and doctrine of Christ; because Galilee was a contemned country, where Christ dwelt, though he was born at Bethlehem of David's line. 3. One man's words may sometimes divert a persecution.

CHAP. VIII.

JESUS went unto the mount of Olives: 2. And early in the morning he came again into the temple, and all the people came unto him; and he sat down and taught them.

1. Note, 1. He left the city at night, lest they should surprise him. 2. He chose the temple as a place of God's consecration, and of best opportunity for auditors. 3. The Jews used to let them teach, who professed themselves to be teachers. 4. His sitting in teaching, is not an obligatory example to us, but an indifferent circumstance.

3. And the scribes and Pharisees brought unto him a woman taken in adultery; and when they had set her in the midst, 4. They say unto him, Master, this woman was taken in adultery, in the very act. 5. Now Moses in the law commanded us, that such should be stoned: but what sayest thou?

3. Note, That the last verse of the foregoing chapter, and the eleven first verses of this chapter were not in divers of the old books in the Greek, and the divers of the most credible fathers either have them not, or take them for apocryphal; and so do many protestants besides Beza: So that it is uncertain to us, whether it be any part of God's word: But we have enough besides of which we may be certain.

Suppose the text current, it seems they would have drawn Christ into a snare, by getting him either to speak against the law, or against Cæsar, who had taken from them the power of putting offenders to death, which the law giveth them.

6. This they said, tempting him, that they might have to accuse him. But Jesus stooped down, and with *his* finger wrote on the ground, as though he heard them not.

6. Beza taketh this writing on the ground to be improbable, and part of the apocryphal story. If it was otherwise, it signified but a discerning of their snare, and a putting off the answer by a seeming neglect or disregard.

7. So when they continued asking him, he lift up himself, and said unto them, He that is without sin among you, let him first cast a stone at her.

7. Note, Thus he evaded the snare of their question, as not belonging to him to judge.

8. And again he stooped down, and wrote on the ground. 9. And they which heard *it*, being convicted by their own conscience, went out one by one, beginning at the eldest, *even* unto the last: and Jesus was left alone, and the woman standing in the midst.

8, 9. Note, It is so improbable that Christ should be left alone in the temple, that this increaseth Beza's suspicion that it is apocryphal: But if it be true, it meaneth that those went away who came to accuse the woman, and left him with his auditors and the woman.

10. When Jesus had lift up himself, and saw none but the woman, he said unto her, Woman, where are those thine accusers? hath no man condemned thee? 11. She said, No man, Lord. And Jesus said unto her, Neither do I condemn thee: go and sin no more.

10, 11. Note, Those that hence take encouragement to connive at adultery, must note, 1. That the text itself is of uncertain authority, 2. If it were certain, it signifieth not that Christ would have adultery unpunished; but that he disclaimed the office of a judge in matters of corporal punishment, as being no magistrate.

12. Then spake Jesus again unto them, saying, I am the light of the world: he that followeth me, shall not walk in darkness, but shall have the light of life.

12. Note, Here begins the certain text: q. d. I am that teacher sent from God, who shew all my followers that light that quickeneth and leadeth to everlasting life, and others live and walk in darkness.

13. The Pharisees therefore said unto him, Thou bearest record of thyself; thy record is not true. 14. Jesus answered and said unto them, Though I bear record of myself, yet my record is true: for I know whence I came, and whither I go; but ye cannot tell whence I come, and whither I go.

13, 14. Thy own testimony of thyself is not credible. Jesus said, Even my testimony of myself is true and credible, because I know what I say, and whence I come, &c. But your denial of it is not credible, because you know not whence I come, &c. but speak against what you know not.

15. Ye judge after the flesh, I judge no man. 16. And yet if I judge, my judgment is true: for I am not alone, but I and the Father that sent me.

15, 16. You see no further than my fleshly part and original; I do not so rashly judge of any: But yet my judgment is true and credible, for you have not my bare word, but therewith the works of the power of my Father that sent me, and his attestation.

17. It is also written in your law, that the testimony of two men is true. 18. I am one that bear witness of myself, and the Father that sent me, beareth witness of me.

17, 18. Your law alloweth two witnesses to be credible, I am one, who may be allowed to witness about other men's interest, that I am sent by the Father to save lost sinners; and the Father is the other, whose voice and works bear witness of me.

19. Then said they unto him, Where is thy Father? Jesus answered, Ye neither know me, nor my Father: if ye had known me, ye should have known my Father also.

19. Where is thy Father: Is not Joseph thy father? He said, You know neither Me nor my Father: Had you by my doctrine and works known Me and my office, I should have taught you to know my Father.

20. These words spake Jesus in the treasury as he taught in the temple: and no man laid hands on him, for his hour was not yet come.

20. Note, Till God's appointed time of trial and suffering, among the fiercest enemies there is safety.

21. Then said Jesus again unto them, I go my way, and ye shall seek me, and shall die in your sins: whither I go, ye cannot come.

21. I come to you as a Saviour, and ye reject me, and I will accordingly depart from you, and your sin shall bring destruction on you, and I will send the gospel to the Gentiles, and will ascend to heaven, whence your sin will exclude you.

22. Then said the Jews, Will he kill himself? because he saith, Whither I go, ye cannot come. 23. And he saith unto them, Ye are from beneath, I am from above: ye are of this world, I am not of this world. 24. I said therefore unto you, that ye shall die in your sins: for if ye believe not that I am he, ye shall die in your sins.

22. Ye are of this lower world: I am of above, and thither I go. And if you believe not that I am the Christ, your nation shall be destroyed for rejecting me, and you shall die unpardoned in your sin.

25. Then said they unto him, Who art thou? And Jesus said unto them, Even the same that I said unto you from the beginning. 26. have many things to say, and to judge of you: but he that sent me is true; and I speak to the world those things which I have heard of him.

25. Even the Messiah as I have always told you. I have much to say against your infidelity, but I will now only appeal to my Father's testimony, whose words I speak.

27. They understood not that he spake to them of the Father.

27. Note, Gross ignorance is the parent and nurse of unbelief.

28. Then said Jesus unto them, When ye have lift up the Son of

Man, then shall ye know that I am *he,* and *that* I do nothing of myself; but as my Father hath taught me, I speak these things.

28. When ye have crucified me, then I shall convince many of you by fuller evidence, that I am the Christ, and the rest shall feel it to their destruction; and these my words shall be confirmed.

29. And he that sent me, is with me: the Father hath not left me alone: for I do always those things that please him.

29. My Father that sent me; never deserted me, for I do but fulfil his will, and do what he appointed me.

30. As he spake these words, many believed on him. 31. Then said Jesus to those Jews which believed on him, If ye continue in my word, *then* are ye my disciples indeed; 32. And ye shall know the truth, and the truth shall make you free.

30, 31. I cannot take you for my disciples, unless your faith be rooted so, as to persevere and proceed to learn what yet you have not learned: And if ye do this, you shall know more of that truth that will save you, and deliver you from the greatest of your bondage.

33. They answered him, We be Abraham's seed, and were never in bondage to any man: how sayest thou, Ye shall be made free?

33. Some present answered him, We be Abraham's seed, and though the Romans master us, we are no men's slaves: What then is the freedom which thou dost promise us?

34. Jesus answered them, Verily, verily, I say unto you, Whosoever committeth sin, is the servant of sin. 35. And the servant abideth not in the house for ever: *but* the Son abideth ever. 36. If the Son therefore shall make you free, ye shall be free indeed.

34, 35, 36. Can you boast of your freedom, who by your sinful practice shew that you are the servants of sin, and by it are liable to the judgment of God, as slaves are to stripes: And if you have thus enslaved yourselves to sin, and to God's judgments, he may turn you out of his house you know not how soon: But the son and heir is not turned away: Therefore if you will be free indeed from the guilt of sin, and the wrath of God, and the malice of Satan, come in by the Son, and so you may be free.

37. I know that ye are Abraham's seed: but ye seek to kill me, because my word hath no place in you. 38. I speak that which I have seen with my Father: and ye do that which you have seen with your father.

37, 38. I know that you are the seed of Abraham by the flesh. But were you his seed as he is the father of the faithful, you would not seek to kill me, and reject my word. Even that word of truth which I have received of my Father, which you reject, and obey the will of your father.

39. They answered and said unto him, Abraham is our father. Jesus saith unto them, If ye were Abraham's children, ye would do the works of Abraham. 40. But now ye seek to kill me, a man that hath told you the truth, which I have heard of God: this did not Abraham.

39, 40. If ye were Abraham's children, you would be like him, and do as he did. But to seek to murder me for telling you the truth, which I have heard from God, is not like Abraham's works of faith.

41. Ye do the deeds of your father. Then said they to him, We be not born of fornication; we have one Father, *even* God. 42. Jesus said unto them, If God were your Father, ye would love me: for I proceeded forth and came from God; neither came I of myself, but he sent me.

41. Ye shew by your deeds, whose nature you have, and so who is your father. 42. If God were your father, you would be like him, and then you would love me, who came from him, as sent by him.

43. Why do you not understand my speech? *even* because ye cannot hear my word. 44. Ye are of *your* father the devil, and the lusts of your father ye will do: he was a murderer from the beginning, and abode not in the truth, because there is no truth in him. When he speaketh a lie, he speaketh of his own: for he is a liar, and the father of it.

43, 44. Why is my doctrine rejected by you, but because your corrupt natures, and sin are contrary to it? To speak plainly to you, As the child's nature is like the father's, from whom it is received, so yours is so like the devil's nature, that I may say you received it from him, and he is the father of it, and so far of you. For you love to do that which he loveth and desireth: These are his great characters: 1. He was from the beginning A MALICIOUS MURDERER. 2. He is A LIAR; a deserter of the truth, and an enemy to it: His business in the world is to deceive by lying; and when he thus lieth and deceiveth, he doth according to his corrupt nature: for he is a liar, and the father of lies.

Note, 1. By these three characters of LYING, MALIGNITY, and MURDER, or hurtfulness, the devilish nature and seed is known: And no boasting of Abraham or Christianity, is any disproof of it. 2. Devilism is the universal pravity of the malignant world: And it is no wrong or railing so to say that the devil is their father.

45. And because I tell *you* the truth, ye believe me not.

45. Though nature love the truth as truth, yet because the truth that I tell you is cross to your prejudice and carnal minds and lusts, ye reject it as if it were error.

46. Which of you convinceth me of sin? And if I say the truth, why do ye not believe me?

46. If ye know any falsehood or sin by me, prove it if you can; but if it be truth that I say, why doth prejudice and malice hinder you from believing it.

47. He that is of God, heareth God's words: ye therefore hear *them* not, because ye are not of God.

47. The children of God have a mind and nature like him: And therefore they favour and love his word: Therefore your rejecting God's word doth prove that ye are not the children of God.

48. Then answered the Jews, and said unto him, Say we not well, that thou art a Samaritan, and hast a devil?

48. They said, do we not call thee as thou art, in saying, thou art a distracted Samaritan heretic.

49. Jesus answered, I have not a devil; but I honour my Father, and ye do dishonour me. 50. And I seek not mine own glory: there is one that seeketh and judgeth.

49. I am not a distracted demoniac, (but you calumniators:) My doctrine and works honour my Father, and as for your dishonouring of me, though I can bear it, who seek not my own glory, my Father will secure my honour, and judge you for your reproach.

51. Verily, verily, I say unto you, If a man keep my saying, he shall never see death.

51. I tell you that reject my word, that to believe and keep it, is the way to everlasting life, and to be saved from death spiritual, temporal, (by resurrection,) and eternal.

52. Then said the Jews unto him, Now we know that thou hast a devil. Abraham is dead, and the prophets; and thou sayest, If a man keep my saying, he shall never taste of death. 53. Art thou greater than our father Abraham which is dead? and the prophets are dead: whom makest thou thyself?

52, 53. Now we know that thou art a distracted demoniac: when thou talkest of men's not dying, when Abraham and the prophets are dead: Art thou so much greater than all they?

54. Jesus answered, If I honour myself, my honour is nothing: it is my Father that honoureth me, of whom ye say, that he is your God: 55. Yet ye have not known him; but I know him: and if I should say, I know him not, I shall be a liar like unto you: but I know him, and keep his saying.

54. It is not my own testimony that I plead with you, it is my Father that honoureth me, whom you should believe, because you call him your God. But indeed you know him not, and therefore understand not his testimony: But I know him, and should I deny his witness, and say, I know him not, I should be a liar like you: But I know him and his word, and keep it.

56. Your father Abraham rejoiced to see my day: and he saw *it*, and was glad.

56. Your father Abraham joyfully believed the promise of the Messiah, and so by faith foresaw my coming, and was glad.

57. Then said the Jews unto him, Thou art not yet fifty years old, and hast thou seen Abraham?

57. They understanding all carnally, thought Christ spake like a distracted fanatic.

58. Jesus said unto them, Verily, verily, I say unto you, Before Abraham was, I am.

58. I tell you that before Abraham's days, (as I was from eternity, so) in time I was the promised

Messiah, in whom Abraham in his days believed: I am not so young as you imagine.

58. Then took they up stones to cast at him: but Jesus hid himself, and went out of the temple, going through the midst of them, and so passed by.

59. At these words they took him for a blasphemer, and attempted to stone him to death: But he some way hid himself, and went out from among them.

Note, That the last part of this verse, is of uncertain authority, being not in some ancient copies.

CHAP. IX.

AND as *Jesus* passed by, he saw a man which was blind from *his* birth. 2. And his disciples asked him, saying, Master, who did sin, this man, or his parents, that he was born blind?

2. Was it for any foreseen sin that he would after commit, or for his original sin, or for any sin of his parents? Or, It is commonly held that all punishment is for sin: How could that be in this man? Not for his own sin, for he had none besides his original sin: not for his parents; for God punisheth not one for another's sin. What then was it for?

Note, 1. It is improbable that Christ's disciples thought that his soul sinned in another body, and Christ not reprove them. 2. The disciples knew that Adam's sin, and our original pravity, or our parents' sin, might be punished with as great a punishment as blindness, but they seemed to think that so miserable a punishment must be for some extraordinary sin, which Christ denieth.

3. Jesus answered, Neither hath this man sinned, nor his parents: but that the works of God should be made manifest in him.

3. Note, Christ meant not to deny, 1. That he had original sin. 2 Or his parents had actual sin. 3. Nor that these were a cause of his punishment. 4. But it was none of these that was the differencing cause why this man was punished rather than others. q. d. Though all punishment be for sin, and this man's had such a common cause, yet no sin was the reason why he was singled out for this suffering: But God designed it for an advantage to glorify him in the man's miraculous cure.

4. I must work the works of him that sent me, while it is day: the night cometh when no man can work.

4. God in this man giveth me an opportunity to do the work for which he hath sent me, for the sealing of the gospel and convincing the world: And I will take the opportunity, for I shall shortly be gone hence: And hereby I give you warning to work while you have day: for the night is at hand, when you shall on earth have time to work no more; therefore take your present time.

5. As long as I am in the world, I am the light of the world.

5. God who made me the light of the world, will have me shine to it while I am here.

6. When he had thus spoken, he spat on the ground, and made clay of the spittle, and he anointed the eyes of the blind man with the clay, 7. And said unto him, Go wash in the pool of Siloam (which is by interpretation, Sent). He went his way therefore, and washed, and came seeing.

6, 7. Note, This dirty means was no more than no means, as to the sufficiency of Christ's commanding power; but he will have us use the unlikeliest means, that we may be fit receivers.

8. The neighbours therefore, and they which before had seen him, that he was blind, said, Is not this he that sat and begged? 9. Some said, This is he: others *said*, He is like him: *but* he said, I am *he*.

8. They were struck with admiration, and had much ado to believe that he was the same man, till he himself told them that he was the man.

10. Therefore said they unto him, How were thine eyes opened? 11. He answered and said, A man that is called Jesus, made clay, and anointed mine eyes, and said unto me, Go to the pool of Siloam, and wash: and I went and washed, and I received sight. 12. Then said they unto him, Where is he? He said, I know not. 13. They brought to the Pharisees him that aforetime was blind. 14. And it was the sabbath-day when Jesus made the clay, and opened his eyes. 15. Then again the Pharisees also asked him how he had received his sight. He said unto them, He put clay upon mine eyes, and I washed, and do see. 16. Therefore said some of the Pharisees, This man is not of God, because he keepeth not

the sabbath-day. Others said, How can a man that is a sinner, do such miracles? And there was a division among them.

10, &c. Note, 1. They first attempted to disprove the matter of fact, and when they could not do that, they pretended God's law to prove him a bad man, and consequently that it was not by God that he did his miracles. 2. They that will try the spirits and miracles by the scripture, must not misunderstand the scripture.

17. They say unto the blind man again, What sayest thou of him, that he hath opened thine eyes? He said, He is a prophet.

17. Note, The benefit prepared the man to judge better than they. It is a double sin if those should judge ill of Christ who have been delivered by him.

18. But the Jews did not believe concerning him, that he had been blind, and received his sight, until they called the parents of him that had received his sight. 19. And they asked them, saying, Is this your son, who ye say was born blind? how then doth he now see? 20. His parents answered them, and said, We know that this is our son, and that he was born blind: 21. But by what means he now seeth, we know not; or who hath opened his eyes, we know not: he is of age, ask him, he shall speak for himself. 22. These words spake his parents, because they feared the Jews: for the Jews had agreed already, that if any man did confess that he was Christ, he should be put out of the synagogue. 23. Therefore said his parents, He is of age, ask him.

18, &c. Note, 1. Unjust judges resolve first what to do, and inquire after. 2. Though excommunication be God's ordinance, the devil oft useth it by wicked men, against the just that own Christ and the truth.

24. Then again called they the man that was blind, and said unto him, Give God the praise: we know that this man is a sinner.

24. They said, ascribe thy cure to God, but think never the better of this man; for we know by his breaking the sabbath that he is a bad man.

Note, Wicked persecutors that speak against God's servants, dare not directly speak against God, but pretend to give him his praise, while they persecute his servants.

25. He answered and said, Whether he be a sinner *or no*, I know not: one thing I know, that whereas I was blind, now I see.

25. Though you say you know him to be a sinner, I know it not, nor am bound to believe you: But I well know that he hath cured me of my blindness.

26. Then said they to him again, What did he to thee? how opened he thine eyes? 27. He answered them, I have told you already, and ye did not hear: wherefore would ye hear *it* again? will ye also be his disciples. 28. Then they reviled him, and said, Thou art his disciple; but we are Moses's disciples. 29. We know that God spake unto Moses: as for this fellow, we know not from whence he is. 30. The man answered and said unto them, Why, herein is a marvellous thing, that ye know not from whence he is, and *yet* he hath opened mine eyes. 31. Now we know that God heareth not sinners: but if any man be a worshipper of God, and doeth his will, him he heareth.

27. Sure you do it not because you would be his disciples. 28. They took it for a reproach to be Christ's disciples. 30. You are strangely ignorant that know not whence a man is, that doth such miracles: Reason and common consent tell us, that God heareth not the prayers of wicked men, so far as to signify his approbation of them; but rejecteth them: But it is godly worshippers of him, and them that obey his will, that he heareth and approveth. (This none that owneth a God dare deny.)

32. Since the world began was it not heard that any man opened the eyes of one that was born blind. 33. If this man were not of God, he could do nothing.

32. Never man did this before (much less by human power.) He could never do it but by God's power and approbation.

34. They answered and said unto him, Thou wast altogether born in

sins, and dost thou teach us? And they cast him out.

34. Note, It is the way of proud wicked men, to scorn to learn, but to lord it, and revile and turn to violence on pretence of discipline, when they cannot answer with reason.

35. Jesus heard that they had cast him out; and when he had found him, he said unto him, Dost thou believe on the Son of God? 36. He answered and said, Who is he, Lord, that I might believe on him?

35. Note, Christ receiveth those whom false church-governors unjustly cast out. 2. Christ taketh advantage of men's injuries, to convert the persons injured. 3. The man was willing to believe, as soon as he could be instructed whom he should believe in.

37. And Jesus said unto him, Thou hast both seen him, and it is he that talketh with thee. 38. And he said, Lord, I believe. And he worshipped him.

37, 38. He believed and bowed, or fell down to him.

39. And Jesus said, for judgment I am come into this world: that they which see not, might see; and that they which see, might be made blind.

39. It is part of my judicial office in this world to open the eyes of many that are now ignorant and blind in sin, and to give up many to their wilful blindness, who think themselves the wisest men, but resist the light of saving truth.

40. And *some* of the Pharisees which were with him, heard these words, and said unto him, Are we blind also?

40. Note, Proud men (especially if rulers or teachers of others) cannot endure to be told of their sin, especially of their ignorance and error.

41. Jesus said unto them, If ye were blind, ye should have no sin: but now ye say, We see; therefore your sin remaineth.

41. If your ignorance were, as blindness is, a necessary natural disease, you would not be voluntary in your error and guilt of sin: Or, if you knew yourselves to be ignorant and erroneous, you would learn and be cured: But your error being wilful, and you conceited of your knowledge, you are guilty and unexcusable, and settled in your sin.

CHAP. X.

VERILY, verily I say unto you, He that entereth not by the door into the sheepfold, but climbeth up some other way, the same is a thief and a robber. 2. But he that entereth in by the door, is the shepherd of the sheep.

1. I say to you who have cast out this man for believing in me, you take upon you to be the true guides of the people, and you look for the Messiah agreeable to your minds: But God's testimony and mission is the door to the Messiah, and the Messiah is the great shepherd and the door to the inferior pastors and the flocks: he that entereth any other way, climbeth in as a thief: but the true shepherd (principal and ministerial) cometh in by the door.

3. To him the porter openeth; and the sheep hear his voice: and he calleth his own sheep by name, and leadeth them out:

3. To the Messiah God will open the door, and to sub-pastors, they that by office are door-keepers to the church, must open it, as to men sent of God: and God's spirit teacheth Christians to know the voice of Christ, and under him of those that speak his word: and as shepherds there regarded every sheep distinctly, and called them by several names (as plough-men now do their oxen,) and did not drive them with clubs like swine, but go before them and call them to their pasture by name, so doth Christ and true pastors now know every member of their flocks, and lead them by name as willing followers to their own salvation, and not drive men into the church or heaven against their wills.

4. And when he putteth forth his own sheep, he goeth before them, and the sheep follow him: for they know his voice.

4. And as the sheep using to find that their shepherd hurteth them not, but feedeth them and bringeth them to pasture, therefore follow him willingly as one that loveth them and is for their good; so do Christ's sheep believe that he loveth them and is their Saviour, and therefore follow him and know his voice.

5. And a stranger will they not follow, but will flee from him: for they know not the voice of strangers.

5. And as sheep (like our dogs) have no such confidence in a stranger, but fly from him in fear, so will true Christians do from false Christs and from false pastors, for their voice is strange to them, and contrary to the new nature that is in them, and to their good.

6. This parable spake Jesus unto

them: but they understood not what things they were which he spake unto them. 7. Then said Jesus unto them again, Verily, verily I say unto you, I am the door of the sheep. 8. All that ever came before me, are thieves and robbers: but the sheep did not hear them. 9. I am the door: by me if any man enter in, he shall be saved, and shall go in and out, and find pasture.

7. As my Father's mission and witness is the door by which I enter, so I being hereby made the shepherd of the flock, am the door by which all others, pastors and flocks must enter. All that before me pretended to be Christs, were but thieves and robbers, and the chosen flock of God did not believe in them nor follow them. I am the true Christ and head of the church: They that believe in me and follow me, shall as my sheep be safe and plentifully fed.

10. The thief cometh not, but for to steal, and to kill, and to destroy: I am come that they might have life, and that they might have *it* more abundantly.

10. False Christs and false prophets have but sought themselves, and seduced the people to destruction of soul and body: I am come to give men spiritual and eternal life, and to raise them higher in light, life, and love, than was vouchsafed to the church before my incarnation.

11. I am the good shepherd: the good shepherd giveth his life for the sheep.

11. As he that keeps the sheep not as an hireling, but as his own, will venture himself to defend them from thieves and wolves: so will I lay down my life for my sheep.

12. But he that is an hireling, and not the shepherd, whose own the sheep are not, seeth the wolf coming, and leaveth the sheep, and fleeth: and the wolf catcheth them, and scattereth the sheep. 13. The hireling fleeth, because he is an hireling, and careth not for the sheep.

12, 13. He that seeketh his own worldly interest by deceit, will shift for himself, and for that interest expose the people to destruction, as not seeking their salvation but his vain-glory.

14. I am the good shepherd, and know my *sheep,* and am known of mine.

14. I know mine own, their persons, their hearts, and all their concerns; with the love and care of a good shepherd: And my grace hath taught them to know me and my word.

15. As the Father knoweth me, even so know I the Father: and I lay down my life for the sheep.

15. As my Father knoweth me with love, and I know the Father, so with a special love I lay down my life for their redemption and salvation.

16. And other sheep I have, which are not of this fold: them also I must bring, and they shall hear my voice; and there shall be one fold, *and* one shepherd.

16. And besides the Jews, I have chosen people among the Gentiles: Them I must call and gather to me: and Jews and Gentiles shall be one Catholic church under me their only universal head and shepherd.

17. Therefore doth my Father love me, because I lay down my life, that I might take it again.

17. Note, 1. It is not unfit to assign causes in man of God's love. 2. Yet nothing real in God is caused by any creature. 3. But as God's love is taken for its effects, our qualifications are a receptive cause or disposition. 4. And so a cause extrinsical of the relative denomination of God himself. So Christ's consent to do the full work of a mediator, was the condition of his peculiar reward, which is called the Father's loving him for it.

18. No man taketh it from me, but I lay it down of myself: I have power to lay it down, and I have power to take it again. This commandment have I received of my Father.

18. Note, 1. Christ foreknew his death and resurrection: 2. It was the law of mediation proper to him, that he should consent so to die, and then rise and reign as his reward.

19. There was a division therefore again among the Jews for these sayings. 20. And many of them said, He hath a devil, and is mad; why hear he him? 21. Others said, These are not the words of him that hath a devil: Can a devil open the eyes of the blind?

20. When they understood not Christ, they said, The man is a distracted demoniac: Why stand you to hear him? But others were better convinced both by his words and miracles.

22. And it was at Jerusalem the

feast of the dedication, and it was winter.

22. Note, Christ refused not to be present at this solemn feast, though appointed but by Maccabeus for a thankful commemoration of the repairing of the temple.

23. And Jesus walked in the temple in Solomon's porch. 24. Then came the Jews round about him, and said unto him, How long dost thou make us to doubt? If thou be the Christ, tell us plainly.

24. Put us out of doubt.

25. Jesus answered them, I told you, and ye believed not: the works that I do in my Father's name, they bear witness of me.

25. Why ask you me to tell you, who believe me not? My miracles done in the name and by the power of God, are a more satisfying testimony than my words.

26. But ye believe not; because ye are not of my sheep, as I said unto you. 27. My sheep hear my voice, and I know them, and they follow me.

26, 27. But no wonder that you believe not me; for you are not my chosen flock, nor qualified to believe: Were you my sheep you would understand, believe, and obey my word.

28. And I give unto them eternal life, and they shall never perish, neither shall any pluck them out of my hand.

28. To my true flock, I will give eternal life, and they shall never be condemned, lost, or forsaken: nor shall any power prevail against me, who will save them.

29. My Father which gave *them* me, is greater than all: and none is able to pluck *them* out of my Father's hand. 30. I and *my* Father are one.

29, 30. God my Father, who gave them me to be saved, is Almighty, and none can overcome him, and take them from his saving love. And he and I being one, they are safe with me.

31. Then the Jews took up stones again to stone him. 32. Jesus answered them, Many good works have I shewed you from my Father; for which of those works do ye stone me? 33. The Jews answered him, saying, For a good work we stone thee not; but for blasphemy, and because that thou, being a man, makest thyself God.

31. Note, No good work could secure the Lord himself from the rage of ignorant men nor from their accusation.

34. Jesus answered them, Is it not written in your law, I said, Ye are gods? 35. If he called them gods, unto whom the word of God came, and the scripture cannot be broken; 36. Say ye of him, whom the Father hath sanctified, and sent into the world, Thou blasphemest; because I said, I am the Son of God?

34, 35, 36. If they may be called God's that are but magistrates, and men in dignity and power, how can you say, It is blasphemy for me to say, I am the Son of God who am by the Father sanctified to the office of mediator, and sent into the world thereunto?

Note, That Christ here by his pleading for his right to his title, only from his office, doth not deny his title as from eternal generation, but only tell them what they were then fit to hear.

37. If I do not the works of my Father, believe me not. 38. But if I do, though ye believe not me, believe the works: that ye may know and believe that the Father *is* in me, and I in him.

37. If I do not such works as certainly signify God's attestation, believe me not: but if I do, believe what those works do surely evidence, and then you will confess that God is in me and worketh them by me, and that I am in him and approved and acted by him.

39. Therefore they sought again to take him: but he escaped out of their hand, 40. And went away again beyond Jordan, into the place where John at first baptized; and there he abode. 41. And many resorted unto him, and said, John did no miracle: but all things that John spake of this man, were true. 42. And many believed on him there.

39. He avoided their persecution by flight: and in the wilderness where John first baptized, many believed on him, seeing all fulfilled by him, which John had foretold of him.

CHAP. XI.

NOW a certain man was sick, *named* Lazarus, of Bethany, the town of Mary and her sister Martha. 2. (It was *that* Mary which anointed the Lord with ointment, and wiped his feet with her hair, whose brother Lazarus was sick.) 3. Therefore his sisters sent unto him, saying, Lord, behold, he whom thou lovest, is sick.

Note, It is a doubt whether Bethany be the name of a town, or only of a tract of ground where the town was. 2. It is like that this Mary is not the same with Mary Magdalen. 3. It is a word of comfort in all troubles, if we can say, It is on one that Christ loveth.

4. When Jesus heard *that*, he said, This sickness is not unto death, but for the glory of God, that the Son of God might be glorified thereby.

4. God's end in this sickness of Lazarus, is not to remove him by death from this world, but to prepare an advantage for the glorifying of himself in me.

5. Now Jesus loved Martha, and her sister, and Lazarus. 6. When he had heard therefore that he was sick, he abode two days still in the same place where he was. 7. Then after that, saith he to *his* disciples, Let us go into Judea again.

6. His love to them inclined him to help them: yet he moved not that his advantage might be the greater, to shew his love and power by raising the dead. Note, We must not misinterpret God's delays.

8. *His* disciples say unto him, Master, the Jews of late sought to stone thee; and goest thou thither again? 9. Jesus answered, Are there not twelve hours in the day? If any man walk in the day, he stumbleth not, because he seeth the light of this world. 10. But if a man walk in the night, he stumbleth, because there is no light in him.

9. As a man that walketh in the twelve hours of day-light is kept from stumbling by that light: So while my day of work continueth I am safe.

11. These things said he: and after that, he saith unto them, Our friend Lazarus sleepeth; but I go that I may awake him out of sleep. 12. Then said his disciples, Lord, if he sleep, he shall do well. 13. Howbeit Jesus spake of his death: but they thought that he had spoken of taking of rest in sleep. 14. Then said Jesus unto them plainly, Lazarus is dead. 15. And I am glad for your sakes, that I was not there (to the intent ye may believe) nevertheless, let us go unto him.

15. To raise him will more convince you, than it would have done merely to cure him.

16. Then said Thomas, which is called Didymus, unto his fellow-disciples, Let us also go, that we may die with him.

16. Whether Thomas spake this in mere passion, [Let us die with grief,] or as expecting Christ's death and theirs by the persecuting Jews, is to us uncertain.

17. Then when Jesus came, he found that he had lain in the grave four days already. 18. (Now Bethany was nigh unto Jerusalem, about fifteen furlongs off). 19. And many of the Jews came to Martha and Mary, to comfort them concerning their brother.

18. Note, A furlong is six hundred feet.

20. Then Martha, as soon as she heard that Jesus was coming, went and met him: but Mary sat *still* in the house. 21. Then said Martha unto Jesus, Lord, if thou hadst been here, my brother had not died. 22. But I know, that even now whatsoever thou wilt ask of God, God will give *it* thee.

21, 22. Note, She believed that Christ could have prevented his death, and could yet raise him. 2. And that it must be by prayer to God.

23. Jesus saith unto her, Thy brother shall rise again. 24. Martha saith unto him, I know that he shall rise again in the resurrection at the last day.

24. Note, The resurrection of the body was then believed as an undoubted truth.

25. Jesus said unto her, I am the resurrection, and the life: he that believeth in me, though he were dead, yet shall he live: 26. And whosoever liveth and believeth in me, shall never die. Believest thou this?

25. I am the principle and cause of life and resurrection. The dead that believe in me shall be raised: and the living that believe in me shall live for ever, their souls first, and their bodies after, raised to blessedness.

27. She saith unto him, Yea, Lord: I believe that thou art the Christ, the Son of God, which should come into the world.

27. Yes, for I believe that thou art the Christ, and therefore hath power of life and death.

28. And when she had so said, she went her way, and called Mary her sister, secretly, saying, The Master is come, and calleth for thee. 29. As soon as she heard *that*, she arose quickly, and came unto him. 30. Now Jesus was not yet come into the town, but was in that place where Martha met him. 31. The Jews then which were with her in the house, and comforted her, when they saw Mary that she rose up hastily, and went out, followed her, saying, She goeth unto the grave, to weep there.

29. Note, Faith, love, and necessity will make all haste.

32. Then when Mary was come where Jesus was, and saw him, she fell down at his feet, saying unto him, Lord, if thou hadst been here, my brother had not died. 33. When Jesus therefore saw her weeping, and the Jews also weeping which came with her, he groaned in the spirit, and was troubled. 34. And said, Where have ye laid him? They say unto him, Lord, come and see. 35. Jesus wept.

32, 33. Note, Christ wept in compassion with his servants' sorrows: and he loveth us no less now, than when he wept with mourners.

36. Then said the Jews, Behold how he loved him.

36. Love can express itself by grief for the hurt of those whom we love.

37. And some of them said, Could not this man which opened the eyes of the blind, have caused that even this man should not have died? 38. Jesus therefore again groaning in himself, cometh to the grave. It was a cave, and a stone lay upon it. 39. Jesus said, Take ye away the stone. Martha, the sister of him that was dead, saith unto him, Lord, by this time he stinketh: for he hath been *dead* four days.

39. Note, How vile a thing will less than four days, shew the body of man to be? Is pride and vain pampering fit for such a body?

40. Jesus saith unto her, Said I not unto thee, that if thou wouldest believe, thou shouldest see the glory of God?

40. Note, The effect of God's power in his glory; and unbelief hinders the effect in us.

41. Then they took away the stone *from the place* where the dead was laid. And Jesus lift up *his* eyes, and said, Father, I thank thee that thou hast heard me. 42. And I knew that thou hearest me always: but because of the people which stand by, I said *it*, that they may believe that thou hast sent me.

41, 42. He looked up towards heaven as the place of God's glory, the spring and end of earthly blessings: Note, Christ knew before that God would do this miracle by him: but begged it by prayer to convince the hearers that it was of God. 2. It is our comfort that Christ's intercession is always heard.

43. And when he had thus spoken, he cried with a loud voice, Lazarus, come forth. 44. And he that was dead came forth, bound hand and foot with grave-clothes: and his face was bound about with a napkin. Jesus saith unto them, Loose him, and let him go.

43. Note, It was not the loud voice, but the invisible power that revived him: yet Christ

would suit his voice thereto. 2. It is vain to ask how could he go when his feet were bound? As if all sort of binding disabled from rising, or Christ could not enable him, who revived him.

45. Then many of the Jews which came to Mary, and had seen the things which Jesus did, believed on him.

45. This miracle convinced many, (and it is strange that it convinced not all.)

46. But some of them went their ways to the Pharisees, and told them what things Jesus had done.

46. Some hardened spectators turned all this but to information against him to the Pharisees.

47. Then gathered the chief priests and the Pharisees a council, and said, What do we? for this man doeth many miracles. 48. If we let him thus alone, all men will believe on him; and the Romans shall come and take away both our place and nation. 49. And one of them *named* Caiaphas, being the high priest that same year, said unto them, Ye know nothing at all, 50. Nor consider that it is expedient for us, that one man should die for the people, and that the whole nation perish not.

47. Note, 1. The greater Christ's miracles were, the more they thought they ought to destroy him, because the people would the more follow him: and still the wiser and better any minister of Christ is, the more worldly, wicked men endeavour to destroy them, because the people follow them. 2. The fear of great men's power more than God's, causeth wicked politicians to destroy the best. 3. But thereby they bring on themselves that very destruction which they thought to avoid.

51. And this spake he not of himself: but being high priest that year, he prophesied that Jesus should die for that nation: 52. And not for that nation only, but that also he should gather together in one, the children of God that were scattered abroad.

51. And though he meant this of saving them from the Romans though by injustice, yet he being priest that year (though by unlawful entrance by the Roman power,) God honoured the office so far as to make him utter those words, which should be a just prophecy as meant by God,

though not by him; and should signify that Christ's death should tend to the conversion also of the chosen people of God in all the Gentile world, who should thereby be made his children, and one church.

53. Then from that day forth, they took counsel together for to put him to death.

53. The greatest miracle and good work of Christ, fixed their resolution to murder him.

54. Jesus therefore walked no more openly among the Jews; but went thence into a country near to the wilderness, into a city called Ephraim, and there continued with his disciples.

54. Note, Christ yet fled from persecution, and spent most of the three years and a half of his public ministry among remote, poor people in Galilee or near the wilderness.

Note, Qu. It is strange that Matthew, Mark, and Luke say nothing of this great miracle.

Answ. 1. No one was to say all: but all together to say sufficient. 2. And John tells us, that even all together, have said but little of all that Christ said and did: but only so much as should be enough to convince unbelievers.

Qu. Where was Lazarus' soul while he was dead? If in heaven, was it not a wrong to him to come thence? And did he remember what he saw there? And tell it to any? If not, doth it not make for the sleepy inactivity of souls departed? Answ. Souls go not to heaven, by necessitation as a stone descendeth; but are disposed of by God as the supreme governor; those that are for heaven to heaven, and those that serve devils to the devils; and those that are not yet judged to either, but are to live presently again on earth (as Lazarus and others raised) are reserved by God accordingly, whether yet in the body (as in a swoon) or near it, or where God pleased, and vouchsafed no other knowledge and memory than is meet for such as are to revive and live yet on earth.

55. And the Jews passover was nigh at hand: and many went out of the country up to Jerusalem before the passover, to purify themselves.

55. The legally unclean were not to celebrate the passover.

56. Then sought they for Jesus, and spake among themselves, as they stood in the temple, What think ye, that he will not come to the feast?

56. For all were bound to come to it, that were not unavoidably hindered.

57. Now both the chief priests

and the Pharisees had given a commandment, that if any man knew where he were, he should shew it, that they might take him.

57. Note, 1. Christ's ministers use God's ordinances to save men, and the devil's clergy use them for snares, mischief, and murder. 2. They will not let the people be neuters between God and the devil, but force them to be informing persecutors.

CHAP. XII.

THEN Jesus, six days before the passover, came to Bethany, where Lazarus was which had been dead, whom he raised from the dead. 2. There they made him a supper and Martha served: but Lazarus was one of them that sat at the table with him.

1. Note, 1. Christ was not against festival entertainment. 2. This is the same history mentioned, Luke x. Where you may see more of it.

3. Then took Mary a pound of ointment, of spikenard, very costly, and anointed the feet of Jesus, and wiped his feet with her hair: and the house was filled with the odour of the ointment.

3. Note, 1. It is not unlike that such an action was twice done, that is, by two several Mary's; and that this is not the same with that Luke vii. But yet it is very hard to judge where this was done: that it was thrice done is not probable: and that it was done in the house of Simon the leper other evangelists notify: yet here it seemeth to have been done in Martha's own house, compared with Luke x. It is most likely to me that Simon and Martha dwelling in the same village at Bethany, joined their purses and labour, and feasted him in Simon's house where this anointing was done: but that he was also entertained at Martha and Mary's house, where that was done; which is recorded, Luke x.

4. Then saith one of his disciples, Judas Iscariot, Simon's *son*, which should betray him, 5. Why was not this ointment sold for three hundred pence, and given to the poor?

4, 5. Note, That as piety is oft pretended by hypocrites against charity, so is charity here by Judas against piety: and there is no work so good but may be opposed by very fair pretences.

6. This he said, not that he cared for the poor; but because he was 'a thief, and had the bag, and bare what was put therein.

6. Judas being purse-bearer, falsely pretended a care of the poor, for his selfish covetousness.

7. Then said Jesus, Let her alone: against the day of my burying hath she kept this. 8. For the poor always ye have with you; but me ye have not always.

7. This which she gave shall be as it were for my funeral embalming; that may be best on such an extraordinary occasion, which ordinarily is not so. You may always give to the poor.

9. Much people of the Jews therefore knew that he was there: and they came, not for Jesus sake only, but that they might see Lazarus also, whom he had raised from the dead. 10. But the chief priests consulted, that they might put Lazarus also to death. 11. Because that by reason of him many of the Jews went away, and believed on Jesus.

9. Note, 1. To be put to death by such wicked priests and rulers, is no dishonour or note of guilt in the sufferer. 2. We see here how much Dives was deceived, Luke xvi. That though his brethren would have been persuaded by Lazarus sent from the dead: it is like they would have indicted him for a *scandalum magnatum*, or put him to death again.

12. On the next day, much people that were come to the feast, when they heard that Jesus was coming to Jerusalem, 13. Took branches of palm-trees, and went forth to meet him, and cried, Hosanna blessed *is* the king of Israel that cometh in the name of the Lord.

12, 13. They honoured him by this applauding solemnity as the Messiah sent from God to be the king of Israel.

14. And Jesus when he had found a young ass, sat thereon: as it is written, 15. Fear not, daughter of Sion: behold, thy King cometh, sitting on an ass's colt.

14, 15. Thus Zach. ix. 9. was fulfilled.

16. These things understood not his disciples at the first: but when

Jesus was glorified, then remembered they that these things were written of him, and *that* they had done these things unto him.

16. Note, Many things are said and done by Christ, which shall not be presently understood, but in their season.

17. And the people therefore that was with him, when he called Lazarus out of his grave, and raised him from the dead, bare record. 18. For this cause the people also met him, for that they heard that he had done this miracle.

17, 18. Note, It was the people that had seen, and heard of his raising Lazarus, that there met him as king, with hosannas.

19. The Pharisees therefore said among themselves, Perceive ye how ye prevail nothing? behold the world is gone after him.

19. Note, They thought their danger imminent, that the people would proclaim him king, and then the Romans would destroy their country as rebels; for they could not trust God to save them from the Romans, though miracles should have taught it them.

20. And there were certain Greeks among them, that came up to worship at the feast:

20. These Greeks were not the Jews of Alexandria that used the Greek tongue, (elsewhere called Greeks) but the proselytes of the gates, who worshipped but as catechumens did with Christians.

21. The same came therefore to Philip, which was of Bethsaida of Galilee, and desired him, saying, Sir, we would see Jesus. 22. Philip cometh and telleth Andrew: and again, Andrew and Philip told Jesus. 23. And Jesus answered them, saying, the hour is come, that the Son of Man should be glorified. 24. Verily, verily, I say unto you, Except a corn of wheat fall into the ground, and die, it abideth alone: but if it die, it bringeth forth much fruit.

21. When Greeks by the fame of Christ's miracles desired to see him, he tells them, that indeed the time of his glory in the world by men's believing on him, was at hand: but that he must die first, and then the Catholic church should be gathered. A grain of wheat is said to die, because the dissolution and change maketh it no longer a grain of wheat, but the seed of many new grains with the straw.

25. He that loveth his life shall lose it: and he that hateth his life in this world, shall keep it unto life eternal.

25. And as it is with me it will be with you: he that so overloveth his life, as that he cannot forsake it for my sake and his salvation, shall lose it by keeping of it: and he that casteth it away as men do a hated thing, rather than deny me and sin, shall live for ever.

26. If any man serve me, let him follow me; and where I am, there shall also my servant be: if any man serve me, him will *my* Father honour.

26. If any man will be a Christian, let him not stick to do and suffer as I do; but believe that he shall fare no worse than I, but if he die, he shall be with me where I am: for my father will honour those that serve me.

Note, 1. To be a Christian, and to be one that serveth Christ are all one. 2. Salvation is promised to all that serve Christ. 3. They that serve him, shall be with him where he is: Therefore the spirits of the just made perfect are in paradise, and heaven; for Christ is there. This is our great comfort in life and at death: And we must then thus think of our godly departed friends, they are all with Christ.

27. Now is my soul troubled; and what shall I say? Father, save me from this hour: but for this cause came I unto this hour. 28. Father, glorify thy name. Then came there a voice from heaven, *saying*, I have both glorified *it*, and will glorify *it* again.

27, 28. I am a man, and my soul is troubled at the foresight of my death and suffering, and nature inclineth me to say, Father, save me from it: but I must not take up with that natural desire; for I came on purpose thus to suffer: therefore my choice and prayer is, Father, glorify thy name; then came there a voice, &c.

29. The people therefore that stood by, and heard *it*, said that it thundered: others said, An angel spake to him.

29. They heard the sound, but understood not the words.

30. Jesus answered and said, This voice came not because of me, but for your sakes. 31. Now is the

judgment of this world; now shall the prince of this world be cast out. 32. And I, if I be lifted up from the earth, will draw all men unto me. 33. (This he said, signifying what death he should die.)

30. This voice though spoke to me, was for your conviction, and not for my sake only: for now the time is at hand when the wickedness of this world shall be detected and punished, and Satan the prince of this world cast out of his possession by the gathering of my church: and when I am lifted up from the earth by crucifixion, I shall be lifted up to heaven in glory, and will by my word and Spirit draw many nations to me their Saviour: by being lift up, he meant his crucifixion as in order to his resurrection and ascension.

34. The people answered him, We have heard out of the law, that Christ abideth for ever: and how sayest thou, The Son of Man must be lift up? who is this Son of Man?

34. We have been taught that Christ dieth not, but shall have an everlasting kingdom: who then is that Son of Man that thou sayest must be lift up?

35. Then Jesus said unto them, Yet a little while is the light with you: walk while ye have the light, lest darkness come upon you: for he that walketh in darkness, knoweth not whither he goeth. 36. While ye have light, believe in the light, that ye may be the children of light. These things spake Jesus and departed, and did hide himself from them.

35, 36. Though Christ abide for ever; he will not for ever abide visible with you: it is but a little while that he who is the light will continue among you: obey the light while you have it, lest darkness surprise you: and he that walketh in darkness knoweth not whither he goeth, nor whether he do well or ill. Before I be taken from you, believe in me, that ye may be illuminated; adopted, and enjoy the light.

37. But though he had done so many miracles before them, yet they believed not on him: 38. That the saying of Esaias the prophet might be fulfilled, which he spake, Lord, who hath believed our report? and to whom hath the arm of the Lord been revealed.

37. All his miracles caused them not to believe: And so Isaiah's prophecy was fulfilled in them, &c.

39. Therefore they could not believe, because that Esaias said again, 40. He hath blinded their eyes, and hardened their heart; that they should not see with *their* eyes, nor understand with *their* heart, and be converted, and I should heal them. 41. These things said Esaias, when he saw his glory, and spake of him.

39. And no wonder that they believed not, for it could not be; it being foretold by Isaiah, that God would forsake them: which Isaiah, foreseeing Christ's day by inspiration, did mean in that prophecy.

Note, To understand this, 1. We must distinguish between a caused necessity, and a necessity of consequence in order of arguing. 2. Between men that have forfeited God's grace by rejection, and those that grace is newly offered to; and so, 1. God is not the efficient cause of any sin: 2. But he deserteth many that abuse his grace, and leaveth them to their blindness and obstinacy: 3. And for it he causeth their destruction. 4. And he oft foretelleth this: 5. And his prediction maketh the thing foretold hypothetically necessary, or a certain consequence in order of arguing: it being impossible that God should lie: and so all that is foreknown by God or man will come to pass; when foreknowledge doth not cause it, but prove it: 6. And deserted souls have a moral impotency to repent, that is, an indisposition which nothing in their depraved nature will overcome.

42. Nevertheless, among the chief rulers also many believed on him; but because of the Pharisees they did not confess *him*, lest they should be put out of the synagogue, 43. For they loved the praise of men more than the praise of God.

42. Many of the chief rulers had a secret belief, but not enough to make them openly own and confess him, lest they should be excommunicated and reproached; for the love of their reputation with men, did prevail in them against their love of God's approbation.

44. Jesus cried, and said, He that believeth on me, believeth on him that sent me. 45. And he that seeth me, seeth him that sent me.

44. To believe in me is not to take my own testimony, but God's that sent me, and so is ultimately, to believe on him: and it is God's power that you see, when ye see my works.

46. I am come a light into the world, that whosoever believeth on me, should not abide in darkness.

46. The world is in darkness, and I am sent to be their light and teacher, to bring them out of it; even from the darkness of atheism, heathenism, infidelity, and unrighteousness.

47. And if any man hear my words, and believe not, I judge him not: for I came not to judge the world, but to save the world. 48. He that rejecteth me, and receiveth not my words, hath one that judgeth him: the word that I have spoken, the same shall judge him in the last day.

47. It is not the work that I came for into the world to accuse men as their enemy for rejecting my word: the final rejecters of it will be condemned, but not so much by my accusation, as by the evidence of truth and divine attestation in the word which they rejected.

Note, It is usual in the gospel, for a comparative negation to be expressed positively: as [I judge him not] that is, not chiefly; [Care not; labour not for the food that perisheth] that is, comparatively, let it be least and last. Many such there are.

49. For I have not spoken of myself; but the Father which sent me, he gave me a commandment, what I should say and what I should speak. 50. And I know that his commandment is life everlasting: whatsoever I speak therefore, even as the Father said unto me, so I speak.

49, 50. It is not the mere word of me as a man, but God's word spoken by me by his command, which I have preached: and his word is the cause of, and guide to everlasting life.

Note, Christ as man was under a peculiar law of mediation, proper to himself.

CHAP. XIII.

NOW before the feast of the passover, when Jesus knew that his hour was come, that he should depart out of this world unto the Father, having loved his own which were in the world, he loved them unto the end.

1. The foreknowledge of his approaching departure to the Father, caused him in this special manner to shew his love to his disciples.

2. And supper being ended, (the devil having now put into the heart of Judas Iscariot, Simon's *son*, to betray him.)

2. Note, Sin is the offspring of a wicked heart and the devil together.

3. Jesus knowing that the Father had given all things into his hands, and that he was come from God, and went to God. 4. He riseth from supper, and laid aside his garments, and took a towel and girded himself. 5. After that he poureth water into a bason, and began to wash the disciples feet, and to wipe *them* with the towel wherewith he was girded.

3. Jesus knowing that he was presently to take possession of his universal dominion, and return to God from whom he came, did humble himself to this work of LOVE and SERVICE, for an example to them;. He riseth from supper, &c.

Note, What is meant by Christ's coming from God is before opened.

6. Then cometh he to Simon Peter: and Peter saith unto him, Lord, dost thou wash my feet? 7. Jesus answered and said unto him, What I do, thou knowest not now; but thou shalt know hereafter.

6, 7. Note, 1. We must not refuse God's mercies on pretence of humility or unworthiness. 2. We must obediently submit to those commands and dealings of God, the reason of which we cannot yet understand, because it is God's will, and we shall understand them hereafter.

8. Peter saith unto him, Thou shalt never wash my feet. Jesus answered him, If I wash thee not, thou hast no part with me. 9. Simon Peter saith unto him, Lord, not my feet only, but also *my* hands and *my* head.

8, 9. Note, 1. It was Peter's rashness to resolve against that which he understood not. 2. Christ washeth all that have part in him from the guilt and filth of sin. 3. It is lawful and a duty to change a purpose taken up upon mistakes, and to break that word which did but express such a purpose: There are three sorts of affirming words. 1. Assertions, saying, this or that is true, or is not true: To violate these wilfully, is lying; and in witness bearing, it is a heinous sin. We must assert nothing but truth.

2. Promises: Which if made to God are vows: if to man, it giveth them right to what we promise. These bind us as far as we had power to make them. And if we had such power, and it be about

lawful things, we may not break them: without his consent to whom the promise was made, or some one that hath full power over him in that concern.

9. There is a pollicitation, or rather, a bare utterance of a man's resolution, As [This or that I will do, or give, &c] This ever in all rational men supposeth many conditions, As [if God will] [if I live and be able,] [If the change of things alter not my case.] [If I find not my reason mistaken, &c.] No Christian may be supposed to say [I will do this whether God will or not : whether I live or die: whatever befal me, or though I find that my reason is an error.] As in all such cases it is a duty to change a resolution, so it is a duty to go against that word by which we expressed our resolution: to change mind, word, and work for the better, is a duty. So Peter doth here.

10. Jesus saith unto him, He that is washed, needeth not, save to wash *his* feet, but is clean every whit: and ye are clean, but not all. 11. For he knew who should betray him; therefore said he, Ye are not all clean.

10, 11. The washing of the feet only may be as a sufficient ceremony to signify your cleansing, as if I had washed you all over. I have done this according to the custom of this country, where with going bare legged, the feet gather dust; to shew you, that as you have need of daily cleansing from the polution that you are liable to gather from this world, so I am he that condescend to cleanse you from it, &c.

12. So after he had washed their feet, and had taken his garments, and was set down again, he said unto them, Know ye what I have done to you? 13. Ye call me Master, and Lord, and ye say well: for *so* I am. 14. If I then *your* Lord and Master, have washed your feet, ye also ought to wash one another's feet. 15. For I have given you an example, that ye should do as I have done to you.

12, 13, &c. Knowing what pride and uncharitableness man's nature is capable of, and what must be the spirit and life of my ministers, I have given you this example to teach you to stoop to the feet of the lowest, to the lowest offices of love and service. And now if you, or any of my ministers shall either disdain this by pride, and instead of it domineer, and menace, or persecute the weak, or by sloth or uncharitableness neglect such ministerial offices of love, my example shall condemn all such.

16. Verily, verily, I say unto you, The servant is not greater than his Lord, neither he that is sent, greater than he that sent him. 17. If ye know these things, happy are ye if ye do them.

16, 17. Make not light of what I say to you; and pretend not your superiority or episcopal power to excuse you from this ministerial service and condescension to the lowest: you are not greater than I that send you: you are but my servants, and this is your service. If you not only know this but do it, you shall be blessed in your reward: But if you pretend learning and knowledge, and neglect this work, your guilt and misery will be double.

18. I speak not of you all, I know whom I have chosen: but that the scripture may be fulfilled, He that eateth bread with me, hath lift up his heel against me.

18. I do not equal you by this speech: I know you all whom I have chosen to follow me; and I know that in one of you that scripture will be fulfilled, He that eateth bread, &c.

19. Now I tell you before it come, that when it is come to pass, ye may believe that I am *he*.

19. I tell you before, that when you see that I know what will come to pass, it may confirm your faith.

20. Verily, verily, I say unto you, He that receiveth whomsoever I send, receiveth me: and he that receiveth me, receiveth him that sent me.

20. But you that are my faithful messengers, shall not fail of success, or of reward: I will take the receiving of you and your message as the receiving of myself, and as the receiving of God himself that sent me.

21. When Jesus had thus said, he was troubled in spirit, and testified and said, Verily, verily, I say unto you, that one of you shall betray me.

21. Then Jesus with a troubled mind, in a just sense of the traitor's sin and misery, and his own approaching suffering told them more plainly, that one of them would betray him to death.

22. Then the disciples looked one on another, doubting of whom he spake.

22. They were troubled, and were thinking who this should be.

23. Now there was leaning on Jesus bosom, one of his disciples whom Jesus loved. 24. Simon

Peter therefore beckoned to him, that he should ask who it should be of whom he spake. 25. He then lying on Jesus breast, saith unto him, Lord, who is it?

25. John at the desire of Peter asked him secretly, who it was.

26. Jesus answered, He it is to whom I shall give a sop, when I have dipped it. And when he had dipped the sop, he gave it to Judas Iscariot, *the son* of Simon.

26. Jesus told John secretly, it is he to whom I give the next piece of bread dipped: Which he did to Judas.

27. And after the sop, Satan entered into him. Then said Jesus unto him, That thou doest, do quickly.

27. As his hypocrisy, and thieving, and covetousness gave Satan power over him before: so now upon his obdurateness after all warnings, he had greater power to hurry him to the execution. And Christ by saying [What thou dost, do quickly] intimated to him that he knew his mind.

28. Now no man at the table knew for what intent he spake this unto him.

28. None of them (unless perhaps John) understood what he meant.

29. For some *of them* thought, because Judas had the bag, that Jesus had said unto him, Buy *those things* that we have need of against the feast: or that he should give something to the poor. 30. He then having received the sop, went immediately out: and it was night.

29. Judas had the purse, and that occasioned their mistake. 30. Note, This immediate going out, maketh it uncertain whether he received the sacramental part of the supper.

31. Therefore when he was gone out, Jesus said, Now is the Son of Man glorified, and God is glorified in him. 32. If God be glorified in him, God shall also glorify him in himself, and shall straightway glorify him.

31, 32. Now is the time at hand that I shall be glorified by my death and resurrection; and God shall be glorified in me, and because God is glorified in me, he will glorify me speedily in myself.

33. Little children, yet a little while I am with you. Ye shall seek me: and as I said unto the Jews, Whither I go, ye cannot come; so now I say unto you.

33. Dear children, the time is now at hand, when I must depart from you, and you cannot now follow me.

34. A new commandment I give unto you, That ye love one another; as I have loved you, that ye also love one another.

34. And being to part from you, I leave this with you as my last and great command in my testament, that you truly love one another; even as I have loved you who lay down my life for you.

35. By this shall all men know that ye are my disciples, if ye have love one to another.

35. It is not bare names and words that make men my true disciples, but learning of me, and obeying me: And this is the great lesson and command which you must learn as the symbol of my religion and church, by which all must know that you are my disciples, even by true practical love to all true Christians.

Note, To hate, malign, hurt, and persecute Christ's servants doth as truly prove men to be no Christians, as to deny the faith, how fair pretences soever may be their cloak.

36. Simon Peter said unto him, Lord, whither goest thou? Jesus answered him, Whither I go, thou canst not follow me now; but thou shalt follow me afterwards.

36. Thou shalt go to the same place in time, and the like way.

37. Peter said unto him, Lord, why cannot I follow thee now? I will lay down my life for thy sake. 38. Jesus answered him, Wilt thou lay down thy life for my sake? Verily, verily, I say unto thee, The cock shall not crow, till thou hast denied me thrice.

38. As confident as thou art of thy fidelity, I know thy heart better than thou dost, and I know that before cock-crowing be past, thou wilt thrice deny thou knowest me.

CHAP. XIV.

LET not your heart be troubled: ye believe in God, believe also in me. 2. In my Father's house are

CHAP. XIV. ST. JOHN. 225

many mansions; if it *were* not *so*, I would have told you: I go to prepare a place for you.

1. Let not my departure trouble your hearts: trust God and trust me with your souls and bodies. In my Father's house there are rooms enough to receive all mine as well as me: If it were not so, I would not have drawn you to hope for it in vain, but have told you the truth: I go before you to prepare for your entertainment.

3. And if I go and prepare a place for you, I will come again, and receive you unto myself, that where I am, *there* ye may be also.

3 Fear not that I should leave you desolate: I do not prepare a place for you in vain, but will come again and take you and all believers to myself as a glorified society. Note, Did not many other texts assure us of the soul's reception to Christ at our death, this would be sad to us, and make us think he would not take us to himself till his return to judgment. But it being then that our felicity will be consummate, in the consummation of the whole church in one body, therefore Christ putteth this promise of the fullest perfection for their comfort.

4. And whither I go, ye know, and the way ye know.

4. And you are not utter strangers to the God and place that I go to, or to the way.

5. Thomas saith unto him, Lord, we know not whither thou goest, and how can we know the way? 6. Jesus saith unto him, I am the way, and the truth, and the life: no man cometh unto the Father but by me.

5, 6. It is to the Father I am going: And think not carnally of the place or state, or way; I am your way and guide, and I am the truth signified by all ceremonial shadows; and I am your life both efficiently, directively, and finally: you must come to God as your end, by me as the only way, if ever you will be happy.

7. If ye had known me, ye should have known my Father also: and from henceforth ye know him, and have seen him.

7. You see me in my bodily presence: But if you had known me better in my spiritual being, and in the works which I have done by my Father's power; you would better have known my Father also. But as you have seen him in me and my works, so henceforth you shall know him more.

8. Philip saith unto him, Lord, shew us the Father, and it sufficeth us.

2.

8. If we might but see the Father, it would satify us. Note, Man in flesh would fain live by sight as more satisfying to him than mere faith.

9. Jesus saith unto him, Have I been so long time with you, and yet hast thou not known me, Philip? he that hath seen me, hath seen the Father; and how sayest thou *then*, Shew us the Father? 10. Believest thou not that I am in the Father, and the Father in me? the words that I speak unto you, I speak not of myself: but the Father that dwelleth in me, he doeth the works.

9, 10. God is invisible, and to be seen only in his works, effects, and appearances: And in what or whom canst thou expect to see him more apparently than in me? Have I been so long with you, and hast thou not seen and known me? If thou hast seen me, thou hast seen the notifying appearance of the Father? And what other sight of the Father canst thou expect? Believest thou not that God the Father is so in me and I in him, as that he appeareth to the world by me? and (though his greatness shine more conspicuously in sun and stars, heaven and earth, yet) his holiness, wisdom, and ruling will, and his saving love to sinful man shew themselves most in me, in the words that I speak and the works that I do, which it is the Father that worketh in me.

11. Believe me that *I am* in the Father, and the Father in me: or else believe me for the very works sake. 12. Verily, verily, I say unto you, He that believeth on me, the works that I do, shall he do also, and greater *works* than these shall he do; because I go unto my Father.

11. If you will not believe my own testimony, believe me for my works, that I am in the Father and acted by him, and he is in me, and his power acteth by me. And this power shall be so manifested, that I will enable those that believe in me, to do greater miracles than I have done, when I ascend to my Father, and send down my Spirit on them, by which you shall see that I was acted by the power of the Father.

13. And whatsoever ye shall ask in my name, that will I do, that the Father may be glorified in the Son. 14. If ye shall ask any thing in my name, I will do *it*.

13. And you shall find by experience in the answer of your prayers, that I am in God and actuate you by his power; for whatever you ask in my name, which is fit to be asked and received, I will do it as the Mediator between the Father and you, that the Father may be glorified in and by the

Q

office of my mediation and administration. When you find that asking in my name procureth your desire, you may know that it is by me.

15. If ye love me, keep my commandments. 16. And I will pray the Father, and he shall give you another Comforter, that he may abide with you for ever; 17. *Even* the Spirit of truth, whom the world cannot receive, because it seeth him not, neither knoweth him: but ye know him, for he dwelleth with you, and shall be in you.

15, 16, 17. If you do but love me, and shew it by sincere keeping my commandments, I will pray the Father, and he shall give you the Holy Ghost in an eminent peculiar manner, to be a paraclete, or an agent and advocate, and intercessor between me and you, pleading my cause with you and the world, and pleading your cause in prayer with me and my Father; To which end he shall, as a vital principle, abide with you for ever. Even God's Spirit of truth, who shall teach you the truth, and confute the lying deceiver; the world cannot receive him as an illuminator and comforter, because not knowing him, and being prepossessed with contrary malignant inclinations, it resisteth him: But he hath in some measure taken possession of you already, and ye know and obey him, and he dwelleth with you, and shall be in you, as sent by me, and as my witness.

18. I will not leave you comfortless; I will come to you.

18. Let not my departure too much trouble you. I will not leave you as destitute orphans, but I will rise and see you, and when ascended, I will come to you by my Spirit, and at last come and take all the church unto my glory.

19. Yet a little while, and the world seeth me no more: but ye see me: because I live, ye shall live also.

19. Though I shall shortly depart out of the sight of this world, yet ye shall see me: For I am your head and principle of life, and as I shall live with God in glory, so shall ye live by communication of life from me. Note, Here we have security for the soul's immortality and heavenly felicity. If Christ live, we shall live.

20. At that day ye shall know that I *am* in my Father, and you in me, and I in you.

20. In that measure that this Spirit of life is from me communicated to you, ye shall experimentally find, that as I am in the Father and act by his power, so you are in me acted by my love and power, and I in you, thus acting you by my Spirit.

21. He that hath my command-ments, and keepeth them, he it is that loveth me: and he that loveth me shall be loved of my Father, and I will love him, and will manifest myself to him.

21. This Holy Spirit which I promise you, is the Spirit of love: And he that loveth and keepeth my commandments, is he that truly loveth me: And (though with the love of benevolence and beneficence I love many enemies, to their conversions, yet) it is only they that thus love me that shall be loved of my Father with complacence and felicitation. And I will delight, bless, and glorify them with my love, and make myself fully known to them.

22. Judas saith unto him, not Iscariot, Lord, how is it that thou wilt manifest thyself unto us, and not unto the world? 23. Jesus answered and said unto him, If a man love me, he will keep my words: and my Father will love him, and we will come unto him, and make our abode with him.

22, 23. The manifestation of myself is not to be by monarchial outward pomp, which the world expecteth, but by spiritual gifts and comforts, and rewards: And none are prepared for these but they that love me and keep my words: These my Father will love, and my Father and I will come to him by the Spirit, and make our abode with him for ever.

24. He that loveth me not, keepeth not my sayings: and the word which you hear, is not mine, but the Father's which sent me.

24. But the world that loveth me not, keepeth not my words: And it is the Father's word, and not mine only, which they reject.

25. These things have I spoken unto you, being *yet* present with you. 26. But the Comforter, *which* is the Holy Ghost, whom the Father will send in my name, he shall teach you all things, and bring all things to your remembrance, whatsoever I have said unto you.

25, 26. I tell you all these things with my own mouth, while I am present with you: But they shall be better understood, and take deeper rooting in your memory and affections, by the work of the Paraclete, the Holy Ghost, whom my Father will send in my name, my agent, advocate, and witness! he shall more fully teach you all things, and bring all things that ever I said, to your remembrance, that you may teach and record them to the world.

27. Peace I leave with you, my peace I give unto you: not as the world giveth, give I unto you. Let not your heart be troubled, neither let it be afraid.

27. And taking my farewell of you, I do not only wish, but give and leave with you my grace and benediction: Not such an uneffectual or delusory peace in sin as the world giveth: But the beginning of everlasting felicity. Therefore let not your hearts be troubled or afraid at my departure, as if ye were deserted.

28. Ye have heard how I said unto you, I go away, and come *again* unto you. If ye loved me, ye would rejoice, because I said, I go unto the Father: for my Father is greater than I.

28. Ye have heard with trouble my words, that I go away and come again to you. If ye understood this aright, your love to me would make you rejoice, because as I told you, it is my Father that I go to, and he is greater than I, whom he hath made mediator; and the presence of his glory is better than this base wicked world.

29. And now I have told you before it come to pass, that when it is come to pass, ye might believe.

29. I have foretold you of my departure, and my sending the Spirit, that when it is come to pass, your faith may be helped by remembering my predictions.

30. Hereafter I will not talk much with you: for the prince of this world cometh, and hath nothing in me.

30. I shall not speak much more to you before my death: For the devil, the prince of the world, and the Romish and Jewish powers, his agents, are ready to execute what I came to suffer, but shall find in me no guilt, or desert of suffering.

31. But that the world may know that I love the Father, and as the Father gave me commandment, even so I do. Arise, let us go hence.

31. But that I may shew to mankind, that my love to my Father, and my perfect obedience to his commands, are more powerful in me than the love of this life, I shall willingly suffer for man an undeserved cursed death. Arise, and let us go to the place where I know Judas will come to apprehend me.

CHAP. XV.

I AM the true vine, and my Father is the husbandman.

1. I am to you like the vine that giveth forth her vital juice for man's life and delight: And my Father is as the husbandman that planteth, owneth, and disposeth of the vine and fruit. Note, Whether Christ spake this before they rose from supper, or as they went by the way, is uncertain.

2. Every branch in me that beareth not fruit, he taketh away: and every *branch* that beareth fruit, he purgeth it, that it may bring forth more fruit.

2. All that manifest themselves Christians, and are baptized and grafted into my church, are to me, as the branches are to the vine; as to covenant-insition. And every such professing Christian that is not sincerely fruitful and obedient, shall be cut off as a superfluous branch: And the sincere and fruitful shall be pruned by instruction, discipline, and correction, that they may be yet more fruitful.

3. Now ye are clean through the word which I have spoken unto you. 4. Abide in me, and I in you. As the branch cannot bear fruit of itself, except it abide in the vine: no more can ye, except ye abide in me.

3, 4. You are now in some measure cleansed and sanctified by my word and grace: But do ye think that all your work is done, or all your danger over; it must be still your care to abide in me by continued faith and love, and that I may abide in you by my Spirit and grace: For as the branch can bear no fruit of itself, but by virtue communicated from the stock, and therefore must abide in it: no more can you, except you abide in me.

5. I am the vine, ye *are* the branches: he that abideth in me and I in him, the same bringeth forth much fruit: for without me ye can do nothing.

5. Your insition and continuance in me, must make you fruitful: For out of me, and without my communicated Spirit of grace, you can do nothing that will save you.

6. If a man abide not in me, he is cast forth as a branch, and is withered; and men gather them, and cast *them* into the fire, and they are burned.

6. He that being grafted into my church and me, and apostatizeth, shall be damned. Quest. Is this spoken of the sincere, or of the unsound and hypocrites? If of the sincere, do they fall away to damnation? If of others, would they not be burned or damned if they should persevere in their hypocritical, dead profession? Answ. First, Christ tells us how we may judge of them, we know them not to be hypocrites till they fall off, and then we may discern their misery. Secondly. The sincere that shall never fall quite away, have need of promises and threatenings, hopes and fears, to be the means of their perseverance: For God fulfilleth his decrees by means. Thirdly, Whether there be not an initial unconfirmed degree of grace (like Adam's) which may be lost, which else would save (though confirmed grace be never totally lost) is a controversy so ancient and among the wisest and best of men, as that it requireth great modesty in the deciders.

7. If ye abide in me, and my words abide in you, ye shall ask what ye will, and it shall be done unto you,

7. If ye abide in me, and my words abide practically in you, you shall be so accepted with God for your union with me, and interest in me, that for my sake all your just requests shall be granted: But this privilege your sin may interrupt.

8. Herein is my Father glorified, that ye bear much fruit, so shall ye be my disciples.

8. It is not your barren profession, but your greater fruitfulness in doing good, which is the honouring of God who is the author of religion, and must prove you to be my true disciples.

9. As the Father hath loved me, so have I loved you: continue ye in my love.

9. As God the Father hath set his special love on me, and sent me on his work, so have I set my special love on you, and chosen you for my service; see that you forfeit not my love by forsaking me, or being unfaithful in my service.

10. If ye keep my commandments, ye shall abide in my love: even as I have kept my Father's commandments, and abide in his love.

10. The way to continue in my love, is to keep my commandments; for thus I abide in my Father's love, even his complacency in me as his servant, by keeping his commandments.

11. These things have I spoken unto you that my joy might remain in you, and *that* your joy might be full.

11. My end in all this counsel to you is but that I may still have joy in your fidelity and fruitfulness, and you may have fulness of joy in me, and in the reward of your fidelity.

12. This is my commandment, That ye love one another, as I have loved you.

12. The sum of my command and doctrine is love, even that in your entire love to one another,

and the fruits and expression of it, you imitate my love to you.

13. Greater love hath no man than this, that a man lay down his life for his friends.

13. Man's love of friendship hath no higher expression, than laying down one's life for his friends.

14. Ye are my friends, if ye do whatsoever I command you.

14. I lay down my life for you, and that as for my beloved friends who shall enjoy my friendly love for ever, if you prove my friends indeed; and that must be by doing whatsoever I command you, and not by bare words and boasts of friendship.

15. Henceforth I call you not servants; for the servant knoweth not what his lord doeth: but I have called you friends: for all things that I have heard of my Father, I have made known unto you.

15. Though you are my servants I have a higher name to call you by, even my friends: For mere service signifieth not that endeared intimacy which I have used with you. Love and friendship is higher than mere service and obedience. I have made known to you the mysteries of God, which signify my love and friendship.

16. Ye have not chosen me, but I have chosen you, and ordained you, that you should go and bring forth fruit, and *that* your fruit should remain: that whatsoever ye shall ask of the Father in my name, he may give it you.

16. You did not first begin in love to me, and choose me for your Saviour, but I began in love of benevolence to you, and chose you to be my friends, the objects of my complacency: And ordained you to be my apostles to convert the world, that you may see the Catholic church gathered, as the settled fruit of your labours. And that whatever power you ask of God, by miracles or other gifts to promote your labour, he may give it you.

17. These things I command you, that ye love one another.

17. I mention all this to you to enforce my last and great command, that ye love one another. Note, Alas, how far are the accusing, slandering, reviling, backbiting, and persecuting teachers, rulers, and sects, from the nature and practice of this love, which Christ so vehemently urgeth.

18. If the world hate you, ye know that it hated me before *it* hated you.

18. When you meet with hatred from ungodly

men, remember that I, that am the Son of God, and never sinned, was hated by them before you, and you do but follow me, and suffer for and with me.

19. If ye were of the world, the world would love his own: but because ye are not of the world, but I have chosen you out of the world, therefore the world hateth you.

19. If you were mere ungodly worldlings or infidels, the world would not hate you for godliness or faith, but love you for being like them. But they hate you for that Christian excellency in which my chosen ones excel them: And would you not be better and happier than they, though you be hated for it?

20. Remember the word that I said unto you, The servant is not greater than the lord. If they have persecuted me, they will also persecute you: if they have kept my sayings, they will keep yours also.

20. If you take me for your Lord indeed, remember that I have told you that you are not greater than I, and look for no better usage of the world than I have found: If they have persecuted me, they will persecute you: And if the unbelieving part reject my word, wonder not if they do so by yours, and if the chosen only do receive it.

21. But all these things will they do unto you for my name's sake, because they know not him that sent me.

21. It is for my sake that they will persecute you, because they know not God, and his testimony of me.

22. If I had not come, and spoken unto them, they had not had sin: but now they have no cloak for their sin.

22. If I had not spoken to them and confirmed my word by my works, their sin had not been so great, but had had excuse. (Note, Here [not had sin] a positive is put for a comparative): Or if I had not come with sufficient evidence, it had not been their sin not to believe me to be the Christ: But now their unbelief and persecution hath no pretence.

23. He that hateth me, hateth my Father also.

23. The hatred that is against me, is consequently against God my Father, it being his word, works, and witness which they reject.

24. If I had not done among them the works which none other man did, they had not had sin: but now have they both seen, and hated both me and my Father.

24. They had not been bound to believe me to be the Christ, if I had not shewed God's attestation, such works as no man else can do, or if any one had done the like. Note, Yet it is a false inference of the infidels, that therefore none are bound to take him for the Christ, where he never came and did such works: for history may as infallibly transmit the notice of his works, as sight and hearing could receive them.

25. But *this cometh to pass*, that the word might be fulfilled that is written in their law, They hated me without a cause.

25. But the word written in Ps. lii. 19. which in a large sense is part of their law is thus fulfilled.

26. But when the Comforter is come, whom I will send unto you from the Father, *even* the Spirit of truth which proceedeth from the Father, he shall testify of me.

26. But when the Holy Ghost my advocate and your comforter is sent down upon you, whom after my resurrection I will send to you, for his eminent signal gifts, from the Father, even that Holy Spirit of Truth which proceedeth from the Father, he shall be my great prevailing witness both to you, and by you to the world, and shall cause belief.

27. And ye also shall bear witness, because ye have been with me from the beginning.

27. And you on whom this Spirit shall come down, shall by his operation be made my effectual witnesses of what I have said and done and suffered, because you have been with me, as eye and ear witnesses from the beginning of my public ministration.

CHAP. XVI.

THESE things have I spoken unto you, that ye should not be offended. 2. They shall put you out of the synagogues: yea, the time cometh, that whosoever killeth you, will think that he doeth God service.

1, 2. I foretel you what you must expect, that when it cometh, you may not be scandalised and turned back. They shall cast you by excommunication out of their sacred and civil assemblies, as a reproach, yea, they that kill you, shall do it as an acceptable offering, or service to God. Note, How little do the religious pretences of persecutors deserve regard.

3. And these things will they do

unto you, because they have not known the Father, nor me.

3. Did they know the Father and me, they would do otherwise: wilful ignorance is the cause.

4. But these things have I told you, that when the time shall come, ye may remember that I told you of them. And these things I said not unto you at the beginning, because I was with you.

4. Remember I foretold you all this: which I said not from the beginning, because I was with you to encourage you, and your time of trial was not come, and at first you could not so well bear it.

5. But now I go my way to him that sent me, and none of you asketh me, Whither goest thou? 6. But because I have said these things unto you, sorrow hath filled your heart.

5, 6. But now I am going to him that sent me, and though it be on your business, and for your interest, you ask me not whither and for what I go? but sorrow oppresseth you to hear of my departure,

7. Nevertheless, I tell you the truth, It is expedient for you that I go away: for if I go not away, the Comforter will not come unto you; but if I depart, I will send him unto you.

7. Believe it, my departure is for your benefit: For the Holy Ghost whom I will then send, will be better to you than my bodily presence on earth.

8. And when he is come, he will reprove the world of sin, and of righteousness, and of judgment: 9. Of sin, because they believe not on me; 10. Of righteousness, because I go to my Father, and ye see me no more: 11. Of judgment, because the prince of this world is judged.

8—11. And it will be his work effectually to plead my cause. And first, to convince the world of their sin in accusing, rejecting, and murdering me, in whom they should have believed, which he will do by his gifts, miracles, and inward operations: And, Secondly, to convince them of the truth and righteousness of my person and doctrine, and my right to be the head of the church, and the righteousness of my government of it; Because I go into heaven to take fuller possession of my plenipotency and administration, and by my Spirit in you and on the hearers, shall more effectually convince men and gather my church, than I did while I was with you: And Thirdly, He shall convince them, that God hath exalted me to the power of conquering Satan and his kingdom, and punishing rebellious adversaries, when they shall see that by my Spirit, the kingdom of Satan falleth, and the powers that served him are partly converted, and partly confounded and destroyed.

12. I have yet many things to say unto you, but ye cannot bear them now.

12. I have many things more to make known to you, which you are not yet prepared to receive.

13. Howbeit, when he the Spirit of truth is come, he will guide you into all truth: for he shall not speak of himself; but whatsoever he shall hear, *that* shall he speak: and he will shew you things to come.

13. But when the Holy Spirit of Truth is come upon you, he will make you capable, and will guide you into all truth (which you must preach and record for the propagating and ordering my church, preaching to the Gentiles, laying by the Mosaic law, &c.) For he shall speak but that which is of God, and things to come, and which you are not yet fit to receive.

14. He shall glorify me: for he shall receive of mine, and shall shew it unto you.

14. It is this extraordinary gift of the Holy Ghost which shall be my great convincing witness in the world that shall prove me to be the Saviour: For it is from me that he is sent, and my word that he shall teach you, whether it be remembering or expounding what I have already spoken, or teaching you more by inspiration. What he saith and doth in and by you my chosen apostles, that I do by him and you.

15. All things that the Father hath, are mine: therefore said I, that he shall take of mine, and shall shew it unto you.

15. I say he shall take of mine: For the wisdom, grace, and gifts that come from the Father, come from me; that which is his is mine, and the Spirit is sent by the Father, and by me.

16. A little while and ye shall not see me; and again, a little while and ye shall see me, because I go to the Father.

16. As it is but a little while till I that am now with you shall depart from your sight, so it will be but a short time till I shall return from heaven to which I am ascending or (as some expound it) [I shall be a little while dead, and a little while with you after my resurrection.]

17. Then said *some* of his disciples among themselves, What is this that he saith unto us, A little while and ye shall not see me; and again, a little while and ye shall see me: and, Because I go to the Father? 18. They said therefore, What is this that he saith, A little while? we cannot tell what he saith. 19. Now Jesus knew that they were desirous to ask him, and said unto them, Do ye inquire among yourselves of that I said, A little while and ye shall not see me: and again, a little while and ye shall see me?

17, 18, 19. Jesus perceived that they understood him not.

20. Verily, verily, I say unto you, That ye shall weep and lament, but the world shall rejoice: and ye shall be sorrowful, but your sorrow shall be turned into joy. 21. A woman when she is in travail, hath sorrow, because her hour is come; but as soon as she is delivered of the child, she remembereth no more the anguish, for joy that a man is born into the world. 22. And ye now therefore have sorrow: but I will see you again, and your heart shall rejoice, and your joy no man taketh from you.

20. You shall have a time of suffering sorrow, while bad men are triumphing over you and rejoicing; but your sorrow shall be turned into joy, in the sense of my resurrection and the comforts of the Holy Ghost, and the success of your labours, and your own salvation: As a woman delivered hath joy in her birth, instead of the sorrows of her travail. I myself will again see you, when I am risen, and finally glorify you. And then you shall have a joy which none can deceive you of, or diminish.

23. And in that day ye shall ask me nothing: Verily, verily, I say unto you, Whatsoever ye shall ask the Father in my name, he will give it you. 24. Hitherto have ye asked nothing in my name: ask, and ye shall receive, that your joy may be full.

23, 24. You shall not then learn by asking me questions, as now: But you shall petition the Father in my name, and he will give you what you need, both for your own instruction and for your ministry. You have not hitherto understood and used my intercession so fully as you must do hereafter, and have not used to ask in my name so explicitly as you must do. But hereafter you must ask in my name to be heard for my merits and sake as your intercessor, as thus by fervent prayer; and fuller answers and gifts shall cause your greater joy.

25. These things have I spoken unto you in proverbs: but the time cometh when I shall no more speak unto you in proverbs, but I shall shew you plainly of the Father.

25. I have hitherto spoken to you in parables, letting in the light by such degrees as you were fit to bear. But when I send you the Holy Ghost, you shall know more plainly the mysteries of God.

26. At that day ye shall ask in my name: and I say not unto you, that I will pray the Father for you: 27. For the Father himself loveth you, because ye have loved me, and have believed that I came out from God.

26, 27. You shall then put up all your prayers in my name, which I would not have you so to understand, as if the Father himself did not love you, but must be moved to it by me: I say more than that I will pray for you; even that the Father himself loveth you, because ye have loved me, and believed in me, &c. Note, First, (I say not that I will pray, is but Christ's ordinary use of a positive phrase for a comparative: it is, I say, not this only, but more. Secondly, our love to Christ as well as our faith is called the cause why God loveth us. Thirdly, but this [because] signifieth no efficient cause of any thing in God, but a moral qualification of the receiver, called a material dispositive receptive cause.

28. I came forth from the Father, and am come into the world: again, I leave the world, and go to the Father.

28. Note, I have before shewed that this coming from the Father, signifieth not any local removal of the deity, but its conjunctive operation on the human nature, and its miraculous conception or production.

29. His disciples said unto him, Lo, now speakest thou plainly, and speakest no proverb. 30. Now are we sure that thou knowest all things, and needest not that any man should ask thee: by this we believe that thou camest forth from God.

29, 30. We now perceive that thou knowest the secrets of our hearts, and what thoughts and doubts they were that troubled us; which thou hast now plainly resolved: Therefore we believe thou comest from God.

31. Jesus answered them, Do ye now believe? 32. Behold, the hour cometh, yea, is now come, that ye shall be scattered every man to his own, and shall leave me alone: and yet I am not alone, because the Father is with me.

31, 32. As confidently as you speak, I tell you the hour is now at hand, in which you shall every man be afraid to own me, and shall shift for yourselves, and fly to your houses, and shall leave me forsaken of you all alone: But I will not call it alone; for the Father will not forsake me.

33. These things I have spoken unto you, that in me ye might have peace. In the world ye shall have tribulation: but be of good cheer, I have overcome the world.

33. I have told you what is to befal you hereafter, that though you will be grieved at my departure, you may fetch your peace and joy from the assurance of what I will do for you after my resurrection. You shall have tribulation to the flesh in the world: But let not that dismay you, but take comfort in me, who have overcome the world, even its flattering temptations, and its malicious persecutions. And my victory is virtually yours, who shall overcome by my intercession, Spirit, and grace.

CHAP. XVII.

THESE words spake Jesus; and lift up his eyes to heaven, and said, Father, the hour is come; glorify thy Son, that thy Son also may glorify thee.

1. This prayer Christ made to his Father, lifting up his eyes to heaven, to teach us to look thither as the place whence God appeareth in glory; [Father, the hour of my death undertaken for man's redemption is at hand: Glorify thy Son by thy attestation and his resurrection, that his glory may be the glory of thy power, wisdom and love to man.]

2. As thou hast given him power over all flesh, that he should give eternal life to as many as thou hast given him.

2. As thou hast advanced him to this power, to be the owner and Lord of all flesh, for disposals, legislation, judgment and execution, to order all things, so as may secure the possession of an eternal life of happiness, to all that thou hast given him by effectual decree to be certainly, eventually saved: All things being for the good of thine elect.

3. And this is life eternal, that they might know thee the only true God, and Jesus Christ whom thou has sent.

3. And what is life eternal, but that perfect knowledge of thee, which fills the soul with love and joy, and knowledge of thy glory, shining forth in thy Son Jesus Christ with his body the heavenly society. And the beginning of this knowledge is the beginning and way to perfection.

4. I have glorified thee on the earth: I have finished the work which thou gavest me to do.

4. My doctrine, example, and miracles, have here shewed forth thy glory: I am near the end, and have almost finished that work on earth for man's redemption, which I undertook.

5. And now, O Father, glorify thou me with thine own self, with the glory which I had with thee before the world was.

5. As I have almost performed my part, perform thou thy part of the covenant of my mediation; and give me, the Son of Man, a due participation of that glory, which my divine nature had with thee from eternity. Note, This text is by divers diversly expounded. First, some say that Christ's human soul was glorified before the world was. Secondly, the Arians say that he had a superangelical nature only before the world was, which united itself to a human soul (say some) or only animated a human body, (say others.) Thirdly, others of late say, he hath three natures uniting itself to the prime created superangelical nature: And this uniting itself to a human soul and body (say some) or to a human body alone (say others:) Fourthly, but the plain paraphrase which I have given, is the doctrine of the orthodox universal church.

6. I have manifested thy name unto the men which thou gavest me out of the world: thine they were, and thou gavest them me; and they have kept thy word.

6. I have made known thee and thy will, to them whom thou gavest me out of the world, to be my peculiar disciples: they were thine as their creator, and thou gavest them me to be their Redeemer, and I have taught them thy word and they have kept it.

7. Now they have known that all things whatsoever thou hast given me, are of thee.

7. They have known this fundamentally, that I and my doctrine and works are all of thee.

8. For I have given unto them the words which thou gavest me: and they have received them, and have known surely that I came out from thee, and they have believed that thou didst send me.

8. Note, That Christ insisteth so much on this, because to believe that he, and his doctrine, and works are all of God, is virtually to believe, that they are all true, without searching after any other reason of yours. For he is mad that believeth not that there is a God, and he believeth not a God, who believeth him not to be perfect, and therefore to be just, good, and true, and not the deceiver of the world.

9. I pray for them: I pray not for the world, but for them which thou hast given me, for they are thine. 10. And all mine are thine, and thine are mine, and I am glorified in them.

9, 10. It is out of special love to them, for the salvation and welfare of these, that I now pray to thee, and not for the mere worldlings and enemies of thy kingdom, (though for them also I have such desires and prayers as signify my common love; and the elect among them yet unconverted, I have such requests for, as are suited to their state.) But these that thou hast given me peremptorily to save, are the people of thy peculiar love as well as mine. And all that I so love thou lovest also, and it is in them that I am glorified and my person, office, and grace is honoured, which others do but swinishly despise.

11. And now I am no more in the world, but these are in the world, and I come to thee. Holy Father, keep through thine own name, those whom thou hast given me, that they may be one, as we *are*.

11. And now I am leaving the world, but must leave them in it to trials and persecutions, while I am with thee. And seeing their union, by one faith and love, is their character, strength, and safety, without which they will fall into scandal and dissolution, O keep them by concentring in thee and thy will (and not distracted by human devices and interests) that they may be one in faith, hope, and practice, as we are one.

12. While I was with them in the world, I kept them in thy name: those that thou gavest me I have kept, and none of them is lost, but the son of perdition: that the scripture might be fulfilled.

12. All that thou gavest to be my adherent followers, I have kept in thy name, save the son of perdition, in whose revolt and treachery the scripture is fulfilled.

13. And now come I to thee, and these things I speak in the world, that they might have my joy fulfilled in themselves.

13. I come to thee, but I leave them my word, to fortify them with that joy which they will need in their afflictions.

14. I have given them thy word; and the world hath hated them, because they are not of the world, even as I am not of the world.

14. It is not all the world that will be saved by me, but a select people to whom I effectually give thy word, and the world hateth them, because their doctrine, mind, and life do differ from the world, and they are of another spirit and society, of which I am the head.

15. I pray not that thou shouldest take them out of the world, but that thou shouldest keep them from the evil. 16. They are not of the world, even as I am not of the world.

15. They have work to do in the world, from which I do not pray thou shouldest take them, but that thou keep them pure from the sins, temptation, and malice of the world, as those that are separated from it to obey thee, as I their leader am.

17. Sanctify them through thy truth: thy word is truth.

17. Qualify and separate them by thy truth, to propagate thy truth, even thy word which is truth.

18. As thou hast sent me into the world, even so have I also sent them into the world.

18. As thou sentest me for the work of a Redeemer into this sinful world, so have I sent them, for the work of apostleship.

19. And for their sakes I sanctify myself, that they also might be sanctified through the truth.

19. For their sakes I become a sacrifice offered to thee, that they may by my doctrine, example, and spirit, be also totally devoted to serve thee.

20. Neither pray I for these alone, but for them also which shall believe on me through their word:

20. But it is not for them only that I pray, but for all that by their ministry shall become true Christians.

21. That they all may be one, as thou Father *art* in me, and I in thee; that they also may be one in us: that the world may believe that thou hast sent me.

21. And the sum of my prayer for them is, that as I am united to thee, that what thou speakest I speak, and what thou lovest I love, and thy works are my works, wrought by thee, so they may be one in us (and not in any uncapable centre of human invention and usurpation) and may all speak the same thing which they have heard from thee by me, and may love what we love, and do our work and not their own: that by their concord in faith, love, and practice, the world may be won to Christianity, and not scandalized by their discord and factions, or by forsaking the true unity, and combining for worldly interest on worldly terms.

22. And the glory which thou gavest me, I have given them: that they may be one, even as we are one.

22. And as thou hast glorified me in the world by the power of working miracles, and gathering sinners home to thee, I have glorified them by giving them the same power to work miracles, and to call and convert the world: that they may be one body, of one mind, and do one work, as I have done thy work alone.

23. I in them, and thou in me, that they may be made perfect in one, and that the world may know that thou hast sent me, and hast loved them, as thou hast loved me.

23. That while I work in them, by my word and spirit, as thou workest in me, they may be perfected into one concordant harmonious body, united in faith and love, that this lustre of their excellency and concord may convince the world, that thou hast sent me to restore them that are so much restored, and that thou lovest them as thy redeemed, sanctified ones, as thou lovest me their Redeemer.

24. Father, I will that they also whom thou hast given me, be with me where I am; that they may behold my glory which thou hast given me: for thou lovedst me before the foundation of the world.

24. Father, as it was thy covenant with me as my reward for redemption, it is now my will and desire, that all that thou givest me by conversion as true Christians, to be saved, may be after death with me where I am, that they may see the glory which thou givest me, the sight of which is part of their glorification: for thou lovedst me before the foundation of the world, and wilt communicate glory to them by me.

25. O righteous Father, the world hath not known thee; but I have known thee, and these have known that thou hast sent me.

25. O righteous Father, that world of men whom thou hast created, have not known thee, but I that have known thee have declared thee to them, and these my disciples having known that thou hast sent me, have believed my word concerning thee.

26. And I have declared unto them thy name, and will declare it: that the love wherewith thou hast loved me, may be in them, and I in them.

26. And I have by my word and works made thee and thy will known to them, and will do so yet more; that the holy spirit of love with which thou hast filled me, may be in them, and by that spirit I may be in them.

CHAP. XVIII.

WHEN Jesus had spoken these words, he went forth with his disciples over the brook Cedron, where was a garden, into the which he entered, and his disciples. 2. And Judas also which betrayed him, knew the place: for Jesus ofttimes resorted thither with his disciples.

1. This sermon and prayer being spoken after sacrament, Jesus went to the garden where he knew he should be apprehended: Judas knew the place, because Christ oft went thither, &c.

3. Judas then having received a band *of men*, and officers from the chief priests and Pharisees, cometh thither with lanterns, and torches, and weapons.

3. Note, Judas was the informer that led the officers (such as constables,) and the chief priests and the Pharisees of their party were they that (like justices) furnished them with commissions and armed men,

4. Jesus therefore knowing all things that should come upon him, went forth, and said unto them, Whom seek ye? 5. They answered him, Jesus of Nazareth. Jesus saith unto them, I am *he*. And Judas also which betrayed him, stood with them.

4, 5. Note, Christ fled not when his hour was come. **2.** What a stony heart had Judas all this while.

6. As soon then as he had said unto them, I am *he*, they went backward and fell to the ground.

6. Some of them went backward and fell. Note, This stopped not them or their companions.

7. Then asked he them again, Whom seek ye? And they said, Jesus of Nazareth. 8. Jesus answered, I have told you that I am *he*, If therefore ye seek me, let these go their way. 9. That the saying might be fulfilled which he spake, Of them which thou gavest me, have I lost none.

7, 8, 9. Note, Christ was careful for the bodily safety of his disciples till their hour came. 2. His words of [losing none,] are here expounded as reaching to the body as well as to the soul.

10. Then Simon Peter having a sword, drew it, and smote the high priest's servant, and cut off his right ear. The servant's name was Malchus. 11. Then said Jesus unto Peter, Put up thy sword into the sheath: the cup which my Father hath given me, shall I not drink it?

10, 11. Note, Peter that before trusted too much to his own constancy, now trusted too much to his sword, without commission. 3. Christ would not be rescued from his undertaken sufferings by human strength.

12. Then the band, and the captain, and officers of the Jews took Jesus, and bound him.

12. The colonel with his soldiers and officers bind Jesus as a malefactor, being slavish executioners.

13. And led him away to Annas first (for he was father-in-law to Caiaphas, which was the high priest that same year). 14. Now Caiaphas was he which gave counsel to the Jews, that it was expedient that one man should die for the people.

13. The power was in Caiaphas, but his father-in-law was made the way to him, no doubt being a forward actor.

15. And Simon Peter followed Jesus, and *so did* another disciple. That disciple was known unto the high priest, and went in with Jesus into the palace of the high priest. 16. But Peter stood at the door without. Then went out that other disciple which was known unto the high priest, and spake unto her that kept the door, and brought in Peter.

15 Note, It seems acquaintance made them bear with John, and yet pretended they knew him not to be a disciple.

17. Then saith the damsel that kept the door, unto Peter, Art not thou also *one* of this man's disciples? He saith, I am not. 18. And the servants and officers stood there, who had made a fire of coals, (for it was cold) and they warmed themselves: and Peter stood with them, and warmed himself.

17, 18. Note, Whenever we have business in bad company, we should foresee what temptations we may there expect and be forewarned.

19. The high priest then asked Jesus of his disciples, and of his doctrine.

19. Note, The perversion and confusion of this blinded world, man examineth and judgeth God; an ignorant high priest who pretendeth no honour, but to be an officer of God, judgeth his master.

20. Jesus answered him, I spake openly to the world; I ever taught in the synagogue, and in the temple, whither the Jews always resort, and in secret have I said nothing. 21. Why askest thou me? ask them which heard me, what I have said unto them: behold, they know what I said.

20, 21. Note, Christ that came to die for our sins, yet would not accuse himself, but referred the ensuaring prelate to his auditors, and bid him produce his witness if he had any thing to accuse him of: giving us an example how to answer such malicious high priests. Secondly, By [in secret have I said nothing] he meaneth, I have not fraudalently concealed my doctrine. Thirdly, Christ did not separate from the temple or synagogue, and yet they could not bear him while he put them but to prove their accusations: they expected that his obedience to their demands should have furnished their malice with matter against him, while they were breaking God's commands.

22. And when he had thus spoken, one of the officers which stood by, struck Jesus with the palm of his hand, saying, Answerest thou the high priest so?

22. Note, It is no wonder if wicked high priests have wicked officers, ready to say and do as they. Rebels against God charge God himself for not obeying them in iniquity; and expect more than due submission from God's servants while they war against God himself.

23. Jesus answered him, If I have spoken evil, bear witness of the evil: but if well, why smitest thou me?

23. If I have by my answer broken the law, prove it: if not, why art thou executioner without trial or desert?

24. (Now Annas had sent him bound unto Caiaphas the high priest). 25. And Simon Peter stood and warmed himself: they said therefore unto him, Art not thou also one of his disciples? He denied it, and said, I am not. 26. One of the servants of the high priest, (being his kinsman whose ear Peter cut off) saith, Did not I see thee in the garden with him? 27. Peter then denied again, and immediately the cock crew.

24, 25, &c. All this was done in Caiaphas' house, whither Annas had sent Christ bound. There Peter then denied Christ: though one denial be here omitted.

28. Then led they Jesus from Caiaphas unto the hall of judgment: and it was early, and they themselves went not into the judgment-hall, lest they should be defiled; but that they might eat the passover.

28. Note, Thus those hypocrite priests make conscience of a ceremony, while they are shedding holy blood.

29. Pilate then went out unto them, and said, What accusation bring you against this man? 30. They answered and said unto him, If he were not a malefactor, we would not have delivered him up unto thee.

29, 30. Note, The wicked priests expected that Pilate should have taken their bare word against Christ to condemn him.

31. Then said Pilate unto them, Take ye him and judge him according to your law. The Jews therefore said unto him, It is not lawful for us to put any man to death: 32. That the saying of Jesus might be fulfilled, which he spake, signifying what death he should die.

31, 32. If he must be condemned upon your bare word, be you the judges of him by your own law: for the Romans use not to condemn men so unjustly.

Note. The Romans having conquered the Jews allowed them the use of their own law for lesser punishments, but not for death (though some think otherwise:) crucifying was the Roman punishment.

33. Then Pilate entered into the judgment-hall again, and called Jesus, and said unto him, Art thou the king of the Jews? 34. Jesus answered him, Sayest thou this thing of thyself, or did others tell it thee of me?

34. I perceive thy question implieth accusation: Who is the accuser? Is it thyself or any other?

35. Pilate answered, Am I a Jew? Thine own nation, and the chief priests have delivered thee unto me: What hast thou done?

35. I am no Jew, nor judge of your prophecies, pretences, and quarrels: it is thy own nation, and those that should best understand the matters of it, even the high priests that have delivered thee to me: how hast thou offended them.

36. Jesus answered, My kingdom is not of this world: if my kingdom were of this world then would my servants fight, that I should not be delivered to the Jews: but now is my kingdom not from hence.

36. I know it is as the usurper of the crown against Cæsar that they intend to accuse me: but of that they have no just cause. For it is no earthly kingdom that I claim; nor do I raise men to fight for me, as I should do if I claimed an earthly kingdom.

37. Pilate therefore said unto him, Art thou a king then? Jesus answered, Thou sayest that I am a king. To this end was I born, and for this cause came I into the world,

that I should bear witness unto the truth. Every one that is of the truth, heareth my voice. 38. Pilate saith unto him, What is truth?

37. And art thou a king indeed! Jesus answered, I am a king, (though I claim no man's crown) it was to this end that I was born and came into the world, that the truth might reign, and that I might reign in the minds of men by the light of truth: and every one that is thus enlightened to obey the truth, obeyeth me: Pilate said, in disdain, What is that truth which thou pretendest to be thy reign?

And when he had said 'this he went out again unto the Jews, and saith unto them, I find in him no fault at all.

38. I find not that he breaketh any of our laws, by any capital crime.

39. But ye have a custom, that I should release unto you one at the passover : will ye therefore that I release unto you the king of the Jews? 40. Then cried they all again, saying, Not this man, but Barabbas. Now Barabbas was a robber.

39. Note. Pilate derided Christ, but was loath to murder him, judging him innocent.

Note, Whereas other writers of the gospel often tell us, that Christ answered not a word, and John tells us of his most pertinent answers, it only signifieth that to many other questions not here mentioned, he gave no answer; and that he forbore, partly as seeing it was in vain with such unrighteous men, and being not over regardful of self-defence, and partly that he might not give them matter against him, wrested from his own words: but the answers omitted by others John reciteth.

CHAP. XIX.

THEN Pilate therefore took Jesus, and scourged *him*. 2. And the soldiers platted a crown of thorns, and put it on his head, and they put on him a purple robe, 3. And said, Hail king of the Jews : and they smote him with their hands.

1, 2. Note, When the unjust ruler had once led the way by scourging him, all the rabble and soldiers make great sport in deriding and abusing him; such are the frolics of wicked ignorance.

4. Pilate therefore went forth again, and said unto them, Behold, I bring him forth to you, that ye may know that I find no fault in him. 5. Then came Jesus forth, wearing the crown of thorns, and the purple robe. And *Pilate* saith unto them, Behold the man.

4. In scorn.

6. When the chief priests therefore and officers saw him, they cried out, saying, Crucify *him*, crucify *him*. Pilate saith unto them, Take ye him, and crucify *him:* for I find no fault in him.

6. Thus Christ is the foot-ball of cruelty and heathen scorn. Pilate saith, let it be your own doing if you will needs have it done, for by our law he deserveth it not.

7. The Jews answered him, We have a law, and by our law he ought to die, because he made himself the Son of God. 8. When Pilate therefore heard that saying, he was the more afraid; 9. And went again into the judgment-hall, and saith unto Jesus, Whence, art thou? But Jesus gave him no answer.

7, 8, 9. Note, The name of the Son of God, was used by the priests against Christ to accuse and murder him, and yet to a heathen judge caused fear and further inquiry: and to this day it is matter of scorn to such, that the faithful are called the children of God.

10. Then saith Pilate unto him, Speakest thou not unto me? knowest thou not that I have power to crucify thee, and have power to release thee? 11. Jesus answered, Thou couldest have no power at all against me, except it were given thee from above; therefore he that delivered me unto thee hath the greater sin.

10. Note, 1. Christ would not tell him whence he was by words, that would not know it by his works. 2. Pilate thought that the power of life and death, should have forced Jesus to answer him. And Christ saith [Whatever proud men may claim or pretend to, no man can have more governing right or authority than God the absolute sovereign giveth him (who giveth none against himself) Therefore the archpriests that deliver me to thee to be crucified, are so much the greater sinners that would turn God's ordinances of magistracy against himself.]

12. And from thenceforth Pilate

sought to release him: but the Jews cried out, saying, If thou let this man go, thou art not Cæsar's friend: whosoever maketh himself a king, speaketh against Cæsar.

12. Then the priests used that argument with Pilate which he had not strength to overcome; as if they would question his life or office, as a traitor to Cæsar, if he would not condemn Christ as such. Though Christ had told him that he pretended not to a kingdom of this world: yet for the name of a king either Christ must die as an enemy to Cæsar, or Pilate go for such. Thus though all royal authority be of God, yet it is often the strength and most prevailing argument, that wicked men use against God and his law and servants.

13. When Pilate therefore heard that saying, he brought Jesus forth, and sat down in the judgment-seat, in a place that is called the Pavement, but in the Hebrew, Gabbatha. 14. And it was the preparation of the passover, and about the sixth hour: and he saith unto the Jews, Behold your king. 15. But they cried out, Away with *him*, away with *him*, crucify him. Pilate saith unto them, Shall I crucify your king? The chief priests answered, We have no king but Cæsar.

13. When Pilate saw that there was no resisting them without danger to himself, he sat in judgment on Christ in a place called in the Syriac Gabbatha.

Note, The controversy of the day, (whether it was that called by us Friday, or Wednesday, or Thursday) and that of the hour, (whether it was the sixth hour, (as John saith it was about) or the third hour, as Mark saith) and whether in John it should be read the third (as Beza and some others think), are both too hard for vulgar readers, and therefore I leave them to controversial writers: much is said on both sides.

Note, 2. These arch-priests, that at the heart were much against Cæsar, yet to murder Christ as a rebel, pretended to be the greatest Cæsarian royalists.

16. Then delivered he him therefore unto them to be crucified, And they took Jesus, and led him away. 17. And he bearing his cross, went forth into a place called *the place* of a skull, which is called in the Hebrew, Golgotha.

17. He bare his cross (till his strength failed, and then they made Simon of Cyrene to bear it)

to a place called in Syriac Golgotha, or the place of a skull.

18. Where they crucified him, and two other with him, on either side one, and Jesus in the midst. 19. And Pilate wrote a title, and put it on the cross. And the writing was, JESUS OF NAZARETH THE KING OF THE JEWS.

18, 19. Note, The title signifieth his accusation.

20. This title then read many of the Jews: for the place where Jesus was crucified was nigh to the city: and it was written in Hebrew, *and* Greek, *and* Latin.

20. Written in Syriac or Chaldee words with Hebrew letters, and in Greek and Latin.

21. Then said the chief priests of the Jews to Pilate, Write not, The king of the Jews; but that he said, I am the king of the Jews. 22. Pilate answered, What I have written, I have written.

21, 22. The title which Pilate made in scorn, and God over-ruled as real truth, displeased the arch-priests: but Pilate would not alter it.

23. Then the soldiers when they had crucified Jesus, took his garments (and made four parts, to every soldier a part) and also *his* coat: now the coat was without seam, woven from the top throughout. 24. They said therefore among themselves, Let us not rent it, but cast lots for it, whose it shall be: that the scripture might be fulfilled, which saith, They parted my raiment among them, and for my vesture they did cast lots. These things therefore the soldiers did.

23. Not that the prophecy made them do it, but was fulfilled by their doing it.

25. Now there stood by the cross of Jesus, his mother, and his mother's sister, Mary *the wife* of Cleophas, and Mary Magdalene. 26. When Jesus therefore saw his mother, and the disciple standing by, whom he loved, he saith unto his mother, Woman, behold thy son.

CHAP. XX. ST. JOHN. 239

27. Then saith he to the disciple, Behold thy mother. And from that hour that disciple took her unto his own *home*.

25, 26, 27. Note, Christ on the cross had a care of his mother's future comfort in the world: which consisted in her entertainment and converse with his beloved disciple.

28. After this, Jesus knowing that all things were now accomplished, that the scripture might be fulfilled, saith, I thirst. 29. Now there was set a vessel full of vinegar: and they filled a spunge with vinegar, and put it upon hyssop, and put it to his mouth. 30. When Jesus therefore had received the vinegar, he said, It is finished: and he bowed his head, and gave up the ghost.

28. As other scriptures of him were fulfilled, so he would have that Psal. lxix. 22. And having drunk the vinegar, he said, my sacrifice on the cross is performed, and the prophecies of it fulfilled, and he bowed his head and resigned his soul. Many passages are omitted by John, because written by others.

31. The Jews therefore, because it was the preparation, that the bodies should not remain upon the cross on the sabbath-day, (for that sabbath-day was an high day) besought Pilate that their legs might be broken, and *that* they might be taken away. 32. Then came the soldiers, and brake the legs of the first, and of the other which was crucified with him.

31, 32. Note, What day it was, whether the seventh day sabbath, or another so called by the Jews' superstition, expositors varying, I have before said, I will not trouble the vulgar reader with the controversy.

33. But when they came to Jesus, and saw that he was dead already, they brake not his legs. 34. But one of the soldiers with a spear pierced his side, and forthwith came there out blood and water.

33, 34. They made sure, since that he was dead.

35. And he that saw it bare record, and his record is true: and he knoweth that he saith true, that ye might believe. 36. For these things were done, that the scripture should be fulfilled, A bone of him shall not be broken.

35, 36. John that saw it, is a true witness, and that Psal. xxxiv. 20. which speaketh God's care of all his people, was specially meant of Christ, whether David so understood it or not.

37. And again another scripture saith, They shall look on him whom they pierced.

37. Thus also that of Zach. xii. 10. was fulfilled.

38. And after this, Joseph of Arimathea (being a disciple of Jesus, but secretly for fear of the Jews) besought Pilate that he might take away the body of Jesus: and Pilate gave him leave: he came therefore and took the body of Jesus.

38. Joseph that durst not own Christ openly alive, begs and obtaineth his body for burial.

39. And there came also Nicodemus, (which at the first came to Jesus by night) and brought a mixture of myrrh and aloes, about an hundred pound *weight*. 40. Then took they the body of Jesus, and wound it in linen clothes with the spices, as the manner of the Jews is to bury.

39. The myrrh and aloes were to keep the body from putrefaction: but it seems they did for haste (being late) but rudely lay them to the body with the clothes, deferring the full embalming to the first day of the week, when the women came with spices to have done it.

41. Now in the place where he was crucified, there was a garden, and in the garden a new sepulchre, wherein was never man yet laid. 42. There laid they Jesus therefore, because of the Jews preparation-day, for the sepulchre was nigh at hand.

41, 42. It was Joseph's sepulchre which he had prepared for himself, cleanness and nearness made it convenient.

CHAP. XX.

THE first *day* of the week cometh Mary Magdalene early when it was yet dark, unto the sepulchre, and seeth the stone taken away from the sepulchre.

1. Mary and other women first see it.

2. Then she runneth, and cometh to Simon Peter, and to the other disciple whom Jesus loved, and saith unto them, They have taken away the Lord out of the sepulchre and we know not where they have laid him. 3. Peter therefore went forth, and that other disciple, and came to the sepulchre. 4. So they ran both together: and the other disciple did outrun Peter, and came first to the sepulchre. 5. And he stooping down, *and looking in,* saw the linen clothes lying; yet went he not in. 6. Then cometh Simon Peter following him, and went into the sepulchre, and seeth the linen clothes lie: 7. And the napkin that was about his head, not lying with the linen clothes, but wrapped together in a place by itself. 8. Then went in also that other disciple which came first to the sepulchre, and he saw, and believed.

2, 3, &c. Peter and John moved by Mary's words, went and saw, &c.

9. For as yet they knew not the scripture, that he must rise again from the dead.

9. Though the scripture (and Christ himself often) foretold them his resurrection, they yet believed it not.

10. Then the disciples went away again unto their own home. 11. But Mary stood without at the sepulchre, weeping: and as she wept, she stooped down, *and looked* into the sepulchre, 12. And seeth two angels in white, sitting, the one at the head, and the other at the feet, where the body of Jesus had lain; 13. And they say unto her, Woman, why weepest thou? She saith unto them, Because they have taken away my Lord, and I know not where they have laid him.

10, 11, &c. Though some evangelists mentioned but one angel, that denieth not that there were two, which is here affirmed.

14. And when she had thus said, she turned herself back, and saw Jesus standing, and knew not that it was Jesus. 15. Jesus saith unto her, Woman, why weepest thou? whom seekest thou? she supposing him to be the gardener, saith unto him, Sir, if thou have borne him hence, tell me where thou hast laid him, and I will take him away. 16. Jesus saith unto her, Mary, She turned herself, and saith unto him, Rabboni, which is to say Master.

14. Note, Whether her not knowing him was not by reason of distance, darkness, or Christ's not appearing in full notoriety, is uncertain. Secondly, Christ's first words are full of compassion to a weeping sinner that loved him. Thirdly, it is easy to think with what passionate joy this sight and word surprised her.

17. Jesus saith unto her, Touch me not: for I am not yet ascended to my Father: but go to my brethren, and say unto them, I ascend unto my Father and your Father, and to my God and your God.

17. I am not risen for such familiar conduct and converse as 1 had with you before my resurrection, but must ascend to my Father, where my body shall be a glorified spiritual body. And though I will allow you as much familiarity as shall convince you of my resurrection, yet no more, nor such as formerly. But go to my disciples, and tell them, I take them as my brethren, and am shortly to ascend where I shall be better to them than on earth, even to him, that is [my Father,] (by nature and merit) and [their Father,] (by adopting grace and union with me through my merit) to [my God] (as I am mediator and man,) and [their God] (through my mediation.)

Note, All true believers should labour to get this most comfortable text deeply imprinted on their minds, and never think of God or come to him but as here described; my Father and your Father, my God and your God. And thus only to think of heaven, and our change at death, we are ascending to our ascended Saviour called our brother, and to his Father and our Father, to his God and our God.

Note, That there seemeth a great differrnce between the evangelists in describing these passages and appearances to the women and apostles: but it is but because one leaveth out what another mentioneth, but not that they contradict each other. And if you take them altogether as one history, the order seemeth to be this, first, Mary Magdalene, Johanna, Mary of James, and Salome, having bought spices, and going to embalm the body, said, who will roll away the stone for us. Secondly, when they came they found

CHAP. XX. ST. JOHN.

hat the stone was rolled away; for an angel had done it, and with his appearing and earthquake ffrighted away the soldiers. Thirdly, That angel with another saith to the women, fear not, I know ou seek Jesus that was crucified: why seek ye he living among the dead: he is not here, he is isen, come, see the place, &c. 4. Then the women run and tell the disciples, They have taken way the Lord we know not where they have aid him. 5. Then Peter and John run to see: Mary being come back stood weeping at the ntrance and looked back and saw two angels, as hen reciteth it. 7. Then Mary looked back and w Christ, and at first knew him not, and he ake to her as here. 8. Then she runs and tells he disciples, that she had seen the Lord: 9. ither then or when she was gone, Jesus met the st of the women, and said to them, All hail, ad they laid hold on his feet and worshipped im; and he said, Fear not, Go tell my brethren, c.

Or perhaps we may make it shorter: As 1. The one rolled away, and the keeper affrighted away. Mary and the other women come and find it . 3. They go in and miss the body. 4. Mary ins and tells Peter and John. 5. They run to e. 6. The women staying see first one angel a the stone on the right side and then two, one the head and one at the feet of the place. 7. hese angels say all that is mentioned, to Mary d the rest. 8. Mary seeth Jesus and so do the st, who holding him by the feet, he restraineth rther corporal contract, and speaketh to Mary ad the rest all that is mentioned. 9. Then she od they tell the disciples that they had seen im, and what he said. This seemeth the order f all together.

18. Mary Magdalene came and old the disciples, that she had seen he Lord, and that he had spoken hese things unto her. 19. Then be same day at evening, being the rst *day* of the week, when the oors were shut, where the disciples were assembled for fear of the ews, came Jesus and stood in the idst, and saith unto them, Peace e unto you.

18, 19. Note, Christ rose and first appeared on e first day of the week. If any should question by cavilling at the text as doubtful, the prac- te of the universal church, ever since observing at day without any contradicting party, proveth past doubt to all that use sober reason in the se. 2. Christ owned their private meeting, t reproving the cautelous fears of persecuters. The first word that he spake to them together r after his words to Mary) was [peace be unto u] (little understood by many churchmen.)

20. And when he had so said, he hewed unto them *his* hands and his ide. Then were the disciples glad hen they saw the Lord.
2.

20. Several appearances are past by because mentioned by others.

21. Then said Jesus to them again, Peace *be* unto you: as *my* Father hath sent me, even so send I you. 22. And when he had said this, he breathed on *them*, and saith unto them, Receive ye the Holy Ghost. 23. Whose soever sins ye remit, they are remitted unto them; *and* whose soever *sins* ye retain, they are retained.

21, 22, &c. Peace is the sum of my gift and benediction to you, and the sum of your duty to others; as my Father sent me into the world to gather, guide, and save his church as their head and mediator, so I send you to gather, guide, and save the church as my apostles: and breathing on them, he said, as my Father sent me not with a bare title unfurnished for his work, but filled with the spirit of life and power, of light and wisdom, of love and goodness, so I will give you the same holy Spirit, and send you furnished with power, knowledge, and love, and not with mere names and titles, as images:) I give you power to preach the gospel so effectually as shall open men's eyes, and turn them from darkness to light, and from the power of Satan unto God, that they may receive really from God, and by sacramental investiture in baptism, and from your remission of sins, a right to the inheritance among the sanctified by faith in me: to be the guides of my church entrusted with witnessing and recording my doctrine, laws, and promises for their government to the end of the world; and with the keys of church order, as authorized judges in your several charges, who is capable of church communion to be received by baptism, restored by repentance, or as incapable apostates cast out; together with an extraordinary power to inflict or to remit bodily punishment by my rule, not at your pleasure, but as it shall please the Holy Ghost, which he shall give you. And I do breathe on you, to communicate now some beginnings of that spirit which I will send down on you after my ascension: and so signify to you that it is a real qualification and spiritual that I will give, (as God when he made man, breathed into him a living soul) that you deceive not yourselves and the church by dead, imaginary, and powerless names: the witness of Jesus is the spirit of prophecy, and of sanctification. And if any man have not the spirit of Christ, he is none of his, by what name or title soever he be dignified.

24. But Thomas, one of the twelve, called Didymus, was not with them when Jesus came. 25. The other disciples therefore said unto him, We have seen the Lord. But he said unto them, Except I shall see in his hands the print of the nails, and put my finger into
R

the print of the nails, and thrust my hand into his side, I will not believe.

25. Note, All Christ's disciples were not equally inclined to believe. 2. This obstinate resolution deserved a desertion, yet Christ in mercy overcame it, and forsook him not.

26. And after eight days, again his disciples were within, and Thomas with them: *then* came Jesus, the doors being shut, and stood in the midst, and said, Peace *be* unto you.

26. The next first day of that week, they being assembled, &c. Note, Coming in when the doors were fast shut, whether he opened them (as some groundlessly think) or not, was a miracle, he whose body was quickly, to be a glorious spiritual body, when it came to that glorious spiritual region, no doubt had after his resurrection a change preparatory thereto, by which he could appear and disappear and vanish from their sight, and come in when the door was shut, and at last ascend to heaven: and the carnal objections against this are all vain.

27. Then saith he to Thomas, Reach hither thy finger, and behold my hands; and reach hither thy hand, and thrust it into my side: and be not faithless, but believing.

27. Note, Wonderful is the condescension of Christ to those that he will save.

28. And Thomas answered and said unto him, My Lord and my God.

28. Note, The convincing condescension of Christ turns unbelief into a rapture of adoration: now Thomas crieth, My Lord and my God.

29. Jesus saith unto him, Thomas, because thou hast seen me, thou hast believed: blessed *are* they that have not seen, and *yet* have believed.

29. I have condescended to thy sight and feeling: but this shall not be the common way to blessedness, but they that have not seen shall believe and so be happy.

30. And many other signs truly did Jesus in the presence of his disciples, which are not written in this book. 31. But these are written, that ye might believe that Jesus is the Christ the Son of God, and that believing ye might have life through his name.

30, 31. These and many more not recited he did; and it being by believing that Christ is the Son of God, and Saviour, that you must come to life, and by the evidence of those miracles that you must believe that he is the Christ, therefore these miracles are recorded to convince you, that you may believe.

CHAP. XXI.

AFTER these things, Jesus shewed himself again to the disciples at the sea of Tiberias; and on this wise shewed he *himself:* 2. There were together Simon Peter, and Thomas called Didymus, and Nathanael of Cana in Galilee, and the *sons* of Zebedee, and two other of his disciples. 3. Simon Peter saith unto them, I go a fishing. They say unto him, We also go with thee. They went forth, and entered into a ship immediately; and that night they caught nothing.

1, 2, 3. Note. The disciples went home to their trades when Jesus was crucified. 2. Their unsuccessfulness was to prepare for the miracle.

4. But when the morning was now come, Jesus stood on the shore: but the disciples knew not that it was Jesus.

4 His appearance after his resurrection was with some change from what he appeared before.

5. Then Jesus saith unto them, Children, have ye any meat? They answered him, No. 6. And he said unto them, Cast the net on the right side of the ship, and ye shall find. They cast therefore, and now they were not able to draw it for the multitude of fishes.

5, 6. Christ taketh occasion of their frustration to shew his power and help their faith.

7. Therefore that disciple whom Jesus loved, saith unto Peter, It is the Lord. Now when Simon Peter heard that it was the Lord, he girt *his* fisher's coat *unto him,* (for he was naked) and did cast himself into the sea.

7. When the miracle convinced him upon John's words that it was the Lord, he put on his fisher's coat, and leaped into the sea, to shew that he trusted Christ with his life.

8. And the other disciples came in a little ship (for they were not far from land, but as it were two hundred cubits) dragging the net with fishes. 9. As soon then as they were come to land, they saw a fire of coals there, and fish laid thereon, and bread. 10. Jesus saith unto them, Bring of the fish which ye have now caught. 11. Simon Peter went up, and drew the net to land full of great fishes, an hundred and fifty and three: and for all there were so many, yet was not the net broken.

8 Here are two miracles conjoined: The fish caught, and the fish, and bread, and fire prepared for them.

12. Jesus saith unto them, Come *and* dine. And none of the disciples durst ask him, Who art thou? knowing that it was the Lord. 13. Jesus then cometh, and taketh bread, and giveth them, and fish likewise.

12, 13. They knew him more by the miracle than by his visage. Though it be not said that he did eat and drink with them, it is improbable though uncertain.

14. This is now the third time that Jesus shewed himself to his disciples, after that he was risen from the dead.

14. This was the third time that he appeared to many of them together, or the third that John recordeth, and the third day of his appearing, though the sixth appearance made: And whether that on a mountain in Galilee, mentioned by others was at this time, is doubted.

15. So when they had dined, Jesus saith to Simon Peter, Simon son of Jonas, lovest thou me more than these? He saith unto him, Yea, Lord; thou knowest that I love thee. He saith unto him, Feed my lambs.

15. Thou didst lately profess that if all men forsook me, yet thou wouldst not, as if thou hadst loved me more than all the rest: And yet did three times deny me: Art thou now of the same resolution more confirmed?... If thou be, What love thou hast to me, shew it by thy ministerial love and labour for the souls even of the lowest.

16. He saith to him again the second time, Simon *son* of Jonas, lovest thou me? He saith unto him, Yea, Lord; thou knowest that I love thee. He saith unto him, Feed my sheep.

16. Thou knowest the heart, and therefore knowest that I love thee, &c.

17. He saith unto him the third time, Simon *son* of Jonas, lovest thou me? Peter was grieved, because he said unto him the third time, Lovest thou me? And he said unto him, Lord, thou knowest all things; thou knowest that I love thee. Jesus saith unto him, Feed my sheep.

17. Note, Peter's three-fold denial required a three-fold confession, and engagement to future fidelity and obedience; and this told him what discipline he was to use by the power of church government towards others that so offend. 2. Ministers that are to require confession and promises of obedience to Christ from offenders, in order to their restoration, must lead the way in the same themselves, if they scandalously sin. 3. The great evidence of our love to Christ must be in serving the church and souls.

18. Verily, verily, I say unto thee, When thou wast young, thou girdest thyself, and walkedst whither thou wouldest: but when thou shalt be old, thou shalt stretch forth thy hands, and another shall gird thee, and carry *thee* whither thou wouldest not.

18. Thou wast at thy free dispose, &c. But hereafter others shall bind thee, and carry thee to prison against thy will, and also unto death. By these words he signified that he should be martyred.

19. This spake he, signifying by what death he should glorify God. And when he had spoken this, he saith unto him, Follow me.

19. Follow me in labour and sufferings unto glory.

20. Then Peter turning about, seeth the disciple whom Jesus loved, following; which also leaned on his breast at supper, and said, Lord, which is he that betrayeth thee? 21. Peter seeing him, saith to Jesus, Lord, and what *shall* this man do?

20. What shall become of John?

22. Jesus saith unto him, If I will that he tarry till I come, what *is that* to thee? Follow thou me.

22. What is that to thee how long he shall live, if it were till my coming, or if he live till he see my Catholic church settled under my proper government, when the Jews' law and policy are fully dissolved at the destruction of their temple and nation?

23. Then went this saying abroad among the brethren, that that disciple should not die: yet Jesus said not unto him, He shall not die: but, If I will that he tarry till I come, what *is that* to thee?

23. Note, A false tradition may pass amongst Christ's own disciples by misunderstanding in some things.

24. This is the disciple which testifieth of these things, and wrote these things: and we know that his testimony is true.

24. This is John the disciple who was an eye and ear witness of all this, and who wrote this history of Christ; And whose testimony the church doth justly receive as true.

Note, Though some take these words to be the Bishop's of Asia that published John's gospel, (at whose request they say he wrote it about thirty two years after Christ's resurrection,) yet it is no less probable that the words are his own, and that [we know] signifieth only [it is well known to the churches.]

25. And there are also many other things which Jesus did, the which if they should be written every one, I suppose that even the world itself could not contain the books that should be written. Amen.

25. Though this history be written to record divers things which others have omitted, yet all together are far from containing all the miracles that Christ did: which were so many, that should they all be written, the many and great volumes would as it were overload the world.

Note, 1. That therefore it is not to be matter of offence, if any one evangelist pass by divers particulars.

2. That though multitudes of Christ's words and miracles may be unknown to us, as much is recorded as he would have taken as needful to the notice of the church through all generations: And none of his laws or promises, the objects of our obedience and faith are omitted: yea all that is essential to Christianity is contained in baptism or a very narrow room.

3. It is in vain to pretend oral tradition for any needful thing omitted in the scripture records, though the essentials and greatest practical matters of religion are most certainly delivered both ways, even by the scriptures, and by the universal public practice of the churches.

THE ACTS
OF THE
HOLY APOSTLES.

NOTE, *That this History written by Saint Luke, is not to be supposed to contain all the Miracles, Preaching and Success of all the Apostles; but only the History of Peter and Paul, and some few others their companions, and that but for a short space of time: not mentioning what the other ten Apostles and their helpers did in other parts of the world; nor what Peter and Paul did to the end of their lives, (supposed to be ten years after the ending of this history:) yea, Peter's history is here recorded but for a far shorter time than Paul's, with whom Luke travelled. And though this history of Luke have more infallibility than other histories of church affairs since written, yet all other credible notice of matter of fact and church practice from the beginning, is of great use to us, and not to be despised.*

CHAP. I.

THE former treatise have I made, O Theophilus, of all that Jesus began both to do and teach, 2. Until the day in which he was taken up, after that he through the Holy Ghost had given commandments unto the apostles whom he had chosen.

1. I wrote the gospel history as a record of Christ's birth, miracles, and doctrine, reaching to the day of his ascension, after he had by breathing on his disciples, given them the Holy Ghost, and their commissions.

3. To whom also he shewed himself alive after his passion, by many infallible proofs, being seen of them forty days, and speaking of the things pertaining to the kingdom of God:

3. That their faith should not waver, but have full assurance, he shewed himself to them by unquestionable manifestation, at several times in the forty days space, in which he abode on earth before his ascension, instructing them in the matters of his kingdom.

4. And being assembled together with them, commanded them that they should not depart from Jerusalem, but wait for the promise of the Father, which, *saith he,* ye have heard of me. 5. For John truly baptized with water; but ye shall be baptized with the Holy Ghost, not many days hence.

4, 5. And when he was among them, he bid them wait at Jerusalem for the great gift of the Father, even the Holy Ghost, the promise of which ye have heard of me: which shall be your full solemn initiation into your apostolical and extraordinary ministry, and a few days hence you shall receive.

Note, The Holy Ghost given by Christ's breathing on them, was not a mere title, name, or relation, but yet it was not that full effusion which they were to have after his ascension; but a previous earnest of it, to shew them from whom the fuller communication was to come, differing from this latter, as his own resurrection-victory differed from his ascension, majesty, and kingdom. They were not to set upon the public ministry without this necessary previous qualification: nor should any now take up the ordinary ministry, without holy suitable qualifications by Christ's Spirit.

6. When they therefore were come together, they asked of him, saying, Lord, wilt thou at this time restore again the kingdom to Israel?

6. They were now in hope of earthly dominion, and said, Wilt thou now deliver Israel from captivity, and reign in visible glory over them, as the Messiah?

7. And he said unto them, It is not for you to know the times or the seasons, which the Father hath put in his own power. 8. But ye shall receive power after that the Holy Ghost is come upon you: and ye shall be witnesses unto me: both in Jerusalem, and in all Judea, and in Samaria, and unto the uttermost part of the earth.

7. Presume not to inquire into God's secrets, of which this is one, at what time God will advance

246 THE ACTS. CHAP. I.

you and his Israel to visible reign and glory. But such power as is fittest for you at present, ye shall receive by the coming of the Holy Ghost upon you: by which you shall be enabled to declare your testimony of what you have seen and heard of me, throughout the earth.

Note, It may seem strange that Christ confuteth not their conceit of an Israelitish kingdom restored, but only their demands about the season. But they were so far in the right, as that Christ would advance believing Israelites with the rest of the Catholic church, though not restore the Mosaic policy, nor set the Israelites over others in a local monarchy at Jerusalem. Therefore Christ intimateth, that they shall have better than they expected; which the Spirit should teach them better to understand.

9. And when he had spoken these things, while they beheld, he was taken up, and a cloud received him out of their sight.

9. Note, No doubt but Christ's body at its entrance in the celestial region of spirits, became glorious and spiritual eminently, such as Paul saith ours shall be. 1 Cor. xv.

2. The sight of Christ's ascension must needs be as full an ascertaining of the apostles' faith as his resurrection; and it must be no wonder that four evangelists mention it not, it being enough that any mention it, God's Spirit making their several histories indited by him to be as one book.

10. And while they looked stedfastly toward heaven, as he went up, behold, two men stood by them in white apparel; 11. Which also said, Ye men of Galilee, why stand ye gazing up into heaven? this same Jesus which is taken up from you into heaven, shall so come in like manner as ye have seen him go into heaven.

10, 11. While they looked up after him, two angels in the likeness of men, in white stood by them, saying, Ye men of G lilee, gaze no more after the body of Jesus as ended into heaven: know ye not that he must there reign in glory, and thence send you down the grace and blessings purchased by his life on earth? and yet he shall come again at the day of judgment, attended with his glorious angels, and does not forsake you by his remove.

12. Then returned they unto Jerusalem, from the mount called Olivet, which is from Jerusalem a sabbath-day's journey.

12. Note, Mount Olivet at the nearest part is but five furlongs from Jerusalem, (a furlong is six hundred feet, and five furlongs a thousand yards.) And Christ is said, Luke xxiv. to lead them out as far as Bethany, which is said to be fifteen furlongs from Jerusalem, John xi. 18. To understand this, some say, 1. That Bethany was the name of a large space of ground (as Hackney, where some houses are far nearer London than others.) 2. And that Christ ascended not from the nearest part of Mount Olivet, but from the top: And it is possible that Christ might lead them as far as Bethany, and in the house of Lazarus instruct them, and go forth again with them to the top of the mount, and thence ascend

13. And when they were come in, they went up into an upper room, where abode both Peter and James, and John, and Andrew, Philip, and Thomas, Bartholomew, and Matthew, James *the son* of Alpheus, and Simon Zelotes, and Judas *the brother* of James. 14. These all continued with one accord in prayer and supplication with the women, and Mary the mother of Jesus, and with his brethren.

13. Note, The sight of Christ ascending confirmed their faith. 2. And that faith presently caused constant prayer in concord and communion.

15. And in those days Peter stood up in the midst of the disciples, and said, (the number of the names together were about an hundred and twenty,)

15. An hundred and twenty being assembled for prayer and mutual encouragement in faith.

16. Men *and* brethren, this scripture must needs have been fulfilled, which the Holy Ghost by the mouth of David spake before concerning Judas, which was guide to them that took Jesus. 17. For he was numbered with us, and had obtained part of this ministry.

16. Note, This must needs signify no necessity of constraint, put on Judas, but a necessity hypothetical, and of consequence, that is, it cannot but be true which God foretelleth or foreseeth. 2. Judas, though a thief and a devil, had by Christ's own choice a part or office in the apostolic order: But not after Christ's breathing on them and evening them the Holy Ghost for the proper work of his universal kingdom, as it began after his resurrection, but only as one sent to offer grace to the twelve tribes of Israel that mostly refused it, such may be ministers to the condemnation of themselves and others; and God may bless their doctrine to his elect.

18. Now this man purchased a field with the reward of iniquity: and falling headlong, he burst asunder in the midst, and all his bowels gushed out.

18. Note, Matt. xxvii. saith he strangled himself; Some expositors suppose strangling was not by hanging himself, but the rage of his conscience and passion did suffocate or strangle him, and that he fell down and burst; or, rather that he was

himself headlong from some high place and burst: Others think that the rope or bough broke where he was hanged; and it is possible without hanging he might at once strangle himself with a cord on the brow of some precipice, and fall, or cast himself down it.

19. And it was known unto all the dwellers at Jerusalem; insomuch as that field is called in their proper tongue, Aceldama, that is to say, The field of blood.

19. This is commonly known, and the field to this day is as a record of it

20. For it is written in the book of Psalms, Let his habitation be desolate, and let no man dwell therein: and, His bishopric let another take.

20. What is said in Ps. lxix. 25. and cix. 8. is ultimately to be verified of him: his office another must take.

21. Wherefore, of these men which have companied with us, all the time that the Lord Jesus went in and out among us, 22. Beginning from the baptism of John, unto that same day that he was taken up from us, must one be ordained to be a witness with us of his resurrection.

21, 22. Note, Many besides the twelve did constantly accompany Christ. 2. Quest. Why must the number of the twelve apostles be yet kept up, were not others good witnesses without being chosen apostles? Answ. The Israelitish polity was not utterly demolished till near forty years after Christ's resurrection: Therefore till then the Jews were to be preached to, and the twelve apostles, suited to the twelve tribes; though after the number was changed by Paul's conversion, when the gospel was to be principally sent unto the Gentiles.

23. And they appointed two, Joseph called Barsabas, who was surnamed Justus, and Matthias. 24. And they prayed, and said, Thou Lord, which knowest the hearts of all men, shew whether of these two thou hast chosen. 25. That he may take part of this ministry and apostleship, from which Judas by transgression fell, that he might go to his own place.

23, 24, 25. Note, 1. The apostleship was not only the qualification of eye witnesses of Christ's works, but a special pre-eminent office of some of those many who saw His works: All that saw them were not apostles. Therefore Christ did set diversity and disparity of ministerial offices in his church.

2. Peter's speech was to all the disciples, ver.

15, 16. It is therefore to be supposed that the two were chosen by all the company, but by the conduct of the apostles. And God by lot chose one of the two, it being his prerogative to make apostles. And I know no reason why the chief pastors of the church (at least in cases of doubt) should not now be so chosen.

26. And they gave forth their lots; and the lot fell upon Matthias, and he was numbered with the eleven apostles.

26. Note, How casual soever it seemed, God was the undoubted determiner of it. But solemnly to appeal to his determination in ludicrous toys, or things already determined by his word, is but profanely to take his name in vain.

CHAP. II.

AND when the day of Pentecost was fully come, they were all with one accord in one place.

1. It is by most expositors taken to be on the Lord's day, though some few contradict it. 2. Christ chose the time to send the Spirit, when they were unanimously assembled for his worship.

2. And suddenly there came a sound from heaven, as of a rushing mighty wind, and it filled all the house where they were sitting. 3. And there appeared unto them cloven tongues, like as of fire, and it sat upon each of them:

2, 3. Note, It is likely it was only on the apostles.

4. And they were all filled with the Holy Ghost, and began to speak with other tongues, as the Spirit gave them utterance.

4. They that were unlearned men, were all suddenly filled with the Holy Ghost, who inspiring their minds with sacred light of knowledge, and fervour of affection, caused them to utter words in various languages which they had never learnt, in the praises of God and his works.

Note, As baptism entereth man into the state of Christianity, this effusion of the Spirit solemnly invested the apostles in the full state and power of their offices.

5. And there were dwelling at Jerusalem, Jews, devout men, out of every nation under heaven.

5. Then were at Pentecost Jews out of many nations whore they were dispersed, that came up to the feast.

6. Now when this was noised abroad, the multitude came together, and were confounded, because that every man heard them speak in his own language. 7. And they were all amazed, and mar-

velled, saying one to another, Behold, are not all these which speak, Galileans? 8. And how hear we every man in our own tongue, wherein we were born? 9. Parthians, and Medes, and Elamites, and the dwellers in Mesopotamia, and in Judea, and Cappadocia, in Pontus, and Asia, 10. Phrygia, and Pamphylia, in Egypt and in the parts of Libya about Cyrene, and strangers of Rome, Jews and proselytes, 14. Cretes and Arabians, we do hear them speak in our tongues the wonderful works of God.

6, 7, &c. The word of Christ and of his gospel, was that which they spake in the tongues of all these countries.

12. They were all amazed, and were in doubt, saying one to another, What meaneth this? 13. Others mocking, said, These men are full of new wine.

12, 13. Some derided them as drunken.

14. But Peter standing up with the eleven, lift up his voice, and said unto them, Ye men of Judea, and all ye that dwell at Jerusalem, be this known unto you, and hearken to my words: 15. For these are not drunken, as ye suppose, seeing it is but the third hour of the day.

14, &c. It is but nine o'clock at which time men use to pray fasting, (and drunkenness will not enable a man to speak various languages.)

16. But this is that which was spoken by the prophet Joel, 17. And it shall come to pass in the last days, (saith God) I will pour out of my Spirit upon all flesh; and your sons and your daughters shall prophesy, and your young men shall see visions, and your old men shall dream dreams: 18. And on my servants, and on my handmaidens I will pour out in those days of my Spirit, and they shall prophesy:

16. &c. This is the fulfilling of what Joel prophesied of the times of the Messiah, &c.

19. And I will shew wonders in heaven above, and signs in the earth beneath; blood, and fire, and vapour of smoke. 20. The sun shall be turned into darkness, and the moon into blood, before that great and notable day of the Lord come. 21. And it shall come to pass, *that* whosoever shall call on the name of the Lord, shall be saved.

19, 20, 21. Many prodigies in heaven and earth, as if the frame of nature did shake or were altered, shall go before the destruction of the temple and nation of the Jews, but faithful, praying Christians shall be saved.

22. Ye men of Israel, hear these words, Jesus of Nazareth, a man approved of God among you, by miracles and wonders and signs, which God did by him in the midst of you, as ye yourselves also know: 23. Him being delivered by the determinate counsel and foreknowledge of God, ye have taken, and by wicked hands have crucified and slain: 24. Whom God hath raised up, having loosed the pains of death: because it was not possible that he should be holden of it.

22, 23, 24. You deny not the fact of those miracles done by Jesus, which are the infallible works of God's attestation: God's determinate counsel having appointed him to die as a sacrifice for the sins of the world, and he foreknowing all that your wicked hearts do in it hereto, accordingly with wicked hands you have murdered him, (not at all excusable by the said decree or foreknowledge of God.) But God raised him from the dead having loosed the bonds of death, it being impossible he should be held and conquered by it.

Note, The word translated pains of death, may be also translated bonds: But if it must be read [pains] death as a separation of soul and body is by privation a penal state; though not dolorous by positive evil; yet some think that the article of descent into hell signifieth some positive penalty on Christ's soul, called here the pains of death. But most think otherwise.

25. For David speaketh concerning him, I foresaw the Lord always before my face, for he is on my right hand, that I should not be moved. 26. Therefore did my heart rejoice, and my tongue was glad: moreover also, my flesh shall rest in hope. 27. Because thou wilt not leave my soul in hell, neither

wilt thou suffer thine Holy One to see corruption.

Note, Though David spake this partly of himself, the Holy Ghost spake it by him of Christ, That God would not leave him in the state of death, nor suffer his body to be corrupted.

28. Thou hast made known to me the ways of life; thou shalt make me full of joy with thy countenance. 29. Men *and* brethren, let me freely speak unto you of the patriarch David, that he is both dead and buried, and his sepulchre is with us unto this day: 30. Therefore being a prophet, and knowing that God had sworn with an oath to him, that of the fruit of his loins according to the flesh he would raise up Christ to sit on his throne: 31. He seeing this before, spake of the resurrection Christ, that his soul was not left in hell, neither his flesh did see corruption.

30. *Qu.* How is Christ said to sit on David's throne, which was of a visible earthly kingdom? *Answ.* It is that which was principally meant in the promise to David: And the eminent and the highest reign containeth the lower under its power.

2. The article of Christ's descent into hell, is so largely handled by many, that I will not here interpose any more of it, than to say, that I take it to be best expounded by Archbishop Usher, in his answer to the Jesuits challenge. And this text speaking first of David, and ultimately of Christ, seemeth to mean no other hell for Christ, but what David meant of himself, which is *hades,* the state of separated souls, as such.

32. This Jesus hath God raised up, whereof we all are witnesses. 33. Therefore being by the right hand of God exalted, and having received of the Father the promise of the Holy Ghost, he hath shed forth this which ye now see and hear.

32. We being all witnesses of his resurrection and ascension, he being in glory in the fulness of his power, and having promised thus to send down the Holy Ghost, hath performed his promise, as ye see and hear: 1. To prove by this miracle, the truth of his power to convince unbelievers, 2. And to enable us to teach the gospel to the people of divers languages in the world.

Note, The apostles were credible witnesses of fact: 2. The Holy Ghost is the infallible evidence that Christ's mission and power is of God.

34. For David is not ascended into the heavens: but he saith himself, The LORD said unto my Lord, Sit thou on my right hand, 35. Until I make thy foes thy footstool.

34. David went not up to heaven bodily as Jesus did, (but only his soul) but he prophesied of Christ's ascension and glory.

36. Therefore let all the house of Israel know assuredly, that God hath made the same Jesus whom ye have crucified, both Lord and Christ.

36. All of you, therefore, believe these divine attestations, and know assuredly, that this Jesus whom you crucified is in glory, exalted by God to be the Lord, King, and Saviour.

37. Now when they heard *this,* they were pricked in their heart, and said unto Peter, and to the rest of the apostles, Men *and* brethren, what shall we do?

37. These words accompanied with so great evidence, and the work of the Spirit now poured out, they could not resist, but their hearts convinced, were pricked or wounded with grief and fear, to find that they had crucified the Messiah whom they expected; and they cried out, Is there yet no hope or remedy? If there be, what shall we do?

38. Then Peter said unto them, Repent, and be baptized every one of you in the name of Jesus Christ, for the remission of sins, and ye shall receive the gift of the Holy Ghost.

38. There is yet hope and remedy. Repent of this and all your sins, and give up yourselves by faith to Christ in the baptismal covenant, and your sins shall be remitted, and this Holy Ghost which you now admire shall also be given unto you.

39. For the promise is unto you, and to your children, and to all that are afar off, even as many as the Lord our God shall call.

39. For the Messiah with his grace of remission, and the Spirit, is promised and is offered to you that are Jews, and your whole nation and children in the first place, and shall be yours yet, if you accept the offer; and not to you only, but to as many as God shall call of the Gentiles in the remotest parts of the world: for Christ is now to be the universal King and Saviour of all nations and persons that accept him.

40. And with many other words did he testify and exhort, saying,

Save yourselves from this untoward generation.

40. And with many more exhortations he persuaded them to believe and repent, and not to imitate the unbelieving, persecuting, hardened part of the Jews, lest they perish with them.

41. Then they that gladly received his word, were baptized: and the same day there were added *unto them* about three thousand souls.

41. Then they that believed and gladly consented to be Christians, were baptized: And that day about three thousand were converted to Christianity.
1. These Jews were before instructed in much of the law and prophets, and therefore their baptism was not delayed so long as the following churches delayed the baptizing of the Gentile Catechumens. 2. Yet though all were converted that day, it is not certain that all were baptized that day. 3. None were baptized that did not profess to believe the essentials of the baptismal covenant (That Jesus is the Christ, sent of God to reconcile us to him, and give us remission of sin, and his Spirit and everlasting salvation) and profest not willing consent to the covenant.

42. And they continued steadfastly in the apostles doctrine and fellowship, and in breaking of bread, and in prayers.

42. And being thus convinced, converted, and sacramentally bound and devoted to Christ, they continued united in communion with the apostles, in learning their doctrine, and in brotherly communication and love, and in celebration of the Lord's Supper, and in conjunct prayer: the apostles conducting the society in all this.

43. And fear came upon every soul: and many wonders and signs were done by the apostles.

43. The wonder amazed all men, and the miracles wrought by the apostles increased men's conviction.

44. And all that believed were together, and had all things common, 45. And sold their possessions and goods, and parted them to all men, as every man had need.

44. The greatness of the thing raised them above the world, and the Holy Ghost filled them with such love, as made every one to be to another as himself, and so made all common, not by destroying property but selfishness, and causing charity: And God that moved them to it, knew that they were quickly to be driven from their possessions in Judea.

46. And they continued daily with one accord in the temple, and breaking of bread from house to house, did eat their meat with gladness and singleness of heart.

46. In the temple was the meeting of the multitude, and from house to house they had their lesser meetings, where they did eat together and sacramentally communicate, and all with great joy and singleness of heart.

Note, Breaking bread sometimes signifieth common eating together, and sometimes sacramental communicating. And it is likest here to signify both conjunct, because there the church used the sacrament at the end of a meal, and not alone as now.

47. Praising God, and having favour with all the people. And the Lord added to the church daily such as should be saved.

47. Praising God and applauded by all, (for in charity to all:) God daily added to the church new converts, saved from unbelief and sin, and to be saved by further grace and glory.

CHAP. III.

NOW Peter and John went up together into the temple at the hour of prayer, *being* the ninth hour.

1. Note, They conformed to the Jews' ordinary way of choosing the temple for a place of prayer, and choosing the common hour.

2. And a certain man lame from his mother's womb, was carried, whom they laid daily at the gate of the temple which is called Beautiful, to ask alms of them that entered into the temple. 3. Who seeing Peter and John about to go into the temple, asked an alms. 4. And Peter fastening his eyes upon him, with John, said, Look on us. 5. And he gave heed unto them, expecting to receive something of them. 6. Then Peter said, Silver and gold have I none; but such as I have give I thee: in the name of Jesus Christ of Nazareth, rise up and walk.

2. Note, 1. They that have not money may have much better: holiness and spiritual riches are found most with poverty. 2. God gave the cripple better than he asked.

7. And he took him by the right

hand, and lift *him* up, and immediately his feet and ancle bones received strength. 8. And he leaping up, stood, and walked, and entered with them into the temple, walking and leaping, and praising God.

7. Note, This and such miracles were not at the mere will of the apostles: but when God would work them, his spirit by inspiration made it known to them, and put them on.

9. And all the people saw him walking and praising God. 10. And they knew that it was he which sat for alms at the Beautiful gate of the temple: and they were filled with wonder and amazement at that which had happened unto him.

9, 10. He had so long used to be there begging, that they well knew him, and wondered at the change.

11. And as the lame man which was healed, held Peter and John, all the people ran together unto them in the porch that is called Solomon's, greatly wondering.

11. The miracle made the people crowd to gaze at them.

12. And when Peter saw *it*, he answered unto the people, Ye men of Israel, why marvel ye at this? or why look ye so earnestly on us, as though by our own power or holiness we had made this man to walk?

12. After all the miracles that Christ himself did, why make you so strange a matter of this: or why gaze you with wonder on us, as if you thought we did it by our own power or holiness.

13. The God of Abraham, and of Isaac, and of Jacob, the God of our fathers hath glorified his Son Jesus; whom ye delivered up, and denied him in the presence of Pilate, when he was determined to let *him* go. 14. But ye denied the Holy One, and the just, and desired a murderer to be granted unto you. 15. And killed the prince of life, whom God hath raised from the dead; whereof we are witnesses,

13. Thus is the work of Jesus glorified, whom ye murdered, though he was the Holy One and Just, and the Lord of Life, now raised to glory.

16. And his name, through faith in his name hath made this man strong, whom ye see and know: yea, the faith which is by him, hath given him this perfect soundness in the presence of you all.

16. Quest. Whose faith was it? The lame man shewed no belief in Christ before he was healed. Answ. 1. It was by the apostles' faith. 2. And for the generating faith in others.

17. And now brethren, I wot that through ignorance ye did *it*, as *did* also your rulers.

17. Note, Ignorance is the common cause of error and all sin: but some men's ignorance is more wilful than others, and against more light, and hath less excuse: And so was the rulers worse than the people.

18. But those things which God before had shewed by the mouth of all his prophets, that Christ should suffer, he hath so fulfilled.

18. God who decreed Christ's sufferings for man, foretold it and permitted your sin that did it, and his prophesies and promises of our redemption are thus fulfilled.

19. Repent ye therefore, and be converted, that your sins may be blotted out; when the times of refreshing shall come from the presence of the Lord. 20. And he shall send Jesus Christ, which before was preached unto you:

19, 20. Repent therefore of your rejecting Jesus Christ, and be converted to true Christianity and godliness, that your sins may be forgiven, and so found to your comfort, when the time of Christ's glorious return, shall rejoice all true believers, and God shall send Jesus visibly to justify and glorify them, whom we now preach to you, and who was designed to be our Saviour.

21. Whom the heaven must receive, until the times of restitution of all things, which God hath spoken by the mouth of all his holy prophets, since the world began.

21. Who must be in the heavens in glory (not visible here) till the great and blessed change shall come which God hath promised by all his prophets, and sin and curse shall be taken away, and the creation shall be delivered from the bondage of corruption, into the glorious liberty of the sons of God, and there shall be a new hea-

ven and a new earth, in which shall dwell righteousness: even the time of our actual full redemption and salvation.

22. For Moses truly said unto the fathers, A prophet shall the Lord your God raise up unto you of your brethren, like unto me; him shall ye hear in all things whatsoever he shall say unto you. 23. And it shall come to pass, *that* every soul which will not hear that prophet, shall be destroyed from among the people.

22, 23. Note, Though Moses immediately spake of the species of the Jewish government, by a prophetical theocracy, that God would not rule them by elective or hereditary kings, but by prophets or men prophetically called (till they cast off this theocracy;) yet the Holy Ghost here tells us that Moses eminently prophesied this of Christ, who must be universally obeyed as our sovereign, and not to obey him will be sure condemnation, of which the Jews' destruction was a foretaste.

24. Yea, and all the prophets from Samuel, and those that follow after, as many as have spoken, have likewise foretold of these days.

24. The sum of all the prophets was to foretel the sufferings and the kingdom of Christ now begun.

25. Ye are the children of the prophets, and of the covenant which God made with our fathers, saying unto Abraham, And in thy seed shall all the kindreds of the earth be blessed.

25. According to the flesh ye are the posterity of the prophetical nation, and first in that covenant which God made with Abraham, pronouncing all nations blessed in his seed, as thence deriving their blessedness.

26. Unto you first, God having raised up his Son Jesus, sent him to bless you, in turning away every one of you from his iniquities.

26. Accordingly God having raised up his Son, doth first offer him and his grace to you before he be preached to the Gentiles; we declare to you his miracles, resurrection, and doctrine, that you may be turned from your unbelief and other sins, and be a people first blessed, as pardoned, and sanctified, and saved by his grace.

CHAP. IV.

AND as they spake unto the people, the priests, and the captain of the temple, and the Sadducees came upon them, 2. Being grieved that they taught the people, and preached through Jesus the resurrection from the dead. 3. And they laid hands on them, and put them in hold unto the next day: for it was now eventide.

1. Note, The great persecutors and silencers were the priests (who should have been the holiest) and the Sadducees that believed no life but this, and next the soldiers that were mercenary. One would wonder what should make such brutists as the Sadducees to be such furious silencers and persecutors: if there were no life to come, what harm can other men's hopes of it do them? But in depraved souls all faculties are vitiated. A blind mind hath a malignant heart and a cruel hand, to this day: who persecute men more for preaching and seeking the heavenly glory, than atheists and brutists who believe there is none such?

4. Howbeit, many of them which heard the word, believed; and the number of the men was about five thousand.

4. The assembly that owned Christianity was increased to above five thousand, and that success grieved the malignants.

5. And it came to pass on the morrow, that their rulers, and elders, and scribes, 6. And Annas the high priest, and Caiaphas, and John, and Alexander, and as many as were of the kindred of the high priest, were gathered together at Jerusalem.

5. Their rulers, the high priests and their consorts met in council.

7. And when they had set them in the midst, they asked, By what power, or by what name have ye done this?

7. Who gave you power and authority to set up us miracle workers and preachers to the people?

8. Then Peter filled with the Holy Ghost, said unto them, Ye rulers of the people, and elders of Israel, 9. If we this day be examined of the good deed done to the impotent man, by what means he is made whole: 10. Be it known unto you all, and to all the people of Israel, that by the name of Jesus Christ of Nazareth, whom ye cru-

cified, whom God raised from the dead, even by him doth this man stand here before you whole.

8. It is Christ's power that did the cure, and to his glory they proclaim it.

11. This is the stone which was set at nought of you builders, which is become the head of the corner. 12. Neither is there salvation in any other: for there is none other name under heaven given among men whereby we must be saved.

11, 12. He whom you rejected, is made the leader and head over all: and it is only by trusting and obeying him that man can be saved.

13. Now when they saw the boldness of Peter and John, and perceived that they were unlearned and ignorant men, they marvelled, and they took knowledge of them, that they had been with Jesus.

13. When they perceived their freedom of speech, and that they had not been bred up to learning, but were vulgar persons untaught, they marvelled, and took notice that they had seen them with Jesus.

14. And beholding the man which was healed standing with them, they could say nothing against it.

14. The evidence of the fact silenced them at present, but did not cure their hardened hearts.

15. But when they had commanded them to go aside out of the council, they conferred among themselves, 16. Saying, What shall we do to these men? for that indeed a notable miracle hath been done by them, is manifest to all them that dwell in Jerusalem, and we cannot deny it. 17. But that it spread no further among the people, let us straitly threaten them, that they speak henceforth to no man in this name.

15. Note, O the blindness and devilish malignity of these silencers of Christ's ministers! While they confess the miracle, and should consult how to repent of their former wickedness, they go on to consult how to silence the preachers, and think the apostles so cowardly, that their threatening would serve to hinder them from preaching.

18. And they called them, and commanded them not to speak at all, nor teach in the name of Jesus. 19. But Peter and John answered and said unto them, Whether it be right in the sight of God, to hearken unto you more than unto God, judge ye.

18, 19. The hardened wretches called them, and silenced them by their pretended authority, commanding them not to speak at all, nor teach in the name of Jesus: but Peter and John answered, the miracle proveth God's attestation, and we know it by his spirit, and dare you say that you are greater than God, and that we should obey you against his command? None but an atheist dare affirm it.

Ques. But may not Christian rulers and prelates silence ministers, though the Jewish might not? Answ. Either of them may silence blasphemy and wickedness: but sure Christian rulers have no more power to fight against Christ and his gospel, and silence his ministers than heathens, but much more obligation to encourage them.

Ques. But must not ministers, called by men, obey men that silence them, though apostles called by Christ, might not? Answ. They that are called justly by men, are called by Christ, who that way signified his will: and Timothy that was called by men, is charged before God and the Lord Jesus Christ, who shall judge, &c. to preach the word, and be instant in season and out of season, &c. Which way soever Christ call men, they are bound to be true to him. Christian rulers must be obeyed in the determination of circumstances (as time, places, maintenance, &c.) which are left to them as judges of edification; but not when they forbid Christ's ministers the work to which they are vowed, and consecrated, unless they be unable, or forfeit their commission. The pastors or bishops preached three hundred years against the will of emperors and kings, and long after against the will of Christian emperors, called Arians, Eutychians, Monothelites, &c.

20. For we cannot but speak the things which we have seen and heard.

20. We are not so blind and hardened as to go against all the divine evidences, which we have seen and heard, and to silence what God bids us speak, of which we have been the eye and ear witnesses ourselves.

21. So when they had further threatened them, they let them go, finding nothing how they might punish them, because of the people: for all men glorified God for that which was done.

21. The common people were not so blinded, hardened, and malignant, as the chief priests and rulers but glorified God for that which did but stir.

up the rulers' malice. 2. God made the people a restraint to the priests' and rulers' rage.

22. For the man was above forty years old, on whom this miracle of healing was shewed.

22. For the case was past all doubt, the man having been thus lame forty years. chap. iii. 2.

23. And being let go, they went to their own company, and reported all that the chief priests and elders had said unto them. 24. And when they heard that, they lift up their voice to God, with one accord, and said,

23. Note, Not that all are supposed with conjunct voice to say just the same words, but either some of them one part and some another; or some said these words with others' acclamations and consent: or they all spake by turns to the same sense.

Lord, thou *art* God which hast made heaven and earth, and the sea, and all that in them is: 25. Who by the mouth of thy servant David hast said, Why did the heathen rage, and the people imagine vain things? 26. The kings of the earth stood up, and the rulers were gathered together against the Lord, and against his Christ.

24. God prophesied by David, that the rulers of the nations, Gentiles and Jews, should in vain join their counsels and powers against Christ, his gospel, and his kingdom.

27. For of a truth against thy holy child Jesus, whom thou hast anointed, both Herod and Pontius Pilate, with the Gentiles, and the people of Israel were gathered together. 28. For to do whatsoever thy hand and thy counsel determined before to be done.

27. All combined by their own wickedness to do that which God hath fore-determined: God fore-decreed that Christ should be a sacrifice for sin; but the wicked determinations of their wills that did it, God only foresaw and permitted, but did not cause.

29. And now, Lord, behold their threatening: and grant unto thy servants, that with all boldness they may speak thy word. 30. By stretching forth thine hand to heal: and that signs and wonders may be done by the name of thy holy child Jesus.

29, 30. Note, 1. That the threatenings of malignant people are a fit opportunity for God's grace to his servants. 2. Boldness to preach when unjustly forbidden, is a great effect of God's grace to his servants. 3. The gift of convincing miracles, though promised, must be prayed for by them.

31. And when they had prayed, the place was shaken where they were assembled together; and they were all filled with the Holy Ghost, and they spake the word of God with boldness.

31. The Spirit caused them thus to pray, and more of the Spirit was poured on them, in answer to those prayers; giving the boldness which they asked, and that with a signal shaking of the place.

32. And the multitude of them that believed, were of one heart, and of one soul: neither said any *of them*, that ought of the things which he possessed, was his own, but they had all things common.

32. They were all of one mind, and will, and practice, united in fervent love, which made all common to them.

Note, It was not a commonness by levelling titles, but by voluntary fervent love. 2. And the Spirit did this in the beginning to give the world an example what true Christianity and the Spirit's operation is, even such fervent love to each other for Christ's sake, as destroyeth all sinful selfishness, and maketh others interest to be to us as our own, and so uniteth us in one body.

33. And with great power gave the apostles witness of the resurrection of the Lord Jesus: and great grace was upon them all.

33. And with evident miracles and wonderful gifts of the Spirit, did the apostles perform their testimony of Christ's resurrection: and the favour of God and man was upon them, or great charity prevailed among them.

34. Neither was there any among them that lacked: for as many as were possessors of lands, or houses, sold them, and brought the prices of the things that were sold, 35. And laid *them* down at the apostles feet: and distribution was made unto every man according as he had need.

34. This was neither to be the constant practice, nor yet was it an unwise excess of zeal: but it was a present effect of the Spirit, to shew what a degree of love all Christians should desire, and what self-denial and contempt of riches it should cause.

36. And Joses, who by the apostles was surnamed Barnabas (which is, being interpreted, The son of consolation), a Levite, *and* of the country of Cyprus, 37. Having land sold *it*, and brought the money, and laid *it* at the apostles feet.

36, 37. To signify his renouncing the world and selfishness in love to Christ and his church; he himself being after to go abroad the world to preach the gospel.

CHAP. V.

BUT a certain man named Ananias, with Sapphira his wife, sold a possession, 2. And kept back *part* of the price, his wife also being privy *to it*, and brought a certain part, and laid *it* at the apostles feet. 3. But Peter said, Ananias, why hath Satan filled thine heart to lie to the Holy Ghost, and to keep back *part* of the price of the land?

1. They pretended to give the whole price, but brought a part and said it was all....Why hast thou let Satan put so great a sin into thy heart, as to think to deceive the Holy Ghost in us apostles, as if he knew not when thou liest.

Note. The sin consisted, 1. In hypocrisy, pretending to give more than he did. 2. In the remnant of a worldly distrustful mind, that could not trust God with all. 3. In blasphemy against the Holy Ghost implied, as if he knew not the heart. 4. In reserving what he pretended to devote, which was a kind of sacrilege.

4. Whiles it remained, was it not thine own? and after it was sold, was it not in thine own power? why hast thou conceived this thing in thine heart? thou hast not lied unto men, but unto God.

4. While it was unsold, it was thy own and in thy power, and so was the money when thou hadst sold it: why did thy heart conceive so great a sin, as to play the hypocrite and lie? Didst thou not know that it was to God who knew thy heart?

5. And Ananias hearing these words, fell down and gave up the ghost: and great fear came on all them that heard these things.

5. Note, This was by part of the apostolical power, to [retain sin] or punish it in the time and manner that the Spirit in them did choose; which made believers see that Christ hath punishments and is to be feared, when mercy and holy things are abused.

6. And the young men arose, wound him up, and carried *him* out, and buried *him*. 7. And it was about the space of three hours after, when his wife, not knowing what was done, came in. 8. And Peter answered unto her, Tell me whether ye sold the land for so much. And she said, Yea, for so much. 9. Then Peter said unto her, How is it that ye have agreed together to tempt the Spirit of the Lord? behold, the feet of them which have buried thy husband *are* at the door, and shall carry thee out. 10. Then fell she down straightway at his feet, and yielded up the ghost: and the young men came in and found her dead, and carrying *her* forth, buried *her* by her husband.

6. Note, This was to confirm the honour of the Holy Ghost in the apostles, and the certainty of their testimony sealed by him; and to do that which magistrates, by the sword, afterwards were to do. As the prophetical theocracy under Moses and Joshua, differed from the monarchy of Saul; so more did the apostles, punishing men by the power of the Holy Ghost, from Christian magistrates who came after.

11. And great fear came upon all the church, and upon as many as heard these things.

11. Note, Under the most joyful tidings of love, mercy, and salvation, God seeth that some fear is needful.

12. And by the hands of the apostles were many signs and wonders wrought among the people; (and they were all with one accord in Solomon's porch.

12. A large porch in the temple was the place of their unanimous assembling.

13. And of the rest durst no man join himself to them: but the people magnified them.

13. Note, Though the gospel invite all, it flattereth none; but will tell hypocrites and liars of their danger, to drive them from entering deceitfully into the church. As there is more hope in the church to the sincere, there is more danger there to hypocrites, than to those without.

14. And believers were the more added to the Lord, multitudes both of men and women)

14. Yet these judgments frightening away hypocrites, hindered not the increase of the church: but the powerful works of the Holy Ghost, external and internal, converted multitudes of both sexes.

15. Insomuch that they brought forth the sick into the streets, and laid *them* on beds and couches, that at the least, the shadow of Peter passing by, might overshadow some of them.

15. As nature taught them to desire the healing of their bodies, experience taught them to expect miracles from the apostles, and that the very shadow of Peter should tend to heal them.

16. There came also a multitude *out* of the cities round about unto Jerusalem, bringing sick folks, and them which were vexed with unclean spirits: and they were healed every one.

16. Note, Reader, that all this was done as well for us at this day, as for them then: all our hopes, comforts, and holiness dependeth on our belief of the promises of the life to come by Christ: the things are unseen and much above us: had we not God's own testimony from heaven, by many uncontrouled miracles, our reason would be puzzled and in doubt, and our faith might fail: but God knoweth our weakness, and by all the miracles that they were then convinced by, who saw them, we also are convinced, to whom, by infallible record they are transmitted; as if we had stood by and seen all these things.

17. Then the high priest rose up, and all they that were with him (which is the sect of the Sadducees) and were filled with indignation, 18. And laid their hands on the apostles, and put them in the common prison.

17, 18. Note, So horridly corrupted was the arch-priesthood in those times, that the atheistical brutish Sadducees were their party: priesthood and prophane brutists were of one body; malignity filled these with indignation, and made them persecute and imprison the apostles.

19. But the angel of the Lord by night opened the prison-doors, and brought them forth, and said, 20. Go, stand and speak in the temple to the people, all the words of this life.

19, 20. God will be above man: angels can do more than devils and persecutors: they can open the prison-doors, and say, Go and fear not these proud tyrants, but preach to the people in the temple, all the doctrine of Christ's resurrection, and of our resurrection and salvation by him, and let priests, and Sadducees, and infidels do their worst to you.

21. And when they heard *that*, they entered into the temple early in the morning, and taught. But the high priest came, and they that were with him, and called the council together, and all the senate of the children of Israel, and sent to the prison to have them brought.

21. The priest and his council sent to have them brought out of prison before them.

22. But when the officers came, and found them not in the prison, they returned, and told, 23. Saying, The prison truly found we shut with all safety, and the keepers standing without before the doors: but when we had opened, we found no man within.

22. It was not owing to the keepers that they got out.

24. Now when the high priest, and the captain of the temple, and the chief priests heard these things, they doubted of them whereunto this would grow.

24. Note, They saw that God overcame their malice, and that the gospel would not be so easily suppressed as they imagined.

25. Then came one and told them, saying, Behold, the men whom ye put in prison, are standing in the temple, and teaching the people. 26. Then went the captain with the officers, and brought them without violence: (for they feared the people, lest they should have been stoned:)

26. Note, It is strange that they accused not the people of sedition, or rebellion, or a riot; and the apostles of heading it.

27. And when they had brought them, they set *them* before the council: and the high priest asked them, 28. Saying, Did not we straitly command you, that you should not teach in this name? and behold, ye have filled Jerusalem with your doctrine, and intend to bring this man's blood upon us.

27. Note, O the blindness and madness of proud worms! What are your commands against God? Did not God command you not to murder, and them to preach his word? Did not you bring his blood upon yourselves?

29. Then Peter and the *other* apostles answered and said, We ought to obey God rather than men.

29. Note, This none of them durst deny. But it is conscience and obedience to God that diabolists fight against.

30. The God of our fathers raised up Jesus, whom ye slew and hanged on a tree. 31. Him hath God exalted with his right hand, *to be* a Prince and a Saviour; for to give repentance to Israel, and forgiveness of sins.

30. That God of our fathers, whom you profess to obey, hath raised up Jesus, whom ye crucified, from death, and hath exalted him by and at his right hand, to be the Lord of all, and the Saviour of his people, to give them converting grace, and repentance, and forgiveness of sins.

32. And we are his witnesses of these things; and *so is* also the Holy Ghost, whom God hath given to them that obey him. 33. When they heard *that*, they were cut to the heart, and took counsel to slay them.

32. And of his resurrection and ascension we are entrusted witnesses, and must not silence our testimony, and of his present power and glory, is gift of the Spirit is a full proof, whose effects ye see yourselves, and which God giveth to them that obey his gospel.

34. Then stood there up one in the council, a Pharisee, named Gamaliel, a doctor of law, had in reputation among all the people; and commanded to put the apostles forth a little space, 35. And said unto them, Ye men of Israel, take heed to yourselves, what ye intend to do as touching these men. 36. For before these days rose up Theudas, boasting himself to be somebody, to whom a number of men, about four hundred, joined themselves; who was slain, and all as many as obeyed him, were scattered and brought to nought.

34. Note, This Pharisee is not so mad as the beastly Sadducees: who this Theudas was, we have no other notice, but by the words of Gamaliel.

37. After this man rose up Judas of Galilee, in the days of the taxing, and drew away much people after him: he also perished, and all even as many as obeyed him, were dispersed.

37. This Judas pretended to be a captain of the people against submitting to the Roman taxing; which he called servitude and insufferable.

38. And now I say unto you, Refrain from these men, and let them alone: for if this counsel, or this work be of men, it will come to nought:

38. By God's providence without your violence.

39. But if it be of God, ye cannot overthrow it: lest haply ye be found even to fight against God.

39. You will overthrow yourselves and not it. If it be of God: it is madness to fight against him.

Note, O that the malignant world would but examine which cause God is for.

40. And to him they agreed: and when they had called the apostles, and beaten *them*, they commanded that they should not speak in the name of Jesus, and let them go. 41. And they departed from the presence of the council, rejoicing that they were counted worthy to suffer shame for his name.

40. Note, Causeless stripes were the mercy of these men. The Holy Ghost did not work miracles to revenge these injuries to the apostles: but taught them to rejoice in this reproach for preaching Christ, as their great honour.

42. And daily in the temple, and in every house they ceased not to teach and preach Jesus Christ.

42. And no commands, threats, or cruelties made them cease preaching Christ publicly, and from house to house.

CHAP. VI.

AND in those days, when the number of the disciples was multiplied, there arose a murmuring of the Grecians against the Hebrews, because their widows were neglected in the daily ministration.

1. Note, Those Jews that understood the Greek tongue, and used the Greek translation of the scripture, were called Greeks: who were some at Jerusalem, most at Alexandria, and some scattered abroad the world. 2. Even in the greatest exemplification of Christian love, concord, and self-denial, the interest of the body, and its provisions, began a murmuring among this chosen flock that had all things common. And can we now expect to live without murmuring at each other upon cross interests and bodily wants. The suffering party will think themselves injured, and will complain.

2. Then the twelve called the multitude of the disciples unto them, and said, It is not reason that we should leave the word of God, and serve tables.

2. We must prefer the greater before the less; the preaching of God's word before the charge of distributing to love-feasts and to the poor; and we are not sufficient for both.

3. Wherefore brethren, look ye out among you seven men of honest report, full of the Holy Ghost and wisdom, whom we may appoint over this business.

3. Note, 1. This is the first call of officers immediately by men: yet the Holy Ghost in the apostles instituteth the office; but yet they give a reason for it. A divine institution, and reason from necessity and convenience, well agree. 2. The apostles fix the number. 3. The congregation must choose the persons. 4. God by his Spirit in the apostles limited them to certain qualifications: 1. Good report: 2. Full of the Holy Ghost: 3. And of wisdom. The chosen persons must be appointed or authorized and directed by the apostles, incapable matter maketh both election and men's ordination void. But yet the electors still are trusted whom to elect, and the ordainers whom to ordain; and every error is not a nullity, where there are the essential qualifications.

4. But we will give ourselves continually to prayer, and to the ministry of the word.

4. Wherever God will bless his church with bishops indeed, this will be their life and their description.

5. And the saying pleased the whole multitude: and they chose Stephen, a man full of faith, and of the Holy Ghost, and Philip, and Prochorus, and Nicanor, and Timon, and Parmenas, and Nicolas, a proselite of Antioch.

5. The reason of the motion, the authority of the apostles, and the spirit of God, made them all unanimously consent.

6. Whom they set before the apostles: and when they had prayed, they laid *their* hands on them.

6. Prayer to God to accept and bless them, and the authorizing them by the sign of imposition of hands, was the apostles' way of ordination (supposing them instructed for their office.)

7. And the word of God increased; and the number of the disciples multiplied in Jerusalem greatly; and a great company of the priests were obedient to the faith.

7. And the success of the word increased, and the number of the disciples in Jerusalem grew very great, and a great company of the priests (or a great company, and of the priests some) were obedient to the doctrine of Christ by believing.

8. And Stephen full of faith and power, did great wonders and miracles among the people.

8. Stephen having a great measure of the Spirit, was full of faith and power, and wrought great miracles.

9. Then there arose certain of the synagogue, which is called *the synagogue* of the Libertines, and Cyrenians, and Alexandrians, and of them of Cilicia, and of Asia, disputing with Stephen.

9. Jerusalem being the place where the scattered Jews of all nations used at certain times to worship, no wonder if several countries had their several synagogues. Libertines are by most supposed to be Jews made free: though some derive the name from a country, thinking one letter is changed.

10. And they were not able to resist the wisdom and the spirit by which he spake. 11. Then they suborned men which said, We have

heard him speak blasphemous words against Moses, and *against* God.

10. Note, On such terms we dispute with malignant men. When they cannot resist the truth they turn diabolists, and suborn men to swear to false accusations: malignity, blood-thirsty cruelty, and lying are the three essentials of a diabolist. 2. It is next to a miracle of providence, that no greater numbers of religious persons have been murdered in the world by the way of perjury, and pretence of law, when so many thousands hate them, who make no conscience of false oaths.

12. And they stirred up the people, and the elders, and the scribes, and came upon *him*, and caught him, and brought *him* to the council,

12. Note, When informers, and perjured witnesses, and council, or judges were all of a mind, else malignants, blood-thirsty men, it was easy to foreknow the sentence.

13. And set up false witnesses, which said, This man ceaseth not to speak blasphemous words against his holy place, and the law. 14. For we have heard him say, that this Jesus of Nazareth shall destroy this place, and shall change the customs which Moses delivered us.

13, 14. Note, It is very likely that they heard Stephen say some words of Christ's abrogation of the law, from which the perjured gathered their testimony, and putting their own sense on his words made blasphemy of them, and did not think they were perjured: and what man is there at judges, jury, and witnesses may not condemn, if they will but put their own sense on their words: Christ so suffered, before Stephen: and it is no wonder or dishonour to be condemned as the greatest malefactors by such men: therefore judge of history accordingly, where wicked men are the accusers and judges.

15. And all that sat in the council, looking steadfastly on him, saw his face as if it had been the face of an angel.

5. With a splendor which might amaze them, did not change them. So much was Dives hell deceived that one from the dead would avert his sensual brethren, when it is like that Lazarus had come to them as he prayed, they would have put him to death again: for so they resolved to do by another Lazarus whom Christ raised. But where are these judges and gentlemen now?

CHAP. VII.

THEN said the high priest, Are these things so?

The arch-priest is the arch-malignant, and his seeming gravity doth but inquire after sin.

2. And he said, Men, brethren, and fathers, hearken, The God of glory appeared unto our father Abraham, when he was in Mesopotamia, before he dwelt in Charran, 3. And said unto him, Get thee out of thy country, and from thy kindred, and come into the land which I shall shew thee.

2, 3. Obey me in forsaking thy idolatrous country and go to another, which I will direct thee to.

4. Then came he out of the land of the Chaldeans, and dwelt in Charran: and from thence, when his father was dead, he removed him into this land wherein ye now dwell. 5. And he gave him none inheritance in it, no not *so much as* to set his foot on: yet he promised that he would give it to him for a possession, and to his seed after him, when *as yet* he had no child. 6. And God spake on this wise, that his seed should sojourn in a strange land, and that they should bring them into bondage, and entreat *them* evil four hundred years. 7. And the nation to whom they shall be in bondage, will I judge, said God: and after that shall they come forth, and serve me in this place.

4, &c. Note, Obedience to God must be performed, by the hope of what he promiseth, though it be many hundred years after, and not only for present possession. 2. The four years began at the birth of Isaac, and not at the going into Egypt.

8. And he gave him the covenant of circumcision: and so *Abraham* begat Isaac, and circumcised him the eighth day: and Isaac *begat* Jacob, and Jacob *begat* the twelve patriarchs. 9. And the patriarchs moved with envy, sold Joseph into Egypt: but God was with him, 10. And delivered him out of all his afflictions, and gave him favour and wisdom in the sight of Pharaoh king of Egypt; and he made him governor over Egypt, and all his house.

8. Note, This history Stephen reciteth to convince them of the greatness of their forefathers sin and theirs, in still hardening their hearts against God's mercies.

11. Now there came a dearth over all the land of Egypt and Canaan, and great affliction; and our fathers found no sustenance. 12. But when Jacob heard that there was corn in Egypt, he sent out our fathers first. 13. And at the second *time* Joseph was made known to his brethren; and Joseph's kindred was made known unto Pharaoh. 14. Then sent Joseph, and called his father Jacob to him, and all his kindred, threescore and fifteen souls. 15. So Jacob went down into Egypt, and died, he and our fathers,

14. Gen. xlvi. 27. saith they were but seventy: some say that Stephen included some born in Egypt, with Joseph, and his sons, and sons' sons: others say, that the Septuagint which Stephen followed hath a mistaken word which caused the difference.

16. And were carried over into Sychem, and laid in the sepulchre that Abraham bought for a sum of money of the sons of Emmor *the father* of Sychem.

16. Some difference from the Hebrew history here raiseth difficulty: the truth seemeth to be, Jacob was carried and buried in the field of Macpelah bought by Abraham of Ephron the son of Zoar, or of the Sons of Heth, Gen. xxiii. 8. and xlix. 32. But Joseph's bones were carried from Egypt to Sychem, Jos. xxiv. 31, 32. and buried in the field bought by Jacob of the sons of Hemer; and in which place his brethren were buried is uncertain.

17. But when the time of the promise drew nigh, which God had sworn to Abraham, the people grew and multiplied in Egypt, 18. Till another king arose, which knew not Joseph. 19. The same dealt subtilly with our kindred, and evil entreated our fathers, so that they cast out their young children, to the end they might not live.

17. Note, Man's cruelty and subtlety fighting in vain against God's providence and mercy to his people, is the common case of the world.

20. In which time Moses was born, and was exceeding fair, and nourished up in his father's house three months: 21. And when he was cast out, Pharaoh's daughter took him up, and nourished him for her own son.

20. See Exod. ii.

22. And Moses was learned in all the wisdom of the Egyptians, and was mighty in words and deeds.

22. And being by Pharaoh's daughter educated as her son, he had the advantage of getting all the Egyptian sort of learning, in which he excelled.

23. And when he was full forty years old, it came into his heart to visit his brethren the children of Israel. 24. And seeing one of *them* suffer wrong, he defended *him*, and revenged him that was oppressed, and smote the Egyptian:

23. Note, Though Moses' age and learning be not mentioned in the Old Testament, it might be otherwise known. 2. And whether he was warranted to slay the Egyptian by any special revelation is doubtful.

25. For he supposed his brethren would have understood, how that God by his hand would deliver them; but they understood not.

25. What notice he had then of this purpose of God, we read not: but saith Dr. Hammond. "This lawfully he might do, in the defence of an "innocent person's life, against an unjust assault "or violence, which could not be averted but by "this means."

26. And the next day he shewed himself unto them as they strove, and would have set them at one again, saying, Sirs, ye are brethren; why do ye wrong one to another?

26. Note, Even while they are oppressed by the common tyranny of the king, they forbear no quarrelling and wronging one another.

27. But he that did his neighbour wrong, thrust him away, saying, Who made thee a ruler and a judge over us? 28. Wilt thou kill me as thou didst the Egyptian yesterday?

27. 28. Note, 1. It is the injuring party that is usually readiest to rise up against peace-makers. 2. He that will reconcile peace-breakers and re-

prove the injurious, must expect to be accused as a peace-breaker, and injurious, and arrogant himself. 2. Self-avengers love not rulers.

29. Then fled Moses at this saying, and was a stranger in the land of Madian, where he begat two sons.

29. He knew then that the killing this Egyptian would be known to Pharaoh, and therefore fled.

30. And when forty years were expired, there appeared to him in the wilderness of mount Sina, an angel of the Lord in a flame of fire in a bush.

30. The same appearance is said to be God and an angel in fire: God speaking by an angel in fire.

31. When Moses saw *it*, he wondered at the sight: and as he drew near to behold *it*, the voice of the Lord came unto him, 32. *Saying*, I *am* the God of thy fathers, the God of Abraham, and the God of Isaac, and the God of Jacob. Then Moses trembled, and durst not behold.

31. If so small an appearing of God will make man tremble, why are we not constantly awed by the belief of his glory?

33. Then said the Lord to him, Put off thy shoes from thy feet: for the place where thou standest is holy ground.

33. Note, 1. The holiness of places is their separate relation to some holy work of God, or some appearance of him. God will have outward bodily expressions of inward reverence to him, and to that which is specially related to him.

34. I have seen, I have seen the affliction of my people which is in Egypt, and I have heard their groaning, and am come down to deliver them. And now come, I will send thee into Egypt.

34. Note, God is not ignorant or regardless of his people's sufferings: 2. But his usual season of deliverance, is when their sufferings are at the greatest.

35. This Moses, whom they refused, saying, Who made thee a ruler and a judge? the same did God send *to be* a ruler and a deliverer by the hands of the angel which appeared to him in the bush.

35. God sent by his angel the same man to rule and deliver them, whom they refused to be their ruler and deliverer; even as you now have done by Jesus Christ whom God hath sent.

36. He brought them out, after that he had shewed wonders and signs in the land of Egypt, and in the Red Sea, and in the wilderness forty years.

36. God wrought many miracles by him for their deliverance, who had rejected him, (as he hath done by Jesus for your deliverance.)

37. This is that Moses which said unto the children of Israel, A prophet shall the Lord your God raise up unto you of your brethren, like unto me; him shall ye hear.

37. This Moses of whom ye boast, thus prophesied of Christ, a prophet, &c.

38. This is he that was in the church in the wilderness, with the angel which spake to him in the mount Sina, and *with* our fathers: who received the lively oracles to give unto us. 39. To whom our fathers would not obey, but thrust *him* from them, and in their hearts turned back again into Egypt, 40. Saying unto Aaron, Make us gods to go before us; for *as for* this Moses, which brought us out of the land of Egypt, we wot not what is become of him.

38. This is he whose name you honour, who was in the congregation in the wilderness, who received the oracles of God by voice, which he gave you then as the way of life, (in subordination to faith in his promises) whom yet your ancestors would not obey, but rebelled against him, and refused him, and unthankfully would have returned to that Egyptian bondage, from which by so many miracles they were delivered; yea, rebelled against God and turned idolaters, and made Aaron make them feigned gods to go before them.

41. And they made a calf in those days, and offered sacrifice unto the idol, and rejoiced in the works of their own hands.

41. So sottish were they as to honour that as God which they had made themselves.

42. Then God turned, and gave

them up to worship the host of heaven; as it is written in the book of the prophets, O ye house of Israel, have ye offered to me slain beasts, and sacrifices, by the space of forty years in the wilderness? 43. Yea, ye took up the tabernacle of Moloch, and the star of your god Remphan, figures which ye made to worship them: and I will carry you away beyond Babylon.

42. That the text Amos v. meaneth by Moloch and Rempham, a deified Egyptian king and Saturn. See Dr. Hammond's annot. and other conjectures in Bexa, &c. whether this last idolatry was included in the golden calf, or the text only meant they fell to it after Joshua's days, is uncertain: Though the Hebrew say beyond Damascus, and Luke's Greek beyond Babylon, the sense is the same. And Luke writing in the Greek, it is like used not the same word as Stephen in Chaldee.

44. Our fathers had the tabernacle of witness in the wilderness, as he had appointed, speaking unto Moses, that he should make it according to the fashion that he had seen.

44 Our ancestors had the tabernacle of the testimony where was the ark of God that had the tables of the law, and where God used by signs to signify his presence, and give his oracles: This Moses was to make according to the pattern which God shewed him.

45. Which also our fathers that came after, brought in with Jesus into the possession of the Gentiles, whom God drave out before the face of our fathers, unto the days of David.

45.This tabernacle our fathers after brought into Canaan with Joshua, and it continued till David's time.

46. Who found favour before God, and desired to find a tabernacle for the God of Jacob. 47. But Solomon built him an house.

46. Who being beloved of God, desired to have built him a temple. But God chose Solomon to build it.

48. Howbeit the Most High dwelleth not in temples made with hands; as saith the prophet, 49. Heaven *is* my throne, and earth *is* my footstool: what house will ye build me? saith the Lord: or what *is* the place of my rest? 50. Hath not my hand made all these things?

48, 49, 50. Temples are for God's worship, and not for God's confinement or necessary abode: Heaven is the place of his glory, and earth of his lower blessings, and all the world of his presence: He made all things, and needeth not your temple, but may forsake it for your sins.

51. Ye stiff-necked, and uncircumcised in heart and ears, ye do always resist the Holy Ghost: as your fathers *did*, so *do* ye.

51. Ye are an unruly obstinate people, whose hearts are unreformed and uncircumcised, and your ears stopped against the truth, while you glory in your circumcision: you have in all ages resisted the Spirit and word of God, and while you disown your fore-fathers' actions, you are like them and do the very same.

52. Which of the prophets have not your fathers persecuted? and they have slain them which shewed before of the coming of the Just One, of whom ye have been now the betrayers and murderers: 53. Who have received the law by the disposition of angels, and have not kept *it*.

52, 53. You boast of the law and the prophets, and the expected Messiah: But which of the prophets did not your fathers persecute? And those that prophesied of the Messiah, they murdered: And so have you done by the Messiah himself, and outdone all your ancestors in wickedness; and the law which you boast of delivered by angels, you have neither understood nor kept.

54. When they heard these things, they were cut to the heart, and they gnashed on him with *their* teeth.

54 At these words their very hearts were enraged against him, &c.

Reproof, which convinceth and humbleth them whom God converteth, enrageth proud, obdurate sinners, and turneth them to persecute the reprovers; which presageth their destruction.

55. But he being full of the Holy Ghost, looked up steadfastly into heaven, and saw the glory of God, and Jesus standing on the right hand of God. 56. And said, Behold, I see the heavens opened, and the Son of Man standing on the right hand of God.

55, 56. God gave him so extraordinary a presure of the Spirit, as when he looked steadfastly toward heaven he had an appearance of the glory of God and Christ standing at his right hand, which in this rapture he declared to them all.

Note, Christ saw it meet by such a glorious miraculous sight to encourage and honour his first dying martyr. Who would fear suffering for Christ? Martyrs may expect the Spirit's greatest help, and afterward the most glorious crown.

57. Then they cried out with a loud voice, and stopped their ears, and ran upon him with one accord, 58. And cast *him* out of the city, and stoned *him*: and the witnesses laid down their clothes at a young man's feet, whose name was Saul.

57, 58. Note, Holiness and miracles do but increase their rage: They will run when malignity and the devil instigates: Sinners are never so mad as against Christ, and mercy, and their own salvation. They that were the accusers for blasphemy, were by the law to cast the first stone as the executioners.

59. And they stoned Stephen, calling upon *God*, and saying, Lord Jesus, receive my spirit.

59. Note, He that gave up himself to Christ in life and death, might comfortably expect to be received. 2. The spirit liveth after the body's death: and Christ receiveth it to himself. This is part of Christ's office now in heaven. See my printed sermon on this text.

60. And he kneeled down, and cried with a loud voice, Lord, lay not this sin to their charge. And when he had said this, he fell asleep.

60. He died praying, and that for his persecutors, as Christ did: And its like the conversion of Saul was an answer to this prayer. Qu. How far may we pray in faith for wicked men, or others, and expect the thing prayed for? Answ. For that which is absolutely promised, we may pray accordingly in assurance: For that which supposeth a qualifying condition in the receiver, we must believe that they shall have it if they are so qualified: For that which hath no promise to it, but is merely at God's unrevealed will, we must pray with submission to that will, and accordingly take the event for uncertain.

CHAP. VIII.

AND Saul was consenting unto his death. And at that time there was a great persecution against the church which was at Jerusalem; and they were all scattered abroad throughout the regions of Judea and Samaria, except the apostles.

1. Note, Saul's persecution must be recorded before his conversion. 2. The purest church was not free from the malice of wicked men. 3. God used malignant persecutions for the spreading abroad his word.

2. And devout men carried Stephen *to his burial*, and made great lamentation over him.

2. They made a funeral for Stephen with solemn mourning.

3. As for Saul, he made havock of the church, entering into every house, and haling men and women, committed *them* to prison.

3. By haling people to prison out of their houses Saul wasted the gathered church.

4. Therefore they that were scattered abroad, went every where preaching the word.

4. Note, It was a tolerable hurt to their bodies, which brought good to others' souls, and so enlarged the church by scattering it, as seed is scattered that is sown. 2. All Christians may and must publish the gospel where they come, if there be need, though only called ministers must make an office and calling of it, as separated to it.

5. Then Philip went down to the city of Samaria, and preached Christ unto them.

5. Philip the deacon preached at the city of Samaria, after by Herod called Sebasto.

6. And the people with one accord gave heed unto those things which Philip spake, hearing and seeing the miracles which he did. 7. For unclean spirits, crying with loud voice, came out of many that were possessed *with them*: and many taken with palsies, and that were lame, were healed. 8. And there was great joy in that city.

6. The Samaritans received the gospel with great joy, convinced by miracles, and pleased by many cures.

Note, The gospel wherever it cometh is cause of great joy.

9. But there was a certain man called Simon, which before time in the same city used sorcery, and bewitched the people of Samaria, giving out that himself was some great one. 10. To whom they all gave heed, from the least to the greatest, saying, This man is the

great power of God. 11. And to him they had regard, because that of long time he had bewitched them with sorceries.

9. One Simon had long been reputed among them some great man, even the great power of God, as he boasted of himself; because by sorcery he had long bewitched, and done some strange things among them: and they all admired and regarded him.

Note, Deceivers have usually many followers.

12. But when they believed Philip, preaching the things concerning the kingdom of God, and the name of Jesus Christ, they were baptized both men and women.

12. Note, This sudden baptizing yet implicith time for instruction, and profession of all essential to Christianity.

13. Then Simon himself believed also: and when he was baptized, he continued with Philip, and wondered, beholding the miracles and signs which were done.

13. Simon saw the reality of Philip's miracles, being conscious of the fallacy of his own, and he believed that Jesus was the Christ, and was baptized into his name, and stayed with Philip, admiring his works.

Note, 1. Simon had a superficial opinionative belief, that was not clear and sound, nor effectual to renew his soul. 2. The ministers of Christ baptized not as heart-searchers, as knowing men's sincerity, but as taking their profession for their title to baptism.

14. Now when the apostles which were at Jerusalem, heard that Samaria had received the word of God, they sent unto them Peter and John.

14. Note, As Peter or John were no rulers of the rest of the apostles, so the rest sent not them as rulers of them by vote, but by brotherly request and consent.

15. Who when they were come down, prayed for them that they might receive the Holy Ghost. 16. (For as yet he was fallen upon none of them: only they were baptized in the name of the Lord Jesus.) 17. Then laid they *their* hands on them, and they received the Holy Ghost.

15. Note, 1. It was at first the eminent privilege of the apostles, that the Holy Ghost should be given by their ministry. 2. Imposition of hands being an usual act of authoritative benediction, was used as the sign herein. 3. Yet prayer to God must first prevail for his grant thereof, before the sign was used. 4. This gift of the Holy Ghost was not that which is regenerating and necessary to pardon and salvation (else all these baptized persons must be supposed till so long after unpardoned:) but it was that extraordinary gift which was for the first sealing and propagating of the gospel, of which others could be discerning judges, (such as languages, prophecy, healing, miracles, &c.) which they were not, of sincere inward holiness.

18. And when Simon saw that through laying on of the apostles hands, the Holy Ghost was given, he offered them money, 19. Saying, Give me also this power, that on whomsoever I lay hands, he may receive the Holy Ghost.

18. Note, 1. It was such a thing as Simon could see in the present effects: 2. He desired this power in pride for his own advancement, and not for Christ and souls. 3. He over-valued money, and blasphemously vilified God, as if he set his gifts to sale.

20. But Peter said unto him, Thy money perish with thee, because thou hast thought that the gift of God may be purchased with money.

20. Unless thou repent thou shalt perish with thy money, for this blasphemous thought of God.

21. Thou hast neither part nor lot in this matter: for thy heart is not right in the sight of God.

21. Though thou art baptized, thou art no true Christian, nor hast any part in the grace and Spirit of Christ: for thy heart is unsound and false in the sight of God.

22. Repent therefore of this thy wickedness, and pray God, if perhaps the thought of thine heart may be forgiven thee. 23. For I perceive that thou art in the gall of bitterness, and *in* the bond of iniquity.

22. Presently repent therefore of that wicked heart and blasphemous thought; and pray to God for mercy and forgiveness, while it is possible to be obtained.

Qu. Is not the prayer of the wicked abominable? Answ. Yes, the wicked prayer of the wicked; which is to serve his wickedness: And his best prayers are not qualified for any certain grant: But if he truly repent, he is no longer wicked: And the prayers a common repentance (like Ahab's and the Ninevites) may tend towards better, and is better than none. Qu. Doth Peter mean that Simon's heart was false at his baptism, or that he received grace and pardon then, and lost it after by apostasy. Answ. Simon's sin made Peter newly perceive that his heart was false before, though his body was washed; but not that it now began to be false by a sudden apostasy. 1 Pet. iii. 21, 22. He was in the gall of bitterness and bond of iniquity, through the wickedness of his unsanctified heart, even when he was baptized. Yet all this hypocrisy and wickedness was pardonable upon repentance.

24. Then answered Simon, and said, Pray ye to the Lord for me, that none of these things which ye have spoken come upon me.

24. Note, His sight of their miracles and fear of destruction humbled him so far as to beg their prayers that the threatened judgments might not befal him. But whether the report of some old writers be true, that after all this he pretended to be God the Father, and had a conflict with Peter, and flying in the air fell down, and was destroyed by his prayers, and had a statue at Rome inscribed, Simoni Deo Sancto, &c. of this many doubt, though others believe it: And if it was he that Paul, 2 Thes. ii. and John in the Revelation speak of, as the man of sin, &c. and the head of heresies so much decried by Paul, (as Dr. Hammond thinks) it is strange that neither Luke, nor Paul, nor Peter, nor Jude, nor James, nor John, who all inveigh against heresies would never once name him, when Nicolaitanus, Diotrephes, Hymenæus, Philetus, &c. are named.

25. And they, when they had testified and preached the word of the Lord, returned to Jerusalem, and preached the gospel in many villages of the Samaritans. 26. And the angel of the Lord spake unto Philip, saying, Arise, and go toward the south, unto the way that goeth down from Jerusalem unto Gaza, which is desert. 27. And he arose and went: and behold, a man of Ethiopia, an eunuch of great authority under Candace queen of the Ethiopians, who had the charge of all her treasure, and had come to Jerusalem for to worship, 28. Was returning, and sitting in his chariot, read Esaias the prophet.

25, 26, &c. Note, God shewed a notable proof in this of his free electing grace.
2. Angels minister towards the conversion of God's elect.
3. He that was a proselyte before, and came so far to worship, was better prepared for the gospel than the heathens.
4. He that would lose no time, but was reading God's word on his journey in his chariot, was in God's way for further mercy, which was sent after him.

29. Then the Spirit said unto Philip, Go near, and join thyself to this chariot.

29. By inspiration. Note, The chariot was driven slowly that he might read, and so Philip on foot could accompany it. God's Spirit directeth his word to the elect.

30. And Philip ran thither to him, and heard him read the prophet Esaias, and said, Understandest thou what thou readest? 31. And he said, How can I, except some man should guide me? and he desired Philip that he would come up, and sit with him.

30. Note, God directed him to the text: And God gave him the sense of his own ignorance and insufficiency to understand, and of his need of a teacher. And God gave him an humble mind, to condescend to ask a stranger on foot, to come sit with him in his chariot and teach him. All these were happy preparatives to Christianity and further grace.

32. The place of the scripture which he read, was this, He was led as a sheep to the slaughter, and like a lamb dumb before his shearer, so opened he not his mouth: 33. In his humiliation his judgment was taken away: and who shall declare his generation? for his life is taken from the earth.

32. He suffered innocently and patiently by unrighteous cruel men; He humbled himself to undergo their unjust judgment: They wickedly triumph over him, as cutting off his life from the earth.

34. And the eunuch answered Philip, and said, I pray thee, of whom speaketh the prophet this? of himself, or of some other man? 35. Then Philip opened his mouth, and began at the same scripture, and preached unto him Jesus. 36. And as they went on *their* way, they came unto a certain water: and the eunuch said, See, *here is* water; what doth hinder me to be baptized?

34, 35. Note, 1. He first craveth instruction and then baptism, and is not forced to be baptized against his will.

37. And Philip said, If thou believest with all thine heart, thou

mayest. And he answered and said, I believe that Jesus Christ is the Son of God.

37. If thou believe with a serious, well-grounded, resolved faith, thou mayest be baptized, and have the present remission of sin, as a Christian.

Note, The belief that Jesus is the Son of God, includeth all the rest that is necessary to salvation, that is, That there is a God whom we offended, to whom he reconcileth us, and who gave him to us in love, and that his word is true, and that by the word and by the Holy Ghost he sanctifieth and prepareth us for heaven.

38. And he commanded the chariot to stand still: and they went down both into the water, both Philip and the eunuch; and he baptized him. 39. And when they were come up out of the water, the Spirit of the Lord caught away Philip, that the eunuch saw him no more: and he went on his way rejoicing.

38, 39. The angel or power of God caught away Philip.

Note, A converted man hath great cause of rejoicing. The gospel proclaimed, much more heartily received, is matter of great joy. 2. The tradition of Abassiah (where is a great empire of Christians) is that they received the Christian faith by this man who was the queen's lord treasurer. And some learned men conjecture that it was rather by Frumentius and Edosius, and that it was Abassiah that was by historians miscalled India: but if these first brought in church government by a bishop, the eunuch might bring lay Christianity before.

40. But Philip was found at Azotus: and passing through, he preached in all the cities, till he came to Cesarea.

CHAP. IX.

AND Saul yet breathing out threatenings and slaughter against the disciples of the Lord, went unto the high priest, 2. And desired of him letters to Damascus to the synagogues, that if he found any of this way, whether they were men or women, he might bring them bound unto Jerusalem.

1. Ignorant zeal made Saul set himself to destroy the Christians, and he sought to the high-priest for power, and travelled toward Damascus to do it,

that he might find them out and bring them in bonds.

3. And as he journeyed, he came near Damascus: and suddenly there shined round about him a light from heaven.

3. God, the Father of light, useth to shew himself to man by light, external and internal, and so do his angels, when the devil is the prince of darkness.

4. And he fell to the earth, and heard a voice, saying unto him, Saul, Saul, why persecutest thou me?

4. The power of God went forth with that light, and cast him to the ground, &c. Note, 1. Love and mercy in Christ expostulate with a blinded furious sinner, in order to his conversion. 2. But till power had cast him down, the expostulation came not: God can soon lay proud persecutors on the earth, and tame them, and make them fear and hear. 3. Whatever is done against Christians for any thing that Christ commandeth them, he taketh as done against himself. If we are bound by the law of Christ to preach, to pray, to edify each other, to live a holy life, and we be reviled, scorned, called all manner of evil names, imprisoned, fined, banished, or murdered, for the Christ will judge the doers of it as doing it against him.

5. And he said, Who art thou, Lord? And the Lord said, I am Jesus whom thou persecutest; *It is hard for thee to kick against the pricks.*

5. Note, Did wicked persecutors know Christ, it would restrain them from persecution, (but the subtle devil hath taught hypocrite Christians to persecute him as by his own authority and commission, and in his own name, and for his church. that is, themselves.) 2. Christ's servants should no more doubt of their seasonable vindication when persecuted for their duty, than if Christ were personally persecuted in their stead. 3. O how terrible will it at last prove to persecutors, that they have kicked with their bare feet against the pricks or thorns of God's displeasure? Who hath hardened himself against him and hath prospered? Or who hath conquered the Almighty?

6. And he trembling and astonished, said, Lord, what wilt thou have me to do? And the Lord *said* unto him, Arise, and go into the city, and it shall be told thee what thou must do.

6. Note, God can make the fiercest persecutor tremble: And then, O how they are changed, ready to do any thing that God will bid them, which before they persecuted! And if the change be true, this will hold and come to practice. 2. O

CHAP. IX. THE ACTS. 267

then what need have proud persecutors to be cast down, and how great a mercy to them it may prove!

7. And the men which journeyed with him, stood speechless, hearing a voice, but seeing no man.

7. Note, In Acts xxii. 9. it is said, [They that were with him saw the light and were afraid, but heard not the voice or words of Christ, which in that sound were uttered to him, nor saw any similitude of Christ. Though we have only Paul's witness of this, his after life of labour, suffering, and miracles, proveth it to be true.

8. And Saul arose from the earth; and when his eyes were opened, he saw no man: but they led him by the hand, and brought *him* into Damascus.

8. This stroke of blindness, was to convince him of the blindness of his persecuting fury.

9. And he was three days without sight, and neither did eat nor drink.

9. Note, This was some conformity to Christ's being three days and three nights in the darksome grave.

10. And there was a certain disciple at Damascus, named Ananias, and to him said 'the Lord in a vision, Ananias. And he said, Behold, I *am here*, Lord. 11. And the Lord *said* unto him, Arise, and go into the street which is called Straight, and inquire in the house of Judas, for *one* called Saul of Tarsus: for behold, he prayeth. 12. And hath seen in a vision a man named Ananias, coming in, and putting *his* hand on him, that he might receive his sight.

10. Ananias was a Christian appointed by God to this work on Saul. 2. Praying was (next to resolved obedience and submission) the first fruits of Saul's conversion.

13. Then Ananias, answered, Lord, I have heard by many of this man, how much evil he hath done to thy saints at Jerusalem: 14. And here he hath authority from the chief priests, to bind all that call on thy name.

13. Note, Ananias objecteth what he had heard of Saul, as rendering his conversion improbable.

15. But the Lord said unto him, Go thy way: for he is a chosen vessel unto me, to bear my name before the Gentiles, and kings, and the children of Israel. 16. For I will shew him how great things he must suffer for my name's sake.

15. Obey me who know man, and my own decrees, and object not former things against me, I have chosen him, &c.

17. And Ananias went his way, and entered into the house; and putting his hands on him, said, Brother Saul, the Lord, *(even* Jesus that appeared unto thee in the way as thou camest) hath sent me, that thou mightest receive thy sight, and be filled with the Holy Ghost.

17. God hath made known to me, what he did to thee by the way, and hath sent me that thou mightest be restored to thy sight, and filled with the Holy Ghost, for gifts necessary to the ministry.

18. And immediately there fell from his eyes as it had been scales; and he received sight forthwith, and arose, and was baptized.

18. He was miraculously struck blind, and miraculously cured, and then baptized.

19. And when he had received meat, he was strengthened. Then was Saul certain days with the disciples which were at Damascus. 20. And straightway he preached Christ in the synagogues, that he is the Son of God.

19, 20. Being strengthened with food, he conversed certain days with the Christians at Damascus whom he purposed to have persecuted, and forthwith preached Christ in the synagogue to the Jews, that he is the Son of God, and consequently all his gospel true. (And then going into Arabia, returned to Damascus again before he went to Jerusalem.)

21. But all that heard *him* were amazed, and said, Is not this he that destroyed them which called on this name in Jerusalem, and came hither for that intent, that he might bring them bound unto the chief priests?

21. The sudden change from being a destroying

persecutor to be a preacher, made the people wonder.

22. But Saul increased the more in strength, and confounded the Jews which dwelt at Damascus, proving that this is very Christ.

22. Proving Jesus to be the true Christ, inferreth all the rest to be believed.

23. And after that many days were fulfilled, the Jews took council to kill him:

23. If one of the leaders of the persecutors or malignant wicked men should be converted and persuade his companions to turn, they would but seek to kill him also, till God convert them.

24. But their laying await was known of Saul: and they watched the gates day and night to kill him. 25. Then the disciples took him by night, and let *him* down by the wall in a basket.

24. Note, It is lawful to avoid the violence of bloody persecutors by secret flight.

26. And when Saul was come to Jerusalem, he assayed to join himself to the disciples: but they were all afraid of him, and believed not that he was a disciple.

26. Note, 1. Conversion will shew itself by joining with the converted. 2. Known persecutors and wicked men are not too hastily to be trusted, when they profess conversion.

27. But Barnabas took him, and brought *him* to the apostles, and declared unto them, how he had seen the Lord in the way, and that he had spoken to him, and how he had preached boldly at Damascus in the name of Jesus. 28. And he was with them coming in, and going out at Jerusalem.

27, 28. This evidence was satisfactory, and they received him to their constant society of the church.

29. And he spake boldly in the name of the Lord Jesus, and disputed against the Grecians: but they went about to slay him. 30. *Which* when the brethren knew, they brought him down to Cesarea, and sent him forth to Tarsus.

29, 30. He preached Christ boldly, and confuted the unbelieving Jews that used the Greek tongue, But they sought to kill him, &c.

31. Then had the churches rest throughout all Judea, and Galilee, and Samaria, and were edified, and walking in the fear of the Lord, and in the comfort of the Holy Ghost, were multiplied.

31. Saul being converted who was a chief persecutor, and he being removed whom they afterward most maligned, the Christian churches were quiet a while from persecution, and were edified in knowledge and holiness of heart and life, living in obedience to God, and in the comfort of the inward grace, and outward gifts and miracles of the Holy Ghost, by which they were multiplied.

32. And it came to pass, as Peter passed throughout all *quarters*, he came down also to the saints which dwelt at Lydda.

32. Note, He was no Christian who was not a saint, by dedication to God, and by profession.

33. And there he found a certain man named Eneas, which had kept his bed eight years, and was sick of the palsy. 34. And Peter said unto him, Eneas, Jesus Christ maketh thee whole: arise, and make thy bed. And he arose immediately.

33. Note, The length and nature of the disease made the miracle the more notable and convincing.

35. And all that dwelt at Lydda, and Saron, saw him, and turned to the Lord.

35. The undeniable miracle caused a general conviction and conversion of them.

36. Now there was at Joppa a certain disciple named Tabitha, which by interpretation is called Dorcas: this woman was full of good works and alms-deeds which she did. 37. And it came to pass in those days, that she was sick and died: whom when they had washed, they laid *her* in an upper chamber. 38. And forasmuch as Lydda was nigh to Joppa, and the disciples had heard that Peter was there, they sent unto him two men, desiring *him* that he would not delay to come to them.

36. A laborious charitable woman being dead, the Christians had faith to believe that by Peter's ministry she might be raised to life.

39. Then Peter arose, and went with them. When he was come, they brought him into the upper chamber: and all the widows stood by him weeping, and shewing the coats and garments which Dorcas made while she was with them.

39. Note, It is like they were poor widows, that shewed the fruit of her labour and charity to them and others.

40. But Peter put them all forth, and kneeled down and prayed, and turning *him* to the body, said, Tabitha, arise. And she opened her eyes: and when she saw Peter, she sat up. 41. And he gave her his hand, and lift her up; and when he had called the saints and widows, presented her alive.

40. Note, This was not a miracle to be done without fervent prayer: and it is like Peter had assurance of raising her, as an answer to his prayer, before he said, Arise.

42. And it was known throughout all Joppa; and many believed in the Lord.

42. Thus miracles made Christians, and fully sealed the testimony of the apostles.

43. And it came to pass, that he tarried many days in Joppa with one Simon a tanner.

CHAP. X.

THERE was a certain man in Cesarea, called Cornelius, a centurion of the band called the Italian *band*,

1. In Cesarea the chief city of the country about seventy miles from Jerusalem, where was a Roman garrison, was one Cornelius captain of an hundred in the Italian regiment, or legion.

2. *A* devout *man*, and one that feared God, with all his house, which gave much alms to the people, and prayed to God always.

2. A proselyte that was a godly man and fearing God, with all his household, liberal in giving alms, and constant in prayer.

2. Note, We must not think this man under

mere common grace, but in a state of saving grace, such as the faithful Jews had before Christ's incarnation; such being prepared above others to believe in Christ personally, when he was come and preached to them. This is notified, 1. In that he was a proselyte of justice, though not circumcised. 2. He is called a godly man (or devout.) 3. He kept no other in his house. 4. He was full of works of charity. 5. And constant in prayer with due fasting. 6. God testified his acceptance of him.

3. He saw in a vision evidently, about the ninth hour of the day, an angel of God coming in to him, and saying unto him, Cornelius.

3. Being fasting and at prayer at three o'clock in the afternoon, an angel appeared to him.

4. And when he looked on him, he was afraid, and said, What is it, Lord? And he said unto him, Thy prayers and thine alms are come up for a memorial before God.

4. The sight of the angel struck him with dread, &c. He said, Thy prayers and alms coming from faith and a sincere heart, are so acceptable to God, that he hath sent me to give thee this notice of it, and to reward thee with a farther blessing.

5. And now send men to Joppa, and call for *one* Simon whose surname is Peter: 6. He lodgeth with one Simon a tanner, whose house is by the sea-side: he shall tell thee what thou oughtest to do.

5. Note, God will honour his appointed qualified instruments in the giving of his mercies.

7. And when the angel which spake unto Cornelius was departed, he called two of his household-servants, and a devout soldier of them that waited on him continually: 8. And when he had declared all *these* things unto them, he sent them to Joppa.

7, 8. Note, O what a blessing to a family is a good master that will keep such about him as he can trust, and also deserve his special love! And what happy society are such families! This man had even godly soldiers, who use to be the worst of men.

9. On the morrow as they went on their journey, and drew nigh unto the city, Peter went up upon the house-top to pray, about the sixth hour.

9. Note, God doth no great things usually, but by men of prayer, at least accepteth no other.

10. And he became very hungry, and would have eaten: but while they made ready, he fell into a trance, 11. And saw heaven opened, and a certain vessel descending unto him, as it had been a great sheet knit at the four corners, and let down to the earth: 12. Wherein were all manner of four-footed beasts of the earth, and wild beasts, and creeping things, and fowls of the air. 13. And there came a voice to him, Rise, Peter; kill, and eat.

10. The clean and the unclean, noted the Jews and Gentiles, and also the abrogation of the ceremonial laws of meats.

14. But Peter said, Not so, Lord; for I have never eaten any thing that is common or unclean. 15. And the voice *spake* unto him again the second time, What God hath cleansed, *that* call not thou common. 16. This was done thrice: and the vessel was received up again into heaven.

16. What meats or what persons God hath cleansed, do not thou call polluted and unclean, to be rejected.

17. Now while Peter doubted in himself what this vision which he had seen, should mean; behold, the men which were sent from Cornelius, had made inquiry for Simon's house, and stood before the gate, 18. And called, and asked whether Simon which was surnamed Peter, were lodged there.

17. The same God directeth both the vision, and the messages of Cornelius to concur.

19. While Peter thought on the vision, the Spirit said unto him, Behold, three men seek thee. 20. Arise therefore, and get thee down, and go with them, doubting nothing: for I have sent them.

20. Note, How this speaking of the Spirit was done and known, they only that have it can fully conceive.

21. Then Peter went down to the men which were sent unto him from Cornelius; and said, Behold, I am he whom ye seek: what *is* the cause wherefore ye are come? 22. And they said, Cornelius the centurion, a just man, and one that feareth God, and of good report among all the nations of the Jews, was warned from God by an holy angel, to send for thee into his house, and to hear words of thee.

22. God commanded Cornelius to send for thee to hear thee.

23. Then called he them in, and lodged *them*. And on the morrow Peter went away with them, and certain brethren from Joppa accompanied him. 24. And the morrow after they entered into Cesarea: and Cornelius waited for them, and had called together his kinsmen and near friends.

23, 24. Note, This good man had a care that his kindred and friends might all be saved as well as he.

25. And as Peter was coming in, Cornelius met him, and fell down at his feet, and worshipped *him*. 26. But Peter took him up, saying, Stand up; I myself also am a man.

25. Note, It was not a divine worship that Cornelius gave him; but yet Peter would not accept of any that was so extraordinary, as was unmeet for an humble man to own.

27. And as he talked with him, he went in, and found many that were come together.

27. Note, As evil as those times were, such conventicles were then allowed.

28. And he said unto them, Ye know how that it is an unlawful thing for a man that is a Jew, to keep company, or come unto one of another nation: but God hath shewed me that I should not call any man common or unclean. 29. Therefore came I *unto you* without gainsaying, as soon as I was sent for: I ask therefore for what intent ye have sent for me.

28. God hath satisfied me to come to you, though Gentiles.

CHAP. X. THE ACTS. 271

30. And Cornelius said, Four days ago I was fasting until this hour, and at the ninth hour I prayed in my house, and behold, a man stood before me in bright clothing, 31. And said, Cornelius, thy prayer is heard, and thine alms are had in remembrance in the sight of God. 32. Send therefore to Joppa, and call hither Simon whose surname is Peter; he is lodged in the house of one Simon a tanner, by the sea-side; who when he cometh, shall speak unto thee. 33. Immediately therefore I sent to thee; and thou hast well done that thou art come. Now therefore are we all here present before God, to hear all things that are commanded thee of God.

30. I was thus commanded by an angel of God to send for thee; and now I and my friends are all here ready as in God's presence, obediently to hear whatever message or command God sendeth by thee to us; (some copies have [before thee] not [God.]

34. Then Peter openeth his mouth, and said, Of a truth I perceive that God is no respecter of persons: 35. But in every nation, he that feareth him, and worketh righteousness, is accepted with him.

34. I do by this instance more fully than before perceive, that God respecteth not men for their country sake, or any common worldly privileges, but for their real goodness; and whatever nation a man be of, if he so sincerely believe in God and his mercy, as to fear and serve him, or to work righteousness, or truly obey his laws, he shall be mercifully accepted by him, who is the rewarder of them that diligently seek him.

36. The word which God sent unto the children of Israel, preaching peace by Jesus Christ (he is Lord of all). 37. That word (*I say*) you know which was published throughout all Judea, and began from Galilee, after the baptism which John preached; 38. How God anointed Jesus of Nazareth with the Holy Ghost, and with power; who went about doing good, and healing all that were oppressed of the devil: for God was with him.

36, &c. The word which God sent to the children of Israel was not like Moses's law confined to them, but it was the proclaiming of reconciliation to all Jews and Gentiles that will believe in him, who is by redemption Lord of all (and not only of the Jews.) This word you cannot but have heard hath been published throughout all Judea, &c. How God endued Jesus with the Holy Ghost and with power who went about doing good, and healing, &c.

39. And we are witnesses of all things which he did both in the land of the Jews, and in Jerusalem; whom they slew and hanged on a tree: 40. Him God raised up the third day, and shewed him openly, 41. Not to all the people, but unto witnesses, chosen before of God, *even* to us, who did eat and drink with him after he rose from the dead.

39. We are witnesses of his doctrine and miracles, and of his resurrection, and did eat and drink with him, being chosen to this office.

42. And he commanded us to preach unto the people, and to testify that it is he which was ordained of God *to be* the judge of quick and dead.

42. Judge of all that are alive at his coming, and that were dead before and are then raised.

43. To him give all the prophets witness, that through his name, whosoever believeth in him, shall receive remission of sins.

43. All the prophets foretold that through the merits of this the Messiah, God by his covenant of grace, would give remission of sins to all that truly believe in him.

44. While Peter yet spake these words, the Holy Ghost fell on all them which heard the word.

44. Even while Peter was thus speaking, the great miraculous gift of the Holy Ghost, came down on all that heard, which broke out in the effects before them all.

45. And they of the circumcision which believed, were astonished, as many as came with Peter, because that on the Gentiles also was poured out the gift of the Holy Ghost. 46. For they heard them speak with tongues, and magnify God. Then answered Peter,

45. This was astonishing news to the Jewish Christians, to hear Gentiles speak tongues not learned, and to be wrapt up in the praise of God.

47. Can any man forbid water, that these should not be baptized, which have received the Holy Ghost, as well as we?

47. Can any reason be given why these, though Gentiles, should not be baptized, when God hath thus signally owned them by his miraculous gift of the Spirit, as he hath done us.

48. And he commanded them to be baptized in the name of the Lord. Then prayed they him to tarry certain days.

48. He caused them to be entered by baptism into the Christian covenant and church: And they prayed him to stay awhile with them, to confirm and comfort them.

CHAP. XI.

AND the apostles and brethren that were in Judea, heard that the Gentiles had also received the word of God. 2. And when Peter was come up to Jerusalem, they that were of the circumcision contended with him, 3. Saying, Thou wentest in to men uncircumcised, and didst eat with them.

1, 2. Note, 1. Even in the pure apostolical first church there were wrangling contending Christians. 2. Even that which should have been their rejoicing was their matter of censorious contention. 3. These weak ones charged sin on the apostle as if they had been wiser and holier than he. 4. It was the separating and self-honouring vice which caused this censorious contention.

4. But Peter rehearsed *the matter* from the beginning, and expounded *it* by order unto them, saying, 5. I was in the city of Joppa, praying; and in a trance I saw a vision, A certain vessel descend, as it had been a great sheet let down from heaven by four corners; and it came even to me. 6. Upon the which when I had fastened mine eyes, I considered, and saw fourfooted beasts of the earth, and wild beasts, and creeping things, and fowls of the air. 7. And I heard a voice saying unto me, Arise, Peter; slay, and eat. 8. But I said, Not so, Lord: for nothing common or unclean hath at any time entered into my mouth. 9. But the voice answered me again from heaven, What God hath cleansed, *that* call not thou common. 10. And this was done three times; and all were drawn up again into heaven. 11. And behold, immediately there were three men already come unto the house where I was, sent from Cesarea unto me. 12. And the Spirit bade me go with them, nothing doubting. Moreover, these six brethren accompanied me, and we entered into the man's house: 13. And he shewed us how he had seen an angel in his house, which stood, and said unto him, Send men to Joppa, and call for Simon, whose surname is Peter: 14. Who shall tell thee words, whereby thou and all thy house shall be saved.

4. Of all this we have spoken on the former chapter.
Note, 1. God who hath ordained the ministry of men, will use it for men's salvation. 2. How greatly should the gospel and men's preaching be valued, when it is God's means of saving men. 3. God used then to covenant and save whole households together. And it seems Cornelius's house was prepared for it.

14. And as I began to speak, the Holy Ghost fell on them, as on us at the beginning. 16. Then remembered I the word of the Lord, how that he said, John indeed baptized with water; but ye shall be baptized with the Holy Ghost.

15, 16. I remembered Christ's promise of the Spirit, and saw that he owned them by fulfilling it.

17. Forasmuch then as God gave them the like gift as *he did* unto us, who believed on the Lord Jesus Christ, what was I that I could withstand God?

17. Seeing God so evidently owned them as he had done us, I was neither able nor willing to oppose God in his way of mercy to the Gentiles, which should rather be our joy.

18. When they heard these things, they held their peace, and glorified

God, saying, Then hath God also to the Gentiles granted repentance unto life.

18. Note, 1. God's miraculous gift of the Spirit was an undeniable evidence of his approbation. 2. Censorious separating contention came from hasty rash judging of things unknown, and before they heard what could be said. 3. When contentious censorious Christians come to hear and know what may be said, they may yield and change their minds.

19. Now they which were scattered abroad upon the persecution that arose about Stephen, travelled as far as Phenice, and Cyprus, and Antioch, preaching the word to none but unto the Jews only.

19. Note, The calling of the Gentiles was not yet well understood by them.

20. And some of them were men of Cyprus, and Cyrene, which when they were come to Antioch, spake unto the Grecians, preaching the Lord Jesus.

20. Note, Whether by the Grecians be meant the Jews that speak Greek, or Gentile proselytes, is doubtful.

21. And the hand of the Lord was with them: and a great number believed, and turned unto the Lord.

21. God blessed their ministry to the conversion of a great number to Christianity.

22. Then tidings of these things came unto the ears of the church which was in Jerusalem: and they sent forth Barnabas, that he should go as far as Antioch.

22. To confirm them and carry on the work.

23. Who when he came, and had seen the grace of God, was glad, and exhorted them all, that with purpose of heart they would cleave unto the Lord. 24. For he was a good man, and full of the Holy Ghost, and of faith: and much people was added unto the Lord.

23. It rejoiced him to see what God's grace had done.

Note, Every good man will be glad at the conversion of souls, and the increase of the church, (as diabolists are grieved at it, and fight against it.)

2. Young converts need counsel and exhortation

to be confirmed and persevere. 3. Confirmation consisteth in an habitual fixed resolution, or full purpose to cleave to the Lord.

25. Then departed Barnabas to Tarsus, for to seek Saul. 26. And when he had found him, he brought him unto Antioch. And it came to pass, that a whole year they assembled themselves with the church, and taught much people; and the disciples were called Christians first in Antioch.

25. Barnabas having sought Saul, and drawn him to Antioch for more public service, they two did, for a whole year, teach much people in the church-assembly (which it seems was then but one:) And the disciples were then first called Christians, who before were called by reproachers but Galileans and Nazarites: (and since by heresy and by hereticating reproaches, are called by a multitude of dividing and disgraceful names.)

27. And in those days came prophets from Jerusalem unto Antioch. 28. And there stood up one of them named Agabus, and signified by the Spirit, that there should be great dearth throughout all the world: which came to pass in the days of Claudius Cesar.

28. In divers countries, especially in Judea, should be a dearth.

29. Then the disciples, every man according to his ability, determined to send relief unto the brethren which dwelt in Judea. 30. Which also they did, and sent it to the elders by the hands of Barnabas and Saul.

29, 30. The famine being most in Judea (the country being dry and poor) and having frequent famines, and many converts, to shew the power of love, having sold their possessions heretofore for common use, the Christians of other countries, sent them relief, by Paul and Barnabas, to the elders of the church to be justly distributed, as there was need.

Note, Whether by elders here be meant the unordained seniors of the people, or the Presbyters ordained, as such, or, as Dr. Hammond thought, Diocesan bishops, who yet had never a Presbyter under them, and therefore were the single pastors of single congregations; is sufficiently elsewhere considered.

CHAP. XII.

NOW about that time Herod the king stretched forth *his* hands to vex certain of the church.

2. And killed James the brother of John with the sword. 3. And because he saw it pleased the Jews, he proceeded further to take Peter also: (Then were the days of unleavened bread:)

1. Note, 1. Kings bear the image of God's dominion, and have their power from him, and not against him, and above all men are bound to serve him to the utmost. Therefore such persecutors as Herod being the greatest traitors against God, no doubt have answerable punishment in hell.
2. James that was one who sought to be chief, was the chief or first of all the apostles in martyrdom, and drank of Christ's cup, and was baptized with his baptism. 3. To please wicked men, this king murdered saints, and displeased God.
4. The holy days of unleavened bread, or Easter, are celebrated with the murder of Christ first, and of James after. This is the hypocrites' holiness.

4. And when he had apprehended him, he put him in prison, and delivered him to four quaternions of soldiers, to keep him, intending after Easter to bring him forth to the people.

4. He set sixteen soldiers to keep him, that after the passover he might sacrifice him to the people.

5. Peter therefore was kept in prison; but prayer was made without ceasing of the church unto God for him.

5. The church for so great a minister in so great danger, betook themselves to their great remedy, even constant, importunate prayer to God.

6. And when Herod would have brought him forth, the same night Peter was sleeping between two soldiers, bound with two chains; and the keepers before the door kept the prison.

6. Just when the tyrant intended his execution, &c.
Note, Chains and keepers are nothing to God.

7. And behold, the angel of the Lord came upon him, and a light shined in the prison: and he smote Peter on the side, and raised him up, saying, Arise up quickly. And his chains fell off from *his* hands.

7. Note, O how powerful are God's invisible agents in comparison of mortal worms. 2. It was a gentle harmless stroke that the angel gave him, and such are God's awakening strokes.

8. And the angel said unto him, Gird thyself, and bind on thy sandals; and so he did. And he saith unto him, Cast thy garment about thee, and follow me. 9. And he went out and followed him, and wist not that it was true which was done by the angel: but thought he saw a vision.

8. Note, Implicit obedience by following God's call even when we know not whither, is acceptable and safe.

10. When they were past the first and the second ward, they came unto the iron gate that leadeth unto the city, which opened to them of his own accord: and they went out, and passed on through one street, and forthwith the angel departed from him.

10. Note, Nothing can hold those that God will deliver. 2. Angels are ministering spirits for our good.

11. And when Peter was come to himself, he said, Now I know of a surety, that the Lord hath sent his angel, and hath delivered me out of the hand of Herod, and *from* all the expectation of the people of the Jews.

11. Note, We seldom understand what God is doing for us in the beginning of our deliverances as we do at last.

12. And when he had considered *the thing*, he came to the house of Mary the mother of John, whose surname was Mark, where many were gathered together, praying.

12. When he considered what God had done for him, he went to the house of Mark's mother, and there in the night was a godly conventicle of many Christians met to pray (no doubt in a special manner for his deliverance.) God sent him to them as answer to their prayers.

13. And as Peter knocked at the door of the gate, a damsel came to hearken, named Rhoda. 14. And when she knew Peter's voice, she opened not the gate for gladness, but ran in, and told how Peter stood before the gate.

13. This poor maid that shewed so much love

to Peter by her joy, hath her name recorded in the scripture.

15. And they said unto her, Thou art mad. But she constantly affirmed that it was even so. Then said they, it is his angel.

15. Note, The word [mad] doth but express that they thought her grossly mistaken, as mad folk use to be; only speaking it in such coarse phrase as men use to speak to servants. 2. Whether by his angel they meant an angel of God representing him, or only a human messenger sent by him, is uncertain.

16. But Peter continued knocking: and when they had opened *the door*, and saw him, they were astonished. 17. But he beckoning unto them with the hand to hold their peace, declared unto them how the Lord had brought him out of the prison. And he said, Go shew these things unto James, and to the brethren. And he departed, and went into another place.

16. God having first sent him to them that were praying for him in answer to their prayers, he first tells them to God's glory how he was delivered, and then sends the notice of it to James (Christ's kinsman) and to the brethren for their encouragement. Our mercies are not given us only for ourselves.

18. Now as soon as it was day, there was no small stir among the soldiers, what was become of Peter. 19. And when Herod had sought for him, and found him not, he examined the keepers, and commanded that *they* should be put to death. And he went down from Judea to Cesarea, and *there* abode.

18. Note, Whether it was death or imprisonment that the soldiers were put to, is doubtful in the Greek text: But it tells us that the innocent may be a prey to tyrants' cruelty and injustice.

20. And Herod was highly displeased with them of Tyre and Sidon: but they came with one accord to him, and having made Blastus the king's chamberlain their friend, desired peace; because their country was nourished by the king's country.

21. And upon a set day, Herod arrayed in royal apparel, sat upon his throne, and made an oration unto them. 22. And the people gave a shout, *saying, It is* the voice of a god, and not of a man. 23. And immediately the angel of the Lord smote him, because he gave not God the glory: and he was eaten of worms, and gave up the ghost.

20, 21. Note, A lively instance of the case of worldly tyrants. To-day countries are crouching to them, and flatterers applauding them, and the persecuted fearing them, and to-morrow they are the stinking food of worms: As gods to-day, and as dung to-morrow.

24. But the word of God grew and multiplied. 25. And Barnabas and Saul returned from Jerusalem, when they had fulfilled *their* ministry, and took with them John, whose surname was Mark.

24. Note, Both the deliverance of Peter, and the death of Herod, furthered the success of the gospel.

CHAP. XIII.

NOW there were in the church that was at Antioch, certain prophets and teachers: as Barnabas, and Simeon that was called Niger, and Lucius of Cyrene, and Manaen, which had been brought up with Herod the tetrarch, and Saul.

1. The church assembled at Antioch, had then in it many men of eminent gifts for prophecy and teaching.

2. And as they ministered to the Lord, and fasted, the Holy Ghost said, Separate me Barnabas and Saul, for the work whereunto I have called them.

2. Note, To whom the Holy Ghost manifested this, whether to many or to few, is uncertain.

3. And when they had fasted and prayed, and laid their hands on them, they sent *them* away. 4. So they being sent forth by the Holy Ghost, departed unto Seleucia; and from thence they sailed to Cyprus. 5. And when they were at Salamis, they preached the word of God in

the synagogues of the Jews: and they had also John to *their* minister.

_{3. Note, This was not the first authorising of them to be ministers by office; for they were called and preached before. But it was their call or mission to this particular work, to go abroad preaching to many nations. To be separated to the ministry is to be done but once; But to be appointed to this or that place, charge or flock, may be oft done, and that by fasting, prayer, and imposition of hands. 2. They began their preaching usually in the Jews' synagogues in all countries, where there were such where they came, they being expectants of the Messiah.}

6. And when they had gone through the isle unto Paphos, they found a certain sorcerer, a false prophet, a Jew, whose name *was* Barjesus: 7. Which was with the deputy of the country, Sergius Paulus, a prudent man; who called for Barnabas and Saul, and desired to hear the word of God.

_{7. Note, His prudence made him willing to be instructed, and to hear men that said they were sent by God.}

8. But Elymas the sorcerer (for so is his name by interpretation) withstood them, seeking to turn away the deputy from the faith.

_{8. Elymas (which signifieth a magician) opposed them to hinder the deputy's conversion.}

9. Then Saul (who also *is called* Paul) filled with the Holy Ghost, set his eyes on him, 10. And said, O full of all subtlety and all mischief, thou child of the devil, thou enemy of all righteousness, wilt thou not cease to pervert the right ways of the Lord? 11. And now behold, the hand of the Lord *is* upon thee, and thou shalt be blind, not seeing the sun for a season. And immediately there fell on him a mist and a darkness; and he went about seeking some to lead him by the hand.

_{9. The Holy Ghost inspired Paul to pass this sentence when he was resolved to execute it: it came not by the will of man primarily.}

12. Then the deputy when he saw what was done, believed, being astonished at the doctrine of the Lord.

<sub>12. Whether the deputy was baptised is uncertain, but being converted to the faith, we may say to his honour that Sergius Paulus was the first Christian magistrate.(unless you will call the Jewish converted priests, magistrates: Constantine was not the first.) But he had no power to use magistracy for Christianity, save obliquely.
2. The judgment of God on Elymas was for the deputy's conversion: what he did himself is unknown.</sub>

13. Now when Paul and his company loosed from Paphos, they came to Perga in Pamphylia: and John departing from them, returned to Jerusalem: 14. But when they departed from Perga, they came to Antioch in Pisidia, and went into the synagogue on the sabbath day, and sat down.

_{13. Note, They began with the despised Jews still, as understanding each others' languages, and as the most prepared to hear the news of the Messiah: miraculous language was like miraculous works: not constant and at the speaker's will, as if they still spake by miracles.}

15. And after the reading of the law and the prophets, the rulers of the synagogue sent unto them, saying, Ye men *and* brethren, if ye have any word of exhortation for the people, say on.

_{15. Note, Thus were their rulers like church justices, that disposed of order, that were no teachers themselves. 2. It was among the Jews allowed any man, that professed to be a wise man and a teacher, though not in office, to teach the people by the consent of the ruler of the synagogue. 3. The reading of the law and prophets was the chief part of their liturgy.}

16. Then Paul stood up, and beckoning with *his* hand, said, Men of Israel, and ye that fear God, give audience. 17. The God of this people of Israel chose our fathers, and exalted the people when they dwelt as strangers in the land of Egypt, and with an high arm brought he them out of it. 18. And about the time of forty years suffered he their manners in the wilderness. 19. And when he had destroyed seven nations in the land of Canaan, he divided their land to them by lot. 20. And after that, he gave *unto them* judges about the space of four hundred and fifty

years, until Samuel the prophet. 21. And afterward they desired a king: and God gave unto them Saul the Son of Kis, a man of the tribe of Benjamin, by the space of forty years. 22. And when he had removed him, he raised up unto them David to be their king: to whom also ne gave testimony, and said, I have found David the *son* of Jesse, a man after mine own heart, which shall fulfil all my will.

16, &c. Note, The recital of the history of the Jews, was by Peter, and Stephen, and Paul, judged the meetest way to introduce the tidings of Christ as come, it being that which the Jews believed and understood, and on which they grounded their privileges and expectations.

23. Of this man's seed hath God according to *his* promise raised unto Israel a Saviour Jesus: 24. When John had first preached before his coming, the baptism of repentance to all the people of Israel.

23. This Jesus is the son of David whom you expect, and John by preaching and baptizing foreshewed you.

25. And as John fulfilled his course, he said, Whom think ye that I am? I am not *he*. But behold, there cometh one after me, whose shoes of his feet I am not worthy to loose.

25. John told you that he was not the Christ, but that this Jesus was he.

26. Men *and* brethren, children of the stock of Abraham, and whosoever among you feareth God, to you is the word of this salvation sent.

26. To you Jews and Proselytes who are prepared by the fear of God and expectation of the Messiah, we are sent to tell you that he is come, that you may believe in him to salvation.

27. For they that dwelt at Jerusalem, and their rulers, because they knew him not, nor yet the voices of the prophets which are read every sabbath-day, they have fulfilled *them* in condemning *him*. 28. And though they found no cause of death in *him*, yet desired they Pilate that he should be slain. 29. And when they had fulfilled all that was written of him, they took *him* down from the tree, and laid *him* in a sepulchre; 30. But God raised him from the dead.

27. The chief of your nation, not believing in him, nor understanding the prophets, fulfilled the prophecy by killing him, but God raised him.

31. And he was seen many days of them which came up with him from Galilee to Jerusalem, who are his witnesses unto the people.

31. He shewed himself to those that he chose to be his witnesses to the world.

32. And we declare unto you glad tidings, how that the promise which was made unto the fathers, 33. God hath fulfilled the same unto us their children, in that he hath raised up Jesus again; as it is also written in the second psalm, Thou art my son, this day have I begotten thee.

32. To you expectants we bring joyful news, the Messiah is come, the promise of him is fulfilled to us, and Christ is risen. Note, Seeing all men love glad tidings, the gospel should be welcome to all.

33. And as David the type is called God's begotten son, because he exalted him to the throne, so is that word fulfilled now in Christ, indeed begotten of God, and raised to glory.

34. And as concerning that he raised him up from the dead, *now* no more to return to corruption, he said on this wise, I will give you the sure mercies of David.

34. And this everlasting kingdom which Christ is raised to, is that called the sure mercies of David, Isa. lv. 3.

35. Wherefore he saith also in another *psalm*, Thou shalt not suffer thine Holy One to see corruption. 36. For David, after he had served his own generation, by the will of God, fell on sleep, and was laid unto his fathers, and saw corruption: 37. But he whom God raised again, saw no corruption.

35. This must be meant of Christ, &c.

38. Be it known unto you therefore men *and* brethren, that through

this man is preached unto you the forgiveness of sins: 39. And by him all that believe are justified from all things, from which ye could not be justified by the law of Moses.

38, 39. By his sacrifice, and merits, and intercession, and kingly power, all sins shall be pardoned to all that truly believe in him, and take him for their Saviour and King; And by him all such are acquit from damning guilt and punishment (initially now by his pardoning law of grace, and finally hereafter by his judgment and execution) from which the law of Moses can never justify or acquit you, by all its sacrifices, and your observances.

40. Beware therefore, lest that come upon you which is spoken of in the prophets. 41. Behold, ye despisers, and wonder, and perish: for I work a work in your days, a work which you shall in no wise believe, though a man declare it unto you.

40. Take heed lest your obstinate unbelief cause God to cast you off, and take in the Gentiles in your stead.

42. And when the Jews were gone out of the synagogue, the Gentiles besought that these words might be preached to them the next sabbath.

42. Some dislike these words, but others, especially proselytes, desired to hear them again. By the same words is meant the same doctrine: Note, They grossly mistake that say it is the 'Lord's day, as such, that is here called the next Sabbath.

43. Now when the congregation was broken up, many of the Jews, and religious proselytes, followed Paul and Barnabas; who speaking to them, persuaded them to continue in the grace of God.

43. Beginners newly convinced must be followed with persuasions to proceed and persevere.

44. And the next sabbath-day came almost the whole city together to hear the word of God. 45. But when the Jews saw the multitudes, they were filled with envy, and spake against those things which were spoken by Paul, contradicting and blaspheming.

44, 45. Note, 1. The apostles did use to meet on the Jews' Sabbath in their synagogues, and to observe the outward rest of them while they were among the Jews, both to get an opportunity of preaching to them, and to avoid their offence, till the dissolution of their state had in fact cast down their law and policy, which Christ had before abrogated.

2. The crowds of hearers, and multitude of converts being hateful to Satan, doth usually stir up rage in his servants, and raise greater opposition.

46. Then Paul and Barnabas waxed bold, and said, It was necessary that the word of God should first have been spoken to you; but seeing ye put it from you, and judge yourselves unworthy of everlasting life, lo, we turn to the Gentiles. 47. For so hath the Lord commanded us, *saying*, I have set thee to be a light of the Gentiles, that thou shouldest be for salvation unto the ends of the earth.

46, 47. God did appoint us to offer Christ first to you Jews, and he, or we rejected not you first: But seeing by your obstinate rejecting of Christ and his gospel, you make and shew yourselves unworthy and incapable of so great mercy, we go to the Gentiles; for so is our commission.

48. And when the Gentiles heard this, they were glad, and glorified the word of the Lord: and as many as were ordained to eternal life, believed.

48. Note, It is a controversy what is here meant by [Ordained to eternal life,] whether it be [Ordained by God's decree] or [ordered by preparing grace:] But there is no doctrinal controversy arising from either exposition, those being proselytes or otherwise in the nearest disposition to believe, it is probable at the least were the persons here meant: But that God also doth fore-decree whom he will effectually convert and save, should be past doubt with all sober Christians, the perfection of God, and the words of scripture making it plain: And not only Augustine and protestants, but almost all the papists, doctors, and schoolmen, proving it. And Dr. Hammond confesseth that this preparing grace is God's gift; which therefore he before purposed to give. But when he opposeth [The absolute decree of destinating them, whatsoever they do, to salvation:] It is very ill done so to insinuate that this is the opinion of those that dissent from him: who are so far from it, that they hold that to destinate to holiness and salvation, is one and the same decree of God: Of this see my Catholic Theology, fully handling it: Alas, for this sad disease in church doctors!

49. And the word of the Lord was published throughout all the region. 50. But the Jews stirred

up the devout and honourable women, and the chief men of the city, and raised persecution against Paul and Barnabas, and expelled them out of their coasts.

50. Devout women and men in ignorance may be adversaries to Christianity and truth, and instruments of persecution: And the chief and honourable are oft the chief herein. 2. Powerful successful preaching, useth to stir up violent persecuting, which often driveth the preachers to some other place where God hath some to call.

51. But they shook off the dust of their feet against them, and came unto Iconium.

51. Note, As excommunication was dismal to them that were cut off, so shaking off the dust of their feet against them was a dismal signification of a forsaken people.

52. And the disciples were filled with joy, and with the Holy Ghost.

52. Note, God's grace, and the church's joy, may increase under persecution, and expulsion by men.

CHAP. XIV.

AND it came to pass in Iconium, that they went both together into the synagogue of the Jews, and so spake, that a great multitude both of the Jews, and also of the Greeks, believed. 2. But the unbelieving Jews stirred up the Gentiles, and made their minds evil-affected against the brethren.

1, 2. Still the great success of the ministry is attended with the greatest envy and opposition of bad men.

3. Long time therefore abode they speaking boldly in the Lord, which gave testimony unto the word of his grace, and granted signs and wonders to be done by their hands.

3. Note, Long preaching is needful to root that word which one or two sermons often leaveth loose. 2. Miracles were the convincing cause of the credibility of the apostles' testimony.

4. But the multitude of the city was divided: and part held with the Jews, and part with the apostles.

4. Note, The gospel causeth divisions by saving some, or else all would perish together in concord.

5. And when there was an assault made both of the Gentiles, and also of the Jews, with their rulers, to use *them* despitefully, and to stone them, 6. They were aware of *it*, and fled unto Lystra and Derbe, cities of Lycaonia, and unto the region that lieth round about: 7. And there they preached the gospel.

5. Note, Still persecution disperseth the gospel.

8. And there sat a certain man at Lystra, impotent in his feet, being a cripple from his mother's womb, who never had walked. 9. The same heard Paul speak: who stedfastly beholding him, and perceiving that he had faith to be healed, 10. Said with a loud voice, Stand upright on thy feet. And he leaped and walked.

8. The Holy Ghost, when he would do the miracle, made Paul discern the man's faith, and exciteth him to bid him stand up.

11. And when the people saw what Paul had done, they lift up their voices, saying in the speech of Lycaonia, The gods are come down to us in the likeness of men. 12. And they called Barnabas, Jupiter; and Paul, Mercurius, because he was the chief speaker.

11. They knew that such a miracle must be a supernatural work, and done by God; and they called them by the usual names of their gods.

13. Then the priest of Jupiter which was before their city, brought oxen and garlands unto the gates, and would have done sacrifice with the people.

13. The priest of Jupiter, whose temple, or statue was without the city, brought oxen to sacrifice to them.

Note, Such men are readier for idolatries than to receive God's word.

14. *Which* when the apostles, Barnabas and Paul, heard *of*, they rent their clothes, and ran in among the people, crying out, 15. And saying, Sirs, why do ye these things? we also are men of like passions with you, and preach unto you,

that ye should turn from these vanities unto the living God, which made heaven and earth, and the sea, and all things that are therein.

14. Note, 1. The number of the twelve apostles was fitted to the Jews' twelve tribes, to whom the gospel was first to be preached: but when Christ would gather the Gentile church, he increased the number, and Paul was commissioned by a voice from heaven, and he and Barnabas, by a special mission of Christ, by the Holy Ghost. 2. The significant ceremony of [renting the clothes] is used by these two apostles. 3. All good men hate idolatry, and would not be idolised themselves. 4. The devil would honour the ministers of Christ overmuch, when it is to contradict their doctrine.

16. Who in times past suffered all nations to walk in their own ways. 17. Nevertheless, he left not himself without witness, in that he did good, and gave us rain from heaven, and fruitful seasons, filling our hearts with food and gladness.

16. He hath long connived by patient permissions, at the manifold idolatries and vices of the world, not punishing them as they deserved: yet his common mercies to men's bodies, did both signify, that he is the merciful ruler and benefactor to mankind, and that he useth not sinful man as he deserveth, but in mercy obligeth all to gratitude and repentance.

18. And with these sayings scarce restrained they the people, that they had not done sacrifice unto them.

18. Note, So forward are men to forbidden worship, who are backward to spiritual and true.

19. And there came thither certain Jews from Antioch and Iconium, who persuaded the people, and having stoned Paul, drew *him* out of the city, supposing he had been dead.

19. Note, This is the levity of the vulgar, that one day will sacrifice as to gods, to those, whom after they would kill as malefactors: so little trust is to be placed in them. And though we know not whether most of the same persons were the persecutors, it is likely that many were.

20. Howbeit, as the disciples stood round about him, he rose up, and came into the city: and the next day he departed with Barnabas to Derbe.

20. Note, It is like his recovery was a miracle; else stoning would have disabled him to travel.

21. And when they had preached the gospel to that city, and had taught many, they returned again to Lystra, and *to* Iconium, and *to* Antioch,

21. Note, Persecution made them not forsake the plantations which they had newly made.

22. Confirming the souls of the disciples, *and* exhorting them to continue in the faith, and *saying* that we must through much tribulation enter into the kingdom of God.

22. Confirming them against the temptation of persecution, which must be suffered by those that will be saved.

23. And when they had ordained them elders in every church, and had prayed with fasting, they commended them to the Lord, on whom they believed.

23. They settled the Christians that were converted in these several cities, in church order, ordaining elders in every church, to be the guides and teachers of the rest; and that with fasting and prayer, because of the great importance of the work.

Note, 1. It is made a controversy, whether the Greek word which is rendered [ordained,] signify [by suffrages] or [by laying on of hands.] But it is of small importance: for it is certain, that the apostles forced no elders on the people, but ordained them by the people's choice or consent: and it is certain, that ordination was the apostles' act.

2. And it is a controversy what is here meant by elders; whether diocesan bishops, or mere presbyters, or lay elders, or deacons also. The scripture calls all church guides and teachers, elders, and here maketh no distinction. It is certain, that each church here was but one small assembly, and therefore, if they will call the pastor of one assembly a diocesan, it is a nominal strife: if they say, it is because they had power to govern a diocese of a multitude of churches when they were gathered, 1. They must prove that power given: 2. Then they were no bishops of those churches, till they were indeed churches: 3. And it is probable, that about those near cities, that was not in their life time.

Though it be not certain, that by [elders in every city] is meant more than one in each city, yet by the phrase, it is most probable, especially considering what evidence there is of many at Corinth, Antioch, and Jerusalem.

24. And after they had passed throughout Pisidia, they came to Pamphylia. 25. And when they had preached the word in Perga,

they went down into Attalia: 26. And thence sailed to Antioch, from whence they had been recommended to the grace of God, for the work which they fulfilled.

24. They returned to Antioch in Syria, (not Antioch in Pisidia) to give the church an account of their success.

27. And when they were come and had gathered the church together, they rehearsed all that God had done with them, and how he had opened the door of faith unto the Gentiles. 28. And there they abode long time with the disciples.

27. Note, 1. It was a congregation, and not a diocese of a multitude of congregations, that is called the church, which they congregated. 2. They brought them the glad tidings, that the Gentiles had received the faith: though it was in the Jews' synagogues that they preached, at least for the most part.

CHAP. XV.

AND certain men which came down from Judea, taught the brethren, *and said*, Except ye be circumcised after the manner of Moses, ye cannot be saved.

1. Some Christian Jews thought and taught, that circumcision and keeping the law of Moses is necessary to salvation, both to Jew and Gentile Christians.

Note, 1. The sound doctrine of Christianity was quickly corrupted by erring teachers. 2. The threatening of damnation, and making error seem necessary to salvation, was used to affright timorous Christians into false ways.

2. When therefore Paul and Barnabas had no small dissension and disputation with them, they determined that Paul and Barnabas, and certain other of them, should go up to Jerusalem unto the apostles and elders about this question.

2. Note, To be dissenters and disputants against errors and tyrannical impositions upon conscience, is no fault but a great duty.

2. It is but a groundless fiction of some that tell us that this was an appeal to Jerusalem, because it was the metropolis of Syria and Antioch: as if metropolitan church power had been then settled: when long after, when it was devised indeed, Antioch was above Jerusalem: and it is as vain a fiction that this was an appeal to a general council, as if the apostles and elders at Jerusalem had been a general council, when none of the bishops of the Gentile churches were there, or called thither. It is notorious that it was an appeal to the apostles (taking in the elders) as those that had the certainest notice of Christ's mind, having conversed with him, and being entrusted to teach all nations whatever he commanded them, and had the greatest measure of the Spirit: and also being Jews themselves, were such as the Judaizing Christians had no reason to suspect or reject.

3. And being brought on their way by the church, they passed through Phenice, and Samaria, declaring the conversion of the Gentiles: and they caused great joy unto all the brethren.

3. Note, By the church that brought them on, is neither meant a diocese of churches, nor the mere clergy; but the chief men of the congregation of Antioch. 2. The Gentiles' conversion was joyful news.

4. And when they were come to Jerusalem, they were received of the church, and *of* the apostles and elders, and they declared all things that God hath done with them. 5. But there rose up certain of the sect of the Pharisees which believed, saying, That it was needful to circumcise them, and to command *them* to keep the law of Moses.

4. They first told them of their success on the Gentiles, and then of the doctrine of these Christian Pharisees.

Note, The error, as to the Jews, had a fair religious pretence; for Moses' law was God's own law, and delivered by angels, and confirmed by miracles; and Christ had said that he came not to destroy it, &c. Therefore had not apostolic testimony, and the authority of the Holy Ghost by miracles, proved the abrogation, it would more hardly have been believed by good men, than the substitute canons of bishops that have no such pretence. But the Gentiles were never under Moses's law, as such.

6. And the apostles and elders came together for to consider of this matter.

6. Note, God's inspiration made not consultation needless to themselves, or to convince gainsayers.

7. And when there had been much disputing, Peter rose up, and said unto them, Men *and* brethren, ye know how that a good while ago, God made choice among us that the Gentiles by my mouth should

hear the word of the gospel, and believe. 8. And God which knoweth the hearts, bare them witness, giving them the Holy Ghost, even as *he did* unto us: 9. And put no difference between us and them, purifying their hearts by faith.

7. Those of the Pharisees way that came with Paul and Barnabas, were heard disputing for their cause, and then Peter said, &c.

10. Now therefore why tempt ye God, to put a yoke upon the neck of the disciples, which neither our fathers nor we were able to bear?

10. God never put this yoke on the Gentiles, and we Jews have found it a heavy burden.

11. But we believe that through the grace of the Lord Jesus Christ, we shall be saved, even as they.

11. And it is not by the works of Moses' law, that we Jews are justified and saved, but in the same way that is common to the Gentiles with us, even by the grace of Jesus Christ.

12. Then all the multitude kept silence, and gave audience to Barnabas and Paul, declaring what miracles and wonders God had wrought among the Gentiles by them.

12. The miracles and conversion of the Gentiles, was God's approving testimony in the case.

13. And after they had held their peace, James answered, saying,

13. Note, They were not like the proud magisterial talkers, so full of themselves, that they have not patience to restrain their list of speaking till another hath done, but stop and silence him by rude uncivil interruption, on pretence that he is too long.

13. Men *and* brethren, hearken unto me. 14. Simon hath declared how God at the first did visit the Gentiles, to take out of them a people for his name. 15. And to this agree the words of the prophets; as it is written, 16. After this I will return, and will build again the tabernacle of David which is fallen down: and I will build again the ruins thereof, and I will set it up: 17. That the residue of men might seek after the Lord, and all the Gentiles upon whom my name is called, saith the Lord, who doeth all these things.

13, 14. Note, Some think James meaneth the prophecy of Simeon, Luke ii. 32. A light to lighten the Gentiles; but it is more likely (though not certain) that it is Peter here that he meaneth.

18. Known unto God are all his works from the beginning of the world.

18. God that hath prophesied of this calling of the Gentiles, decreed and foreknew it. They are his works, as well as we, and he is merciful to all.

19. Wherefore my sentence is, that we trouble not them, which from among the Gentiles are turned to God. 20. But that we write unto them, that they abstain from pollutions of idols, and *from* fornication, and *from* things strangled, and *from* blood.

19. Note, It is not agreed by expositors what these words mean, whether it be only things indifferent that are here determined (as Beza and some others think,) and that only to avoid offence for a time: or whether it be the precepts of Noah imposed on the proselytes of the gate, as such, (as Dr. Hammond thought.) They that go the first way, think, that by [fornication] here, is meant idolatry, that is, the countenancing of it by the use of things in themselves indifferent: but most think, that by [fornication] is meant some controverted sorts of it, (as marrying within some prohibited degrees, or using concubines, or second wives, which the Jews scrupled not.) And others think that the ignorance of Jews and Gentiles of the evil of fornication, and some heretics pleading for it, made it, though not indifferent, joined with the rest.

Those that go the second way, say, that to the proselytes of the gate, the seven precepts of Noah were necessary, and therefore when they turned Christians, not to be cast off: and by [blood] they think is meant [bloodshed or murder:] so the two first precepts (saith Dr. Hammond) are, for worshipping the true God; 2. And not idols: both these are included in [abstaining from meats offered to idols.] 3. Abstaining from blood, is the fifth of those precepts against murder. 4. From things strangled is the seventh. 5. From fornication was the fourth. 6. And many ancient Greek copies add here [Thou shalt not do to another what thou wouldst not have done to thee,] and that containeth that against theft and injustice, &c. Which ever of these be right, it maketh no difference as to our obligation. By eating things strangled and blood, can be meant no more than such beastly devouring, either of the blood itself, or the blood in the strangled creature, which signified a bloody mind, and may harden men in cruelty, and more easily dispose them to shed man's blood. And if there be any more that is ceremonious in it, it was temporary to avoid

21. For Moses of old time hath in every city them that preach him, being read in the synagogues every sabbath-day.

21. As for the Jews, the law of Moses belongs to them, and we leave them to it, till God shall dissolve their state and policy (it is preached by the reading of it in the synagogues every sabbath-day.)

22. Then pleased it the apostles and elders, with the whole church, to send chosen men of their own company to Antioch, with Paul and Barnabas; *namely,* Judas surnamed Barsabas, and Silas, chief men among the brethren:

22. Though the apostles were the infallible deciders, the elders and the whole church were unanimous consenters: and to shew the necessity of concord, and that even infallible and miraculous teachers yet guide only volunteers; they sent some of their own company (of the college that guided the church at Jerusalem; or as Dr. Hammond thinketh bishops of some single congregation of Judea) that contending parties might not be the only reporters of their sentence.

23. And they wrote letters by them after this manner, The apostles, and elders, and brethren, send greeting unto the brethren which are of the Gentiles in Antioch, and Syria, and Cilicia. 24. Forasmuch as we have heard, that certain which went out from us have troubled you with words, subverting your souls, saying, *Ye must* be circumcised, and keep the law; to whom we gave no *such* commandment:

23, 24. Note, 1. If false teachers pretended apostolical authority or mission when they were near them, no wonder if they do it now when they are so easily confuted. 2. Tyrannical impositions on conscience, do but trouble the church and subvert souls, by pious pretences.

25. It seemed good unto us, being assembled with one accord, to send chosen men unto you, with our beloved Barnabas and Paul; 26. Men that have hazarded their lives for the name of our Lord Jesus Christ. 27. We have sent therefore Judas and Silas, who shall also tell *you* the same things by mouth.

25. Thus far their letters are credential, to tell them that they may believe the messengers.

28. For it seemeth good to the Holy Ghost and to us, to lay upon you no greater burden than these necessary things;

28. Note, 1. It is prophaneness for any bishops or councils to use those words, who neither have assurance, nor can give any proof that the Holy Ghost guideth them. 2. The Holy Ghost is against imposing unnecessary things as necessary. These things here imposed were necessary, (at least all to those persons, and at that time) and most (if not all) continually.

29. That ye abstain from meats offered to idols, and from blood, and from things strangled, and from fornication: from which if ye keep yourselves, ye shall do well. Fare ye well.

29. It is not Moses' law that ye are bound to keep, but these commoner precepts. Do nothing that scandalously savoureth idolatry, or savoureth of cruelty and bloodiness, not eating strangled creatures in the gore blood. Avoid defilement, by any sort of forbidden fleshly lust and filthiness.

30. So when they were dismissed, they came to Antioch: and when they had gathered the multitude together, they delivered the epistle.

30. Note, The multitude was one assembly, not a diocese, nor only the clergy.

31. *Which* when they had read, they rejoiced for the consolation.

31. Note, Liberty from toilsome ceremonies (though God first instituted them) was matter of joy to the churches; but alas few churches are allowed that joy, by their lordly pastors!

32. And Judas and Silas, being prophets also themselves, exhorted the brethren with many words, and confirmed *them.*

32. Note, By [prophets] is meant such as were inspired by the Holy Ghost, either by revelation of any new thing, or by ability to explain and apply known truth.

33. And after they had tarried there a space, they were let go in peace from the brethren unto the apostles. 34. Notwithstanding it pleased Silas to abide there still. 35. Paul also and Barnabas continued in Antioch, teaching and preaching the word of the Lord, with many others also.

35 Note, The church of Antioch had many excellent teachers, and it is not intimated, that any one was bishop over the rest, or that Paul, Barnabas, Silas, Simeon, Lucius, Manaen, &c. were subjects to any one.

36. And some days after, Paul said unto Barnabas, Let us go again, and visit our brethren, in every city where we have preached the word of the Lord, *and see* how they do.

36. Note, Converted souls and planted churches, must be further visited, observed, and watered.

37. And Barnabas determined to take with them John, whose surname was Mark. 38. But Paul thought not good to take him with them, who departed from them from Pamphylia, and went not with them to the work. 39. And the contention was so sharp between them, that they departed asunder one from the other: and so Barnabas took Mark, and sailed unto Cyprus; 40. And Paul chose Silas, and departed, being recommended by the brethren unto the grace of God. 41. And he went through Syria and Cilicia, confirming the churches.

37. Note, Apostles were not infallible in all things, even about the fitness of their helpers. 2. Small differences even to sharpen contention, may stand with Christian love and unity. 3. There was then no judge of such controversies, either bishop or synod, to avoid and end them. 4. But God turned this to good, for the better spreading of the gospel.

CHAP. XVI.

THEN came he to Derbe and Lystra: and behold, a certain disciple was there, named Timotheus, the son of a certain woman which was a Jewess, and believed; but his father *was* a Greek: 2. Which was well reported of by the brethren that were at Lystra and Iconium. 3. Him would Paul have to go forth with him; and took and circumcised him, because of the Jews which were in those quarters: for they knew all that his father was a Greek.

1. Timothy's mother being a Jewess, he might be circumcised, though his father was a Greek: And because uncircumcised, he might not be admitted to converse with the Jews, he circumcised him, the Jews being yet permitted to use the law of Moses, which he would not have done, had both parents been Gentiles.

4. And as they went through the cities, they delivered them the decrees for to keep, that were ordained of the apostles and elders which were at Jerusalem. 5. And so were the churches established in the faith, and increased in number daily.

4, 5. They delivered them the apostles' decrees, which freed the church from the doubts which the Judaizers had raised, and so they were quieted and settled in judgment, faith, and concord, and daily increased.

6. Now when they had gone throughout Phrygia, and the region of Galatia, and were forbidden of the Holy Ghost to preach the word in Asia.

6. Forbidden by some revelation or inspiration.

7. After they were come to Mysia, they assayed to go into Bithynia: but the Spirit suffered them not. 8. And they passing by Mysia, came down to Troas.

7. The invitation or inspiration of God's Spirit diverted them.

9. And a vision appeared to Paul in the night: There stood a man of Macedonia, and prayed him, saying, Come over into Macedonia, and help us.

9. Note, God's differencing grace plainly appeareth in sending his gospel to some countries rather than to others.

10. And after he had seen the vision, immediately we endeavoured to go into Macedonia, assuredly gathering that the Lord had called us for to preach the gospel unto them.

10. Note, It is the duty of ministers to follow God's call; though all have not visions, all have some notifications of God's will, by men's necessity, opportunity, invitation, &c.

11. Therefore loosing from Troas, we came with a straight course to Samothracia, and the next *day* to Neapolis; 12. And from thence to Philippi, which is the chief city of that part of Macedonia, *and* a colony: and we were in that city abiding certain days.

11. Note, The apostles did choose populous cities to preach in, because there was most matter to work on: It is best fishing in the sea. Besides that, the Jews' synagogues were mostly in such places.

13. And on the sabbath we went out of the city by a river-side, where prayer was wont to be made; and we sat down and spake unto the women which resorted *thither*.

13. Note, Whether here was an oratory or chapel, or only the open field, is uncertain: And whether the assemblies were proselytes of the Jews, or Jews with such, or the better sort of Gentiles, is not certain: But the first is likely, because they kept the sabbath.

14. And a certain woman named Lydia, a seller of purple, of the city of Thyatira, which worshipped God, heard *us:* whose heart the Lord opened, that she attended unto the things which were spoken of Paul.

14. Note, 1. It is like she was a proselyte. 2. They that worship God are best prepared for further grace: 3. God opening the heart maketh the word effectual: 4. Diligent regardful attention to the word, is the beginning of conversion, or a great preparation.

15. And when she was baptized and her household, she besought *us*, saying, If ye have judged me to be faithful to the Lord, come into my house, and abide *there*. And she constrained us.

15. Note, 1. It was the ordinary way of the apostles to baptise households: Not that they could be sure they were all true believers, or that the rulers could make them such. But it was the rulers' duty to devote all in their power to God; and therefore to do their best to persuade them to a true consent, and to rid their house of all unnecessary persons that refused: And God used to bless their endeavours, and their interest and power might do much.

2. Converted persons have so much love to Christ's ministers who converted them, that they greatly desire their company and further help.

16. And it came to pass as we went to prayer, a certain damsel possessed with a spirit of divination, met us, which brought her masters much gain by soothsaying.

16. One possessed with a deluding foretelling devil, who thereby brought him gain for divination.

17. The same followed Paul and us, and cried, saying, These men are the servants of the Most High God, which shew unto us the way of salvation.

17. Note, God constrained the devil to confess Christ against his will.

18. And this did she many days. But Paul being grieved, turned and said to the spirit, I command thee in the name of Jesus Christ to come out of her. And he came out the same hour.

18. Note, 1. Satan must be dispossessed of body, soul, or nation, whenever Christ commandeth it.

19. And when her masters saw that the hope of their gains was gone, they caught Paul and Silas, and drew *them* into the market-place, unto the rulers.

19. Note, It is like her masters being more than one, were some heathen priests, however we see, the love of money is the root of persecution and all evil.

20. And brought them to the magistrates, saying, These men being Jews, do exceedingly trouble our city, 21. And teach customs which are not lawful for us to receive, neither to observe, being Romans.

20, 21. They brought them to the Roman officers, under whose government they were, and accused them as being Jews of a contrary religion, and by their unlawful doctrines causing sedition, and disturbing the public peace. Note, Covetous malignants use the accusation of sedition to hide their malice.

22. And the multitude rose up together against them: and the magistrates rent off their clothes, and commanded to beat *them*. 23. And when they had laid many stripes upon them, they cast *them* into prison, charging the jailer to

keep them safely. 24. Who having received such a charge, thrust them into the inner prison, and made their feet fast in the stocks.

22, &c. Note, Rulers, and rabble, and most, were for the devil against Christ and their own salvation: And the innocent servants of Christ are imprisoned and used as rogues, merely for seeking men's welfare.

25. And at midnight Paul and Silas prayed, and sang praises unto God: and the prisoners heard them.

25. Note, Persecution doth not disoblige us from joyful praise to God, nor destroy believers' comforts.

26. And suddenly there was a great earthquake, so that the foundations of the prison were shaken: and immediately all the doors were opened, and every one's hands were loosed.

26. Note, Luke that wrote this, was one of their company in the city, when this was done; God's power is invincible.

27. And the keeper of the prison awaking out of his sleep, and seeing the prison-doors open, he drew out his sword, and would have killed himself, supposing that the prisoners had been fled. 28. But Paul cried with a loud voice, saying, Do thyself no harm; for we are all here.

27. He would have killed himself to prevent punishment, in the rage of his passion.

29. Then he called for a light, and sprang in, and came trembling, and fell down before Paul and Silas; 30. And brought them out, and said, Sirs, what must I do to be saved?

29. Note, When God's dreadful judgments and his grace join together, no heart can resist them.

31. And they said, Believe on the Lord Jesus Christ, and thou shalt be saved, and thy house.

31. Note, 1. He was resolved to do whatever they required, knowing by this miracle that they were sent by God. 2. Believing in Christ, includeth all the essentials of Christianity. 3. His house would not be saved for his faith, without any of their own. But it is supposed, that God would bless his endeavours to convert them.

32. And they spake unto him the word of the Lord, and to all that were in his house.

32. They instructed him and his household, that they might indeed believe and be saved.

33. And he took them the same hour of the night, and washed *their* stripes; and was baptized, he and all his, straightway.

33. He presently shewed his repentance and faith: For he that had scourged them, washed their sores to heal them; and he and all his household were presently baptized, as having professed their resolved faith in Christ.

Note, The apostles delayed not baptism, when serious profession gave them right: but in doubtful cases of ignorant or unresolved men, it ought to be longer delayed.

34. And when he had brought them into his house, he set meat before them, and rejoiced, believing in God, with all his house.

34. Note, 1. True conversion changeth men's thoughts of God's servants, and causeth men to love and honour them. 2. Conversion puts men into a joyful state.

35. And when it was day, the magistrates sent the serjeants, saying, Let those men go. 36. And the keeper of the prison told this saying to Paul, The magistrates have sent to let you go: now therefore depart, and go in peace. 37. But Paul said unto them, They have beaten us openly uncondemned, being Romans, and have cast us into prison; and now do they thrust us out privily? nay verily; but let them come themselves and fetch us out.

37. Note, It is lawful to plead our right by law against unjust magistrates, Paul was a Roman by enfranchisement (though a Jew).

38. And the serjeants told these words unto the magistrates: and they feared when they heard that they were Romans.

38. Note, The Roman laws forbad all such base usage of any that were of Roman freedom.

39. And they came and besought them, and brought *them* out, and desired *them* to depart out of the city. 40. And they went out of

the prison, and entered into *the house of* Lydia: and when they had seen the brethren, they comforted them, and departed.

39. They spake them fair, for fear, and intreated them to depart. 40. They visited, comforted, and confirmed their converts.

CHAP. XVII.

NOW when they had passed through Amphipolis, and Apollonia, they came to Thessalonica, where was a synagogue of the Jews. 2. And Paul, as his manner was, went in unto them, and three sabbath-days reasoned with them out of the scriptures, 3. Opening and alleging that Christ must needs have suffered, and risen again from the dead: and that this Jesus whom I preach unto you, is Christ.

2, 3. Note, Paul began his preaching usually in the Jews' synagogue, because they were most prepared by expectation of the Messiah, and understood his language: for it is not certain, that the miraculous gift of unlearned tongues, was it which he used in his ordinary preaching, and not only on extraordinary inspirations.

4. And some of them believed, and comforted with Paul and Silas: and of the devout Greeks a great multitude, and of the chief women not a few.

4. And being convinced by proof out of the Old Testament, that Christ must suffer and rise again, many believed; some Jews, but more of the proselytes and chief women.

5. But the Jews which believed not, moved with envy, took unto them certain lewd fellows of the baser sort, and gathered a company, and set all the city on an uproar, and assaulted the house of Jason, and sought to bring them out to the people.

5. Note, The rabble are fit instruments for persecution; for they have sufficient ignorance and malignity, and will rage against reason: But it is legalists that incite them.

6. And when they found them not, they drew Jason, and certain brethren, unto the rulers of the city, crying, These that have turned the world upside down, are come hither also; 7. Whom Jason hath received: and these all do contrary to the decrees of Cæsar, saying, That there is another king, *one* Jesus.

6, 7. Note, Were it not for the false pretence of sedition against rulers, to engage their safety, and honour, in jealousy against Christ and religion, the devil would be posed in his accusation of the faithful. 2. The name of King Jesus falsely expounded, is it that is used to engage princes against Christ.

8. And they troubled the people, and the rulers of the city, when they heard these things. 9. And when they had taken security of Jason, and of the other, they let him go.

8. Note, So solicitous are men of their own safety, from the rulers' power, that all puts them into trouble, which seemeth to bring them into any danger. Fears raise commotions.

10. And the brethren immediately sent away Paul and Silas by night unto Berea: who coming *thither*, went into the synagogue of the Jews.

10. Note, 1. It is good to reserve persecuted ministers for further work, when Satan would destroy them. 2. Again the apostles make the Jews' synagogue their preaching place.

11. These were more noble than those in Thessalonica, in that they received the word with all readiness of mind, and searched the scriptures daily, whether those things were so.

11. These were more ingenious, rational, sober Jews, and did not meet the gospel with rage, but thought it worthy their serious inquiry, whether the scriptures did foretel the death and resurrection of Christ, and whether Paul's proofs of Christianity were valid.

12. Therefore many of them believed: also of honourable women which were Greeks, and of men not a few.

12. This preparation of a sober inquiry after truth, is a reason rendered, why many of them believed. As did many men and women of note.

13. But when the Jews of Thessalonica had knowledge that the word of God was preached of Paul

at Berea, they came thither also, and stirred up the people.

13. Note, Satan sends about his messenger as Christ did his: to stir up the people.

14. And then immediately the brethren sent away Paul, to go as it were to the sea: but Silas and Timotheus abode there still.

14. Note, Not because Paul was more fearful than the rest, but that he was more useful and more maliced.

15. And they that conducted Paul, brought him unto Athens: and receiving a commandment unto Silas and Timotheus, for to come to him with all speed, they departed.

15. Paul passing by many countries between, was conducted to Athens, the great seat or university of philosophy, to Greece and all the learned world.

16. Now while Paul waited for them at Athens, his spirit was stirred in him, when he saw the city wholly given to idolatry.

16. He was much moved to see such abundance of statues, images, and altars, in the city.

17. Therefore disputed he in the synagogue with the Jews, and with the devout persons, and in the market daily with them that met with him.

17. Therefore he did not only dispute for Christianity in the synagogue with the Jews, and devout worshippers (who when converted, were usually the first members of the churches) but also with the heathens where he met them, against their idolatry.

18. Then certain philosophers of the Epicureans, and of the Stoicks encountered him: and some said, What will this babbler say? other some, He seemeth to be a setter forth of strange gods: because he preached unto them Jesus, and the resurrection.

18. The Epicureans a loose sensual sect, and the Stoics a stricter sect, encountered him; and some of them despised him as an unlearned babbler: others thought that he preached some God (by the name of Jesus and the resurrection) not known to them before. Note, The Athenians were not only for liberty for every one to worship what God he would, but thought it the height of religion to take in and worship the gods of all nations: and to please them all, and build them altars.

19. And they took him, and brought him unto Areopagus, saying, May we know what this new doctrine, whereof thou speakest, is? 20. For thou bringest certain strange things to our ears: we would know therefore what these things mean.

19. They brought him to the court of judicature, who were to be judges, before any new God was to be received, that they might hear what God it was that he preached.

21. (For all the Athenians and strangers which were there, spent their time in nothing else, but either to tell, or to hear some new thing.)

21. The very learning and daily business of the Athenian philosophers, students, and sojourners, was but to know news, and tell it, whether speculative or historical: (and what else is all learning, that serveth not to holiness and heaven.)

22. Then Paul stood in the midst of Mars-hill, and said, Ye men of Athens, I perceive that in all things ye are too superstitious.

22. Ye are on pretence of being very religious, addicted to worship multitudes of Gods.

23. For as I passed by, and beheld your devotions, I found an altar with this inscription, TO THE UNKNOWN GOD. Whom therefore ye ignorantly worship, him declare I unto you.

23. Whatever was the occasion of that inscription, you confess you worship an unknown God, I would therefore make known to you that only God, whom you must worship.

24. God that made the world, and all things therein, seeing that he is Lord of heaven and earth, dwelleth not in temples made with hands: 25. Neither is worshipped with men's hands, as though he needed any thing, seeing he giveth to all life, and breath, and all things;

24, 25. Bring not down that God that made and owneth all the world, imaginarily to your temples and images, or think that he needeth, or you can give him any thing, who giveth us all things.

26. And hath made of one blood, all nations of men, for to dwell on all the face of the earth, and hath determined the times before appointed, and the bounds of their habitation:

26. And hath made all men of one human nature (propagated from one root) and ordered them into their several countries, and bounded habitations, determined by him.

27. That they should seek the Lord, if haply they might feel after him, and find him.

27. Making it their duty to seek to know him as their maker by his works, and as their benefactor by his mercies, which palpably declare him, that they might serve, love, and worship him, as their God.

27. Though he be not far from every one of us: 28. For in him we live, and move, and have our being; as certain also of your own poets have said, For we are also his offspring.

27, 28. He is as near us as our souls are to our bodies; Being indeed more than a soul to all the world: For it is in him that we live, and move, and have our being: As your poet Aratus saith, For we are his offspring; for of him, and through him, and to him are all things; and no parent so much causeth us as God doth, nor doth the soul so much to our life, motion, and being, as God doth.

29. Forasmuch then as we are the offspring of God, we ought not to think that the Godhead is like unto gold, or silver, or stone, graven by art and man's device.

29. Our souls being the best image of God our Maker, we must not so much debase him as to make images of him of gold, silver, or stone, as if he were like such shapes.

30. And the times of this ignorance God winked at; but now commandeth all men every where to repent:

30. And as man seemeth by forbearance awhile to connive at faults, so God hath not in the time of this ignorance, either punished the world as they deserved, nor sent them from heaven that notice of his displeasure, and that call to repent and amend, as now he doth, but left them mostly to the light of nature, and the discoveries of his works and providence: but now in hatred of sin and mercy to sinners, he hath sent a special messenger to the world, to call all to repentance, and offer them pardon thereupon.

31. Because he hath appointed a day in the which he will judge the world in righteousness, by *that* man whom he hath ordained; whereof he hath given assurance unto all men, in that he hath raised him from the dead.

31. For he hath certainly determined to judge the world with righteousness, by that man whom he hath ordained to be the Saviour of the faithful and the judge of all: which (though it seem incredible to most, that a man should be so advanced to be king and judge of all the world, yet) God hath given certain proof of it, by evidence sufficient to evince it to true reason, in that he hath raised him from death to life, (and taken him up to heaven.)

32. And when they heard of the resurrection of the dead, some mocked: and others said, We will hear thee again of this matter. 33. So Paul departed from among them.

32, 33. Note, The resurrection seemed so incredible, that some (Epicureans, it is like) scoffed at it.

Note, Paul did wisely in preaching the true God to them first, and reproving their idolatry, and only concluding with the notice of Christ. And yet no sort of men more contemned his doctrine than the learned Athenians. Self-conceit and the prepossession of their vain, though extolled learning, most powerfully kept out the truth: And it did not please God there to work miracles to convince them.

34. Howbeit certain men clave unto him, and believed: among the which *was* Dionysius the Areopagite, and a woman named Damaris, and others with them.

34. This famous university yielded few converts: But those few were precious to God.

CHAP. XVIII.

AFTER these things Paul departed from Athens, and came to Corinth; 2. And found a certain Jew named Aquila, born in Pontus, lately come from Italy, with his wife Priscilla (because that Claudius had commanded all Jews to depart from Rome) and came unto them.

2. That Claudius banished all Jews from Rome is certain; but the cause is uncertain. Suetonius saith, It was their tumults by the impulse or imitation of Christ, (or some read it, of one Crestus.) It is not unlike that the Jews' rage at Rome against the gospel, made them tumultuous against Christians: and thereupon both sorts were banished under the name of Jews: And so there could then be no church left and tolerated at Rome, but Gentiles only. For it is doubtless that the Christian Jews were banished.

3. And because he was of the same craft, he abode with them, and wrought (for by their occupation they were tent-makers).

3. Note, Men separated to the ministry of the gospel, may labour for their living, if needful.

4. And he reasoned in the synagogue every sabbath, and persuaded the Jews, and the Greeks.

4. Note, Still the Jew's synagogue was his preaching-place, to gather the beginnings of a church.

5. And when Silas and Timotheus were come from Macedonia, Paul was pressed in spirit, and testified to the Jews, that Jesus was Christ.

5. He was extraordinarily moved in spirit, more openly and earnestly to testify to the Jews that Jesus is the Christ, to leave them without excuse.

6. And when they opposed themselves, and blasphemed, he shook his raiment, and said unto them, Your blood be upon your own heads; I am clean: from henceforth I will go unto the Gentiles.

6. And when they gainsayed, and railed, and blasphemed Christ, he renounced and deserted them by the ceremony of shaking off the dust, as a witness that their destruction was of themselves, and not by his neglect to convince them. And thenceforth he resolved to leave their synagogue and teach the Gentiles.

7. And he departed thence, and entered into a certain man's house, named Justus, one that worshipped God, whose house joined hard to the synagogue.

7. Note, It is like this Justus was a proselyte; if not, he was one that had learned at least to worship the true God.

8. And Crispus the chief ruler of the synagogue, believed on the Lord with all his house: and many of the Corinthians hearing, believed and were baptized.

8. Note, 1. Still we see households are converted and baptized together; the rulers' power and God's blessing prevailing with them. 2. Though the synagogue drove against Paul, the ruler followed him.

9. Then spake the Lord to Paul in the night by a vision, Be not afraid, but speak, and hold not thy peace: 10. For I am with thee, and no man shall set on thee to hurt thee: for I have much people in this city.

9. Note, 1. It is an ungrounded exposition of them that say that these were God's people, as pious men before, (though some proselytes might be such) or that God only foreknew their conversion, and did not decree to cause it: God had many there whom he decreed to convert; and therefore will have Paul to preach to them, and will secure him from persecutions.

11. And he continued there a year and six months, teaching the word of God among them.

11. Note, 1. Great works must have answerable time and labour. 2. There is mention of Paul, Silas, Timothy, Aquila, Luke, and many other such, at Corinth: but of no one that was sole bishop over the rest.

12. And when Gallio was the deputy of Achaia, the Jews made insurrection with one accord against Paul, and brought him to the judgment-seat,

12. They carried him by force before the Roman proconsul to be judged.

13. Saying, This fellow persuadeth men to worship God contrary to the law.

13. Note, Who would think but these men were very godly men themselves, who were so zealous against worshipping of God contrary to the law. And yet they were mere blind, ungodly, malignant persecutors.

14. And when Paul was now about to open his mouth, Gallio said unto the Jews, If it were a matter of wrong or wicked lewdness, O ye Jews, reason would that I should bear with you: 15. But if it be a question of words and names, and of your law, look ye to it; for I will be no judge of such matters.

14. The Roman law enabled not Gallio to decide the Jewish controversies, but to punish men

that wronged one another, or committed any wicked lewdness.

Note, If Christian magistrates were all as wise as these heathens, and would not lend fiery legalists their swords, nor become the executioners of the fury of blind proud zealots, the business would be soon over, and be but a scuffle among themselves.

16. And he drave them from the judgment-seat. 17. Then all the Greeks took Sosthenes, the chief ruler of the synagogue, and beat him before the judgment-seat: and Gallio cared for none of those things.

16, 17. Note, It is like these Greeks were Christian converts: They did ill in exercising revenge.

18. And Paul *after this* tarried *there* yet a good while, and then took his leave of the brethren, and sailed thence into Syria, and with him Priscilla and Aquila: having shorn *his* head in Cenchrea: for he had a vow.

18. Note, It is uncertain whether it was Paul or Aquila, that is said to cut his hair: but it seemeth like to be Aquila. The vow of Nazarites was not to cut their hair, sometime during life, and sometime for a certain time; when it was ended they cut their hair.

19. And he came to Ephesus, and left them there: but he himself entered into the synagogue, and reasoned with the Jews.

19. Note, His renouncing the Jews at Corinth, was not a forsaking them elsewhere.

20. When they desired *him* to tarry longer time with them, he consented not: 21. But bade them farewell, saying, I must by all means keep this feast that cometh, in Jerusalem: but I will return again unto you, if God will. And he sailed from Ephesus. 22. And when he had landed at Cesarea, and gone up, and saluted the church, he went down to Antioch.

22. He went up from Cesarea to Jerusalem, and after returned to Antioch.

23. And after he had spent some time *there*, he departed, and went over all the country of Galatia and Phrygia in order, strengthening all the disciples.

23. To instruct and encourage those before converted, as well as to gather more.

24. And a certain Jew named Apollos, born at Alexandria, an eloquent man, *and* mighty in the scriptures, came to Ephesus. 25. This man was instructed in the way of the Lord; and being fervent in the spirit, he spake and taught diligently the things of the Lord, knowing only the baptism of John.

24, 25. He was well acquainted with the scriptures, and believed so much of Christ as John had preached, and was baptised with his baptism, but wanted yet much of the further knowledge of Christ, and of the Christian baptism.

26. And he began to speak boldly in the synagogue. Whom when Aquila and Priscilla had heard, they took him unto them, and expounded unto him the way of God more perfectly.

26. Note, An eloquent teacher mighty in the scriptures, yet disdaineth not to be better instructed by a tent-maker and his wife.

27. And when he was disposed to pass into Achaia, the brethren wrote, exhorting the disciples to receive him: who, when he was come, helped them much which had believed through grace.

27. They wrote to them to entertain and encourage him; who when he was come, proved a great helper to them that already by the grace of God were made believers.

28. For he mightily convinced the Jews, *and that* publicly, shewing by the scriptures, that Jesus was Christ.

28. For by the advantage of great acquaintance with the scriptures, and his eloquence, he was too hard for the contradicting Jews, and clearly proved to them from the scriptures which they own, that Jesus is the true Messiah or Christ.

CHAP. XIX.

AND it came to pass, that while Apollos was at Corinth, Paul having passed through the upper coasts, came to Ephesus: and finding certain disciples, 2. He said unto them, Have ye received the

Holy Ghost since ye believed? And they said unto him, We have not so much as heard whether there be any Holy Ghost. 3. And he said unto them, Unto what then were ye baptized? And they said, unto John's baptism.

1. He found some that owned the Christian profession. 2. Note, John's preaching was, that the Messiah is now come, and those that repented and believed this, he baptized, though they knew not that Jesus was he: But to many he also pointed to Jesus and said, this is he. And these disciples, it is like, were such: and had learned no more.

4. Then said Paul, John verily baptized with the baptism of repentance, saying unto the people, That they should believe on him which should come after him, that is, on Christ Jesus. 5. When they heard *this*, they were baptized in the name of the Lord Jesus.

4. Paul said, John baptized those who professed repentance and faith in the Messiah as just now at hand, who indeed was Jesus Christ. When these disciples heard that, they were expressly baptized (again) into the name of the Lord Jesus.

6. And when Paul had laid *his* hands upon them the Holy Ghost came on them; and they spake with tongues, and prophesied. 7. And all the men were about twelve.

6, 7. And the miraculous signal gift came on these men, when Paul had laid his hands on them.

Note, The opinion of Marnixius and Beza, that verse 5, was the speech of Paul concerning John's converts, that they were baptized in the name of the Lord Jesus, 1. Is forced, and therefore to be suspected. 2. It is contrary to the context: For [they] in verse 3, and [they] in verse 5, and [them] in verse 6, all plainly speak of the same persons. 3. It is contrary to the history of John's baptism, who baptized multitudes of the common people, soldiers, publicans, and Pharisees, upon a mere profession or repentance, and belief of the Messiah at hand, and is never said to have baptized any into the name of the Lord Jesus. 4. Their reason for it is contrary to the doctrine of Christianity, as if John's baptism were so much the same with Christ's, that it is not to be perfected by the latter. If any one then or now were baptized only by John's baptism, he ought to be baptized again. It is essential to Christian baptism, to be baptized into the name of the Father, and of the Son, (as buried and risen with him) and of the Holy Ghost. But John's baptism had not all this. Therefore it is not the (now) Christian baptism.

8. And he went into the synagogue, and spake boldly for the space of three months, disputing and persuading the things concerning the kingdom of God.

8. Note, The gospel is the doctrine of God's reign by the Messiah.

9. But when divers were hardened, and believed not, but spake evil of that way before the multitude, he departed from them, and separated the disciples, disputing daily in the school of one Tyrannus.

9. The ears of Christians being unfit to bear their reproaching and blaspheming of Christ, he separated the disciples from the public synagogue of the Jews to a private school.

10. And this continued by the space of two years; so that all they which dwelt in Asia, heard the word of the Lord Jesus, both Jews and Greeks.

10. By two years teaching and disputing, the gospel was spread through all Asia proconsular.

11. And God wrought special miracles by the hands of Paul: 12. So that from his body were brought unto the sick, handkerchiefs or aprons, and the diseases departed from them, and the evil spirits went out of them.

11, 12. So many and great were the miracles and cures done by Paul's means, that his corporal presence could not serve all, but by clothes sent from his body they at a distance were cured.

13. Then certain of the vagabond Jews, exorcists, took upon them to call over them which had evil spirits, the name of the Lord Jesus, saying, We adjure you by Jesus, whom Paul preacheth. 14. And there were seven sons of *one* Sceva a Jew, *and* chief of the priests which did so.

13. Seven sons of one of the Jews' chief priests, being vagabonds, exorcists that pretended to conjure out devils, seeing Paul's miracles, had (like Simon Magus) a desire to do the like, and thought that saying the same words would serve without the same faith and grace (as hypocrites do in the matters of salvation.)

15. And the evil spirit answered and said, Jesus I know, and Paul I know; but who are ye? 16. And

the man in whom the evil spirit was, leapt on them, and overcame them, and prevailed against them, so that they fled out of that house naked and wounded.

15. Words without faith would not work to cast out devils, and Christ would not give power to his name used as a charm: but Satan strengthened the man to wound and shame them.

17. And this was known to all the Jews and Greeks also dwelling at Ephesus; and fear fell on them all, and the name of the Lord Jesus was magnified.

17. This being commonly known, the name of Christ was more reverenced and honoured.

18. And many that believed came, and confessed, and shewed their deeds.

18. Many converts openly confessed their former evil deeds.

19. Many also of them which used curious arts, brought their books together, and burned them before all men: and they counted the price of them, and found it fifty thousand *pieces* of silver. 20. So mightily grew the word of God, and prevailed.

19. To shew the truth of their repentance by the renunciation of their former delusions, and that no men else might be hurt by their ill books, or make an ill use of them, they would not sell but burn their books of magic, and charms, and idolatrous rites, and divination; though the price amounted to a very great sum (not pretending as Judas, that this money might have been given to the poor.) This shewed the power of God's word and grace, which so prevailed against delusions and the love of money.

21. After these things were ended, Paul purposed in the spirit, when he had passed through Macedonia, and Achaia, to go to Jerusalem, saying, After I have been there, I must also see Rome. 22. So he sent into Macedonia two of them that ministered unto him, Timotheus, and Erastus; *but* he himself stayed in Asia for a season.

21. Intending to go to Jerusalem, he sent two that were as servants to him in attending and helping him in his ministry.

23. And the same time there arose no small stir about that way. 24. For a certain man named Demetrius, a silver-smith, which made silver shrines for Diana, brought no small gain unto the craftsmen. 25. Whom he called together with the workmen of like occupation, and said,

23, 24. One whose trade was to make either medals, that had the image of the temple of Diana to sell, or else little boxes in which the image of Diana in her temple was carried about in procession by them.

Note. It is worldly interest and commodity, and love of money, that causeth enmity and persecution against the servants of Christ, who must preach the gospel contrary to this interest.

25. Sirs, ye know that by this craft we have our wealth: 26. Moreover, ye see and hear, that not alone at Ephesus, but almost throughout all Asia, this Paul hath persuaded and turned away much people, saying, that they be no gods which are made with hands: 27. So that not only this our craft is in danger to be set at nought: but also that the temple of the great goddess Diana should be despised, and her magnificence should be destroyed, whom all Asia, and the world worshippeth. 28. And when they heard *these sayings*, they were full of wrath, and cried out, saying, Great *is* Diana of the Ephesians.

25, 26, 27. Note, Arguments from wealth and interest are unanswerable with blinded worldlings, and raise the rage of the rabble against reformation. Here we may see what resisteth reformation in the church of Rome? Can it be hoped that any truth or reason should persuade the pope and cardinals, and all their worldly prelates, to give up their wealth, grandeur, power, and dominion, and all their lay chancellors to surrender with repentance, their gainful usurpation of the power of the keys? And all their courts (called) ecclesiastic, officials, commissaries, surrogates, arch-deacons, and all the multitude of their sub-officers, to become poor by giving over their trade of money-catching? and all their inquisitors to vomit up their blood and gain? And all the crowds of jesuits and friars to lose their revenues and life of ease: and their worldly clergy who live in lazy ignorance and fleshly ease and pleasure, and railing at truth and serious godliness, to become poor and base by renouncing their usurpation, and their maintenances, and domination, which they get by pretending to watch and rule for the saving of the people's souls. What power but God's can overcome all this?

29. And the whole city was filled with confusion: and having caught Gaius and Aristarchus, men of Macedonia, Paul's companions in travail, they rushed with one accord into the theatre. 30. And when Paul would have entered in unto the people, the disciples suffered him not.

29. Interest caused rage and confusion.

31. And certain of the chief of Asia, which were his friends, sent unto him, desiring *him* that he would not adventure himself into the theatre.

31. The theatre was the place where they met to judge offenders, and cast them to wild beasts: And some of the priests or heathen masters of those executions favoured Paul, and dissuaded him from coming.

32. Some therefore cried one thing, and some another: for the assembly was confused, and the more part knew not wherefore they were come together.

32. Note, What reason or justice is to be expected where the ignorant rabble are up and rage?

33. And they drew Alexander out of the multitude, the Jews putting him forward. And Alexander beckoned with the hand, and would have made his defence unto the people. 34. But when they knew that he was a Jew, all with one voice about the space of two hours cried out, Great *is* Diana of the Ephesians.

33. Note, It is like, but not certain, that this Alexander was he that Paul tells Timothy, did him much evil: Whether he were a Jew or a Christian by religion, is uncertain.

35. And when the town-clerk had appeased the people, he said, Ye men of Ephesus, what man is there that knoweth not how that the city of the Ephesians is a worshipper of the great goddess Diana, and of the *image* which fell down from Jupiter? 36. Seeing then that these things cannot be spoken against, ye ought to be quiet, and to do nothing rashly. 37. For ye have brought hither these men, which are neither robbers of churches, nor yet blasphemers of your goddess.

35. Note, It is the office of rulers to appease the rabble's rage by reason and authority. 2. It seems the Christians in wisdom had asserted Christianity without saying much against Diana, which would have enraged the people against them.

38. Wherefore if Demetrius, and the craftsmen which are with him, have a matter against any man, the law is open, and there are deputies: let them implead one another.

38. If they have any action, let it be tried fairly at the judicature by law, and not thus by tumult.

39. But if he inquire any thing concerning other matters, it shall be determined in a lawful assembly.

39. If beside matters of wrong you have any accusation of more public concern, it must be tried in a greater assembly and higher judicature. Note, The higher judicature consisted of fuller assemblies than the lower.

40. For we are in danger to be called in question for this day's uproar, there being no cause whereby we may give an account of this concourse. 41. And when he had thus spoken, he dismissed the assembly.

40. Our superiors are justly jealous of tumults, and we are in danger to be questioned for this, and can give no just reason to excuse it.

CHAP. XX.

AND after the uproar was ceased, Paul called unto him the disciples, and embraced *them*, and departed for to go into Macedonia. 2. And when he had gone over those parts, and had given them much exhortation, he came into Greece. 3. And *there* abode three months:

1 Note, He spared no labour to save souls and gather churches.

3. And when the Jews laid wait for him, as he was about to sail into Syria, he purposed to return through Macedonia. 4. And there accompanied him into Asia, Sopa-

ter of Berea; and of the Thessalonians, Aristarchus, and Secundus; and Gaius of Derbe, and Timotheus; and of Asia, Tychicus and Trophimus. 5. These going before, tarried for us at Troas.

3. Note. The Jews, though nearer in religion than the heathens, yet persecuted the Christians, when the heathens gave them liberty of religion (till Nero's time) even as the Papists do the reformed whom Turks tolerate. 2. Timothy was not now fixed bishop of Ephesus, who travelled with Paul.

6. And we sailed away from Philippi, after the days of unleavened bread, and came unto them to Troas in five days, where we abode seven days. 7. And upon the first *day* of the week, when the disciples came together to break bread, Paul preached unto them, ready to depart on the morrow, and continued his speech until midnight.

7. On the Lord's day when the Christians met as they used to do, to eat a supper together, and the Lord's supper after it, Paul being to depart on the morrow, was the longer in preaching to them even till midnight.

8. And there were many lights in the upper chamber where they were gathered together. 9. And there sat in a window a certain young man, named Eutychus, being fallen into a deep sleep: and as Paul was long preaching, he sunk down with sleep, and fell down from the third loft, and was taken up dead. 10. And Paul went down and fell on him, and embracing *him*, said, Trouble not yourselves; for his life is in him.

8. Note, This accident was to prepare for his delivery.

11. When he therefore was come up again, and had broken bread, and eaten, and talked a long while, even till break of day, so he departed.

11. Note, Grace with persecution made Christians willing of long exercises of religion.

12. And they brought the young man alive, and were not a little comforted.

12. Note, Had he died, some would have said, This is the effect of Christianity; others, This is the fruit of conventicles, and night meetings; others, This is the fruit of long and unseasonable preaching; and they would have been hardened by the scandal.

13. And we went before to ship, and sailed unto Assos, there intending to take in Paul: for so had he appointed, minding himself to go afoot.

13. Note, It was these poor labouring foot preachers that planted the Catholic church, and not mitred pompous princes and lords, or the worldly crew.

14. And when he met with us at Assos, we took him in, and came to Mitylene. 15. And we sailed thence, and came the next *day* over against Chios; and the next *day* we arrived at Samos, and tarried at Trogyllium; and the next *day* we came to Miletus.

16. For Paul had determined to sail by Ephesus, because he would not spend the time in Asia: for he hastened, if it were possible for him to be at Jerusalem the day of Pentecost. 17. And from Miletus he sent to Ephesus, and called the elders of the church.

17. Note, They that tell us that by the elders of the church is meant all the diocesan bishops of Asia, should tell us, 1. Why Luke would not tell us so? 2. Why all Asia is called a church in the singular number, when we never find the churches of Judea, Galatia, or any other country, so called one church? 3. Why the churches of all Asia are summoned as the church of Ephesus? 4. What proof there is of metropolitan churches singularly named in those days? 5. How it would stand with Paul's great haste to congregate all the bishops of Asia; and whether it was done in a day or two? 6. Whether Paul that stayed two or three years at Ephesus did preach through all Asia from house to house, warning every one night and day with tears? 7. Whether this be not good evidence of many elders then at Ephesus alone? 8. Why there is no word of making some one the ruler of all the rest, as their bishop?

18. And when they were come to him, he said unto them, Ye know, from the first day that I came into Asia, after what manner I have been with you at all seasons, 19. Serv-

ing the Lord with all humility of mind, and with many tears and temptations which befel me by the lying in wait of the Jews:

19. Ye know at what rates of danger and suffering I have served God for your salvation, humbly bearing all, &c.

20. *And* how I kept back nothing that was profitable *unto you*, but have shewed you, and have taught you publicly, and from house to house.

20. Not fraudulently concealing any thing profitable to you, nor teaching unprofitable things, but instructing you both in the public assemblies, and from house to house, as I had opportunity.

21. Testifying both to the Jews, and also to the Greeks, repentance toward God, and faith toward our Lord Jesus Christ.

21. The sum of my preaching hath been to draw all men to repent, and turn from sin and vanity to God, as their God, by a lively faith in our Lord Jesus Christ, as the way to the Father.

22. And now behold, I go bound in the spirit unto Jerusalem, not knowing the things that shall befal me there: 23. Save that the Holy Ghost witnesseth in every city, saying, that bonds and afflictions abide me.

22. And now I am going to Jerusalem, by the mission of God's Spirit, who directeth my way in expectation of bonds, not knowing just what and how I shall suffer, but that wherever I come, the Holy Ghost in others that are prophets tells me, that bonds and afflictions must befal me.

24. But none of these things move me, neither count I my life dear unto myself, so that I might finish my course with joy, and the ministry which I have received of the Lord Jesus to testify the gospel of the grace of God.

24. But the expectation of suffering, shaketh not my faith or resolution: for it can but amount to their taking away my life: and I account not my life dear, if I may lay it down in so good a cause, and for so great a benefit, as is the finishing of the race or course of life, which God hath assigned me to, with joy, as one that is past danger and ready to receive the crown, and the full performance of the commission which I have received of the Lord, to proclaim and testify the gospel of grace for the gathering of the church and saving of souls.

Note, 1. Suffering must not shake the trust or resolution of a Christian, especially a minister of Christ. 2. We should not only endeavour to finish our course of Christianity and ministry with fidelity, but also with joy. 3. Good beginnings are not enough without well finishing our course. 4. Life must not be thought too dear to lay down for so desirable an end. 5. Martyrs may end their course with joy.
Qu. How should we finish our course with joy? Answ. 1. Take God and heavenly glory for your all or only happiness, and believe it firmly. 2. Give up yourselves wholly to his love and service without reserve. Live on the meditation of Christ by faith.

25. And now behold, I know that ye all, among whom I have gone preaching the kingdom of God, shall see my face no more.

25. Note, O hear your teachers, as those that shortly shall see their faces on earth no more.

26. Wherefore I take you to record this day, that I am pure from the blood of all men. 27. For I have not shunned to declare unto you all the counsel of God.

26. You are my witnesses, that if any perish it is not long of me, for want of teaching; for I have not concealed from you any truth necessary to your salvation committed to my trust.

28. Take heed therefore unto yourselves, and to all the flock, over the which the Holy Ghost hath made you overseers, to feed the church of God, which he hath purchased with his own blood.

28. Use your greatest care, and watchfulness, and labour, first about yourselves, (that your judgments may be sound, your hearts holy, and your lives exemplary) and then for all the flock (that one flock at Ephesus) over which the Holy Ghost, by his inward qualifying and exciting you, and by his outward call, by the flock and the ordainers, hath made you so many bishops or overseers: spare for no diligence to feed and guide this church of God, which Christ the Son of God hath so much loved, as to purchase it with his own blood.
Note, 1. The work of the ministry is not imperiousness and idleness, but a great care and labour for our own souls and all the flock, whose great danger and necessities require it. O, wo, wo, wo, to idle, worldly, ungodly, treacherous bishops and ministers: 2. He is no true minister as to his own conscience and salvation, who is not made such by the Holy Ghost, though his acts may be valid to the guilty people. 3. Christ's blood hath purchased the church in a fuller sense than he is said to die for all. 4. The blood of Christ may be called the blood of God. 5. The reasons before mentioned make me think that it is the one church of Ephesus, and not all

in Asia that had all these bishops. It is called here the [flock and the church] in the singular number, and I remember not that any church under the gospel is so called, save only a single church, and the universal church, and not a collection of many churches.

29. For I know this, that after my departing shall grievous wolves enter in among you, not sparing the flock.

29. I foreknow that dangerous heretics and tyrannical domineerers will enter, who as wolves, may be known by the mischiefs which they do to the flock.

30. Also of your own selves shall men arise, speaking perverse things, to draw away disciples after them.

30. Even out of your own church (if not of you bishops that hear me) shall some arise, that shall vend unsound and novel doctrines, purposely to draw disciples to admire and follow them : O then, what church can be secure from such hurtful ministers and corruptions?

31. Therefore watch, and remember that by the space of three years, I ceased not to warn every one night and day with tears.

31. Remember my example and imitate it, lest it condemn you, &c. Note, Did Paul warn every one night and day with tears, in a diocese of many hundred parish churches?

32. And now, brethren, I commend you to God, and to the word of his grace, which is able to build you up, and to give you an inheritance among all them which are sanctified.

32. And now brethren, I have no greater benediction for you, nor counsel to you, but that God may be your God, your all, your guide, protector, and reward, and the word of his grace may be your rule, your employment and your trust; which is sufficient in its kind, by the help of the Spirit, to build you yet higher in faith, love, and comfort, and to secure you of the inheritance among the sanctified which it promiseth.

33. I have coveted no man's silver, or gold, or apparel.

33. Note, The worldly self-seekers that cannot say this, are not such as Christ will own or bless.

34. Yea, ye yourselves know, that these hands have ministered unto my necessities, and to them that were with me.

34. Note, Worldly labour for worldly love is sordid in a minister, but in necessity it is laudable.

35. I have shewed you all things, how that so labouring ye ought to support the weak; and to remember the words of the Lord Jesus, how he said, It is more blessed to give than to receive.

35. Note, This labouring of Paul is exemplary to ministers when necessary. 2. If ministers must labour to have to give to the relief of others, how much more others that have not such avocation as the ministerial work? They live wickedly like Sodomites that live idly without any labour profitable to others, merely because they are rich and in no need themselves.

3. It is uncertain whether Paul cite this saying of Christ as verbally told him, though not written, or whether he spake it only as the sense and not the words which are recorded. 4. To be a giver is more honourable than to be a receiver.

36. And when he had thus spoken, he kneeled down, and prayed with them all.

36. Note, Prayer is a meet way of parting with our friends, and shewing our love to them, commending them to God. All things are sanctified by it.

37. And they all wept sore, and fell on Paul's neck, and kissed him, 38. Sorrowing most of all for the words which he spake, that they should see his face no more. And they accompanied him to the ship.

37. Note, Thus love causeth sorrow here, and thus we part at last with our friends with tears and grief with whom we lived with joy. But we shall meet again with greater joy, and never part.

CHAP. XXI.

AND it came to pass, that after we were gotten from them, and had launched, we came with a straight course unto Coos, and the *day* following unto Rhodes, and from thence unto Patara. 2. And finding a ship sailing over unto Phenicia, we went aboard, and set forth. 3. Now when we had discovered Cyprus, we left it on the left hand, and sailed into Syria, and landed at Tyre: for there the ship was to unlade her burden. 4. And finding disciples, we tarried there seven days: who said to Paul through the

Spirit, that he should not go up to Jerusalem.

4. Note, Was the Spirit in Paul and in them contrary? No, but the Spirit in them told them in what danger he would be at Jerusalem, and then they in kindness as men, dissuaded him, but not that the Spirit forbid him, but carried him on to it, and therefore he went on.

5. And when we had accomplished those days, we departed, and went our way, and they all brought us on our way, with wives and children, till *we were* out of the city: and we kneeled down on the shore, and prayed.

5. Note, The loving communion of saints and prayer, are the mark of true disciples. Beza conjectureth that they are called disciples as mere Christians, not ordered into a particular church state: and that they are called the brethren, when associated in church order.

6. And when we had taken our leave one of another, we took ship; and they returned home again. 7. And when we had finished *our* course from Tyre, we came to Ptolemais, and saluted the brethren, and abode with them one day. 8. And the next *day* we that were of Paul's company departed, and came unto Cesarea; and we entered into the house of Philip the evangelist, (which was *one* of the seven) and abode with him.

6. Note, Luke who was one of Paul's ordinary company makes no mention of himself and his own actions and labours, as if he were nobody.

9. And the same man had four daughters, virgins, which did prophesy.

9. Note, Though women were not to speak as teachers in the assemblies, they might have the extraordinary gifts of the Spirit, and speak by inspiration and prediction.

10. And as we tarried *there* many days, there came down from Judea a certain prophet named Agabus. 11. And when he was come unto us, he took Paul's girdle, and bound his own hands and feet, and said, Thus saith the Holy Ghost, so shall the Jews at Jerusalem bind the man that owneth this girdle, and shall deliver *him* into the hands of the Gentiles.

11. Note, God foretelleth his servants' sufferings, not as bidding them avoid them, but as warning them to prepare.

12. And when we heard these things, both we and they of that place, besought him not to go up to Jerusalem.

12. Note, As men, they persuaded him to avoid the danger.

13. Then Paul answered, What mean ye to weep, and to break mine heart? for I am ready not to be bound only, but also to die at Jerusalem for the name of the Lord Jesus.

13. You do but become yourselves the authors of my sufferings: what are bonds, and what is life, that I should not cheerfully entertain them for the name of Jesus my Lord?

Note, The condolence and temptations of compassionate friends, are oft more grievous than persecution.

14. And when he would not be persuaded, we ceased, saying, The will of the Lord be done.

14. We saw by his resolution and unpersuadableness that it was God's will, and we submitted to it.

15. And after those days we took up our carriages, and went up to Jerusalem. 16. There went with us also *certain* of the disciples of Cesarea, and brought with them one Mnason of Cyprus, an old disciple, with whom we should lodge. 17. And when we were come to Jerusalem, the brethren received us gladly.

15. Mnason lodged us, and the church gladly owned us.

18. And the *day* following Paul went in with us unto James; and all the elders were present.

18. Note, They that say, all the elders were all the bishops of Judea, do without proof, feign Paul to have sent word before of his coming, and desired a council to be gathered to entertain him; or else they take all the bishops of Judea to be very gross non-residents, that were all found the first day, so far from their flocks.

19. And when he had saluted

them, he declared particularly what things God had wrought among the Gentiles by his ministry. 20. And when they heard it, they glorified the Lord,

19. They rejoiced and thanked God for the success of the gospel on the Gentiles, and the scattered Jews abroad.

20. And said unto him, Thou seest, brother, how many thousands of Jews there are which believe, and they are all zealous of the law. 21. And they are informed of thee that thou teachest all the Jews which are among the Gentiles, to forsake Moses, saying, that they ought not to circumcise *their* children, neither to walk after the customs.

20, 21. They are told, that thou teachest not only the Gentiles, but the Jews, to forsake circumcision, and Moses' law and the customs.

22. What is it therefore? the multitude must needs come together: for they will hear that thou art come. 23. Do therefore this that we say to thee: we have four men which have a vow on them: 24. Them take, and purify thyself with them, and be at charges with them, that they may shave *their* heads: and all may know, that those things whereof they were informed concerning thee, are nothing, but *that* thou thyself also walkest orderly, and keepest the law.

22. The multitude of Christian Jews will hear of thy coming, deliver them thus from this office; we have four men that made the Nazarites' vows to abstain from some things a certain time, which is now expired, and they are to shave themselves ceremoniously in the temples: go thou with them, and perform there the legal ceremonies of purification, and be at the cost of this solemnity on them, that the people may know that the report of thee is not true, but that thou being a Jew dost thyself keep the law.

Note, The law was by Christ abrogated as to the use of the types and ceremonies, as signifying him that was to come. The political part ceased when their policy was dissolved by their ruin: and the moral natural part Christ continued as his law. And the abrogation of the rest was not fully made known at first, but by degrees; and the exercise of it long tolerated to the Jews.

25. As touching the Gentiles which believe, we have written and concluded, that they observe no such thing, save only that they keep themselves from things offered to idols, and from blood, and from strangled, and from fornication.

25. We intend not this for the Gentiles, nor would bring them under the yoke of Moses' law, &c.

26. Then Paul took the men, and the next day purifying himself with them, entered into the temple, to signify the accomplishment of the days of purification, until that an offering should be offered for every one of them.

26. Paul did as they advised him, and performed all the ceremonies required, and came to the temple to make it known, that the days of purification were accomplished, till they were to offer.

27. And when the seven days were almost ended, the Jews which were of Asia, when they saw him in the temple, stirred up all the people, and laid hands on him, 28. Crying out, Men of Israel, help: this is the man that teacheth all men every where against the people, and the law, and this place: and farther, brought Greeks also into the temple, and hath polluted this holy place. 29. (For they had seen before with him in the city, Trophimus an Ephesian, whom they supposed that Paul had brought into the temple.)

27. Note, Some think that God let out this affliction on Paul, for complying so far to please the people; as if it had been carnal counsel which he followed. But that is not to be supposed, that both the apostles and elders, and he himself, who was guided by the Spirit, should herein err and be misled: this would leave us uncertain of the truth of their writings. But it was the way of fulfilling God's decree; and tells us what a task it is to have to do with such men: whether they be pleased or not, we must suffer by them.

30. And all the city was moved, and the people ran together; and they took Paul, and drew him out of the temple: and forthwith the doors were shut.

30. In blind rage they dragged him out of the temple as a profaner of it.

31. And as they went about to kill him, tidings came unto the chief captain of the band, that all Jerusalem was in an uproar.

31. This sort of zeal maketh men think it no sin but a serving God, to murder the best of saints, as a sacrifice to their holy temple and ceremonies.

32. Who immediately took soldiers, and centurions, and ran down unto them: and when they saw the chief captain and the soldiers, they left beating of Paul.

32. Note, 1. Even a heathen government is better than the popular rage of blind ceremonious superstitious zealots. 2. Heathens are oft the protectors of Christians against the blind rage of those that profess devotion to the same God.

33. Then the chief captain came near, and took him, and commanded *him* to be bound with two chains; and demanded who he was, and what he had done. 34. And some cried one thing, some another, among the multitude: and when he could not know the certainty for the tumult, he commanded him to be carried into the castle.

33, 34. A heathen would hear the cause before he judges it, when superstitious zealots execute before they try or hear.

35. And when he came upon the stairs, so it was, that he was borne of the soldiers, for the violence of the people. 36. For the multitude of the people followed after, crying, Away with him.

35. The heathen soldiers were fain by force, to carry and guard him from these hypocrites.

37. And as Paul was to be led into the castle, he said unto the chief captain, May I speak unto thee? Who said, Canst thou speak Greek? 38. Art not thou that Egyptian which before these days madest an uproar, and leddest out into the wilderness four thousand men that were murderers.

37, 38. The tumult about him made him suspect him to be an incendiary that had lately raised sedition.

39. But Paul said, I am a man which am a Jew of Tarsus. *a city* in Cilicia, a citizen of no mean city; and I beseech thee, suffer me to speak unto the people. 40. And when he had given him licence, Paul stood on the stairs, and beckoned with the hand unto the people: and when there was made a great silence, he spake unto them in the Hebrew tongue, saying,

39, 40. When he had given him leave to speak, and procured silence and audience by his authority, which else the multitude of legal zealots would not have granted him, he spake to them in the Chaldee tongue then called the Hebrew, because it was understood by a greater number than the Greek. This sheweth that Greek was not then most common.

CHAP. XXII.

MEN, brethren, and fathers, hear ye my defence *which I make* now unto you, (2. And when they heard that he spake in the Hebrew tongue to them, they kept the more silence: and he saith,) 3. I am verily a man which am a Jew, born in Tarsus, *a city* in Cilicia, yet brought up in this city, at the feet of Gamaliel, *and* taught according to the perfect manner of the law of the fathers, and was zealous towards God, as ye all are this day.

3. I am a Jew, brought up a disciple of Gamaliel, under the same laws and customs, and as zealous for God in your way, as you now are.

4. And I persecuted this way unto the death, binding and delivering into prisons both men and women.

4. And as you are affected with zealous cruelty now against Christians, so was I then, and persecuted them even to death, binding and delivering them into prison, both men and women.

5. As also the high priest doth bear me witness, and all the estate of the elders: from whom also I received letters unto the brethren, and went to Damascus, to bring them which were there, bound unto Jerusalem, for to be punished.

5. The high priest and all the council of elders (called the Sanhedrim) know this, from whom I

had letters authorising me to bring them prisoners to Jerusalem to be punished.

6. And it came to pass, that as I made my journey, and was come nigh unto Damascus about noon, suddenly there shone from heaven a great light round about me. 7. And I fell unto the ground, and heard a voice saying unto me, Saul, Saul, why persecutest thou me?

6, 7. I saw a light, and heard a voice, &c.
Note, When Christ will speak in power and terror, he will cast down the proudest persecutor. 8. Christ taketh the persecuting of his servants, and striving against his gospel, as persecuting himself, it being against his friends and for his cause.

8. And I answered, Who art thou, Lord? And he said unto me, I am Jesus of Nazareth whom thou persecutest.

8. Note, Did persecutors know Christ aright, and know that it is him in his servants whom they persecute, they durst not, they would not do it.

9. And they that were with me, saw indeed the light, and were afraid; but they heard not the voice of him that spake to me.

9. They saw the light, and heard the sound (like thunder) but saw no man, nor heard the voice and words that were spoken to me, and which I heard.

10. And I said, What shall I do, Lord? And the Lord said unto me, Arise, and go into Damascus, and there it shall be told thee of all things which are appointed for thee to do.

10. I will not this way by voice from heaven, tell thee thy duty, I have established the way of notifying it by my ministers and Spirit: go to Damascus, and I will send thee a teacher.
Note, Souls duly humbled are ready to do any thing that God would have them do.

11. And when I could not see for the glory of that light, being led by the hand of them that were with me, I came into Damascus.

11. Note, God made the light itself to blind him, as an emblem of his persecuting blindness.

12. And one Ananias, a devout man according to the law, having a good report of all the Jews which dwelt *there*, 13. Came unto me, and stood, and said unto me, Brother Saul, receive thy sight. And the same hour I looked up upon him.

12. Ananias a zealous Jew, though a Christian, well spoken of by the Jews themselves, was sent to restore my sight, &c.

14. And he said, The God of our fathers hath chosen thee, that thou shouldest know his will, and see that Just One, and shouldest hear the voice of his mouth. 15. For thou shalt be his witness unto all men, of what thou hast seen and heard.

14, 15. It is the free grace and will of God that hath chosen thee to see Christ, (whom thou persecutest) and to hear his voice from heaven; and to be his witness of what thou hast seen and heard.
Note, Paul is a full instance of God's special electing grace.

16. And now why tarriest thou? arise, and be baptized, and wash away thy sins, calling on the name of the Lord.

16. Delay not, but presently repent and believe in Christ, and give up thyself to him in his baptismal covenant, and as the water washeth his body, his pardoning grace, through the merits of his blood and righteousness, shall wash away the guilt of thy sins: and call on the Lord for mercy and for his Spirit.

17. And it came to pass that when I was come again to Jerusalem, even while I prayed in the temple, I was in a trance; 18. And saw him, saying unto me, Make haste, and get thee quickly out of Jerusalem: for they will not receive thy testimony concerning me.

17. Note, God that foreknew that the Jews would obstinately reject Paul, directed his ministry from them elsewhere.

19. And I said, Lord, they know that I imprisoned, and beat in every synagogue, them that believed on thee. 20. And when the blood of thy martyr Stephen was shed, I also was standing by, and consenting unto his death, and kept the raiment of them that slew him.

19, 20. Lord, sure they will not hear me without prejudice, who have as hotly persecuted thy servants, as they do.

21. And he said unto me, Depart: for I will send thee far hence unto the Gentiles.

21. I have other work for thee to do elsewhere with more success.

22. And they gave him audience unto this word, and *then* lift up their voices, and said, Away with such a fellow from the earth: for it is not fit that he should live.

22. Note, 1. Of how little credit is the judgment of blinded wicked men, of God's servants? When they judge them unfit to live on earth, it signifieth no guilt in them, but their own madness.

23. And as they cried out, and cast off *their* clothes, and threw dust into the air. 24. The chief captain commanded him to be brought into the castle, and bade that he should be examined by scourging: that he might know wherefore they cried so against him.

23, 24. Note, What usage God's servants must look for in the world: the legalists rage as the devils' bedlams, and the heathen judge who was just, and preserved him, yet would scourge him on presumption before he heard his cause, but there is at hand a final judgment, where all these bedlams and tyrants shall be cast.

25. And as they bound him with thongs, Paul said unto the centurion that stood by, is it lawful for you to scourge a man that is a Roman, and uncondemned?

26. As they prepared his body to be scourged, he said, Is it not against your law to scourge a man uncondemned, who is a denizen of the Roman privileges.

26. When the centurion heard *that*, he went and told the chief captain, saying, Take heed what thou doest; for this man is a Roman. 27. Then the chief captain came, and said unto him, Tell me, art thou a Roman? He said, Yea. 28. And the chief captain answered, With a great sum obtained I this freedom. And Paul said, But I was *free*-born.

26. Art thou a Roman, denizen! Note, Tarsus

was a city that was enfranchised with the Roman privileges.

29. Then straightway they departed from him which should have examined him: and the chief captain also was afraid after he knew that he was a Roman, and because he had bound him.

29. Note, The fear of man's laws hath more power with worldly men, than the fear of God.

30. On the morrow, because he would have known the certainty wherefore he was accused of the Jews, he loosed him from *his* bands, and commanded the chief priests and all their council to appear, and brought Paul down, and set him before them.

30. He would hear him and them together.

CHAP. XXIII.

AND Paul earnestly beholding the council, said, Men *and* brethren, I have lived in all good conscience before God, until this day.

1. Quest. Did Paul persecute with a good conscience? Answ. He went according to his conscience, though in sinful ignorance.

2. And the high priest Ananias commanded them that stood by him, to smite him on the mouth.

2. Note, The usual justice of proud archpriests, whose will is instead of reason and equity.

3. Then said Paul unto him, God shall smite thee, thou whited wall: for sittest thou to judge me after the law, and commandest me to be smitten contrary to the law? 4. And they that stood by, said, Revilest thou God's high priest?

3. Note, The gross injustice of the archpriest is not blamed by them, but Paul taken as criminal for reproving it.

5. Then said Paul, I wist not brethren, that he was the high priest: For it is written, Thou shalt not speak evil of the ruler of thy people.

5. Note, Some think that Paul confesseth him

self guilty of rashness or passion: but others rather think that he spake but ironically, Ananias being indeed no high priest but an usurper; but yet it was not prudence for Paul openly to say so: q. d. [I knew not that he was the true high priest, for he was not: and I confess it a sin to revile rulers, for it is forbidden:] but it is no sin to vindicate innocency, and declare the unrighteousness of oppressors, and prophetically to foretel God's judgments against them. Christ said more who never sinned, and was made under the law, rulers are not unreprovable.

6. But when Paul perceived that the one part were Sadducees, and the other Pharisees, he cried out in the council, Men *and* brethren, I am a Pharisee, the son of a Pharisee: of the hope and resurrection of the dead, I am called in question.

6. He took the advantage of their own differences, to draw the Pharisees to favour him, and to turn their opposition against each other. He spake nothing but the truth, but he left out one half of the truth, and so it was a sort of equivocation; which is a speaking part of the truth and concealing another part, knowing that the hearer will thence misunderstand it: this is a fault when we are obliged to declare the whole, or when it is injurious to the hearers or to the truth, but by concealment to occasion other men's error or deceit, is not always a sin.

7. And when he had so said, there arose a dissention between the Pharisees and the Sadducees; and the multitude was divided. 8. For the Sadducees say, that there is no resurrection, neither angel nor spirit; but the Pharisees confess both.

8. How bad a state was the Jewish church in, when men that believed no life but this, had equal power with the rest in priesthood and government! 2. What hypocrites were these Pharisees that could thus embody with damnable heretics, and yet could not endure Christians, but silenced and murdered them, like the Papist prelates, who can endure Jews and Atheists, while they burn and silence Protestants.

9. And there arose a great cry: and the scribes *that were* of the Pharisees part arose, and strove, saying, We find no evil in this man: but if a spirit or an angel hath spoken to him, let us not fight against God.

9. Note, See how partiality will change men's judgments according to the interest of a party or faction.

10. And when there arose a great dissention, the chief captain fearing lest Paul should have been pulled in pieces of them, commanded the soldiers to go down, and take him by force from among them, and to bring him into the castle. 11. And the night following, the Lord stood by him, and said, Be of good cheer, Paul: for as thou hast testified of me in Jerusalem, so must thou bear witness also at Rome.

11. Note, God's encouragements accompany his commands and faithful service.

12. And when it was day, certain of the Jews banded together, and bound themselves under a curse, saying, that they would neither eat nor drink till they had killed Paul.

12. Note, Seeing the Pharisees now spake for him, it seems all or most of these furious men were Sadducees: who were then the strongest party. And even to this day, those that believe no life to come are the most cruel enemies of believers; and what should deter such from bloody vows, conspiracies, and perjuries, when yet only devilish malice doth provoke them?

13. And there were more than forty which had made this conspiracy. 14. And they came to the chief priests and elders, and said, We have bound ourselves under a great curse, that we will eat nothing until we have slain Paul. 15. Now therefore ye with the council, signify to the chief captain, that he bring him down unto you to-morrow, as though ye would inquire something more perfectly concerning him: and we, or ever he come near, are ready to kill him.

15. O what a clergy was this, that must head a confederacy of murdering Sadducees.

16. And when Paul's sister's son heard of their lying in wait, he went and entered into the castle, and told Paul. 17. Then Paul called one of the centurions unto him, and said, Bring this young man unto the chief captain: for he hath a certain thing to tell him. 18. So he took him, and brought him to the chief captain, and said, Paul the prisoner called me unto him,

and prayed me to bring this young man unto thee, who hath something to say unto thee. 19. Then the chief captain took him by the hand, and went *with him* aside privately, and asked *him*, What is that thou hast to tell me? 20. And he said, The Jews have agreed to desire thee, that thou wouldest bring down Paul to-morrow into the council, as though they would inquire somewhat of him more perfectly. 21. But do not thou yield unto them: for there lie in wait for him of them more than forty men, which have bound themselves with an oath, that they will neither eat nor drink till they have killed him: and now are they ready, looking for a promise from thee.

16. Note, 1. No conspiracies are kept secret from God, who can detect and frustrate them. 2. No doubt but these men that could vow to satisfy rage, did break it rather than famish.

22. So the chief captain *then* let the young man depart, and charged *him*, *See thou* tell no man that thou hast shewed these things to me. 23. And he called unto him two centurions, saying, Make ready two hundred soldiers to go to Cesarea, and horsemen threescore and ten, and spearmen two hundred, at the third hour of the night. 24. And provide *them* beasts, that they may set Paul on, and bring *him* safe unto Felix the governor.

Note, Thus God raised forces of heathens to defend his servant.

25. And he wrote a letter after this manner: 26. Claudius Lysias, unto the most excellent governor Felix, *sendeth* greeting. 27. This man was taken of the Jews, and should have been killed of them: then came I with an army, and rescued him, having understood that he was a Roman. 28. And when I would have known the cause wherefore they accused him, I brought him forth into their council: 29. Whom I perceived to be accused of questions of their law, but to have nothing laid to his charge worthy of death or of bonds. 30. And when it was told me, how that the Jews laid wait for the man, I sent him straightway to thee, and gave commandment to his accusers also, to say before thee what *they had* against him. Farewel.

Note, This Colonel, that by a band of soldiers rescued him, judgeth him guiltless as to the Roman law.

31. Then the soldiers, as it was commanded them, took Paul and brought *him* by night to Antipatris. 32. On the morrow they left the horsemen to go with him, and returned to the castle. 33. Who when they came to Cesarea, and delivered the epistle to the governor, presented Paul also before him. 34. And when the governor had read *the letter*, he asked of what province he was. And when he understood that he was of Cilicia; 35. I will hear thee, said he, when thine accusers are also come. And he commanded him to be kept in Herod's judgment-hall.

35. Note, A place called Herod's hall. Not that he was there. Thus God carried on Paul toward Rome to fulfil his will and word.

CHAP. XXIV.

AND after five days, Ananias the high priest descended with the elders, and *with* a certain orator *named* Tertullus, who informed the governor against Paul.

1. Note, Tertullus was the malignant lawyer or orator, who was to plead their charge against Paul, if not of mere malice, at least for his fee. The accusation is given in, and hotly prosecuted by the high priest and elders: Dr. Hammond thought that the word [elders] in the Christian church never signified any but bishops (such as we now call diocesan.) And it is undoubted that the church borrowed that title from the Jews' elders, and therefore meant some similitude of offices (allowing the difference of materials and law.) And then it would follow that the Jews' elders that made their council, were the Jewish bishops of several distant cities gathered together

at Jerusalem: and so, that it was the Jews' archbishop and all the bishops under him, that were these malignant diabolical accusers and persecutors: but the Jewish elders were not such city bishops, but a conjunction of laymen and priests in a supreme council at Jerusalem, and inferior councils in cities, where were synagogues.

2. And when he was called forth, Tertullus began to accuse *him*, saying, Seeing that by thee we enjoy great quietness, and that very worthy deeds are done unto this nation by thy providence, 3. We accept *it* always, and in all places, most noble Felix, with all thankfulness.

2, 3. To win the judge by flattery, hath ever by false accusers, been taken for the surest way for success.

4. Notwithstanding, that I be not further tedious unto thee, I pray thee, that thou wouldest hear us of thy clemency a few words. 5. For we have found this man a pestilent fellow, and a mover of sedition among all the Jews throughout the world, and a ringleader of the sect of the Nazarenes;

5. We have found this man a very plague, &c. Note, This part of the accusation is, 1. In general that he was a very walking pestilence: O what diabolism is it to judge thus of the preachers of love, and mercy, and salvation? 2. Particularly, i. A mover of sedition among all the Jews through the Roman empire: so Christian reformation must be called sedition, to stir up rulers against it, as defenders of the common peace: and this to Felix was a potent argument, for he had been put to conquer and destroy one Eleazar, that came out of Egypt as a pretended prophet, and gathered an army of seditious cutthroats that endangered the peace. 2. The second accusation was, that he was a leader of a sect or schism, calling the Christians Nazarenes in scorn, from Nazareth where Christ dwelt.

6. Who also hath gone about to profane the temple: whom we took, and would have judged according to our law.

6. The third part of the accusation was profaning the temple: Note, Would not these infidels be thought holy men: they were zealous for temple, law, and ceremonies, against Christianity, holiness, innocency, and the lives of the best of men.

7. But the chief captain Lysias came upon us, and with great violence took *him* away out of our hands,

2.

7. Note, To save the innocent from the violence of wicked priests, is accused as violence even in a governor.

8. Commanding his accusers to come unto thee: by examining of whom, thyself mayest take knowledge of all these things, whereof we accuse him. 9. And the Jews also assented, saying, that these things were so.

8, 9. Note, Seeing the judgments of men are so contrary, that he is a seditious plague and sectary to one, that is one of the best on earth to another: alas, how shall the people know who to believe? The histories of liars are stuffed with lies: and how can strangers and posterity know who were the liars? This is a great shake to the credit of most history. But the haters of holiness are seldom to be believed.

10. Then Paul, after that the governor had beckoned unto him to speak, answered, Forasmuch as I know that thou hast been of many years a judge unto this nation, I do the more cheerfully answer for myself: 11. Because that thou mayest understand, that there are yet but twelve days since I went up to Jerusalem for to worship.

10. Thou knowest their customs, had I been such a one as they accuse me to be, what should move me to come so far from other countries, but twelve days ago, to keep the feast of Pentecost, and to worship at Jerusalem.

12. And they neither found me in the temple disputing with any man, neither raising up the people, neither in the synagogues, nor in the city: 13. Neither can they prove the things whereof they now accuse me.

12. I was only worshipping in the temple, and deny that I did any thing to move sedition, as they accuse me.

13. But this I confess unto thee, that after the way which they call heresy, so worship I the God of my fathers, believing all things which are written in the law and the prophets.

14. I am not ashamed to own it, that I worship God as a Christian, in the way that they call a heresy or sect, for I believe the law and the prophets who teach it me

15. And have hope towards God, which they themselves also allow, that there shall be a resurrection of the dead, both of the just and unjust.

15. *The resurrection of Christ confirmeth my belief of the resurrection of the dead, &c.*
Note, 1. The doctrine of a resurrection of the just only, was not then owned by the Jews. 2. It seems by this time the Pharisees joined in his persecution, though before they excused him in contention with the Sadducees.

16. And herein do I exercise myself to have always a conscience void of offence toward God, and toward men.

16. *And in this hope of a resurrection and the Christian faith, my daily care and exercise is, to keep myself from offending God or man by any sin, that my conscience may not be my accuser.*

17. Now after many years, I came to bring alms to my nation, and offerings.

17. *To bring alms and offerings is no prophaneness or sedition, &c.*

18. Whereupon certain Jews from Asia found me purified in the temple, neither with multitude, nor with tumult. 19. Who ought to have been here before thee, and object, if they had ought against me.

18, 19. *These Asian Jews falsely thought that I had brought Trophimus into the temple: and it being they that are the first accusers and witnesses, they should have been here.*

20. Or else let these same here say, if they have found any evil-doing in me, while I stood before the council, 21. Except it be for this one voice, that I cried standing among them, Touching the resurrection of the dead, I am called in question by you this day.

20. *As to any thing that I did in the council let them witness what they can against me: they have nothing to charge me with, but that I said, touching the resurrection of the dead, I am accused: I meant Christ's resurrection as the cause and pledge of ours.*
Note, Some think that Paul here confesseth it a fault, that he equivocated to set them together by the ears, as being an act of carnal wisdom and an obscuring of his confession of Christ. But most expositors rather think that he spake this ironically, as if he had said, unless they will make it a fault, that I said, I am called in question about the resurrection, they can charge me with none there.

22. And when Felix heard these things, having more perfect knowledge of that way, he deferred them, and said, When Lysias the chief captain shall come down, I will know the uttermost of your matter.

22. *He said, when I have got a more perfect knowledge of this way of Christianity, and how far it is against your law, and when I have spoke with Colonel Lysias of the tumults, I will judge the cause, which yet I cannot do.*

23. And he commanded a centurion to keep Paul, and to let him have liberty, and that he should forbid none of his acquaintance to minister or come unto him.

23. *To secure him as a prisoner at large.*

24. And after certain days, when Felix came with his wife Drusilla, which was a Jewess, he sent for Paul, and heard him concerning the faith in Christ. 25. And as he reasoned of righteousness, temperance, and judgment to come, Felix trembled, and answered, Go thy way for this time: when I have a convenient season I will call for thee.

24, 25. *Note, Felix is noted by the historians of those times to be specially guilty of two crimes: injustice through covetousness, and incontinence, taking another man's wife: (This Drusilla the niece of Anthony and Cleopatra.) And so the subject moved his conscience to make him tremble.*
Note, O the strength of sin that will live, even when men tremble for fear of judgment.

26. He hoped also that money should have been given him of Paul that he might loose him: wherefore he sent for him the oftener, and communed with him.

26. *Note, All his trembling overcame not the love of money. Money is the worldlings' great mediator.*

27. But after two years Porcius Festus came into Felix' room; and Felix willing to shew the Jews a pleasure, left Paul bound.

27. *His carnal respects to man and fame, and to please the malicious Jews, prevailed against his conscience, and he leaves Paul a prisoner to be judged by Festus his successor, when Paul had been two years kept a prisoner.*

CHAP. XXV.

NOW when Festus was come into the province, after three days he ascended from Cesarea to Jerusalem. 2. Then the high priest, and the chief of the Jews, informed him against Paul, and besought him, 3. And desired favour against him, that he would send for him to Jerusalem, laying wait in the way to kill him.

1, 2, 3. The malicious priests and rulers continue their murderous design, and cannot get a heathen ruler to be so bad as they.

4. But Festus answered, that Paul should be kept at Cesarea, and that he himself would depart shortly thither. 5. Let them therefore, said he, which among you are able, go down with me, and accuse this man, if there be any wickedness in him. 6. And when he had tarried among them more than ten days, he went down unto Cesarea, and the next day sitting in the judgment-seat, commanded Paul to be brought.

4. After ten days he went down and they with him.

7. And when he was come, the Jews which came down from Jerusalem, stood round about, and laid many and grievous complaints against Paul, which they could not prove; 8. While he answered for himself, Neither against the law of the Jews, neither against the temple, nor yet against Cesar, have I offended any thing at all.

7. The diabolists did pretend that he broke their law, profaned their holy temple, and disturbed the peace, as a seditious breaker of Cesar's law: All which he denied, and they could not prove.

Note, It is strange that the devil had not attained to what he hath done in this age, to enable them to prove any thing by perjured witnesses.

9. But Festus, willing to do the Jews a pleasure, answered Paul, and said, Wilt thou go up to Jerusalem, and there be judged of these things before me?

9. The pleasing of the priests and multitude being more to the ruler's carnal interest, than doing justice for one poor man, he would thus have sacrificed him to them.

10. Then said Paul, I stand at Cesar's judgment-seat, where I ought to be judged: to the Jews have I done no wrong, as thou very well knowest. 11. For if I be an offender, or have committed any thing worthy of death, I refuse not to die: but if there be none of these things whereof these accuse me, no man may deliver me unto them. I appeal unto Cesar.

10. Note, Having the Roman privileges, he might appeal to the Roman laws, which then had not condemned Christianity. But doubtless the Jews would call this heathenish, for him to choose rather to be saved by heathens, than to be murdered by Jews. As at this day he that had rather be saved from murder by a Mahometan than murdered or tormented by a Papist, shall be said to be for Mahometanism. And here let them that grudge at Christ, for requiring us to deny our lives for him, and for the heavenly reward, consider that even church-tyrants require as much, and that for nothing, without any such reward: If under their inquisitions, or other persecutions, men do but, as every living creature will do, strive to escape their malice and live, and do not die without any reluctancy, they call them rebels; yea, if they do but groan and complain, it goeth for sedition to feel when they are hurt; when it is the holy church that doeth it: Christ doth not thus condemn sense and natural love of life, in his hardest laws of self-denial.

12. Then Festus when he had conferred with the council, answered, Hast thou appealed unto Cesar? unto Cesar shalt thou go.

1C. Note, They might have constrained him to be judged there: but God over-ruled it, to spread abroad the gospel.

13. And after certain days, king Agrippa and Bernice came unto Cesarea to salute Festus. 14. And when they had been there many days, Festus declared Paul's cause unto the king, saying, There is a certain man left in bonds by Felix: 15. About whom, when I was at Jerusalem, the chief priests and the elders of the Jews informed me, desiring to have judgment against him.

13. Note, This Agrippa was the son of that Herod that was eaten to death by worms, and Bernice was his sister, the wife of Polemon king of

Cilicia, who left her husband, and lived with this brother.

16. To whom I answered, It is not the manner of the Romans to deliver any man to die before that he which is accused, have the accusers face to face, and have licence to answer for himself concerning the crime laid against him.

16. The Jewish religious tyrants had overcome and cast off this law of nature, which the heathens kept.

17. Therefore when they were come hither, without any delay on the morrow, I sat on the judgment-seat, and I commanded the man to be brought forth. 8. Against whom, when the accusers stood up, they brought none accusation of such things as I supposed: 19. But had certain questions against him of their own superstition, and of one Jesus, which was dead, whom Paul affirmed to be alive.

17, 18, 19. Note, These things he made light of, and not understanding them.

20. And because I doubted of such manner of questions, I asked *him* whether he would go to Jerusalem, and there be judged of these matters. 21. But when Paul had appealed to be reserved unto the hearing of Augustus, I commanded him to be kept till I might send him to Cesar.

20. I would have had him tried by the Jews, who understood their own law, &c.

22. Then Agrippa said unto Festus, I would also hear the man myself. To-morrow, said he, thou shalt hear him. 23. And on the morrow when Agrippa was come, and Bernice, with great pomp, and was entered into the place of hearing, with the chief captains, and principal men of the city, at Festus' commandment, Paul was brought forth. 24. And Festus said, King Agrippa, and all men which are here present with us, ye see this man, about whom all the multitude of the Jews have dealt with me, both at Jerusalem, and also here, crying that he ought not to live any longer.

24. Note, The lives of God's best servants are a grief to the malignants.

25. But when I found that he had committed nothing worthy of death, and that he himself hath appealed to Augustus, I have determined to send him.

25. Note, What an odious scandal did these priests cast on God's law, to make it seem worse than heathens' laws!

26. Of whom I have no certain thing to write unto my lord. Wherefore I have brought him forth before you, and specially before thee, O king Agrippa, that after examination had, I might have somewhat to write. 27. For it seemeth to me unreasonable to send a prisoner, and not withal to signify the crimes *laid* against him.

26. Note, Justice is a part of the law of nature known to all.

CHAP. XXVI.

THEN Agrippa said unto Paul, Thou art permitted to speak for thyself. Then Paul stretched forth the hand, and answered for himself.

1. Note, It was the custom by the motion of the hand to give notice when one was beginning to speak, to procure silent audience.

2. I think myself happy, king Agrippa, because I shall answer for myself this day before thee, touching all the things whereof I am accused of the Jews: 3. Especially, because I know thee to be expert in all customs and questions which are among the Jews: wherefore I beseech thee to hear me patiently.

2. It is a great favour for great men so much as to hear an innocent good man speak for himself.

4. My manner of life from my youth, which was at the first among mine own nation at Jerusalem, know all the Jews, 5. Which knew me from the beginning, (if they

would testify) that after the most strictest sect of our religion, I lived a Pharisee. 6. And now I stand and am judged for the hope of the promise made of God unto our fathers: 7. Unto which *promise* our twelve tribes instantly serving *God* day and night, hope to come: for which hope's sake, king Agrippa, I am accused of the Jews.

4. Note, He supposed Agrippa acquainted with the Jewish affairs, of their expectation of the Messiah, and the preaching of Christianity, and the stirs about it. And if the hopes of a Messiah be sedition, all the Jews are guilty of it, that pray for it continually. Qu. Did the ten tribes pray for it, who were carried away by the Assyrians, and idolaters put in their country? Answ. 1. In such captivating transplantation, they never carry away all the poor people that must till the ground, but the rulers, soldiers, great men, and men of note; else it would be the conquerors' loss: So it hath been here, at the conquests made by the Romans, Saxons, and Danes, and Normans: The greater number of the country people still staid as tenants or servants to the conquerors. 2. The neighbourhood of the Jews, did by degrees shame away much of the idolatry of the Israelites: As Josiah's power extended to pull down their idols and altars, and burn men's bones on them. 3. And afterward the Israelites' country, wanting some inhabitants, the Jews by degrees possessed much of their country. And the speech of the Samaritan woman, John iv. sheweth that they commonly expected Christ to come, and tell them all things.

8. Why should it be thought a thing incredible with you, that God should raise the dead?

8. The great point of our controversy now is, Whether Christ rose from the dead? And why should this seem an incredible thing to you? Is it too hard for God who upholdeth all the world, and giveth life to all that live.

9. I verily thought with myself that I ought to do many things contrary to the name of Jesus of Nazareth.

9. I once was of your mind, and did not only set light by the name of Jesus, but thought I ought to set myself against it, and oppose them that preached and professed it.

13. Which thing I also did in Jerusalem: and many of the saints did I shut up in prison, having received authority from the chief priests; and when they were put to death, I gave my voice against them.

10. In this blindness, I was a persecutor of the saints.

11. And I punished them oft in every synagogue, and compelled *them* to blaspheme; and being exceedingly mad against them, I persecuted *them* even unto strange cities.

11. Note, Whether Paul prevailed with any to blaspheme Christ through fear, or only endeavoured it, is uncertain. 2. He now knew that his persecution was from exceeding madness, when yet before he took it for his duty! So blind are persecutors' judgments.

12. Whereupon as I went to Damascus, with authority and commission from the chief priests, 13. At mid-day, O king, I saw in the way a light from heaven, above the brightness of the sun, shining round about me, and them which journeyed with me. 14. And when we were all fallen to the earth, I heard a voice speaking unto me, and saying in the Hebrew tongue, Saul, Saul, why persecutest thou me? *It is* hard for thee to kick against the pricks.

12. I was convinced by this miracle and voice from heaven........ Ignorant man! Dost thou know whom thou persecutest, and why? It will prove to thee but like spurning at thorns with thy bare feet.

Note, Here we find that all Paul's company fell to the ground with him, which is not mentioned chap. ix. or xxii.

15. And I said, Who art thou, Lord? And he said, I am Jesus whom thou persecutest.

15. It is me in my cause and servants that thou persecutest.

16. But rise, and stand upon thy feet: for I have appeared unto thee for this purpose, to make thee a minister and a witness both of these things which thou hast seen, and of those things in the which I will appear unto thee;

16. My appearing to thee is to make thee a preacher of that thou hast persecuted, to witness what thou now hast seen, and what I shall further tell thee by my Spirit and works.

17. Delivering thee from the people, and *from* the Gentiles, unto whom now I send thee, 18. To

open their eyes, and to turn *them* from darkness to light, and *from* the power of Satan unto God, that they may receive forgiveness of sins, and inheritance among them which are sanctified by faith that is in me.

17, 18. Delivering thee both from the Jews and Gentiles, to whom now I command thee to preach, to open the eyes that are blinded in gross ignorance and idolatry, and to turn them from that darkness to the light of the saving knowledge of God and their Redeemer; from the power of Satan whom they serve by sin, to the belief, love, and obedience of God; that they may hereupon receive the forgiveness of all their past sins, and right to the inheritance among the sanctified: Which is here begun in holiness and communion with God and his saints, and hereafter perfected in glory; and all this by believing, trusting, and obeying me, and my gospel, (or by being Christians.)

Note, These words were omitted by Luke, in chap. ix. and xxii. Here is a promise to be trusted, and a command to be obeyed.

19. Whereupon, O king Agrippa, I was not disobedient unto the heavenly vision.

19. I did not, I durst not, rebel against such a vision, and a command from heaven.

20. But shewed first unto them of Damascus, and at Jerusalem, and throughout all the coasts of Judea, and then to the Gentiles, that they should repent and turn to God, and do works meet for repentance.

20. And the gospel which I preached at Damascus, &c. is, That men should repent and turn to God, and shew the sincerity of their repentance by a holy, righteous, charitable and sober life, (and all this in hope of glory, purchased and promised by Christ who thus sent me.)

21. For these causes the Jews caught me in the temple, and went about to kill *me*.

21. This is the true cause why the Jews would have killed me, as crossing their unbelief.

22. Having, therefore, obtained help of God, I continue unto this day, witnessing both to small and great, saying none other things than those which the prophets and Moses did say should come: 23. That Christ should suffer, *and* that he should be the first that should rise from the dead, and should shew light unto the people, and to the Gentiles.

22. God hath kept me through many dangers to this day, while I testify this gospel to all, which is but what was prophesied that Christ should die for our sins, and rise from death and convert the Gentiles.

24. And as he thus spake for himself, Festus said with a loud voice, Paul, thou art beside thyself: much learning doth make thee mad.

24. Thou art a crazed fanatic; much learning or bookishness hath distracted thee.

25. But he said, I am not mad, most noble Festus; but speak forth the words of truth and soberness. 26. For the king knoweth of these things, before whom also I speak freely: for I am persuaded that none of these things are hidden from him; for this thing was not done in a corner.

25, 26. I am not mad, but soberly speak that truth which I supposed the king knoweth; I do not think that the fame of Christ's miracles, death, and resurrection, no, nor of this vision of mine, is unknown to him, being things openly done and famed abroad.

27. King Agrippa, believest thou the prophets? I know that thou believest.

27. If thou believe the prophets, thou mayest see that they prophesied this of Christ.

28. Then Agrippa said unto Paul, Almost thou persuadest me to be a Christian.

28. A little thou persuadest, &c.

Note, It is uncertain whether he spake this seriously as inclining to believe in Christ; Or in contempt. Thou would persuade me that I am almost a Christian.

29. And Paul said, I would to God, that not only thou, but also all that hear me this day, were both almost, and altogether, such as I am, except these bonds.

29. Note, True ministers thirst for men's conversion and salvation.

30. And when he had thus spoken, the king rose up, and the governor, and Bernice, and they that sat with them. 31. And when they were gone aside, they talked between themselves, saying, This man doeth nothing worthy of death,

or of bonds. 32. Then said Agrippa unto Festus, This man might have been set at liberty, if he had not appealed unto Cesar.

30. They acquit him, but discharge him not.

CHAP. XXVII.

AND when it was determined that we should sail into Italy, they delivered Paul and certain other prisoners, unto one named Julius, a centurion of Augustus' band. 2. And entering into a ship of Adramyttium, we launched, meaning to sail by the coasts of Asia, one Aristarchus a Macedonian of Thessalonica, being with us. 3. And the next *day* we touched at Sidon. And Julius courteously entreated Paul, and gave *him* liberty to go unto his friends to refresh himself.

3. Heathen soldiers are less cruel than Jewish superstitious priests and hypocrites.

4. And when we had launched from thence, we sailed unto Cyprus, because the winds were contrary. 5. And when we had sailed over the sea of Cilicia and Pamphylia, we came to Myra *a city* of Lycia. 6. And there the centurion found a ship of Alexandria sailing into Italy; and he put us therein. 7. And when we had sailed slowly many days, and scarce were come over against Cnidus, the wind not suffering us, we sailed under Crete, over against Salmone: 8. And hardly passing it, came unto a place which is called, The fair havens, nigh whereunto was the city of Lasea.

Note, God caused these difficulties to manifest his merciful providence.

9. Now when much time was spent, and when sailing was now dangerous, because the fast was now already past, Paul admonished *them,* 10. And said unto them, Sirs, I perceive that this voyage will be with hurt and much damage, not only of the lading and ship, but also of our lives.

9. At the time of the Jews' yearly fast of expiation, which was in part of our October, sailing used to be very dangerous on those seas.

11. Nevertheless, the centurion believed the master and the owner of the ship, more than those things which were spoken by Paul. 12. And because the haven was not commodious to winter in, the more part advised to depart thence also, if by any means they might attain to Phenice, *and there* to winter; which is an haven of Crete, and lieth toward the south-west, and north-west.

12. Note, Phœnice a haven-town is described, to distinguish it from the country called Phœnice.

13. And when the south-wind blew softly, supposing that they had obtained *their* purpose, loosing *thence* they sailed close by Crete. 14. But not long after there arose against it a tempestuous wind, called Euroclydon. 15. And when the ship was caught, and could not bear up into the wind, we let *her* drive. 16. And running under a certain island which is called Clauda, we had much work to come by the boat: 17. Which when they had taken up, they used helps, undergirding the ship; and fearing lest they should fall into the quicksands, strake sail, and so were driven. 18. And we being exceedingly tossed with a tempest, the next *day* they lightened the ship; 19. And the third *day* we cast out with our own hands the tackling of the ship.

Note, They cast away all to save themselves: All that a man hath will he give for his life. And yet the ungodly sell their souls for nothing.

20. And when neither sun nor stars in many days appeared, and no small tempest lay on *us,* all hope that we should be saved, was then taken away.

20. All hope that could be grounded on visible probability.

21. But after long abstinence, Paul stood forth in the midst of them, and said, Sirs, ye should have hearkened unto me, and not have loosed from Crete, and to have gained this harm and loss.

21. To have escaped this loss.

22. And now I exhort you to be of good cheer: for there shall be no loss of *any man's* life among you, but of the ship. 23. For there stood by me this night the angel of God, whose I am, and whom I serve, 24. Saying, Fear not, Paul; thou must be brought before Cesar: and lo, God hath given thee all them that sail with thee.

23. Note, 1. God useth his angel for the safety and comfort of his servants; 2. Paul mentioneth God in his relations to us; 1. He is our owner, whose we are? 2. Our ruler, whom we serve; and it is implied, our father, and protector, in whom we trust.
3. Many bad men fare the better, for one good man that is among them.

25. Wherefore sirs, be of good cheer: for I believe God, that it shall be even as it was told me. 26. Howbeit we must be cast upon a certain island.

25. I trust my God, and would have you trust him.

27. But when the fourteenth night was come, as we were driven up and down in Adria about midnight, the shipmen deemed that they drew near to some country: 28. And sounded, and found it twenty fathoms: and when they had gone a little further, they sounded again, and found it fifteen fathoms. 29. Then fearing lest they should have fallen upon rocks, they cast four anchors out of the stern, and wished for the day.

29. They stopped the ship and durst go no further.

30. And as the shipmen were about to flee out of the ship, when they had let down the boat into the sea, under colour as though they would have cast anchors out of the foreship, 31. Paul said to the centurion, and to the soldiers, Except these abide in the ship, ye cannot be saved.

30. Note, God that decreed that they should not perish, decreed also that the skilful seamen should abide in the ship. Means and end are in the same decree.

32. Then the soldiers cut off the ropes of the boat, and let her fall off. 33. And while the day was coming on, Paul besought them all to take meat, saying, This day is the fourteenth day that ye have tarried, and continued fasting, having taken nothing. 34. Wherefore I pray you to take *some* meat; for this is for your health: for there shall not an hair fall from the head of any of you.

33. Note, Not that they had eat nothing in fourteen days; But say some expositors, no set meal, or so little as was next to nothing; but others more probably say, [you have eaten nothing all this (one) day, expecting the fourteenth day as critical.]

35. And when he had thus spoken he took bread, and gave thanks to God in presence of them all, and when he had broken *it*, he began to eat.

35. Note, If those in England that scorn at open thanksgiving to God, even at noble tables and great feasts, and think it deserveth a prison for more than four to be present at such a religious exercise, had been in this ship, or in Jonas', fear might have taught them better.

36. Then were they all of good cheer, and they also took *some* meat. 37. And we were in all in the ship, two hundred threescore and sixteen souls.

37. Note, And thou Paul preached to them, the honest heathens accused him not for a conventicle; what shall we think the priests would have done, had they been now among them.

38. And when they had eaten enough, they lightened the ship, and cast out the wheat into the sea.

38, Note, Even future provision is cast away to save life at present. That is a duty in such a case of necessity, which in other cases would have been a great sin.

39. And when it was day, they

knew not the land: but they discovered a certain creek with a shore, into the which they were minded, if it were possible to thrust in the ship. 40. And when they had taken up the anchors, they committed *themselves* unto the sea, and loosed the rudder-bands, and hoisted up the main-sail to the wind, and made toward shore. 41. And falling into a place where two seas met, they ran the ship aground; and the forepart stuck fast, and remained unmoveable, but the hinder part was broken with the violence of the waves.

39. This was a shallow near a neck of land called an isthmus, where the sea is on both sides of it. The Malthasses call it to this day St. Paul's landing place.

42. And the soldiers' counsel was to kill the prisoners, lest any of them should swim out and escape.

42. Note, Lest they should have been punished for letting them escape, they would have killed them.

43. But the centurion willing to save Paul, kept them from *their* purpose, and commanded that they which could swim, should cast *themselves* first into the sea, and get to land: 44. And the rest, some on boards, and some on *broken pieces* of the ship: and so it came to pass, that they escaped all safe to land.

43. Note, God gave them their lives for a prey.

CHAP. XXVIII.

AND when they were escaped, then they knew that the island was called Melita, 2. And the barbarous people shewed us no little kindness; for they kindled a fire, and received us every one, because of the present rain, and because of the cold.

1. Note, There are two islands of this name: and it is a controversy which is meant: but Beza and others shew great probability that it is that called Maltha, now possessed by Christians, as a fort against the Turks.

3. And when Paul had gathered a bundle of sticks, and laid them on the fire, there came a viper out of the heat, and fastened on his hand.

3. Note, Not that Paul carried the adder or viper among the sticks into a chimney; but they made the fire in some open place where the adder lay, and was forced out by the heat.

4. And when the barbarians saw the venomous beast hang on his hand, they said among themselves, No doubt this man is a murderer, whom though he hath escaped the sea, yet vengeance suffereth not to live.

4. Note, Even these barbarians believed God to be the revenger of murder: and yet the priests took the murder of Christ and his disciples for a meritorious work, and zealously pursued it.

5. And he shook off the beast into the fire, and felt no harm. 6. Howbeit they looked when he should have swollen, or fallen down dead suddenly: but after they had looked a great while, and saw no harm come to him, they changed their minds, and said that he was a god.

5. Note, So mutable is vulgar judgment.

7. In the same quarters were possessions of the chief man of the Island, whose name was Publius, who received us and lodged us three days courteously. 8. And it came to pass that the father of Publius lay sick of a fever, and a bloody flux: to whom Paul entered in, and prayed, and laid his hands on him, and healed him. 9. So when this was done, others also which had diseases in the Island, came, and were healed, 10. Who also honoured us with many honours, and when we departed, they laded us with such things as were necessary.

7. Note, If we could pray as Paul did, and heal all the sick by it; Qu. Whether men would imprison us for it? Answ. The sick or the healed would not, but it is not unlike that Jewish priests would do it; for so they did.

11. And after three months we departed in a ship of Alexandria, which had wintered in the isle,

whose sign was Castor and Pollux. 12. And landing at Syracuse, we tarried *there* three days. 13. And from thence we set a compass, and came to Rhegium: and after one day the south wind blew, and we came the next day to Puteoli: 14. Where we found brethren, and were desired to tarry with them seven days: and so we went toward Rome.

14. Note, It appeareth by this that the gospel had been received before Paul's coming thither, in the Italian country about Rome. Whether these brethren entertained all the soldiers and prisoners seven days, or Paul and his company only, as trusted by the centurion to come after him, is uncertain.

15. And from thence, when the brethren heard of us, they came to meet us as far as Appiforum, and the Three Taverns: whom when Paul saw, he thanked God, and took courage.

15. Note, By this it appeareth also that Paul found a church in Rome. No doubt these brethren lived not without assembling to worship God, being then not forbidden. But who first brought Christianity thither, or planted a church, or was their first pastor, no history tells us; but it is most probable that it was neither Peter nor Paul. Circumstances have persuaded me, that Christianity came first into England by Christian soldiers that were in the Roman army, (such as built the church called St. Martin's near Canterbury, which Beda mentioneth.) And it is more probable that such as Cornelius being converted in Judea, and having their dependance on Rome, and business there, were like to be the first introducers of Christianity there. (As such were in Helvetii.)

16. And when we came to Rome, the centurion delivered the prisoners to the captain of the guard: but Paul was suffered to dwell by himself, with a soldier that kept him.

16. One soldier was his guard.

17. And it came to pass that after three days, Paul called the chief of the Jews together. And when they were come together, he said unto them, Men *and* brethren, though I have committed nothing against the people, or customs of our fathers, yet was I delivered prisoner from Jerusalem into the hands of the Romans. 18. Who when they had examined me, would have let *me* go, because there was no cause of death in me. 19. But when the Jews spake against *it*, I was constrained to appeal unto Cæsar; not that I had ought to accuse my nation of.

17. Note, Though Paul preached against the Gentiles' subjection to Moses' law, yet to the Jews he only spake against the imposing it as necessary on others, and against its justifying power without Christ. 19. I appealed in my own necessary defence, and not as an accuser of the Jews.

20. For this cause therefore have I called for you, to see *you*, and to speak with *you*: because that for the hope of Israel I am bound with this chain.

20. It is for preaching that Messiah who hath long been expected and prayed for, as the hope of Israel, that I am come hither a prisoner in this chain.

21. And they said unto him, We neither received letters out of Judea concerning thee, neither any of the brethren that came, shewed or spake any harm of thee. 22. But we desire to hear of thee what thou thinkest; for as concerning this sect, we know that every where it is spoken against.

21. We have had no accusation of thee: but that we may be able to judge of thee, we would hear thee ourselves, what it is that thou holdest and teachest. For Christians are every where spoken against, as an evil sect.

Note, He that would know how far to regard common fame against any man or party, must know what sort of people they be that report it, whether men of truth, sobriety, and conscience, or debauched, ungodly, malignant scoundrels; and by what motives they are set on work, whether by God's word and will, or by carnal interests, and flattery of great and ungodly worldlings, or enmity to holy doctrine and practice: and what evidence they give to prove their accusations.

23. And when they had appointed him a day, there came many to him into his lodging; to whom he expounded and testified the kingdom of God, persuading them concerning Jesus, both out of the law of Moses, and *out of* the prophets, from morning till evening.

23. He proved to them out of the law and prophets, that Christ was the Messiah, whose king-

dom is spiritual, and is now begun, as foretold, upon his resurrection and ascension, and gathering an universal church by the miracles, gifts, and grace of the Holy Ghost.

24. And some believed the things which were spoken, and some believed not. 25. And when they agreed not among themselves, they departed, after that Paul had spoken one word, Well spake the Holy Ghost by Esaias the prophet, unto our fathers, 26. Saying, Go unto this people, and say, Hearing ye shall hear, and shall not understand; and seeing ye shall see, and not perceive. 27. For the heart of this people is waxed gross, and their ears are dull of hearing, and their eyes have they closed; lest they should see with *their* eyes, and hear with *their* ears, and understand with *their* heart, and should be converted, and I should heal them.

26. You verify the words of the prophets, being like your fore-fathers, of whom Isaiah saith, that though they have their natural faculties of seeing, hearing, and understanding, yet they have wilfully so indisposed and corrupted them, that as to the knowledge and obedience of God, they are as if they had neither eyes, ears, or understanding, from whence it is that my resisted and rejected grace doth not convert and heal them.

28. Be it known therefore unto you, that the salvation of God is sent unto the Gentiles, and *that* they will hear it.

28. Be it known to you that the Christ whom you reject shall be preached to the Gentiles, and they will believe in him, and receive him for their Saviour: and Christ will set up among them the Catholic church and kingdom of God, which you reject, and which shall therefore be none of yours, that boasted in your expectation of it.

29. And when he had said these words, the Jews departed, and had great reasoning among themselves.

29. Note, But so many of them believed at Rome, Jerusalem, and many countries, as were a considerable part of the Christian church at that time: and within four hundred years, Christianity was the professed national religion in Judea.

30. And Paul dwelt two whole years in his own hired house, and received all that came in unto him, 31. Preaching the kingdom of God, and teaching those things which concern the Lord Jesus Christ, with all confidence, no man forbidding him.

30. And Paul was so free a prisoner, that he was allowed to live in his own hired house, and there for two years received all, how many soever great or small, who came to him, preaching even in imperious Rome the kingdom of God, as ruling souls to salvation by the Redeemer, teaching all the doctrines and practices of Christianity, (the history of Christ, his person, office, acts, grace, and glory) and this with all boldness and freedom, NO MAN FORBIDDING HIM, silencing him, or condemning them for conventicles, or any way hindering him, even in proud, powerful, heathen Rome: when the religious Jewish priests and rulers, hunted Christ's ministers as bloodhounds, forbidding them to preach to the Gentiles that they might be saved, and so wrath is come upon them to the uttermost, as it will in due time on all that imitate them.

Note, 1. What Paul preached: not vain jangling, or envious railing, but the kingdom of God, and the things concerning Jesus Christ and his salvation.

2. Where: in Rome, and in his own hired house.

3. To whom: to all that come to him.

4. How long: two years, at that time.

5. How: with all confidence, openness, and boldness.

6. How tolerated: no man, emperor, or senate, or inferior officer, soldiers, or magistrates, priests, or people, hindering or forbidding him, in the capital heathen city of the world, which yet was devoted to idolatry, and captivated the church of God both Jews and Gentiles. But had Paul preached immorality, rebellion, abusive injury to others, no doubt they would have punished him: and verily many preachers whose doctrine is tolerable, are so abusive in false reviling application, that we may say, some orthodox churches have need of church justices to keep the peace.

THE EPISTLE OF PAUL THE APOSTLE,

TO THE

ROMANS.

INTRODUCTION.

FOR the understanding of Paul's Epistle to the Romans, it is necessary, I. To understand his main design and subject. II. To that end, to know what parties he had to do with. III. And what their several errors were, or their temptations to error. IV. And by what arguments he opposed them, and what he granteth them.

I. Paul's great design is to establish the Roman Christians in the faith of the gospel, and in holiness of life, and in mutual love and concord against all the temptations which then assaulted them.

II. The adversaries of their stability, and his design, whom he noteth, are, 1. The Roman heathens, especially the learned sort. 2. Especially the Jews, and the Judaizing Christians. 3. Some erroneous heretical Christians, who were inclined both to libertinism, and to divisions.

III. The errors opposed by him were, 1. The heathens, who while they scorned the faith of a crucified Christ, shewed how little they were to be regarded, by their sins against the light of nature.

2. The Jews had all these following errors: (1.) Because God had made them a peculiar people, by special privileges and promises, they were over-proud of it, as if they had been the only servants that God had in the world, and that none but Jews and their proselytes were saved. (2.) And so, that their law was to be received by all the world.

(3.) That this law, given to, and by Moses, for their government as a peculiar republic, was so excellent, because thus divine, that the keeping of it was the sufficient and only way of salvation. (4.) Herein they overlooked the promise which was before the law, and pre-supposed in the law, as its foundation, and its very life; both the common promise made to lapsed mankind, in Adam and Noah, and the spiritual part of the special promise made to Abraham. And 2. they overlooked the signification of their types and ceremonies; and looked at the law merely as a law of works, rewarding or punishing for the doing or not doing it.

(5.) Therefore they mistook the promised Messiah to be a king of David's line, who was to restore their commonwealth, and subdue the nations to it, and rule them in earthly glory by that law; and so made him subservient to Moses' law, as to be restored by him.

(6.) And so they thought that this law must endure for ever, and that to talk of its abrogation was blasphemy against God.

3. The Judaizing Christians conjoined Christianity and the law, and thought, that though Christ's miracles, resurrection, and Spirit, proved him to be the Messiah, who died for their sins, yet he came not to change their law, but to establish it: and first, they were long before they could be convinced, that it was not necessary to the Gentiles to be proselytes to it: and when they were forced to grant that they still held, that it was necessary to all the Jews. And therefore they kept up their ceremonies, and separated too far from the Gentile Christians: and the Gentile Christians too much despised these.

4. Besides these, there were some that heretically took it to be a part of their extraordinary knowledge, to hold, That Christianity delivered men not only from the Jews' law, but from subjection to men, and from necessary strictness in outward actions: and they made a party for these opinions.

5. The Apostle, (1.) Dealeth but briefly with the heathens, and argueth against them from their own errors and crimes; 1. Telling them of the light of nature, and then of their odious sins against it; that the Christians might not be moved by the scorns and opposition of such a blinded incapable sort of adversaries.

(2). But the chief work of his epistle is to confute the Jews and Judaizers, and to establish the Gentile Christians against their errors and opposition. To which end, he proveth all these things;

1. That the Gentiles are not bound to receive the law of Moses, and become Jews. 2. That they may be justified and saved by the faith of Christ, as well as the Jews. 3. That God foretold their calling by the prophets, and the promise to Abraham extended to them, as the spiritual believing seed or children. 4. That if this were not true, none could be justified or saved; because by the deeds of the law, as such, no man can be justified. The Jews themselves must be justified by faith, or not at all. 5. That the law of Moses, as such, came long after the promise, and the justification of Abraham by faith, and therefore could not null that promise, or way of life. 6. That the law required such a degree of works, or strict obedience, as no man kept; and therefore none could be justified by it. 7. That the law was given but to the Jews, and God is not only the God and governor of the Jews, but of the Gentiles also. 8. That the law forbiddeth sin, and curseth the sinner, and condemneth him, and therefore doth not justify him. 9. That the law, as such, giveth not grace and strength to keep it, but supposeth ability: but the grace and Spirit of Christ enableth. 10. That the law by accident irritateth lust, and increaseth it, and doth not mortify and overcome it. 11. That the law was given to another end, than to justify the sinner by its bare works; even to convince men of sin, and the need of grace, and as a schoolmaster to lead them to Christ, who is the end of the law. 12. That pardon, justification, and salvation must needs be God's free gift to the guilty and condemned, and not the reward of meritorious works of the law; nor can any pretend the title of innocency or debt. 13. That Christ is designed to gather a more large and excellent church than the Jewish nation, even a Catholic church through all the world, and that more spiritual and holy; into which the Jews, if they will believe, shall be all grafted, which will be to them a higher privilege than to live under the Mosaic polity. 14. That the

Jewish law was so strict, shadowy, burdensome, and terrible, that it is part of the office of a Saviour to deliver men from it, and to bring them under a far better law and covenant of grace.

By many such arguments he confuteth the Jews, and Judaizing Christians.

3. How he confuteth the censorious dividers, who agreed in the essentials of Christianity, but differed about some Jewish rites; and also the erroneous, that inclined to licentiousness, and unjust separation from the orthodox, will be sufficiently shewn in the particular expositions.

IV. But the apostle denieth none of these following truths, but implieth some, and expressly asserteth others of them, as concessions:

1. According to the promise made to Abraham, the Israelites were a holy nation, and a peculiar people, separated to God out of all the world.

2. God's government first settled over them was eminently a theocracy the supremacy being exercised by extraordinary revelation, by angelical or signal notices, and by prophecy.

3. Their law was eminently divine, the law of God; their princes being but executioners, and not having power of legislation, to add, abrogate, or diminish.

4. This law was wholly political; that is, The rule of the subjects' obedience, and the rewards and punishments, to be exercised by God as supreme, and by magistrates as his officers, in the government of that people, as a holy commonwealth. Even the decalogue and ceremonies were such laws of polity.

5. But this law supposed the law of nature, and the antecedent law of mercy made to fallen mankind in Adam and Noah, and the special promise made to Abraham, and all the nations of the earth in his seed: and the Jews ought not to have separated any part of their law from these, which were as its very life and soul, and principally respected things spiritual, and heavenly, and everlasting.

6. The law presupposing these, and being given to men that had immortal souls, and bound to know so much, doth not much mention such matters of the life to come, as being pre-supposed; and Moses adding specially the distinguishing laws of Jewish government.

7. The breach even of a political law, where God was the legislator, deserved future everlasting punishment, though as men were the official executioners, it was but corporal punishment that it inflicted.

8. The sacrifices were obsignations of that law of grace which was elder than Moses, and so they should have been understood.

9. The sincere keeping of that law, while it was in force, was the material part of the Jews obedience as they were under the law of grace.

10. Even the decalogue itself, as Mosaical and political, delivered in stone to the Jews only, is done away with all the rest by Christ, their peculiar commonwealth being ended: but as it is (1.) The law of nature, (2.) And the law of Christ, it still continueth.

There are three controversies that I will here briefly speak to, rather than by inserted annotations afterwards. I. Whom Paul describeth in the first and second chapters. II. What law it is that he speaketh of. III. How he meaneth, that faith is imputed to righteousness and justification.

I. A late writer hath laboured hard to persuade us, that Rom. i. and a great part of the epistles speak of the Gnostics, which have usually been otherwise expounded. Of this chapter I think otherwise, (and of many other texts) because, 1. The philosophers, and other heathens, were so much more potent, numerous, and famous adversaries to Christianity, that we have great reason to suspect, that Paul doth not so much pass them by, to pelt at a few heretics, as this writer imagined.

2. The text agreeth more to the heathens. It was to them that the gospel was a matter of shame, and counted foolishness. It was not by the works of creation chiefly, that the Gnostics pretended to know God, or should have known him; but this was the only book to the heathens. The Gnostics were unexcusable, as professors of faith; but it was the heathens that were left without excuse by the mere works of God's creation. The heathen philosophers were they that professed the greatest wisdom, deriding all Christians, as fools. It was the heathens that were the authors of all that imagery and idolatry, named ver. 23. The Gnostics were but for involuntary compliance in case of danger: They renounced worshipping the creature more than the Creator. The sodomy, and all the other sins by which they are described, belong far more to the heathens than to the Gnostics. Chap. 2. Paul distributeth them that he speaks of, into [Jews and Gentiles,] and so doth the whole scope of his discourse, 1 Cor. i. and ii. It is the same sort that he there speaketh of, as the wise, and great, and noble of the world, who counted the wisdom of the gospel foolishness, and whose wisdom was foolishness, which God would confound, and bring to nought, &c. which is the plain description of the philosophical heathens. A great deal more such evidence is at hand.

3. The writers of church-history and heresies, tell us of many sorts of heretics in the beginning, that went before those called Gnostics; yet none of these are named in scripture, but the Nicolaitans, and the woman Jezebel, Rev. ii. and iii. And why should we think then that the Gnostics are meant more than they?

4. Those that Paul oft singleth out seem to be them mentioned Acts xv. against whom he reasoneth to the Galatians, &c. Had he meant others, as their crimes were greater, he would have as plainly notified them. Indeed 2 Pet. ii. and Jude, seem to mean the Nicolaitans as much like the Gnostics; but Paul had much more to do with the heathen opposition.

II. Some have thought that it is the *law of innocency* made first to Adam, which Paul meaneth, when he speaks against justification by the works of the law. Their chief reasons are, 1. Because it saith, *Cursed is he that doth not all things written, &c.* And hence they gather, That the Jews' law was of the same tenor. 2. But others give this reason, Because the Jews' law was a covenant of grace, and therefore could not be that here described.

But it is evident all along, that it was Moses's law that Paul here meaneth. It would be tedious to cite the proofs all along visible. And as to the reasons for the contrary, (1.) It is certain, that the law of innocency was not then in being and force, but ceased with man's innocency, upon Adam's fall; not by mutability in God, but in man. God's law is the present obligation of his will to duty or punishment. Shall we imagine God to say to the sinful world, 1. *I command thee, that art a guilty sin-*

ner, to be sinless? (contrary to the hypothetical necessity of existence.) 2. And, *thou shalt be rewarded if thou be innocent*, (when he is guilty already?) 3. And, *if thou be a sinner, thou shalt die*, (when he is a sinner already, and the *conditional* is become *absolute*, and passed into a sentence of judgment?)

 2. The law of Moses granteth sacrifice and pardon for many sins but the law of innocency pardoneth none.

 3. The meaning of [*Cursed be he that doth not all things*] is not, *Cursed be he that hath any sin;* but, *he that keepeth not all this law:* (And only the Jews were under that law, and its curse.) And this law of Moses was so strict, that no man did perfectly fulfil it: And if they had, it would not procure their pardon for the common sin of nature, nor merit any thing of God, by the benefit he received by their works.

 4. And as to the other objectors, It is true, that Moses's law was given to them as a material peculiar part of the law of grace. But those, that Paul disputed against, had in conceit separated the law, as such, from the promise or covenant of free grace, and thought to be justified by the merit of their obedience to it.

 III. Perverse engagement against one anothers' opinions, as dangerous, hath made Paul's doctrine of faith and justification seem much more difficult than it is. 1. It is certain, That by [*faith*] he meaneth no one single act only, as is [The believing that Christ's righteousness is imputed to us] as if we were not justified by believing in God the Father, or the Holy Ghost, or trusting the promise of glory, or believing that Christ died for our sins, rose, ascended, intercedeth, reigneth, and will judge us, and glorify us, or by consenting to his covenant of grace, accepting offered mercy, &c. Faith is a moral act, containing many physical acts of understanding and will; like a covenant consent to a king, a husband, a physician, &c. It is all that is essentially required in baptism, to the collation of the grace there given. It is Christianity in consent.

 2. This faith is commanded by God, and grace and glory promised to them that by believing obey this command: which maketh it the condition, or moral receptive qualification for this gift. And though God's grace cause men to believe, yet the command and conditional promise are the means by which God worketh this effect. And that the *promise* be *conditional*, joined with *threatening* to disobedience, is no more needless than the *command* or *preaching* is.

 3. Hence men may claim *pardon* upon *believing;* but none can claim *faith* by virtue of any absolute promise of God, before he have it.

 4. Though no creature can *merit* of God in *commutative justice*, as giving him a benefit, yet they may merit of him as in *governing justice*, or *distributive:* But this is various, as the governing law is.

 According to the law of *innocency* no man meriteth; nor justification according to the law of Moses; save Christ alone. Christ's merit was in the fulfilling the undertaken mediatorship, which was fulfilling the law of innocency, (which he only was capable of) and Moses's law, and the peculiar acts of a mediator: This merit of Christ is the valuable, procuring, meritorious cause of all our deliverance, (pardon, justification, adoption, &c.) of which our own habits or acts are no parts, nor are at all to be judged to be instead of any part of the office of Christ.

 5. But we are not *lawless*, but under a *pardoning* and *justifying law.*

or *covenant* of *grace*, which giveth grace and glory (as is said) to them that believe and repent; that is, pardoneth them, and giveth them the indwelling spirit of love, and right to life, if they sincerely trust Christ's mediation and promise for it, and give up themselves for that end to God their reconciled Father, to Christ as their Saviour, and his Spirit as their Sanctifier.

And because God will not give us the free gift of Christ, and life with him, but as first qualified by this condition of faith, therefore faith is said to be imputed to us for righteousness: that is, This acceptance of his free gift in Christ, is all that the law of grace, by which we shall be judged, requireth of us that we may be accounted righteous, without innocency, or the works of Moses's law, or any that make not the gift of pardon and life to be of free grace. To have *righteousness imputed*, is to be *accounted righteous*.

6. To call faith a *justifying instrument*, is an unapt speech of man's vain invention; but may be tolerated, if they mean but [*A moral receptive disposition*] unfitly called, *A receptive instrument*: But not in proper sense.

7. But though Christ is our surety, and *vicarius poenæ* in some sense, and properly a sacrifice for our sin, and merited all that we have, by his righteousness; yet it subverteth the gospel and Christianity, to teach, as some do, That Christ did so properly personate every one of the elect, that in the sense of God and the law (though not physically) they all perfectly fulfilled the law of innocency in and by him, and so are justified by that law, as imputatively being sinless: As if that law had said, [*Thou or thy surety shall die if thou sin*] and we are justified by the same law that condemned us; and no death, or suffering, or permitted sin, were any penalties on us: And as if we were at once reputed sinless from birth to death, and yet must have a Christ to die for our sin, and must daily beg forgiveness of it.

CHAP. I.

PAUL, a servant of Jesus Christ, called *to be* an apostle, separated unto the gospel of God;

1. By an immediate appearance of Christ from heaven, by voice and inspiration, sent to publish the glad tidings of redemption and salvation by Christ.

2. (Which he had promised afore by his prophets in the holy scriptures.) 3. Concerning his Son Jesus Christ our Lord, which was made of the seed of David according to the flesh, 4. And declared *to be* the Son of God with power, according to the Spirit of holiness, by the resurrection from the dead:

3. Having his human nature from his mother of David's line.

4. But the power of God, which owned him, by the Spirit of holiness, and his resurrection from the dead, did demonstrate that he was not a mere man, but God's own son, sent from heaven, and miraculously incarnate.

5. By whom we have received grace and apostleship, for obedience to the faith among all nations for his name:

5. By whose own heavenly mission I received this favour and honour, to be his special messenger, sent to call all nations to believe and obey the gospel, and proclaim the glory of his name.

6. Among whom are ye also the called of Jesus Christ.

6. Of whom God hath vouchsafed you to be a part, being the called followers of Jesus Christ.

7. To all that be in Rome, beloved of God, called *to be* saints: Grace to you, and peace from God

our Father, and the Lord Jesus Christ.

7. To all in Rome that are the beloved of God, called out of the world, into the holy Christian state, I salute you by this benediction and prayer, That the grace of God, our Father, and the Lord Jesus Christ, and that true peace and welfare which is its special fruit, may be yet more upon you.

8. First, I thank my God through Jesus Christ for you all, that your faith is spoken of throughout the whole world.

8. And first, I thank my God through Jesus Christ, that (as you dwell in that city which is most eminent in the world, which is an advantage to the lustre and communication of your faith, so) your profession of that faith is so illustrious, as to be famous throughout the world.

9. For God is my witness, whom I serve with my spirit in the gospel of his Son, that without ceasing I make mention of you always in my prayers, 10. Making request (if by any means now at length I might have a prosperous journey by the will of God) to come unto you.

9. For God, whom I serve with a devoted soul, doth know, that this your honourable profession of the Christian faith, doth make me the more constantly remember you in my prayers.

10. And request of God, if it seem good to him, that I may come to you, for the furtherance of my joy, and your edification.

11. For I long to see you, that I may impart unto you some spiritual gift, to the end you may be established; 12. That is, that I may be comforted together with you, by the mutual faith both of you and me.

11, 12. For I long to see you, that by communicating to you what God hath given to me, you may be further established, and you and I may be comforted in the mutual manifestation of our concordant faith.

13. Now I would not have you ignorant, brethren, that oftentimes I purposed to come unto you (but was led hitherto) that I might have some fruit among you also, even as among other Gentiles.

13. I would have you know, that as God hath called me to be an apostle to the Gentiles, I oft purposed to come to you, (though hitherto hindered) that I might reap some fruit of that my office among you, as well as among other Gentiles.

14. I am debtor both to the Greeks, and to the barbarians, both to the wise, and to the unwise.

14. By this my mission and office, it is my duty to preach the gospel, both to the learned Greeks and Romans, and to unlearned barbarous nations.

15. So as much as in me is, I am ready to preach the gospel to you that are at Rome also.

15. Therefore, if it be the will of God, that I shall come unto you, I am ready, as the apostle to the Gentiles, to exercise mine office, by preaching to you, as I have done to others.

16. For I am not ashamed of the gospel of Christ: for it is the power of God unto salvation, to every one that believeth, to the Jew first, and also to the Greeks.

16. For though a crucified Christ be to the Jews a stumbling-block, and to the Gentiles foolishness, I am not ashamed most openly to own and preach this gospel: For the power of God, by this called weakness and foolishness by men, is manifested in it, and by it, in the conversion, comfort, and salvation of every true believer, whether Jews, with whom it began, or Greeks, to whom it is now preached.

17. For therein is the righteousness of God revealed from faith to faith: as it is written, The just shall live by faith.

17. For that sort of righteousness which God hath made the necessary and acceptable way to salvation, is therein revealed to the world; even righteousness by faith, is revealed to beget faith in men; by which it is that men must be justified and saved, as was foretold.

18. For the wrath of God is revealed from heaven against all ungodliness, and unrighteousness of men, who hold the truth in unrighteousness.

18. For that gospel which pardoneth penitent believers, doth reveal God's wrath against the impenitent and unbelievers, who by the love of sin, resist and reject the truth, and continue in ungodliness and unrighteousness.

19. Because that which may be known of God, is manifest in them; for God hath shewed it unto them.

19. For they may know much of the nature and attributes of God, as manifested by the light of nature in them, and by the providence of God among them; by which God sheweth it unto them.

20. For the invisible things of him from the creation of the world are clearly seen, being understood

by the things that are made, *even* his eternal power and Godhead; so that they are without excuse:

20. For though God and heavenly things be invisible, even his eternal power, and his Godhead, yet are they clearly to be seen in the glass of his works; so that their sin against God, thus revealed, leaveth them without all just excuse.

21. Because that when they knew God, they glorified him not as God, neither were thankful, but became vain in their imaginations, and their foolish heart was darkened. 22. Professing themselves to be wise, they became fools: 23. And changed the glory of the uncorruptible God, into an image made like to corruptible man, and to birds, and four-footed beasts, and creeping things.

21. Because, when by his works, and the light of nature, they were forced to confess the divine perfections, they yet lived not to his glory, or in holy thankfulness to the God whom they acknowledged, but dishonoured him, and corrupted their minds by vain imaginations, and their foolish hearts were darkened by gross errors. 22. And professing themselves to be the learned philosophers, and wise men of the world, and contemning others as ignorant and barbarous, they shewed by their practice that they were fools. 23. For when their tongues acknowledged the glory of the incorruptible God, they worshipped him as in and by the images of corruptible man, and of birds, beasts, and creeping things; as if God had been like these.

24. Wherefore God also gave them up to uncleanness, through the lusts of their own hearts, to dishonour their own bodies between themselves: 25. Who changed the truth of God into a lie, and worshipped and served the creature more than the Creator, who is blessed for ever. Amen.

24. Wherefore, as a just punishment for their wilful sins, God left them to the lust of the flesh, to base unnatural uncleanness. 25. Seeing they confessing the perfections of the true God, yet represented him in the image of vain shadows and creatures, and so offered their worship to such creatures, and to the stars, rather than to the true and blessed Creator, whom they acknowledged.

26. For this cause God gave them up unto vile affections: for even their women did change the natural use into that which is against nature: 27. And likewise also the men, leaving the natural use of the woman, burned in their lust one toward another, men with men working that which is unseemly, and receiving in themselves that recompence of their error which was meet.

26, 27. For this sin, God gave them to base lusts against nature, who in their religion sinned against the light of nature; both women and men burning in worse than beastly unnatural lusts towards those of their own sex, and by being left to that unnatural filthiness, were justly punished for their unnatural idolatry.

28. And even as they did not like to retain God in *their* knowledge, God gave them over to a reprobate mind, to do those things which are not convenient:

28. And as their wicked hearts refused to obey and honour God practically, though they did in words acknowledge him; God gave them over to a reprobate mind, to do those things which the light of nature, and common reason do condemn.

29. Being filled with all unrighteousness, fornication, wickedness, covetousness, maliciousness; full of envy, murder, debate, deceit, malignity, whisperers, 30. Backbiters, haters of God, despiteful, proud, boasters, inventors of evil things, disobedient to parents. 31. Without understanding, covenant-breakers, without natural affection, implacable, unmerciful.

29. So far is their learning and arts from making them just and happy, that they abound with all manner of odious shameful sin (here named.)

32. Who knowing the judgment of God, that they which commit such things are worthy of death, not only do the same, but have pleasure in them that do them.

32. And all their knowledge (of good and evil) is so far from justifying or sanctifying them, that they live in the practice of that which they know God doth condemn, and in their societies and conversation make it their delight.

CHAP. II.

THEREFORE thou art inexcusable, O man, whosoever thou art that judgest: for wherein thou judgest another, thou condemnest thyself; for thou that judgest, doest the same things.

1. Therefore thou that thinkest highly of thyself, for thy knowledge, and basely of others, as ignorant or barbarous, art so far from being justified by this, that it aggravateth thy sin, and leaveth thee without excuse: For thou livest in as great sin as those whom thou condemnest as ignorant.

2. But we are sure that the judgment of God is according to truth, against them which commit such things.

2. But we know that God will judge all men in truth and righteousness, according to their works; and will condemn evil doers, whatever their knowledge and profession be.

3. And thinkest thou this, O man, that judgest them which do such things, and doest the same, that thou shalt escape the judgment of God?

3. Is it not then thy manifest error, to think that thy knowledge, and condemning sin in others will justify and save thee, that livest in sin?

4. Or despisest thou the riches of his goodness, and forbearance, and long-suffering, not knowing that the goodness of God leadeth thee to repentance? 5. But after thy hardness and impenitent heart, treasurest up unto thyself wrath against the day of wrath, and revelation of the righteous judgment of God; 6. Who will render to every man according to his deeds.

4, 5, 6. While thou boastest of wisdom, and livest in wickedness, thou shewest the more contempt of God, even of the riches of his goodness, and forbearance, and long-suffering, not knowing practically, that the goodness of God which thou dost acknowledge in words, should lead thee to repentance, and forsaking of sin. 5. But thy heart being hardened in impenitency, by sin against knowledge, thou dost but treasure up certain punishment against the day when God will shew his righteousness by his judgment; 6. And will judge and use men according to their deeds.

7. To them, who by patient continuance in well-doing, seek for glory and honour, and immortality; eternal life:

7. To them, who by a life of true obedience, and patient waiting for his reward, do seek first for future glory, and honour, and immortal happiness, he will give eternal life.

8. But to them that are contentious, and do not obey the truth, but obey unrighteousness, indignation, and wrath; 9. Tribulation and anguish upon every soul of man that doeth evil, of the Jew first, and also of the Gentile.

8, 9. But to them that resist the light, and contend against the revealed truth, and obey it not, but live in the practice of unrighteousness, while they boast of knowledge, God will pour forth his indignation, and wrath, tribulation, and anguish, even on every one that liveth in sin and wickedness, first on the Jews, who sin under their boasting of their peculiarity, law, and Jewish knowledge; and the Greeks and Romans, who sin under their boasting of learning and philosophy, and conceited wisdom.

10. But glory, honour, and peace to every man that worketh good, to the Jew first, and also to the Gentile. 11. For there is no respect of persons with God.

10. 11. But glory, honour, and peace, to every man that liveth a life of true obedience and welldoing; to the Jew first, according to their covenant prerogative, and also to the Gentiles, as being in the same covenant of grace, for God saveth not men partially, for their outward privileges, or their barren knowledge and profession.

12. For as many as have sinned without law, shall also perish without law: and as many as have sinned in the law, shall be judged by the law,

12. For all men shall be judged according to the obligations which they were under. They that sinned against the law of nature and common mercies, and were never under the Mosaical law, or supernatural revelation, shall be condemned by the law which they sinned against, and not by that which was never given them. But the Jews, that sinned under Moses's law, shall be judged by it.

13. (For not the hearers of the law *are* just before God, but the doers of the law shall be justified.

13. For no law of God doth justify men merely for having it, and hearing it, but for doing it, so far as they do it.

14. For when the Gentiles which have not the law, do by nature the things contained in the law, these having not the law, are a law unto themselves: 15. Which shew the work of the law written in their hearts, their conscience also bearing witness, and *their* thoughts the

mean while accusing, or else excusing one another.)

14, 15. For when the Gentiles, which have not the Jewish, or any written law of God, do by nature that which that law commandeth, these having not that supernatural written law, have God's law of nature in themselves, and shew the effects of this natural revelation written in their hearts, their conscience naturally having some conviction of God's sovereign government and man's duty, tells them, as a witness, whether they do well or ill; and their reason accusing or defending them accordingly.

16. In the day when God shall judge the secrets of men by Jesus Christ, according to my gospel.

16. I mean not by any mistaken self-judging in this world; but even at the bar of Christ, when God shall open all men's secret acts, and rectify all mistaken judgings, as I have preached in foretelling that judgment of Christ.

17. Behold, thou art called a Jew, and restest in the law, and makest thy boast of God: 18. And knowest his will, and approvest the things that are more excellent, being instructed out of the law. 19. And art confident that thou thyself art a guide of the blind, a light of them which are in darkness, 20. An instructor of the foolish, a teacher of babes, which hast the form of knowledge, and of the truth in the law.

17, 18, &c. And that you may know that the law will justify no man for having or knowing it, but for doing it, consider that it is but self-deceit to think that thou shalt be justified for being called a Jew, and resting in the divineness and perfection of your law, and boasting that you are God's peculiar people, and that his will and excellent things are known by you, which the world knoweth not; and that it is you that by that law, must be the lights and guides of the dark and ignorant, to whom all others as children should come to school, because you have the only true knowledge by the means of your law.

21. Thou, therefore, which teachest another, teachest thou not thyself? thou that preachest a man should not steal, dost thou steal? 22. Thou that sayest a man should not commit adultery, dost thou commit adultery? thou that abhorrest idols, dost thou commit sacrilege? 23. Thou that makest thy boast of the law, through breaking the law dishonourest thou God?

21, 22, 23. Will the law justify thee, that condemnest thyself by breaking it, while thou boastest of it? Will teaching others justify thee, who teachest not thyself? Will it justify a thief to preach against stealing, or an adulterer to preach against adultery, or the sacrilegious to abhor idols?

24. For the name of God is blasphemed among the Gentiles through you, as it is written.

24. For as the prophets truly told your forefathers, I may tell you, that you are so far from keeping your law to justification, that the scandal of your sin occasioneth the Gentiles to speak evil of your law, and blaspheme God that made it.

25. For circumcision verily profiteth, if thou keep the law: but if thou be a breaker of the law, thy circumcision is made uncircumcision.

25. Indeed God made not the law in vain: To keep it is required of the Jews, as the matter of their obedience: And if you keep it as the covenant of circumcision obligeth you, you shall not lose the promised reward. But if you are breakers of the law, you will be no more justified than the uncircumcised, but more condemned for violating your duty and covenant with God.

26. Therefore if the uncircumcision keep the righteousness of the law, shall not his uncircumcision be counted for circumcision? 27. And shall not uncircumcision which is by nature, if it fulfil the law, judge thee, who by the letter and circumcision dost trangress the law?

26, 27. Therefore it being performance which the law requireth, if uncircumcised persons do that good which the law requireth, it is them that the law will so far justify; and such obedient uncircumcised persons, that by obeying the law of nature, perform the matter of your laws, shall condemn those that have the letter of the law, and are by circumcision engaged to keep it, and yet transgress it.

28. For he is not a Jew, which is one outwardly: neither *is that* circumcision, which is outward in the flesh: 29. But he *is* a Jew which is one inwardly; and circumcision *is that* of the heart, in the spirit, *and* not in the letter, whose praise *is* not of men, but of God.

28, 29. But the Jew that God will accept and justify as the seed of believing Abraham, and that answered the end of the law, is not he that is only visibly one in the outward ceremony: nor is that the acceptable circumcision, which is only outward in the flesh: but he is the accepted person with God, as his peculiar, who is such at the heart as the law required Jews to be; and that is the acceptable circumcision, which cleanseth and sanctifieth the heart in spirituality, and not only in outward letter, form, and ceremony: which is approved of the most holy heart-searching God, and not that which is but approved of men.

CHAP. III.

WHAT advantage then hath the Jew? or what profit *is there* of circumcision? 2. Much every way: chiefly, because that unto them were committed the oracles of God.

1, 2. You will say, If this be so, what advantage hath the Jew above the Gentile, or what profit doth circumcision afford them? I answer, Much every way: as first, That God committed his oracles of supernatural revelation principally to them; (and from them it is that others have received them.)

3. For what if some did not believe? shall their unbelief make the faith of God without effect?

3. It is true, that the most of the present Jews do not believe in Christ, nor yield to the persuasions of the gospel. But still God's word is sure and true, and his fidelity will perform all his promises.

4. God forbid: yea, let God be true, but every man a liar; as it is written, That thou mightest be justified in thy sayings, and mightest overcome when thou art judged.

4. Far be it from us to think that God is untrusty, or can lie: all men are untrusty, and may deceive by lies; but God's fidelity is his perfection, which cannot fail. As David saith, His word shall be justified, and all be silenced that dare accuse him of untrustiness or lying.

5. But if our unrighteousness commend the righteousness of God, what shall we say? Is God unrighteous who taketh vengeance? (I speak as a man.)

5. But if all our sin do but occasion the manifestation of God's righteousness, and so his honour and end is secured, is it not unjust for God to punish and destroy men for unbelief and sin? I object as a man.

6. God forbid: for then how shall God judge the world?

6. Far be it from us so to think: for sure the judge of all the world is righteous, and will righteously judge.

7. For if the truth of God hath more abounded through my lie unto his glory, why yet am I also judged as a sinner? 8. And not *rather*, as we be slanderously reported, and as some affirm that we say, Let us do evil, that good may come? whose damnation is just.

7, 8. But, say they, If my falsehood and sin do occasion the glorifying of God and his truth, why should I be judged a sinner against God, who is glorified by all that I do; and not rather conclude (as some falsely say we do) that we should never fear sinning, seeing the effect is always good? But just is the damnation of such, that pretend God's glory to embolden them in sin.

9. What then? are we better *than they*? No, in no wise; for we have before proved both Jews and Gentiles, that they are all under sin;

9. What shall we then conclude from this unbelief and punishment of the Jews? Is it, that we who are Christians, Jews, and Gentiles, were so much better antecedently than the unbelieving part, that God therefore gave us his grace for our better deserts? No, in no wise: for we have before proved, that the Jews and Gentiles are all under the guilt and reign of sin, till grace recover them.

10. As it is written, There is none righteous, no not one: 11. There is none that understandeth, there is none that seeketh after God. 12. They are all gone out of the way, they are together become unprofitable, there is none that doeth good, no not one. 13. Their throat *is* an open sepulchre; with their tongues they have used deceit; the poison of asps *is* under their lips; 14. Whose mouth is full of cursing and bitterness. 15. Their feet *are* swift to shed blood. 16. Destruction and misery *are* in their ways, 17. And the way of peace have they not known: 18. There is no fear of God before their eyes.

10, 11, &c. David truly describeth the state of corrupted nature, and of all men till grace restrain or change them, in Ps. xiv. and liii. &c. that, There is not one of them that are righteous men: they understand not practically the matters of true wisdom, and chief concerns, but are a blind and sottish generation; and therefore they seek not seriously to know God, or to please him, and enjoy his love. They are turned from the way of truth, and obedience, and happiness: they are all but hurtful, or unprofitable in the world, and none of them that set themselves to a life that may do good to themselves or others, or to please God. They are so like Satan, who seeketh whom he may devour, that their throat is like an open sepulchre, greedily gaping to devour the just and godly: their tongues serve the father of lies, in slandering God's truth and servants; and their words are like adders' poison, that tends to do mischief, and destroy the good and innocent. Cursing and false deceitful words, are the fruit of their lips. They are ready to shed the blood of the godly and innocent: the way of their life is destruction and misery to the faithful, and to the societies where they live, and finally to themselves. Nature and custom may teach them to talk for peace, and unity, and love; but they do not, and will not know the true nature of them, or the way by which they must be attained: for they are not governed by the law and fear of God, but by their carnal deceived wit, and worldly interest, which God condemneth.

19. Now we know that what things soever the law saith, it saith to them who are under the law: that every mouth may be stopped, and all the world may become guilty before God.

19. All this is written in the Jews' laws, and therefore is spoken to and of the Jews as well as others; for the law speaketh to none but those that are subjects, and obliged by it: so that neither Jew nor Gentile can be justified as innocent; but all such self-justifiers will be confuted, and all the world proved guilty of sin and punishment before God when he shall judge them.

20. Therefore by the deeds of the law there shall no flesh be justified in his sight. For by the law is the knowledge of sin.

20. By all this therefore it is clear, that seeing all that are under Moses' law, are sinners against the law, and none are innocent, no flesh shall be justified in God's sight by that law: for as they are sinners, so it is the law which notifieth their sin, and condemneth them for it.

21. But now the righteousness of God without the law is manifested, being witnessed by the law and the prophets; 22. Even the righteousness of God *which is* by faith of Jesus Christ unto all, and upon all them that believe; for there is no difference.

21. But there is another way of righteousness ordained of God for our justification, and the glory of his grace and justice, without the keeping of Moses' law, or being justified by it. 22. Even the righteousness prescribed by God, and given by his grace, which is by the way of faith in Christ, even our believing trust in him, and adhering to him; and this is prescribed and given to, and found in all true believers, without difference.

23. For all have sinned, and come short of the glory of God; 24. Being justified freely by his grace, through the redemption that is in Jesus Christ.

23, 24. For all men are sinners, and therefore have come short of obtaining the glory which God had appointed to the innocent that never brake his law; and cannot be saved or justified by the law which they have broken: but must be justified by his free grace, forgiving their sin, and giving and accepting their sincere faith and repentance, through the redemption of lost sinners, which Jesus Christ hath wrought for them and in them.

25. Whom God hath set forth *to be* a propitiation, through faith in his blood, to declare his righteousness for the remission of sins that are past, through the forbearance of God; 26. To declare, *I say,* at this time his righteousness: that he might be just, and the justifier of him which believeth in Jesus.

25, 26. Whom God hath by his unsearchable, counsel, decree, and ordination, set forth to be the great reconciler and propitiation, by the way and means of faith in his blood as a propitiatory sacrifice, and the seal of his truth and love; and this was (as well as by justifying the innocent) to demonstrate that he is a holy, just, and merciful God, and no friend to sin, but a lover of holiness and truth, in pardoning to such believers all their past sins, to which his forbearance and reprieve was a preparation. I say, to declare that he is (as merciful, so) just, while he will have so precious a sacrifice for sin, and by pardon and grace doth make, and judge the faithful righteous, which is it that is now fully declared by our preaching the gospel.

27. Where *is* boasting then? It is excluded. By what law? of works? Nay: but by the law of faith.

27. Grace, therefore, must have the glory of our justification: For who can boast that he hath it by innocency, because he deserved not death by sin? No, this is utterly shut out: By what law? Is it by the law of Moses, or any law which justifieth men because they sinned not against it, nor deserved death? No; but by another law, even the law of faith, which grace hath brought us under, which pardoneth and saveth true penitent believers.

28. Therefore we conclude, that a man is justified by faith without the deeds of the law.

28. Therefore against the Jews and all self justiciaries, we conclude, that the law of Moses, (much less the first law of pure innocency) is so far from being necessary to the Gentiles for justification and salvation, that no man, Jew or Gentile, is otherwise justified by God, but by his free grace given through Jesus Christ, to all true believers, who accept it as a free gift.

29. *Is he* the God of the Jews only? *is he* not also of the Gentiles? Yes, of the Gentiles also:

29. And how absurd is it to think that God is a God, that is, a merciful governor, to no more in the world, than that little sorry people of the Jews! Doth not his actual mercies, and his government, obliging all the world to the use of some means for recovery, pardon, and salvation, confute this, and shew that he is the God, and merciful governor also of the Gentiles?

30. Seeing *it is* one God, which shall justify the circumcision by faith, and uncircumcision through faith.

30. It is the same God who will justify circumcised believers, and uncircumcised believers, by one and the same way: even by the way of grace and faith.

31. Do we then make void the law through faith? God forbid: yea, we establish the law.

31. Can the Jews then say that we dishonour and make void their law, as if God had given it in vain, and they had not been bound to keep it: far be this from us, yea, by the doctrine of Christianity, we set the law in its proper place, (as consequent and subordinate to the promise and law of grace that went before it, and as preparatory to the fuller edition of the law of grace which cometh after it.) And so we assign it its due office, and honour, and end, that God may have the glory of making it; though the Jews misunderstand it.

CHAP. IV.

WHAT shall we say then, that Abraham our father, as pertaining to the flesh, hath found?

1. Let us consider Abraham's case, the father of the Israelites according to the flesh: for sure his prerogative must be as great as theirs that claim it as his fleshly seed.

2. For if Abraham were justified by works, he hath *whereof* to glory, but not before God.

2. If Abraham was justified by the merit of his righteousness, as having never deserved death by sin, then he may boast that life and impunity was his due on that account, though yet even that did not merit by any benefit to God: (or, but towards God, he could have no matter to boast of, as his own.)

3. For what saith the scripture? Abraham believed God, and it was counted unto him for righteousness,

3. For what account doth the Scripture give us of his righteousness? Abraham believed God, (viz. That he would perform his free promise of grace and peculiarity made to him and his seed, and all nations of the earth in him,) and it was counted to him for righteousness. And though God made his promises to him also for his obedience, [Because he spared not his only son,] yet this was not because he never deserved death by any sin, but as it was a work of faith, and so a consequent part of the righteousness of a believer, accepted, though imperfect, through the merits and righteousness of Christ, forgiving his sin, and freely adopting him an heir of life.

4. Now to him that worketh, is the reward not reckoned of grace, but of debt.

4. Now to him that meriteth by the perfection of his obedience, or that never deserved death by sin, (much more to him that benefiteth another by his work) the reward is not reckoned to be the free gift of a benefactor, but the just giving a man that which is his deserved due (in the first case by governing justice; and in the second by commutative justice.)

5. But to him that worketh not, but believeth on him that justifieth the ungodly, his faith is counted for righteousness.

5. But to him that hath no such meritorious work for the value of which the reward should be his due, but trusteth wholly to his free grace, who first maketh and then judgeth them just, that were before ungodly and unjust, (or, who justifieth them that by sin have deserved death, and never merited life by the worth of their good works) his faith is counted for righteousness, by the covenant of grace; that is, God accepteth it as the qualification or condition, which must be found in him, (without such meritorious works) to make him partaker of that pardon, adoption, and salvation, freely given by grace, upon the consideration of the meritorious righteousness of Christ. (Indeed faith, repentance, prayer, confession, love, &c. are acts that may be called works in another sense; but it is works deserving life for their perfection, or not deserving punishment by the law, which are here spoken of.)

6. Even as David also describeth the blessedness of the man unto whom God imputeth righteousness without works, 7. *Saying*, Blessed *are* they whose iniquities are forgiven, and whose sins are covered. 8. Blessed *is* the man to whom the Lord will not impute sin.

6, 7, 8. So David also describeth the qualification of a blessed man (which is a man justified) not that he hath no sin, which deserved death, but that God doth not impute his sin to him for his condemnation, but forgiveth and covereth it, and imputeth righteousness to him; that is, judgeth and useth him as one that is not obliged to punishment, but hath right to salvation: and this, not because his works deserved not death but life; but because he forgiveth him, and freely saveth him for the righteousness and intercession of Christ; and useth him not as he deserved.

9. *Cometh* this blessedness then upon the circumcision *only*, or upon the uncircumcision also? For we say that faith was reckoned to Abraham for righteousness.

9. And are none pardoned and saved but the circumcised? Are not the uncircumcised pardoned and blessed also? If faith was imputed for righteousness to Abraham, will it not be so to all that have it?

10. How was it then reckoned? when he was in circumcision, or in uncircumcision? Not in circumcision, but in uncircumcision.

10. And the time when this was said of Abraham will clear up all this; for it was not after he was circumcised, but before; even uncircumcised, as the Gentile Christians be.

11. And he received the sign of circumcision, a seal of the righteousness of the faith, which *he had yet* being uncircumcised: that he might be the father of all them that believe, though they be not circumcised; that righteousness might be imputed unto them also:

11. And he after received the sign of circumcision, not as a legally justifying sign, but as a seal of that righteousness which God before imputed to him as a believer; that so he might be, by promise and example, the father, not only of his carnal and circumcised seed, but of all them that believe, throughout the world, that so, righteousness might be imputed to them as believers, as it was to him.

12. And the father of circumcision to them who are not of the circumcision only, but also walk in the steps of that faith of our father Abraham, which *he had* being *yet* uncircumcised.

12. And might be the father of the ends, and spiritual benefits of circumcision, conveyed to them who are not of the circumcision only, but also to them that walk in the steps of that faith of our father Abraham, which he had, being yet uncircumcised as they are.

13. For the promise that he should be the heir of the world, *was* not to Abraham or to his seed through the law, but through the righteousness of faith.

13. For the promise to Abraham and his seed, That he should be heir of the world, was not made to him by the law, which was long after, nor for the keeping of it; but upon his believing God's merciful promise, and trusting him, for which he was accounted and pronounced righteous.

14. For if they which are of the law *be* heirs, faith is made void, and the promise made of none effect.

14. For if this great promise of inheritance was made to men for keeping Moses' law, as such, (and so only to them) then it was null to Abraham, and it is of no effect to any.

15. Because the law worketh wrath: for where no law is, *there is* no transgression.

15. Because, as the law is made to forbid and condemn sin, so it obligeth sinners to undergo the punishment; which were no obligation, were there no obliging law: and Abraham was not under Moses' law, and so transgressed it not.

16. Therefore *it is* of faith, that *it might be* by grace; to the end the promise might be sure to all the seed, not to that only which is of the law, but to that also which is of the faith of Abraham, who is the father of us all,

16. Therefore this great promise and blessing is made to believers, as such, that it may be free, and of mere grace, that so it may be sure and firm to all the seed or children of promise; not only to the Jews that had the law, and were the natural seed, but to the Gentiles also, who have Abraham's faith, and so are his spiritual seed, who is the father of all believers.

17. (As it is written, I have made thee a father of many nations) 'before him whom he believed, *even* God who quickeneth the dead, and calleth those things which be not, as though they were:

17. As it is written, I have made thee a father of many nations, and not of the Israelitish nation only: so that though the Gentiles were not then called, as now they are, by the gospel, yet that God who promised this to Abraham, when his body and Sarah's were naturally past generation, and to Isaac when he was unborn; and again, when God demanded him as an offering, and thence, as it were, raised him from the dead; that God, I say, did decree the calling of the Gentiles, and spake of that in promise which was long after to be done.

18. Who against hope believed in hope, that he might become the father of many nations; according to that which was spoken, So shall thy seed be.

18. This was the meaning of God's promise to Abraham, who against all natural probability, trusted God's promise, and believed and hoped that accordingly he should become the father of many nations: and that, as he was promised, his seed should be as the stars in heaven.

19. And being not weak in faith, he considered not his own body now dead, when he was about an hundred years old, neither yet the deadness of Sarah's womb.

19. And his faith was not weak and shaken with the consideration that his aged body was almost dead, and unfit for procreation, or that Sarah's womb was so also.

20. He staggered not at the promise of God through unbelief; but was strong in faith, giving glory to God: 21. And being fully persuaded, that what he had promised, he was also able to perform.

20, 21. He was not staggered by unbelief into a distrustful doubting: but was strong in faith, whereby he gave God the glory of his power, wisdom, love, and truth, being fully persuaded, that though nature shewed no probability of it in second causes, the Almighty God could perform all that he had promised.

22. And therefore it was imputed to him for righteousness.

22. And therefore this way of glorifying God by the trusting belief of his free promise, was so suitable to God's end and honour, that he accepted it as righteousness, or a sufficient qualification of him that should partake of his free-given mercy, though Abraham had no sinless innocency, nor could say that he never deserved death.

23. Now it was not written for his sake alone, that it was imputed to him; 24. But for us also, to whom it shall be imputed, if we believe on him that raised up Jesus our Lord from the dead.

23. And certainly, God did not leave this on record for Abraham's sake only: as if there had been a righteousness and right to life, which he only must have, and belonged to no other, and he must be justified by some odd way proper to himself. 24. But this is written also for all us, to tell us what righteousness God requireth and accepteth to our salvation; and that if we believe with trust on his power, truth, and mercy, who raised up our Lord from the dead, this faith shall be imputed to us for righteousness, and we shall be saved by the sacrifice, merits, and mediation of Christ, though our sins deserved death, and neither the law of innocency, or of Moses, justify us.

25. Who was delivered for our offences, and was raised again for our justification.

25. Even our faith in God by Christ and in him, who for our sins was made a propitiatory sacrifice, to procure us free forgiveness of them, and was raised again to cause our justification, by uniting us to himself, and pardoning our sin, and giving us his Spirit and right to impunity and salvation, and justifying this right and us as our advocate, and by his sentence as our judge.

CHAP. V.

THEREFORE being justified by faith, we have peace with God, through our Lord Jesus Christ.

1. Therefore I may conclude, that being constituted, accounted of God, and judged righteous by faith, we have peace with and towards God, as reconciled and adopted through our Lord Jesus Christ, (notwithstanding we are not justifiable as fulfillers of the law.)

2. By whom also we have access by faith into this grace wherein we stand, and rejoice in hope of the glory of God.

2. By whose mediation it is that we came or had access by faith, into this blessed state of grace and God's favour wherein we now are; and greatly rejoice in hope of the promised glory of God.

3. And not only so, but we glory in tribulations also, knowing that tribulation worketh patience; 4. And patience, experience; and experience, hope; 5. And hope maketh not ashamed, because the love of God is shed abroad in our hearts, by the Holy Ghost, which is given unto us.

3, 4, 5. Yea, more than so, but also in all our tribulations which we undergo in the world for Christ and righteousness, we exult with glorying and joy; knowing that this tribulation doth by exercise increase our patience, and being tried, our patient and constant suffering maketh us the more certain by experience that our faith is sound, and giveth us experience of God's supporting grace. And this experience much confirmeth our hope of God's acceptance, and our salvation, which we should be apt to doubt of, if our faith and God's grace had not been thus tried; it being easy by self-flattery to think untried faith is better than it is. And this confirmed hope will never leave us to shame by disappointment, for

CHAP. V. ROMANS. 331

it is accompanied and sealed by that special gift of the Holy Ghost, which sheddeth abroad in our hearts the effects and sense of the love of God through Christ, and so replenisheth us with reflecting love to God, (even as the summer rains and sunshine moisten and warm the earth, and replenish it with pleasant fruits.)

6. For when we were yet without strength, in due time Christ died for the ungodly.

6. For when we were worthless, helpless, lost, and miserable, in the fittest season, Christ died even for the ungodly, guilty sinners; to recover them to God, and save them.

7. For scarcely for a righteous man will one die: yet peradventure for a good man some would even dare to die.

7. For among men, few (or scarce any one) would die for an innocent man; though perhaps some few of rare charity and self-denial, would venture on death for a man of eminent worth and goodness.

8. But God commendeth his love towards us, in that while we were yet sinners, Christ died for us.

8. But the love of God to us was so transcendantly declared and magnified, that while we were yet sinners against his law and him, Christ died to reconcile and save us.

9. Much more then being now justified by his blood, we shall be saved from wrath through him.

9. And if he loved us so far, as to give his Son to die for us when we were mere guilty sinners, we may be sure that now he hath made and accepted us as righteous, pardoning all our sin for the sacrifice of the blood of Christ, he will certainly save us from damnation.

10. For if when we were enemies, we were reconciled to God by the death of his Son: much more being reconciled, we shall be saved by his life.

10. For if God reconciled us to himself by his Son's death, when we were his enemies, doubtless he will save them that are now reconciled, and pardoned believers, by the intercession of him that liveth in glory, and is now our head, the Lord of life, by giving us his Spirit, and justifying us at last, and receiving us to himself in glory. He that loved his enemies, will not damn his beloved children.

11. And not only so, but we also joy in God, through our Lord Jesus Christ, by whom we have now received the atonement.

11. And now moreover, through this reconciliation by Christ, which we have received upon our believing, God is so far from being our terrifying, avenging judge, that he is become our greatest glorying and joy: he being our God and we his people, and he being our father, and all-sufficient portion and felicity.

12. Wherefore as by one man sin entered into the world, and death by sin; and so death passed upon all men, for that all have sinned.

12. In all this we have notice of this great mystery, that as Adam was the root or first cause of man's sin and death, and by that one man sin entered into the world, and death by sin, and so all being sinners, death passed upon all, even temporal death actually, and eternal death by the sentence of the violated law, as being our due.

13. For until the law sin was in the world: but sin is not imputed when there is no law. 14. Nevertheless, death reigned from Adam to Moses, even over them that had not sinned after the similitude of Adam's transgression, who is the figure of him that was to come:

13, 14. For it is certain that sin was in the world before Moses' law, even from Adam's fall; and whereas that is no sin, nor imputed to guilt and punishment, which is against no law; yet death reigned from Adam's fall till Moses; and therefore all were under some law, sin being so far imputed to them: though they sinned not themselves as Adam did, against an express particular command and penal threatening by supernatural revelation from heaven, nor all that died (e. g. infants) did actually and personally transgress: therefore it was from him as his vitiated guilty seed, that they derived original sin, and by this vitious nature they at age sinned actually, against that law which they were under, and by both were the children of death; so that we may compare Adam as the root of sin and death to all, with Christ, who is to all true Christians the root of holiness and life.

15. But not as the offence, so also is the free gift. For if through the offence of one many be dead; much more the grace of God, and the gift by grace *which is* by one man, Jesus Christ, hath abounded unto many.

15. But the disparity must be noted: For if the sin of one man had such malignant power and pernicious efficacy as to procure the guilt and death of many, we may be sure that the grace and mercy of God, and the gift of that saving grace which is from the merits, intercession, and Spirit of Christ, shall be more effectual to the life of many.

16. And not as *it was* by one that sinned, *so is* the gift: for the judgment *was* by one to condemn,

tion; but the free gift is of many offences unto justification.

16. And there is this further difference, that Adam, one man by one sin, brought the sentence of death on all the world, which had not passed else upon us. But it is many sins of many men, which Christ doth deliver us from in the free gift of our justification.

17. For if by one man's offence, death reigned by one; much more they which receive abundance of grace, and of the gift of righteousness, shall reign in life by one, Jesus Christ.

17. For if one offence of one man made all men subjects to death by that one; much more powerfully and effectually, they which receive from one Redeemer abundance of grace, and the gift of righteousness, in the healing and pardoning of all their sins, shall certainly reign in the purchased and promised life of glory, by that one Saviour Jesus Christ.

18. Therefore as by the offence of one, *judgment came* upon all men to condemnation: even so by the righteousness of one, *the free gift came* upon all men unto justification of life.

18. Therefore, as by the offence of one the sentence of death was passed upon all his posterity; so also by the righteousness of one, as the meritorious and procuring cause, the free gift came on all men, for justification and life: that is, a free gift is made and offered promiscuously to all, on condition of believing, suitable acceptance, and actually justifieth all to life, who so believingly accept it, and unthankfully reject it not.

19. For as by one man's disobedience many were made sinners: so by the obedience of one shall many be made righteous.

19. For as by one, Adam's disobedience, all men, as receiving their nature from him, are made guilty and corrupt, and punishable as sinners, so by the procuring meritorious obedience of one (in performing all that was required of him as our Redeemer, in perfect holiness of soul and life, fulfilling the law of innocency, and of Moses, and the peculiar law of mediation, being obedient to the death on the cross) shall the many that by faith receive him, be constituted righteous, and so accounted and judged of God, even reconciled, pardoned, adopted, and made the heirs of life.

20. Moreover, the law entered, that the offence might abound: but where sin abounded, grace did much more abound:

20. And Moses' law, which came in afterward, was made to increase men's obligation against sin,

and more expressly and terribly forbid it, that, if the Jews would sin, their guilt and punishment should be the greater (as alas, they did even to abundance:) but when guilt was increased (and sin by man's abuse of the law) grace did superabound, being victorious against sin, and guilt, and the curse, in all true believers, and extending to many more than Moses' law did, even to all the called nations of the world.

21. That as sin hath reigned unto death, even so might grace reign through righteousness unto eternal life, by Jesus Christ our Lord.

21. That as sin hath had its reign and sad effects in the death and miseries of the sons of Adam, even so shall grace have its more victorious dominion, and reign by the meritorious righteousness of Christ, in making all his members or spiritual offspring righteous, by his pardoning, adopting, sanctifying mercy, and bringing them to eternal life, by the power and efficacy of Jesus their Redeemer.

CHAP. VI.

WHAT shall we say then? Shall we continue in sin, that grace may abound?

1. Perhaps some may gather from all this, that we preach a doctrine of licentiousness; and seeing grace abounded, where sin abounded that we infer that men may continue in sin that grace may abound.

2. God forbid: how shall we that are dead to sin, live any longer therein?

2. Far be it from us so to think: For though Christ came to save sinners, it was not to favour sin, but to destroy it, and save men from it. And therefore as he died for sin, he causeth us to die to sin; and how then shall we live in it that are dead to it?

3. Know ye not that so many of us as were baptized into Jesus Christ, were baptized into his death?

3. Know ye not, that when men are baptized, they are by vow, covenant, and profession, listed into the belief of a crucified Saviour, who died for sin to save us from it, and do profess that repentance by which we renounce it, as dead to it for the time to come?

4. Therefore we are buried with him by baptism into death; that like as Christ was raised up from the dead by the glory of the Father, even so we also should walk in newness of life.

4. Therefore in our baptism we are dipped under the water, as signifying our covenant profes-

tion, that as he was buried for sin, we are dead and buried to sin, that as the glorious power of God raised him from the dead, so we should rise up to live to him in newness and holiness of life.

5. For if we have been planted together in the likeness of his death, we shall be also in *the likeness of his* resurrection:

5. For as we have covenanted and professed our belief in him and conformity to him as dead, so we have covenanted and professed, and must practise our conformity to his resurrection, or else it is not true baptism, and Christianity, and conformity to Christ.

6. Knowing this, that our old man is crucified with *him*, that the body of sin might be destroyed, that henceforth we should not serve sin.

6. Knowing that as his body was crucified for sin, so we have herein covenanted and professed to be, as our old dispositions and sinful conversations, as it were crucified with him, that the body of sin, that is, our fleshly corrupt disposition and conversation, might be destroyed, that henceforth we should not serve sin, but be as dead to it.

7. For he that is dead, is freed from sin.

7. For as a dead man is absolved from all service obligations to his master, so he that is by the death of sin conformed to the death of Christ, is freed from the dominion of sin.

8. Now if we be dead with Christ, we believe that we shall also live with him:

8. And if we be indeed what we are by baptismal profession, conformed thus to Christ's death, we have cause to believe that we must and shall be conformed to his resurrection and life.

9. Knowing that Christ being raised from the dead, dieth no more; death hath no more dominion over him. 10. For in that he died, he died unto sin once: but in that he liveth, he liveth unto God. 11. Likewise reckon ye also yourselves to be dead indeed unto sin; but alive unto God through Jesus Christ our Lord.

9, 10, 11. For as we know that Christ being raised from the dead, dieth no more. His death for sin was but once, but he being risen, liveth to God for ever; so must you reckon that you are by conversion from sin to God, once dead to sin by covenant, consent, and profession, that you may ever after live to God, by the mediation, spirit, and grace of Christ.

12. Let not sin, therefore, reign in your mortal body, that ye should obey it in the lusts thereof.

12. Therefore, unless you will renounce your baptism and Christianity, you must not let sin reign in those bodies, which as they die for sin, so are professedly dead to sin: its lusts may tempt and trouble you, but must not be obeyed.

13. Neither yield ye your members *as* instruments of unrighteousness unto sin: but yield yourselves unto God, as those that are alive from the dead; and your members *as* instruments of righteousness unto God.

13. Nor must you yield the members of your bodies, as instruments of unrighteousness unto sin, though you should pretend that you keep your hearts clean to God; but give up yourselves to the government and will of God, as these that are risen and alive from your dead state of sin, that you may live to him, and so give up the members of your bodies as the soul's instruments of righteousness in serving God.

14. For sin shall not have dominion over you: for ye are not under the law, but under grace.

14. For sin must not, and shall not have dominion over you, to rule you or condemn you ; for you are not under the law which merely forbad it, and condemned the sinner, but under grace which mortifieth and forgiveth it.

15. What then? Shall we sin because we are not under the law, but under grace? God forbid.

15. What then? shall we turn this argument of our deliverance from sin to encourage us in sin, and be the bolder to sin, because we are not under the law that condemneth sinners, but under grace that pardoneth them. Far be it from us.

16. Know ye not, that to whom ye yield yourselves servants to obey, his servants ye are to whom ye obey; whether of sin unto death, or of obedience unto righteousness?

16. Know ye not, that as your engagement to be servants of Christ bindeth you to obey him; so your obedience will shew whose servants you are indeed; whether you obey sin, which is the way of death, or obey Christ unto righteousness and life.

17. But God be thanked, that ye were the servants of sin; but ye have obeyed from the heart that form of doctrine which was delivered you.

17. But God be thanked for your change and

deliverance; that though you were formerly the servants of sin, you have obeyed, not only bodily, but from the heart, that form of Christian doctrine, which was delivered to you, and to which you did consent.

18. Being then made free from sin, ye became the servants of righteousness.

18. In your conversion and baptism, you being delivered from the servitude and guilt of sin, you then by consent and covenant, became Christ's servants for the way and works of righteousness.

19. I speak after the manner of men, because of the infirmity of your flesh. For as ye have yielded your members servants to uncleanness and to iniquity, unto iniquity; even so now yield your members servants to righteousness, unto holiness.

19. I use this familiar speech by similitude and allegory, as fitted to your capacity: As you did formerly use your bodies in uncleanness and iniquity, as servants of iniquity; so now use your bodies as servants of righteousness, devoted to God, and sanctified to obey him.

20. For when ye were the servants of sin, ye were free from righteousness.

20. For when you lived in the servitude of sin, you were not the servants of God and righteousness, you lived not a life of holiness and obedience to God.

21. What fruit had ye then in those things whereof ye are now ashamed? for the end of those things *is* death.

21. Review now those works, and think what you got by them, you are justly now ashamed of them and of their fruits: For whatever sin seem in the committing, misery and death is the end and fruit of it, where grace doth not recover and forgive.

22. But now being made free from sin, and become servants to God, ye have your fruit unto holiness, and the end everlasting life.

22. But now having by conversion changed your master and life, and being delivered from the slavery of sin, and become the servants of God, the fruit is a life of holiness here, and hereafter at the end, everlasting happiness.

23. For the wages of sin *is* death; but the gift of God *is* eternal life, through Jesus Christ our Lord.

23. For the service of sin is rewarded with death, and this the law obligeth the sinner to; but the free gift of God through the mediation of Christ is eternal life: And this is it which in the gospel covenant is proclaimed and bestowed: And do you not now see both how necessary it is to have a Saviour, and a better covenant and way of life than Moses's mere law, or man's own meritorious works; and that our gospel is so far from favouring sin, that it declareth the only way to be delivered, both from the guilt and power of it, and to be made holy here, and happy for ever.

CHAP. VII.

KNOW ye not brethren, (for I speak to them that know the law) how that the law hath dominion over a man as long as he liveth?

1. I have used the similitudes of a dead man, and one raised from death, and of a servant, and one set free and under another master: I will now add the similitude of a married woman and a dead husband. You know (who know the law) that the law of superiority, which giveth one power over another, obligeth only until death.

2. For the woman which hath an husband, is bound by the law to *her* husband so long as he liveth: but if the husband be dead, she is loosed from the law of *her* husband.

2. The law bindeth a wife to be a subject to her husband till he die: but then she is thereby no longer bound to him:

3. So then if while *her* husband liveth, she be married to another man, she shall be called an adulteress: but if her husband be dead, she is free from that law; so that she is no adulteress, though she be married to another man.

3. So that though she be an adulteress who marrieth another, while her husband liveth, yet when her husband is dead, she is free from that obligation, and is no adulteress for marrying with another.

4. Wherefore, my brethren, ye also are become dead to the law by the body of Christ; that ye should be married to another, *even* to him who is raised from the dead, that we should bring forth fruit unto God.

4. So death hath separated the law and the believing Jews. The law being abrogated by the coming, and death, and grace of Christ, is dead to it; that so you should be married to him that caused this by his death, and is raised from the dead, and hath raised you from the death of sin and guilt, and legal condemnation to a new and holy life, that regeneration may cause you to generate the holy fruit of love and good works, and live hereafter unto God.

5. For when we were in the flesh, the motions of sin which were by the law, did work in our members to bring forth fruit unto death.

5. For when we were in our mere corrupted nature, and only under a forbidding and condemning law, without the gospel and its grace, the law did but irritate and shew our carnal lusts, and cause our guilt and condemnation, and did not either heal or pardon us.

6. But now we are delivered from the law, that being dead wherein we were held; that we should serve in newness of spirit, and not *in* the oldness of the letter.

6. But now we are delivered from that law, and so from its manifold difficult impositions, all which we could not fulfil, and also from its curse of those that fulfil it not: For it is abolished, and bindeth us no more. That now we may serve God with new hearts, and lives, by the Spirit of Christ, according to the law of grace, and not carnally in the bondage and terror of the old law.

7. What shall we say then? *Is* the law sin? God forbid. Nay, I had not known sin, but by the law: for I had not known lust, except the law had said, Thou shalt not covet.

7. But think not by this that we infer, that the law is bad or culpable, or the cause of sin: Far be it from us, so far am I from such a thought, that I testify that the law is the forbidder, and discoverer, and condemner of sin: For I had not known my heart's inordinate desires or lusts to be so bad, if the law had not said, Thou shalt not covet; For corrupt nature hardly discerneth the evil of its own inclination, so be it break not out into act, but is ready to think it is blameless, because it is natural.

8. But sin taking occasion by the commandment, wrought in me all manner of concupiscence. For without the law sin *was* dead.

8. But my own soul hath sinful inclinations and imperfections, by original corruption and the evil habits increased by actual sin. And by these I am so backward to good, and prone to evil, that a law of such a multitude of difficult, positive precepts and prohibitions, making me so much work, and so hard, is become morally impossible for me perfectly to fulfil: Had I been only under the law made to fallen Adam and Noah, and all mankind, a great number of legal positives and ceremonials had never obliged me; but this law being made, and all these things laid upon me which my corrupt nature could not fulfil, presently my badness and disability appeared in a great number of acts, which now became forbidden sin, and in the omission of things commanded: even as if you command ignorant, weak, and ill disposed men, a multitude of such particulars as none but the wise and well-disposed will keep, it will occasion them to be guilty of a multitude of sins, which without those canons, or laws would have been no sin; so my sinful nature made this law of works an occasion of my guilt of a multitude of actual sins; which without the law would have been no sin, or not so culpable. Besides that the prohibition stirred up my ill inclination, and also that I sinned against more knowledge.

9. For I was alive without the law once: but when the commandment came, sin revived, and I died.

9. For if you suppose me only under the common law made to Noah and all mankind, and the promise made to him and to Abraham, before the law of Moses was made, I had not then been under either that sentence of a temporal, or an eternal death, which by Moses's law are the wages of many sins, not before forbidden: But when I am under all those laws which curse or cut off all that do not the numerous tasks and ceremonies there imposed, I am then become a dead man in law, and the law and sin rise up in power against me, and condemn me.

10. And the commandment which *was ordained* to life, I found *to be* unto death.

10. And the commandment which promised life to them that keep it, proved the occasion of death to me.

11. For sin taking occasion by the commandment, deceived me, and by it slew me.

11. For my sinful nature called out to so much duty, and forbidden so many things, being unable to do the duties, and prone to the things forbidden, by occasion of this law, became the guilty cause of many actual sins of omission and commission; and as ill humours stirred by a purge oft rage the more, so did the pravity of my nature, and so I was made guilty of death.

12. Wherefore the law *is* holy; and the commandment holy, and just, and good.

12. Wherefore I testify, that the law is pure, and holy, and just, and good: God justly made it: His wisdom and holiness shine forth in it: If men be bad and ill disposed, God may justly give them such laws as their badness is averse to keep. And he had good and gracious ends in giving it: He made it indeed very operous, somewhat like the law of innocency to Adam, though not that same but yet conjunct and subordinate to the law and promise of grace; which the Jews should have noted and used it accordingly.

13. Was then that which is good, made death unto me? God forbid. But sin that it might appear sin, working death in me by that which is good; that sin by the commandment might become exceeding sinful.

13. What then? Is the law guilty of my sin and death? By no means: But the inward pravity of my soul, which else would have been more latent, unknown, and not have brought forth so much actual sin and death, did by the good law of God, appear in its proper evil nature, and shew how pregnant it was of actual sin, and how averse to full obedience, and so by producing these actual sins, appeared and became exceeding sinful.

14. For we know that the law is spiritual: but I am carnal, sold under sin.

14. For we all confess that the law being God's own law, is divine, spiritual, and pure. And the reason why I do not fulfil it, and so cannot be justified by it, is in myself, who in my corrupt nature am carnal, and under a moral necessity of sinning against it; predominantly before grace, and in part after.

15. For that which I do, I allow not: for what I would, that do I not; but what I hate, that do I.

15. I may well call a captivity, or a kind of necessity, when my knowledge and unfeigned (though imperfect) willingness and desire and my hatred of the sin, yet will not enable me to be so free from sin; and fulfil the law, as to be justified by it (much less will the uneffectual convictions and wishes of the unregenerate do this.) For though I do not in judgment approve my sin ; and I have a desire perfectly to fulfil the law of God, and I would be freed from all sin, yet I attain not this perfection which I desire.

16. If then I do that which I would not, I consent unto the law, that it is good.

16. Now if I did not justify the law as good, I should not thus condemn myself for breaking it, nor desire thus perfectly to keep it.

17. Now then it is no more I that do it, but sin that dwelleth in me.

17. And because the understanding and will are the highest faculties, and a man is in God's account what he truly would be, therefore I may say, that (though it be my sin to have so inordinate a sensitive inclination, and so imperfect a mind and will which should better rule it,) yet it is not such a sin as sheweth the predominant disposition of my soul, and denominateth the man, but is contrary to the resolved bent of my heart and life; and therefore the Lord of Grace will not judge me according to that which is but my imperfection, and which I more hate than love, and would unfeignedly be rid of, for it is no reigning sin that I confess.

18. For I know that in me (that is, in my flesh) dwelleth no good thing: for to will is present with me, but *how* to perform that which is good, I find not.

18. For I know that so far as I have any corruption and carnality, I am prone to evil and not to good: For by the grace of God I do truly desire perfection itself; but I am not able to attain my desire, and to be perfect in my obedience.

19. For the good that I would, I do not: but the evil which I would not, that I do.

19. For my nature being corrupt, and my will but imperfectly renewed, though sincere, I cannot be as good as I would be, nor do all the good which I would do, nor avoid all the evil which I would avoid, and so cannot be sinless and perfectly obedient.

20. Now if I do that I would not, it is no more I that do it, but sin that dwelleth in me.

20. Now seeing the main bent of my mind and will is for perfect obedience, and against all sin, and it is by the instigation of the remnant of carnality, that I am not sinless and free from all culpable infirmities, God will not impute that to me which I hate, and is contrary to the bent of my heart and life, so much as that which I love and live for.

21. I find then a law, that when I would do good, evil is present with me.

21. I find then in my carnal part, an inclination, which is a contradicting law, which striveth so much against the law of God, that I oft sin contrary to my predominant will, and when I would be sinless and perfect, yet I cannot.

22. For I delight in the law of God, after the inward man. 23. But I see another law in my members, warring against the law of my mind, and bringing me into captivity to the law of sin, which is in my members.

22, 23. For I delight in the law of God, after the inward man, which is the bent of my mind and will. But my corrupt sensual inclination is like a contrary law, which warreth against my judgment and will, and like a captive I am brought by it under a necessity of sinning, so far as that my obedience is imperfect, and so unjustifiable by the law of works, (as in the unregenerate sin doth reign.)

24. O wretched man that I am,

who shall deliver me from the body of this death!

24. So far am I then from being justified by this law that while it calleth for more perfect obedience to its hard and numerous precepts, that my sinful soul can perform, and so condemneth me, it doth but shew me how bad and miserable I am, and make me cry out, O wretched man, who shall deliver me from this sinning deadly flesh?

25. I thank God, through Jesus Christ our Lord. So then with the mind I myself serve the law of God; but with the flesh the law of sin.

25. But as I have told you of my misery by nature, under the law, I will tell you of my remedy: I rejoice in thankfulness to God that hath abrogated the law, and sanctified my nature by Jesus Christ: And so I conclude, that my renewed mind and will so desireth perfection, that I would be sinless, and keep all the law which God shall impose and continue; but my fleshly inclination maketh this sinless perfection too hard for my attainment, and therefore I cannot be justified by so hard and rigorous a law.

ANNOTATIONS.

Though expositors are much disagreed whether St. Paul here describes a man unregenerate under the mere law, or an imperfect man, how sincere soever; yet no such doctrinal controversy dependeth on this difference, as the ignorant and contentious do imagine. For they that think that he describeth the case of a carnal legalist, or Jew, suppose that he speaketh of their committing against knowledge, and uneffectual wishes, the reigning sins called mortal, and live an ungodly life; and that [It is not I, but sin] signifieth only [my superior faculties have some uneffectual reluctancy, and are convinced that the law is good;] and that by [Captivity to the law of sin] is meant, a slavish life of predominant sensuality. And doubtless such there are, of whom all this is true.

And those that think that he speaketh of himself even in his regenerate state, and so of all men, do think that it is not a life of wickedness, or mortal sin, that he describeth, nor a captivity to it, but unavoidable imperfection, called venial sin; to the same sense as St. John saith, [If wo say that we have no sin, there is no truth in us.] And that [It is not I, but sin] signifieth but that a man shall be accounted and judged by God, according to what is predominant in his mind, will, and life.

And I most incline to this exposition, 1. Because the other seemeth forced, which must not be received without necessity. 2. Because the apostle is not only proving that the law will not justify an unregenerate legal Jew, but that it will justify no man, how good soever. 3. And I do not believe that the unregenerate can truly say as he, [I delight in the law of God,] and [It will is present with me,] and [I myself in mind serve the law of God. 4. Many passages are plainly applicable to Paul in his Christian state.

2.

CHAP. VIII.

THERE is, therefore, now no condemnation to them which are in Christ Jesus, who walk not after the flesh, but after the Spirit.

1. It is not then the law that justifieth us, but faith in Christ; and all that are in him are acquit from the curse and condemnation of the law, (and also of the law of nature) for their sin is pardoned, and they are regenerate, and live not now after the fleshly inclination or law, but under the spiritual law of grace, by a spiritual inclination wrought in them by the Holy Ghost, which is given them by Christ.

2. For the law of the Spirit of life in Christ Jesus, hath made me free from the law of sin and death.

2 For the covenant of grace which giveth the Spirit, and the Spirit so given me by Christ, being not a killing but a quickening law, giving me internal and spiritual life, and title to eternal life, hath made me free from the power and rule of my carnal inclination, and from the obligation and condemnation of Moses's law.

3. For what the law could not do, in that it was weak through the flesh, God sending his own Son in the likeness of sinful flesh, and for sin condemned sin in the flesh:

3. For when the mere law could neither justify nor regenerate us, because our fleshly pravity was incapable hereof, God sending his own Son in flesh like ours which is sinful, though without sin, as a sacrifice for sin, and example of perfect holiness, thereby shewed his enmity to sin, and began the holy enterprize of its destruction.

4. That the righteousness of the law might be fulfilled in us, who walk not after the flesh, but after the Spirit.

4. That the true righteousness which the law was made to lead men to, might be found in us, and the true ends of the law obtained by us, who live now by the spiritual principle and rule, and not by the carnal principle and letter.

5. For they that are after the flesh, do mind the things of the flesh: but they that are after the Spirit, the things of the Spirit.

5. For the unregenerate who are under the dominion of a carnal disposition, though they may be under the terror of a threatening law, do still favour, love, and mind nothing so much as fleshly interest and pleasure: But they whose souls are renewed by the Holy Spirit, and live by faith on spiritual promises, do mind, love, and seek most spiritual welfare and felicity.

Z

6. For to be carnally minded, *is* death; but to be spiritually minded, *is* life and peace;

6. For the true state of misery called death in the soul, which is the way to everlasting misery, consisteth in its being turned from the love of God and holiness, to the love of carnal interest and pleasure; and the true state of spiritual life and felicity, consisteth in the love of God and holiness, and the soul's perfection.

7. Because the carnal mind *is* enmity against God: for it is not subject to the law of God, neither indeed can be.

7. Because the carnal unregenerate mind, having a predominant inclination to inferior sensual interests and delights, and a privation, yea, and enmity to things spiritual and holy, hath thereby an enmity to the holy laws and ways of God, and consequently to God as holy: For it is not subject to the law of God, which is quite against their sinful life and inclination, nor indeed can be, while it so continueth; there being a contrariety between their inclinations and the law of God.

8. So then they that are in the flesh, cannot please God.

8. So that they that are unregenerate and carnal, cannot please God while they are such; because they cannot, through the perverseness of their own wills, do the things that please him, what legal restraint soever they be under.

9. But ye are not in the flesh, but in the Spirit, if so be that the Spirit of God dwell in you. Now if any man have not the Spirit of Christ, he is none of his.

9. But you are not in this carnal state, and under the dominion of the flesh, if the Spirit of God do not only provoke you towards goodness, but also dwell in you and possess you; For it is a powerful Spirit, and will overcome the flesh: But if any man have not this indwelling, illuminating, quickening, sanctifying Spirit, he is not a true Christian, and saved by Christ: He may be baptised, and deceive the church, and pass for a visible member of it, and so for a Christian among men, but Christ will not own him as a living member to justification and salvation.

10. And if Christ *be* in you, the body *is* dead because of sin; but the spirit *is* life, because of righteousness.

10. And if Christ by his Spirit and government be and rule in you, the body which hath still some inordinate sinful inclinations, and backwardness to good, shall die for sin; but your spirits being quickened by the Spirit of God, unto holiness and justification, are in a state of life begun, and shall not die as the body doth, but live with Christ, by whom they live.

11. But if the Spirit of him that raised up Jesus from the dead, dwell in you; he that raised up Christ from the dead, shall also quicken your mortal bodies, by his Spirit that dwelleth in you.

11. But if the Spirit of him that raised up Jesus from the dead dwell in you, he that by this same Spirit of life and power raised up Christ from the dead, as he hath begun to raise you from spiritual death in sin, and sanctify both soul and body to himself, will not only glorify your souls, but also raise and save your mortal bodies, by that same Almighty Spirit which raised Christ, and sanctified you.

12. Therefore, brethren, we are debtors not to the flesh, to live after the flesh. 13. For if ye live after the flesh, ye shall die: but if ye through the Spirit do mortify the deeds of the body, ye shall live.

12, 13. By all which you may see, that it is not to the flesh that we owe our chief respect, care, and obedience, nor after the lusts of which we should live: For it is this sinful fleshly life that causeth death, and tendeth unto future misery: But if by the Spirit you mortify those fleshly lusts and deeds, which carnal men obey and practise, this beginning of spiritual life will end in future life and happiness.

14. For as many as are led by the Spirit of God, they are the sons of God.

14. For as many as are principled and ruled by God's Spirit, and spiritual law of grace, are God's children: And God will not forsake, lose, or destroy his spiritual children.

15. For ye have not received the spirit of bondage again to fear; but ye have received the Spirit of adoption, whereby we cry, Abba, Father.

15. For the Spirit which you have now received is not that of a slave, which doth no good but for fear of punishment; (and the mere law without grace could give no better) but you have received the Spirit of adoption, which giveth you an inclination of dependance, love, and trust in God, much like that which a child hath by nature to his father, to the collation of which child-like love, trust, and nature, the wondrous revelation of God's love in Christ, and the free gifts of his grace, were spiritually fitted.

16. The Spirit itself beareth witness with our spirit, that we are the children of God.

16. And to have this Spirit of God dwelling in us, and sanctifying us, is a certain evidence or testimony in and with our own spirits and con-

sciences, that God doth specially love us, and take us for his children, having set this special mark upon us: For we could not love him as a father, and he not love us as his children. And this Spirit also helpeth our consciences to discern and exercise this sealing grace, and to rejoice therein.

17. And if children, then heirs; heirs of God, and joint-heirs with Christ: if so be that we suffer with *him*, that we may be also glorified together.

17. And if this seal of the Spirit prove us sons, it proveth us heirs of the purchased kingdom, or heavenly inheritance, for such are all the sons of God; heirs of God, and co-heirs with Christ; but, so that there is a further condition of our possession, even that we take up the cross and follow him, submitting to be conformed to him in his sufferings, if God call us to it, that so by the same way we may come to be glorified together with him.

18. For I reckon, that the sufferings of this present time, *are* not worthy *to be compared* with the glory which shall be revealed in us.

18. For though we must suffer in this life, with Christ, and for his sake, and by God's correction for our sins, having in my reckoning compared them with the promised effects and end, I fully resolve the case, that they are not worthy to be compared with the glory which in the saints shall be shortly manifested; nor should they stop any man from entertaining the doctrine of the cross, and pursuing his celestial hopes.

19. For the earnest expectation of the creature waiteth for the manifestation of the sons of God.

19. For all the frame of nature strongly tending to its own perfection, (and God annihilateth not the natural or sensitive creatures, though he dissolve the composition) they do, as it were, wait for their better state and deliverance from the curse caused by man's sins, till the manifestation of the glory of the sons of God; with whom, and for whom they shall have their restoration, as with men they fell under the curse.

20. For the creature was made subject to vanity, not willingly, but by reason of him who hath subjected *the same* in hope:

20. For so much of the world as was made for man, and marred or cursed for man's sake, so was made subject to this curse and mutation, not for its own sin, nor by its own choice, but by the sin of man, even by that God who subjected its condition to the free will and state of man, and so to suffer with and for him, but with a purpose to restore it with him unto its integrity.

21. Because the creature itself also shall be delivered from the bondage of corruption, into the glorious liberty of the children of God.

21. Because the natural and sensitive parts of the world, that were subjected to the use of man, and fell under a curse by man, shall be delivered with man from that curse and bondage, and corruptibility, into a state of liberty and useful perfection, suitable to the glory of the children of God, for whom they were made.

22. For we know that the whole creation groaneth and travaileth in pain together until now:

22. For it is evident, that the whole natural and subjective world which was thus subjected to man, and cursed for him, is like a woman in the pangs or expectation of child-birth, and groaneth till it be delivered with us at that time of restoration.

23. And not only *they*, but ourselves also, which have the first-fruits of the Spirit, even we ourselves groan within ourselves, waiting for the adoption, *to wit*, the redemption of our body.

23. And if this be their case, much more do we who have the Spirit of God, which is the pledge, earnest, and first fruit of glory, feeling ourselves burdened with sin, temptations and sufferings in the world, and yet short of our expected glory, feel ourselves as a woman in travail, groaning for deliverance, and longing for the blessed inheritance, yea, even the resurrection of the body itself, to which we were adopted.

24. For we are saved by hope: But hope that is seen, is not hope: for what a man seeth, why doth he yet hope for?

24. For our present state of salvation is not in sight and full possession, but in the hope of unseen things that are promised, and this hope will bring us possession. But if we had sight and possession of it, we could not be said to live by the hopes of it, for why should we be said to hope for that which we see and possess.

25. But if we hope for that we see not, *then* do we with patience wait for it.

25. But hoping for that which we never saw or possessed, we do with patience under all delays wait for the desired attainment and possession.

26. Likewise the Spirit also helpeth our infirmities: for we know not what we should pray for as we ought: but the Spirit itself maketh intercession for us with groanings which cannot be uttered.

26. And the Spirit which God hath given us, helpeth us against our infirmities of hope and

prayer; and under our sufferings and distresses; for we are unmeet judges of our own necessities and condition, and the flesh is too prone to desire its own ease and safety: But the Spirit of Christ in us, teacheth and inclineth us to go to God as a merciful all-sufficient Father, and to pour out our souls' complaints before him, at least with groans, when we cannot utter them with words; and to cry, Abba, Father, and to refer ourselves unto his wisdom, and cast our case in trust on him.

27. And he that searcheth the hearts, knoweth what *is* the mind of the Spirit, because he maketh intercession for the saints, according to *the will of* God.

27. And God that searcheth the heart, knoweth the meaning of these very groans, excited by his Spirit, which we want words to express: For he knoweth what his own Spirit moveth us to ask, and what desires come from himself; for as Christ is in heaven our intercessor with the Father, so the Holy Spirit sent down into our hearts, is our intercessor with the Father and the Son; for as he is Christ's agent and witness in us, to communicate spiritual life, light, and love to us, so he is a Spirit of supplication and adoption in us; and the spring of all our holy desires and motions Godward, and that only which is of him is accepted of God; for he moveth us to ask what pleaseth God, and to submit to his will, and returneth us the answer of our prayers in inward strength and consolation.

28. And we know that all things work together for good, to them that love God, to them who are called according to *his* purpose.

28. For we know that all the course of God's providence, and particularly all our sufferings for him, do by God's over-ruling ordination, work together for our good, even to carry on them that love him to salvation; who are called hereto according to the gracious benevolent purpose of his own will.

29. For whom he did foreknow, he also did predestinate *to be* conformed to the image of his Son, that he might be the first-born among many brethren.

29. For those whom he fore-knew and purposed to glorify, he also predestinated as the way to their glory, to be conformed to the image of his Son, in holiness and patient suffering, that his church as brethren, might be like their head and eldest brother.

30. Moreover, whom he did predestinate, them he also called: and whom he called, them he also justified: and whom he justified, them he also glorified.

30. And those whom God thus predestinateth to be conformed to Christ, them in time he effectually called to repent and believe in Christ; and those whom he thus called, and made true Christians, he justified, both making them just by pardoning their sin, and giving them his indwelling Spirit of love and holiness, and accounting them just, for the merits of Christ; and those whom he thus justifieth, he will glorify with Christ.

31. What shall we then say to these things? If God *be* for us, who *can be* against us?

31. What then shall we say, when we consider all this, but with joyful thankfulness conclude, that God is in for his saints, their Father and Protector, and therefore they have no cause to fear any that are against them, how great, or many, or strong soever; that is, not fear their power, so be we take heed that they draw us not to sin.

32. He that spared not his own Son, but delivered him up for us all, how shall he not with him also freely give us all things?

32. He that spared not his own Son, not thinking him too precious a gift, but delivered him up to suffer as a sacrifice to procure the pardon of sin and salvation, to be given to all by a conditional covenant of faith and acceptance, and actually to pardon and save all true believers, that accept him, how can it be that he should think any thing else, which we need, too good for us, and not freely give all other things with Christ to us that believingly accept him? See 1 John i. 11, 12.

33. Who shall lay any thing to the charge of God's elect? *It is* God that justifieth:

33. Of how little moment is it what erroneous and malignant men lay to the charge of God's elect (accusing them as breakers of their laws) whilst God himself doth justify them?

34. Who *is* he that condemneth? *It is* Christ that died, yea rather that is risen again, who is even at the right hand of God, who also maketh intercession for us.

34. What, or who is he that condemneth those whom Almighty God doth justify? What is the sentence of a worm, a sinner, and a blinded enemy to be set against God's sentence? It is Christ that died for our sins, to deliver us from the law and curse, that justifieth believers here on earth; yea, I say more to our consolation, It is Christ that is risen again, and advanced in glory, head over all things to his church, who effectually intercedeth for us, and will finally justify us as our judge.

35. Who shall separate us from the love of Christ? *shall* tribulation, or distress, or persecution, or famine, or nakedness, or peril, or sword?

35. And when God, by such an incomprehensi-

CHAP. VIII. ROMANS. 341

his miracle of mercy, declared such unspeakable love to us in Christ, who or what can be supposed to have power to dissolve this bond of mutual love? viz. to separate us from God's love to us, and our thankful return of love to him? Shall tribulation, or distress, or famine, or nakedness, or peril, or sword, or any thing that men can do; which are little matters, and all work to our good, and none of them signify or cause God's forsaking us, nor shall cause us to forsake him.

36. (As it is written, For thy sake we are killed all the day long: we are accounted as sheep for the slaughter.)

36. We may say as the Psalmist doth, xliv. 22. [For thy sake we are killed all the day long, &c.]

37. Nay in all these things we are more than conquerors, through him that loved us.

37. Yes, all these are but the occasions of our triumph, when we overcome them all as they are temptations. It were not so much to us to conquer all our enemies and persecutors in fight, as it is by faith and patience to overcome their persecutions.

38. For I am persuaded, that neither death, nor life, nor angels, nor principalities, nor powers, nor things present, nor things to come, 39. Nor height, nor depth, nor any other creature, shall be able to separate us from the love of God which is in Christ Jesus our Lord.

38, 39. For I am persuaded that the band of love between God and all true confirmed Christians, made in and by our Mediator Christ, is so strong and sure, that it will never be dissolved by the terrors of death, or the love of this life, nor by malignant spirits, by principalities or powers, Satan or his instruments of strength and violence, by what now doth, or what hereafter shall befal us, or assault us; by any things above us, or beneath us, exaltation, or dejection, nor by the power of any creature: Nothing hath power to cause God to cease loving us, or us to cease loving God.

ANNOTATIONS.

I. The controversies raised about the first fourteen verses, of the fulfilling of the righteousness of the law; of the carnal and spiritual state of mind, &c. are sufficiently decided in the paraphrase.

II. So is that of the spirit of bondage and adoption, and that of the witness of the Spirit with our spirits, &c. in the paraphrase on the 15th and 16th verses.

III. His exposition on the 19th, 20th, 21st, and 22d verses, which feigneth them to speak of the heathen world, hath so many and palpable violences, that I think it not worth the labour to give a particular confutation of them. But if many things about the creatures' restoration be yet unknown and unrevealed to us, it followeth not that therefore it is unknown whether a restoration there shall be. The heavens must contain Christ till the time of this restoration. And his violence is as gross about the words of St. Peter, That we look for a new heaven and a new earth, in which dwelleth righteousness. What God doth with the souls of brutes, when they die hence, may be unknown to us, and yet their restoration known. It is not hard, by the most probable principles of philosophy, to shame their opinion who confidently say, that their souls are no spiritual substances, but evanid, accidents, qualities, or motions. And as they may easily be proved substances, that have an essential power of vital action, perception, and appetite; so it is most improbable that God annihilateth them, or changeth their essential form or nature. But whether they are continued individuate, or only in one or more universal form; and if individuate, whither, or to what use God disposeth of them, and what alteration there will be in the state of restoration, mortals know not.

IV. Those that say, That by the [Spirit that helpeth our infirmities,] verse 26, is meant Christ by his Spirit praying for us in heaven, can neither make it agree with the context, nor prove that the Spirit groaneth in heaven, or is called our intercessor there, but within us.

V. They that feign the 28th verse to say, That all the sins of believers shall work for their good, dangerously pervert the text: It is contrary to the context, and to the tenor of all the scripture, and the wisdom and holiness of God, and the safety of believers, to feign God to promise them, that how much soever they sin, they shall be gainers by it; when he still useth the clean contrary means to save them from it, even by his threatenings. And it is contrary to the very terms of the text, [To them that love God, &c.] which implieth, that the defects or decay of their love to God is not for their good. And it is contrary to common experience, which tells us, that many Christians by sin lose some degrees of love to God, and other grace, and die worse than once they were, (and so have a less degree of glory.) And is this for their good? Yes, all men die in some sin of omission, as in a culpable defect of some due act or degree of faith, hope, love, joy, patience, of which they have no more time to repent. And what good doth that do them? Indeed some sin to some men God maketh an occasion of good, and an object of repentance, &c. But as an occasion is not a cause, and to be an object of repentance is to be a duty, and not a sin; so even this much is none of the meaning of this promise, which speaketh but of sufferings, or at most of God's providential works, of which sin is none.

VI. The controversies about predestination, raised from the 28th and 29th verses, might be ended by the text itself, if we could be content to know no more than God doth teach us, and to be no wiser than St. Paul was.

1. He teacheth us, That there are some called according to God's purpose and foreknown by him, that is, to be such as he will use as is after mentioned: He knoweth them to be those whom he purposeth to call and save; but Paul was not so presumptuous and profane, as to dispute, How God foreknoweth them, or why he purposeth to call them rather than others.

2. And whereas profane men do foolishly say, If God decree and foreknow my salvation, I shall be saved whatever I do; and if he do not I shall not: St. Paul tells us, That those whom God purposeth or decreeth to save, he predestinateth to be conformed to the image of his Son, even to the means, as well as to the end. So that, to say, That God doth predestinate men to salvation, and not to holiness of heart and life, is to contradict God's doctrine of predestination. As God doth decree how long we shall live, and withal that we shall live by meat and drink; so he decreeth that we shall be saved, and that by faith and sincere obedience. And sure they know not what they say, who call this doctrine of election licentious. Doth it encourage men to impenitency or disobedience, to tell them, that God doth predestinate men to repent, and obey, and be saved? Will it tempt men to live after the flesh, in worldliness, or sensuality, to believe that God hath decreed to make them to live after the Spirit, and to mortify the deeds of the flesh, and to avoid such sins?

3. And Paul tells us, That this chain of causes is all decreed of God, from the first to the last: and therefore that it is God's purpose which secureth the event of our glorification. And it is strange that any should think, that God should undertake so great a work as man's redemption, and not effectually secure the success by his own will and wisdom, but leave all to the lubricous will of man.

4. But the apostle tells us of no such decrees of the causes of men's damnation. God causeth and giveth grace, and foreknoweth that which he will give: But he doth not cause or give men sin, nor necessitate any to commit it; and therefore decreeth not to cause it, nor foreknoweth it as his own work, but as man's. So that election and non-election, or reprobation, are not of the same kind, degree, and order.

VII. The sense of the terms of the 30th verse, expositors much differ about; but there is no great doctrinal controversy depending on it. 1. It is doubted, whether by [calling] here be meant only effectual calling and conversion, or only general calling antecedent to its efficacy. But it is confessed, that both these are asserted in the scripture. 2. It is doubted, why sanctification is omitted, or where it is included: But it is agreed, that it is one link of the chain of the causes of salvation. 3. And so it is doubted, what the word [justify] doth mean: But the thing is agreed on. 4. And the greatest doubt is, whether every one of these causes will infer the rest, or only the connexion of all the foregoing will infer that which followeth.

1. There is small reason to doubt, but that by [calling] is meant [effectual calling]: Else it would neither prove predestination, nor infer justification.

2. Sanctification is a word which signifieth many acts. As it signifieth the gift of our first faith and repentance, and our covenant-devotedness to God in baptism, it is the same with effectual vocation, regeneration, and conversion. But as it signifieth the after gift of the indwelling Spirit, to habituate the soul with fixed holiness and love, and the practice of these, it followeth vocation, at least in order of nature.

3. Justification sometime signifieth making us righteous; sometime, accounting us righteous; sometime, by apology, maintaining us to be righteous; sometime, by judicial sentence, pronouncing us righteous; sometime, executively, using us as righteous; usually, many of these together, all the rest being implied. It is certain, that God maketh men righteous; before he account or judge them righteous. Now to make a man righteous (and justifiable in judgment) all these concur. 1. The merit of Christ's righteousness, as the deserving matter and cause. 2. The act of the new covenant, giving him a part in Christ, and with him pardon of sin, and right to the Spirit of grace, and unto glory. 3. The gift of faith and repentance, that Christ and his further grace may be ours; and for continuance, the holy habits and acts of sanctification. And seeing all sound expositors confess (with Beza) that at least three texts by justification mean, or include sanctification, we have reason to judge, that part of sanctification is here included in vocation, and part in justification, and some think the triumphant part in glorification. And certainly this inferreth no unsound doctrine.

4. Augustine thought, that the links of this are separable, unless you include the first as the qualification of all the rest, by way of distinction; and the meaning is, That [God will call all the predestinate or elect, and will justify all the predestinate that are called, and will glorify all the justified that are predestinate and called;] but that there are some justified and sanctified, that were not predestinate, nor shall be glorified, but fall away. What the sense of the ancient fathers was about perseverance, Ger. Vossius hath so truly opened in his Theses, that I may thither refer the inquisitive. My own sense of it I have opened in my Catholic Theology; and it is too long a case to be handled here. But I think no confirmed Christian doth totally and finally fall away; and that the rest of the doubt should not be thought enough to break the love and peace of Christians.

VIII. As to the doubt, Whether the 38th and 39th verses speak [of God's love to us, or ours to him,] as they are in themselves inseparable, so I think that the context giveth us reason to think that it is both, even the bond of mutual love which is here spoken of. All the doubt is, whether it be spoken of every true Christian, or only of the elect and confirmed; of which before.

CHAP. IX.

I SAY the truth in Christ, I lie not, my conscience also bearing me witness in the Holy Ghost, 2. That I have great heaviness, and continual sorrow in my heart. 3. For I could wish that myself were accursed from Christ for my brethren, my kinsmen according to the flesh:

1, 2, 3: I am so far from saying all that I have said in contempt of the Jews, or triumph over them in their misery, that I protest as a Christian, I lie not, my conscience bearing me witness, which is illuminated and actuated by the Holy Ghost,

CHAP. IX. ROMANS. 343

that in the midst of all my rejoicing in Christ, I have great heaviness and continual sorrow of heart, for the sin and misery of the Jews, who are my brethren and kinsmen according to the flesh; yea, so great, that were my own misery a means by which God would save their nation, I could consent to be deprived of my part of blessedness with Christ, and used as a cursed man, for their conversion, that all the grace fore-described might be theirs. I say not that I do wish it, for it is no means to any such end; but that I could wish it, if God had made it such a means: Because the happiness of a nation, and the glory of God's grace in so many, is much better than my single welfare, and if God had set them in competition, the best should have been preferred.

4. Who are Israelites; to whom *pertaineth* the adoption, and the glory, and the covenants, and the giving of the law, and the service *of God*, and the promises; 5. Whose *are* the fathers, and of whom as concerning the flesh, Christ *came*, who is over all, God blessed for ever. Amen.

4, 5. Who are the posterity of Abraham, Isaac, and Jacob, adopted of God to be to him a holy nation above all people of the earth; who had the ark and temple, where God oft showed his presence by a glory, and with whom the covenant of peculiarity was made, and oft renewed: To whom God gave the law from heaven, and appointed all the services or worship therein commanded, and gave them the promise of the Messiah, and his grace and kingdom (though now they understand them not:) The beloved fathers were their ancestors, for whose sakes they were first taken into this covenant of peculiarity; and (which is their greater honour) Christ is of their flock and nation according to the flesh, in whom all nations of the earth are blessed, being himself over all, God blessed for ever. These are their great and excellent privileges.

6. Not as though the word of God hath taken none effect. For they *are* not all Israel, which are of Israel: 7. Neither because they are the seed of Abraham, *are they* all children: but in Isaac shall thy seed be called.

6, 7. But what, doth it follow, that all God's promises to the Jews of a Saviour had taken no effect, because the most of them believe not? for many thousands of them are converted, besides the Gentiles; And it is not all that were the offspring of Jacob, that God ever promised to save; but as he made the promises to Abraham and Isaac, and yet took not Ishmael nor Esau into the state of peculiarity, so he may distinguish of the seed of their posterity, as well as he did of theirs; without breaking his promise to them. They are not all the children of the promise of life, that are Abraham's natural seed; Isaac's seed had the peculiarity; and so have now the believing part.

8. That is, They which are the children of the flesh, these *are* not the children of God: but the children of the promise are counted for the seed.

8. That is, They which are the children of the flesh, are not, as such, the children of God, but only those to whom he made the special promise of grace and glory; these are the seed of promise indeed.

9. For this *is* the word of promise, At this time will I come, and Sara shall have a son. 10. And not only *this*, but when Rebecca also had conceived by one, *even* by our father Isaac,

9, 10. For the promise plainly distinguisheth of the natural seed, and is made to Sara's son, and not to Hagar's; to Jacob, and not to Esau; and therefore, it is not to the natural seed as such, and to them all.

11. (For *the children* being not yet born, neither having done any good or evil, that the purpose of God according to election might stand, not of works, but of him that calleth.) 12. It was said unto her, The elder shall serve the younger.

11, 12. For before the children were born, or had done good or evil, (that God's purpose might stand, by which he chose or preferred one before the other, not because of the difference of their works, but by the absolute will of him that is the Lord of all, and may freely distribute his bounty as he please) it was said to her, [The elder shall serve the younger,] (as expressing God's differencing power and purpose.)

13. As it is written, Jacob have I loved, but Esau have I hated.

13. As the prophet Malachi, i. ii. iii. saith of the Edomites and the Israelites long after, Jacob and his Israelites I have loved, and chosen into the covenant of peculiarity; but the Idumean posterity of Esau, I have rejected out of that privilege of peculiarity, and have exposed their country to waste and ruin; even as God preferred the person of Jacob before Esau's, who was the first-born, and was rejected from the birth-right and peculiarity.

14. What shall we say then? *Is there* unrighteousness with God? God forbid.

14. But what, doth it hence follow, that God is unjust, for making such an unmerited difference? Not at all.

15. For he saith to Moses, I will

have mercy on whom I will have mercy, and I will have compassion on whom I will have compassion.

15. For he saith by Moses, I will have mercy and compassion on whom I will; so, no doubt, but he may and doth as he pleaseth, without giving us any reason but his will, give his free gifts, with difference and disproportion, to some that deserve them not, passing by others; And if he call the undeserving Gentiles, our eye must not be evil because he is good.

16. So then *it is* not of him that willeth, nor of him that runneth, but of God that sheweth mercy.

16. So that the reason why the sinful Gentiles, (or any unworthy sinner) is called, while the Jews and other sinners are left in their chosen unbelief and sin, it is not because that these sinful Gentiles (or such others) were first more willing, or more worthy by their previous seeking of grace, but from God's free differencing grace and mercy.

17. For the scripture saith unto Pharaoh, Even for this same purpose have I raised thee up, that I might shew my power in thee, and that my name might be declared throughout all the earth.

17. And that he giveth not his free mercies equally to all, is proved in his words to Pharaoh. As if he had said, I well foreknew all thy sin and obstinacy, but I will serve the honour of my name by it all; for I have raised thee, and made thee king with this intent, to manifest my power in triumphing over all thy rebellion, and to proclaim the fame of my works against thee, through all the earth.

18. Therefore hath he mercy on whom he will *have mercy*, and whom he will, he hardeneth.

18. So that, though as rector he do equal justice unto all, according to his laws and their works, yet he hath two other relations, even as our lord or owner, and as benefactor, and according to these he is a free distributer of his undeserved mercies, and may do with his own as he list, and giveth them arbitrarily in great inequality. He giveth his mercy to whom and in what degree he pleaseth; and whom he will, he leaveth in their wilful sin, and even occasioneth (though he cause it not) their obduration, by such mercies and providential dispensations as he knows they will abuse to harden themselves in sin.

19. Thou wilt say then unto me, Why doth he yet find fault? For who hath resisted his will?

19. It is like you will say, If this be so, why doth he find fault with men, that want but what he will not give them, and are not what he will not make them? Doth not all this proceed according to his will? If he would give them all his grace, they would be better.

20. Nay but O man, who art thou that repliest against God? shall the thing formed say to him that formed *it*, Why hast thou made me thus?

20, (God's laws and governing will which make man's duty, is resisted by sin) but as to the disposing and donative will of God as our owner and free benefactor, can man that is a dark and sinful worm, think himself meet to call God to account, and demand a reason of his free gifts, why he giveth them to this man and not to another? Darest thou thus dispute with God, and ask a reason of his will, which is absolute, and the spring and reason of all created good? Hath the unformed matter an antecedent right to any subsequent shape or use? and may it say, Why hast thou made me thus, and not in a nobler form for higher use?

21. Hath not the potter power over the clay, of the same lump to make one vessel unto honour, and another unto dishonour?

21. The power that a potter hath over his clay, is incomparably less than God hath over man; and yet none accuseth him for making one vessel to serve at the table, and another for a baser use. As God hath done thee no wrong if he had made thee a dog or a toad, and not a man; so be doth thee none, if he give thee not that undeserved abused grace which he freely giveth to others that as little deserve it.

22. *What* if God, willing to shew *his* wrath, and to make his power known, endured with much longsufferings the vessels of wrath fitted to destruction:

22. Shall man accuse God, because he resolveth to shew his punishing justice and power on these self-hardening, wilful sinners, who made themselves vessels of wrath, and fitted to destruction, when he hath in long patience and forbearance endured them, while they abused mercy?

23. And that he might make known the riches of his glory on the vessels of mercy, which he had afore prepared unto glory?

23. And because he will make known the riches of his glory in the felicity of those whom he hath freely made vessels of mercy, and had by grace prepared them for glory.

24. Even us whom he hath called, not of the Jews only, but also of the Gentiles.

24. I mean, on all us that are true Christians, both Jews and Gentiles, effectually called by his free grace.

25. And he saith also in Osee, I will call them my people, which

were not my people; and her, beloved, which was not beloved.

25. Which purpose of free mercy to undeserving sinners, he expresseth in Hosea ii. 23. saying, (I will call them, &c.]

26. And it shall come to pass, *that* in the place where it was said unto them, Ye *are* not my people; there shall they be called, the children of the living God.

26. And as the words, Hosea i. 10. shew, that God will call even unworthy outcasts, and make them his people by free grace.

27. Esaias also crieth concerning Israel, Though the number of the children of Israel be as the sand of the sea, a remnant shall be saved.

27. Which differencing grace, God expresseth even of the Israelites, Isa.x. 3t, 33. that of all their number, it is but a remnant that shall escape his judgment, and return from captivity, signifying the like difference as to their salvation by the faith of Christ.

28. For he will finish the work, and cut *it* short in righteousness: because a short work will the Lord make upon the earth.

28. Or the consumption decreed shall overflow in justice; for the Lord God of Hosts shall make a consumption, even determined in the midst of all the land, &c.

29. And as Esaias said before: Except the Lord of sabaoth had left us a seed, we had been as Sodoma, and been made like unto Gomorrha.

29. And that differencing mercy decreed to save a little remnant; the other words of Isay prove, (Except the Lord, &c.]

30. What shall we say then? That the Gentiles which followed not after righteousness, have attained to righteousness, even the righteousness which is of faith:

30. What shall we say then to this mystery of grace (the calling of the Gentile world, and the abscission of the most of the present nation of the Jews) which so much offendeth them? That the Gentiles who lived in darkness and unrighteousness, have attained righteousness (in reality and imputation) even that which is by faith in Christ?

31. But Israel, which followed after the law of righteousness, hath not attained to the law of righteousness.

31. But Israel, who had God's own righteous law, and trusted to be justified by keeping it, have not understood the true law, and terms of justification, nor have attained that justifying righteousness to which their law did point them.

32. Wherefore? Because *they sought it*, not by faith, but as it were by the works of the law: for they stumbled at that stumblingstone;

32. And wherefore have they not attained it? Because they understood not that the promise and covenant of grace was the very life and foundation, and end of the law, by which they should by faith have expected justification, as God's free gift to true believers; but thought it must be had by the righteousness of their own works, in keeping all the ceremonies and precepts of that law: For Christ became to them a stumbling-stone, in whom they should have believed.

33. As it is written, Behold, I lay in Sion a stumbling-stone, and rock of offence: and whosoever believeth on him, shall not be ashamed.

33. As it is written, Isa. xxviii. 16. Behold I lay in Zion a stone which many will stumble and fall upon, though it be the precious foundationstone, and a rock that many shall be split upon, though that on which my church is built; and whosoever believeth on him, shall not be disappointed nor ashamed of his hopes.

So that the cause why Israel is cast off, is not because God sent not his Son and gospel to them, nor invited them to believe, nor gave them evidence of the truth of Christ, which was sufficient to convince a well-disposed mind; much less, because he hindered them from believing, or because he shewed mercy to the Gentiles; but because by error they hardened themselves against Christ, as not answering their carnal erroneous expectations, For though God would glorify the riches of his grace by Jesus Christ, yet was it not his will to reveal him in such visible majesty and glory, as should of itself necessitate and force men to believe in him: For then faith would have been no work of trial, nor fit for a reward, but such as the wicked and sensual might perform. But God would so reveal his Son, as that faith might have sufficient encouragement and help, and yet such difficulties as might make it proper to honest souls, and fit for a reward; so that those that will be blinded by prejudice and worldly interest, will stumble and fall on the rock which they should be built on; but to them that sincerely trust and obey him, he might be the author of eternal salvation, and be the power and wisdom of God.

ANNOTATIONS.

1. This chapter is ordinarily misunderstood; 2. Because men observe not what it is that Paul is proving. 2. And because they distinguish not God's acts which he doth as an owner and benefactor, from those acts of justice which he doth as rector to subjects under his laws and covenants,

3. And because they distinguish not the common law of grace made to fallen mankind, from the covenant of peculiarity proper to the Jews.

1. Many think that Paul here giveth the reason from God's mere will and reprobating decree, why some are unbelievers and hardened in sin, and are not pardoned and saved, when others are. 2. And so they think, that God pardoneth and justifieth and saveth men, without any reason or cause fetched from their different qualifications, but merely from his will. 3. And they think, that Esau was not only shut out from the covenant of peculiarity, but also from the commoner covenant or law of grace, and was hated to damnation, merely from the antecedent will of God. But contrarily.

I. It is evident, that St. Paul is but proving and justifying God's free mercy in calling the Gentiles, while he permitted the obstinate part of the Jews to cut off themselves by unbelief, and wilfully rejecting Christ.

II. And that he speaketh not at all of any arbitrary inequality in his rewards and punishments, but only in his free gifts; all men should understand, that God is to man, 1. Our owner. 2, Our benefactor. 3. Our rector. 1. As an owner, he may do with his own as he will. 2. As our benefactor, he giveth many things antecedently to his laws, and many things besides what he there promiseth. And as a Lord and benefactor, he distributeth his gifts with incomprehensible arbitrary variety; and none have cause to accuse him for giving another more than them. He wrongs not the stars, by not making them suns; nor the clouds, by not making them stars; nor men, by not making them angels; nor beasts, in not making them men; nor worms, or toads, by making them no better. And scarce two things in the world are alike, without any dissimilitude or inequality.

But when he hath made a law of precepts, prohibitions, rewards and punishments, it is his justice equally to perform them to all, according to their qualifications and titles. He pardoneth all believers and none else: he glorifieth all that are justified and sanctified, and none else: and giveth the reason of the different sentences, from their qualifications and works, Matt. xxv. &c. which he doth not in his gifts as mere benefactor. So that he doth not say, that the reason why some are pardoned and saved, is not in him that willeth, and him that runneth; but the reason why, of two ill-deserving persons or nations, one is overcome by decreed effectual grace, and the other hath not that grace that so overcometh his wilful resistance.

III. And when Paul speaketh of Esau being hated, the text alleged meaneth no more but that the Edomites were exposed to God's overflowing punishments on earth, and that Esau was less loved than Jacob, and he and his seed rejected from the covenant of peculiarity: but as it is certain that they were under the law of mercy made to mankind in fallen Adam and Noah, so it is not said in scripture, that Esau was damned, or void of saving grace.

II. As to the hardening of Pharaoh and others, it being agreed by all sober Christians, that God causeth not sin, we need to debate it no further, whether the sense be, that he denieth them softening converting grace when they have forfeited it by wilful resistance, and so permitteth them to be hardened; or, whether it be, that he doth these good and righteous acts which he knows they will be wilfully hardened by, as occasions and objects, or both these.

Here is not the least hint, that damneth any, or decreed so to do, merely because he will do it, without any reason taken from their own deserts; or, that he maketh some men sinners; or damneth them, merely as the potter differenceth his vessels of clay: but only, that when all have deserved to be forsaken and condemned, and be giveth common grace for their recovery to all, why he freely giveth more, which shall be infallibly effectual to some, rather than to others, when those some were no better than the rest.

It is said by some schoolmen, that men's damnation is caused by sin, but God's decree to damn them is not, nor hath any cause. But this must be more distinctly answered. By God's decree to damn men, is meant, 1. Either the effects of his will. 2. Or his will itself: 3. Or his will as extrinsically denominated from the object correlated to it.

1. No doubt but punishment, which is the effect of his will, hath a meritorious cause, in man's sin.

2. The will of God, or his decree, considered as in God, is nothing but his essence, which hath no cause; and is not in itself called a decree to damn men.

3. The denomination of God's will from its relation to the extrinsic object, hath objective cause the object qualified.

Whoever truly repenteth and believeth, may be sure of his justification: and it is sinful to doubt of it on pretence that God may condemn whom he will, when he hath told whom he will not condemn: and whoever is unregenerate and ungodly, may be sure he is unjustified, and unpardoned, and in a damnable state; for God hath assured us of this in his word.

CHAP. X.

BRETHREN, my heart's desire, and prayer to God for Israel is, that they might be saved. 2. For I bear them record, that they have a zeal of God, but not according to knowledge.

1, 2. My great desire and prayer to God for Israel, is, that they may be converted and saved: and it is laudable in them that they have a zeal of God, and his law and worship; but it is frustrate, because misguided by error.

3. For they being ignorant of God's righteousness, and going about to establish their own righteousness, have not submitted themselves unto the righteousness of God.

3. For they being ignorant of God's way of justification and righteousness, intended as the end of the law, and freely given by grace, and fully

now revealed in the gospel by Jesus Christ, and trusting to their own works of the law as a sufficient righteousness to justify them, have by their error rejected God's free gift of justification by faith in Christ.

4. For Christ *is* the end of the law for righteousness to every one that believeth.

4. For they should have understood, that the sense and use of the law is to lead them for righteousness to Christ, who is its end, and prefigured in its sacrifices and other types.

5. For Moses describeth the righteousness which is of the law, That the man which doeth those things, shall live by them.

5. For though the law do point men to a better righteousness, yet in itself as a law, it owneth nothing as a righteousness sufficient to justification, but that which Moses thus describeth, Lev. xviii. 5. The man that doth these things, and breaketh not this law, shall live by them.

6. But the righteousness which is of faith, speaketh on this wise, Say not in thine heart, Who shall ascend into heaven? (that is to bring Christ down *from above*;) 7. Or, Who shall descend into the deep? (that is to bring up Christ again from the dead;) 8. But what saith it? The word is nigh thee, *even* in thy mouth, and in thy heart: that is the word of faith which we preach,

6, 7, 8. But I may describe the righteousness which is of faith in the words of Moses, Deut. xxx. [Say not in thy heart, Who shall ascend into heaven], (or how can we know God's will, that never were in heaven? Or who shall bring us thence a messenger of it?) Or, [Who shall descend into the deep?] (or, it is hid from us like the depths of the sea, and who shall fetch it to our knowledge?) But as it saith, [The word is nigh thee:] God hath not concealed it, but sent it from heaven: Christ is come down to make known God and his word; and he is risen, and gone to intercede for us in heaven: and he hath brought his gospel both to our eyes, mouth, and ears, and writeth it by his Spirit in our hearts. And Moses there seemeth to intend such a way of righteousness by free grace to the repenting Israelites. And this is it which our preaching fuller revealeth to you.

9. That if thou shalt confess with thy mouth the Lord Jesus, and shalt believe in thine heart, that God hath raised him from the dead, thou shalt be saved.

9. That if thou confess Christ before men, notwithstanding persecution, and own him as Christ before the world, and believe truly and heartily that God raised him from the dead, and thereby witnessed that he owned him, and justified the truth of his gospel, thou shalt be saved (as well as justified. For to justify a man, is partly to justify his right to salvation.)

10. For with the heart man believeth unto righteousness, and with the mouth confession is made unto salvation.

10. For these two make up the gospel terms of life: to give up soul and body to Christ; if thou believe sincerely in him with thy heart, thou wilt be accepted for his merits by God as righteous; and if thou constantly confess and own him, whatever thou suffer by it, from men, by word and deed, in obedience and patience, thou shalt possess the salvation to which thy justification initially gave thee right.

11. For the scripture saith, Whosoever believeth on him, shall not be ashamed.

11. For Isa. viii. 16. God hath promised us in his word, that whoever believeth on him, and trusteth him on his promise, and practically placeth his hope accordingly, shall never be disappointed and ashamed of that hope.

12. For there is no difference between the Jew and the Greek: for the same Lord over all, is rich unto all that call upon him.

12. For God is no respecter of persons, and saveth not men, or rejecteth men, because they are Jews or Greeks. The law of grace doth equally pardon and justify Jew and Gentile that truly repent and believe, and no other: he is the same Lord over all, and is rich in mercy to all that call on him in faith, (for when he proclaimed his name to Moses, Exod. xxxiv. [as gracious and merciful, forgiving iniquity, transgression, and sin, &c.] it was his very nature and decree by which he would be known to all the world, and not only by the Jews.

13. For whosoever shall call upon the name of the Lord shall be saved.

13. For as it is said, Joel ii. 32. [Whosoever shall call on the name of the Lord, shall be saved;] that is, of what nation soever he be, if he truly seek God, he will be found of him; and if he fear God and work righteousness by faith, he shall be accepted of him; for he is the rewarder of them that diligently seek him, Heb. xi. 6.

14. How then shall they call on him in whom they have not believed? and how shall they believe in him of whom they have not heard? and how shall they hear without a preacher?

14. And this sheweth you this necessity of

preaching the gospel; for how shall men seek, and worship, and call on that God and Saviour in whom they have not believed? And how shall they believe in him of whom they have never heard? And how shall they hear, if no one tell them, or preach to them? (Even the works of nature, and providence that reveal God darkly, must be told men by instructors, to make them capable of understanding them: much more the gospel of Christ.)

15. And how shall they preach, except they be sent? As it is written, How beautiful are the feet of them that preach the gospel of peace, and bring glad tidings of good things!

15. And how shall men preach the mysteries of salvation, that are not called and sent of God, by his qualifications and commission? for who can be such a light in the world, that is not taught and gifted by the Father of lights? And who can in God's name proclaim the word of reconciliation as his messenger, who is not authorized by him so to do? We love glad tidings, and welcome the messengers of them; and this should be the entertainment of Christ's apostles and ministers in the world, who bring the most joyful tidings of salvation. As it is written, [How beautiful are the feet of them that, &c.] Isa. lii. 7.

16. But they have not all obeyed the gospel. For Esaias saith, Lord, who hath believed our report?

16. But you may say, why then doth not this preaching convert more of the Jews? This excellence of the gospel, and the preaching of it, doth not suppose that all that have it will be converted by it: for of the Jews, Isaiah saith, [Lord who hath believed our report?] Few did hearken to the prophets, Isa. liii. 1.

17. So then faith *cometh* by hearing, and hearing by the word of God,

17. It is evident, that they must hear, that they may believe; and God's word must be preached to them, or made known, that they may hear it.

18. But I say, Have they not heard? Yes verily, their sound went into all the earth, and their words unto the ends of the world,

18. But is not the world excusable then in their sin, for want of preaching? I answer, As God tells us, Ps. xix. That the visible works of God do preach him, (even his power, wisdom, and goodness) to all the world which will leave it without all just excuse! (See Rom. i. 20, 21.) So Christ sent his apostles with a commission to preach to all nations; and many nations have already heard his gospel.

19. But I say, Did not Israel know? First Moses saith, I will provoke you to jealousy by *them*

that are no people, *and* by a foolish nation I will anger you.

19. But have not the Jews had notice of the gospel, when it was first preached to them, and rejected by them? The very conversion of the Gentiles, receiving that Christ whom they rejected, which is matter of envy to them, shall leave them without excuse; as Moses saith, Deut. xxxii. 21. [I will provoke you to jealousy by, &c.

20. But Esaias is very bold, and saith, I was found of them that sought me not; I was made manifest unto them that asked not after me. 21. But to Israel he saith, All day long I have stretched forth my hands unto a disobedient and gainsaying people.

20, 21. But Isaiah boldly and plainly foretels God's calling the Gentiles by free grace, and seeking them that first sought not him; and his rejecting the Jews as a people, that after his long suffering did continue obstinately to reject his word and grace, saying, [I was found of them that sought me not, &c.] and, [All day long have I stretched forth, &c.]

ANNOTATIONS.

1. The 16, 13, 14, and 15 verses are controverted by expositors, as to the question, whether they assert or deny the salvation of any that hear not of Christ; because (on one side) it is said, That whoever doth call on the name of the Lord shall be saved; and the 19th Psalm is cited, which tells us how God's works do preach him to all the world, &c. And on the other side, [How shall they hear without a preacher? &c.]

First, We must not confound the doubt of the sense of this text, with the doubt of the matter, which is the salvation of men that hear not the gospel; as to the former, I have said what I thought needful in the Paraphrase and leave it to the judgment of the reader.

As to the matter, I think thus much following may satisfy the sober. 1. We must first know what law of God such men are under, and then how far it justifieth them. It is certain, that the world (once guilty of sin and death) is not under the law of innocency, which maketh innocency the only condition of life (now it is lost to all.) And it is certain, that they are neither lawless, or shut up as devils in despair; but that they have duties and means of repentance, recovery, mercy, and salvation, imposed on them, which they are bound to use for those ends in hope; and they have much forfeited mercy given to them all, which proveth that God useth them not according to the law of innocency. And it is certain, that God made to all mankind, in fallen Adam and Noah, a law of mercy and grace; and that when he proclaimed his name to Moses, Exod. xxxiv. [The Lord gracious and merciful, forgiving, &c.] it was his nature, and his way of governing of mankind, which he proclaimed. And so that all the world is under a law which offereth pardon and life on other terms than sinless innocency.

2. It is certain, that the superadded covenant of peculiarity to the Jews, or the preaching of the gospel of Christ incarnate to part of the world only, repealed not any of the merciful law, or terms before given to all the world: Christ added more mercy, but took away none; much less so much from most of the world: he came not to condemn the world but to save.

3. It is certain, that all men shall be judged according to the law that they were under, and obliged by, and no other.

4. It is certain that the apostles themselves, though in a state of grace, believed not till Christ was risen, that he must die a sacrifice for sin, rise from the dead, ascend and intercede in heaven, send down the eminent gift of the Holy Ghost, call the Gentiles, gather a Catholic church, &c. Therefore it was not all our articles of faith that were necessary before Christ's coming; but the belief of so much as was then revealed.

But 2. What others do, that hear not of Christ, in fact, who repenteth, and believeth, and be saved, God is only fit to judge; it belongeth not to us. But we may say that the case of Melchisedec, Job and his friends, and many others, prove, that grace and salvation were not confined to the Jews. And that Abraham thought that even Sodom had fifty righteous persons, when it was worse than other places of the world. And he that will well read Psa. xix. Prov. i. Acts xiv. & xvii. Rom. i. & ii. may yet receive fuller satisfaction from God.

II. About ministers' mission, verse 15. It is doubted whether we may hear any, till we know that God sent them; and it is the device of the Roman clergy, to puzzle the ignorant, by objecting against the mission and ordination of Protestant ministers, to draw men from hearing them as ministers of Christ, claiming to themselves the peculiarity of divine commission and authority, as the only church that have uninterrupted succession of canonical ordination. But as the interruption of theirs is easily proved, so it is most certain, that God hath not made it an antecedent necessary thing to the belief of his gospel, for all men and women to be first so well acquainted with history, as to know what continuance or interruption there hath been in all countries of canonical ordination.

In short, 1. A lay-man is to be heard that brings the gospel. 2. He that wanteth some circumstances of order, necessary ordinarily to the right ordering of the church, may yet have all that is essential to the ministry.

3. He that hath just abilities; and mutual consent of him and a Christian flock that need him, hath all that is essentially necessary.

4. He that is ordained by concordant senior pastors of that church, hath all that is necessary essentially to ordination.

5. He that seemeth to have such qualifications or ordination, but hath not, but is in possession upon deceiving probability, is a pastor to that church, so far that his ministrations shall be valid to the people, though not to justify himself from the guilt of profane usurpation.

6. The people that love their souls, must be more careful what doctrine a minister preacheth, than what ordination he hath.

7. In divers cases the magistrates' authority may serve without ordination, and in some the people's choice alone, though, where it may lawfully be had, just and regular ordination should not be neglected, seeing none may be himself the sole judge of his own call and fitness.

CHAP. XI.

I SAY then, Hath God cast away his people? God forbid: For I also am an Israelite, of the seed of Abraham, *of* the tribe of Benjamin.

1. But what? Do I by all this conclude, that God hath broken his covenant with Abraham, and utterly cast off the people of Israel? Not at all. For I, and all believing Jews, are the seed of Abraham, not cast off.

2. God hath not cast away his people which he foreknew. Wot ye not what the scripture saith of Elias? how he maketh intercession to God against Israel, saying, 3. Lord, they have killed thy prophets, and digged down thine altars; and I am left alone, and they seek my life.

2, 3. God hath among the Israelites his foreknown and chosen people: and these he doth not cast off, though he leave the rest in their rebellion. Know ye not what Elias thought and said of the Israelites in his time, That he was left alone, as if they had been all revolters?

4. But what saith the answer of God unto him? I have reserved to myself seven thousand men, who have not bowed the knee to *the image of* Baal.

4. But God knew of more than Elias did: he had seven thousand that were no idolaters.

5. Even so then at this present time also there is a remnant according to the election of grace.

5. So now also God hath his chosen remnant, whom his grace hath brought to faith in Christ.

6. And if by grace, then *it is* no more of works: otherwise grace is no more grace. But if *it be* of works, then is it no more grace: otherwise work is no more work.

6. And if they are chosen and made his justified people by grace and free gift for the merits of Christ, then it cannot be by the merit of our own performance of the law. And if it be by the merit of such performance, deserving not death but life, then it is not of mere grace or free gift. For what need a man pardon, who deserveth not

punishment? Or, to have life freely given him, which is his due for the merit of his works? (For I here give you notice, that it is no works that I speak of and exclude, but that which excludeth free gift and grace, and not that which subordinately obeyeth grace, and doth suppose it.)

7. What then? Israel hath not obtained that which he seeketh for; but the election hath obtained it, and the rest were blinded.

7. The whole nation of the Jews have not obtained deliverance by the Messiah, though they sought, and hoped, and waited for him: but God's elect ones have obtained it, and the rest miss of it, because their sin and prejudice blindeth them.

8. According as it is written, God hath given them the spirit of slumber, eyes that they should not see, and ears that they should not hear, unto this day.

8. As it is written, Isa. xxix. 10. Because they would not obey the Spirit of God, that would have awakened and enlightened them, God hath justly given them up to the seduction of the spirit of slumber, stupidity, and blindness; from whence it is no wonder that they see not and hear not to this day, being deprived of his Spirit's illumination.

9. And David saith, Let their table be made a snare, and a trap, and a stumbling-block, and a recompence unto them. 10. Let their eyes be darkened, that they may not see, and bow down their back alway.

9, 10. And David prophetically prayed for such judgments on the obstinate enemies of the just, that for a recompence of their malice God would turn their comforts into punishments, and forsake them, saying, &c.

11. I say then, Have they stumbled that they should fall? God forbid: but *rather* through their fall salvation *is come* unto the Gentiles, for to provoke them to jealousy.

11. But what? Are they utterly forsaken and cast off? And had God no better end herein than their destruction? No such thing. But the greater part were permitted justly to drive away the gospel from them to the Gentiles, that these being converted, might after occasion their conversion in the universal church.

12. Now if the fall of them *be* the riches of the world, and the diminishing of them the riches of the Gentiles: how much more their fulness?

12. And if the Gentiles have been so great gainers by occasion of the sin and fall of the Jews, how much more when they shall become Christians, will they add to the glory and greatness of the Catholic Christian church.

13. For I speak to you Gentiles, in as much as I am the apostle of the Gentiles, I magnify mine office:

13. I speak this to my own and the Gentile' comfort, as their apostle, as well as for the Jews, as improving and glorying in that my office, that the case of the Jews is not wholly desperate.

14. If by any means I may provoke to emulation *them which are* my flesh, and might save some of them.

14. And that by glorying in your faith, and hoping yet for their conversion, I might provoke them to emulation, and win and save more of them.

15. For if the casting away of them *be* the reconciling of the world; what *shall* the receiving *of them be,* but life from the dead?

15. For if the Gentiles have received the gospel, and so are reconciled to God, by occasion of the Jews expelling it, what a blessed state will the church be in, and what a mercy like a resurrection will it be to the Jews, when they shall come into the Catholic church?

16. For if the first fruit *be* holy, the lump *is* also *holy*: and if the root *be* holy, so *are* the branches.

16. For if God hath accepted those Jews that are believers, who are to the whole nation but as the first fruits to the lump, he will accordingly accept the nation when they come into Christ as we have done: and as he accepted Abraham and their believing ancestors, he will also accept them: and if those apostles be honoured of God as holy, who from them are sent with the gospel into the world, so shall the broken branches be when they are restored.

17. And if some of the branches be broken off, and thou being a wild olive tree, were graffed in amongst them, and with them partakest of the root and fatness of the olive tree; 18. Boast not against the branches: but if thou boast, thou bearest not the root, but the root thee.

17, 18. The Catholic church I compare to an olive tree: the covenant of peculiarity is their constituting charter: it was made first with Abraham the father of the Jews, and next, of all the faithful: it was sent to all the world by apostles from Judea: these two are the root: the Jews and Gentiles are branches; the Jews are the first branches, and the Gentiles the branches of a wild olive here graffed in. If the Jews be cut off, boast not against them, for the covenant and gospel was not first given to you (that now receive its benefits) but to them, and from them to you.

19. Thou wilt say then, The branches were broken off, that I might be graffed in. 20. Well; because of unbelief they were broken off, and thou standest by faith. Be not high-minded, but fear.

19, 20. If you say, That God more esteemed me than them, because he broke them off, that I might be graffed in. Be not deceived. It was for their own unbelief, and by it, and not undeservedly, that they were broken off: and it is by faith, and not for any worldly pre-eminence, that thou art graffed in: therefore be not puffed up, but fear that sin that cut off them.

21. For if God spared not the natural branches, *take heed* lest he also spare not thee.

21. For if God cast off them with whom he first made the covenant of peculiarity, take heed of sinning as they did by pride and unbelief against his gospel, lest he also cut off thee.

22. Behold, therefore, the goodness and severity of God: on them which fell, severity; but towards thee, goodness, if thou continue in *his* goodness: otherwise thou also shalt be cut off.

22. Rather here reverently admire God's goodness and severity. On the sinful rejected Jews, severity of justice: but mercy to thee; which shall continue, if thou continue in the faith, and obedience and gratitude to him: otherwise thou also shalt be cut off. (As, alas! most of the Eastern churches are.)

23. And they also, if they bide not still in unbelief shall be graffed in: for God is able to graff them in again.

23. And God hath not excluded them from the grace of the gospel, so, as to make their recovery impossible. If they be converted from unbelief, which God can effect, they shall be graffed into the Catholic church.

24. For if thou wert cut out of the olive tree which is wild by nature, and wert graffed contrary to nature into a good olive tree; how much more shall these which be the natural *branches*, be graffed into their own olive tree?

24. For if thou wert cut off from the wild olive tree which was natural to thee; and besides or

above nature, and contrary to thy desert, was taken into God's covenant and church; how much more will God take them in when they believe, who were Abraham's natural seed, and first in his covenant?

25. For I would not, brethren, that ye should be ignorant of this mystery (lest ye should be wise in your own conceits) that blindness in part is happened to Israel, until the fulness of the Gentiles be come in. 26. And so all Israel shall be saved:

25, 26. For I would not have you ignorant of this mystery of God's providence, lest ignorance puff you up with false self-conceits; that part of the Jews are now left in this blindness, till the Gentile churches be advanced to an honourable state and fulness: and then all the Israel of God, the true faithful seed of Abraham, and therein the main body of the Jews, shall make up the Catholic church, and be saved from their state of unbelief

26. As it is written, There shall come out of Sion the deliverer, and shall turn away ungodliness from Jacob.

26. As Isa. lix. 20. it was prophesied, That out of Sion a Saviour should arise for Israel, to turn them from iniquity.

27. For this *is* my covenant unto them, when I shall take away their sins.

27. As he saith, That his covenant made with them is to take away their sin.

28. As concerning the gospel, *they are* enemies for your sake: but as touching the election, *they are* beloved for the father's sakes.

28. For your conversion they were permitted as enemies to Christ to drive away the gospel from them to you: but yet God hath not quite nailed his covenant with their fathers, but will perform it in the conversion of all of them that are elect.

29. For the gifts and calling of God *are* without repentance.

29. For God is not mutable, and will not for the sin of these men, forget his covenant with their fathers, but will yet perform it in the full sense of it, and not repeat of it and null it.

30. For as ye in times past have not believed God, yet have now obtained mercy through their unbelief: 31. Even so have these also now not believed, that through your mercy they also may obtain mercy.

30, 31. For as you were formerly in unbelief, and disobedient, and yet now are converted by occasion of their unbelief; so the unbelieving Jews shall be brought by mercy into the church, by the preaching that shall be sent from the Gentile churches, and by the power and glory of the church under Christian emperors and governors, and by your good example.

32. For God hath concluded them all in unbelief, that he might have mercy upon all.

32. For God in justice and wisdom hath for a time left the main body of the Jews in unbelief, as formerly he did the Gentiles, that in his time he might in mercy call in the main body of them into the Catholic church, as he hath done you.

33. O the depth of the riches both of the wisdom and knowledge of God! how unsearchable *are* his judgments and his ways past finding out!

33. When we think of these mysterious providences of God (freely shewing mercy to the unworthy, and permitting presuming men to miscarry, and yet making use of their sin for good) we should be so far from questioning God's mercy or justice herein, that we should admire the depth of the riches of his wisdom, whose judgments are unsearchable, and his counsels and ways not to be traced, and fitly judged of by the wit of man.

34. For who hath known the mind of the Lord, or who hath been his counsellor? 35. Or who hath first given to him and it shall be recompensed unto him again?

34, 35. How little know men of the mind of God? Nothing but what he freely tells them. He is not guided by the counsel of man, nor is man acquainted with his secret counsels. Who can oblige him to recompense by his gifts, or hath any thing but what God giveth him?

36. For of him, and through him, and to him, *are* all things: to whom *be* glory for ever. Amen.

36. For as all creatures have three sorts of extrinsic causes, viz. the efficient, dirigent, and final, God is all these; the chief efficient, chief dirigent, and chief final cause of all things: all is of him, by him, and to him, and he of none: he is all in all things: and as he made and doth all things for his glory, his glory shall for ever shine forth to all, which angels and saints shall intelligently see, and praise for ever. Amen.

ANNOTATIONS.

The great doubt about this chapter is, what it prophecies of the full conversion of the Jews. Concerning which, I shall only speak so much as is certain, and leave the rest to the judgment of others.

1. It is certain, that God never meant to restore the Jewish polity under Moses' law: for that law is abrogated by Christ, and so that polity. It is Jewish contradiction of Christianity to expect such a restoration.

2. Much less will God ever confine the church and covenant of peculiarity to the Jewish nation, and take it from the Gentiles, and cease Catholicism.

3. Nor will God restore and confine the Jews to their ancient country in Palestine; which being such a country as Wales, now barren, and about half as big as England, would be far from making them a people of eminent glory in the world, but rather contemptible in that respect.

4. Nor hath God promised to make the Jews lords and rulers over the rest of the nations of the earth, as the carnal sort of them did expect.

5. Therefore no other calling of the Jews can be expected, but that they become parts of the Catholic church.

6. It seems to me by history, that this is performed long ago, the main body of their nation being turned to Christianity. To which purpose, consider these things,

1. Myriads were converted in Judea by the apostles.

2. In all other countries of the Roman empire, the scattered Jews had synagogues, to which the apostles first preached, and where they first gathered the rudiments of the Christian churches.

3. A vast number of the unbelieving Jews were destroyed by Vespasian and Titus, when Jerusalem was besieged and destroyed.

4. Many more Jews were then converted, when they saw God's judgments executed on them, and the Christians spared. And many turned Christians then.

5. Vast numbers of the remainder of the unbelievers were destroyed by Adrian, and the Christians spared.

6. Since then many have been converted by solemn disputes, and many Jews become eminent doctors in the church.

7. They were ever fond of their own country and therefore we may suppose, that as many as could, lived there. And it is known, that all conquerors use to transplant only the rich and ruling men, and leave the multitude of the poor labourers to manure the ground, that it may yield them tribute. So did Nebuchadnezzar; and so in England did the Romans, Saxons, Danes, and Normans: they left the vulgar to possess the land under them, or else the land would have been unprofitable to them. It was the rich and the soldiers that they drove into Wales; so that we are mostly of a British offspring. Now it is known, that in the days of Constantine, and the following Christian emperors, (though no country wholly turned Christian of a long time) Judea turned as other provinces did; and had their bishops, and their patriarch, in councils: and proportionably rather more than in other countries, were Christians there. So that Judea was Christian, as other provinces were.

CHAP. XII.

1 BESEECH you, therefore, brethren, by the mercies of God, that ye present your bodies a living sacrifice, holy, acceptable unto God, *which is* your reasonable service.

1. Now to make application of all this doctrine fore-written, I beseech you, as you have a due sense of Christ's offering himself a sacrifice for our sins, and of the great mercy of the Gentiles' salvation by grace, and of our deliverance from the burdens of the Jewish law, those costly sacrifices of beasts being abrogated by Christ, that you will resign and dedicate yourselves to God, and as a living holy sacrifice, give up your own bodies wholly to him, even to the obedience of his commands, and to suffer what he calls you to, even to death, which will be better than a sacrifice of beasts, even a reasonable, holy, acceptable service of God.

2. And be not conformed to this world: but be ye transformed by the renewing of your mind, that ye may prove what *is* that good, and acceptable, and perfect will of God.

2. And now you are called out of the world, and made a peculiar people to God, conform not yourselves to the sinful practices of the world; but be transformed from your former errors and sins, by the renewing of your minds by truth and holiness; that you may know by experience the goodness of God's ways to which you are called, and the greatness of his love.

3. For I say, through the grace given unto me, to every man that is among you, not to think of *himself* more highly than he ought to think; but to think soberly according as God hath dealt to every man the measure of faith.

3. And specially because that the proud overvaluing of men's own understandings, and thinking that they know more than they do, is the common cause of errors and sins, of censures, divisions, and heresies in the churches, I do, as an apostle sent and taught of God, admonish and charge you all, every one to think humbly of himself, and not to think yourselves wiser or better than you are; but with wise self-suspicion, and consciousness of your ignorance and great imperfection, to think soberly of yourselves, according to truth, and to the degree of faith and wisdom given you of God.

4. For as we have many members in one body, and all members have not the same office: 5. So we being many are one body in Christ, and every one members one of another.

2.

4, 5. For as the members of the same body have great diversity in number and office; so we, though many individual persons make up one body or church, in Christ the head, in whom we are united, and are related to each other as members of the same body.

6. Having then gifts, differing according to the grace that is given to us, whether prophecy, *let us prophesy* according to the proportion of faith: 7. Or ministry, *let us wait* on *our* ministering; or he that teacheth, on teaching;

6, 7. Seeing it pleaseth God to give various degrees of gifts, according to the dispensation of his free grace, and not to make all equal in gifts or office, let all confine themselves to their measure and office, and that let them faithfully execute. Let those that are inspired to speak as from God, by prediction or instruction, speak what God hath revealed to them, according to the proportion of their revelation and knowledge, and no more; and not pretend special revelation against the sealed word of faith. Let those that are called to any special service for the church, perform their own office faithfully therein; and let those that are called to teach, be faithful teachers. Neglect not your own part, and invade not others.

8. Or he that exhorteth, on exhortation; he that giveth, *let him do it* with simplicity; he that ruleth, with diligence; he that sheweth mercy, with cheerfulness.

8. He that is to exhort men to practise what is taught, let him do it diligently, (for men's corrupt wills and affections have need of excitation and persuasion, as well as their understandings of information.) He that giveth, (his own, or the churches) let him do it sincerely and impartially. He that is intrusted to govern church or family, let him do it carefully and diligently. He that sheweth mercy to any in distress, let him do it cheerfully.

9. *Let* love *be* without dissimulation. Abhor that which is evil, cleave to that which is good.

9. Let Christian love, which is the great duty of the gospel, be hearty and sincere, appearing in its fruits, and not in barren words alone. Be not indifferent and cold towards evil or good: but avoid evil with abhorrence, and resolutely stick to that which is good.

10. *Be* kindly affectionate one to another; with brotherly love, in honour preferring one another;

10. Love each other as brethren, and live in the kind affectionate expression of it, (and not as selfish, uncharitable, peevish, quarrelsome, censorious, or persecuting men:) be forwarder to prefer others in esteem, praise, or practice (according to their worth and rank) than to set up

A a

yourselves, or seek esteem, applause, or preferment. Strive not to be thought wisest or best, or to be highest; nor envy others.

11. Not slothful in business: fervent in spirit; serving the Lord:

11. Do not your duties slothfully, unwillingly, and heavily; but diligently: and serve God in all the duties of your places and times, with a fervent, zealous mind.

12. Rejoicing in hope; patient in tribulation; continuing instant in prayer:

12. In all your present tribulation, rejoice in hope of promised deliverance and felicity hereafter; and patiently endure it: and continue instantly to pray.

13. Distributing to the necessity of saints; given to hospitality.

13. Freely distributing to the necessity, especially of holy persons; and not living in superfluity, and shutting up your compassion from those that are in want: delight to give the needy entertainment in your houses, and seek them to that end.

14. Bless them which persecute you: bless, and curse not.

14. And though the sin of persecution be heinous, it is God that is the avenger of it: avenge not yourselves in word or deed: pray for them, and curse them not.

15. Rejoice with them that do rejoice, and weep with them that weep.

15. Be not like those selfish persons, that are little affected with the case of any but themselves: not like the dividers, that affect to go cross to others by proud singularity: but rejoice with rejoicers, and weep with weepers, as being of the same body, and as regarding their case as if it were your own.

16. *Be* of the same mind one towards another. Mind not high things, but condescend to men of low estate.

16. Affect not to be odd and singular from other Christians; but to be of one mind and way with them, (so it be not in sin) and mind their case as if it were your own; mind not preferment, nor riches and vain-glory, nor put yourselves for these into the company and favour of those above you: but be content with a low condition in the world, and go along in society with the lower sort.

16. Be not wise in your own conceits.

16. Have humble thoughts of your own knowledge, and think it not greater than it is; but be conscious of your ignorance, and uncertainties, and weakness, and rather as doubters stay and learn, than too hastily judge and conclude.

17. Recompense to no man evil for evil.

17. If others do ill to you, do not you do ill to them, nor requite them with revenge.

17. Provide things honest in the sight of all men.

17. Be diligent in your outward labours, that you may avoid base dependance as much as may be, and may provide for a decent living for yourselves, and help to others.

18. If it be possible, as much as lieth in you, live peaceably with all men.

18. Though it is not in your power to make the malignant, persecutors, contentious, and proud, to be peaceable towards you, nor must you purchase peace, by sinning against God; yet see that you be peaceable towards all men, to the utmost of your power; that the distance may not be your fault, but theirs, who make peace impossible.

19. Dearly beloved, avenge not yourselves, but rather give place unto wrath: for it is written, Vengeance *is* mine; I will repay, saith the Lord.

19. Passion is so unruly, and so blindeth the judgment of selfish men, that I again beseech you, to avoid self-righting by revenge; but when men are wrathful, and wrong you, give place, by departing, submission, or patience; and leave God's work of revenge to himself, which he will execute soon enough, and severely enough, partly by himself, and partly by his officers entrusted with the sword.

20. Therefore if thine enemy hunger, feed him; if he thirst, give him drink: for in so doing thou shalt heap coals of fire on his head.

20. As Christ hath won us by love, so hath he taught us to win our enemies. Love is our nature and duty, and that to which we would win all: and therefore love is the means or weapon by which we must overcome them; and particularly, by such bodily kindness which they can value: therefore if they hunger, feed them; supply their want; let not their enmity stop your kindness By this means, as fire melts metals, the hardest heart may be melted: for love kindleth love, which strangeness and revenge destroyeth. At least, this will aggravate his sin, and shame him, and justify you against his calumnies.

21. Be not overcome of evil, but overcome evil with good.

21. Satan by your enemies tempteth you to sin: they overcome you, if you yield, by passion, or revenge, or any sin; but not, if they do but hurt your bodies. Therefore keep your charity and innocency, and you are the conquerors: and by your love and good works overcome their evil, as it would draw you to sin, and as it is the malady

of their souls, which you would overcome for them, that they may be saved.

CHAP. XIII.

LET every soul be subject unto the higher powers. For there is no power but of God: the powers that be, are ordained of God.

1. And one of the duties that are necessary to your peace, and required of God, is your due subjection to governors: take heed therefore of their opinion who think, that Christ hath set us free from human government: for God is the God of order: and as in natural effects he useth natural means, so in politic government he useth officers. I speak not of mere strength, but of authority, or right to govern: and as subordinate magistrates have no such power, but what is given them by the supreme; so it is impossible that supreme rulers on earth can have true authority, but what is given them by God, the universal sovereign; even as impossible, as for any creature to be what it is, without a Creator: for of him, and through him, and to him, are all things. Even where you must not obey a sinful command, yet you must be subject still. None are exempted from this duty; for government is the ordinance of God.

2. Whosoever therefore resisteth the power, resisteth the ordinance of God: and they that resist, shall receive to themselves damnation.

2. Whosoever therefore will not be subject to human government, but resisteth true authority, resisteth a needful ordinance of God, and deserveth punishment from God and man.

3. For rulers are not a terror to good works, but to the evil. Wilt thou then not be afraid of the power? Do that which is good, and thou shalt have praise of the same.

3. For as God is the ordainer of government in general, so he hath specified their office, as to the universally necessary part, and bound them as his officers to see to the execution of his universal laws, as the king binds justices to execute his laws: and therefore their office and authority received from God, is not to be persecutors, or a terror to good works, but to punish the evil, for God giveth no authority against himself, or his laws. If therefore thou fear this power given of God, do that which is good, and it will further thy encouragement and praise. Even heathens, by seeing to the execution of the law of nature, will promote natural virtue, and suppress and punish vice.

4. For he is the minister of God to thee for good. But if thou do that which is evil, be afraid; for he beareth not the sword in vain: for he is the minister of God, a revenger to *execute* wrath upon him that doeth evil.

4. And let not bad men's abuse of government make thee think evil of the office: for they are but God's servants or officers, not authorized to destroy and to do mischief, but to do good, even to see to the execution of God's laws by their own, and to take care of the common welfare. But if thou do evil, fear them; for God hath not entrusted them with the sword in vain, (much less for mischief.) For they are God's officers, revengers of sin, to execute God's wrath and man's on sinners: and so to resist them, is to resist the officers of God; and to honour and obey them, is to honour and obey God that hath authorised them.

5. Wherefore ye must needs be subject not only for wrath, but also for conscience sake.

5. Wherefore you ought to be subject (even when you may not obey) not only for fear of punishment from man, but in conscience of your duty to God who ordaineth them.

6. For, for this cause pay you tribute also: for they are God's ministers, attending continually upon this very thing.

6. Therefore honourable maintenance and tribute is their due: for they are God's servants, whose very office and daily care and labour is to do his service for the common good.

7. Render therefore to all their dues: tribute to whom tribute *is due*, custom to whom custom, fear to whom fear, honour to whom honour.

7. I am not persuading you to own usurpation, or to give men that which is not their due; nor yet do I determine among several claimers, which is the supreme: but that you give all their proper due; tribute, custom, fear, and honour, to every one to whom they are due. And let not covetousness or disobedience hinder you.

8. Owe no man any thing, but to love one another: for he that loveth another, hath fulfilled the law.

8. Discharge your debts, and give all men the due which you owe them, (else you are unjust, and rob them:) only love we shall still owe to one another, and shall thus owe it even while we pay it. And to pay this debt of sincere love, is to fulfil all the law to man.

9. For this, Thou shalt not commit adultery, Thou shalt not kill, Thou shalt not steal, Thou shalt not bear false witness, Thou shalt

not covet; and if *there be* any other commandment, it is briefly comprehended in this saying, namely, Thou shalt love thy neighbour as thyself.

9. For all our duty to men is virtually comprehended in loving them as ourselves: for a man will not wrong the life, the estate, the marriage-right, the honour of himself, nor falsely accuse or prosecute himself, or covet from himself, or those that he loveth as himself. Bring men once to this unfeigned love; and hurtfulness, covetousness, fraud, false accusation, persecution, and all injustice, will cease.

10. Love worketh no ill to his neighbour: therefore love *is* the fulfilling of the law.

10. As we are not apt to hurt ourselves, so true love would not hurt others, in their lives, liberties, estates, or good names, (much less studying to destroy them.) Therefore love is the virtual fulfilling of all our duty to them.

11. And that, knowing the time, that now *it is* high time to awake out of sleep: for now *is* our salvation nearer than when we believed.

11. And we should increase in this careful discharge of our duty of love and justice, though in the state of infidelity we lived in such sins: for by this time we should be better acquainted with our duties, and awaked to all conscionable performance of them, we being nearer our reward and salvation than when, we were first converted to the faith; and God expecteth now more from us.

12. The night is far spent, the day is at hand: let us therefore cast off the works of darkness, and let us put on the armour of light.

12. We are now got farther from our former state of darkness: we are now come to the daylight of illuminating grace, and under the increase thereof. The church is growing to a more honourable state by its increase. Let us therefore more resolvedly cast off all the works of heathenish darkness, and, as Christ's soldiers, put on our sacred armour, and use it as in the day-light of grace.

13. Let us walk honestly as in the day; not in rioting and drunkenness, not in chambering and wantonness, not in strife and envying.

13. Seeing we are in the light, let us walk modestly and decently, as becometh our condition; not as the heathens, in rioting and drunkenness; not in lasciviousness, and uncleanness, and fleshly lusts; not in proud, selfish, or covetous strife and envy.

14. But put ye on the Lord Jesus Christ, and make not provision for the flesh, to *fulfil* the lusts thereof.

14. But let Christ, his spirit and love, his doctrine and example, his interest and kingdom, take you up, and be to you as the clothing which you daily wear: and do not as carnal men, (whose fleshly pleasure and prosperity is their choice and best) that live to the said fleshly pleasure, and make provision to satisfy the carnal will and lust. instead of preferring the heavenly treasure.

ANNOTATIONS.

Qu. I. What is meant here by Powers? Answ. Not mere strength, but authority or right to govern. It is not δύναμις, but ἐξουσία: an usurper's strength may be resisted; but rightful power or authority may not.

Qu. II. Doth St. Paul determine here either of the species, or individually, who it is that hath the highest power? Answ. Not at all. In those ages, and long after, sometime the senate claimed the supremacy wholly, and sometime a part of it; sometime they pretended to make emperors, and some emperors yielded them more than others: but whether the senate or the emperor were the highest power, or the supremacy in both conjunct, or which *de specie* was most just, Paul medleth not.

Qu. How then would he have the Christians know whom to obey? Answ. He leaveth that to be known by its proper evidence, and not by divine revelation by him.

Qu. III. Is no power to do wrong ordained of God? Or is all such ordained by him? Answ. Power here being right to govern, no man hath right to do wrong, that is a contradiction; but God hath ordained that right which may be abused to do wrong, and yet not resisted.

Qu. IV. What is meant by subjection? Answ. A state of consent and obligation to obey. Obedience is the practice of subjection.

Qu. V. Hath the universal [every soul] no exception? Answ. The higher powers themselves are excepted: and neither foreigners, nor those that have no governors, are bound to be subject to other princes; It is only their own subjects that are meant. And the Pope could have no pretence to except his clergy, if he did not feign himself to be the highest power over them, and above the kings and states.

Qu. VI. Is obedience to go as far as subjection? Answ. No: we must not obey any by disobeying God: But yet we must continue subjection and due honour to them, and not deny them their due, because we must not give them more by sin.

Qu. What then are the limits of our obedience to men? Answ. 1. Materially, we must not obey any by sin, nor yet against the common good, to do more hurt than good, when they command without the due power or right. 2. As to formal obedience, which is to act by the obligation of their authority, the limits of their power are the limits of that obligation and obedience.

Qu. What are the limits of their power? Answ. In general, they have no more from God than he giveth them. 1. They have no power against any of his laws, of nature or scripture, nor against his kingdom, or himself. 2. They have no right or power to overthrow personal, or family, or church government; nor to deprive any of any thing which God hath given them, without forfeiture or consent, explicit or implicit; nor to destroy the common good.

2. Therefore, that propriety which God hath given man as man, (in life, and limbs, and the use of his faculties for his welfare and his duty to God, and his wife and children) are such objective limitations of this power that no man hath right to take them from any, but on forfeiture, or valid consent.

Qu. VII. How far is all power of God, and how far of man? Answ. 1. It is of God's ordination in nature, that there be government and subjection in general. 2. And the specification is so far of God, that he hath made them his officers; 1. To promote obedience to his own law; 2. For his glory, and the common good. So that no people can make a power that shall not have right to promote God's law; 2. Or that shall destroy the common good. 3. God's providence doth so manage the affairs of the world, as shall point out the man or families that the people should accept of first while free, as qualified by strength, wisdom, and goodness for authority. 4. Monarchy and aristocracy in specie are both of divine allowance.

2. But it is of men, 1. Which of these sorts (monarchy, or aristocracy, or mixed) shall by a free people be chosen. 2. And who (by such a free people) shall be chosen for the persons or families. 3. And what degree of power they shall have over their properties, (which are antecedent to regiment) in undetermined cases. So that government is partly from God, and partly from man.

Qu. VIII. By what right doth one person or family claim it before all others? Ans. The foregoing words decide this. 1. Not by mere worth, wit, or virtue: For these may be without such authority. 2. Not by mere strength or conquest: For then every rebel, or foreign prince, that can conquer kings, will have the right; which would tempt them to attempt such conquest. 3. Not every conquest made just by some injury: For that giveth right but to reprisal or damages, and over the injuries: And all wars usually are on pretence of right. 4. Not a succession of primogeniture from Noah, nor from the first founding of the commonwealth: This is not necessary; nor may any rebel against all the kings on earth, if they can but disprove such an uninterrupted succession of primogeniture: Else kings were dangerously exposed. 5. Nor is revelation from heaven necessary to notify the person: For who but fanatics now pretend to that? I knew, therefore, no remaining title, but mutual consent (free or forced) of persons made capable by the providence of God, at the forming of the government.

Qu. IX. Are not [the powers that be] all that have present possession? Answ. Yes, all that possess the right of government; but not all that usurp it, or possess mere strength.

Qu. How then? Shall all the vulgar be made judges of the prince's right? Answ. They are bound to judge as far as they can know; else they could not tell whom to obey or defend: But misjudging will not excuse them from guilt. And in difficult cases; appearance and probability must serve them that can have no more. And submission and patience under usurpers, is not subjection and consent.

Qu. X. What is meant by resistance? Answ. Not only fighting against them, but all that is contrary to subjection and due obedience: But most eminently libertinism, which pretendeth, that God hath freed Christians from subjection.

Qu. XI. How doth the description, verse 3, agree with heathens and persecutors? Are they none of God's ministers who are a terror to good works? Answ. If they are not in the general course of their government for virtue and against vice, and for the common good, they want the essence of the office. But they that are a terror to some particular good works, not essential to the end of the office, and that through error, may yet be against vice, and for goodness, in the main. And a heathen may execute the law of nature, and be so far for the common good. But persecuting the just is no exercise of divine ministry or power.

Qu. XII. Verse 5. How is conscience bound by man's laws? Answ. All men must be conscious of God's obligations on them, to obey the just laws of men.

Qu. XIII. Verse 6, 7. May we give none more tribute, custom, fear, or honour, than their due? And are all judges of the Prince's due? Answ. All is not due that may be claimed: Materially men may, for their own safety and just ends, give rulers or others more than their due, or which they have right to: But as to formal obedience or justice, we are not bound to give any one more than his due. And of this we are discerners, though not deciding public judges: but misjudging will excuse no injury.

Qu. XIV. What sort of debt is sinful? Verse 8. Answ. It is injustice not to give every man his due, if we are able. And to promise or borrow what we know we cannot pay, or when we acquaint not the lender with the weakness and doubtfulness of our estate, that the hazard may be by his own consent, is to defraud him, and is a stealing of one of the worst sorts.

Qu. XV. Verse 13. When is provision for the flesh unlawful? Answ. When it is sought more to satisfy its appetite, or lust, or inordinate desires, than to strengthen and fit us (and others) for our duty to God and man.

CHAP. XIV.

HIM that is weak in the faith receive you: but not to doubtful disputations.

1. And as your subjection to government is necessary to a life of Christian love and concord, so also is the mutual forbearance and reception of such brethren, as are weak in the faith, and differ in disputable tolerable points. Therefore see that you receive such to your love and communion, without searching their opinions, and racking them by doubtful disputations, about the points wherein they differ.

2. For one believeth that he may

eat all things: another who is weak eateth herbs.

2. For instance, one truly believeth'—that all meats are now lawful; another either thinks that he should not live on the life and flesh of his fellow-creatures, or that he should at least abstain from that which by the law of Moses was forbidden: This is his weakness.

3. Let not him that eateth despise him that eateth not: and let not him which eateth not judge him that eateth: for God hath received him.

3. Let not him that understandeth, that eating all things is lawful, set at nought or vilify him (as a humourous, scrupulous fool) who is of another opinion, and thinks it unlawful to eat flesh, (as many are too apt to do) and let not him that dare not eat such flesh or meat forbidden by Moses's law, take him for an ungodly sinner that doth otherwise, nor separate from him as profane: For God that is most holy, and hateth all sin, yet receiveth both these sorts; and therefore so must you, if you will please God.

4. Who art thou that judgest another man's servant? To his own master he standeth or falleth: Yea, he shall be holden up, for God is able to make him stand.

4. Dost thou know thyself while thou so judgest others? Who art thou, a sinful man, that thou presumest to judge and condemn God's servants? It is his sentence and not thine to which they shall stand or fall, as justified or condemned: and these differences shall not hinder God's acceptance of him and his salvation: for God that is just and merciful can justify, confirm, and save him.

5. One man esteemeth one day above another: another esteemeth every day *alike:* Let every man be fully persuaded in his own mind.

5. So one man makes conscience to keep the Jewish feasts and fasts: Another knoweth that Christ hath abrogated them. Let every one labour as well as he can to know God's will, and then be true to his upright conscience; as knowing that he may not in these things follow the judgment of others against his own, which he thinks is according to the mind of God, whom he intendeth herein to obey.

6. He that regardeth *the* day, regardeth *it* unto the Lord, and he that regardeth not the day, to the Lord he doth not regard *it:* He that eateth, eateth to the Lord, for he giveth God thanks, and he that eateth not, to the Lord he eateth not, and giveth God thanks.

6. He that maketh conscience to keep such days, and not so to eat, he intendeth it as an act of obedience to God; and so doth he that is contrarily minded; and both of them pray for God's acceptance, and give him thanks: And dare you for such things discourage or reject men, that as they are able study to please God: Is pleasing God so light in your esteem.

7. For none of us liveth to himself, and no man dieth to himself.

7. For we are all convinced that we are not our own, and therefore may not do what we list ourselves, and fit our practice to carnal self-interests, but to the pleasing of the will of God; as all men die at his will and into his hands, and not their own.

8. For whether we live, we live unto the Lord; and whether we die, we die unto the Lord: Whether we live therefore, or die, we are the Lord's.

8. For our lives are of God, and must be for him to do his will, and when we die, his will therein is done, in which we must contentedly acquiesce: For living and dying we are his.

9. For to this end Christ both died, and rose, and revived, that he might be Lord both of the dead and living.

9. For this being the very end of Christ's dying, rising, and reviving, that he might be Lord of all both dead and living, who shall presume to take the governing or judging power out of his hands, and take men's souls and consciences from subjection to him, and expect to be obeyed or pleased before him?

10. But why dost thou judge thy brother? Or, why dost thou set at nought thy brother? For we shall all stand before the judgment-seat of Christ.

10. Why then doth one party call their brethren sinners, or profane, for not being against such lawful things as they call unlawful? And why do the other part vilify their brethren for conscionable scrupling and avoiding such a lawful thing? Do you not all know our common imperfection of knowledge, and that we have no authority for such judgment or contempt? And are you not afraid thus to usurp the judgment which belongs to Christ, and fear lest he will judge you for your uncharitableness to his servants?

11. For it is written, *As* I live, saith the Lord, every knee shall bow to me, and every tongue shall confess to God. 12. So then every one of us shall give account of himself to God.

11, 12. God hath told us in his word that he

will be first obeyed and pleased before all men: It is he that is our supreme absolute Lord: and to him we must all give our great account, and from him receive our final doom: And would you wish any then to obey or humour you, when he is persuaded that it displeaseth God, and would condemn him? Or will you anticipate God's judgment, and tempt men out of the fear of sinning by your fallible censures or contempt.

13. Let us not, therefore, judge one another any more: but judge this rather, that no man put a stumbling-block, or an occasion to fall, in *his* brother's way.

13. Let not us therefore (pastors or neighbours) thus uncharitably judge or use each other for such tolerable differences in things that are done conscientiously, as for God: But instead of this discouraging conscience, and the fear of sin, let this be your true judgment, that no man (clergy or lay) do either by command or his own practice, put a stumbling-block, scandal, or occasion of sinning or hurt, in his brother's way, pretending the lawfulness of the thing, or his own authority to impose it, souls must not be so driven upon sin.

14. I know, and am persuaded by the Lord Jesus, that *there is* nothing unclean of itself: but to him that esteemeth any thing to be unclean, to him *it is* unclean.

14. I (that am an apostle, and therefore want not knowledge, nor authority to command what should be commanded in such cases,) do know and am persuaded in and by the Lord Jesus, that none of the meats, counted unclean and avoided by the Jewish Christians, are unlawful in themselves, and that they mistake that think otherwise. But it is unclean, and unlawful to him that thinks it so (or else men must do that which they think God forbiddeth, which were formal disobedience to him.)

15. But if thy brother be grieved with *thy* meat, now walkest thou not charitably. Destroy not him with thy meat, for whom Christ died. 16. Let not then your good be evil spoken of,

15, 16. But if by thy unnecessary practice of an indifferent lawful thing (and much more if by thy compulsion) thy mistaken brother be hurt and galled, and discouraged in religion, now thou art guilty of the great sin of uncharitableness, when he was guilty but of a pardonable unwilling mistake: and see to it, that thou do not thus by (the practice, or urging of) any things indifferent, destroy him for whom Christ died, by drawing or driving him to that which to him is sin: Christ purchased souls by a dearer price than things indifferent. It is good in you to know more than he, and lawful to use such meats as he scrupleth: But turn not your knowledge into a scandal, and offence, and mischief.

17. For the kingdom of God is not meat and drink, but righteousness, and peace, and joy in the Holy Ghost.

17. For it is not every lawful indifferent thing (no, nor every truth or smaller duty) which Christianity and salvation, and right to our love and communion, lieth on: These are not essential to the acceptable subjects of Christ's kingdom: Think not so unworthily of him that came to free us from the Mosaical ceremonies, that he hath made such things as these the necessary terms of love and communion in his church. But it is in righteousness before God and man, and in the love and practice of peace with all, and in the joyful sense of the love of God, and hope of glory shed abroad on our hearts by the Holy Ghost, taking pleasure to help and comfort our brethren in the way to heaven. This is Christianity.

18. For he that in these things serveth Christ, *is* acceptable to God, and approved of men.

18. For notwithstanding such difference in lesser things, he that is such a one, and in these things sincerely serveth Christ, is acceptable to God, whoever censure him, despise him, or excommunicate him; and he is approved of wise and charitable men, and is one whose life, even the natural conscience of men, will secretly be forced to approve, and condemn them that condemn and vilify him.

19. Let us therefore follow after the things which make for peace, and things wherewith one may edify another.

19. Instead, therefore, of excommunicating, abusing, or despising one another, for such ceremonies, or small differences as these, if we are Christians, let us lay by these matters of contention, and earnestly pursue the things that make for the common peace of all Christians, though thus differing, and the things by which we may further each others' edification and salvation, and not obtrude our own opinions, or things unnecessary, to the hurt of others, and division of the church.

20. For meat destroy not the work of God. All things indeed *are* pure; but *it is* evil for that man who eateth with offence.

20. Obtrude not your scrupled meat, or ceremonies, or small things, to the destroying of men's souls, by driving or drawing them to sin: All such indifferent things are pure to the pure; but it is your sin if you use them (much more if you impose them) to the scandal, offence, or hurt of others.

21. *It is* good neither to eat flesh, not to drink wine, nor *any thing* whereby thy brother stumbleth, or is offended, or is made weak.

21. It is thy duty to forbear even flesh and wine when they are not necessary, if the use of them

will occasion sin or more hurt to thy brother than good to thee; much more to avoid obtruding thy indifferent things on him who takes them to be sins.

22. Hast thou faith? have it to thyself before God. Happy *is* he that condemneth not himself in that thing which he alloweth.

22. Hast thou more knowledge than he, to believe those things to be lawful, which he judgeth sin? Keep thy knowledge and belief to thyself, to justify thy judgment to God; but use it not to the hurt of others. Happy is he that useth not his knowledge of good and evil to his own condemnation. It is a sad kind of knowledge which is used to destroy others, and condemn thyself.

23. And he that doubteth, is damned if he eat, because *he eateth* not of faith: for whatsoever *is* not of faith, is sin.

23. I may well call it destroying thy brother: For if he do the indifferent thing, who rather thinketh it to be unlawful, it tendeth to his damnation, because it is sin in his opinion and interpretation, while he believeth it to be so, or not to be lawful. For whatever a man doth, believing it to be sin, and not believing that God alloweth it, is certainly a sin in him.

CHAP. XV.

WE then that are strong ought to bear the infirmities of the weak, and not to please ourselves.

1. We then (even church-governors as well as others) that are more knowing, (instead of driving men of weaker understanding to go against their consciences in unnecessary things) ought to bear their weakness with compassion, and in love, and patience, and not to practice what we think lawful, on pretence that we are in the right, when it tendeth to their hurt, (much less to force them to our way.)

2. Let every one of us please *his* neighbour for *his* good to edification. 3. For even Christ pleaseth not himself, but as it is written, The reproaches of them that reproached thee, fell on me.

2, 3. Let every one of us (not excepting myself that am an apostle) lay by his own humour and self-will, and choose the way by which he may edify his brother, by bearing with his weakness. For even Christ so condescended and accommodated himself to the good of others. As it is written, The reproaches, &c. He suffered for men's sin against God.

4. For whatsoever things were written aforetime, were written for our learning; that we through patience and comforts of the scriptures might have hope.

4. Which saying was primarily David's indeed; but all such are written in scripture to teach us also patience, and imitation of such examples of charity, and so to confirm our hope.

5. Now the God of patience and consolation, grant you to be like-minded one towards another, according to Christ Jesus:

5. I know the danger of this selfish uncharitable humour of imposing men's own opinions on all others as terms of their communion with them; and therefore as I have used this long and plain exhortation against it, I shall also pray for you, that the God who is patient with the weak, and is their comforter and yours, will grant you so much grace and charity, as to make you imitators of him, and of the love and condescension of Christ, and to bear with others, and do by them, as you would be borne with and used yourselves.

6. That ye may with one mind and one mouth glorify God, even the Father of our Lord Jesus Christ.

6. That you may with unity and concord hold your holy communion for worshipping God, without uncharitable excommunications or separations, vilifying or censuring each other; which can never be expected by driving each one to agree in small unnecessary things, or without bearing with the mistakes and differences of one another; when all are guilty of many mistakes, and such differences must still be expected.

7. Wherefore receive ye one another, as Christ also received us, to the glory of God.

7. I conclude, therefore, by beseeching you to receive one another with love, to your communion and kindness, as you would be Christian imitators of Christ, and as you are sensible of his needful mercy to yourselves, in receiving us that once were enemies, and still have manifold sins and errors, to the glorifying of God's love and mercy: And pretend not your knowledge, or authority, or piety, against so commanding a motive and example.

ANNOTATIONS

On Chapters Fourteen and Fifteen.

The subject of the former chapter is handled on thus far, and here that chapter should have ended. He that understandeth the former and present state of the Christian churches, and the pride and ignorance to which man is liable, will easily perceive, that it was not in vain that the Spirit of God did by the apostle handle and decide this case, of receiving dissenters in tolerable cases, into love and communion. The Jews were so tied up from legislation in God's matters, by the knowledge of God's prerogative in their Theocracy, that they had less room for the canons and engines of man's making, to exercise their pride and uncharitableness by, than the Romanists have since done. And yet the Pharisees played their part, and by their traditions made void the law of God, and preferred their ceremonies before the weighty matters of the law, and would not understand what that meaneth, [I will have mercy, and not sacrifice;] and did thereby condemn the guiltless. And Christ found the Samaritans and Jews at the debate, [whether in this mountain, or at Jerusalem, men ought to worship?] overlooking that worship which is [in spirit and in truth.] And, alas! what work hath domination, unnecessary canons and censures made in the Christian churches these 1300 years? And it is an instance what power, blindness, and prejudice, and worldly interest have, to frustrate the plainest decisions of God's word, that so full and express a decision as these two chapters make, (with 1 Cor. xii. and Eph. iv. and James iii.) hath signified as little with the dividers and proud, almost as if there had been no such written. And yet such men call for a judge of controversies, because of the pretended obscurity of the scriptures, when nothing can be plainer than this, which they despise. They mean, that such as they must be judges, and God shall make the words, if they may make the sense.

How great is the number that go on the two sides of uncharitableness here reproved; especially on that which is most largely insisted on? One side saith, all God's truths are precious, and none must be sold for peace; and we must not partake of other men's sins: As if our great duty of love, forbearance, and communion, were our sin, or a partaking of the faults of all that we join with. The other side pretend, 1. That Paul only requireth forbearance in things indifferent, undetermined by governors, and not after such a command or determination. 2. Or; that he giveth only a temporary rule for the present concord of Jews and Gentiles, till the settled church should take a contrary course.

I will not here answer these at large, having done it in my book called, ' The only Way of the Church's Concord': But I say, that I despair of reducing that man to the truth herein, who shall continue of either of these opinions, after he hath seriously perused the text, and hath considered, 1. That St. Paul here useth, I think, above twenty arguments, from morality and common Christian duty, which he would not do for a mutable case, which bishops may change when they will. 2. That Rome was then a famous church, and therefore had pastors, or one at least; and that he writeth to the whole church, and therefore to the pastors; and sure he never meant, [The clergy shall receive such Dissenters to communion, and neither by canon or practice cast them out, till they think meet to do otherwise, and till they have made such canons.] Paul doth not so play with contradictions, in so long and grave a reprehension. 3. That St. Paul oft puts himself in, as under the same obligation with the rest: And if an apostle called from heaven, may not do what is here forbidden, what bishops can pretend a right to do it by greater authority or wisdom? But they that have not known the way of peace, may say something against the fullest and plainest description of it, and the sharpest reproofs of God himself. But he will expound these chapters to their consciences, if ever he makes them healers of his church.

As to those that say, it is not church communion that Paul here speaks of; I refer them to the plain text, and Dr. Hammond's annotations, which they value. The God of love and peace hath given laws for love and peace, so strict, and full, and clear, that all the world may see, that it is not he that alloweth the canons or censures which have so long torn the churches.

8. Now I say, that Jesus Christ was a minister of the circumcision for the truth of God, to confirm the promises *made* unto the fathers: 9. And that the Gentiles might glorify God for *his* mercy;

8, 9. And that you may understand my argument from the example of Christ, I say, that it was his office to reconcile both Jews and Gentiles to God, who will receive them both: And therefore they should live as reconciled to each other. Christ was a minister of God, circumcised being a Jew, and personally exercised his ministry among them, to perform God's true promises to the fathers: And yet his gospel extendeth to the Gentiles also, that they may glorify God with the Jews.

9. As it is written, For this cause I will confess to thee among the Gentiles, and sing unto thy name. 10. And again he saith, Rejoice ye Gentiles with his people. 11. And again, Praise the Lord all ye Gentiles, and laud him all ye people. 12. And again Esaias saith, There shall be a root of Jesse, and he that shall rise to reign over the Gentiles; in him shall the Gentiles trust.

9, 10, &c. This is also prophesied, That Christ shall call and save the Gentiles: It is written, &c.

13. Now the God of hope fill you with all joy and peace in believing, that ye may abound in hope through the power of the Holy Ghost.

13. Now that God who is our common hope, fill you with that holy inward joy, and that peace with God and one another, which are the blessings which your faith doth tend to, that your hope in God may more abound, by the seal and working of his Spirit.

14. And I myself also am persuaded of you, my brethren, that ye also are full of goodness, filled

with all knowledge, able also to admonish one another.

14. And though I am persuaded that you yourselves are replenished with grace, goodness, and knowledge, and able to admonish one another, (and so my letter may seem less necessary;)

15. Nevertheless, brethren, I have written the more boldly unto you, in some sort, as putting you in mind, because of the grace that is given to me of God. 16. That I should be the minister of Jesus Christ to the Gentiles, ministering the gospel of God, that the offering up of the Gentiles might be acceptable, being sanctified by the Holy Ghost.

15, 16. Yet I have written the more boldly to you, of what I found most suitable, to put you in mind of that which I hope you know already; because God hath vouchsafed me freely the favour and honour to be Christ's minister to the Gentiles, to minister to them the gospel of God: And therefore I do but perform my office, that I may present to him the converted and edified Gentiles, as an acceptable offering, sanctified (not ceremoniously only) but by the Holy Ghost, by whom I preach, and which is poured out on them that believe.

17. I have therefore whereof I may glory through Jesus Christ, in those things which pertain to God.

17. And in the honour and success of this my office, I have just matter of glorying and joy; not as it is a worldly dignity, but spiritual in the great things that belong to God.

18. For I will not dare to speak of any of those things which Christ hath not wrought by me, to make the Gentiles obedient, by word and deed.

18. For I will not feign that God hath done more by me than he hath, but speak the truth of the words and deeds which were wrought by me, to bring the Gentiles to believe in Christ, and obey him, and my success herein.

19. Through mighty signs and wonders, by the power of the Spirit of God; so that from Jerusalem and round about into Illyricum, I have fully preached the gospel of Christ.

19. Not by mere words, but by such signs and wonders by the power of the Spirit, as bear the proof of God's approbation, and were convincing evidences to the hearers. So that from Jerusalem round to Illyricum, I have fully preached the gospel of Christ.

20. Yea, so have I strived to preach the gospel, not where Christ was named, lest I should build upon another man's foundation:

20. And I specially chose to preach the gospel, where Christ was not known, that I might not only come after others, to finish the work which they had begun.

21. But as it is written, To whom he was not spoken of they shall see: and they that have not heard, shall understand.

21. Which God foretold, saying, &c.

22. For which cause also I have been much hindered from coming to you. 23. But now having no more place in these parts, and having a great desire these many years to come unto you; 24. Whensoever I take my journey into Spain, I will come to you: for I trust to see you in my journey, and to be brought on my way thitherward by you, if first I be somewhat filled with your *company*.

22, 23, 24. And by such work I have been hindered from coming to Rome; but now being more vacant from it here, I hope to see you as I go to Spain, and to be brought on my way, when I have had first the comfort of your company there.

(Note, That Paul knew not how God would send him to Rome, and stop him from going to Spain.)

25. But now I go unto Jerusalem to minister unto the saints.

25. Now I am going to Jerusalem, to serve Christ, in bringing his poor saints, which were under a famine, such relief as I have collected for them.

26. For it hath pleased them of Macedonia and Achaia, to make a certain contribution for the poor saints which are at Jerusalem. 27. It hath pleased them *verily*, and their debtors they are.

26, 27. For the Christians of Macedonia and Achaia have cheerfully made a contribution for them, &c.

27. For if the Gentiles have been made partakers of their spiritual things, their duty is also to minister unto them in carnal things.

27. And though they have obliged them hereby, it was but what they owed them: For if from Jerusalem the gospel of salvation hath been sent

abroad to the Gentiles, it is meet that they should communicate to their wants, in the small matters of bodily relief.

28. When, therefore, I have performed this, and have sealed to them this fruit, I will come by you into Spain.

28. When I have done this, and have delivered this fruit of the Gentiles' love and communion, I purpose to take you in my way to Spain. (Note, Which God disappointed.)

29. And I am sure that when I come unto you, I shall come in the fulness of the blessing of the gospel of Christ.

29. And I am sure that when I come to you, I shall come with such great assistance and evidence of God's Spirit, as will have great and comfortable success among you.

30. Now I beseech you, brethren, for the Lord Jesus Christ's sake, and for the love of the Spirit, that ye strive together with me in your prayers to God for me; 31. That I may be delivered from them that do not believe in Judea; and that my service which *I have* for Jerusalem, may be accepted of the saints.

30, 31. I beseech you for his sake whom we all serve and trust, and as the Spirit of love hath taught you to love all saints that, you will be very earnest as well as I, in prayer to God for me, that I may be preserved from the unbelievers in Judea, and my work of relief may be so accepted as may help to reconcile the Jews, and Gentile Christians. (Note, 1. That earnest conjunct prayer is God's appointed means for his servants' safety and success: 2. And that the strongest believers must so much see and regard their dangers, as to move them earnestly to pray for deliverance.)

32. That I may come unto you with joy by the will of God, and may with you be refreshed.

32. That I may not be hindered from my desired coming to you, and comfort among you. Note, That when we would fain serve God in peace, God oft chooseth otherwise, that we shall serve him (as Paul there did) in prison: (And his will is best.)

33. Now the God of peace *be* with you all. Amen.

33. And it is my prayer for you, that God, who is the lover and giver of peace, may dwell among you with the great blessing of love, peace, and concord. Amen.

CHAP. XVI.

I COMMEND unto you Phebe, our sister, which is a servant of the church which is at Cenchrea: 2. That ye receive her in the Lord as becometh saints, and that ye assist her in whatsoever business she hath need of you: for she hath been a succourer of many, and of myself also.

1, 2. I pray you kindly receive and assist Phebe, &c. For she hath been a great help and reliever of many saints, and me.

3. Greet Priscilla and Aquila, my helpers in Christ Jesus: 4. (Who have for my life laid down their own necks: unto whom not only I give thanks, but also all the churches of the Gentiles).

3, 4. Salute in my name Priscilla and her husband Aquila, eminent in helpfulness, and willing hazards, by which all the Gentiles take themselves beholden to them, as means of my deliverance. Note, The preserving and helping an eminent minister, may oblige many churches.

5. Likewise *greet* the church that is in their house.

5. Salute all their Christian family, and the saints that use there to assemble in communion.

5. Salute my well-beloved Epenetus, who is the first-fruits of Achaia unto Christ. 6. Greet Mary, who bestowed much labour on us.

5, 6. Note, That God would have the good works and service of his saints to be valued and praised.

7. Salute Andronicus and Junia, my kinsmen and my fellow prisoners, who are of note among the apostles, who also were in Christ before me.

7. Noted for their sufferings and service among the apostles.

8. Greet Amplias my beloved in the Lord. 9. Salute Urbane our helper in Christ, and Stachys my beloved. 10. Salute Apelles approved in Christ. Salute them which are of Aristobulus' *household*. 11. Salute Herodion my kinsman.

364　　　　　ROMANS.　　　　CHAP. XVI.

Greet them that be of the *household* of Narcissus, which are in the Lord. 12. Salute Tryphena and Tryphosa, who labour in the Lord. Salute the beloved Persis, which laboured much in the Lord. 13. Salute Rufus chosen in the Lord, and his mother and mine. 14. Salute Asyncritus, Phlegon, Hermas, Patrobas, Hermes, and the brethren which are with them. 15. Salute Philologus, and Julia, Nereus, and his sister, and Olympas, and all the saints which are with them.

8, 9, &c. That you may see that I mind them in particular, salute specially these whom I have notice of.

16. Salute one another with an holy kiss. The churches of Christ salute you.

16. And exercise such love one to another, expressed by (not an immodest and lascivious, but) an holy kiss (the usual expression of friendship in those times:) The churches which have notice of my writing salute you.

17. Now I beseech you, brethren, mark them which cause divisions and offences, contrary to the doctrine which ye have learned; and avoid them.

17. And though I seem to have ended, I will re-assume my exhortation for love and concord, for which I have said so much in this epistle, beseeching you to mark those men, that bring false and new doctrines which the apostles never taught you, and to promote them, and for other sinful ends, draw parties, and make divisions and scandals among you; avoid these, and turn from them.

18. For they that are such, serve not our Lord Jesus Christ, but their own belly; and by good words and fair speeches deceive the hearts of the simple.

18. For though this sort of men pretend to be the chiefest servants of Christ, and promoters of truth, and holiness, and happiness; yet it will be found, that it is not Christ, and his gospel, kingdom, and interest, which indeed they serve: For these are much dissevered by divisions and scandals: But it is their own belly, and fleshly interest in some carnal design, for to escape suffering, or prosper, or be followed and cried up as excellent persons: And though it is usual with them to have good words and fair pretences of wisdom and excellency, and to use subtile arguments, which the simple are much taken with, as if they were clear truth, and holy zeal; yet indeed they do not edify them, but deceive the hearts of such ignorant undiscerning persons.

19. For your obedience is come abroad unto all men. I am glad therefore, on your behalf; but yet I would have you wise unto that which is good, and simple concerning evil.

19. Think not that I accuse you, but warn you: I rejoice that you are famous for your obedience to the apostolical doctrine of faith, love, peace, and concord: But yet I know so much of the way of dividing seducers, and of the weakness and injudiciousness of many zealous Christians, that I see cause to warn you and all others, and to tell you, that there is need of much wisdom to escape this snare, and to discern good from evil; and to wish that you may be wise, as well as zealous, to all that is good; and simple or unacquainted with sinning and heresies.

20. And the God of peace shall bruise Satan under your feet shortly. The grace of our Lord Jesus Christ be with you. Amen.

20. And to encourage you, I foretel you, That God, who would be known to us as the God of peace, and hath promised that the holy seed shall break the serpent's head, will ere long bruise Satan under your feet, overcoming his temptations, and subduing the tyrannical and persecuting instruments that serve him against the church. That the great riches of all Christ's grace may be with you, is the best benediction and wish that I can have for you. Amen.

21. Timotheus my work-fellow, and Lucius, and Jason, and Sosipater, my kinsmen, salute you. 22. I Tertius, who wrote *this* epistle, salute you in the Lord.

23. Gaius mine host, and of the whole church, saluteth you. Erastus the chamberlain of the city saluteth you, and Quartus a brother.

21, 22, 23. The brethren here with me salute you, &c.

24. The grace of our Lord Jesus Christ be with you all. Amen.

24. From the abundance of my affection to you, I again repeat my great benediction and desire, The grace of our Lord Jesus Christ be with you all. Amen.

25. Now to him that is of power to establish you according to my

gospel, and the preaching of Jesus Christ, (according to the revelation of the mystery which was kept secret since the world began. 26. But now is made manifest, and by the scriptures of the prophets according to the commandment of the everlasting God, made known to all nations for the obedience of faith.) 27. To God only wise, *be* glory through Jesus Christ for ever. Amen.

25, 26, 27. I conclude (as Christ taught us in his prayer) with that which is the end of all religion, and of our lives, and salvation itself, the glorifying of God. To him that can make all our exhortations effectual, and is of power to establish you according to that gospel which we preach, as it is now a mystery openly revealed, which was more darkly delivered from the beginning, and not clearly understood by Jews or Gentiles; but now is openly made manifest by Christ the light of the world, and his Spirit in his servants, and by the scriptures of the prophets now opened, and agreeing with our gospel, which by God's command we make known to all nations, to bring them to this faith, which now is the eminent and necessary obedience to the command and covenant of grace: I say, To God only be glory, (as the end of all our grace and glory) through Jesus Christ, (whom he hath ordained to be the chief means and glass in whom his glory shall shine forth to man) for ever. Amen.

ANNOTATIONS.

Why do we read so much in the scriptures [of the obedience of faith?] Some would not have faith called [obedience] lest that signify [works.] Answ. God hath not made believers or unbelievers lawless, or under no command. No act of man pleaseth God, which is not obedience to his will. When God sendeth abroad the gospel, or word of faith, he commandeth men to hear it, believe it, and obey it: But bare commanding is not all: but with it he giveth convincing evidence of its truth, and persuading reasons and motives to obey it. Therefore we translate the same word sometime [believing,] and sometime [being persuaded;] and the same sometime [unbelieving] and sometime [unpersuaded] and [disobedient.] And Christ is called, The author of eternal salvation to all them that obey him. To say, that [faith as it is obedience,] is the condition or qualification for salvation, but [not for pardon or justification,] is a perverse invention of man's brain. But cannot men distinguish between obeying the law of innocency or of Moses, and obeying the law of faith and grace? yea, and between obeying this gospel initially by believing, repenting, and entering into the baptismal covenant, (which entereth into a state of justification and right to life) and the progressive obedience of performing that covenant to the end, which is necessary to survivors for actual glory? Christ knew what he said to the Jews, [This is the work of God, that ye believe on him whom the Father hath sent: and Paul was sent to the Gentile world to preach the obedience of faith; that is, that obedience which consisteth in actual faith performed to the doctrine and command of faith; and which hath the promise of pardon, grace, and glory, freely given for the merits of Christ.

THE FIRST EPISTLE OF PAUL THE APOSTLE,

TO THE

CORINTHIANS.

INTRODUCTION.

WHEN it was that Paul wrote this epistle, and when these Corinthians were converted to Christianity, and what wealth and reputation Corinth (a chief city of Achaia) was then of, I pass by, as things presupposed. The occasion of writing this, is of nearer concern to be known, for the understanding of it. It was not unusual with him (as to visit the churches which he had planted, so) to write to them for their establishment, when he could not be present with them. But as to the *matter* and *manner* of his writing, the case of the Corinthians was the occasion.

1. There were several cases which it seems they proposed to him, which he resolveth; (as about church-order, and prophecy, and prayer; about eating things offered to idols; about marriage and separation, &c.)

2. There were many scandals among them, which he endeavoureth to heal by convincing reproof; as, 1. Factions and schisms, by setting up teachers in envious competition. 2. Conceitedness of more wisdom than they had. 3. Hearkening to envious teachers, that vilified him, and defamed his person and ministry. 4. The favouring of incest and scandal, and neglect of discipline. 5. Going to law against one another, and that before heathen judges, when they should have decided their differences by amicable arbitration. 6. Defrauding and wronging one another. 7. Too easy thoughts of fornication. 8. Scandalous eating things offered to idols. 9. Too much backwardness to maintain the ministers, and the charges of their work. 10. Profane disorder at their love-feasts and sacrament, even to partiality, and excess of drink, and scandalous unreverence, for which God punished some in the flesh. 11. Overvaluing gifts, and undervaluing lower Christians that wanted them; as not enough sensible of the necessity and extent of Christian unity. 12. Disorder in their sacred assemblies in the exercise of their gifts. 13. Some erring about and against the resurrection, and others too much hearkening to them.

These things Paul reproveth, and blameth them for not reforming; but persuadeth none to separate from that church for all these corruptions. But by this we may know what must be expected from young unskilful Christians; and what faults will be in such churches as ours, though the pastors were the best, when the churches were so faulty in the apostles' time and presence; and how far they are from the apostolic spirit, skill, love, and lenity, who would excommunicate all as intolerable schismatics, who conform not to all their devised unnecessary additions, and dare not subscribe their justification or approbation of all their forms. And they also that quarrel with their teachers, and forsake them, when men of new opinions and zealous confidence tempt them. And they that instead of doing their own part to reform the corruptions of such a church, and in love and tenderness to draw sinners to repentance, to take the dividing lazy course, to separate from such churches with a few counted the best, who will put them to least labour and trouble in discipline. Paul himself held communion with this and other such churches, notwithstanding all these faults: And we find not that he excommunicated any one, though he require them to do it, and decreed to do it but on one, 1 Cor. v. and reversed that purpose. I find not in all the New Testament that there was ever two Christian churches in any one town or city, upon any difference among them, unless you will call the condemned nests of heretics such.

CHAP. I.

PAUL called *to be* an apostle of Jesus Christ, through the will of God, and Sosthenes *our* brother, 2. Unto the church of God which is at Corinth, to them that are sanctified in Christ Jesus; called *to be* saints with all that in every place call upon the name of Jesus Christ our Lord, both theirs and ours.

1, 2. Paul, a called apostle by the special electing will and favour of God, and brother Sosthenes; To the church of God at Corinth, being sanctified to God in Christ, and so are called saints; with all such as faithfully call on the name of Christ, our common Lord.

3. Grace *be* unto you, and peace from God our Father, and *from* the Lord Jesus Christ.

3. I wish the great blessings of grace and peace, inward and outward welfare from God the Fountain of all good, and Jesus Christ the mediator and donor of all to us.

4. I thank my God always on your behalf, for the grace of God which is given you by Jesus Christ; 5. That in every thing ye are enriched by him, in all utterance, and in all knowledge: 6. Even as the testimony of Christ was confirmed in you. 7. So that ye come behind in no gift; waiting for the coming of our Lord Jesus Christ.

4, 5, &c. I am thankful for what you have received, that you abound in the gifts of utterance and knowledge, as among you the gospel of Christ was confirmed to you by the miraculous gifts of the Spirit, which you saw and received, so that you have attained to such an eminency, as fitteth you for the perfection of all at the coming of Christ, which you hope and wait for.

8. Who shall also confirm you unto the end, that *ye may be* blameless in the day of our Lord Jesus Christ.

8. Who will not deny you his confirming grace, that you may be found holy and justifiable at that day.

9. God *is* faithful, by whom ye were called unto the fellowship of his Son Jesus Christ our Lord.

9. For God is faithful, who freely called you to the state of communion with and in Christ, when you were aliens to it, and therefore will not fail you when you are called and reconciled.

10. Now I beseech you, brethren, by the name of our Lord Jesus Christ, that ye all speak the same thing, and *that* there be no divisions among you; but *that* ye be perfectly joined together in the same mind, and in the same judgment. 11. For it hath been declared unto me of you, my brethren, by them *which are of the*

house of Chloe, that there are contentions among you.

10, 11. But notwithstanding all your gifts, I find cause to beseech you, even by the authority and precious name of Christ, that you will take heed of divisions, sidings, and contentions, and be as in one mind and judgment. For I have been credibly told of your contentions, &c.

Note, 1. That churches and persons of eminent gifts may be liable to sinful divisions and strife. 2. That unity and concord must improve all our gifts, if we would have them profit ourselves and others. 3. Therefore it must be in the necessary things that we must unite, and be of the same mind and judgment, and not in things doubtful and unnecessary: else it would be as vain, as to beseech them to be all men of learning or highest understanding.

12. Now this I say, that every one of you saith, I am of Paul, and I of Apollos, and I of Cephas, and I of Christ.

12. I hear that you name yourselves as the followers or party of this and that man, as if you set your teachers and their doctrine against one another, and even Christ against his ministers.

13. Is Christ divided? was Paul crucified for you? or were ye baptized in the name of Paul?

13. Will ye make Christ, who is our common head and Saviour, to be the head of a faction? Or will you set Paul against Christ? As if Paul had been crucified for you, or you baptised into his name? Know ye not that we have no head of the church but Christ?

14. I thank God that I baptised none of you, but Crispus and Gaius: 15. Lest any should say that I had baptized in my own name. 16. And I baptized also the household of Stephanas: besides, I know not whether I baptized any other.

14, 15, 16. Though baptising be Christ's ordinance, I thank God that he so overruled my actions, that I baptised none of you, but Crispus and Gaius, and the household of Stephanas, but that it was done by others, because thereby I have escaped this scandal, which might have done more harm, than my baptising would have done good.

Note, That as Abraham and others were to bring all their households with them into the covenant, who were their own, and not free servants; so were those that had households bound to bring all their own into God's covenant, as far as they were able.

17. For Christ sent me not to baptize, but to peach the gospel: not with wisdom of words, lest the cross of Christ should be made of none effect.

17. For though baptizing be within my commission, it was not that, but preaching the gospel to convert soul's to Christ, that I was most expressly and principally commissioned to: and that not by such human arts of philosophy and oratory as now pass for wisdom, lest these should carry the praise from the doctrine, cross, and miracles, which Christ doth work by, to convert the world.

Note, How grossly they err, that say, that God converteth and giveth grace by sacraments only, or rather than by preaching.

18. For the preaching of the cross is to them that perish foolishness: but unto us which are saved, it is the power of God.

28. For to them that thus pass for wise men in the world, but are unsaved and perish in their wisdom, it seemeth great folly to trust in a crucified Christ for salvation, and suffer for him: but the power and wisdom of God are this way eminently manifested to us, who have felt its saving efficacy on ourselves, and shall be saved by it.

19. For it is written, I will destroy the wisdom of the wise, and will bring to nothing the understanding of the prudent.

19. For God, who is against the pride of man, did prophesy, that he would frustrate the carnal wisdom of ungodly men, saying, [I will destroy,] &c.

20. Where *is* the wise? where *is* the scribe? where *is* the disputer of this world? hath not God made foolish the wisdom of this world?

20. Doth not the gospel of a crucified Christ now vanquish and shame the learned philosophy and oratory, heathen and Jewish artificial learning, counted the chief wisdom? And doth it not silence and shame the wrangling logicians, and shew the folly and utter impotency and vanity of their learning?

21. For after that, in the wisdom of God, the world by wisdom knew not God, it pleased God by the foolishness of preaching to save them that believe.

21. For when as the world, by God's wise permission, lived in such ignorance, that they had not the practical knowledge of the true God, but disobeyed him, and worshipped idols, it pleased God by that preaching of Christ which they count foolishness, to convert and save believers, and do that which all their learning could not do.

22. For the Jews require a sign, and the Greeks seek after wisdom: 23. But we preach Christ crucified, unto the Jews a stumbling-block, and unto the Greeks, foolishness;

24. But unto them which are called, both Jews and Greeks, Christ, the power of God, and the wisdom of God.

22, 23, 24. For besides all the miracles and resurrection of Christ, the Jews require some sign from heaven, to prove to them that Christ was sent from God: and the Greeks look for eminent learning to prove it, (some eminent learning in philosophy, logic, or oratory.) But we, that convert and save the world, do it by preaching salvation by a crucified Christ, though it be to the Jews a scandal which they cannot receive; and to Gentiles seeming folly: but to them that are converted and saved by it, Christ is the power and the wisdom of God.

25. Because the foolishness of God is wiser than men; and the weakness of God is stronger than men.

25. For that of God which men count foolishness and weakness, and deride, doth overcome their pretended wisdom and strength, and do that which they cannot do, and proveth them to be but folly and weakness.

26. For ye see your calling, brethren, how that not many wise men after the flesh, not many mighty, not many noble, *are called*.

26. As Christianity is the true wisdom, you see by experience, that not many learned men, or great men that rule in the world, or noble men that abound in wealth, pleasures, and honour, become Christians.

27. But God hath chosen the foolish things of the world, to confound the wise; and God hath chosen the weak things of the world, to confound the things which are mighty; 28. And base things of the world, and things which are despised, hath God chosen, *yea*, and things which are not, to bring to nought things that are: 29. That no flesh should glory in his presence.

27, 28, 29. But it pleaseth God to chuse that which the world counts foolish, and weak, and base, to confound, shame, and overcome, that which is accounted by them wise, and mighty, and honourable; and the things which they despise, God will use and honour: yea, by that which seemeth nothing to them, or which yet is not in being, to vanquish those which seem great and real to them; that so the pride of man may be shamed, and the impotency of man manifested, and all flesh may be humbled, and driven from their self-confidence, and none may glory of any thing of his own, against his glory.

2.

30. But of him are ye in Christ Jesus, who of God is made unto us wisdom, and righteousness, and sanctification, and redemption: 31. That, according as it is written, He that glorieth, let him glory in the Lord.

30, 31. But it is by his power and work that you are made Christians, united to Christ, who of God is made to us the object and teacher of the truest wisdom; (to know him, and to be taught by him the great things of salvation, excelleth all the heathen philosophy.) He is made of God our righteousness, the merits of his perfect righteousness procuring our free pardon and adoption, which our works could not do. He is made our sanctification, we being purified by virtue of his sacrifice, and by his Spirit, and by him separated as a peculiar people to God. And by him it is that we have redemption and deliverance from sin, and Satan, and the law, and death, and hell: that, as it is written, God and not man may be all our glorying and trust.

ANNOTATIONS.

This chapter doth so plainly describe the same sort of wise men that are described Rom. i. and several other such places, as yet is confessedly meant of heathen philosophers, and learned and great men, including the Jewish scribes; and therefore confuteth the misapplication of many such texts to the Gnostics only.

CHAP. II.

AND I, brethren, when I came to you, came not with excellency of speech, or of wisdom, declaring unto you the testimony of God.

1. Accordingly, I myself being sent by Christ to preach to the world, did not come to you with the admired philosophy and oratory of the world, in declaring the gospel mystery, and God's attestation of it.

2. For I determined not to know any thing among you, save Jesus Christ, and him crucified.

2. For I resolved to make no ostentation of any other learning, and to teach you no other, than the knowledge of a crucified Christ, in an humble manner preached.

3. And I was with you in weakness, and in fear, and in much trembling.

3. And accordingly I was humbled among you, by persecutions, and abuse, and continual dangers and sufferings, in conformity to the cross of Christ, which I preached.

B b

4. And my speech, and my preaching, *was* not with enticing words of man's wisdom, but in demonstration of the Spirit, and of power:

4. And my manner of preaching was, not by the witty insinuations of artificial learning, (oratory or logic;) but so, as did demonstrate the supernatural gift of the Spirit of God, and in the power thereof, manifested by miracles and success.

5. That your faith should not stand in the wisdom of men, but in the power of God.

5. That your faith, the effect, which will be like its cause and motives, might not be merely human, founded on and resolved into the art of the speaker; but divine, grounded on and resolved into the evidence of divine revelation and authority.

6. Howbeit we speak wisdom among them that are perfect: yet not the wisdom of this world, nor of the princes of this world, that come to nought.

6. Yet we are not without useful learning, and sublimity and accurateness of speech, but use such with those that are knowing and capable of it: but not the vain and frothy learning which is now most applauded in the world by men of name and power, which perisheth as a bubble, and saveth not them that have it.

7. But we speak the wisdom of God in a mystery, *even* the hidden *wisdom* which God ordained before the world unto our glory.

7. But we speak the mystery of redemption, the product and discovery of the wisdom of God, which hath been kept in much darkness, and little known, but ordained before the world was, to be opened in the fulness of time to our glory.

8. Which none of the princes of this world knew: for had they known *it*, they would not have crucified the Lord of glory.

8. Which none of the rulers of this age of the world knew; else they had not crucified Christ, &c.

9. But as it is written, Eye hath not seen, nor ear heard, neither have entered into the heart of man, the things which God hath prepared for them that love him.

9. For the great gifts of God's grace, decreed and prepared for all that love him, are such as man seeth not, and hardly believeth, and cannot comprehend; as it is written, [Eye hath not seen, &c.]

10. But God hath revealed *them* unto us by his Spirit: for the Spirit searcheth all things, yea, the deep things of God.

10. But God by his Spirit hath revealed them to us his apostles (and to others that have his Spirit in the measure that they have it:) for the Spirit of God is given us (in our several measures) to teach us all things fit for us to know, even the depths of God.

11. For what man knoweth the things of a man, save the spirit of man which is in him? even so the things of God knoweth no man, but the Spirit of God.

11. As a man's spirit is conscious of its own secret actings and thoughts, which no man else can know; so the Spirit of God knoweth the secret things of God, and maketh us know them in our measures, which they that have not the Spirit cannot by all their learning know.

12. Now we have received, not the spirit of the world, but the Spirit which is of God; that we might know the things that are freely given to us of God.

12. And this Spirit God hath given to us; not the spirit of the world, to make us carnally and worldly wise; but the Spirit of God, to make us savour and know God's great mysterious gifts of grace.

13. Which things also we speak, not in the words which man's wisdom teacheth, but which the Holy Ghost teacheth; comparing spiritual things with spiritual.

13. And these are the things which we preach to you, not in words and manner now counted by the heathens to be learned and wise, nor after their vain arts; but in the very words and manner which God's Spirit teacheth us, who teacheth us the matter, fitting spiritual words to spiritual things, that all may be of God.

14. But the natural man receiveth not the things of the Spirit of God: for they are foolishness unto him; neither can he know *them*, because they are spiritually discerned.

14. But they that have not the Spirit themselves, but mere nature, cannot with all their learning receive these spiritual mysteries revealed to us by God; for they will seem but fanatic dreams and foolishness to them, not to be believed. Nor can they understand them; for only a mind illuminated by God's Spirit doth discern them.

15. But he that is spiritual, judg-

eth all things; yet he himself is judged of no man.

15. But he that is spiritual discerneth these revealed things of the Spirit in his measure; when yet he himself, and his own spiritual apprehensions and affections, are unknown to carnal men that hear him.

16. For who hath known the mind of the Lord, that he may instruct him? But we have the mind of Christ.

16. For who hath pried into God's secret counsels, or known his mind, further than he hath opened it to him? But Christ our teacher hath told us his own and his Father's mind, which we are to preach to the world for man's salvation.

ANNOTATIONS.

1. It is none of Paul's meaning here, to vilify true philosophy, logic, or oratory, or any useful knowledge or art: and all knowledge is useful to one that referreth it to right ends, which is knowledge indeed: for God hath made nothing knowable in vain. True physics is the knowledge of the knowable works of God, and God in them, that we may admire, love, serve and trust him. True logic is but the skill of using our reason truly and orderly. True grammar and oratory are but fitting words to things, and to the hearer's minds, as most tendeth to their edification. God is against none of these, which are his precious gifts. But carnal men have carnal ends, and fit all these abusively to their ends, to wrangle against truth, and divert their minds from things to words and from great and everlasting things to trifles, and to feed their pride, and ambition, and covetousness, and to make their malignity more keen and hurtful. And such was the learning of these heathens, which then past for wisdom in the world.

2. Nor doth Paul here favour false pretences of the spirit, or true fanaticism; when men take the delusions of Satan, or every strong imagination, or the boiling of their pride and erroneous passions, fed by prejudice, for the work of God's Spirit. These sin more dangerously than many others, by charging their sin and error upon God, and tempting men to deride the Spirit. Even as false prophets are most sharply reproved, and the counterfeit use of Christ's name by the sons of Sceva, did but strengthen the devil against them. Therefore we are bid to try the spirits.

CHAP. III.

AND I, brethren, could not speak unto you as unto spiritual, but as unto carnal, even as unto babes in Christ.

1. But this spiritual wisdom, of which I have said such great things, is not in all Christians alike. Though the apostles had the Spirit to lead them into all needful truth, and record it for the church, yet some weak Christians are still so much carnal, that their spiritual wisdom is but such as babes in Christ have, who have still need to be fed and taught by others: and as to such, I am constrained to speak to you.

2. I have fed you with milk, and not with meat: for hitherto ye were not able *to bear it*, neither yet now are ye able.

2. I feed you with the food of babes, and not of strong understanding men; or else I had lost my labour by your incapacity: for harder things you could not, nor yet can bear.

3. For ye are yet carnal: for whereas *there is* among you envying, and strife, and divisions, are ye not carnal, and walk as men?

3. For ye are yet in a great measure carnal: do not your envy, and strife and divisions, prove that you are so far carnal, and live according to the corrupt nature of man, and not by the Spirit of God?

4. For while one saith, I am of Paul, and another, I *am* of Apollos, are ye not carnal?

4. For while you divide into factions for your several teachers, are ye not so far carnal?

5. Who then is Paul, and who *is* Apollos, but ministers by whom ye believed, even as the Lord gave to every man?

5. What are any of us but Christ's ministers, by whose ministry you were brought to believe in Christ, even as God gave us various degrees of success.

6. I have planted, Apollos watered: but God gave the increase.

6. I first preached to your conversion, and Apollos to your further edification: but the success and fruit of all was not from our power, but from the free grace of God.

7. So then, neither is he that planteth any thing, neither he that watereth: but God that giveth the increase.

7. If then you would know to whom to ascribe your conversion and salvation, we poor ministers that plant and water are but as God's tools, and to be accounted as nothing in comparison of him, who (as he sent us, and enabled us, so) caused freely all the success, which is our joy, and your welfare.

8. Now he that planteth, and he that watereth, are one: and every man shall receive his own reward, according to his own labour.

8. Now it is by the same ministerial grace and office that one of us planteth, and another watereth; and it is the same Spirit that moveth us, and the same gospel which we preach: but we also have our different measure of gifts, grace, and labour; and so shall we have our reward.

9. For we are labourers together with God: ye are God's husbandry, *ye are* God's building.

9. For we are all but God's ministers, fellow labourers each with other, having our several parts to do: ye are not our husbandry, and building, and church, but God's.

10. According to the grace of God which is given unto me, as a wise master-builder, I have laid the foundation, and another buildeth thereon. But let every man take heed how he buildeth thereupon.

10. As God gave me an extraordinary call and grace, my work hath been that of an architect or chief builder; and accordingly I have laid the foundation of many churches, preaching Christ where none before believed; and another hath come after me to build them up: but let every man take heed that he teach nothing but what is true and sound.

11. For other foundation can no man lay, than that is laid, which is Jesus Christ.

11. Let him not alter the foundation which I have laid: for there is no other but Christ, or the essentials of Christianity.

12. Now if any man build upon this foundation, gold, silver, precious stones, wood, hay, stubble: 13. Every man's work shall be made manifest. For the day shall declare it, because it shall be revealed by fire: and the fire shall try every man's work, of what sort it is.

12, 13. And what following teachers build on this foundation, God will bring to trial and manifest. If it be sound and holy, gold, silver, precious stones, God will approve and bless it: if it be error, and carnal policy, or corrupt mixtures, or things unprofitable, God will try and disown it, by his Spirit, and by the fire of persecution.

14. If any man's work abide which he hath built thereupon, he shall receive a reward.

14. If his labour and doctrine prove sound, and endure God's furnace in trial, he shall be rewarded.

15. If any man's work shall be burnt, he shall suffer loss. But he himself shall be saved, yet so, as by fire.

15. If it prove that such teachers have erred, and misled the people, God's trial will turn such labour to their grief, as worse than lost: but if he practically hold the foundation, he shall be pardoned and saved; yet not without the trying furnace, which shall detect his error, and teach him better, to his cost.

16. Know ye not that ye are the temple of God, and *that* the Spirit of God dwelleth in you?

16. Know ye not that your souls severally, and your church collectively, are the temple of God, and that the Spirit of God dwelleth in you and among you; and therefore you must be holy?

17. If any man defile the temple of God, him shall God destroy: for the temple of God is holy, which *temple* ye are.

17. God will destroy them that profane his holy temple, and defile it with the things which he abhorreth: and you and your churches are this holy temple, if you are holy, and his indeed.

18. Let no man deceive himself: If any man among you seemeth to be wise in this world, let him become a fool, that he may be wise.

18. Let none of you deceive himself by pretended wisdom, which is not spiritual, and doth not purify heart and life: like these that boast of wisdom, and live in the filth of sin. If any man among you be puffed up with the conceit of this philosophical worldly wisdom, let him know, that it is but folly, and be convinced of his ignorance, that he may humbly learn of Christ, and be made truly wise.

19. For the wisdom of this world is foolishness with God: for it is written, He taketh the wise in their own craftiness. 20. And again, The Lord knoweth the thoughts of the wise, that they are vain.

19, 20. For all that men call learning and wisdom, which doth not serve a worldly interest, and saveth not the soul from sin and hell, is mere foolishness in God's account: for it proveth but a snare to themselves, and vapoureth away as idleness and vanity; as it is written, &c.

21. Therefore let no man glory in men: for all things are yours: 22. Whether Paul, or Apollos, or Cephas, or the world, or life, or death, or things present, or things to come, all are yours; 23. And ye are Christ's; and Christ is God's.

21. Therefore think not over-highly of any man

especially for his worldly wisdom and learning, or boasting that he knoweth more than others: for all teachers and their wisdom, are but God's gifts for your good; apostles, providence, life, or death, all are for your salvation; and that is best to you, that maketh you best: the end must direct you to judge of the means, and so of teachers: they are for you, and your salvation; and you are Christ's, and for his glory; and Christ, as man and mediator, is God's, and for his glory.

ANNOTATIONS.

We see here, that sects, factions, and divisions, are the works of the flesh, and signify a mind that is so far carnal; and that this cometh usually by preferring and setting teacher against teacher; not but that the great difference of worth and grace must be acknowledged and valued, but not made an occasion of division, but of concord, all being God's ministers for the church's common good, in the various measure of their gifts. The carnal are headed by man, and the spiritual by Christ only, though men be their helpers. And Cephas is here named, as if it were on foresight that the Roman bishop would make himself such a head, on pretence of being his successor.

CHAP. IV.

LET a man so account of us, as of the ministers of Christ, and stewards of the mysteries of God.

1. I speak not all this to draw you from the due honour of faithful ministers: account us neither more nor less, but as the ministers of Christ for your salvation, and stewards called and trusted with the just ministration of the mysteries of God; that is, the sound preaching of his word, and the due application of it, and administration of his sacraments, and power of the keys, to judge who shall be baptized, and live, as fit, in holy communion with his visible churches.

2. Moreover it is required in stewards, that a man be found faithful.

2. And it is required of stewards, especially that have so great a trust, that they be faithful and answer that trust, in matter, and manner, and application; and that they falsify not God's word, nor corrupt his worship, or church, nor betray or neglect souls, nor turn over their proper trust and work to others.

3. But with me it is a very small thing that I should be judged of you, or of man's judgment: Yea, I judge not mine own self.

3. And if any among you censure me, I account it a very small matter; though I despise no man's just admonition, man's judgment signifieth little as to myself, further than it may be hurtful to others: for my case will not be finally determined by any man's judgment, nor by my own.

4. For I know nothing by myself, yet am I not hereby justified: but he that judgeth me is the Lord.

4. For my conscience is witness of my sincerity, and I know no unfaithfulness in my stewardship, though I am yet imperfect; but this is not my deciding justification, nor is my conscience any public or final judge, but only the discerner of my case. It is Christ only whose judgment must publicly and finally pass my doom.

5. Therefore judge nothing before the time, until the Lord come, who both will bring to light the hidden things of darkness, and will make manifest the counsels of the hearts: and then shall every man have praise of God.

5. Therefore usurp not God's part in uncalled, bold, and peremptory judging: stay till God's day come; he will bring works of darkness into light, and open the secrets of men's hearts; and then those that indeed are excellent persons shall have God's approbation and praise, which is better than the applause of factions and partial followers.

6. And these things, brethren, I have in a figure transferred to myself, and to Apollos, for your sakes; that ye might learn in us, not to think *of men* above that which is written, that no one of you be puffed up for one against another.

6. All this I have spoken as if the case had been my own and Apollos's, to warn you of the sin and danger of making men the heads of factions and divisions, by thinking over-highly of yourselves, or them; and that you think of all ministers but as God's stewards for your good, as I wrote here before, and use them for concord and not for sects.

7. For who maketh thee to differ *from another?* and what hast thou that thou didst not receive? now if thou didst receive *it*, why dost thou glory, as if thou hadst not received *it?*

7. And if really any of you are wiser than others, who gave thee that wisdom which maketh the difference? And what hast thou which was not freely given thee without desert? And if it was so given thee, why art thou puffed up and boastest, as if it had been deserved, or were from thyself?

8. Now ye are full, now ye are rich, ye have reigned as kings without us: and I would to God ye did reign, that we also might reign with you.

8. You take yourselves to be grown much wiser and better under your exalted envious teachers, than you were under us, and so set light by those that converted you: you are as kings in your fulness and prosperity in your own conceits, since I was with you: and I would you were so indeed, that we might rejoice and partake with you, and be refreshed with you under all the persecution which we yet endure.

9. For I think that God hath set forth us the apostles last, as it were appointed to death. For we are made a spectacle unto the world, and to angels, and to men.

9. For God seemeth to have called us apostles, to be exposed on the theatre of the world, as last, and appointed to greater sufferings than the prophets were, who suffered before us, in our martyrdom, to be made public spectacles to the world, both angels and men.

10. We *are* fool's for Christ's sake, but ye *are* wise in Christ: we *are* weak, but ye *are* strong: ye *are* honourable, but we *are* despised.

10. While you are conceited of yourselves as wise in the things of Christ, and as strong and honourable, we are despised by the boasters of the world, as fools and weak.

11. Even unto this present hour we both hunger, and thirst, and are naked, and are buffeted, and have no certain dwelling-place; 12. And labour working with our own hands:

11, 12. Your prosperous state, and our suffering state much differ; formerly, and to this day, we are taken for contemptible vagabonds, and live in hunger and thirst, and poor clothing, abused and buffeted without justice or relief, having no fixed habitation of our own, and put to get our bread by our handy labour, while we preach to others.

12. Being reviled, we bless: being persecuted, we suffer it: 13. Being defamed, we intreat: we are made as the filth of the world, *and are* the off-scouring of all things unto this day.

12, 13. Being reviled by opprobrious words, we wish them well that do it: being unjustly persecuted, we put all up, and patiently bear it: being defamed by vilifying false accusers, we intreat and speak them fair; we are esteemed and used as the filth of the world, and the off scouring, refuse, and scum of the earth, as unworthy of human society or peace to this day.

14. I write not these things to shame you, but as my beloved sons I warn *you*.

14. And though we suffer all this for you, and such others, and some of you have added to my afflictions, which you should have eased, I write it to warn you, and not to reproach you with it; even as to my sons, and not mine enemies.

15. For though you have ten thousand instructors in Christ, yet *have ye* not many fathers: for in Christ Jesus I have begotten you through the gospel.

15. For though you have never so many teachers you owe some special respect to me, who am your father, or first converter by my ministry.

16. Wherefore I beseech you, be ye followers of me.

16. Wherefore I beseech you, let no teachers draw you from the doctrine which I delivered to you from Christ, but constantly adhere to it.

17. For this cause have I sent unto you Timotheus, who is my beloved son, and faithful in the Lord, who shall bring you into remembrance of my ways which be in Christ, as I teach every where in every church.

17. And till I can come myself, I have sent Timothy, who is my son and faithful, who knoweth my doctrine and practice, in the things of Christ, and will faithfully remember you of them.

18. Now some are puffed up as though I would not come to you.

18. Some envious teachers vaunt as if, I durst not come to you, and stand before them.

19. But I will come to you shortly, if the Lord will, and will know, not the speech of them which are puffed up, but the power.

19. But I will come shortly if the Lord will, and will try your boasting, envious teachers, not who hath the smoothest tongue, but who hath the greatest power of the Spirit.

20. For the kingdom of God *is* not in word, but in power.

20. For the kingdom of Christ is not raised, nor distinguished from the world, or carried on by smooth words, but by works of divine efficacy and power.

21. What will ye? shall I come unto you with a rod, or in love, and *in* the spirit of meekness?

21. And had you not rather that I come in love and meekness, than with punishing power, to deliver any offenders to Satan as God's executioner on their bodies?

CHAP. V.

IT is reported commonly *that there is* fornication among you, and such fornication as is not so much as named amongst the Gentiles, that one should have his father's wife.

1. It is not a doubtful fame, but a credible report that there is such fornication among you, as civil heathens do abhor; that one should have his father's wife.

2. And ye are puffed up, and have not rather mourned, that he that hath done this deed, might be taken away from among you.

2. And you have made light of it, and not as sensible of the sin and shame, bewailed it, that he that is impenitent in this may be cut off from your society.

3. For I verily as absent in body, but present in spirit, have judged already, as though I were present *concerning* him that hath so done this deed; 4. In the name of our Lord Jesus Christ, when ye are gathered together, and my spirit with the power of our Lord Jesus Christ, 5. To deliver such an one unto Satan for the destruction of the flesh, that the spirit may be saved in the day of the Lord Jesus.

3, 4, 5. For though I be absent in body, yet present in spirit, I have by the power given me by Christ, determined already, when you are assembled, and my spirit with you, to deliver this man to Satan, by casting him out of the church, and leaving him to God's executioner, to inflict destructive punishment on his body, to bring him to repentance for the saving of his soul.

Note, 1. That Paul himself was the judge. 2. Yet he would do it when they were assembled, for order; to shew them what they should have done. 3. That it was in a church-assembly of men present for holy communion, and not in a lay-court, or a consistory of the pastors of other assemblies, who knew not the man, nor had any special over-sight of him. 4. That Satan is God's executioner on the bodies even of Christians, specially of sins to death. The church having then no Christian magistrates, was put to appeal to God, to punish capital crimes miraculously. 5. That yet this is to save the sinner by repentance, as well as to be a warning to others.

6. Your glorying *is* not good: Know ye not that a little leaven leaveneth the whole lump?

6. You do not well to bear up such a man in his sin, and to make light of it: the whole church so far as it is guilty of such a conniving or consent, is thus defiled with guilt, and may be tempted to the like sin.

7. Purge out therefore the old leaven, that ye may be a new lump, as ye are unleavened. For even Christ our passover is sacrificed for us.

7. As the Jews when they kept the passover were to cast all leavened bread out of their houses, so we assemble to commemorate the sacrifice of Christ our Pascal lamb. Purge out of your assemblies the old leaven of scandalous sins, that you may approve yourselves a society acceptable to God through Christ.

Note, 1. That, as Dr. Hammond observes out of Chrysostom and Theodoret, there was a tradition, that this offender was a bishop. 2. And the assembly was to purge the church of such a one, whoever he was, by forsaking him.

8. Therefore let us keep the feast, not with old leaven, neither with the leaven of malice and wickedness; but with the unleavened *bread* of sincerity and truth.

8. Therefore let our Christian assemblies be kept as holy feasts before God, not with the vices of our old natural or heathen state, nor with the odious leaven of naughtiness and wickedness; but with the unleavened bread of purity, sincerity, and truth.

9. I wrote unto you in an epistle, not to company with fornicators. 10. Yet not altogether with the fornicators of this world, or with the covetous, or extortioners, or with idolators; for then must ye needs go out of the world.

9, 10. I did indeed write to you before (In this or some other epistle) to avoid familiarity with fornicators, covetous, extortioners, idolaters, &c. I meant, that you shew your abhorrence of this sin, and shame the sinner, by shunning his company, when it is unnecessary, and it is in your power so to do: but I meant not that you should have no company or converse at all with any that are such; for you live among unbelievers, and cannot go out of the world.

11. But now I have written unto you, not to keep company, if any man that is called a brother be a fornicator, or covetous, or an idolater, or a railer, or a drunkard, or an extortioner; with such an one no not to eat.

11. But my meaning and your duty is, that you shun all company which may signify owning or brotherly familiarity with any called Christians,

who are such scandalous sinners, that the church and religion may not be thought to favour them, and that shame may humble them. And though it belong not to every Christian, but the church, to cast such out of public societies, nor to separate from the church because such are there; yet as the church ought to purge out such, so every private man should avoid that familiarity which is in their power, even that which lieth in friendly eating, or the like.

12. For what have I to do to judge them also that are without? do not ye judge them that are within?

12. For we are not authorized to call those without the church before us, to try and judge their cases, who never submitted to our authority, and are not a scandal to the Christian profession. It is them that have consented to our power and discipline, that you judge.

13. But them that are without, God judgeth. Therefore put away from among yourselves that wicked person.

13. Those that are without the church we must leave to the judgment of God; they are not under our government: but that wicked person who is as one of you, disown, and put away from your communion.

CHAP. VI.

DARE any of you, having a matter against another, go to law before the unjust, and not before the saints?

1. Another scandal I hear of among you, is, That you go to law against one another before heathen judges, when you might decide your differences among yourselves. How dare you do this, when heathens are unjust, and will deride you?

2. Do ye not know that the saints shall judge the world? and if the world shall be judged by you, are ye unworthy to judge the smallest matters?

2. Know ye not that Christ will commit that honour to his saints, with him to judge the world of the ungodly? And you should be all saints yourselves: And if the world shall be judged by you, are you not meet to decide your own little differences?

3. Know ye not that we shall judge angels? how much more things that pertain to this life?

3. And as Christ is the judge of the evil angels, we shall be honoured to join with him in that judgment also, when all his enemies shall be put under his feet and ours. How much more are we meet to decide these worldly strifes?

4. If then ye have judgments of things pertaining to this life, set them to judge who are least esteemed in the church.

4. If then it be a thing belonging to you, though you are no magistrates, to arbitrate your own differences, if you have no wise men and elders among you whom you will trust, chuse the weakest; for the lowest of you should be fitter than unjust heathens.

5. I speak to your shame. Is it so, that there is not a wise man amongst you? no not one that shall be able to judge between his brethren?

5. I speak ironically, to your shame. Are you the men that boast of wisdom? and is there not one man among you wise enough to judge of the differences of Christians?

6. But brother goeth to law with brother, and that before the unbelievers.

6. But you must take the contentious and chargeable way of public judicatures, and that before infidels, that are unjust, and will deride you?

7. Now therefore there is utterly a fault among you, because ye go to law one with another: why do ye not rather take wrong? why do ye not rather suffer yourselves to be defrauded?

7. Why have ye not learnt of Christ to put up injuries, and let go your right, rather than violate the laws of love and peace? It is your sin to be uncharitable, and contentious seekers of your own right. Is patience, and forbearing, and forgiving, a strange thing to you? Is it not your pertain duty?

8. Nay, you do wrong and defraud, and that *your* brethren.

8. Nay, you that are bound to forgive wrongs, do wrong others, even your Christian brethren.

9. Know ye not that the unrighteous shall not inherit the kingdom of God? Be not deceived: neither fornicators, nor idolaters, nor adulterers, nor effeminate, nor abusers of themselves with mankind, 10. Nor thieves, nor covetous, nor drunkards, nor revilers, nor extortioners, shall inherit the kingdom of God.

9, 10. Think not you can be saved either by the righteousness of Christ, or by a dead belief, or profession of Christianity, without a personal righteousness, consisting in sincere obedience to God: and you are not such, if you live in such sins as these here named. Let no deceivers persuade you otherwise: you may, by neglect of discipline, be in the church visible; but you are, while such, incapable of salvation.

11. And such were some of you: but ye are washed, but ye are sanctified, but ye are justified, in the name of the Lord Jesus, and by the Spirit of our God.

11. Though some of you were such in your heathen state, you have since been baptised unto Christ and the holy Spirit, and renouncing these sins, have been sacramentally washed from them, and dedicated as holy to God, and numbered with the just; and if you are sincere believers, you are such indeed, as well as sacramentally, by the merits of Christ, and the Spirit's sanctification.

12. All things are lawful unto me, but all things are not expedient: all things are lawful for me, but I will not be brought under the power of any.

12. As to them that say, That there is no law against the pleasing of our appetites, or simple fornication, they take notice only of political laws, with human executions. I confess that Moses' law, as such, being political, left some excesses and fornications, as polygamy, &c. unpunished, or but lightly punished; and the Roman laws neglect them; and Moses' law, as such, is abrogated, and so I am under no political law which punisheth these: but I am a servant of Christ, whose law of grace forbiddeth all things that are inexpedient, and contrary to the purity and hopes of Christianity, or to the law of love. And if you plead Christian liberty, I answer, 1. As to meats, and other things indifferent, though they are in themselves lawful, yet it is not indifferent how we use them, whether we do hurt or not, when they are inexpedient and hurtful. 2. And I will not be so enslaved to my fleshly appetite, as to obey it to my own or others hurt.

13. Meats for the belly, and the belly for meats: but God shall destroy both it and them. Now the body *is* not for fornication, but for the Lord; and the Lord for the body.

13. And I further answer, That you do ill to join fornication with things indifferent: meats indeed are to feed flesh and appetite, and the belly and appetite are for them; but both must be used as perishing things; but our bodies are not made for fornication, but to serve the Lord, who also will take care of them as his redeemed.

14. And God hath both raised up the Lord, and will also raise up us by his own power.

14. And accordingly, God that raised up the body of Christ, will also raise us by his power.

15. Know ye not, that your bodies are the members of Christ? shall I then take the members of Christ, and make them the members of an harlot? God forbid.

15. It is so far from being lawful, that it hath this odious aggravation, to make those bodies the united members of an harlot, which are united and related to Christ as his members, that is, of the holy society of which he is the head.

16. What, know ye not that he which is joined to an harlot, is one body? for two (saith he) shall be one flesh.

16. Fornication is a sort of union with a harlot; for to generation they are as one flesh.

17. But he that is joined unto the Lord is one spirit.

17. But those that by a true faith are joined to Christ, are quickened and acted in holiness by the very Spirit of Christ, and so are one spirit with him, by a union which destroyeth not their personal individuation, nor maketh them Christ, but maketh them more blessedly one with him than we can now comprehend: (even plants live by the sun-beams, and yet are not the sun.)

18. Flee fornication. Every sin that a man doeth, is without the body: but he that committeth fornication, sinneth against his own body.

18. Hate and avoid fornication also on this account: most other sins in their outward acts, are but the abuse of things without you (as your money, lands, houses, friends, enemies, power, &c.) but fornication is the abusive polluting and debasing your own bodies.

19. What, know ye not that your body is the temple of the Holy Ghost *which is* in you, which ye have of God,

19. When God giveth his Spirit to believers to sanctify them to himself, he thereby maketh them as temples, holy, for his holy Spirit to dwell in and actuate.

19. And ye are not your own?
20. For ye are bought with a price: therefore glorify God in your body, and in your spirit, which are God's.

19, 20. And seeing you are not at all your own, you may not do with your bodies what you list; God is your absolute owner, (not only by the right of creation and preservation, but) by that of redemption, by the price of the blood and merits of Christ: Therefore you rob and wrong him (though you cannot hurt him) if you alienate his own, and glorify not that God whose you wholly are, by the faithful love and service of soul and body which are his. (And to be thus his, is your honour, safety, and felicity.)

CHAP. VII.

NOW concerning the things whereof ye wrote unto me: *It is* good for a man not to touch a woman.

1. As to the question about marriage, of which you wrote, I say, that if a man have no kind of intrinsic or extrinsic reason to make it best for him, it is for a man's own ease and quietness in the world to live single, and safest to avoid temptations, to keep at sufficient distance from women, especially to avoid all tempting and immodest touches, or familiarity.

2. Nevertheless, *to avoid* fornication, let every man have his own wife, and let every woman have her own husband.

2. But the state of man on earth is such, that men cannot always do that which is most for their own quietness and ease. Some have so strong lust, that marriage is necessary to them, to avoid fornication: And to those that need it, it is God's ordinance for the propagation of mankind on earth.

3. Let the husband render unto the wife due benevolence: and likewise also the wife unto the husband.

3. And let husband and wife perform to each other all the duties of marriage which they promised.

4. The wife hath not power of her own body, but the husband: and likewise also the husband hath not power of his own body, but the wife.

4. By the marriage covenant, you have given each other power of your bodies for regular congress.

5. Defraud you not one the other, except *it be* with consent for a time, that ye may give yourselves to fasting and prayer; and come together again, that Satan tempt you not for your incontinency.

5. To deny this to each other, is injury and fraud: except when you are called to humbling, fasting, and prayer, and then you should consent to that sort of abstinence: but after use due matrimonial conversation, lest your forbearance give Satan advantage to tempt you.

6. But I speak this by permission, *and* not of commandment.

6. But mistake me not, as if I hereby imposed marriage on all men as their duty, though allowed when necessary, or gave this my counsel as a law.

7. For I would that all men were even as I myself: but every man hath his proper gift of God, one after this manner, and another after that.

7. For I could wish that all men, for their own advantage, had the gift of continence as well as I have: But God, who will have the world yet continued, hath not given it to all; but some have one measure and sort of gift, and some another.

8. I say therefore to the unmarried and widows, It is good for them if they abide even as I.

8. It is most for their own ease, and liberty, and quiet, if they can, to abide single as I do.

9. But if they cannot contain, let them marry: for it is better to marry than to burn.

9. But if they cannot, let them use marriage, as God's appointed remedy for such; which is better than sinful lust.

10. And unto the married I command, *yet* not I, but the Lord, Let not the wife depart from *her* husband:

10. But though it be no sin to marry, it is a sin to depart when married: Herein I lay God's command upon you, and offer it not to your choice, as a thing indifferent.

11. But and if she depart, let her remain unmarried, or be reconciled to *her* husband; and let not the husband put away *his* wife.

11. But to marry upon departure, is a double sin. If any intolerable abuse, or passion, provoke her to depart, let her remain unmarried, and be reconciled to her husband: And so let not the husband put away his wife.

12. But to the rest speak I, not the Lord, if any brother hath a wife that believeth not, and she be pleased to dwell with him, let him not put her away. 13. And the woman which hath an husband that believeth not, and if he be pleased to dwell with her, let her not leave him.

12, 13. But as to the case of separation from an

infidel (which some may think necessary by the Israelites case in Ezra, &c.) I bring you not this as a flat command of Christ, but as my best advice: though you may let an infidel go, and may live without him that will not stay with you, but is the deserter, in enmity to your religion; yet I think it best for you to do your best, first to make such willing to continue, and, though it be to your great trouble, to live with such; yet if they be willing to stay, be not you the deserters, no not for a time, nor omit due means to make them willing; though some such will by tyrannical and malicious adversaries.

14. For the unbelieving husband is sanctified by the wife, and the unbelieving wife is sanctified by the husband: else were your children unclean; but now are they holy.

14. For though the case in Ezra may make you doubt how it was with the Israelites; yet to Christians, under the law of grace, your abode with an infidel doth not make your conjugal state, or converse, or family, to be unholy. The state and interest of a believer maketh your relation and cohabitation holy, as separated to God for holy use, which the believer can improve, as all things else are sanctified to him, for the service of God. Else your children would be like those of the infidels, unclean, as not in the covenant and church of God: but now they are holy, and numbered with his peculiar people. For the Christian devoteth to God himself, and all that is in his power and disposal, which is accepted according to the capacity and use of that which is devoted; and this he doth by God's command, and therefore with his acceptance; as the seed of the faithful always were.

15. But if the unbelieving depart, let him depart. A brother or a sister is not under bondage in such *cases*: but God hath called us to peace.

15. But (to resolve your doubt) I say, If the unbeliever depart, and will not be persuaded to stay, you are not bound to follow them whither ever they go. Marriage was made for mutual help, and you are not bound in such cases to be enslaved by a sinner's implacability and desertion. But yet omit nothing that tendeth to a peaceable cohabitation: for God hath called us all to peace.

16. For what knowest thou, O wife, whether thou shalt save *thy* husband? or how knowest thou, O man, whether thou shalt save *thy* wife?

16. And as the relation and marriage-converse is sanctified to the believer, so you know not but by loving and peaceable behaviour the unbeliever may be converted and saved.

17. But as God hath distributed to every man, as the Lord hath called every one, so let him walk; and so ordain I in all churches.

17. But let none on pretence of Christianity desert the relation that God hath set him in, but do his duty in the place that God hath distributed and called him to: And this order I appoint to all the churches.

18. Is any man called being circumcised? let him not become uncircumcised: is any called in uncumcision? let him not become circumcised.

18. Think not that Christianity requireth any needless changes, to circumcision or uncircumcision, as to the external ceremony: It is a change from sin to God which it requireth.

19. Circumcision is nothing, and uncircumcision is nothing, but the keeping of the commandments of God.

19. To be one that was or that was not circumcised, is no part of the Christian religion; but to keep those commandments which God hath given us, either in the law of nature, or by Jesus Christ. Do God's work, and make it not more than it is.

20. Let every man abide in the same calling wherein he was called.

20. Pretend not religion for breaking away from the state of relation which the gospel found you in, without a just discharge, or cause of change.

21. Art thou called *being* a servant? care not for it; but if thou mayest be made free, use *it* rather.

21. If thou was a servant when thou wast converted, be contented with thy condition; for it is not contrary to thy deliverance by Christ. But if thou mayest be set free from a servile life, on lawful terms, it is rather to be chosen: (For it is not all change of relation, or outward state that I forbid.)

22. For he that is called in the Lord, *being* a servant, is the Lord's free man: likewise also he that is called, *being* free, is Christ's servant.

22. A Christian servant hath that sort of freedom which Christ hath purchased: He is freed from guilt, and the curse, and the slavery of sin and Satan: And the freest and greatest that is a Christian, is devoted absolutely to the service of Christ.

23. Ye are bought with a price, be not ye the servants of men.

23. And if you are free, make not yourselves needlessly the servants of men, especially of infidels; nor serve any man before Christ, or against him: For He hath brought you to be his servants.

380   I. CORINTHIANS.   CHAP. VII.

24. Brethren, let every man wherein he is called, therein abide with God.

24. To conclude, Serve God in the calling that grace found you in, till he remove you.

25. Now concerning virgins, I have no commandment of the Lord: yet I give my judgment as one that hath obtained mercy of the Lord to be faithful.

25. As to your question about virginity, God hath made no universal law for it, or against it; and I pretend not to give you any such. But it being a case to be variously resolved, according to persons' various conditions, I shall give you faithfully my judgment how to decide it severally for yourselves.

26. I suppose, therefore, that this is good for the present distress, I say, that it is good for a man so to be.

26. Christians being now under persecution and distress, no doubt but it is much more for their ease and quiet to be single, than to have a wife or husband, and children to care for, in poverty or in flight.

27. Art thou bound unto a wife? seek not to be loosed. Art thou loosed from a wife? seek not a wife.

27. If thou be bound, to seek to be loosed is a sin: But if thou art loosed, that thou seek not to be bound without necessity, is my advice.

28. But and if thou marry, thou hast not sinned; and if a virgin marry, she hath not sinned; nevertheless, such shall have trouble in the flesh; but I spare you.

28. But to marry, as such, is no sin: (Though it be a sin to do it when there is clear reason against it.) But such must reckon upon trouble in the flesh. But though I forewarn you to prevent your trouble, I would not by urgency, be your snare.

29. But this I say, brethren, the time is short. It remaineth, that both they that have wives, be as though they had none: 30. And they that weep, as though they wept not; and they that rejoice, as though they rejoiced not; and they that buy, as though they possessed not; 31. And they that use this world, as not abusing it: for the fashion of this world passeth away.

29, 30, 31. But this none should forget, that this life is so short, and the end of all so near and sure, that there is little difference between having a wife or no wife, weeping or not weeping, rejoicing or not rejoicing, possessing and not possessing: And therefore you should have wives, and weep, and rejoice, and possess, and use this world as if you did it not, with such an indifferency through the sense of greater things, as that you may not be overmuch affected with the getting, or enjoying, or loss, of any transitory thing: For all these things are in continual change, and the fashion of them passeth away.

32. But I would have you without carefulness. He that is unmarried, careth for the things that belong to the Lord, how he may please the Lord.

32. Carefulness about the world is so bad a thing, that I would have you escape it if you can. The unmarried hath less worldly care to divert him from caring how to please God, and to do good to others, and secure his soul.

33. But he that is married, careth for the things that are of the world, how he may please his wife.

33. But he that is married hath made himself so much more duty, temptation, and trouble, as must needs increase those cares which will much divert his thoughts and cares from the pleasing of God: Particularly, the care of pleasing his wife will take him up; because there is in all persons much unsuitableness, and difference in judgment, temper, and inclinations; and in the weaker sex usually much passion and impatience, and difficulty in bearing that which crosseth their will; so that the wisest man can hardly please some, with all his skill, and kindness, and diligence, without violating his duty to God.

34. There is difference also between a wife and a virgin: The unmarried woman careth for the things of the Lord, that she may be holy, both in body and in spirit: but she that is married, careth for the things of the world, how she may please her husband.

34. And the difference is great also on the woman's part, (whose weakness usually can less bear difficulties, troubles, and temptations.) The unmarried is free from abundance of troubles and temptations, which would turn away her care from the things of God, and so she is more free to keep close to God, and to keep both spiritual and corporal sanctity: But she that is married must needs care for worldly things, for children, and family, and specially to please her husband, (who possibly may be unsuitable, and tyrannical, and hardly pleased without displeasing God.) And to live in mutual displeasure, how sad and tempting a condition will that be? (Christ told Martha how bad a choice it was to be cumbered about many

things, though lawful, in comparison of choosing a free attendance on the better part.)

35. And this I speak for your own profit, not that I may cast a snare upon you, but for that which is comely, and that you may attend upon the Lord without distraction.

35. If any of you think that I wrong you, by debarring you from the comforts of marriage, let such know, that I speak but comparatively, and for your profit tell you, that many ignorantly rush upon it, without consideration, and so miscarry by unexpected troubles. I forbid not marriage nor make a law for you, to ensnare you; but I would have you prudently to prefer the condition which is best for yourselves, in which you may serve God without distracting cares.

36. But if any man think that he behaveth himself uncomely toward his virgin, if she pass the flower of *her* age, and need so require, let him do what he will, he sinneth not: let them marry.

36. But in these things about which there is no common law, men should themselves best judge what is suitable, convenient, and best for themselves. If, therefore, you find that your daughters have need, and that it will be inconvenient to them to pass the flower of their age, let them marry; it is no sin in itself, nor to such as so need it.

37. Nevertheless, he that standeth steadfast in his heart, having no necessity, but hath power over his own will, and hath so decreed in his heart, that he will keep his virgin, doeth well. 38. So then he that giveth *her* in marriage, doeth well: but he that giveth *her* not in marriage, doeth better.

37, 38. But yet he that being urged by no necessity of his own or of his daughter, hath fixed his resolution to preserve the freedom of a single life, (not by vows, which bind those whose condition God may alter, and so make laws and snares to themselves, but) by well-grounded reason submitting to God, that can change their state; this man taketh the way to his daughter's greatest peace and advantage. So then, he that giveth her in marriage, doth that which is in itself good, and no sin: But he that giveth her not in marriage, doth that which is better for her, if she have no necessity.

39. The wife is bound by the law as long as her husband liveth: but if her husband be dead, she is at liberty to be married to whom she will; only in the Lord.

39. God's law and man's bind the wife to her husband during his life: But if her husband be dead, she may marry another, if nothing in her condition forbid it; but it must be to a believer, that is fit for her.

40. But she is happier if she so abide, after my judgment: and I think also that I have the Spirit of God.

40. But as I am giving you no common law against marriage, or for it, but directing you how every one may discern what is best for themselves, my judgment is, That ordinarily, where there is no necessity, a single life is more for the person's peace and quietness, and freedom from hindrances in serving God, and therefore better for them.

ANNOTATIONS.

Divers errors have risen from the misunderstanding of some passages in this chapter.

I. Of them that make Paul to speak at uncertainty, without the Spirit of God, when they read, [by permission, and not by commandment,] and [I, and not the Lord]: When as he only disclaimeth the giving them a law instead of particular direction.

II. The error of them that hence gather, that God hath given us in scripture his counsels, which are no commands, and make not duty, nor is it sin to violate them, but a work of supererogation to do them. Whereas the apostle only distinguisheth of a proper universal law, and a consequential obligation from other general laws. A common law is rule of societies: If such a law had commanded or forbidden marriage, it would be a duty or sin to all: But yet God's law bindeth all to choose that which most tendeth to their own good, and the escape of evil; and to break this law is sin to him that doth it, though the same thing be lawful to another. e. g. To marry against parents' consent, to an unmeet person, without necessity, and oblige ones self to instruct and maintain a family, when one is unable for it, and many such cases, may make it a great sin to marry. A common law, and a personal obligation, resulting from another general law, much differ.

III. The error of them that say, By holiness of children, verse 14, is meant either legitimation only, or mere baptism, and not an interest according to their capacity, in the covenant of peculiarity, I have so far confuted, in my Treatise of Infant Baptism, that here I. pass it by.

IV. One excellent divine hath hence taken occasion to speak so much against changing any trade or calling, as affrighteth some from lawful changes, which do more good than hurt.

V. From verse 37, many unjustly commend absolute vows of celibate; which is to make a law to God, that he shall not bring them into necessity by any change, and to make snares and self-binding laws for themselves, as if they were their own rulers, when God hath made them work enough, and for ought they know, may bring them under a necessity to marry.

VI. On the other side, by a blind opposition to this extreme, thousands rashly run into marriage without considering the difficulties, cares, sufferings, troubles, and temptations, that attend it: And being surprised and unprepared, live accordingly in worldly cares, impatience, and discontent.

CHAP. VIII.

NOW as touching things offered unto idols, we know that we all have knowledge. Knowledge puffeth up, but charity edifieth.

1. As to your case about things offered to idols, they that, to defend their licentious practice herein, pretend to know more of their liberty than we do, must understand, that we have knowledge as well as they; and knowledge without charity is not an excellency to be boasted of; it doth but puff men up with pride and self-conceitedness: but charity is necessary to true edification.

2. And if any man think that he knoweth any thing, he knoweth nothing yet as he ought to know.

2. And this conceitedness of their great knowledge and wisdom, proveth that they knew nothing at all as they ought. If they knew themselves, or man, they would know the weakness of man's understanding, and how little they know. If they knew God, or any of his works, they would know their incomprehensibleness. Indeed though we know somewhat of God, and his works, and word, we have no adequate knowledge of any thing in the world; we know not the whole of any thing, but some part of it. And to be ignorant of our ignorance, is a double ignorance. It is this false conceit, That men know more than indeed they know, which is the grand cause of all the pernicious errors of the world; And confident error is far more dangerous and hurtful than mere nescience.

3. But if any man love God, the same is known of him.

3. But he that hath such knowledge as habituateth his soul to the true love of God and holiness, is one that God owneth and knoweth as his own, and attaineth the true end of knowledge: For our happiness is better secured by God's loving beneficent knowledge of us, and all our concerns, than by our own wisdom.

4. As concerning therefore the eating of those things that are offered in sacrifice unto idols, we know that an idol is nothing in the world, and that there is none other God but one.

4. And as to the case of eating things offered to idols, we know, as well as these pretenders to great wisdom, that idols are nothing but fictions of deceived men, and that there is no God but one.

5. For though there be that are called gods, whether in heaven or in earth, (as there be gods many, and lords many.) 6. But to us *there is but* one God, the Father, of whom *are* all things, and we in him, and one Lord Jesus Christ, by whom *are* all things, and we by him.

5, 6. For though the world hath feigned many deities, supreme and subordinate ones, as mediators; yet we know that there is but one God the Father, of whom all creatures have all their beings, and for and to whom we and all things are; and one Lord Jesus Christ, by whom all things were at first created, and ordered, and by whom we are redeemed, and who only is our mediator with this one God.

(Note, That this text, which the Arians greatly boast of, and mistake, as if it expressly confined the deity to the Father, as distinct from Christ, is variously expounded against them by two sorts of expositors. I. The ordinary exposition is, 1. That though there be but one God the Father, the same God is also the Son. 2. But (more probably) that in scripture God the Father, (as *Fundamentum Trinitatis*, as the schoolmen speak) is oft put for the deity, as such, comprehending the three persons. II. Theirs that hold three natures in Christ, viz. 1. The second person in the divine nature. 2. Unitively producing the first of creatures, a superangelical being, by whom he made all other creatures, and who appeared to the fathers of old. And 3. The human nature assumed into personal union by the superangelical and divine. These say, that Christ is called [One Lord, by whom are all things] as in his first created superangelical nature, distinct from one God the Father, but not divided from him. (But, besides Peter Story, and some such of late, few have entertained this.)

7. Howbeit *there is* not in every man that knowledge; for some with conscience of the idol unto this hour, eat it as a thing offered unto an idol; and their conscience being weak, is defiled.

7. But when every man knoweth not this, that an idol is nothing, but custom hath fixed in men the conceit of many subordinate demi-gods, to whom they think they owe some worship, some novices and corrupted professors of Christianity are not yet cured of these dangerous opinions, and really intend some honour to the idol; and their diseased souls will be more defiled, when they are herein encouraged by your example, and see you do the same outward act, though you do it not with the same opinion and intention.

(Note, Some expositors rather think that this is the sense; [Some know not that an idol is nothing, but think them real demons that are worshipped, and that eating things offered to them is real worship; and are tempted to it by fear to save themselves, and will be hardened and defiled by the encouragement of your example.] But this seemeth not so agreeable to the phrase.)

8. But meat commendeth us not to God: for neither if we eat are we the better; neither if we eat not, are we the worse.

8. It is not the mere eating or not eating the meat, that is any great matter, nor maketh one better and more acceptable to God, and another worse.

9. But take heed lest by any means this liberty of yours become a stumbling-block to them that are weak.

9. But take heed, though the eating of that meat, as such, be lawful, lest by outward symbolising with idolaters, you seem to worship the idol, and so tempt others both to the mutual error and corporal sin, (against charity and piety, viz. the second commandment:) For weak unsettled persons are too easily seduced.

10. For if any man see thee which hast knowledge, sit at meat in the idol's temple, shall not the conscience of him which is weak be emboldened to eat those things which are offered to idols:

10. For though thou say, that thou dost not offer it to an idol, but eat it in that temple, to avoid danger, as a common meal; yet thy action will persuade the weak, that that is lawful, which so knowing a man doth seem by his own practice to approve.

11. And through thy knowledge shall the weak brother perish, for whom Christ died?

11. And whereas Christ died, rose, and revived, that he might be Lord of the dead and living, and hath a right of propriety unto all, having purchased for them a conditional gift of salvation, thou wilt now rob Christ of his right, and them of their salvation, by the abuse of thy pretended knowledge.

12. But when ye sin so against the brethren, and wound their weak conscience, ye sin against Christ.

12. Know, therefore, that thus ensnaring the consciences of the weak by temptation, is not only uncharitable wrong to them, but sin and injury against the very blood and right of Christ.

13. Wherefore if meat make my brother to offend, I will eat no flesh while the world standeth, lest I make my brother to offend.

13. I conclude then, That I do not make so light of another's sin, nor set so light by the soul of a weak brother, or by the blood and right of Christ, as for flesh, or any unnecessary thing, to abuse my liberty, when it will prove to them a dangerous temptation to sin. Though it be their culpable weakness that maketh them in such danger, I will forbear flesh as long as I live, if that conduce to save them from sin, (unless God lay on me a necessity to do otherwise, and leave it no longer to my liberty as indifferent.) To prefer my liberty or commodity in the use of things otherwise lawful, before the saving of the soul, even of the erroneous, from sin, is to despise both Christ and souls.

Note, O then what have those Papal church-tyrants to answer for, that by their numerous, vain, yea, noxious canons, to shew their usurped dominion over souls, will rather tempt men, and excommunicate Christians, and burn them, and keep the Christian world in scandalous pernicious strife, than they will give men leave to deny obedience to their usurpation in such things? And how unlike Paul are they that say, They will not deny their own liberty or convenience in an unnecessary humour or pleasure, for any man, whose error or weakness is the cause of his offence or stumbling?

And many good Christians mistake this and such texts, thinking that by offending the weak, is meant displeasing them, and doing that which others take for sin: When as by offending, is meant laying a stumbling-block, or causeless occasioning or tempting men to sin and ruin.

CHAP. IX.

AM I not an apostle? am I not free? have I not seen Jesus Christ our Lord? are not you my work in the Lord?

1. It seems some among you object against me, 1. That I am no apostle. 2. That I get my living by tent-making. 3. That I am none of those that knew Christ. 4. That my knowledge is lower than theirs. To all which I say, 1. That Christ made me an apostle by his mission. 2. That I may use my own liberty, either to live on the church, or on my labour, as is most for the furtherance of the gospel. 3. That I have seen Christ from heaven, though not on earth. 4. That you are the fruit and seal of my ministry, which therefore is not to questioned by you.

2. If I be not an apostle unto others, yet doubtless I am to you: for the seal of my apostleship are ye in the Lord.

2. You of all men should not question my apostleship, who were converted by it.

3. Mine answer to them that do examine me, is this, 4. Have we not power to eat and to drink? 5. Have we not power to lead about a sister, a wife, as well as other apostles, and as the brethren of the

Lord, and Cephas? 6. Or I only and Barnabas, have not we power to forbear working?

3—6. And as to my labour, I answer, That I own my power to live on the church: And I that persuade you to forbear the use of your liberty when it would do hurt, do go before you by my own example. I have right to be maintained by my hearers, and to put the church to the charge of a wife and family with me, as other apostles do. I and Barnabas have power to forbear working for our living.

7. Who goeth a warfare any time at his own charges? who planteth a vineyard, and eateth not of the fruit thereof? or who feedeth a flock, and eateth not of the milk of the flock?

7. Soldiers are paid by those who use them; and the husbandman and shepherd live on the fruit of their labour: and so may I.

8. Say I these things as a man? or saith not the law the same also? 9. For it is written in the law of Moses, Thou shalt not muzzle the mouth of the ox that treadeth out the corn. Doth God take care for oxen? 10. Or saith he it altogether for our sakes? for our sakes, no doubt, *this is* written: that he that ploweth should plow in hope; and that he that thresheth in hope, should be partaker of his hope.

8, 9, 10. Do I speak this as a man pleading his own interest? Doth not God say it in his law, &c. And doth God make laws chiefly for the good of oxen, or for men? For men, no doubt, to encourage them by just expectations of the fruit of their own just labours.

11. If we have sown unto you spiritual things, *is it* a great thing if we shall reap your carnal things?

11. The spiritual things which we sowed with you, are far greater than the carnal things which we may reap: And if you maintain others, you owe more to us.

12. If others be partakers *of this* power over you, *are* not we rather? Nevertheless, we have not used this power; but suffer all things, lest we should hinder the gospel of Christ.

12. Yet have I not claimed or taken that which is my due, lest it should hinder the success of my ministry.

13. Do ye not know that they which minister about holy things live *of the things* of the temple? and they which wait at the altar, are partakers with the altar?

13. You know that the Levites and priests live on the things that are offered in the temple, and at the altar.

14. Even so hath the Lord ordained, that they which preach the gospel, should live of the gospel.

14. So is it the Lord's own appointment (who said, The labourer is worthy of his hire,) that they who are called to preach the gospel as a stated office; (and not only occasionally) should be maintained in and for that labour, and not be taken off by cares and worldly labour.

15. But I have used none of these things. Neither have I written these things, that it should be so done unto me: for *it were* better for me to die, than that any man should make my glorying void.

15. But as I have not made use of this my due, so I write not as expecting it: For I value my advantages for the gospel as my glory, above my right, and above my life.

16. For though I preach the gospel, I have nothing to glory of: for necessity is laid upon me; yea, woe is unto me, if I preach not the gospel.

16. For my bare preaching would have nothing singular, to vindicate me from calumny, or extraordinarily further the success of my labours: Even bad men preach, and I am under a command or law of Christ, which will punish me if I do not.

17. For if I do this thing willingly, I have a reward: but if against my will, a dispensation *of the gospel* is committed unto me.

17. For if my preaching, and that without maintenance from you, be done willingly, God will reward me (who accepteth no unwilling service:) But if I preach but for fear of punishment, and take not maintenance because men will not give it, I do but a task imposed on me, and forfeit my reward so far as I am unwilling.

18. What is my reward then? verily, that when I preach the gospel, I may make the gospel of Christ without charge, that I abuse not my power in the gospel.

18. What then is that qualification of my service which God will specially reward? Not the mere task of preaching; but that I so do it, as to devote all my own rights and interest to the great ends of the gospel; and whatever I lose or suffer

19. For though I be free from all men, yet have I made myself servant unto all, that I might gain the more.

19. I am no man's slave or bondman, to serve him against my will; but I am a voluntary servant to all men, in charity to save them, and in obedience to Christ.

20. And unto the Jews, I became as a Jew, that I might gain the Jews; to them that are under the law, as under the law; that I might gain them that are under the law; 21. To them that are without law, as without law, (being not without law to God, but under the law to Christ) that I might gain them that are without law. 22. To the weak became I as weak, that I might gain the weak: I am made all things to all men, that I might by all means save some.

20, 21, 22. To the Jews, and those whose education and consciences keep them under Moses's law, I behaved myself by all lawful compliance and conformity to that law, that I might win them, (preserving the truth of the gospel, and my own and the Gentiles' liberty.) When I converse with the Gentiles that are not under the law of Moses, and have no written law of God, as the Jews have, but only the law of nature, and men's laws, I fit myself and doctrine to their state and capacity, to win them, not pleading the written law with them, as I do with the Jews; (though I am far from thinking or living as lawless; for I am under Christ's own government and law.) To the scrupulous ignorant sort of Christians, and those that are yet unsettled, and liable to temptation, I behaved myself with all winning compliance and pleasingness; knowing that stiff singularity, and affected or unnecessary crossness to others, is not the way to gain, but to alienate them. And though I know that all will not be won by such compliance, yet I am made all things lawful towards all men, that by this my duty I may save some.

23. And this I do for the gospel's sake, that I might be partakers thereof with *you*.

23. All this I do, not as a man-pleasing flatterer, for lucre or repute; but to promote the ends of the gospel with you, that you and I may rejoice therein together.

24. Know ye not that they which run in a race, run all, but one receiveth the prize? So run that ye may obtain.

24. As it is not every one that runneth that wins the prize; so it is not every one that preacheth, or professeth Christianity, that is accepted to salvation. Therefore so preach, and so live, as answereth your covenant and profession, and as God hath promised to accept and reward.

25. And every man that striveth for the mastery, is temperate in all things: Now, they *do it* to obtain a corruptible crown, but we an incorruptible.

25. Even in ludicrous plays, races, combats, &c. Men prepare their bodies by abstinence and strict diet, and this but for a withering garland, applause, or prize: And shall not we do much more for the heavenly glory?

26. I therefore so run, not as uncertainly; so fight I, not as one that beateth the air:

26. I, therefore, do not run in vain, as not knowing for what, or as by sloth to lose the prize; nor fight I as fencers, for mere show and ostentation.

27. But I keep under my body, and bring it into subjection: lest that by any means when I have preached to others, I myself should be a cast away.

27. But my first work is about myself, to mortify and subdue all my fleshly desires, which stand against my duty, and to keep my body in constant subjection, lest when by preaching I have won others, I should as a carnal man be lost and cast away myself.

(And if you are true to the gospel, and to your own souls, and would not prove self-deceiving hypocrites, take you the same course, and devote all your interests to the ends of your profession, and the saving of your souls, instead of pleading for and abusing your real or pretended liberties to the tempting of others, and hindering their salvation, and boasting of this pernicious folly, as the knowledge wherein you excel others.)

ANNOTATIONS.

1. The darkness of this chapter comes from the uncertainty in matter of fact, what was the accusation that was made by the envious proud teachers against Paul: 1. Whether it were that he laboured like a secular man, and lived not on the church. 2. Or, that he was a poor mechanic fellow, that at last must be cast on their charge or charity. 3. Or, that he solicited them for contributions to the poor at Jerusalem, or for others; and they suggested, that he partly meant himself. It were easier to expound many verses, did we certainly know the case objected.

II. They that from verse 16, 17, 18, gather a sort of counsels which make no duty or sin, and a state of perfection which is no duty, utterly abuse the text, which intimateth no such thing; and are sufficiently before confuted, on chap. vii. about the case of marriage.

III. Though Paul's becoming all things to all men, condemn their humour that in converse, congregations, opinions, practices, do proudly affect unnecessary oddness, that they may seem wiser and better than the rest, and justify Austin's resolution, to do as the church doth wherever he cometh, in all lawful things, to win men by approach, and not to alienate them by crossness; yet it no way countenanceth them, who were temporizers, man-pleasers, or for worldly ends, or an indifferency in religion, for want of judgment, or tender consciences and true obedience to God, will conform themselves to any sin which men's laws or customs shall make needful to their carnal interest. And yet in things antecedently indifferent, law and custom may weigh down lighter motives that are on the other side, but not weightier motives. True prudence here must hold the scales, and determine what is duty, and what is sin.

CHAP. X.

MOREOVER, brethren, I would not that ye should be ignorant, how that all our fathers were under the cloud, and all passed through the sea; 2. And were all baptized unto Moses in the cloud, and in the sea: 3. And did all eat the same spiritual meat; 4. And did all drink the same spiritual drink: (For they drank of that spiritual rock that followed them: and that rock was Christ.)

1, 2, &c. And because your boast of knowledge, and your scandalous uncharitable abuse of your liberty, and insulting therein, give me cause to be jealous of many among you, let me further remember you, That it is not your being baptized, and being partakers of outward privileges, and being eminent in the church, that will save you, if you live in sin: For all the Israelites passed through the sea, and were under the cloud, and so were typically baptized by covenant to Moses's law; and they did all eat the passover, which was sacramentally spiritual meat, and typically as our eucharist; and they all drank of miraculous rock-water oft in the wilderness, which rock and water were typically or spiritually Christ and his sacramental blood.

5. But with many of them God was not well pleased; for they were overthrown in the wilderness.

5. And yet with many, yea, most of them, God was so offended by their sin, that he overthrew them in the wilderness.

6. Now these things were our examples, to the intent that we should not lust after evil things, as they also lusted.

6. Now these were admonishing types to us, and written to warn us, that we lust not after forbidden gratifying of the flesh, as they did: (If they are accused as lusting in the wilderness for flesh, when they had only manna for forty years, what excess of lust is it in them that take it for their liberty and wisdom to serve their flesh and appetite, to the scandal of others by their ill example.

7. Neither be ye idolaters, as *were* some of them; as it is written, The people sat down to eat and drink, and rose up to play.

7. And take warning by them, and do not partake of idol's feasts, and make a sport of that which God is jealous in.

8. Neither let us commit fornication, as some of them committed, and fell in one day three and twenty thousand.

8. And take warning by their destruction, Numb. xxv. 1, 2, 3, to avoid fornication, which some of you make light of.

9. Neither let us tempt Christ, as some of them also tempted, and were destroyed of serpents.

9. And be warned by their plagues, that you make not your fleshly lusts, and your impatience of sufferings, to be the law and measure of your expectations from God, as if he must needs do what your flesh would have him, and allow you to do what you desire.

10. Neither murmur ye, as some of them also murmured, and were destroyed of the destroyer.

10. And let not the life of self-denial, and sufferings in the flesh which Christ calls you to, provoke you to murmur and be impatient under the cross, or weary of Christianity, lest you be destroyed by the executioners of God's justice, as they were by the plague.

11. Now all these things happened unto them for ensamples; and they are written for our admonition, upon whom the ends of the world are come.

11. The history of them, and their sins and punishments, are written for the use of all following generations, even for us that live in the last age of the world, to warn us to avoid the like.

12. Wherefore let him that thinketh he standeth, take heed lest he fall.

12. Therefore instead of self-conceitedness and self-confidence, let even those that think best of themselves for wisdom and stability, take heed lest they fall to sin and misery.

13. There hath no temptation

taken you, but such as is common to man: but God *is* faithful, who will not suffer you to be tempted above that ye are able: but will with the temptation also make a way to escape, that ye may be able to bear *it*.

13. There hath yet no tempting trial befallen you but such as men in your state of humanity ordinarily undergo; so that your sufferings have been no justification of any self-saving compliance with idolaters: And you have no cause to distrust God for the time to come; for he is faithful, and will not let your trials be intolerable, but with the trial will shew you a safe passage out of it at last, that by the foresight of that, and the brevity, you may be safe to undergo it.

14. Wherefore, my dearly beloved, flee from idolatry. 15. I speak as to wise men: judge ye what I say.

14, 15. As you plead for wisdom, I will suppose I speak to men of wisdom, who can judge of reason; and I offer the reason of my exhortation to your wisest judgment.

16. The cup of blessing which we bless, is it not the communion of the blood of Christ? The bread which we break, is it not the communion of the body of Christ?

16. Is not our communion in the Lord's supper, in wine and bread blessed, a common reception sacramentally of the blood and the body of Christ? Do we not join in a professed reception of these, communicated to us by Christ?

17. For we being many are one bread, and one body: for we are all partakers of that one bread.

17. For we that are many persons, are one church or body of Christ, by covenant union with him the Bread of Life, of whom we all sacramentally and professedly partake; as many grains of corn make one loaf, and many members one body.

18. Behold Israel after the flesh: are not they which eat of the sacrifices partakers of the altar?

18. Do not they that eat of the sacrifices of the Jews, thereby profess worship to the God they sacrifice to?

19. What say I then? that the idol is any thing, or that which is offered in sacrifice to idols is any thing? 20. But *I say*, that the things which the Gentiles sacrifice, they sacrifice to devils, and not to God: and I would not that ye should have fellowship with devils.

19, 20. And now do not we know as well as others, that an idol or image is nothing, (but wood, stone, gold, &c.) and that the meat that is offered them is not in itself at all changed from what it was? But I say, that it is devils that seduce the heathens to this idolatry, and devils whom they thereby obey, and devils whom they worship, as supposed demi-gods, there represented; and consequentially, devils with whom they have this federal communion. And I would not have you Christians to be subjects and communicants with devils.

21. Ye cannot drink the cup of the Lord, and the cup of devils: ye cannot be partakers of the Lord's table, and of the table of devils.

21. Think not that you may do both: You cannot lawfully, acceptably, or effectually, sacramentally, and federally, communicate in the blood and body of Christ, or receive that sacred cup and bread, and be made members of him and his church, and also communicate in the federal sacrifices to devils; no, not with your bodies, though you never so much despise them in your hearts.

22. Do we provoke the Lord to jealousy? are we stronger than he?

22. Shall we provoke God by that which in the second commandment, and often, he hath told us, he will be a jealous avenger of? Are we strong enough to overcome him, or to bear the wrath of the Almighty?

23. All things are lawful for me, but all things are not expedient: all things are lawful for me, but all things edify not.

23. As I am from under Moses's law, and not bound by it, as such; so also I know that all meats are in themselves now clean, and lawful to me: But lawful things may be used contrary to the will of God, the ends of Christianity, and the edification of others; and the law of Christ forbiddeth us so to use them.

24. Let no man seek his own: but every man another's wealth.

24. We are bound by Christ to love others as ourselves, and therefore not to prefer our own small and bodily interest or safety, before the spiritual, greater good of others; nor to do only what we think best for ourselves, but also what is best for others, (especially for the church of Christ.)

25. Whatsoever is sold in the shambles, that eat, asking no question for conscience sake. 26. For the earth *is* the Lord's and the fulness thereof.

25. If it be sold in the shambles, it is common food to you; your consciences need not ask whether it be unclean, or whether it was ever offered to any idol. 26. God that is the Lord of all the earth, hath allowed us all that is fit for food.

27. If any of them that believe not, bid you *to a feast*, and ye be disposed to go; whatsoever is set before you, eat, asking no question for conscience sake.

27. As it is not unlawful when invited, to go to a feast to unbelievers; so, when you see cause to go, eat what is set before you, and question not the lawfulness of it yourselves.

28. But if any man say unto you, This is offered in sacrifice unto idols, eat not, for his sake that shewed it, and for conscience sake. For the earth *is* the Lord's, and the fulness thereof.

28. But if any man say, This is part of the meat that was an idol sacrifice, eat not of it, for his sake that told thee so, lest thou tempt him to venture on idol-sacrifices; and for conscience sake, that thou uncharitably seduce not his conscience. God hath allowed thee lawful meats enough; thou needest not eat to others hurt.

29. Conscience, I say, not thine own, but of the others: for why is my liberty judged of another man's conscience?

29. When I say conscience, I mean, that you wrong not another's conscience. I mean not that this meat is unlawful to you, had you not been told it was offered to idols, or had eaten it privately, where no one was hurt by it: For another man's conscience is not my guide, nor makes lawful food unlawful to me. But uncharitableness, and hurtfulness to others, (as well as corporal idolatry) I must make conscience to avoid myself, as against the great commands of Christ.

30. For, if I by grace be a partaker, why am I evil spoken of for that for which I give thanks?

30. For if I neither seem to worship the idol myself, nor hurt another, but with thanksgiving eat what is set before me at a common feast, though another expect that I should inquire whether it was not an idol's sacrifice, I sin not, nor ought he to speak evil of me as a sinner.

31. Whether, therefore, ye eat or drink, or whatsoever ye do, do all to the glory of God.

31. Therefore, as in all that you do, so in these things, where God hath made no particular, common, determining law, the interest of our great end, the glory of God, must be our common and most obliging law; neither eat, nor drink, nor do any thing against the glory of God, and your religion, and the good of others, in which God is glorified. Yea, do nothing but what, as some means, hath its tendency to his glory; nothing that is either hurtful or vain.

32. Give none offence, neither to the Jews, nor to the Gentiles, nor to the church of God:

32. Avoid all unnecessary things, which will be a stumbling or hurtful temptation, to Jews or heathens, or the church of God, or any members of it.

(So dangerously are abundance of religious persons mistaken, that scruple not offending or hardening the ungodly by sour contempt, and causeless singularity, and that take displeasing mistaken censorious Christians to be the offence here meant, when pleasing them by seeming to own their mistakes (as Peter did, Gal. ii. by his separation) is a usual hurtful way of scandalising them.)

33. Even as I please all men in all things, not seeking mine own profit, but the *profit* of many, that they may be saved.

33. Imitate me in this, who in things which God hath left undetermined to my power, do choose that part which pleaseth other men, so far as is for their profit, and do not humour or please my own self-will for any carnal interest of my own, but do that which tendeth to the good of most, even their salvation.

Note, O happy had it been with the Christian world, if the bishops had been of Paul's mind, and had not chosen to silence, banish, burn, and murder thousands of God's faithful servants, for not humouring their wills, and obeying unnecessary canons, imposed by Papal usurpation.

CHAP. XI.

BE ye followers of me, even as I also *am* of Christ.

1. In all this self-denial which I tell you I have used, I follow Christ, who denied his very life for us. Therefore, follow me, as I follow Christ.

2. Now I praise you, brethren, that you remember me in all things, and keep the ordinances, as I delivered *them* to you.

2. It is your praise (as well as your duty and safety) that you remember what doctrine and orders we apostles of Christ at first delivered to you, and keep that which then we taught you.

3. But I would have you know, that the head of every man is Christ; and the head of the woman, *is* the man; and the head of Christ, *is* God.

3. And now to your case about church-order, I first remember you, that the due subordination

of persons must be kept: Christ is the head of all men, high and low; and the man is the head of the woman, who therefore must shew subjection; and God is the head of Christ, as man and mediator.

4. Every man praying or prophesying, having *his* head covered, dishonoureth his head.

4. It being the custom then to cover the faces of those that were put to any great shame, a man that shall vail his head and face, doth thereby take reproach unto himself.

5. But every woman that prayeth, or prophesieth with *her* head uncovered, dishonoureth her head: for that is even all one as if she were shaven.

5. But for a woman to be uncovered in the assembly at public worship, prayer, or prophesying, is a dishonour to her, as contrary to the sign of subjection which is her duty.

Note, That the woman is said to pray or prophesy, that joineth with the church therein.

As custom maketh it a shame to her to be shaven, so also to be unvailed.

Note, That this was a changeable custom, and is contrary now with us.

6. For if the woman be not covered, let her also be shorn: but if it be a shame for a woman to be shorn or shaven, let her be covered.

6. The custom of long hair as a kind of covering, pleads also for the custom of vailing.

7. For a man indeed ought not to cover *his* head, for as much as he is the image and glory of God: but the woman is the glory of the man.

7. The man's face is used well to be uncovered, as being made first in the image of God, and so a beam of his splendour: But the woman made out of man, is subject to him and his splendour.

8. For the man is not of the woman: but the woman of the man.

8. For at the creation, the man was first made, and the woman was made out of the man.

9. Neither was the man created for the woman: but the woman for the man.

9. And so God made the woman after, to be a meet help for the man; and not the woman first, and then the man, as a helper to her: (Though they must now be mutual helpers.)

10. For this cause ought the woman to have power on *her* head, because of the angels.

10. Therefore the woman ought to be vailed, to signify her subjection to the power of man, yea, and especially her reverence to the ministers of God, (and perhaps of the angels that are spectators of the church assemblies: Doctrinally both are true; though which is here meant, cannot be proved.)

11. Nevertheless, neither *is* the man without the woman, neither the woman without the man in the Lord.

11. Yet men have no being but by women, nor without men do women exist or propagate; and this is by the ordination of the Lord.

12. For as the woman *is* of the man, even so *is* the man also by the woman: but all things of God.

12. For as at the first creation, the woman was taken out of the man, so in generation the man is the woman, and all things are of God.

13. Judge in yourselves: is it comely that a woman pray unto God uncovered?

13. The signification of being uncovered, being by custom a note of superiority, judge in yourselves whether such be decent for a woman at the church's prayers.

14. Doth not even nature itself teach you, that if a man have long hair, it is a shame unto him?

14. And when common custom hath made the wearing of hair at length the note of the female sex, doth not nature itself tell you, that it is a shame for man to be so like a woman? (when God forbiddeth us so much as to be clothed as women, to confound the sexes, which must needs be visibly distinguished.)

15. But if a woman have long hair, it is a glory to her: for her hair is given her for a covering.

15. But use tells us, that for women to let their hair grow out at length, is a signification of modesty, as a kind of covering, and so is decent to them.

16. But if any man seem to be contentious, we have no such custom, neither the churches of God.

16. But if any will contentiously dispute against what I say, though I would make no greater a matter of such things, than the nature of them requireth, let this answer suffice to resolve sober minds: The custom of all the churches is against women's being uncovered, as an unseemly thing; and you should not easily be different from all the churches, in a matter which depends on the signification of an action, which use and common opinion must interpret. We, that must be as concordant as we can, must not affect dissimilitude.

17. Now in this that I declare *unto you*, I praise *you* not, that you come together, not for the better, but for the worse.

17. But about your church assemblies, I have a greater matter, of which I must blame you; that you come together for holy communion, not as you ought, but in sinful sort.

18. For first of all, when ye come together in the church, I hear that there be divisions among you; and I partly believe it.

*18. For first, when you come together in one church, to profess union and communion, as members of one body in holy love, I hear credibly, that you even there shew your divisions, and are of dissenting minds, and parties, and practices.

19. For there must be also heresies among you, that they which are approved, may be made manifest among you.

19. For God will permit heresies, or sects and divisions, to rise among you, to try you, that it may be seen who are sound, well-settled, approved Christians, (when the chaff flieth away.)

20. When ye come together, therefore, into one place, *this* is not to eat the Lord's supper. 21. For in eating, every one taketh before *other*, his own supper: and one is hungry, and another is drunken.

20, 21. When you meet in one place, as a church, to profess unity in Christ, it is not like the supper of the Lord, which is a holy feast of sacramental unity, where all had the same food, and the same sacramental body and blood of Christ: For you first bring to the church every one his own supper for himself, instead of a common feast of love, and the rich eat and drink to the full, and the poor are hungry.

22. What, have ye not houses to eat and to drink in? or despise ye the church of God, and shame them that have not? What shall I say to you? shall I praise you in this? I praise *you* not.

22. If you must differ according to your riches, do it in your own houses, and pretend not a holy love-feast in such disparities; and abuse not church assemblies and feasts, by your fulness, and uncharitable propriety; and shame not the poor that should be feasted with you. This is a practice worthy to be blamed in you.

23. For I have received of the Lord, that which I also delivered unto you, That the Lord Jesus, the *same* night in which he was betrayed, took bread: 24. And when he had given thanks, he brake *it*, and said, Take, eat; this is my body, which is broken for you; this do in remembrance of me.

23, 24. For I have not taught you of my own invention the doctrine of the sacrament, but I received it from Christ (partly by them that were present, and partly by his inspiration,) to wit, that the same night in which he was, &c.

Note, 1ˢᵗ It was bread that he took, it was bread which he brake, after thanksgiving or benediction, it was bread which he gave them.

2. Yet it was his body which he gave them, sacramentally and relatively: As the same thing which is materially gold and silver, may formally be the king's coin, and current money, or a badge of honour, or the king's image, &c.

3. That Christ gave it them together plurally, and bid them take it as personal appliers, each to himself.

4. That it is his will and institution that this use should be continued to the church, in commemoration of his sacrificed body and blood.

25. After the same manner also *he took* the cup, when he supped, saying, This cup is the new testament in my blood: this do ye, as oft as ye drink *it*, in remembrance of me.

25. So also he took the cup after supper, saying, The wine in this cup is by sacramental signification, my blood, as it purchaseth (as a sacrifice) and sealeth the new covenant or statute: Use it thus frequently in your holy communion, in remembrance of my bloodshed.

26. For as often as ye eat this bread, and drink this cup, ye do shew the Lord's death till he come.

26. For by the frequent use of this bread and cup, ye are to represent and declare the sacrificing of Christ for our sins, till he come in glory.

27. Wherefore, whosoever shall eat this bread, and drink *this* cup of the Lord unworthily, shall be guilty of the body and blood of the Lord.

27. And it being so sacred an institution, for so high a use, whoever shall profane it, and use it but as common food, or contrary to the holy ends of it, which is the signification of God's love to us by the sacrifice of Christ for our sins, and our signification and covenant of love and union with him and one another, he partaketh in guilt with them that despise and crucify him.

28. But let a man examine himself, and so let him eat of *that* bread, and drink of *that* cup.

28. But let men try and examine themselves, whether their hearts and practice do answer the necessary ends of this holy institution, [coming to it as reverent partakers of the sacramental or representative sacrificed body and blood of Christ in the penitent and believing sense of their sin

and need of a Saviour, and of his pardoning and healing grace: trusting the hopes of their salvation on him, and sincerely renewing their self-dedication to him, and covenant of new obedience to him, in love and unity with his church, even all sincere believers] and so let them comfortably herein communicate.

29. For he that eateth and drinketh unworthily, eateth and drinketh damnation to himself, not discerning the Lord's body.

29. For he that eateth and drinketh otherwise than thus, that is profanely, and not to the ends of the institution, doth but draw judgment on himself, instead of grace.

30. For this cause many *are* weak and sickly among you, and many sleep.

30. For this very sin of profaning the holy ordinance, God hath inflicted on many of you weakness and sickness, and death on some. (For God useth paternal castigation, justice, and punishments, even on his family.)

31. For if we would judge ourselves, we should not be judged.

31. And if we would examine and judge ourselves and so come to this feast as true penitent believers, with a right intent, and holy reverence, we should escape such castigatory penalties, and the judgment of God.

32. But when we are judged, we are chastened of the Lord, that we should not be condemned with the world.

32. But these judgments of God on his family are not by destructive revenge, but fatherly chastisements, to bring us to repentance, that we may not be condemned with the unholy world.

33. Wherefore, my brethren, when ye come together to eat, tarry one for another.

33. Wherefore, as brethren, do all in that impartial unity and love, as answereth your profession and Christ's institution, and not in selfishness, division, or profaneness.

34. And if any man hunger, let him eat at home; that ye come not together unto condemnation. And the rest will I set in order when I come.

34. Let the hungry eat at home, and not disorder the sacred communion, and use it carnally, or as a common feast, and that with uncharitable inequality; lest your profanation of so holy a thing bring down God's judgments on you. As for other points of church order, I will determine them when I come.

ANNOTATIONS.

I. As to the custom of men and women's covering and hair, mentioned ver. 13, 14, &c.

1. It is certain, that the significancy is the thing that must decide the case; and that as words, so this action is an arbitrary sign, and depends upon the custom and opinion of the country as the expositor: and that with us, where men's being uncovered signifieth reverence and submission to a superior, the case quite differeth from that of the Corinthians.

2. And yet the custom is so common in most nations for women to wear their hair at full length, and men to cut it, that it seems there is somewhat in nature that tendeth to this difference, (as there is in kneeling and prostration, to shew humiliation and submission:) and to confound the difference of sexes in habits, is a great sin, tending to debauchery, and to hide unclean and beastly conversation. And therefore though a man may in such things, of themselves indifferent, do as the worst do in an undecent fashion, to avoid some great evil, (as among thieves or persecutors to escape unknown; as one may wear woman's clothes to escape from unjust imprisonment, or death:) yet sober godly persons should not without such necessity imitate the fashions, which are the ensigns of pride, debauchery, or any sinful self-distinguishing sort of men or women. Apply this to our case of men's wearing great perriwigs, and that of women's hair, who sell it for that use; and to the fashion of women's naked breasts, and gowns with long superfluous trains, while the poor want necessary clothing, &c. What would Paul have said, if any of these had been then the case?

II. It is a most doleful case, that Satan hath prevailed to turn this sacred institution of Christ's supper into the matter of bloody contention with some, and of uncomfortable distracting scruples and fears with others; when as Christ ordained it to be the firm bond of constant love and unity, and the great comfort of the souls of penitent believers.

1. On one side, by over-doing in the dogmatical and ceremonious part, it is turned into the monsters of transubstantiation, the priests communing alone while the people look on, a half sacrament without the cup, a Latin mass not understood, a real sacrifice offered for the dead, instead of a representative commemorative sacrifice; the adoration of bread as God, supposed to be no bread, but the body of God indeed, &c. And it is made an engine to rack men's consciences, and tear the church, by excommunicating all that dare not conform to all the dresses which usurping domination hath painted this sacrament withal: And the blood of Christ's faithful servants is shed, for not following all these opinions and antic ceremonies that the sacrifice of Christ's body and blood is abused by: So that, alas! how many churches are torn, and persecute one another, for not using this sacrament of love and communion according to those devices of men, which Peter or Paul never used or approved?

2. On the other side, many godly persons, quite misunderstanding the words of Paul, about [un-

worthy receiving,) come with such an excess of reverence and fear, lest they eat and drink their own damnation, that either they seldom venture to communicate, (which the old Christians did oftener than every Lord's day) or else they are more terrified far, than comforted: And looking that God should suddenly comfort them in the very act of receiving, while they fight against their own comforts by mistakes and unbelieving fears, when they feel not their expectation answered, they are ready to despair, as having received unworthily. And should they do so by prayer and hearing, what a torment and slavery would they make of religion, by their error!

3. And yet the ignorant and ungodly, who truly receive unworthily, can from the bare doing of the outward act, steal to themselves that deceitful comfort by which they are emboldened to go on in sin, supposing that now God pardoneth all. Thus Satan hath turned Christ's sacred ordinance against himself, and the peace of the church, and the comfort of some, and the reformation of others; and carrieth on these most horrid depravations with such odious success, that without wonders of gracious providence, there appeareth no probability of deliverance from these heavy effects of sacrament distraction.

CHAP. XII.

NOW concerning spiritual *gifts*, brethren, I would not have you ignorant. 2. Ye know that ye were Gentiles, carried away unto these dumb idols, even as ye were led.

1, 2. As to your case of discerning spirit and spiritual gifts, it is of great importance that you should not be ignorant, lest you should take evil spirits for the Spirit of God, or not distinguish the various gifts of God's own Spirit in believers: In your heathen state you were carried away with idol oracles and worship.

3. Wherefore, I give you to understand, that no man speaking by the Spirit of God, calleth Jesus accursed: and *that* no man can say, that Jesus is the Lord, but by the Holy Ghost.

3. First, in general you may be sure, that none of those, idol oracles or blasphemers that speak against Christ, and anathematise him, as infidels do, speak by the Spirit of God. (For God's Spirit bore uncontroulable witness to Christ, by prophecies, resurrection, miracles, and holiness.) And on the contrary side, he that believeth and confesseth that Jesus is the Lord, the true Son of God, and our mediator, hath surely learnt this of the Holy Ghost, his outward testimony in the foresaid evidence, and his inward teaching. (For do but truly believe the truth of Christ himself, and the truth of all his doctrine will undeniably follow.)

4. Now there are diversities of gifts, but the same Spirit. 5. And there are differences of administrations, but the same Lord. 6. And there are diversities of operations, but it is the same God, which worketh all in all.

4, 5, 6. And as gifts are ascribed to the Holy Ghost, and administration to the Son, and operations to the Father Almighty; so in all these there is great diversities, both of kinds and of degrees.

7. But the manifestation of the Spirit is given to every man to profit withal.

7. But all the gifts of the Spirit are given for the churches' edification, or to do good with. (Though some of them are found in unholy men, who perish in their sin.)

8. For to one is given by the Spirit, the word of wisdom; to another the word of knowledge by the same Spirit;

8. The same Spirit maketh one eminently wise and prudent in applying sacred truth to the case of the hearers: and it giveth another an eminent knowledge of sacred mysteries.

9. To another faith by the same Spirit; to another the gifts of healing by the same Spirit;

9. Another he maketh eminently strong in faith, for extraordinary effects; and another hath the gift of miraculous healing of the sick, (when the Spirit will have it done.)

10. To another the working of miracles; to another prophecy; to another discerning of spirits; to another *divers* kinds of tongues: to another the interpretation of tongues.

10. To another, other sorts of powerful miracles: to another, to speak by immediate inspiration, either predictions, or powerful explications and applications of God's word; to another, a quick and sure discerning whether men pretending to the Spirit, speak from God, or not: to another, the speaking of divers languages; to another, the interpretation of those languages to them that understand them not.

11. But all these worketh that one and the-self-same Spirit, dividing to every man severally as he will.

11. And though these are very various, and greatly difference man from man, yet it is the same Spirit that worketh them all, diversifying as he freely and wisely pleaseth.

12. For as the body is one, and hath many members, and all the

members of that one body, being many, are one body: so also *is* Christ.

12. For here one and many well consist: as the natural body is but one body, but made of many members, differing in number, excellency, and office; so is Christ and his church.

13. For by one Spirit are we all baptized into one body, whether *we be* Jews or Gentiles, whether *we be* bond or free; and have been all made to drink into one Spirit.

13. For as sacramentally all visible members are baptized into one universal church of professed Christians, and drink the cup of holy union and communion in the Lord's supper; so all true, living, saved members are baptized by one Spirit into one universal church of true spiritual Christians, and drink the true uniting spirit of communion.

14. For the body is not one member, but many. 15. If the foot shall say, Because I am not the hand, I am not of the body; is it therefore not of the body? 16. And if the ear shall say, Because I am not the eye, I am not of the body; is it therefore not of the body? 17. If the whole body *were* an eye, where *were* the hearing? if the whole *were* hearing, where *were* the smelling?

14—17. The body is not one member as to number, kind, or office; but many united: and so in Christ's body the church: if a mistaken Christian himself should say, Because I am low in place, grace or gifts, I am none of the church; this will not prove or make him none; much less, if others, by false censure or church-tyranny, say he is none, or excommunicate him for dissenting from their vain appendages or opinions. If all were of one office, stature, complexion, or degree of grace or knowledge, who would be rulers, and who subjects? who teachers, and who learners? How many offices of piety and charity would be unperformed? God hath not a church on earth where all members are so wise, as besides the essentials of Christianity, to know all the integrals; much less, to know the numerous little accidents of forms and ceremonies, and all that is really or pretendedly indifferent and lawful (which domineerers can invent) to be so indeed, and so to be all united in such things indifferent.

18. But now hath God set the members, every one of them in the body, as it hath pleased him. 19. And if they were all one member, where *were* the body? 20. But now *are they* many members, yet but one body.

18, 19, 20. But as the wise Creator in nature, so as our redeemer, governor, and regenerator by grace, God hath chosen great diversity of members, as to office and gifts: and he himself, as it pleased him, hath set them in his church. (And who are they that presume against him, to censure or cast out the meanest of such?) Were they all numerically, or in office, or degree of knowledge and grace, but one, or equal, the church would not be such a thing as God hath made it. But now God, that freely delighteth in the variety of his works, hath made it one body of Christ, composed of variety of members.

21. And the eye cannot say unto the hand, I have no need of thee: nor again, the head to the feet, I have no need of you.

21. As the principal members of the body need the less principal; so the rulers, pastors, and wisest members of the church, need even those weak and inferior Christians, whom surly censurers, and proud or contentious usurpers, will cast out.

22. Nay, much more those members of the body which seem to be more feeble, are necessary.

22. Yea, the parts which are least honoured, and feeble, have a peculiar necessary office, which none of the rest is able to perform or supply.

23. And those *members* of the body, which we think to be less honourable, upon these we bestow more abundant honour, and our uncomely *parts* have more abundant comeliness.

23. And those parts which we account shameful, we most carefully clothe and cover, to hide either deformity or shame, (and do not reproach, neglect, or cast away.)

24. For our comely *parts* have no need: but God hath tempered the body together, having given more abundant honour to that *part* which lacked: 25. That there should be no schism in the body; but *that* the members should have the same care one for another.

24, 25. Our comely parts need not our care to adorn and cover them from shame? But God hath so contempered the parts, that we should more care to secure from dishonour the parts that need our care; that unity and love of the whole should cause such love and care for every part, that the parts should not envy, or strive against, or cut off, or divide, from one another.

Note, 1. O how clean contrary to this are the tearing canons and cruelties that cut off all members that think any of their needless impositions unlawful?

c. And here Paul tells us the true cause of schism: not weakness of Christians, but the butchery of that clergy that cut off the weak, when they should carefully hide their dishonour in love; and that revile them whom they should love as themselves.

26. And whether one member suffer, all the members suffer with it: or one member be honoured, all the members rejoice with it.

26. As all the body condoleth or rejoiceth with the pain or welfare of every member, even the weakest; so is it with the living members of Christ.

Note, Therefore they are but hypocrites, like wooden legs, that have no such sense, and traiterous enemies of Christ, that hate, and reproach, and destroy his true members.

27. Now ye are the body of Christ, and members in particular.

27. Thus must it be with you, that are the several members of Christ's church.

28. And God hath set some in the church, first apostles, secondarily prophets, thirdly teachers, after that miracles, then gifts of healing, helps, governments, diversities of tongues.

28. And God hath set in his church diversity and disparity, both in qualifying gifts and offices: as, in the first place, are apostles, sent immediately by Christ, to be the chief witnesses and recorders of his works and words. Next them, prophets, immediately inspired to reveal his will: and next them, settled teachers of his recorded word: and then, workers of miracles, for convincing infidels, and confirming believers: then, extraordinary gifts of healing; and eminent helpers of the churches by charity and special care, especially for ministers and the poor; and governments to arbitrate differences, and keep order; and languages, to spread and confirm the word.

29. *Are* all apostles? *are* all prophets? *are* all teachers? *are* all workers of miracles? 30. Have all the gifts of healing? do all speak with tongues? do all interpret? 31. But covet earnestly the best gifts:

29, 30, 31. None of all these gifts or offices are common to all. But desire most that which is best and most edifying.

Note, That even apostles are but chief members, and Peter himself not the head, but one of them.

31. And yet shew I unto you a more excellent way.

31. Yet true Christian love excelleth all these gifts and offices.

CHAP. XIII.

THOUGH I speak with the tongues of men and of angels, and have not charity, I am become *as* sounding brass, or a tinkling cymbal.

1. Lest you should too much trust to any of these forementioned gifts, which Christ giveth to some that perish, you must know, that the true divine nature, proper to saints, consisteth in charity, (which is the predominant love of God, and of saints as a ints, and men as men, as God is in them, and served by them.) And if I be without this, could I preach, discourse, and pray in better language and oratory than any mortal man, even as well as angels, what were this voice to God, that is a spirit, and looketh to the heart, but even as the tinkling of a musical instrument?

2. And though I have *the gift of* prophecy, and understand all mysteries, and all knowledge; and though I have all faith, so that I could remove mountains, and have not charity, I am nothing.

c. And though I could speak by inspiration (as Balaam did) of things present or things to come, and could understand all the deep and difficult points in God's word and works, and were the most excellent philosopher, and could truly open all the principles and compositions in nature; and though I could believe even to the production of the most miraculous effects, and yet have not this predominant love of God, and of saints, and of men, as to God's acceptance, and my own salvation, I am as a mere nothing: none of these shadows will do my work.

3. And though I bestow all my goods to feed the poor, and though I give my body to be burned and have not charity, it profiteth me nothing.

3. And though I give all that I have to the poor, either to be well spoken of, or through fear of hell, or a conceit of obliging God by merit, or out of mere natural pity, or any other cause, which includeth not love, it will not profit me to salvation. Yea, if for these lower ends I should forsake life itself, without the predominant love of God and man, it would be as nothing to me.

4. Charity suffereth long, *and* is kind; charity envieth not; charity vaunteth not itself, is not puffed up.

4. Love is kind, inclining to do good, and is patient, and can bear much wrong from others, (as self-love maketh us bear much more from ourselves.) Love envieth not the reputation, applause, precedency, or profit of others. Love doth not vaunt and lift up a man's self in his own esteem, or desire to be lifted up by others, above

CHAP. XIII.   1. CORINTHIANS.   395

our worth and place, but in honour preferreth others.

5. Doth not behave itself unseemly, seeketh not her own, is not easily provoked, thinketh no evil,

5. Love doth not break out into injurious reflections, or passions, or uncomely deportment towards others; it is not selfish, and seeketh not our own inordinately, to the injury, neglect or greater hurt of others: is not provoked to any uncharitable thought, word, or deed, by small injuries or occasions, but beareth, forbeareth, and forgiveth; and doth not think evil of any groundlessly, or till constrained, nor design evil or hurt against any unnecessarily or unjustly.

6. Rejoiceth not in iniquity, but rejoiceth in the truth:

6. It doth not rejoice in the sins that others commit, nor in the wrongs they undergo, nor themselves to do unjustly against any, or to be prosperous therein against them.

7. Beareth all things, believeth all things, hopeth all things, endureth all things.

7. It doth by others as we feel we do by ourselves; that is, it beareth with the faults of men so far as is not against their own or others good: it is inclined to believe the best of all men till evidence constrain us to know the worst, (not neglecting such cautelous suspicion, as may save us from rash and foolish trust.) It still hopeth well of others, as far as there is any ground of hope: it endureth hurt and wrong from others, when it is for their own or others greater good.

8. Charity never faileth: but whether *there be* prophecies, they shall fail; whether *there be* tongues, they shall cease; whether *there be* knowledge, it shall vanish away.

8. Holy love is an everlasting quality and employment, and shall not cease, but be perfected at death, and in heaven: but prophesying, languages, sciences, and all the artificial and imperfect sort of knowledge which now we have, shall cease, as useless there.

9. For we know in part, and we prophesy in part. 10. But when that which is perfect is come, then that which is in part shall be done away.

9, 10. For here the manner of our knowing in the body is imperfect, and the measure is all inadequate: we know nothing wholly, but some part of things: and so we speak, even in prophesying and preaching; but perfection will end all this imperfection.

11. When I was a child, I spake as a child, I understood as a child, I thought as a child: but when I became a man, I put away childish things.

11. As manhood, and increase of wit and experience, change the childish speech, understanding, and thoughts, into that which is true and more perfect; so much more will the life to come do.

12. For now we see through a glass darkly; but then face to face: now I know in part; but then shall I know even as also I am known.

12. For our knowledge now in this body and world, is by imperfect *media* as we see things in a glass; and know by riddles, parables, or similitudes, a superficial glimpse: but then we shall know as men that see each others faces, by intuition. Now we know but little parts, and outsides, and accidents of things, and nothing adequately: but then we shall know in the world of spirits, as those spirits now know us; which is better than we know of ourselves.

13. And now abideth faith, hope, charity, these three; but the greatest of these *is* charity.

13. I conclude therefore, That though now our state of grace consist of faith, hope, and love, the greatest of these is love: (for it is the divine nature, the everlasting work, the soul's felicity, even its complacency in God, and in all his saints, and in all his works: and it is the end to which faith and hope are but the means.

ANNOTATIONS.

1. Yet faith and hope have their peculiar offices, which love alone cannot perform; As the heart cannot do the work of the hand or eye.

2. By faith is meant, believing and trusting in God through Christ for grace and glory. And by hope is meant, a desirous comforting expectation of the good promised and believed.

3. It followeth, that he hath the most excellent knowledge, who hath most holy love; and all the learning that kindleth not this love, is but dreaming, doating, diverting, and deceiving vanity.

4. The English abuse of the word [charity] deceiveth many, as if it were nothing but giving to the poor! But it is the love of God and holiness, and of holy persons, and of our neighbours as ourselves; and specially of the holy celestial society, Christ, angels, and saints.

5. By this we see, that those church rulers, preachers, writers, disputers, and all other malignants, who zealously labour to destroy love, and to persuade Christians to hate, and persecute, and destroy one another, for their selfish interests, opinions, or factions, whatever they think of themselves, are diabolists and Cainites, the devil's slaves, and in his image do his work.

6. It is made a doubt by some, Whether faith and hope continue not in heaven; because, say they, How shall we know things past, (as the creation, flood, &c.) but by believing? And shall we not believe and hope for the perpetuity of glory?

But, 1. We know not now in what manner God will make known things to us there: whether in seeing him, we shall see all things? Or how? 2. However, it will not be the same things that are called faith and hope, which are exercised on promises, and are but means to that perfection which is their end; so that if you call them by the same names, they will be but equivocal.

7. Thus much tells us what measure of faith and hope are necessary to salvation, viz. so much as shall cause in us sincere love to God and holiness, and heaven, and to one another.

8. This tells us what those texts do mean, which promise the spirit of sanctification to penitent believers, viz. The Holy Ghost doth but prepare us, and open the door by faith and hope, that by them, as means, he may excite holy love, and as a spirit of love dwell in us, and possess us.

9. This teacheth ministers how to preach, and people what and how to hear, read, meditate, and confer and live; and what true religion is, viz. To all as may most kindle holy love, as we use the bellows to kindle the fire. [Pure religion, and undefiled, is to visit the fatherless and widows in adversity, and keep ourselves unspotted of the world.]

10. This teacheth us what fear of God to use: none that breedeth hard thoughts of God, or quencheth holy love; but a reverence of him, and a fear lest by sin we make ourselves unlovely to him, and fall under that justice which is holy and good, even when it destroys the wicked. Other fear of God is sinful superstition.

CHAP. XIV.

FOLLOW after charity, and desire spiritual *gifts*, but rather that ye may prophesy.

1. The sum of my advice is, That above all you value and pursue charity, (or holy love:) but desire also spiritual gifts, in subordination to it, and for the profitable exercise of it; and therefore prefer prophesy, (which is speaking by immediate inspiration, to the instruction and edification of others) as most profitable.

2. For he that speaketh in an *unknown* tongue, speaketh not unto men, but unto God: for no man understandeth *him;* howbeit in the spirit he speaketh mysteries.

2. For he that speaketh in an unknown language, speaketh not to the understanding of man, though God understand him: for though he speak never so high and excellent mysteries, no man that knoweth not that language understandeth him.

3. But he that prophesieth, speaketh unto men to edification, and exhortation, and comfort.

3. But he that intelligibly applieth God's word to the hearers, speaketh so as conduceth to their edification, and exhortation, and comfort, which are the ends of your assemblies.

4. He that speaketh in an *unknown* tongue, edifieth himself; but he that prophesieth, edifieth the church.

4. It is supposed, that he that speaketh in a language unknown to the people, understandeth it himself, and so may be edified himself: (for the Spirit of God did not move men to speak like parrots, they knew not what.) But he that by God's Spirit, instructeth and exhorteth others, edifieth the church; for which end you meet.

5. I would that ye all spake with tongues, but rather that ye prophesied: for greater *is* he that prophesieth, than he that speaketh with tongues, except he interpret, that the church may receive edifying.

5. I would you had all such knowledge of languages, as is useful to propagate the gospel: but I more wish, as Moses, that all the Lord's people were prophets, that is, inspired to speak wisely and zealously the will of God to men. For he is the greatest in the church, who is most edifying; and that is he that prophesieth, more than he that speaketh strange language, unless he interpret it to the church's edification.

6. Now brethren, if I come unto you speaking with tongues, what shall I profit you, except I shall speak to you either by revelation, or by knowledge, or by prophesying, or by doctrine?

6. What the better will you be for speaking languages to you, except I either reveal to you something immediately from God, or open to you some truths which you knew not before, or from God urge you to some needful duty, or doctrinally expound to you the matters of faith and obedience recorded in the gospel.

7. And even things without life giving sound, whether pipe or harp, except they give a distinction in the sounds, how shall it be known what is piped or harped?

7. Even the sounds of lifeless things, as musical instruments, being used for some signification, are useless, if by distinction their signification be not perceptible.

8. For if the trumpet give an uncertain sound, who shall prepare himself to the battle?

8. You may learn this of soldiers, how vain the unintelligible sound of the trumpet is.

9. So likewise you, except ye utter by the tongue words easy to be understood, how shall it be

known what is spoken? for ye shall speak into the air.

9. So if you speak not intelligibly to the hearers, what the better are they? You do but speak into the air.

10. There are, it may be, so many kinds of voices in the world, and none of them *is* without signification.

10. Even the voices of birds and beasts have their usual significancy to man, and to one another: much more of men.

11. Therefore if I know not the meaning of the voice, I shall be unto him that speaketh, a barbarian; and he that speaketh *shall be a barbarian* unto me.

11. Therefore what I understand not, is of no more use to me, than to a barbarian of another language.

12. Even so ye, for as much as ye are zealous of spiritual *gifts*, seek that ye may excel to the edification of the church.

12. Therefore as you much desire spiritual gifts, prefer those that most edify, and seek them not for vain glory.

13. Wherefore let him that speaketh in an *unknown* tongue, pray that he may interpret.

13. Let him that hath the gifts of languages, pray for the gift of edifying interpretation.

14. For if I pray in an *unknown* tongue, my spirit prayeth, but my understanding is unfruitful.

14. If I pray in an unknown tongue, my spirit prayeth, but others understand me not, and can not profitably join with me.

15. What is it then? I will pray with the spirit, and I will pray with the understanding also: I will sing with the spirit, and I will sing with the understanding also.

15. Therefore when I pray or sing by the gift of unknown tongues, I will also pray and sing intelligibly, for edification.

16. Else when thou shalt bless with the spirit, how shall he that occupieth the room of the unlearned, say Amen, at thy giving of thanks, seeing he understandeth not what thou sayest?

16. If others join not with thee, it is but a private exercise, and not a church exercise: and how shall the vulgar join by consent, and say, Amen, to what they do not understand?

17. For thou verily givest thanks well, but the other is not edified.

17. Thy thanksgiving is a good work; but what is another, or the church the wiser for it?

18. I thank my God, I speak with tongues more than you all:

18. I thank God he hath given the gift of more languages to me, than to any of you.

19. Yet in the church I had rather speak five words with my understanding, that *by my voice* I might teach others also, than ten thousand words in an *unknown* tongue.

19 Yet in the worshipping assembly, (which is the church) I prefer a few intelligible words, which may teach others, before all that can be said for ostentation, and are unintelligible.

20. Brethren, be not children in understanding: howbeit, in malice be ye children, but in understanding be men.

20. Be not like children, that love unedifying gingles; but imitate them in harmlessness: but as men, value and use that which increaseth wisdom and understanding.

21. In the law it is written, With *men of* other tongues and other lips, will I speak unto this people: and yet for all that will they not hear me, saith the Lord.

21. It is spoken, in Isa. xiv. 11. by God, That with men of, &c. to shew their hard-heartedness, that would neither hear their own prophets, nor strangers sent to them by the providence of God.

22. Wherefore tongues are for a sign, not to them that believe, but to them that believe not, but prophesying *serveth* not for them that believe not, but for them which believe.

22. So that the miraculous gift of languages is to convince unbelievers, of that which the church believeth already: but prophetical opening the doctrine of Christ, for farther edification, is appointed for them that are already believers.

23. If therefore the whole church be come together into one place, and all speak with tongues, and there come in those that are unlearned, or unbelievers, will they not say that ye are mad?

23. Surely you should not meet or worship God scandalously, like mad men: but if the whole church do meet in one place, (as churches then did) and all speak in unknown tongues, the unlearned and unbelievers will take you all for mad fanatics.

24. But if all prophesy, and there come in one that believeth not, or *one* unlearned, he is convinced of all, he is judged of all:

24. But if all that speak, do by God's Spirit use convincing evidence in explication and application, they all convince him and shew him his condition.

25. And thus are the secrets of his heart made manifest; and so falling down on *his* face, he will worship God, and report that God is in you of a truth.

25. And this searching convincing light will make them join with you in the reverent worship of God, and make them report that God is in your church, as a holy assembly.

26. How is it then, brethren? when ye come together, every one of you hath a psalm, hath a doctrine, hath a tongue, hath a revelation, hath an interpretation. Let all things be done to edifying.

26. Therefore let all your gifts, whether of psalmody, or doctrine, or languages, or revelation, or interpretation, be used to edification, which is the true end of church assemblies. And the end is your directory, in the use of all undetermined accidents of the means.

27. If any man speak in an *unknown* tongue, *let it be* by two, or at the most *by* three, and that by course: and let one interpret.

27. If you will use your gift of languages, let it be done by no more than two or three, one after another; and let some interpret it to the unlearned in the church.

28. But if there be no interpreter, let him keep silence in the church; and let him speak to himself, and to God.

28. That which only God and yourselves understand, let none but God and yourselves hear; and speak not that in the church which they cannot understand.

29. Let the prophets speak two or three, and let the other judge.

29. And the prophets also must do all to edification, and therefore must speak no more than may edify the church, which is but two or three at an assembly, the rest judging.

30. If *any thing* be revealed to another that sitteth by, let the first hold his peace.

30. If God immediately inspire another then to speak, let the first give way to him by silence.

31. For ye may all prophesy one by one, that all may learn, and all may be comforted.

31. For all that are prophets, or are then prophetically inspired, may prophesy in order, that all in the church may learn, and be exhorted, and comforted.

32. And the spirits of the prophets are subject to the prophets.

32. And whereas men may pretend to be inspired of God, and that to speak just at that time, when it is not so (as their own understanding must judge of the edifying season and order, so) the prophets that are hearers, having the Spirit of God, are fit judges whether it be that Spirit, or a delusion and passion of their own, that order may be kept in the assemblies, at least as to the time.

33. For God is not *the author* of confusion, but of peace, as in all churches of the saints.

33. For pretended inspirations and mandates are not to be believed against God's common law to all the churches, which have a surer notification than a single man can give us: but God's common law is against confusion, and for peace and order; and therefore it is certain, that confusion is not of divine inspiration.

34. Let your women keep silence in the churches: for it is not permitted unto them to speak; but *they are commanded* to be under obedience, as also saith the law.

34. And it is one of the rules of order, That women be no public teachers or speakers in the church: God permitteth it not, who hath commanded them subjection by the law.

35. And if they will learn any thing, let them ask their husbands at home: for it is a shame for women to speak in the church.

35. Not but that they should learn; but it must be with modesty, asking their husbands, if they have such as are able to teach them, (as they ought; else they have other private helps.) It is a shame to the church and her, for a woman there to speak except in common singing psalms, or other common acts.

36. What? came the word of God out from you? or came it unto you only?

36. I ask them that contradict this: Did God's word come out from you, or from intrusted apos-

ties? Or did it come to you only, that you contradict the churches?

37. If any man think himself to be a prophet, or spiritual, let him acknowledge that the things that I write unto you, are the commandments of the Lord. 38. But if any man be ignorant, let him be ignorant.

37, 38. If any be indeed a prophet, or inspired, and not pretendedly only, he will confess, that these canons or decisions are God's own commandments, and not my device. But if men will be obstinate in their ignorance, let them look to it.

39. Wherefore, brethren, covet to prophesy, and forbid not to speak with tongues.

40. Let all things be done decently, and in order.

39. Prophesy for the church's edifying is to be coveted, and languages there not forbidden.

40. That sacred things be all done decently, and not with uncomely negligence; and orderly, and not in confusion, or as every man's fancy leads him; this is a general law of God, according to which, undetermined modes and circumstances must be regulated and done.

ANNOTATIONS.

I. It is a doubt oft put, How it could be that God's Spirit should inspire men with tongues or prophesy, and yet not tell them when and how to use them? But it is not to be thought, that he that was before without the habit, had the actual use of them, then suddenly inspired; but that, as the learned, so the inspired had the habitual knowledge of tongues before they assembled, and so for the actual use and time, were to exercise their own discretion.

II. The description of the church here, oft named as meeting in one place with their officers and guides, tells us, that then a church of this rank was not a diocese of many hundred assemblies, which had all but one bishop, their constitutive head; but that it was a company associated for personal communion, that usually met in one place; though necessity might make them meet in many, and though some general guides might take care of many such churches.

III. The greater number of prophets, and teachers, &c. that were here in one assembly, whose exercises the apostle was put to restrain, doth fully confute Dr. Hammond's oft-repeated opinion, That in scripture-times there is no proof that there were any more presbyters to one church, than one, who was a bishop, and had deacons under him; and that for want of capable persons. But his opinion inferreth, That then a church was no greater than could meet in one place: for one bishop could not be at once in many. And if no subject-presbyters were made in scripture-times,

it must be proved by what just power they were after made, even a sort of pastors never made by the apostles.

IV. The arguments of the apostle against the uninterrupted use of tongues not understood in the church, are so many cogent, plain, and vehement, that I will not lose time to answer the Papists' cavils against them, when they defend their Latin masses and prayers; but only note, That nothing can be so plainly spoken by God's own Spirit, which carnal prejudiced men cannot pervert: and that it is no wonder if they will not be judged and ruled by God's word, unless they themselves may be judges of the sense of it; and how little God's word signifieth to the people, where it must have such expositors and judges. One that knew no more against the Papal kingdom, called the church of Rome, than 1. Their Latin service, and cherishing of ignorance: 2. And that as leeches they live on blood, and keep up their religion by violent cruelty; if he have but read this 1 Cor. xiv. and Christ's commands for loving each other; yea, if he have not lost much of humanity itself, I think, can hardly be a Papist.

V. The pretence that some fetch hence, for any man that will to speak in the church, if he think he is inspired, is utterly vain: for that leave is here restrained to inspired prophets, and those to be regulated by the laws of order, decency and edification. And God hath made it the office of the pastors, to be rulers in the assemblies.

VI. The abuse of the general rules by Papists usurping church-lords and canonists, is notorious; who, because God's own ordinances must, as to modes and circumstances, be managed decently, orderly, and to edification, thence plead for a dominion to add many symbolical rites and ordinances of their own, which Peter and Paul never knew, to make God's ordinances seem decent, orderly, and to edification, even things that in *specie et genere* are needless at the best; and then they silence, excommunicate, and ruin all that refute such corrupting inventions: Like Zedekiah Ahab's prophet, who (with his brethren) spake by a lying spirit; and then made it decent, orderly, and edifying, by wearing a pair of horns, to tell Ahab how he would push down his enemies, and then smote Michaiah, for pretending to have more of the Spirit and truth than he had: that Micaiah might be fed in prison with the bread and water of affliction, till experience shewed who had the truth? how these men would have used the apostles of Christ if they now lived, and worshipped God but as then they did, their canons teach us to conjecture.

CHAP. XV.

MOREOVER, brethren, I declare unto you the gospel which I preached unto you, which also you have received, and wherein ye stand; 2. By which also ye are saved, if ye keep in memory what I preached unto you, unless ye have believed in vain.

1, 2. And because some endeavour to subvert your faith, I will recite the sum of that gospel which I preached to you, and in which you have since continued, and which is the sure and sufficient doctrine of salvation, (though the articles be few) without all the corrupt additions invented by proud erroneous men, unless your belief of them have been unsound and superficial, and so in vain. See that your unsound belief deceive you not, and this gospel will not deceive you.

3. For I delivered unto you first of all, that which I also received, how that Christ died for our sins according to the scriptures:

3. For I told you, that Christ died as a voluntary sacrifice for our sins, therein fulfilling what was promised of him. This I received from God by inspiration, and from the certain witnesses by just report and evidence.

4. And that he was buried, and that he rose again the third day according to the scriptures: 5. And that he was seen of Cephas, then of the twelve. 6. After that, he was seen of above five hundred brethren at once: of whom the greater part remain unto this present, but some are fallen asleep.

4, 5, 6. And as the scripture foretold, he was buried, and rose again the third day, and appeared to Peter, and after to the special disciples, who were twelve before Judas defection, and after. And after that [it is like, in Galilee] he was seen of five hundred, &c.

7. After that he was seen of James; then of all the apostles.

7. Note, That it is not to be wondered at, that this appearance to James, and to the five hundred, are not before distinctly mentioned in the gospel, when St. John tells us how small a part of what Christ did, is written. And as one evangelist hath some things which the other omit, so if Paul, have some which all four omitted, the same spirit recordeth them all.

8. And last of all he was seen of me also, as of one born out of due time.

8. And after all these he appeared to me from heaven, as to one that was too late converted.

9. For I am the least of the apostles, that am not meet to be called an apostle, because I persecuted the church of God.

9. For my persecuting God's church maketh me so unworthy to be numbered with the apostles, that though God called us to be one, I must esteem myself as the last, so the least of them, or below the twelve.

10. But by the grace of God I am what I am: and his grace which *was bestowed* upon me, was not in vain; but I laboured more abundantly than they all: yet not I, but the grace of God which was with me.

10. But God's free grace hath called me to this honour and work: and his grace given hath not been in vain; for (though I came late in, and was a persecutor) I have since been more laborious than any of them all: which I ascribe not to myself, but to God's free grace, which chose, called, instructed, excited, and strengthened me.

11. Therefore, whether *it were* I or they, so we preach, and so ye believed.

11. But whether the conversion of so many of several nations was by me or by them, is not material to the thing in question. These same articles of faith were they that we all unanimously preached, and into the belief of which, as the Christian verity, you were baptized.

12. Now if Christ be preached that he rose from the dead, how say some among you, that there is no resurrection of the dead?

12. And how then can the same that say they believe the resurrection of Christ, deny the resurrection of the dead, and the life hereafter:

13. But if there be no resurrection of the dead, then is Christ not risen. 14. And if Christ be not risen, then *is* our preaching vain, and your faith *is* also vain.

13, 14. If none rise, Christ is not risen: and if Christ be not risen, then is it falsehood and deceit which we preach, and which you have believed, and not the glad tidings of salvation.

15. Yea, and we are found false witnesses of God; because we have testified of God that he raised up Christ: whom he raised not up, if so be that the dead rise not.

15. And then it will follow, not only that we deceive the world, but that we belie God himself, when we witness that he hath raised Christ; which would be a most heinous crime.

16. For if the dead rise not, then is not Christ raised: 17. And if Christ be not raised, your faith *is* vain; ye are yet in your sins.

16, 17. If the dead rise not, and Christ rose not,

what hope have you of salvation from sin and death?

18. Then they also which are fallen asleep in Christ are perished.

18. Then dead Christians are perished: that is, If their souls live not when the body is dissolved, their souls perish; and if the body rise not, that perisheth for ever; and the martyrs would be great losers, and martyrdom folly.

19. If in this life only we have hope in Christ, we are of all men most miserable.

19. And if there be no resurrection or life after this, but our hope of benefit by Christ were only in the things and time of this present life, none were so miserable as Christians, who must forsake all, even life itself for Christ.

Note, That the thing denied by the heretics, was not only the resurrection of the body, but also all life after this for soul or body: and so the apostle joineth the confutation of both under the name of resurrection.

20. But now is Christ risen from the dead, and become the first-fruits of them that slept.

20. But we have full proof even from sense, that Christ is risen; and therefore as the first-fruits consecrate the whole, so Christ's resurrection being to purchase ours, doth prove to our comfort, that the dead shall rise.

21. For since by man came death, by man came also the resurrection of the dead. 22. For as in Adam all die, even so in Christ shall all be made alive.

21, 22. For as by man came death corporal, as well as spiritual and eternal, by man also came our deliverance by a resurrection. For as by Adam's sin the sentence of death came on all his posterity, as such; so all that are in Christ shall by him be delivered to an everlasting happy life.

Note, That the resurrection of all men, good and bad, is an effect of Christ's death and resurrection, antecedently to differencing grace, as appeareth, John v. 24, 25, &c. But that it proveth a resurrection to condemnation, is consequently caused by men's sin: and the apostle here speaketh of the elect's resurrection to felicity.

23. But every man in his own order: Christ the first fruits, afterward they that are Christ's, at his coming.

23. But Christ the cause of our resurrection must rise before us, and all Christians at his coming.

24. Then cometh the end, when he shall have delivered up the kingdom to God, even the Father; when he shall have put down all rule, and all authority, and power.

2.

24. Then cometh the end of his acquired mediatorial kingdom, when he shall have reduced us perfectly to God his Father, and we shall need his reducing, healing government no more, and so God shall govern us in the state of perfect innocency, and Christ shall have put down all rebelling powers, authority, and rule.

Note, This is a sad intimation that so much of rule, authority, and power as is here called [All] will be against Christ.

25. For he must reign till he hath put all enemies under his feet.

25. For these powers now mentioned being enemies to Christ, he must reign till they are all subdued.

26. The last enemy that shall be destroyed, is death.

26. By enemies, I mean all that resist his saving works: And of these death is the last.

27. For he hath put all things under his feet. But when he saith all things are put under him, it is manifest that he is excepted which did put all things under him.

27. Only God is evidently excepted, who is he that thus puts all things under him.

28. And when all things shall be subdued unto him, then shall the Son also himself be subject unto him that put all things under him, that God may be all in all.

28. When Christ hath subdued all that opposed his saving mediatorial work, Christ, as a creature shall be for ever himself subject to the deity, and shall give up his recovering work (though still it will be our glory to see his glory:) so that the pure blessed deity will be the felicity of saints, and be all in all.

29. Else what shall they do which are baptized for the dead, if the dead rise not at all? why are they then baptized for the dead?

29. And if the dead rise not, to what purpose do we in baptism profess our belief of the resurrection, and resign our bodies a living sacrifice to die when Christ requireth it, and this in hope of a resurrection signified by our rising from under the water.

30. And why stand we in jeopardy every hour? 31. I protest by your rejoicing which I have in Christ Jesus our Lord, I die daily.

30, 31. What folly were it in us Christians to choose a religion and course of life, for which we are in continual danger from the malignant world! I protest by the joy which I have in your Christianity, that I live continually a dying life, that is, in daily sufferings, and danger of death, and preparation for it.

D d

32. If after the manner of men I have fought with beasts at Ephesus, what advantageth it me, if the dead rise not? let us eat and drink, for to-morrow we die.

32. If as men combat one with another, I was put at Ephesus to strive with beasts (or beasts in the shape of men) what get I by such hazards and sufferings, if there be no life to come? Then will it follow, that those sensual fools are the wise men, who say, Let us eat and drink, and take pleasure to the flesh while we may, for we shall shortly die.

33. Be not deceived: evil communications corrupt good manners.

33. Let no such evil principles, and proverbs, and talk, deceive you. Ill words deceive many, and draw to ill deeds and conversations.

34. Awake to righteousness, and sin not; for some have not the knowledge of God: I speak this to your shame.

34. Such lewd opinions shew that men's reasons and consciences are in a sleep and stupidity; awake them, and they will lead you from sin to righteousness. By this it appeareth that some among you that call themselves Christians, have not yet the true knowledge of God and his will; which I say, to humble you by shame.

35. But some man will say, How are the dead raised up? and with what body do they come?

35. But some of you may the hardlier believe the resurrection, because they cannot tell how the dead are raised, and with what body they shall rise.

36. Thou fool, that which thou sowest is not quickened except it die.

36. This is the objection of a fool: for in sowing (though a seed truly dead be unfruitful, yet) the seed is buried, and by a sort of rotting or corruption seemeth as dead, before it spring up unto fruit.

37. And that which thou sowest, thou sowest not that body that shall be, but bare grain, it may chance of wheat, or of some other *grain*.

37. The corn which thou sowest hath not the blade or stalk, and ear, and flower, and chaff. It is not formally, but virtually or seminally the same, whether it be wheat, or other grain.

38. But God giveth it a body as it hath pleased him, and to every seed his own body.

38. But out of this seed, and by its seminal virtue, God, by the addition of attracted nutriment, giveth it a body, with straw, flowers, chaff, and seed, as pleaseth him; it being his power and will, to which nothing is impossible, which must satisfy our inquisitive minds; resurrection, as generation, being unsearchable to us.

39. All flesh is not the same flesh: but *there is* one *kind of* flesh of men, another flesh of beasts, another of fishes, *and* another of birds.

39. But you must allow a difference of bodies: for even here there is much difference.

40. *There are* also celestial bodies, and bodies terrestrial: but the glory of the celestial *is* one, and the *glory* of the terrestrial *is* another. 41. There is one glory of the sun, and another glory of the moon, and another glory of the stars; for *one* star differeth from *another* star in glory. 42. So also *is* the resurrection of the dead. It is sown in corruption, it is raised in incorruption.

40, 41, 42. The celestial bodies greatly differ from the earthly bodies; and so do even the celestial among themselves; as the sun from the moon, and one star from another, &c. And so shall our bodies at the resurrection greatly differ from these that we have now; particularly, by being incorruptible.

43. It is sown in dishonour, it is raised in glory: it is sown in weakness, it is raised in power: 44. It is sown a natural body, it is raised a spiritual body. There is a natural body, and there is a spiritual body.

43, 44. It is now so vile a body, that it must rot and corrupt in darkness in the earth; but it shall rise in glory. It is buried in utter impotency, like the common earth; but God's power shall raise it a powerful body. It is buried like the body of a beast, that was passive, and only acted by the living soul; but it shall rise a spiritual body, more suited to the nature of the soul, and having also an active nature (like as fire hath,) in itself. There are natural bodies of passive matter, in daily flux, repaired by food, and acted only by other natures, or souls: and there are spiritual bodies, (either such as the sun and light hath, or higher) which are incorruptible, and of themselves not inclined to death, dissolution, or change, and besides the soul, are so like it, that they are themselves active natures.

45. And so it is written, The first man Adam was made a living soul, the last Adam *was made* a quickening spirit.

45. That is, The first Adam was made by God

a living soul, put into a corruptible body, not having an unchangeable state in himself, nor power to make his posterity such: but the second Adam had in himself unchangeable life, suited to a spiritual, glorious state, and was the root of such to his believing posterity; enabled as the Lord of life, to raise himself, ascend to heaven, and to raise them to life, and take them to himself, and to make them a spiritual, holy people, capable thereof.

46. Howbeit, that *was* not first which is spiritual, but that which is natural; and afterward that which is spiritual.

46. But the animal person from whom, by generation we have but mere nature, was to us in causality, before him that conveyeth to us spiritual and everlasting life. Our nature derived from Adam was before the reparation, spiritual holiness, resurrection, or glory given by Christ; even as Adam was before Christ's own incarnation and resurrection. Perfection is the last and ripe state of God's work in our salvation.

47. The first man *is* of the earth, earthy: the second man *is* the Lord from heaven.

47. Adam was made out of the dust of the passive elements; though God breathed into him a living soul, yet earth was his first abode: but Christ is the Lord from heaven; his divine nature being there from everlasting, assumed the human by the overshadowing of the Holy Ghost.

48. As *is* the earthy, such *are* they also that are earthy; and as *is* the heavenly, such *are* they also that are heavenly.

48. And as Adam was a natural man, and the root of such; so it is but nature which we have from him: and as Christ is heavenly and spiritual, so will he make all the holy seed to be like him, spiritual and heavenly.

49. And as we have borne the image of the earthy, we shall also bear the image of the heavenly.

49. And as we are born of Adam, men as he was; so we shall be made by Christ spiritual and heavenly, as he is.

50. Now this I say, brethren, that flesh and blood cannot inherit the kingdom of God; neither doth corruption inherit incorruption.

50. And this I tell you, That these bodies must not come to heaven in the proper form of flesh and blood, nor can as such, possess it; for, as such, they are corruptible, and cannot so inherit heaven, which is incorruptible.

51. Behold, I shew you a mystery; We shall not all sleep, but we shall all be changed,

51. And I will tell you that which is commonly unknown: though the just shall not die that are alive at Christ's coming, they shall all be changed, as well as those that rise from the dead, from being proper flesh and blood, to have spiritual bodies.

52. In a moment, in the twinkling of an eye, at the last trump (for the trumpet shall sound) and the dead shall be raised incorruptible, and we shall be changed.

52. In a moment Christ's potent call will be like a trumpet, calling men together: and the dead shall be raised, and the living saints changed into an incorruptible state.

53. For this corruptible must put on incorruption, and this mortal *must* put on immortality.

53. For this mortal body and composition, which is now corruptible by dissolution, must be changed into an incorruptible and immortal state of being and habitation.

54. So when this corruptible shall have put on incorruption, and this mortal shall have put on immortality, then shall be brought to pass, the saying that is written, Death is swallowed up in victory.

54. And death being conquered by Christ, (being a fruit of sin, from which he saveth us) we shall die no more.

55. O death, where *is* thy sting? O grave, where *is* thy victory?

56. The sting of death *is* sin; and the strength of sin *is* the law.

55. Though now death seem to conquer us, we triumph over it by faith in Christ, foreseeing our resurrection: being saved from sin, which is the sting, and the penal law or curse, which is sin's condemning strength.

57. But thanks *be* to God, which giveth us the victory, through our Lord Jesus Christ.

57. But by faith which seeth things to come we give God thanks, that will raise us from the dead, and give us final victory over death through Christ.

58. Therefore my beloved brethren, be ye steadfast, unmoveable, always abounding in the work of the Lord, forasmuch as ye know that your labour is not in vain in the Lord.

58. And now, brethren, make this necessary use of all. Seeing our faith and hope of a resurrection and future life assureth us, that none of our Christian labour or suffering shall be in vain, or

to our loss, or without a glorious reward; what remaineth, but that against all temptations you be stedfast and unmoveable, and do God's work with all your power, abounding in labour and patience to the end?

ANNOTATIONS.

As this chapter is of great use for our instruction, so it is not without many difficulties to our understanding.

I. It is needful to be observed, into how narrow a room Paul reduceth the gospel, or articles of faith concerning Christ; and how greatly herein they differ from him, that condemn, excommunicate, or persecute those who believe these, and all the Bible besides, if they subscribe not to the truth of all their articles and forms superadded, and the justness of their numerous canons.

II. The apparition of Christ to the five hundred, and to James, seemeth part of that which St. John saith was not by him written. So that part of the evidence of Christ's resurrection should be enough to cause us to believe it.

III. Though it was but some at Corinth that denied the resurrection, the church was faulty in bearing with them; yet separation from that church for their sakes, is not required, nor allowed by the apostle.

IV. The Socinians from the 19th verse, and divers others, gather, That Paul denieth the felicity of our souls before the resurrection, because he intimateth, That if there were no resurrection, (but only an immortality of the soul) Christians were the most miserable men, and their faith and sufferings vain, and they were yet in their sins, &c. The matter is weighty, and the solution hath its difficulty. Some say, That because the heretical denied the immortality of the soul, as well as the resurrection of the body, Paul supposeth this, and answereth them as to both: and they say, That ἐγείρω, signifying but to stand up, that is, to live again, includeth the life of the separated soul, as well as the resurrection of the body. Others say, That Paul speaketh only of the man, and not of the soul alone, which is but part of the man. Soul and body are essential to a man: and as a man he may be miserable, because part is so, (as a tooth-ach is to the whole body) though the soul be happy. Others say, That the felicity of perfect man at the resurrection will be so much greater than that of the separated soul before, and also that this separate state is so darkly revealed to us, that the apostle maketh light of it in comparison of the latter. The first of these opinions is not inconsiderable; but the chief answer is by a stricter exposition of the particular texts. And, 1. verse 19 argueth thus. (If we believe in, and suffer for a Christ as risen, who is not risen, then he cannot save us either as to soul or body; and then we are the most miserable sort of men. For our hopes in him for the time and things of this life only, affords us less than others have, his kingdom being not of this world:) this argument is not against, but for the immortality of the soul.

So verse 32. [What advantageth it me if the dead rise not?] i. e. Neither soul nor body is advantaged by suffering for a Christ as risen, who is not risen.

V. The comparison of Adam and Christ is so hard, seeming to mean, that Adam's soul, and his posterity's, as such, are not immortal. But indeed it implieth no more than this: 1. That it is called, Gen. ii. A living soul, but Christ the Lord of life. 2. That Adam had but a soul breathed into him by creation on earth; but Christ was in heaven from everlasting, the living God. 3. That Adam propagated only humanity; but Christ also sanctity and felicity. 4. That Adam by nature had but a loseable capacity of bodily life continued, and heavenly felicity; and by sin came short of both: but Christ hath life in himself, as the root of holiness and happiness in heaven, which he will give believers, both to their souls and bodies, and will give a bodily resurrection to all men.

VI. Ver. 24. The kingdom delivered up to the Father, is but that government which Christ useth to recover and save sinners, and is no addition to the Father, nor diminution to Christ: but as a prince undertaking to reduce rebels, layeth down his commission and arms when he hath done his work, and yet increaseth his own honour; or as a physician giveth up his hospital, when he hath healed all the sick. And it is like, yea, certain, that when Christ's acquisitive mediation is finished, he will still be some sort of mediator of our fruition: for we shall still behold his glory.

VII. Ver. 37, 38, seem to intimate, That the body that shall rise is not the same that was sowed, but such a body as God pleaseth anew to give. Doubtless it is the same in some respect, and not the same in all respects: and to be able to know just how far it is or is not the same, is too hard for us, and may be quietly left to the will of God. The seminal part of the grain (matter and form) liveth in the new fruit, in which it springeth up, (as the seminal part of man begins his being in the womb) but the added mass which makes up the root, the stalk, and ear, and new grains, are all drawn from without, from the water, earth, and air, by God, and by the seminal spirit. We see that men oft grow fleshy, fat, and lean again, and at last die with little but a skinned skeleton: I think few believe, that either men dying fat shall rise fat, or men dying lean shall rise lean; or yet that every man shall rise with all the flesh which he ever lived or sinned in, and which daily passed away, or consumed in sickness. To know how much, and what goeth to identify the body, we must leave to God, if we will not pretend to the knowledge we have not. Nor is it necessary to believe, that all fowls, beasts, and fishes, rise again, and go to heaven, which are ever digested, and made human flesh.

The apostle, likening our bodies to seed, maketh some to doubt whether the dead body hath a resurrection by any seminal virtue, as a natural cause, or only rise by miracle. The latter is most commonly held: and yet it is certain, that the soul taketh with it a love and inclination to its body, which is a sort of seminal disposition. And no mortal man knoweth whether the soul take not with it some of the igneous spirits by which it here operated as such a body, as seminal virtue in inferior things is lodged in them; and whether at the resurrection God use that composition of igneous matter (or ethereal) and spiritual form, for the aggregation of so much more such matter as shall be needful to make up the glorious, spiritual, incorruptible body. But all this, and how much of the flesh we lived in God will raise, is to us unknown.

VIII. Ver. 50. That flesh and blood cannot enter into the kingdom of God, is grossly perverted by them that say, That it is only sinful flesh that is meant, or them that say, That flesh and blood shall enter, but incorruptible, it is proper formal flesh and blood that the apostle mentioneth. Flesh is the blood, and other nutritive juice, coagulated into that fibrous substance so called, and is the matter of food digested and assimilated unto this. It is made of earth, water, and air; and so is blood. Define them, and nothing that is in heaven will agree with that definition. If such earth shall be placed in heaven, it will cease by transmutation to be earth. To call a spiritual, incorruptible, glorious body, earth and water, flesh and blood, and place these with the blessed spirits, is but to equivocate, and not to use the words univocally. The two general councils (Nice second, and Constance before it) differing in other things, agree, That Christ's true body is in heaven, but that there it is not flesh and blood: (and yet the Papists feign, that he hath still real flesh and blood in the sacrament.)

Doubtless by a spiritual body is meant one that is so near the nature of a spirit, as is fittest for spiritual and glorious work; which made many of the fathers say, That it will be an ethereal, or igneous, or luminous body. But God's knowledge must be implicitly rested in, when we have no explicit knowledge.

CHAP. XVI.

NOW concerning the collection for the saints, as I have given order to the churches of Galatia, even so do ye.

1. I come next to your order for collections for the poor Christians in the present famine at Jerusalem: in which I would have you, as most convenient, to observe this order, which I give to the churches of Galatia.

2. Upon the first *day* of the week, let every one of you lay by him in store, as *God* hath prospered him, that there be no gatherings when I come.

2. The Lord's day being separated for sacred works, of which holy charity is a great part, let every one willingly lay by, as devoted to God for this service, according to the proportion of his increase, that I may find it ready, and not stay when I come for your collections.

3. And when I come, whomsoever you shall approve by *your* letters, them will I send to bring your liberality unto Jerusalem.

3. And then, that you may be satisfied of the faithful delivery, you shall choose the messenger yourselves.

4. And if it be meet that I go also, they shall go with me.

4. And if I find cause to go myself, your own trustees shall go with me.

5. Now I will come unto you, when I shall pass through Macedonia: (for I do pass through Macedonia), 6. And it may be that I will abide, yea, and winter with you, that ye may bring me on my journey, whithersoever I go. 7. For I will not see you now by the way, but I trust to tarry awhile with you, if the Lord permit.

5, 6, 7. Note, That a wise fore-contrivance of our own course of labour is lawful, but only with submission to God's will.

8. But I will tarry at Ephesus until Pentecost. 9. For a great door and effectual is opened unto me, and *there are* many adversaries.

8, 9. Hope of great success, and the opposition of many adversaries, persuade me to stay at Ephesus.

Note, That great success of the gospel oft consisteth with many adversaries.

10. Now if Timotheus come, see that he may be with you without fear: for he worketh the work of the Lord, as I also *do*.

10. See that Timothy, when he cometh, be not discouraged by distrust or abuse; for he is my faithful helper in the same work of the Lord, in which I serve him.

11. Let no man therefore despise him: but conduct him forth in peace, that he may come unto me: for I look for him with the brethren.

11. Despise him not, but give credit to his message, and respectfully conduct him at his return to us.

12. As touching *our* brother Apollos, I greatly desire him to come unto you with the brethren: but his will was not at all to come at this time; but he will come when he shall have convenient time.

12. Note, That Paul left him to his choice, and did not suspend or silence him for disobeying an apostle.

13. Watch ye, stand fast in the faith, quit you like men, be strong.

13. Finally, Your cause is so weighty, and trial so great, as require your constant watch, your resolved steadfastness in the faith, a manlike strength, endeavour, and defence.

14. Let all your things be done with charity.

14. The sum and chiefest rule that I give you, is, Do all that you do in love, or endearedness to one another; and this will cast out selfishness, pride, envy, and division, and keep you from rash censuring, separating, despising, or abusing one another.

15. I beseech you, brethren, (ye know the house of Stephanas, that it is the first-fruits of Achaia, and that they have addicted themselves to the ministry of the saints) 16. That you submit yourselves unto such, and to every one that helpeth with us and laboureth.

15, 16. The house of Stephanas being the first converted in Achaia, and addicted to further Christians with their estates and labour, and he being now my fellow-labourer, submit yourselves to him, and to all such.

17. I am glad of the coming of Stephanas, and Fortunatus, and Achaitus: for that which was lacking on your part, they have supplied. 18. For they have refreshed my spirit and yours: therefore acknowledge ye them that are such.

17, 18. For they have performed such respectful offices as you were wanting in. Therefore let such be respected by you.

19. The churches of Asia salute you. Aquila and Priscilla salute you much in the Lord, with the church that is in their house. 20. All the brethren greet you. Greet ye one another with an holy kiss. 21. The salutation of me Paul with mine own hand.

19, 20, 21. The Christians of their family, (or the assembly that used to meet there for church communion.)

22. If any man love not the Lord Jesus Christ, let him be Anathema, Maran-atha.

22. Those that love the Lord Jesus as their Saviour and hope, will stick to him, and confess him in temptation and sufferings; and if any man love him not, let him, as accursed, be delivered to Satan, and cut off from God.

23. The grace of our Lord Jesus Christ, *be* with you. 24. My love *be* with you all in Christ Jesus. Amen.

23, 24. The best benediction I can give you, is by praying, that the grace of our Lord Jesus Christ may be with you, (for that will render you holy and acceptable to God, and save you from evil, and bring you to glory.) I am sure my love is with you all: may your loveliness so continue it. Amen.

THE SECOND EPISTLE OF PAUL THE APOSTLE,

TO THE

CORINTHIANS.

CHAP. I.

PAUL an apostle of Jesus Christ by the will of God, and Timothy our brother, unto the church of God which is at Corinth, with all the saints which are in all Achaia: 2. Grace *be* to you, and peace from God our father, and *from* the Lord Jesus Christ.

1, 2. When it is read to the church at Corinth, to whom it is specially directed, to be communicated to others in Achaia by them.

3. Blessed *be* God, even the Father of our Lord Jesus Christ, the Father of mercies, and the God of all comfort; 4. Who comforteth us in all our tribulation, that we may be able to comfort them which are in any trouble, by the comfort wherewith we ourselves are comforted of God.

3, 4.—[By the same reasons that comforted me, and by the experience of his mercies, which giveth me a comforting frame of mind.]

5. For as the sufferings of Christ abound in us, so our consolation also aboundeth by Christ.

5. As I suffer more than others for Christ, so I have proportionable comfort by Christ.

6. And whether we be afflicted *it is* for your consolation and salvation, which is effectual in the enduring of the same sufferings which we also suffer: or whether we be comforted, *it is* for your consolation and salvation.

6. So great is the love of God to you, that both our afflictions and our comforts are intended as means to your comfort; that you may the easilier suffer as we do, and hope for that comfort that we enjoy, and that all may further your salvation.

7. And our hope of you *is* steadfast, knowing that as you are partakers of the sufferings, so *shall ye* be also of the consolation.

7. Therefore I hope that suffering will not overthrow your faith, while you look for the same consolation.

8. For we would not, brethren, have you ignorant of our trouble which came to us in Asia, that we were pressed out of measure, above strength, insomuch that we despaired even of life.

8. I would have you know how great our sufferings were in Asia, even beyond our own strength to bear them, and such as put me in expectation of death.

9. But we had the sentence of death in ourselves, that we should not trust in ourselves, but in God, which raiseth the dead.

9. But God brought me to this expectation of death, that I might not trust to my present life, but unto God alone, and that as one that can raise the dead, and give them a better life hereafter than that which they lay down for Christ.

10. Who delivered us from so great a death, and doth deliver; in whom we trust that he will yet deliver *us:* 11. You also helping together by prayer for us, that for the gift *bestowed* upon us by the means of many persons, thanks may be given by many on our behalf.

10, 11. Who hath delivered us from so terrible a kind of death, and still doth deliver us, and we hope will do till our work be done: but your prayers must concur as the means, that God also may have all your thanks.

12. For our rejoicing is this, the testimony of our conscience, that in simplicity and godly sincerity, not with fleshly wisdom, but by the grace of God we have had our conversation in the world, and more abundantly to you-wards.

12. Note, 1. That the Christian must have rejoicing not only in Christ's merits, but in the conscience of his own sincerity. 2. Sincerity is much in simplicity, and contrary to self-seeking fleshly wisdom. 3. It is God's grace that giveth this sincerity. 4. Where it is used in eminent self-denial it may lawfully be gloried in against detractors.

13. For we write none other things unto you, than what you read or acknowledge, and I trust you shall acknowledge even to the end.

13. For I willingly expose myself and doctrine to your trial: I write but the same things which you have received and own, and I hope will own even to the end.

14. As also you have acknowledged us in part, that we are your rejoicing, even as ye also *are* ours in the day of the Lord Jesus.

14. As I myself have been owned by you as your comfort, though I have some accusers, even as you are my comfort when I render an account of my ministry to Christ.

15. And in this confidence I was minded to come unto you before, that you might have a second benefit:

15. And in confidence of this our mutual love, I purposed to come to you, for the increase of your graces.

16. And to pass by you into Macedonia, and to come again out of Macedonia unto you, and of you to be brought on my way toward Judea.

16. When I carry the contribution to Judea.

17. When I therefore was thus minded, did I use lightness? or the things that I purpose, do I purpose according to the flesh, that with me there should be yea, yea, and nay, nay. 18. But *as* God *is* true, our word toward you, was not yea and nay.

17, 18. What I purposed was with submission to God's providence and will. Had any cause then to accuse me of levity and falsehood in my promises, as if my word were not to be credited? I take God to witness, that I spake my real purpose in truth, though I was hindered from performance.

19. For the Son of God, Jesus Christ, who was preached among you by us, *even* by me, and Silvanus, and Timotheus, was not yea and nay, but in him was yea. 20. For all the promises of God in him *are* yea, and in him amen, unto the glory of God by us.

19, 20. And more abusive is it hence to gather my incredibility in preaching, and the uncertainty of my doctrine: for Christ whom we preached is a certain Saviour, and his promises all sure, and are sealed, confirmed, and proved to God's glory, in the power of our ministry.

21. Now he which stablisheth us with you in Christ, and hath anointed us, *is* God: 22. Who hath also sealed us, and given the earnest of the Spirit in our hearts.

21, 22. And it is God himself who stablisheth both us and you in Christ, and hath anointed us, and given us the earnest of his Spirit, which is his pledge and our security.

23. Moreover, I call God for a record upon my soul, that to spare you I came not as yet unto Corinth.

23. I do by oath call God himself to witness, that my not coming yet to you, was not out of any such falsehood, levity, or self-respect, as my accusers intimate; but I delayed, as foreseeing how unpleasing it would be to have exercised the severity among you, which your sin, before repentance, required.

24. Not for that we have dominion over your faith, but are helpers of your joy: for by faith ye stand.

24. Not that we are lords over your faith, or have any power to change it; but our preaching and discipline is to help your joy by casting out sin, and by stablishing you in faith, in and by which you must stand and live.

CHAP. II.

BUT I determined this with myself, that I would not come again to you in heaviness. 2. For if I make you sorry, who is he then that maketh me glad, but the same which is made sorry by me?

1, 2. But the true cause of my delay to come to you, was, that having reproved you for many sins, which required sharper censure if you had not disowned them, I was not forward to grieve you by such displeasing work, and stayed to hear of your repentance. For your grief is my own; and none can take it from me, but yourselves by your repentance.

3. And I wrote this same unto you, lest when I came, I should have sorrow from them of whom I ought to rejoice, having confidence in you all, that my joy is *the joy* of you all.

3. And I gave you my reproof by a letter, that it might cause that reformation which might prevent my sorrow when I came myself; for I ought to have joy in you, as I hope also my joy is yours.

4. For out of much affliction and anguish of heart, I wrote unto you with many tears; not that you should be grieved, but that ye might know the love which I have more abundantly unto you.

4. For I was so far from insulting over you, or desiring your hurt, that I performed that necessary part of my office with great grief and anguish, and wrote to you with many tears; not delighting to grieve you, but to shew my love for your reformation and salvation.

5. But if any have caused grief, he hath not grieved me, but in part: that I may not overcharge you all.

5. But the grief which I had by the sins of some particular persons, I am far from charging on all the church.

6. Sufficient to such a man *is* this punishment, which *was inflicted* of many.

6. The churches' censure and rejection of such a sinner, is as much punishment as I judged meet.

Note, That the punishment was not only in the presence of many, (that is, the assembly) but also [by many :] For though the pastor had the keys, the people were consenting executioners, by avoiding communion with the excommunicate.

7. So that contrariwise, *ye ought* rather to forgive *him*, and comfort *him*, lest perhaps such a one should be swallowed up with overmuch sorrow.

7. But now he is penitent, ye ought to forgive, and comfort him with the notice of pardoning mercy from God, lest too much sorrow overwhelm him.

Note, That sorrow for sin may be too much; and it is so, when it swalloweth us up, and doth more hurt than good.

8. Wherefore I beseech you, that ye would confirm *your* love towards him.

8. I that judged him for his sin, now absolve him, and intreat you in love to receive him.

9. For to this end also did I write, that I might know the proof of you, whether ye be obedient in all things.

9. I wrote to you to cast him out, to exercise your obedience: and so I now do to take him in.

·10. To whom ye forgive any thing, I *forgive* also: for if I forgave any thing, to whom I forgave *it*, for your sakes *forgave I it*, in the person of Christ;

10. As you forgive him, and desire his restoration, so do I: And I absolve him by Christ's authority, as his minister, for your own good and comfort; discipline being for the church's good.

11. Lest Satan should get an advantage of us: for we are not ignorant of his devices.

11. For we know that Satan hath his stratagems, and would turn our justice and discipline to our hurt, (either by too much dejecting the sinner, or by exasperating and dividing the church:) And we would not be over-reached by him: The means are for the end.

12. Furthermore, when I came to Troas to *preach* Christ's gospel, and a door was opened unto me of the Lord, 13. I had no rest in my spirit, because I found not Titus my brother: but taking my leave of them, I went from thence into Macedonia.

12, 13. At Troas I had great encouragement in my ministry; but not hearing of you by Titus, disquieted me, &c.

14. Now thanks *be* unto God, which always causeth us to triumph in Christ, and maketh manifest the favour of his knowledge by us in every place.

14. To God I give thanks, who causeth me to rejoice in the success of my ministry for Christ; and wheresoever I come communicateth to men the knowledge of his gospel.

15. For we are unto God a sweet savour of Christ, in them that are saved, and in them that perish. 16. To the one *we are* the savour of death unto death; and to the other the savour of life unto life:

15, 16. For our service to God is an acceptable sacrifice, for the sake of Christ, both about them that are saved, and them that perish; to them that abuse and reject the gospel to their own destruction, and them that are converted and saved by it: For God will be glorified in both, and accepteth our ministry to both, notwithstanding the various success.

16. And who *is* sufficient for these things?

17. For we are not as many, which corrupt the word of God: but as of sincerity, but as of God, in the sight of God speak we in Christ.

16, 17. So great is this work, that neither I nor any is sufficient for it, in our own strength, without God's suitable help and grace. But I have the conscience of my sincerity, that I do not as do the corrupters of the word of God; but I speak the things of Christ in truth, as God inspired me, and as in his sight.

CHAP. III.

DO we begin again to commend ourselves? or need we, as some *others*, epistles of commendation to you, or *letters* of commendation from you?

1. And seeing the reputation of our persons is so needful to the ends of our ministry, let me expostulate with you, why you should hearken to them who make it needful to vindicate yourselves? Am I a stranger to you? Do I need, as some others, to be recommended to you by other men's letters? Or by your letters to be recommended to other churches? Do I not bring with me the proof of mine apostleship?

2. Ye are our epistle written in our hearts, known and read of all men:

2. Your own conversion by my ministry, which is the rejoicing of my heart, is more than a commendatory epistle; and this may be read of all that know you.

3. For *as much as ye are* manifestly declared to be the epistle of Christ, ministered by us, written not with ink, but with the spirit of the living God; not in tables of stone, but in fleshly tables of the heart.

3. For your conversion openly proveth, that you are, as it were, Christ's own epistle by our ministry, written by the quickening Spirit of the living God, and not with ink; not as Moses's law, on tables of stone; but on your very hearts.

And therefore, as you are the epistle or testimony of the work of Christ, so of me, as his minister.

4. And such trust have we through Christ to God-ward: 5. Not that we are sufficient of ourselves to think any thing as of ourselves: but our sufficiency *is* of God.

4, 5. It is of God that I have this confidence and glorying; far be it from me to think that I have any such sufficiency of myself, to convert souls; but my sufficiency and the success is all of God.

6. Who also hath made us able ministers of the new Testament not of the letter, but of the spirit: for the letter killeth, but the spirit giveth life.

6. It is he that hath made me an able minister of the new covenant; not a preacher of the law of Moses written in stone, but of the gospel of Christ, who sendeth us forth by his Spirit, and giveth his Spirit by our ministry: for the law of Moses curseth sinners, and sheweth them sin, and condemneth them: but the Spirit of Christ doth quicken them, and kill their sin, and lead them in the way of life.

7. But if the ministration of death written *and* engraven in stones was glorious, so that the children of Israel could not steadfastly behold the face of Moses, for the glory of his countenance, which *glory* was to be done away:

7. For if that ministry of Moses, which by consequence was of death, (or of a law that condemned, but gave not the Spirit of life) written and engraven by God in stones, was accompanied with so great glory, that the Israelites could not endure to look Moses in the face, for the glory of his countenance, which yet is now done away;

8. How shall not the ministration of the spirit be rather glorious?

8. Must not the more excellent ministry of a durable gospel, by which God giveth men his Spirit, be more glorious? (though we the ministers seem contemptible.)

9. For if the ministration of condemnation *be* glory, much more doth the ministration of righteousness exceed in glory.

9. The different covenants shew the different glory of the ministry; For if Moses's ministration of a condemning law was glory, our ministration of a justifying, saving gospel-covenant, must needs exceed his ministry in true glory.

10. For even that which was made glorious, had no glory in this

respect, by reason of the glory that excelleth.

10. For as a greater light maketh the lesser seem as none, so the Mosaic ministry of the law had as it were, no glory, being clouded by the glory of the gospel.

11. For if that which is done away was glorious, much more that which remaineth is glorious.

11. For if the law of Moses (considered formally as such, and given to the Jews to rule their commonwealth, and lead them to Christ) which was to cease when the gospel came, to which it was a schoolmaster, was yet given in glory; much more is the gospel, which is to continue, and its ministration glorious.

12. Seeing then that we have such hope, we use great plainness of speech.

12. Wonder not then that we speak boldly to you, when we can shew such authority.

13. And not as Moses, *which* put a vail over his face, that the children of Israel could not steadfastly look to the end of that which is abolished.

13. We do not as Moses vail our faces, signifying that the Israelites could not well look to the true end and meaning of their own law, which is Christ, to whom by types is pointed them; nor see that it was to be abolished by his better covenant, as it now is. We speak freely to you with open face.

14. But their minds were blinded: for until this day remaineth the same vail untaken away, in the reading of the old testament; which *vail* is done away in Christ.

14. But the minds of the unbelieving Jews were blinded, and to this day the vail remaineth by this their blindness, so that they understand not the end and design of the Old Testament when they read it. But it is taken away by Christ to true believers.

15. But even unto this day, when Moses is read, the vail is upon their heart.

15. Their unbelief sheweth us, that the vail and blindness is on them to this day.

16. Nevertheless when it shall turn to the Lord, the vail shall be taken away.

16. But when they shall be converted to Christianity, the vail shall be taken away, and they shall understand the meaning and tendency of the law.

17. Now the Lord is that Spirit: and where the Spirit of the Lord *is*, there *is* liberty.

17. And as the letter doth but point unto the Spirit, without which it doth but kill; so it is Christ who is that Spirit which is the sum and end of the letter and types: And where the Spirit of the Lord is, there is freedom and power of speech as well as deliverance; and therefore we use that freedom with you.

18. But we all with open face, beholding as in a glass the glory of the Lord, are changed into the same image, from glory to glory, *even* as by the Spirit of the Lord.

18. And so all true Christians, not vailed as the Jews, but with open face, in the open light, though yet but as in a glass, behold the glory of the Lord; and by our spiritual renovation are changed into the image of Christ, from one degree of glory to another, by the Spirit of the Lord, who will perfect his work.

ANNOTATIONS.

The fear of favouring Antinomianism hath tempted some to pervert this chapter, about the abolishing Moses's law. I know of no man that hath written so much against the Antinomians as I have done, nor with so much success, in casting down their libertine errors in this land: and yet I abhor running into the contrary extreme. And therefore I say, that it is evident to any unprejudiced considering reason, that Paul here affirmeth, That the very law written in stone is abolished and done away. To say, it is only the glory of the burning mount, or of Moses's face, that is done away, is plainly contrary to verse 7, 9, 10, 11, 13. I will not tire the reader with arguments from so plain words. The truth is this:

1. The law of nature is not done away by Christ, but made part of his own law, into whose hands that and all things are given.

2. The Ten Commandments, except the preface, and a word or two in the second commandment, and the determination of the seventh day in the fourth commandment, are the common law of nature.

3. Christ also hath expressly made them his law, by reciting them preceptively: and so they bind all Christians now, as the law of nature and the law of Christ.

4. God by giving the Jews their laws, gave us directions to know in the like cases what is equal or wrong to us.

5. But formally, as it was God's law delivered by Moses to the Jews, it binds not us, and it is done away.

For, 1. It never, as such, bound any but the Jews, and the few proselytes among them. For it was never promulgated to the world: and even the decalogue was political, and all made for that commonwealth. And all the world was never bound to turn Jews, nor to dwell or come into a remote country, no bigger than half England.

2. The Jews' own commonwealth is dissolved, and so are their peculiar laws.
3. The apostle expressly saith, That the law written in stone, that was glorious, is done away, verse 7, and 11, 12, compared.
4. Moses was no ruler or mediator to the whole world.
5. If one part of Moses's law, as such, bind, then all of it bindeth, *a gustanne ad omne*; and so we must turn Jews.
6. Paul expressly nameth sabbaths as abolished; that is, A day of ceremonial rest, which the fourth commandment ordaineth as a type of spiritual rest by Christ.

The sum is, That we are bound to the law commonly called moral, as it is the law of nature, and of Christ; but not formally, as the law given the Jews by Moses, or as written in stone.

CHAP. IV.

THEREFORE seeing we have this ministry, as we have received mercy we faint not.

1. Therefore having received a more honourable ministry than that of Moses, God's mercy encourageth us, and keepeth us from fainting in our labours and sufferings.

2. But have renounced the hidden things of dishonesty, not walking in craftiness, nor handling the word of God deceitfully, but, by manifestation of the truth commending ourselves to every man's conscience in the sight of God.

2. But have renounced those things which cannot endure the light, lest they should be ashamed, but are craftily carried on in the dark; nor do we use deceiving arts in handling the word of God, but in the open light, by evidence of truth, we expose ourselves to trial, and expect success.

3. But if our gospel be hid, it is hid to them that are lost:

3. So that if our preaching be not yet understood and believed, it is not for want of our clear delivery, but from the miserable case of lost uncapable hearers.

4. In whom the God of this world hath blinded the minds of them which believe not, lest the light of the glorious gospel of Christ, who is the image of God, should shine unto them.

4. Because the devil, by the love of worldly things, ruling the hearts of worldly men, hath blinded them, that they may not believe the gospel, and see that glory which shineth in Christ, who is the image of God.

5. For we preach not ourselves, but Christ Jesus the Lord: and ourselves your servants for Jesus' sake.

5. It is not ourselves that we commend by preaching to you, or set up for you to believe in; but it is Christ Jesus the Lord, (else indeed our ministry were inglorious;) and we only manifest ourselves to be faithful servants for your salvation by Christ, who hath called us hereto, and whose glory we proclaim.

6. For God who commanded the light to shine out of darkness, hath shined in our hearts, to give the light of the knowledge of the glory of God, in the face of Jesus Christ.

6. For God, who by his word created light, hath shined by spiritual light into our hearts, giving us that knowledge of God which gloriously appeareth in the person, doctrine, and works of Christ, which he commandeth us to communicate to others.

7. But we have this treasure in earthern vessels, that the excellency of the power may be of God, and not of us,

7. But we that are thus trusted and honoured of God, are ourselves poor, frail, afflicted mortals, that it may appear, that it is by the power of God, and not of men, that the gospel prospereth.

8. We are troubled on every side, yet not distressed; we are perplexed, but not in despair; 9. Persecuted, but not forsaken; cast down, but not destroyed.

8, 9. We are many ways troubled, but not brought to any extreme distress; in straits, but not in despair; persecuted by men, but not forsaken of God; cast down low, and yet upheld, and not destroyed.

10. Always bearing about in the body, the dying of the Lord Jesus, that the life also of Jesus might be made manifest in our body.

10. We still bear in our bodies a memorative conformity to our suffering, dying Lord, that our delivered bodies also might have some conformity to his life, by whom we live, and whom we preach.

11. For we which live, are alway delivered unto death for Jesus' sake, that the life also of Jesus might be made manifest in our mortal flesh.

11. For we that yet live are in continual danger of death by persecutors, for Jesus' sake: that we may be emblems of Christ's resurrection and life, and a proof that he liveth, who preserveth

us, while we preach that blessed life which he possesseth, and hath purchased, and promised.

12. So then death worketh in us, but life in you.

12. So that in our sufferings Christ's death is resembled; but his life in your conversion and preservation.

13. We having the same spirit of faith, according as it is written, I believed, and therefore have I spoken; we also believe, and therefore speak.

13. But we have the same spirit of faith as you have, and therefore say with David, That we speak because we believe.

14. Knowing that he which raised up the Lord Jesus, shall raise up us also by Jesus, and shall present us with you.

14. For he that raised up Christ shall raise us up both from our sufferings and death, and present us with you, who are the blessings of our labours.

15. For all things are for your sakes, that the abundant grace might, through the thanksgiving of many, redound to the glory of God.

15. For it is for you that we suffer, and labour, and are preserved; that as many have the benefit, so God may be glorified by the thanksgiving of many.

16. For which cause we faint not, but though our outward man perish, yet the inward man is renewed day by day.

16. Therefore we are not tired in our labour or suffering: but while our bodies suffer and perish, our souls receive daily new supplies of strength and comfort.

17. For our light affliction, which is but for a moment, worketh for us a far more exceeding and eternal weight of glory.

17. For all our sufferings for Christ, and bodily afflictions, are very tolerable and light, and so short as to be but as for one moment; and so gainful, that they are the means appointed to procure us a crown of glory, which is weighty, and of exceeding worth, and everlasting.

18. While we look not at the things which are seen, but at the things which are not seen, for the things which are seen, are temporal; but the things which are not seen, are eternal.

18. For we intend no worldly end, nor fix our eyes and mind on these transitory things, which now are here seen; but on the glory and kingdom which is unseen: For the things which are seen are temporary, mutable, and fly away, and therefore are not to be much regarded; but the things which are now to us unseen, are unchangeable and everlasting.

CHAP. V.

FOR we know, that if our earthly house of *this* tabernacle were dissolved, we have a building of God, an house not made with hands, eternal in the heavens.

1. For by faith we know, that if our bodies, which are as a tent or tabernacle to the soul, were dissolved, we have in the heavens, a building of God's providing for the blessed, not like our houses here made by man, but celestial and everlasting.

Note, 1. That faith is a sort of knowledge: We know what God saith is true; and we know this to be his word.

2. That our happiness will not be only in the new earth, and at the resurrection; but it is a dwelling in heaven, now existent, and such as shall be everlasting: And, therefore, no hope of Christ's reign on earth, should take down our hopes and desires of heaven.

2. For in this we groan earnestly, desiring to be clothed upon with our house which is from heaven:
3. If so be that being clothed, we shall not be found naked.

2, 3. For in this body we are under a constant uneasiness, which maketh us groan with earnest desire to be better clothed, even with the incorruptible celestial glory: For when death uncloatheth us, we shall not be found naked and destitute, or, as some expound it, [So be it we be not found as Adam, naked in our guilt, when we enter into the future state.]

4. For we that are in *this* tabernacle do groan, being burdened: not for that we would be unclothed, but clothed upon, that mortality might be swallowed up of like.

4. For our burdens in this body are so great, as make us groan: not that we desire death as death; or to be unhoused, or without clothing to the soul: but we would be better clothed with a heavenly glory, that that which is mortal, may be swallowed up by immortal glory.

5. Now he that hath wrought us for self-same thing, *is* God, who also hath given unto us the earnest of the spirit.

5. And we have good evidence for the certain

ty of this hope: For God himself, who doth nothing in vain, hath made and formed as hereunto: It is he that gave us immortal souls, and faculties to prepare for a better life: And it is he that hath redeemed us to it, and hath promised it, and provided and commanded us the means that lead to it, and hath given us by his Spirit those holy affections, desires, and endeavours, which are the earnest of it, and which he will not frustrate.

6. Therefore *we are* always confident, knowing that whilst we are at home in the body, we are absent from the Lord: 7. (For we walk by faith, not by sight.)

6, 7. Therefore we go on in the confidence and boldness which beseem believers, being above the fear of death; knowing, that while we dwell here in these bodies, we are absent from the glory where God is fully manifested to the blessed: For it is not things seen which are the motives, hopes, and comfort of our lives; it is things believed and unseen.

8. We are confident *I say*, and willing rather to be absent from the body, and to be present with the Lord.

8. I say, we are bold and comfortably confident in all our labours and danger of death, and rather willing to go from the body, and to be at home or present with the Lord.

8. Wherefore we labour, that whether present or absent we may be accepted of him.

9. Whether we shall yet live or die, we live to God; but it is our earnest desire, care, and labour, that whether we live here or die, or wherever we are, we may please God, and be accepted by him.

10. For we must all appear before the judgment-seat of Christ, that every one may receive the things *done* in his body, according to that he hath done, whether *it be* good or bad.

10. For we must all appear at the judgment-seat of Christ, where all that we have done will be brought to light, and every man shall be sentenced and rewarded according as he hath lived and done in the body, whether it be good or evil, according to that law which pardoneth penitent believers.

11. Knowing therefore the terror of the Lord, we persuade men: but we are made manifest unto God, and I trust also are made manifest in your consciences.

11. It is the knowledge of the terrors of the Lord, and how woeful it will be to be found there unjustified under guilt, and sentenced to damnation, which causeth us to make so much ado in the world, to persuade men to believe and repeat, that they may be saved: And God that knoweth our hearts and ways, will justify us herein, and I hope so do your convinced consciences.

12. For we commend not ourselves again unto you, but give you occasion to glory on our behalf, that you may have somewhat to *answer* them which glory in appearance, and not in heart.

12. I say not all this to get your praise by my self-commendation, but to give you the matter of an answer to them that would draw you from the truth, by drawing you into a disesteem of us that were your first teachers, and by boasting of themselves by outward appearances, without an answerable inward worth.

13. For whether we be besides ourselves, *it is* to God: or whether we be sober, *it is* for your cause.

13. And if any tell you that our zeal is but crazy melancholy, (as Festus thought of Paul) it is in obedience to God's command, and for his work and glory; (and dare any accuse this of madness?) And if we be thought to do it soberly, it is not for our glory, but for your stability and safety.

14. For the love of Christ constraineth us, because we thus judge, that if one died for all, then were all dead; 15. And *that* he died for all, that they which live, should not henceforth live unto themselves, but unto him which died for them, and rose again.

14, 15. If any think we are too zealously transported, let them know, that the greatness of Christ's love to us, and ours to him, constraineth us, and will bear no cold indifferency: For we have cause to judge, that they are great things which our redemption intimateth, even that Christ, who died for all, found all men dead in sin and misery; and that he, therefore, redeemed them by his death, that they who are recovered by him should not hereafter live to themselves, but to him that died for them, and rose again.

16. Wherefore henceforth know we no man after the flesh: yea, though we have known Christ after the flesh, yet now henceforth know we *him* no more.

16. Wherefore it is the great things of spirituality and eternity which we now look at in our ministry and life: We value no man on mere carnal advantages or account; yea, if we had been of those that conversed with Christ on earth in the body, and had eat and drank in his presence, such corporal familiarity is ended, and it is not

that our faith, and hope, and preaching, most respecteth, but his spiritual kingdom, and glorious presence, and the means thereto.

17. Therefore if any man *be* in Christ, *he is* a new creature; old things are past away, behold, all things are become new.

17. Therefore if any one be a Christian indeed, a true member of Christ, he is a new man, as it were new made by regeneration. The old legal and carnal mind and conversation are ceased; his old mind, and will, and life, are changed; his fleshly and earthly mind is become spiritual, and heavenly, and all is new.

18. And all things *are* of God, who hath reconciled us to himself by Jesus Christ, and hath given to us the ministry of reconciliation.

18. The divine revelation, and the divine nature in us, now causeth us to mind and use all things as they belong to God, and as they are all of him, and by him, and to him; and to overlook comparatively carnal interest: and as reconciled and brought home to God by Jesus Christ, and placing all our interest and hopes in him, who also hath committed to us his ministry, to draw home the world into this reconciled state.

19. To wit, that God was in Christ, reconciling the world unto himself, not imputing their trespasses unto them: and hath committed unto us the word of reconciliation.

19. To tell them, that it was God himself that sent Christ to redeem us, and was in Christ, reconciling the lapsed world to himself, by the doctrine, merits, and sacrifice of Christ, which was performed by his gracious will for that end; purchasing their pardon, and not using them as their sin deserved, but giving them an act of oblivion, on condition of believing acceptance; and hath committed to us the ministry, to preach this reconciliation to the world.

20. Now then we are ambassadors for Christ, as though God did beseech *you* by us: we pray *you* in Christ's stead, be ye reconciled to God.

20. By all this they that contemn us may see what is the nature and dignity of our apostleship: We are sent to men from God as his ambassadors, to persuade them to believe in Christ. As though God himself did beseech you by us his messengers, we pray you in Christ's stead, who is the prime and great apostle from the Father, to be reconciled to God, even thankfully to accept his grace, and to give up heart and life to him.

21. For he hath made him *to be* sin for us, who knew no sin; that we might be made the righteousness of God in him.

21. For God hath made Christ to be a sacrifice for sin, who himself was sinless; and this in our stead, and for our pardon and salvation, that so in him we might have the righteousness which is freely given us of God, and be partakers of the divine nature.

ANNOTATIONS.

1. The Socinians strive hard to distort the first part of this chapter, as if it spake of no heavenly house till the resurrection: Their first reason is, Because διωδομιον [Domicilium] is opposed to the body here, and therefore it must mean the future body. But 1. by [the tabernacle of our earthly house] Paul seemeth to me to mean both this body and earth together; our present worldly state in the flesh. 2. Were it otherwise, yet their conclusion would not follow: For the heavenly state of glory without a body may be called an house, as contradistinct to this body. 3. Nor is this objection any thing to the old fathers, and some present divines (as Dr. More, &c.) who think that departed souls have a pure sort of bodies above, to us invisible: either taking with them some tenacious, igneous spirits hence, or passing into some ethereal vehicle there; as even Mimmerius thought, and others, who yet assert, that souls are immaterial.

2. Their second reason is from verse 2, because it is called τὸ ἐξ ἐρανῦ, our house which is from heaven, and not [which is in heaven.] But ἐξ oft signifieth the substance, matter, or thing, of which another thing is made; as we say, some things are made from or of, earth, stone, iron, silver, &c. So here τὸ ἐξ ἐρανῦ doth necessarily signify no more, but that our house or building after death will be heavenly, that is, of heavenly substance, quality, and state.

3. And the context doth confute the perverters. For 1. The first verse intimateth, that we shall have the eternal building in heaven, when the earthly tabernacle is dissolved; for the conditional ἐην intimateth the time.

2. Verse 3, signifieth, that we shall not be found naked; which none could suspect after the resurrection that believed it: but the putting off the body might make men fear.

3. What else can be meant, verse 6, 8, by being absent from the Lord while we are in the body, and being absent from the body, and present with the Lord? And verse 9, by being accepted of him as the height of our ambition when we die?

II. Verse 19, is mistaken by many, as if by [the world] were meant only [the elect] because reconciliation, and not imputing trespasses, are mentioned: But the text most plainly tells us of a general reconciliation and non-imputation to mankind, and a particular to believers. God did so far reconcile and forgive the world, as not to deal with them merely on the terms of the violated law of innocency, but to give them a redeemer, and a law of grace, and a sealed pardon of all sin, and free gift of salvation by Christ, on condition of believing acceptance; and that is commonly said to be given, which is freely by a deed of gift conferred, though acceptance be implied or expressed as the condition of enjoyment, and a man may yet wilfully refuse it or neglect it; yea, such conditions are so naturally necessary, that they use not to be expressed. Yet no man is actually (but only conditionally) possessed of pardon and reconciliation, till that condition be performed: Yet God was forgiving them on his part, and was not imputing sin and unworthiness of redemption to them, when he gave them a Saviour. And yet the work of the ministry remaineth, even to intreat men to believe and accept this pardon and reconciliation as offered; and it is then actually theirs, when they thus accept it. To say, that then their faith doth more than Christ's did, or God's grace, is but mere cavil. Their faith, or acceptance, is no efficient cause at all of their pardon or justification: It is but a necessary receptive qualification. He that shuts the window causeth darkness; but it is absurd to say, that he that openeth it doth more than the sun to cause light; which he cometh not at all, but removeth the impediment of reception; and faith itself is God's gift of grace, though preaching and persuasion be the means of working it.

CHAP. VI.

WE then, *as* workers together *with him*, beseech *you* also, that ye receive not the grace of God in vain.

1. We then whose office is to subserve Christ for your salvation, beseech you that ye take care that all the mercy which he hath shewed you in the gospel, and you profess to have received, be not in vain, and frustrated by any deceit.

2. (For he saith, I have heard thee in a time accepted, and in the day of salvation have I succoured thee: behold, now *is* the accepted time; behold, now *is* the day of salvation.)

2. It is of exceeding great moment to know your time and day of grace: God hath his accepted time, and special day of mercy, which all should watch and take; as it is written, [I have heard thee, &c.] And certainly this is your time and day of mercy, while mercy is so freely and fully preached to you.

3. Giving no offence in any thing, that the ministry be not blamed:

3. Our care is to give no occasion of falling to any, nor expose the ministry to blame, or to the hard thoughts of those that should be saved by it.

4. But in all things approving ourselves as the ministers of God in much patience, in afflictions, in necessities, in distresses, 5. In stripes, in imprisonments, in tumults, in labours, in watchings, in fastings,

4, 5. Note, What an approved minister of Christ must endure and do, for the ends of his ministry, if he be called to it.

6. By pureness, by knowledge, by long-suffering, by kindness, by the Holy Ghost, by love unfeigned, 7. By the word of truth, by the power of God, by the armour of righteousness, on the right hand and on the left, 8. By honour and dishonour, by evil report and good report:

6, 7, 8. Note, By how many means the work of the ministry is promoted, and how we must be qualified thereto.

8. As deceivers, and yet true; 9. As unknown, and yet well known; as dying, and behold, we live; as chastened, and not killed; 10. As sorrowful, yet alway rejoicing; as poor, yet making many rich; as having nothing, and yet possessing all things.

8, 9, 10. Our life is made up of seeming, but not real, contradictions. As deceivers use craft to hurt men, we use our wit and skill (or wiles) to save men; and yet we deliver nothing but the truth: Our spirit and spiritual condition is unknown; and yet our outside known to many. We daily are exposed to the danger of death, and die daily; and yet you see we are alive. We are oft chastened, and yet not killed; we are under many sorrows in the flesh, and yet we continually rejoice in God; we are poor, and yet God useth us to make many rich in grace; we have nothing, and yet by faith all the world is ours, as ordered by God, and used by us for our spiritual good. Love maketh all other men's estates comfortable to us as our own, and God useth all things for our good.

11. O ye Corinthians, our mouth is open unto you, our heart is enlarged. 12. Ye are not straitened in us, but ye are straitened in your own bowels.

11, 12. Our mouth hath been opened to you in full communication of the gospel, and our heart enlarged towards you, in love and zeal for your salvation If yet there be any straitness and defects in you of knowledge and love, it is of yourselves, and your own deficiency.

13. Now for a recompence in the same, (I speak as unto my children) be ye also enlarged.

13. And justice requireth, that (as children to a father) your love and kindness be large towards us, and that the fruits of our ministry in you be not narrow and defective.

14. Be ye not unequally yoked together with unbelievers: for what fellowship hath righteousness with unrighteousness? and what communion hath light with darkness? 15. And what concord hath Christ with Belial? or what part hath he that believeth, with an infidel?

14, 15. Let not seducers, or carnal interest, draw you to communion with infidels, and idolaters, as if you were inclined to their way, or were yet indifferent in religion. Partake not externally of their sacrifices, as if you were of their society: For how can such contraries as righteousness and unrighteousness, light and darkness, Christ and Belial, a believer and an infidel, be united, or have special communion, even symbolical, in the things wherein they are contrary?

16. And what agreement hath the temple of God with idols? for ye are the temple of the living God; as God hath said, I will dwell in them, and walk in *them*; and I will be their God, and they shall be my people.

16. Will you join the temple of God and idols together? God hath made you his temple and peculiar people, and promised specially to own you in communion as your God: And will you go to idols' temples, as if your God had concord and communion with them?

17. Wherefore come out from among them, and be ye separate, saith the Lord, and touch not the unclean thing; and I will receive you. 18. And will be a Father unto you, and ye shall be my sons and daughters, saith the Lord almighty.

17, 18. Wherefore, go not to the idols' temples, and symbolize not with them in religion to avoid persecution; but come out from among them, as a holy people segregate to the Lord, and defile not yourselves with their unclean things, and then God will own you as his sons and daughters, while you are pure, and cleave to him.

1. Note, That this command for the church to avoid communion with idolaters and infidels, is perverted by them that feign it to forbid communion with Christians and their churches, if they do but differ in some tolerable opinion or practice from them, which their censorious ignorance will falsely call idolatry. They call such differences or defects false worship, and then say we must not join in false worship: Whereas every faulty manner of worship may be called false, because it is so far disagreeable to the rule: And no man offers any worship to God that is not false, if all faultiness be falseness. But it is no false worship that will allow us to separate from churches or Christians, further than they separate from Christ,

2.

and Christ disowneth them for that faultiness, or than they make any sin to be to us necessary to any part of their communion. They were very foul sins, even in worship, that the Corinthians were guilty of; and yet none was commanded to come out from them.

And much more are those Papists displeasing to God, who cast out and violently persecute good Christians, that do but avoid, as sinful, some circumstances or forms which their canons impose as things indifferent, or made necessary merely by themselves.

Yet it is not the name of a Christian church that will make it lawful for us to communicate in idolatry, or to commit any sin for their communion, or to own such worship as we know God rejecteth: But as he pardoneth the faulty imperfections of other men's and church's worship, and of our own, so must we bear with our own and the church's tolerable fastings, so far as we cannot cure them.

II. They are mistaken that think it is unequal marrying with infidels, which the apostle here only or chiefly meaneth. The word translated [yoked] signifieth here rather inclined towards them, as the balance is by weight: And that which Paul chiefly pleads against all along, is that, Rev. ii. and iii. called the doctrine of Jezebel and the Nicolaitans, which God hateth, which taught the lawfulness of fornication, and eating things offered to idols; and this on pretence of greater wisdom and revelation than Paul had.

CHAP. VII.

HAVING therefore these promises, (dearly beloved) let us cleanse ourselves from all filthiness of the flesh and spirit, perfecting holiness in the fear of God.

1. Having these promises, that God will be your God, and own you, and dwell in you, on this condition, that you keep yourselves pure to him, from fleshly vice and idol-communion; let us avoid all defilement of the flesh, by fornication, or outward symbolizing with idolaters; and of the spirit, by entertaining the doctrines of seducers, or suffering our hearts to depart from God.

2. Receive us; we have wronged no man, we have corrupted no man, we have defrauded no man.

2. And let not seducing teachers turn you from receiving the ministry of us by whom you were converted: We have not done by you as they do; we have wronged none, corrupted none, nor covetously over-reached or defrauded any.

3. I speak not this to condemn *you*: for I have said before, that *you* are in our hearts, to die and live with *you*.

3. It is not censoriously, or for your reproach that I say this, for you are dear unto me.

E e

4. Great *is* my boldness of speech toward you, great *is* my glorying of you: I am filled with comfort, I am exceeding joyful in all our tribulation.

4. It is my love that makes me use so much freedom of speech to you, and maketh me boast of you. I am full of comfort and joy, to think of your continuance in the faith.

5. For when we were come into Macedonia, our flesh had no rest, but we were troubled on every side; without *were* fightings, within *were* fears.

5. And our condition needed such consolation: for in Macedonia our flesh had no rest from labour and trouble; we had persecution and opposition without, and fears within.

6. Nevertheless, God that comforteth those that are cast down, comforted us by the coming of Titus:

6. But God who comforteth them that are humbled, made the coming of Titus a comfort to me.

7. And not by his coming only, but by the consolation wherewith he was comforted in you, when he told us your earnest desire, your mourning, your fervent mind toward me; so that I rejoiced the more.

7. Not so much for his company and welfare, as for the glad tidings which he brought of you, even of your earnest desire of me, your sorrow for the sin which I reproved, and your zeal in my just vindication against accusers, which were joy for you.

8. For though I made you sorry with a letter, I do not repent, though I did repent: for I perceive that the same epistle made you sorry, though *it were* but for a season.

8. For though, till I heard of the success, I was troubled myself that I must trouble you; yet now I repent not of it: for I perceive, that the sorrow which it caused in you was but short, till the reproved sinner did repent.

9. Now I rejoice, not that ye were made sorry, but that ye sorrowed to repentance: for ye were made sorry after a godly manner, that ye might receive damage by us in nothing.

9. And now I rejoice, not in your grief, as such; for sorrow is but to prepare for joy by reformation) but that your sorrow was godly, and wrought repentance; which is so necessary to forgiveness and salvation, that I am satisfied my plain dealing with you was not to your damage, but to your gain.

10. For godly sorrow worketh repentance to salvation not to be repented of: but the sorrow of the world worketh death.

10. For godly sorrow, as it is commanded of God for your own good, so it worketh repentance and recovery from sin, and so the saving of the sinner: But the sorrow for losses and crosses, which proceedeth from the over-much love of the world, is sinful; and as it doth but hurt the soul, so doth it the body, and hasteneth death.

11. For, behold, this self-same thing that ye sorrowed after a godly sort, what carefulness it wrought in you, yea, *what* clearing of yourselves, yea, *what* indignation, yea, *what* fear, yea, *what* vehement desire, yea, *what* zeal, yea, *what* revenge! in all things ye have approved yourselves to be clear in this matter.

11. Of this you have now experience in yourselves; for your godly sorrow for the scandal that rose among you, hath wrought great carefulness to search out the case, and to reform it; great care to clear yourselves from partaking in the guilt; great indignation against the sin; great fear of God, lest he should avenge it; great desire after a reformation; great zeal against any church-pollution in the things of God: yea, and just revenge on the offenders by way of penitence, and on yourselves for any degree of guilt: so that you have by all means shewed, that you are clear from the guilt.

12. Wherefore though I wrote unto you, *I did it* not for his cause that had done the wrong, nor for his cause that suffered wrong, but that our care for you in the sight of God might appear unto you.

12. And my sharp writing to you was not merely to right one man against the injuries of another, as an act of justice between man and man; but it was in love to you, and care of your souls, that you might not be found guilty before God.

13. Therefore we were comforted in your comfort: yea, and exceedingly the more joyed we for the joy of Titus, because his spirit was refreshed by you all.

13. Therefore in these fruits which tend to your own comfort, I also am comforted; to which much is added by the comfort that Titus had among you.

14. For if I have boasted any thing to him of you, I am not ashamed; but as we speak all things to you in truth, even so our boasting which *I made* before Titus is found a truth.

14. For you have confirmed to him all the good which I boastingly spake of you; so that I have no cause to be ashamed of it: But as I spake truly to you, so I did of you.

15. And his inward affection is more abundant toward you, whilst he remembereth the obedience of you all, how with fear and trembling you received him.

15. And he is greatly affected towards you, by finding you so obedient, and how you received him and his message with a careful fear of God's displeasure, and the guilt of sin.

16. I rejoice therefore that I have confidence in you in all things.

16. My expectation, therefore, of your obedience, dispersing my fear of you, and increasing my confidence of your stability, doth increase my joy.

CHAP. VIII.

MOREOVER, brethren, we do you to wit of the grace of God bestowed on the churches of Macedonia:

1. And I think it meet here to give you notice of the grace of God on the churches of Macedonia, which appeared in their willing liberality in our collections for Judea.

2. How that in a great trial of affliction, the abundance of their joy, and their deep poverty, abounded unto the riches of their liberality.

2. How, that while they were themselves under a great trial of affliction, and in deep poverty, yet they joyfully abounded in liberality.

3. For to *their* power (I bear record) yea, and beyond their power, *they were* willing of themselves.

3. For they were voluntarily ready, even beyond their power, which they extended to the utmost.

4. Praying us with much intreaty, that we would receive the gift, and *take upon us* the fellowship of the ministering to the saints.

4. Earnestly entreating us to receive their contribution, and undertake the administering of it to the saints at Jerusalem, as an expression of their communicating love.

5. And *this they did*, not as we hoped, but first gave their own selves to the Lord, and unto us by the will of God.

5. And in this they exceeded our hope, first giving themselves to God, and to us as his ministers, as ready to help us with their persons, as well as with their purses.

6. Insomuch that we desired Titus, that as he had begun, so he would also finish in you the same grace also.

6. And so we desired Titus, that as he had begun the motion of this charity to you, he would be at the labour to travel to you, and bring it to perfection.

7. Therefore as ye abound in every thing, in faith, in utterance, and knowledge, and in all diligence, and in your love to us ; *see* that ye abound in this grace also.

7. Therefore as you are a church eminent for gifts of faith, knowledge, speech, diligence, and love to us, see that your charitable contribution abound in answerableness to your gifts.

8. I speak not by commandment, but by occasion of the forwardness of others, and to prove the sincerity of your love.

8. I do not this as the master of your purses, by way of command; but I set before you the good example of others, and I invite you to give this proof of the sincerity of your love to me, and to the brethren: (for hypocrites will afford us a cheap sort of love, but not a costly one.)

9. For ye know the grace of our Lord Jesus Christ, that though he was rich, yet for your sakes he became poor, that ye through his poverty might be rich,

9. And what can be a stronger motive to you, than the example of Christ; who, though he was Lord of all the world, for our sakes lived in the body, in the condition of the poor; and this was to procure us the heavenly riches: so that you relieve him reputatively, in relieving his members: and you imitate him, when you forsake your own abundance for the good of others.

10. And herein I give *my* advice: for this is expedient for you who have begun before not only to do, but also to be forward a year ago.

10. And I am the bolder herein to advise you, because you yourselves have herein begun, and resolved to go on, a year ago; and therefore it is but agreeable to your own resolves.

11. Now therefore perform the

doing of it; that *as there was* a readiness to will, *so there may be a performance* also out of that which you have.

11. Therefore now perform what then you readily resolved on, according to your ability.

12. For if there be first a willing mind, *it is* accepted according to that a man hath, *and* not according to that he hath not.

12. For if there be a true willingness, it will be performed according to a man's ability: and God requireth no more, but accepteth the will for that which we are unable for.

13. For *I mean* not that other men be eased, and you burdened: 14. But by an equality, *that* now at this time, your abundance *may be a supply* for want, that their abundance also may be *a supply* for your want, that there may be equality.

13, 14. Not that I would lay more on you than your proportion, to ease others: but that now you abound, you may supply their want; and that when you are in want, the abundance of others may supply your wants.

15. As it is written, He that *had gathered* much, had nothing over; and he that *had gathered* little, had no lack.

15. In which I may allude to what is said of the Israelites gathering manna; [He that, &c.] Obey God, and you shall not want; and if you abound, what enjoy you of it more than they that have but food and raiment? God will reduce all his servants to an equality suitable to them severally, in the use and end.

16. But thanks *be* to God, which put the same earnest care into the heart of Titus for you. 17. For indeed he accepted the exhortation, but being more forward, of his own accord he went unto you.

16, 17. I thank God that Titus was as forward to move you to this work as I; for he did not only yield to it at my request, but of his own accord was forward to go to you about it.

18. And we have sent with him the brother, whose praise *is* in the gospel throughout all the churches.

18. And with him we sent Luke, whose service for the gospel hath made him honoured in all the churches.

19. (And not that only, but who was also chosen of the churches to travel with us with this grace which is administered by us to the glory of the same Lord, and *declaration of* your ready mind.)

19. And who was chosen by the churches to go with us in this ministration of your charity to the Jews, that God may have the glory of this notified concord of Jewish and Gentile Christians, and of your ready minds to so good a work.

20. Avoiding this, that no man should blame us in this abundance, which is administered by us; 21. Providing for honest things, not only in the sight of the Lord, but also in the sight of men.

20. 21. For I took care to avoid all occasion of suspicion, that I should detain any of this large contribution to myself, or unfaithfully distribute it: providing that all be done decently and blamelessly in the sight of men, as well as faithfully in the sight of God.

22. And we have sent with them our brother, whom we have oftentimes proved diligent in many things, but now much more diligent upon the great confidence which *I have* in you.

22. And with them I have sent another brother, whose diligence I have oft tried, but now find him much more willing, being encouraged by my confidence of your forwardness.

23. Whether *any do inquire* of Titus, *he is* my partner, and fellowhelper concerning you: or our brethren *be inquired of, they are* the messengers of the churches, *and* the glory of Christ.

23. If any doubting of their trustiness, inquire what these brethren are, let them know, that Titus is my partner and helper, even for your service, and the other two brethren are messengers of the churches (who would not trust untrusty men) and an honour to the Christian faith.

24. Wherefore shew ye to them, and before the churches, the proof of your love, and of our boasting on your behalf.

24. So far therefore regard them, as to let them see, and the churches, that sent them, hear the proof of your love to me, and to all saints, by your liberality, and that I have not boasted of you in vain.

Note, 1. That Paul's importunity for this collection sheweth that the case was much altered, since, in Acts iv. &c. they sold all and laid at the apostles' feet, and had all things common. And as men were quickly grown more cold, so that was not intended for a constant and universal practice, but to shew with the gift of tongues, the marvellous degree of holy love and unity which the Holy Ghost was given to effect: for to continue it every where, would have disabled them all to do much future good with riches, when all was gone. And perhaps the Christians at Jerusalem were then in greater want by that.

2. We see, that even among Christians costly duties come hardly off, (else Paul had not needed all this ado) even where gifts and parts are eminent.

3. And yet it is costly duties of charity that must prove the truth of our faith and love, which are dead, if barren.

4. We see, that a minister who seeth cause obstinately to avoid being chargeable to any of his hearers himself, lest they contemn or suspect him as a self-seeker, may yet put on confidence, and be bold and importunate in urging them to charity for others, and collections for the service o' the church and gospel.

CHAP. IX.

FOR as touching the ministring to the saints, it is superfluous for me to write to you. 2. For I know the forwardness of your mind, for which I boast of you to them of Macedonia, that Achaia was ready a year ago; and your zeal hath provoked very many.

1, 2. But to use many arguments with you, for the duty of relieving the needy saints in general, or for his contribution in particular, I suppose it needless, you being yourselves so forward to it, that I have boasted of your readiness a year ago, which hath quickened the zeal of many others.

3. Yet have I sent the brethren, lest our boasting of you should be in vain in this behalf; that, as I said, ye may be ready:

3. Yet to make sure, I have sent the brethren, lest it be to do when I come, and my boasting of you fail.

4. Lest haply if they of Macedonia come with me, and find you unprepared, we (that we say not you) should be ashamed in this same confident boasting.

4. For I would not have them of Macedonia, if they come with me, by finding your collection unready, think that you are unwilling, to your dishonour and mine that boasted of you.

Note, That it is lawful to use an honest craft to draw men to their duty, 1. By engaging their reputation in it: 2. And by alluring them by just praise.

5. Therefore I thought it necessary to exhort the brethren, that they would go before unto you, and make up beforehand your bounty, whereof ye had notice before, that the same might be ready as a *matter of* bounty, and not as of covetousness.

5. Therefore I sent these three brethren, to desire you that it might be ready, (you having notice of it also heretofore) that it may appear to be of willing liberality, and not extorted from covetous men.

6. But this *I say*, He which soweth sparingly, shall reap also sparingly; and he which soweth bountifully, shall reap also bountifully.

6. As to the proportion, I will say but this; all shall reap in that measure that they sow.

Note, That Paul's disclaiming justification by works, consisteth with this doctrine, That all men shall be rewarded not only according to the sincerity of their hearts, but also according to the degrees of their obedient will and works.

7. Every man according as he purposeth in his heart, *so let him give;* not grudgingly, or of necessity: for God loveth a cheerful giver.

7. Let your will command you in the proportion: do it not grudgingly, and as urged and constrained against your wills; but as you are truly willing: for God loveth a cheerful giver, and not the outward deed only, which is against or without the will.

8. And God *is* able to make all grace abound towards you; that ye having always all sufficiency in all things, may abound to every good work:

8. And it should take off all unwillingness, to consider, that God is all sufficient to give you by his blessing such abundance, that you shall always have enough to furnish you for good works, as well as to supply your own necessities.

9. (As it is written, He hath dispersed abroad; he hath given to the poor: his righteousness, remaineth for ever.

9. For God hath promised in his description of the righteous, Psal. cxii. That he will so bless him that is charitable and liberal in good works, that he shall prosper, and have supply from God, for all that he requireth of him, and shall for ever be rewarded for it, as for that which is part of his personal righteousness.

10. Now he that ministereth seed to the sower, both minister bread for your food, and multiply your

seed sown, and increase the fruits of your righteousness.).

10. And this is my benediction and prayer for you, That God. who giveth both seed and increase, will supply all your wants, and bless your liberality with the increase of his gifts, and the fruits of this your righteousness to yourselves.

11. Being enriched in every thing to all bountifulness, which causeth through us thanksgiving to God.

11. That you may be enriched by him in all things, so as to feed your bounty, which when we distribute, will make many thankful to God.

12. For the administration of this service, not only supplieth the want of the saints, but is abundant also by many thanksgivings unto God;

12. For the distribution of your charity will not only supply the saints' necessities, but also cause them to give thanks to God, who sendeth them his mercies by the hands of men.

13. (Whiles by the experiment of this ministration, they glorify God for your professed subjection unto the gospel of Christ, and for your liberal distribution unto them, and unto all men.)

13. The distribution of your gift will be a convincing experiment to the Jews, that the Gentiles are converted to a loving union with them, and are sincerely subject to the gospel, and that your faith is not barren, but effectual and fruitful.

14. And by their prayer for you, which long after you, for the exceeding grace of God in you.

14. And it will provoke them to pray for you, who greatly value you, for the abundant grace of God, which sheweth itself by such evident fruit.

15. Thanks *be* unto God for his unspeakable gift.

15. And as gifts and grace, wealth and willing minds, are all the unspeakable gifts of God, to him we return our chiefest thanks.

CHAP. X.

NOW I Paul myself beseech you, by the meekness and gentleness of Christ, who in presence *am* base among you, but being absent am bold toward you. 2. But I beseech you that I may not be bold when I am present, with that confidence wherewith I think to be bold against some which think on us, as if we walked according to the flesh.

1, 2. And having pleaded with you for the poor Christians in Judea, let me next speak for myself. Though some among you report, that my bold speech to you is only by letters, and that my presence is contemptible; I will by this letter also use the meekness and gentleness which is according to the command and example of Christ, in beseeching you not to put me to use that boldness that else I must do against them that calumniate my ministry as carnal and self-seeking.

3. For though we walk in the flesh, we do not war after the flesh:

3. For though we yet dwell in the body, our ministry and life are not from carnal principles, to carnal ends, nor by carnal means.

4. (For the weapons of our warfare *are* not carnal, but mighty through God, to the pulling down of strong holds)

4. For it is not bribes, or swords, or outward violence, but more powerful arms, by which we better and cast down the fortresses of sin and Satan.

5. Casting down imaginations, and every high thing that exalteth itself against the knowledge of God, and bringing into captivity every thought to the obedience of Christ;

5. It is not men's estates or bodies that we conquer by fines, imprisonments, or captivity; but even the conceits. opinions, and imaginations of men's minds, the logic of cavillers, the philosophy of opposers, the pride of Jews and Gentiles, and all their misapprehensions of the Christian verity, and opposition against it, and bringing their thoughts and minds into subjection to Christ.

6. And having in readiness to revenge all disobedience, when your obedience is fulfilled.

6. And though we call not for fire from heaven to revenge ourselves, and gratify our passions; yet when the church is settled in their obedience, so that the wheat may be separated from the tares, God who hath furnished me with authority, will not deny me ability to inflict such penalties as he judgeth fit for the impenitent, by delivering them to Satan.

7. Do ye look on things after the outward appearance? if any man trust to himself that he *is* Christ's, let him of himself think this again, that as he *is* Christ's, even so *are* we Christ's.

7. Do you judge by means outward appearance and ostentation, and judge of me by the meanness of my garb, and bodily stature, and aspect? If it be pretence of any gifts or authority from

Christ, which puffeth up these men, let them consider whether we have not as much of these from Christ to shew as they?

8. For though I would boast somewhat more of our authority, (which the Lord hath given us for edification, and not for your destruction) I should not be ashamed:

8. If I should say, that I can shew more authority from Christ than they can, I should not be ashamed, as unable to prove it: (yet we pretend to none that is destructive and hurtful to the church, or any of the brethren; but only to such power as is to edify and do good.)

9. That I may not seem as if I would terrify you by letters. 10. For *his* letters (say they) *are* weighty and powerful, but *his* bodily presence *is* weak, and *his* speech contemptible.

9, 10. I will not seem to terrify you by letters, contrary to what I say in presence; though my accusers say, that my bodily presence and speech are contemptible, and not answerable to my letters.

Note, That tradition tells us, that Paul, (according to his name) was a man of a very little stature, and his voice answerably small; and it may be that hence they raised this report of his presence and speech.

11. Let such an one think this, that such as we are in word by letters, when we are absent, such *will we be* also in deed when we are present.

11. But let such believe, that when I come, my deeds shall be as awful as my words are.

Note, That the thing which Paul would have his accusers fear, was, that by the miraculous gift of the Holy Ghost they should speed as Elymas did.

12. For we dare not make ourselves of the number, or compare ourselves with some that commend themselves: but they measuring themselves by themselves, and comparing themselves amongst themselves, are not wise.

12. I will not imitate them in self-commendation and comparisons: but it is their folly and self-deceit, to measure themselves by their own self-conceit, and compare themselves with their own followers, not knowing the grace of God in others.

13. But we will not boast of things without *our* measure, but according to the measure of the rule which God hath distributed to us, a measure to reach even unto you.

13. But I will not boast of any thing done beyond the province and measure of gifts assigned, and vouchsafed to us of God, as those that would reap the praise of other men's labours; but of that which God hath really done by us, of which yourselves are part of our witnesses.

14. For we stretch not ourselves beyond *our measure*, as though we reached not unto you; for we are come as far as to you also, in *preaching* the gospel of Christ:

14. You know, that when I extend my boasting even to you, that I boast not of that which I never performed: for you are my witnesses, as being the fruits of my ministry.

15. Not boasting of things without *our* measure, *that is*, of other men's labours: but having hope when your faith is increased, that we shall be enlarged by you according to our rule abundantly,

15. I boast not of labour in another man's province, and of other men's performance (as these do;) but I hope that the increase of your faith will be the increase of my advantage, and of my comfort and reward, whoever helpeth you, it being the fruit and increase of the seed which I sowed.

16. To preach the gospel in the *regions* beyond you, *and* not to boast in another man's line of things made ready to our hand.

16. I hope by your increase to have the better opportunity to carry the gospel beyond you, to the regions that have not yet received it; and not to boast, as entering on other men's labours.

17. But he that glorieth, let him glory in the Lord.

17. But let us all take heed that we glory not in ourselves, but purely in God, and for God, that we do his work, and promote his kingdom and honour in the world.

18. For not he that commendeth himself is approved, but whom the Lord commendeth.

18. Self-condemnation is no just praise, (but a detection and shame of pride and folly.) But it is God's approbation and praise which is our real honour.

CHAP. XI.

WOULD to God you could bear with me a little in *my* folly; and indeed bear with me. 2. For I am jealous over you with godly jealousy: for I have espoused you to one husband, that I may present *you as* a chaste virgin to Christ.

1, 2. I would you could bear a little with that which is like to foolish boasting: yea, you must bear with me, because it is from a godly jealousy of love to you, for Christ's sake, to whom I did espouse you as chaste and peculiar to him.

3. But I fear, lest by any means as the serpent beguiled Eve through his subtilty, so your minds should be corrupted from the simplicity that is in Christ.

3. But I fear, lest by the craft and fair pretences of them that tell you of a more sublime degree of knowledge, as the serpent by subtilty beguiled Eve, by telling her that they should be as God, knowing good and evil: so your minds should be corrupted, while you think that they are edified, by forsaking that Christian simplicity and purity, which is the true wisdom.

Note, 1. That fair promises and beginnings may end in foul corruptions.

2. Forsaking Christian simplicity, is the corruption of minds and churches. That is, 1. Turning from the simple doctrine of the creed, and things necessary and sure, to vain curiosities, and uncertain assertions and contentions, on pretence of orthodoxness, or of higher knowledge. 2. From the simplicity of worship, to ludicrous human ceremonies and formalities. 3. From the simplicity of discipline, to tyranny and domination, and ensnaring unnecessary canons and customs, imposed on the churches. 4. From the simplicity of Christian love and conversation, to segregate sects, and to partiality, and self-seeking worldly craft.

3. Pretended extraordinary knowledge is one of Satan's methods to corrupt the church.

4. For if he that cometh, preacheth another Jesus whom we have not preached, or *if* ye receive another spirit, which ye have not received, or another gospel, which ye have not accepted, ye might well bear with *him.*

4. It is one Christ, one spirit, and one gospel, that we have preached, and you received: if your new pretended teachers have another Christ, and spirit, and gospel to preach, and can give better proof of what they say, than I have done for the Christ, Spirit, and Gospel which I have preached, let them shew it, and let them be borne with and received.

5. For I suppose I was not a whit behind the very chiefest apostles. 6. But though *I be* rude in speech, yet not in knowledge; but we have been throughly made manifest among you in all things.

5, 6. I suppose that I have no way come short of those that are the most eminent apostles: If my speech be as mean and rude as they object, so is not my knowledge, (which is the thing that they pretend to excel in.) But sure I need not tell you of this, who have had the proof of it in my ministry to yourselves.

7. Have I committed an offence in abasing myself, that you might be exalted, because I have preached to you the gospel of God freely?

7. Is it my offence, that forbearing the ostentation of learning called wisdom, I have preached the gospel of the cross according to your capacity, and that without putting you to charge, by taking any maintenance from you?

8. I robbed other churches, taking wages *of them* to do you service. 9. And when I was present with you and wanted, I was chargeable to no man: for that which was lacking to me, the brethren which came from Macedonia supplied: and in all things I have kept myself from being burdensome unto you, and *so* will I keep *myself.*

8, 9. I did that which had been partiality and robbing, had there not been just cause, &c.

Note, That 1, One church ought to contribute to the furtherance of the gospel to others.

2. This is a close reproof of the Corinthians, whom Paul saw so covetous, or suspicious of him, that if he had made himself beholden to them, he had crossed the ends of his ministry.

10. As the truth of Christ is in me, no man shall stop me of this boasting in the regions of Achaia.

10. And that you may not think I am covetous, or like to burden you, I solemnly protest, that I will not in Achaia give away this advantage of serving you freely knowing what occasion some among you would else take to reproach my ministry.

Note, If it was so meritorious in Paul to serve them freely, what a sort of people are they among us, that reproach that ministry that would, instead of burdening them, give oven their own estates to the poor, as well as their labours?

11. Wherefore? because I love you not? God knoweth. 12. But what I do, that I will do, that I may cut off occasion from them which desire occasion, that wherein they glory, they may be found even as we.

11, 12. This it not, God knoweth, because I love you not; but because I know how some men watch for an occasion to accuse us; which I will cut off from them, that they may not have an advantage to boast on this account.

CHAP. XI.   II. CORINTHIANS.   425

Note, It is most likely that these accusers of Paul were some rich men, that complied with the times for interest, and took no pay of the churches, but deceived them freely, and reproached Paul as a poor indigent fellow, that preached for bread.

13. For such *are* false apostles, deceitful workers, transforming themselves into the apostles of Christ.

13. For these false apostles are deceitful workers, pretending that they are Christ's apostles, and acting as if they were such indeed.

Note, It is no wonder then if there be swarms of false ministers, pretending to be the true ministers of Christ.

14. And no marvel; for Satan himself is transformed into an angel of light.

14. And no marvel, when Satan doth but teach them to do as he doth, who counterfeiteth an angel of light, and bringeth in error and sin by boldly pretending that it is light, and extraordinary knowledge and virtue.

15. Therefore *it is* no great thing if his ministers also be transformed as the ministers of righteousness; whose end shall be according to their works.

15. Therefore it is not an incredible thing, that men should be really the devil's ministers, animated and taught by him to do his work, against the interest of Christ, and truth, and godliness; and yet pretend to go beyond Christ's own apostles in preaching righteousness, wisdom, and godliness.

Note, That the pretences of truth, orthodoxness, righteousness, free grace, unity, peace, &c are no sufficient evidences of true ministers. The devil's ministers may pretend them all, and may cry down Christ's ministers as carnal, heretics, legal, schismatics, &c.

16. I say again, Let no man think me a fool: if otherwise, yet as a fool receive me, that I may boast myself a little.

16. Take it not for folly to vindicate my ministry: but if you do, yet hear me, try, and judge.

Note, That Paul meaneth, that boasting is the usual mark of a fool; but it is no folly, when the interest of God and souls require it: it was seemingly, not really, his folly.

17. That which I speak, I speak *it* not after the Lord, but as it were foolishly in this confidence of boasting.

17. That which I speak of myself, I speak not as I do the gospel by inspiration; and I confess that materially it hath the appearance of folly in ostentation.

18. Seeing that many glory after the flesh, I will glory also. 19. For ye suffer fools gladly, seeing ye *yourselves* are wise. 20. For ye suffer if a man bring you into bondage, if a man devour you, if a man take *of you,* if a man exalt himself, if a man smite you on the face.

18, 19, 20. You can easily bear with a fool, because you are wise yourselves: so bear with me, while I do that necessarily, which they do vainly. You can bear with greater provocations, even with them that would captivate you to error and the law, and would make a prey of you, and make themselves your lords and masters and abuse you.

21. I speak as concerning reproach, as though we had been weak: howbeit, wherein soever any is bold (I speak foolishly) I am bold also.

21. I speak of them that reproach me of contemptible weakness: though I confess, that boasting usually signifieth folly, I will say, that I have as much as them to boast of.

Note, That Paul is so cautious lest any by his example should be tempted by proud boasting, that materially he calls it folly, though formally it was not so in him.

22. Are they Hebrews? so *am* I: are they Israelites? so *am* I: are they the seed of Abraham? so *am* I: 23. Are they ministers of Christ? (I speak as a fool) I *am* more: in labours more abundant, in stripes above measure, in prisons more frequent, in deaths oft.

22, 23. They boast that they are Hebrews, Israelites, Abraham's seed, and ministers of Christ: and am not I so too? Yea, though my words be like those of a fool, I say, that I have laboured and suffered more for Christ, by stripes, prisons, and daily dying, than they have done.

24. Of the Jews five times received I forty *stripes* save one. 25. Thrice was I beaten with rods; once was I stoned; thrice I suffered shipwreck; a night and day I have been in the deep:

24, 25. Scourged by the Jews to the utmost severity, beaten by the Romans, stoned by the rabble, thrice shipwrecked, a night and a day in some darksome dangerous passage at sea, (or a dungeon so called, as some think.)

26. In journeying often, in perils of waters, in perils of robbers, in perils by mine own countrymen, in

perils by the heathen, in perils in the city, in perils in the wilderness, in perils in the sea, in perils among false brethren; 27. In weariness and painfulness, in watchings often, in hunger and thirst, in fastings often, in cold and nakedness.

26, 27. *Note,* That the sufferings which deter carnal men from religion by shame and fear, are the honour of believers.

28. Besides those things that are without, that which cometh upon me daily, the care of all the churches.

28. Besides the things that are without my body, even the case of all the churches, which are my daily care.

29. Who is weak, and I am not weak? who is offended, and I burn not?

29. Every man's weakness and sufferings are to me as my own: the danger of the tempted and scandalized is my pain and care for their preservation.

30. If I must needs glory, I will glory of the things which concern mine infirmities.

30. If you will put me to boast, it shall be of that which worldly men will turn to my reproach; not of any pre-eminence, but of my sufferings.

31. The God and Father of our Lord Jesus Christ, which is blessed for evermore, knoweth that I lie not. 32. In Damascus the governor under Aretas the king, kept the city of the Damascenes with a garrison, desirous to apprehend me: 33. And through a window in a basket was I let down by the wall, and escaped his hands.

1. *Note,* That through all this chapter Paul calls his boasting folly, not formally and really, but materially and seemingly, because it is fools that boast unnecessarily; when the false apostles made it his duty.

2. *Note,* That it was no small quarrel of brethren, (like that of Barnabas) which put him upon all this apology, (which else would not have savoured of humility;) but it was the intrusion and envious accusation of such Jewish, heretical, false apostles, as he calleth the ministers of Satan, who endeavoured to subvert the gospel, and by disgracing him, to frustrate all his labours, and destroy the church: it is like to be those called Nicolaitans, Rev. ii. and iii.

CHAP. XII.

IT is not expedient for me doubtless to glory: I will come to visions and revelations of the Lord.

1. I know that boasting is unseemly for an humble minister of Christ: but seeing it is put upon me, I proceed to a higher matter, even visions and revelations from God.

2. I knew a man in Christ, above fourteen years ago (whether in the body, I cannot tell: or whether out of the body, I cannot tell: God knoweth) such an one caught up to the third heaven. 3. And I knew such a man (whether in the body, or out of the body, I cannot tell: God knoweth) 4. How that he was caught up into paradise, and heard unspeakable words, which it is not lawful for a man to utter.

2, 3, 4. I knew a man that was acted by the Spirit of Christ above himself, who above fourteen years ago (whether bodily, or only by mental ecstasy and rapture, I know not, God knoweth) was caught up to that place of glory, called the third heavens, and caught up there into paradise, a place of joys, and heard that which neither can nor must be uttered, being unsuitable to the ears of mortals, and proper to possessors.

5. Of such an one will I glory: yet of myself I will not glory, but in mine infirmities.

5. I think this foretaste of the heavenly glory, worthy to be gloried in: but (though I be the man) I will not glory in it as my own, who was but passive, and advanced to it by God, to whom all the glory is due. It is my infirmities, or debasing sufferings in the world, which I will call my own, and boast of.

6. For though I would desire to glory, I shall not be a fool; for I will say the truth: but *now* I forbear, lest any man should think of me above that which he seeth me *to be,* or *that* he heareth of me.

6. Should I boast of this so great a gift, to the glory of the giver, it would be no folly: but I lay it by, expecting that no man judge more highly of me, than by what himself shall see or hear.

7. And lest I should be exalted above measure through the abundance of the revelations, there was given to me a thorn in the flesh, the messenger of Satan to buffet me, lest I should be exalted above measure.

7. And lest this revelation should too much lift me up, there was given me a thorn in the flesh, the messenger of Satan put me to pain, and keep me from too much exaltation.

Note, 1. It is most unlikely which some *feign* to be the sense of these words, viz. That it was a temptation to lust: it is most likely it was such a pain as the stone, or at least some bitter persecution.

2. Even the holiest Christians, after their most heavenly acquaintance, are not out of danger of pride, or being too much exalted.

3. This spiritual pride is so dangerous a sin, that it is a mercy to be saved from it, even by bodily pain.

4. God will hurt the bodies, to save the souls, even of his dearest children.

5. Satan, that intendeth hurt, is oft God's instrument to do us good.

6. Bodily pains are oft the messengers of Satan, and yet of God.

8. For this thing I besought the Lord thrice, that it might depart from me.

8. Note, 1. That it is lawful to pray for the removal of pain; 2. Yea, to be oft in prayer for it.

9. And he said unto me, My grace is sufficient for thee: for my strength is made perfect in weakness?

9. And the answer which I had was not a present removal of the thorn, but a word for patience and trust in God, viz. That his favour and grace was sufficient for me, to support and comfort me till deliverance came; and that it is his way, in our weakness to manifest most his helping power.

9. Most gladly, therefore, will I rather glory in my infirmities, that the power of Christ may rest upon me. 10. Therefore I take pleasure in infirmities, in reproaches, in necessities, in persecutions, in distresses for Christ's sake: for when I am weak, then am I strong.

9, 10. It is therefore in sufferings that I will glory, as being the occasion of my greater experience of the love and power of Christ: yea, I even take pleasure in abasing sufferings for him, though not as painful, yet as an advantage to his grace that strengtheneth me; so far am I from being ashamed or impatient of them.

11. I am become a fool in glorying, ye have compelled me: for I ought to have been commended of you: for in nothing am I behind the very chiefest apostles, though I be nothing.

11. I have said all this as in the habit of a fool: but it is you that put it on me, by necessity, who should have vindicated me and my ministry against seducing accusers.

12. Truly the signs of an apostle were wrought among you in all patience, in signs, and wonders, and mighty deeds.

12. Are not you my witnesses? I appeal to yourselves: Among you my apostleship was fully proved, by patient suffering, and by miraculous gifts, and signs, and wonders, and works, done by the power of God.

13. For what is it wherein ye were inferior to other churches, except *it be* that I myself was not burdensome to you? forgive me this wrong.

13. For what gifts of the Spirit poured out among you? what signs and miracles have other churches excelled you in? The difference between you and others was, that I spared your purses, and put you to no charge: If that be a wrong, I hope you can easily forgive it.

14. Behold, the third time I am ready to come to you; and I will not be burthensome to you; for I seek not yours, but you: for the children ought not to lay up for the parents, but the parents for the children.

14. A third time I purpose to come to you, and not to burthen you, but as to my children, to give, rather than to receive.

15. And I will very gladly spend and be spent for you, though the more abundantly I love you, the less I be loved.

15. I will gladly spend my time and labour, and be spent myself, even as to my strength and life, for your salvation, though my love should be requited with neglect.

16. But be it so, I did not burden you: nevertheless being crafty, I caught you with guile. 17. Did I make a gain of you by any of them whom I sent unto you?

16, 17. But be it as some object, that though I took no money of you, I craftily caught you with guile, that getting your affections, I might hereafter make advantage of you for myself: But my craft was but to win you to Christ. Did I make a gain of you, by any of them whom I sent unto you? Will you judge of my design contrary to my practice?

18. I desired Titus, and with *him* I sent a brother: did Titus make again of you? walked we not in the same spirit! *walked we* not in the same steps?

18. Did Titus, or the brother whom I sent to you, make a gain of you? Did we not all agree in mind and practice?

19. Again, think you that we

excuse ourselves unto you? we speak before God in Christ; but *we do* all things, dearly beloved, for your edifying.

19. Think not that I say all this to insinuate myself into your esteem for any by ends of my own: I speak it as before God in Christ; it is your edification that is my end in this and all things that I do concerning you.

20. For I fear, lest when I come I shall not find you such as I would, and *that* I shall be found unto you such as ye would not: lest *there be* debates, envyings, wraths, strifes, backbitings, whisperings, swellings, tumults: 21. *And* lest when I come again, my God will humble me among you, and that I shall bewail many which have sinned already, and have not repented of the uncleanness, and fornication, and laciviousness which they have committed.

20, 21. For I fear lest when I come I shall find among you these sins, which are the characters of factious minds, debates, &c. and lest God will humble me among you with grief for you, and mourning over the impenitent, that have been guilty of those filthy sins, which deceivers and idol feasts have drawn them to; and lest I be forced to be unwelcome to such persons.

Note, 1. Though Paul seems to contradict himself in praising the Corinthians so largely in the beginning of this epistle, and describing them so ill in the end: yet, 1. It is not the same persons that he praiseth and dispraiseth, though of the same church. 2. We must praise all that is good in men, when we reprove the evil.

Note, 2. That the very characters of factious seduced professors, are the sins here named, which therefore we should specially abhor: 1. Debates, 2. Envying zeal, 3. Wraths, 4. Strifes, 5. Backbitings, 6. Whisperings, 7. Swellings against each other, 8. Tumults, Yet it is very notable, that notwithstanding all these corruptions, and abuses, and filthy scandals, Paul neither separateth, nor persuadeth any to separate; but leaveth that to the heretical, who used to separate themselves into distinct bodies, for the promoting of their opinions and parties.

CHAP. XIII.

THIS *is* the third time I am coming to you: In the mouth of two or three witnesses shall every word be established.

1. As the testimony of two or three witnesses confirmeth questioned truth, so my second and third admonition warneth you, to prevent severity.

2. I told you before, and foretel you as if I were present the second time, and being absent, now I write to them which heretofore have sinned, and to all other, that if I come again I will not spare:

2. Though I be absent, my writing may pass for warning as if I were present, by which I foretel you, that if I come, I will not forbear to exercise on the impenitent the power given me by Christ.

3. Since ye seek a proof of Christ speaking in me, which to you-ward is not weak, but is mighty in you.

3. And seeing you call for a proof of Christ's speaking in me, you shall have this farther proof (the corporal punishment of the impenitent by miracle or Satan's execution:) Though sure the power of Christ attesting my ministry, hath been so fully manifested among you, that you should have been thereby convinced.

4. For though he was crucified through weakness, yet he liveth by the power of God: for we also are weak in him, but we shall live with him by the power of God toward you.

4. For as Christ in the state of human weakness was crucified, but by divine power was raised, and liveth; so, as we are conformed to him in weakness and suffering, we shall shew you that we partake of the power of God in our life and ministry.

5. Examine yourselves, whether ye be in the faith, prove your ownselves: know you not your ownselves, *how* that Jesus Christ is in you, except ye be reprobates?

5. If you question my ministry, do but examine yourselves, whether you be Christians or not: If you are, was it not by the convincing power of God's attestation to my ministry? and do you question that which converted you? If not, you are yet without a Saviour, and in your sins: And if you deny Christ in you, and his power shewed among you, you may expect that he will deny you.

6. But I trust that ye shall know that we are not reprobates.

6. And I trust that you shall be convinced that we have not forsaken Christ, nor shall be cast off or forsaken by him.

7. Now I pray to God that ye do no evil; not that we should appear approved, but that ye should

do that which is honest, though we be as reprobates.

7. My prayer is, that you may be saved from sin and seduction, not so much that you may think well of us, but that you may do that which is right, how ill soever you think of us.

8. For we can do nothing against the truth, but for the truth.

8. For as we have no authority or commission to do any thing against the truth, but only for it; so we have no desire to do otherwise.

9. For we are glad when we are weak, and ye are strong: and this also we wish, even your perfection.

9. For how much soever we be vilified or afflicted, it is our joy that you are strong, and that it is better with you: yea, it is your perfection that is our desire.

10. Therefore I write these things being absent, lest being present I should use sharpness, according to the power which the Lord hath given me to edification, and not to destruction.

10. It is to prevent severity when I am present, and the trouble that you and I shall have in penalties on you, that I give you this admonition by letter: still professing, That Christ hath given me no power of tyranny, or against your own good, but only for your edification. Should I claim any other, it is not of Christ.

11. Finally, brethren, farewel: Be perfect, be of good comfort, be of one mind, live in peace; and the God of love and peace shall be with you.

11. My concluding valediction is, Be compact together in holy union; Rejoice in the Lord; Be of one mind in faith and love, though you cannot in lesser things; Live in peace; and then he that would be known to us as the God of love and peace, will be among you.

12. Greet one another with an holy kiss. 13. All the saints salute you. 14. The grace of our Lord Jesus Christ, and the love of God, and the communion of the Holy Ghost, be with you all. Amen.

12, 13, 14. Express Christian love to one another. The saints here salute you. The highest blessing I can wish you, is, The grace of Christ, the love of God, and communication of, and communion in the Holy Spirit. Amen.

Note, Out of all this epistle, That though proud tenderness of our reputation be a sin, yet it is a duty to vindicate it when the interest of the gospel and of souls requires it; which it did more with an apostle, than an ordinary minister.

THE EPISTLE OF PAUL THE APOSTLE, TO THE GALATIANS.

INTRODUCTION.

THE scope of this epistle is to reduce the Galatians, who began to be seduced by those Judaizers, that would have not only joined Moses's law to Christianity, but also would have put that yoke on the Gentile Christians; and it is most likely some heretics joined with them. To which end he sharply reproveth the unsteadfastness of the Galatians; evinceth the non-obligation of that law, and the carnality of judaizing, and the spirituality of the gospel; and that he had his gospel by immediate inspiration from Christ; and that it is not singular from the other apostles, nor dissonant to itself, nor to his condescending practice with the Jews.

CHAP. I.

PAUL an apostle (not of men, neither by man, but by Jesus Christ, and God the Father, who raised him from the dead) 2. And all the brethren which are with me, unto the churches of Galatia: 3. Grace *be* to you, and peace from God the Father, and *from* our Lord Jesus Christ.

1, 2, 3. Paul an apostle, not of men, nor called by men, but by Christ from heaven, and by his revelation, attested by the power of God the Father, who raised him from the dead; and all the brethren with me: To the churches of Galatia we wish grace and peace from God the Father, and our Lord Jesus Christ.

Note, That Paul mentions not [the church of Galatia,] but [the churches;] every city that had Christians (like our corporations) having then a church, not then put down to settle one only church, called diocesan, instead of multitudes.

4. Who gave himself for our sins, that he might deliver us from this present evil world, according to the will of God and our Father: 5. To whom *be* glory for ever and ever. Amen.

4, 5. Who by dying for our sins, designed to call us out of the world, and save us from the temptations, vices, examples, and practices of wicked and worldly men. To him be glory for ever and ever. Amen.

6. I marvel that ye are so soon removed from him that called you into the grace of Christ, unto another gospel:

6. I marvel that you, who voluntarily received the truth from me, are so soon turned from the gospel of the grace of Christ, to another doctrine contrary to this grace, as if it were the gospel.

7. Which is not another; but there be some that trouble you, and would pervert the gospel of Christ.

7. Which is far from being Christ's gospel, contrary to my preaching, as they pretend; but it is the doctrine of men that would trouble you, and would pervert the gospel of Christ.

8. But though we, or an angel from heaven, preach any other gospel unto you, than that which we have preached unto you, let him be accursed. 9. As we said before, so say I now again, If any *man* preach any other gospel unto you, than that you have received, let him be accursed.

8, 9. But I pronounce and repeat it, If I, yea or an angel from heaven, if any man pretend to preach to you any other gospel than that which we have preached, or you received, let him be

Anathema, renounce him as an excommunicate and accursed person.

Note, 1. That there is no other gospel to be expected, besides that communicated to us by the apostles, and recorded in the scripture. The dream of a more perfect gospel of the Holy Ghost, is wicked.

2. That this gospel has fuller evidence than if an angel spake from heaven, and is to be believed before, or against such an angel.

3. That it is the people's duty to reject and forsake any teacher that would bring another gospel or pervert this: not as church governors, but as subjects of Christ, that must be loyal to him, and save themselves.

10. For do I now persuade men, or God? or do I seek to please men? for if yet I pleased men, I should not be the servant of Christ.

10. Do I now preach the doctrine of men, on man's authority, to please men; or the word of God, by his authority, to please him? Am I the messenger and preacher of man, or of God? Which do I serve, and seek to please? For if I please men as their servant, I am none of Christ's servant.

11. But I certify you, brethren, that the gospel which was preached of me, is not after man.

11. I would have you know, that the gospel which I preach is not human, from man, nor on man's authority, nor to gratify the will or worldly interest of man.

12. For I neither received it of man, neither was I taught it but by the revelation of Jesus Christ.

12. I learned it not from any human teacher, nor took it on human authority, but from Christ's revelation.

13. For ye have heard of my conversation in time past, in the Jews religion, *how* that beyond measure I persecuted the church of God, and wasted it: 14. And profited in the Jews religion, above many my equals in mine own nation, being more exceeding zealous of the traditions of my fathers.

13, 14. You have heard how I formerly unmeasurably persecuted and wasted the church, through excess of zeal for the tradition of my fathers, and religion of the Jews, &c.

15. But when it pleased God, who separated me from my mother's womb, and called *me* by his grace, 16. To reveal his son in me, that I might preach him among the heathen.

15, 16. But when it pleased God, who by his free electing grace decreed me to know Christ first myself, and then preach him to the heathens, which was a kind of separating me to it from the womb, and when he called me hereto by his mere grace.

16, 17. Immediately I conferred not with flesh and blood: Neither went I up to Jerusalem, to them which were apostles before me; but I went into Arabia, and returned again unto Damascus.

16, 17. I stayed not to consult with any man, but presently preached the gospel; nor went I up to Jerusalem, to learn of the apostles there what to preach, but, &c.

18. Then after three years I went up to Jerusalem, to see Peter, and abode with him fifteen days. 19. But other of the apostles saw I none, save James the Lord's brother.

18, 19. It was three years after before I went to Jerusalem, and stayed fifteen days with Peter, &c.

Note, 1. That though Luke, Acts ix. 26, put Paul's coming up to Jerusalem near his conversion, and mentions not expressly his three years absence, or being in Arabia; yet the brevity of the history proveth not the shortness of the time: And it was not three years after his going from Damascus, but after his conversion. And Luke, Acts ix. 23, saith, that it was after much time that he went from Damascus (which belonged to Arabia;) so that it is like that he spent the three years at or near Damascus; and when he was escaped, went presently to Jerusalem.

2. And though it may seem that three years had been time enough to have satisfied the church at Jerusalem of Paul's conversion, yet it seems that he spent that time in Arabia and Damascus, to avoid the rage of his countrymen at Jerusalem, and so his remoteness occasioned their dissatisfaction.

20. Now the things which I write unto you, behold, before God, I lie not. 21. Afterwards I came into the regions of Syria and Cilicia; 22. And was unknown by face unto the churches of Judea, which were in Christ: 23. But they had heard only, That he which persecuted us in times past, now preacheth the faith which once he destroyed. 24. And they glorified God in me.

Note, All this Paul writeth to prove that he received not the gospel from the apostles, or any man, but immediately from Christ.

CHAP. II.

THEN fourteen years after, I went up again to Jerusalem, with Barnabas, and took Titus with me also. 2. And I went up by revelation, and communicated unto them that gospel which I preach among the Gentiles, but privately to them which were of reputation, lest by any means I should run, or had run in vain.

1, 2. Fourteen years after my conversion, I went again to Jerusalem, &c. and told them what doctrine I preached, and with what success: But severally and privately to the eminent apostles, that avoiding offence both of Jews and Gentiles, I might not frustrate my labours to either of them.

3. But neither Titus, who was with me, being a Greek, was compelled to be circumcised. 4. And that because of false brethren unawares brought in, who came in privily to spy out our liberty which we have in Christ Jesus, that they might bring us into bondage.

3, 4. And I would not yield that Titus should be circumcised, because some false brethren crept in to take advantage of the liberty I used in compliance with the Jews, to take occasion by it to bring us into bondage to the Mosaic law, and turn our liberty into necessity, and to plead, that conformity to it is our duty, because in some degree and case we yielded to it as lawful, at the present, to avoid a greater hurt.

5. To whom we gave place by subjection, no not for an hour: that the truth of the gospel might continue with you.

5. Note, That an outward act of compliance, which in some cases may be lawful, must not be done when it will strengthen church-tyrants and deceivers, who by making it necessary, would turn Christian liberty into bondage.

6. But of these, who seemed to be somewhat (whatsoever they were, it maketh no matter to me: God accepteth no man's person) for they who seemed *to be somewhat*, in conference added nothing to me.

6. But even Peter, James, and John, who were the chief men, and of reputation, (God tieth not his grace to the dignity of men's persons, therefore my case dependeth not on their worth:) I say, in conference they added nothing to me, much less taught me any other gospel than I had learned of Christ, nor found me faulty or defective in my doctrine.

7. But contrariwise, when they saw that the gospel of the uncircumcision was committed unto me, as *the gospel* of the circumcision was unto Peter; 8. (For he that wrought effectually in Peter to the apostleship of the circumcision, the same was mighty in me towards the Gentiles.) 9. And when James, Cephas, and John, who seemed to be pillars, perceived the grace that was given unto me, they gave to me and Barnabas, the right hands of fellowship; that we *should go* unto the heathen, and they unto the circumcision.

7, 8, 9. But they being satisfied that I was sent to preach to the Gentiles, as Peter was to the Jews; and that God wrought powerfully in me for the conversion of the Gentiles, as he did in Peter for the conversion of the Jews, even by many miracles; these who are justly reputed pillars, perceiving God's grace, agreed to take me and Barnabas for their fellow-labourers, and that we should preach to the heathens, and they to the Jews.

Note, That Dr. Hammond thus paraphraseth it; [into what city either of us enter,———and so constitute several congregations in each city, of Jews and Gentiles.] And he, with Grotius, say, That the two witnesses, Rev. xi. are the bishops and churches of these two sorts at Jerusalem, if so, cities had then more bishops and churches than one.

10. Only *they would* that we should remember the poor; the same which I also was forward to do.

10. That we should make collection in the Gentile churches for the Christian Jews.

Note, That besides the extraordinary famine, the Jews were generally poorer than the Gentiles; 1. Living in a poor and narrow country; 2. And having at first sold and given their lands to the common stock.

11. But when Peter was come to Antioch, I withstood him to the face, because he was to be blamed.

11. I withstood him face to face, because he was blamed (or, to be blamed) as dissembling.

12. For before that certain came from James, he did eat with the Gentiles: but when they were come he withdrew, and separated himself, fearing them which were of the circumcision. 13. And the other Jews dissembled likewise with him; insomuch that Barnabas also

was carried away with their dissimulation.

12, 13. Note, 1. That it appeareth by this, that it was then the ordinary practice of the apostles and Christians at Jerusalem to observe the law of Moses; though they absolved the Gentiles from it.

2. That Peter did this to avoid the displeasure and censure of the Jewish Christians, in compliance with their weakness, which is a lawful end.

3. That his fault lay in letting this weigh down a far greater evil on the other side, viz. the danger of bringing the Gentiles under the law of Moses, by making it seem necessary. This case is much like as if some doubtful thing should by reason or custom be imposed on Christians; and one party saith, You may do it; and another saith, You must do it, or you sin: And they that say, we may, though they know it be unnecessary, for fear of displeasing the imposers, separate from the refusers, and forbear communion with them, and thereby harden them in their error, and would ensnare the rest.

14. But when I saw that they walked not uprightly, according to the truth of the gospel, I said unto Peter before *them* all, If thou being a Jew livest after the manner of Gentiles, and not as do the Jews, why compellest thou the Gentiles to live as do the Jews?

14. When I saw that this cause was not according to the plain simplicity of the gospel, nor answered the ends of our preaching, but was the way to seduce the Gentiles to Judaism, I said to Peter before all (because the case concerned all) seeing thy own practice before the Jews came, sheweth that thou thinkest not that the Gentiles are bound to live as the Jews do after Moses's law, why dost thou now seem to tell them the contrary by thy contrary practices, as if Judaising were necessary to them.

15, 16. We *who are* Jews by nature, and not sinners of the Gentiles, knowing that a man is not justified by the works of the law, but by the faith of Jesus Christ, even we have believed in Jesus Christ; that we might be justified by the faith of Christ, and not by the works of the law: for by the works of the law shall no flesh be justified.

15, 16. We ourselves who are Jews by birth, and not the seed of heathen idolaters, yet knowing that it is not by the works of the law, but by faith in Christ, that we must be justified, have become Christians, that we might be justified by this, and not by the works of the law, which none are justified by: And shall our practice now seem to intimate the contrary, and gainsay our faith?

17. But if while we seek to be justified by Christ, we ourselves also are found sinners, *is* therefore Christ the minister of sin? God forbid.

17. For if you feign us to be sinners, and guilty of Gentilism, because we communicate with the uncircumcised, you hereby would make Christ to be our leader and teacher to sin; for it is he that taught us this: And dare you charge Christ with sin?

18. For if I build again the things which I destroyed, I make myself a transgressor.

18. For if we that have preached deliverance from the law, and that it doth not justify us, do now intimate the contrary by our practice, we confess ourselves sinners in teaching such doctrine heretofore.

19. For I through the law am dead to the law, that I might live unto God.

19. The law itself hath taught me not to trust it for justification, nor to live in the bondage of it, but to look for life towards God by Christ.

20. I am crucified with Christ: Nevertheless I live; yet not I, but Christ liveth in me: and the life which I now live in the flesh, I live by the faith of the Son of God, who loved me, and gave himself for me.

20. As Christ was crucified, and took away this wall of separation, and yoke of bondage; so I am now a member of his body, the Catholic church, and am dead to the law, and it to me: But I have a better life, by which Christ liveth in me, both objectively, as trusted, and loved; and efficiently by his Spirit. And now it is by faith in him, who loved me, and gave himself for me, that I live.

21. I do not frustrate the grace of God: for if righteousness *come* by the law, then Christ is dead in vain.

21. I do not by returning to the law, make void all the design of grace in our redemption: Christ is dead in vain, if righteousness must be by our performance of the law of Moses; for what need we then any other sacrifice for sin, or to be redeemed from its curse.

CHAP. III.

O Foolish Galatians, who hath bewitched you, that you should not obey the truth, before whose eyes Jesus Christ hath been evidently set forth, crucified among you.

1. So great is your folly in inclining to Judaism, that you seem in it as men bewitched, and deprived of reason, to turn from grace to the law so soon, when Christ crucified for your deliverance hath been so plainly preached, and set forth before you.

2. This only would I learn of you, Received ye the Spirit by the works of the law, or by the hearing of faith?

2. Do but answer me from your own experience: Have you not received the Spirit yourselves? (some for miracles, or tongues, and the sincere for sanctification:) If not, you are none of Christ's: If yea, then by what means did you receive it? Was it by the works of the law? (you will not say it:) or was it by hearing the gospel of faith?

3. Are ye so foolish? having begun in the Spirit, are ye now made perfect by the flesh?

3. Are you so foolish, as having received a spiritual doctrine, and having received and seen the gifts of the Spirit by it, which are its seal, that you should think it your growth or perfection to turn to the carnal ceremonies of the law, which gave you not the spirit?

4. Have ye suffered so many things in vain? if it be yet in vain.

4. Will you lose all the sufferings which you have undergone? If you turn to the law, you lose them all.

5. He therefore that ministereth to you the Spirit, and worketh miracles among you, *doth he it* by the works of the law, or by the hearing of faith?

5. Are the miracles that are wrought among you, and the Spirit communicated to yourselves, given from God by the ministry of the law or its works, or by the preaching of the gospel?

Note, That here is a strong evidence for the matter of fact, That the gift of the Spirit, and the working of miracles, were then things certainly existent: Else when Paul appealed to these seduced Galatians themselves, as to men that had the Spirit and these miracles among them, and that with the provoking words of [foolish and bewitched,] how easily would they have confuted him, and said, They knew of no such thing? This had been the most likely way to turn them from Christianity with scorn, to make that his proof, which, if false, must be so known to them all.

6. Even as Abraham believed God, and it was accounted to him for righteousness. 7. Know ye therefore, that they which are of faith, the same are the children of Abraham.

6, 7. As it was by believing and trusting God's promise, that Abraham was accounted righteous; so it followeth, that it is believers that are his seed as heirs of the promise.

8. And the scripture foreseeing that God would justify the heathen through faith, preached before the gospel unto Abraham, *saying*, In thee shall all nations be blessed.

8. And the scripture foretelling that God would justify the heathen, as he did Abraham, by faith, did in effect preach this gospel to him then, when it is said, [In thee shall all nations be blessed,] and therefore not the Jewish nation only.

9. So then they which be of faith, are blessed with faithful Abraham.

9. So that if the promise be made to them in Abraham, they that have the same qualification of faith, must needs be they that are blessed in him, though they keep not the law of Moses, which Abraham did not, nor the Gentile believers.

10. For as many as are of the works of the law, are under the curse: for it is written, Cursed *is* every one that continueth not in all things which are written in the book of the law to do them.

10. For all that trust for justification and life to their own doing the works of that law, and not to the free grace of God in Christ, must needs be cursed, and not justified by it: For it saith, [Cursed is every one that continueth not, &c.] which no man doth.

11. But that no man is justified by the law in the sight of God, *it is* evident: for, The just shall live by faith. 12. And the law is not of faith: but, The man that doth them, shall live in them.

11, 12. It is evident, that before God none is justified by the law: For it is said, [That the just by faith shall live:] But the law considered in itself, as distinct from the promise, doth not give life on condition of faith's receiving it as a free gift, but on condition of doing all that it commandeth. (Though the law, as subordinate to the promise, be of faith.)

13. Christ hath redeemed us from the curse of the law, being made a curse for us: for *it is* written, Cursed is every one that hangeth on a tree:

13. That law which curseth us, doth not justify us: But so doth Moses's law: and therefore came Christ to redeem us from that curse, suffering as a sacrifice for us a cursed death.

14. That the blessing of Abraham might come on the Gentiles through Jesus Christ; that we might receive the promise of the Spirit through faith.

14. That the blessing which was pronounced to Abraham as a believer, might come on all (Jews and) Gentiles, who are believers; and we might through faith, receive the promised gifts of the Holy Ghost, (as we have done.)

15. Brethren, I speak after the manner of men; Though it be but a man's covenant, yet if it be confirmed, no man disannulleth or addeth thereto. 16. Now to Abraham and his seed were the promises made. He saith not, And to seeds, as of many; but as of one. And to thy seed, which is Christ.

15, 16. Even men presume not to violate covenants: And God's promise to Abraham was to him and his seed, which immediately was Isaac, prefiguring Christ eminently: (though as all the carnal seed also sprang from Isaac, so all believers be included as springing from Christ.)

17. And this I say, *that* the covenant that was confirmed before of God in Christ, the law which was four hundred and thirty years after, cannot disannul, that it should make the promise of none effect.

17. And so the covenant to Abraham, as the father of the faithful, including a promise of Christ and his seed by faith, was not nulled by the law, which was four hundred and thirty years after; But if justification before was by faith, it must be so still, and so all true believers justified.

18. For if the inheritance *be* of the law, *it is* no more of promise: but God gave it to Abraham by promise.

18. For if the blessing meant in that covenant with Abraham be given on condition of keeping Moses's law, then cometh it not by free gift, as it did to Abraham by that promise: But God gave it freely by promise to Abraham, without his keeping that law.

19. Wherefore then *serveth* the law? It was added because of transgression, till the seed should come, to whom the promise was made; *and it was* ordained by angels in the hand of a mediator.

19. To what use then was the law given? To convince men of sin, and restrain them from it, and make them know the need of a mediating Saviour; whom Moses typified as a Mediator, in receiving the law from the ministry of Angels.

20. Now a mediator is not a mediator of one, but God is one.

20. Now mediation is between two parties:

Of these, that God is one who made the promise to Abraham, and justified him by faith, and surely is not mutable.

21. *Is* the law then against the promises of God? God forbid: for if there had been a law given which could have given life, verily, righteousness should have been by the law.

21. And hath this One God contradicted his promises by his law? By no means: Therefore he intended not that the works of the law should be our justifying righteousness; which it must have been, if it could have given life by the meritorious keeping of it: and so God should have overthrown his former way of justification.

22. But the scripture hath concluded all under sin, that the promise by faith of Jesus Christ might be given to them that believe.

22. But the scripture tells us, that all men are under the guilt of sin, and the law doth not justify sinners that break it; therefore none can be justified by it. And this it doth, to teach us to look for life by a promised Christ.

23. But before faith came, we were kept under the law, shut up unto the faith which should afterwards be revealed.

23. But before the gospel, and Christ incarnate came, which now as objects constitute our faith, we Jews were under the restraint and tutorage of the law, to teach us to wait for Christ, who is the truth and end of the law.

24. Wherefore the law was our school-master *to bring us* unto Christ, that we might be justified by faith.

24. And so the law to us Jews was suited to our youth and rudeness, to keep us as a schoolmaster in a learning and restrained state, and prepare us for the gospel, and teach us to look for justification by faith in Christ alone.

25. But after that faith is come, we are no longer under a school-master.

25. But now Christ is fully revealed to our faith, we are no longer under that preparatory tutorage of Moses's law.

26. For we are all the children of God by faith in Christ Jesus.

26. For now all you that are sincere believers, are from under the bondage of legal servile tasks and fears, and are taken into the family of God, as his adopted children by Christ, whom you believe in. And all of you profess yourselves to stand in this relation and hope.

27. For as many of you as have been baptized in Christ, have put on Christ.

27. For as many of you as have sincerely consented to the baptismal covenant, and so been baptised into the faith of Christ, and relation to him, have thereby even put him on as your garment, and wholly given up yourselves to him, and so as his members are united to him: And all that are baptised have professed this, which the sincere perform.

28. There is neither Jew nor Greek, there is neither bond nor free, there is neither male nor female: for ye are all one in Christ Jesus.

28. So that the difference between Jew and Greek, bond and free, male and female, maketh no difference in your relation to Christ, and your justification and salvation by him.

29. And if ye *be* Christ's, then are ye Abraham's seed, and heirs according to the promise.

29. And if ye be Christ's, who was eminently Abraham's seed, in whom all nations by faith are blessed, then it must needs follow, that you also are Abraham's seed in and through Christ, and so are justified as Abraham was, by faith, without the keeping of Moses's law.

CHAP. IV.

NOW I say, *that* the heir, as long as he is a child, differeth nothing from a servant, though he be lord of all; 2. But is under tutors and governors, until the time appointed of the father.

1, 2. As heirs enjoy not their estates in minority, but under guardians are used like servants till maturity;

3. Even so we, when we were children were in bondage under the elements of the world.

3. So the state of legal ceremonial bondage was suited to our rude minority.

4. But when the fulness of the time was come, God sent forth his Son made of a woman, made under the law, 5. To redeem them that were under the law, that we might receive the adoption of sons.

4, 5. But when God, who carrieth on his works from low beginnings to perfection, saw it meet to use us at maturity, he sent his Son into the world, whose humanity was made of a woman, made un- der the law, which he perfectly fulfilled, that he might redeem those that were under the law from its bondage and curse, that they might henceforth serve him as sons, not in legal terror, but in love and joy.

6. And because ye are sons, God hath sent forth the Spirit of his Son into your hearts, crying, Abba, Father.

6. And as fathers communicate their natures to their children, (and not only their names and inheritance) so God, having called you in Christ by grace into this state of adoption, from the servitude of sin and the law, hath sealed you with his sanctifying Spirit, whereby in the belief of his fatherly love to you in Christ, your new natures are inclined to love and trust him, and depend on him, and seek to him in all your wants and straits, as children to their parents. This is your mark of adoption.

Note, That as adoption is taken in two senses and degrees, so is the gift of the Spirit. 1. To be so far redeemed by Christ, as to be brought from under sin, and the law, and curse, into a state of sonship and life, by a conditional deed of gift or promise, that is, so men will accept and not reject the gift; this is a conditional adoption, and with this there goeth a measure of the Spirit's operation which should draw all, and doth draw the elect to the first true faith and repentance, by vocation.

2. But to those that thus actually believe and repent, and so receive Christ, and are united to him, is given with him the gift and relation of actual adoption; and these have actually the Spirit of holiness, love, and adoption, even possessing them.

7. Wherefore thou art no more a servant, but a son; and if a son, then an heir of God through Christ.

7. So that now you are not slaves, or mere servants, ruled by constraint of fear, and so not under the bondage of that law, which doth work by cursing terror; but you are sons, and under a fatherly government; and if sons, then have you right to the inheritance by Christ.

8. Howbeit, then when ye knew not God, ye did service unto them which by nature are no gods.

8. But before you were brought to the true knowledge of God, you Gentile Christians were the worst of slaves, serving them that are no gods at all; and the Jews thought there was no hope of you, but by becoming proselytes to them: And now Christ hath delivered both you and them.

9. But now after that ye have known God, or rather are known of God, how turn ye again to the weak and beggarly elements, whereunto ye desire again to be in bondage?

9. And now you have learned the knowledge

of God, or rather were by his free mercy known first of him, and called home by him, what should move you to incline to forsake this state of liberty, and of sons, to become servants under either Jewish or Gentile bondage, or that law whose ceremonies were suited to a poor kind weak sort of people?

10. Ye observe days, and months, and times, and years. 11. I am afraid of you, lest I have bestowed upon you labour in vain.

10, 11. You keep the Jewish ceremonial sabbaths, feasts, and fasts, as if that law were obligatory to you: This maketh me fear lest I have preached the gospel to such in vain.

12. Brethren, I beseech you, be as I am; for I am as ye are: ye have not injured me at all.

12. Brethren, reject not my counsel and example, for it is for your own interest and liberty that I speak, and not for any gain of my own: Your dissent doth not hurt me, but yourselves.

13. Ye know how through infirmity of the flesh, I preached the gospel unto you at the first. 14. And my temptation which was in my flesh ye despised not, nor rejected; *but* received me as an angel of God, even as Christ Jesus.

13, 14. You know that I was so far from seeking any ends of my own, when I first preached the gospel to you, that it cost me suffering in the flesh from persecutors: And though by this I was rendered vile in the eyes of the world, and few will own men in their sufferings, yet you did not for this despise me, or reject my doctrine; yea, you received me as you would have done an angel, or Christ himself, with kindness.

15. Where is then the blessedness you spake of? for I bear you record, that if it had been possible, ye would have plucked out your own eyes, and have given them to me.

15. How happy did you then think yourselves in the comfort of the gospel? And how is the case now altered? For I testify for you, that your respect to me was so great that you would not have thought your very eyes too dear to have given me, had it been needful.

16. Am I therefore become your enemy, because I tell you the truth.

16. And have I forfeited all your love, by telling you the truth, which speaketh your liberty and peace with God, though it may expose you to some suffering from the Jews.

17. They zealously affect you, *but* not well; yea, they would ex-

clude you, that you might affect them.

17. They solicit you with zealous expressions of love; but it is not to do you good; nor is erroneous zeal and kindness profitable; Yes, they would cast you out of your spiritual liberty and grace, that they might obtain a mastery in your erroneous affections to them.

18. But *it is* good to be zealously affected always in a good thing, and not only when I am present with you.

18. Zealous affections are good when they are laid out on that which is good: But when it should be constant, and not liable to be changed by seducers, if your teachers be but absent from you, and not at hand to confute them.

19. My little children, of whom I travail in birth again, until Christ be formed in you, 20. I desire to be present with you now, and to change my voice, for I stand in doubt of you.

19, 20. You are to me as my children, and I am again in painful care of your salvation, till I hear that you are resolved Christians in sincerity. I desire, and did purpose to come to you: For being in suspicion and fear of you, I would know better what to say to you, than at this distance I can.

21, 22. Tell me, ye that desire to be under the law, do ye not hear the law? For it is written, that Abraham had two sons; the one by a bond-maid, the other by a free-woman.

21, 22. Did you mark and understand the law which you hear, you would not desire to be under it. You may read, that Abraham had two sons, one by Hagar a bond-servant, the other by Sarah his free and lawful wife.

23. But he *who was* of the bond-woman, was born after the flesh: but he of the free-woman *was* by promise.

23. Ishmael was born of Hagar by ordinary carnal generation; but Isaac was born of Sarah, by God's promise, and his power above the ordinary course of nature.

24. Which things are an allegory; for these are the two covenants; the one from the Mount Sinai, which gendereth to bondage, which is Agar.

24. Which are to be allegorically understood, as denoting the two covenants; One, that of the law, given at Mount Sinai, which bring a law of servitude and fear, is well signified by Agar.

25. For this Agar is Mount Sinai in Arabia, and answereth to Jerusalem which now is, and is in bondage with her children.

25. For Hagar signifieth Mount Sinai in Arabia, and prefigureth the present state of Jesusalem, which is outwardly in bondage to the Romans, and inwardly to their law.

26. But Jerusalem which is above is free, which is the mother of us all.

26. But the Jerusalem above in heaven, of which true Christians on earth are heirs, and to which they belong by promise, initiation, and relative union with Christ, which is the mother of us all that are children of promise, (the gospel and Spirit coming from heaven, and our inheritance being there) is fully freed from all bondage, and so are we all initially in our gospel liberty.

27. For it is written, rejoice, thou barren that bearest not; break forth and cry, thou that travailest not: for the desolate hath many more children than she which hath an husband.

27. For it is written, &c. The Christian church, which before Christ's coming was but in obscure rudiments, and after was but as a grain of mustard-seed, a little flock, shall become Catholic, and be incomparably greater than was the Jewish church.

Note, That whereas many expositors take [Jerusalem which is above,] or [supernal,] to mean only [the church on earth,] because it is caused by grace and revelation from heaven, and tendeth to it, they causelessly give away a plain text which proveth the immortality of the soul, and its felicity presently upon our death: As if [Jerusalem above] were but [Jerusalem on earth, caused from above;] and so was Moses's law, and the old Jerusalem. The heavenly society containeth the spirits of the just made perfect, with the innumerable company of angels, &c. Heb. xii. To this we are joined in the relation of heirs. When it is said, That this shall come down with Christ at judgment, it implieth, that it was with Christ in heaven before; and he hath promised, that where he is, there his servants shall be also, John xii. 26. And that some expressions here signify the church on earth, is not against this; for the church on earth, is but the lower part of that in heaven.

28. Now we, brethren, as Isaac was, are the children of promise.

28. We are children by adoption and free-gift, and of a free-given inheritance.

29. But as then he that was born after the flesh, persecuted him *that was born* after the Spirit, even so *it is* now.

29. As Ishmael persecuted Isaac, so now the Jews and carnal seed do persecute Christians, the spiritual seed.

30. Nevertheless, what saith the scripture? Cast out the bond-woman and her son: for the son of the bond-woman shall not be heir with the son of the free-woman.

30. But as the scripture saith [Cast out, &c.] so the unbelieving Jews, that trust to the works of the law for life, shall not inherit the saving privileges of the Christian church.

31. So then, brethren, we are not children of the bond-woman, but of the free.

31. So then we that are the children of promise, saved by faith, are not under the bondage of the law, but delivered from sin and curse by Christ.

CHAP. V.

STAND fast, therefore, in the liberty wherewith Christ hath made us free, and be not entangled again with the yoke of bondage.

1. It is not a vain thing which Christ hath purchased for us; undervalue not this freedom, and cast it not away, but hold it fast, and do not causelessly return to the yoke of Jewish bondage.

2. Behold, I Paul say unto you, that if ye be circumcised, Christ shall profit you nothing. 3. For I testify again to every man that is circumcised, that he is a debtor to do the whole law.

2, 3. I Paul tell you, That if you be circumcised, as these men tell you must be, (Acts xv.) that is, as it binds you to Moses's law as the condition of salvation, you renounce the deliverance purchased by Christ, and so he will be no Saviour to you: For, to be so circumcised, is to bind yourselves under that whole law and covenant of works.

Note, That as baptism physically taken is but washing, and is not baptism in the moral sense, which is, a sacramental covenanting with Christ by that figure; just so the physical act of circumcising is not circumcision in the proper moral sense, but using it as a covenanting sign: And as Abraham used it as a seal of the promise to him as a believer, it is in specie morali another thing from that used by the carnal Jews, as signing another covenant: For they used it as a covenanting sign that they would keep Moses's law as the condition of life; whereas they ought to have used it as a seal of the promise made to Abraham and his seed, and also to bind them sincerely to keep that law as the matter of their obedience, trusting to the promise for grace and pardon. So that Paul doth not say, that the Abyssines that are circumcised for other ends, or Timothy, or such believing Jews as were circumcised only to win the Jews, had no profit by Christ: but only such as believed those that taught them, (Except you be circumcised, and keep the law of Moses, you cannot be saved.)]

4. Christ is become of no effect unto you, whosoever of you are justified by the law; ye are fallen from grace.

4. What use is Christ of to you? If you trust to your fulfilling the law for justification, you renounce justification by grace, and so are fallen from Christianity, and the covenant of grace.

5. For we through the Spirit wait for the hope of righteousness by faith.

5. For the Spirit of Christ, which is poured out on the faithful, causeth them to wait in hope of that blessedness, of which we are made heirs by the righteousness of faith.

6. For in Jesus Christ neither circumcision availeth any thing, nor uncircumcision, but faith, which worketh by love.

6. For in our state of Christianity, as subjects of Christ's kingdom, a man shall not be accepted and justified as circumcised, or as uncircumcised, (though circumcision, as binding him to the law of works, may undo him:) But the qualification necessary to salvation is, faith working by love; that is, such an effectual belief of the future heavenly blessedness, purchased and promised by Christ, as causeth us to place our trust and hope on God's love, and Christ's merits, and promise to attain it; and in the sense hereof to love God, and that glory, above all this world, and our neighbours sincerely as ourselves.

7. Ye did run well, who did hinder you, that ye should not obey the truth?

7. You began your race of Christianity well: who hath stopped and perverted you from the belief and obedience of the truth of the gospel, which you then received?

8, 9. This persuasion *cometh* not of him that calleth you. A little leaven leaveneth the whole lump.

8, 9. This Judaizing was never taught you by me, that first preached to you, or by God: But a few corrupted men among you, have brought all your churches into danger of defection.

10. I have confidence in you through the Lord, that you will be none otherwise minded: but he that troubleth you, shall bear *his* judgment, whosoever he be.

10. I trust God will keep the churches from revolting: but those persons, whoever they be, that by seduction trouble and endanger you, shall not escape God's judgment, and our just rebukes and censures.

11. And I, brethren, If I yet preach circumcision, why do I yet suffer persecution? then is the offence of the cross ceased.

11. And as for me, what need I suffer much if I could conform to the Judaism which these men would impose? And then how are we still bound to take up the cross, and suffer with and for Christ? These conditions, imposed by Christ on those that will reign with him, are then ceased, and the church is no more a persecuted society.

Note, That the Jews, who took themselves to be not only God's peculiar, but his only people, and thought all others contemptible and profane, were yet far greater persecutors than the heathens, and that as in zeal for God and his law. And so are the worldly, papal, tyrannical clergy, at this day, who appropriate the name of the church to themselves.

12. I would they were even cut off which trouble you.

12. The hurt that these men do, who would unsettle and pervert you, is so great, that I would they were even cut off from the church, if upon personal admonition they repent not, and so left to God's judgment, who oft maketh Satan his executioner on such men's bodies.

13. For, brethren, ye have been called unto liberty; only use not liberty for an occasion to the flesh, but by love serve one another.

13. Christ hath called you to a state of freedom from Mosaical rites, and from the curse: Use it, therefore, thankfully; but yet abuse it not to any sin, to despise the weak that yet scruple the forsaking of those rites, or to serve any carnal lust or interest, as if you had liberty to sin.

14. For all the law is fulfilled in one word, *even* in this; Thou shalt love thy neighbour as thyself.

14. You are still under a law; but it is the law of love, which, in the duties that you owe to man, is fulfilled, if you do but love your neighbours as yourselves, (supposing that you love yourselves with a well-guided love.)

15. But if ye bite and devour one another, take heed that ye be not consumed one of another.

15. But if selfishness and faction conquer brotherly love, and set you on hurting one another, you will stir up those whom you hurt to self-defence and revenge, and make yourselves so many enemies, that you will be consumed each of the other.

Note, How sottish or malignant are they that preach down love and gentleness, and preach to stir up men to wrath, hatred, and hurtfulness, that they consider not this, and lay it not to heart with fear?

16. *This* I say then, Walk in the Spirit, and ye shall not fulfil the lust of the flesh.

16. If you say, 'That without the law there will be no restraint of fleshly sins; I say, Walk in the Spirit of Christ, that is, by his spiritual law, and his Spirit's sanctifying inclinations, and then you will overcome your fleshly lusts, without the carnal rites and corporal penalties of that law.

17. For the flesh lusteth against the Spirit, and the Spirit against the flesh: and these are contrary the one to the other; so that ye cannot do the things that ye would.

17. For the flesh and Spirit are more contrary than the flesh and Moses's political and ritual law. It is the Spirit that the flesh lusteth against; and it is the Spirit that is contrarily inclined, and must overcome it. These contrary inclinations keep you in such imperfection, that you cannot be as good and blameless as you would be, (and therefore grace must pardon you.)

18. But if ye be led by the Spirit, ye are not under the law.

18. But if the sanctifying Spirit of Christ be it that ruleth you, then as you are above the childish rites, so you so far are above the need of terrifying penalties; for love will be your powerful principle.

19, 20. Now the works of the flesh are manifest, which are these, adultery, fornication, uncleanness, lasciviousness, idolatry, witchcraft, hatred, variance, emulations, wrath, strife, seditions, heresies, 21. Envyings, murders, drunkenness, revellings, and such like: of the which I tell you before, as I have also told you in time past, that they which do such things, shall not inherit the kingdom of God.

19, 20, 21. Perhaps you will say, How shall we know sin but by the law? To which I say, That they being works of the flesh, against true reason, and the Spirit of God, the very light of nature, and Christ's Spirit and spiritual word doth make them manifest, such as adultery, fornication, &c. of which I have told you, and yet tell you, that such shall not inherit the kingdom of God.

22. But the fruit of the Spirit, is love, joy, peace, long-suffering, gentleness, goodness, faith, 23. Meekness, temperance: against such there is no law.

22, 23. But the fruits of the Spirit of Christ in all true Christians (them that are not under the law of Moses) are love to God and men, joy in the hope of salvation and in doing good, peace with conscience, and as much as in us lieth with men, patience under sufferings and wrongs, kindness and gentleness, doing all the good we can, trustiness and trusting God, meekness and tameness of disposition, temperance and chastity, &c. The Spirit of God giveth us a love to all these; so that such need not penal terror to force them to it, nor doth the law condemn any of these.

24. And they that are Christ's have crucified the flesh, with the affections and lusts.

24. And all true Christians whom Christ will own, have by his Spirit crucified the flesh, with its inordinate affections and lusts, in conformity to the crucified body of their Lord, (though he had no sin.) And this is more effectual against sin, than all the curses of Moses's law.

25. If we live in the Spirit, let us also walk in the Spirit.

25. If the Spirit be the principle of our new life, let us do the works of it.

26. Let us not be desirous of vain glory, provoking one another, envying one another.

26. If you be spiritual, shew it by avoiding vain-glorious boasting of your own knowledge and goodness, and provoking others by proud contempt, or contentious opposition. See James iii.

CHAP. VI.

BRETHREN, if a man be overtaken in a fault, ye which are spiritual, restore such an one in the spirit of meekness; considering thyself, lest thou also be tempted.

1. If any of you be surprised in faultiness, contrary to the bent of his heart and life, you that are indeed spiritual and free yourselves, shew it by that meekness which is the fruit of the Spirit, in restoring him by repentance; and use not rough severity and contempt, considering how uncertain you are what temptation may do upon yourselves.

2. Bear ye one anothers' burdens, and so fulfil the law of Christ.

2. Let other men's burdens, hurts, and dangers, be to you as if they were your own; help each other to deliverance and ease, and not add to the load that is upon them: And by this you shall fulfil the law of Christ, which is the law of love.

3. For if a man think himself to be something, when he is nothing he deceiveth himself.

3. Alas! Man is a poor nothing, unable of himself to stand in trial: and the self-confident, who roughly handle the faulty, or contemn them, and

so think themselves to be something, do but deceive themselves, as the event will manifest.

4. But let every man prove his own work, and then shall he have rejoicing in himself alone, and not in another.

4. The way of wisdom is, not to lift up yourselves as wise and good, by sharply censuring the faults of others; but closely to try and prove yourselves, and your own doings, that so your own consciences may speak comfort to you, and not to seek honour by insulting over the weak, that others may exalt you.

5. For every man shall bear his own burden.

5. For it is not other men's goodness or sins for which men shall be rewarded or punished, but their own: And therefore they are most concerned to judge themselves.

6. Let him that is taught in the word, communicate unto him that teacheth in all good things.

6. And to your teachers, it is the hearers' duty to maintain them, and communicate according to your own ability for their provision and supply.

7. Be not deceived; God is not mocked: for whatsoever a man soweth, that shall he also reap.

7. Let not men deceive themselves by a barren profession; for God will not be deceived: All men shall reap as they sow, and be judged according to their works.

8. For he that soweth to his flesh, shall of the flesh reap corruption; but he that soweth to the Spirit, shall of the Spirit reap life everlasting.

8. They that seek first provision for their own flesh, do live but for a body that will rot in the grave; and where then is the fruit of their life? (besides the ruin of their soul.) But they that in obedience to the Spirit, do live a spiritual life, for spiritual felicity, shall receive everlasting life as their reward.

9. And let us not be weary in well-doing: for in due season we shall reap if we faint not.

9. And let us not be tired with length of labour, or delay of the reward: Harvest cometh not as soon as we have sown: When God's due season is come, we shall certainly reap the blessed fruit, if fainting make us not come short of it.

10. As we have therefore opportunity, let us do good unto all men, especially unto them who are of the household of faith.

10. Let us, therefore, according to our several abilities, do all the good to all men that we can, but especially to Christians, who are the household or church of Christ.

11, 12. Ye see how large a letter I have written unto you with mine own hand. As many as desire to make a fair shew in the flesh, they constrain you to be circumcised; only lest they should suffer persecution for the cross of Christ.

11, 12. You see how large a letter your own danger hath drawn me to write. They that would draw you to conformity to the Jews, are a carnal sort of men, that will keep their worldly reputation and safety; and because they cannot suffer persecution from the Jews themselves, they would draw you to this conformity with them, that you may seem to justify them in their sin, and pretend that all others are ignorant of Christian liberty.

13. For neither they themselves who are circumcised keep the law, but desire to have you circumcised, that they may glory in your flesh.

13. For they keep not the law themselves, but would keep up their reputation by getting you on their side, to strengthen their interest, and make you their defence.

14. But God forbid that I should glory, save in the cross of our Lord Jesus Christ, by whom the world is crucified unto me, and I unto the world.

14. But my glorying shall not be in worldly prosperity, and freedom from sufferings; but in following a crucified Christ in cross-bearing, by whom the world to me is a dead condemned thing, as Christ on the cross seemed to the men of the world; and my esteem and love of the world are crucified and dead in me, so that I can spare its ease and honours.

15. For in Christ Jesus neither circumcision availeth any thing, nor uncircumcision, but a new creature.

15. For in the judgment of Christ, the Christianity which is accepted to salvation, is neither circumcision, nor uncircumcision, (though Judaizing circumcision be now contrary to grace;) but it is a new creature, by the Spirit regenerated to God.

16. And as many as walk according to this rule, peace be on them, and mercy, and upon the Israel of God.

16. And the peace and mercy of God will be on all them that walk as new creatures, by the guidance of his Spirit, placing acceptable religion in this, and not in circumcision or uncircumcision. This benediction I pronounce on them that are the true Israel of God, and so will be accepted by him, however judged of by man.

17. From henceforth let no man trouble me; for I bear in my body the marks of the Lord Jesus.

17. *Let not those that profess themselves Christians any more trouble me by their emulations and calumnies, and by seducing the churches: For I carry with me the marks of my faithfulness to Christ, even the sufferings which I undergo for him; which are a better evidence of his acceptance, than avoiding persecution is to my accusers that would seduce you.*

18. Brethren, the grace of our Lord Jesus Christ *be* with your spirit. Amen.

18. *My benediction and prayer for you is, that the grace of our Lord Jesus Christ may be with your spirit, to guide, justify, and sanctify you, (which will save you, when Judaism, and trusting to the works of the law will fail you.) Amen.*

THE
EPISTLE OF PAUL THE APOSTLE,
TO THE
EPHESIANS.

CHAP. I.

PAUL an apostle of Jesus Christ, by the will of God, to the saints which are at Ephesus, and to the faithful in Christ Jesus: 2. Grace be to you, and peace from God our Father, and from the Lord Jesus Christ.

1, 2. *Paul an apostle of Jesus Christ, called and sent by his appearance and voice to preach his gospel, to which God had chosen me; to the saints and faithful Christians at Ephesus, my benediction and prayer is, that they may have grace and peace, holiness and consolation, from God our Father, and Christ our Saviour.*

3. Blessed *be* the God and Father of our Lord Jesus Christ, who hath blessed us with all spiritual blessings in heavenly places in Christ:

3. *Thanks and praise be given to God the Father of our Lord Jesus Christ, who hath blessed us with all spiritual blessings in celestials, or heavenly things which tend to glory, which Christ doth purchase, promise, prepare, and possess for us.*

4. According as he hath chosen us in him before the foundation of the world, that we should be holy and without blame before him in love:

4. *As he chose us as members of Christ, whom he chose to be our head, before the world was made, that we should be holy and blameless, both which summarily consist in holy love.*

5. Having predestinated us unto the adoption of children by Jesus Christ to himself, according to the good pleasure of his will, 6. To the praise of the glory of his grace, wherein he hath made us accepted in the beloved:

5, 6. *Having predestinated us to become his adopted children to him in and by Jesus Christ, of his own free and good will, that so his grace, wherein he hath made us accepted in his beloved Son, might have the praise and glory.*

Note, 1. That the election is from before the foundation of the world. 2. That it is one decree or election of God by which he chooseth Christ to be our head, and us to be his members. 3. It is one and the same election by which God hath chosen us to the praise and glory of his grace, to be saved, and to be holy and blameless in love. On God's part it is by one act, and on our part it is to one state of blessedness, (as generation maketh one man) though as objectively that one have many parts, it may accordingly be named many, and distinguished. And the essentials are given at once, though the integrals and augmentation be after given by degrees. 4. That love is the sum of that holiness and blamelessness to which we are predestinated. 5. That we are not only predestinated to life on condition of holiness, but are predestinated to holiness itself; and consequently, to faith and repentance, and not only on condition that we believe and repent: and so election is of individual persons, to faith, holiness, and salvation, and not only of believers to salvation, or of persons to be saved if they believe. A conditional puts nothing into being or act. Were the scripture dark in the point of God's free electing of some to faith and repentance, more than others of equal guilt and pravity, experience might fully satisfy us of it.

7, 8. In whom we have redemption through his blood, the forgiveness of sins, according to the riches of his grace; wherein he hath abounded toward us in all wisdom and prudence.

7, 8. In whom we have deliverance by redemption, through the sacrifice of his blood for our sins, even the forgiveness of all our sin, which manifesteth the riches of his grace and bounty, from which this gift proceedeth; in which he abounded toward us in the exercise of that wonderful divine wisdom and prudence in the way of our salvation by Christ, which to search and know, is the greatest wisdom and prudence of man.

9. Having made known unto us the mystery of his will according to his good pleasure, which he hath purposed in himself:

9. Having now opened to us the mystery of his own will and good pleasure, which he purposed in himself, but was little known by Jews or Gentiles.

10. That in the dispensation of the fulness of times he might gather together in one all things in Christ, both which are in heaven, and which are on earth, even in him.

10. That when he saw the fit time fully come, he might gather into one universal church, united to Christ the head, as his kingdom and body, both Jews and Gentiles, yea angels and men, the departed souls and those on earth, to be one, I say, in him their Head and King.

Note, Those that confine this to Jews and Gentiles, yea, and those that exclude angels, force the text without proof. For though angels sinned not, Christ may gather us into one heavenly society with them, and make us like them, himself being the head.

11. In whom also we have obtained an inheritance, being predestinated according to the purpose of him, who worketh all things after the counsel of his own will:

11. In whom also we have our lot of inheritance, being thereto predestinated by God, who calleth whom he pleaseth, and worketh all things according to his own counsel, wisdom, and will.

12. That we should be to the praise of his glory, who first trusted in Christ.

12. That we, who were first called, and made believers in Christ, might be the first-fruits of his church, and bring him much praise and glory by our service.

13. In whom ye also *trusted* after that ye heard the word of truth, the gospel of your salvation: in whom also after that ye believed, ye were sealed with that Holy Spirit of promise.

13. In whom you trusted, when you had heard the true gospel of your salvation; and in and by Christ, after you believed, you received the great gift of the promised Spirit, which is God's seal upon you, and the seal of the truth of his promise to you.

14. Which is the earnest of our inheritance, until the redemption of the purchased possession, unto the praise of his glory.

14. Which Spirit is given us by God as the ascertaining earnest of our inheritance, to fit us for and assure us of our attaining the possession of that which Christ hath purchased for those whom he had redeemed to be his peculiar people.

15. Wherefore I also, after I heard of your faith in the Lord Jesus, and love unto all the saints. 16. Cease not to give thanks for you, making mention of you in my prayers;

15, 16. Hearing of the continuance and increase of your faith, and your love to all the saints, (and not only to those that conform to your minds in small or indifferent things) do constantly give thanks to God for your stability, and daily pray for you.

17. That the God of our Lord Jesus Christ, the Father of glory, may give unto you the Spirit of

wisdom and revelation, in the knowledge of him :

17. That he that is the God of our Lord Jesus as man, who sent him, and raised him from the dead, and glorified him, would give you yet more of the spirit of wisdom and revelation, that you may know yet more of the mystery of his love in our redemption by Christ.

18. The eyes of your understanding being enlightened; that ye may know what is the hope of his calling, and what the riches of the glory in his inheritance in the saints.

18. That your minds being yet more illuminated, you may more fully and clearly know, to what glorious hopes he hath called us, and what treasures of glory he hath promised to his saints, in whom he will be glorified for ever.

19. And what *is* the exceeding greatness of his power to us-ward who believe, according to the working of his mighty power; 20. Which he wrought in Christ when he raised him from the dead, and set him at his own right hand in the heavenly *places.*

19, 20. And how wonderfully God hath manifested his power in us that believe, in giving us the spirit of miracles, tongues, prophecy, &c. and the spirit of illumination, faith, hope, love, joy, patience, to go on in labour and suffering for Christ, suitable to the power which he shewed in raising Christ from death, and advancing him to the heavenly glory, where he is Lord of all.

21. Far from all principality, and power, and might, and dominion and every name that is named, not only in this world, but also in that which is to come :

21. Far above all the princes, states, and powers on earth, the greatest conquerors or monarchs, whether those that persecuted him and us, or any other, even those above us in the world that we are going to, angels, or any sort of spirits.

22. And hath put all things under his feet, and gave him *to be* the head over all things to the Church.

22. And hath given him power over all things, and made him head of the church, and Lord over all things, for his church's good, and ends of redemption.

23. Which is his body, the fulness of him that filleth all in all.

23. Which church is his body mystical, the celestial, political society, united to and under him,

in which he attaineth fully the ends of his redemption, and in whom, as glorified with him, he is effectively a full and perfect Saviour, in whom he will delight, and be glorified: and God, that in all in all things, fully manifesteth his love and glory.

Note, 1. That the text distinguisheth Christ's relation to his church, and to all things else. He is head to the church by vital influx, as his body. He is over all things, some as utensils for the church, and some as conquered rebels, or enemies.

2. How little reason the church hath to fear malicious principalities or powers, or great names, or devils, any further than we fear ourselves, lest we yield to sin by their temptations; seeing they are all in the power of Christ, and under his feet: and therefore our sinful fear doth plainly prove our unbelief, in that degree that it prevaileth.

3. As the same love, so the same power of God, that was glorified in the miracles and resurrection of Christ, is engaged for, and glorified on the church: and this glory we shall see in the fulness of time, though now the church (as Christ on the cross, or in the grave) seem a forsaken, shattered, desolate thing.

4. It is no wonder that Christ taketh what is done to his church and members as done to himself, and will judge men accordingly.

5. The great service that Christ requireth of us in the world, is to contribute our utmost labour and help for the church; he himself needing nothing that we can do.

CHAP. II.

AND you hath he quickened who were dead in trespasses and sins.

1. And you who are members of this church hath he revived and quickened by his mortifying and sanctifying grace, and by absolving you from the guilt of death, who were in and by your sin as dead to spiritual saving good, and liable by guilt to everlasting death : your state of sin was such a state of death.

2. Wherein in time past ye walked according to the course of this world, according to the prince of the power of the air, the spirit that now worketh in the children of disobedience.

2. In this sin you lived in your former Gentile state, according to the temptations and will of Satan, who is by God's permission the prince of the power of the air, and by his temptations worketh in the unpersuadable unbelievers, and ungodly, against God's grace and their salvation.

3. Among whom also we all had our conversation in times past, in the lusts of our flesh, fulfilling the desires of the flesh and of the mind; and were by nature the children of wrath, even as others.

3. And we ourselves were formerly such as they, and lived among them in fleshly lusts, fulfilling the desires of our flesh, and our own thoughts and false reasoning, and were by natural corruption (not only as children of Adam, but also the progeny of heathens) the heirs of God's wrath, obliged to punishment by his justice, as other men, and especially heathens, be.

4. But God who is rich in mercy, for his great love wherewith he loved us, 5. Even when we were dead in sins, hath quickened us together with Christ, (by grace ye are saved.) 6. And hath raised us up together, and made us sit together in heavenly places in Christ Jesus.

4, 5, 6. But God, who is very merciful, to manifest his own free love to us, when we were as others dead in sins, hath by his own grace begun our salvation, conforming us to the resurrection and exaltation of Christ, by delivering us from the death of sin and guilt, and making us alive to holiness, and giving us the earnest and foretaste of glory.

7. That in the ages to come he might shew the exceeding riches of his grace, in his kindness towards us, through Christ Jesus.

7. That in these latter days he might shew forth the glory of his grace in our redemption by Christ, in which his love and kindness to us is resplendent.

8. For by grace are ye saved, through faith; and that not of yourselves: it is the gift of God: 9. Not of works, lest any man should boast:

8, 9. For your salvation is of God's mere grace and gift, through your faith in Christ: and this is not of your own contriving, meriting, seeking, or effecting; but all of God's own gift, who hath chosen this way, rather than that of works, that none may boast, and ascribe that to themselves which is due only to God.

10. For we are his workmanship created in Christ Jesus unto good works, which God hath before ordained that we should walk in them.

10. Not that we hereby exclude good works, by excluding man's boasting of his own power or merits: for we ourselves are God's work, new made by regeneration, which planted us into Christ, purposely to do those good works, which neither the law nor mere nature enabled and inclined us to do: these God hath fore-ordained and prescribed for us to live in, and by grace inclined us to do them.

11. Wherefore remember that ye being in time passed Gentiles in the flesh, who are called uncircumcision by that which is called the circumcision in the flesh made by hands; 12. That at that time ye were without Christ, being aliens from the commonwealth of Israel, and strangers from the covenants of promise, having no hope, and without God in the world:

11, 12. And that you may duly value the mercy of your vocation, you must never forget, that you were of the Gentiles, called uncircumcised by the Jews, and had no knowledge of Christ as promised, or as incarnate, and were no part of that peculiar people the Jews, but aliens, whom they justly refused communion with, and were strangers from the covenant which promised peculiarity, and so had none of the hope of redemption, which those promises gave, nor knew how, as reconciled, to be accepted of God, and lived as Atheists, without the true knowledge of God, or trust in him, or obedience to him, (though you had many idols.)

13. But now in Christ Jesus, ye who sometimes were far off, are made nigh by the blood of Christ.

13. But now ye are Christians, you are brought as nigh God as the believing Jews, the partition being taken down, and the covenant of grace founding an universal church, purchased and sealed by the blood of Christ, whose peculiar people now ye are.

14. For he is our peace who hath made both one, and hath broken down the middle wall of partition between us;

14. For he is the maker of our peace with God and one another, and he hath taken away, the division between Jews and Gentiles, which was like the wall which kept the Gentiles in the outer court of the temple, and opened to us all a way into the sanctuary.

15. (Having abolished in his flesh the enmity, even the law of commandments, contained in ordinances, for to make in himself, of twain, one new man, so making peace.

15. Being man in the common nature of man, and offering his body a sacrifice for the sins of all, he hath abolished the law of Moses, which contained ordinances ceremonial, typical, and political, with severe penalties, and maketh us all one Catholic church, united in himself the head.

16. And that he might reconcile both unto God in one body by the cross, having slain the enmity thereby.

16. And as his one body was crucified for both,

so be thereby reconcileth both to God in one body or society, which is his church, having abolished the enmity.

17. And came and preached peace to you which are afar off, and to them that were nigh.

17. And this gospel of reconciliation and unity he hath by himself and his apostles preached, and offereth grace and peace, both to Gentiles and Jews.

18. For through him we both have an access by one Spirit unto the Father.

18. For through his merits, intercession, and covenant, all believers, Jews and Gentiles, are made the children of God, and are sealed by his Spirit of adoption, which is an intercessor within us, by whom we have access to God.

19. Now therefore ye are no more strangers and foreigners, but fellow-citizens with the saints, and of the household of God;

19. And now this reconciliation being made by Christ, you Gentiles are no longer strangers or foreigners to the church or peculiar people of God; but are free denizens, burgesses, or enfranchised citizens, with the rest of the holy society, even members of the holy Catholic church, of adopted ones, which is as the household of God.

20. And are built upon the foundation of the apostles and prophets, Jesus Christ himself being the chief corner-*stone*;

20. And I may liken you not only to the household, but to the house of God, of which you are a living part, built on the doctrine of the apostles and prophets, qualified by the Holy Ghost, and authorised by Christ to call and gather his Catholic church, and so may secondarily be called its foundation, Christ himself being the primary foundation, or chief corner stone.

21. In whom all the building fitly framed together, groweth unto an holy temple in the Lord.

21. In whom, as the head of union, all the church of God being compact into one holy society, as it were, of living stones, is built, riseth and groweth up to be an holy temple to the Lord, increasing to its perfection.

22. In whom you also are builded together for an habitation of God through the Spirit.

22. And as God called the temple at Jerusalem his dwelling, so by the Spirit of Christ, you also, with all the rest of the faithful, are built up as a holy temple, in which, by the same Spirit, God will dwell.

Note, That 1. The Catholic church is not only that which was once by the policy of emperors and bishops called Catholic, as national, being in that empire only, and under its laws; but as it containeth all Christians in the world. 2. That it is headed only by Christ, the centre of its unity. 3. That inspired apostles and prophets being the messengers of new divine revelation, are its secondary foundation, by an authority and qualification proper to them, and not extending to bishops or their councils, who come after them. 4. Note the great dignity of the church, as resulting from this foundation Christ, and the reconciliation wrought by him. 5. That they that would destroy this unity and superstruction, fight against Christ, and would destroy the church; which is most notably done by setting up a false head or foundation, or making false incapable terms of union, by the presumptuous canons and laws of usurpers. 6. That though this church have no uniting head but Christ, yet it must be compact, as the members of his body, and have one faith, hope, baptism, and spirit of love, and abhor division as destruction.

CHAP. III.

FOR this cause, I Paul, the prisoner of Jesus Christ for you Gentiles.

1. Having those great encouragements, I feel even glory that I am Christ's prisoner for the Gentiles' sake, even for preaching the gospel for their conversion and salvation.

Note, That at once Paul was the Jews' prisoner, as his accusers and persecutors; and the heathen Romans' prisoner, as his judges; and Christ's prisoner, both finally, as suffering for his sake, and obligatorily, as commissioned for a persecuted work; and the Gentiles' prisoner finally, as suffering for his labours for their salvation.

2. If ye have heard of the dispensation of the grace of God, which is given me to you-ward:

3. How that by revelation he made known unto me the mystery, (as I wrote afore in few words,

2, 3. For I suppose you have heard how, for your good, God hath commissioned me to declare and dispense to you the gospel of grace and gifts of the Spirit, and by revelation from heaven by the voice of Christ, and inwardly by his Spirit, made known to me the mystery of man's redemption, and the calling of the Gentiles, (as I wrote briefly before.

4, 5. Whereby when ye read ye may understand my knowledge in the mystery of Christ) which in other ages was not made known unto the sons of men, as it is now revealed unto his holy apostles and prophets by the Spirit; 6. That the Gentiles should be fellow-heirs, and of the same body, and partakers of his promise in Christ by the gospel.

4, 5, 6. In which you may read my explication of this mystery, and perceive that Christ hath acquainted me with it, which in former ages was not openly and clearly made known to men, as it is now by the Spirit revealed to the holy apostles and prophets who preach the gospel; even that Christ would call and take in the Gentiles, into the Catholic church and covenant, as his peculiar people, and make them partakers of his promise and gift of life in Christ, by the gospel preached to them.

7. Whereof I was made a minister according to the gift of the grace of God given unto me by the effectual working of his power.

7. Of which gospel I was made a minister, to dispense it according to that measure of the gift of the Spirit by grace given to me, which wrought effectually in me, and by me, by doctrine and miracles to convert the Gentiles.

8. Unto me, who am less than the least of all saints, is this grace given, that I should preach among the Gentiles the unsearchable riches of Christ:

8. To me, who am by my former persecution of the church the lowest or most unworthy of all saints, in this favour and honour freely vouchsafed, that I should preach to the Gentiles the unsearchable riches of Christ.

9. And to make all men see what is the fellowship of the mystery which from the beginning of the world hath been hid in God, who created all things by Jesus Christ:

9. And to notify to all men the communication and communion of this mysterious grace, which from the very creation was secretly included (as a tree in the seed) in God's making the whole world by Jesus Christ, even that he would redeem and new-make us all by him.

10. To the intent that now unto the principalities and powers in heavenly *places* might be known by the church the manifold wisdom of God, 11. According to the eternal purpose which he purposed in Christ Jesus our Lord:

10, 11. That now in this collection of the universal church in Christ, as in a glass, or as in the clear effects, the very spiritual principalities and powers above us in the heavens might see more of God's eternal counsel opened, and manifold wisdom displayed, than they knew before.

Note, 1. That superior spirits are principalities and powers, either over political societies there,

or as rulers over us here below, as guardians: see Josh. v. 14. Exod. xxiii. 20, 23. & 32, 34. Numb. xx. 16. Gen. xxiv. 7, 40. Psal. xxxiv. 7. Dan. x. 13, &c. It is like it is both.

2. That even superior powers are not omniscient, but may by new means have new increased knowledge; and therefore saints in heaven are not more knowing.

3. That it is in heaven that the great ends of God, in redeeming and gathering his church, are attained.

12. In whom we have boldness and access with confidence by the faith of him.

12. In whom we all that trust in him, may come with boldness and confident hope of acceptance to God.

13. Wherefore I desire that ye faint not at my tribulations for you, which is your glory.

13. Wherefore, I beseech you, be not discouraged by my sufferings for preaching to you: for it is your honour to have the ministry of your salvation thus attested by me.

14. For this cause I bow my knees unto the Father of our Lord Jesus Christ, 15. Of whom the whole family in heaven and earth is named, 16. That he would grant you according to the riches of his glory, to be strengthened with might by his Spirit in the inner man;

14, 15, 16. For this end I beg of God the Father of our Lord Jesus Christ, of whom all the blessed society in heaven and earth is named his family, (or of which Christ, Jews and Gentiles are named Christians) that of his abundant grace, in which he will be glorified, he will by his Spirit fortify your souls.

Note, 1. It is uncertain whether [of whom] relate to the Father, or to Christ.

2. Though Paul speak specially of the Catholic church of Jews and Gentiles, there is no reason to exclude the glorified souls; no, nor the angels, from being part of God's family, united in and under Christ.

17. That Christ may dwell in your hearts by faith; that ye being rooted and grounded in love, 18. May be able to comprehend with all saints, what is the breadth, and length, and depth, and height; 19. And to know the love of Christ, which passeth knowledge, that ye might be filled with all the fulness of God.

17, 18, 19. That Christ may by the constant exercise of your faith upon him, even dwell objectively in your hearts, (as one friend by love and trust doth in another's) and effectively possess and actuate you by his Spirit; that by his Spirit and your faith, you may be so deeply possessed with the sense of God's love, that you may be filled with love to him and one another, and it may be the very habit of your souls, and a rooted nature in you; that so being qualified by this faith and love, you may be able and fit to measure and understand, as all saints in their several degrees do, the vast and wonderful dimensions; and to know the love of Christ, and of the Father in him, which exceedeth our comprehensive and adequate knowledge, (or which is more excellent than all the sciences which heathens and heretics boast of;) that so by faith and love your souls may be filled with the highest degrees of grace, and the Spirit of God.

20, 21. **Now unto him that is able to do exceeding abundantly above all that we ask or think, according to the power that worketh in us, unto him be glory in the church by Christ Jesus, throughout all ages, world without end. Amen.**

20, 21. Now to that Almighty God who can do for his people exceeding abundantly, above all that we can desire or ask, believe or conceive in our narrow thoughts, as it is intimated even in the power of sanctity and miracles, which he exerciseth in and among us now; to him, I say, be glory in the church, by the mediation of Jesus Christ, (in whom the glory of God's love shineth to us, and by whom we render praise to God) throughout all ages, world without end. Amen.

CHAP. IV.

I Therefore the prisoner of the Lord, beseech you that ye walk worthy of the vocation wherewith ye are called.

1. Seeing then the riches of God's grace in Christ is so abundant to you converted Gentiles, I that am a prisoner for declaring this grace of Christ to you, exhort you that you live according to the great obligation of your vocation.

2. With all lowliness and meekness, with long-suffering, forbearing one another in love;

2. Such a Christian life must be in all lowliness, or humble thoughts of yourselves, your knowledge, your goodness, and your power, and in all meekness or gentleness towards others: love must cause you with long-suffering to forbear one another.

Note, 1. That forbearance is to be exercised towards evil, that is, imperfections in knowledge, virtue, and duty, and tolerable faults, and injuries against each other: therefore it supposeth us to be all faulty, needing forbearance.

2. That proud high thoughts of ourselves, and contempt, censoriousness, and hurtfulness to others, and not forbearing tolerable offenders, is contrary to Christianity, and the cause of divisions in the church: and by these the carnal persecuting seed, especially when they invade the sacred office, are differenced from true Christians, as wolves from sheep, even when, as the false prophets, they pretend the cause and name of Christ.

3. That all this is for want of Christian love, and the dominion of carnal self-love; and love to God, and to others as ourselves, must be the proper cure.

3. Endeavouring to keep the unity of the Spirit in the bond of peace.

3. This love and forbearance must specially be exercised to preserve the unity of the Christian church; which all must endeavour faithfully to keep. And this unity inwardly consisteth in being all possessed and governed by one holy Spirit, as all the parts of the body are by one soul; and outwardly, by living peaceably towards each other, especially in our church communion.

4, 5, 6. There is one body, and one Spirit, even as ye are called in one hope of your calling; one Lord, one faith, one baptism, one God and Father of all, who is above all, and through all, and in you all.

4, 5, 6. More particularly in these seven respects our unity doth consist. 1. The church, which is as the body of Christ, is one universal church. 2. The Spirit of God, which as it were animateth it, is one and the same Spirit. 3. The grace and heavenly glory which is the hope of believers, which they seek, and for which they forsake the world, is one. 4. The Head, Lord, and Saviour of the church, is one and the same to all. 5. The essentials of the Christian faith or creed, are one and the same. 6. The baptismal vow, and covenant, and profession, in which we are devoted to God, the Father, Son, and Holy Ghost, and united sacramentally to Christ his church, is one and the same to all in the essentials. 7. And all have one God and Father in Christ, who is, 1. Transcendently and absolutely above and over all; 2. And inconceivably penetrateth all: and 3. Is in his essence most intimately in you all, and to all in all things.

Note, That in these seven things, that unity of the church consisteth, which is God's prescribed and conferred qualification for Christian communion in love and peace. And that as Satan seeketh to undo by over-doing (and the Pharisees had more laws, traditions, and strictness therein, as needful to communion, than Christ had, who would have mercy rather than sacrifice.) So it is by adding a multitude of ensnaring customs, and opinions, as necessary to communion, that he hath corrupted and torn the visible church, and turned love and communion into wrath and persecution.

And yet this unity must be kept in peace; and therefore, both persecuting, and contentious, turbulent unpeaceableness, against those that own these seven points of union, should be avoided by Christians, and restrained by magistrates; who must keep the peace. And whenever God in mercy will heal the lacerated church, it will be on these terms.

7. But unto every one of us is given grace according to the measure of the gift of Christ.

7. But though we have all one spirit, and are one in all the foresaid essentials of our religion, yet this unity is found in very great diversity of degrees of grace, and both degrees and kind of gifts, (see 1 Cor. xii.) as it pleaseth Christ to distribute them.

8. Wherefore he saith, When he ascended up on high, he led captivity captive, and gave gifts unto men.

8. As it is said in Psal. lxviii. 18. When, &c. So when Christ ascended, he triumphed over Satan, death, and hell, and sent down from heaven the gifts of his Spirit.

9. (Now that he ascended, what is it but that he also descended first into the lower parts of the earth? 10. He that descended, is the same also that ascended up far above all heavens, that he might fill all things.)

9, 10. And when it is said, that he ascendeth, it implieth, that he first descended into this lower world, into a low condition, and into the grave. And therefore it is the same Jesus who was here humbled in his descent, who is exalted by his ascent, far above all heavens which man doth see or know, that thence (as the sun by the influence of its heat, and light, and motion, filleth all below, according to the receptive capacity of each, so) our glorified Lord, by his administering influx, might fill all with common or special grace, according to their various receptivity.

11. And he gave some, apostles: and some prophets: and some evangelists: and some, pastors and teachers: 12. For the perfecting of the saints, for the work of the ministry, for the edifying of the body of Christ:

11, 12. And he gave, by qualification and mission, some apostles, sent by his own mouth, to be the most eminent attesters of his miracles, doctrine, and resurrection, and founders of the churches; some prophets, by revelation and inspiration to confirm the Christian faith; some evangelists, whose work was as eminently qualified to go abroad, to preach the gospel, and gather churches, or confirm them, without being fixed to a special place or flock; and some pastors and teachers, (called also bishops and elders) who were set over the particular churches as their guides and instructors, as being their special flocks and charge. And all these gifts and offices are given for that ministerial work which God (who worketh by means) will use, to bring on all his saints towards the perfection of themselves and of the church, and by the increase, concord, and sanctity of the members, to edify or build up this body of Christ.

13. Till we all come in the unity of the faith, and of the knowledge of the Son of God, unto a perfect man, unto the measure of the stature of the fulness of Christ:

13. Till by this increase of number and holiness, and concord, we all Jews and Gentiles make up that church, which in the unity of faith, and knowledge and acknowledgment of Christ, attaineth to that degree of perfection, in which consisteth the measure of grace, and fulness of stature, which Christ will bring his church unto, which is that maturity which imitateth our natural growth from infancy to full manhood.

14. That we henceforth be no more children, tossed to and fro, and carried about with every wind of doctrine, by the sleight of men, and cunning craftiness, whereby they lie in wait to deceive:

14. That being by God's blessing by such a ministry brought up to manhood, we may no longer be like children, who through weakness cannot stand in the wind, but are carried about by it; so childish Christians are by every wind of plausible doctrine, by the sleight subtlety and craft of men, that by pretences of knowledge, holiness, power or love, lay snares and lie in wait to deceive the weak.

15. But speaking the truth in love, may grow up into him in all things, which is the head, even Christ:

15. But (though we know but in part, yet) speaking and keeping the necessary truth or essentials of our religion in love and concord, in this faith and love, may in all things grow up to greater measures by degrees, even into a fuller communion with Christ our head, and likeness to him.

16. From whom the whole body fitly joined together and compacted by that which every joint supplieth, according to the effectual working in the measure of every part, maketh increase of the body, unto the edifying of itself in love.

16. From whom the whole church receiveth both that vital influence, and that conduct and government, to its own intensive and extensive increase in love, which is its spiritual life, which the natural body doth from the head and heart, by communication of vital and animal spirits and heat: and this life and increase is received and commu-

nicated to each part from Christ, by that coagmentation and due connexion of all the members of the church together, while each keepeth his place, and performeth his own office, by the exercise of faith and love effectually for the good of all: even as the body is kept in life and health, while every inferior part and joint is receptive and active according to its proper place and office.

Note, There is no text which is so plausibly wrested to maintain Popery, that is, One universal human government of the whole church on earth, monarchical or aristocratical, (by Pope, counsel, or combined metropolitans, as one sovereignty) as this: it seeming, to forestalled men, to speak of the church as compacted in one universal policy so governed: and it is a text which must be greatly studied against dividers, and yet vindicated from Roman perverters.

I. Doubtless the text speaketh strongly for universal concord, and not only for a uniting of members in several congregations, which shall each be independent. which would be but like so many limbs cut off from the body; but for a uniting of congregations, yea, of all through the world, in one compacted body: and therefore all Christians must abhor dissection and separation, or schism.

II. Yet it is evident that Paul speaketh of no one head but Christ, and of no sort of universal sovereign on earth as under him. And indeed it is an office that human nature here is not capable of, either in monarchy or aristocracy; it is impossible for any church-sovereign-power, save divine, (or angelical at least) to rule the church by legislation, judgment, and execution, all over the earth; much of it being out of our reach, as the moon is; and the church is under contrary, enemy, militant, civil governors, which maketh it the more impossible. And the only pretenders have been the great dividers and destroyers. What then is here meant, and to be done for unity?

Not to feign impossible terms, such as are an universal sovereignty, and multitudes of human, doubtful, unnecessary canons; which are the most effectual causes of discord. But, 1. To take up with Christ's own prescribed terms of union here laid down, verse 3, 4, 5. If Christ have not made the laws of church union, he is not the maker of the church; for unity is essential to it (as to a house or body.) 2. To be one in love, and to repress all tyranny that would destroy love and peace. 3. As in the several assemblies they must exercise the same faith and hope, and love and worship the same God and Saviour by the same Spirit; so that these churches must live in love to each other, and avoid all discord: and if any breach be made between them in faith or love, they must use all reasonable means to heal it; which is by writing or messengers giving to each other an account of their faith and practice; and when need is, consulting in synods, of one or of divers nations: not that such synods are governors of many churches by a major vote, or by metropolitan power (save as they may exercise the magistrate's power of the sword by his commission, which (were such fit) can be given only in his own dominions, out of which synods and metropolitans can have no political governing power: but the major vote must be regarded for concord, which is the use of synods; yet so that it prevail not against divine authority and law, nor against reason, or the churches' good. And therefore, 1. Synods are but for counsel and agreement. 2. And general councils impossible and needless, it being impossible and needless that all the world have notice of the cases of every particular church, much less that they meet for the redress. 3. And when corruption and tyranny (as under the Arians and Papists) have got the major vote, the minor are not bound to agree with them, but to dissent. As the earth is God's kingdom, and all kings are his officers in their several kingdoms, but neither any one man, or many conjunct in one aristocracy or council, are one sovereign governing power over all the earth; but only should by consultations seek to keep the common love and peace; even so all churches and Christians on earth are Christ's kingdom or church universal, and all true pastors are his officers in their several churches, but neither one man, or many conjunct as one political person, or aristocracy, are one *summa potestas* over all Christians on earth; but those that are within the reach and notice of each other should, when it is needful, by synods and consultations, keep up unity of faith and love, and all needful concord. Had not princes been made too capable of abuse, they would not take well the doctrine of a late learned and triumphant writer, who tells us, that though *de facto*, princes do not, yet they ought to unite their power in one council, which should be the brightest governor of them all: and so, 1. All kings must be subjects. 2. Aristocracy must rule monarchy. 3. How shall all kings from the antipodes, or over all the earth, meet? 4. Who shall call them? 5. Where must they meet? 6. Shall they trust their crowns to delegate subjects? 7. What if the most be Heathens and Mahometans, and most Christian heretics, in each others account? 8. If he condescend to limit this sovereign diet, who shall limit it, and how? And then the universal sovereign is still wanting.

They that dare plead for no more than universal communion, should have understood that communion as such belongs but to a community; and a mere community is no body politic, or governed society, but a confederacy of equals (as to rule.) With respect to God only the world is one governed kingdom, and with respect to Christ, the church is one ruled body politic: but neither of them is one as united in any vicarious sovereign, but in their several provinces must keep communion in faith, love, and peace.

17. This I say, therefore, and testify in the Lord, that ye henceforth walk not as other Gentiles walk in the vanity of their mind.

17. Therefore I charge you as from Christ, that you that are Christians live not henceforth as the unconverted heathen, that follow their own false imaginations.

18. Having the understanding darkened, being alienated from the life of God, through the ignorance that is in them, because of the blindness of their heart: 19. Who being past feeling, have given themselves over unto lasciviousness, to work all uncleanness with greediness.

18, 19. Their understanding being darkened, and they being mere strangers to a holy living on and unto God, because of the ignorance and blindness of their minds, which have lost the very light of nature, and being stupified by pravity and custom in sin, have given themselves up to fleshly lusts, to do the filthiest acts with greedy desire and delight.

20. But ye have not so learned Christ; 21. If so be that ye have heard him, and have been taught by him, as the truth is in Jesus:

20, 21. But Christ has taught you, and you have learned a clean contrary course of life; if indeed you have heard what he teacheth, and have been taught the true doctrine of Christ.

22. That ye put off concerning the former conversation, the old man, which is corrupt according to the deceitful lusts: 23. And be renewed in the spirit of your mind;

22, 23. That you put off the old fleshly mind and life, which is corrupt in disposition and practice, by the deceit of sensual lusts; and that you be made new men, in the very bent and habits of your mind, with new judgment and affections.

24. And that ye put on the new man, which after God is created in righteousness and true holiness.

24. And that you become new men, possessed of new dispositions, wrought in you by God, according to his word, and for his glory, consisting in righteousness and true holiness.

25. Wherefore putting away lying, speak every man truth with his neighbour: for we are members one of another.

25. And in particular, as parts of your righteousness, see that you avoid all lying and fraud, and speak the plain truth to one another; for we are all fellow members of one body, and therefore should not be false and fraudulent to each other.

26. Be ye angry and sin not: let not the sun go down upon your wrath:

26. Anger is given us for the due resisting of evil; but use it not blindly, rashly, and inordinately to sin; much less may you lie down and continue in such sin.

27. Neither give place to the devil.

27. And do not yield to Satan, who by men's provocations would draw you to sin.

28. Let him that stole, steal no more: but rather let him labour, working with his hands the thing which is good, that he may have to give to him that needeth.

28. If any have by want or error been tempted to steal, or take any thing that is another's against his will, let him do so no more, nor by idleness continue his necessities, but as he is able labour in some profitable work, and that not only to supply his own wants but to relieve as many others as he well can.

29. Let no corrupt communication proceed out of your mouth, but that which is good to the use of edifying, that it may minister grace unto the hearers.

29. Let no sinful, rotten, or filthy discourse, come out of your mouths, (which will signify a polluted heart, and may corrupt the hearers) but let your words be such as are not only harmless to others, but profitable, even that which is useful to edification, (for useless truth itself is not to be chosen.)

30. And grieve not the holy Spirit of God, whereby ye are sealed unto the day of redemption.

30. For the Spirit of God, which is his mark and seal upon you, to prepare you for the day of salvation, is a hater of all filthiness and vanity, and a lover of purity and holiness, and mutual edification: and though he have not passion and grief as men have, yet as offended men will in displeasure forsake that which is filthy and abhorred, so will the Spirit of God in displeasure forsake a filthy sinner: and that is one of the sorest kinds of punishment.

31. Let all bitterness, and wrath, and anger, and clamour, and evil-speaking, be put away from you, with all malice.

31. And God's Spirit being the spirit of love, cast away malice and all that savoureth of it; bitterness, wrath, and hurtful anger, clamorous, fierce, and ill and hurtful words.

32. And ye be kind one to another, tender-hearted, forgiving one another, even as God for Christ's sake hath forgiven you.

32. As having the same spirit in the same body, be kind and tender-hearted one to another, taking the good or hurt of each other as your own: and as you can easily forbear and forgive yourselves, and be willing that others forgive you, so forgive one another, and that out of the belief and thankful sense of God's forgiving you much more, for the sake of Jesus Christ.

CHAP. V.

BE ye therefore followers of God, as dear children;

2. And walk in love, as Christ also hath loved us, and hath given himself for us, as an offering and a sacrifice to God for a sweet smelling savour.

1, 2. Having therefore so obliging an example of your heavenly Father, shew that you are his true beloved children by imitating him; and let love be your very nature and course of life, remembering still how Christ hath loved us, and given himself for us, an offering and sacrifice for our sins, with which God was highly pleased in him.

3. But fornication, and all uncleanness, or covetousness, let it not be once named amongst you, as becometh saints: 4. Neither filthiness, nor foolish talking, nor jesting, which are not convenient: but rather giving of thanks.

3, 4. But let not fornication or any uncleanness, or filthy lust, be once named amongst you, unless by necessary opposition and detestation; for this is the course beseeming all Christians, who must be pure, or saints: nor yet use any ribald talk, or filthy action, nor foolish speaking, nor vain jesting or drollery, the foam of a light, vain wit; for these are unbeseeming holy persons; but rather employ your tongues in thanks and joyful praise to God, and in holy edifying discourse.

5. For this ye know, that no whoremonger, nor unclean person, nor covetous man who is an idolater, hath any inheritance in the kingdom of Christ, and of God.

5. Let none pretend that Christianity by freeing them from the law, giveth them liberty to sin unpunished: for if you are Christians, the word and law of Christ hath taught you, that no whoremonger, or unclean person, or covetous person, who is an idolater by loving the world more than God (or one that imitateth idolaters in lusts,) hath right of inheritance in heaven, or in the holy church on earth.

6. Let no man deceive you with vain words: for because of these things cometh the wrath of God upon the children of disobedience. 7. Be not ye therefore partakers with them.

6, 7. Let no heretics or libertines deceive you with false pretences of liberty; for these are the sins for which God's wrath cometh on the unbelievers, and therefore will do so on all the disobedient that live in them: therefore be not you partakers in the sin, if you would not partake also of the punishment.

8. For ye were sometimes darkness, but now *are ye* light in the Lord: walk as Children of light,

8. For you were in darkness formerly yourselves, but Christ hath brought you into the light of saving knowledge; live then as in the light according to the gospel and Spirit of Christ, and do that of which you need not be ashamed.

9, 10. (For the fruit of the Spirit *is* in all goodness, and righteousness, and truth) proving what is acceptable unto the Lord.

9, 10. For Christ ruleth all true Christians by his Spirit of illumination and sanctification; and the fruits of that Spirit and light are goodness, love, and kindness, righteousness, truth, and faithfulness; trying and choosing what is pleasing to the Lord.

11. And have no fellowship with the unfruitful works of darkness, but rather reprove them.

11. Communicate not with these heathens and heretics' works of darkness, and fleshly lusts, but rather do your best to save men from them by reproof.

12. For it is a shame even to speak of those things which are done of them in secret.

12. For their secret filthiness, which cannot bear the light, is such as modesty is loath to name.

13. But all things that are reproved, are made manifest by the light: for whatsoever doth make manifest, is light.

13. But all things, when the light discovereth them, are manifest, and, if approvable, need not fear it; for the doctrine and Spirit of Christ are a manifesting light.

14. Wherefore he saith, Awake thou that sleepest, and arise from the dead, and Christ shall give thee light.

14. Which is the sense of Isa. lx. 1. which calleth the people that slept in darkness to awake, that the Lord may shine upon them; which Christ now doth to true believers.

15. See then that ye walk circumspectly, not as fools, but as wise, 16. Redeeming the time, because the days are evil.

15, 16. See then that you live not carelessly, but with watchfulness and accurate circumspection, not as fools that see not, or mind not their danger, but as wise men, that look on every side, and are careful to avoid all sorts of evil: and therefore take hold of the present opportunity, and use well the light of the gospel while you have it: for the world is round about you full of snares

CHAP. V. EPHESIANS. 453

and dangers, which without wise circumspection cannot be avoided.

17. Wherefore be ye not unwise, but understanding what the will of the Lord is.

17. Wherefore let not ignorance and folly prepare you for deceit, but labour to be well acquainted with the will of God concerning your duty.

18. And be not drunk with wine, wherein is excess; but be filled with the Spirit: 19. Speaking to yourselves in psalms, and hymns, and spiritual songs, singing and making melody in your heart to the Lord.

18, 19. And do not, like heathens and sensual libertines think that the exhilaration of excess of wine, which causeth sottishness and lust, is either lawful, or suitable to devotion; but be you exhilarated by the Spirit of God, whose grace you must excite and exercise by psalms, and hymns of praise to God, and spiritual songs, which you must use in holy manner to the Lord, with the inward melody of the heart.

Note, 1. That Paul here leaveth it to Christian wisdom, whether we shall use David's psalms, or others more fitted to gospel times and worship.

2. That hence it is evident, that it is lawful to use some forms of worship, invented and imposed by man; for hymns and songs cannot be used without invention: and the church, or many, cannot join in them, unless some one lead and impose them on the rest. It would be mad work for a congregation to sing extempore songs, and every one a separate one of his own. And if prayer and praise in metre may be invented and imposed, the same reasons will hold as to prose, when uniformity is needful (as in baptism, &c.)

20. Giving thanks always for all things unto God and the Father, in the name of our Lord Jesus Christ;

20. Cheerfully thanking God continually on all occasions, for all his mercies, which are found in all things that he doth; offering this to the Father in the name of Christ.

Note, That psalms and thanksgiving to God through Christ, must be the most constant part of Christian worship.

21. Submitting yourselves one to another in the fear of God.

21. And let God's command move you to be yielding and submissive, and not stout and stiff towards one another; but especially to your superiors: but so as to fear and obey God before men.

22, 23. Wives, submit yourselves unto your own husbands, as unto the Lord. For the husband is the head of the wife, even as Christ is the head of the church: and he is the Saviour of the body.

22, 23. Let wives shew their subjection to Christ, by submitting to their husbands, as by his command. For the husband is under Christ the head or ruler of the wife, to govern her in love, and protect her, as Christ is the supreme head and ruler of the church, and the Saviour of it as his body.

24. Therefore as the church is subject unto Christ, so let the wives be to their own husbands in every thing.

24. Therefore, as the church is in all things to be subject to Christ, so must the wives be to their husbands, in all things belonging to that relation, under Christ.

25. Husbands, love your wives, even as Christ also loved the church, and gave himself for it: 26. That he might sanctify and cleanse it with the washing of water, by the word,

25, 26. Husbands, imitate Christ, in loving your wives, as Christ did his church, for which (in a special sense he gave himself by death, that he might sanctify it to God, and cleanse it from sin, by washing away their guilt and filth, signified and sealed in baptism, and by the promises and preaching of his word.

27. That he might present it to himself a glorious church, not having spot or wrinkle, or any such thing; but that it should be holy, and without blemish.

27. That he may prepare it for the great marriage-day, and then present it to himself, cleansed and beautified, without sin, guilt, or blemish, but perfect in holiness, and glorious.

28. So ought men to love their wives, as their own bodies: he that loveth his wife, loveth himself.

28. As Eve was taken out of Adam, so the union between husband and wife is so near, that men should love their wives in a sort as their own bodies; and to love a wife should be as the loving of ourselves.

29. For no man ever yet hated his own flesh; but nourisheth and cherisheth it, even as the Lord the church.

29. And as nature causeth all men to love, nourish, and cherish their own flesh, and not to hate it; so must men do by their wives, as Christ doth by the church.

30. For we are members of his body, of his flesh, and of his bones.

30. And as Eve was said to be to Adam, flesh of his flesh, and bone of his bone: so by allusion, we may say of the church and Christ in a spiritual sense.

31. For this cause shall a man leave his father and mother, and shall be joined unto his wife, and they two shall be one flesh.

31. And as it was then said, [A man shall leave, &c.] so must believers leave all for Christ, as Christ laid down his life for them; and they shall be made as one.

32. This is a great mystery: but I speak concerning Christ and the church.

32. That which is said of Adam and Eve, and of marriage, did mystically prefigure the marriage of Jesus Christ and the church: and of this it is that I now speak.

33. Nevertheless, let every one of you in particular, so love his wife even as himself; and the wife *see* that she reverence *her* husband,

33. But though I have turned my speech to Christ and the church, I repeat my counsel; let every man love his wife, with such an entire, constant, and forbearing love, as he loveth himself; and let the wife see that she live in loving subjection and reverence to her husband.

CHAP. VI.

CHILDREN, obey your parents in the Lord: for this is right.

1. Let children be obedient to their parents under God, in obedience to him; for he hath commanded it.

2. Honour thy father and mother, (which is the first commandment with promise.)

2. Saying, honour thy father and mother: and though general promises be intimated in the first and second commandment, this is the first commandment that hath annexed the promise of the land which God was then leading the Israelites to; as it is said.

3. That it may be well with thee, and thou mayest live long on the earth.

3. That thou mayest live long, and prosper, in the promised land of Canaan; which intimateth also to us Christian Gentiles a promise of more prosperity on earth than disobedient children shall have, and an earthly curse to the disobedient.

Note. That accordingly, God's curse on earth doth usually follow children that dishonour and wrong their parents, and rebel against them; and usually even earthly blessings are given to those that honour and obey parents (under God.)

4. And ye fathers, provoke not your children to wrath: but bring them up in the nurture and admonition of the Lord.

4. And let parents remember, that childrens' corrupt nature and weakness are liable to such passions as may pervert them; and therefore let not your sour and provoking government and carriage tempt them hereto, beyond their strength; but govern them with fatherly love, and bring them up to the knowledge and obedience of the Lord, by wise and diligent teaching, example, admonition, and discipline.

5. Servants, be obedient to them that are your masters according to the flesh, with fear and trembling, in singleness of your heart, as unto Christ.

5. And let not servants think that Christianity freeth them from service, or from obedience, diligence, or reverence to their masters, though they be unbelievers: but give them all due obedience, and reverent submission, and this in conscience and sincerity, as part of your obedience to Christ, who doth command it, and will reward you.

6. Not with eye-service as menpleasers, but as the servants of Christ, doing the will of God from the heart;

6. Not deceitfully, when your masters see and know what you do, merely to please men; but as the true servants of Christ, with heartiness, and in secret things as well as open, doing service to men in obedience to the will of God, and to please him.

7. With good will doing service, as to the Lord, and not to men.

7. I repeat it, because it greatly concerneth you, that you do all your service faithfully and willingly, without grudging; and that not as a bare service to man, but as a part of your service to the Lord himself, which he hath prescribed, and will accept.

8. Knowing that whatsoever good thing any man doth, the same shall he receive of the Lord, whether *he* be bond or free.

8. Be sure of this, That your lowest and hardest service being your duty, is a good work; and such works of fidelity in the lowest bond-servants are accepted of God, as well as the more honoured servants of the greatest.

9. And ye masters, do the same things unto them, forbearing threatening: knowing that your master also is in heaven, neither is there respect of persons with him.

9. And you that are masters, see that you be as careful of your part to your servants, as you would have them be of their duty to you; and use them not tyrannically, by insulting and pas-

sionate menaces and reproaches: knowing that Christ in heaven is equally the Lord of them and you, and will not be partial to you for your wealth or superiority, but will equally do justice unto all.

10. Finally, my brethren, be strong in the Lord, and in the power of his might.

10. To conclude, Behave yourselves in the discharge of all your duties, and resistance of all the temptations of your warfare, as resolved valiant Christians, strong in the faith and love of Christ, by his powerful assisting grace.

11. Put on the whole armour of God, that ye may be able to stand against the wiles of the devil.

11. And with skill and care put on and use the grace and helps which God vouchsafeth you, (which are to a Christian like complete armour to a soldier) that you may be able to stand fast against all the stratagems and plots of the devil, who seeketh to overthrow you.

12. For we wrestle not against flesh and blood, but against principalities, against powers, against the rulers of the darkness of this world, against spiritual wickedness in high places.

12. For the great conflict which Christians are engaged in, is not merely against men, but against devils, who by God's ordination, and the success of their temptations, are principalities and powers, and the rulers of the persons and ways of darkness, ignorance, and unbelief in the world, and are spiritual wickedness, above us in the air.

13. Wherefore take unto you the whole armour of God, that ye may be able to withstand in the evil day, and having done all, to stand.

13. Therefore neglect no part of the armour afforded you by God, but use it all, that in the time of temptation you may be able to resist and conquer the assaults of men and devils, and when they have done their worst, and you have withstood them, you may stand fast in faith, and holiness, and hope.

14. Stand, therefore, having your loins girt about with truth, and having on the breast-plate of righteousness; 15. And your feet shod with the preparation of the gospel of peace.

14, 15. Stand, therefore, to your obligations to faith and holiness. 1. See that the firm belief of the truth of the gospel, against all deceivers, be to you as a military girdle about your loins. 2. And that universal sincere obedience to God, and uprightness of life towards all men, joined to your pardon through the merits of Christ, may be to you as a breast-plate is to soldiers in fight, that no adversary may have matter of just accusation against you. 3. And that the gospel of Christ, which speaketh peace to the world, and to yourselves, may so dwell in your hearts, to make you men of peace, and in your mouths to invite others to peace with God and one another, that it may be to you as those shoes were to soldiers, which they put on when they went to war, to keep their feet from hurt and danger.

16. Above all, taking the shield of faith, wherewith ye shall be able to quench all the fiery darts of the wicked.

16. Above all, see that you firmly believe and trust to the word and promises of God, which will be to you as a shield or target to a soldier, by which he is preserved from all the darts or shot that is made against him. And though Satan's darts be fiery persecution and fierce temptations, this will defend you, and frustrate all.

17. And take the helmet of salvation, and the sword of the Spirit, which is the word of God:

17. And trust fully in Christ as your saviour for salvation, and this will, as an helmet (or headpiece) to a soldier, defend your chiefest part from danger. And skilfully use the word of God, indited and sealed by his Spirit, which will serve you for defence and conquest by the help of the same Spirit, as a sword doth to a soldier.

18. Praying always with all prayer and supplication in the Spirit, and watching thereunto with all perseverance, and supplication for all saints;

18. And because you must do all in dependance on God, see that you be constant in all sorts of prayer, for yourselves and others; even such prayer as God's Spirit directeth you to by his word, and exciteth you to by his grace: and for that end, keep your minds by watchfulness in a serious praying temper, and be not cold or weary, but hold on; and forget not to pray for all holy persons (and holy things).

Note, That 1. They that scorn praying in or by the Spirit, scorn the work of the Spirit in all acceptable prayer to God.

2. They that forbid prayer, forbid that which God commandeth, and his Spirit in us as an intercessor performeth.

3. When God commandeth [all prayer and supplication] we must obey him, though many men would confine us to the fetters of their narrow defective words and books.

4. They that hate, revile, excommunicate unjustly, and persecute those saints whom God commandeth us to love and pray for, fight under Satan, against Christ.

19. And for me, that utterance may be given unto me, that I may open my mouth boldly, to make known the mystery of the gospel.

19. And let me have a special part in your prayers, that I may be freed from silencing imprisonments and restraints, and may have liberty and ability boldly to make known the mystery of man's salvation by Christ.

20. For which I am an ambassador in bonds: that therein I may speak boldly as I ought to speak.

20. For I am in bonds by men, though Christ's ambassador, even for preaching to men this gospel of salvation: but pray for me, that whatever it cost me, I may do my duty, and speak (though forbidden) as I ought to speak.

Note, That as God worketh by men, so doth the devil: and therefore it is no wonder that Paul was in bonds for preaching salvation; and that men make laws against praying and preaching, and if the devil call it sedition: for really praying and preaching do more to destroy his kingdom, and save souls, than arms can do.

21. But that ye also may know my affairs, and how I do, Tychicus, a beloved brother and faithful minister in the Lord, shall make known to you all things;

21. And that you may know how all things go with me, Tychicus will tell you whom you may trust.

22. Whom I have sent unto you for the same purpose, that ye might know our affairs, and that he might comfort your hearts.

22. I have sent him, that he may represent things truly to you, and help to keep you from discouragement, or undue trouble for my sufferings.

23. Peace be to the brethren, and love with faith from God the Father and the Lord Jesus Christ.

23. I conclude with this benediction and prayer for you, That God the Father of our Lord Jesus Christ will give, maintain, and increase in you all that confirmed faith which may fill you with love, and keep you in peace and welfare.

24. Grace be with all them that love our Lord Jesus Christ in sincerity. Amen.

24. And let the grace, favour, and blessing of God be still with all them who love our Lord Jesus Christ with sincere, incorruptible, confirmed love. Amen.

THE
EPISTLE OF PAUL THE APOSTLE,
TO THE
PHILIPPIANS.

CHAP. I.

PAUL and Timotheus the servants of Jesus Christ, to all the saints of Christ Jesus, which are at Philippi, with the bishops and deacons: 2. Grace be unto you, and peace from God our Father, and from the Lord Jesus Christ.

1, 2. I Paul, and Timothy now with me, send greeting with this epistle to all the saints (or Christians) which are at Philippi, with the bishops and deacons there; wishing to them grace and peace, which are all blessings in sum, from God our Father, and Jesus Christ our Lord.

Note, 1. That Dr. Hammond affirming, That Paul meant here all the bishops and deacons in Macedonia, or a whole province, doth this without any cogent proof; as he saith the like of Corinth, Ephesus, &c. though it may be granted, that consequently they to whom these epistles were written, were to communicate them to as many as they could.

2. That he contradicteth himself in saying, there was but one bishop in a city: when elsewhere he saith, there was one of the Jews' church, and another of the Gentiles'.

3. That Paul saith it was [the saints, which are at Philippi, with the bishops and deacons,] to wit,

which were at Philippi with them. But sure all that were in a province so great, were not at Philippi.

And his conclusion, That every church in scripture-times had but one bishop, with deacons his servants, [there being then no middle order in use;] and that in all the New Testament the words [bishop and presbyter] signifieth only such as we now call bishops, 1. Is contrary to the descriptions of the churches of Jerusalem, Antioch, Corinth, &c. where, in one assembly there were so many prophets fit for the public ministry, that they needed regulating restraint in ministering. 2. But thus he must maintain, That *de facto* no church had then more than one presbyter, and so no bishop more than one fixed congregation, (being but in one place at one time:) and so that there was no bishop that governed presbyters, nor any presbyters subject to bishops, (but only to itinerant apostles.) So that all that remaineth in controversy will be, Who instituted this middle order of presbyters after scripture-times? and, *Quo jure?* and, How it is proved that they had power so to do?

3. I thank my God upon every remembrance of you, 4. (Always in every prayer of mine for you all, making request with joy.)

3, 4. Whenever I remember you, it is with thankfulness to God; and in all my prayers for you, I do it with joy.

5. For your fellowship in the gospel from the first day until now:

5. For the hearty communion and communication in, and for the gospel, which you have exercised from the first day of your conversion until now.

6. Being confident of this very thing, that he which hath begun a good work in you, will perform it until the day of Jesus Christ.

6. Not doubting but God, who hath been the author of this good beginning, will carry it on, till you are presented perfect in the day of the coming of Christ.

7. Even as it is meet for me to think this of you all, because I have you in my heart inasmuch as both in my bonds, and in the defence and confirmation of the gospel, ye all are partakers of my grace.

7. It is meet that I think this of you all; for you have, a great room in my heart, because in my bonds and sufferings, and in all that we do for the defence and confirmation of the gospel, you have manifested the same grace, and by your communication and co-operation have your part in the blessing and reward of my ministerial grace and labours.

8. For God is my record, how greatly I long after you all, in the bowels of Christ Jesus.

8. For God is my witness, with what earnest love I long for your welfare; even with that love which Christ hath kindled in me for his own sake who loveth you.

9. And this I pray, that your love may abound yet more and more in knowledge, and in all judgment;

9. And my prayer for you is, That you may increase and abound in holy love to Christ and his gospel, and each other, and in all spiritual wisdom and discerning judgment.

10. That ye may approve things that are excellent; that ye may be sincere, and without offence till the day of Christ:

10. That you may yet more grow up in the approbation and love of the excellent things of Christian faith, and life, and hope, and may be sound and sincere in faith and life, without warping in judgment, or scandal in practice, till the day of judgment.

11. Being filled with the fruits of righteousness, which are by Jesus Christ unto the glory and praise of God.

11. And that you may abound with all that righteousness towards God and man, which is the true fruit of faith and of the Spirit, by which you may praise and glorify God.

12. But I would ye should understand, brethren, that the things which happened unto me, have fallen out rather unto the furtherance of the gospel.

12. I think meet to give you notice, lest misinformation discourage you, that my imprisonment and sufferings have not hindered but furthered the gospel.

13. So that my bonds in Christ are manifest in all the palace, and in all other places;

13. For my imprisonment for Christ, hath but made me, and consequently my preaching, to be known in the court, and places of judicature, and abroad to others.

14. And many of the brethren in the Lord, waxing confident by my bonds, are much more bold to speak the word without fear.

14. And the example of my patience, boldness, and success in suffering, hath emboldened many of the brethren, confidently, without fear, to preach and profess the gospel.

15. Some indeed preach Christ even of envy and strife; and some also of good will. 16. The one preach Christ of contention, not sincerely, supposing to add affliction to my bonds: 17. But the other of love, knowing that I am set for the defence of the gospel.

15, 16, 17. There be some here at Rome, and elsewhere, that because I reprove them for Judaizing, by obtruding the law and ceremonies of Moses on the Gentiles, and such other causes, are quarrelsome with me, and seek my defamation; and while they preach Christ, it is with the mixture of spleen and bitterness against me, and in an envious, striving, and reproachful manner, against me, and such as I, who conform not to their ceremonious impositions. Thus some preach the same Christ that I do, but contentiously, and not in sincerity, and love, and meekness, but to add to my bonds the affliction of men's contempt and disaffection, to turn the hearts of people from me and my ministry. But there are others that preach in Christian love, and carry it with kindness towards me, knowing that I am called to propagate and defend Christ's gospel, and that it is it that I suffer for, and not for my fault and error, as the other would persuade the people.

18. What then? notwithstanding every way, whether in pretence, or in truth, Christ is preached; and I therein do rejoice, yea, and will rejoice.

18. But though some seek pre-eminence, and their own honour and interest, and envy me, and join too much self-seeking with the preaching of the gospel, and do it not with the love and sincerity that they ought; yet every way Christ is preached, and I therein rejoice, yea, and will rejoice.

Note, 1. That they mistake who think Paul speaketh of the preachers of false doctrine in any great point: for he would not rejoice in that. It is but preaching with corrupt passions and purposes, perhaps for little differences, in a splenetic manner, contrary to love and peaceableness.

2. Paul here entereth his professed dissent, both against church-tyranny, that would forbid those who preach them and their opinions or interest, and against those separatists who cry down the ministry of those that are faulty in tolerable things, yea that cross them in their way.

19. For I know that this shall turn to my salvation through your prayer, and the supply of the Spirit of Jesus Christ.

19. For I doubt not but even this accumulating affliction on me, by envious brethren, with heathen persecutors, shall through your prayer, and Christ's Spirit, all turn to good, and but further my own and other men's salvation.

20. According to my earnest expectation, and my hope, that in nothing I shall be ashamed, but that with all boldness, as always, so now also Christ shall be magnified in my body, whether it be by life or by death.

20. For, as it is my earnest expectation, so it is my comfortable hope, that whether it be by my life or death, all that befals my body shall be to the honour of Christ, and then I have my end.

21. For me to live is Christ, and to die is gain.

21. For to me to live, is to serve and honour Christ; he is the end of my life, and his work the business; it is for Christ that I live; and if I die, it will be my gain.

22. But if I live in the flesh, this is the fruit of my labour: yet what I shall choose I wot not.

22. But if God will have me live longer, it will be time given for my fruitful labour, (or, it will be worth desiring, for my labour sake;) or, as Beza [whether it will be worth my labour and suffering], and what to choose (if God would leave it to my choice) I know not.

23. For I am in a strait betwixt two, having a desire to depart, and to be with Christ; which is far better.

23. For it is to me a great difficulty to know which is more desirable: I would fain be with Christ, which is far better for me than to be here.

24. Nevertheless to abide in the flesh, is more needful for you.

24. But my life seemeth more needful for your farther service.

25. And having this confidence, I know that I shall abide and continue with you all, for your furtherance and joy of faith,

25. And being assured of this, (and knowing withal Christ's love to his church) I am persuaded that I shall yet longer continue in life, for your furtherance, and comfort, and confirmation in your Christian faith and hope.

36. That your rejoicing may be more abundant in Jesus Christ for me by my coming to you again.

26. That when you see me with you again, you may greatly for my sake rejoice in Christ.

27. Only let your conversation be as it becometh the gospel of Christ: that whether I come and see you, or else be absent, I may hear of your affairs, that ye stand

fast in one Spirit, with one mind, striving together for the faith of the gospel:

27. But I beseech you look to this one thing on your own part, that your conversation may be such as becometh the belief and profession of the gospel of salvation; that whether I come to you again, or not, I may hear that you stand fast, in one spirit actuating you, and with one mind and loving concord, (not striving against one another, as persecutors and sectaries do, but) co-operating and striving together to defend and propagate the belief of the gospel, (though you may differ about many lesser things.)

28. And in nothing terrified by your adversaries: which is to them an evident token of perdition, but to you of salvation, and that of God.

28. And that you be in nothing terrified by your adversaries' power or rage; for their persecuting, and your patience, are an evident prognostic of their perdition, but of your salvation, even by God, who will condemn the wicked, and justify the just.

29. For unto you it is given in the behalf of Christ, not only to believe on him, but also to suffer for his sake;

29. For it is a great addition to your honour and felicity, that God hath given you this blessing, not only to believe on Christ as Christians, but to suffer for him as martyrs. (For by this you have the promise of the greatest reward.)

30. Having the same conflict which ye saw in me, and now hear *to be* in me.

30. Having the same kind of conflict with opposers and persecutors, which you saw me have when I was with you, and now hear that I have at Rome when I am from you.

Note, It is mere violence to the text, which the Socinians use with verse 21, 23, while they expound verse 21, of [Gain to the church by my martyrdom, and not to me only as I shall be rewarded as a martyr at Christ's coming;] and verse 23, of [A desire to depart by martyrdom, that I may be with Christ at the resurrection:] or, [which is far better for the church, that will gain more by my martyrdom, than my preaching:] clean contrary to what he saith, verse 24, 25, and to the plain text. Men that can thus use the scripture, may believe what they list, let God say what he will. Christ hath expressly promised all his servants, John xii. 26. as well as the dying thief, that they shall be with him where he is, even in paradise.

CHAP. II.

IF *there be* therefore any consolation in Christ, if any comfort of love, if any fellowship of the Spirit, if any bowels and mercies; 2. Fulfil ye my joy, that ye be likeminded, having the same love, being of one accord, of one mind.

1, 2. I adjure or beseech you, therefore, as ever you take Christ, our common head, for your hope and comfort, and look to find comfort in the exercise of Christian love to all saints, and if you are indeed united in the communion of the same Spirit, (without which you are none of Christ's) and if you have any bowels of mercy to others, (as all Christians must have,) that you yet make me more joyful by your increased unanimity, that you have all one and the same affection and design of life, that you all love one another as yourselves, and be of one accord in your doctrine and converse, and of one mind and judgment.

Note, 1. That Paul here supposeth that all Christians should live in this unanimity, love, and concord, who do but know and agree in the great things which constitute true Christianity, though they may not have skill enough to know right from wrong in many small, indifferent or circumstantial things. The church tyrants' exposition maketh Paul to scorn them, rather than counsel them; as if he said, [I adjure you by all the comforts of Christ and his Spirit, that you be all so wise as to know all that is in the Bible, yea more, all that any bishops in council and all their canons shall tell you, or command you; yea, that you know not only all the essentials and integrals of religion, but even all the things indifferent, which canons shall impose on you, to be really indifferent, that is, that every man and woman know more than any doctor on earth knoweth, or else you cannot live in Christian love and comfort.] It is this diabolical exposition of the scripture, that hath torn and ruined the Christian world.

2. And yet Paul here implieth, that no Christian should affectedly scruple any lawful command of their superiors, or custom of the church, but should so avoid singularity and disobedience, as to do any thing, save sin, for peace and concord.

3. Let nothing *be done* through strife, or vain-glory, but in lowliness of mind let each esteem other better than themselves.

3. Let not pride make you vain-glorious and contentious: but let Christian humility make you so low in your own eyes, as to be more inclinable to think highly of other men's wisdom and goodness than of your own, further than evidence constraineth you to think more meanly of any.

Note, That Paul knew that it was pride of men's own knowledge and goodness, (especially in the clergy) setting them in a vain-glorious striving against each other, that was like to cause schism in the church.

4. Look not every man on his own things, but every man also on the things of others.

4. Specially take heed of selfishness which maketh men over-regardful of all that is their own, their own interest in honour, or profit, or opinion;

and to set too light by other men's, yea, to set against the interest of others to advance their own.

Note, That self-denial and love (or, to love others as ourselves) are the great means to keep and cast out schism: and the want of them in clergy and laity, is the common mischief and ruin of the churches.

5, 6. Let this mind be in you, which was also in Christ Jesus; who being in the form of God, thought it not robbery to be equal with God.

5, 6. Learn this of Christ, who being God, the brightness of his Father's glory, and the express image of his subsistence, (or person) Heb. i. 3. thought it no robbery to be equal with God the Father, being one with him.

7. But made himself of no reputation, and took upon him the form of a servant, and was made in the likeness of men:

7. But yet condescended to assume human nature, and so in that which was visible was a man, and a servant, obliged to obedience in the most humble instance, and so made himself, by this humble self-denial, of no reputation with the unbelieving world, that knew not his divinity thus veiled, yea, counted him a malefactor.

8. And being found in fashion as a man, he humbled himself, and became obedient unto death, even the death of the cross.

8. And being visible only in his human nature, like other men, he yet further humbled himself obeying his Father, by submitting to the reproachful, cursed death of being crucified, as accused of blasphemy and treason against Cesar.

9. Wherefore God also hath highly exalted him, and given him a name which is above every name:

9. Wherefore God hath highly exalted him in that manhood, in which he suffered, and hath given him greater dignity, and honour, and renown, than any creature ever had over them all.

10. That at the name of Jesus, every knee shall bow, of *things* in heaven, and *things* in earth, and *things* under the earth.

10. That to his dignity and power all creatures should be subject, and angels, men, and devils, should by their submission respectively honour his name.

11. And that every tongue should confess that Jesus Christ is Lord to the glory of God the Father:

11. And that all reasonable creatures acknowledge Christ's dominion, to the glory of the Father.

12. Wherefore, my beloved, as ye have always obeyed, not as in my presence only, but now much more in my absence; work out your own salvation with fear and trembling.

12. Wherefore as you have always lived in obedience to Christ, both while I was with you, and much more since, go on, and finish or perfect that holy obedience which God requireth of you, for the obtaining of salvation, and that with holy care and diligence, and watchful cautelous fear of miscarrying.

13. For it is God which worketh in you, both to will and to do of *his* good pleasure.

13. Which I may the more confidently exhort you to in hope, because you are not the prime agents required to do this merely of yourselves, but only under God, the prime cause of all good, both of nature and grace, who doth not only give you power, but worketh in you both the act of willing and of working, of his own good pleasure.

14. Do all things without murmurings and disputings.

14. And do all your works of obedience to God, in love and peace with one another, without murmuring at your work, at one another, and without provoking wranglings.

15. That ye may be blameless and harmless, the sons of God without rebuke, in the midst of a crooked and perverse nation, among whom ye shine as lights in the world:

15. That you may be unreproveable and sincere, the blameless sons of God, in the midst of a naughty, crooked, and perverse generation, or sort of men, among whom ye shine as lights in the world.

16. Holding forth the word of life; that I may rejoice in the day of Christ, that I have not run in vain, neither laboured in vain.

16. That in the day of Christ's judgment, I may rejoice not only in the sincerity of my labour but in the success, that I have not preached and laboured, and suffered, without fruit.

17. Yea, and if I be offered upon the sacrifice and service of your faith, I joy, and rejoice with you all.

17. Yea, if I suffer death as a sacrifice for the service of your faith, your constancy and welfare will make it matter of joy to me for your sakes.

18. For the same cause also do ye joy, and rejoice with me.

18. And if my suffering be my joy, let it be yours also; be not discouraged, but rejoice with me.

19. But I trust in the Lord Jesus, to send Timotheus shortly unto you, that I also may be of good comfort when I know your state.

19. But I hope by the mercy of the Lord, to send Timothy shortly to you, that when by him I know your state, I may have comfort in you, as you may have in me.

20. For I have no man like-minded, who will naturally care for your state.

20. For I have no man equal to him in love to you, who will care for your state with such affection, even as nature teacheth men, to care for their children as themselves.

21. For all seek their own, not the things which are Jesus Christ's.

21. For all are so much set on minding their own matters, and seeking their own interest, that it abateth their zeal and diligence in seeking the interest and things of Christ.
Note, 1. That selfishly to prefer their own carnal interests to Christ's, is a certain mark of a graceless hypocrite. 2. Therefore Paul meaneth not that all are such predominantly, but that all too much seek their own, and Christ's too little. 3. But that this self-seeking is the plague of the clergy and church, culpably in all in various degrees, and predominantly in false-hearted hypocrites.

22. But ye know the proof of him, that as a son with the father, he hath served with me in the gospel.

22. But you know what experience you and I have had of him, that with the love of a son, and the diligence of a servant, he hath assisted me in my ministry of the gospel.

23. Him therefore I hope to send presently, so soon as I shall see how it will go with me.

23. Him I hope to send as soon as I know, and can by him tell you, how it is like to go with me.

24. But I trust in the Lord, that I also myself shall come shortly.

24. And I trust that the Lord's mercy will deliver me, and I shall shortly come myself.

25. Yet I supposed it necessary to send to you Epaphroditus, my brother, and companion in labour, and fellow-soldier, but your messenger, and he that ministered to my wants.

25. But I thought good to send you back Epaphroditus, who is my brother and fellow-labourer, and messenger, who from you supplied my wants.

26. For he longed after you all, and was full of heaviness, because that ye had heard that he had been sick.

26. He longed to be with you, and comfort you by the sight of his health, bearing that his sickness made you sad.

27. For indeed he was sick nigh unto death; but God had mercy on him; and not on him only, but on me also, lest I should have sorrow upon sorrow.

27. He was nigh to death, but God in mercy to him and me recovered him, not adding his death to my affliction.

28. I sent him therefore the more carefully, that when ye see him again, ye may rejoice, and that I may be the less sorrowful.

28. Note, That mercies restored after danger, affect us more than those continued in prosperity.

29. Receive him therefore in the Lord with all gladness, and hold such in reputation: 30. Because for the work of Christ he was nigh unto death, not regarding his life to supply your lack of service toward me.

29, 30. Receive him gladly as returned to you by God, and account such honourable; for it was for the work of Christ, that he willingly hazarded his life by his travels and labour to be serviceable to me as your messenger in your stead.

CHAP. III.

FINALLY, my brethren, rejoice in the Lord. To write the same things to you, to me indeed *is* not grievous, but for you *it is* safe.

1. Finally, brethren, serve God with joyful hearts: That I write to you the same things which I have formerly taught you, and warned you of, is not through sloth or cowardice in me, but for your own safety, as fittest for you.

2. Beware of dogs, beware of evil workers, beware of the concision.

2. To wit, that you take heed of the worrying hurtful sort of men, who live in wickedness, and calling themselves the Circumcision, are indeed the Concision, that cut and rend the churches.

3. For we are the circumcision,

which worship God in the Spirit, and rejoice in Christ Jesus, and have no confidence in the flesh.

3. For we are the children of circumcised Abraham, who worship God in spirit and truth, and have no confidence in fleshly privileges, or carnal ceremonious Jewish worship.

4. Though I might also have confidence in the flesh. If any other man thinketh that he hath whereof he might trust in the flesh, I more:

4. Though if Judaism were matter of trust or boasting, I have more such cause than any of them.

5. Circumcised the eighth day, of the stock of Israel, *of* the tribe of Benjamin, an Hebrew of the Hebrews; as touching the law, a Pharisee; 6. Concerning zeal, persecuting the church; touching the righteousness which is in the law, blameless.

5, 6. I was circumcised as the law required, I was an Israelite, a Benjamite, an Hebrew, a Pharisee, the strictest sect in religion; not cold in religion, but a zealous persecutor of the church, which I thought had been against it. And as to the outward observance of the law of Moses, I seemed to men so just and harmless, that none accused me.

7. But what things were gain to me, those I counted loss for Christ.

7. But I willingly disclaim all confidence in these, and reject all as loss that would keep me from Christ.

8. Yea doubtless, and I count all things but loss, for the excellency of the knowledge of Christ Jesus my Lord; for whom I have suffered the loss of all things, and do count them but dung that I may win Christ.

8. Yea, I reject all as loss and hurtful to me, which stand against the excellency of the knowledge of Christ, for whom I have readily suffered the loss of all things, and count them but as dung in order to my part in Christ, and that I may be found in him.

9. And be found in him, not having mine own righteousness, which is of the law, but that which is through the faith of Christ, the righteousness, which is of God by faith:

9. Not having, and trusting not in that righteousness which consisteth in keeping the law of Moses, which is of my own works, and I account-

ed formerly to be my justifying righteousness: but that which is of faith in Christ, even the righteousness which is of God's free gift by believing acceptance of his purchased and offered grace.

10. That I may know him, and the power of his resurrection, and the fellowship of his suffering, being made conformable unto his death.

10. By which I shall gain the knowledge of Christ, and of the great mystery of salvation by him, and the powerful work of his grace and quickening Spirit, and preserving providence, answering in his members that power that raised him from the dead, and a communion with him in sufferings, by which I shall be made conformable to him as crucified for our sins; and thus in all be made as a member suitable to him that is my head.

11. If by any means I might attain unto the resurrection of the dead:

11. In hope that by all these means and methods (which I account not too dear) I may at last attain that blessed perfection in which I shall be also like him, as he is now risen from the dead, and glorified in the state of immortality.

12. Not as though I had already attained, either were already perfect: but I follow after, if that I may apprehend that for which also I am apprehended of Christ Jesus.

12. Not that I have already attained this conformity to my glorified Lord, or were already perfect by reaching all that I pursue; But I run as for this prize, and earnestly strive, that at last I may lay hold on and attain the state of glory, to bring me to which Jesus Christ did elect, redeem, and call me to himself.

13. Brethren, I count not myself to have apprehended: but *this one* thing *I do*, forgetting those things which are behind, and reaching forth unto those things which are before, 14. I press toward the mark, for the prize of the high calling of God in Christ Jesus.

13, 14. I know I have not yet attained the end that I ran for, even glorious perfection: But this I do, not minding things of the world which I have forsaken, but neglecting and forgetting them, and with all my might and diligence striving towards the things which are before. I press or hasten towards the mark, or that glorious crown and prize, for obtaining whereof, the high calling of God by Jesus Christ hath encouraged me to seek and hope.

15. Let us therefore, as many as be perfect, be thus minded: and if in any thing ye be otherwise mind-

ed, God shall reveal even this unto you.

15. And let all that are sound and sincere Christians, holding these things that are necessary to salvation, be thus minded, and with joint endeavour confessing our defects, thus press toward the end of our faith in love: And then, if through imperfection of knowledge you come short, and differ in other things, while you wait on God in humility, love, and peace, God will in time make you know what yet is wanting to you.

16. Nevertheless, whereto we have already attained, let us walk by the same rule, let us mind the same thing.

16. But let all that have attained soundness in these necessary essentials of Christianity, still live according to these gospel-truths which we all acknowledge, and in love and concord practise and promote these things in which we are agreed.

Note, How directly Paul condemneth both church-tyrants and sectaries, the former silencing, reviling, and persecuting, and the other reproachfully censuring and separating from those that agree in all here instanced, for not consenting to needless trifles of the clergy's imposition, or to the errors of superstitious ignorant men.

17. Brethren, be followers together of me, and mark them which walk so, as ye have us for an ensample.

17. God that hath sent me to teach you, hath herein also made me an ensample to you; I beseech you therefore herein follow me, (in humble striving towards perfection, uniting in sincere Christianity, and bearing in other things with each other, till God teach you the rest.)

18. (For many walk, of whom I have told you often, and now tell you even weeping, *that they are* the enemies of the cross of Christ: 19. Whose end *is* destruction, whose God *is their* belly: and *whose* glory *is* in their shame, who mind earthly things.)

18, 19. For many, of whom I have oft told you, and now mention them with tears, for their own sakes and the churches, do so live, as that while they are called Christians, they are such enemies to the bearing of the cross, in following a crucified Christ, that they will suffer nothing for their faith: For taking up Christianity notionally in their brains, without the life and power on their hearts, the world was never overcome, or their lust mortified by it; so that their belly, or fleshly lust, is the god which they most love and obey; and while they glory that they know more of Christian liberty than we do, and so may lawfully please fleshly lusts, it is their shame and brutishness which they glory in: And therefore destruction will be their end.

20. For our conversation is in heaven, from whence also we look for the Saviour, the Lord Jesus Christ: 21. Who shall change our vile body, that it may be fashioned like unto his glorious body, according to the working whereby he is able even to subdue all things to himself.

20, 21. But our city-freedom, relation treasure, converse, and business, is in heaven, among the heavenly society, in the Jerusalem above: From thence, by faith and joyful hope, we look for the Saviour, the Lord Jesus, who is our Head and Intercessor there; and who will not only receive our souls at death, but will also change these vile bodies, (which being made of the low dissoluble elements, are a clog to our souls, and must corrupt like the flesh of brutes) and will make them like his own now glorious body, (spiritual, incorruptible, and glorious,) and this he can and will do, how unlikely soever it appears to us, by the exercise of his omnipotency, by which he can conquer all difficulties and enemies, for the accomplishing of the work of the salvation of his church.

Note, 1. That the great difference between miserable hypocrites and sound Christians is, that the former set most by flesh and earth; and the latter by the hopes of heaven, to which they subject all worldly interest, and on which and for which they live and labour most, as worldlings do for a worldly welfare.

2. That a false, sensual, worldly, unmortified heart, betrayeth hypocrites into worldly sensual opinions and heresies, and they easily believe all to be lawful which maketh for their fleshly worldly interests and lusts, because their false hearts would have it to be lawful.

CHAP. IV.

THEREFORE, my brethren, dearly beloved and longed for, my joy and crown, so stand fast in the Lord, *my* dearly beloved.

1. Note, That the most amiable Christians have need of warning and earnest exhortation against backsliding by temptation and deceivers.

2. I beseech Euodias and beseech Syntyche, that they be of the same mind in the Lord.

2. Note, It is like he heard of contentions between these two, which he beseecheth them to cease.

3. And I intreat thee also, true yoke-fellow, help those women which laboured with me in the gospel, with Clement also, and with other my fellow-labourers, whose names *are* in the book of life.

3. And I intreat thee, my true fellow-labourer, (it is like he meaneth Epaphroditus, but uncertain:) take care of those women that furthered our work, (by entertaining us, and suffering for the faith,) with Clement, and other helpers, who are of the number of those that God will own.

4. Rejoice in the Lord alway, *and* again I say, Rejoice.

4. Rejoice in the interest you have in the Lord, his grace, and protection, and promise of glory: Yea, I again urge it on you, Always rejoice.

Note, 1. That Christians even in a state of opposition from the world, have always greater cause of rejoicing in God, than of sorrow for the world, (though if they wilfully sin, it may interrupt their joy, by making them unfit for it, as wounds and sickness do the body.

2 That holy joy in the Lord is that flower of religion which all Christians should desire, and chiefly labour to attain.

5. Let your moderation be known unto all men, The Lord *is* at hand.

5. Let all men see, that you put the best sense on all that befals you from God and man, and that you take nothing by impatience or uncharitableness at the worst, but can suffer injuries: For God is with you, and the day of his delivering you is near.

6. Be careful for nothing, but in every thing by prayer and supplication with thanksgiving, let your requests be made known unto God.

6. Let no want nor danger disturb your mind with anxious distrustful cares; but in every case go and open it to God in prayer, for yourselves and others, with thanksgiving for what you have received, as beseemeth those who truly trust in God.

7. And the peace of God which passeth all understanding, shall keep your hearts and minds through Christ Jesus.

7. And by this lenity of mind, and trust in God by prayer, the peace which you shall have in God's love to you, in your own souls, and in concord with the church, which is of inestimable value, above much notional knowledge, shall, as a garrison, keep your affections from disturbance, and your judgments from error, through the grace of Christ.

8. Finally, brethren, whatsoever things are true, whatsoever things *are* honest, whatsoever things *are* just, whatsoever things *are* pure, whatsoever things *are* lovely, whatsoever things *are* of good report; if *there be* any virtue, and if *there be* any praise, think on these things.

8. In general, to conclude, Be sure that you cleave to truth, against falsehood; to things seemly and venerable, against things shameful; to things just against injustice; to things pure, against lust and pollution; to things truly amiable, against deceiving paint, and flattering allurements; to things deservedly of good report and approved by men, against scandal. In a word, Let all things that are truly virtuous and praiseworthy, be faithfully minded and followed by you.

9. Those things which ye have both learned and received, and heard and seen in me, do: and the God of peace shall be with you.

9. Practice the doctrine which you have heard and received from me; and the good example which you have seen in me; and the God of love and peace will be with you, thus walking in love and peace.

10. But I rejoiced in the Lord greatly that now at the last your care of me hath flourished again, wherein ye were also careful, but ye lacked opportunity.

10. I was glad, and thanked God, that your care of my supply at last revived; not that I supposed it dead before, but that you lacked opportunity of sending to me, rather than will, and care of me.

11. Not that I speak in respect of want: for I have learned in whatsoever state I am, *therewith* to be content.

11. I mean not that I so much rejoice that my wants were supplied: For I have learned to be of a quiet and contented mind, in whatever condition God shall bring me.

12. I know both *how* to be abased, and know *how* to abound; every where, and in all things I am instructed, both to be full and to be hungry, both to abound and to suffer need.

12. I know how to be in a low and poor condition, without repining; and how to have plenty, without sensuality and abuse: I have learned how to live in every place and case, both to be fully provided, and to be in hunger through poverty, to abound, and to suffer need, and glorify God in all.

13. I can do all things through Christ which strengtheneth me.

13. All this is but my duty; and Christ will strengthen me for all that he calls me to.

14. Notwithstanding, ye have well done, that ye did communicate with my afflictions.

14. But this communication for my supply is my suffering for the gospel, was your duty, and you did well in doing it.

15. Now ye Philippians know also, that at the beginning of the gospel when I departed from Macedonia, no church communicated with me, as concerning giving and receiving, but ye only.

15. I suppose you know that this honour of contributing to me was due only to you, when I first had preached the gospel in Macedonia, no other church doing the like at my departure.

16. For even in Thessalonica ye sent once and again unto my necessity.

16. Note, How much professed Christians differ in liberality, as they do in charity.

17. Not because I desire a gift: but I desire fruit that may abound to your account.

17. Not that I am craving more by commending you, or value most my own supplies; but I commend and desire your fruitfulness in good works, that it may abound to your own consolation, when you must be accountable for all to God.

18. But I have all, and abound: I am full, having received of Epaphroditus the things *which were sent* from you, an odour of a sweet smell, a sacrifice acceptable, well-pleasing to God.

18. But I certify you, that I received your gift from Epaphroditus, and it was a very liberal supply to me; and to encourage you, I add. That under and through Christ, the great propitiating sacrifice, such works are the sweet incense and sacrifice acceptable and pleasing to God.

19. But my God shall supply all your need, according to his riches in glory, by Christ Jesus.

19. And my God, who employeth me in his work, will see that you shall lose nothing by furthering his service, but, out of the riches of his glory by Christ, will give a more excellent supply of all your wants.

20. Now unto God and our Father *be* glory for ever and ever. Amen.

20. Now to God, who is love, and a Father to us through Christ, be glory for all his mercies, and for and by all his works, for ever. Amen.

21, 22, 23. Salute every saint in Christ Jesus. The brethren which are with me greet you. All the saints salute you, chiefly they that are of Cesar's household. The grace of our Lord Jesus Christ *be* with you all. Amen.

Note, 1. That Christians were all then called saints, because they were by profession and vow devoted to God in the covenant of holiness, and were not debauched, as multitudes now are.

2. That God had his saints, even in a heathen persecuting emperor's family.

3. That the grace of Christ is the sum of all benediction on earth.

THE EPISTLE OF PAUL THE APOSTLE,

TO THE

COLOSSIANS.

CHAP. I.

PAUL an apostle of Jesus Christ, by the will of God, and Timotheus *our* brother. 2. To the saints and faithful brethren in Christ, which are at Colosse; Grace *be* unto you, and peace from God our Father, and the Lord Jesus Christ. 3. We give thanks to God, and the Father of our Lord Jesus Christ, praying always for you: 4. Since we heard of your faith in Christ Jesus, and of the love *which ye have* to all the saints;

3, 4. Note, 1. That faith and love are the sum of religion, and greater riches than all earthly things.
2. Love must extend to all saints, and not only those that are of one party.

5. For the hope which is laid up for you in heaven, whereof ye heard before in the word of the truth of the gospel: 6. Which is come unto you, as *it is* in all the world, and bringeth forth fruit, as *it doth* also in you, since the day ye heard of it, and knew the grace of God in truth.

5, 6. Note, 1. It is the hope of heavenly felicity, which is the end, and effectual motive, of Christian love and duty. 2. It is the true word of the gospel that giveth us this hope. 3. This gospel divulged to the world is fruitful extensively in the number of converts, and intensely in their holiness, when it is so heard as to cause men to know God's grace in truth.

7. As ye also learned of Epaphras our dear fellow-servant, who is for you a faithful minister of Christ; 8. Who also declared unto us your love in the Spirit.

7, 8. Note. It is like Epaphras was he by whom they were converted, or at least their present bishop.

9. For this cause, we also, since the day we heard it, do not cease to pray for you, and to desire that ye might be filled with the knowledge of his will, in all wisdom and spiritual understanding.

9. True converts have need to be prayed for, that they may have spiritual and practical wisdom to know the will of God.

10. That ye might walk worthy of the Lord unto all pleasing, being fruitful in every good work, and increasing in the knowledge of God;

10. That you may live suitably to your professed faith, sincerely obeying and pleasing God in all things, which is your worthiness in a gospel sense, bringing forth the fruits of all sorts of good works, and increasing in the knowledge (or acknowledging) of God.

11. Strengthened with all might, according to his glorious power, unto all patience and long-suffering with joyfulness.

11. Note, 1. The glorious power of God appeareth in his servants' strength. 2. The strength of Christians appeareth most in suffering long and patiently for Christ with joy, and not in overcoming men by strength.

12. Giving thanks unto the Father, which hath made us meet to be partakers of the inheritance of the saints in light:

12. Note, 1. The inheritance of the saints is in the state and world of light, that is, of vision and

glory. 2. God's way of bringing men to this glory, is by fitting them for it now by holiness. 3. This is the gift which obligeth us to the greatest thankfulness to God.

13. Who hath delivered us from the power of darkness, and hath translated us into the kingdom of his dear Son.

13. Note, The world is divided into two societies: One under the power of darkness, that is, Satan the prince of darkness, who leads men by the way of ignorance, error, unbelief, and lies, to the utter darkness of misery. The other is the kingdom of Christ, led by him who is the light of the world, by truth, knowledge, and faith, to the heavenly light.

2. When men are truly converted to Christ, they are initially delivered from the power, state, and way of darkness, into the kingdom of Christ and light.

14. In whom we have redemption through his blood, even the forgiveness of sins.

14. Note, Christ's blood is the price of our redemption, and remission of sin is much of the collation and application. Redemption signifieth deliverance from bondage.

15. Who is the image of the invisible God, the first born of every creature:

15. In whose human nature, doctrine, and works, the invisible God, whose image he is, is manifested to man; and who in his divine nature was begotten of the Father before any creature was made, (even from eternity,) and in his person, as Godman, is most excellent, and is Lord of all.

(This [First-born] numbereth him not with creatures, but sets him above them.)

16. For by him were all things created that are in heaven, and that are in earth, visible and invisible, whether *they be* thrones, or dominions, or principalities, or powers; all things are created by him, and for him. 17. And he is before all things, and by him all things consist.

16, 17. By him, as God, were all things created, and for him; and he is from eternity before them all, and by him they are upheld in being.

Note, 1. Some by [things in heaven and earth,] and [thrones, dominions, &c.] understand only [Jews and Gentiles,] and [the powers of men:] But this forced exposition is groundless: it being certain, that all heavenly powers and orders were created by the eternal word, and Paul being here extolling his magnificence, why should we feign him to leave out the highest part, which he so plainly expresseth? That celestial spirits have potent superiority both over us and one another, is no doubt.

II. The ancient churches and heretics had so great contentions about the right notions of the nature and person of Christ, and with such dismal effects, as maketh many lovers of peace to wish, that such points had been handled more cautiously, reverently, and peaceably. Four notable opinions there be about the natures and person of Christ.

1. The orthodox hold, that he hath only two natures in one person, the divine and human. And of these, the subtle philosophers say, that the human nature is no part of his person, but an adjunct, because God cannot be a part. But others avoid this as dangerous.

2. The Arians think Christ is but a creature, is but a superangelical spirit, the first created, by whom God made all the rest; and that he assumed the human nature, and may be well called God, but not as the Father is, nor of the same substance: And so, that he hath two natures, superangelical and human. Of these, 1. Some think that the superangelical, as a soul, assumed only a human body: And, 2. Some that he assumed a soul and body.

3. A third sort say, Christ hath three natures; 1. The Divine, producing by emanation the first created superangelical nature, united to itself, and by it creating all other things; and both these natures in the fulness of time assuming the human nature, (entire, say some; and a body only, say others.)

4. The last and worst is that of the Socinians, that count Christ a mere glorified man. This text seemeth to speak but the first, though the favourers of the third think it is for them; and that other texts are so also. They think it was was not only the divine nature, but the superangelical, which appeared to Abraham, Moses, &c. in a visible body, before the incarnation: And by asserting these three natures in Christ, they would reconcile the orthodox and the Arians. The controversies also whether Christ be two persons or but one, and have two wills and operations, or but one, and whether it may be said, That Mary was the mother of God, and that one of the Trinity was crucified, &c. did grievously rend the church; of which I have spoken elsewhere, and plainly shewed in what sense Christ is two, yea, many persons (relatively,) and in what sense but one; in what sense his wills are two, and in what sense but one.

18. And he is the head of the body, the church: who is the beginning, the first-born from the dead; that in all things he might have the pre-eminence.

18. And he is now the Head, both by government and quickening influence, of the church, which is his body politic, and united to him incomprehensibly; the spring of life to us, and the first that rose from death to glorious immortality, triumphantly, by his own power; by whom it is that we live, and shall be raised: For in all things he is highest, above all creatures.

19. For it pleased *the Father*, that in him should all fulness dwell:

19. For it seemed good to the Father that Jesus Christ should be filled with all created perfection, as well as he hath divine perfection, and be the spring and treasure of all good, as the head over all things to his church, and the Universal Administrator.

20. And (having made peace through the blood of the cross) by him to reconcile all things unto himself, by him, *I say*, whether they be things in earth, or things in heaven.

20. And having accepted his sacrifice on the cross for a general atonement and propitiation, by him to reconcile the guilty, sinful, and cursed world, to him, so far as that their guilt and enmity should not hinder the tenders of free mercy and salvation to Jews and Gentiles, nor keep his elect and faithful flock from that heavenly glory, where angels and saints shall be one blessed society, united in love to God and each other.

21. And you that were sometimes alienated, and enemies in your mind by wicked works, yet now hath he reconciled.

21. And you, who were not only, as all others, originally guilty, as the seed of Adam, but also of the race and society of Gentiles, by your wicked works estranged from God, and out of the way of his saving grace, and enemies to it and him, yet now hath he reconciled by Christ, and taken you for his children.

22. In the body of his flesh through death, to present you holy and unblameable, and unreproveable in his sight.

22. By giving up his body of flesh to death, as a propitiatory sacrifice; and by justifying and sanctifying you, to present you holy, and blameless, and justified at last before him.

23. If ye continue in the faith, grounded and settled, and be not moved away from the hope of the gospel, which ye have heard, *and which was preached to every creature which is under heaven; whereof I Paul am made a minister.*

23. I say, you shall be thus perfected at last, if you prove sound confirmed Christians, continuing in the faith, grounded and settled, and by no temptation be ever turned from the hope which Christ hath given you in his gospel; which by Christ's commission we preach to all men in this lower world, which is already happily begun, the church being no more confined to Jews, but gathered out of all the earth; to which work Christ hath commissioned me, who am labouring therein.

Note, That how true soever it be, that sound believers shall be finally justified in judgement, and glorified, the promise giveth them right to it but on condition of perseverance; and God useth conditional promises to engage us rationally to our duty, and as a means to accomplish his absolute decrees.

24. Who now rejoice in my sufferings for you, and fill up that which is behind of the afflictions of Christ in my flesh, for his body's sake, which is the church.

24. And I rejoice that God honoureth me to suffer for his church in so excellent a work: for it is by the cross, or suffering, that God will bring the church to glory: And as Christ hath perfectly done his own part, as the only propitiating sacrifice; so I, with the rest of his members, must undergo and make up the rest, even for the same church's sake for which he died, though not as a mediator, to reconcile God and man, as he was.

25. Whereof I am made a minister according to the dispensation of God, which is given to me for you, to fulfil the word of God.

25. Of which church I am made a servant, by God's appointment and commission, given me for you, as well as for others, that I may fully divulge the word of God.

26. *Even* the mystery which hath been hid from ages, and from generations, but now is made manifest to his saints:

26. The great mystery of redemption, (God manifested in the flesh, as the head and Saviour of the church) which (though not wholly, yet comparatively) hath been hid from Jews under dark types, as well as more from Gentiles by greater darkness, in all foregoing ages: but now is more plainly made known to God's saints.

27. To whom God would make known what is the riches of the glory of this mystery among the Gentiles; which is Christ in you, the hope of glory:

27. To whom God of his good pleasure would specially make known the riches and glory of the mystery of calling the whole world of Gentiles. The sum of it is, Christ among you, and in you, purchasing, giving, and assuring to you the heavenly glory, for which he hath commanded you joyfully to hope. Christ the way, glory the end.

28. Whom we preach, warning every man, and teaching every man in all wisdom; that we may present every man perfect in Christ Jesus:

28. To preach this Christ is the work of our office, warning and teaching every man as we have opportunity, neglecting none of any rank, in all the saving wisdom of the gospel, that we may present as many as possible, perfect to salvation.

29. Whereunto I also labour, striving according to his working, which worketh in me mightily.

29. In this labour I am employed; in which with diligence I strive, according to the grace of him that called me, which wrought in me (or worketh by me) in power, (confirming my ministry by miracles and success, as well as qualifying me for it.)

CHAP. II.

FOR I would that ye knew what great conflict I have for you, and for them at Laodicea, and for as many as have not seen my face in the flesh:

1. [Conflict] by prayer, and care, and study, to do them good.
Note, Good men long for the good of them whom they never saw.

2. That their hearts might be comforted, being knit together in love, and unto all riches of the full assurance of understanding, to the acknowledgment of the mystery of God, and of the Father, and of Christ.

2. That they may grow up to a state of joy, by holy union and communion in love, and to be yet richer and happier in the full and assured understanding and acknowledgment of the mystery of God's love, and of Christ's grace, in the promises, prefigurations, and performance of our redemption.

3. In whom are hid all the treasures of wisdom and knowledge.

3. Though it be not discerned by carnal men, who search more after other knowledge in the world, the depth, excellency, and benefit, of all true wisdom and knowledge, are comprised in the knowledge of God manifested in Christ: this is the true philosophy, in comparison of which, all other is vanity and folly.

4. And this I say, lest any man should beguile you with enticing words.

4. I tell you this, lest any delude you by the specious ostentation of any other sort of knowledge, called philosophy, or oracular, or enthusiastical, or pharisaical traditions, as if it were somewhat more excellent than the knowledge of Christ.

5. For though I be absent in the flesh, yet am I with you in the Spirit, joying and beholding your order and the steadfastness of your faith in Christ.

5. For though I see you not, I am in the Spirit as if I was present with you, affected with joy to hear of your order, and steadfastness of faith: but yet I know where your danger lieth.

6. As ye have therefore received Christ Jesus the Lord, so walk ye in him;

6. Let it be then your care to hold fast and practise the gospel of Christ, as you have already received him and his word, and turn not to any other way.

7. Rooted and built up in him, and stablished in the faith, as ye have been taught, abounding therein with thanksgiving.

7. As growing downwards in the roots is necessary to trees, for steadfastness and fruit; and as the house must be built up, when the foundation is laid: so must you now be more and more rooted, and built up, and stablished in the same faith which you were taught at first, and must abound with joyful thanks to God, in the increased knowledge, love, and practice of that, instead of hearkening to novelties or errors.

8. Beware lest any man spoil you through philosophy and vain deceit, after the tradition of men, after the rudiments of the world, and not after Christ:

8. The danger of which I advise you to beware, is, lest any by pretending that the heathen philosophy is a higher sort of wisdom and learning (more methodical, accurate, extensive) than the gospel of Christ, should deceive you from the true wisdom of Christianity, or heretics draw you by philosophical pretences to their heresies; and they should set up the tradition, books, or opinions of any sect of philosophers, against the heavenly doctrine of Christ.

Note, That as Moses' law was very useful in subordination to the covenant of grace, and to Christ; but pernicious to them that set it in opposition to Christ, or in separation from him: so is true philosophy; which is the knowledge of the knowable part of God's works, useful in subordination to Christ: but the heathen sect of philosophers were the most dangerous adversaries to Christianity, by deriding its simplicity, and pretending to far greater learning, and despising Christians as ignorant and credulous, and using against them their logical art and sophistry, and the reputation of all their sciences.

9. For in him dwelleth all the fulness of the Godhead bodily.

9. For as the divine nature itself hath united itself to, and so dwelleth in his human nature; so in the person, doctrine, and works of Christ incarnate, God hath treasured up, and by that indwelling, placed the fullest manifestation of himself to mankind, that ever he will give them in this life on earth.

10. And ye are complete in him,

who is the head of all principality and power.

10. You need not seek after wisdom in the oracles or knowledge of demons or angels; for in Christ you have complete wisdom, (if you truly receive him, and learn of him) who is not only above all philosophers and rabbies, but above the highest angels or celestial powers, and is the chief revealer of God to man.

11. In whom also ye are circumcised, by the circumcision made without hands, in putting off the body of the sins of the flesh, by the circumcision of Christ.

11. Nor need you go to Judaism for circumcision: for you have the true saving circumcision in Christ, even that of the heart, made without hands by the Spirit of Christ, cutting off and casting away the body of sin, or fleshly lusts.

12. Buried with him in baptism, wherein also you are risen with him through the faith of the operation of God, who hath raised him from the dead.

12. And it is more than a circumcision of your lusts that you have in Christ; they are dead and buried with him: for so your baptism signifieth, in which you are put under the water, to signify and profess, that your old man, or fleshly lust, is dead and buried with him; and you rise thence, to signify and profess, that you rise to newness of life, and heavenly hopes, through the belief of God's works that raised Christ from the dead.

13. And you being dead in your sins, and the uncircumcision of your flesh, hath he quickened together with him, having forgiven you all trespasses.

13. And you, that were as dead in the guilt and power of your sins, your hearts and lusts, as your flesh, being uncircumcised, hath God made spiritually alive, as Christ was quickened and raised, and hath absolved you by pardon of all sin, from the obligation to everlasting death which you had contracted.

14. Blotting out the hand-writing of ordinances that was against us, which was contrary to us, and took it out of the way, nailing it to his cross,

14. Cancelling the legal imposition of Mosaical rites and ceremonies, even to us Jews, which might have been produced against us breakers of the law to our condemnation, and as it were, nailed it to his cross, while by dying he disabled it: so that you need not think that Judaizing is necessary to your salvation.

15. And having spoiled principalities and powers, he made a shew of them openly, triumphing over them in it.

15. And when his crucifiers triumphed over him on the cross, as if they had utterly overcome him, it was but his conquest and spoils of all principalities and powers, of devils or men, that were adversaries to his grace and kingdom, and his open ostentation of his victory, and triumph over them, in that his crucifixion.

16. Let no man therefore judge you in meat or in drink, or in respect of an holy-day, or of the new-moon, or of the Sabbath-*days:*

16. Seeing then that Christ hath abrogated the Mosaical law, none ought to censure you as sinners, for not keeping the ceremonies of the law, about meat, or drink, or in the point of festivals called holy-days, or of the new moon, or of the Sabbath-days.

17. Which are a shadow of things to come; but the body *is* of Christ.

17. For these were but shadows of the things to come, even Christ and Christianity, which are the substance shadowed.

Note, That sabbaths are abolished with the rest of Moses' law. As to the Lord's day, consider these things distinctly. 1. That all Moses' law, as such, bound only the Jews, to whom it was promulgated, and is now abolished, even (saith Paul) that written in stone. 2. That all the law of Christ in nature and revelation still bindeth us. 3. That the word [sabbath] in scripture properly signifieth a day of ceremonial rest, in which the bodily rest was a duty directly in itself, (as sacrificing and other ceremonies were.) 4. That the Lord's day is never called a sabbath in scripture, (however some mistake a text or two.) 5. That the Lord's day is separated by divine appointment to the holy commemoration of Christ's resurrection and our redemption, especially in sacred assemblies for church worship. 6. That it is of greater dignity than the sabbaths were, as being far more substantial, spiritual, excellent work. 7. That on it, rest is not a ceremonial due, as it was on sabbaths, for itself; but only a subordinate duty, that soul and body (even of servants) may be vacant and free for spiritual worship: and no breach of rest is now a sin, but. 1. That which hindereth this spiritual work; 2. Or is scandalous, encouraging others to sin 8. That therefore the seventh-day sabbath is abolished, 1. Because Moses' law is abolished: 2. And all proper sabbaths are abolished. 9. That yet (with the ancient churches) we may well call the Lord's day [the sabbath], (when it tendeth not to error.) but only by allusion, or metaphorically, as they then called the table an altar, the ministers, priests, and the sacrament, and alms, and thanksgiving, sacrifices. This is the full truth, as I have proved in a set treatise.

13. Let no man beguile you of your reward, in a voluntary humility, and worshipping of angels, in-

COLOSSIANS.

truding into those things which he hath not seen, vainly puffed up by his fleshly mind;

18. Let no man beguile you of the reward of Christianity, by pretending greater self-humbling than God commandeth, by worshipping angels, intruding into, and pretending to know the things which he never saw, nor God revealed to him, vainly puffed up by the imaginations of his fleshly mind, and building on his deluded conjectures and self-conceits.

19. And not holding the head, from which all the body by joints and bands having nourishment ministered, and knit together, increaseth with the increase of God.

19. By which they depart from their due dependance on Christ the head, whose office it is to be the sole immediate mediator between God and man, and the law-giver to the church, who hath given us sufficient notice what worship God accepteth. It is from him the head (of life and government) that the body even the church, receiveth its nourishment and holy increase by the blessing of God, it being by joints and ligaments of faith, love, and ministry and communion for concord, conjoined and made a meet receiver.

20. Wherefore if ye be dead with Christ from the rudiments of the world; why as though living in the world, are ye subject to ordinances, 21. (Touch not, taste not, handle not: 22. Which all are to perish with the using) after the commandments and doctrines of men?

20, 21, 22. If then you be dead to the rudiments of all other masters and customs in the world, of Jews or heathens, in conformity to your crucified Lord, why, as though yet you were not separated from the world to Christ, are you subject to such ordinances, which Christ never made you, but hath abolished? as, Touch not, taste not, meddle not with such and such meats, as unclean, and the like: which were all temporary things, and consist in transient unprofitable actions, having no reward of God, as being but the products of the commands and doctrines of unauthorized men.

23. Which things have indeed a shew of wisdom in will-worship, and humility, and neglecting of the body, not in any honour to the satisfying of the flesh.

23. Which are the things for which, as deceitful shews, the heretical and heathen seducers pretend to be wiser men than the apostles and Christians, and to be more pious men, and so would draw you to their errors, as being stricter in voluntary worship and greater humility, and neglecting of the body on pretence of being more for the soul, and not, as sensual men do, setting up and pampering the flesh.

Note, The description of Paul and church historians notify to us, that these heretics made up a religion of three parts: 1. Of the name and some parts of Christianity, to keep in with the Christians. 2. Of many Jewish rites, to keep fair with the Jews. 3. But the main substance which they boasted of, was Pythagorean heathenism, in which they pretended great knowledge of spirits, demons, and invisible things, their orders, powers, offices, durations, &c. which God never revealed, but the deluded imaginations of themselves and the said Pythagorean and Platonic philosophers taught them. In many which superstitions, of will-worship, angel-worship, laws of penance on the flesh, (while the vain mind usurpeth Christ's legislative power) too many of the carnal corrupt church do imitate them to this day.

CHAP. III.

IF ye then be risen with Christ, seek those things which are above, where Christ sitteth on the right hand of God.

1. If then you be true Christians, risen with Christ, as you profess to the hope of a celestial glory, and to a holy life, shew it by seeking the things which are above, where Christ, who you trust in, is as your head, over all in glory.

2. Set your affection on things above, not on things on the earth.

2. Let the heavenly things, and not the things on earth, have your strongest affections, your love, your desire, your hope, your joy, your care, your very hearts.

3. For ye are dead, and your life is hid with Christ in God. 4. When Christ who is our life shall appear, then shall ye also appear with him in glory.

3, 4. For ye are dead to the world and sin, and the root of your spiritual life is not in yourselves; but both your objective life, which is your happiness, and the root of all your spiritual life, are out of sight with Christ in God. It is by him that you live, and it is with him and on him that you must live in glory for ever.

5. Mortify therefore your members which are upon the earth: fornication, uncleanness, inordinate affection, evil concupiscence, and covetousness, which is idolatry: 6. For which things sake, the wrath of God cometh on the children of disobedience.

5, 6. Therefore, though your lusts are as it were the very members of your corrupt fleshly nature, kill them all, even fornication, uncleanness, inordinate affections of love or delight, all evil lustings or desires, and covetousness, which loveth the creature above God, and which is idolaters' sin. For it is for these things that the unbelieving rebellious world is under the wrath of God.

7. In the which ye also walked sometime when ye lived in them.

7. Those sins were formerly your own practices, when you were heathens among them.

8. But now you also put off all these: anger, wrath, malice, blasphemy, filthy communication out of your mouth. 9. Lie not one to another, seeing that ye have put off the old man with his deeds;

8, 9. But now you must not only cast off all these filthy sins, but also all that is contrary to love and peace, all sinful wrath and malice, and evil speaking and ribaldry, and lying: for all these are the members and deeds of the old man, or state which you have renounced.

10. And have put on the new *man*, which is renewed in knowledge, after the image of him that created him.

10. And you have by conversion become new men, renewed in saving knowledge unto the image of that God and Saviour who is the Maker of this new creature.

11. Where there is neither Greek nor Jew, circumcision nor uncircumcision, barbarian, Scythian, bond *nor* free: but Christ *is* all, and in all.

11. Where the interest and union that we have all in one Christ, who is all in all, doth swallow up all the little differences, of Greeks and Jews, &c. And so must do in our communion.

12. Put on therefore (as the elect of God, holy and beloved) bowels of mercies, kindness, humbleness of mind, meekness, long-suffering;

12. Let these therefore be your very habit, and nature, and practice, as becometh God's chosen, holy and beloved ones, bowels of mercy, kindness, &c.

13. Forbearing one another, and forgiving one another, if any man have a quarrel against any: even as Christ forgave you, so also *do ye*.

13. Note, 1. That it is supposed that we are wronged, else there is no need of forgiving. 2. True Christians are known by this spiritual nature, as well as by religious exercises.

14. And above all these things *put on* charity, which is the bond of perfectness.

14. But as the most necessary and excellent of all, put on true endeared love to others as yourselves, for the sake of God, who must be most loved: for as this is the highest grace which Christ's Spirit worketh in us, so it is that bond which by uniting believers to Christ and each other, tendeth to the perfect compagination, growth, and welfare of the church, and every member of it.

15. And let the peace of God rule in your hearts, to the which also ye are called in one body; and be ye thankful.

15. And let that peace which God both giveth you within, and calleth you to exercise, by dwelling in your hearts, bear rule in your lives towards all men, as being of the same body; and live in continual thankfulness to God.

16. Let the word of Christ dwell in you richly in all wisdom; teaching and admonishing one another in psalms and hymns, and spiritual songs, singing with grace in your hearts to the Lord.

16. Let the word of God so possess your souls, that you may by it have plenteous holy wisdom to instruct and admonish one another, and holy affections, that those who have the gift of composing holy psalms, and hymns, and spiritual songs, for themselves and others use, may do it wisely, and all of you use them with holy joy in singing to the Lord.

17. And whatsoever ye do in word or deed, *do* all in the name of the Lord Jesus, giving thanks to God and the Father by him.

17. And let all that you offer to God in word or deed, in worship or obedience, be done in the name of the Lord Jesus, trusting for acceptance to his mediation, and offer your daily thanksgiving to God the Father, by him our high priest in the heavens.

18—23. Wives, submit yourselves unto your own husbands, as it is fit in the Lord. Husbands, love *your* wives, and be not bitter against them. Children, obey *your* parents in all things: for this is well-pleasing unto the Lord. Fathers, provoke not your children *to anger*, lest they be discouraged. Servants, obey in all things *your* masters according to the flesh; not with eye-service as men-pleasers, but in singleness of heart, fearing God: And whatsoever ye do, do it heartily, as to the Lord, and not unto men; 24. Knowing that of the Lord ye shall receive the reward of the inheritance; for ye serve the Lord Christ.

18, 19. &c. See all this before paraphrased, Eph. v. and vi.

25. But he that doth wrong, shall receive for the wrong which he hath done: and there is no respect of persons.

25. But if masters or servants do wrong to the other, though they may escape the punishment of man, God who respecteth no man's person will judge and punish them.

CHAP. IV.

MASTERS, give unto *your* servants that which is just and equal, knowing that ye also have a master in heaven.

1. Let not your power over your servants embolden you to abuse, oppress, or wrong them, but give them all wages and usage which justice and equity require; for you have a master in heaven, who will judge you as you are and do.

2. Continue in prayer, and watch in the same with thanksgiving;

2. Be constant in prayer, and not cursory or cold, and watch in it against your corruptions and temptations, joining thanksgiving with your requests.

3. Withal, praying also for us, that God would open unto us a door of utterance, to speak the mystery of Christ, for which I am also in bonds:

3. Praying for us ministers of Christ, that God would give us freedom from men's restraints and our own infirmities, that we may with enlargedness and boldness preach the gospel, for which I suffer.

4. That I may make it manifest, as I ought to speak.

4. That I may open and apply it, as the work and the souls of men require.

5. Walk in wisdom toward them that are without, redeeming the time.

5. Use the wisdom toward them that are without the church, which is needful to keep you from receiving hurt by them, or in doing good to them.

6. Let your speech *be* always with grace, seasoned with salt, that ye may know how ye ought to answer every man.

6. Let all your speech be the exercise of God's grace in your hearts, not rotten, filthy, or vain, but wise and savoury, that you may speak pertinently and fruitfully to every man, especially in the necessary defence of the truth, against gainsayers, and resolving of the doubtful.

7. All my state shall Tychicus declare unto you, *who* is a beloved brother, and a faithful minister, and fellow-servant in the Lord:

7. Tychicus a faithful brother, fully shall acquaint you with my concerns.

8, 9. Whom I have sent unto you for the same purpose, that he might know your estate, and comfort your hearts: With Onesimus a faithful and beloved brother, who is one of you. They shall make known unto you all things which *are done* here. 10. Aristarchus my fellow-prisoner saluteth you, and Marcus, sister's son to Barnabas (touching whom ye received commandments; if he come unto you, receive him:) 11. And Jesus which is called Justus, who are of the circumcision. These only *are my* fellow-workers unto the kingdom of God, which have been a comfort unto me.

8, 9, &c. These are all that have helped me here at Rome in my suffering, and have much comforted me.

12. Epaphras, who is one of you, a servant of Christ, saluteth you, always labouring fervently for you in prayers, that ye may stand perfect and complete in all the will of God. 13. For I bear him record, that he hath a great zeal for you, and them that are in Laodicea, and them in Hierapolis.

12, 13. Note, 1. That prayer should be a work of fervent labouring. 2. That ministers should long for the people's increase in grace and universal obedience, more than to promote their own interest with them.

14, 15. Luke the beloved physician, and Demas greet you. Salute the brethren which are in Laodicea, and Nymphas, and the church which is in his house.

15. Which use to meet there.

16. And when this epistle is read amongst you, cause that it be read

also in the church of the Laodiceans, and that ye likewise read the epistle from Laodicea.

16. Note. 1. It was the duty of the churches to communicate the epistles written to them by the apostles. 2. What that epistle written to Laodicea was, it concerneth us not to know. It is vain to think that Paul and other apostles wrote, no more epistles than be in the Bible; or, that God is bound to bring down all that they wrote to us.

17. And say to Archippus, take heed to the ministry which thou hast received in the Lord, that thou fulfil it.

17. Note, That bishops, or pastors may have need to be admonished by the people to take heed to the ministry which God calleth them to, and not to slubber it over, (much less pervert it) but fulfil it.

18. The salutation by the hand of me Paul. Remember my bonds. Grace *be* with you. Amen.

18. In conclusion, I subscribe my salutation to you. Let the remembrance of my bonds, remember you of your duty to me, in prayer, and receiving of this word. Grace be with you, is the summary benediction. Amen.

THE
FIRST EPISTLE OF PAUL THE APOSTLE,
TO THE
THESSALONIANS.

CHAP. I.

PAUL, and Silvanus, and Timotheus, unto the church of the Thessalonians, *which is* in God the Father, and *in* the Lord Jesus Christ: Grace *be* unto you, and peace from God our Father, and the Lord Jesus Christ.

1. To the assembly of Christians associated in the professed belief of God the Father, and the Lord Jesus Christ, &c.

2, 3. We give thanks to God always for you all, making mention of you in our prayers, remembering without ceasing your work of faith, and labour of love, and patience of hope in our Lord Jesus Christ, in the sight of God, and our Father.

2, 3. We thankfully remember your working faith, your laborious love, and patient hope in Christ, which is all seen and accepted by God our Father.

4, 5. Knowing, brethren beloved, your election of God. For our gospel came not unto you in word only, but also in power, and in the Holy Ghost, and in much assurance; as ye know what manner of men we were among you for your sake.

4, 5. For I was assured, that God had freely elected you to be honoured as a church of Christ, in that he sent me particularly to you, and that with power of miracles, and pouring out of the Holy Ghost, he confirmed my ministry, and caused me to fulfil it, as your experience telleth you.

6. And ye became followers of us, and of the Lord, having received

the word in much affliction, with joy of the Holy Ghost:

6. And because he blessed all with such success, that you obeyed our word, and were converted to God, receiving the word in the trial of sharp affliction and opposition, and yet with joy, and the participation of the Holy Ghost.

7. So that ye were ensamples to all that believe, in Macedonia and Achaia.

7. So that your example tended to the happy imitation of all that now believe in Macedonia and Achaia.

8. For from you sounded out the word of the Lord, not only in Macedonia and Achaia, but also in every place your faith to God-ward is spread abroad, so that we need not to speak any thing.

8. For from you the word of God spread abroad, even in many other countries it is known; so that I need not tell it them, to your praise, and their imitation.

9. For they themselves shew of us, what manner of entering in we had unto you, and how ye turned to God from idols, to serve the living and true God.

9. They tell abroad themselves, what success we had in your conversion from idolatry to the true God.

10. And to wait for his Son from heaven, whom he raised from the dead, even Jesus, which delivered us from the wrath to come.

10. And to wait in faith and hope, that his Son, that is raised from death, and ascended, will come from heaven for our salvation, even Jesus, who delivereth us from the wrath that will come on unbelievers.

CHAP. II.

FOR yourselves, brethren, know our entrance in unto you, that it was not in vain.

1. For you are my witnesses, that I came not to you in deceit, or any false design or manner.

2. But even after that we had suffered before, and were shamefully entreated, as ye know at Philippi, we were bold in our God to speak unto you the gospel of God with much contention.

2. But our shameful usage at Philippi did not discourage us; but our trust in our God did embolden us to preach his gospel to you, though in a conflict of great opposition.

3. For our exhortation *was* not of deceit, nor of uncleanness, nor in guile: 4. But as we were allowed of God to be put in trust with the gospel, even so we speak, not as pleasing men, but God, which trieth our hearts.

3, 4. For I came not to you to deceive you into error, nor to plead for fleshly lusts, nor craftily to make advantage of you to our gain: But as God approved and chose me to be put in trust with the preaching of the gospel, I do it to please him who trieth our hearts, and not to please the humours and lusts of men.

5. For neither at any time used we flattering words, as ye know, nor a cloak of covetousness; God is witness.

5. For you yourselves know, that I flattered you not, nor indulged fleshly pleasures; and God knoweth, that I made not the gospel a cloak to hide any covetous design.

6. Nor of men sought we glory, neither of you, nor yet of others, when we might have been burthensome, as the apostles of Christ.

6. Nor did I preach up myself, for vain-glory (power or profit), neither with you, or any others; though as Christ's apostle I might have pleaded my power, and demanded maintenance.

7. But we were gentle among you, even as a nurse cherisheth her children:

7. But we sought not our gain and glory, but your good; and that with all the love and tenderness to you, as a nurse cherisheth her children in self-denial.

8. So being affectionately desirous of you, we were willing to have imparted unto you, not the gospel of God only, but also our own souls, because ye were dear unto us.

8. So my strong love to you made me not only willingly to preach the gospel to you, (without any selfish, proud, or covetous design) but you are so dear to me, that I think not my life too dear for you.

9. For ye remember, brethren, our labour and travail: for labouring night and day, because we would not be chargeable unto any of you, we preached unto you the gospel of God.

9. Ye cannot but remember my great toil and labour, how working at my trade night and day, because I would not be chargeable to any of you, I preached the gospel to you freely.

10. Ye *are* witnesses, and God *also*, how holily, and justly, and unblamably, we behaved ourselves among you that believe.

10. I appeal to yourselves, and to God, as witnesses, that our behaviour with you was holy, just, and blameless.

11. As you know how we exhorted and comforted, and charged every one of you (as a father *doth* his children.) 12. That ye would walk worthy of God, who hath called you unto his kingdom and glory.

11, 12. As you know how tenderly I exhorted, and comforted, and charged, not only the assemblies, but every one that I could speak to, even as a father will do to every child; that now you are Christians, you will live as suitable to the God you serve, and the kingdom and glory to which he hath called you.

13. For this cause also thank we God without ceasing; because when ye received the word of God which ye heard of us, ye received *it* not *as* the word of men, but (as it is in truth) the word of God, which effectually worketh also in you that believe.

13. And it is the matter of our incessant thanks to God, that you received not the gospel as mens' word, with a mere human faith and obedience; but as God's word, with a divine: which it appeareth to be, by the powerful efficacy of it on yourselves, who are true believers.

14. For ye, brethren, became followers of the churches of God, which in Judea are in Christ Jesus: for ye also have suffered like things of your own country-men, even as they have of the Jews.

14. Ye follow the churches in Judea, in suffering by your own neighbours, as well as in the same faith.

Note, The same faith, hope, and holiness, will meet with the same enmity in all countries.

15. Who both killed the Lord Jesus, and their own prophets, and have persecuted us; and they please not God, and are contrary to all men: 16. Forbidding us to speak to the Gentiles, that they might be saved, to fill up their sins alway, for the wrath is come upon them to the uttermost.

15, 16. Note, 1. That the carnal church hath been more persecuting and bloody than the heathens.

2. That Christ himself seemed not to them good enough to live, or to be endured among them; but was murdered as a traitor and blasphemer, by pretended law and justice. And prophets and apostles had the like usage.

3. That bloody persecution oft goeth with the carnal church for a great duty.

4. That God is not pleased with the persecutors of his servants, though they do it as to please him.

5. That malignant persecutors are oft so mad as to be contrary to all men, or engage themselves against the common interest of mankind, that they may persecute the faithful.

6. It is the silencing of the best preachers of the gospel, which hath the heat of their malignant zeal.

7. It is that preaching which would save souls, which they forbid: And because this preaching is the means to save souls, it is that Satan aimeth his militia against it.

8. Persecuting and silencing faithful preachers, is the way to fill up the sins of the malignant enemies.

9. God useth not to bring the utmost wrath on men, till they have filled up their sins.

10. How long soever they prosper, wrath will come at last to the uttermost on malignant sinners and persecutors of the faithful preachers of the gospel.

17. But we, brethren, being taken from you for a short time, in presence, not in heart, endeavoured the more abundantly to see your face with great desire.

17. But our constrained absence from you, (in person, not in heart) made us the more earnestly desire to see you.

18. Wherefore we would have come unto you, (even I Paul) once and again, but Satan hindered us.

18. I would oft have come to you, and attempted it: but by God's permission Satan hindered me, (by stirring up persecution and restraints, and making me work elsewhere by opposition.)

19. For what *is* our hope, or joy, or crown of rejoicing? *are* not even ye in the presence of the Lord Jesus Christ at his coming? 20. For ye are our glory and joy.

19, 20. For what is that hope, and joy, and crown, for which I labour so hard, and suffer so much? Is it not your conversion and salvation, which before Christ at his coming will be my joy? Yes, ye are our glory and joy, that God hath so blessed our labours to your salvation.

Note, 1. True ministers of Christ thirst and labour far more for men's conversion and salvation, than for reputation, honour, riches, preferment, or domination.

2. Though God will reward faithful preachers, though they have small success, yet to have great success to the saving of many, is far more comfortable, not only now, but at the coming of Christ.

CHAP. III.

WHEREFORE when we could no longer forbear, we thought it good to be left at Athens alone: 2. And sent Timotheus our brother and minister of God, and our fellow-labourer in the gospel of Christ, to establish you, and to comfort you concerning your faith.

1,2 Note, That in the time of trying persecutions, Christians have special need of confirming and comforting helps.

3. That no man should be moved by these afflictions: for yourselves know that we are appointed thereunto.

3. Note, Sufferings for Christ should be so expected, that they should seem no strange surprising thing.

4. For verily when we were with you, we told you before, that we should suffer tribulation; even as it came to pass, and ye know.

4. God's foretelling us of suffering, should forearm us for it.

5. For this cause when I could no longer forbear, I sent to know your faith, lest by some means the tempter have tempted you, and our labour be in vain.

5. Note, That though censorious suspicions of men be forbidden, yet man is so mutable and weak a thing, that loving suspicions for preventing hurt, are necessary to them that have the care of men.

6. But now when Timotheus came from you unto us, and brought us good tidings of your faith and charity, and that ye have good remembrance of us always, desiring greatly to see us, as we also *to see* you: 7. Therefore, brethren, we were comforted over you in all our affliction and distress by your faith.

6, 7. Note, That they that by affliction are not drawn to sin, are matter of joy to themselves and their friends, notwithstanding their sufferings.

8. For now we live, if ye stand fast in the Lord.

8. Your steadfastness and victory is the joy or life of our lives.

9. For what thanks can we render to God again for you, for all the joy wherewith we joy for your sake before our God.

9. We can never be thankful enough to God, for the comfort which we have in you.

10. Night and day praying exceedingly that we might see your face, and might perfect that which is lacking in your faith?

10. Note, That the faith of good Christians is wanting (in act and object,) and needeth increase and help thereto.

11. Now God himself, and our Father, and our Lord Jesus Christ direct our way unto you: 12. And the Lord make you to increase and abound in love one towards another, and towards all men, even as we *do* towards you.

11, 12. Note, That to abound in love to saints as saints, and to all men as men, is the state of true increase in grace.

13. To the end he may establish your hearts unblamable in holiness before God even our Father, at the coming of our Lord Jesus Christ, with all his saints.

13. Note, That it is confirmed faith working by abounding love, which is the qualification in which we may stand uncondemned, as truly holy, before God, at the coming of Christ to judgment.

CHAP. IV.

FURTHERMORE then we beseech you, brethren, and exhort you by the Lord Jesus, that as ye have received of us how you ought to walk, and to please God, so ye would abound more and more.

1. Note, That Paul's doctrine against justification by the works of the law, consisteth with vehement urgency, for men to please God, by doing their duty, and abounding therein.

2—5. For ye know what commandments we gave you by the Lord Jesus. For this is the will of

God, *even* your sanctification, that ye should abstain from fornication: That every one of you should know how to possess his vessel in sanctification and honour; not in the lust of concupiscence, even as the Gentiles which know not God:

2--5. You know how we charged you from Christ, as that which God requireth in you, that you be a holy people, and therefore that you be no fornicators, but be careful to use your bodies in purity and honour, and not in fleshly lust, like the ignorant heathens.

6. That *no man* go beyond, and defraud his brother in any matter: because that the Lord is the avenger of all such, as we also have forewarned you, and testified.

6. That no man tread upon or defraud his brother in any matter, &c.

Note, Some think that it is unnatural lust that is here obscurely named by modesty: But that it forbids all forcible or fraudulent wrong to another in body or estate, is most probable. And note, That God is especially the avenger of such wrongs, in which the power and fraud of oppressors leaveth men no other help but God's.

7. For God hath not called us unto uncleanness, but unto holiness.

7. It is to holiness, and from all uncleanness, that God hath called us by Christ: And we must live according to our vocation, if we are converted indeed.

8. He therefore that despiseth, despiseth not man, but God, who hath also given unto us his Holy Spirit.

8. Those, therefore, that plead for such sins as harmless, and despise these bounds of lust, despise God's own commandments and him, and not only us that preach them; and they despise the Spirit of Holiness, given by God to all the faithful, which condemneth these lusts.

9. But as touching brotherly love, ye need not that I write unto you; for ye yourselves are taught of God to love one another.

9. As for brotherly love, you have not such need to be taught it as those that know it: For God (who hath a way of teaching by efficiency, beyond that of words) hath taught you to love one another, by giving you this love, by his holy Spirit.

10. And indeed ye do it towards all the brethren which are in all Macedonia: but we beseech you, brethren, that ye increase more and more:

10. Note, 1. That it is a wise way to make men better, to praise so much good as is in them.

2. Even those whom God hath taught by his own operations, have need to be entreated by men to increase, even in the duty of loving others.

11. And that ye study to be quiet, and to do your own business, and to work with your own hands, (as we commanded you.)

11. And to that end, that you make it your earnest care and study to avoid all strife, and to live in quietness with all men: and for this, that you avoid meddling in other men's matters unnecessarily, but mind and meddle with the business which is your own; and that idleness cast you not upon others for supply, but that you work for yourselves, as I commanded you.

Note, That he that will increase in love, must, 1. Study quietness: 2. And not meddle uncalled with other men's matters: 3. Not make himself need the help of others: 4. And therefore not live in impoverishing idleness.

12. That ye may walk honestly toward them that are without, and that ye may have lack of nothing.

12. That so your condition in the world may enable you to live in a comely sort, with reputation, and not expose you to contempt, and that want may not afflict you.

13. But I would not have you to be ignorant, brethren, concerning them that are asleep, that ye sorrow not, even as others which have no hope.

13. And lest you be tempted to doubtful or over-sorrowful thoughts of the dead, like them that believe not a better life hereafter, I would not have you cherish such sorrows by ignorance of their case.

14. For if we believe that Jesus died, and rose again, even so them also which sleep in Jesus, will God bring with him.

14. For how can we believe that Christ died and rose, but we must also believe the resurrection of those that are the departed members of Christ? He will bring their souls with him, for they are with him now; and he will raise their bodies, and so bring the entire man with him in judgment.

Note, That death is called a sleep to the faithful, with respect to the body, and the rest of the soul from sorrow: but not as if the soul were but in a sleepy inactivity.

15. For this we say unto you by the word of the Lord, that we which are alive and remain unto the coming of the Lord, shall not prevent them that are asleep.

15. For I say this not as my word, but God's, That such of us believers as shall be found alive then, shall not go before them that are dead to Christ at his coming.

16. For the Lord himself shall descend from heaven with a shout, with the voice of the archangel, and with the trump of God: and the dead in Christ shall rise first:

16. For the Lord himself coming down in his visible humanity from heaven, shall call the world together, as men call assemblies, by shout, by voice, or by a trumpet; so shall Christ, by his unknown way, called the voice of an archangel, and the trumpet of God; and first the dead Christians shall be raised to life.

17. Then we which are alive and remain, shall be caught up together with them in the clouds, to meet the Lord in the air: and so shall we ever be with the Lord. 18. Wherefore comfort one another with these words.

17, 18. Then those of us who shall be alive and remain, shall by his power be caught up with them, to meet Christ in the air; who will adjudge us to everlasting life, and so we shall ever after that be with Christ in glory where he is: therefore encourage and comfort yourselves, and each other, with the lively belief, the joyful hopes, and the frequent mention of this most blessed time and state.

Note, 1. That though Paul knew not the time, it is a groundless reproach of Paul by them that say, he thought that he should have lived here till the coming of Christ to judgment. Had Paul made men believe that Christ should come again in that very age, what a delusion would it have been to the churches; and what false expectations and religious duties would it have enticed them to? and have tempted the next age, that saw the frustration, to have revolted to infidelity.

2. Though we are told, that we must meet the Lord in the air, and then be ever with him; it pleased not God to give us yet a distinct knowledge of the place, nor what he will do with the new earth in which righteousness will dwell: but wherever it is, it will be in heavenly glory with Christ.

3. They that will have true Christian comfort, must fetch it from the daily and lively belief and consideration of this, That we shall for ever be in happiness with Christ our Lord, and the holy society of the blessed.

4. Qu. Why doth not Paul comfort them with the mention of the soul's immortality and happiness before the resurrection of the body? Ans. Because, 1. It was the body that suffered by persecution, and that slept, and that they mourned for too much; and therefore it was about it that they needed comfort. 2. And the soul's immortality was a more undoubted thing, (without which a resurrection of the same man had been impossible.) 3. And the felicity or perfection of entire man is greater than that of the soul alone, the state of which God hath less clearly revealed to us.

CHAP. V.

BUT of the times and the seasons, brethren, ye have no need that I write unto you. 2. For yourselves know perfectly that the day of the Lord so cometh as a thief in the night.

1, 2. But to write to you of the particular time of Christ's coming, I suppose you expect not; for you have been told, that he cometh as a thief in the night, unexpected, men not foreknowing when.

3. For when they shall say, Peace and safety; then sudden destruction cometh upon them, as travail upon a woman with child; and they shall not escape.

3. So much must the time be unknown, that it will surprise them with sudden unavoidable destruction, when they most presume that all is well with them, and safe.

4. But ye, brethren, are not in darkness, that that day should overtake you as a thief. 5. Ye are all the children of light, and the children of the day: we are not of the night, nor of darkness.

4, 5. But though you know not the time, it will not so surprise you, as thieves do men asleep in the night: for ye are all in the day-light, and not unprepared, in a state of darkness.

6. Therefore let us not sleep as do others; but let us watch and be sober.

6. Therefore let this remember you to avoid the careless presumption, the vices and unprepared state of the sleepy world; and to live as awake, and in sobriety.

7. For they that sleep, sleep in the night; and they that be drunken, are drunken in the night.

7. For the night is the time of sleep, and to hide the shame of drunkenness by darkness.

8. But let us who are of the day, be sober, putting on the breastplate of faith and love, and for an helmet the hope of salvation.

8. But let us, whom God hath brought out of darkness into the Christian light, live soberly, wearing faith and love as soldiers do a breast-

plate, and the hope of salvation as they down helmet, to save heart and head from all assaults.

9. For God hath not appointed us to wrath; but to obtain salvation by our Lord Jesus Christ.

9. For it is not us, that are his faithful servants, but his rebellious enemies, whom God hath appointed to wrath; but us he appointeth to obtain salvation by Christ.

10. Who died for us, that whether we wake or sleep, we should live together with him.

10. Who died for us, that whether we wake or sleep in body, live or die, we should live with him.

11. Wherefore comfort yourselves together, and edify one another, even as also ye do.

11. Therefore continue as you do to assemble and comfort yourselves together with these hopes, and to edify one another thereby.

Note, Paul knew that rulers were against such assemblies and exercises. Qu. But must they not be 'forborne, if men forbid them'? Ans. Not as an act of obedience, when God commandeth us to use them: but force may make it impossible to us: as it is to relieve the poor, when men disable us, and take away all that we have to give them.

12. And we beseech you, brethren, to know them which labour among you, and are over you in the Lord, and admonish you; 13. And to esteem them very highly in love for their work's sake. *And be at peace among yourselves.*

12, 13. Acknowledge their office and worth, and your obligations, to them that are truly called to be your bishops, or spiritual guides and rulers, and labour among you in that office, and admonish you: and as their office is high, their labour and your benefit great, let them be greatly esteemed by you, and dearly loved for their work. This due love and submission to them, and living in peace among yourselves, will make you a happy church.

Note, 1. That every church should have their proper overseers and guides among them.

2. That these pastors are over them in the Lord, and not to be ruled by the people.

3. That the work of bishops is to labour among them, and admonish their particular churches.

4. That their authority must be owned, and they highly esteemed and loved.

5. That it is for their work's sake that this is due to them, and therefore not to those that work not.

6. The bishops whom in this text they were intreated to own, honour, and love, were those that laboured among them, and not only those that lived far off, and never laboured among them.

7. Due love and respect between the pastors and the flock, and being at peace among themselves, are the way to establish a church in a prosperous state.

14. Now we exhort you, brethren, warn them that are unruly, comfort the feeble-minded, support the weak, be patient towards all men.

14. Those that are disorderly and unruly, warn: those that are feeble-minded, comfort: those that are weak, support, and help them to bear their burdens: and be gentle, and patient to all.

Note, How contrary to this is reviling and destroying all these sorts? yea, silencing the strongest, that fear sinning against God, by swearing, subscribing, and conforming to the needless and wicked canons of Papal usurpers.

15. See that none render evil for evil unto any man: but ever follow that which is good, both among yourselves, and to all men.

15. Though men by doing evil to you, deserve evil, return it not by revenge, by word or deed: but set yourselves to do good, both to Christians, and to all men.

16, 17, 18. Rejoice evermore. Pray without ceasing. In every thing give thanks: for this is the will of God in Christ Jesus concerning you.

16, 17, 18. Whatever you suffer, always rejoice, because still your cause of joy remaineth: and let prayer be your constant practice, and your habit of holy desire be a continued virtual prayer. And in every case give thanks to God, because your mercies are still greater than your sufferings: and this God hath made your duty, by the great blessings which he hath given you in Christ.

19, 20. Quench not the Spirit. Despise not prophesyings.

19, 20. Quench not divine operations of the Spirit, by neglect, or by wilful sin. Set not light by those instructing gifts which any exercise by the special assistance of the Spirit of God: for the witness of Jesus is the spirit of prophecy.

21. Prove all things: hold fast that which is good.

21. Receive not hastily or rashly, without sufficient proof, any doctrines, or pretended revelations, or practices; but the good that is tried and proved, hold fast.

22. Abstain from all appearance of evil.

22. Avoid all sin so carefully, as not to venture on that which ye have just cause to suspect to be sinful, till you have tried whether it be so or not.

23. And the very God of peace sanctify you wholly: and *I pray God* your whole spirit and soul and body be preserved blameless unto the coming of our Lord Jesus Christ.

23. And God who giveth and loveth the peace and prosperity of his servants, sanctify you wholly: and I pray God that you may wholly, in spirit, soul, and body, be so preserved from sin, that you may stand uncondemned, approved as faithful, at the coming of Christ.

Note, 1. It is of great use for our comfort and imitation, to know God to be the God of peace.

2. Paul meaneth not that their bodies should live till Christ's coming, or that they should be without all sin and blame; but without all condemning sin, and so justified and forgiven as to their imperfections.

3. He doth not make spirit, soul, and body, three substantial compounding parts of man, (as far as can be proved;) but seemeth only to mean, that he desireth that they may stand approved in all these three respects: 1. In the spirit, that is, the habits and disposition of the soul, looking beyond itself to its end. 2. In the soul, as it actuateth the body which it animateth. 3. In the body, as it is the instrument of the soul. But of these things even Christian philosophers differ. 1. Some think, man hath three distinct souls, intellectual, sensitive, and vegetative. 2. Some, that he hath two, intellectual and sensitive; and that the vegetative is a part of the body. 3. Some, that he hath but one, with these three faculties. 4. Some, that he hath but one, with these two faculties, intellectual and sensitive. 5. Some, that he hath but one, with the faculty of intellection and will; and that the sensitive is corporeal. So little do we know ourselves. What I think most probable, I have opened in *Methoda Theologiæ*; that man hath but one substantial soul, with both intellectual and sensitive faculties; and that it is uncertain whether the vegetative be its faculty, or only the faculty of the igneous or etherial substance, which is the immediate vehicle of the soul. It is enough for us to know so much of our souls as our duty in using them, and our felicity do require: as he may know to use his clock, watch, house, horse, who knoweth not how to make them, nor can anatomise them.

24. Faithful is he that calleth you, who also will do it.

24. Note, God's faithfulness may give the sanctified great hope of their perseverance.

25. Brethren, pray for us. 26. Greet all the brethren with an holy kiss.

25, 26. Note, 1. Apostles needed the prayers of weak Christians.

2. The ceremony of kissing, and such other, are mutable, fit or unfit, as the custom of countries varieth the signification.

27. I charge you by the Lord, that this epistle be read unto all holy brethren. 28. The grace of our Lord Jesus Christ be with you. Amen.

27, 28. Note, That the epistles written to single churches were not confined to their use, but by them to be communicated to as many as they well could.

THE
SECOND EPISTLE OF PAUL THE APOSTLE,
TO THE
THESSALONIANS.

CHAP. I.

PAUL, and Silvanus, and Timotheus, unto the church of the Thessalonians, in God our Father, and the Lord Jesus Christ. 2. Grace unto you, and peace from God our Father, and the Lord Jesus Christ. 3. We are bound to thank God always for you, brethren, as it is meet, because that your faith groweth exceedingly, and the charity of every one of you all towards each other aboundeth.

3. Note, That it is the growth of the church in faith and love, which is the matter of their true prosperity, and the pastors' joy and thanks to God, rather than their riches, honour, or notional contending knowledge.

4. So that we ourselves glory in you in the churches of God, for your patience and faith in all your persecutions, and tribulations, that ye endure.

4. Note, When worldly men are ashamed of Christians in persecution, godly men rejoice in their faith and patience as being then most honourable.

5. *Which is* a manifest token of the righteous judgment of God, that ye may be counted worthy of the kingdom of God, for which ye also suffer.

5. Which is a plain prognostic, that God, the righteous Judge will reward you with a part in that kingdom for which you suffer, as being worthy of it, in a sense of grace, that is, qualified as those to whom it is promised, and freely given.

6. Seeing *it is* a righteous thing with God to recompense tribulation to them that trouble you; 7. And to you who are troubled, rest with us.

6, 7. For God ruleth righteously; and it is the way of his justice, to punish your persecutors, and give you who are persecuted rest with us his apostles.

Note, That they who think this is meant of the destruction of Jerusalem, must think that Paul thought he should live to see it, and that he and they should then have rest on earth; which were to be deceived, and to deceive them.

7, 8. When the Lord Jesus shall be revealed from heaven with his mighty angels, in flaming fire, taking vengeance on them that know not God, and that obey not the gospel of our Lord Jesus Christ:

7, 8. Note, By [them that know not God] is usually meant the heathens; which confuteth them who distort this to signify but the destruction of the Jews. And to them in Macedonia it was more to be delivered from the heathens, who were the rulers, than from a handful of scattered despised Jews.

2. Christ will appear with his angels to judge and punish the ungodly.

9. Who shall be punished with everlasting destruction from the presence of the Lord, and from the glory of his power:

9. Note, That the phrases [everlasting destruction] and [from the presence of the Lord] and [from the glory of his power] agree to the usual scripture-description of damnation, and not to the destruction of Jerusalem, without distortion. Nor was it much ascribed then to an appearance of Christ in glory, that the heathen who despised him, and killed him, and persecuted his cause and servants, did also destroy the Jews.

10. When he shall come to be glorified in his saints, and to be admired in all them that believe (because our testimony among you was believed) in that day.

10. Note, The end of Christ's glorious coming will be to be glorified and admired in holy believers, as having by his merit, intercession, and Spirit, made them by holiness fit for glory, and in justice set them above their persecutors.

2. So far were the poor Christians from being then such a glory and admiration, that they continued above two hundred years after this to be persecuted and made the scorn of the world.

11. Wherefore also we pray always for you, that our God would count you worthy of *this* calling, and fulfil all the good pleasure of *his* goodness, and the work of faith with power.

11. We pray, that God will fit you by his grace for this, and make you suitable to your holy calling, and fully perform to you all the purposes of his love and powerfully finish your work of faith.

Note, Worthiness, in the gospel-sense, is that moral qualification by grace, to which, as a moral condition, God hath promised the blessing.

12. That the name of our Lord Jesus Christ may be glorified in you, and ye in him, according to the grace of our God, and the Lord Jesus Christ.

12. Note, That sanctifying grace maketh Christians a glory to the name of Christ, declaratively, as the cause is honoured in the effect; and they are glorified in Christ possessively, as the means in the end obtained, and the runner in the prize; and relatively, as an adopted son in a prince that adopted him.

CHAP. II.

NOW we beseech you, brethren, by the coming of our Lord Jesus Christ, and by our gathering together unto him, 2. That ye be not so soon shaken in mind, or be troubled, neither by spirit, nor by word, nor by letter, as from us, as that the day of Christ is at hand.

1, 2. I vehemently beseech you, that no pretence either of Spirit, word, or apostolical letter, persuade you that Christ's coming is near at hand, and so trouble you, and your faith be shaken when that is disappointed.

Note further, That it is more than the destruction of Jerusalem that is here meant; For it will be the churches gathering together to Christ at his coming. 2. And it neither agreeth with the following long persecutions of the church by the heathens, nor with Paul's usual pity to the Jews, thus to insult in their destruction, as if it brought a felicity to the church like heaven itself.

3. Let no man deceive you by any means: for *that day shall not come*, except there come a falling away first, and that man of sin be revealed, the son of perdition; 4. Who opposeth and exalteth himself above all that is called God, or that is worshipped; so that he as God sitteth in the temple of God, shewing himself that he is God.

3. It is dangerous deceit for any to persuade you, that the day of Christ is at hand: for there are many things that must first come to pass: there must first be a falling away of many from the faith; and that notable man of sin must appear, who is to be destroyed. 4. Who arrogantly opposeth true Christianity, and exalteth himself above all, &c.

5, 6, 7. Remember ye not, that when I was yet with you, I told you these things? And now ye know what withholdeth, that he might be revealed in his time. For the mystery of iniquity doth already work: only he who now letteth, *will let*, until he be taken out of the way. 8. And then shall that wicked be revealed, whom the Lord shall consume with the spirit of his mouth, and shall destroy with the brightness of his coming: 9. *Even him* whose coming is after the working of Satan, with all power, and signs, and lying wonders, 10. And with all deceivableness of unrighteousness, in them that perish, because that they received not the love of the truth, that they might be saved. 11. And for this cause God shall send them strong delusion, that they should believe a lie: 12. That they all might be damned who believed not the truth, but had pleasure in unrighteousness.

Note, 1. That forewarning should be fore-arming. 2. Both the rise and fall of sin and sinners must have their proper seasons: God's delays are but staying till the due time. 3. Removing impediments is the preparatory work for future events. 4. This great enemy of Christ is a man lawless, and made up of wickedness. 5. He must be first revealed, and then consumed, even by his word, Spirit, and coming. 6. Satan will promote this enemy of Christ, with power, signs, and lying wonders, and deceivableness of unrighteousness. 7. Not receiving the love of the truth of the gospel, nor heartily believing it, but taking pleasure in unrighteousness, prepare men for damning delusions. 8. God is said to send them such delusions, by penal desertions and permissions.

Readers, I dare not take on me to teach you that as true, which I know not myself; nor yet to pretend that I know more than I do, I confess, that I am uncertain who it is that Paul here describeth: and merely to know what other men say of it, is no satisfaction to me, especially when they so greatly differ as they do.

1. Most of the fathers and Papists think, that Antichrist here described is some odious false Christ, who is yet to come before the end of the world. I have much to say against that opinion.

2. Grotius thought that this chapter speaks of the emperor Caius Caligula chiefly, and partly of Simon Magus. So much may be said against that, as that his follower Dr. Hammond rejecteth it.

3. Dr. Hammond thinks it speaketh only of Simon Magus. I cannot believe that: 1. Because really this Simon was no such considerable formidable person as he describeth him. The few scraps of history of Simon recited by him, are very dubious. No great or public history of those times mention him. He was affrighted into submission and supplication to Peter, Acts viii. He was not thought worthy the naming after, in all the sharp charges against heretics in the epistles. The Judaizers are reproved; the concision called dogs; the troublers Paul wisheth cut off; the Nicolaitans named; and the woman Jezebel, and many antichrists, mentioned by John; the grosser sort of heretics smartly described, and condemned by Peter and Jude: John forbids us to bid them good-speed: Paul bids men avoid them as self-condemned: the Revelation speaketh yet more fully. And none of them all mention Simon as the god and ring-leader of them. If the Nicolaitans, and all those that the Doctor calleth Gnostics, were known to be the disciples of Simon, why is that concealed in such large reproofs? and why not called Simonians, as well as Nicolaitans? If they were not then known to be his offspring, it seems these heresies had other fathers before him, more noted and followed. 3. Simon was revealed before the writing of this epistle, Acts viii. and the heresies before too common. 3. There were seven or eight other heresies described by Epiphanius, as early as the Simonians and Gnostics, and as bad. 4. Sure Gnosticism was not then an unrevealed mystery, if it be mentioned as oft as the Doctor thinketh. 5. And through God's mercy the falling away first was comparatively but of few, and not of so great a number of churches or Christians, as was a stop to their expectation of the coming of Christ. It is not noted in Acts viii. that the Samaritans were seduced by him after they believed. If it were true, that they, and some at Rome were, what is that to all the churches? 6. It is above sixteen hundred years since Simon was revealed, and yet Christ is not come; how then is that made an occasion of men's delayed expectation? 7. That Christ's coming signifieth but the destruction of Jerusalem, is before shewed to be very improbable, and more fully might be. How many hot persecutions of Christians after that, do all church histories describe, in another manner than Simon's pranks? And what could the Jews do through all the empire, being condemned vagabonds, but by way of rabble-tumult, which the Roman power restrained? 8. And it seemeth mere violence to the text, to make [him that withholdeth] to signify not [him], but [that thing] which withholdeth, even the Christians not yet separating from the Jews. For, 1. There was no set time of separation: Paul did it long before the apostles that conversed with them in Judea, and when they did, none knew. And Paul withdrew from them as obstinacy gave him cause, in one place sooner than in others; and never so far, but that he laboured for their conversion. Nor were any such direful persecutions an effect of that separation, as far as just history informeth us: it was the scattered Jews that were the rudiments of most of the Christian churches in the empire, to whom the Gentiles were added. And this Doctor himself oft asserteth, That Rome, Alexandria, Antioch, and such other great cities, had two bishops, and two churches, one of the Jews, and one of the Gentiles. And the Christian Jews did not separate from their countrymen of a long time.

That which the apostle mentioneth, the whole Catholic church seemeth to be concerned in: whereas the little pranks of Simon Magus were like John of Leyden's, and Knipperdolling's, and James Naylor's, which had a few contemned followers, in a few towns, a little while, and then ended in shame—like the boy's squibs, compared to a war.

8. And what mystery was there in so gross iniquity, as for Simon to call himself God the Father, &c. any more than to have seen a Hacket or bedlamite rave.

9. And if such wonders of deceit had been wrought by him, as here mentioned, as should delude those that received not the love of the truth to salvation, history would have more fully recorded his miracles, and this success: even on all them that believed not the truth, but had pleasure in unrighteousness.

4. Some think that Paul here speaketh of a seditious ring-leader of the Jews, that drew them into rebellion, to their destruction; and that the fear of some Roman governor was it that for a time restrained him. But this opinion few follow.

5. Lyra and some other Papists think, that it was Mahomet that was this great deceiver, and the antichrist, and the empire that withheld. His reasons are rendered in his annotations on the Revelations, and on this text: and Zanchy was much of the same mind, though he thought the Pope was a kind of a second antichrist.

6. But the far greatest number of Protestants think, that it is the Pope that is here spoken of, as the [Man of Sin,] and [Son of Perdition,] &c. and that it is the Roman empire that withheld his revelation: but some few think that it was the godly bishops of Rome, that for some ages possessed that seat, (and many were martyrs) that withheld this revelation of antichrist, till they were taken away by death: for men would not believe that the successors of so good men could

be antichrist. Abundance of volumes are written to prove the Pope to be the antichrist; and one of the chief, by bishop George Downame.

For myself, 1. I can better try him by the plain parts of scripture, than by the hard prophecies. And I can easily see many and great points in which Popery is contrary to the word of God, and I am most moved by such moral arguments as Dr. H. Moore useth in his Mystery of Iniquity. And I find enough to settle me against Popery. 2. But whether it be he that this text meaneth, or those applied to him in the Revelation, I have not skill enough to be sure, or very confident. And, 3. I think a Christian may be very safe without understanding these obscure texts: I long to know God and Jesus Christ better, more than to know antichrist: his name is not in the creed, nor is it an article of the ancient necessary faith to know who he is; so we know the false doctrines and practices which we must avoid. Perhaps, those that have more thoroughly studied these texts may know more; (though I must say, that their real disagreement of opinion discourageth my hopes of full understanding them.) I think it my duty to confess my ignorance, and not pretend to the knowledge which I have not. They that are offended at this gap or defect in my paraphrase, may turn to many others that know more, or are more confident.

If you say, why were these prophecies written, if not to be understood? I answer, To be understood by them that can, and not to be expounded by them that cannot. And I add, that the great beloved prophet Daniel thus concludeth, chap. xii. 8, 9. [I heard but understood not.]—And the angel said, [Go thy way, Daniel, for the words are closed up and sealed to the time of the end.] And I take it to be no excess of humility to confess, that in expounding prophecies, I am not so wise as Daniel. That Popery is a heinous corruption of Christianity, I am past doubt: and that it is aggravated by the profession of the gospel, and fathering their sin on Christ.

But for the help of those that are more capable of arriving at certainty than I am, I will distinctly tell the reader the paraphrase of the three most considerable sort of expositors.

I. "Ver. 3. Let no man persuade you that Christ's coming is at hand, for it will not be till a great part of the church fall away from Christianity, and Mahomet that wicked man and seducer be revealed, who is a destroyer, and shall be destroyed. 4. Who opposeth and exalteth himself, not only above all earthly powers, but above all sorts of divine worship, both heathenish and Christian. So that as if he were a God, he will set up his own worship as next to the supreme only God, both in the temple at Jerusalem, and throughout all the now Christian eastern empire, and a great part further of the world; and under the title of God's greatest prophet, will put down God's own institutions, and laws, and gospel, and set up his own in the stead. 6. What it is that stops him is a thing known to you all, even the imperial power; which as it falls he will rise. For as he is to make his false religion by a composition of Arianism, Judaism, and his own inventions, so the swarm of heresies now among us, (Nicolaitans, Ebionites, Corinthians, Gnostics, &c.) are secretly a mysterious iniquity preparing for him: only that empire that now letteth, must give place to him, by diminution at his first rising, and by its total overthrow in the east, at his full possession. And so he shall in his time become the open seducer and captivater of the church and world; and must stay till Christ diminish and consume Mahometanism by his word preached, and utterly destroy it with the glory of his more full appearance before the end. 9. Even that Mahomet's kingdom, whose coming is by satanical, murdering wars, and deceitful pretences of heavenly signs and revelations; and with the unrighteous deceit of pretended opposition to idolatry, and to Christians, as if they worship two or three Gods, and their laws were not so good as his: and those superficial, hypocrite Christians, that had but the name and form, and not the hearty belief, love, and obedience to the truth, shall turn Mahometans, and be damned."

II. The commonest Protestant paraphrase is thus, "Ver. 3. Christ's coming shall not be till there be a general apostacy of the whole visible church, say some, or of most or much of it, say others, unto idolatrous worship, and subjection to the Papacy, and that man of sin, the Pope, be revealed, the active and passive son of perdition, the Abaddon, the head of this apostacy given up to all sin himself, and to promote it. 4. Who claimeth Christ's prerogative under the name of his universal vicar, and overthrows his officers and laws, and sets up his own against them, and overtoppeth and subjecteth all princes and magistrates; and this in the church of God, say most, or in that idolatrous church of his own, falsely called, The Church of God, say others, as if he were there chief lord himself, and arrogating names of blasphemy. I told you formerly of all this. And now you know what hindereth his speedy arising: even the empire, as such, (say some) including both the Pagan and Christian: or (as others) the empire, as Pagan only. 6. For the beginnings of antichristianity are secretly and mysteriously already working, which will bring him forth in time, even the pride and ambition of ministers seeking superiority, and the people's excess of factious respects to some above others, and falling into sects and heresies in following them. Only the empire that now hindereth must first be taken out of the way: 8. And then shall the Pope, that man of wickedness, arise, (say some) or be openly discovered to be antichrist (say others): whom the Lord shall consume by the power of his word preached by the two witnesses, and then destroy by pouring out the vials of his wrath upon him at his latter coming to restore his church. 9. Even that Pope with his Roman church of Papists, whose coming to the Papacy is after that way of working, by force, and cheats, and feigned miracles, which Satan teacheth and giveth them to seduce the Christian world. 10. And with all the deceiving arts of falsehood, by which unrighteousness is upheld and promoted, to delude those that shall perish for ever: because they received not sound doctrine when it was delivered, nor held the Christian faith in love, and in its power, but in custom, hypocrisy, and form, that it might sanctify and save them.

"Therefore God justly gave them up by desertions, to deceivers and delusions, to believe a lie. 11. That all these Papists might be damned who believed not the truth that is contrary to Popery, but had pleasure in its unrighteous principles and practices, and in that sensual life which is contrary to the Christianity which they profess."

III. The third considerable opinion runs thus, in the paraphrase exposition.—

1. Paul's words have relation both to Daniel's words, of Antiochus, say most, but of the Roman power rather, say Calvin and Brightman (who largely proveth it).

2. It is so far from being true, that the Christians rejoiced in Christ's sending the Romans to destroy Jerusalem, that they grealy lamented it: the city's name was precious to them, the first Christians being all Jews, and the Gentiles receiving the gospel from Jerusalem, Christ wept over them when he prophesied their ruin: Paul's lamentation was great for them. The ruin was dreadful, 111,000 killed, and 700,000 carried captive: and the apostles were all Jews; and there was a common expectation among the Jews of the Messiah's glorious kingdom at Jerusalem, and they called it The Holy City, and Land.

3. The abomination and desolation is by Christ himself compared to that spoken of by Daniel the prophet, which was the destroying the holy place and worship, and setting up idolatry in its stead. And the authors themselves of the second exposition (as against the Pope) expound the desolating abomination in Matt. xxiv. to be the Roman heathen army coming to lay waste the holy city and temple : for that abomination of desolation was to go before the flight of men from Jerusalem, or to concur. And this text, ver. 3, &c. seemeth plainly to follow Christ, and speak of the same that he speaketh of.

4. Vespasian, and his son Titus, by his command, were the men that destroyed the holy city, temple, and nation, and the idolatrous heathens and their worship there took present possession, and to set up the desolation and abomination : and his younger son Domitian destroyed the Christians, and proclaimed himself to be God, and to be worshipped with altars and sacrifices as God.

5. This Vespasian took on him to work miracles, healing a blind man, and many others: so that some foolish Jews called him the Messiah: and he and his son Titus by their flattery and fair lives got great esteem as excellent men : and their learned orators, &c. promoted the honour of idolatry by theirs.

6. This way of self-deifying and promoting idolatry, and captivating, the Jews and all Christians, went on, though not equally, through all the emperors almost, till Constantine.

7. The attempt of Caius Caligula told the Christians what further to expect, when he commanded Petronius to set up his image in the temple to be worshipped as Jupiter.

Nero's cruelty prognosticated much.

8. But Vespasian and Titus were stopped from the desolation first attempted by the life of Claudius, Galba, Otho, Vitellius, till he was made emperor himself.

9. And Christ consumed their idolatry by his gospel, and destroyed it by Constantine. These things premised, their paraphrase is. " ver. 3. The day of the Lord will not come till the Jews' rebellion and revolt from the Romans provoke them to destroy them, and then will the wicked destroyer appear, even the Romans' imperial pride and rage, who exalt themselves above all human power, and will arrogate the name and worship of gods, and put down God's own instituted worship, and will have altars and images erected to themselves. 6. What delayeth them yet you know: they are killing one another for empire at Rome; and the sin of the poor Jews against Christ and his apostles is not yet ripe for utter ruin; and then next the destroyer will appear: for their self-idolising is already at work, as Caligula's attempt assureth us, with Nero's pride and cruelty : only the foresaid impediments at Rome, &c. do stop the desolation and abomination till it be removed, and then it will invade the holy city and temple, and Judea shall feel the Roman pride and idolatry. Who come as from Satan with all help that he can give them, by powerful armies, and with the countenance of the Roman idolaters' learning, and magic, and lying oracles and wonders, such as Vespasian pretended to work, and the virtues that his son Titus made ostentation of. And with all the deceitful learning and arts, which may countenance idolatry and wickedness, and beguile men fitted to destruction: because these poor Jews received not the gospel in love, that they might be saved by Christ, and many Christians proved hypocrites, and formalists, and heretics, and therefore God penally will let loose upon them the learned Roman idolaters with their arts and subtlety, and advantages of power to delude them to worship idols which are lying vanities : and so they that would not believe the truth, but had pleasure in unrighteousness, might be left to be their own destroyers, by believing and practising the idolatry and wickedness which will damn them.

The matter of all these three expositions is itself, hath a great deal of truth, that is, Mahomet is an antichrist (most notorious): the Pope as pretended universal head of the church, corrupting Christianity in doctrine, worship, and discipline, and bloodily destroying sounder Christ, is one sort of antichrist. The Roman Pagan idolaters that set up the desolating abomination were no less : but, which this text meaneth, I know not. But I detest that opinion that maketh all the visible church idolatrous and antichristian since Constantine delivered it from Pagan persecution. Sure such should not now complain of persecution, but fear deliverance and prosperity.

12. But we are bound to give thanks alway to God for you, brethren, beloved of the Lord, because God hath from the beginning chosen you to salvation, through sanctification of the spirit, and belief of the truth.

13. But when I speak of this pernicious apostacy of the followers of this man of sin and perdition, it mindeth me to be thankful to God for you, that from the beginning he hath chosen and marked you out for salvation, by sanctifying you by his Spirit, and giving you a sound belief of that truth, which these apostates do deny.

Note, That God's election connecteth the end and means ; whom he chooseth to salvation, he at once chooseth to sanctification and confirmed faith.

14. Whereunto he called you by our gospel, to the obtaining of the glory of our Lord Jesus Christ.

14. And I am thankful that my preaching the gospel was the means by which he called you hereto, and to obtain your part with Christ in glory.

15. Therefore, brethren, stand fast, and hold the traditions which ye have been taught, whether by word, or our epistle.

15. Therefore stand fast, and hold the same doctrine which I have delivered to you, whether by preaching, discourse, or writing, against all innovating seducers.

16. Now our Lord Jesus Christ himself, and God even our Father, which hath loved us and hath given us everlasting consolation and good hope through grace, 17. Comfort your hearts, and stablish you in every good word and work.

16, 17. And I have great encouragement to pray for you, in hope that you may be comforted and established in all that is good, because it is to that Christ that is our Saviour, and God who is our Father, and hath already shewed that he loveth us, and hath by his grace given us solid hope, and the foretaste of the everlasting consolation.

CHAP. III.

FINALLY, brethren, pray for us, that the word of the Lord may have *free* course, and be glorified even as *it is* with you.

1. And as I pray for you, pray ye for us, that the word of God, may run abroad with speed and prosperous success, and not to be stopped or hindered by persecutors' contradictions, or scandalous seducers, but may be honoured by free and full reception and obedience, as it is with you (which praise I give you to encourage you.)

2. And that we may be delivered from unreasonable and wicked men: for all men have not faith.

2. And that our persons may be preserved, and our preaching prosper, against all the endeavours of absurd and wicked men, who are our adversaries. For faithless men are every where against us.

3. But the Lord is faithful, who shall stablish you, and keep *you* from evil.

3. But though men be faithless who resist me, we have a faithful God, who will confirm you, and keep you from Satan and from evil.

4. And we have confidence in the Lord touching you, that ye both do, and will do the things which we command you.

4. And we have good hope that you will still follow the precepts which we give you from the Lord.

5. And the Lord direct your hearts into the love of God, and into the patient waiting for Christ.

5. To which end I pray, that God would direct your hearts to love himself, and patiently to wait for Christ, and these two graces will keep you in obedience from backsliding.

6. Now we command you brethren, in the name of our Lord Jesus Christ, that ye withdraw yourselves from every brother that walketh disorderly, and not after the tradition which he received of us.

6. And this is one of the commands which in the name of Christ I have to deliver you, to preserve you from revolting, viz. to keep your society clean from scandal, by avoiding the familiar company of every one professing Christianity, who liveth disorderly, and not according to the law of Christ which we delivered to him.

Note, 1. That there is a degree of avoiding familiarity with a disorderly Christian, to shame him into repentance, and to preserve ourselves, and the honour of Christianity, which is short of a public declarative, excommunication, and casting out of the church. It is justly called [suspension] because a man is not to be excommunicate till he be proved obstinately impenitent: But a man that is guilty of a notorious scandalous sin, may be suspended while he is under trial whether he will repent or not.

2. Note, That this command of withdrawing from the disorderly, doth not require that we withdraw from the church when such intrude, or are there permitted. No more than you must forsake your own house and family if he intrude: you have right and command to be there, though he have no right.

3. Nor doth it make all to be of equal power in church matters, nor bind any to go beyond his power. 1. Of man's capacity for public church communion, the pastors are judges: and if they be negligent, it is their sin, which will not allow private men to forsake the public communion, till the church so far forsake God as to be forsaken by him. 2. But private familiarity is in private men's power, where they may discountenance the scandalous by withdrawing from them.

7. For yourselves know how ye ought to follow us: for we behaved not ourselves disorderly among you, 8. Neither did we eat any man's bread for nought: but wrought with labour and travel night and

day, that we might not be chargeable to any of you:

7, 8. You know what our example was, that ought to be imitated: I did not live idly, and look that the church should maintain me, nor basely hang on any, or needlessly burden them: nor take their bread which I paid not for: but while I taught you, I laboured and toiled at my trade, that I might be chargeable to none of you.

9. Not because we have not power, but to make ourselves an ensample unto you to follow us.

9. My ministerial office and labour made maintenance from you my due; but idleness I saw was a sin, that had need of example as well as doctrine to subdue it.

10. For even when we were with you, this we commanded you, that if any would not work, neither should he eat.

10. Note, Poor men that will not work when they can, do forfeit the bread of charity from men; but rich men that live idly do by that sin forfeit their food, (and more, even their lives and souls) to God; but men may not therefore take it from them.

11. For we hear that there are some which walk among you disorderly, working not at all, but are busy-bodies.

11. By disorderly persons I specially mean such as I hear some among you are, who live not in any profitable trade and labour, but yet are busy, but it is about circumstantial, unnecessary or unprofitable bye-matters.

Note, That as idleness is a base sin, which equals life and death, so unnecessary and unprofitable labour is a mis-spending time, and a forfeiture of maintenance as well as idleness: and to make a trade or daily employment of vain or unprofitable business, is but a cloak of deceit for an idle life: the slothful and unprofitable servants forfeit wages. Oh what a deal of business to little purpose hath the world to answer for, by not labouring, but busily trifling; men will find that God gave them life and reason for greater things.

12. Now them that are such we command and exhort by our Lord Jesus Christ, that with quietness they work, and eat their own bread.

12. To live on the labours or cost of others, through base, indulging fleshly ease, or unprofitable trifling, is so great a sin, that I do command you, and exhort you, by the authority of Christ, and as you will obey him, that you avoid it, and that you quietly and willingly get your own living by some profitable labour, and eat not other men's bread, but your own, and that not the bread of idleness.

13, 14. But ye, brethren, be not weary in well doing. And if any man obey not our word by this epistle, note that man, and have no company with him, that he may be ashamed. 15. Yet count him not as an enemy, but admonish him as a brother.

13, 14, 15. If after all this the slothful will not labour, though you are not to cut him off from the church, as if it were for rejecting an essential part of Christianity, yet there is a discipline to be used in the church towards its members: set a note of shame upon that man, by avoiding familiarity with him; but yet take him not for an enemy or heathen, but an offending Christian, and continue to call him to repentance.

Note, Qu. But what if it be a son? must the parents deny him food? Ans. If he be obstinate in an idle or unprofitable life, being able for a better, 1. The parents should mark him out to shame: 2. And should so far straiten him in the quality of his food and maintenance, as may make his sloth a penal suffering to him, and signify their abhorrence of his sin, though they may not famish him to death.

16. Now the Lord of peace himself give you peace always by all means. The Lord *be* with you all. 17. The salutation of me Paul with mine own hand, which is the token in every epistle: so I write; 18. The grace of our Lord Jesus Christ be with you all. Amen.

16, 17, 18. Note, We may boldly trust him for our peace and safety, who will be called The Lord of Peace, and by the grace of Christ will be with us, and give us peace always, and by all means. Amen.

THE
FIRST EPISTLE OF PAUL THE APOSTLE,
TO
TIMOTHY.

CHAP. I.

PAUL, an apostle of Jesus Christ by the commandment of God our Saviour, and the Lord Jesus Christ, *which is* our hope; 2. Unto Timothy, *my* own son in the faith: Grace, mercy, *and* peace from God our Father, and Jesus Christ our Lord.

1, 2. Note, 1. Apostleship was by God's call and command.
2. Christ is the believer's hope.
3. It is meet to have some special endeared love to those that are our sons in the faith, converted by our ministry.
4. As the desire of worldlings is to worldly prosperity, so the sum of all holy Christian desires, is grace, mercy, and peace, from God the Father, and from Christ.

3. As I besought thee to abide still at Ephesus when I went into Macedonia, that thou mightest charge some that they teach no other doctrine, 4. Neither give heed to fables, and endless genealogies, which minister questions, rather than godly edifying, which is in faith; *so do.*

3, 4. Note, 1. Whether this imply that Timothy was bishop of Ephesus, is a question of small moment to them that know what a bishop then was. A bishop, as Dr. Hammond maintaineth, had then but one congregation, and no subject-presbyter under him. He certainly had no power of the sword to force men. He was only a guide to volunteers and consenters; and not to any against their will. It is certain, that every church had at least one such bishop, (I think usually more.) And no doubt Ephesus had such, (either Timothy, or others.) If it be archbishops that are made the matter of this doubt, it is certain, that an archbishop had no power of the sword, nor was a bishop to any but consenting volunteers, and worked only on conscience, and not immediately on body or purse. And I believe that Timothy and Titus, and the apostles, were so far archbishops, as that they had by office the care of gathering many churches, and then taking care of their preservation and increase, by urging the doctrine and commands of Christ, and ordaining bishops over particular churches *(Episcopos gregis)* by their own and the flocks' consent, and not otherwise; and then exhorting such pastors and churches on just occasions to do their duties. And who can be against such archbishops.

But some that now feign the idea of a bishop to be one that hath many score or hundred churches under him, which have no bishop but himself, and one that is set over them without their consent, and that ruleth them by force, of the adjoined sword, imprisonment, or ruin, are ready to dream that Timothy and Titus were such bishops. Doubtless every city or corporation where were Christians, had then a church (at least) and every church a bishop (at least.) And whether it was Timothy or another, Ephesus was not without. Though it is true that we find him so constantly with Paul, almost every where, where he was, that it is hard to believe that he was very long at Ephesus.

2. Note, That churches are in danger of corruption by other doctrines than those delivered by the apostles. And their doctrines were so sufficient, that no other should be taught.

3. Though some think it is still the Gnostics that are here described by fables and genealogies, it is most like to be all the Judaizers. And though genealogies be part of scripture, it is perverseness to make too great a stir about them, and to turn religion into endless questions, and divert from matter of faith, in which our edification chiefly doth consist. Multitudes sin by too much stir about lesser scripture verities, when by wrangling or long study it hindereth them from greater.

5. Now the end of the commandment is charity out of a pure heart, and *of* a good conscience, and *of* faith unfeigned:

5. The holy scripture is a complete body, which hath its accidents and ornaments, as well as essential and integral parts, (as hair, nails, colour), &c. But it is the end that is the chief part, and must be preferred: and the end of all Christ's doctrine and law is, [charity] or to bring men's souls to the love of God, and man, and goodness, as its very nature: and the grand means to this are, 1. A heart purified by God's Spirit. 2. A good conscience, not guilty of reigning sin, and justified from the guilt of former sin and present infirmity by Christ. 3. An unfeigned faith in Christ, by which we are united to him, and have our part in the foresaid benefits. And this is the sum of true Christian religion in few words, which is more profitably insisted on than jangling controversies.

6. From which some having swerved, have turned aside unto vain jangling; 7. Desiring to be teachers of the law, understanding neither what they say, nor whereof they affirm.

6, 7. And some that have roved from this mark, (not placing religion finally in love, to be promoted aforesaid) have turned aside to vain jangling, or vain chat: as if religion lay in being doctors of Moses' law; when as they understand not what they say themselves, nor what the things are which they pretend to teach.

Note, 1. They that shoot not at this mark, and place not religion as aforesaid, have ever since corrupted it by vain jangling, though not about the same subjects: some setting the churches together by the ears about unnecessary curious notions, concerning the person of Christ, or concerning God's decrees, and concourse, and some about the clergy's universal domination, and about their canon law (worse than was that of Moses) and their dunghill of corruptions and ensnaring ceremonies, and some about quibbling notions concerning justification, faith, and works. Satan hath religious diversions for them that are above sensuality. And ignorant confidence (with rage) is the usual character of all such.

8. But we know that the law *is* good, if a man use it lawfully;

8. We praise the law as well as they: it is God's law, and therefore good, if lawfully used: which is to lead men to Christ, and typify spiritual things to come, and to condemn and restrain sin; but not to justify men instead of grace, nor to be imposed on the Gentiles, or continued, when a better doth displace it.

9. Knowing this, that the law is not made for a righteous man, but for the lawless and disobedient, for the ungodly and for sinners, for unholy and profane, for murderers of fathers and murderers of mothers, for man-slayers, 10. For whoremongers, for them that defile themselves with mankind, for men-stealers, for liars, for perjured persons, and if there be any other thing that is contrary to sound doctrine, 11. According to the glorious gospel of the blessed God, which was committed to my trust.

9, 10, 11. It must be foreknown, 1. That the world was not lawless that had not Moses' laws: they had the law of nature, and the common law of grace which was given to mankind after the fall: and Christ hath now brought us the holy spiritual law of grace in the most perfect edition. So that sin is condemned where Moses' law is not received or known. 2. That Moses' laws, as such, were all political for the government of that republic, even the Ten Commandments, and had penalties to be executed by men annexed, as an essential part of it. Now of this law, saith Paul, [It was not made with these penalties either to bridle or to punish them that without it were righteous men,] that is, who were obedient to the law of nature, and of grace, and whose hearts were ruled with the love of righteousness, and needed not to be frightened to it by corporal penalties; much less for us Christians, who have Christ's law of grace, and are sanctified by his Spirit writing it in our hearts by love of goodness: but God knowing the corruption of man's heart, did make it for the Israelites, to restrain them by fear from living like lawless, disobedient men, &c. and to punish them by the magistrate, who were ungodly, sinners, unholy, profane, murderers, &c. which the gospel, and Christ's law, which I preach, is as much against as Moses' law, and more powerfully overcometh: so that we that have better, even Christ's law without us, need not the countenance of Moses law.

12. And I thank Christ Jesus our Lord, who hath enabled me, for that he counted me faithful, putting me into the ministry;

12. Note, It is a great mercy to be entrusted with the ministry of the gospel, with ability and faithfulness.

13. Who was before a blasphemer, and a persecutor, and injurious. But I obtained mercy, because I did *it* ignorantly in unbelief:

13. Note, 1. The great mercy of God to great sinners; even persecutors and blasphemers may be converted.

2. That God giveth the greatest mercy without previous merit.

3. The word [because] here meaneth not that ignorance was a proper cause of God's mercy: but that it made Paul a more capable receiver of mer-

cy, than he should have been, if he had maliciously sinned against knowledge.

14. And the grace of our Lord was exceeding abundant, with faith, and love which is in Christ Jesus.

14. And this mercy which called me, hath poured out on me, by the Holy Ghost, an abundant measure of faith in Christ, and love to him and his, which carrieth me on in his work with zeal and unwearied diligence.

15. This *is* a faithful saying, and worthy of all acceptation, that Christ Jesus came into the world to save sinners; of whom I am chief.

15. This is the great article of our Christian faith, which we may trust to, and of great comfort to us all, and worthy of our thankful acceptation, That Christ came into the world to save sinners; which I, that am one of the chief, must therefore predicate with chiefest thanks.

16. Howbeit, for this cause, I obtained mercy, that in me first Jesus Christ might shew forth all longsuffering, for a pattern to them which should hereafter believe on him to life everlasting.

16. But it pleased God to shew mercy to me, so great a sinner, to magnify his grace, and encourage all sinners against despair, that in me Christ might exemplarily shew his gracious patience and forbearance, and confirm all sinners in the hope of everlasting life, who after shall believe and be converted.

17. Now unto the king eternal, immortal, invisible, and only wise God, *be* honour and glory for ever and ever. Amen.

17. The sense of this unspeakable mercy calleth up my soul (and should do all) to speak with joy the praises of our God, who is eternal, immortal, invisible, the only God, absolutely wise, over angels, and all creatures: to him be honour and glory, for ever and ever. Amen.

18. This charge I commit unto thee, son Timothy, according to the prophesies which went before on thee, that thou by them mightest war a good warfare. 19. Holding faith, and a good conscience;

18. Note, 1. By [charge] is meant holding faith and a good conscience, and keeping the doctrine committed to him by Paul, as a faithful minister and soldier of Christ, against all opposition.

2. It seems some particular prophecy (such as Agabus had of Paul, and many then had) had foretold that Timothy should be a faithful minister.

19. Which some having put away, concerning faith have made shipwreck. 20. Of whom is Hymeneus and Alexander; whom I have delivered unto Satan, that they may learn not to blaspheme.

19, 20. Which some have cast away, and lost the Christian faith: such are Hymeneus and Alexander, whom I have delivered to Satan, as God's executioner of some bodily punishment, to see whether correction will convince them of their blasphemy.

Note, 1. What their blasphemy was, is after shewn, 2 Tim. ii. 17. and iv. 14.

2. That Satan is oft God's executioner in correction and destruction, is certain; and that such is the delivery here meant (for want of Christian magistrates): but it was none of Satan's desire, but God's, hereby to teach them not to blaspheme.

CHAP. II.

I Exhort therefore, that first of all, supplications, prayers, intercessions *and* giving of thanks, be made for all men:

1. As I have oft said, that charity is the end and sum of religion, I exhort, that this may be sincerely manifested in your religious worship; and that you heartily pray for all sorts of men, that God would save them from sin and misery, and give them grace and mercy; and be thankful for their welfare as if it were your own.

2. For kings, and for all that are in authority; that we may lead a quiet and peaceable life in all godliness and honesty.

2. For kings, and for all that are in pre-eminence or superiority, that they may so govern, that we may be protected in the quiet serving of God, in godliness and decent conversation with men, without reproach and persecution.

Note, 1. That the character of the rulers that we are to pray for, is not only ἰσυρία, *jus regendi*, right; but ὑπεροχὴ, pre-eminence.

Pray for him that hath the right of governing, as far as you can know it; but submit to him that hath settled possession, so far as it wrongeth not another's right; and so far pray for such, that we may live a quiet and peaceable life in all godliness and honesty.

3. For this *is* good and acceptable in the sight of God our Saviour: 4. Who will have all men to be saved, and to come unto the knowledge of the truth.

3, 4. For this is agreeable to the great mercy manifested in man's redemption by Jesus Christ, who by his death, and covenant of grace, and preaching, hath shewed us how willing he is that all men should be saved, and come to the knowledge of his gospel.

Note, 1. That while we obediently pray as God commandeth us, we may confidently expect God's acceptance. 2. An extensive charity rendereth us like Christ. 3. It is not only all sorts of men that Christ would have to be saved; but he willeth the salvation of all men in general, so far as to make a sacrifice sufficient for all, if all will believe; and to make an act of oblivion, or general pardon, and gift of life, to all, on condition of acceptance; and to send his messengers promiscuously to all, with the word of reconciliation, to beseech them to be reconciled to God. That Christ giveth to all, he willeth and purchased for all: but he giveth to all a pardon, and right to life, on condition of acceptance: therefore he is so far willing of their salvation.

5. For *there is* one God, and one Mediator between God and man, the man Christ Jesus; 6. Who gave himself a ransom for all, to be testified in due time.

5, 6. For it must move us to pray for all, in compliance with this will of God, that would have all men saved: because there is one God who is good to all, and one Mediator between God and mankind, who took upon him the common nature of all men, and gave himself a ransom for all, revealed in the season appointed of God, (or to be preached to all in due time, as God pleaseth.)

Note, The controversy about universal redemption, too hotly agitated by Beza, Piscator, and others, on one side, and by many on the other, I have fully handled in my Catholic Theology, and Methodus Theologiæ; and it needs no more than as aforesaid: 1. Whoever is damned, it is not because no ransom was made for him, or because it was not sufficient for him. 2. By God's will to save all, is meant the effects of his will that have a tendency to their salvation. 3. It is notorious, that God hath made an universal act of grace or oblivion, giving pardon of all sin, and right to life in Christ, to all men, without exception, on condition of believing's acceptance, and hath commissioned his ministers to offer this gift to all men, to the utmost of their power, and intreat them to accept it; and doth by many mercies intimate to them, that he useth them not according to the mere violated law of innocency, but on terms of grace. 4. Few Christians have the face to affirm that this universal conditional pardon and gift (or law of grace) is no fruit of the death of Christ. 5. If therefore this act of pardon was purchased by Christ, and given to all, no modest face can deny, that he so far died for all, as to purchase for them all that he actually giveth them. 6. It is usual to say that we give a man a benefit, (e. g. life to a condemned malefactor) if it be given him on the fair condition of his acceptance, and brought to his own will, and he intreated to receive it. 7. If any wrangler say, that this is unfit language, (to say, He is willing that men shall be saved, who offereth them salvation freely, unless he also make them willing;) let him confess, that it is but the name that he denieth, and none of the gifts in question. 8. And be it known, that unwillingness cometh not from a physical impossibility, through the want of natural faculties (as it is with brutes) but from a voluntary pravity, which aggravateth the sin. 9. And the mutable will of man is to be changed by reason: And God giveth men reasons in their kind sufficient to persuade them to accept of Christ and life. 10. And lastly, No man can say, that Adam when he fell had not grace enough to make him able to have stood, which he might have done, to his actual standing: nor, that God never giveth such a power to believe (or at least to come nearer the state of a true believer) to many that might bring it into act, and do not. This much is enough to end this controversy with modest wits.

7. Whereunto I am ordained a preacher and an apostle, (I speak the truth in Christ, *and lie not*) a teacher of the Gentiles in faith and verity.

7. This gospel I am appointed to preach to the Gentiles, (Christ knoweth that I feign not this commission) and faithfully and truly to be their teacher.

8. I will therefore that men pray every where, lifting up holy hands without wrath and doubting.

8. According to this my commission, I give these directions following to all sorts. First, That all men be much in prayer to God, not only in the assemblies, but in all convenient places wheresoever, open or secret: but that they lift not up to God hands defiled with any wilful sin, but pure and clean by harmless conversation; and that they come not to God with wrath against others, or with a quarrelsome, disputing, contentious disposition; but in Christian love.

Note, That the ceremony of lifting up the hands in prayer, (which was an act of corporal ceremony worship) is lawful, and fit where custom maketh it so, and yet is not necessary by institution; as kneeling also is.

9. In like manner also, that women adorn themselves in modest apparel, with shamefacedness and sobriety; not with broidered hair, or gold, or pearls, or costly array:

9. And for women, I forbid them not all ornaments, especially when they come to the sacred assemblies; but let them be adorned only with attire which expresseth gravity, modesty, and sobriety; not like proud, vain, or alluring persons, with curious dressings of their hair, embroidery, jewels, gold, or any over-costly apparel, as those that would seem either richer or comelier than they are.

10. But (which becometh women professing godliness) with good works.

10. But let them take good works (of piety to God, and charity to man) for their chiefest ornament; as they will do, if they are true professors of godliness. It is these in which they must ex-

cel the ungodly, and not in ostentation of wealth or beauty.

11. Let the women learn in silence with all subjection.

11. Let them be learners, rather than teachers; and let them use silence and humble subjection, and not be over-talkative and masterly; specially silent in the church.

12. But I suffer not a woman to teach, nor to usurp authority over the man, but to be in silence.

12. I forbid women to be public teachers, and to usurp an authority over their husbands, or over men in church-government; but to be quiet, silent, and obedient.

Note, 1. That Paul forbiddeth not women to teach their children or servants, or the elder women to teach the younger. 2. Nor doth he meddle with cases of civil government; as, whether a woman may govern a kingdom, or a city, or a multitude of her own tenants and men-servants.

13, 14. For Adam was first formed, then Eve. And Adam was not deceived, but the woman being deceived, was in the transgression.

13, 14. For God made the woman for subjection, by making Adam first, and then making her to be for his help: and the woman subjected.herself yet lower, by being first in the transgression deceived by the serpent, and then tempting her husband.

15. Notwithstanding she shall be saved in child-bearing, if they continue in faith and charity, and holiness with sobriety.

15. Yet though her sin hath brought her low, and even under a curse in the pain and peril of child-bearing, she is, even in that low and sad condition under God's merciful protection, and saving covenant of grace, which containeth the promise of this life, and that to come, if they continue in faith, charity, and purity, with sobriety.

Or, [Though sin and sorrow in travail came in by the woman, yet by a woman's child-bearing a Saviour came into the world, (which is some reparation of the honour of the sex;) and so the women may be saved as well as the men by Christ, if they continue in faith, charity, purity, and sobriety.]

CHAP. III.

THIS is a true saying, if a man desire the office of a bishop, he desireth a good work.

1. As for the office of a bishop, believe it, he that desireth it, doth desire a very great and excellent work: It is not a bare name, title, dignity, or place of honour and command; but a work, and a work of great importance, and labour, and difficulty, which every desirer is not fit for: Take heed, therefore, whom thou dost admit.

2. A bishop then must be blameless, the husband of one wife, vigilant, sober, of good behaviour, given to hospitality, apt to teach;

2. A bishop must be one, 1. That is not guilty of any scandalous sin since his conversion. 2. One that hath not put away his wife, except for fornication, and married another; much less that hath two at once. 3. One that is vigilant, and wholly addicted to do what he shall undertake. 4. One that is of a sober, moderate temper, and not guilty of levity and temerity. 5. One that is an orderly composed, decent temper and carriage. 6. By charity to be ready to entertain strangers, and to take in those that are exposed to want. 7. One that is fit by ability and zealous willingness to teach the flock the necessary things communicated to the ministry to communicate.

3. Not given to wine, no striker, not greedy of filthy lucre, but patient, not a brawler, not covetous;

3. 8. One that is not inordinately in love with wine or strong drink. 9. One that useth no violence, nor hurteth others. 10. One that studieth not after gain, nor useth dishonest, unseemly ways of getting. 11. One that by lenity taketh all things in the best sense, and is not rigorous. 12. One that is against strife, contention, and fighting. 13. One that is not in love with money.

4. One that ruleth well his own house, having his children in subjection with all gravity: 5. (For if a man know not how to rule his own house, how shall he take care of the church of God?)

4, 5. 14. One that ruleth well his own house, (if he have any) and by his success sheweth it, and that God blesseth his labours, his children being in subjection with all comely, grave, and pious behaviour. For if either he have not skill and care enough to rule his family well, or the badness of his children shew that God blesseth not his labour, how should the church judge him fit to rule them, and likely to succeed.

6. Not a novice, lest being lifted up with pride, he fall into the condemnation of the devil.

6. Not a late young convert; for such are more in danger of pride than others, when they are set up as teachers, and so fall as the devils did.

Note, That young, raw Christians made teachers are in great danger of falling into condemnation by pride, even like to devils. Because, 1. They have less knowledge of their own ignorance, and how much yet they want. 2. The suddenness of the light which they have received so transporteth them, that they think it to be greater in them than it is. 3. They have stronger passions in them than the aged; and those puff them up, as if they signified answerable judgment. 4. They have weaker degrees yet of humility, self-denial, and all grace, than riper Christians have. 5. They have had less time to learn the great things which should balance them. 6. They want that experience which fully convinceth riper Christians of the error of self-exalting, so that none are so apt to rage and be confident as the ignorant and injudicious. 7. And they are themselves as children carried away easily by the applause and flatteries of such as are like them, and cry them up for their injudicious fervour.

7. Moreover, he must have a good report of them which are without; lest he fall into reproach, and the snare of the devil.

7. 16. And he must be one that hath by his parts and conversation got some esteem, even among unbelievers, or at least, is not by the common sort of them made odious or contemptible by any infamy, just or unjust, lest Satan get by his former scandals, or ill name, to make the Christian religion odious, and turn his infamy into a snare to keep men in unbelief.

Note, 1. If all these sixteen things be needful to a bishop, and must be required in one that is offered to the ministry, is he a true bishop or pastor that hath scarce two of all these qualifications? Yea, that hath almost all the contraries? That such are pastors, *de facto*, claiming honour and obedience, is easily proved: what God accounteth them I leave to him: and how the people should esteem them, Cyprian tells us in his epistle against Martial and Basilides.

2. What a bishop then was must be understood by those that would know their divine obligation to obey such: of which see before, 1 Thes. v. 12, 13. The ministerial work was, 1. Indefinite; by itinerants, or unfixed men, viz. 1. To convert those without, and gather churches, and settle pastors over them. 2. And to go and send to them after for their confirmation. These in scripture are called apostles and evangelists, and their helpers, but not bishops. II. But the settled churches had settled pastors (with deacons) these are called bishops and elders. These churches were so many neighbour Christians as could know and converse with one another, and were associated for personal communion, in holy doctrine, worship, and conversation, as distinct from distant communion by mere concord in the species of these, or by delegates: though they did not always meet all in one place; so that the bishops or elders had opportunity to know them personally, teach and oversee them ordinarily: which they did without force, upon none but consenting volunteers. This episcopacy we are for, and not against the pre-eminence of some one, as a senior and guide to the rest of the elders in a church that hath many: nor yet against the foresaid general ministers or evangelists inspection and care of many churches of such consenters. But if one such general pastor will put down all the bishops of single churches, and have none over many hundred parishes but himself alone, who cannot possibly do the hundredth part of the true episcopal work, and will do some of the rest by curates that are no bishops, and by laymen, his episcopacy is not to be justified. Much less when the clergy or people choose them not, nor consent to them, but are governed by them forcibly, and as constrained Dissenters.

8. Likewise must the deacons be grave, not double-tongued, not given to much wine, not greedy of filthy lucre. 9. Holding the mystery of the faith in a pure conscience.

8, 9. The deacons also must be well-qualified persons; grave and pious; not double tongued, to say and unsay, as interest leadeth them; not addicted to much wine or strong drink; not greedy of filthy gain, as lovers of money used to be: and they must be sound believers and of an upright life.

Note, 1. That here are but two sorts of fixed church officers noted by Paul, bishops and deacons. 2. As every church had its own bishop (one or more), so had they their own deacons. For, as Dr. Hammond noteth, [the deacons were every where constituted to attend the bishop.] But antiquity never knew what a deacon of a diocese of many churches (or hundreds of churches) was, till archdeacons were first new-made. Therefore, as no man was a deacon of more than one single church, so no man was a bishop of more (distinct from archbishops), as the said doctor *de facto* maintaineth, in scripture times.

10. And let these also first be proved: then let them use the office of a deacon, being found blameless.

10. And even deacons must not be made, till they are tried and proved fit, and found blameless.

11. Even so must their wives be grave, not slanderers, sober, faithful in all things.

11. So also must the women (or wives) be grave, &c.

Note, 1. It is uncertain whether by [women] here be meant the deacons' wives, or the deaconesses that then were appointed to some care of women, which men were less fit for. 2. The qualifications imply, that women are most in danger of the contrary sins, that is, of unstayed levity, forwardness to backbite and speak evil falsely, as accusers of those that distaste them, not sober and careful of their business, not trusty in all things.

12. Let the deacons be the husbands of one wife, ruling their children and their own houses well.

12. The deacons must not be such as have more wives than one, or that have injuriously put away one and married another: the good government of their own children, and houses also, must shew that they are fit to serve in the church.

13. For they that have used the office of a deacon well, purchase to themselves a good degree, and great

boldness in the faith *which is* in Jesus Christ.

13. For though the deacons be as servants to the pastors, they that have used that office well, are in a degree above the vulgar, and have matter of confident boldness and freedom in the management and defence of the affairs of Christianity.

14. These things write I unto thee, hoping to come unto thee shortly: 15. But if I tarry long, that thou mayest know how thou oughtest to behave thyself in the house of God, which is the church of the living God, the pillar and ground of the truth.

14, 15. I hope to come to thee shortly: but lest I should be delayed, I write these things to thee, that thou mayest know how thou oughtest to converse in the house of God (which is the church of the living God) as (in it) a pillar and firm buttress (or basis) of the truth.

Note, Though it be true, that the truth of God is most safely preserved in his church, yet I (with Gataker) marvel that so many apply these words to the church, which are spoken of Timothy. That it is he that is called here [a pillar and buttress of the truth] seemeth to me evident: 1. In that in the allegory it is not like that Paul would in the very next words call the church a pillar and buttress in the house, when he calleth it [the house itself.] He plainly differenceth [a part] from [the whole.] The church is the whole, a pillar is a part. 2. It is the very sum of Paul's exhortation to Timothy, that according to his office he should be [a pillar and buttress of truth in the church.] 3. The preposition [in the house] agreeth to him, and the word [pillar, &c. which is in the house.] 4. It should rather be translated [a pillar, &c.] than [the pillar] which it is most likely would have been put in, had it been the church's peculiar privilege that had been meant. 5. The apostle useth the same word of James, Cephas, and John, Gal. ii 9. And the very same phrase as here, is used Rev. iii. 12. He that overcometh, I will make him a pillar in the temple of God. But the church is never called [a pillar that is in the church.] 6. As to them that feign it would be false construction, because the words in the original are in the nominative case, this hath no pretence from the text: so that I doubt not but the plain sense is as it is paraphrased; and all the fabric is built on a mere mistake, which the Papists raise upon this text: though, were it otherwise, it would not serve their turn.

16. And without controversy, great is the mystery of godliness: God was manifest in the flesh, justified in the Spirit, seen of angels, preached unto the Gentiles, believed on in the world, received up into glory.

16. And confessedly the mystery of godliness,

which requireth such great abilities in thee, as to make thee a pillar and buttress of it in the church is exceeding great and high. 1. God himself appeared to man in the flesh of our Redeemer, to manifest his love, and will for our salvation. 2. The Spirit was Christ's witness, which by its inimitable holy impressions, miracles, his resurrection, and communication to his followers, did justify Christ to be truly what he did profess to be, and sealed his doctrine to the world. 3. Angels beheld, proclaimed, and obeyed him. 4. The wall of separation being broken down, he was preached by his commissioned apostles to the Gentile world. 5. The world, that knew him not, or despised him, is by a few poor unlearned men brought to believe in him, and submit to him as Lord and Saviour. Philosophy submitteth, and wit is silenced, and policy and power stoop to him in part, and more will do. 6. He was taken up into heaven in glory, angels attending him, his apostles looking on. Those six articles are that great mystery which requireth the ablest preacher, and the soundest faith: and he that firmly believeth these, doth see into a more excellent mystery than philosophy, and will be a stable pillar in the church.

CHAP. IV.

NOW the Spirit speaketh expressly, that in the latter times some shall depart from the faith, giving heed to seducing spirits, and doctrines of devils;

1. The spirit of prophecy plainly foretelleth us, that in the latter times some who professed themselves Christians, shall depart from either the whole, or some essential parts of the Christian faith, turning apostates, or heretics; and this by giving heed to false revelations of seducing spirits (in themselves or others, and to doctrines of devils.)

Note, Whether it mean effectively doctrines taught by devils, or (as Mr. Mead largely maintaineth) objectively, doctrines concerning demons, or the nature, order, and minds of the spirits, like the Valentinians, Aiones, &c. I leave to the judgment of others.

2. Speaking lies in hypocrisy, having their conscience seared with a hot iron;

2. Covering their lies or false doctrine by hypocritical pretences of piety, or divine revelation, or some great excellency; having consciences seared and branded as the perfidious use to be, by their flagitious lives.

3. Forbidding to marry, *and commanding* to abstain from meats, which God hath created to be received with thanksgiving of them which believe and know the truth.

3. Note, I think it far more probable, that Paul here speaketh of those heretics which made up a

religion of Judaism and Pythagorean fancies, who taught, that marriage was of the devil, to propagate sinful miserable men; and that flesh was not to be eaten, especially the unclean beasts; than of those erroneous Christians, who only forbid marriage to the clergy, and flesh on certain days of abstinence, or that affect the total avoiding of marriage, and eating flesh, as a state of special strictness, not required of most: for Paul seemeth plainly to speak of a doctrine taught to all; and he describeth Christian knowledge herein to be, that God hath made such meat in kind to be received with thanksgiving; and not that all men, or any at all times, must use such meats.

4. For every creature of God is good, and nothing to be refused, if it be received with thanksgiving: 5. For it is sanctified by the word of God, and prayer.

4, 5. For all that God hath made for food is good and clean, and not to be received as in kind unlawful, if it be received lawfully, as from God's gift, to fit us for his service; for to such as do thus, it is more than lawful, even a sanctified means to fit them to serve God, God's word allowing and giving it them, and prayer craving his blessing to that end.

6. If thou put the brethren in remembrance of these things, thou shalt be a good minister of Jesus Christ, nourished up in the words of faith, and of good doctrine, whereunto thou hast attained.

6. These things thou must suggest to the brethren as their teacher, that thou mayest approve thyself a good minister of Christ, bred up in sound faith and doctrine, &c.

7. But refuse profane and old wives' fables, and exercise thyself *rather* unto godliness.

7. But as for the Jewish and heretical fancies of abstinence from marriage and meats, and the idle reasons from tradition, or Pythagorean dotage, which they give for them, avoid them; and let it be thy business to preach, promote, and practise plain doctrine and duties of godliness; and guide the flock therein.

8. For bodily exercise profiteth little: but godliness is profitable unto all things, having the promise of the life that now is, and of that which is to come.

8. For no corporal austerities or exercises in religion must be overvalued: the best of them are of small profit, in comparison of that godliness, which consisteth in spiritual exercises (of faith, hope, love, and their expressions:) but this true spiritual stubstantial godliness is profitable to all that we can justly desire, having from God the promise of all the good of this life which is meet for us, and we meet for it; and of that which is to come, after this life is ended.

9. This *is* a faithful saying, and worthy of all acceptation. 10. For therefore we both labour, and suffer reproach, because we trust in the living God, who is the Saviour of all men, specially of those that believe.

9, 10. And what I say of the promise to godliness for this life and that to come, is a truth most sure, and of greatest moment, and worthy of our greatest acceptation. For it is on the belief of this, that we labour, strive, and suffer, trusting on the goodness and promises of God, who is life, and the Lord of life, and as their Saviour giveth the mercies of this life, and that to come, as men are fitted for each, to all men; all good being from him to all the world: but eternal good being by his promise secured to all true believers, (which others reject when it is offered them, for temporal good.)

11, 12. These things command and teach. Let no man despise thy youth, but be thou an example of the believers, in word, in conversation, in charity, in spirit, in faith, in purity.

11, 12. These things teach commandingly, so necessary, with authority, and so behave thyself, that thy youth expose thee not to contempt. Be thou an example, in whom all the believers may see how they should live, in thy speech, and thy conversation, in love and spirituality, in sound faith, and spotless purity.

13. Till I come, give attendance to reading, to exhortation, to doctrine.

13. Till I come, be diligent in reading the scripture, (privately for thyself, and publicly to expound it to the church) to apply it by exhortation, and sound doctrine.

14. Neglect not the gift that is in thee, which was given thee by prophecy, with the laying on of the hands of the presbytery.

14. Neglect not diligently to use and improve those eminent gifts which were given thee, even with prophecy of thee, as one that would be faithful, by the laying on of the hands of the presbytery, or elders of the church, when thou wast called and ordained to the ministry. (For neglect quencheth the Spirit.)

15. Meditate upon these things, give thyself wholly to them; that thy profiting may appear to all.

15. Note, That even those that are extraordinarily inspired and qualified, must study hard, and

wholly give themselves to that, and all their ministerial work, if they would appear good proficients; therefore those that have no such inspiration, have need of hard study. And they that wholly addict themselves to the ministry, have no leisure for magistracy or worldly avocations: nor can do that for many hundred churches, which required the whole of a Timothy for one.

16. Take heed unto thyself, and unto thy doctrine: continue in them: for in doing this, thou shalt both save thyself and them that hear thee.

16. In sum, Take greatest heed. First, that thy own soul and life be sound, and holy, undefiled; and next, that thy doctrine be so, and thou diligently labour in it: continue in this two-fold care and diligence, and thou shalt secure thy own salvation, and in all likelihood thy hearers; for God will not deny his blessing to such labours.

CHAP. V.

REBUKE not an elder, but entreat him as a father, and the younger men as brethren; 2. The elder women as mothers, the younger as sisters, with all purity.

1, 2. When elders (in age or office) transgress, use not magisterial roughness of reproof, but humble exhortation, as to fathers: and speak to the younger with love and gentleness, as to brethren: and speak to the elder women, as mothers, with due respect; and to the younger, as sisters, carefully shunning all that savoureth of immodesty or unchastity in thought, or speech, or looks, or behaviour.

3, 4. Honour widows that are widows indeed. But if any widow have children or nephews, let them learn first to shew piety at home, and to requite their parents; for that is good and acceptable before God.

3, 4. Let those that are widows indeed, at once, deprived of husbands and maintenance, being aged and unable to work, be maintained by the church with due respect. But if any of them have children and nephews that can maintain them: let these their offspring be taught piety and gratitude for all their parents' care of them; oblige them to maintain their widows, and not to cast them on the church, and that this is a duty that God requireth of them, and will accept.

Note, That it is doubted, whether these widows were deaconesses, or merely kept for poverty. I think that it was the custom of the ancient churches to maintain all that are poor and aged, and unable to get their own livings, but not to maintain them in idleness, but to appoint them to employ much of their time, in visiting the sick

2,

and poor women, and counselling the younger sort, and giving notice of their wants and cases to the elders; so that the same women were also as deaconesses, though some that were wiser and fitter than the rest might be more specially thus employed.

5. Now she that is a widow indeed, and desolate, trusteth in God, and continueth in supplications and prayers night and day.

5. By a widow indeed, I mean one that is desolate, having neither maintenance, nor ability to get it, nor kindred to relieve her, but liveth by faith and trust in God, who as she is to live upon the church, so she is bound to serve the church, by constant prayers both alone and with these women whom she visiteth and instructeth.

6. But she that liveth in pleasure is dead while she liveth.

6. But she that liveth delicately, and sportingly, and wantonly, with gaudy ornaments, is a living carcase.

7. And these things give in charge, that they may be blameless.

7. Acquaint them with these canons, that the church and they may be kept from misdoing.

8. But if any provide not for his own, and specially those of his own house, he hath denied the faith, and is worse than an infidel.

8. But if any of the church that is able, maintain not his own near kindred, especially those that have right to be kept in his own family, (as parents have) he liveth so contrary to the Christian faith, that he forfeits the reputation of true Christians, and doth that which the infidels themselves will condemn, and in that is worse than they.

9. Let not a widow be taken into the number under threescore years old, having been the wife of one man.

9. Because such widows, 1. Must be maintained as those that cannot labour. 2. And do resolve against marrying again, being past the need of it. 3. And must be staid monitors to the younger women, therefore take in none into the church's charge, that is under threescore years old, and none that hath separated from her husband, and married another.

10. Well reported of for good works; if she have brought up children, if she have lodged strangers, if she have washed the saints' feet, if she have relieved the afflicted, if she have diligently followed every good work.

10. It is her Christian behaviour before her pa-

K k

verty, that must be rewarded with the church's maintenance. Therefore she must be one, 1. That is known to have done good to others while she was able. 2. Who hath piously educated her own children. 3. Lodged strangers, &c.

Note, That in that hot and poor country, those here called saints usually travelled on foot, and were bare-legged, wearing only sandals, or shoes, and had not inns for entertainment, with that convenience as we have here, nor money for such charges; therefore it was one of the great works of godly charity, for Christians to take travellers and strangers into their houses, and wash their feet from the dust contracted daily in their travel: and to relieve all in want and affliction according to their power.

11. But the younger widows refuse: for when they have begun to wax wanton against Christ, they will marry; 12. Having damnation, because they have cast off their first faith.

11, 12. But receive not a young widow into the number of those that serve the church, and are maintained by it: for as they are not by age past labouring for themselves, or fit to resolve on a single life for the church's service, so when they grow lustful and wanton, and weary of the yoke of chastity and church-service, they will marry; and so prove criminal sinners against Christ, by violating that sort of devotedness to his service.

13. And withal they learn to be idle, wandering about from house to house; and not only idle, but tatlers also, and busy-bodies, speaking things which they ought not.

13. And being idle, they learn to go about to houses, and there not only idly pass their time, but spend it in tattling, or in idle and unfit chat, and busying themselves with other men's matters, and talking of that which they ought not to talk of.

Note, Qu. But are not women prone to this, though they be not devoted to chastity and church service? Ans. Yes, 1. And therefore Paul speaketh this as the vice that most women are strongly by nature addicted to: and that all may see the danger of it, and fear it. And indeed, how rare are those women, even that profess to be most religious, that use not to venture on this chat, and backbiting, and busily judging those that are absent, and meddling with things which they should not meddle with. 2. But yet those that are taken up with family business of their own, are not so vacant and liable to these crimes, as the idle are. And therefore what Paul saith of these young church widows, all rich women should read with application: for riches tempt them to be idle; and idleness tempts them to the same sins, to spend their time in going from house to house, on pretence of civil visits, and there to talk venturously without a call, of all things and persons that come into their minds.

14. I will therefore that the younger women marry, bear children, guide the house, give none occasion to the adversary to speak reproachfully. 15. For some are already turned aside after Satan.

14, 15. My advice therefore is, That young women marry (that have not some special reason against it); and by bearing children, and educating them religiously, and guiding their houses piously and diligently, they may so do the church the greatest service, and give no occasion to malicious adversaries to speak evil of the church, as if it were a society of idle twatlers, and lustful wantons. For some have already forsaken Christianity, tempted partly by some such scandals; or at least are ready to believe and report them.

16. If any man or woman that believeth, have widows, let them relieve them, and let not the church be charged; that it may relieve them that are widows indeed.

16. Let all Christians keep the widows that nature bindeth them to keep, if able, and not cast them on the church, and rob widows indeed, by disabling the church to maintain them.

17. Let the elders that rule well, be counted worthy of double honour, especially they who labour in word and doctrine.

17. It being the office of church-elders to be the church's guides or rulers, by the canon of God's laws; let those that do this well, be counted worthy of double honour, above the common rank of the faithful, and to be accordingly maintained and obeyed; but especially those of them who are laborious preachers, expounding and applying the word and doctrine of Christ.

Note, That elders or bishops were the fixed guides of single churches, (no bigger than our parishes for number of souls.) 2. That they had very much work to do besides public preaching: as to judge who was to be taken in by baptism, or to be openly rebuked, or cast out, or reconciled; to teach from house to house on just occasion, to visit the sick, take care of the poor, resolve doubts, oversee manners, &c. 3. That usually one church had many of these, and all found work enough; some maintained themselves, and some the church-offerings maintained. 4. As all these could not publicly preach at once, so all were not fitted for it by skill and free utterance: but some one or few that were most able for it were the ordinary preachers: and these being the ablest, and of most reputation, were quickly made and called the bishops, being such presidents and guides to the rest, as the presidents of colleges of men in the same office, (physicians, philosophers, &c.) are, or as the chief justice among the judges. 5. Yet all the rest were of the same office, essentiated by church guidance in the word, worship, sacraments, and discipline; and were not mere lay-men, but were ordained and separated to the sacred ministry, and wanted not authority to preach and to minister sacraments, and did these on just occasions, though the ablest did it most usually. 6.

18. For the scripture saith, Thou shalt not muzzle the ox that treadeth out the corn: and, The labourer *is* worthy of his reward.

18. Note, 1. That honour here includeth maintenance. 2. That it is the labour of church guides which giveth them right to honour and maintenance. 3. That the greatest honour and maintenance is due to them that are laborious preachers and instructers of the flock, and not to them that seldom so labour: much less to them that unjustly silence such.

19. Against an elder receive not an accusation, but before two or three witnesses.

19. Seeing no private man should believe an accusation against a grave ancient person, much less against a person of the church, without sufficient proof; much less must thou that art president in the presbytery admit any publicly to defame an elder in office by entering his accusation against him without two or three witnesses; and much less mayest thou believe such an accusation. Note, For, 1. It is to be supposed that such are more unlikely to be guilty than other men. 2. And that for their works sake, the wicked or reproved sort will be more malicious and forward to accuse such; and they shall never want false accusers, if such can but find judges that are willing to believe them. 3. And their defamation is most injurious to religion, and to the church.

20. Them that sin, rebuke before all, that others also may fear.

20. Those that sin scandalously, either openly, or after reproof for private sin, before two or three, and repent not, rebuke before the church (or community of the people, saith Dr. Hammond), that others may be warned to avoid such sins and such impenitence.

21. I charge *thee* before God and the Lord Jesus Christ, and the elect angels, that thou observe these things without preferring one before another, doing nothing by partiality.

21. So heinous is the sin of unjust judging in a guide of the church, and so great a mischief to the church, that I do hereby most solemnly charge thee before God, and the Lord Jesus Christ, and the elect angels, that thou observe these rules of justice, without a hasty or forestalled judgment or prejudice, and that thou do nothing according to a partial inclination to one party.

Note, 1. There are elect angels, both as respecting reprobate devils, and as chosen to the service of distinct churches. 2. Though we know not just how far, and when angels are present, we may so far presume of their notice of church affairs, and their regard thereof, as to adjure even the pastors of the church to avoid sin, as before the elect angels. 3. O how heinous then is the sin of those who under the name of bishops cast out and silence Christ's faithful ministers, and are prejudiced and partial against the most godly Christians, who dare not obey all their questionable canons? The honour of bishops being due to them for their work, it is Satan's design to bring them into dishonour by engaging them in contrary odious work.

22. Lay hands suddenly on no man, neither be partaker of other mens' sins: keep thyself pure.

22. Lay not hands in ordination rashly on any unworthy candidate; nor for absolution too hastily on those that profess not repentance credibly: lest thou make thyself partaker of the guilt of the sins of unworthy ministers, and unsound penitents. Keep thyself pure from the sins which thou must reprove in others.

23. Drink no longer water, but use a little wine for thy stomachs' sake, and thine often infirmities.

23. Note, 1. That diet must be fitted to health; and men should know what is fittest for it. To use wine, yea, much wine or strong drink for mere appetite, instead of a little for health, is sinful sensuality. 2. Even then the apostles that had the gift of healing could not use it commonly, but must help infirmities by ordinary means.

24. Some mens' sins are open before-hand, going before to judgment; and some men they follow after. 25. Likewise also the good works *of some* are manifest beforehand; and they that are otherwise cannot be hid.

24, 25. I know that when the best is done, church discipline will not cleanse out all sin. It dealeth not with secret, but with open sins: some men's sins are open and proveable, of which God will have the church judge them before his final judgment: and some men's are unknown, and those not we, but God must judge. And so men's good works and sincerity of repentance and obedience are manifested to the church to judge of; and hypocrites that counterfeit such, God will open in his time.

CHAP. VI.

LET as many servants as are under the yoke, count their own masters worthy of all honour; that the name of God, and *his* doctrine, be not blasphemed.

1. Let all that are servants under that yoke whether their masters be Christians or heathens account it their duty to give them all the honour and obedience which is due in that relation, and

not think that Christianity giveth them liberty to disobey them, nor despise them, because of their defect of religion: else heathens will reproach religion and Christ, and say, that we teach men to be unfaithful, disobedient, and proud.

2. And they that have believing masters, let them not despise *them*, because they are brethren, but rather do *them* service, because they are faithful and beloved, partakers of the benefit. These things teach and exhort.

2. And let none despise their masters, because they are both believers, and so brethren in Christ, for Christian brotherhood consisteth with inequality of place and relation, and with subjection, and doth not level men in other things, nor encourage pride or disobedience: but such must the more willingly do service to their Christian masters, because they are faithful, and partakers of all the same blessings of Christianity with themselves, and so more amiable, and therefore should be served out of special love, and not only for fear, or wages. These duties are of great moment; therefore teach and press them earnestly.

3. If any man teach otherwise, and consent not to wholesome words, *even* the words of our Lord Jesus Christ, and to the doctrine which is according to godliness: 4. He is proud, knowing nothing, but doting about questions and strifes of words, whereof cometh envy, strife, railings, evil surmisings, 5. Perverse disputings of men of corrupt minds, and destitute of the truth, supposing that gain is godliness.

3, 4, 5. There be some risen up that teach otherwise, on pretence of Christian liberty, and excellency above heathens: but they go contrary to the words of Christ our Lord, which are the words of truth and life, and to the doctrine which is formed to true godliness; and they are a sort of proud, self-conceited men, puffed up with a false opinion that they know more than others, and are but brain sick, doting about unprofitable questions, and striving about words; and instead of edifying men to salvation, the fruit of all their proud contention is but the increase of envy and strifes, and railings at one another, and evil surmisings, and ill thoughts of one another, (or ill opinions) paltry and frivolous disputings against each other, coming from minds corrupted by pride and error, that are void of true knowledge, and fly further from the truth, striving for victory, and for their own conceits; taking the side that is most for their worldly and fleshly advantage, preferring gain before true godliness, and fitting their cloak of pretended godliness and wisdom to their worldly gain.

5, 6. From such withdraw thyself. But godliness with contentment is great gain.

5, 6. Such men as these, being not only heretics, but also proud defenders of their heresy, are neither fit for thy communion, nor to be disputed with, but to be avoided, if they repent not. But resolve thou to adhere to sincere godliness, which, with contentedness with God's allowance of daily bread, is the true and great gain, and better than the wealth of the world, which those hypocrites prefer.

7. For we brought nothing into *this* world, *and it is* certain we can carry nothing out.

7. As for bodily provision and wealth, as we brought none of it with us into the world, so it is certain that we can take none of it away with us; and therefore truly have no more than we profitably and well use while we are alive.

8. And having food and raiment, let us be therewith content.

8. If we have food and raiment, and what is needful to the well-doing of our work, we have enough, and must be contented with it; for, desire of more, except to do good with it to others, is but the sinful disease of the mind.

9. But they that will be rich, fall into temptation, and a snare, and *into* many foolish and hurtful lusts, which drown men in destruction and perdition.

9. But they that love and set their hearts on riches, and seek after them, do thereby cast themselves into dangerous temptations and snares, and kindle and pursue such desires as shew their gross folly, and instead of gain, do but hurt themselves, and cast themselves into the gulf of destruction and damnation.

Note, 1. Oh how little then do the most of the world, that study and scramble for riches, think what they are doing all their lives, against themselves! 2. And is it not doleful blindness in those Roman prelates, that for wealth and worldly greatness have corrupted Christian doctrine, worship, discipline, and conversation, and overthrown the church's peace, that yet they can say, That Paul here condemneth the Gnostics and heretics, for that in which they incomparably exceed them.

10. For the love of money is the root of all evil: which while some coveted after, they have erred from the faith and pierced themselves through with many sorrows.

10. For very much evil springeth from the love of money: (from hence is sinful care, and desire, and grief, and anger, and malice, and envy, and oppression, and deceit, and lying, and theft, and murders, and wars, and persecutions, and church-corruptions, and divisions, needless law-suits, bribery, false witness, perjury, slander, railings, and much more such.) And by coveting money,

many have been their own tormentors, piercing themselves through in body and mind with many sorrows, (vexatious labours, cares, fears, trouble for disappointments, and torment of conscience for their guilt, and oft come to an untimely death.) Yes, it hath drawn them to forsake or corrupt the faith, for worldly ends.

11. But thou, O man of God, flee these things: and follow after righteousness, godliness, faith, love, patience, meekness.

11. But thou, that art devoted to God, and his special service, abhor and avoid this love of money, and all these its odious fruits; and follow after the spiritual riches, righteousness, godliness, &c.

Note, That is best which is most divine, likest to God, and most pleasing to God, and which is the welfare of our best part, the soul, which will never die and fail us, as worldly riches will.

12. Fight the good fight of faith lay hold on eternal life, whereunto thou art also called, and hast professed a good profession before many witnesses.

12. Go on by faith to overcome all temptations, difficulties, sins, and adversaries, and to propagate and defend the faith: press towards the mark, till thou lay hold on eternal life, which is the prize. This is the life that thou art called out to hope for, to seek, and to obtain, and the work thou art to do, and hast well begun, and before many witnesses openly and manfully stood to the truth.

13. I give thee charge in the sight of God, who quickeneth all things, and *before* Christ Jesus, who before Pontius Pilate witnessed a good confession; 14. That thou keep *this* commandment without spot, unrebukable, until the appearing of our Lord Jesus Christ.

13, 14. I must urgently charge thee, before God, in whose power are all our lives; and before Christ, who went before us by the example of a good confession, not denying the truth to save his life, that thou keep this necessary law of thy ministry, as spotless and unrebukable, that thou mayest be found such at the coming of Jesus Christ.

15. Which in his times he shall shew, *who is* the blessed and only potentate, the king of kings, and Lord of Lords; 16. Who only hath immortality, dwelling in the light which no man can approach unto, whom no man hath seen, nor can see: to whom *be* honour and power everlasting. Amen.

15, 16. Which in his due appointed season God will shew, who is the blessed and only potentate, &c. who only is essentially and necessarily of himself immortal, whose glorious abode is in the light inaccessible to us men, and who is to us invisible: to him be honour and power for ever. Amen.

17. Charge them that are rich in this world, that they be not highminded, nor trust in uncertain riches, but in the living God, who giveth us richly all things to enjoy:

17. And knowing to what sins riches most tempt men, charge the rich that they be not highminded, nor think highly of themselves for their wealth, nor look to this for their safety and chief comfort, as if it were their best: but that they take God for their portion and security, and wholly trust him for soul and body, who will give us enough for our comfort and content.

18. That they do good, that they be rich in good works, ready to distribute, willing to communicate; 19. Laying up in store for themselves a good foundation against the time to come, that they may lay hold on eternal life.

18, 19. That they use their riches to do all the good that they can in the world, that so they may be rich in good works, which are a far more excellent sort of riches than bare money; that they distribute to others necessity with readiness, and communicate with a willing, forward mind, and not with grudging or backwardness, as against their wills; that so they may not lose their riches, but as they love themselves, will lay up by them a treasure for themselves, even a good fund and security by coming under God's faithful promise, for the time to come, that so as good runners lay hold on the prize, they may lay hold on eternal life.

20. O Timothy, keep that which is committed to thy trust, avoiding profane *and* vain babblings, and oppositions of science, falsely so called: 21. Which some professing, have erred concerning the faith. Grace *be* with thee. Amen.

20, 21. O Timothy, be sure to hold fast and keep safe these necessary precepts which I have given thee, as from God by his Spirit, containing the true wisdom, tending to salvation, in trust that thou teach them others: but avoid those frivolous tricks, and wordy arts, and disputing strife about their falsely named science, even the logical and philosophical triflings of Stoics, Peripatetics, and all the sects of heathen philosophers, in which they think the excellency of learning consisteth, (despising the simplicity of Christianity as ignorance). Some Christians being taken with this sort of learning, have been tempted to corrupt religion by it, and to turn such heretics as are but mongrel Christians, and not sound and truly such. The grace of God preserve, sanctify, and save thee. Amen.

Note, I have before shewed, that it was philosophers, who by their pretence of greater learning were then the despisers, and most powerful adversaries of Christianity: and the generality of them were taken up with mere useless quibbling and trifling, and striving about words, and barren notions, instead of needful, useful knowledge; so that their famed sciences were but like dreams and childish babbling: so that it was the honour of Socrates to call them off to the study of virtues and things of use, whom Plato followed with a mixture of vanity: and a smattering of these sciences bewitched the heretics in that age. But Paul doth not hereby condemn the true philosophical knowledge of God in his works, nor a carefulness of exact speaking, as to words and method, or the accurate fitting of words to things, and using art in due measure, and in subservience to great and saving truth. But further than it thus subserveth to the saving truth of God in Christ, and our duty and hopes of life eternal, all that is called learning and wit, is but folly.

ANNOTATIONS.

Paul's epistles to Timothy and Titus are the church-canons, which the Holy Ghost indited, and sufficient to their proper use and end, though still there will be use for pastoral determination of such circumstances, as must be varied according to variety of persons, occasions, times, and places. And no canons of men that are contrary to any of these divine rules, (I mean such of them as are of universal, fixed obligation) are obligations to the faithful. O how happy had the churches been if these had been better observed, and the churches not corrupted or torn, by such as by men are destructively or needlessly added, by badness, doubtfulness, or numbers answering or overwhelming the consciences of those that are most obedient to God.

THE
SECOND EPISTLE OF PAUL THE APOSTLE,
TO
TIMOTHY.

CHAP. I.

PAUL an apostle of Jesus Christ by the will of God, according to the promise of life, which is in Christ Jesus: 2. To Timothy *my* dearly beloved son: Grace, mercy, *and* peace from God the Father, and Christ Jesus our Lord.

1. Note, 1. It is God's calling will, and not only his permitting will, which must warrant any to assume the sacred ministry, and prove him a true minister of Christ.

2. The promise of life in Christ must have ministers to proclaim it, and to preach this is their work.

3. I thank God, whom I serve from *my* forefathers with pure conscience, that without ceasing I have remembrance of thee in my prayers night and day:

3. Note, It seemeth strange, that a persecutor, and the chief of sinners, should say, That from his forefathers he served God with pure conscience; and to the high priest, That he had lived in all good conscience to that day. Answ. 1. Some think he meaneth, [Since I was a Christian, I have served God sincerely, as Abraham, Isaac, and Jacob did.] Others think he meaneth, [Not only since my conversion, but before, I designed only to serve God;] and though through ignorance I mistook the matter, I did it in zeal to please God, and faithfully obeyed my conscience. Whichever be the sense, there is no doctrinal difference dependeth on the controversy.

4. Greatly desiring to see thee,

being minded of thy tears, that I may be filled with joy: 5. When I call to remembrance the unfeigned faith that is in thee, which dwelt first in thy grandmother Lois, and thy mother Eunice; and I am persuaded that is thee also.

4, 5. Note.1.Though we must love all Christians with a special love, yet with great difference, as they differ. Choice Christians, and very loving friends, must be loved above the rest.

2. The more unfeigned and free from hypocrisy in faith and godliness, he appears to be, the more amiable is that Christian.

3. God often blesseth the labours and examples of godly women, to raise up excellent instruments in his church.

4. It rendereth a good Christian more amiable and honourable, to be the offspring of godly parents.

6. Wherefore I put thee in remembrance, that thou stir up the gift of God, which is in thee by the putting on of my hands.

6. Note, 1. God's spiritual gifts must be used by our own stirring them up.

2. It is here controverted, 1. Whether it be the gift of the ministry, and its proper necessaries, that is here meant, or the foregoing gift of the Holy Ghost? 2. Whether it be meant of Paul's laying on his hands for the former, or the latter?

To these, it may suffice us to know, 1. That Timothy was converted by Paul; and then it was usual for converts to receive the Holy Ghost for some wonderful gifts, by the laying on of the apostles' hands: And it is not to be doubted, but so did Timothy, long before his ordination to the ministry. And who was so likely to do this as Paul? 2. It is not to be doubted, but Timothy, after this, had imposition of hands at his ordination. 3. It is certain,that it was then by the hands of the presbytery. 4. It is probable, that Paul was one of them, and the chief: 5. Therefore, as the next verse sheweth, that he speaketh of the spirit or gift of sanctification, not proper to ministers; so it is certain, that Paul meant this, but not improbable that he meant the other also, but comprehendeth both.

7. For God hath not given us the spirit of fear; but of power, and of love, and of a sound mind.

7. For though Jews are under the spirit of legal fear and bondage, and unbelievers have a cowardly fear of men, this is not the spirit given us by the gospel, but it is the sanctifying of the three great faculties of the soul, the executive faculty by holy power, the will, by holy love, and the intellectual by sound and sober judgment: This is the Spirit of Christ.

8. Be not thou therefore ashamed of the testimony of our Lord, nor of me his prisoner: but be thou partaker of the afflictions of the gospel, according to the power of God;

8. Be not therefore ashamed of preaching and owning the gospel, or of any suffering that this will bring, nor of me, who am Christ's prisoner, as suffering for his work: but whatever hard usage men exercise against the gospel, and the preachers of it, be content to bear thy part with others as strengthened by the power of God.

9. Who hath saved us, and called us with an holy calling, not according to our works, but according to his own purpose and grace which was given us in Christ Jesus, before the world began.

9. Who hath saved us from our servitude to sin and Satan, and called us out of the world to be a holy people, separated to himself; not because by our works we were a more deserving people before than others, but according to his own purpose and gracious decree of saving us by Christ, which he had for us before the world or ages began.

10. But is now made manifest by the appearing of our Saviour Jesus Christ, who hath abolished death, and hath brought life and immortality to light, through the gospel:

10. But now this purpose is opened by Christ's appearing in flesh, who hath now delivered us from the power of that death which was the wages of sin, assuring us of a resurrection, and hath brought future life and immortality to our more full assured notice by his gospel.

Note, That though the soul's immortality, and a life of retribution, be knowable by the light of nature, yet, 1. It is with far less certainty than the gospel giveth us. 2. And nature tells us not with any clearness of a resurrection of the body. 3. Nor doth it give men clear notice of the conditions of our attaining that felicity. But Christ by the gospel hath given us assured notice of all this. And this is the chief thing in which Christ's plain teaching excelleth all the subtleties of the trifling, heathen philosophers.

11. Whereunto I am appointed a preacher, and an apostle, and a teacher of the Gentiles.

11. To preach this, and teach the Gentiles, I am a commissioned apostle, and for this I suffer.

12. For the which cause I also suffer these things; nevertheless I am not ashamed; for I know whom I have believed, and I am persuaded that he is able to keep that which I have commi ted unto him against that day.

12. But I am not ashamed of my preaching or suffering; for I know whom I have trusted, and am persuaded that he can and will keep me in safety, who have committed myself wholly to him, even to the great day (in which all his promises shall be performed.)

13. Hold fast the form of sound words, which thou hast heard of me, in faith and love which is in Christ Jesus.

13. Keep before thee the form or summary of sound doctrine which thou heardest of me, which consisteth in the articles of faith, and the precepts of love, of both which Christ is the object and sum, (or which form of sound doctrine thou must hold fast by a firm belief, and practical love of Christ and his cause.)

14. That good thing which was committed unto thee, keep by the Holy Ghost which dwelleth in us.

14. That good and sure summary of sound doctrine which I committed to thy keeping, hold close to, by the Spirit of God who dwelleth in us, to help our memory, love, and practice.
Note, Though it be not certain that Paul meaneth our creed in the very words as now we have them, it is more than probable that he meaneth the same articles in sense, which he reciteth, 1 Cor. xv. 3, 4, 5. and elsewhere.

15. This thou knowest, that all they which are in Asia be turned away from me; of whom are Phygellus and Hermogenes.

15. I suppose thou knowest that all the bishops or teachers in Asia have forsaken me in my sufferings, and rejected my apostolic authority, or neglect it; of whom are, &c.
Note, 1. That he accuseth them not of apostacy from Christ, but forsaking him. 2. That those that forsake not Christ or his church, may forsake a particular ruler of it, even an apostle, especially if he be in prison. 3. That all the churches or bishops in Asia were conjoined in this sin: Sin may have the major vote of the bishops. 4. It is like then Timothy was no bishop of Ephesus, which was in Asia, for Timothy forsook not Paul.

16, 17. The Lord give mercy unto the house of Onesiphorus; for he oft refreshed me, and was not ashamed of my chain. But when he was in Rome, he sought me out very diligently, and found me. 18. The Lord grant unto him that he may find mercy of the Lord in that day: And in how many things he ministered unto me at Ephesus, thou knowest very well.

16, 17, 18. Note, That the particular acts of Christian charity are here rewarded with the most hearty prayers of the saints, and in the day of the Lord with special mercy. 2. That it is no sinful selfishness to return a special gratitude, love, and prayer, for those that have been specially kind to us in distress; especially when by it they manifest a special degree of love and fidelity to Christ.

CHAP. II.

THOU therefore my son, be strong in the grace that is in Christ Jesus.

1. Let other men's cases provoke thee to grow more strong, confirmed and resolved in the doctrine, practice, comfort, and patience of that grace which is treasured up for us in Christ.

2. And the things that thou hast heard of me among many witnesses, the same commit thou to faithful men, who shall be able to teach others also.

2. Note, 1. That the senior pastors must train up others to preach the gospel: And this seemeth the original of eminent episcopacy: The elders introducing their own scholars, were as fathers to them, and fit to be their guides. 2. None should be trusted with the ministry, but men faithful, and able to teach others. 3. It is the same doctrine which was delivered by the apostles which must be committed to ministers to teach the people. 4. While the scriptures were yet unwritten or unfinished, the words which men heard from the apostles, were to be their rule and doctrine.

3. Thou therefore endure hardness, as a good soldier of Jesus Christ.

3. Note, The life of a minister or bishop is not a life of ease, and idleness, and safeness, and dominion, and fulness; but like a soldier's, a life of hardship, hard labour: hard usage by the world, hard sufferings, requiring resolution, fortitude, and patience.

4. No man that warreth intangleth himself with the affairs of this life; that he may please him who hath chosen him to be a soldier.

4. A bishop or minister must be like a soldier who maketh it his whole business, and doth not join any other trade of life that would take up any of his time.

5. And if a man also strive for masteries, yet is he not crowned except he strive lawfully.

5. And in the games in which men strive for masteries for a prize (as running, wrestling, fencing, fighting) it is not every one that striveth that hath the crown or prize, but only he that winneth it by getting the better: And so must a minister of Christ strive for the crown of life, by putting forth all his care and strength.

6. The husbandman that laboureth, must be first partaker of his fruits.

6. The husbandman must labour (plow, sow, &c.) before he reap and gather the fruit.
Note, God will reward no pastors but the laborious, though men may advance the proud and idle.

7. Consider what I say, and the Lord give thee understanding in all things.

7. Note, They that will have God's word and good counsel blest by God to their understanding, must consider of it, even of its meaning, truth, and use.

8. Remember that Jesus Christ of the seed of David was raised from the dead.

8. If thou deeply consider and remember that Christ was raised from the dead, as it will infer the truth of all the rest of the gospel to thee, so it will be to thee a powerful example of patience and hope in all thy sufferings for Christ.

8, 9. According to my gospel: Wherein I suffer trouble as an evil doer, even unto bonds; but the word of God is not bound.

8, 9. This resurrection of Christ is it I preach, for which I suffer as reputed a malefactor, and that even to imprisoment and bonds, but God's word still prospereth and is not bound.
Note, So blind and devilish is malignant enmity to truth and godliness, that Christ's best servants are reputed and used as malefactors and rogues, even for the best of their duty to God, and that which is most profitable to the world.

10. Therefore I endure all things for the elect's sakes, that they may also obtain the salvation which is in Christ Jesus, with eternal glory.

10. And I think not any suffering too dear for the sake of God's elect, (though the rest of the world reject the gospel) that it may but further the salvation of them by the grace of Christ, to bring them to eternal glory.

11. It is a faithful saying: For if we be dead with him, we shall also live with him: 12. If we suffer, we shall also reign with him:

11, 12. Believe this as a gospel maxim, if we be dead to the world for him, as he died for us, we shall live in glory with him: And if we suffer for and with him, we shall follow him also in exaltation unto glory.

12, 13. If we deny him, he also will deny us; If we believe not, yet he abideth faithful; he cannot deny himself.

12, 13. If for fear of suffering we deny him, he will disown us, and deny us his salvation: And if we be unfaithful, and forsake him and our own salvation, yet he will be true of his word, and will not deny and forsake his own cause, but make good his threatening against them that forsake his mercies.

14. Of these things put them in remembrance, charging *them* before the Lord, that they strive not about words, to no profit, but to the subverting of the hearers.

14. Note, Bishops and ministers have great need to call men to the serious study of fundamental practical truths, from vain diverting kinds of study: 2. Such are the disputes and contentions about words or grammatical criticisms, and barren speculations in arts and sciences, which profit not by their due subserviency to saving truths, but subvert men, by diverting their thoughts, love, and labour.

15. Study to shew thyself approved unto God, a workman that needeth not to be ashamed, rightly dividing the word of truth.

15. Study not for applause, and to humour sick brains, but to please God, and do all as approved to him; with such skill, and care, and diligence, as beseemeth a good workman that need not be ashamed of his work, and disgrace not the work by an ignorant bungling, confused handling; but take great care rightly to order, methodize, and distribute the word of truth.
Note, That though curious unprofitable trifling with words be sinful, yet the more accurate ordering, methodizing, or distributing truth, setting each in its proper place, and giving every hearer his due part, is the part of a skilful teacher.

16. But shun profane and vain babblings; for they will increase unto more ungodliness. 17. And their word will eat as doth a canker:

16. But avoid profane and vain clamours and babblings of heathen philosophers or heretics, who set up a course of ostentation of their wit by unprofitable disputes; for the fruit will be but the increase of ungodliness: And vain proud wits are so liable to the infection, that their words will eat like a gangrene.

17, 18. Of whom is Hymeneus and Philetus: who, concerning the truth have erred, saying, That the resurrection is past already: and overthrow the faith of some.

17, 18. Note, It is not certain on what account they said the resurrection was past, 1. Whether as the Familists and Quakers by pretending, that it is but an inward resurrection from sin, that is meant, Or, 2. As Pythagoreans, saying, That it is but the transition of souls into other bodies, which is done here, and no more to be expected.

I incline most to this last; It is that which Paul disputeth against, 1 Cor. xv. that is here meant. And the doctrine of transmigration was then so common, and the heretics had so much from the Pythagorean philosophers, that it is most likely to be this.

19. Nevertheless, the foundation of God standeth sure, having this seal, The Lord knoweth them that are his. And, Let every one that nameth the name of Christ depart from iniquity.

19. But whoever falls away, God's foundation on which we build our hope is sure, and hath a seal as it were, with this double inscription; on one side [The Lord knoweth them that are his] for he hath decreed their salvation, and will not lose them; and he hath marked them out by his Spirit and written on them, [Holiness to the Lord:] And therefore on the other side is written, [Let every one that nameth the name of Christ depart from iniquity] For God's decree conjoineth the end and means, and he decreeth none to salvation that are not at once decreed to sanctification: As his covenant on his part promiseth us life, so our covenant to him obligeth us to holiness.

20. But in a great house there are not only vessels of gold, and of silver, but also of wood, and earth; and some to honour, and some to dishonour.

20. But it is not to be wondered at, if in God's house, which is his church visible, or the professors of Christianity, there be errors and scandals, and some backslide. For it is usual in great men's houses to have some wooden and earthen vessels for low and base usage, as well as silver and gold for the table, &c.

21. If a man therefore purge himself from these, he shall be a vessel unto honour, sanctified and meet for the master's use, *and* prepared unto every good work.

21. All that (by God's grace) do purge themselves from heresy and iniquity, are vessels of honour, sanctified, and meet to serve and honour God, and disposed to all good works.

22. Flee also youthful lusts: but follow righteousness, faith, charity, peace, with them that call on the Lord out of a pure heart.

22. Note, 1. That the flesh and its lusts, especially in youth, are such dangerous enemies to our holiness and salvation, that we have great need to be warned to avoid those lusts; and consequently, all that cherisheth them, (fulness, idleness, loose company, &c.) 2. Righteousness, faith, charity, and peace, are the sum of a holy life. 3. Charity and peace must extend to all that call on the Lord out of a pure heart, (though not in our forms or ceremonies.)

23. But foolish and unlearned questions avoid, knowing that they do gender strifes.

23. But whereas the more ignorant and unsound professors are apt to turn practical godliness into self-conceited, ignorant controversy and disputes, avoid this ill practice, as knowing that such wranglings do but breed strifes.

24. And the servant of the Lord must not strive; but be gentle unto all men, apt to teach, patient, 25. In meekness instructing those that oppose themselves; if God peradventure will give them repentance to the acknowledging of the truth: 26. And that they may recover themselves out of the snare of the devil, who are taken captive by him at his will.

24, 25, 26. But God's servants, especially bishops and teachers, must not provoke dissenters by striving debates, but be gentle to all men, even the erroneous; apt to teach them, and patient with them in error, instructing them in meekness, and in a gentle sort, even when they oppose the truth; and thus to wait in the right use of God's means, to see whether God will convince them, and turn them by repentance to the acknowledging of the truth, and that by consideration of what you teach them, they may recover themselves out of the snare of the devil, who captivateth them alive to do his will.

Note, 1. If men will not hear gentle teaching, much less will they yield to provoking disputes. 2. Yet disputes, like defensive wars, are oft necessary to the defence of the truth and church, though it be not the way to win the opponent. 3. Till sinners by consideration can be brought to be agents in recovering themselves, no teaching or disputing is like to recover them. 4. Fire and water are not more contrary than this word of God, and the way of the Romish prelates, who hereticate, imprison, silence, ruin, and murder true Christians, for not conforming to all their superstitious canons and ceremonies, and not swearing obedience to their usurped domination.

CHAP. III.

THIS know also, that in the last days perilous times shall come.

1. Before the end, the times will grow yet harder, more difficult and dangerous.

2, 3. For men shall be lovers of their ownselves, covetous, boasters, proud blasphemers, disobedient to parents, unthankful, unholy, without natural affection, truce-breakers,

II. TIMOTHY.

false accusers, incontinent, fierce, despisers of those that are good, 4. Traitors, heady, high-minded, lovers of pleasures more than lovers of God; 5. Having a form of godliness, but denying the power thereof; from such turn away.

2, 3, &c. The sins which abound are these: 1. They will be enslaved by selfishness, and little care for any but themselves. 2. Lovers of money and covetous. 3. Open boasters and vain-glorious. 4. Proud. 5. Blasphemers and reproachful. 6. Disobedient to their own parents. 7. Unthankful. 8. Without holiness, profane. 9. Having no true, friendly love, no, not natural. 10. Men that will not live in peace, but are unreconcilable. 11. Devils, or false accusers of others, especially of the best. 12. Distempered, ill-conditioned, incontinent. 13. Fierce and cruel. 14. Having no love to goodness, or good men. 15. Betrayers of others, or treacherous. 16. Rash, precipitate, heady men. 17. High-minded, puffed up with self-conceit, instead of solid knowledge. 18. Lovers of pleasure, (sensual and fantastical, as carnal men) more than lovers of God. 19. Having an image, or form of godliness, a shew and outside, in words, gestures, liturgies, ceremonies, and professions: 20. But the power of it for sanctification, mortifying the flesh, and overcoming the world, and living above, they savour not, but deny and do oppose. From this sort of men turn away, and have no communion with them.

Note, If the apostle had written thus in these latter ages of the church, guilt would have made many accuse him as describing and defaming them and their church rulers.

6. For of this sort are they which creep into houses, and lead captive silly women laden with sins, led away with divers lusts, 7. Ever learning and never able to come to the knowledge of the truth.

6, 7. This evil spirit is already gone forth, and these mischiefs are begun, (and will increase) for such are they that thrust themselves into houses, and there by deceit lead captive silly women, who being under a heap of their own sins, and acted and led by divers lusts, or ill desires, come to the Christian assemblies, and are still learning, but grow not in sound religion, nor come to any sound knowledge of the truth, and so are very capable receptive objects for any such deceivers to draw away.

Note, That all the said twenty foresaid vices, which cleave to creeping heretics while they are low, do work with greater power and confidence in them, when they get into domination.

8. Now as Jannes and Jambres withstood Moses, so do these also resist the truth: men of corrupt minds, reprobate concerning the faith.

8. And as the Egyptian magicians withstood Moses to keep Pharaoh from believing him, and that by magic, so do these resist the true preachers of the gospel, by their magic and arts now, and by the sword and cruelty when they can get into power: Men of corrupt minds, reprobate concerning the faith, unbelievers under the name of Christians.

Note, That the names of Jannes and Jambres are taken by Paul from the tradition of the Jews.

9. But they shall proceed no farther: for their folly shall be manifest unto all men, as theirs also was.

9. But as Moses's miracles overcame the magicians, and shamed them, so these shall be stopped in the pursuit of their deceit and heresy and opposition to the truth, and shall not proceed much further: But God will confound them, and manifest all their folly.

10. But thou hast fully known my doctrine, manner of live, purpose, faith, long-suffering, charity, patience, 11. Persecutions, afflictions which came unto me at Antioch, and Iconium, at Lystra, what persecutions I endured:

10, 11. But for thy establishment, I set before thee the example of my ministry: Thou hast been fully acquainted with the doctrine which I have taught, with the course and ordering of my life, my purpose and design, my faithfulness in my work, my long-suffering and freedom from wrath, my love to others, my patient suffering, my persecutions and sufferings at Antioch, and other places where I have preached, and what the ministry hath cost me.

11, 12. But out of them all the Lord delivered me. Yea, and all that will live godly in Christ Jesus shall suffer persecution.

11, 12. But out of them all God delivered me, so that I went on to do his work: Yea, such is the malignity of the carnal world, against that which crosseth their lusts and errors, and carnal interest, that all that resolve in a throughly godly life, and not by flattery or sin to comply with the wiles of proud ungodly men, but to be true to Christ, shall suffer some sort of persecution.

13. But evil men and seducers shall wax worse and worse, deceiving, and being deceived.

13. But the sin which hardeneth these wicked men to be persecutors of godly Christians, will harden them so far as to justify it, and stand to it impenitently, and think they do God service by persecuting his servants, pretending that it is they that are erroneous and bad men, and do deserve it; and being deceived themselves, will by deceit draw others to do the like.

14. But continue thou in the things which thou hast learned, and hast been assured of, knowing of whom thou hast learned *them:*

14. But do thou continue in that doctrine which I have taught, and thou hast received as assured truth, as knowing that thou hadst it from Christ by an authorized apostle.

15. And that from a child thou hast known the holy scriptures, which are able to make thee wise unto salvation, through faith which is in Christ Jesus.

15. And from thy childhood thou hast been trained up in the knowledge of the Old Testament, whose prophecies of Christ, and sacred precepts now illustrated by the gospel of Christian faith, are sufficient to make thee wise (by the Spirit of grace) in all that is needful to salvation.

16, 17. All scripture is given by inspiration of God, and *is* profitable for doctrine, for reproof, for correction, for instruction in righteousness : That the man of God may be perfect, throughly furnished unto all good works.

16, 17. All those writings which are of divine inspiration, are also profitable for doctrine, for reproof, for amendment and correction, and for education and discipline in righteousness, that so all God's servants, and especially teachers, may be complete and fully instructed and furnished for every good work required of God, for the ministerial service, and for men's salvation.

Note, Though this exclude not the use of any subservient arts of knowledge, yet certainly this is little understood or believed by the Roman clergy, who have made it necessary to a tolerated minister to know and observe their numerous canons, and oaths, subscriptions, and ceremonies, besides many books of theirs, while they admit priests that are ignorant of the scripture, and forbid the reading of them to the people.

CHAP. IV.

I CHARGE *thee* therefore before God, and the Lord Jesus Christ, who shall judge the quick and the dead at his appearing, and his kingdom: 2. Preach the word, be instant in season, out of season: reprove, rebuke, exhort with all long-suffering and doctrine.

1, 2. So dreadful is the sin sacrilegiously to deny Christ the service which thou hast vowed him, and art ordained to, and to betray the gospel, and men's souls, by so doing, that I do adjure thee with all possible earnestness, as before God, and as thou wilt answer it to Christ in judgment, when he cometh in the kingdom of his glory, that thou forbear not by any persecution, as far as possibly thou canst, to preach the word, be instant and urgent, in season, or fair opportunities, yes, out of season, (necessity must take place of convenience and circumstantial decencies), reprove the faulty, rebuke gross sinners, exhort all men, with unwearied long-suffering and sound doctrine.

Note, How dreadful a thing it is to cease preaching the gospel while we can, whatever we suffer for it, and whoever forbiddeth it. Let them that think that the apostles only were exempted from yielding to men's prohibition, remember that Timothy had his call and commission from men. Qu. But may not church-rulers silence ministers? Ans. Yes, when they so deserve it, by doing more hurt than good, that Christ's law doth silence them; else not; though they may determine of place and circumstances, and magistrates may also dispose of their own free encouragements, and may restrain men from evil doing.

3. For the time will come when they will not endure sound doctrine; but after their own lusts shall they heap to themselves teachers, having itching ears.

3. Note, 1. That the foresight of evil times by tempting teachers, should make faithful ministers labour the harder in their time.

2. It is 'no new thing for professed Christians not to endure sound doctrine, but to follow false teachers.

3. It is by their own lusts, or erroneous wills and choice, that professors are seduced by false teachers.

4. Itching ears is a dangerous disease.

5. False teachers may be heaped up, and to have the major vote, when sound teachers cannot be endured.

4. And they shall turn away their ears from the truth, and shall be turned unto fables.

4. Note, That churches, pastors, and people, may turn away from the truth to fables.

5. But watch thou in all things, endure afflictions, do the work of an Evangelist, make full proof of thy ministry.

5. Note, That great watchfulness, patient labouring and suffering, and fulfilling their ministry approvedly in all trials, is the description of a true minister of Christ.

6. For I am now ready to be offered, and the time of my departure is at hand. 7. I have fought a good fight, I have finished my course, I have kept the faith. 8. Henceforth there is laid up for me a crown of righteousness, which the

Lord the righteous judge shall give me at that day: and not to me only, but unto all them also that love his appearing.

6, 7, 8. Note, That, 1. Our ministry and life is like a battle, combat, or race, for life or death. 8. Only they that overcome shall be crowned. 3. Faithful men may take great comfort when death is at hand, in the conscience, and review of a well spent victorious life and ministry. 4. Their reward will be a crown of righteousness, given by God as a righteous judge, on gospel worthiness, though not on legal merit, but supposing free grace in Christ.
5. To love Christ's appearing, is the effect of a saving faith.

9, 10, 11. Do thy diligence to come shortly unto me. For Demas hath forsaken me, having loved this present world, and is departed unto Thessalonica; Crescens to Galatia, Titus unto Dalmatia. Only Luke is with me. Take Mark and bring him with thee: for he is profitable to me for the ministry. 12. And Tychicus have I sent to Ephesus.

9—12. Note, 1. It is not Christ that Demas is said to forsake, but Paul; and not to turn worldling, but to go about his worldly business unseasonably. 2. Timothy was not then at Ephesus.

13. The cloak that I left at Troas with Carpus, when thou comest bring *with thee*, and the books, but especially the parchments.

13. Note, The word translated [the cloak] is very probably by others translated [the roll] viz. of parchment.

14, 15. Alexander the coppersmith did me much evil: the Lord reward him according to his works. Of whom be thou aware also; for he hath greatly withstood our words.

14, 15. Alexander an excommunicate man hath much wronged me; God will reward him according to his works.
Note, Excommunication enrageth impenitent, bad men.

16. At my first answer, no man stood with me, but all men forsook me: *I pray God* that may not be laid to their charge.

16. Note, 1. This was not a forsaking Paul's cause, but his person in danger, which is too usual a case: herein he followed Christ, whose disciples all forsook him and fled. 2. It is like Peter was not then at Rome among the forsakers of Paul.

17. Notwithstanding the Lord stood with me, and strengthened me; that by me the preaching might be fully known, and *that* all the Gentiles might hear: and I was delivered out of the mouth of the lion.

17. But God forsook me not when all men forsook me, but was with me, and strengthened me, in vindicating my person and cause; that while I was permitted to answer for myself, the hearers might know, and fame might tell abroad, what doctrine it is that I suffer for preaching, and so all the city of Rome, and others by their report, might hear and have notice of it: and so I was delivered from the present danger of death by the Roman persecutors, as from the jaws of a lion.
Note, 1. Some think that the words [that the preaching might be fully known] refer to Paul's longer time to preach: I exclude not this, but prefer the other sense.
2. It was no treason nor sin for Paul to call his deliverance from the unjust judgment of the civil power, his being delivered out of the mouth of the lion.

18. And the Lord shall deliver me from every evil work, and will preserve *me* unto his heavenly kingdom, to whom *be* glory for ever and ever. Amen.

18. And I doubt not but God will still keep me from the ill designs and attempts of men against me, at least so far, that they shall not draw me to do evil, and will keep me in a state of right and preparation to his heavenly kingdom: in the hopeful sense whereof I rejoicingly desire that he may be glorified for ever. Amen.

19, 20. Salute Prisca and Aquila, and the household of Onesiphorus. Erastus abode at Corinth: but Trophimus have I left at Miletum sick.

19, 20. Note, That Trophimus was sick, though Paul had the gift of healing; because it was not to be common, nor at the will of man.

21. Do thy diligence to come before winter. Eubulus greeteth thee, and Pudens, and Linus, and Claudia, and all the brethren.

21. Make haste to come, &c.

22. The Lord Jesus Christ *be* with thy spirit. Grace *be* with you. Amen.

22. The Lord Jesus Christ, who is our mediator and head, and hath purchased, chosen, and called thee, performed for thee his saving office, in keeping thy soul in holiness and peace: his grace (which is the greatest treasure on earth) be with you, to keep you and prepare you for glory Amen.

Note, The subscriptions to the epistles, are no part of the holy scriptures.

ANNOTATIONS.

Faithful ministers, whose work is to preach the gospel of salvation, should have so much of the form, belief, and power of it in themselves, as to pass triumphantly out of the world in suffering for it, and not to think that God useth them hardly: and to be satisfied in God's acceptance, though their brethren and coverts should forsake them, as the bishops and churches of Asia did Paul.

THE
EPISTLE OF PAUL THE APOSTLE,
TO
TITUS.

CHAP. I.

PAUL a servant of God, and an apostle of Jesus Christ, according to the faith of God's elect, and the acknowledging of the truth, which is after godliness: 2. In hope of eternal life, which God that cannot lie, promised before the world began.

1, 2. Paul, &c. for the propagating of the faith of God's elect, and the acknowledgment of that sound doctrine, which is suited to the promoting of godliness, (in opposition to profaneness and heresy;) in hope of eternal life, which is the end of all our faith and godliness, and all our preaching and suffering; which God, that cannot lie, promised before many ages past.

3. But hath in due times manifested his word through preaching, which is committed unto me according to the commandment of God our Saviour.

3. But what he so long ago purposed, and darkly promised, he hath in the fittest appointed season manifested by his gospel through preaching, which is committed to me by the commission and commandment of God our Saviour.

Note, That it is doubtful whether by God's promise, be meant only his secret purpose; or by πρὸ χρόνων αἰωνίων be meant [many ages ago.] One of the two it must be; for we cannot feign an actual promise before the world began, distinct from his purpose.

2. It is not unlikely that he meaneth the promise first made to fallen man, of the woman's seed, and after often renewed; and this obscure word was made plain by the preaching of the gospel upon Christ's incarnation, life, and resurrection, &c.

4. To Titus *mine* own son after the common faith, grace, mercy, *and* peace from the Father, and the Lord Jesus Christ our Saviour.

4. Note, The church hath but one faith (or creed) common in the essentials to every Christian.

5. For, this cause left I thee in Crete, that thou shouldest set in order the things that are wanting, and ordain elders in every city, as I had appointed thee.

5. Note, 1. That Titus is not said to be settled in Crete as their fixed bishop, but left there in his travels, to settle fixed bishops there. The scriptures tell us that Timothy and Titus were itinerant evangelists, that went about where Paul sent them to plant and settle churches. But the plain truth is, that apostles, and such evangelists as these, wherever they came, had as great autho-

rity as any mere bishops, and more; and that they staid in some countries longer than in others, to settle the churches; and that the churches after their age thought it an honour to be their charge, and so called them their bishops. In which sense one apostle might have twenty or forty bishoprics, as he planted and settled so many churches; but none of them were bishops fixed and confined to one church, as those usually called bishops then were; so that to controvert whether Peter, Paul, Timothy, Titus, Luke, &c. were bishops, is a mere ignorant strife *de nomine*, about the name, while we are, or easily may be, agreed of the thing, what work for those churches they performed. They were bishops *eminenter*, transient from church to church; but he degradeth them, that feigneth them affixed to any one as their sole and proper flock.

2. Note further, That Titus ordaining elders, (that is, bishops, as Dr. Hammond noteth) implieth the people's consent; for Titus had no forcing power.

3. That Crete is said to have an hundred cities in it, being but a small island; and so must have an hundred bishops, if every city had one. But doubtless Paul meaneth every city that had Christians in it enough to be a church.

4. That by πόλις, is meant any big town, such as our corporations are, and κατα πόλιν, *oppidatim*, is meant from town to town, where there is matter for a church.' And Paul never meant by this to confine bishops to cities, and forbid them to villages, but he nameth cities or towns, because then no other places had Christians enow for a church.

5. Dr. Hammond thinks that these bishops then were only the single pastors of congregations, having no sub-presbyters, but deacons.

6. The ordering of things wanting, was not adding to their faith and religion, or making them a book of canons; but seeing them reduced to the obedient and orderly practice of that which the apostles every where taught and settled.

6. If any be blameless, the husband of one wife, having faithful children, not accused of riot or unruly.

6. Note, If God bless not the education of his own children, 1. The church would doubt of his fidelity, or whether God will bless his greater undertaking. 2. And his family would be a scandal to religion.

7. For a bishop must be blameless, as the steward of God : not self-willed, not soon angry, not given to wine, no striker, not given to filthy lucre :

7. Note, That the same man is called a bishop here, who was called an elder, verse 5. If then they were distinct officers, Paul neglected to describe one of them, which is not credible, when he describeth deacons and deaconesses. Dr. Hammond confesseth that there were in scripture-times no subject-presbyters, save bishops, that were under the apostolic order; but he thinks that bishops had power from the apostles to institute another order of presbyters under them afterwards: but, 1. Where is there any proof of that? Must church-government cast out all ministers who believe not such an unproved assertion? 2. It is thus disproved : Paul giveth Timothy and Titus sufficient instructions what officers to ordain in the church (which canons were to be a guide to all after ages.) But Paul gave them no instruction or canon for the instituting of any new order between bishops (or elders) and deacons: therefore it is not credible that any such power was then given to other bishops, which he gave not to Timothy and Titus.

But as to others, who say that the apostles and evangelists were then the only bishops, I answer, *de re*, we confess that these had power to go about to gather and settle churches; and *de nomine*, whether such may be called bishops, let them quarrel that have nothing else to do. But besides them, every town or church had then their own fixed bishop, (one or more) and deacons. If diocesans or metropolitans will be successors of the itinerant apostles and evangelists, or general bishops, let them restore to every church their particular proper bishops, and not make pastors that have not the power of the keys.

As for them that say, Paul includeth both orders under the same names, bishops and presbyters; I answer, Paul useth not only the same name, but the same description, and so the order or office also must be the same: and both name and thing the same.

2. Bishops are God's stewards, entrusted to govern by his law; and not lords of his church, or of their faith.

3. By [self-willed] is meant [self-conceited, proud men, that must be pleased, and have their own will] and cannot become all things lawful to all men, for their good, but will silence, and excommunicate, and reproach those that are most careful to do God's will, if they do but cross their wills, and canons.

4. Not [soon angry] rather [an angry, Wrathful man.] The rest see on 1 Tim. iii.

8. But a lover of hospitality, a lover of good men, sober, just, holy, temperate.

8. But one that loveth to entertain men in his house, a lover of goodness, and good men, of a sound and sober mind, righteous, holy, as devoted to God, continent, and abstemious.

9. Holding fast the faithful word, as he hath been taught, that he may be able by sound doctrine both to exhort and to convince the gainsayers.

9. Faithfully holding fast the word of faith, even that which we have preached and taught from Christ, that so he may be able to use sound doctrine, both in exhortation, and in confutation of opposers.

10. For there are many unruly and vain talkers and deceivers, specially they of the circumcision, 11.

Whose mouths must be stopped, who subvert whole houses, teaching *things* which they ought not, for filthy lucre's sake.

10, 11. For there are many disorderly and unruly, foolish vain talkers, deceivers of men's judgments, specially those Jewish corrupt Christians, (before often described.)

Note, That here it appeareth whom Paul meaneth in his invectives in many epistles, even those mentioned, Acts xv. that would have made Christianity but a supplement to Moses' law; and not Gnostics only or chiefly: Ebion and Cerinthus were of the worser degenerate sort of them, and the Nicolaitans next.

2. Note, That Paul meaneth not stopping the seducers' mouths by force. but by confutation by the word: for Titus had no power of the sword.

3. Note, That so great is the weakness and unsteadfastness of many Christians, that whole households may be subverted by the most gross deceivers. If the apostles' converts were such, no wonder if ours be so.

12, 13. One of themselves, *even* a prophet of their own, said, The Cretians *are* always liars, evil beasts, slow bellies: This witness is true;

12. Epimenides, an esteemed poet of their own, saith, that the Cretians are false, bad, and savage, gluttonous and idle; and his words are true, of too many of them, who are not converted from these sins.

13. Wherefore rebuke them sharply, that they may be sound in the faith:

13. Note, That sharp and cutting rebukes are necessary to some, that they be sound in faith and religion.

14. Not giving heed to Jewish fables and commandments of men, that turn from the truth.

14. Not believing the Jewish fables, and traditions, and commands of men, which the Pharisees uphold, and which turn men from sound faith.

Note, Do you think that Paul then was for introducing all the vast body of the Popish canons, and all their corrupt traditions and ceremonies?

15. Unto the pure, all things *are* pure, but unto them that are defiled, and unbelieving, *is* nothing pure: but even their mind and conscience is defiled.

15. They pretend that men are defiled by eating things unclean, not keeping their days, traditions, &c. But to believers who are purified from guilt and sin, all meats, and days, and things of that nature, are clean and lawful, yea sanctified, to further them in serving God. But all things are made unclean, as abused to sin and evil ends,

by them that are unclean and unbelievers; their defiled minds and consciences defile all to them.

16. They profess that they know God, but in works they deny *him*, being abominable, and disobedient, and unto every good work reprobate.

16. It is not these Judaizers and heretics' profession, that they know more of God, and his will, than others, that will prove them wise or good: for their deeds contradict their tongues: they are practical Atheists, while they deny God by their works, and lives, as if they knew not God to be the holy and righteous governor and judge of all: for they are abominable and disobedient, and averse and unmeet for all good works.

CHAP. II.

BUT speak thou the things which become sound doctrine: 2. That the aged men be sober, grave, temperate, sound in faith, in charity, in patience.

1. Note, Sound doctrine is practical, teaching men their duties.

2. It was so ordinary with the Jews for the younger to reverence and obey the elder, that officers being chosen by seniority (*cæteris paribus*) it is of no great moment whether we here expound this of office or age (as most do.) They that take [aged] to signify rulers, some mean deacons, some elders, that ruled only, either as some, not ordained to preach, or as others, not ordinary preachers: but all unproved.

3. The aged women likewise, that *they be* in behaviour as becometh holiness, not false accusers, not given to much wine, teachers of good things,

3. That the aged women who are in the church catalogue or list, that they behave themselves as becometh holiness, not to diabolize or calumniate, not addicted to wine, teachers of the younger sort in good things.

Note, Whether these were deconesses by office or not, it is certain, 1. That all aged women should instruct the younger. 2. But because few do their duty to purpose, it is of great use in a well ordered church, that some few of the fittest be by office chosen to this work, that the ministers may direct these aged women in it, and not be themselves too often with the younger sort in private.

4. That they may teach the young women to be sober, to love their husbands, to love their children, 5. *To be* discreet, chaste, keepers at home, good, obedient to their own husbands, that the word of God be not blasphemed.

4, 5. It is their work to teach the younger women to be wise, and of sound judgment, to love their husbands, and children, and shew it in their care and behaviour, to be discreet and chaste in mind and behaviour; to keep at home, and look to their household business, and not affect to be needlessly abroad in idleness, or under temptations; to be good, and subject to their husbands, for there is danger that the miscarriages of young women may bring reproach on religion and the gospel which they profess.

6. Young men likewise exhort to be sober-minded.

6. Note, 1. By sober mindedness, is meant a mind settled in the truth, guided by sound judgment, and not by passion, not seduced by sense and appetite, or evil company, or proud self-conceit, or hasty judging, into evil ways. 2. By Paul's warnings we may note, what the vices are that young men, and all sorts, are most in danger of.

7. In all things shewing thyself a pattern of good works: in doctrine *shewing* uncorruptness, gravity, sincerity; 8. Sound speech that cannot be condemned, that he that is of the contrary part, may be ashamed, having no evil thing to say of you.

7, 8. In all the good which thou wouldest persuade thy hearers to, be an eminent visible pattern *thyself*, that they may see in thyself what thou meanest in thy preaching: let thy doctrine be entire and sincere, without corrupt mixture, and grave without levity, sound words that deserve not blame, and cannot be confuted; that gainsayers (for such you must expect) may be ashamed, having no ill to charge on your doctrine or life.

9, 10. *Exhort* servants to be obedient unto their own masters, *and* to please *them* well in all things, not answering again: Not purloining, but shewing all good fidelity, that they may adorn the doctrine of God our Saviour in all things.

9, 10. Servants, even the lowest, are thy charge, and must be taught to be obedient to their masters, and in all things lawful belonging to their government, to make it their care to please them, not crossing and contradicting them, nor stealing the least thing, nor taking any thing that is theirs, which is not allowed them by their consent, but shewing all conscionable trustiness; that while Christian servants thus excel all others, it may honour the gospel and religion (more than opinionative proud professors do.)

11, 12. For the grace of God that bringeth salvation, hath appeared to all men, teaching us,

That denying ungodliness and worldly lusts, we should live soberly, righteously, and godly, in this present world.

11, 12. For the grace of God by a Redeemer, which bringeth salvation, is made known now to all sorts of men, and extendeth to servants as well as masters, teaching us all (not the vain speculations of the world, but) to deny all doctrines and practices which are ungodly, and all worldly lusts, of sensuality or covetousness, and that we should live in this present world, soberly and temperately to ourselves, righteously and charitably to others, and holily and obediently to God.

13. Looking for that blessed hope, and the glorious appearing of the great God, and our Saviour Jesus Christ.

13. Animated herein by our believing expectation of our hoped blessedness, and the appearing of the glory of that great God, and our Saviour Jesus Christ, (according to his faithful promise.)

14. Who gave himself for us, that he might redeem us from all iniquity, and purify unto himself a peculiar people, zealous of good works.

14. Who gave himself as our Saviour a sacrifice for our sins, and a ransom for our deliverance, that thereby he might redeem and save us from the guilt, punishment, and power of all our sins, and purify and sanctify a church to himself, as his body and spouse, for his glory, and delightful communion with them, a peculiar people segregate from the polluted wicked world, and by his Spirit made zealously devoted in love and diligence, to all good works, of holiness to God, and justice and beneficence to man.

Note, 1. It was to redeem us from our own sin, and its effects, that Christ gave himself as our Saviour to be a sacrifice for us. 2. The redeemed of Christ (not only as to sufficiency, but efficacy) differ not from the polluted world only by name and profession, and common things, but are a purified and peculiar people, possessed by Christ's Spirit with a zeal for good works. 3. True zeal is for good works, and not for dead ceremony, or worldly interest, or odd opinions, and dividing sects. It is not furious, and hurtful, and envious, but first pure, and then peaceable, and sets men upon earnest endeavour to do good. 4. It is not only for us that Christ redeemeth and purifieth a church and chosen people, but ultimately for himself, and for his own and his Father's glory and complacence. As he made the world not as needing it, but as pleased in his own expressed glory.

15. These things speak and exhort, and rebuke with all authority. Let no man despise thee.

15. These necessary practical saving truths must be the matter of thy preaching: and according to

the authority of thy office, rebuke gain-sayers, and the disobedient: and let thy doctrine and behaviour in wisdom and gravity, keep thee from all men's contempt.

CHAP. III.

PUT them in mind to be subject to principalities and powers, to obey magistrates, to be ready to every good work.

1. Teach them oft to live in due subjection to chief rulers or princes, and those that have governing authority, and to obey magistrates, in all things which belong to their office and authority to command under God; and to do all the good they can to all men.

2. To speak evil of no man, to be no brawlers, *but* gentle, shewing all meekness unto all men.

2. To avoid all reproachful and evil speaking of any men, without a necessary cause upon sufficient evidence, to be no contentious strivers, but apt to take all things in the most favourable sense, using all meekness to all men.

3. For we ourselves also were sometimes foolish, disobedient, deceived, serving divers lusts and pleasures, living in malice and envy, hateful, *and* hating one another.

3. In our dealing with others we must use compassion, remembering that before our conversion to Christ, we ourselves had those vices which are reproachful in others; we were witless, unpersuadable, and disobedient, deceived in the greatest things, the servants of divers lusts and pleasures, living in malice and envy against others, odious ourselves, and with hatred-pursuing one another. This was the Gentile life.

4. But after that the kindness and love of God our Saviour toward man appeared, 5. Not by works of righteousness, which we have done, but according to his mercy he saved us by the washing of regeneration, and renewing of the Holy Ghost. 6. Which he shed on us abundantly, through Jesus Christ our Saviour.

4, 5, 6. But when the saving kindness and love of God our Saviour to fallen man appeared to us by the communication and illumination of his grace, not for any good works or deserts of ours (for we were as bad, as aforesaid) but of his mere free mercy he saved us from that state of sin and misery, by regeneration signified and sealed in baptism, and by the renewing work of the Holy Ghost, which he poured out upon us in the extraordinary measure promised after Christ's resurrection, both for sanctification and confirming miracles.

7. That being justified by his grace, we should be made heirs according to the hope of eternal *life*.

7. That thus by his grace, being of wicked enemies made acceptably righteous, by pardon of sin, and renovation by the merit and Spirit of Christ, we should be adopted sons and heirs of eternal life, according to his promise, on which we safely build our hope.

8. *This is* a faithful saying, and these things I will that thou affirm constantly, that they which have believed in God, might be careful to maintain good works: these things are good and profitable unto men.

8. This is a point of great importance, which I require thee often to press upon them, that they which are Christians think not that they have nothing to do, but to mind heaven, and pray, and worship God; but that they live in such callings or trades in the world, in which labouring diligently, they may be profitable to others, and the public good, and not make religion a cloak for idleness, but spend their time in that which is good and profitable to men.

9. But avoid foolish questions and genealogies, and contentions, and strivings about the law; for they are unprofitable and vain.

9. Note, That though some of these things were pretended to be learned speculations, and others to be parts of God's own word, yet to be employed in controversial strivings and disputings, or study, or talk about such little things, to the diverting of us from the study, discourse, and exercise of practical godliness, is fruitless vanity.

10. A man that is an heretic, after the first and second admonition, reject: 11. Knowing that he that is such, is subverted and sinneth, being condemned of himself.

10, 11. The over-valuing of such conceits, and trifling disputes, and thinking themselves more wise men for these, and gathering parties to themselves from the church, to propagate them in separation, and to draw disciples after them, is the way of heretics: whoever is such a one (supposing private men do their part) do thou that art a public minister duly admonish him by meekness and convincing evidence of truth, once and again; and if he hear not, reject him from the communion of the flock: for such a man is fixed in his sin by pride, self-conceit, and a depraved judgment; and being subverted into a sinful separation, is self-condemned, both by the open profession of his sin, as if it were some glorious truth and duty, and by casting himself out of the communion of the church, so that he needeth neither witness nor judge to cast him.

12, 13. When I shall send Artemas unto thee, or Tychicus, be diligent to come unto me to Nicopolis: for I have determined there to winter. Bring Zenas the lawyer, and Apollos, on their journey diligently, that nothing be wanting unto them.

12, 13. Note, God's ministers must further all others in his work, as well as work themselves.

14. And let ours also learn to maintain good works for necessary uses, that they be not unfruitful.

14. And let all that keep in our communion, as sound Christians, see that they live not idly or unprofitably, or on other men's cost and labour, but that they live in some trade and diligent labour, by which they may be themselves maintained, and be fruitful in pious and charitable communications.

15. All that are with me salute thee: Greet them that love us in the faith, Grace be with you all. Amen.

15. Note, Mutual kind salutations, and benedictions, are meet expressions of Christian love.

THE
EPISTLE OF PAUL THE APOSTLE,
TO
PHILEMON.

CHAP. I.

PAUL a prisoner of Jesus Christ, and Timothy our brother, unto Philemon our dearly beloved, and fellow labourer, 2. And to our beloved Apphia, and Archippus our fellow-soldier, and to the church in thy house: 3. Grace to you, and peace from God our Father, and the Lord Jesus Christ.

1. Note, That to be a labourer, and soldier, and a prisoner for Christ, are the titles that Paul glorieth in, and not in worldly dignities.

4. I thank my God, making mention of thee always in my prayers. 5. Hearing of thy love and faith, which thou hast toward the Lord Jesus, and toward all saints;

4, 5. Note, That 1. Paul made particular mention of persons and churches, yea many of both, in his prayers. 2. True faith in Christ will produce love to him, and to all saints, and not only to those of a party with us.

6. That the communication of thy faith may become effectual, by the acknowledging of every good thing, which is in you in Christ Jesus.

6. That thy faith may be manifest to be effectual by the evident production of all sorts of good fruits, which Jesus Christ hath taught thee, and wrought in and by thee.

7. For we have great joy and consolation in thy love, because the bowels of the saints are refreshed by thee, brother.

7. Note, That when faith bringeth forth the fruits of liberal charity to the relief of others, it makes it and the agent much more amiable, than when it doth not, though it should be sincere and want only ability (as a good tree laden with choice fruit is more lovely than in the winter:) much more than when hypocrisy maketh faith fruitless.

8. Wherefore, though I might be much bold in Christ, to enjoin thee that which is convenient, 9. Yet for love's sake I rather beseech thee, being such a one as Paul the aged, and now also a prisoner of Jesus Christ.

8, 9. Church-rulers must not plead and use mere commanding authority, when love and intreaty is more fit for the end, as usually it is with brethren, and worketh more kindly and effectually.

10, 11. I beseech thee for my son Onesimus, whom I have begotten in my bonds: Which in time past was to thee unprofitable, but now profitable to thee and to me.

10, 11. Note, 1. That true conversion maketh good servants, as well as good Christians. 2. That the faults of converted servants should be pardoned by us, as ours be of God. 3. That God's word by a prisoner may save souls. 4. That a converted servant should be valued by the greatest apostle.

12. Whom I have sent again: thou therefore receive him that is mine own bowels.

12. Note. How dear are the souls of the meanest to a faithful minister, and how lovely when converted!

13. Whom I would have retained with me, that in thy stead he might have ministered unto me in the bonds of the gospel.

13. Even thou thyself owest me service while I suffer bonds for the gospel's sake; and I would have kept him to do it for me in thy stead.

14. But without thy mind would I do nothing, that thy benefit should not be as it were of necessity, but willingly.

14. But I would not, without thy consent, so dispose of one who is rightfully thy servant, though a fugitive; that thy kindness to me may not be necessitated by my will, but be free as of thy own will.

15. For perhaps he therefore departed for a season, that thou shouldest receive him for ever. 16. Not now as a servant, but above a servant, a brother beloved, specially to me, but how much more unto thee, both in the flesh and in the Lord?

15, 16. His temporary departure may end in a durable reception and entertainment; and that not only as a servant, but a brother, beloved specially by me who converted him, much more by thee to whom now he is doubly related, both as a servant, and as a fellow-member of Christ.

17, 18. If thou count me therefore a partner, receive him as myself. If he hath wronged thee, or oweth *thee ought,* put that on mine account.

17, 18. If thou judge me to have right in thy affairs, by the bonds of Christian friendship, receive him if thou wouldst receive me: set thy losses by him and wrongs on my account, and I will give thee satisfaction.

19. I Paul have written it with mine own hand, I will repay it; albeit I do not say to thee how thou owest unto me even thine own self besides.

19. Rather than money-matters shall continue a breach, I here give thee a bill under my hand, that I will repay all that he oweth thee; though I might tell thee that thou owest me even *thyself.*

20. Yea, brother, let me have joy of thee in the Lord: refresh my bowels in the Lord.

20. I pray thee, brother, comfort me with this expression of thy Christian love and forgiveness.

21. Having confidence in thy obedience, I wrote unto thee, knowing that thou wilt also do more than I say.

21. I write this as encouraged by a strong persuasion that thou wilt not only obey my desire, but do more for him than I think meet particularly to urge thee to.

22. But withal prepare me also a lodging, for I trust that through your prayers I shall be given unto you.

22. Note, That our deliverances must be expected by the means of the prayers of the faithful.

23, 24, 25. There salute thee Epaphras, my fellow-prisoner in Christ Jesus: Marcus, Aristarchus, Demas, Lucas, my fellow-labourers: The grace of our Lord Jesus Christ *be* with your spirit. Amen.

23, 24, 25. Note, Paul was not without fellow-prisoners, or fellow-labourers, in his bonds.

THE EPISTLE TO THE HEBREWS.

[*Whether by Paul, Luke, or whom, is uncertain.*]

CHAP. I.

GOD, who at sundry times, and in divers manners, spake in time past unto the fathers by the prophets, 2. Hath in these last days spoken unto us by *his* Son,

1. God who hath not left us only to the light of nature, to know him by his works of creation, but in mercy hath more fully informed us by supernatural revelation, was pleased to do this variously as to times, and manner, and degree, and of old spake to our ancestors by several prophets, who were the messengers of his word: but in these last days he hath spoken to us by his Son (greater than all prophets.)

2. Whom he hath appointed to be heir of all things, by whom also be made the worlds.

2. Whom he hath appointed to be owner and Lord of all things, as he is God and man, not only by the prime right of creation, but as the Redeemer of man, all power in heaven and earth, and all things are delivered to him for the ends of redemption: and by him, (his wisdom and word) he made the worlds, and all therein.

3. Who being the brightness of his glory, and the express image of his person, and upholding all things by the word of his power, when he had by himself purged our sins, sat down on the right hand of the majesty on high:

3. Who being the shining beam, or splendor of his glory, by whom God shineth forth, or giveth the knowledge of himself to us (as the sun is known to us by its light) and the character of his subsistence, and upholding and ruling all things by the word of his power (as by that word of God's power they were made) when he had by his own merits, and sacrifice, and covenant, made a sufficient purgation to take away the guilt of our sins, and so far purged them away, as to enact a pardoning covenant for all that will believingly accept it in him. So that now the general pardon wants nothing but acceptance, (and none shall perish for want of sufficiency in the sacrifice or covenant) he then ascended, and is in heavenly glory, at the right hand of God's supreme celestial majesty, head over all things to his church, that thence he may send down the Holy Ghost, to gather his chosen, and bring his mystical body to glory.

4. Being made so much better than the angels, as he hath by inheritance obtained a more excellent name than they.

4. Being in excellency and superiority set above the angels, as he hath by lot or inheritance obtained higher titles, power, and offices than they.

5. For unto which of the angels said he at any time, Thou art my son, this day have I begotten thee? And again, I will be to him a Father, and he shall be to me a son. 6. And again, when he bringeth in the first begotten into the world, he saith, And let all the angels of God worship him.

5, 6. He calls Christ his son in divers texts, (which, though it spake partly of David, yet ultimately meaneth Christ;) and he commandeth the angels to worship him. But none of this is said of angels.

7. And of the angels he saith, Who maketh his angels spirits, and his ministers a flame of fire:

7. But he calls his angels spirits, and servants, and a flame of fire.

8. But unto the Son, *he saith,* Thy throne, O God, *is* for ever and ever; a sceptre of righteousness *is* the sceptre of thy kingdom. 9. Thou hast loved righteousness, and hated iniquity, therefore God,

even thy God, hath anointed thee with the oil of gladness above thy fellows.

8, 9. But to the Son he ascribeth the name of God, and an everlasting throne and kingdom, and a sceptre of righteousness, and a superiority by divine unction, above all others.

10. And, thou Lord, in the beginning hast laid the foundation of the earth; and the heavens are the works of thine hands. 11. They shall perish, but thou remainest; and they shall wax old as doth a garment. 12. And as a vesture shalt thou fold them up, and they shall be changed: but thou art the same, and thy years shall not fail.

10, 11, 12. He is said to be the Lord who made earth and heaven; and who will remain when they perish, and be the same when they are changed.

13. But to which of the angels said he at any time, sit on my right hand, until I make thine enemies thy footstool?

13. He never said to any angel, what he said to Christ of his kingdom, and the subduing of his enemies, &c.

14. Are they not all ministering spirits, sent forth to minister for them, who shall be heirs of salvation?

14. All those spirits that are properly called angels or messengers, are spirits appointed and sent forth by God, to minister for them who shall be heirs of salvation, under Jesus Christ.

ANNOTATIONS.

The great difficulty here is, to understand how this description belongeth to the person of Christ, Whether it be the divine nature that is said to be [appointed heir, &c. the brightness of God's glory, the character of his subsistence, or person, made better than angels, begotten this day, set on God's right hand in power, &c.] or the human: or whether it be spoken of the person of Christ as in both natures: and we must not inquire according to which nature the words are spoken of Christ? I have before said, on Col. i. 15, 16. how many opinions about the person and natures of Christ have been pleaded for. 1. That of the orthodox, who assert but one person of Christ, and two natures; though the word [person] was long refused by many, as not meaning the same with hypostasis. And subtle philosophers say, that the human nature can be no part of Christ's person, but an adjunct; because his person was complete from eternity, and the Deity cannot be a part. But if it were not that the hereticates will quarrel with it, it may be said, that the word person is equivocal; and that as hypostasis is a person, the divine nature is the whole person; but not as it is ερωπος, or a relative person.

2. That of the wretched Socinians, who feign Christ to be mere man advanced.

3. That of the Arians, who make him only the first creature, or emanation of God incarnate, super-angelical, light of lights, very God of very God, begotten by emanation; not made, as other creatures, but making them all, but yet not [of] the same essence or substance with the Father, but [from] the same, as a beam or light from the sun. This the church hath condemned these thirteen hundred years, and more.

4. That of some, who say that Christ hath three natures: 1. The divine. 2. The aforesaid super-angelical, assumed by the divine to nearest union. 3. The human, assumed by both. And they think that this text speaketh chiefly of the second, as assuming the third. As it is dangerous to err about any necessary point concerning Christ's person, so it is dangerous to be rash in taking up any unnecessary opinion about so incomprehensible a mystery, and worse to urge it with pride and fury, to the dividing of the church, and the damning of dissenters. To say about many cases that have torn the churches, I know not, is more pardonable than turbulent error.

CHAP. II.

THEREFORE we ought to give the more earnest heed to the things which we have heard, lest at any time we should let them slip.

1. Therefore we that have heard the gospel of Christ, and especially who have professed to receive it, should with great earnestness set our minds and hearts unto it, lest by negligence or unbelief we should lose what we have heard, and be as leaking vessels, and be lost ourselves.

2. For if the word spoken by angels was steadfast, and every transgression and disobedience received a just recompence of reward:

2. For if the law which God delivered to Moses, by the ministry of the voice and appearance of angels, was not yet firm and sure, and every sin against it, and threatened by it, was punished:

3. How shall we escape, if we neglect so great salvation, which at the first began to be spoken by the Lord, and was confirmed unto us by them that heard *him*, 4. God also bearing them witness, both with signs and wonders, and with divers miracles, and gifts of the Holy Ghost, according to his own will?

CHAP. II. HEBREWS. 519

3, 4. Much less shall we escape, if we neglect this far greater salvation, and more excellent manifestation of the will of God; even that gospel which Christ first preached himself, and those that heard him confirmed by their testimony and preaching; God also confirming to us their testimony from heaven, by many such signs and wonderful works, and with many sorts of miracles or acts of power, and distributions of the Holy Ghost to others when they believed, as were a certain proof of God's attestation, and the approbation of his own will.

Note, That here we have the true evidence of the truth of the gospel, on which believers may build their faith.

5. For unto angels hath he not put in subjection the world to come, whereof we speak.

5. God hath not made angels the sovereigns of the world to come, and put the kingdom of glory so under them, that all must be their subjects.

6. But one in a certain place testified, saying, What is man, that thou art mindful of him: or the son of man, that thou visitest him? 7. Thou madest him a little lower than the angels, thou crownedst him with glory and honour, and didst set him over the works of thy hands: 8. Thou hast put all things in subjection under his feet.

6, 7, 8. But the psalm is ultimately to be understood of Christ and his church, which saith, [What is man, &c.] Though Christ was a while on earth, in a state of humiliation, below angels as to the flesh; yet it was in order to the glory, and victorious power of his kingdom.

8. For in that he put all in subjection under him, he left nothing that is not put under him. But now we see not yet all things put under him.

8. By this it is sure that all things are to be subdued to Christ, though yet we see it not done.

9. But we see Jesus, who was made a little lower than the angels, for the suffering of death, crowned with glory and honour, that he, by the grace of God should taste death for every man.

9. But we see that Jesus, who was made lower than angels, for and in his state of humiliation and crucifixion, is already ascended up into heaven, where he is crowned with glory. And as his death was suffered in the common nature of men, and the sins of all men had a causal hand in it, and it was by God's grace the purchasing cause of the conditional covenant of grace, and of all the good that men receive, so he died to bring men to glory with himself. And therefore that text may be understood of the advancement of man both in Christ, and his church, that shall be advanced by him.

10. For it became him, for whom are all things, and by whom are all things in bringing many sons unto glory, to make the captain of their salvation perfect through sufferings.

10. For it seemed meet to the God of wisdom, for whom, and by whom all things are, to make Christ the captain of their salvation, a perfect performer of his saving office, and to obtain his own glory in heavenly perfection by the way of suffering, and to bring all God's adopted sons to glory by the merit of it, and by following him in the same suffering way.

11. For both he that sanctifieth, and they who are sanctified, are all of one: for which cause he is not ashamed to call them brethren, 12. Saying, I will declare thy name unto my brethren, in the midst of the church will I sing praise unto thee. 13. And again, I will put my trust in him; and again, behold, I, and the children which God hath given me.

11, 12, 13. And that it is in and by Christ, that human nature is advanced, as Psal. viii saith, is proved by the union that is between Christ and us. He that sanctifieth us, and we that are sanctified, are of the same human nature, and are as one body; and therefore, as we must suffer with him, we shall reign with him. Therefore in the texts that, under other typical persons, speak of Christ, he calls us his brethren, and children given him, to whose trust we are committed.

14, 15. Forasmuch then as the children are partakers of flesh and blood, he also himself likewise took part of the same, that through death he might destroy him that had the power of death, that is the devil: And deliver them, who through fear of death, were all their life-time subject to bondage.

14, 15. And that he might bring us to glory with him, as we have flesh and blood, he would first be so far made one with us, as to take also flesh and blood, that he might be capable of suffering and dying for us; and so, by undergoing death, which we by sin have brought ourselves under, and by rising from the dead, he might conquer Satan and death, and destroy his kingdom and power of death, which he had obtained by conquering man by his temptations, and by God's letting him be the executioner, where he had been the conquering tempter; and so that

Christ might deliver the faithful by his conquest of Satan and death, from continuance under death, and from the danger of hell, and from the slavish fear of both (death temporal and everlasting;) who else, by their guilt, and liableness to both these, must be all their lifetime in bondage, both by their danger and their fears.

16. For verily he took not on him the *nature of* angels: but he took on *him* the seed of Abraham.

16. For it is not angels that he took hold of, or whose natures he assumed, and came to save; but he took on him the nature of man, the seed of Abraham, to save man.

17. Wherefore in all things it behoved him to be made like unto his brethren, that he might be a merciful and faithful high priest, in things *pertaining* to God, to make reconciliation for the sins of the people.

17. So that he must be in all things like man, whom he would save, that he might be fit for his undertaken office, to be an high priest for us to Godward, and to be merciful and faithful therein, to make reconciliation for our sins.

18. For in that he himself hath suffered, being tempted, he is able to succour them that are tempted.

18. For he himself having been tempted and tried by sufferings, and having overcome them all, he is now more meet to be a compassionate helper, the example, the teacher, and the trust of them that must follow him through temptations; and by his merit and victory hath obtained power to deliver them.

CHAP. III.

WHEREFORE, holy brethren, partakers of the heavenly calling, consider the apostle and high priest of our profession, Christ Jesus, 2. Who was faithful to him that appointed him, as also Moses *was faithful* in all his house.

1. Wherefore you who are holy brethren, by faith and dedication given up to Christ, and in him made partakers of that calling from heaven, which maketh you heirs of heaven, study and consider Jesus Christ, the great apostle, sent of God to be the prime preacher of the gospel, and the high priest and chief guide and mediator to Godward, of our religion and profession; who faithfully did all that belonged to his undertaken office (in sacrificing himself for our sins, and fulfilling all righteousness, and conquering Satan and death, and ascending to intercede for us in glory, and sending down the Holy Ghost, and making and

sealing the law of faith) even as Moses in his time was faithful, though with disparity of honour and work; Christ in his own house by a more perfect administration, and Moses but as a steward.

3. For this *man* was counted worthy of more glory than Moses, inasmuch, as he who hath builded the house, hath more honour than the house.

3. For Christ is as much more honourable than Moses, as the maker and master is than the house; for Moses was but a member of the family, but Christ the maker and master of it.

4. For every house is builded by some man: but he that built all things *is* God.

4. All families or houses are founded by some man, but he that built the church, is the same that built or made all things; and that is God.

5. And Moses verily *was* faithful in all his house as a servant for a testimony of those things which were to be spoken after. 6. But Christ, as a son over his own house,

5, 6. And Moses, as a servant was faithful for the delivery and confirmation of so much of God's word as was to be spoken to the Jews by him: but Christ, as the son and heir, and master of the house, as his own.

6. Whose house are we, if we hold fast the confidence, and the rejoicing of the hope firm unto the end.

6. This house is the church, of which we are parts, so be it we hold fast the confident profession of our faith, and the joy and glorying in our hopes of the promised blessedness, firm to the end?

7. Wherefore, as the Holy Ghost saith, To-day, if ye will hear his voice, 8. Harden not your hearts, as in the provocation, in the day of temptation in the wilderness: 9. When your fathers tempted me, proved me, and saw my works forty years. 10. Wherefore I was grieved with that generation, and said, They do always err in their hearts, and they have not known my ways. 11. So I sware in my wrath, They shall not enter into my rest.

7, 8, &c. But seeing he will take none to dwell with him in glory, but those that persevere, hear, and consider what the Holy Ghost said to, and of the Israelites; [To-day, &c.] Neglect not his present call, and your present day, to the hardening of your hearts, as your fathers did in the wilderness: by which God's justice was engaged against them, as a people whose hearts were habituated to evil, and have not the obedient knowledge of his ways, and works, and will: so that he sware in his just displeasure, that that generation should not enter into the promised land.

12. Take heed, brethren, lest there be in any of you an evil heart of unbelief, in departing from the living God.

12. Take warning by these Israelites, and see that there be not in any of you an evil unsound heart, that is prepared by secret unbelief, to depart in trial from the living God.

13. But exhort one another daily, while it is called, to-day, lest any of you be hardened through the deceitfulness of sin.

13. To this end, one means appointed by God for your perseverance is, speedily and daily to exhort and stir up one another; the pastors in the church and assemblies, and all in their places and converse: and the rather, because sin, of which you are in danger, is a deceitful thing; and they that revolt are made believe, that it is but a receiving of the truth, or a necessary self-saving, and no forsaking of Christ, or truth, or godliness.

N. Ques. But what if rulers forbid us to meet daily for such exhortation? Ans. God commandeth you to do it in the manner and time that the end requireth, and no man can dispense with his law. The Christians, for three hundred years assembled, when forbidden.

Ques. But what if Christian rulers forbid it? Ans. Christians have more obligation than heathens to do good, but no more authority to do evil, or null God's laws.

Ques. But what if violence or prisons restrain us? Ans. God requireth not impossibilities.

14. For we are made partakers of Christ, if we hold the beginning of our confidence steadfast unto the end.

14. We are initially made partakers of Christ as our Saviour: but if we will attain salvation by him, we must hold the subsisting faith (or the confidence) in which we have begun (or which is our principle) firm to the end: (for perseverance is made a condition of the promise of salvation.)

15. While it is said, To-day if ye will hear his voice, harden not your hearts, as in the provocation. 16. For some, when they had heard, did provoke: howbeit not all that came out of Egypt by Moses.

15, 16. The words tell us, that some that heard, after deliverance from Egypt, provoked God; but it was not all.

17. But with whom was he grieved forty years? was it not with them that had sinned, whose carcases fell in the wilderness?

17. With whom was God so displeased, as grief here signifieth? Nothing displeaseth him but sin. It was with backsliding, disobedient, unthankful murmurers, that would not rest in the will, and word, and providence of God, but must have their own carnal will fulfilled, and so God in justice killed them in the wilderness, after so many miracles had led them many years towards the promised land. Take heed lest you follow them in the like sin, to greater punishment, for abusing greater mercies.

18, 19. And to whom sware he that they should not enter into his rest, but to them that believed not? So we see that they could not enter in because of unbelief.

18, 19. It was the sinning unbelievers that he sware should not enter: and it was because of their unbelief, that they could not enter. Take heed, therefore, lest ye fall by unbelief in trial: for there is more required to our complete salvation, than to our first part in Christ.

CHAP. IV.

LET us therefore fear, lest a promise being left us of entering into his rest, any of you should seem to come short of it.

1. Seeing then that this promise of rest is conditional, if we persevere, and among so many trials we are in so much danger of our own heart, let careful fear prevent your falling, and missing the benefit of that promise.

Note, Ques. Why should we fear that which God's decree and grace have made impossible? Ans. 1. God hath not made it impossible in itself, but only hypothetically, or by consequence from his decree and foreknowledge, to any man. 2. His decree and foreknowledge conjoin the end and means; as if he had said [This man shall be saved by persevering faith, and shall persevere by fearing to fall away, and avoiding the occasions.] 3. Weak Christians have not the assurance of God's election, and therefore can gather no such consequence. 4. So few (if any known) did for many hundred years hold, that no initial right to salvation is lost; or that all true Christians, besides strong confirmed ones, did persevere; that it is not safe for doubting persons to lay their salvation on such a controversy, specially when it tendeth to abate necessary fear. The fathers of the first four hundred years thought, that some beginnings of justifying faith were loseable, as Adam's innocency was. And Calvin saith, *Semen qualecunque fidei perditur.*

2. For unto us was the gospel preached, as well as unto them; but the word preached did not pro,

it them, not being mixed with faith in them that heard it.

2. They heard God's word, and so do we: but it did not profit and save them, because they received it not by a sound, confirmed, practical belief.

3. For we which have believed, do enter into rest, as he said, As I have sworn in my wrath, if they shall enter into my rest: although the works were finished from the foundation of the world.

3. There is a rest promised to us believers, as well as the typical rest was to the Israelites, and the seventh day separated for a sabbath from the creation, which signified our better rest.

4, 5. For he spake in a certain place of the seventh *day* on this wise, And God did rest the seventh day from all his works. And in this place again, If they shall enter into my rest.

4, 5. The text tells us, that besides the sabbath-rest, there was another promised.

6. Seeing therefore it remaineth that some must enter therein, and they to whom it was first preached, entered not in because of unbelief: 7. Again, he limited a certain day, saying in David, To-day, after so long a time: as it is said, To-day, if ye will hear his voice, harden not your hearts. 8. For if Jesus had given them rest, then would he not afterward have spoken of another day.

6, 7, 8. It is plain then that some must enter into rest; and unbelief kept out them to whom it was then preached; and David, long after their entering into Canaan, sets them a day for their further entrance, which he would not have done, if Joshua's bringing them into Canaan had been the full obtainment of the promised rest; it followeth, that more than that was promised.

9. There remaineth therefore a rest to the people of God.

9. The great Sabbatism or rest then promised to the people of God is yet to come.

Note, This Sabbatism or rest, no doubt, is all the state of the church's deliverance and felicity by Christ incarnate and glorified, which in the first-fruits is all the grace which he giveth us on earth, but in the proper full performance, it is the state of glory.

I have before said why I assent not to Dr. Hammond, who maketh it to be the deliverance of Christians from persecution, and enjoying peaceable assemblies by the destruction of Jerusalem, as if this were the main sense of the text. 1. How little a thing was that in comparison of saving grace and glory? 2. Most of the Christians to whom Paul wrote, were to die before that, and so not to see and enjoy it. 3. The apostles themselves were not to see it and enjoy it. 4. Christianity continued, after that, a persecuted hated thing under the heathen, till above three hundred years, till Constantine's time, though with intermissions between the ten persecutions. Multitudes more were martyred by the heathens than by the Jews, who were in servitude themselves. 5. And if any apply it to the time after Constantine, the mercy indeed was unspeakable, but those that were here written to, were not to see it: and the voice that is reported to say, Hodie veneramus funditur in ecclesiam, hath by experience been so far credited, that we must not prefer the political grandeur and power, which shortly was set up, before the better rest of saints; while we think how much peaceable assemblies (which the Doctor calls that rest) through a great part of the Christian world, have been hindered and persecuted by violence, inquisitions, prisons, and the blood of many hundred thousands more than the Jews killed, by the canons, and executions of Papal greatness, and for its interest.

And it is incredible that to the suffering believers of that age, the Holy Ghost, comforting them with this great promise of a Sabbatism or rest, should not principally mean the great and glorious final rest.

10. For he that is entered into his rest, he also hath ceased from his own works, as God did *from his.*

10. For as God is said to rest and sanctify the sabbath, when he ended his six days work: so our sabbatism or rest must be a ceasing from our own works, that is, 1. From sin. 2. From those wilderness labours, or troublesome means, (as sorrow, fear, conflict, &c.) which are short of the end. And 3. From suffering.

Note, This verse shews that it is the heavenly rest, with the beginning of it by holiness, which is here meant, for church grandeur, and felt prosperity, have been the cherishers of our own works, and not the ceasing of them.

11. Let us labour therefore to enter into that rest, lest any man fall after the same example of unbelief.

11. Let it then be the care and diligence of heart and life, to attain that rest, and not to lose it by apostasy, but to take warning by these unbelievers.

Note, Is it more likely to be the destruction of the Jews, and freedom from this persecution, that should be meant, by an apostle that gloried in suffering, rather than that glory which is indeed the end of Christian care and labour?

12. For the word of God is quick, and powerful, and sharper than any two-edged sword, piercing even to the dividing asunder of soul

and spirit, and of the joints and marrow, and is a discerner of the thoughts and intents of the heart.

12. For though some may be deceived by a self-flattering heart, and seducing reasonings, and some think to conceal their sin, God's word is quick and powerful, and sharper than a two-edged sword, being fitted by the all-seeing God, to search hearts to the bottom, and to discover and separate evil from good, in the most secret thoughts and intents of the heart.

13. Neither is there any creature that is not manifest in his sight, but all things are naked and opened unto the eyes of him with whom we have to do.

13. It is (as the light from the sun) the word of that God, before whose eyes all hearts and things are in open view, as a dissected body; and such a searching light is his word with whom we have to do (or which we are speaking of.)

14. Seeing then that we have a great high priest, that is passed into the heavens, Jesus the Son of God, let us hold fast *our* profession.

14. Having then so great a high priest ascended into heaven (the Eternal Word, who sendeth forth his searching word) who is able to save, and help us, or destroy us, if we revolt; let us hold fast our professed faith and hope through all our trials.

15. For we have not an high priest which cannot be touched with the feeling of our infirmities: but was in all points tempted like as we are, *yet* without sin.

15. For we have not a high priest that is so far from our natures and case, as to be unconcerned, and void of compassion towards us, as much as we are towards the brutes; but one that was man, and tempted, and persecuted, as much as we, but without sin.

Note, That temptation may be without sin: it is not our sin merely to be tempted.

16. Let us therefore come boldly unto the throne of grace, that we may obtain mercy, and find grace to help in time of need.

16. Let us therefore so fully trust to the sufficiency and mercy of our high priest in the heavens, as to come (though with filial reverence, yet) with boldness in the belief of our acceptance, that we may obtain mercy, and find suitable and seasonable help in all our dangers and needs. (For God will yet be sought unto for all.)

CHAP. V.

FOR every high priest taken from among men, is ordained for men in things *pertaining* to God, that he may offer both gifts and sacrifices for sins.

1. For among men, the high priest, that is one of them, is a person consecrated to officiate for them Godwards, or in things of their concernment towards God, specially in offering gifts and sacrifices for sin.

2. Who can have compassion on the ignorant, and on them that are out of the way, for that he himself also is compassed with infirmity.

2. Who can the more compassionately offer for those sins of ignorance, error, and weakness, which the law alloweth sacrifice for, as being liable to infirmity himself.

3. And by reason hereof he ought, as for the people, so also for himself, to offer for sins.

3. And being liable to sin himself, he must offer for his own sin as well as others.

4. And no man taketh this honour unto himself, but he that is called of God, as *was* Aaron.

4. And so sacred an office was not to be invaded by usurpers, without God's call, for by it Aaron was made priest.

5. So that Christ glorified not himself to be made an high priest: but he that said unto him, Thou art my Son, to-day, have I begotten thee.

5. And Christ usurped not this honour, but God gave it him, who said, [Thou art my son, &c.]

6. As he saith also in another *place*, Thou *art* a priest for ever after the order of Melchisedec.

6. And Psal. cx. he saith, [Thou art, &c] Thou art a king and priest, as Melchisedec was, and that for ever.

7. Who in the days of his flesh, when he had offered up prayers and supplications, with strong crying and tears, unto him that was able to save him from death, and was heard in that he feared:

7. Who in the garden, and on the cross, when he had offered prayers with agony, sweating like water and blood, and cried out on the cross, [Why hast thou forsaken me?] to him that could have prevented his death, and all the pains which he feared not with any sinful distrust in God, nor

any opposition to his Father's will, but from that strong aversion to suffering and death, as such, which is a property of human nature, and did consist with a full submission to his Father's will, and consent to be a sacrifice for us); and he was heard in that he feared, though he must first suffer before he was raised.

8. Though he were a Son, yet learned he obedience, by the things which he suffered:

8. Though he was a Son, (and sinless) yet did he by his suffering, experimentally know and shew what it is to obey at the dearest rate, as absolutely subject to the will of God.

9. And being made perfect, he became the author of eternal salvation unto all them that obey him,

9. And being consummate, or made by the perfection of his performed part on earth, a perfect Redeemer, he is in the fulness of power in heaven become the author of eternal salvation, by intercession, pardon, communication of his Spirit, and by actual glorification, to all that hearken to him, and obey him.

Note, 1. That these texts do not intimate any privative imperfection in Christ's knowledge or obedience, or any qualification before; but a negative imperfection cannot be denied to his human nature. As Adam, new made, knew not all sensible objects remote, as he did when they came before his senses; so Christ in his infancy, and in the stable at Bethlehem, must not be supposed to know as a man, all that after he knew: yea himself saith after, that he knew not the day and hour, &c. so he had no sensible experimental knowledge of passive obedience before. 2. He is said to be made perfect in two respects. 1. In the perfect performance of his work on earth; as any undertaker is called perfect when he hath perfected his undertaking. 2. In his own perfection in heaven. 3. Obeying Christ is part of the condition of final justification and salvation.

10, 11. Called of God an high priest after the order of Melchisedec: Of whom we have many things to say, and hard to be uttered, seeing ye are dull of hearing.

10, 11. Of which priesthood of Christ, as compared to Melchisedec, we have much to say, which it is not easy to make intelligible by words, to those that are so unprepared, as you are, by ignorance, and a dull and slow understanding.

Note, 1. All great scripture truths be not equally easy to be understood.

2. It is the incapacity of hearers, through dulness and want of preparatory knowledge, which maketh scripture and teaching not understood.

3. It is no uncharitable dishonouring of professed Christians, but an undeniable thing, to say, that great numbers of them are dull hearers, and by ignorance incapable at the present of hard things.

12. For when for the time ye ought to be teachers, ye have need that one teach you again which be the first principles of the oracles of God, and are become such as have need of milk, and not of strong meat.

Note, 1. Men ought to grow in knowledge, according to the time they have to learn. 2. Many after long teaching are ignorant, and must be taught again the same things which they have long ago heard. 3. God's oracles have principles which must be first learnt.

13. For every one that useth milk is unskilful in the word of righteousness: for he is a babe. 14. But strong meat belongeth to them that are of full age; even those who by reason of use have their senses exercised to discern both good and evil.

13, 14. Milk is the diet for babes, and plain things for young and dull Christians; harder things will but hurt them: these are for them that by long study and practice have got a preparatory knowledge, and a habit of quick, clear, and sound discerning truth and error, good and evil.

Note, 1. People must be taught but according to their capacity. 2. Harder things in divinity must be taught them that have learned the easier and are fit for them. But by [hard things] is not meant unnecessary curiosities of human arts, nor unprofitable words, or trifling controversies: but, 1. A more clear, distinct, and satisfying knowledge of the evidence of the truth and sense of the essentials. 2. A more orderly knowledge of their method and mutual dependance as one system, that as in a table or scheme we may set each member in its proper place. 3. A more extensive knowledge of the useful consequences of the essentials and principles.

CHAP. VI.

THEREFORE, leaving the principles of the doctrine of Christ, let us go on unto perfection, not laying again the foundation of repentance from dead works, and of faith towards God, 2. Of the doctrine of baptism, and of laying on of hands, and of resurrection of the dead, and of eternal judgment.

1, 2. Therefore supposing the principles of Christian doctrine, I now pass over such discourse, and will go to lead you to some additional knowledge belonging to the more perfect; not now discoursing of these principles as to men that have not received them; I mean, 1. Repentance and conversion from a state of death, and from infidelity, and a wicked ungodly life. 2. A lively belief and trust in God the Father, Son, and

Holy Ghost. 3. The preparatory baptism of John and the baptism of Christ, which constituteth us professed Christians; what profession is pre-requisite in the adult, and what covenant it solemnizeth, what duties it binds us to, and what benefits it delivereth and sealeth. 4. The great gift to Christ's apostles and ministers of authoritative imposition of hands, by which the same Holy Ghost was given to others, and miracles wrought for the confirmation and propagation of the Christian faith. 5. The certainty of a resurrection, and future life, including the immortality of souls. 6. The final judgment which will sentence men to their everlasting state, and use them accordingly.

3. And this will we do, If God permit.

3. And so I will now pass to some additional further truths, by God's assistance.

4. For it is impossible for those who were once enlightened, and have tasted of the heavenly gift, and were made partakers of the Holy Ghost, 5. And have tasted the good word of God, and the powers of the world to come: 6. If they shall fall away, to renew them again unto repentance; seeing they crucify to themselves the Son of God afresh, and put *him* to an open shame.

4, 5, 6. I will not now go back to preach regeneration to you that profess to be already regenerate, though you are tempted to apostacy: for it is impossible for those that were illuminated to believe in Christ, and were baptized, and have not only heard of the signal gifts of the Holy Ghost from heaven, but have themselves had an experimental taste thereof, and been themselves partakers of the Holy Ghost, as well as seen his miraculous gifts in the church, and have had an inward experimental taste of the truth and goodness of the gospel, and the powerful preparations and hopes of the world to come: if they shall really lose all this, and fall from the belief of Christianity, to regenerate or renew these men again to saving repentance, seeing after believing Christ to be the Messiah, they are turned to take him for a deceiver and blasphemer, and consent to the pretended justness of his crucifixion, and so expose him by slander to the same reproach as his crucifiers did.

Note, 1. That the apostle speaketh of no other falling away, but to infidelity, denying Jesus to be the Christ. 2. That it is not temptations to unbelief, nor a degree of unbelief mixed with faith, or doubting, that he speaketh of, but a forsaking and renouncing Christ. 3. He speaketh not of the mere denial of the tongue in a passion or fear, but of the renouncing Christ by heart and tongue. 4. He speaketh not of the act of a man in madness, or melancholy, who is not himself, but of a man's deliberate act, that hath free use of reason. 5. He speaketh of no infidels, or total

apostates, but those that had themselves been partakers of the signal gifts of the Holy Ghost, and were convinced by experimental gust of the truth. 6. Therefore it must be noted, that not only truly holy persons, but abundance (if not the greatest part) that did but so believe as to imbody with the church, had then one sort or other of those miraculous, or rare gifts for confirmation of the gospel, which made Christ, Matt. vii. bring in the workers of iniquity as wonder-workers in his name; and Paul, Gal. iii. 3, 4, 5, appealeth to the quarrelsome Galatians, which way they had the Spirit and miracles. 7. That this must needs be the same blasphemy of the Holy Ghost, which Christ pronounceth unpardonable: for they who had not only seen the miracles, but had the Holy Ghost themselves for some such wonders, could not doubt of the matter of fact, whether such miracles were extant or not: so that there was no possible way for such to turn infidels, but by believing that this witness of the Spirit of miracles, was a false, deceiving testimony of Satan, and not God's testimony: and this was the blasphemy against the Spirit, Matt. xii. 8. That it is not all that is here meant, that such are not to be absolved by the church (which ought but to forejudge, as God will judge, as far as they can :) but that also such can never truly be regenerate and saved. 9. The reason is, because God giveth faith by means, and the witness of the Spirit's signal gifts is the last means for proof that God will give them; and they that after receiving this, reject it by such blasphemy, are forsaken by the grace of the Spirit, whom they blasphemously renounce. 10. Crucifying Christ afresh importeth charging him to deserve crucifixion, as guilty of the deceit and blasphemy for which he was crucified: so that none that believe not the Spirit's miracles in fact, are guilty of this sin, though they be infidels. Some ancients, and most Papists expound [impossible] by [difficult;] but I think ungroundedly. 11. Yea, the Jews that crucified him were not such as here are described: for they had not before believed and received the Holy Ghost: it is the worst reproach of Christ for a professed Christian to say, (I did believe in him, and had the Spirit myself, and saw and did signal works or miracles, and I found at last that he was but a deceiver, and all these gifts were the operations of evil spirits.)

7, 8. For the earth which drinketh in the rain that cometh oft upon it, and bringeth forth herbs meet for them by whom it is dressed, receiveth blessing from God. 8. But that which beareth thorns and briars, *is* rejected, and *is* nigh unto cursing, whose end *is* to be burned.

7, 8. For as the earth is blessed, or justly praised, which bringeth fruit when it is watered and manured; but that is called cursed, and bad, whose fruit must be for the fire, which bringeth forth but thorns and briars: so God will bless and reward them who fruitfully answer the means which he useth in them; but will curse and burn those who, after the greatest means, and experimental partaking of the signal gifts of the Spirit, shall turn to reproach and blaspheme him whom they believed in.

9. But beloved, we are persuaded better things of you, and things that accompany salvation, though we thus speak.

9. But though, in the dangerous times, and temptations to apostacy, I think meet to tell you the dreadful case of such, for your safety, do not interpret it, as though I thought this is, or would be your case: we have reason to hope better of you, that you have the grace which will bring you to salvation.

10. For God *is* not unrighteous to forget your work and labour of love, which ye have shewed toward his name, in that ye have ministered to the saints, and do minister.

10. For God, who is our most righteous governor, even in this life distributeth rewards and penalties in justice: and as, in justice, he forsaketh the foresaid apostates, who scorn his mercy, so he will reward your faithful use of his grace with more grace, and will not forsake you who have shewed so much fidelity to his name, and charity to his saints.

Note, That the additional grace, which is necessary to perseverance, is given (oft) by way of reward for former fidelity, and not merely without such respects.

11. And we desire that every one of you do shew the same diligence, to the full assurance of hope unto the end;

11. Therefore, seeing this is God's ordinary way, to reward well used grace with more, I desire that you will hold on in the same diligence, till you reach to the consummation, or full assurance of your hope of perseverance and salvation, which every young beginner did not attain.

12. That ye be not slothful, but followers of them, who through faith and patience inherit the promises.

12. And that tired, weary sluggishness make you not desist, and lose your reward; but that in unwearied diligence to the end, you follow them, who, through faith and enduring patience, have won the prize, and possess the promised felicity.

13, 14. For when God made promise to Abraham, because he could swear by no greater, he sware by himself, Saying, Surely, blessing I will bless thee, and multiplying, I will multiply thee. **15.** And so after he had patiently endured, he obtained the promise.

13, 14, 15. So God, who sware by himself to Abraham (having no greater to swear by), confirmed his promises of the multiplication of his seed, which yet Abraham lived not to see fulfilled; but he patiently waited and died in faith, and all the promises were fulfilled in due time.

16. For men verily swear by the greater, and an oath for confirmation *is* to them an end of all strife.

16. For men use, by oath, to appeal to him that can discern and revenge perfidiousness; and when other evidences fail, they end their strifes by the confirmation of an oath.

17. Wherein God, willing more abundantly to shew unto the heirs of promise the immutability of his counsel, confirmed it by an oath:

17. And God knowing our weakness of faith, to confirm the faithful, who are the heirs of his promised happiness, of the truth and immutability of his decrees, confirmed his word to us by his oath, that we might be put quite out of doubt.

18. That by two immutable things, in which it *was* impossible for God to lie, we might have a strong consolation, who have fled for refuge to lay hold upon the hope set before us.

18. That so, by his word and his oath, which are both immutable, and therefore infallible security, seeing it is impossible for God to lie, we who are fled for refuge from guilt, and sin, and danger, and misery, to lay hold on the proposed hope of everlasting life, might have well-grounded and strong consolation, and not be shaken by any doubts of the fidelity or promises of God.

Note, God would have us to have strong consolation in our faith and hope.

19. Which *hope* we have as an anchor of the soul, both sure and steadfast, and which entereth into that within the vail.

19. Though the things of this life are much uncertain, this hope, which is our support and comfort, is founded on firm and steadfast security; and is fetched, by faith, from the most holy and invisible things, which the vail of mortality yet hideth from our sight.

20. Whither the forerunner *is* for us entered, *even* Jesus, made an high priest for ever after the order of Melchisedec.

20. Into which invisible heavenly glory, Christ is entered, not only for himself, and his own consummation, but as a forerunner for us, to intercede, and prepare felicity for us, and from his fulness of power, to send down his Spirit, and consummate all that concerneth our salvation, as a royal priest, typified by Melchisedec.

CHAP. VII.

FOR this Melchisedec king of Salem, priest of the most high God, who met Abraham returning from the slaughter of the kings, and blessed him: 2. To whom also Abraham gave a tenth part of all: first, being by interpretation king of righteousness, and after that also king of Salem, which is king of peace:

1, 2. This Melchisedec, to whom Abraham gave the tenths of the spoils, was king of righteousness by the signification of his name; and king of peace, interpreting his place: which Christ is eminently, whom he typified.

3. Without father, without mother, without descent: having neither beginning of days, nor end of life: but made like unto the Son of God, abideth a priest continually.

3. The history of him maketh no mention of his father, or mother, or descent, nor of his birth or beginning, nor of his death or end; but describeth him like a continuing priest, and a type of the Son of God, who abideth a priest continually.

Note, The Jews think he was Shem, whose beginning was not seen by the new world, nor his end by the old, nor his death mentioned: but this is a presumption: had it been good for us to know more of him, God would have told us more.

4. Now consider how great this man was, unto whom even the patriarch Abraham gave the tenth of the spoils.

4. When Abraham, from whom the Levitical priesthood, and the peculiar seed, sprung, gave him the tenths of all the spoils, it tells us how great a man Melchisedec was.

5. And verily they that are of the sons of Levi, who receive the office of the priesthood, have a commandment to take tithes of the people, according to the law, that is, of their brethren, though they come out of the loins of Abraham.

5. The law allowed Aaron, and the other priests, to take tithes of their brethren that sprung from Abraham.

6. But he whose descent is not counted from them, received tithes of Abraham, and blessed him that had the promises. 7. And without all contradiction, the less is blessed of the better.

6, 7. But Melchisedec received tithes of Abraham, who was none of his people; and blessed him who had from God the promise of a peculiar offspring: which is a certain sign that he was greater than Abraham: and so is Christ greater than the Jewish priests.

8. And here men that die receive tithes: but there he receiveth them, of whom it is witnessed that he liveth. 9. And as I may so say, Levi also, who receiveth tithes, payed tithes in Abraham. 10. For he was yet in the loins of his father, when Melchisedec met him.

8, 9, 10. And here it is mortal men that take tithes; but Melchisedec is mentioned as if he had not died: and Levi, who received tithes, paid them, then being in Abraham's loins.

11. If therefore perfection were by the Levitical priesthood (for under it the people received the law) what further need was there that another priest should rise after the order of Melchisedec, and not be called after the order of Aaron?

11. This proveth that the Levitical priesthood (and consequently the law) was not perfect, nor gave perfection: else what need had there been of another more excellent royal priesthood which was promised.

12. For the priesthood being changed, there is made of necessity a change also of the law.

12. And if there must be a more excellent priesthood than the legal, there must needs be some more excellent laws, appointing them their work: for the old priesthood had their work prescribed them by the law of Moses.

Note, That they who deny Christ to be a lawgiver, deny his royal priesthood, and deny him to be Christ.

13. For he of whom these things are spoken, pertaineth to another tribe, of which no man gave attendance at the altar. 14. For it is evident that our Lord sprang out of Judah, of which tribe Moses spake nothing concerning priesthood.

13, 14. And the translating the priesthood to Judah, the ruling tribe, of which Christ was, proveth the change of the law.

15. And it is yet far more evident; for that after the similitude of Melchisedec there ariseth another priest. 16. Who is made not after the law of a carnal commandment,

ment, but after the power of an endless life.

15, 16. And it is yet more evident, that there must be a higher priesthood than Aaron's, because he must be made as Melchisedec, not by lineal succession, according to the law of Moses, but with reference to a state of immortality, as to its rise and end.

17. For he testifieth, *Thou art a priest for ever after the order of Melchisedec.* 18. For there is verily a disannulling of the commandment going before, for the weakness and unprofitableness thereof.

17, 18. And this express testimony of another sort of priesthood sheweth, that the law, which they were to execute, was to cease, as weak, insufficient, and unprofitable.

Note, Ques. Is not the gospel priesthood then, in conformity to Christ, to be kingly, and above all kings, under Christ the king? or kings and priests to be the same? Ans. 1. Let them here on earth follow Christ in his humiliation, who said, [My kingdom is not of this world;] and then when they come to him in heaven, they shall reign as kings. 2. Our uncertain collections are not so sure a way to know Christ's will, as his own words; who hath plainly forbidden secular dominion to his ministers, and given them a far other description and canon. 3. But by the use of the church keys, they have the government of church communion; which, as it hath a nearer relation to the heavenly kingdom, is therein nobler than secular power.

19. For the law made nothing perfect, but the bringing in of a better hope *did;* by the which we draw nigh unto God.

19. For the law of Moses did all as an imperfect thing, which was not, of itself, to make man, or his service, perfect, or his hopes and comforts, but to lead him towards a better revelation; which bringeth a fuller notice of pardon and grace, life and immortality, advanceth us nearer to God, and giveth us more bold and comfortable access to him, in order to our heavenly fruition.

20, 21. And in as much as not without an oath, *he was made priest,* (For those *priests* were made without an oath; but this with an oath, by him that said unto him, The Lord sware, and will not repent, Thou art a priest for ever after the order of Melchisedec;)

20, 21. And this change God sweareth to, which was not done by Aaron's priesthood: which sheweth its certainty and immutability.

22. By so much was Jesus made a surety of a better testament.

22. Note, 1. The word here translated [testament] signifieth, God's statute-law, proposed to us for our covenant-consent and obedience, and promising us grace and glory; and signifieth the same thing as [the law of grace.] And not a mere absolute promise, without precepts, conditions or penalty.

2. The word translated [surety] signifieth an interceding administrator and mediator, giving man assurance of the will of God (as Moses did in delivering the law) and consenting to receive God's terms and promises in the nature of man, and to perform his own part and undertaking, for the gathering and glorifying his church thereby: but not that he undertook that all that he mediated for, should do all that is their duty.

23. And they truly were many priests, because they were not suffered to continue, by reason of death. 24. But this man, because he continueth ever, hath an unchangeable priesthood.

23, 24. And so the Levitical priesthood was in many successively, because they were mortal: but Christ living for ever, is only one and the same, and there is no other.

Note, Therefore Christ hath no mortal Vicar, to be an universal high priest.

25. Wherefore he is able also to save them to the uttermost, that come unto God by him, seeing he ever liveth to make intercession for them.

25. And this is the great comfort of believers, that he is able to save us in all extremities, even at death, and to eternity of blessedness, seeing he ever liveth, by his intercession, to finish his saving work for all that come by him to God. Friends die, and all worldly helps may fail, but Christ will never die.

26. For such an high priest became us, who *is* holy, harmless, undefiled, separate from sinners, and made higher than the heavens.

26. For our condition required such an high priest, who is holy, free from doing ill, or suffering any more from any enemies, clean from all sin of his own, and is separated from the condition of sinful man that dwells on earth.

27. Who needeth not daily, as those high priests, to offer up sacrifice, first for his own sin, and then for the people's: for this he did once, when he offered up himself.

27. Who had no sin of his own, as the high priests had; and therefore, for his own sin he needed not to offer any sacrifice, though he did it to perfect his undertaken work for us. Nor needed he offer often for the sins of the people; for his once offering up himself, was a sufficient expiatory sacrifice.

28. For the law maketh men high priests, which have infirmity; but the word of the oath, which was since the law, *maketh* the Son, who is consecrated for evermore.

28. For the law had none to make high priests of, but mortal sinners: but the word of the oath, Psal. cx. which was since the making of the law, maketh the Son of God high priest, who is holy, sinless, immortal, and consecrated to an everlasting priesthood.

CHAP. VIII.

NOW of the things which we have spoken, *this is* the sum: we have such an high priest, who is set on the right hand of the throne of the majesty in the heavens: 2. A minister of the sanctuary, and of the true tabernacle, which the Lord pitched, and not man.

1. The sum of all that is said is this, We have such an high priest, who is advanced to the highest honour and power in glory, called God's throne of majesty in the heavens. As man, a minister indeed, or the prime administrator; but it is of the true and heavenly sanctuary and tabernacle, not like that which was made by man, but which the Lord hath made for the glorifying of himself in his glorified saints with Christ, where we shall in presence worship him for ever.

3. For every high priest is ordained to offer gifts and sacrifices: wherefore it is of necessity that this man have somewhat also to offer.

3. And he were no high priest, if he had nothing as gift or sacrifice to offer.

4. For if he were on earth, he should not be a priest, seeing that there are priests that offer gifts according to the law.

4. And if he were on earth, he should not be a priest according to the law, because there are such already, and it was entailed on the line of Aaron: (and Christ's sacrifice when he was on earth, was not according to the law, but superlegal.)

5. Who serve unto the example and shadow of heavenly things, as Moses was admonished of God, when he was about to make the tabernacle. For see (saith he) that thou make all things according to the pattern shewed to thee in the mount.

5. And the Levitical priesthood on earth, was made to perform those administrations, which are but shadows of the heavenly things, having some notifying and instructing resemblance to them as figurative; which God darkly intimated to Moses when he charged him to make the tabernacle in the wilderness according to the pattern which he had seen in the mount. So that the earthly tabernacle and worship is but a figure or shadow of the heavenly.

6. But now hath he obtained a more excellent ministry, by how much also he is the mediator of a better covenant, which was established upon better promises.

6. But Christ's priestly ministry is more excellent, as he is the mediator of a better covenant, than the mere law of Moses was. (Though the promise that went before and with the law, was an obscure gospel.) It is better, as having better promises; even clearer and fuller, and more confirmed by God's oath, and seal, and earnest. It hath promises of fuller pardon, greater grace and privileges, and surer and greater glory.

Note, That both the Mosaical and the Christian are named in scripture, both a law and a covenant; for they have the same parts, viz. precepts, promises, and threats, and obedience must be consented to. As proposed by God, with his antecedent mercy, it is a law, and a proposed covenant. As consented to by man, it is a law accepted by subjects, and a mutual covenant. See Grotius' preface to annotations on the New Testament of the names.

7. For if that first *covenant* had been faultless, then should no place have been sought for the second.

7. For if the first covenant had been perfect, God would not have made the second better.

Note, 1. That it is not sinful faultiness, but such imperfection as the beginnings of art and nature have, compared with the perfection that is here meant.

2. It is not here called, the first covenant, as if no other had gone before it; for there was a former with Adam, Noah, Abraham: but as it is the first of these two. And it was a covenant of peculiarity, distinct from the common one, and the promise.

8. For finding fault with them, he saith, Behold, the days come (saith the Lord) when I will make a new covenant with the house of Israel, and the house of Judah: 9. Not according to the covenant that I made with their fathers, in the day when I took them by the hand to lead them out of the land of Egypt, because they continued not in my covenant, and I regarded them not, saith the Lord.

8, 9. For he intimateth the defect of the Mosaical covenant, when he saith, [Behold, the days come, &c. I will make with them a new covenant,] of greater and surer mercy; for the former they quickly forsook, and I forsook them.

10. For this is the covenant that I will make with the house of Israel after those days, saith the Lord, I will put my laws into their mind, and write them in their hearts: and I will be to them a God, and they shall be to me a people.

10. But this is my new covenant which I will make with all Abraham's believing seed: I will sanctify them by my Spirit, and thereby give them a saving knowledge and love of all my necessary laws, and their duties, as if they were written in their minds and hearts; and I will be to them a God (which is their all), and will love and cherish them as my peculiar people.

Note, That this promise is not made to Israel, as a peculiar, political body (for their policy was to be dissolved); but as a part of the Catholic church, which are Abraham's believing seed. 2. Therefore it being supposed that it is to believers that this promise is made, it followeth, that it is a promise on condition of preceding faith: as vocation giveth faith, which is the condition of consequent justification and sanctification. Though all be of grace, God's wisdom maketh the condition a means to introduce the rest.

11. And they shall not teach every man his neighbour, and every man his brother, saying, Know the Lord: for all shall know me, from the least to the greatest.

11. And it shall not be doubtful to them, whether the Lord or Baal be the true God, as it hath been with this unsteadfast people, who have so long lived in idolatry: for all the church of believers, from the least to the greatest, shall know and own me to be their God, and not need to be again taught it, as an unknown thing.

Note, That this speaketh not against the necessity of human teaching: for it is by such teaching that God is supposed to give them the knowledge of himself. Nor doth it mean that it shall be needless to teach the best to know God better; for to know him is the sum and perfection of knowledge, and it is life eternal. But the meaning is, That it shall not be an unknown thing, that the Lord is our God.

12. For I will be merciful to their unrighteousness, and their sins and their iniquities will I remember no more.

12. For the greatness of my mercy shall forgive all the sins of their unconverted state, and not charge them upon them, to their destruction, and all the infirmities of their regenerate state.

Note, That this promise of justification, as well as the former of sanctification, supposeth them to be believers in order of nature first, as the condition.

13. In that he saith, A new covenant, he hath made the first old. Now that which decayeth and waxeth old, is ready to vanish away.

13. This term of a new covenant implieth, that the old one must then be abolished: and the time is come.

CHAP. IX.

THEN verily the first *covenant*, had also ordinances of divine service, and a worldly sanctuary.

1. The Mosaical covenant had its proper ordinances of service to God, and an earthly, temporary tabernacle.

2. For there was a tabernacle made, the first wherein *was* the candlestick, and the table, and the shewbread, which is called the sanctuary.

3. And after the second vail, the tabernacle which is called the holiest of all.

2, 3. This made tabernacle had two parts: is the first called the sanctuary, was the candlestick, &c. And within the second vail was the holiest of all.

Note, Some out of Philo say, that the tabernacle (and the temple after) was made as an image, or figure of the world, and therefore called worldly: the outward part figuring the lower world, in which was the candlestick with six branches; and one in the midst, signifying the planets; and twelve loaves on the table, signifying the fruits of the earth: the inmost signifying the highest heavens. But it is presumptuous to trust our wit too far in feigning divine significations: and it is groundless hence to gather, that it was called a worldly sanctuary.

4, 5. Which had the golden censer, and the ark of the covenant overlaid round about with gold, wherein *was* the golden pot that had manna, and Aaron's rod that budded, and the tables of the covenant; and over it the cherubims of glory shadowing the mercy-seat; of which we cannot now speak particularly.

4, 5. In it was the golden censer, for incense brought when the priest went in; and the ark overlaid with gold, in which, or near it, was the pot of manna, and Aaron's rod, and in it the table of the commandments of the covenant; and over it, the images of angelical cherubims, shewing God's glory, when it appeared to men; which also shadowed the covering of the mercy-seat.

6. Now when these things were thus ordained, the priests went al-

ways into the first tabernacle, accomplishing the service *of God*. 7. But into the second *went* the high priest alone once every year, not without blood, which he offered for himself, and for the errors of the people.

6, 7. Into the first part of this tabernacle, the priests went to perform the ordinary service: but into the second went only the high priest once a year, but not without the blood of calves and goats, which he offered for such sins of himself and the people, as were expiable.

8. The Holy Ghost this signifying, that the way into the holiest of all, was not yet made manifest, while as the first tabernacle was yet standing:

8. By this the Holy Ghost signified, that under that law, or tabernacle state, the access of sinners to God, for assured acceptance here, and glory hereafter, was not yet clearly, fully, and with satisfying assurance revealed, nor by that law, as such, conferred: for it was reserved to the coming of the Messiah: (though the promise, or law of grace, saved men then.)

9. Which *was* a figure for the time then present, in which were offered both gifts and sacrifices, that could not make him that did the service perfect, as pertaining to the conscience.

9. Which figuratively signified the time then (or now) present, when the gifts and sacrifices were offered, which could not suffice to perfect the acceptance of the offerer, with God, or to cleanse him from the conscience and guilt of sin.

10. *Which stood* only in meats and drinks, and divers washings, and carnal ordinances imposed on *them* until the time of reformation.

10. I speak not of the laws of nature, of godliness, charity, justice, and sobriety, which are common to the Jews, with us, and other people, but of the positive institutions of bodily service to God, proper to Moses' law. And these laws, in such outwards as the body performeth, called rights and ceremonies, meats, drinks, washings, which God indeed imposed on them, as a material part of their obedience; but it was as suited to their carnality and minority, till the Messiah's reformation set up a better law and worship.

11. But Christ being come an high priest of good things to come, by a greater and more perfect tabernacle, not made with hands, that is to say, not of this building:

11. But Christ is come a high priest of the future felicity, promised in the gospel, even to procure us grace and glory, officiating in a greater and more perfect tabernacle, even his body, now glorified in heaven (having done his preparatory work on earth) which was not built as tabernacles are on earth.

12. Neither by the blood of goats and calves: but by his own blood he entered in once into the holy place, having obtained eternal redemption *for us*.

12. And not as the Levitical priests, by the blood of goats and calves, offered for expiation; but by obedient and voluntary offering his own blood a sacrifice for the sins of the world, he obtained his entrance into the state of glorious exaltation, there to intercede for us, and rule us, having here, by his merit and sacrifice, purchased eternal redemption for us, which thence he will bestow.

13. For if the blood of bulls, and of goats, and the ashes of an heifer sprinkling the unclean, sanctifieth to the purifying of the flesh:

13. If these be by divine institution effectual against corporal legal uncleanness, by a ceremonial sanctification, the figure of the spiritual.

14. How much more shall the blood of Christ, who through the eternal Spirit, offered himself without spot to God, purge your consciences from dead works to serve the living God?

14. Most certainly then shall the blood of Christ, who by the eternal Spirit offered himself, soul and body, a spotless sacrifice to God the sovereign righteous Judge, to cleanse soul and conscience from the power and guilt of dead works (which signify a death in sin, and tend to death for sin,) to serve the living God, who will accept us to an everlasting life.

Note, By the Eternal Spirit, by which Christ offered himself, some expositors understand Christ's immortal soul voluntarily resigning his life. 2. Others understand the Holy Ghost, the third person in the Trinity, by whom Christ is said to be conceived, and to do his miracles. 3. Others understand his own divine nature, as the second person. It is hard to be sure which is meant; but it is of no great moment, seeing it is certain that indeed he did it by all these three. There is a fourth opinion of some that understand it of a prime superangelical nature of Christ, which they think, by eternal emanation, cometh from the deity united to it, which they make a middle third nature in Christ; and in which they suppose it is that, as a creature, he is advanced above all angels; because they take angels and men to be specie distinct; and that if human nature must be set above angels, in itself, it must thereby change its species, and be no more human.

But to be wise to sobriety in such mysteries is safe, and not to presume.

15. And for this cause he is the mediator of the New Testament, that by means of death, for the redemption of the transgressions *that were* under the first Testament, they which are called might receive the promise of eternal inheritance.

15. And for this cause Christ became Mediator between God and man, to procure, seal, and promulgate the new covenant, or law of grace, that his death doing that which no other sacrifice could do in expiation of the Jews' sins, committed under the Mosaical covenant, (as well as of the rest of the world) they which are by his call made sound believers, might by promise be secured of the eternal inheritance, and possessed of it in due time.

16. For where a testament *is*, there must also of necessity be the death of the testator. 17. For a testament *is* of force after men are dead: otherwise it is of no strength at all whilst the testator liveth.

16, 17. And Christ being by his sponsion to be a sacrifice, his donation doth pre-suppose his purchase; and thence his covenant hath also the nature of a testament, which supposeth the death of the testator, and is not of efficacy till then, to give full right to what he bequeatheth.

Note, That the eminent evangelical kingdom of the Mediator, in its last full edition, called the kingdom of Christ, and of heaven, distinct from the obscure state of promise before Christ's incarnation, began at Christ's resurrection, ascension, and sending of the eminent gift of the Holy Ghost, and was but as an embryo before.

18. Whereupon, neither the first *testament* was dedicated without blood.

18. Therefore the first as figurative of the second, was consecrated and sealed in blood.

19. For when Moses had spoken every precept to all the people, according to the law, he took the blood of calves and of goats, with water and scarlet-wool, and hyssop, and sprinkled both the book and all the people, 20. Saying, This *is* the blood of the testament which God hath enjoined unto you. 21. Moreover, he sprinkled likewise with blood both the tabernacle, and all the vessels of the ministry. 22. And almost all things are by the law purged with blood; and without shedding of blood is no remission.

19—22. Note, 1. God purposely instituted all these bloody purifications to prefigure Christ. 2. The custom of sacrificing from the fall, must arise from divine institution, and not without it from natural invention, as some now affirm. And no doubt but it is propagated among all idolaters through the world; 1. By tradition from Adam; 2. Corrupted by devils, who would be worshipped as God, and to that end promote the imitation of God; 3. The Papists sprinkling of holy water, is such another corrupt imitation, setting up their ceremony instead of God's, which Christ abolished.

23. *It was* therefore necessary that the patterns of things in the heavens should be purified with these, but the heavenly things themselves with better sacrifices than these.

23. These ceremonies being ordained to prefigure and notify things that are in heaven, and belong to heaven, it was meet that such blood should be the purifying ceremony: but the heavenly things themselves must be purchased, and the souls fitted for it purified, and the covenant consecrated by a more precious sacrifice, even the blood of the Lamb of God, who taketh away the sins of the world.

24. For Christ is not entered into the holy places made with hands, *which are* the figures of the true, but into heaven itself: now to appear in the presence of God for us.

24. For it was not to officiate in a tabernacle made by man, that Christ became our high priest, but (though his sacrifice was offered on earth) it was to officiate by continued intercession for us in the heavens, in the presence of God's glory, of which the other was but a type.

25. Nor yet that he should offer himself often, as the high priest entereth into the holy place, every year with blood of others. 26. For then must he often have suffered since the foundation of the world: but now once in the end of the world, hath he appeared to put away sin by the sacrifice of himself.

25, 26. Note, 1. Christ's once offering was sufficient: it may oft be commemorated, but only once done. 2. It is unspeakable joy to believers, that Christ is for us, as our high priest, entered into heaven. For he hath promised, that we shall be with him where he is. And where else now shall we desire to be? 3. The days of Christ here, were the declining latter part of the world, called the end, as fifty or sixty years old is the end; that is, the latter part of man's life. How near then is it now to an end, 1666 years after.

27, 28. And as it is appointed unto men once to die, but after this the judgment: so Christ was once offered to bear the sins of many, and unto them that look for him shall he appear the second time, without sin, unto salvation.

27, 28. And as it is with the common state of man on earth, who must all once die, and then be doomed to their endless state; so Christ was once to die as a sacrifice for the sins of many; and to them that wait for him in the prepared state of faith, hope, obedience, and patience, he shall appear again, but not any more to bear the punishment of their sins, but to justify them publicly, and take them to his glory.

CHAP. X.

FOR the law having a shadow of good things to come, *and* not the very image of the things, can never with those sacrifices which they offered year by year continually, make the comers thereunto perfect.

1. For the law having but in its ceremonies a shadow of the great heavenly blessings of the gospel, and not the clear image (or draught, or map) of the things themselves, doth shew by the frequent yearly iteration of those sacrifices, that it doth not perfect the sacrificers.

2. For then would they not have ceased to be offered: because that the worshippers once purged, should have had no more conscience of sins.

2. For then they would have ceased to be offered, because the worshippers once pardoned and cleansed, should have no more conscience of guilt, or remaining pravity.

3. But in those sacrifices *there is* a remembrance again *made* of sins. every year. 4. For it is not possible that the blood of bulls and of goats, should take away sins.

3, 4. Note, 1. This text doth not deny, that the faithful Jews were then forgiven, nor that the law conduced to it, as used in subordination to the antecedent promise and law of grace: but without this promise, the law could not do it. 2. Nor doth this infer, that we may not mention, lament, and beg pardon for our old sins, while we live on earth; nor that renewed sins have no need of a renewed pardon; but no need of a new sacrifice.

5. Wherefore when he cometh into the world, he saith, Sacrifice and offering thou wouldest not, but a body hast thou prepared me. 6. In burnt-offerings, and sacrifices for sin thou hast had no pleasure: 7. Then said I, Lo, I come (in the volume of the book it is written of me) to do thy will, O God. 8. Above, when he said, sacrifice, and offering, and burnt-offerings, and offering for sin thou wouldest not, neither hadst pleasure *therein*, which are offered by the law; 9. Then said he, Lo, I come to do thy will, (O God) he taketh away the first, that he may establish the second.

5, 6, &c. David, as a prophet, personating Christ, saith, &c. taking down sacrifices as insufficient, and introducing Christ's obedient sacrifice of himself.

10. By the which will we are sanctified through the offering of the body of Jesus Christ once *for all*.

10. And by this decree of God, giving us a Saviour to be a sacrifice for our sins, we are, (as far as belongeth to the expiating sacrifice,) made a holy people unto God, the sins of the faithful, by this price being pardoned, and reconciliation made.

11. And every priest standeth daily ministering and offering oftentimes the same sacrifices, which can never take away sins.

11. And the priests must be still sacrificing the same things, never finishing the expiation.

12. But this man, after he had offered one sacrifice for sins, for ever sat down on the right hand of God: 13. From henceforth expecting till his enemies be made his footstool.

12, 13. But Christ having offered but one sacrifice for sins, as sufficient, for ever sat down in the possession of glory, and universal dominion in the heavens, on the right hand of God, where he will reign, till he hath subdued all his enemies, even all that opposeth the perfecting of his work of the salvation and glory of his church.

14. For by one offering he hath perfected for ever them that are sanctified.

14. For all the faithful and sanctified are by that one offering, as a sufficient expiatory sacrifice, freed from all guilt and sin now initially, and shall be perfectly without any other expiatory sacrifice, for ever.

15, 16, 17. *Whereof* the Holy Ghost also is a witness to us: for after that he had said before, This is the covenant that I will make with them after those days, saith the Lord, I will put my laws into their hearts, and in their minds will I write them: and their sins and iniquities will I remember no more. 18. Now, where remission of these is, *there is* no more offering for sin.

15, 16, &c. Note here, 1. That when the price is given and taken, and a free act of oblivion made on the bare condition of thankful acceptance, the crime is said to be pardoned in the common custom of speech, it being done as far as belongeth to the satisfier and the rector, as such, though yet the refuser, be all actually unpardoned: for a conditional gift puts nothing in act, till the condition be performed. 2. That here in the promise, pardon is not in time before renovation, and so not actually of any infidels, or unconverted, though elected thereto. 3. That even the pardon of the sanctified is but such as excludeth any more sacrifice, but not any more faith, repentance, watching, praying, &c.

19. Having therefore, brethren, boldness to enter into the holiest by the blood of Jesus, 20. By a new and living way which he hath consecrated for us, through the vail, that is to say, his flesh; 21. And having an high priest over the house of God:

19, 20, 21. And now I come to the use of all that I have said in all the foregoing doctrine: we are not now deterred from access to God by unexpiated guilt, but may come to him as a Father, with comfortable, reverent boldness and hope, as reconciled by Christ; even in confidence of the merit of his righteousness and sacrifice, which is as a new and still effectual living way, through the vail of his flesh consecrated for us: and we have now in the heavens a glorified high priest, who is head over all things to his church, which is the house of God, and ever liveth to do all for us in heaven, which belongeth to a perfect high priest.

22. Let us draw near with a true heart, in full assurance of faith, having our hearts sprinkled from an evil conscience,' and our bodies washed with pure water.

22. Let us therefore draw near to God in holy worship, and heavenly desires and aspirings, with a heart that is sound, sincere, and true to Christ, and our convictions, and abounding with full belief and trust in Christ, for all that he hath promised, having our hearts cleansed by Christ's blood (which is the sprinkling figured under the law) from the conscience of guilt, and the love and power of sin, and our bodily practice purified from uncleanness, (typified by the washings under the law, and fœderally signified by our baptism.)

23. Let us hold fast the profession of our faith without wavering; (for he *is* faithful that promised.)

23. Let us against all subtle, deceitful adversaries, and against all cruel persecutors, under all trials and sufferings, hold fast both our hope and faith, and the open profession of it; for he is faithful who hath promised us the endless felicity, which will pay for all, and exceed all our expectations.

24. And let us consider one another, to provoke unto love, and to good works.

24. Let none of us live merely to ourselves, but set ourselves with studious diligence to promote the sanctity and salvation of each other, which is not done by vain janglings and faction, but by provoking one another to love, and to good works, and each to be a common blessing in his place, by profiting others.

25. Not forsaking the assembling of ourselves together, as the manner of some is: but exhorting *one another*, and so much the more, as ye see the day approaching.

25. Not forsaking either the more full church-assemblies, or any Christian converse and communion, by which ye may excite and edify one another; as some do out of cowardly fear of suffering, and some through selfishness and want of brotherly love, and through coldness in religion. And the more resolved should you be in this, because the time of suffering is short, and the day of your deliverance draws on, and cannot be far off.

Note, Ques. 1. What if the rulers forbid church-assemblies, or at least inferior edifying converse? Ans. So they did for three hundred years, when yet Christians used it by command from Christ. And Christian princes (as is said heretofore) must do more good, but are not authorized to do more mischief, and forbid good, than heathens. But yet, though we may not statedly forbear the duties of piety and charity, (no more than Daniel did praying, or the old Christians preaching and meeting) when we can perform them; 1. We may forbear this or that particular meeting or action, when it would do more hurt than good; 2. And when imprisonment or banishment make it impossible, it can be no duty.

Ques. 2. Who be they that must exhort one another? Ans. Not every one that hath a proud self-conceit, or masterly talkative disease, may needlessly gather assemblies to ease his stomach, on pretence of duty: but the truly qualified and called pastors must exhort in church-assemblies, by office, and occasionally such other well-qualified men as he shall there call forth or allow: and in inferior occasional converse or meetings, such qualified persons as have best ability and opportunities to do good: even as overseers by office relieve the poor, but every man that can, must do

CHAP. X. HEBREWS. 535

it in charity. And as the physician by calling must heal the sick and wounded; but any in charity may offer such help as others need, and he is able, not usurping the function of the physician.

26. For if we sin wilfully after that we have received the knowledge of the truth, there remaineth no more sacrifice for sins, 27. But a certain fearful looking for of judgment, and fiery indignation, which shall devour the adversaries.

26, 27. And the dreadful case of apostates must deter you: for if you wilfully forsake Christ, and Christianity, after you have received the knowledge of the truth of it, by the Spirit, and all those miraculous evidences by which it hath prevailed hitherto, you must never look for another Saviour, nor that Christ should come again to be sacrificed for you: reject him now, and nothing remaineth, but a dreadful expectation of his vindictive judgment, when his enemies that refused his reign, shall be brought forth to destruction, Luke xix. 27.

Note, Of this see before on chap. vi. what this sin is.

28. He that despised Moses' law, died without mercy, under two or three witnesses. 29. Of how much sorer punishment, suppose ye, shall he be thought worthy, who hath trodden under foot the Son of God, and hath counted the blood of the covenant wherewith he was sanctified, an unholy thing, and hath done despite unto the Spirit of grace?

28, 29. Capital, presumptuous sins, and contempt, were punished by death, by Moses' law. And as Christ bringeth greater mercy, the contempt of him deserveth far greater punishment, when men, by renouncing Christianity, tread under foot the Son of God, by calling him a crucified deceiver, and count the blood of the covenant (which was shed to sanctify them, and reconcile them to God) which they professing to believe, were joined with the saints, to be the blood of a justly crucified malefactor, and a profane thing, and thus do despite also to the Spirit of grace, which is Christ's witness on earth, and by the testimony of whose miraculous and sanctifying gifts they once professed to believe in Christ, and receive his doctrine: and now they will reproach these gifts and testimonies of the Spirit, as delusions, and not of the Spirit of God.

Note, The falseness of their doctrine, who say, that the gospel is a bare absolute promise, and no law, and hath no proper threatening of penalty.

30. For we know him that hath said, vengeance *belongeth* unto me, I will recompense, saith the Lord: and again, The Lord shall judge his people. 31. It is a fearful thing to fall into the hands of the living God.

30, 31. Note, Grace puts us not out of fear of danger. 2. None so dreadful as a vindictive God. And, 3. Apostates, who reject Christ and his salvation, fall into the hands of God's terrible justice.

32. But call to remembrance the former days, in which after ye were illuminated, ye endured a great fight of afflictions: 33. Partly whilst ye were made a gazing-stock, both by reproaches and afflictions, and partly whilst ye became companions of them that were so used.

32, 33. But remember what you have formerly suffered for Christ: Will you lose all that? Or cannot God strengthen you now, when you should be grown stronger? Remember how you endured to be made the common spectacle and scorn of men, by your own sufferings (for sufferers are usually disdained by the baser multitude) and also by being the companions of those that suffered, and openly owning them, and bore part of their afflictions.

34. For ye had compassion of me in my bonds, and took joyfully the spoiling of your goods, knowing in yourselves that ye have in heaven a better and an enduring substance.

34. For I, for one, must bear you witness, that in my bonds, you did partake in my sufferings, by compassion; and also you took not only patiently, but joyfully, the loss and spoiling of your goods and bodily maintenance, by the plunder and distraining of persecutors: and what made you do this, but that you firmly believed, yea, knew, by the witness in yourselves, attesting the promises of Christ, that you have (as to right) in heaven a treasure incomparably better than that which you lose, and such as is endless, and none can rob you of.

35. Cast not away therefore your confidence, which hath great recompence of reward.

35. Do not then for nothing at last, cast away the open, bold owning of your faith and hope (and with it all your hope, labour, and sufferings); for the recompence of reward is great.

36. For ye have need of patience, that after ye have done the will of God, ye might receive the promise.

36. For it is not enough to begin well: it is like God will yet try you with sharper persecutions; so that you have need, not only of conversion, but of patience, to hold out, and overcome temptations, that having done the will of God, in all your trials, and fully manifested your sincerity

by your constancy, you might receive the promised reward.

37. For yet a little while, and he that shall come, will come, and will not tarry.

37. For (though to unbelief and impatience it seem long) it is but a very little time, till Christ will come to end your fears and sufferings, and fulfil your hopes: and he will not delay or tarry at all, beyond the due approaching time.

38. Now the just shall live by faith: but if *any man* draw back, my soul shall have no pleasure in him.

38. It is by the firm belief of the promise of glory (purchased by Christ) that the just do overcome temptations, hold on in duty and comfortable hope, and are finally saved: but if any man forsake this faith, and its profession, either through fraud, flattery, or fear of men, God will forsake him, and have no pleasure in him.

Note, Dr. Hammond applieth it to [forsaking public worship] as the Gnostics did; which indeed backsliders use to do when such assembling is persecuted: and his note should warn them to take heed of such forsaking public worship, who live where men are tolerated to be Atheists, and not to worship God at all, but not to be Christians, and to assemble for God's worship, unless they will be stigmatized with the profession or practice of some imposed wickedness; though this Atheism and persecution pretend Christian order.

39. But we are not of them who draw back unto perdition: but of them that believe, to the saving of the soul.

39. But I hope you will approve yourselves faithful Christians, and not of the loose unsteadfast sort, who by sophistry or persecution are drawn to revolt, and turn back to their own destruction; but of them who believe with sincerity, firmness and constancy, to the saving of their souls.

CHAP. XI.

NOW faith is the substance of things hoped for, the evidence of things not seen.

1. And seeing it is by faith that you must obtain all this victory, and perseverance, and salvation, it greatly concerneth you to understand rightly what that faith is by which the just must live, and how it differeth from that living by sight and sense on worldly things, which is the case and life of the children of perdition. This faith is the subsistence, or firm and confident expectation from God of the things which we believing, hope for, and which maketh them by the security of his faithful promise, to be effectual motives to us, as if they were even present: And it is the convincing evidence, or demonstration in the mind, of the unseen things which God revealeth, by which they prevail with us against all the visible vanities of this world. This realising things future and unseen as certain by God's promise, and overcoming temptations from things seen and present, is our saving faith.

2. For by it the elders obtained a good report.

2. It was by this effectual belief and trust in God's promise for things unseen, preferred before things seen and present, that the ancients are said to be approved of God.

3. Through faith we understand that the worlds were framed by the word of God, so that things which are seen were not made of things which do appear.

3. How can we know but by believing God's revelation, that heaven and earth were compacted and formed by the word of God, so that all this great and well-ordered frame which is seen, was made not of things which appear.

Note, This latter part is diversly expounded. 1. Some, as Calvin, expound it thus, [The things that are seen were made to be as a glass or image of the things that are unseen.] That they are so, is true; but few receive this as the sense of these words.

2. Others expound it as equal to [the seen worlds were made not of things seen, therefore of nothing, or no pre-existent matter.] This most Protestants receive.

3. Others take [framing or compacting] to presuppose existent matter to be compact, and say, that was the chaos in which the form was unseen.

4. Others, following the vulgar Latin, Erasmus, &c. translate it, [the things which are seen, were made of things unseen:] And on the text and supposition, some build a frame of philosophy, viz. that all things are made or flow from God; so as that the nearest effects are the most pure and noble, and the remotest most gross, and made by transmutation and condensation, and so that earth is but incrassate humour, and humour (or water) incrassate air, and air incrassate fire, and fire incrassate vegetative spirit, and that incrassate intellectual spirit: And so that all visible bodies are made of invisible spirit debased, which again may be refined to invisibility. But these are the frothy dreaming presumptions of unhumbled wits; and wise men will rest in the measure of God's revelations.

4. By faith Abel offered unto God a more excellent sacrifice than Cain, by which he obtained witness that he was righteous, God testifying of his gifts: and by it he being dead, yet speaketh.

4. By this faith it was that Abel offered to God a more excellent, and therefore more acceptable sacrifice than Cain: by which he obtained God's judgment and record, that he was righteous (and so far was justified by it in God's account) God by some notable sign shewing, that

when he rejected Cain's offering, he accepted Abel's: And by this sacrifice, and God's attestation, though his malignant brother murdered him, his acceptance, recorded by God in scripture, yet speaketh his honour, and our imitation.

Note, 1. That Abel's faith producing his offering, was not any other, but that for which God judged him righteous.

2. That the brief history maketh it not fully clear, wherein the difference of their offerings lay, save that, 1. Abel's being of the firstlings of living creatures, was in its nature more excellent than Cain's of vegetables. 2. And the nobler effect shewed a nobler cause, or faith.

But seeing, 1. That it is most probable that the duty of sacrificing came from no original, but Adam's tradition of God's command. 2. And that the use of it under Moses's law, expoundeth it after, we may conceive, 1. That it was to signify that man was to believe that death was deserved by man's sin: 2. That by death the mediator was to redeem him: 3. And that as the beast was offered to God, they offered their own lives to him, in hope of the immortality of the soul, and a better life, which death was the way to. And in this faith Abel excelled Cain.

5. By faith Enoch was translated, that he should not see death, and was not found, because God had translated him: for before his translation he had this testimony, that he pleased God.

5. It was by trusting God for a better, unseen life, that Enoch was made fit for, and obtained to be translated by God without dying, and so was no more seen on earth: For before it is recorded of him, that he pleased God, who thus rewarded him.

Note, 1. That though Enoch died not by any corruption of his body, no doubt but it had such a change at its entrance into heaven, as the bodies of the living saints shall have at Christ's second coming (which proveth a transmutation of elements by scripture testimony) and as Christ's own body had, which made it suitable to the heavenly region: For flesh and blood cannot enter into the kingdom of God, it is made a spiritual, incorruptible body, as ours shall be.

2. It is like this intimateth, how God would have used man, if he had not by sin contracted the guilt of threatened death.

3. But it is certain, that it is recorded to tell us whither it is that faith and holiness do tend, and that there is a better life.

6. But without faith it is impossible to please him: for he that cometh to God must believe that he is, and that he is a rewarder of them that diligently seek him.

6. Those that please God must needs be happy; for that is happiness itself. But it is impossible to have a heart or life that pleaseth God, without a trusting belief of these two articles; 1. That God is the very and only God, infinite in all perfection; 2. And that he is, as our ruler and benefactor, the full rewarder of all them that with sincere diligence seek to please him, in the obedience of his governing will, or his law revealed to them.

Note, He that thinks there is no God, can neither love, trust, or obey him: And he that thinks he is impotent, ignorant, or bad, or any way imperfect, thinks that he is not God, and giveth him but the name of God, while he denieth and blasphemeth him. And he that thinketh that he is not man's ruler morally by law, but only physically by motion, like lifeless engines, will never obey his laws; and therefore will live after his lusts, and be far worse than savage brutes, as abusing a nobler nature. And he that thinks that God will let men be losers by their most costly and diligent obedience, takes him to be none of our governor, or to be unjust, and so not to be God indeed: Nay, if he believe not that his holiness and goodness will be pleased with, and abundantly reward such sincere diligence. And he that believeth not a life of great reward after this, cannot well believe that God is such a rewarder of them that diligently seek him, seeing what they suffer here.

Qu. But are these two articles enough to salvation?

Answ. He that sincerely and trustingly believeth and practiseth these, shall not perish: but what more is necessary, God will make known to him: For of a truth (whoever deny it) God is no respecter of persons, but in every nation, he that feareth God, and worketh righteousness, is accepted of him. And if a soul that truly loveth God, and is accepted of him, should be in hell, heaven itself should be in hell.

7. By faith Noah being warned of God of things not seen as yet, moved with fear, prepared an ark to the saving of his house, by the which he condemned the world, and became heir of the righteousness which is by faith.

7, Note, 1. God's revelation was Noah's warning. 2. The flood neither seen, nor likely in itself was the thing revealed and believed, with the way to escape. 3. True belief will be affectual in an obedient use of God's appointed means of salvation. 4. The belief of God's threatenings is a part of saving faith. 5. Faithful obedience to God condemneth the unbelieving, rebellious world. 6. All these acts of faith go to make us heirs of the righteousness of faith, that is, to be saved, as those that God accounteth acceptably righteous. 7. To be moved with the promised glory, and threatened misery that is unseen, is the life of faith.

8. By faith Abraham, when he was called to go out into a place which he should after receive for an inheritance, obeyed, and he went out, not knowing whither he went.

8. Why did Abraham go, when God called him into an unknown land, but that he practically trusted and believed God, that he would give it his seed for an inheritance.

9. By faith he sojourned in the land of promise, as *in* a strange country, dwelling in tabernacles with Isaac and Jacob, the heirs with him of the same promise. 10. For he looked for a city which hath foundations, whose builder and maker is God.

9, 10. And why did he (and Isaac and Jacob) sojourn there in tents as strangers? but because he believed that God would give his posterity cities there (such as Jerusalem) strong and walled, instead of tents, and would give him, in the mean time, a place in the heavenly Jerusalem, for his faith and obedience to God.

11. Through faith also Sarah herself received strength to conceive seed, and was delivered of a child when she was past age, because she judged him faithful who had promised.

11. And Sarah, past age, brought forth Isaac, because she trusted God's promise against natural probability.

12. Therefore sprang there even of one, and him as good as dead, *so many* as the stars of the sky in multitude, and as the sand which is by the sea-shore, innumerable.

12. Thus the numerous seed of Israel sprang from one, dead to generating, by believing God.

13. These all died in faith, not having received the promises, but having seen them afar off, and were persuaded of *them*, and embraced *them*, and confessed that they were strangers and pilgrims on the earth.

13. Both Abraham and his posterity long lived as strangers, before the promised land was given to their successors, which they received not themselves. And Abraham, who foresaw Christ's day and rejoiced, and his believing seed, died in that faith, which saw him afar off, (and the heavenly glory promised by him) and yet lived not to see the promised Messiah, but confessed that they were pilgrims on earth, though they believed and embraced the promises.

14. For they that say such things, declare plainly that they seek a country.

14. And as their taking themselves for strangers in Canaan, shewed that they were not yet at home, and were but seekers of a country promised; so those that were true believers, confessing that they were but strangers and pilgrims on earth, declare that it was a better place than earth, that they sought and hoped for.

15. And truly if they had been mindful of that *country* from whence they came out, they might have had opportunity to have returned.

15. And it was not Chaldea, whence they came, which they sought: for they might have returned to that.

16. But now they desire a better *country*, that is, an heavenly: wherefore God is not ashamed to be called their God; for he hath prepared for them a city.

16. But it was a better country which they desired; and though the carnal seed looked but to Canaan, the true believers took Jerusalem but as a type of the Jerusalem above, and chiefly desired an heavenly country; and it was specially in relation to heaven, that God condescended to be called The God of Abraham, Isaac, and Jacob, and the God of Israel; for it is there where he will gloriously own and govern them.

Note, 1. The force of Christ's argument against the Sadducees, from God's relation to Abraham, &c. is here expounded. 2. They err, that think believers of old expected not a heavenly felicity; Though Moses's law, as it was political, to be the rule of magistrates' judgment, reached not so high, yet as subordinate to the promise or covenant of grace, it did.

17. By faith Abraham, when he was tried, offered up Isaac; and he that had received the promises offered up his only begotten *Son*. 18. Of whom it was said, That in Isaac shall thy seed be called.

17, 18. It was by believing and trusting the promise of God concerning his seed in Isaac, that Abraham, when God thereby tried him, offered up even that son to death, to whom the promise of multiplication was made, and the nations to be blessed in his seed.

19. Accounting that God was able to raise *him* up, even from the dead: from whence also he received *him* in a figure.

19. For he believed that God's promise must be fulfilled, and could not be broken for want of power, no more than for want of wisdom or goodness; and that he would rather raise him from the dead, than break his word: And indeed he received him again as it had been from the dead (in which he prefigured Christ's resurrection and ours.)

Note, The great difficulty of Abraham's case was, how he was bound to take that to be God's voice, which bid him murder the innocent, and so break God's law of nature: Must not we try the spirits by the standing law of God in nature? Answ. 1. God is the absolute Lord of all lives, and can do no man wrong; and Abraham knew that he could make both Isaac and himself amends yea, that he could and would presently raise him to life again. 2. And by full evidence and experimental proof, he knew that it was God that spake to him: But we are supposed to have more cause of doubting, where we must try the spirits. We must believe no pretended revelation against certain foreknown truth; nor yet disbelieve God upon a proud pretence that we know that to be truth, which indeed we know not.

20. By faith Isaac blessed Jacob and Esau concerning things to come.

20. It was by believing God's promise of things to come, yet unseen, that Isaac blessed Jacob and Esau, foretelling what God would do with them.

21. By faith Jacob, when he was a dying, blessed both the sons of Joseph, and worshipped, *leaning* upon the top of his staff.

21. It was by believing unseen future things, that Jacob, when he could scarce sit up, and was ready to die, foretold what God would do with the posterity of Joseph's sons.

Note, Qu. When Isaac and Jacob both ignorantly preferred the younger before the elder; how could that be said to be done by faith, which they understood not?

Ans. 1. They believed the promised blessing to both. 2. And they believed the inward inspiration of God, which told them, [This person on whom thou layest thy hands, shall have this particular blessing] though they knew not which of them it was by name: It was to a determinate individual.

22. By faith Joseph, when he died, made mention of the departing of the children of Israel, and gave commandment concerning his bones.

22. How could Joseph foretel the Israelites' going out of Egypt, and give them order to carry his bones with them, but by believing unseen, future things, on the credit of God's testimony, by inward prophetical inspiration (which was his word to him.)

23. By faith Moses, when he was born, was hid three months of his parents, because they saw *he was* a proper child, and they were not afraid of the king's commandment.

23. It was by believing some intimation from God, partly inward, and partly in his personal appearance, what Moses should prove, as to unseen future things, which encouraged his parents to hide him, notwithstanding the murderous commandment of the king.

24. By faith Moses, when he was come to years, refused to be called the son of Pharaoh's daughter. 25. Choosing rather to suffer affliction with the people of God, than to enjoy the pleasures of sin for a season. 26. Esteeming the reproach of Christ greater riches than the treasures in Egypt: for he had respect unto the recompence of the reward.

24, 25, 26. It was by trusting God's intimations of unseen future things, that Moses, being grown up, refused the wealth and honour of an adopted son of Pharaoh's daughter, preferring affliction among the people of God, before the short enjoyment of sinful pleasures; yea, esteeming such reproach, as we Christians now undergo for Christ, and as the believers of the future kingdom of Christ, then suffered, to be not only tolerable, but greater riches than all the treasures of Egypt; because he had a believing respect to the recompence of reward, to which such sufferings did conduce.

27. By faith he forsook Egypt, not fearing the wrath of the king; for he endured, as seeing him who is invisible.

27. Why left he Egypt to go into a foreign land and wilderness, and after fearlessly faced a wrathful king, when he spake from God? but because, as his eyes saw the flaming tokens of the presence of God, so his faith was instead of a sight of him that is invisible: He believed in an unseen God for unseen future things.

28. Through faith he kept the passover, and the sprinkling of blood, lest he that destroyed the first-born should touch them.

28. Why kept he the passover, and sprinkled the door posts with blood, but because he believed God for unseen future things, even that the destroying angel should spare such houses?

29. By faith they passed through the red sea, as by dry land: which the Egyptians assaying to do were drowned.

29. How durst they have ventured into, and through the red sea, but that they believed God, that he would there deliver them by that miracle; when the Egyptians were drowned, who went not in by faith, but by presumption.

Note, It is a great controversy among expositors, whether the Israelites passed quite through the sea to the other side, or rather went in and came out, as in a semi-circular course on the same side; because their journies are after said to be on the same side where they entered, and so they think it was but to draw in the Egyptians.

30. By faith the walls of Jericho fell down, after they were compassed about seven days.

30. How came the people to go about Jericho seven days, and the walls to fall, but because they

believed and trusted the promises of Almighty God?

31. By faith the harlot Rahab perished not with them that believed not, when she had received the spies with peace.

31. How came Rahab (who was formerly a heathen harlot, and then kept an inn, or house of entertainment) to escape when Jericho was destroyed, but because she believed that the God of Israel was the true God, and would deliver them that trust him?

32. And what shall I more say? for the time will fail me to tell of Gideon, and of Barak, and of Samson, and of Jephtha, of David also, and Samuel, and of the prophets. 33. Who through faith subdued kingdoms, wrought righteousness, obtained promises, stopped the mouths of lions.

32, 33. By believing and trusting God for unseen future things, some conquered the nations of their enemies, (as Joshua, the judges, David, &c.) the truly faithful lived righteously in a sinful world, obtained what God had conditionally promised, and promises of yet further mercies, for their fidelity (as Abraham, Phineas, &c.) and God stopped the mouths of lions to deliver them (as he did by Daniel.)

34. Quenched the violence of fire, escaped the edge of the sword, out of weakness were made strong, waxed valiant in fight, turned to flight the armies of the aliens. 35. Women received their dead raised to life again: and others were tortured, not accepting deliverance, that they might obtain a better resurrection.

34, 35. God made the fire harmless to them, (as Dan. iii.) Divers escaped the sword of bloody persecutors, (as David, &c.) recovered from sickness, (as Job, Hezekiah, &c.) fought valiantly, trusting on God for victory, and so overcame: Had their dead raised, (as 1 Kings, xvii. xxi. 2 Kings, iv.) Others endured torment, and would not sin to be delivered; believing and hoping for resurrection to a better life, (as 2 Maccab. xix. 30. and vii. 9.)

36. And others had trial of cruel mockings and scourgings, yea moreover, of bonds and imprisonments. 37. They were stoned, they were sawn asunder, were tempted, were slain with the sword: they wandered about in sheep-skins, and goat-skins, being destitute, afflicted, tormented:

36, 37. And by believing the promises, unseen reward, others endured the trial of cruel mockings, and scornful reproach, and to be whipt as rogues, and bound and laid in gaols as malefactors; some were stoned, some sawn asunder, others tried by hot irons, and other fiery torments; some slain with the sword, others, like contemned vagabonds, wandered in base clothing of sheepskins, and goat-skins, destitute of outward things, afflicted and tormented.

38. Of whom the world was not worthy: they wandered in deserts, and in mountains, and in dens and caves of the earth.

38. All these were accounted and used as bad men, unworthy to live, as others, peaceably in the world. But were they such indeed? No; but such, of whom the world was not worthy. And many of them retired from the converse of the world, into dens, caves, and mountains.

Note, Oh, the difference between God's judgment of a saint, and man's! The world is not worthy of those scorned, persecuted saints, whom their persecutors call rogues, unworthy to live. They are not worthy of their company, example, counsel, or other benefits: For they know not what a saint is, nor the worth of a saint, nor how to use him; yea, they hate him, and drive such away, as they do the offer of Christ and his grace.

39. And these all, having obtained a good report through faith, received not the promise: 40. God having provided some better thing for us, that they without us should not be made perfect.

39, 40. And all these true believers were justified by God's own testimony, left on record to their praise. But still it was things unseen and future which they believed, and for which they suffered all this martyrdom and pain: And though God gave them their reward in heaven, they lived not to see the incarnate Saviour, and the kingdom of the Messiah, the Catholic church advanced by the pourings out of the Spirit of Christ; which were the promised blessings, which God had told them, he would give in the fulness of time. For God had provided these greater blessings, of the kingdom of Christ in its more perfect state, and the fulness of that Spirit, for this age of the world in which we live, and would not let them, in those former ages before our time, partake of this more perfect church state: Even as we now believe Christ's glorious coming, and wait, and suffer persecution in hope; and yet must not live on earth to see it, as the last age will do; but must die first, and be raised to enjoy that sight.

CHAP. XII.

WHEREFORE seeing we also are compassed about with so great a cloud of witnesses, let us lay aside every weight, and the sin which doth so easily beset us, and let us run with patience the race that is set before us.

1. Seeing then we that are now called out to trial, have before us the instances of all the faithful that have been before us, who have conquered all the impediments of their salvation, by the effectual belief of God's promise of unseen things let us quit ourselves like men; and as runners in a race, let us be so far from turning to the world, as to cast off all worldly incumbrances which would hinder us, and to avoid all sin, in which, without great care, we shall be entangled, and let us run with patience and perseverance the race, in which by God and our covenant, we are engaged; (for it is for our salvation.)

2. Looking unto Jesus the author and finisher of our faith, who for the joy that was set before him, endured the cross, despising the shame, and is set down at the right hand of the throne of God.

2. Let us fix our eyes on Jesus, the author and leader of our Christian faith and course, and the perfecter of it; who hath by his doctrine and example, proposed it to us in that perfect form which he will own and crown; who himself was moved by the future proposed joy, which was to be the reward of all his mediatorial works; for which he endured the pains of his cross and sufferings, and despised the shame and reproach that attended it, in comparison of the desired end, which he hath now attained; and is set down in triumph and glory, next the throne of God.

3. For consider him that endured such contradiction of sinners against himself, lest ye be wearied, and faint in your minds.

3. If you will well study Christ, and consider how, and why he endured such opposition and contradiction of wicked men, who by sin, falsely accused him of sin, it will greatly strengthen you against weary tiredness, or fainting cowardice.

4. Ye have not resisted unto blood, striving against sin.

4. It is but little which you have yet been put to. If you will be crowned, you must be prepared to lay down your lives, rather than wilfully to sin.

5. And ye have forgotten the exhortation, which speaketh unto you as unto children, My son, despise not thou the chastening of the Lord, nor faint when thou art rebuked of him.

5. Have ye forgotten the Lord's gentle words, as of a father to his children, My son, &c. Prov. iii. 11.

6. For whom the Lord loveth, he chasteneth, and scourgeth every son whom he receiveth. 7. If ye endure chastening, God dealeth with you as with sons; for what son is he whom the father chasteneth not? 8. But if ye be without chastisement, whereof all are partakers, then are ye bastards and not sons.

6, 7, 8. Note, 1. Chastisement is one sort of punishment, distinguished from destructive punishment, in that it is not only for a warning to others, but also for the amendment of the offender. No man correcteth another but for a fault, and that maketh it a punishment. 2. It is not any derogation from the perfection of Christ's satisfaction, that we are punished; for he never intended to make us lawless, or that our sins should not be punished at all: His law of grace hath penalties annexed. A father hath fatherly justice and punishment for his children; and Christ it not a king without such justice. 3. Even the sufferings of martyrs are of a mixed nature, partly for sin, even Adam's and their own, (God not on earth taking off all the first curse, but making a medicine of it for good) and partly for the trial and reward of faith. 4. Pardon of sin is not perfect in this life; else, no chastising penalty would remain.

9. Furthermore, we have had fathers of our flesh, which corrected us, and we gave them reverence; shall we not much rather be in subjection unto the Father of spirits, and live?

9. We reverently submitted to the correction of our parents (whose authority was less, and they were liable to do it amiss:) And shall we not much more submit to God, who is the Infinite Spirit, and Father of Spirits, as well as of our flesh (and is of infallible wisdom, and never doth amiss) and will fit our spirits by suffering, for a better life.

10. For they verily for a few days chastened us after their own pleasure, but he for our profit, that we might be partakers of his holiness.

10. For they chastened us as fallible and passionate men, as they thought good, though sometimes in causeless anger; but God doth all in wisdom and mercy, for our good, to make us more holy, which is to be more happy, as most like himself.

11. Now no chastening for the present seemeth to be joyous, but grievous: nevertheless, afterward it yieldeth the peaceable fruit of righteousness unto them which are exercised thereby.

11. Indeed, suffering, as such, is grievous, as a

hurt to nature (and a fruit of sin to be chastised:) It is not to be expected that pain should be pleasant; but it is the fruit of it which is good, which is peaceable righteousness, making us more righteous and holy, which is peace to the soul, as health is to the body. This is the fruit when we have been tried and exercised by it.

12. Wherefore lift up the hands that hang down, and the feeble knees: 13. And make straight paths for your feet, lest that which is lame be turned out of the way, but let it rather be healed.

12, 13. Therefore seeing nature is weak, and young unsettled Christians are apt to discouragement, and fear, and fainting, labour to strengthen and encourage yourselves and one another, and avoid tempting seducers, and keep under the helps in public and private, which God hath appointed for you; and avoid all scandals which may turn the weak out of the way, who already go but lamely in it; but rather labour to heal such weakness.

14. Follow peace with all men, and holiness, without which no man shall see the Lord.

14. Let peace with all men, as much as in you lieth, be (not only your desire, but) your study, care, and diligent pursuit; and holiness and purity of heart and life, without which, none are capable of the blessed sight of God's pleased face, either here by faith, or hereafter in glorious fruition, Matt. v. 8.

15. Looking diligently, lest any man fail of the grace of God, lest any root of bitterness springing up, trouble *you*, and thereby many be defiled.

15. Make it your diligent care that none of you fail of sound believing, obeying and enjoying that grace which is offered you by Christ in the gospel, and you have professed to accept; lest any ill and dangerous doctrine, or fleshly lust or practice, spring up among you, and cast you into trouble and danger, and the churches be defiled by them, while the weak and unsteadfast are carried away, and catch the infection.

16. Lest there *be* any fornicator, or profane person, as Esau, who for one morsel of meat sold his birth-right.

16. Lest seducers and fleshly lust draw any to fornication; or any be so profane, and set so light by Christ and grace, and glory, as to lose them all for the base things of the world, and to prefer wealth and sensual delights before them: Like Esau, that set so light by his birth-right, as to sell it for one dish of meat.

Note, What a base price all ungodly men do get on Christ and their own salvation! What hath the fornicator, the drunkard, the glutton, the worldling, the ambitious, proud, and oppressor, for all, but the base portion of a beast?

17. For ye know how that afterward, when he would have inherited the blessing, he was rejected: for he found no place of repentance, though he sought it carefully with tears.

17. For the text tells you, that after, when he would fain have had the blessing of primogeniture, which he sold, and sought it of Isaac with tears, Isaac rejected him, and would not retract what he had said of Jacob.

Note, This intimateth a warning of the danger of the contempt of grace, lest God withdraw the offers, or leave men to the power of temptation as deserted. But, 1. It determineth not any thing about the damnation of Esau. 2. Nor that he truly repented of his sin against God (but only of his loss of the privilege of the elder brother;) and yet could not be forgiven (but that this loss could not be recalled.) 3. Nor that any one that truly repenteth, and is converted, shall not be forgiven: For the contrary is a great part of the doctrine of the gospel.

18. For ye are not come into the mount that might be touched, and that burned with fire; nor unto blackness, and darkness, and tempest, 19. And the sound of a trumpet, and the voice of words, which *voice* they that heard, intreated that the word should not be spoken to them any more.

18, 19. For ye are not in the infant and wilderness state of Israel, when they must bear from God out of a mountain on earth, which was touchable (but must not be touched) and which terrified them with flames of fire, and blackness, and darkness, and tempest, signifying the distance of unreconciled man from God: where they heard the sound of a trumpet, and a terrible voice of words, which fear made them desire that they might hear no more.

20, 21. For they could not endure that which was commanded: and if so much as a beast touch the mountain, it shall be stoned, or thrust through with a dart. 2. And so terrible was the sight, that Moses said, I exceedingly fear and quake.

20, 21. This signified, how little they could bear the things commanded. And the distance and dreadfulness was such, that a beast must die if it touched the mountain. And Moses himself (as we may gather by consequence and tradition) did fear and quake.

22. But ye are come unto mount Sion, and unto the city of the living

God, the heavenly Jerusalem, and to an innumerable company of angels: 23. To the general assembly, and church of the first-born, which are written in heaven, and to God the judge of all, and to the spirits of just men made perfect: 24. And to Jesus the mediator of the new covenant, and to the blood of sprinkling, that speaketh better things than that of Abel.

22, 23, 24. But the state of relation to which ye are brought, as Christians, is more spiritual and sublime: You are come in faith, relation, hope, and initial participation, to that state of holy worship which mount Zion typified, and to that blessed church which is gathering on earth, and consummate in heaven, which Jerusalem typified and may well be called the heavenly Jerusalem, the blessed city of immortal ones, dwelling with the living God: And to myriads, or numberless multitudes of angels, inhabiting those vast and glorious regions (where you shall see that the number of glorified spirits were not few:) And to that advanced state of the church, in its triumphant, joyful communion, which answereth a general assembly of the princes of the tribes of Israel, who had the honour of primogeniture; even those who are the enrolled citizens of heaven; (here they have right and there possession.) And more than all this, you are come as adopted sons to God the judge of all; and to the spirits of the consummate, or perfected, just men, with whom, as we are here united by one spirit and love into one body, so there we shall live in the perfection of this love, and union, and communion: And to our glorified Saviour, the mediator of the new covenant; by whom it was purchased, made, sealed, and executed; and who, according to the tenor of it, mediateth for us with God, and from God to us: And as the way hereto, to the real purification by his sprinkled blood, which the blood of the passover and sacrifices typified; and which crieth not against us, as Abel's blood did, for revenge, but saveth us by satisfying vindictive justice. This is the society and state of the faithful.

25. See that ye refuse not him that speaketh: for if they escaped not, who refused him that spake on earth, much more shall not we *escape*, if we turn away from him that *speaketh* from heaven.

25. Therefore your motive, both of fear and hope, being so exceeding great, with your greatest care, see that no temptation draw you to refuse him that is the great teacher and author of salvation; for if they escaped not who rejected Moses, and the law delivered by him, who was but a man like us on earth, certainly we shall not escape, if we turn away from God, who sent his Son from heaven, and thence also speaketh to us by his Spirit.

26. Whose voice then shook the earth, but now he hath promised, saying, Yet once more I shake not the earth only, but also heaven. 27. And this *word*, Yet once more, signifieth the removing of those things that are shaken, as of things that are made, that those things which cannot be shaken may remain.

26, 27. Whose voice shook the earth, when he delivered the law. But now he hath promised, once more to shake even heaven, as well as earth. Which signifieth, that he will remove the things so shaken, as made to be transitory in their use; that the things, whose designment, use and nature, are perpetual, may remain without them: that is, that the law of Moses shall be removed, to make way for grace; and the corrupted form of heaven and earth to make way for glory, even the new heaven and earth that must follow.

28. Wherefore we receiving a kingdom which cannot be moved, let us have grace, whereby we may serve God acceptably with reverence and godly fear. 29. For our God is a consuming fire.

28, 29. Seeing therefore that the gospel is the doctrine and gift of an unmoveable kingdom of Christ in glory, which we receive in right when we are true believers, and in possession at the last; and so we have the strongest motives to holiness and perseverance; let us serve God with the greater diligence and reverence, that we may be meet for his acceptance, and with a godly fear of falling off, and of his displeasure if we should prove hypocrites or apostates. For the gospel is not only a word of promises, but hath its threatenings and terrors, as well as the law, against all refusing unbelievers, hypocrites, and apostates, to whom even our God, so rich in grace, will yet prove a consuming fire.

CHAP. XIII.

LET brotherly love continue. 2. Be not forgetful to entertain strangers, for thereby some have entertained angels unawares.

1, 2. And as to your particular duties, I subjoin these brief precepts of Christian morality. 1. Be sure to keep up that special love which Christians owe to one another (notwithstanding tolerable infirmities and differences) above the common love which they owe to all men: and avoid all that would destroy this love.

2. Shew this among other means, by your hospitality, entertaining travellers that need entertainment: For so Abraham, Lot, and others, have

entertained angels, thinking that they were men: (And Christ, at judgment, will say, I was a stranger, and ye took me in.)

Note, That in those countries, inns were not so ready as with us; and Christians were mostly poor men, not able to bear their own charges in their travel.

3. Remember them that are in bonds, as bound with them: *and* them which suffer adversity, as being yourselves also in the body.

3. Seeing all the members of Christ's body must suffer if one suffer, think of those that are prisoners, especially for Christ or righteousness, with such compassion, as if their case were your own; and so in all other cases of adversity, remembering also, that you are yet in a body liable to as great affliction.

4. Marriage is honourable in all, and the bed undefiled: but whoremongers and adulterers God will judge.

4. Account and use marriage as God's institution, honourably, and keep the marriage bed undefiled: For fornicators and adulterers God hateth, and will judge.

5. Let your conversation be without covetousness, and be content with such things as ye have. For he hath said, I will never leave thee, nor forsake thee.

5. Let your hearts be kept free from the love of money, and the sinful desires, cares, fears, and troubles which thence arise; and be content with God's allowance, be it less or more: for his promise to Joshua is applicable to all the faithful; [I will never fail thee, nor forsake thee.]

6. So that we may boldly say, The Lord is my helper, and I will not fear what man shall do unto me.

6. And so to our dangers or sufferings from men, on the same account we may say as David did, having the same relation to God, and the same promises, The Lord is my helper, I will not fear man, &c. (further, my sin giveth me cause to fear, that God may use them as the chastising instruments of his displeasure.

7. Remember them which have the rule over you, who have spoken unto you the word of God, whose faith follow, considering the end of their conversation. 8. Jesus Christ the same yesterday, and to-day, and for ever.

7, 8. Remember your bishops, or guides (both the dead and living) who have spoken to you the word of God: Remember what doctrine they taught you, and how faithfully they preached, and owned it in suffering: and consider what was the main end of all their doctrine and life; even Jesus Christ, who is, and will be still the same, and no new gospel, or doctrine, which corrupters do cry up.

9. Be not carried about with divers and strange doctrines: for it is a good thing that the heart be established with grace, not with meats, which have not profited them that have been occupied therein.

9. Be not carried about (as children in a strong wind, Ephes. iv. 14.) with various doctrines, or such as are new and strange to the church of God; for Christ and his gospel being but one and the same still, your duty and interest lieth in establishing your hearts in the doctrine and covenant of grace through Christ, which is your strength, and the bread of life; and not to Judaize and turn back to the shadowy, abolished ceremonies, in sacrifices and difference of meats, which did not truly purify, save, and profit those that used them.

10. We have an altar, whereof they have no right to eat which serve the tabernacle.

10. We are not without a more holy and profitable sacrifice and sacred food than theirs, even Christ, (who is The Lamb of God that taketh away the sins of the world) whose saving sacrifice we feed on by faith, and commemorate in our communion, whose broken body, and his shed blood, they did not partake of, who offered beasts in sacrifice, in the service of the tabernacle, as we now do; but were employed about the shadows of it: And those that stick still in those abrogated rites, have no right to our altar.

11. For the bodies of those beasts, whose blood is brought into the sanctuary by the high priest for sin, are burnt without the camp. 12. Wherefore Jesus also, that he might sanctify the people with his own blood, suffered without the gate.

11, 12. For as the beasts slain for atonement, whose blood was brought into the sanctuary, was not to be eaten by the priest, but burnt without the bounds of the camp of Israel: So Christ, when he was to be offered, to sanctify the people with his blood, went without the gates of Jerusalem to suffer, signifying that (as they rejected him, as unworthy to live with them, so) he departed from them, and their political and legal state.

13. Let us go forth therefore unto him without the camp, bearing his reproach. 14. For here have we no continuing city, but we seek one to come.

13, 14. So let us go out to him, from the Jewish state, and ceremonial law (and also from the heathen world) and submit to the reproach of the cross, which must be expected: We must forsake both the Jewish polity, and the world, or else we cannot follow Christ; for the Christian church is not fixed, as the Jewish church was to Jerusalem, to one city; nor have we any fixed state on earth, in which we may glory, as our home or abiding place; but by faith in God's promises, through Christ, we hope and seek for one to come, even the new and heavenly Jerusalem.

15. By him therefore let us offer the sacrifice of praise to God continually, that is the fruit of *our* lips, giving thanks to his name.

15. Therefore, instead of Jewish sacrifices, let us by Christ, our great interceding high-priest, offer daily to God the sacrifice of praise from a believing, thankful heart, and give thanks to him for Christ and all his gifts; and this hearty, sincere fruit of our lips will be more acceptable than the fruits of the earth, or any bloody sacrifice of beasts.

16. But to do good, and to communicate forget not, for with such sacrifices God is well pleased.

16. But there is another sort of sacrifice very pleasing to God also, which you must not forget, even beneficence and bounty; doing all the good you can, and communicating to the relief of those that need.

Note. The name of Sacrifice and Altar, as well as Priests, used, as here, by allusion, or similitude to those of old, may lawfully be used, as here they are, and were by the primitive Christians, even as the Lord's day was called the Christian-sabbath. It is no dishonour to Christ, to say that we may offer sacrifices acceptable unto God, so it be but in subordination to his sacrifice, as our gospel-worthiness is but subordinate to his meritorious righteousness.

17. Obey them that have the rule over you, and submit yourselves, for they watch for your souls, as they that must give account, that they may do it with joy, and not with grief: for that is unprofitable for you.

17. God that hath made the bishops or pastors to be your guiding rulers in church affairs, obligeth you to obey them, and to submit yourselves to their government, and not to live as unruly, or in confusion: for the charge of watching for your souls is committed to them, so far as belongeth to their office, by teaching publicly and privately, and personally watching over the state and conversation of every single person to their power, and instructing, exhorting, reproving, comforting; intrusted with the administration of the seals of God's covenant, and with your public church communion, by judging of men's capacity; and receiving or excluding, binding or loosing, by the power of the keys. And of all this they must give account to God; which, as it will be terrible to them if they be unfaithful, so it will be to you if their faithfulness be without success; which else will be to the joy of them and you. And they have not any constraining power of the sword, and can govern and profit you only as voluntary, by your own consent; and therefore, as you love your comfort, and regard them, and their labours and comfort, obey them, by obeying God's word, which they preach.

Note, 1. That those bishops which God commandeth men to obey, are those that watch for the souls of all the flocks, as men that must give account of all; and not those that have many hundred, or score of churches, without any other bishop, save one, and never see, or know, or once hear the names of one of many hundred, called their flock; much less ever taught them, or gave them the sacrament.

2. That God having trusted the pastors by office, with church-government by the keys, it is very false that the people should govern it by vote: Though it is true, that being governed but as volunteers by the pastors, their consent is needful to their subjection, and to their profit and salvation.

18. Pray for us: for we trust we have a good conscience in all things, willing to live honestly.

18. Our work and charge being so great, and of such importance to yourselves, while some revile and persecute us, and some turn from us, and disobey our doctrine, do you pray for us, that God will guide, strengthen, support, and prosper us: For our conscience is our witness, that we are faithful in our ministry and our lives.

19. But I beseech you the rather to do this, that I may be restored to you the sooner.

19. And put up this one request also for me, that I may the sooner be restored to the comfort of your service.

20. Now the God of peace that brought again from the dead our Lord Jesus, that great shepherd of the sheep, through the blood of the everlasting covenant, 21. Make you perfect in every good work to do his will, working in you that which is well-pleasing in his sight, through Jesus Christ, to whom be glory for ever and ever. Amen.

20, 21. My chief benediction and prayer for you is, that God, who will be called The God of Peace, as being the giver, the lover, and the objective end of love and peace, who raised our Lord and Saviour from death, whose resurrection is the great encouragement of our hope, even him who is the chief pastor of all his holy flock, by the purchase of the blood of the everlasting covenant; compact, frame, and fit you by holiness and union, for every good work, to do his will, and work in you (by his Spirit, as he commandeth you in his word) that which is well-pleasing in his sight: (To please him being the ultimate end of the whole creation, and as here begun, the way thereto.) To whom be glory in this perfect fulfilling of his will, for ever and over. Amen.

22. And I beseech you, brethren, suffer the word of exhortation, for I have written a letter unto you in few words. 23. Know ye that our brother Timothy is set at liberty, with whom, if he come shortly, I will see you. 24. Salute all them that have the rule over you, and all the saints. They of Italy salute you. 25. Grace be with you all. Amen.

22, 23, &c. Note. 1. So bad is man, even Christians, through the relics of their corruption, that when the most important, comfortable doctrine is delivered to them, for their own good, and that with the most convincing evidence, there is need of earnest entreaty and exhortation that they would bear it, and not fall out with it, neglect it, or reject it.

2. For people to know and regard their faithful pastors, or church-guides, or rulers, is of so great importance to their salvation, and the church's union, strength, and safety, against ignorance, unbelief, error, and unruliness, that they are three times reminded of it in this one chapter.

THE

GENERAL (OR CATHOLIC) EPISTLE

OF

ST. JAMES

(The Apostle, say most Copies.)

Whether the writer was one of the Twelve, called the son of *Alpheus*; or rather, the son of *Cleophas*, cousin-german to Jesus, and called his brother, is uncertain.

The drift of the epistle is; 1. To establish the Christian Jews in a well-ordered, religious course of life, and fortify them against tribulations, 2. To shame a sort of sectaries, who misunderstood, and abused the doctrine of justification by faith, and turned religion into opinion; and yet were not only magisterial boasters of their great knowledge, but did it by a censorious, contentious contempt of others, and making ostentation of their supposed wisdom, as heretics use to do, by a proud and wrangling self-exalting way. 3. To reprove the over-valuing of the rich, and their contempt of the poor, and the guilt of sensuality, worldliness, and pride, that had corrupted some among them.

CHAP. I.

JAMES, a servant of God, and of the Lord Jesus Christ, to the twelve tribes which are scattered abroad, greeting.

1. Note, 1. Ten of the tribes, ever since the reign of king Hoshea, were scattered by captivity, and the rest were in great numbers dispersed through much of the Roman empire; partly, by the many insurrections and wars which had brought them to ruin by conquerors; and partly by the smallness and poverty of their country; so that at first the apostles, when they travelled into heathen countries, began their preaching, and church-gathering with the Jews' synagogues, which they found there.

2. My brethren, count it all joy when ye fall into divers temptations. 3. Knowing *this*, that the trying of your faith worketh patience.

2, 3. Note, 1. He speaketh not of direct temptations to sin, as cast into us by the devil, or carnal allurements, and fleshly appetites and lusts; but of trial by suffering for Christ and righteousness chiefly; and partly next for such correcting trials from God, as tend to our amendment.

2. It is not the suffering that is matter of joy, in itself, but the good effects of a proved faith, and increased patience. Trials, because they tend to this, should be received with joy; but when they cause this, much more.

4. But let patience have *her* perfect work, that ye may be perfect and entire, wanting nothing.

4. Note, 1. The care of a tried, suffering Christian, should be to look to his faith and patience (as the goldsmith doth to his gold in the fire); and to see that they be duly and fully exercised, and have their perfect work.

2. A full or perfect exercise and use of patience in great trials, sheweth a strong, intire Christian, and hath great joy; when a lame use of patience mixed with much impatience, sheweth a lame Christian, and giveth but little joy.

3. To despair, or fret, or swell, with bitter, revengeful thoughts against our persecutors or enemies, is contrary to sound Christianity.

5. If any of you lack wisdom, let him ask of God, that giveth to all men liberally, and upbraideth not, and it shall be given him.

5. Wisdom is necessary both for the guidance of you in all your difficulties and duties, and in the management of all your religious affairs: And all parties pretend to the greatest wisdom, to draw people to be their disciples. But if you would be truly wise, seek it not by running unto heretics, but by sincere prayer unto God, who is the bounteous giver of it, and doth not, as heretics, reproach you with your weakness, but mercifully vouchsafeth to teach the humble.

Note, 1. Prayer is a great and necessary means to get true wisdom. But as for outward things, so for wisdom, we must not only pray, but labour, and use God's other helps. Study without prayer maketh but ungodly talkers, whose dreaming knowledge will but condemn them: And prayer without study, and learning of the wise, is but a self-deceiving idle tempting of God.

6. But let him ask in faith, nothing wavering: for he that wavereth is like a wave of the sea, driven with the wind, and tossed. 7. For let not that man think that he shall receive any thing of the Lord.

6, 7. But see that your belief of God's power and goodness, and the truth of his promises to faithful supplicants, be firm and sound; for if you doubt and waver in this, you will be but tossed about like a wave in the sea: When you cannot trust God, every temptation and difficulty will overthrow both your hope and your innocency: And such have no promise that God will hear them; it is but presumption to expect it.

Note, That the faith here mentioned is not an assurance of our own sincerity, and that God will give us what we ask, as being surely fit to receive it: But it is a resolute cleaving to the Christian verity, and a sound belief that God is most able, and faithful in performing all his promises, and will give all the good which we ask, and are meet to receive. Distrusting ourselves is not distrusting God.

8. A double-minded man *is* unstable in all his ways.

8. A man whose mind and heart hangs doubtful and unresolved between God and the world, Christ and infidelity, heaven and earth, holiness and sin, is fickle, and still untrusty.

9, 10. Let the brother of low degree rejoice in that he is exalted: But the rich, in that he is made low:

9, 10. You must not judge of your felicity by your outward things, but take that for best which God, as a father, provideth for you. If he advance you, gladly and thankfully acknowledge it; if he take you down, and deprive you of riches, be not only patient, but thankful that God will choose for you, according to his wisdom, who knoweth better what you are fit for, and what is fit for you, than you can know.

10, 11. Because as the flower of the grass, he shall pass away. For the sun is no *sooner* risen with a burning heat, *but* it withereth the grass, and the flower thereof falleth, and the grace of the fashion of it perisheth: so also shall the rich man fade away in his ways.

10, 11. For riches are too inconsiderable things to make any great, just alteration in our minds:

They are transitory, and so is man, like the flower, whose sweetness you may use for a moment, but it fadeth presently before the heat of the scorching sun.

12. Blessed *is* the man that endureth temptation, for when he is tried he shall receive the crown of life, which the Lord hath promised to them that love him.

12. It is the tried Christian that is the blessed man, who, after suffering and temptation, holds fast his integrity. God will give him that crown of life, which he hath promised to all that sincerely love him.

13. Let no man say when he is tempted, I am tempted of God: for God cannot be tempted with evil, neither tempteth he any man.

13. But as to the seducing sort of temptation, which is not to try our constancy, but to draw men to sin and ruin; let no man charge that on God as his doing; for as God cannot be tempted to sin, nor possibly love it, so he tempteth no man to it, (much less forceth them to it, or unresistibly, by determining premotion, makes them sin.)

14. But every man is tempted when he is drawn away of his own lust, and enticed. 15. Then when lust hath conceived, it bringeth forth sin: and sin, when it is finished, bringeth forth death.

14, 15. But the course of temptation, sin, and death, is this: First, fleshly appetite, lust, and phantasy, by strongly inclining men to their carnal objects and interests, prevail with their judgments, either to take part with these lusts, or not to oppose them; and so, by these lusts, Satan, the great tempter, doth his work, which he could not do without them. And when these lusts, or carnal affections, have bribed the understanding to be erroneous or remiss, and have drawn the will to a sinful yielding or consent, this sin conceived by lust in the heart, doth bring forth the fruits of a sinful practice in the life, and then God's justice punisheth it with death, when it hath resisted and driven away his offered grace.

16, 17. Do not err, my beloved brethren. Every good gift, and every perfect gift is from above, and cometh down from the Father of lights, with whom is no variableness, neither shadow of turning.

16, 17. Be not deceived about the causes of good and evil; sin and death are from ourselves; but every good and perfecting gift is of God's free grace and donation, even from above, from the Father of lights, who (as the sun is the same in its nature and action, though earth and clouds oft interposing, make it seem to us as varying by its rising and setting, and turning away its light into shadows, when the change is not in it, so) God is unchangeable, and our changes and shadows are not from any mutability, or shadowy alteration in him, but from ourselves.

18. Of his own will begat he us with the word of truth, that we should be a kind of first-fruits of his creatures.

18. It was of his own good will and grace that he hath regenerated us by the true word of the gospel (and not of any desert of ours) and hath made us as the first fruits sanctified to him (so that all good is of God, and all evil of ourselves and the devil.)

19. Wherefore, my beloved brethren, let every man be swift to hear, slow to speak, slow to wrath.

19. Therefore, watch over yourselves, if you would be safe; and particularly observe these three rules: 1. Be swift to hear as humble learners, while proud men are forward to be teachers, before they were ever profitable learners. 2. Be slow to speak, and not as proud men, full of words, because of self conceit, readier to teach than to learn, telling what they think they know, while the humble are learning to know more; and when in multitude of words there is seldom innocency; but the rash and talkative say that which must be repented of. 3. Be slow to wrath.

20. For the wrath of man worketh not the righteousness of God.

20. For a wrathful mind is very unfit for that righteousness which God requireth in and of us: It puts the mind out of a composed, holy frame, and unfits it for communion with God: It blindeth and perverteth the judgment, and destroyeth holy love and peace. A wrathful man scarce loveth his neighbour as himself, nor doth as he would be done by.

21. Wherefore lay apart all filthiness, and superfluity of naughtiness, and receive with meekness the ingrafted word, which *is* able to save your souls.

21. Also cast away all filthiness out of your thoughts, affections, speech, and practice, and all excrementitious naughtiness, (or that superfluity, which is but provision for the flesh, to satisfy its lust;) and with humble, tractable meekness, receive God's word, not only opinionatively, but as the graff is taken into the tree, or your food, when it is digested into blood and flesh, thus made an innaturalized word; and so received and digested, it will save your souls.

22. But be ye doers of the word, and not hearers only, deceiving your ownselves.

22. But to think that bare hearing the word will save you, is but self-deceit: There must be inward practice by meditation, and outward practice in true obedience.

23. For if any be a hearer of the word, and not a doer, he is like unto a man beholding his natural face in a glass: 24. For he beholdeth himself, and goeth his way, and straightway forgetteth what manner of man he was.

23, 24. An unprofitable custom of bare hearing, and not doing, is but like a man's looking at his face in a glass, who so goeth away, and minds it no more, or forgets it, which neither feedeth nor clotheth him, nor cureth his diseases; such are these customary, dull speculators.

25. But whoso looketh into the perfect law of liberty, and continueth *therein*, he being not a forgetful hearer, but a doer of the work, this man shall be blessed in his deed.

25. But he that well considereth the covenant of grace, or the gospel, which is Christ's law of liberty, or liberation, giving us deliverance from the Jewish law, and from sin, and guilt, and wrath, and death, and dwelleth in the study of it, till it turn to spiritual life digested and ingraffed in him, and is not a forgetful hearer, but a doer of that which is required to salvation, even sound faith, repentance, sincere obedience, and patience, this man shall be blessed in so doing.
Note, 1. They grossly deny Christ to be king, which say that he hath no law. 2. His gospel covenant hath precepts, rewarding promises, and penal threats, and therefore is a proper law. 3. It giveth pardon on condition of faith and repentance (to be performed by divine grace) and salvation, on condition of added obedience and perseverance, and so is a law of liberty. Christ is the author of eternal salvation to all them that obey him. 4. This doing his commands, which is made his imposed condition, is the necessary entitling qualification for blessedness, Rev. xxii. 14. Blessed are they that do his commandments, that they may have right to the tree of life, and may enter in by the gates into the city.

26. If any man among you seem to be religious, and bridleth not his tongue, but deceiveth his own heart, this man's religion *is* vain.

26. If any man among you seem to others, or himself, to be religious, (and perhaps of a higher form than others) and yet bridleth not his tongue from backbiting, slandering, or reproaching his brethren, to render them contemptible and unlovely, and from speaking ill of men without either truth, or a just call; this man's sinful practice doth shew that his religion is but ineffectual and vain, and doth but serve to deceive his own heart: For that which doth not save men from sin, will not save them from justice.

27. Pure religion and undefiled before God and the Father, is this, to visit the fatherless and widows in their affliction, *and* to keep himself unspotted from the world.

27. There is great contending among Christians, whose way of religious worship is the purest, and best pleasing to God. That is the pure and undefiled religion in God's sight, who is our Father, which is effectual to sound practical charity, and to a pure, unspotted, holy life; even with true love and liberality, to relieve those that are in distress, and to keep heart and life clean from the love of the world, and the temptations of wicked, worldly men, (as seeking in hope for a better world.)

CHAP. II.

MY brethren, have not the faith of our Lord Jesus Christ, *the Lord* of glory, with respect of persons.

1. And you that profess to believe the glory of our Lord Jesus Christ, which the poorest Christians shall partake of, equally with the rich, and to which all worldly glory is but vanity, must not now make a great difference in the church between rich men and the poor, by a worldly respect of persons for their riches.

2. For if there come into your assembly a man with a gold ring, in goodly apparel, and there come in also a poor man in vile raiment, 3. And ye have respect to him that weareth the gay clothing, and say unto him, Sit thou here in a good place; and say to the poor, Stand thou there, or sit here under my footstool: 4. Are ye not then partial in yourselves, and are become judges of evil thoughts?

2, 3, 4. If in your church-assemblies you inordinately shew respect to men for gay clothing, as rich, and set light by men, that by their garb seem poor, do you not shew a carnal partiality, by overvaluing wealth, and a judgment misguided by evil estimation?
Note, 1. That this speaketh not against honouring magistrates, but riches. 2. Nor against a prudent respect to the rich, so far as by their wealth they may be engaged to do more good than others. 3. And I think those mistake, that rather expound this of meetings of bishops for judicature (as Dr. Hammond) than other church assemblies: For, 1. If they mean any forcing judicatures, Christians had none such, there being then no Christian magistrates that had the power of the sword. 2. And if bishops had been like our diocesans, and so distant, they could not have travelled so far as such must do to keep up ordinary judicatures, without a total deserting their chief work for their flocks. 3. And as they truly were (congregational bishops) ever no more than one of our parishes, their dis-

tance between city and city was too great for this, without the like omissions. 4. Christians having then no judicial power but as arbitrators, the contenders chose what arbitrators they thought best. 5. Their public church government was exercised in the same assemblies which met for worship, which therefore are more like here to be mentioned with respect to their most usual business, and not the rarer. 6. It is the whole church, and not the bishops only, that is here admonished. 7. It is too hard a censure for such men to use, as are pleading for too much honour to bishops, to suppose them so early guilty of so much partiality and carnal respect to fine clothes and riches, and so much injustice in judging as this doctor's expositiou doth suppose: It is more like to be the vulgar's fault.

5. Hearken, my beloved brethren, hath not God chosen the poor of this world, rich in faith, and heirs of the kingdom, which he hath promised to them that love him?

5. Consider how God himself confuteth your over-valuing rich men, and vilifying the poor: Is it not mostly of the poor that your churches consist? Is it not them that God hath chosen, poor in the world, but rich in faith, to be here made heirs, and hereafter possessors of that kingdom of glory, which he hath promised to them that truly love him.

6, 7. But ye have despised the poor. Do not rich men oppress you, and draw you before the judgment-seats? Do not they blaspheme that worthy name, by the which ye are called?

6, 7. Yet you despise the poor, whom God himself chooseth and honoureth: And doth not your own experience and suffering condemn you? Who is it but rich men that oppress you by tyranny, and draw you, like malefactors, before their courts of judicature? Do they not blaspheme the name of Christ, and reproach your religion?

8. If ye fulfil the royal law, according to the scripture: Thou shalt love thy neighbour as thyself, ye do well.

8. I persuade you not to hate men for their riches, but not to think that these allow you so partial a differencing: If you obey God's great command, as the scripture teacheth you; to love all sorts of your neighbours as yourselves, according to the various degrees of their truest amiableness (be they rich or poor) you then do well.

9. But if ye have respect unto persons, ye commit sin, *and* are convinced of the law as transgressors.

9. But if you thus inordinately respect men differently for their wealth, not only the gospel of love, but the law of Moses convinceth you as sinners. Exod. xxiii. 3. Lev. xxx. 15. Deut. i. 16,17.

10. For whosoever shall keep the whole law, and yet offend in *one point,* he is guilty of all. 11. For he that said, Do not commit adultery; said also, Do not kill. Now, if thou commit no adultery, yet if thou kill, thou art become a transgressor of the law.

10. 11. And that law condemneth all that continue not in all things therein written, to do them; and we are bound by God's law in force to universal obedience. If you keep all other commands, and presumptuously break one, you are contemners of the law, and so interpretatively break all.

12. So speak ye, and so do, as they that shall be judged by the law of liberty.

12. And though you are delivered from Moses's law, and the covenant of works, remember that Christ is your King and Lawgiver, and you are not lawless; therefore so speak and so do, as they that are under his law of liberty and grace, and shall be judged by it, by justification or condemnation.

13. For he *shall have* judgment without mercy, that hath shewed no mercy; and mercy rejoiceth against judgment.

13. For though this be a law of mercy, it will condemn the unmerciful without mercy: It hath its conditions of life or death, though none but what consist with grace: But the merciful shall obtain mercy at judgment: And God's mercy in Christ as the cause, and their mercy to men for his sake, as the condition, will prevail against condemning judgment.

14. What *doth* it profit, my brethren, though a man say he hath faith, and have not works? can faith save him?

14. Is not a mere wordy profession an unprofitable thing to yourselves, as well as to others? Will professing Christianity, and saying, you believe, profit you to salvation, if you obey not Christ, and live not according to the gospel.

15, 16. If a brother or sister be naked and destitute of daily food, and one of you say unto them, Depart in peace, be you warmed and filled: notwithstanding ye give them not those things which are needful to the body: what *doth* it profit?

15, 16. Will good words clothe the naked, or feed the hungry? Is it not like a mocking of them

17. Even so faith, if it hath not works, is dead, being alone.

17. Even so your notional knowledge and belief, and the bare profession of faith, if it produce not the fruits of obedience, love, and mercy, is but an ineffectual, dead thing in itself, shewing a dead soul, and is dead as to your justification and salvation.

18. Yea, a man may say, Thou hast faith, and I have works: shew me thy faith without thy works, and I will shew thee my faith by my works.

18. Any one may say to this man, If thy religion be sound, it will have life and power, and be known by its fruits: Canst thou shew and justify thy religion or belief, without any good works or fruits, as I can do mine by them?

19. Thou believest that there is one God, thou doest well: the devils also believe, and tremble.

19. It is part of thy religion to believe that there is one God: This is well done; it is a most fundamental truth, but it saveth not the devils that believe it and tremble.

20. But wilt thou know, O vain man, that faith without works is dead? 21. Was not Abraham our father justified by works, when he had offered Isaac his son upon the altar?

20, 21. But art thou not a vain man, that knowest not that faith is but a dead opinion, ineffectual to justify and save, if it be ineffectual to works? Dost thou not discern how plainly the scripture confuteth thee? Was it not doing in faith, or a faith that caused working obedience, by which Abraham was justified, who was the father of the faithful? when he offered his son Isaac, and God said, Gen. xxii. 16. [Because thou hast done this thing, and hast not withheld thy son, thy only son, in blessing I will bless thee, &c.]

22. Seest thou how faith wrought with his works, and by works was faith made perfect?

22. You may see that his faith made him obey God's command, and the obedient working of it did constitute it a sound, effectual faith, without which it could not justify him.

23. And the scripture was fulfilled, which saith, Abraham believed God, and it was imputed unto him for righteousness; and he was called the friend of God.

23. And this is the true sense of the scripture, which saith, Abraham believed, &c. that is, he so far believed and trusted God, as to offer up his son; and this trust working by such obedience, or this practical effectual trust, was so accepted by God, that though he was not perfect without sin, God accounted him a righteous man, that we meet for the free salvation of his grace, and to called The friend of God.

24. Ye see then how that by works a man is justified, and not by faith only.

24. You see then that by such necessary doing God's will, which is the product of an effectual faith, and sheweth it to be lively and sincere, and not a dead opinion, a man is accounted just by God, according to the covenant of grace through Christ, and not only by bare believing, or not by believing only without obeying.

25. Likewise also, was not Rahab the harlot justified by works, when she had received the messengers, and had sent them out another way?

25. And was it not by doing by faith, or a faith causing obedience, that Rahab was justified?

26. For as the body without the spirit is dead, so faith without works is dead also.

26. For as it is a dead spiritless body that cannot stir, so it is a dead, notional, ineffectual belief, that commandeth not a man's life and action: It is dead in itself, and dead as to men's justification and salvation.

ANNOTATIONS.

Nothing but men's misunderstanding the plain drift and sense of Paul's epistles, could make so many take it for a matter of great difficulty to reconcile Paul and James, where there is no considerable show of contradiction. I have shewn the scope and sense of Paul before the epistle to the Romans, 1. That his arguing is to prove that it is not the law of Moses that can justify any man, as a mere doer of it; nor any works at all in commutative justice, making the reward to be of debt for the value of the works, and not of free grace; but that justification must needs be of God's free gift, and therefore by the merits of our Redeemer; and therefore that a fiducial accepting practical belief of God's free gift, covenant, or promise of grace and glory, for, in, and with Christ, is the condition on our part (to be performed by his grace) which is our moral qualification, or receptive disposition, on which God by his covenant giveth us right to the foresaid free gifts (Christ's grace and glory.) This faith Paul never described by some one single physical act of the soul, but as a moral act of the man; as we use the word in human converse: as if one say, if you will trust me as your physician, I will cure you; if you take me for your tutor, I will teach you. Here to trust or take him, signifieth a consenting trust to be medicined and to be taught by such a one. If one say to a condemned beggar, trust me, and I will give thee a lordship in a foreign land; it signifieth a trust consenting practically to go with him, and trust his convoy, and forsake his own country. And James never questioned this doctrine: but some vain men (as James calls them) misunderstood this, and spin out a web of their own vanity, and feign it to be Paul's doctrine. 1. They say that Paul by faith meaneth not faith, by which we are said to be justified, but only Christ (who doubtless is a chief object of that faith.) 2. That God the Father, or the Holy Ghost, are none of the object of faith, as it is justifying. 3. That it is not Christ himself, as prophet or king, but only as priest, that is this object. 4. That it is not all Christ's priesthood, but only sacrifice and righteousness, that is this object, and not his heavenly intercession. 5. That it is not Christ's sacrifice and righteousness as merely meritorious of our pardon and life, but as it was paid and performed by Christ as our surety in our legal reputative person, and so is imputed to us as our own, because done by another in our name and stead, as one paying a debt by another that was bound for him. 6. That so far as faith is here meant, it is but one single physical act of faith in species; and there they are utterly disagreed. 1. Whether it be an act of the understanding, or will, or both? 2. Whether one act can be the belief of many objects, viz. of Christ's sacrifice, obedience, promise, pardon, heaven? &c. 7. Yet many say that it is but one individual act that we are justified by (which no mortal man can know, the individuation of the soul's acts being obscure, and the objects being always many conjunct) and they say that it is only our first act of faith, and that all following acts of the same species, finding us justified, cannot justify us any more than works. 8. They say that faith justifieth only as an instrumental cause, and not as a moral qualifying receptive condition, or disposition. 9. They say that believing in the Father and the Holy Ghost, and hoping for heaven, and praying for mercy, and repenting of sin, and loving God and our Saviour, and his word and saints, and thankfulness for grace, and obedience to Christ, and patience, and forsaking all for him, are the works which Paul meaneth to exclude from justification, and so is faith in Christ's righteousness as an act, but not as an instrument. 10. They are utterly disagreed whether faith justify by appropriating only Christ's active righteousness, or also his passive, or also his divine righteousness and perfection. 11. They say that by [imputing faith for righteousness] is meant, that not our faith, but Christ's righteousness, is imputed in itself (and not in its effects only) to be our own, because we performed it by him. 12. They say, that is the very law of innocency and works that justifieth us, as having perfectly fulfilled it in and by Christ. 13. They (most) hold that in Christ we have both perfectly kept the law, from birth till death, by imputed obedience, and yet satisfied for not keeping it by his sufferings, as if perfect obedience imputed, could consist with sin. 14. They say that God's correctious are no punishments, because else Christ's suffering was insufficient, and God should punish one sin twice. 15. And that our pardon and justification is perfect as soon as we believe. 16. And that no more is needful to our continued justification, than to its beginning. 17. And that yet more is needful to our salvation than to our final justification. Many such human inventions man's brain hath spun out, and made a doctrine of their own, and called it Paul's.

And James, having to do with carnal gospellers, that thought to be saved for being of a right opinion, and calling this faith, doth, 1. Tell them, that this is not that true Christian faith which hath the promise of justification and salvation, but that that is a powerful, practical belief, and trust. 2. Therefore their doing that which faith consents and engageth them to do, must justify that faith to be sound, which must justify them as the condition of life. 3. And that therefore this efficiency or doing of this practical faith, is part of the condition of their justification, and it justifieth the man himself, 1. As it justifieth his faith, and so justifieth him to be a sound believer, and not an infidel or hypocrite. 2. In that the effectual, operative nature, and consent to obey, is essential to that faith itself. 3. In that as a faith accepting Christ, and consenting to obey him as the author of eternal salvation, is the condition of our first entering into a state of life and justification, so our performance of that consent by sincere obedience and perseverance, is the condition of our justification, as continued and consummate at judgment, and so of our final salvation. 4. In that sincere holiness and obedience is the very matter that must justify men, against the virtual or actual accusation of Satan, that they were not holy and obedient, but ungodly or hypocrites: as faith itself is the matter of our justification against the accusation, that we were not believers. Now James speaketh of no other faith than Paul doth: but, 1. He speaketh of another thing under the name of [works.] 2. And he speaketh of a working nature in faith for our justification begun, and of the deeds themselves, as needful to its continuance. And, in a word, he speaketh of such justification by no sort of works. 1. In opposition to Christ or free grace; or 2. In co-ordination with him; 3. But in mere instituted subordination to him. And no Christian must ascribe to any faith, works, or act of man, the least part of the office of Christ.

CHAP. III.

MY brethren, be not many masters, knowing that we shall receive the greater condemnation.

1. And as I thus admonish you against the error of hypocrites, who take their dead opinions and professions for a justifying faith; so must I do against another vice, which that sort of hypocrites are guilty of: their pride and self-conceit maketh them think that their knowledge is much higher than other Christians; and that they are the fittest men to be teaching masters, and reprovers; and so they are all more forward to teach, and magisterially censure others, and use their tongue to contemn others as short of them in knowledge, and to boast of themselves; and all their talk runs in a teaching, and not a learning way. But I warn you to avoid this proud and masterly spirit; for it will make your sin the greater, and without excuse, and increase your condemnation.

2. For in many things we offend all. If any man offend not in word, the same is a perfect man, and able also to bridle the whole body.

2. Your zeal goeth out by censuring others, as great sinners in comparison of you (perhaps for not observing your ceremonies and traditions, and not taking you for their teaching masters;) but fear sin in yourselves; yea, lest your censorious, reproachful, unbridled tongues, should prove worse than that which you censure others for. He that hath most power to rule his tongue, and sinneth not in words, is like to be the most perfect Christian, and can rule his actions by the same obedience and wisdom which doth rule his tongue.

3. Behold, we put bitts in the horses' mouths, that they may obey us, and we turn about their whole body.

3. As we rule the whole bodies of horses by a bridle in the mouth; so, could you bridle your mouths, it would both signify a power to rule your lives, and much promote this.

4. Behold also the ships, which though they be so great, and are driven of fierce winds, yet are they turned about with a very small helm, whithersoever the governor listeth.

4. So the pilot, by so small a thing as the helm, ruleth great ships, that are under the force of winds.

5. Even so the tongue is a little member, and boasteth great things:

5. And man's tongue is but a small part of the body, though it boast great things; and the government of that little member, is a great part of the government of the man.

5, 6. Behold, how great a matter a little fire kindleth! and the tongue is a fire, a world of iniquity: so is the tongue amongst our members, that it defileth the whole body, and setteth on fire the course of nature, and it is set on fire of hell.

5, 6. The tongue in the body, and the world, is like fire among much combustible matter. As a little fire kindleth much; so this little member doth both kindle defiling passions and guilt in our own bodies, and also kindle hatred, rage, and strife in the world, and set on fire the societies and affairs of mankind in the world, being itself set on fire by the devil, and used by hellish temptations to hellish designs in diabolical employment.

7. For every kind of beasts and of birds, and of serpents, and things in the sea, is tamed, and hath been tamed of mankind: 8. But the tongue can no man tame,

7, 8. For all sorts of animals have been mastered by man: but the tongue of another who can master? [when we have so much ado to subdue our own.]

8, 9. It is an unruly evil, full of deadly poison. Therewith bless we God, even the Father; and therewith curse we men, which are made after the similitude of God. 10. Out of the same mouth proceedeth blessing and cursing:

8, 9. It is to us, and in the world, an unruly evil (till grace shall tame it) und infecteth ourselves and the societies where we live, with the mortal poison of many great sins. The same hypocrites, who praise God, and worship him with it, do reproach their brethren with it: not only men that have some of God's image in their natural faculties, but those that are God's true servants, better than themselves, who are renewed to God's image in holiness by grace.

10, 11. My brethren, these things ought not so to be. Doth a fountain send forth at the same place sweet water and bitter? 12. Can a fig-tree, my brethren, bear olive-berries? either a vine, figs? so can no fountain both yield salt water and fresh.

10, 11, 12. Do you not perceive that your ill reproachful tongues, which vilify, speak evil of, and condemn good Christians, for not being of your minds, do confute themselves, when the same tongues profess to honour God, and boast of wisdom and religion in yourselves: if you were as wise and godly, as you profess, your tongues would not, by speaking ill of your brethren, shew the contrary. No fountain sends forth sweet water and bitter, fresh and salt; no fig-tree brings forth olives: the tree is known by its fruit.

13. Who is a wise man and endued with knowledge amongst you? let him shew out of a good conversation his works with meekness of wisdom.

13. Are any among you, indeed, as much wiser, and knowing and excelling others, as you would be thought when you censure or despise them: shew it, if you would have any wise man believe you, not by proud boasting or talking against others, but by the true fruits of the spirit, even a better conversation than theirs in all your dealings, and by more good works, with that humble meekness, which signifieth true wisdom.

14. But if ye have bitter envying and strife in your hearts, glory not, and lie not against the truth. 15. This wisdom descendeth not from

above, but *is* earthly, sensual, devilish.

14, 15. But if you have a bitter zeal and envy, and uncharitable heart-rising and strife against your brethren, pretending truth, orthodoxness, or religion, for your swelling envy and emulation, and talking and preaching down love and peace, to make those that differ from your side, to seem hateful, or contemptuous, in comparison of you, your profession of greater knowledge and religiousness is but proud boasting, and lying against the truth: this wisdom, and this preaching and course, is not of God, not such as he will own. It is from an earthly and sensual principle, your own praise or profit, or magisterial will, or some carnal interest is at the root; if you could know yourselves, you might see this: yea, it is so far from excelling others, that it is a devilish wisdom, a devilish zeal, and devilish preaching and disputing, which you glory in.

16. For where envying and strife *is*, there *is* confusion, and every evil work.

16. For where envious zeal and strife prevail, there is still faction and unquietness, (or sedition, tumults, and unsettledness still for change;) and this cherisheth all sorts of evil works, which men will think to be all good or lawful, to serve their contentious zeal, and to further their changes and carnal ends.

17. But the wisdom that is from above is first pure, then peaceable, gentle, *and* easy to be intreated, full of mercy and good fruits, without partiality, and without hypocrisy. 18. And the fruit of righteousness is sown in peace of them that make peace.

17, 18. But if you would know among the several pretenders, whose knowledge, and religiousness, and zeal, is from above, the fruit of the Spirit, which God will own, these are the sure marks of it. 1. It is first for true purity of heart and life: it will not choose sin, on any pretence, so far as men can know it. If any be for wilful, deliberate conformity to sin, or for a loose and sensual life, or against serious godliness, and a holy, heavenly, sober, and just life, this is not from the Spirit of God. 2. It is next to this, addicted to peace, and will seek it by all lawful means. 3. It is addicted to put the best sense of another man's case, and to a gentle, and not a rigid, censorious judgment. 4. Easily yielding to good persuasions, and not stiff in ill opinions or ways. 5. Full of mercy to others, and of all good works or fruits to his power, as being devoted to do good. 6. Without censorious partiality, as sectaries, that can see nothing but what seemeth to make for their own party and opinions, (or, without a wavering unresolvedness in the Christian religion.) 7. Without hypocrisy, or false pretendings. And though the erroneous and contentious in both extremes, do use to vilify or abhor peace-makers, who serve God according to this supernal wisdom,

yet these men, who labour to make peace, are sowing, in this work of peace, the fruit of true righteousness, as guiltless of the crimes of the extreme contenders, and of the tumults caused by them: and when the harvest of God's judgment cometh, they shall reap this fruit to themselves: and if the countries, where they live, are worthy of such fruit, they must reap it from this seed of peace-making labours.

CHAP. IV.

FROM whence come wars and fightings among you? *come they* not hence, *even* of your lusts, that war in your members?

1. The Jews are in frequent seditions and fightings among themselves, in which many erroneous Christians join with the unbelievers, in a blind zeal for their law and nation. And do you think it is from true zeal that their wars arise? No, it is from their own sensual, worldly lusts, that first war in themselves, and then disturb the common peace.

2. Ye lust, and have not: ye kill and desire to have, and cannot obtain: ye fight and war, yet ye have not, because ye ask not.

2. You covet, and fight, and kill, in your mistaken desires of your law and liberties; and you do but lose your blood and labour, by going your own sinful way, and not seeking to God for counsel, conduct, and success, who must give all good, and that in his own way.

3. Ye ask, and receive not; because ye ask amiss, that you may consume it upon your lusts.

3. Yea, you will be religious in your sin, and make your prayers to God for deliverance from the Roman power, and for your country's liberty. But they are carnal prayers; and God rejecteth them; for it is but that you may live in great plenty, power and pleasure, enjoying sensual prosperity, that you pray to God for your deliverance.

4. Ye adulterers, and adulteresses, know ye not that the friendship of the world is enmity against God? whosoever therefore will be a friend of the world, is the enemy of God.

4. You that by your perfidiousness to God, are like perfidious adulterers, loving the world best, whilst God is in your mouths, know ye not that this love of the world, as his competitor, is enmity to God; and that he is God's enemy that so loveth it predominantly?

5. Do you think that the scripture saith in vain, The spirit that dwelleth in us lusteth to envy?

5. Is it not true, which the scripture saith of

the evil inclination of man's heart, as lusting after worldly pomp and pleasure, and to envy and strife, that they may obtain it?

6. But he giveth more grace: wherefore he saith, God resisteth the proud, but giveth grace unto the humble.

6. But God's grace is of a contrary tendency, and would teach you better things; but he giveth it to the humble, and not to the proud; for he is against such, as it is said, &c.

7. Submit yourselves therefore to God: resist the devil, and he will flee from you.

7. If ye would be delivered and live in safety, submit yourselves to God's government and will, and go the way which he prescribeth: conquer Satan, and you need not fear his forces; and do but resolutely resist him, and you conquer him.

8. Draw nigh to God, and he will draw nigh to you: cleanse *your* hands, ye sinners, and purify *your* hearts, ye double-minded. 9. Be afflicted, and mourn, and weep: let your laughter be turned into mourning, and *your* joy to heaviness. 10. Humble yourselves in the sight of the Lord, and he shall lift you up.

8, 9, 10. Draw nigh to that God against whom you have rebelled, and he will draw nigh to you for your deliverance, and will not forsake you. Cleanse your hands by reformation from your sins, and your hearts from your halting between God and the world: bewail your former sin, by self-afflicting, mourning, and weeping. Turn your sensual pleasures into godly sorrow, and your carnal mirth into penitent tears: humble yourselves before that God whom you have offended, and then he will lift you up, and save you better than your seditions.

11. Speak not evil one of another (brethren.) He that speaketh evil of *his* brother, and judgeth *his* brother, speaketh evil of the law, and judgeth the law: but if thou judge the law, thou art not a doer of the law, but a judge.

11. And give over your reproach and censoriousness against the Gentile Christians, that do not observe your ceremonial law, by which you encourage their persecutors; for both the law of Christ, and the law of Moses, which you profess to own, do bid you love your neighbour as yourself, and forbid such uncharitable censures; so that by condemning your brethren, you condemn the law: and this is not to keep either Moses' law, or Christ's, but to set yourselves above both, by making yourselves reproving judges of them.

12. There is one law-giver, who is able to save, and to destroy: who art thou that judgest another?

12. Christ, and none else (saith Dr. H.) hath authority to give laws to us: there is but one lawgiver, who hath the absolute and final power of life and death eternal, salvation and damnation. Who art thou that darest arrogate this judgment? Or what power hast thou to judge or anathematize another, any further than truly to tell men whom Christ will judge and cast away?

13. Go to now, ye that say, Today or to-morrow we will go into such a city, and continue there a year, and buy and sell, and get gain: 14. Whereas ye know not what *shall be* on the morrow: for what is your life? it is even a vapour that appeareth for a little time, and then vanisheth away.

13, 14. You are too much set on worldly prosperity; and you plot for gain, as if you were secured of long abode on earth; and you lay your designs with presumptuous confidence, where and how long you will dwell, trade, and gain, whereas your life on earth is a mere uncertain fugitive vapour, quickly gone.

15. For that ye *ought* to say, If the Lord will we shall live, and do this, or that. 16. But now ye rejoice in your boastings: all such rejoicing is evil.

15, 16. Whereas ye should remember the uncertainty and shortness of your lives, and design and do all in submissive dependence on the will of God: but you fetch your comfort from worldly things by your own vain presumption of long life, and hope of worldly prosperity: all such presumptuous carnal comforts are evil.

17. Therefore to him that knoweth to do good, and doth it not, to him it is sin.

17. And the brevity of man's life, and the vanity of worldly gain, are things so notorious and undeniable to all men, especially to Christians, that to let these vanities loosen you from Christ and your obedience, is utterly inexcusable.

CHAP. V.

GO to now, ye rich men, weep and howl for your miseries that shall come upon you.

1. But as do those that will yet cleave to the world, and take no warning, let me tell you to your sorrow, that dreadful miseries are coming upon you, the foresight of which should make you weep and howl, instead of your deceitful joy.

2. Your riches are corrupted,

and your garments are moth eaten. 3. Your gold and silver is cankered, and the rust of them shall be a witness against you, and shall eat your flesh as it were fire: Ye have heaped treasure together for the last days.

2, 3. What are these vanities which you have so inordinately affected? Your beloved riches are not only corruptible, but corrupted by you, to your own sin and hurt; your rich clothing is a moth-eaten vanity: the gold and silver, which you have treasured up, is cankered and rusty, and the guilt signified by that rust, shall condemn you, and corrode your consciences as fire. At great cost and labour you have treasured up riches, but it is in effect, to be a prey to your enemies in the day of your destruction, and a witness in God's day of the judgment against yourselves to your own confusion.

4. Behold the hire of the labourers, which have reaped down your fields, which is of you kept back by fraud, crieth: and the cries of them which have reaped, are entered into the ears of the Lord of sabaoth (or hosts.)

4. You Jews are addicted to covetousness, and by that to injury and oppression; and you deny poor labourers their wages, and defraud them; and God heareth their cries, and will revenge them on you.

5. Ye have lived in pleasure on the earth, and been wanton: ye have nourished your hearts as in a day of slaughter.

5. Your riches have been provision for your sensuality: you have by them made provision for the lusts of the flesh, and lived in pleasure, revelling, and luxury, and lasciviousness, and have fed and cherished the flesh, and its delights, as in a continual feast.

6. Ye have condemned and killed the just, and he doth not resist you.

6. Your riches have lift you up into power, which you have abused to condemn and kill innocent men, who have not resisted you, but endured all.

Note, 1. Some think that the Jewish Christians are here meant, to whom James wrote; but sure they were not so degenerate. 2. Some think it was the Gnostic heretics. 3. I think it much more probable, that by an apostrophe he speaks to the rich infidels, to introduce his exhortation to the Christians to patience.

7. Be patient therefore, brethren, unto the coming of the Lord: behold the husbandman waiteth for the precious fruit of the earth, and hath long patience for it, until he receive the early and latter rain. 8. Be ye also patient, establish your hearts: for the coming of the Lord draweth nigh.

7, 8. But as for you, persecuted Christians, bear all this patiently, without discouragement, tiredness, or wavering in your faith: for the time is short, and the coming of Christ for your deliverance is not far off: if in your husbandry or tillage you look not to reap as soon as you have sowed, but wait for the harvest and fruit, and for the showers that must ripen it; should you not more patiently wait for greater things, when the time will quickly come?

9. Grudge not one against another, brethren, lest ye be condemned; behold, the judge standeth before the door.

9. Make not too great a matter of your wrongs, nor quarrel among yourselves, (as the Jewish zealots, mentioned by Josephus, did) lest while you condemn one another, all condemn themselves; and biting and devouring one another, you be devoured one of another: stay but a little, and the judge, who is at hand, will avenge you of your enemies, and end all your quarrels, which ignorance and pride have made, and kept up among yourselves.

10. Take, my brethren, the prophets, who have spoken in the name of the Lord, for an example of suffering affliction, and of patience.

10. You justly honour the prophets, who have spoken, as sent from God: remember how they were used, and how they suffered, and let them be your example, and imitate them in patience.

11. Behold, we count them happy which endure. Ye have heard of the patience of Job, and have seen the end of the Lord: that the Lord is very pitiful, and of tender mercy.

11. It is part of our faith, to believe that they are happy who patiently suffer for righteousness sake: you have heard of Job's patience, and of the end which God intended and accomplished, which tells us, that God is full of pity and mercy to us, when he afflicteth us.

12. But above all things, my brethren, swear not, neither by heaven, neither by earth, neither by any other oath: but let your yea, be yea: and your nay, nay: lest ye fall into condemnation.

12. And I must especially exhort you to avoid customary, needless swearing by heaven or earth, or any oath: but let yea and nay serve you, and be true of your word, that you be not drawn into a just suspicion of falsehood, (or condemned for profaning the name of God.)

Note, That this is so far from forbidding necessary oaths, for ending strife, that it is but to confirm them, by preserving the due reverence of them.

2. The true nature of an oath is by our speech [to pawn the reputation of some certain or great thing, for the averring of a doubted lesser thing;] and not only (as is commonly held) an appeal to God, or other judge. As to swear [by the fire, by the temple, by my faith or truth, by the life of Pharaoh, by the heavens, &c.] is as much as to say [if this be not true, then the fire burneth not, the temple is not holy, I am a liar, Pharaoh is no king, as sure as heaven is heaven, &c.] so [the Lord liveth] is [this is as true as that God liveth.]

13. Is any among you afflicted? let him pray. Is any merry? let him sing psalms.

13. In your affliction, have present recourse to God by prayer (in faith and hope) and when you are cheerful and merry, turn it to God's praise and thanksgiving for his mercies, in singing holy songs to God.

Note, That it is not only David's psalms that they are tied to, but such as are by men fitted to their proper cases; which confuteth them that condemn all human forms of composed words in God's service.

14. Is any sick among you? let him call for the elders of the church, and let them pray over him, anointing him with oil in the name of the Lord. **15.** And the prayer of faith shall save the sick, and the Lord shall raise him up; and if he have committed sins, they shall be forgiven him.

14, 15. When any of you is sick, let him send for the bishops or pastors of the church, and let them pray over him, anointing him, with oil in the name of the Lord, as a sign and means which he hath appointed for miraculous cures: and if it be the prayer of faith, and he be a person capable and fit for that deliverance, it shall recover him from his sickness, and God shall raise him; and if his sickness be a corrective punishment for any sin that he hath committed, God will forgive him, and take off that penalty, if he repent.

Note, 1. That this implieth, that each church hath divers elders: and whereas Dr. H. thinks it meaneth one single bishop, who, the ancients say, visited all the sick, you may see then how great their dioceses were. Should all the sick men in London, or in many countries, send for the bishop, he would come but to a few of them, at least forty or eighty miles off: but it will be said, he will do it for others: and why not give orders and sacraments by others, (as laymen now use the keys?) And if the work be proper for bishops, those others then are made bishops; if not, others may do it.

2. Anointing (being healthful to dry bodies in those hot countries) was used by Christ's appointment for miraculous cures, and never made a duty or sacrament to continue when miracles cease.

3. Sicknesses are usually corrective punishments for sin; and to forgive the sin as to that penalty, is to remit the punishment, and heal the sick.

4. The promise of pardon and recovery pre-supposeth the person penitent, and fit for that deliverance.

16. Confess *your* faults one to another, and pray one for another, that ye may be healed: the effectual fervent prayer of a righteous man availeth much.

16. Therefore penitently confess your faults to one another (especially to the elders that visit you), and pray one for another; for this is the likely way of your recovery: the effectual, fervent instant prayer of a righteous man is of great force or prevalence.

Note, 1. An impenitent man is unfit for pardon, and therefore, for deliverance from punishment: and he that doth not penitently confess and bewail his sin, cannot be judged a true penitent; and therefore cannot be prayed for with that faith and hope as we may do for the penitent. 2. This is not to be a customary thing, or only to a priest, but it is a duty both in sickness and health, wherever the expression of repentance to others is a duty. By which, alas! we know how rare true repentance is, when even professors of zeal in religion are sharp in censuring and blaming others; and except a very few humble souls, if they be never so justly blamed or reproved, do swell against the reprover with pride and indignation, as if he were their enemy: and they that separate from the churches for want of discipline, are earnest for it for others, but cannot bear it on themselves; nor so much as endure a confutation of their errors, but take him to speak against godliness, who speaketh against their mistakes and faults; and too many (like the profane) will turn again and all to rend him.

17. Elias was a man subject to like passions as we are, and he prayed earnestly that it might not rain: and it rained not on the earth by the space of three years and six months. **18.** And he prayed again, and the heaven gave rain, and the earth brought forth her fruit.

17, 18. Think not that prayer is a vain or ineffectual thing, though we be frail and faulty men: Elias was but a man, liable both to sufferings, and to a troubled mind in them; as we are; yet on his earnest prayer, it rained not on an idolatrous persecuting country for three years and a half; and at his prayer, it rained again, and the land was fruitful.

19, 20. Brethren, if any of you do err from the truth, and one convert him; Let him know, that he which converteth the sinner from the error of his way, shall save a soul from death, and shall hide a multitude of sins.

19, 20. I beseech you, brethren, be neither negligent or despairing to the cure of men in error, nor yet impatient with those that would detect your errors, and convince you and bring you to repentance (as proud impenitent persons are: but know, that (as all men alas are too prone to error) if any man err from the truth (through ignorance or a corrupted will) and one convert him, he that converteth a sinner from his error in mind or life, doth not only do that which tendeth to save his life from God's punishing stroke, but also shall save his soul from everlasting death, and procure the pardon of his manifold sin, not only so far that the church, but God himself, shall receive him into a reconciled state.

Note, 1. That error and sin are the way to death and misery. 2. Converting the erroneous sinner, is the way to save him. 3. One man may be said to save another, (much more a man himself) by converting him, without derogating from Christ's salvation, but in subordination to it. 4. Therefore all Christians, but especially ministers, should be diligent and skilful to convert erroneous sinners, and the erroneous patient and thankful for their help.

Note, If it be the Gnostics, as Dr. H. saith, that James here, and Paul in his epistles so greatly warn the Christians against, alas, too great a part of the church governors, bishops and their clergy, abroad on earth, seem turned very like these by him described Gnostics. 1. In being for worldly interest, wealth, and pleasure. 2. In being for ceremonies. 3. In joining with the ungodly enemies of piety. 4. In being latitudinarians, or licentious against strictness and tenderness of conscience, and adiaphorists in things not adiaphorous. 5. In being persecutors. And if base underling Gnostics or Nicolaitans, could so trouble the churches then, what a case must those countries be in, where they are got into the episcopal chair, and claim the keys of the kingdom of heaven, to execute their pride and lusts over princes and people of all sorts, sure Borborites or Gnostics are not the less such, nor the less dangerous, for being called bishops, and having power, wealth, and interest.

THE FIRST EPISTLE GENERAL

OF

ST. PETER.

CHAP. I.

PETER, an apostle of Jesus Christ, to the strangers scattered throughout Pontus, Galatia, Cappadocia, Asia, and Bythinia, 2. Elect according to the foreknowledge of God the Father, through sanctification of the spirit unto obedience and sprinkling of the blood of Jesus Christ: grace unto you, and peace be multiplied.

1. Peter an apostle (not called the universal bishop or head, or governor of the church) to the dispersed Jews throughout Pontus, &c. chosen by grace out of that unbelieving forlorn nation, according to God's foreknowledge and unsearchable counsel, to sanctification by the Holy Ghost, and to obedience, and to a state of reconciliation and justification, by the merit of the blood of Christ applied; grace and peace multiplied to you, is my prayer and benediction.

3. Blessed be the God and Father of our Lord Jesus Christ, which according to his abundant mercy, hath begotten us again unto a lively hope, by the resurrection of Jesus Christ from the dead,

3. Blessed be God the Father of our Lord Jesus Christ, who out of his abundant mercy, for the manifestation and glory of it, hath regenerated us to a living hope, even a hope of glorious life, procured, notified, and secured to us, by the resurrection of Christ from the dead.

4. To an inheritance incorruptible, and undefiled, and that fadeth not away, reserved in heaven for you: 5. Who are kept by the power of God through faith unto salvation, ready to be revealed in the last time.

4, 5. Not to such a corruptible, defiled, fading inheritance, as earth is to its lovers, but to an inheritance incorruptible, undefiled, and holy, never fading, reserved by the divine love and decree, and by the possession, intercession, and promise of Christ, for you who are true believers, and are kept by the power of God through that faith, which he hath given you, and you keep and exercise to salvation, which ere long will be gloriously revealed to your sight and possession, the last time being not far off.

Note, It is revealed already in the gospel, and will be fully revealed to separated souls : but the full glorious revelation is when the whole church is consummated.

6. Wherein ye greatly rejoice, though now for a season (if need be) ye are in heaviness through manifold temptations :

6. In the belief and hope of this glorious inheritance, you now live in great joy, though for a little time, when God seeth it needful for your good, he let out upon you those trying sufferings which are heavy and grievous to the flesh.

7. That the trial of your faith, being much more precious than of gold that perisheth, though it be tried with fire, might be found unto praise, and honour and glory at the appearing of Jesus Christ.

7. For as your faith is more a precious thing than gold, and refined gold is the most precious gold; so tried faith, is the most precious faith, and the trial of it a greater work than the trying and refining of gold by the fire; that so it may be found at the coming of Christ, a qualification meet for your own praise, honour, and glory, and in you also unto Christ's.

8. Whom having not seen, ye love, in whom though now ye see *him* not, yet believing, ye rejoice with joy unspeakable, and full of glory.

8. Whom though you never saw in the flesh, as we did that followed him, yet you truly love and honour: and though now you see him not in his glory, nor his coming, yet your effectual faith doth so far serve instead of seeing him, that you rejoice by it with unspeakable triumphant joy, in hope of that which you shall see.

9. Receiving the end of your faith, even the salvation of your souls.

9. And shall shortly receive that great salvation, for which you have believed.

10. Of which salvation the prophets have inquired, and searched diligently, who prophesied of the grace *that should come* unto you. 11. Searching what, or what manner of time the Spirit of Christ which was in them did signify, when it testified beforehand the sufferings of Christ, and the glory that should follow.

10, 11. Of this great salvation and kingdom of Christ incarnate, which is dated from his resurrection, and perfected at his next coming, many prophets foretold in their manner and degree ; and they inquired, and diligently searched, more explicitly to have known it, and the time when it should be, when the Spirit in them foretold that the Messiah must suffer, and in general, that glorious things should follow.

12. Unto whom it was revealed, that not unto themselves, but unto us they did minister the things which are now reported unto you by them that have preached the gospel unto you, with the Holy Ghost sent down from heaven, which things the angels desire to look into.

12. And it was revealed to them, that it was not to come to pass in their days, and that it was not they, but we that should see the Messiah, and his special kingdom, and the things which since his resurrection, are now preached to you by us his ministers, with the seal of the Holy Spirit sent down in a special abundance from heaven, to be the witness of Christ, and the sanctifier of souls ; a mystery so great, and of so excellent importance, that the angels think it worthy their search.

13. Wherefore gird up the loins of your mind, be sober, and hope to the end, for the grace that is to be brought unto you at the revelation of Jesus Christ.

13. Wherefore, as runners gird their clothes to them, that they trouble them not; do you fortify your minds with holy resolution, and soberly watch, and keep up your hope until the end; for that glorious effect of redemption and grace, which

14. As obedient children, not fashioning yourselves according to the former lusts, in your ignorance.

14. And as obedient children of God, to whom you are reconciled, no more living as you did in the time of your ignorance, in fleshly lusts, and worldly vice.

15. But as he which hath called you is holy, so be ye holy in all manner of conversation; 16. Because it is written, Be ye holy, for I am holy.

15, 16. And, as children must be like their father, and they must please God, who will be saved by him; therefore, as he that hath called you is a holy God and Saviour, be ye a holy people; for so God requireth; [Be ye holy, for I am holy.]

17. And if ye call on the Father, who without respect of persons, judgeth according to every man's work, pass the time of your sojourning here in fear.

17. And if you call God your father, and call on him, who, without respect of persons, for any worldly difference, judgeth all men according to their works, let the thoughts of his holiness and future judgment, cause you to pass the time that you, as sojourners, wait for Christ's coming, in holy carefulness, obedient fear.

18. Forasmuch as ye know that ye were not redeemed with corruptible things, as silver and gold, from your vain conversation received by tradition from your fathers; 19. But with the precious blood of Christ, as of a Lamb without blemish and without spot.

18, 19. For the preciousness of the price which redeemed us, tells us the great worth of our salvation from sin and misery, which was not with silver and gold, or any corruptible price, but it was with the precious blood of Christ, the spotless Lamb of God, that ye were redeemed from the vain ceremonies and traditions which you were bred up in, and from your sinful conversation.

20. Who verily was fore-ordained before the foundation of the world, but was manifest in these last times for you: 21. Who by him do believe in God that raised him up from the dead, and gave him glory, that your faith and hope might be in God.

20, 21. Whom God had fore-ordained to this blessed office before the foundation of the world; but (though oft prophesied of) was not incarnate and manifest in the flesh, till these last times, even for you that live since his coming, who are not by him drawn, as we are falsely accused, from the true and only God, but by him are taught the true knowledge of God, and to believe that God to be God indeed, wise, good, and almighty, who raised Christ from the dead, and gave him glory; and so that your faith and hope might be ultimately in God alone, by Christ's mediation.

22. Seeing ye have purified your souls in obeying the truth through the Spirit, unto unfeigned love of the brethren: see that ye love one another with a pure heart fervently.

22. And as you have purified your souls from former error and sin, by obeying the gospel, by the work of God's Spirit, unto unfeigned love of Christian brethren, be sure to keep up that love, and with a pure heart, and deep affection, to love each other.

23. Being born again, not of corruptible seed, but of incorruptible, by the word of God, which liveth and abideth for ever.

23. Seeing you are not only brethren by corruptible generation and relation, but of incorruptible seed, by the word of God, who liveth and abideth for ever, and so must your incorruptible love to each other, which is part of your incorruptible nature.

24. For all flesh is as grass, and all the glory of man as the flower of grass: the grass withereth, and the flower thereof falleth away: 25. But the word of the Lord endureth for ever. And this is the word which by the gospel is preached unto you.

24, 25. For all flesh, and all its glory, is a fading, dying thing, like the grass and flower: but God's word is everlasting truth, as Christ the author is, and is our guide to an everlasting life: and this true word is it which we preach to you by the gospel, and bespeaketh endless constancy in your holy love and obedience.

CHAP. II.

WHEREFORE laying aside all malice, and all guile, and hypocrisies, and envies, and all evil speakings, 2. As new born babes, desire the sincere milk of the word, that ye may grow thereby:

1, 2. Lay aside therefore, and renounce all

naughtiness, and all deceit, and hypocrisy, or counterfeiting, and all envy, and all speaking evil of others. And as new born babes, desire, and seek, and drink in the rational milk, (or intellectual) without fraud and mixture) that you may grow up to salvation by it; which the mixture of heresy, or hypocrisy, would vitiate, and invectives against others would but turn it against yourselves.

3. If so be, ye have tasted that the Lord is gracious. 4. To whom coming, *as* unto a living stone, disallowed indeed of men, but chosen of God and precious. 5. Ye also, as lively stones, are built up a spiritual house, an holy priesthood, to offer up spiritual sacrifices, acceptable to God by Jesus Christ.

3, 4, 5. And if you are Christians indeed, and have had a spiritual relish of the love of God in Christ, you must suppose his church to be like an house, in which every stone is a living man, and Christ is the chief foundation-stone, as the Lord of Life, on whom all the building is erected; rejected indeed by the Jewish and heathen rulers, but chosen of God to this blessed office, and more precious than any pearl: and so coming to him the foundation, as so many living stones yourselves, you being cemented to him, and to one another, ye are made one spiritual house of God; yea, as a temple, in which you are all priests, to offer daily sacrifice to God; which he will accept through the intercession of the great high priest Jesus Christ: for your prayer and praise may be thus accepted: (think thus of God's house, and you may be for sweeping and repairing it, but you will never be for dividing, dismembering, or separating from it.)

6. Wherefore also it is contained in the scripture, Behold, I lay in Sion a chief corner-stone, elect, precious; and he that believeth on him shall not be confounded.

6. This the scripture foretold, saying, [I lay in Sion, &c.] that is, I set over the church a Saviour, and a King, on whom the church shall be founded: and none shall be put to shame, by the frustration of their faith, hope, and obedience, who put their trust in him.

7. Unto you therefore which believe he is precious: but unto them which be disobedient, the stone which the builders disallowed, the same is made the head of the corner, 8. And a stone of stumbling, and a rock of offence, *even to them* which stumble at the word, being disobedient, whereunto also they were appointed.

7, 8. To you who believe, as he is esteemed precious, so will he be in the riches of his grace to you: but to them that obey not the gospel, but are unbelieving rejecters of him, he whom the builders, the Jewish rulers, did refuse, is made the foundation of the church, and they shall feel his kingly power: he is that stone on which they stumble and fall, and that rock on which the adversaries dash themselves in pieces, even they that unbelievingly reject, and quarrel against the gospel, and disobey it; to which destruction (not to their sin) the righteous God appointed them.

9. But ye are a chosen generation, a royal priesthood, an holy nation, a peculiar people, that ye should shew forth the praises of him, who hath called you out of darkness into his marvellous light:

9. But as the Israelites were, by their proper covenant of peculiarity, separated to God from the rest of the world, and called a chosen generation, a royal priesthood, an holy nation, a peculiar people, especially as typifying the Christian church; so are you more eminently a chosen seed of Christ by his Spirit, a dignified kingdom of priests, who are all designed to reign with Christ: and all may have access to God, a nation or sort of men sanctified by dedication to God; though all the world be his, you are his peculiarly, and have the covenant and privileges of peculiarity, having greater mercies than the rest of the world, that as priests, you may stand daily before God, and celebrate his praises, who hath called you out of the darkness of ignorance, and unbelief, and wickedness, into that marvellous light, by which you know him the Father of lights.

10. Which in time past were not a people, but are now the people of God: which had not obtained mercy, but now have obtained mercy.

10. Who were under the Roman captivity, and scattered over the earth, and alienated from God by unbelief, but now are made Christ's free-men, and fellow-citizens with the saints, and have obtained that mercy, which unbelievers do reject.

11. Dearly beloved, I beseech you as strangers and pilgrims, abstain from fleshly lusts, which war against the soul.

11. But you are yet strangers and sojourners in the countries where you are scattered, and indeed on earth; therefore I earnestly beseech you to abstain from that fleshly pleasure and life, which are usually the fruit of wealth and prosperity in the world, and are warring enemies, against the holy inclinations, motions, and works, of the holy Spirit.

12. Having your conversation honest among the Gentiles, that whereas they speak against you as evil-doers, they may by *your* good

works which they shall behold, glorify God in the day of visitation.

12. And let your conversation among the heathens, be so just, and decent, and exemplary, that they that now speak against you, as if you were a sort of bad, deluded, contemptible men, through prejudice and malicious fame, may, by your excelling all others in good works, rejoice, and give glory to God, when he shall visit you with deliverance from your oppressors, and shall exalt you.

13. Submit yourselves to every ordinance of man for the Lord's sake, whether it be to the king, as supreme. 14. Or unto governors, as unto them that are sent by him for the punishment of evil-doers, and for the praise of them that do well.

13, 14. Be subject to every civil, human ruler, though heathen, whether it be to Cæsar as supreme, or those subordinate rulers, who are sent by him for that which is truly the office of magistrates, to which God empowereth them, which is, to be punishers of evil-doers, and praisers or encouragers of them that do well.

15. For so is the will of God, that with well-doing ye may put to silence the ignorance of foolish men.

15. Your peace and safety is not to be looked for by resisting and conquering the powers that are over you, but by due subjection and patience while you obey God, to silence those ignorant, foolish men, who falsely reproach you as a turbulent and unruly sort of people, for differing from them in religion, and obeying God before men.

16. As free, and not using your liberty for a cloke of maliciousness, but as the servants of God.

16. You are indeed Christ's free-men, delivered from true servitude to sin and Satan; but you are God's servants, and must obey him, in using your Christian liberty to his glory, in your appointed way of duty; and not as a covering for any evil.

17. Honour all men. Love the brotherhood. Fear God. Honour the king.

17. In short, give all men their due respect: love all Christians, especially Christian societies or churches, with a special love: fear God above all, with reverent obedience; and under him give that eminent obedient honour to kings and rulers, which is their due.

18. Servants be subject to your masters with all fear, not only to the good and gentle, but also to the froward.

18. Christian servants must be subject to their masters, whether Christian or heathen, with due respect and reverence, even to those that are froward, and watchful, and abuse them, and not only to the good and gentle.

Note, That this binds not free servants to continue with such masters, when they may have better; but only slaves, that may not change, and also voluntary servants, till their time of servitude be at an end.

19. For this is thank-worthy, if a man for conscience toward God endure grief, suffering wrongfully. 20. For what glory is it, if when ye be buffeted for your faults, ye shall take it patiently? but if when ye do well and suffer for it, ye take it patiently, this is acceptable with God.

19. For this God accepteth as a rewardable act of obedience, when in conscience of God's commanding patience, you endure wrongful suffering. 20. Can you think it a rewardable thing, as of any special worth, to take it patiently when you are beaten for your faults? &c.

Note, What then shall we think of those servants, even the religious sort, that can neither bear strokes nor words when they deserve them, but will repine, and swell with passion, if they be but reproved for their faults, yea, for their sins against God, and will not humbly confess them?

21. For even hereunto were ye called: because Christ also suffered for us, leaving us an example, that ye should follow his steps,.

21. For your very calling of Christianity bindeth you to this obedient patience, in imitation of Christ, who in his suffering for us, became our example, whom we must follow.

22. Who did no sin, neither was guile found in his mouth. 23. Who when he was reviled, reviled not again, when he suffered, he threatened not, but committed himself to him that judgeth righteously.

22, 23. Who never did ill, in word or deed; and yet being scorned and reviled, he returned not to them the like, nor gave them one ill word for another; nor threatened revenge when he suffered by them, but prayed for the pardonable, and committed all to God the righteous Judge.

24. Who his ownself bare our sins in his own body on the tree, that we, being dead to sin, should live unto righteousness; by whose stripes ye were healed.

24. And never think much to imitate the patience of your Lord, considering what he did therein for us: for it was the punishment of our sins, which, as a sacrifice, he bore in his suffering

body upon the cross, that he being dead to sin, as he died for sin, might live to righteousness, as he revived and rose; and he that healed you by his own stripes, will not let you be finally losers by any stripes which you endure in obedience to him.

25. For ye were as sheep going astray, but are now returned unto the shepherd and bishop of your souls.

25. For in your state of ignorance and unbelief, you were like wandering, lost sheep, but now you are converted, and come home to the true Shepherd and Bishop of your souls, who keepeth you, and will feed and save you.

CHAP. III.

LIKEWISE, ye wives, be in subjection to your own husbands, that if any obey not the word, they also may without the word be won by the conversation of the wives.

1. And though wives be not servants, yet a loving subjection and obedience to their husbands is their duty; so that if their husbands be unbelievers, and are not converted by ministers preaching, yet the conversation of their wives may be such as may convince them of the goodness of religion, and may win them to a liking of the word, till by it they are fully converted.

Note, This winning conversation of wives, is, their excelling all other sorts of women in love, prudence, meekness, patience, humility, diligence in educating children, in holiness, &c.

2. While they behold your chaste conversation coupled with fear.

2. While they see your pure and chaste conversation, joined with the true fear of God (or reverence to them.)

3. Whose adorning, let it not be that outward *adorning* of plaiting the hair, and of wearing of gold, and of putting on of apparel:

3. And do not inordinately mind that sort of adorning, which consisteth in following the fashions of proud, vain or lascivious persons, such as plaiting or knotting the hair, and wearing ornaments of gold, to make you seem rich, or extraordinarily comely; and costliness, neatness, or curiosity of apparel.

Note, That the thing forbidden, is the signifying a vain, proud, procacious, tempting mind, and the imitation of such vain persons: and that the rule to be observed in apparel by the rich, is to choose, 1. That which is best for bodily health, as warm and suitable. 2. Least hindering, and most useful for labour and business. 3. Decent, without curiosity, or too much costliness. 4. Not scandalous, either imitating those above our rank, or humourously and sordidly singular, but imitating those above our rank. 5. But the command

of a husband, though he should be mistaken, may oblige a wife or child to somewhat differing from their own inclination or judgment, 6. And young persons desiring marriage, may go further in adorning than graver women, so they deceive none thereby.

4. But *let it be* the hidden man of the heart, in that which is not corruptible *even the ornament* of a meek and quiet spirit, which is in the sight of God of great price.

4. But labour to excel in that which is the truest and most precious ornament, which is the new creature, of a right frame of heart, which is not like beauty, or apparel, or gold, a corruptible thing; and especially an humble, meek, and quiet spirit, void of pride, and passion, and of an unquiet mind, that troubleth itself, and those that are about such; that is hardly pleased, nor can live pleasingly to others, but keep themselves, and their families, in discontent, and uncomfortableness, God is the judge of our amiableness, whom you must specially please: and he highly valueth this meek and quiet spirit.

5. For after this manner in the old time, the holy women also who trusted in God, adorned themselves, being in subjection unto their own husbands.

5. This was the chief adorning of those holy women, whose praises you read of in the scripture, who trusted in God, being in reverent and loving subjection to their husbands.

6. Even as Sarah obeyed Abraham, calling him Lord, whose daughters ye are as long as ye do well, and are not afraid with any amazement.

6. And thus Sarah, the believing wife of Abraham, the father of the faithful, obeyed and reverenced her husband, and spake of him as her superior; and you will be the daughters and successors of her faith and blessing, as long as you do well, and are obedient to God and your husbands, and give not way to those vexatious, causeless fears, which your sex is much liable to, and which signify too little trust in God, especially when they would fright you from your duty.

7. Likewise ye husbands, dwell with them according to knowledge, giving honour unto the wife as unto the weaker vessel, and as being heirs together of the grace of life, that your prayers be not hindered.

7. And you husbands must dwell with them, as beseemeth those that should teach and guide them, and therefore should excel them in knowledge, and help to edify them; and because their parts are supposed to be lower than yours, do not contemn them for it, but contribute your authori-

ty and wisdom to maintain their honour, and keep them from being contemned by children or servants; as being so nearly united, that you should live together as joint heirs of all the mercies of God, for this life, and a better; that so, in this concord, you may daily pray together, as with one mind and mouth, and that discord and discontent unfit you not for such united prayers.

8. Finally, *be ye* all of one mind, having compassion one of another, love as brethren, be pitiful, be courteous: 9. Not rendering evil for evil, or railing for railing: but contrariwise blessing, knowing that ye are thereunto called, that ye should inherit a blessing.

8. Yea, let all Christians be of one mind, and live in concord, not exagitating, but compassionating, each others infirmities and sufferings, loving as Christian brethren ought; pitiful to those that need you, and humble and courteous to all; not hurting those that hurt you, nor railing at those that rail at you, as if you might lawfully revenge evil with evil: but contrarily, bless those and give them good words who give you evil ones: for Christ by his word, example, and mercies, hath called and obliged you to this, that you may be blest of God.

10. For he that will love life, and see good days, let him refrain his tongue from evil, and his lips, that they speak no guile. 11. Let him eschew evil, and do good, let him seek peace, and ensue it.

10, 11. For as it is said, Psal. xxxiv. [He that will love life, &c.] seeing you love life, and would live in peace and quietness, the likeliest means to attain this is, 1. To keep your tongues from speaking evil of any man, and from all other evil: 2. And from falsehood, deceit, and dissimulation, (for it is men's own unbridled tongues which bring most of their troubles on them, and false words that hide faults, at last detected, expose men more.) 3. Avoid all real evil, and then your righteousness will appear through the vail of malicious slanders, and falsehood will be detected, and not long hide your innocency. 4. And do all the good you can to all men, as well as your immediate duty to God: and nature having a love to such as do us good, and a reverence of God, such good works, and well-doing, will powerfully justify you in the consciences of most men, 5. And stand not contentiously on your right, but whatever men are or do, seek peace with all; and be not soon weary, but follow after it still in hope.

12. For the eyes of the Lord are over the righteous, and his ears *are* open unto their prayers: but the face of the Lord is against them that do evil.

12. And this is not mere policy to please men, but whatever they be, it is God that your lives and peace depend on; and he that commandeth this, is pleased with it: and his eyes watch over you for good, to save you from unreasonable men, and he heareth their prayers in all distress: while evil speakers and doers, God himself is more against, than men.

13. And who is he that will harm you, if ye be followers of that which is good.

13. If your zeal in religion be a zeal of good works, to set yourselves earnestly, as to obey God, so to do good to all men; he must be a very impious diabolical man, that will for this set against you: it is the likeliest way to your quietness.

14. But, and if ye suffer for righteousness sake, happy *are ye*, and be not afraid of their terror, neither be troubled.

14. But I confess such blinded, unreasonable, malignant slaves and executioners, Satan hath, that will persecute you, even for righteousness sake: but this is the way to, and prognostic of your reward and happiness: and therefore let not men's threats, rage, or cruelty, terrify or trouble you, seeing you shall be unspeakably gainers by it.

15. But sanctify the Lord God in your hearts, and *be ready* always to give an answer to every man that asketh you a reason of the hope that is in you, with meekness and fear:

15. But let God always be in your hearts with the highest respect, obedience, and honour, and be still furnished with those reasons of your faith and hope, that you may be ready to profess them, and to give a good account of them to any that demandeth it; and this with meekness and due reverence to superiors, and not with passionate upbraiding them, or with disdain.

16. Having a good conscience, that whereas they speak evil of you, as of evil-doers, they may be ashamed that falsely accuse your good conversation in Christ.

16. Keeping your consciences clear from guilt, that they may justify you when men accuse you; and whereas men slander you as bad men, and seditious and unpeaceable, your good conversation, according to Christ's law and example, may shame their false accusations, (a better defence than bare words, and disputing with them.)

17. For it is better, if the will of God be so, that ye suffer for well-doing than for evil-doing.

17. For if God will have you suffer, it is far better that it be for well-doing, than for ill-doing: better for you, though worse for your persecutors:

CHAP. IV. I. PETER. 565

for now the body only suffereth, while the soul is free, which else would suffer far worse than persecution.

18. For Christ also hath once suffered for sins, the just for the unjust : (that he might bring us to God.)

18. For Christ himself had greater sufferings in the body than we; but he suffered not in the conscience of any guilt of his own, but was just, and suffered for the unjust, to reconcile and bring us to God.

18, 19, 20. Being put to death in the flesh, but quickened by the Spirit : By which also he went and preached unto the spirits in prison : Which sometime were disobedient, when once the long-suffering of God waited in the days of Noah, while the ark was a preparing, wherein few, that is eight souls, were saved by water.

18, 19, 20. Being put to death indeed as to the flesh, but made alive as to the spirit, (or by the spirit;) in which (or by which) he went and reached to the spirits in prison, which heretofore, in the days of Noah, were refractory, and hardened in sin and disobedience, while the long-suffering of God endured them, and waited for their repentance, while the ark was making and preparing, and Noah preaching to them; yet so impenitent were they to the last, that only eight were saved by the ark.

Note, It is no wonder that expositors of this text differ: some think that by [the Spirit] should rather be [in the spirit] or [as to it] put in direct distinction from the body, and that it is an argument for the immortality of the soul, by [quickened] being meant only that his soul was alive, while his body was dead; and that in that soul he went then and preached to imprisoned sinners, that were drowned in the flood; say some, to shew them his triumph, and what salvation they lost; and say they, this is it that is called his descending to hell; say others, to offer them mercy once again; say others, to bring some penitents from their long imprisonment: but others think, that [by spirit] is meant the power of God, or the divine nature of Christ, or the Holy Ghost, (not Christ's soul again entering into his body) and that the preaching meant, was by Christ's Spirit in Noah before the flood, and not after his death. To name other expositions, or the reasons given for each, would but perplex the reader, unless I were able so clearly to assert one of the expositions, as to confute all the rest. They that think Christ's soul and godhead preached to spirits while his body lay in the grave, suppose that those spirits knew it whom it concerned; but if it had been necessary for us to know not only Christ's preaching to ourselves, but to them, he would surely have more clearly told it us.

21. The like figure whereunto,

even baptism, doth also now save us, (not the putting away of the filth of the flesh, but the answer of a good conscience towards God) by the resurrection of Jesus Christ :

21. And that salvation from the deluge by the ark, prefigured our salvation in the church from God's wrath by baptism, and that through the power of Christ's resurrection, to which we begin our conformity, when we are raised to holiness by his Spirit, as we rise out of the water in baptism: but by baptism I mean not that the outward act of washing the body serveth to this salvation; nor must you think that God layeth it on any outward ceremony, save as it is the exercise of our obedience and faith: but it is the faithful answer to God of a resolved soul in the covenant of baptism, who when asked, doth profess and promised to believe in, and give up itself, to God the Father, Son, and Holy Ghost, and to renounce the world, the flesh, and the devil, baptism is but the celebration of this saving covenant; and it is covenanting sincerely that is the condition of salvation, and washing is but the sign.

22. Who is gone into heaven, and is on the right hand of God, angels, and authorities, and powers, being made subject unto him.

22. And well may I say, that Christ's resurrection saveth sincere baptized covenanters, as God by the ark did Noah, &c. when Christ thus risen, is gone into heaven, advanced to the highest authority and honour, all angels, and all authorities and powers in heaven or earth, being made subject, as his enemies to their woe, and his servants to their joy, shall shortly find; so that he is fully able to give and do for us whatever he hath promised, and we need.

CHAP. IV.

FORASMUCH then as Christ hath suffered for us in the flesh, arm yourselves likewise with the same mind : for he that hath suffered in the flesh, hath ceased from sin :
2. That he no longer should live the rest of his time in the flesh, to the lust of men, but to the will of God.

1, 2. Let then the sufferings of Christ have their due effect on you, in conforming you to his death, that you may, as crucified or dead men, give over sinning, being as dead to fleshly lusts; that ye no longer live the rest of your time in the flesh, according to the lusts of yourselves, or any tempting men, but wholly live to the will of God, as your rule and end.

3. For the time past of our life may suffice us to have wrought the

will of the Gentiles, when we walked in lasciviousness, lusts, excess of wine, revellings, banquetings, and abomiuable idolatries:

3. Alas, we did too long live according to heathen sensuality (and that time cannot be called back) even in lasciviousness and lusts, (either in fornication or immodesties that tend thereto) and in excess of wine or strong drinks, in revellings, and banquetings or unnecessary feastings, to gratify fleshly appetite and lusts, and in the Bacchanals and jovialties of their idolatry.

4. Wherein they think it strange that you run not with them to the same excess of riot, speaking evil of you.

4. And though it is monstrous and against humanity, that reasonable men should thus live like brutes, yet they stand and wonder at you, as if you were the monsters, or strange people, because you will not be as bad and mad as they, and run with them brutishly against God, and faith, and reason, into this sensual excess of sports, lust, and riot.

5. Who shall give account to him that is ready to judge the quick and the dead.

5. But the time is near when, for all this, they must come to judgment, and a sad account they must shortly give to the righteous Judge of the world.

6. For, for this cause was the gospel preached also to them that are dead, that they might be judged according to men in the flesh, but live according to God in the Spirit.

6. But wonder not at their obloquy, nor imitate them; but look to the example of the martyrs, and those that are dead in Christ, who received and obeyed the gospel preached to them, that while they were judged and persecuted in the flesh according to the rage of men, they might live in the Spirit unto God, and obtain his glory through all such suffering.

7. But the end of all things is at hand: be ye therefore sober, and watch unto prayer.

7. But the time of their foolish rage, and of your patient suffering, will be but short: The end of all earthly things is near; therefore let soberness be to you instead of lusts, and revelling, and fleshly pleasure; and by watching and prayer, seek and wait for grace and glory.

8. And above all things have fervent charity among yourselves: for charity shall cover the multitude of sins.

8. And above all things, be sure that you have and carefully preserve and exercise (not only peace and mutual forbearance, but) a special love, yea, fervent love to one another, even to all Christians, and especially in your societies and relations: For as love covereth, and not aggravateth faults towards one another; so God who hath said [Blessed are the merciful, for they shall obtain mercy; and if ye forgive, you shall be forgiven,] will cover and forgive the many sins of sincere, loving Christians.

Note, 1. The two extremes that in all ages have torn the church, should have regarded these words of Peter.

1. The Papal church-tearers, that persecute all that consent not to their canons, forms, and shadows, should have remembered [above all things] (even above your pretended plea for obedience to you, and decency and order) [have fervent love:] 2. And the passive separatists, that can find faults enough in the orders, and forms, and ceremonies, of churches, to separate from the communion of almost all on earth, should have more deeply received such texts as this [above all your superstitious pretences to more purity of churches, and better discipline, have fervent charity.] 3. It is but partiality and jealousy of the cause of justification against the Papists, which maketh some excellent expositors distort this text, so as to exclude from its sense God's covering of our sins; because they consider not aright. 1. That pardon, as continued, and as renewed for daily renewed sins, hath more for the condition of it required in us, than the first pardon and begun justification hath: the first act of sound faith serveth for the beginning, but the continuance of it, with its necessary fruits, is necessary to the continuance and renewing of pardon. 2. That the faith which is required to justification and pardon, is giving up ourselves to God the Father, Son, and Holy Ghost, in the baptismal covenant: that is, our Christianity, which is not put in opposition to that love or repentance, which is still implied as part of the same covenant consent, or its necessary fruit, but to the works of the law of Moses, or of works, or any that are set in competition with Christ, and free grace.

If prejudice hindered not men, the reading of the angel's words to Cornelius, and of Christ's [forgive, and you shall be forgiven] and the parable of the pardoned debtor cast into prison for not pardoning his fellow-servant, with Jam. ii. and Matt. xxv. would end all this controversy.

9. Use hospitality one to another without grudging. 10. As every man hath received the gift, even so minister the same one to another, as good stewards of the manifold grace of God.

9, 10. As God hath given more or less of riches or any of his gifts to any one, let him proportionably use them by free communication to those that need, remembering that all you have is freely given you of God, and that you are but his stewards, and receive it not for provision for your pride, or fleshly lusts, but for your Master's use, of which you must give an account.

11. If any man speak, *let him*

speak as the oracles of God: if any man minister, *let him do it* as of the ability which God giveth, that God in all things may be glorified through Jesus Christ; to whom be praise and dominion for ever and ever. Amen.

11. Let your discourse be holy, grave, and true, especially when you speak of divine things: let your contribution and bounty to all good uses, be proportioned to the estate and ability which God giveth you, that God may be glorified in all you do, by the exercise of your faith in Christ, &c.

12. Beloved, think it not strange concerning the fiery trial, which is to try you, as though some strange thing happened unto you.

12. Note, 1. Persecutions are for the trial of our sincerity and strength; and therefore our use of them is, to come out approved and refined. 2. No Christians should count them strange, because Christ taught us to expect them, and calls us to count our cost, and forsake all. And counting them strange, sheweth that we came not to Christ on his terms of taking up the cross, and self-denial as we ought.

13. But rejoice inasmuch as ye are partakers of Christ's sufferings; that when his glory shall be revealed, ye may be glad also with exceeding joy.

13. But instead of dejection, let it be your joy, that you are now partakers of Christ's sufferings, that you are conformed therein to him, and suffer for him, that so you may have assurance that you shall be glorified with him; and meet him with exceeding joy at his great appearing.

14. If ye be reproached for the Name of Christ, happy *are ye,* for the spirit of glory and of God, resteth upon you: on their part he is evil spoken of, but on your part he is glorified.

14. Your patient suffering reproach for Christ, is a part and prognostic of your happiness: and should they that believe this, be impatient of their own good? For the Spirit of God, which is your glory, and glorifieth him, and proveth his love to you, is it that fortifieth you: and as he is dishonoured by their reproaches, for which they will suffer; so he is glorified by your fortitude and fidelity, for which you shall be fully rewarded.

15. But let none of you suffer as a murderer, or a thief, or as an evil-doer, or as a busy-body in other men's matters.

15. But sin is worse, and more shameful than suffering; and therefore be sure that you avoid guilt, and that none of you suffer, 1. As a murderer, or hurter of others; 2. Or as a thief or defrauder of any; 3. Or for any evil deed; 4. Nor for playing the bishop in other men's charges, or meddling in other men's matters without a just call.

16. Yet if *any man suffer* as a Christian, let him not be ashamed, but let him glorify God on this behalf.

16. But if any suffer patiently for Christ, or for well-doing, take it not for a shame, but for an honour, and so behave yourselves in it, as to honour God who honoureth you.

17. For the time *is come,* that judgment must begin at the house of God: and if it first begin at us, what shall the end be of them that obey not the gospel of God?

17. As it is said, Ezek. xliii. 4, 5. So now God, being entering on a course of judgment, will begin with the correction and trying of children, in which the infidels will by execution, increase their guilt: And our sufferings now are a dreadful prognostic of theirs that follow in the end.

Note, How little cause wicked men have to be glad of the churches' sufferings; when it prognosticateth a far more heavy judgment on themselves!

18. And if the righteous scarcely be saved, where shall the ungodly and the sinner appear?

18. And if the righteous be saved (though certainly, yet) by so much labour, cost, and suffering in this life, O how will ungodly sinners stand in judgment before a just condemning Judge?

19. Wherefore let them that suffer according to the will of God, commit the keeping of their souls *to him* in well doing, as unto a faithful Creator.

19. Therefore, let us see that, if we suffer, it be for matter and manner according to God's will, and let our duty and well-doing be our care; and so let us wholly commit our souls to the keeping and love of our faithful Creator, and quietly trust him to preserve and save them.

CHAP. V.

THE elders which are among you I exhort, who am also an elder, and a witness of the sufferings of Christ, and also a partaker of the glory that shall be revealed. 2. Feed the flock of God which is among you, taking the oversight *thereof,* not by constraint, but willingly: not for filthy lucre, but of a ready mind.

1, 2. The elder and wiser sort being usually made pastors of the churches, I, who am an elder in age and apostleship, and a witness of Christ's sufferings, and, on the mount, had a glimpse of the glory which shall be fully revealed and communicated, and have my right to it, and part in its foretaste, do exhort and beseech them faithfully to oversee, and feed, and take care of all the flock which is among you; taking the over-sight, or episcopacy, of it, not as a burthen unwillingly, but willingly, not for filthy lucre, because the pastors have double honour and maintenance, but out of love to Christ and the church, with a ready cheerfulness to undergo all the trouble and danger of it.

Note, 1. The office of true bishops is to [feed and guide the flock that is among them.] What are they then, that have the name and title of being sole bishops over a thousand, or many hundred, or score of flocks, which are so far from being among them, or being fed by them, that the hundredth person never heard them teach, or saw their faces?

2. Though most expositors apply μη αναγκαστως αλλ' εκουσιως, not by constraint, but willingly, to the bishop's willingness of his work, yet Dr. Hammond applieth it to the bishop's manner of guiding the flock, as not constraining them by force, nor using violence in an active sense. And whether these words prove it or not, other scriptures, and the nature of the case, prove that bishops have no power of corporal force, but of ruling by God's word, and that none but volunteers are capable of church-privileges and communion, and pastoral conduct.

3. They that seek and take a bishopric for filthy lucre of the benefice, wealth, and worldly honour, are intruders that come not in Christ's way: And they that also cast out the use of the keys from the particular churches among them, and instead of it, rule secularly, by destructive force, and profane the power of the keys, by committing them to uncapable laymen, to be used *suo modo*, contrary to their nature and ends, yea, against men for obeying God; do take God's name and their sacred titles in vain, for which God will not hold them guiltless.

3. Neither as being lords over God's heritage: but being ensamples to the flock.

3. Nor, as if they were lords of the church, to domineer over the people of God, and rule them by the sword, or outward force, or command them by laws or impositions of their own, besides the ordering of Christ's own ordinances in subservient circumstances, for the churches' edification, nor to extort from them a large maintenance: But as becoming ensamples to the flock, of all the humility, self-denial, love, and patience, and all other virtues which they preach.

Note, How can men be such visible examples to many hundred flocks that never knew them?

4. And when the chief Shepherd shall appear, ye shall receive a crown of glory that fadeth not away.

4. And though you have no reward from men, when Christ the redeemer, and owner, and chief ruler, lover, and defender of his church, shall come to judgment, you shall receive from him your full reward, even a never fading crown of glory.

5. Likewise ye younger, submit yourselves unto the elder: yea, all *of you* be subject one to another, and be clothed with humility: for God resisteth the proud, and giveth grace to the humble.

5. And as juniors are usually fittest to be subject, yea that are young, and inferiors, submit yourselves to the teaching and guidance of the elder, especially the pastors: Yea, let all Christians be as teachable, and willing to learn, and to please the righteous wills of one another, as if they were your rulers, and you their subjects; not insisting too much on your self-will, and self-interest, or liberty. And let humility, which will cause this condescension and complaisance, be to you as your very clothing and ornaments, instead of proud ostentation in garb and carriage: for God sets himself against proud men, to bring them down; but the humble he doth countenance and exalt.

6. Humble yourselves therefore under the mighty hand of God, that he may exalt you in due time: 7. Casting all your care upon him, for he careth for you.

6,7. Seeing then that God's judgments are abroad in the earth, and it is the Almighty God in whose hand we and all things are, humble yourselves under his hand, that he may exalt you in his appointed time: And wholly trust him with all your concerns, and cast away all distrustful care, for his love and providence will be your full security.

8. Be sober, be vigilant; because your adversary, the devil, as a roaring lion, walketh about, seeking whom he may devour.

8. Be sober, and not entangled with baits of fleshly pleasure; and be not careless, but as always watching: for the devil, who pleadeth against you as your accuser, is unwearied in ravenous, murderous rage, seeking night and day to deceive you with his temptations, and destroy you.

9. Whom resist steadfast in the faith, knowing that the same afflictions are accomplished in your brethren that are in the world.

9. Be steadfast, therefore, in the faith, from which, Satan, by temptations, would discourage you; and resist his ill suggestions, occasioned by your sufferings, remembering that it is not your case alone, but others also suffer with you: Yea, all that will live godly in Christ, shall suffer persecution.

10. But the God of all grace, who hath called us unto his eternal

CHAP. V.   I. PETER.   569

glory by Christ Jesus, after that ye have suffered a while, make you perfect, stablish, strengthen, settle you.

11. To him be glory and dominion for ever and ever. Amen.

10, 11. But the God of all grace, who hath already effectually called us into that state of grace, in which we have right and comfortable hope of attaining his eternal glory by the redemption and intercession of Christ Jesus, after you have suffered the short time of his appointment, compaginate and perfect you, and your several churches, and stablish, strengthen, and settle you more firmly by the shaking of these trials, blessed by his grace. And the glory and dominion which are his, be acknowledged in his praise for ever. Amen.

12. By Sylvanus, a faithful brother unto you, (as I suppose) I have written briefly, exhorting and testifying, that this is the true grace of God wherein ye stand.

12. By Sylvanus, a trusty brother to you, as I reckon, I have written with sufficient brevity; the scope of all being to exhort you to stand fast, and to testify to you, that this Christian faith which we have preached, and you profess, is that true state or kingdom of grace, foretold by the prophets, and expected by your forefathers, and that there is no other Saviour, or way of life; and therefore let no deceivers or persecutors shake you.

13. The *church that is* at Babylon, elected together with *you*, saluteth you, and *so doth* Marcus my son.

13. Note, Some by Babylon, understand Rome: But being forced senses are not to be received without cogent reasons, I rather take it plainly for Babylon in Assyria, or that in Egypt.

14. Greet ye one another with a kiss of charity: peace *be* with you all that are in Christ Jesus. Amen.

14. Let the constancy of your mutual Christian love be, on all meet occasions, expressed, by friendly kissing of men with men, and women with women (being now the ordinary expression of it.) Holy peace (the summary of prosperity) be with you all, that are the true members of Christ, the great peace-maker. Amen.

Note, 1. That the thing made a common Christian duty, is not kissing, which is a mutable signification: but it is indeared love expressed. 2. But kissing being then the common signification of love, was a duty where that signifying use, by custom, was continued as needful. 3. That it is doubtless, that all significant actions, even in worship, which are mentioned in scripture, are not of standing duty; nor such forbidden, that are not there mentioned or commanded in particular. For when God commandeth in general the expressions of love, humility, reverence, consent, &c. he leaveth it to the custom of the countries, or natural aptitude of the action, or the consent of many, or the conduct of rulers, by what fit action these things shall be expressed: As love, by this kiss, or by embracing, or shaking hands; and humility, by putting off the hat, bowing, kneeling,&c. or reverence, by the same actions (even in worship) kneeling, bowing, standing, prostration, being uncovered,&c. Consent, by holding up the hand, standing up, writing, &c. But this is no warrant for them who will invent many practices, or things, which have no such signifying aptitude, and put on them a signification of their own devising, and command this to be used as a badge and symbol of Christianity, and fœderal sign with God and man, like Christ's own sacraments, at least in a great part, and then to make these the test and condition of Christian communion, ejecting and silencing all Christ's ministers, and cutting off all Christians from church communion, who dare not use them, lest thereby they break the law of God.

THE
SECOND EPISTLE GENERAL
OF
ST. PETER.

CHAP. I.

SIMON Peter, a servant and an apostle of Jesus Christ, to them that have obtained like precious faith with us, through the righteousness of God, and our Saviour Jesus Christ. 2. Grace and peace be multiplied unto you through the knowledge of God, and of Jesus our Lord.

1, 2. Simon Peter, &c. to all Christians who have obtained the same precious faith with us, which is founded in the precious price of our redemption, and advanceth us to the dignity of being sons of God, through the righteousness of God, which is manifested in his way of justifying us by the merits of Christ's perfect righteousness. Grace and peace, which are the greatest blessings that man is capable of on earth, be multiplied to you, which must be only through the knowledge of God, and of Jesus our Lord.

3. According as his divine power hath given unto us all things that *pertain* unto life and godliness, through the knowledge of him that hath called us to glory and virtue.

3. As his divine power hath, in and by Christ, provided and given us all things necessary to life, present and everlasting, and to godliness, which is the right use of this life, and the way to a better: and this through the knowledge of Christ, who hath called us to future glory, and present virtue.

Note, Some read it [by glory and virtue] and expound it [by the voice from heaven that called Christ, the Beloved Son, and the virtue or power of signal miracles.]

4. Whereby are given unto us exceeding great and precious promises; that by these you might be partakers of the divine nature, having escaped the corruption that is in the world through lust.

4. By which calling are given to us exceeding great and precious promises, even God's covenant of grace, sure and sealed, that by these, as his deed of gift, or instrument, conveying to us our right to Christ, and grace, and glory, we may be made partakers as it is in Christ, but also inherently of the divine nature, not only relatively, as it is the renovation of our own souls, to a holy inclination godward, by the spirit of adoption, like the love and likeness of a child to the father; being advanced hereby above the sensual corrupt nature, and escaping the pollutions of fleshly lusts, which the world is defiled with, and would defile us by.

Note, Though a nature strictly signify some essential part, or inseparable inclination, it here signifieth a holy inclining habit, called, a Nature, by resemblance; it being not the effect of a mere art or opinion, but a fixed complacency, love and bent of the soul towards God, and holiness, and heaven.

5. And besides this, giving all diligence, add to your faith, virtue; and to virtue, knowledge; 6. And to knowledge, temperance; and to temperance, patience; and to patience, godliness; 7. And to godliness, brotherly-kindness: and to brotherly-kindness, charity.

5, 6, 7. And having the divine nature, let diligent exercise reduce it to particular holy habits. As you are believers, let your faith shew itself in holy strength and fortitude in all that is your duty; and to that add a daily increase of knowledge in godly things, and a careful mortifying all fleshly lusts, and abstaining from all forbidden sensuality; and to that add, patience of mind under all wrongs, crosses, and afflictions; and to that add, a zealous, holy, heavenly observance of all the duties of the first table, or of religion, public and private; and to that add, a special love to all Christian brethren and friends: And let all grow up to that highest love to God, and to all men, as he is interested in them, with an addictedness to do them all the good you can, which is the top of all our graces.

8. For if these things be in you, and abound, they make *you that ye shall* neither be barren nor unfruitful in the knowledge of our Lord Jesus Christ.

8. If you have these blessed graces of sanctification, you will be clearly differenced from formal hypocrites, whose faith and religion is but a barren, unfruitful speculation; an art, and not the divine nature.

9. But he that lacketh these things is blind, and cannot see afar off, and hath forgotten that he was purged from his old sins.

9. But he that boasteth of his faith, without these virtues, is like a purblind man, that can see nothing, but what is just near to him. Could they, with a lively faith, foresee the things to come, it would waken their sluggish souls to all this: And could they rightly look back to their baptism, they would remember that they there virtually vowed all this, and were sacramentally washed from their old sins.

10. Wherefore the rather, brethren, give diligence to make your calling and election sure: for if ye do these things, ye shall never fall.

10. Therefore see that ye use your utmost diligence in the things aforesaid, that your calling and election may thereby be made firm, stablished and sure: For if you do these things, you shall not miscarry, nor come short of salvation.

Note, It is a frivolous contention that is raised about this text; some disputing that it is only meant of sure notification to our consciences; and some, that it is to make us meet objects of God's decretive election, and to make an uneffectual calling turn to a more effectual. By Election is oft meant God's actual taking us out of the world, into the church; and is the same with Calling. The Greek here signifieth, to [make firm] and not only to make known. God's promise is our title to salvation: This promise maketh faith the condition of our first right; but the fruits of faith, the condition of our continued and final right to salvation. Therefore, as there is somewhat on our part necessary to our first justification, besides God's part; so there is something more on our part necessary to our right to salvation, if we survive our initiation which Christ describeth, Matt. xxv. And the doing of this making us capable receivers of God's free gift, may as properly be said to make it sure, as our faith to justify us: that is, it maketh up our title to life, which else would be defective; and so maketh our calling and actual election to be confirmed, and sufficient on their part, and not frustrate as to their end: And then, being made firm and valid in itself, it followeth that our title may the easier be known to us.

11. For so an entrance shall be ministered unto you abundantly, into the everlasting kingdom of our Lord and Saviour Jesus Christ.

11. And your baptismal faith and covenant proving not ineffectual, these performances being the condition of your actual salvation, your covenant title will be complete, and you shall have sure entrance, and full possession of the kingdom of glory.

12. Wherefore I will not be negligent to put you always in remembrance of these things, though ye know them, and be established in the present truth.

12. And holy diligence and improvement being so necessary to you, I must not be negligent to put you in remembrance, and stir you up to it, though you know it already, and believe it.

Note, We have great need to be diligently stirred up to the remembrance and practice of that which we know already, as well as to know more.

13. Yea, I think it meet, as long as I am in this tabernacle, to stir you up, by putting *you* in remembrance: 14. Knowing that shortly I must put off *this* my tabernacle, even as our Lord Jesus Christ shewed me.

13, 14. Note, 1. The body is but the soul's tabernacle. 2. Ministers must never give over pressing known truths while they live. 3. The knowledge of approaching death must quicken us to diligence.

15. Moreover, I will endeavour, that you may be able, after my decease, to have these things always in remembrance.

15. Note, That we must not be careful only for our own life-time, but for a succession and continuance of truth and godliness, when we are dead, lest it die with us. Therefore we write.

16. For we have not followed cunningly devised fables, when we made known unto you the power and coming of our Lord Jesus Christ, but were eye-witnesses of his majesty.

16. For our doctrine of the glorious coming and kingdom of Christ, is not a cunningly devised fable: For we were eye witnesses of a glimpse of that glory in his transfiguration, which he foretold us of as a resemblance of his last coming, and his kingdom.

17. For he received from God the Father, honour, and glory, when there came such a voice to him

from the excellent glory, This is my beloved Son in whom I am well-pleased.

17. For he then received in his human nature a communicated splendor, and celestial honour and glory, when God, from the heavenly magnificent glory, said, This is my, &c.

Note, 1. It is the highest honour and perfection of a creature, to be loved and pleasing to God. 2. God's testimony of his Son from heaven is our great obligation to faith and obedience to him.

18. And this voice which came from heaven we heard, when we were with him in the holy mount.

18. This voice three of us heard, when we were with him in that mount, which was sanctified by this glorious appearance, and may well be called, The Holy Mount.

19. We have also a more sure word of prophecy, whereunto ye do well that ye take heed, as unto a light that shineth in a dark place, until the day dawn, and the day-star arise in your hearts:

19. And we have also in the Old Testament a firm prophetic word, many prophets foretelling the kingdom of Christ: And ye do well to search and take notice of these, as to a light that was set up by God, for the use of those darker ages, to lead them to the knowledge of Christ, and so is very useful still, till the clearer preaching of that gospel come, and the Spirit of Christ, as his agent and witness, possess your hearts.

Note, The word [more sure] signifieth not more sure than the gospel, but [very sure.] Or more sure to the Jews, than Peter's bare word of the transfiguration, and voice, on the mount.

20. Knowing this first, that no prophecy of the scripture is of any private interpretation. 21. For the prophecy came not in old time by the will of man: but holy men of God spake *as they were* moved by the Holy Ghost.

20, 21. But this you must first know, that no prophesy of scripture is to be expounded as speaking only of those persons, whom the speaker first meant, whether himself or others, nor according to the speaker's proper private thought: For the prophecy came not in old time, by the speaker's own wisdom, kmowledge, invention, or will; but holy men of God, were moved by God's Spirit to speak those words, which signifieth more than they designed, or always meant and understood themselves.

Note, It seemeth strange to me that Ιδίας επιλύσεως [proper or private interpretation] should be commonly by excellent expositors, misinterpreted, as if it spake of [proper or private expositors] and so set men on disputing who must be the public expositor; when the words plainly speak of [proper or private sense, or objective exposition.] As when David oft speaketh words which are immediately true of himself, or of Solomon, you must not expound them as meant properly of them who were private persons, and but types: For it was the Holy Ghost speaking in them, whose sense must be known, who meant Christ the public person as typified by the private, of whom they were first verified: And whether David (as in Ps. ii. and xxii. and such other) meant more than himself, and his kingdom, or not, the Holy Ghost meant more. If Grotius were in the right, that Isay meant but Jeremy, or Josiah, in Isa. liii. it is certain that they were but typical, and the HolyGhost meant Christ. So that the plain sense is, that scripture-prophecy receiving its full sense from the Spirit, and not from the speaker, must not in our exposition be appropriated narrowly to those private men, by whom, or of whom, they were proximately meant by the speaker.

CHAP. II.

BUT there were false prophets also among the people, even as there shall be false teachers among you, who privily shall bring in damnable heresies, even denying the Lord that bought them, and bring upon themselves swift destruction.

1. But one of your great trials will be, as theirs of old, by false prophets, so by false teachers, who will rise up among yourselves, and will by secret seducing persons, with whom by familiarity, they have advantage, bring in sects, holding damnable errors, even by plain consequence, denying Christ that bought them, while they deny what is essential to his person and offices (or teaching that he may be denied with the tongue in danger for self-preservation, because God will have mercy and not sacrifice, as long as the heart doth not deny him.

Note, 1. That all Christians have need to be fortified against false teachers, as well as against persecuting enemies.

2. Christ is called, The Lord that bought them, not because they falsely professed that he bought them, as some say, but because he purchased and made to them a deed of gift of Christ, pardon, and life, to be theirs, on condition of believing acceptance. And because they should not perish for want of a sufficient sacrifice for sin.

2. And many shall follow their pernicious ways by reason of whom the way of truth shall be evil spoken of.

2. And many that professed Christianity, shall be seduced by them, and follow their pernicious ways, by reason of whom, malignant enemies will take occasion to speak evil of Christianity, and make a reproach of truth and godliness, as if we were all like this scandalous sect.

3. And through covetousness shall

they with feigned words make merchandise of you; whose judgment now of a long time lingereth not, and their damnation slumbereth not.

3. Note, 1. That it is worldly, covetous men, who are most to be suspected to be traitors to the church, as Judas was against Christ, for [for what will ye give me?] 2. All their seducing, confident harangues, to this end, are but false and feigned words. 3. Their business is to sell souls to the devil for their own worldly benefice, gain, or honour, as Judas did his Master. 4. God is hastening to judge such men with speed, as he did Judas, when his gain was too hot to hold, and he hanged himself for betraying the innocent.

4. For if God spared not the angels that sinned, but cast *them* down to hell, and delivered *them* into chains of darkness, to be reserved unto judgment: 5. And spared not the old world, but saved Noah the eighth *person*, a preacher of righteousness, bringing in the flood upon the world of the ungodly:

4, 5. Note, 1. These angels were not in a fixed, immutable state, but mutable by free will. 2. Their own sin was the cause of their misery. 3. For it they were cast down to hell, that is a state of misery, reserved for more; though they are said to be the powers of the air, and to rule in the children of disobedience. 4. There they have their prince and kingdom. 5. Pride and malice against God and man, and wickedness is their quality, warring against Christ and his kingdom. 6. Tempting men to sin is their employment. 7. Their way against the church is by lying, malice, and murder, in which wicked men are their slaves and instruments. 8. So far as men yield to sin by their temptations, they fall into the fuller power of them, both for further temptations and execution, by God's permission.

6. And turning the cities of Sodom and Gomorrah into ashes, condemned *them* with an overthrow, making *them* an ensample unto those that after should live ungodly.

6. And with fire from heaven destroying Sodom and Gomorrah, and the adjacent villages, both men and houses, that the history of them, and the stinking lake that now possesseth the place, might be a warning to the ungodly.

7. And he delivered just Lot, vexed with the filthy conversation of the wicked. 8. (For that righteous man dwelling among them, in seeing and hearing, vexed his righteous soul from day to day with *their* unlawful deeds.)

7, 8. Note, 1. Lot is called just, from the tenor of his life, though after he fell into very great sin. 2. Just men are grieved at the overspreading wickedness of the times and places where they live, especially their filthiness and their rage against the just. 3. God will deliver the just from the wicked, and from his judgments on them.

9. The Lord knoweth how to deliver the godly out of temptations, and to reserve the unjust unto the day of judgment to be punished:

9. We may well trust, that God, who as he is just, and a hater of sin and a lover of righteousness, to knoweth how to deliver the godly out of temptations, so far as that they should not be conquered by them, though they be tried, and to reserve the wicked and oppressing enemies to a full vindictive punishment at the day of judgment, though they prosper and triumph now.

10. But chiefly them that walk after the flesh, in the lust of uncleanness, and despise government: Presumptuous *are they*, self-willed, they are not afraid to speak evil of dignities.

10. Note, Dr. Hammond, who supposeth this spoken of the Gnostics, would sure think it a heinous aggravation, if governors themselves should prove Borborites or Gnostics, and walk after the flesh, in the lust of uncleanness, and suppress piety by power. To use dignities for sin, is worse than to despise them, or speak evil of them for being evil, though this also is bad, and must be avoided. 2. The Doctor thinks that the dignities here meant are apostles; I rather think it is civil rulers.

11. Whereas angels, which are greater in power and might, bring not railing accusation against them before the Lord.

11. Whereas, the blessed angels, which have more power than men, when they plead against devils themselves, do it not by railing accusation (as the instance in Zachary shews.)

12. But these, as natural brute beasts, made to be taken and destroyed, speak evil of the things that they understand not, *and* shall utterly perish in their own corruption.

12. But these are like wild brute beasts, whom all men seek to destroy for their hurtfulness, and do speak evil in proud ignorance of doctrines, practices, and persons, which they understand not, do stir up men against themselves, and shall be destroyed in their sin.

13. *And* shall receive the reward of unrighteousness, *as* they that count it pleasure to riot in the day-

time: spots *they are* and blemishes, sporting themselves with their own deceivings, while they feast with you; 14. Having eyes full of adultery, and that cannot cease from sin, beguiling unstable souls: an heart they have exercised with covetous practices; cursed children:

13, 14. They shall be doubly punished for living in unrighteousness, and sensual riot, in the light of the gospel, and profession of Christianity. You admit such to feast with you, even as if they were of your societies, at love-feasts and sacraments; but they are disgraceful spots and blemishes in your assemblies, and a dishonour to the Christian name: Their unclean hearts have ungoverned eyes, fed with enticing objects of lust, and let in the impressions of filthy pleasure into their imaginations, deceiving themselves, and sporting away their own souls, while they allure and deceive others. Their imaginations and minds are so habited to such filthy vice, that they cannot cease from it, being unstable, and by the power of sensuality, cannot obey their own convictions; and where lust reigneth, covetousness ruleth to maintain it: They are such as God's word doth pronounce accursed, whatever they profess.

15. Which have forsaken the right way, and are gone astray, following the way of Balaam, *the son* of Bosor, who loved the wages of unrighteousness. 16. But was rebuked for his iniquity: the dumb ass speaking with man's voice, forbade the madness of the prophet.

15, 16. Covetousness hath drawn them from the right way of truth and godliness, and they stray in the way of Balaam the son of Bosor, whom the hire that bribed him to do evil, was prevalent with to attempt it: But he that by reason of the love of money and honour, could not see the evil of his own way, was rebuked by a dumb ass, whom God made speak, to evince and forbid the madness of such a prophet.

17. These are wells without water, clouds that are carried with a tempest, to whom the mist of darkness is reserved for ever.

17. These are like wells that have no water, having a barren profession, that will not save them: Clouds that seem to be for fruitful rains, but are only for tempestuous whirlwinds or hurricanes, dark in themselves, both now and for ever, as well as troublesome and hurtful to others.

18. For when they speak great swelling *words* of vanity, they allure through the lusts of the flesh, through much wantonness, those that were clean escaped from them who live in error.

18. For when they boast of their extraordinary knowledge (of angels, and other unknown things, as the heretics described by Ireneus, Epiphanius, &c. then did) and withal, make fleshly licentiousness to be Christian liberty, their vain boasting words, are but to serve their fleshly lust, alluring by base lasciviousness, some who were quite come off from heathenish and Jewish errors.

19. While they promise them liberty, they themselves are the servants of corruption; for *of whom* a man is overcome, of the same is he brought in bondage.

19. They tell the simple, that flesh-pleasing and lust is part of their Christian liberty, and that we are ignorant that know not such things; when under all these promises of liberty, they are the slaves of lust themselves, being conquered by them, and in bondage to them.

20. For if after they have escaped the pollutions of the world, through the knowledge of the Lord and Saviour Jesus Christ, they are again entangled therein and overcome; the latter end is worse with them than the beginning.

20. For if after they have been convinced of the heathen abominations and filthy practices, and have renounced them in baptism, and forsaken them, and joined in the communion of saints by the acknowledgment of Christ, and Christian verity, they shall again return to the practising of the same sins, on pretence of knowledge and Christian liberty, and so be overcome, their end will be more sinful and miserable, than was their heathen state of ignorant pollution.

21. For it had been better for them not to have known the way of righteousness, than after they have known it, to turn from the holy commandment delivered unto them.

21. For their sin and misery had been less, if they had never known the way of righteousness, revealed by the gospel of Christ, than after they have known it, to forsake the owning or practice of the commands of holy and righteous living, which they received.

Note, Sins against present or former knowledge in great instances, have dangerous aggravations, as coming from contempt of God, or odious depravation of judgment after.

22. But it is happened unto them according to the true proverb, The dog is turned to his own vomit again, and the sow that was washed to her wallowing in the mire.

22. But it is with them according to the proverb, The dog, &c. Their natures were not renewed by the Holy Ghost, and made holy or divine; they were dogs, though they had disgorged their vomit; and swine, though they were washed: No wonder then, if temptation draw them to return to their vomit, and to the mire of filthy sin again.

Note, What sort of men these here described were, is not agreed on by all expositors: But thus much seemeth clear, 1. That they were professed Christians. 2. That they lived in sensuality and fornication. 3. That they taught that these were lawful, and the use of them was Christian liberty. 4. That to make this good, they joined with sectmasters, that boasted of more knowledge than the apostles and their followers had, (as most heretics do.) 5. That yet they did not wholly separate from the Christian churches, nor the churches cast them out (as they ought.) For they are said to [feast with them, to be spots and blemishes to them.] And Rev. ii. and iii. shews, that too many churches had such among them, and did tolerate them; and that whole societies were in danger of being corrupted by them, and the churches threatened to be punished for having such members. 6. Whatever name some put on them, it is plain they were those that are called Nicolaitans in Rev. ii. and iii. Qu. What if bishops, priests, and people, should become such debauched, covetous sensualists, and also set against serious godliness, and seek the reproach of it as hypocrisy and fanaticism, and the silencing and excommunicating of the most godly ministers and people, and so become a Gnostic or Nicolaitan church? Ans. Forsake their local communion, if you can have better; and if you cannot, do not approve or commit any of their sin, nor own any uncapable of the ministry by heresy, or open enmity to godliness, but either worship God only in private, or protest against their sin, when you join with them only in good.

CHAP. III.

THIS second epistle (beloved) I now write unto you; in both which I stir up your pure minds by way of remembrance: 2. That ye may be mindful of the words which were spoken before by the holy prophets, and of the commandment of us the apostles of our Lord and Saviour.

1, 2. This second epistle, with the former, I write to you, as to those that are pure from the evils which I describe, but have need to be remembered of what you have learned from the prophets, and been commanded by us the apostles of Christ.

3. Knowing this first, that there shall come in the last days, scoffers, walking after their own lusts, 4. And saying, Where is the promise of his coming? for since the fathers fell asleep, all things continue as they were from the beginning of the creation.

3, 4. And here I first remember you, that, as you have been foretold in the last days before Christ's coming, there shall arise unbelievers, that shall make a mock at the promise of his coming, and thereby harden themselves in a fleshly wicked life, saying, How long shall we stay ere we see Christ come? What is become of the promise of it, which you so long awed men with? It is long since the fathers, who you say, Believed in him, were dead; and none of them are risen again, nor yet see Christ come; the world continueth as it did from the creation.

5. For this they willingly are ignorant of, that by the word of God the heavens were of old, and the earth standing out of the water and in the water. 6. Whereby the world that then was, being overflowed with water, perished. 7. But the heavens and the earth which are now, by the same word are kept in store, reserved unto fire against the day of judgment, and perdition of ungodly men.

5, 6, 7. For it must belong to themselves, if men, professing Christian's knowledge, do not know what a change was once made since the creation; that God's word made the heavens and the earth, and that this earth being partly in the water, and partly out of it, separated from seas and clouds; by this water, the world of men that lived in the days of Noah, were drowned. But by the same will and word of God, the heavens and the earth that are now, are kept from being drowned, being reserved to another sort of ruin, even by fire, when the time is come, in which God will publicly judge and destroy ungodly men.

Note, It is strange how any expositor can think that this text speaketh only of the destruction of Jerusalem, and the Gnostics, when, 1. It is resembled to the drowning of all the world: 2. And it speaketh of the [heavens and the earth that are now,] which are more than Jerusalem: 3. And it referreth to the promise to Noah, to drown the world no more; 4. And faith, it is reserved to fire; 5. And that at the day of judgment and perdition of the ungodly, and not of the Jews only.

8. But (beloved) be not ignorant of this one thing, that one day is with the Lord as a thousand years, and a thousand years as one day.

8. But you must not ignorantly measure God's time by the measure of us men: for one day is with the eternal God as a thousand years, and a thousand years as one day: time is soon gone with us, but to eternity it is as nothing.

9. The Lord is not slack concerning his promise, as some men count slackness; but is long-suffering to us-ward, not willing that any should perish, but that all should come to repentance.

9. The delay is not because God is slack as to the performing of his promises, (as slackness signifieth some culpable omission among men:) but it is because he is long-suffering to us men, not delighting in, or willing any man's destruction as such, but that all should come to repentance.

Note, 1. God's will, as totally distinct from all effects, is only his essence, and is immutable, and is not denominated his, willing this or that; 2. But his will, which is but the effects of his essential will, is manifold, and doth begin, and end, and change. And, 3. His will, as it is but the relation of his essential will to these effects, and an extrinsic denomination from them, is also manifold and mutable: and it is in these two last senses that Peter saith, that [God is not willing that any should perish, but all come to repentance;] that is, God hath provided a sufficient sacrifice for their sin in Christ; he reprieved them from deserved damnation, and patiently endureth them; he offereth pardon and salvation to all that will accept it, who hear his offer; he giveth all the world undeserved mercy, and obligeth them to repent in hope of more, and bindeth all the world to certain duties as means of their recovery and salvation, and useth none according to the mere terms of the law of innocency [obey perfectly or die.] His daily mercies lead to repentance and hope: he commandeth his ministers to beseech them to be reconciled and saved: he bringeth life to their own wills, and giveth them abundant reasons and motives to accept it, &c. 1. That he doth this *de facto*, no Christian can deny. 2. Therefore, he is said to will their repentance and salvation. 1. As these effects of his will are called his will; 2. Or as his will is named only as related to these effects. Thus much well considered may end this controversy.

10. But the day of the Lord will come as a thief in the night, in the which the heavens shall pass away with a great noise, and the elements shall melt with fervent heat, the earth also and the works that are therein shall be burnt up.

10. But as men sleep, not knowing when a thief will come in the night; so shall Christ's coming surprise men unexpected; in which the heavens, so far as they belong to man, and partake of any of the curse for our sins, shall pass away with a great and dreadful noise like a storm; and the elements shall be dissolved with fervent heat; and all this earth, and all men's works thereon, shall be consumed by this fire.

Note, It is marvellous prepossession that could make any learned man think, that all these words signify nothing but the destruction of Jerusalem.

6. Seeing then that all these things shall be dissolved, what manner of persons ought ye to be in *all* holy conversation and godliness.

11. Note, The true belief of the day of Christ's coming to judgment, and the dissolution of all this lower world by fire, should convince all Christians, that a holy conversation and godliness should be endeavoured with all possible care and diligence. And those men that think they can be truly godly and holy overmuch, do not believe seriously such a change and day.

12. Looking for, and hasting unto the coming of the day of God, wherein the heavens being on fire, shall be dissolved, and the elements shall melt with fervent heat.

12. Looking for, and earnestly desiring the coming of this day of God, when the lower heavens and earth shall thus be dissolved, and the elements melt with the fervent fiery heat. (The joyful day of our perfect deliverance and salvation.)

13. Nevertheless we, according to his promise, look for new heavens and a new earth, wherein dwelleth righteousness.

13. But we, according to his promise, look that God should by these dissolving flames refine heaven and earth, and having consumed with them all sin, and the wicked hence, should make (as he formed this out of the chaos) a new heaven, and a new earth, an habitation for righteous persons; where sin shall prevail no more.

Note, 1. He that maketh this new heaven and earth to succeed the destruction of Jerusalem, surely forgot, 1. That the heathens for near three hundred years after persecuted the Christians far more bloodily than the few poor Jews did, or could, and that church-history saith very little of the Jews' persecution in comparison of the heathens, or of any martyrs that died by them. And sure, if it was the time of the ten heathen persecutions that was the new heaven and earth, it is strange. 2. And if it were at three hundred years after Christ, that the new heavens and earth come, it seems, far short of this here promised. What was in the days of Constantine, Martian, and Theodosius, they in Peter's days must never see. But the day of Christ they were all to see.

14. Wherefore (beloved) seeing that ye look for such things, be diligent that ye may be found of him in peace, without spot, and blameless.

14. Note, 1. It is not before death that Peter would have them look for this change, whatever it was: he lived not himself to see Jerusalem destroyed, and he and Paul died by the heathen power, though the Jews accused them, and Jews were more hated than they.

2. Whether the new heaven and earth be, as many of the old fathers thought, a restitution of

all things to the state they were in before the fall, for which the whole creation groaneth and travaileth in pain to be delivered; and that either for a thousand years, or for perpetuity; and who shall dwell in the new earth, and whether heaven and it shall be made so like, as that the same men shall inhabit both? &c. These are doubts, which I think, it must be the day of performance that must resolve. As also, whether accordingly there were other heavens and earth destroyed for sin before the creation of this. But Christians' care should be to be diligent to be found in a state of safety and peace, and without spot and blameless, and leave unknown things to God; and then whatever this blessed change be, we shall have our part in it.

15. And account *that* the longsuffering of our Lord *is* salvation, even as our beloved brother Paul also, according to the wisdom given unto him, hath written unto you.

15. And think not that God neglecteth you by delays, but that he suffereth the wicked world so long, that he may gather all his chosen to salvation that are yet to be born and called, as Paul hath shewed, Rom. ix.

16. As also in *all* his epistles, speaking in them of these things, in which are some things hard to be understood, which they that are unlearned and unstable wrest, as *they do* also the other scriptures, unto their own destruction.

16. Note, 1. They that refer [in which] to [these things] and not to [his epistles] pervert the text; for it puts [in which] as contradistinct to [other scriptures] and not to [other things.] And it is many other things much more than these, that were wrested to destruction. And Peter himself even here speaketh as hard things of this as ever Paul did. 2. It pleased God to put hard things in the scripture for our exercise. 3. Yet it is men's ignorant instability that wresteth such to their destruction; for there is as much very plain, as may bring men to salvation. And if, as to the difficult parts, they will, 1. But search as humble learners. 2. And not take on them to know before they do, but confess their ignorance, it may stand both with salvation, and the churches' peace. 3. And if they must by men be inclined to either side, let them say plainly, I hold not this by divine faith, as part of my religion, but as an opinion on the trust of man.

17. Ye therefore, beloved, seeing ye know *these things* before, beware lest ye also, being led away with the error of the wicked, fall from your own steadfastness.

17. The scope of what I have said is to warn you, that having timely notice of all these things, ye most diligently take heed, lest any of these sensual professors, or heretical backsliders, or scoffers, deceive you, in wavering and unbelief, or heresy, or sensuality, to fall from your spiritual steadfastness in faith, and hope, and holy living.

18. But grow in grace, and in the knowledge of our Lord and Saviour Jesus Christ: to him *be* glory both now and for ever. Amen.

18. But contrariwise, labour diligently to grow in all grace (in faith, love, holiness, patience, hope, &c.) and in the knowledge of our Lord and Saviour Jesus Christ (his person, office, undertaking, performance, humiliation, resurrection, doctrine, example, spirit, intercession, glory, kingdom, and judgment: that as glory belongeth to him, you may glorify him now, and in sight of his glory, for ever. Amen.

THE
FIRST EPISTLE GENERAL
OF
JOHN THE APOSTLE.

CHAP. I.

THAT which was from the beginning, which we have heard, which we have seen with our eyes, which we have looked upon, and our hands have handled of the word of life.

1. Whereas there are of late many heresies sprung up about the person, doctrine, and works of Christ, I shall declare to you that which was from the beginning (his godhead, or say others, that of him which was decreed from eternity; or as others, that which is true of him from his beginning or incarnation) and [that same Christ whom we have heard, and seen with our eyes, and looked on, and our hands have handled, even the human body of Christ the Word of Life.] Or, as others, [that gospel which we have heard, that person, and those works, which we have seen, and him whom we have handled, as these concern the gospel of life.

2. (For the life was manifested, and we have seen it, and bear witness, and shew unto you that eternal life which was with the Father, and was manifested unto us.)

2. For Christ, who is life in himself, and the fountain of life to us, was manifested in flesh, and we have seen him, and bear witness, and preach to you the eternal divine life and nature of Christ, which was eternally one with the Father, and was manifest to us.

3. That which we have seen and heard, declare we unto you, that ye also may have fellowship with us; and truly our fellowship is with the Father, and with his Son Jesus Christ.

3. I say, we declare to you that of Christ, which we ourselves have seen and heard, that so what we had by seeing and hearing, you may have from our testimony, who have seen and heard Christ himself; and so you may by our communication partake of the same faith and grace, as we ourselves do, and may continue in our communion; and that is no other than to have the same Father and Saviour from, and with whom it is that we have communication and communion, and not to turn from them.

4. And these things write we unto you, that your joy may be full.

4. And the end of my writing this to you, is the completing of your own joy and salvation.

5. This then is the message which we have heard of him, and declare unto you, that God is light, and in him is no darkness at all.

5. The first and great part of Christ's doctrine, and our message, is to teach us to know God himself; and first, that he is light, and in him is no darkness at all.

Note, 1. The apostle telling us what God is, speaketh in the abstract, to let us know that it is his essence, and not a mere accident that he meaneth. And as God's image in man's soul hath three essentiating faculties, vitality, understanding, and will, which are eminently self-motions, light, and heat, or resembled by these; so God is here called LIFE, verse 1. LIGHT, verse 5. and LOVE, chap. iv. 8.

2. When God is called LIGHT, it is spoken but metaphorically, and signifieth his KNOWLEDGE or WISDOM, as it is his essence, and as communicative, giving the light of knowledge to all that have it, and wisely ruling them by his laws: and also the GLORY of this, and all his perfections, as refulgent to the creature: for glory and light are oft the same in sense. 3. When it is said, There is no darkness in him, it meaneth, No ignorance, nor privation, nor uncomfortableness, as darkness is.

6. If we say that we have fellow-

ship with him, and walk in darkness, we lie, and do not the truth: 7. But if we walk in the light, as he is in the light, we have fellowship one with another, and the blood of Jesus Christ his Son cleanseth us from all sin.

6, 7. If we say that we live in communion with God, and yet are in the darkness of unbelief, ignorance, error, and wickedness, we do but lie: but if we walk in the light of holy knowledge, faith and purity, we have mutual communion with God, and with his Son Jesus Christ, whose blood doth cleanse us from all sin.

Note. Qu. Is it not fanaticism to talk of fellowship with God, or communion either? Ans. Fellowship is too harsh an English word: but communion is the thing meant, consisting in receptive participation from God, and accepted returns to God. And this is no fancy, but the only rectitude and felicity of our souls: if you conceive not how, think how the eye hath communion with the sun: really, 1. By receiving its luminous beams or emitted light, by the receptive aptitude of the visive faculty and organs. 2. By such an emission, or active congress, by which the light and sun are seen.

8. If we say that we have no sin, we deceive ourselves, and the truth is not in us.

8. If we say, that we need not Christ thus to cleanse us from guilt and corruption, as having no sin; this is but self-deceiving falsehood.

9. If we confess our sins, he is faithful and just to forgive us our sins, and to cleanse us from all unrighteousness.

9. But if we with true repentance confess our sins (always to God, and humbly to man, when either reparation of any one's wrong, or satisfaction to the church offended, or the curing of scandal, and honour of religion, or the ease or information of our own consciences require it) God that hath promised it, is faithful and just to forgive us our sin, and to cleanse us from its guilt and power.

10. If we say that we have not sinned, we make him a liar, and his word is not in us.

10. But if we will either pretend to sinless perfection, or else break God's command, and say, that it is no sin, but a duty, or an indifferent thing, and so justify ourselves or our sins; this is to give the lie to God's word, which therefore doth not rule such men.

CHAP. II.

MY little children, these things write I unto you, that ye sin not. And if any man sin, we have an advocate with the Father, Jesus Christ the righteous. 2. And he is the propitiation for our sins: and not for ours only, but also for the sins of the whole world.

1, 2. I write to you as to babes, who need help and confirmation, in your temptations by seducers, that you may not be drawn by them to take sensuality, or such like evils, to be lawful, nor to live wilfully or impenitently in any sin: but if any man, contrary to the bent and tenor of his heart and life, be guilty of any sin of infirmity, let him not despair, but fly to our advocate with the Father Jesus Christ, whose perfect righteousness merited our pardon: for he is the propitiation for our sins by virtue of his sacrifice, now interceding for us in heaven: and he is a propitiation sufficient for the sins of the whole world (so far as that none of them shall be damned for want of a sufficient sacrifice, but only for want of accepting his grace) and actually effecting the pardon of all in the world, who believingly trust and accept him and his grace.

3. And hereby we do know that we know him, if we keep his commandments.

3. And because uneffectual faith is but self-deceit, and he pardoneth sin to none but to the sincerely penitent and obedient; it is by this that we must be known to be sound believers, if we sincerely keep his commandments.

4. He that saith, I know him, and keepeth not his commandments, is a liar, and the truth is not in him.

4. He that professeth the knowledge and faith of Christ, and calls himself a Christian, and yet doth not sincerely keep his commandments, is an hypocrite and liar, and is not what he professeth to be.

5. But whoso keepeth his word, in him verily is the love of God perfected; hereby know we that we are in him. 6. He that saith, he abideth in him, ought himself also so to walk, even as he walked.

5, 6. But as true faith worketh by love, so doth love by obedience; and it is they that keep his word, in whom the love of God doth shew its soundness and perfection. We cannot bear fruit, unless we are in him as the branches in the vine: and it is by this fruit that we must know that we are in him. He that professeth to be a Christian, and in Christ, must walk as Christ did (in holiness, love, obedience, and patience.)

7. Brethren, I write no new commandment unto you, but an old commandment, which ye had from the beginning: the old command-

ment is the word which ye have heard from the beginning.

7. It is not novelty that I bring you, as seducers do; but that same old commandment which Christ and his apostles preached when they first brought the gospel to the world: I call it old, because it is the word which you heard from the beginning of Christianity.

8. Again, a new commandment I write unto you, which thing is true in him, and in you, because the darkness is past, and the true light now shineth.

8. Yet it may be called a new commandment which I write, as it is the doctrine of divine love newly and more resplendently shining forth in the work of our redemption by Christ; and there is true and just reason to call it new, both in Christ and in you: in Christ, because he is the newly incarnate, crucified, glorified demonstration of God's love to man, and the eminent messenger of it, accordingly obliging to a new and extraordinary love to God, and one another: and in you, because, as you are renewed by, and to this special love; so as new men you live therein: for the darkness of a life of malice and ungodliness is past, and the true light now shining is ever accompanied, when it is effectual, with the heats of love and obedience.

9. He that saith he is in the light, and hateth his brother, is in darkness, even until now.

9. The true light of knowledge and faith is so inseparable from the heats of love, that whoever pretendeth to that true Christian light, is deceived, and hath it not indeed, if he hate, or do not truly love his brother.

Note. We must love all in the various kinds and measures, as God appeareth in them; that is, 1. All men as men above brutes; 2. All professed Christians (not nullifying that profession) as such. 3. All Christians of eminent wisdom, and goodness, and usefulness, as such. 4. All rulers and teachers, as such. 5. All kindred, friends, and neighbours, as such. But, 1. We must hate all the evil that is in any of them. 2. Not equally, but as it is in various degrees in them. 3. And no hatred to the sin, and to the man as a sinner, must cast out our love to him, so far as he is lovely. 4. But rulers may be obliged to put to death some sinners; but that must be more for love to justice and the commonwealth, than hatred to the man; though yet, as he is bad, some hatred is due to him.

10. He that loveth his brother, abideth in the light, and there is none occasion of stumbling in him. 11. But he that hateth his brother, is in darkness, and walketh in darkness, and knoweth not whither he goeth, because that darkness hath blinded his eyes.

10, 11. He that truly loveth his brother as himself, doth shew that he is indeed a knowing and true Christian: and he will be free from the scandalous mischiefs of persecution, oppression, and other injuriousness, which want of true love doth cause in others. But he that hateth, abuseth, persecuteth, hurteth, or destroyeth his brother, is but a dark, self-deceiving pretender to Christian faith and wisdom, and knoweth not what he doth himself, when he exerciseth his wit or power against his brother, for he is blind in sin.

12. I write unto you, little children, because your sins are forgiven you for his name's sake. 13. I write unto you, fathers, because ye have known him that is from the beginning. I write unto you, young men, because ye have overcome the wicked one.

12, 13. And this command of love and obedience is such, as all sorts of you must receive, I urge it on you that are children in Christ, because, being washed lately in baptism, and the blood of Christ, trom your sins, you should love much, because much is forgiven you. I urge it on you, ancient Christians, because you have long been taught to know this commandment, and to know the love of God in Christ, which doth enforce it. I urge it on you that are strong Christians, because you have conquered the devil, who is the wicked one, and the grand enemy of love.

13, 14. I write unto you, little children, because ye have known the Father. I have written unto you, fathers, because ye have known him that is from the beginning. I have written unto you, young men, because ye are strong, and the word of God abideth in you, and ye have overcome the wicked one.

13, 14. Again I say, that you may not neglect it; I urge this commandment of love and obedience on all sorts among you: on young Christians, because, to know God, as he is love and a father to us, is your chief principle of faith. On you, ancient Christians, because it is your old religion. On you, strong Christians, because you that have most strength and victory over Satan, must have most of this grace of love and obedience.

15. Love not the world, neither the things that are in the world. If any man love the world, the love of the Father is not in him.

15. And I must accordingly warn you against the love that is contrary to this divine, Christian love; which is the carnal, inordinate love of this world, and worldly interest and things. Avoid this with all possible care; for in that measure that you thus love the world, you are so far des-

16. For all that is in the world, the lust of the flesh, the lust of the eyes, and the pride of life, is not of the Father, but is of the world.

16. For, all that is the bait of sensuality in the world, whether it be the pleasures of appetite, lust, and other senses, or the pleasing of a covetous, lustful, or vain imagination by the eyes: or preferment, dominion, pompous living, and pride of life, are none of them, the way to communion with God, and salvation; but are the worldly interest, and temptation of the flesh, which turn men's hearts to the world from God.

17. And the world passeth away, and the lust thereof: but he that doeth the will of God, abideth for ever.

17. And the world, and all its pomp, plenty, and pleasure, and the fleshly lusts that are pleased by it, are hastily passing away, while they seem enjoyed: but the reward and the pleasure of those that do the will of God, will have no end.

18. Little children, it is the last time: and as ye have heard that Antichrist shall come, even now are there many Antichrists, whereby we know that it is the last time.

18. I yet speak to you, as children liable to deceit, it is now the latter part of the age of the world; and, as you have heard that Antichrist shall come, so, even, now there are many false teachers risen up, who, in several sorts and measures, are adversaries to Christ: which shews us that, indeed, it is already the beginning of the last age.

Note, Of the controversy about Antichrist, see the notes on 2 Thess. ii. there are four opinions, very commonly pleaded for; and others, by some few.

1. Most of the old doctors and Christians, that have left us their thoughts, took Antichrist to be a false, pretending Christ, that should rise up towards the end of the world; little dreaming that the Pope was he; much less, that all the visible Christian church was then, in its most flourishing state, idolatrous and Antichristian, as some hold. By which it appeareth, that it is a point that godly men may be ignorant of: for few now, but the Papists are of this opinion.

II. Others think that Mahomet is the great Antichrist, as being that open enemy of Christianity; who by pretending hatred to idolatry, hath set up himself, and won more of the world, than all the Christian part of the earth, by far.

III. Most Protestants hold, that the Pope is the Antichrist; but they greatly disagree of the time when he began to be so; some say, at the churches' deliverance by Constantine, which was three hundred and four years after the birth of Christ: some say, about anno 604, when Phocas named Pope Boniface the third, universal bishop of the empire. And thence riseth a doubt, whether the same claim made not John of Constantinople Antichrist before, and so there be not two Antichrists: and whether the like ambition made not Cyril, Theophilus, and other patriarchs of Alexandria, and divers other bishops, to be so many Antichrists. Some say, he began about Hildebrand's time, when the claim of universal head, and Vice-Christ, over all the world began, with power over princes; which was above one thousand years after Christ. And some few say, he began about Innocent the third: when the general council of the Lateran owned that power, with transubstantiation, and the murder of reformers, as heretics. The reasons for the opinion that the Pope is the Antichrist, you may find in many volumes, and particularly bishop G. Downame's.

IV. Others think that Antichrist was a false Christ, who was to appear in the days of some of the apostles, or that generation, to seduce the Jews into rebellion against the Romans, to their destruction. And they are very confident that John here meant no other than Christ himself meant in Matt. xxiv. and received his notice from none but Christ and that Christ's own words are the surest notification, who is the Antichrist: for, it is mentioned here, not as a thing known only by special inspiration to them, or the apostles, but as a received former prophecy; [as you have heard that Antichrist shall come.] And which way did they hear it, but by the apostles, as from Christ; whose words the evangelists have not omitted? Now Christ's words were, [Many shall come in my name, saying, I am Christ, and shall deceive many.] Here he doth not fix the name on any one, more than on others. And it is certain that Christ was not mistaken; but what he foretold did come to pass: though we read not of any that was expressly called Christ, and commonly so believed, that was not, because none attempted so to deceive men, but because their success was small, and soon stifled, and not like Mahomet's. Beza, on the text, Matt. xxiv. saith, [In my name, is, They shall usurp the name of the Messiah, or Christ. Such was that Dositheus, whom Theophilact speaketh of, and Simon, and Theudas; and after these, Manes, who also chose his twelve apostles. And in our memory, the Munster Anabaptists attempted the same; and after them, David George, the prince of the libertines.] (So James Nailor lately, the quaker, whose tongue the Parliament bored through, whipped him, and imprisoned him till he died, for solemnly personating Christ, riding into Bristol.) But there were others that promised to deliver the Jews, till they drew them into rebellion, to their destruction: and so took on them to redeem Israel, though they called not themselves the Christ. Almost all expositors agree, that these were the Antichrists meant by Christ, Matt. xxiv. But though these were then shortly to arise, it followeth not, but that more such might arise after them; and such was Mahomet, above all others, notorious by his alcoran, kingdom, and success. And, as Ebion, Cerinthus, and some other heretics, were against Christ in some degree, so more notably is the Pope in that degree, as he arrogateth Christ's prerogative, and maketh himself a vicarious head of the whole church on earth. So that these grant, that such Popes are one sort of those Antichrists that should after arise; but that the Pope is not he that is meant by Christ in Matt. xxiv. nor here by John.

And whereas, 2 Thes. ii. is objected for [One Man of Sin, &c.] they say, that it is not Antichrist properly, that is there mentioned; but the Antigod, the Roman idolatrous emperor, that should cause Jerusalem's desolation, and set up there the idol of abomination.

There is the like mention of Antichrist again, chap. iv. 3. [Every spirit that confesseth not that Jesus Christ is come in the flesh, is not of God: and this is the spirit of Antichrist, whereof ye have heard that it should come, and even now already is in the world.]

So, chap. ii. 20. [He is Antichrist, that denieth the Father and the Son.]

And, 2 John. [For many deceivers are entered into the world, who confess not that Jesus Christ is come in the flesh. This is a deceiver, and one Antichrist.]

And (say they) when no other text in scripture hath the name Antichrist, and these four all thus expound it of such as deny Christ's incarnation, and directly oppose him; and such as were then in being, and of many such heresies, and not of one man, or order, alone; and when all this concurreth with Christ's own words, of many false Christs, that should deceive the Jews to their destruction, whence can we expect a surer exposition of Antichristianity, whether we take the name for an adversary to Christ, or for a false Christ.

When Grotius singleth out Barchochebas, as the chief Antichrist, who called himself the Messiah, and seduced thousands, and even the sanhedrim of rulers, into his error, to their destruction, it is answered by some, that this was all done before this epistle was written. To which some reply; 1. That this is utterly uncertain, because that Epiphanius saith, John was first banished under Claudius: and because the contrary tradition hath no good evidence, and because the Apocalyps is the best expositor, whose very stile implieth that, at least, much of it was written before the destruction of Jerusalem; and so may this epistle. 2. Were it certain, John maketh no one to be the only, or grand Antichrist, and therefore Christ's words might be first fulfilled in Barchochebus, and such others; and yet more after may succeed them.

The other two opinions. (1. That it is only Simon Magus. 2. Or Vespasian) I think not worthy the confuting.

In these difficulties, I only advise the reader, that he never forsake great and certain truths, or duties, for any thing uncertain: and that human faith overthrow not divine faith: and no man's opinion draw him to depose Christ, by denying all his visible church, and making it all, in any age, (much less in its best state) to be idolatrous and antichristian: or to be frightened from Christian love, unity, and peace, or from any lawful thing, by the mere name of Antichrist. But to judge of doctrines by scripture, and of persons by their doctrines, practices, and personal qualification; and to hate sin impartially, wherever he findeth it; and to accuse rashly, and unjustly, neither persons, parties, or societies.

19. They went out from us, but they were not of us: for if they had been of us, they would, no doubt, have continued with us; but *they went out* that they might be made manifest, that they were not all of us.

19 These deceivers, (the Nicolaitans, Ebion, Cerinthus, &c.) were indeed in our communion, and went out from us; but they were never sincerely of the same faith and spirit with us; else they would have stayed with us: but they went out, and separated, and set up their heresies, that they might show that they were never sound in the faith.

20. But ye have an unction from the Holy One, and ye know all things.

20 But the most holy God and Saviour hath anointed you with his holy Spirit, which will lead you from pernicious error, into all necessary truth, if you obey him.

21. I have not written unto you, because ye know not the truth: but because ye know it, and that no lie is of the truth.

21. It is not as supposing you ignorant of the truth, that I write to you; but because you know the necessary truth, and therefore may the easier reject all inconsistent falsehoods.

22. Who is a liar but he that denieth that Jesus is the Christ? he is Antichrist that denieth the Father and the Son. 23. Whosoever denieth the Son, the same hath not the Father: *but he that acknowledgeth the Son hath the Father also.*

22, 23. And who is the dangerous liar, but he that denieth that Jesus is the Christ; and consequently, denieth the Father?

Note, The scantiness of history leaveth it uncertain, what sort of seducers John meaneth; whether some that fell to flat infidelity, directly renouncing Christianity; or only such as Ebion, Cerinthus, and others, that denied somewhat of Christ's being, his manhood, or his godhead, or his real suffering: or those that were for Moses' law, and held, that Christ may be denied with the tongue, in case of danger, so that the heart deny him not; pretending that God will have mercy to ourselves, and not sacrifice.

24. Let that therefore abide in you, which ye have heard from the beginning: if that which ye have heard from the beginning, shall remain in you, ye also shall continue in the Son, and in the Father.

24. Hold fast the doctrine which at the first ye received from us, and turn not after novelties: and this will preserve you against seduction, and

continue you in the faith, relation, and love, of the Son and Father.

25. And this is the promise that he hath promised us, even eternal life.

25. And if you live by faith upon his promises, he will give you eternal life, which he hath promised, whatever you suffer or forsake here in the way.

26. These things have I written unto you, concerning them that seduce you.

26. It is the seducing heretics, who occasion my writing these warnings to you.

27. But the anointing which ye have received of him, abideth in you: and ye need not that any man teach you: but, as the same anointing teacheth you of all things, and is truth, and is no lie: and even as it hath taught you, ye shall abide in him.

27. But I hope I need no other argument, to confirm you in the Christian faith, against seducers, than that the Spirit of Christ, which is his witness, agent, and advocate, hath through his apostles' preaching and imposition of hands, been given to you, and among you. His miracles have sealed his truth before your eyes; and his illuminating and sanctifying grace hath been given you, if you be true believers. And I hope you will not deny the Holy Ghost: as he is thus the infallible objective evidence of Christ's truth, so is he in you, an efficient, illuminating teacher, and ready, within you, to plead Christ's cause, and teach you all necessary truth. Therefore you need not any man's testimony and teaching, as those do that have no other, but must take the word of man alone. Use Christ's ministers but in due subordination to the spirit, and quench it not, and he will keep you.

28. And now, little children, abide in him, that when he shall appear, we may have confidence, and not be ashamed before him at his coming.

28. Therefore, children, waver not, but fixedly abide in Christ, and true Christianity; that when he shall appear in judgment, we may see and meet him with joyful confidence, and not with shame unto condemnation, as apostates will.

Note, It is wonderful that he that expounds all this, of Christ's coming to destroy Jerusalem by the Romans (his enemies) should think that all the Christians, to whom the apostles wrote, should then meet Christ or be so much comforted therein, when most were like to die first, and few living to be much the better for it; and Christian compassion would fill them with grief, as Paul had, Rom. ix. and xi. and not make them like men of utter malice, to take it for so great joy, to have the Jews so murdered, when Christ wept over them, that foretold it; and when the Romans were far more to persecute the church, near three hundred years. And this exposition leaveth all the Christian world since, to this day, little more use of the abundance of motives and comforts of the New Testament, than of the fulfilled prophecies of the Old. Do not Christ's and the apostles' words nearly concern us? Or should the church be moved to constancy, patience, and comfort, chiefly, sixteen hundred years after, because a million of Jews were killed then?

29. If ye know that he is righteous, ye know that every one that doeth righteousness, is born of him.

29. And as ye believe that Christ is just, and a lover of righteousness, so all that sincerely live a righteous life towards God and man, are new born, by his sanctifying spirit, to his image, and shall surely be received and owned by him.

CHAP. III.

BEHOLD, what manner of love the Father hath bestowed upon us, that we should be called the sons of God; therefore the world knoweth us not, because it knew him not.

1. Let us, therefore, instead of forsaking Christ, admire the wondrous love of God to us, that hath, in Christ, adopted us to be his sons. Indeed our dignity is unknown to the unbelieving world; for they knew not Christ to be the Son of God, and how then should they know us?

2. Beloved, now are we the sons of God, and it doth not yet appear what we shall be: but we know, that when he shall appear, we shall be like him: for we shall see him as he is.

2. And it is no wonder if our condition be unknown to the unbelieving world; for though we are already the sons of God, and have right, by promise, to future glory, our future glory is yet unseen, and what we shall be, doth not appear to the world, or to our own sight: but we know by faith, that when Christ appeareth, we that are his members, shall, in our several measures, be made like our glorified head, in the perfection both of soul and body, and place and state of blessedness. For he hath promised that we shall be with him, and therefore shall see him as he is, and therefore be made capable of such a sight, and glorious communion.

3. And every man that hath this hope in him, purifieth himself, even as he is pure.

3. And knowing that, without holiness, none can see God; and that it is the pure in heart that

have the promise of seeing him, therefore all that have a true effectual hope of seeing him, will make it their chief care to purify themselves, that such likeness to Christ may render them capable of such a blessed sight.

4. Whosoever committeth sin, transgresseth also the law: for sin is the transgression of the law. 5. And ye know that he was manifested to take away our sins, and in him is no sin.

4, 5. For, to sin, is to transgress, and break God's law: for that is the definition of sin. And ye know that Christ came in the flesh, to be a sacrifice for sin, and to take it away, and destroy it, and never sinned himself; and all this, that he might vindicate God's law and holiness.

6. Whosoever abideth in him sinneth not: whosoever sinneth, hath not seen him, neither known him.

6. So far as any man is in him, and is taught and ruled by him; so far is he freed from all sin: and all his true members are delivered from the predominant love and practice of all known sin; and are willing to know all, that they may avoid it. And he that would not know it, and when he doth know it, doth not hate it, more than love it, and so far forsake it, as to conquer the dominion of it, and live in sincere and willing holy obedience in the course of his life, may boast falsely that he is a Christian; but indeed, hath no true saving knowledge of Christ.

7. Little children, let no man deceive you: he that doeth righteousness, is righteous, even as he is righteous.

7. Be not so childish, as to be deceived by the vain words of any that pretend to be righteous before God, on any account whatsoever, while they live in unrighteousness and predominant sin; as if God would justify the wicked for their opinions or presumptions. It is he that, being called, justified and sanctified by the merits and Spirit of Christ, doth live in a sincere obedience to him, and labours to be like him, in holiness and love to God and man, whom God will call a righteous man, and save him as such, when he is judge.

8. He that committeth sin, is of the devil; for the devil sinneth from the beginning. For this purpose the Son of God was manifested, that he might destroy the works of the devil.

8. So far as any man sinneth, so far he is of the devil, and like him: and he is the servant of the devil, in whom sin is predominant: or that liveth in the love and practice of any sin, not consistent with true hatred of it, and repentance, and the predominant love and practice of holy obedience. And Christ will be no justifying advocate, or judge, of the servants of the devil (though he may by making them just, and holy, turn them from the power of Satan, to God; and judge them just, when he hath made them just, both by conversion and pardon, but not before.) For the Son of God came purposely into the world, to destroy the works of the devil, in all that he will save, and not to call the wicked righteous.

9. Whosoever is born of God, doth not commit sin: for his seed remaineth in him, and he cannot sin, because he is born of God.

9. He that is truly regenerate by the Spirit, is made a hater and forsaker of sin, and therefore doth not live in the ruling love or practice of it; nor indeed, commit any sin, in that degree that he is sanctified; much less, live in wilful, gross sin: for God's word and Spirit, by which he was regenerate, still abide in him. And it is a contradiction to say that, at once, he is a holy person, born of God, and yet liveth in reigning sin.

Note, [Cannot] Here signifieth a hypothetical impossibility, because it is a contradiction, and not a natural impossibility; much less, impotency: for it is sinning, and not forbearing sin, that signifieth impotency. And the contradiction is only on supposition that he continue sanctified.

10. In this the children of God are manifest, and the children of the devil: whosoever doth not righteousness, is not of God, neither he that loveth not *his brother*.

10. It is not by proud boasting, nor barren opinions, that God's children are known from the children of the devil; but by the image of God, which faith in Christ doth cause in his true disciples. He that doth not live in the true love and practice of righteousness towards God and man; abhorring and avoiding ungodliness, injustice, and fleshly lusts, is no child of God, but of the devil: nor he that doth not unfeignedly love all Christians, as Christians; and men, as men; and live in charity to them accordingly.

Note, That wicked men are called, The children of the devil, because they are like him, and do his will. And the world swarmeth with men so like to devils, in lying, malignity, and mischiefs, as maketh it easy to believe, that there are devils, and a hell.

11. For this is the message that ye heard from the beginning, that we should love one another.

11. For this is the message which Christ, the Lord of love, did commit to us, and, from the first, we have preached to you, that love is the very sum and end of law and gospel.

12. Not as Cain, *who* was of that wicked one, and slew his brother: and wherefore slew he him? because his own works were evil, and his brother's righteous.

12. That we be not like wicked Cain, who was of the diabolical disposition and practice, and killed his own brother. And, why did he kill

him? Not for any ill desert, nor for any harm that he had done him: but because he was bad himself, and his works bad; and his brother's righteous, and, by difference, condemned him.

Note, Doubtless, God permitted Adam's first son to be wicked, and murder his righteous brother, to shew the world, what a state we are first in, since the fall, by natural pravity; and that we are. as such, the children of the devil, till grace recover us: and to expound the enmity put between the seed of the woman, and of the serpent; and to tell us, what a war will be continued upon earth, from the days of Cain and Abel, till the end: and that superiority and cruelty will usually be against the righteous, whose victory is mostly by patient suffering and death.

13. Marvel not, my brethren, if the world hate you.

13. If the ungodly successors of Cain, whose own works are evil, do hate godliness and conscience, and hate you for them, take it for no strange or unexpected thing: it hath been so since Cain's days, and will be so, as Christ foretold.

14. We know that we have passed from death unto life, because we love the brethren: he that loveth not *his* brother abideth in death.

14. Love being the great work of God's renewing spirit on the soul, it is by love, especially to all true Christians, that we know that we are changed from the Cainish, corrupt state of death, into the state of holy life. Whatever else men have, if they have not true love to others, especially to godly Christians, they are yet dead in sin. Note, 1. By [the brethren,] here is meant, [Christians are such:] not only those of some party in opinion which we like, nor only those that are friendly to us, nor yet all men, or all called Christians alike; though all men must be loved as men. It is, to love God in man, and man for his sake, so far as God's amiableness shineth in them; especially, to love God's holiness in holy persons.

2. It is not all love to godly Christians, as such, that will prove us translated from death to life, but to love them, and God in them, better than the pleasures and wealth of the world; the cheap love of such as wish men well, but will be at no great cost or danger for any, because they love their money better, is the hypocrite's love.

15. Whosoever hateth his brother, is a murderer: and ye know that no murderer hath eternal life abiding in him.

15. Note, 1. How dreadful a sentence this is against malignant, or factious haters of brethren.

2. But the self-deceit of murderous hypocrites is, by taking brethren for no brethren; but as the Papists, first call them heretics, schismatics, fanatics, puritans, rebels against the Pope or church; that they may justify their hating, murdering, imprisoning, silencing, and ruining them. As the scribes were loath to know who was their neighbour, so are these loath to know who is a brother: but God will know his children, though men call them by reproachful names. Alas for the murderous generation, that preach, write, and strive to destroy the upright, and say, they killed them, or ruined them in love; (that is, they hated them in love.) Woe to them, when God shall judge them.

3. Every degree of unjust hurt or hatred is a breach of the sixth commandment: but the meaning is not every degree, or mistaken wrong, is as bad as actual murder, or as sure a sign of death. Alas! how few else would live.

16. Hereby perceive we the love of God, because he laid down his life for us, and we ought to lay down our lives for the brethren.

16. As God hath manifested his love to us, by laying down for us the life of our Redeemer; so if we be God's children, we must learn of him (as to love our enemies, so) if God should call us to it, as needful to better ends than our lives, to lay down our lives for Christian brethren.

17. But whoso hath this world's good, and seeth his brother have need, and shutteth up his bowels *of compassion* from him, how dwelleth the love of God in him?

17. And if love must make us die for others, surely those have no true love to God, and to the brethren, as God requireth, who cannot lay down part of their abundance (perhaps superfluity) for them; but while they are well able, yet cannot find in their hearts to relieve them, but shut up the bowels of their compassion from them. Note, O the dreadful account that many of the rich must give, that feast all the year, while their poor neighbours hunger! and spend forty times more in (needless) housekeeping, as they call their luxury, than on the poor.

18. My little children, let us not love in word, neither in tongue, but in deed, and in truth.

18. Let not your love be hypocritical, which will bring forth no better fruit, than good wishes, and fair words, but shew the truth of it by your cost and real helps.

19. And hereby we know that we are of the truth, and shall assure our hearts before him.

19. It is by such efficacy and real fruit that we must know that we are true Christians, and not hypocrites, and must have assurance that our hearts are true to God.

20. For if our heart condemn us, God is greater than our heart, and knoweth all things. 21. Beloved, if our heart condemn us not, *then* have we confidence towards God.

20, 21. For if our consciences, tell us that our love is barren and fruitless, and so condemn us of hypocrisy, God is greater, and more acquainted with our hypocrisy than our consciences: but if our conscience truly witness the sincerity of our love by the fruits of it, then this assurance of our sincerity giveth us boldness towards God.

22. And whatsoever we ask, we receive of him, because we keep his commandments, and do those things that are pleasing in his sight.

22. And if we do God's will sincerely, in obeying his commandments, and the things that please him, he will hear our prayers, and grant our just desires, and give us that which is good for us; whereas, if we love iniquity, and live therein, God will not hear our prayers.

Note, They that deny that holy, sincere obedience, is any condition of God's hearing our prayers (because faith hath the promise) contradict the scope of scripture.

23. And this is his commandment, that we should believe on the name of his Son Jesus Christ, and love one another, as he gave us commandment.

23. And the sum of all this acceptable duty is but this, to believe truly in Jesus Christ, our redeemer, our teacher, king, and intercessor, and to obey his great command of loving one another; with all such God is pleased, and heareth them.

24. And he that keepeth his commandments dwelleth in him, and he in him: and hereby we know that he abideth in us, by the Spirit which he hath given us.

24. And if we keep Christ's commands (of fruitful love in faith) there is a near communion between Christ and us; we dwell in Christ as his members, and he dwelleth in us; and his dwelling in us is by the spirit of love and holiness (the seal of his promise) which he hath given us: he that keepeth Christ's commandments (especially of love) hath his Spirit: and Christ dwells where his Spirit dwells.

CHAP. IV.

BELOVED, believe not every spirit, but try the spirits, whether they are of God: because many false prophets are gone out into the world.

1. There be many false teachers, who pretend to revelation as prophets, who teach you the doctrines of sensuality, worldliness, and malice, contrary to the doctrine of holiness and love, which I have taught you: Therefore, believe not that every man speaketh by God's Spirit, who pretendeth to it; nor that every strong suggestion in yourselves is from God's Spirit, which seemeth such before you try it: But try all pretences of the spirit, whether they come indeed from the Spirit of God, or rather from Satan, or men's own imaginations corrupted by pride.

Qu. How shall we justly try spirits, or spiritual pretences? Ans. By somewhat that is more easily known, and no otherwise: And that is two things; 1. The common certain notices of the light and law of nature. 2. By the infallible words of the Spirit in Christ and his apostles, and prophets: For both these are the sure word of God, who doth not contradict himself: Our gifts of the Spirit are lower than the apostles, and must be tried by theirs, which were given them to record a rule for us.

2. Hereby know ye the *Spirit* of God: every spirit that confesseth that Jesus Christ is come in the flesh, is of God. 3. And every spirit that confesseth not that Jesus Christ *is* come in the flesh, is not of God: and this is that *spirit* of Antichrist, whereof you have heard that it should come, and even now already is it in the world.

2, 3. By this you shall know whether these pretenders speak from the Spirit of God: For the Spirit of God is the Spirit of Christ, sent by him to be his advocate, and plead his cause, and do his work in the world, and therefore beareth witness of him: If, therefore, these teachers, truly and openly in the face of danger, do own, profess, and preach Christ Jesus, as the incarnate Word and Son of God, sent from heaven to redeem, teach, rule, and save us; this doctrine is of the Spirit of God. But if they deny the godhead, or manhood of Christ, or that he is indeed the true incarnate Saviour, prophet, priest, and king, or will not own him in hazards or sufferings, but deny him to save the flesh, and teach men so to do; this doctrine and spirit is not of God: But this is the spirit of Antichrist, which you have been foretold should come, and is already in the world.

Note, By the spirit of Antichrist is not here meant, the spirit sent by Antichrist, but the same doctrine that Antichrist will vend, and therefore from the same spirit that acteth Antichrist, which is a spirit of opposition to Christ. And in those times, Ebion, Cerinthus, and many other heretics did, some deny Christ's manhood, some his godhead, some his death, and some his resurrection, and each part of his office was denied: That among all these Simon Magus only should be the Antichrist, I see no reason to believe, of which more before and after.

4. Ye are of God, little children, and have overcome them: because greater is he that *is* in you, than he that is in the world.

4. But your faith in Christ is of the Spirit of God, who dwelleth and worketh in you, and you have overcome the worldly seducing spirit, its doctrines, baits and temptations; for God's Spirit which is in you, is more powerful than the spirit which deludeth the world.

CHAP. IV.   I. JOHN.   587

5. They are of the world: therefore speak they of the world, and the world heareth them.

5. These seducers are men of a worldly interest and mind, and therefore they preach a worldly doctrine, fitted to a worldly interest and ear; and therefore worldly men believe them.

6. We are of God: he that knoweth God, heareth us: he that is not of God, heareth not us. Hereby know we the spirit of truth, and the spirit of error.

6. We are of God, and can prove our mission by his attestation to our doctrine, as being from God: And therefore, all that truly know God, will receive and own our doctrine as God's, and us as his apostles: But he that is not of God, having not the same spirit, receiveth not the same holy doctrine, nor us. Thus differ the Spirit of God, and of error.

7. Beloved, let us love one another: for love is of God; and every one that loveth is born of God, and knoweth God. 8. He that loveth not, knoweth not God: for God is love.

7, 8. And as true faith in Christ, and open confessing him, is one sign; so true Christian love is another, to know that our doctrine and spirit is of God: Therefore be sure that you unfeignedly love one another: Most certainly love is of God; (common love is his common gift, and holy love is his special grace;) and every one that loveth saints as saints, as well as men as men, sincerely for the love of God, and goodness in them, is so far like God (who as the God of nature, loveth nature, and as the God of grace, loveth holiness,) and therefore is a regenerate child of God, and hath true faith and knowledge of God, or else he could not love him in his saints. And whatever they pretend, they have no true effectual love of the most holy God, or of his will, who love not his holiness in his children, and are not dear to one another. For love is not a mere quality in God, but his very essence: GOD IS LOVE.

Note, I know no sentence more worthy to be written in letters of gold, or rather written on all our hearts: But the other two prime attributes written in this epistle must be conjoined, GOD IS LIFE, LIGHT, and LOVE: And love is complacency, and includeth infinite joy or pleasure.

9. In this was manifested the love of God towards us, because that God sent his only begotten Son into the world, that we might live through him.

9. And God's essential love doth tend to communication; he is good, and doth good: He loveth us, not with a barren love, as hypocrites do; but he chose this most wonderful glorifying way of public manifesting his love to us, even by sending his Son into the world, that we might live through him.

10. Herein is love, not that we loved God, but that he loved us, and sent his Son *to be* the propitiation for our sins.

10. And the glory of God's love to us, is not only that he consequently loved us for loving him; but that he antecedently loved us (that we might love him) and (while we were yet in sin and enmity) freely sent his Son to be the propitiation for our sins.

11. Beloved, if God so loved us, we ought also to love one another.

11 And God's great works, and glorious manifestations of himself to us are purposely to be (as the seal to the wax) to make us like him in our degree: And he therefore, chose this astonishing way of revealing his love to us, that by it we might be brought to love him, and one another for him.

12. No man hath seen God at any time. If we love one another, God dwelleth in us, and his love is perfected in us.

12. It is God himself that his love obligeth us to love. But as we see him but in the glass or image of his nature and holiness in man; so we must love him as we see him here, even in the nature and holiness of man: And if we thus holily love one another as God's image, God by his Spirit dwelleth in us, for it is his Spirit of love that maketh us thus love: And his love to us attaineth its end, which was to make us like him in love. (O that Christians would study this well!)

13. Hereby know we that we dwell in him, and he in us, because he hath given us of his Spirit.

13. By this sure evidence we know that God, and we do, as it were, dwell in each other, and have blessed communion, because he hath given us this Spirit of holy love.

14. And we have seen, and do testify, that the Father sent the Son *to be* the Saviour of the world.

14. And we are the preachers of faith and love; as we have seen, so we testify, that God the Father glorified his love, by sending his Son to be the Saviour of the sinful world.

15. Whosoever shall confess, that Jesus is the Son of God, God dwelleth in him, and he in God.

15. It cannot be that any man can soundly believe such astonishing love, that God was manifested in flesh, or that the Father sent his Son into flesh, by his doctrine, example, suffering, merits, resurrection, and intercession, to save us, and shall confess this, whatever suffering it cost him, but that man must needs be possessed by God's Spirit of holy love, and so God dwelleth in that man by

his Spirit, and that man is God as the great object of his faith and love. [For with the heart man believeth to righteousness, and with the mouth confession is made to salvation. Rom. x.]

16. And we have known and believed the love that God hath to us. God is love, and he that dwelleth in love, dwelleth in God, and God in him.

16. And knowing, and by faith believing the love that God hath to us, and hath declared in Christ, we again conclude, that GOD IS LOVE, and he that dwelleth in love (as his ruling habit of soul, and practice of life) dwelleth by communion in God (as the eye in the light; and a friend by love dwells in his friend,) and God by his Spirit of love in him.

Note, I prefer this verse before all the human learning in the world.

17. Herein is our love made perfect, that we may have boldness in the day of judgment: because as he is, so are we in this world.

17. And our love is for this blessed effect, that we may joyfully now foresee, and stand at last before him in judgment, as the Lord, to whom by love we are endeared and united: For as his interest is dearest to us in this world, and we obey and follow him in suffering; so it is that we may come to him in glory, with whom our life is now hid.

18. There is no fear in love, but perfect love casteth out fear: because fear hath torment: he that feareth, is not made perfect in love.

18. For though our darkness and guilt would keep us under terror, lest God should destroy us, or our weakness make us fear the power of man, and bodily calamities and death, yet the love that I speak of, hath none of this terror in it; but were it perfect, it would fully quiet the soul, and cast out all distrustful painful fear; For though cautelous preventing fear of all danger is necessary in this life to our safe avoiding of evil, and the awe and reverence of God is the duty of every creature; yet tormenting, or painful troubling fear cometh from distrust, and sheweth that our love is yet imperfect.

Note, This is spoken both of tormenting fear of God and man, of hell and of death, sicknesses, and crosses here. For he that by faith is fully persuaded of God's great and special love to him, such as he hath manifested by Christ, and thereupon doth love God entirely above all, in that measure, cannot fear that such a God will damn him, or leave him to the malice of men or devils, and by death itself do him any hurt inconsistent with dearest love. If wives and children fear not being murdered by loving husbands or fathers: Perfect love would make us fully quiet in our trust in God. Painful fear of hell, death, sickness, poverty, or persecutors, doth shew a distrust and doubting of God's love (who could sure quickly save us by such a word as made the world) and an imperfection of our love to him as caused by his distrust. Fear may stand with true faith and love, but not with perfect. Only I confess sensitive passion, through bodily disease or disposition, quite differing from rational fear, is a tyrant, which faith and reason will not overcome. As a man bound with chains to the top of a spire steeple is rationally sure that he cannot fall, and yet is terrified with looking down. O how should fearful Christians study [trust and love,] as their only cure, and quieting help.

19. We love him, because he first loved us.

19. And it is the knowledge of God's antecedent love to us, giving us a Christ and grace, and making us love him, which thus delivereth the soul from fear, and turneth us to him with love and boldness: If his love had been a mere dependant consequent of ours, how uncertain should we be of its continuance?

20. If a man say, I love God, and hateth his brother, he is a liar: for he that loveth not his brother whom he hath seen, how can he love God whom he hath not seen?

20. But still, I say, our love to God must be shewn in our hearty love to our brethren: To hate and persecute them, yea, not effectually to love them, proveth him a liar, who saith, he loveth God: It is God in his image that you must love and help: He needeth you not, but he will make you need one another, to try your love and obedience to him. If you love not his visible image, how can you love the invisible God? This doth but detect your self-deceiving hypocrisy.

21. And this commandment have we from him, that he who loveth God, love his brother also.

21. And he that will be the judge who love him truly, hath made this his summary great commandment, that you must love God first, and above all, and your brother or neighbour, for his sake, as yourselves: And you love him not if you keep not his great commandment.

CHAP. V.

WHOSOEVER believeth that Jesus is the Christ, is born of God: and every one that loveth him that begat, loveth him also that is begotten of him.

1. Note, That it is believing God and not man only, a divine faith, and not a human, a sincere faith, and not a doubting opinion, that is here called [believing.] Believing this on the word of our rulers or teachers is good, but it is but preparatory to religion, and the belief of God: And it is a matter of such great importance to believe it sincerely as God's word, that God was manifested

in flesh, and appointed Christ to the office and work of man's sanctification and salvation, that it is not possible but such a sound belief must fill the soul with love to God, and carry it up to a holy and heavenly state, as the regenerate are: Nor is it possible but such should love that Saviour, who is the image of God's love.

2. By this we know that we love the children of God, when we love God, and keep his commandments.

3. For this is the love of God, that we keep his commandments, and his commandments are not grievous.

2, 3. And you must know, that it is not all love to one another, or to good people; that will prove us regenerate (for men may love them as their friends, for loving them, or for being of their opinion, sect, or party, or for their interest, &c.) But your love to men as God's children is sincere and saving, when it is God himself that you love most, and them for his sake: And when his love maketh you keep his commandments. And his commandments are not heavy, nor have any thing in them which men should be unwilling to keep, but should be both our work and pleasure.

4. For whosoever is born of God overcometh the world: and this is the victory that overcometh the world, *even* our faith.

4. God's Spirit is stronger than the evil spirit that ruleth the ungodly world; and therefore all that are truly regenerate, do overcome the love and temptations of the world, though not perfectly, yet in prevalency. And how do we overcome the world, but by firm believing in Jesus Christ, and the love of God, that will bring us to a far better world? The things believed prevail against the things seen, in all that are true believers indeed.

5. Who is he that overcometh the world, but he that believeth that Jesus is the Son of God:

5. Where do you see any truly overcome the love of this world, but by believing in him that overcame it, and is preparing a place for us in heaven, and hath made us the heirs of glory?

6. This is he that came by water and blood, *even* Jesus Christ, not by water only, but by water and blood: and it is the Spirit that beareth witness, because the Spirit is truth.

6. This is he that, as he was baptized, so he instituted baptism for the cleansing of souls: And as he was crucified to be a sacrifice for sin, so doth he, by his sacrament and grace, communicate this sacrifice in its benefits to us; which his crucifixion signified, when both water and blood ran out of his pierced side. He cleanseth us, not by water and baptism alone, but as a sacrifice, by water and blood, and at a dearer rate. And the witness, by

which God attesteth all this to be his truth, is the gift of his Spirit.

7. For there are three that bear record in heaven, the Father, the Word, and the Holy Ghost: and these three are one. 8. And there are three that bear witness in earth, the Spirit, and the water, and the blood: and these three agree in one.

7, 8. For there are three in heaven, who have given us their witness to the gospel on earth; even, the Father, who hath from heaven declared Christ to be his Son: and the Word, or godhead of Christ, which he shewed in his miracles, resurrection, &c. and the Holy Ghost, sent down for infallibility, miracles, and renovation of the faithful. And these are so three, as yet to be one. And on earth, we have seen these three witnesses attesting one thing by agreement, even the Spirit in the souls of believers, in their miracles and holiness sealing the truth; the water of baptism, and the washing of their souls from sin; and Christ's blood and sacrifice, which is our expiation, signified in the Lord's supper; even as Christ, on the cross, first recommended his Spirit into his Father's hands, and then out of his pierced side came water and blood.

Note, Though much of these words, ver. 7, 8. be not in many antient copies of the Bible, we have more reason to think that the Arians left them out, than that the orthodox put them in; (other texts that assert Christ's godhead being so used.) But however, it need not offend the faithful, there being so many other texts which assert the Trinity.

9. If we receive the witness of men, the witness of God is greater: for this is the witness of God, which he hath testified of his Son.

9. If the witness of credible men end controversies among us, much more must the witness of God be believed: And this mentioned, is God's own testimony of Christ.

10. He that believeth on the Son of God, hath the witness in himself; he that believeth not God, hath made him a liar, because he believeth not the record that God gave of his Son.

10. He that is a true believer in Christ, hath the Spirit of Christ, which hath regenerated him; (for if any man have not his Spirit, he is none of his.) And this Spirit of power, wisdom, and holiness, is most certainly from God, and an infallible evidence, that God owneth the gospel: therefore, all these have the witnessing evidence of Christ in themselves. And he that believeth not so sure a testimony of God, doth make him a liar; as if he gave the Holy Spirit as a false witness of Christ, to deceive the world.

11. And this is the record that

God hath given to us, eternal life: and this life is in his Son. 12. He that hath the Son hath life; and he that hath not the Son of God, hath not life.

11, 12. And the sum of the gospel, attested by God and his Spirit, is this, that God hath made a free gift of pardon and salvation to the world, even the life of grace and glory; but so as that this life is given us in and with Christ, who, with all these benefits, is offered to men, on condition of believing acceptance; (As a woman in marriage, hath the man with his estate; and as we choose our physician for physic, our teacher for learning, our ruler for government, &c.) He that hath Christ upon believing acceptance, as his Saviour, hath life initially, and title to salvation: And he that hath not Christ, through his unbelief and refusal, hath not life.

13. These things have I written unto you that believe on the name of the Son of God, that ye may know that ye have eternal life, and that ye may believe on the name of the Son of God.

13. These things I have written to you that are true Christians, that you may know what a treasure you have in and with Christ; even right to eternal life, and its beginning here: and that you may go on confirmed, and constant in the faith.

14. And this is the confidence that we have in him, that if we ask any thing according to his will, he heareth us.

14. And through our interest in Christ, his merits and intercession, we have sufficient ground of confidence that, by and through him, our prayers are heard, and that he will give us whatever we ask, which he hath promised to give, and we are fit to receive.

15. And if we know that he hear us, whatsoever we ask, we know that we have the petitions that we desired of him.

15. And if he thus hear your prayers, we may reckon that, in his time and way, he will give us whatever particular we ask, if we and our prayers be qualified for his promise.

16. If any man see his brother sin a sin, *which is* not unto death, he shall ask, and he shall give him life for them that sin not unto death. There is a sin unto death: I do not say that ye shall pray for it. 17. All unrighteousness is sin, and there is a sin not unto death.

16, 17. And this comfort you have, in your prayers for others, as well as for yourselves: God will hear you for those, who are qualified for the mercy which you beg for them according to his promise. Death temporal and eternal, is the wages of sin; but with great difference. There are many sins of infirmity, which we hate and strive against, (as vain thoughts, words, passions, coldness in duty, imperfection in all good;) and all sins that stand with true repentance, and the predominant love of God and holiness. These the law of grace doth pardon, through Christ, and not damn any for: But pardon must be asked, and shall be obtained, for the faithful, penitent, qualified person. But God hath told us, that he doth not pardon the impenitent and unsanctified, that had rather keep their sin than leave it; and unqualified for pardon. Your prayer to God, to pardon such, shall not prevail, while they are impenitant; much less for them that are infidels, and blaspheme the Holy Ghost. And God's own children may fall into some sins that are to be punished with bodily death, or shame? Magistrates must put to death murderers, and other capital offenders; and when magistrates do it not, God will oft-times do it without them, himself; (as he did on Ananias and Sapphira, and others.) In this case, if one be to be executed by justice, or be under God's justice, that will put him to death, you may pray for his soul, but you must not pray for his life, though he repent; because it is against God's law, and the common good: And if you should pray for the recovery of such a man in sickness, God hath not promised you to recover him: No, nor any of his own children, when their dying time is come.

18. We know *that whosoever* is born of God, sinneth not: but he that is begotten of God, keepeth himself, and that wicked one toucheth him not.

18. We know that all that are born of God, hate sin, and overcome it in the course of their lives; and live in no reigning sin which is predominant, but only hated infirmities, which consist with sincere, predominant faith, obedience, and repentance, (nor have any sin at all, so far as they have the divine nature;) but they watchfully keep themselves from the prevalence of Satan's snares.

19. And we know that we are of God, and the whole world lieth in wickedness.

19. And, though Christ's flocks here be less than the world, we see by experience, that we are of God; guided by his Spirit, obeying his laws, pleasing his will, living to him, and hoping for his glory, and that the unconverted world is wholly set on wickedness and mischief; so notorious is the difference between the faithful, and the ungodly world (which foretels the future difference.)

20. And we know that the Son of God is come, and hath given us an understanding, that we may know him that is true: and we are in him that is true, even in his Son Jesus Christ. This is the true God, and eternal life.

20. In a word, by all aforesaid, we are certain of the truth of our religion: We are sure that the Son of God is come, and Christ is he; and by his doctrine and Spirit, hath enlightened us to know the true and only God, and his will: and we are, by faith and the Spirit, planted into him who is the truth, even into Jesus Christ. So that we are sure it is the true God that we believe and serve, and the gift and title to eternal life, that by Christ we do receive.

21. Little children, keep yourselves from idols. Amen.

21. I speak to you in love, as if you were my own children; but with care of you, as to your weakness, and what temptations the idolatrous world assaults you with: As Christ hath called you out of the world, from idolatry, which you have renounced; as you love God, and your Saviour, and your souls, hold close to Christ, and return not to idols, nor partake of their sacrifices, nor seem to own them by idolatrous communion. Amen.

THE SECOND EPISTLE

OF

ST. JOHN,

(The Apostle, it is most commonly thought.)

THE elder unto the elect lady, and her children, whom I love in the truth: and not I only, but also all they that have known the truth: 2. For the truth's sake which dwelleth in us, and shall be with us for ever.

1, 2. Note, It seems this was some choice woman, that was a great support and helper to the Christians, and eminent in piety, and steadfastness in the faith; though some groundlessly think, that it was some church that he calleth lady.

3. Grace be with you, mercy and peace from God the Father, and from the Lord Jesus Christ, the Son of the Father, in truth and love.

3. Grace, mercy, and peace from God the Father, and Christ the Son, are the true invaluable blessings I wish you, to confirm you in the two great parts of religion, truth, and love.

4. I rejoiced greatly, that I found of thy children walking in truth, as we have received a commandment from the Father.

4. I greatly rejoiced, that I found thy children both holding fast the Christian truth, and living in the practice of it, as the Father commanded us to preach and do.

5. And now I beseech thee, lady, not as though I wrote a new commandment unto thee: but that which we had from the beginning, that we love one another.

5. The sum of my writing to thee is, not any novelty, but the old, great law of Christ: Be sure that we keep up true Christian love (which Satan is an enemy to.)

6. And this is love, that we walk after his commandments. This is

the commandment, that, as ye have heard from the beginning, ye should walk in it.

6. And the love, in which we all must live, is our union and concord in keeping his commandments; even the same gospel, which from the beginning, was committed to us: (For both new and false doctrines, and a sinful life, do break the union and peace of Christians.)

7. For many deceivers are entered into the world, who confess not that Jesus Christ is come in the flesh. This is a deceiver and an Antichrist.

7. For there are many heretics now come to that deceiving pass, that they deny Christ himself; either his godhead, or manhood, or office, or work; yea, his incarnation; as if his body were but fantasm. These are deceivers and Antichrists.

8. Look to yourselves, that we lose not those things which we have wrought, but that we receive a full reward.

8. Look to yourselves with watchful care, that no temptation draw you to backslide, and you lose all your former belief and labour, nor we our ministerial labour on you: but hold on, that you and we may attain that full reward that we seek.

9. Whosoever transgresseth, and abideth not in the doctrine of Christ, hath not God: He that abideth in the doctrine of Christ, he hath both the Father and the Son.

9. As it was by the doctrine of Christ, that you were brought into your blessed knowledge and relation to the Father and the Son, so, if you fall from that doctrine, you will fall from God himself, to whom, by Christ, you are reconciled. But if you abide in Christ's doctrine, you will continue your relation to the Father and the Son.

10. If there come any unto you, and bring not this doctrine, receive him not into your *house*, neither bid him God speed. 11. For *he* that biddeth him God speed, is partakers of his evil deeds.

10, 11. As for those heretics and apostates that deny the gospel, or any essential part of Christianity, shew them no encouraging countenance, familiarity, or communion: otherwise you will be guilty, as partners in their sin.

12. Having many things to write unto you, I would not write with paper and ink; but I trust to come unto you, and speak face to face, that our joy may be full. 13. The children of thy elect sister greet thee. Amen.

12, 13. Note, 1. Presence maketh *friendly* converse the more comfortable. 2. By [elect sister] here again, some think he meaneth another church but it cannot be proved.

THE

THIRD EPISTLE

OF

ST. JOHN,

(It is most likely the Apostle.)

THE elder unto the well-beloved Gaius, whom I love in the truth. 2. Beloved, I wish above all things that thou mayest prosper, and be in health, even as thy soul prospereth.

1, 2. My love to thee for the truth's sake, which thou adherest to, maketh me wish earnestly, that as thy soul prospereth, so may thy bodily health, for the service of God and thy soul.

3. For I rejoiced greatly when *the* brethren came and testified of the

CHAP. I.   III. JOHN.   593

truth that is in thee, even as thou walkest in the truth.

3. Note, 1. Soul-mercies are the greatest mercies, and matters of the greatest joy for one another. 2. Good reports of our brethren is a duty tending to the comfort of ministers and friends.

4. I have no greater joy than to hear that my children walk in truth.

4. Note, True ministers rejoice more for the welfare of men's souls, than in preferments, wealth, or worldly honour.

5. Beloved, thou doest faithfully whatsoever thou doest to the brethren, and to strangers: 6. Which have borne witness of thy charity before the church:

5. It is well done of thee, as a sincere Christian, that thou shewest so much love and help, both to the brethren of the church with thee, and to strangers in their banishment and travels: Which divers have here testified before the church to thy praise.

6. Whom if thou bring forward on their journey after a godly sort, thou shalt do well: 7. Because that for his name's sake they went forth, taking nothing of the Gentiles.

6, 7. And if thou further furnish and help them in their travel, it will be a laudable Christian duty, doing as to God's servants, who, for Christ's name sake, went out of their country to preach abroad (or were persecuted out) and took nothing of the Gentile Christians, towards their maintenance in their travels.

8. We therefore ought to receive such, that we might be fellow-helpers to the truth.

8. To entertain and further such is part of our duty for the propagating of the gospel. (He that receiveth a prophet in the name of a prophet, shall have a prophet's reward.)

9. I wrote unto the church, but Diotrephes, who loveth to have the pre-eminence among them, receiveth us not.

9. I wrote for them, to the church, my testimonial, and desire of their reception: But their bishop, Diotrephes, who loveth to rule as pre-eminent among them, receiveth not us Jews (or my letters and request to the church for them.)

10. Wherefore, if I come, I will remember his deeds which he doeth, prating against us with malicious words: and not content therewith, neither doth he himself receive the

brethren, and forbiddeth them that would, and casteth *them* out of the church.

10. Note, 1. By remembering his deeds and words, is meant sharp rebuking him before all, at least. 2. It is like that this Diotrephes was pastor, (or bishop) else he could not have cast such out of the church: At least, he was some great man that usurped that power: But sure no layman did so early usurp the keys. 3 By this we see that the pride of domineering bishops began early to be schismatical, and divide the church by tyranny: Yea, it grew arrogant to oppose and reject the beloved apostle, and maliciously to prate against him. There is no man or cause so good, but a malicious bishop, or other man may prate against it. As there are few mutinies dangerous in armies, unless headed by some commanders; so there are few schisms much dangerous in the church, but those that are headed by bishops or clergymen. 4. It is uncertain whether it was to receive them to communion, or only to hospitality that Diotrephes opposed: But it is like it was both, because he cast out their receivers from communion. 5. It is uncertain whether he did it on any difference of opinion, or occasional quarrel; but it is most like it was that he was a Gentile Christian, and too much despised the Jews, as they censured and separated too much from the Gentiles, Rom. xiv. Gal. ii. Thus separation on both sides soon began, and even peace-making apostles could not be heard by the dividers.

11. Beloved, follow not that which is evil, but that which is good. He that doeth good, is of God; but he that doeth evil, hath not seen God.

11. Imitate not such proud hurtful, uncharitable dividing examples; whatever it pretend to, a hurtful, uncharitable course is not of God; such are not true believers, and know not God aright. But it is doing good that must shew that we are of God. By their fruit ye shall know them.

Note, Clergy Roman cruelty by inquisitions, prisons, ejecting true ministers, &c. shews that they are not of God, though they pretend power, order, unity, faith, as if it were for God and truth.

12. Demetrius hath good report of all *men*, and of the truth itself: yea, and we *also* bear record; and ye know that our record is true.

12. Both by common report, and his own good works, and our true witness commend Demetrius.

13, 14. I had many things to write, but I will not with ink and pen write unto thee: But I trust I shall shortly see thee, and we shall speak face to face. Peace *be* to thee. Our friends salute thee. Greet the friends by name.

13, 14. Note, Kind remembrances and greetings are suitable to Christian friendship.

2.   Q q

THE GENERAL EPISTLE OF JUDE.

JUDE, the servant of Jesus Christ, and brother of James, to them that are sanctified by God the Father, and preserved in Jesus Christ, *and* called: 2. Mercy unto you, and peace, and love be multiplied.

1, 2. Note, Men being judged of according to their profession, all Christians are called sanctified persons.

3. Beloved, when I gave all diligence to write unto you of the common salvation, it was needful for me to write unto you, and exhort you that ye should earnestly contend for the faith which was once delivered unto the saints.

3. Note, 1. The common salvation signifieth but that way to salvation which all must go in that will be saved, God's high-way to heaven; Christ and his gospel.

2. The apostles writing more against heretics and Jews than heathens, tells us, That the church hath more cause usually to defend the truth against pretended religious zealots, and sects that are erroneous, than against open Pagans, who are not animated by so much blind zeal against them; therefore they know not the churches case, who fear none but profane enemies.

3. Though love and meekness may be predominant in Christians, earnest contending for the faith against corrupting heretics is oft a duty. But if this be pretended for odious censures, excommunications, persecutions, or dividing contentions against Christians of the same faith, for their differences about lesser things, and for tolerable imperfections, or for doubting of unnecessary opinions, ceremonies, forms, or human canons, it will be no cover for the sin.

4. It is the faith first delivered to the churches by the apostles, that corrupters deprave, and we must contend for, and must be the test of our several differences.

5. Keep faith and religion sound among its professors, and it will overcome the world.

4. For there are certain men crept in unawares, who were before of old ordained to this condemnation; ungodly men, turning the grace of our God into lasciviousness, and denying the only Lord God, and our Lord Jesus Christ.

4. For there are crept in by little and little, as in the dark, some men that Christ had before told us should arise (or God decreed to condemn for their sin) ungodly men, that though they did seem Christians, have turned the doctrine of God's grace in Christ, into a doctrine and practice of lasciviousness and licentiousness, and denying Jesus Christ, who is the only Lord God, and our Lord (or the only God and our Saviour, &c.)

Note, 1. One of Satan's chief ways against the church and religion, is to corrupt it by heresies. 2. Corrupters creep secretly into the church, at unawares, and do not openly bring in all at once. 3. Though God ordain or decree no man's sin, he both decreeth and foretelleth their condemnation for sin. 4. It is ungodly men that are usually the great corrupters of the church and doctrine. 5. Libertinism, looseness, and sensuality, are the usual dangerous ways of such corruption, as being the way most suitable to man's corrupt nature, and which will have most followers.

5. I will therefore put you in remembrance, though ye once knew this, how that the Lord having saved the people out of the land of Egypt, afterwards destroyed them that believed not.

5. As the Israelites perished in the wilderness for unbelief, after all their miraculous deliverance

from Egypt; so shall revolters perish, notwithstanding their baptism and fair beginnings.

6. And the angels which kept not their first estate, but left their own habitation, he hath reserved in everlasting chains under darkness, unto the judgment of the great day.

6. And the angels that stood not in their integrity, but fell by sin, God hath shut up as it were prisoners in chains (though they go about all the earth with temptations,) in certain expectation of fuller condemnation at the great day of judgment.

7. Even as Sodom and Gomorrah, and the cities about them, in like manner giving themselves over to fornication, and going after strange flesh, are set forth for an example, suffering the vengeance of eternal fire.

7. As Sodom, &c. were by fire from heaven utterly destroyed, by God's revenging judgment,

8. Likewise also these filthy dreamers defile the flesh, despise dominion, and speak evil of dignities.

8. So these heretics, dreaming of high wisdom, are turned to fleshly lusts, and to despise government, and speak contemptuously or reproachfully of superiors, as if Christ hath freed men from human rule, and made all equal, and all things lawful (when yet they deny even Christ himself, in some essentials of his person or office.)

9. Yet Michael the archangel, when contending with the devil, he disputed about the body of Moses, durst not bring against him a railing accusation, but said, the Lord rebuke thee.

9. Yet Michael, the chief angel, contending with a principal devil about the rebuilding of the Jewish temple, Zech. iii. durst not bring railing accusation, but appealed to God.

Note, 1. There are differences and superiorities among the angels and devils. It seems by Dan. x. 13, 21. that angels have their several earthly provinces in charge, and that Michael was prince of the Jews. 2. The badness and vanity of malignants will not justify railing accusation against them, when it may not be used against devils; yet their evil must be detected that it may be frustrated. 3. By the Body of Moses, some understand his buried body, which Satan would have idolized; and others, his body in the basket, which Satan would have had drowned: but, by Zech. iii. it is more like to be the temple, law, and Jewish policy, called the Body of Moses, as the church is called the Body of Christ.

10. But these speak evil of those things which they know not: but what they know naturally, as brute beasts, in those things they corrupt themselves.

10. But these, pretending to know that they do not, speak evil of the things which they know not, being proud, and ignorant of their ignorance; but what natural sense or reasonableness constraineth them to know, their lust prevaileth against it, and they live in debauchery, as if they knew it not to be evil.

Note, It is the common mark of erroneous men to be confident where they mistake, and to censure and speak evil fiercely of that which they never understood, and to sin against that knowledge which they have, or easily might have.

11. Woe unto them, for they have gone in the way of Cain, and ran greedily after the error of Balaam for reward, and perished in the gainsaying of Core.

11. Woe to them, for they have imitated Cain in offering God a faithless sacrifice, and envying and persecuting them that do better: And they are covetous worldlings, that, like Balaam, would do evil for reward or gain: And they have imitated Core in opposing Moses and Aaron, magistrates, and apostles, and shall perish as they did.

12. These are spots in your feasts of charity, when they feast with you, feeding themselves without fear: clouds *they are* without water, carried about of winds; trees whose fruit withereth, without fruit, twice dead, plucked up by the roots.

12. These are the disgrace of your love-feasts and communion, which they turn into a sensual feast, not fearing profanation or excess: Hypocrites, like empty clouds that water not the earth, but carried about with the winds of worldly interest or seduction; like fruitless trees, twice dead and rooted up by apostasy from their first profession.

Note, It is a wonder that the apostle no more reproveth them for admitting such to their communion, as it seemeth by these words they did.

13. Raging waves of the sea, foaming out their shame; wandering stars, to whom is reserved the blackness of darkness for ever.

13. Unquiet, fierce, and raging persons, who while they pour out ill words of others, do but foam out their own shame: Teachers they will needs be, as stars to the churches; but they are but erratic stars or comets, that shall end in endless darkness to themselves, while they boast of light to others.

14. And Enoch also, the seventh from Adam, prophesied of these, saying, Behold, the Lord cometh

with ten thousand of his saints, 15. To execute judgment upon all, and to convince all that are ungodly among them, of all their ungodly deeds which they have ungodly committed, and of all their hard *speeches* which ungodly sinners have spoken against him.

14, 15. Note, 1. It is like this prophecy of Enoch was received by tradition. 2. This description sure is not of the destruction of Jerusalem, but of the great day of the Lord, terrible to all the wicked, and the malignant adversaries of godliness.

16. These are murmurers, complainers, walking after their own lusts; and their mouth speaketh great swelling *words*, having men's persons in admiration because of advantage.

16. These are men that swell, and murmur, and complain against government, and all that cross their opinion or lusts, after which they walk; and they use big and boasting words, as men that were more knowing than all others (in philosophical fancies, and the orders of angels, and ages, and things above, and of Christian liberty, &c.) and they extol the men for advantage of themselves, and of their sect, who are their leaders and chief favourers.

17. But, beloved, remember ye the words which were spoken before of the apostles of our Lord Jesus Christ; 18. How that they told you there should be mockers in the last time, who should walk after their own ungodly lusts.

17, 18. But remember the words which Peter and other apostles have spoken heretofore, that told you such men should come; and keep to the first doctrine of the apostles.

19. These be they who separate themselves, sensual, having not the Spirit.

19. These separate themselves into a distinct sect, as if they were above the apostolical churches; but their actions shew that they are sensual, carnal men, not all sanctified and guided by God's Spirit, as the faithful be.

10. But ye, beloved, building up yourselves on your most holy faith, praying in the Holy Ghost, 21. Keep yourselves in the love of God, looking for the mercy of our Lord Jesus Christ unto eternal life.

20, 21. But ye, beloved, must be quite other men from these; they build sensuality, temporizing and separation upon error, and proud self-conceit: But you must build up yourselves, and one another, in holiness, upon your divine and most holy faith. They are sensual, having not the Spirit. You must, as men in whom God's Spirit dwells and rules, pray in the Holy Ghost, even with those holy and fervent desires, which the Spirit of God exciteth in you: They are revolted from true faith and love: You must by God's Spirit keep yourselves in unfeigned love to God, and to his truth, and one another, waiting in faith and hope for eternal life by God's mercy in Christ.

22. And of some have compassion, making a difference: 23. And others save with fear, pulling *them* out of the fire: hating even the garment spotted by the flesh.

22, 23. And as to your dealing with such erroneous men, it must be differently as they differ, even tenderly and compassionately with some; and with others you must deal more fervently and sharply, as with Lot in Sodom, or men in a house that is on fire, whose death, if not quickly prevented, you must fear, and therefore be importunate with them: But seek to save them all, (and not to use any violent or hurtful course.) And yourselves must hate and avoid all degrees of filthiness and sensuality.

24. Now unto him that is able to keep you from falling, and to present you faultless before the presence of his glory, with exceeding joy. 25. To the only wise God our Saviour, be glory and majesty, dominion and power, now and ever. Amen.

24, 25. Now to him who is able in all temptations, notwithstanding your own weakness, to keep you steadfast in faith and holiness, from falling into the snares of heresy or ungodliness, and to prevent you faultless (as being faithful and upright, and your sins forgiven) before the presence of his glory at his coming, that you may see him and stand before him with exceeding joy, (when the wicked are condemned) I say, to him, the only God of infinite wisdom, to our Saviour, be glory, and majesty, and dominion, and power, now and ever; so it will certainly be; and such is the prayer of all the faithful.

THE
REVELATION
OF
ST. JOHN THE DIVINE.

CHAP. I.

THE Revelation of Jesus Christ, which God gave unto him, to shew unto his servants things which must shortly come to pass; and he sent and signified it by his angel unto his servant John:

1. Note, 1. It is eminently called the Revelation, as being by Vision and prophetic notice an extraordinary revelation of future things.
2. Beza well observeth hence the order of God's revelation to his church. First, God himself is the fountain; he revealeth it to our Mediator, as man, (who knoweth all things as God) that according to his office he may be the light and teacher to his church. Christ revealeth it to angels; the Holy Ghost and angels reveal it to apostles and prophets; they reveal and record it to the church, where all must learn it, but especially teachers, to tell it to the people.
3. It is things to come that are here revealed; therefore, I cannot receive those two learned men's exposition, who make it a history in a prophetic style, and say, that most, or very much of it was done before it was written.
4. The word [shortly] made them expound almost the whole book of things all fulfilled about Constantine's time, or presently after Alaricus's sacking of Rome. But [shortly] may signify no more than, 1. That these things will shortly be begun, though not so quickly finished; And 2. That a thousand years is with the Lord but as one day. But I confess that so much, as can be proved already done, we must not feign to be yet to come.
5. It is most like that this John was the apostle, but it is not certain.

2. Who bare record of the word of God, and of the testimony of Jesus Christ, and of all things that he saw.

2. Who by this writing truly telleth the churches, what Christ by his angel told him, as a faithful witness of Christ, and of all that he saw and heard in this vision and revelation; some things that then were, may be mentioned, to introduce the prophecy of things to come.

3. Blessed is he that readeth, and they that hear the words of this prophecy, and keep those things which are written therein, for the time is at hand.

3. Note, It is a desirable thing, and an addition to that man's wisdom and happiness, who understandeth this, and all other scripture prophecies; but this concludeth not that no other are blessed, or that many attain that degree of happiness. (For I think I never knew one such :) But the necessary parts of Christianity, which are in this prophecy mixed with darker passages, all must keep that will be blessed.
2. The time of their beginning was at hand, and the end not far off.

4. John to the seven churches in Asia, Grace be unto you, and peace from him which is, and which was, and which is to come, and from the seven spirits which are before his throne.

4. I John, send you this holy greeting and benediction, Grace and Peace (the greatest blessings) be to you from the eternal God, and those angels whom he hath made your special guardians.
Note, 1. That it is angels (and not the Holy Ghost's) seven graces that is here meant, is after manifested.
2. Why they are called seven, some say is, because seven goeth for a number of perfection, whence the seven planets, the seven days of the week, &c. But this is but men's conceit, and no part of God's word. Nor can we prove hence, that God hath set seven angels above all the rest. But all that we can know of it is, that John, being commanded to write to seven churches, numbereth the guardian angels accordingly from their charges.
3. This is no prayer to these angels, but a no-

tice that God's mercies are communicated to those churches by their ministry, and this message sent by them from Christ.

4. The naming of the seven spirits before Christ, is no preferring them as above him: But Christ is after named, because much more is to be said there of him together.

5. Why seven churches only are named, men variously conjecture; some say, because they are spoken of prophetically, as in their names seven states of the universal church, or its notable parts, to the end are signified. But this (being impossible to be proved) is rather to pretend another revelation, than to expound this. Others say, that it being only the Pro-Consular Asia that John wrote to, these seven being the metropolitan city churches, did comprehend all the rest, as parts under them. But, 1. This also is but a human imagination, without any proof. 2. If they meant that these were then made ecclesiastical metropolises, it is a fiction without, and against historical evidence, which tells us of a far later date of metropolitical churches. 3. If they mean that they were metropolises only in a civil sense, and that the apostles, in planting churches there, purposed, or ordained, that afterwards church-power should follow the order of the seats of civil power, I answer, 1. That this is a crude unproved assertion, and therefore of no authority or credit. 2. And it is known, that it was four hundred years after that this was decreed by a council as a new thing. 3. And this was so far from being apostolical, that it confounded the church, setting in superiority the worst men that could but get into a metropolis, and putting all bishops and churches at present under the power of the people, and presbyters of one city, which was a metropolis, and chose their own bishop: Yea, Dr. Hammond thought that then no bishop had any presbyters under him, and so there were none but his people to choose him; (for the neighbour bishops did not, though they ordained him:) Yea, it turned churches upside down at the will of every emperor, heathen, infidel, or Christian, who can enfranchise or disfranchise cities at his pleasure. 4. And there is no proof that these seven were all and only the civil metropolitical cities of Asia.

3. Both these then, being men's unproved imaginations, yea, and unlikely, it remaineth that these seven churches were most eminent in Asia, both for greatness, and those trials, virtues, and faults, which Christ was pleased to note at the occasion of this message; And if he see cause to send a message to seven, it belongs not to us to ask him, why he sendeth to no more.

5. And from Jesus Christ, *who is* the faithful witness, and the first begotten of the dead, and the Prince of the kings of the earth:

5. Note, 1. By [faithful witness] is meant, the faithful and certain messenger and revealer of God's will to man: 2. By [first begotten] is meant, both the greatest and most excellent, and the first in order and casuality, who rising from the dead, is the cause that we shall rise. 3. He is Prince of the kings of the earth, not only as greater than all kings, but as over them all in power, by whom they reign, and who doth dispose of all, Eph. ii.

23. Matt. xxviii. 19. John xvii. 2. John xiii. 3. John v. 22. Eph. i. 21. Col. i. 15, 16, 17. Phil. ii. 9, 10, 11.

5. Unto him that loved us, and washed us from our sins in his own blood, 6. And hath made us kings and priests unto God and his Father; to him be glory for ever and ever. Amen.

5, 6. To this glorious Lord and Saviour, who shewed his wonderful love to us, by his giving up himself a sacrifice for our sins, that the merit of his blood might cleanse us from guilt and sin, and justify us from it before God, and who hath chosen and sanctified us, and made us by his grace, a peculiar holy people to God, dignified in our relation to Christ as kings in honour, and brought us near to God like consecrated priests, to offer him our daily service acceptable through Christ; To him, I say, shall be glory and dominion for ever, in the acknowledgment whereof, let all his saints rejoice.

7. Behold, he cometh with clouds, and every eye shall see him, and they also which pierced him, and all kindreds of the earth shall wail because of him: even so. Amen.

7. I have often before inquired, whether this coming of Christ be, 1. His coming by the Roman armies to destroy Jerusalem. 2. Or his setting up Christianity in the world, and destroying heathenism. 3. Or his coming at last in glory. The matter is true as to all the three: But the text seemeth most strained by the first exposition, and least by the last; Every way he is dreadful to his enemies. But every eye seeth him not the first way; nor did the destroyed Jews acknowledge it to be by him.

8. I am Alpha and Omega, the beginning and the ending, saith the Lord, which is, and which was, and which is to come, the Almighty.

8. I am everlasting, before all worlds, and without end, and he who hath power over all.

Note, These words seem to be the words of Christ, and not of God the Father; And with the sixth verse, which ascribeth to him everlasting glory and dominion, do seem plainly to speak the godhead of Christ.

9. I John, who also am your brother and companion in tribulation, and in the kingdom and patience of Jesus Christ, was in the isle that is called Patmos, for the word of God, and for the testimony of Jesus Christ.

9. I John, who was your brother and companion, undergo the like sufferings as you do, in the same

CHAP. I. REVELATION. 599

belief and subjection as Christ in his kingdom, and in patient enduring for his sake, was in the isle of Patmos, whither I was banished for my testimony, and preaching the faith of Christ.

10. I was in the spirit on the Lord's day, and heard behind me a great voice, as of a trumpet.

10. I was there in a transporting rapture by the Spirit of God, on the first day of the week, called by the church, The Lord's Day, (observed in commemoration of his resurrection:) And I heard a voice call to me as loud as a trumpet.

Note, 1. The vain cavil of those that deny the [Lord's day] here to mean the Christians' day of holy worship, even the first of the week, I have fully confuted in a book called the 'Divine Appointment of the Lord's Day.' And it needs no confutation to those that are acquainted with church history, who know that this day hath been kept holy as of apostolital ordination and practice by the universal church ever since the apostles' days, the heretics themselves consenting.

2. Christ owned his own day, and the suffering of his banished solitary servant, by the communication of these extraordinary revelations, and by the ecstasy of spiritual influence.

11. Saying, I am Alpha and Omega, the first and the last: and what thou seest, write in a book, and send it unto the seven churches which are in Asia, unto Ephesus, and unto Smyrna, and unto Pergamos, and unto Thyatira, and unto Sardis, and unto Philadelphia, and unto Laodicea.

11. Note, 1. The first sentence is out of divers Greek copies; but is before spoken, and is the description of Christ's eternity.
2. This was written by Christ's command.

12. And I turned to see the voice that spake with me. And being turned, I saw several golden candlesticks.

12. To see who that voice came from which I heard.

13. And in the midst of the seven candlesticks, *one* like unto the Son of man, clothed with a garment down to the foot, and girt about the paps with a golden girdle.

13. One in the shape of a man, who was a representation of Christ in splendid clothing like Aaron's.

Note, Whether it was the angel that thus represented Christ, or Christ himself who assumed this appearing shape immediately, is uncertain.

14. His head and his hairs were white, like wool, as white as snow, and his eyes were as a flame of fire.

15. And his feet like unto fine brass, as if they burned in a furnace: and his voice as the sound of many waters.

14, 15. Christ's apparition signifieth his innocency and glory by whiteness; his terrible majesty, by his fiery eyes and feet, and his dreadful voice; to affect all with reverence, and his foes with terror.

16. And he had in his right hand seven stars, and out of his mouth went a sharp two-edged sword, and his countenance was as the sun shineth in his strength.

*16. And in his right hand were held seven stars, which signify the pastors of the seven churches, commissioned and upheld by him: And a two-edged sword, from his mouth, signified his word sent forth with power, to convert and save the elect, and to convince and condemn the obstinate rejecters: And his countenance was glorious as the sun in its clearest appearance.

17. And when I saw him, I fell at his feet as dead: and he laid his right hand upon me, saying unto me, Fear not, I am the first and the last.

17. He laid on me his supporting hand of love, when his terrible glory had cast me at his feet, and bid me not fear, (for his glory is joyful to his servants, though terrible to his enemies:) He is my almighty, eternal God, and my hope.

18. I am he that liveth, and was dead: and behold, I am alive for evermore, Amen, and have the keys of hell and of death.

18. I am Christ who was lately incarnate, on earth, and crucified for your sins, and now live your King and Intercessor in glory, and shall die no more: And death, and all separated souls are in my power, to be taken into happiness, or cast out.

19. Write the things which thou hast seen, and the things which are, and the things which shall be hereafter.

19. Write these Revelations for posterity, which contain what thou seest, and the exposition of some things that already exist, and the prophecy of many things to come.

20. The mystery of the seven stars which thou sawest in my right hand, and the seven golden candlesticks. The seven stars are the angels of the seven churches: and the seven candlesticks which thou sawest, are the seven churches.

20. Note, It is a great controversy what is meant by angels here; 1. Some say, that the prophetical phrase being primarily of proper angels, as the guardians of the churches, yet as in their names intending the message to the churches themselves, so it is here spoken of, and to the churches, but as denominated from their several angels: and this seemeth to me the most likely sense, viz. To the whole churches, pastors, and people, under the name of their guardian angels, though blaming the churches and not the angels: which should not seem strange to them who feign such good men as Timothy to be the angels, who were not guilty of the crimes here reproved. Thus Augustine de Doct. Christ. lib. 3. cap. 30. citeth and seemeth to like Tyconius's exposition, who supposeth the whole church meant under the angel's name.

2. Others suppose the presbytery of each church collectively governing them, are called the angels.

3. Others think that only the metropolitans are meant as heads of presbyters, and other bishops.

4. Dr. Hammond thinks there were no sub-presbyters in scripture times, and so that it is metropolitans that are here meant; but such as were but single pastors of congregations, like a parish-pastor now that hath not so much as a curate under him, save deacons, but was metropolitan over many dioceses of such single bishops.

I am far from believing, 1. That any such metropolitans were then settled; 2. Or that such churches had but one pastor; 3. Or that the single bishop of a metropolis was blamed for the faults of many dioceses of churches; 4. Or that the bishops of the excellent primitive churches, were so quickly degenerate, and guilty of the crimes here mentioned, especially if Timothy was one. And this exposition too grossly slurs episcopacy. But if they were but single pastors of single churches, the difference is of no great moment: what he speaketh of the apostle's intending so great a change afterward as diocesans have made, requireth proof.

CHAP. II.

UNTO the angel of the church of Ephesus, write, These things saith he that holdeth the seven stars in his right hand, who walketh in the midst of the seven golden candlesticks:

1. To the pastors and flock of the church of Ephesus, meant by the name of their angels, These things saith Christ before described; and commandeth me to write them.

Note, 1. I believe not that Timothy was their bishop in the ordinary sense as a fixed pastor of that church alone; but that he in his itinerant course (described in scripture, doing the work of an evangelist) was there some time, and is therefore by the ancients called their bishop, as apostles were called bishops, for planting and taking care for many churches; when as there is not the least proof that they appropriated any diocesses or churches to each, as their proper charge, which other apostles might not use the same authority with, or were fixed to any.

2. I believe it yet less probable, that Timothy was the angel here accused of leaving and falling from his first love.

2. I know thy works, and thy labour, and thy patience, and how thou canst not bear them which are evil, and thou hast tried them which say they are apostles, and are not, and hast found them liars:

2. Thy good works, and great labour in the gospel, and thy patience in suffering for it, are not unknown or disregarded by me: and it is thy praise that thou dost not countenance nor tolerate among you, the seducing heretics and wicked men; and that those that have pretended inspiration, as sent of God, thou hast tried, and rejected them as proved liars, and false apostles.

3. And hast borne, and hast patience, and for my name's sake hast laboured and hast not fainted.

3. Note, Christ loveth and praiseth that which is good in the churches, while he reproveth them for that which is evil.

4. Nevertheless, I have somewhat against thee, because thou hast left thy first love.

4. But for this I reprove thee, that you have not that hearty, fervent love to me, and to one another, which you had at the first; and that you grow colder when you should grow better.

Note, Even good people may fall into a more cold, declining state, by negligence.

5. Remember, therefore, from whence thou art fallen, and repent, and do the first works, or else I will come unto thee quickly, and will remove thy candlestick out of his place, except thou repent.

5. Look back on thy first love and works, and think whether it was not then better with thee, and whether thou hadst any cause to decline; return to thy first works, or else I will shortly visit thee with the heavy punishment, of taking the ministry and gospel from thee.

Note, 1. Declinings from former love and duty are displeasing to God, and tend to worse. 2. It is a grievous punishment to have the gospel and ministry taken away, either by wars, devastations, persecutions, silencing, and worst by wilful expulsion.

6. But this thou hast, that thou hatest the deeds of the Nicolaitans, which I also hate.

6. It is commendable in thee, that thou hatest the deeds of the Nicolaitans, for I hate them.

Note, It is lawful to distinguish such heretics as are not to be tolerated in church communion by the names of their leaders: but this should not be done against tolerable differences, as tending to divide those that should all unite in the Christian name.

2. God hateth licentious doctrines and deeds, and so must we

3. Whence these Nicolaitans had their name is not known certainly, but doubtful tradition in history tells us, that Nicholas the deacon, Acts vi. had a beautiful wife, and he was blamed as jealous of her; and that thereupon he brought her forth, and bid who would take her, to shew that he was above all fleshly lust; and that some people, misunderstanding him, thence took occasion to plead for the lawfulness of fornication. The heresy of these hateful Nicolaitans lay, 1, In making light of fornication, 2. And in despising the heathens' government, as if Christian liberty lay in being from under its power; 3. And in teaching that to avoid suffering, men might deny Christ with the mouth, while the heart denied him not; 4. And that they might eat things offered to idols, so they despised the idol in their hearts. Paul, Acts xx. had before told these Ephesians, that grievous wolves should enter and devour; and that of their own selves men should arise speaking perverse things, to draw disciples after them : and it seems thus warned, they hated the heresies. And St. John himself lived in Asia, and is said to die at Ephesus, who no doubt would warn them (and was above Timothy.)

7. He that hath an ear, let him hear what the Spirit saith unto the churches, To him that overcometh, will I give to eat of the tree of life, which is in the midst of the paradise of God.

7. Let all that hear or read these words of the Spirit to the churches, set their hearts to them with regard, as of great and common importance: To him that in the day of trial and temptation doth overcome, by being true to Christ, and keeping his innocency, I will give a part in everlasting happiness, signified by the tree of life in paradise.

Note, 1. Striving without overcoming in temptation, so far as to keep our uprightness and faithfulness, will not save men (much less lazy wishers.)

2. Though faith put us at first in a state of righteousness and life, to those that survive, perseverance and victory are conditions of salvation.

3. It seems that the sense of the tree of life in paradise, Gen. iii. is here expounded to be, everlasting life of blessedness with God; and so in the New Jerusalem after, chap. xxi, xxii.

8. And unto the angel of the church in Smyrna write, These things saith the First and the Last, which was dead, and is alive.

8. Note, Christ is not barely named, but described by divine properties, to awe the church with reverence to him, and to resolve them to trust him, who can deliver and reward them.

9. I know thy works, and tribulation, and poverty, (but thou art rich) and I *know* the blasphemy of them which say they are Jews, and are not, but are the synagogue of Satan.

9. I know with approbation and praise, thy labour, and sufferings, and worldly poverty; but thou art rich in grace: and I know that blasphemous sect, that tempt and reproach thee, who by obtruding Moses' law on the churches, (or at least seem Jews to avoid their malice) do trouble the churches against purity, unity, and peace, and are Satan's synagogue, as thus doing his work.

10. Fear none of those things which thou shalt suffer : behold, the devil shall cast some of you into prison, that ye may be tried, and ye shall have tribulation ten days : be thou faithful unto death, and I will give thee a crown of life.

10. Fear not though thou must suffer; and I foretel thee what thy sufferings will be: but I will fully reward thee.

Note, 1. Certainty of suffering may consist with the conquest of cowardly fear.

2. It is the devil that imprisoneth and persecuteth Christ's servants, when his wicked servants do it by his temptation.

3. Prisons and persecutions are for the trial of the faithful. Our care therefore must be, that we fall not in the trial.

4. Ten days is a short time, yet seemeth long to the flesh.

5. The crown of life everlasting is the sure reward of true martyrdom and perseverance in trial.

11. He that hath an ear, let him hear what the Spirit saith unto the churches. He that overcometh, shall not be hurt of the second death.

11. These warnings of the Spirit to the churches are recorded as of great concernment for all. It is they that overcome the love of this life and world, even unto death, if God call them to martyrdom, that shall escape that sorer second death that, after this life, will befal the ungodly.

12. And to the angel of the church in Pergamos, write, These things saith he which hath the sharp sword with two edges.

12. To the pastors and people of the church of Pergamos, noted by the word angel, Christ, that hath his dreadful justice, as well as saving mercy sendeth this message.

Note ; Once for all here note, that churches were then named from cities, because proximity was needful to communion : and among Christians, there should be so great unity, that they that live in one proximity (like our parishes or towns) should always be of one church, unless the uncapable multitude force them to divide in one city, into many churches; in which still proximity should be observed; or unless the great corruption, or violence, of any church do necessitate any to congregate by themselves, for their safety and duty. For if the faults of a church, and any of its members, be but tolerable weaknesses, it should not break their communion, but they should bear with, and receive each other: but if they are intolerable, for which God disowneth and forsaketh them, or their worship, they are no true churches, and must be forsaken of all, as no true particular Christians, and must be cast out.

13. I know thy works, and where thou dwellest, *even* where Satan's seat is, and thou holdest fast my name, and hast not denied my faith, even in those days wherein Antipas *was* my faithful martyr, who was slain among you, where Satan dwelleth.

13. I know, with approbation, all thy good works, and that thou dwellest where Satan ruleth in the heathen multitude; having there an idol-temple, and Roman, persecuting powers; and that yet thou hast held fast the profession of Christianity, and not denied me in persecution; even in the days when Satan's instruments murdered my faithful martyr Antipas.

Note, We have no other certain history of Antipas, and his case, but only the uncertain stories of Metaphrastes, and the Menology. No doubt but there were many martyrs, whose history is not come down to us: but Christ hath honoured Antipas by his sacred record: the time of his suffering is unknown.

14. But I have a few things against thee, because thou hast there them that hold the doctrine of Balaam, who taught Balak to cast a stumbling-block before the children of Israel, to eat things sacrificed unto idols, and to commit fornication.

14. Though all this good be found in thee, I am offended that thou so connivest at the heresy of the false teachers, as to admit some of them in your communion, who, as Balaam for gain taught Balak how to ensnare the Israelites into sin by women, so they lay snares and temptations before men, by teaching them, that it is lawful to eat things offered to idols, and to commit fornication.

Note, Had not this church tolerated these filthy heretics in their communion, Christ would not have blamed them for their mere neighbourhood.

15. So hast thou also them that hold the doctrine of the Nicolaitans, which thing I hate.

15. And thou hast yet in thy communion some that hold the doctrine of the Nicolaitans, which maketh light of adulteries, which is hateful to me.

Note, Christ hateth all such false doctrine as corrupteth faith and manners.

16. Repent, or else I will come unto thee quickly, and I will fight against them with the sword of my mouth.

16. Repent of thy connivance at this wicked sect and doctrine, and cast out them that will not be cured; or else with the two-edged sword, which goeth out of my mouth, I will shortly cut off these heretics, and punish thee for bearing with them.

17. He that hath an ear, let him hear what the Spirit saith unto the churches, To him that overcometh will I give to eat of the hidden manna, and will give him a white stone, and in the stone a new name written, which no man knoweth, saving he that receiveth it.

17. Let no man disregard what the Spirit saith to the churches: to him that overcometh the manifold temptations, of persecutors, false teachers, and fleshly lusts, I will give the bread of life, that hidden manna which is laid up in the heavenly sanctuary, even Christ and his Spirit; and in the grace of that Spirit I will give him a pledge and title to eternal life, and that new name and nature, holiness and the divine image, the evidence of right to the heavenly inheritance, whose nature and worth none rightly know, but those who receive it. Thus shall it be done to them whom I will honour.

18. And unto the angel of the church in Thyatira, write, These things saith the Son of God, who hath his eyes like unto a flame of fire, and his feet are like fine brass;

18. To the church of Thyatira, pastors and people represented by their angel, hear and regard this message from the Son of God, whose glory and dreadfulness was signified by his appearing to me, with eyes like a flame, and feet shining as burnished brass.

19. I know thy works, and charity, and service, and faith, and thy patience, and thy works, and the last *to be* more than the first.

19. I know and commend thy good works and charity, and ministration to the saints, and thy fidelity and constant patience in trials, and that thy last works excel thy first.

20. Notwithstanding, I have a few things against thee, because thou sufferest that woman Jezebel, which calleth herself a prophetess, to teach, and to seduce my servants to commit fornication, and to eat things sacrificed unto idols. 21. And I

gave her space to repent of her fornication, and she repented not.

20. Note, 1. Even a few faults in a laudable church may be a provocation to the justice of Christ. 2. Suffering corrupt doctrines and seducers in a church, is a sin which Christ will not pass by. Suffering was not opposite to banishing, imprisoning, killing: for the church had no such power or command. But it was forbearing that sharp reproof, confutation, and excommunication, which was the church's duty. 3. Whether there were really a woman among them that promoted this wickedness, by pretence of prophetic inspiration, or whether, by the woman Jezebel, be meant the whole sect of Nicolaitans or Gnostics, is uncertain. But it is certain thất the heresy tolerated was the same as was before reproved, and that Paul was put so oft to write against, viz. Fornication and idol-sacrifices, pleaded for as lawful for Christians to partake of, so they kept their faith and hearts to God. 4. Impenitence after God's patience and warning, ripeneth men for judgment.

22. Behold, I will cast her into a bed, and them that commit adultery with her, into great tribulation, except they repent of their deeds. 33. And I will kill her children with death, and all the churches shall know that I am he which searcheth the reins and hearts: and I will give unto every one of you according to your works.

22, 23. Instead of a bed of lust, I will cast her, and all the seduced sect, into a bed of great tribulation, except true repentance and reformation prevent it; so that all the churches shall see my heavy plagues on them, and shall know that I discern, and hate, and judge the most secret lusts and sins; and will judge you, and all men, according to your works.

Note, Judging is either justifying or condemning, and executing accordingly. Our first justification, which maketh us just, and so accounts us, is not according to any works strictly so called, unless you will call it a work, believingly to accept a free gift: nor is our justification in judgment according to the works of the law of innocency, or of Moses, or any that can be thought to make the reward not of grace, but of debt: but it is according to our performing the covenant of Christianity, made by Christ the condition of salvation.

24. But unto you I say, and to the rest in Thyatira, as many as have not this doctrine; and which have not known the depths of Satan, as they speak, I will put upon you none other burden. 25. But that which ye have already, hold fast till I come.

24, 25. Note, Some copies have [And] and some leave it out. If it be [you and the rest] it must mean [you pastors, and the faithful people.] And this would shew that it is not one, but many pastors that is meant by [the angel]. But if [and] be left out, then the sense is [All you of the church that are not polluted with this filthy doctrine, which the pretenders to wisdom call profound knowledge, but is indeed the depths of Satan; I will put on you no new doctrine nor burden, but charge you to hold fast that apostolic doctrine which you have received; and wait in fidelity for my coming, who will reward you.

26. And he that overcometh, and keepeth my works unto the end, to him will I give power over the nations: 27. (And he shall rule them with a rod of iron; as the vessels of a potter shall they be broken to shivers) even as I have received of my Father. 28. And I will give him the morning star.

26, 27. This promise is diversely expounded: 1. Some think that it is not the same persons than living to whom it is made, but those, that in Constantine's time are found persevering, then shall be advanced by him to honour and power. Others think that it is to the same persons, and meaneth but, that they shall be made bishops, and convert many heathens. But all the church could not be made bishops; and bishops then were the greatest sufferers; and converting is not ruling, and dashing them in pieces with an iron rod. The phrase is fetched from Psal. ii. Others think that it is meant of the heavenly power of faithful, separated souls; and that after death, the saints join with angels, as invisible rulers of this world. And others think that it is meant of a thousand years reign on earth, before the last judgment. And others think it is meant, of the state after judgment; and that the damned shall be as slaves to the glorified saints. It is certain, that it signifieth a triumphant, glorious state in heaven: but the rest is dark to us.

I think it meaneth, that they shall partake of Christ's royal power subserviently, in their degree; by which they shall now triumph over the world in faith, and in time, be delivered from men's tyranny; and at death, initially, and at judgment, fully shall, with Christ, judge the world of wicked men and angels; which is here called, Ruling them. And it is not improbable that the miserable damned ones will be, in some sort, trod down by Christ and his saints; but how, we yet know not. By the morning-star, seemeth meant, Christ and his Spirit to shine on them in glory.

29. He that hath an ear, let him hear what the Spirit saith unto the churches.

29. Let none take themselves to be unconcerned in Christ's message to his churches; for it is recorded for our common use, and nearly concerneth us all.

CHAP. III.

AND unto the angel of the church in Sardis write, These things saith he that hath the seven spirits of God, and the seven stars, I know thy works, that thou hast a name, that thou livest, and art dead.

1. To the angel, that is, the pastors and people, of the church in Sardis; thus saith he who is the Lord of angels and ministers.

Note, Though the spirits before were named before Christ, it was not as preferring them before him; for he is here said to have them, as he hath the pastors.

I know what thou art and dost: and that thou art reputed by men, to be an excellent church: but thou art declining to a cold and decayed state, even like to death.

Note, Profession, and outward splendor, make churches and persons applauded that, wanting the life and power of the religion they profess, are next to dead.

2. Be watchful, and strengthen the things which remain, that are ready to die: for I have not found thy works perfect before God.

2. Be awakened from thy self flattery and coldness, and revive and exercise that good which yet thou hast, that it may be strengthened; for I find much hypocrisy and formality in thee, and not that soundness, seriousness, and zeal, which God will require.

3. Remember therefore, how thou hast received and heard, and hold fast, and repent. If therefore thou shalt not watch, I will come on thee as a thief, and thou shalt not know what hour I will come upon thee.

3. Remember what doctrine my apostles taught thee, and hold fast that, and receive no other. Repent of thy backsliding; for if thou do not awake and watch in holy preparation, I will come upon thee with my judgment, as a thief cometh on men asleep, when thou art most fearless, and dost least expect me.

4. Thou hast a few names even in Sardis, which have not defiled their garments, and they shall walk with me in white: for they are worthy.

4. Though the greater part of that church be as dead in their declining, some few there are yet in it, who have kept their innocency from heresy, vice, and cowardly shrinking: and these shall have the honourable reward of their uprightness; for they are worthy of it, according to the law of grace, which promiseth it to such alone.

Note, Yet these few names are not commanded to separate from the rest.

5. He that overcometh, the same shall be clothed in white raiment, and I will not blot out his name out of the book of life: but I will confess his name before my Father, and before his angels.

5. He that overcometh in this life of trial, shall be clothed with the glory which signifieth the reward of innocency, and is the mark of dignity and honour; (for such then was white raiment:) and I will own him openly, before my Father and his angels, as one who is enrolled as a denison of heaven, among the elect of God;

Note, If white garments now be seemly for conquering saints, they are unmeet for them that are overcome by the world, and the love of its honour, wealth, and power, and by fleshly lusts.

6. He that hath an ear, let him hear what the Spirit saith unto the churches. 7. And to the angel of the church in Philadelphia, write, These things saith he that is holy, he that is true, he that hath the key of David, he that openeth, and no man shutteth, and shutteth, and no man openeth.

6, 7. Note, Christ is described by his holiness and truth, and absolute power of governing and judging, to awe and to comfort the faithful.

8. I know thy works; behold, I have set before thee an open door, and no man can shut it: for thou hast a little strength, and hast kept my word, and hast not denied my name.

8. I know and approve thy fidelity: and I opened thee a door of advantage, to do good in converting infidels, and to enjoy the comfort of it; and none shall shut this door against thee: for thou hast kept some strength of faith and courage, and hast not denied me by heresy nor cowardice.

9. Behold, I will make them of the synagogue of Satan, which say they are Jews, and are not, but do lie: behold, I will make them to come and worship before thy feet, and to know that I have loved thee.

9. And as for those heretics that, pretending Judaism, corrupt Christianity, and are but the synagogue of Satan; I will make them acknowledge the vanity of their error, and the honour of thy fidelity; and to confess that I have loved and justified thee therein, against their accusations.

10. Because thou hast kept the word of my patience, I also will

keep thee from the hour of temptation, which shall come upon all the world, to try them that dwell upon the earth.

10. I will give thee a special exemption from the persecutions which the heathens will shortly use, to try those on earth, that profess thy name. (Which, no doubt, was performed.)

Note, Though the best are oft singled out for persecution, usually the most obedient churches escape above others, and must have a hand in bringing it on themselves.

11. Behold, I come quickly: hold that fast which thou hast, that no man take thy crown.

11. My performance of all this, is not far off; for the trial of the churches, and thy preservation. But see that thou hold fast still thy innocency, fidelity, and patience, that thou lose not the crown, for want of perseverance.

Note, The best churches and Christians have need to be warned to take heed, lest they backslide, and lose all their labour and reward. Even where God decreeth to cause men to persevere, he decreeth to cause it, by holy fear of falling, and by the use of watchfulness, and diligent obedience.

12. Him that overcometh will I make a pillar in the temple of my God, and he shall go no more out: and I will write upon him the name of my God, and the name of the city of my God, *which is* New Jerusalem, which cometh down out of heaven from my God: and *I will write upon him* my new name.

12. Him that overcometh in all the trials of this life, I will make an honourable member of the glorified church, (called a pillar, as Timothy is called a pillar and basis of truth, in the house of God;) and he shall there dwell for ever: and I will signalize him, as with a written name, both of my God, and of the city of my God, the new Jerusalem, which is now gathering in heaven; and when it is complete, shall thence come, and appear with me in glory: and I will write on him my new name, The glorified Redeemer, &c.

Note, The whole name, thus set together, will be, [An adopted son of God, and an heir of the new Jerusalem from heaven, and a living member of Christ, the glorified Redeemer.]

13. He that hath an ear, let him hear what the Spirit saith unto the churches.

13. All that have ears, and hear what Christ, by his Spirit, saith to all these churches, should lay it deeply to heart, for their own instruction and admonition.

14. And unto the angel of the church of the Laodiceans, write, These things saith the Amen, the faithful and true witness, the beginning of the creation of God.

14. Thus saith he who is the truth, and by whom all God's predictions are, and will be fulfilled; the faithful witness of God, to man, by his word and sufferings; the head and chief of all God's creatures.

Note, This text is diversely expounded, as men's judgments differ. 1. The Arians hence gather, that Christ is but the first of creatures, by whom God made the rest. 2. Peter Sterry, and that party, who hold three natures in Christ; the divine, the prime-created (super-angelical) and the human, say, it is his middle nature that is here called, The beginning of the creation of God. 3. But the commonest judgment of the church is, that it is Christ, as in both natures, thus called; because he is the head, or chief, of all creatures: or, say some, as he is the cause and father of the new creature, by grace.

15. I know thy works, that thou art neither cold nor hot: I would thou wert cold or hot. 16. So then because thou art lukewarm, and neither cold nor hot, I will spew thee out of my mouth.

15, 16. I know thy case and course, that thou art not for open heresy or infidelity, but professest Christianity; but it is with tepidity, without such zeal as the faith and hope of Christians requireth. If thou wert cold, and for downright infidelity or heresy, I would judge thee accordingly: and if you were sound and zealous Christians, I would own you. But being of a lukewarm indifferency, like hypocrites, that profess Christianity, with reserves for worldly safety, I will disown thee with disdain.

Note, 1. Not that God had rather men were stark nought, than half Christians; but, as if he had said, I should sooner have judged thee accordingly, and thou wouldest not have aggravated thy sin with profession of Christianity, nor have dishonoured me so much by it. 2. God will disown luke-warm worldly hypocrites; not all, whose zeal is defective, and are too luke-warm, but all that have not so much zeal, as to prefer Christ before the world.

17. Because thou sayest, I am rich, and increased with goods, and have need of nothing: and knowest not that thou art wretched, and miserable, and poor, and blind, and naked.

17. Note, It is like, The ostentation of this church came from some worldly prosperity; and outward, lifeless formality in religion, with the decay of the power of it. When true religion decayeth in any, it is usually accompanied with self-esteem, and boasting, when they should learn, not to be high-minded, but fear. When they have turned religion into a lifeless image, they dance about that image, and honour it.

18. I counsel thee to buy of me gold tried in the fire, that thou mayest be rich: and white raiment, that thou mayest be clothed, and that the shame of thy nakedness do not appear; and anoint thine eyes with eye-salve, that thou mayest see.

18. I counsel thee to seek earnestly to me for sound understanding in the faith, against all heresy; and for the grace of consummation, against all deceitful wavering and reserves: and for the grace of sincere righteousness and holiness, that thou bear not the shame of hypocrisy, and halting between heresy, or infidelity, and saving truth; and for the illumination of my Spirit, to know the danger of heresy and hypocrisy.

19. As many as I love, I rebuke and chasten: be zealous therefore, and repent.

19. If I forsake you not, but shew my love to you, it will be by chastening you, to revive your care and zeal: if therefore you love not chastening, prevent it by zeal and reformation.

20. Behold, I stand at the door, and knock; if any man hear my voice, and open the door, I will come in to him, and will sup with him, and he with me.

20. I have my time of offering mercy, and desiring you to entertain it: and if any man hear and obey this call, I will come in by my Spirit, and take habitual possession of him, and have spiritual communion with him, and he with me.

Note, Though it be not without the grace of Christ that we open to him when he knocks, and receive his offered special grace; yet, in this, he layeth so much on man, as to make our opening, that is, our accepting faith, the condition of his entering for a fixed habitation by habitual love and holiness. On which account, divines used to say, that faith and repentance, wrought first in conversion, are the conditions or qualifications for consequent justification and sanctification.

21. To him that overcometh will I grant to sit with me in my throne, even as I also overcame, and am set down with my Father, in his throne.

21. To him that overcometh all the temptations of this life, so far as to keep his sincere faith, love, and obedience to the end, I will give a participation in my kingdom, power, and glory; even as I obtained my glory, by overcoming Satan and the world.

Note, This expoundeth what is meant before, by ruling the nations with a rod of iron, &c.

22. He that hath an ear, let him hear what the Spirit saith unto the churches.

22. Note, Let every man that hath an ear and heart, lay close to heart these reproofs, warnings, and promises of Christ, to these seven churches; for it concerneth them all.

Again note, that, notwithstanding all Christ's reproofs and threatenings, to many of these churches, he biddeth no one separate from them.

CHAP. IV.

AFTER this I looked, and behold, a door was opened in heaven: and the first voice which I heard, was as it were of a trumpet talking with me, which said, Come up hither, and I will shew thee things which must be hereafter.

1. After this the vision, that I further saw, was as if a door had been opened into heaven. &c.

Note, 1. Not that heaven hath a door, but the vision was to be suited to the capacity of a soul in flesh. 2. The notices which advance man's understanding on earth, come all from heaven. 3. And thither must we look and seek, if we will know the things of God.

2. And immediately I was in the Spirit: and behold, a throne was set in heaven, and one sat on the throne.

2. And immediately I was in an ecstasy, the spirit acting me as above the body: and God revealing things according to my capacity, I thought I saw a throne, the seat of royal, glorious majesty, and a royal person sat on the throne.

3. And he that sat was, to look upon, like a jasper, and a sardine stone: and there was a rain-bow round about the throne, in sight like unto an emerald.

3. And the power and glory of him that sat on the throne was represented to me, as by the similitude of precious stones, a jasper, and a sardine: and his glory, and faithful keeping of his covenant, was represented to me, by the appearance of a rain-bow, like an emerald in colour, round about the throne.

4. And round about the throne were four and twenty seats, and upon the seats I saw four and twenty elders sitting, clothed in white raiment, and they had on their heads crowns of gold.

4. Note, The apparition, being made to him that was a Jew, was a representation of the Jewish camp in the wilderness, with the tabernacle in the midst; according to which also the temple-worship was formed to bear some similitude; and the Christian assemblies had some resemblance to that: some think it relateth to the church at Jerusalem, which had (say they) twenty-four elders; say some, twelve apostles, and twelve elders;

CHAP. IV. REVELATION. 607

others, that it is to the bishop of Jerusalem, and four and twenty city bishops of Judea, who use to sit in council with him, who yet (saith Dr. H.) were then but the sole pastors of single assemblies, without any other elders under them, but were after to have such: others think it intimateth, that all churches should unite in such synods as consist of twelve teaching elders, and twelve ruling elders that are not teachers. Rather all churches and pastors are signified by twenty-four. But all these are but men's unproved thoughts, save only that in general, the vision appeared in resemblance of such an assembly as is here described: and it clearly intimateth, 1. That the elders have a proper dignity, and honour, and power, signified by their seals, and white raiment, and crowns of gold. I would not have ignorant, proud lads, that can but get a lay-patron to present them to a benefice, where they may live in the guilt of betraying souls, to call themselves these elders, nor to feign in white raiment that they have crowns of gold.

5. And out of the throne proceeded lightnings, and thunderings, and voices: and there were seven lamps of fire burning before the throne, which are the seven spirits of God.

5. Note, 1. The glory and terror of the heavenly apparition is thus expressed: from the similitude of the temple-worship, and more fully of the church-worship and sacred assemblies, whence must proceed the light of doctrine, the thunder of reproof, and just censures, and the voices of common consent and praises to God. Whether it signify the scorching lightnings, and thunderings, and excommunications of lay-chancellors, officials, surrogates, commissaries, &c. that use an absent bishop's name over (not one parish only, but) many score or hundred parish-churches, I leave to the arguments of the affirmers.

2. The seven lamps are expounded of the seven spirits of God, relating, as some suppose, to the lamps which were continually to burn before the tabernacle, Exod. xvii. 20. and after before the temple; and as others think, to the seven deacons at Jerusalem. Others think it is the seven guardian angels of the Asian churches, to whom John specially directeth all this book, though for the use of all others.

But of this, and other such passages, the great doubt is, whether really there be not, in the spiritual world which John saw, such things as he describeth, and the institutions about tabernacle, temple, and church-assemblies, be not formed to some resemblance of these? Or whether all be spoken only of the things below, of which the superior world hath no real similitude, but by fiction?

6. And before the throne there was a sea of glass like unto crystal: and in the midst of the throne, and round about the throne, were four beasts, full of eyes, before and behind.

6. Note, Before the tabernacle and the temple, there was a great broad vessel of water, called a sea, for the priest to wash in, Exod. xx. 18. 1 Kings, vii. 23. signifying the purity required in the worshippers of God; being as crystal, tells us, that no spots or hypocrisy is unseen to God. (Though some make this to signify the multitude of worshippers.)

The four beasts, say some, resemble the four standards and camps of Israel in the wilderness; or as others, the four evangelists: but it is like to mean the executioners by providence and miracles of Christ's will and power, full of eyes, as knowing all the affairs of the sons of men about which they are employed, called living creatures for their executive power.

7. And the first beast was like a lion, and the second beast like a calf, and the third beast had a face as a man, and the fourth beast was like a flying eagle.

7. Note, As these four agree with the apparition in Ezekiel i. 10. in the main (notwithstanding some small difference) so it is observable, which Dr. Hammond noteth from Aben Ezra, that these were the escutcheons on the four ensigns or standards of the camp of Israel, a lion for the camp of Juda, a man for the camp of Reuben, an ox for the camp of Ephraim, and an eagle for the camp of Dan: and an ox and calf are oft used for the same. And these four are noted to be the chief in their several kinds; the lion among wild beasts; the ox among the tame and serviceable; a man among all animals; and an eagle among birds. To conjecture what God would signify by them to Israel must needs be uncertain: I know nothing liker than an intimation of duty and prophecy, that Israel should be victorious over their enemies, and valiant as a lion, wise, and in dominion as man, and should have a fertile and plenteous land, signified by the ox, and seraphic and divine in the holy ! worship of God, signified by the eagle that mounteth heaven-ward in her strength. And it is like such blessings are hereby signified to be conferred on the church; some on ministers: and less probable are theirs that think Peter, John, Paul, and Barnabas, are meant, or they that apply it to the four evangelists, or four patriarchs.

8. And the four beasts had each of them six wings about him, and they were full of eyes within, and they rest not day and night, saying, Holy, holy, holy, Lord God Almighty, which was, and is, and is to come.

8. Note, The beasts resembling the standard-bearer in the camp, are likest to signify both the angels in heaven, who glorify God's attributes, and serve him in the performance of his promises to the church; and also to the apostles, and prophets, and evangelists, and pastors, who do their part herein on earth. See Isa. vi. 2. of their wings.

2. Holy, holy, holy, may relate to the Trinity,

but certainly signifieth that the holiness of God is that for which he is loved and praised by angels and saints. His holiness is his perfection, and transcendency above all creatures, being the end of all, to whom they are to be devoted; and consequently his perfect contrariety to all evil.

3. The celebrating of the praises of the most Holy God, is the incessant work of heavenly spirits, and most of the work of ministers and church-assemblies on earth.

9. And when those beasts gave glory, and honour, and thanks to him that sat on the throne, who liveth for ever and ever, 10. The four and twenty elders fall down before him that sat on the throne, and worship him that liveth for ever and ever, and cast their crowns before the throne. saying, 11. Thou art worthy, O Lord, to receive glory, and honour, and power, for thou hast created all things, and for thy pleasure they are, and were created.

9, 10, 11. Note, With the chief angels concur the heavenly host, in magnifying the holy, eternal God, as shining forth in the glory of all his works, by him, and for him, by his efficient will, and for his complacential will fulfilled, they being all created, preserved, and ordered. And this heavenly work is to be imitated by the churches on earth, whose pastors leading the people, must concur in the praises of the most holy, ever-living God; and those churches that are dry and scant in these praises of God (how well soever the word be there preached) are defective and unlike their pattern. These passages are best expounded in the three first petitions of the Lord's prayer; [Let thy name be hallowed. Thy kingdom come, and thy will be done on earth, as it is in heaven.] Neither heaven nor earth must be left out in the exposition.

CHAP. V.

AND I saw in the right hand of him that sat on the throne a a book written within, and on the back-side, sealed with seven seals.

1. I saw a roll called a book, in his hand who sat on the throne, written on both sides, but the roll was sealed up with seven seals.

Note, The roll contained God's decrees, as they were to be fulfilled according to this prophecy: and it is like they were seven rolls together making one book.

2. And I saw a strong angel proclaiming with a loud voice, Who is worthy to open the book, and to loose the seals thereof?

2. Note, Every angel of man is not worthy or meet to be the expositor and messenger of God's mysteries to man.

3. And no man in heaven, nor in earth, neither under the earth, was able to open the book; neither to look thereon.

3. It was a work and trust too high for any mere creature in all the world: none of them was worthy.

4. And I wept much, because no man was found worthy to open, and to read the book, neither to look thereon.

4. I lamented that the creature should be found so unworthy, and God's mysteries be kept unknown.

5. And one of the elders saith unto me, Weep not: behold the Lion of the tribe of Judah, the Root of David, hath prevailed to open the book, and to loose the seven seals thereof.

5. One of the elders, that were at the throne, comforted me, and told me that Christ, who is called the Lion of the tribe of Juda, and the Son of David, and Root of Jesse, was found worthy by the dignity of his person, and his merits by man's redemption, to open to the church all the mysteries of God, which it was meet for man to know, and to loose the seals.

6. And I beheld, and lo, in the midst of the throne and of the four beasts, and in the midst of the elders stood a Lamb as it had been slain, having seven horns, and seven eyes, which are the seven Spirits of God, sent forth into all the earth.

6. Upon this glad tidings, I looked and saw Christ in the likeness of a Lamb, wounded and bloody, as he was sacrificed, which signified that it was by the merit of redemption that he had his power over all: and he seemed to have seven horns and eyes for the exercise of government, by judgment and victory over his enemies, and illumination of his church, and the full notice of all that concerneth his government; which is done by the spiritual powers, or angels and ministers, whom he sendeth forth from God into all the earth: or, as others, by the manifold gifts of the Holy Ghost, which is his agent or advocate on earth.

7. And he came and took the book out of the right hand of him that sat upon the throne.

7. He that alone was worthy, received power from God, both to open the mysteries, and execute them.

8. And when he had taken the book, the four beasts and four and twenty elders fell down before the Lamb, having every one of them harps, and golden vials, full of odours, which are the prayers of saints.

8. Note, Who were the four living wights (here ill-translated beasts, when one was a man) was before inquired, but it is hard to know, only they seem to signify some greater than the elders. Some Papists think they were the four first patriarchs; and the elders the councils. It is more probable than so, that they were all the sorts of ministers that were intrusted with the first gathering of churches, and sealing the gospel by miracles, as distinct from the fixed church-bishops, allied elders. That is, that they were apostles, prophets, evangelists, and miracle-workers, as such. But all is doubtful.

2. That both the living wights and the elders were men on earth, is plain by their work here described; they are priests that, in the sacred assemblies, do by office speak for and lead the church in offering up the common praises to God, and also the prayers of the congregation. That there are any angels that resemble this office in heaven, we cannot conclude from so obscure a text.

Hence we see, 1. That church guides are the worshippers of Jesus: 2. Though we cannot hence prove that God's praises must be used with harps and musical instruments, they that use such have fairer pretence hence to prove them lawful (as doing God's will on earth, as John saw it resembled in heaven) that any can shew to prove it unlawful. 3. Ministers in offering up the church's praise and prayers, are sub-mediators under Christ.

9. And they sung a new song, saying, Thou art worthy to take the book, and to open the seals thereof: for thou wast slain, and hast redeemed us to God by thy blood, out of every kindred, and tongue, and people, and nation; 10. And hast made us unto our God, kings and priests: and we shall reign on the earth.

9, 10. Note, 1. Christ is to be praised in the church with a new song, or praises suited to his works of redemption and his glory, and not only with the Jewish psalms and worship (though those psalms also may be used.) 2. Though the collective phrase of gathering out of every nation, &c. makes some think that it is an assembly of glorified saints in the heavenly Jerusalem, called the general assembly of the first-born, and the spirits of the perfected just that is here primarily meant, it seems more probable that it is the church on earth alone: and that it is the first ages by faith, and the following also, by some experience of the church's deliverance by Constantine, that mention reigning on the earth: the saints departed indeed shall judge the world. To be kings and

priests to God, is to be endowed with power, and honour, and holiness, and employed accordingly in God's administrations and holy worship.

11. And I beheld, and I heard the voice of many angels round about the throne, and the beasts, and the elders: and the number of them was ten thousand times ten thousand, and thousands of thousands;

11. As I looked, I seemed to hear innumerable angels, joining with the living wights and elders in the praises of Christ for man's redemption.

Note, That this signifies the multitude of believers, or of ministers, through all the world, is not to be proved. But that it is meant properly of angels is most probable. And it is to be noted, that when the living wights are but four, and the elders but twenty-four, the angels that praise Christ are millions and numberless. So Heb. xii. 24. Whence note, that it is ignorance that calls God more severe than merciful, because it is but a few of this world that are sanctified and glorified; when as the vast and glorious regions above seem, to reason and by scripture, to have so many millions of angels, that it is likely the damned are very few to them.

The greatest kingdom is not near so great and glorious, in comparison of one jail and one gallows, as the heavenly regions are in comparison of this spot called earth, or the 'place of execution, called hell.'

12. Saying with a loud voice, Worthy is the Lamb that was slain, to receive power, and riches, and wisdom, and strength, and honour, and glory, and blessing.

12. These angels joined with the churches in the praises of Christ, ascribing to him, in their praises, all power and glory, &c. as deserved by his redemption of the world by his death.

Note, Those angels that join with us in Christ's praises, and are present in our assemblies, and guardians of us and them, and pitch their tents about us, and bear us up in their hands, and rejoice in our conversion, and are ministering spirits for our good, are not so ignorant of us and our concerns, and our prayers, as some imagine. We have many ignorant men that think they know more of our case here below than the angels do; when they scarce know so much as may keep them from being seducers, and dividers of the church. They are sure but ill guardians, who know as little of our affairs as these men think. Christ saith that the least Christians have their angels who behold the face of God; and why are they called their angels, and what do they for them with God, if they know not our condition and concerns? And though this will not warrant praying to them, which themselves in this book seem to disown; yet we ought not to think that mistake of those ancient fathers and churches to be greater than it was, who thought that, as pastors on earth offer up the congregations' prayers and praises to God, so there is an answerable office of angels to offer them, as from them to Christ, who offereth them to God the

Father: and who thought, as a man might pray a minister to pray for him, so he might do an angel, though it be an error, one is no more idolatry than the other.

13. And every creature which is in heaven, and on the earth, and under the earth, and such as are in the sea, and all that are in them, heard I, saying, Blessing, honour, glory, and power *be* unto him that sitteth upon the throne, and unto the Lamb, for ever and ever.

13. And as all the world, which was cursed for man's sin, was according to each creature's capacity redeemed from that curse by Christ, (to be performed in due time) so I seemed to hear all that part of the world, that belonged to man, to magnify Christ, and God by him, for the world's redemption: ascribing to him all perfection, blessing, honour, glory, power, &c.

Note, Whether there be any reasonable creatures in the sea is unknown to us: the reasonable creatures praise God and Christ understandingly; the rest demonstratively and objectively. Those under the earth are the Antipodes on the other side of the earth.

14. And the four beasts said, Amen. And the four *and* twenty elders fell down, and worshipped him that liveth for ever and ever.

14. And the four living wights, who are as the four cherubims mentioned in Ezekiel, joined with the four and twenty elders, (who answer the Jews' sanhedrims) that is, with the churches in the praises of God and of the Redeemer.

Note, If these four cherubims signified only angels, it is no wonder that they join with the church in the praises of Christ when they are of the same society with us, though the higher parts.

CHAP. VI.

AND I saw when the Lamb opened one of the seals, and I heard as it were the noise of thunder, one of the four beasts saying, Come and see.

1. When Christ opened the divine decrees, is a noise like thunder, I heard one of the four living wights, or cherubims, calling me to come and see.

2. And I saw, and behold, a white horse; and he that sat on him had a bow, and a crown was given unto him, and he went forth conquering, and to conquer.

2. Note, Some take this to be Christ going forth to convert men by the gospel: others to be Christ, beginning his judgments on the Jews: others to be the Roman power by their conquests preparing for further execution on the Jews.

3. And when he had opened the second seal, I heard the second beast say, Come and see.

3. The second cherub called me to see, when the second seal was opened.

4. And there went out another horse that was red: and power was given to him that sat thereon, to take peace from the earth, and that they should kill one another: and there was given unto him a great sword.

4. God proceeded further towards his dreadful executions, and gave up the world, and especially the Jews, to divisions, and unpeaceable tumults, and to kill and ruin one another.

5. And when he had opened the third seal, I heard the third beast say, Come and see. And I beheld, and lo, a black horse: and he that sat on him had a pair of balances in his hand.

5. God yet proceeded to the next judgment, which was famine; signified by one on a black horse with a balance to weigh food, to shew its scarcity.

6. And I heard a voice in the midst of the four beasts say, A measure of wheat for a penny, and three measures of barley for a penny; and see thou hurt not the oil and the wine.

6. A man's day-wages for labour shall buy but bread enough for one man, there shall be a scarcity of the necessary part of food; especially in Judea.

7. And when he had opened the fourth seal, I heard the voice of the fourth beast say, Come and see. 8. And I looked, and behold, a pale horse; and his name that sat upon him was Death, and hell followed with him: and power was given unto them over the fourth part of the earth, to kill with the sword, and with hunger, and with death, and with the beasts of the earth.

7, 8. Judgment shall proceed from scarcity to death and ruin, by famine, wars, and plagues, which shall destroy a great part of the Jews at least.

9. And when he had opened the

fifth seal, I saw under the altar, the souls of them that were slain for the word of God, and for the testimony which they held.

9. Note, The heavenly apparition relating to the church on earth, useth the name of an altar, and I think justifieth the use of it now.

2. The souls of martyrs live in heaven, and therefore so do other saints; which proveth the immortality of souls. To be under the altar, is to be in the heavenly communion with them that offer praise to God: and to be commemorated at the altar by the church on earth, that prayeth for deliverance from persecutors.

3. There be not only praises, but prayers in heaven, and that for justice on persecutors on earth; therefore they know that their blood is not revenged.

4. How then are miserable persecutors like to escape, when heaven and earth pray against them?

10. And they cried with a loud voice, saying, How long, O Lord, holy and true, dost thou not judge and avenge our blood on them that dwell on the earth?

10. Note, This was not from uncharitableness, but conformity to God's holiness, justice, and truth: the revenge desired being the vindication of God's holiness and truth, which he had promised.

11. And white robes were given unto every one of them, and it was said unto them, that they should rest yet for a little season, until their fellow-servants also, and their brethren, that should be killed as they were, should be fulfilled.

11. They were clothed in white, which then signified righteousness and dignity, in acknowledgment of their fidelity; but the revenge must be delayed till the rest were killed; especially, say some, by the Jews, that must kill more, that on that generation might come all the righteous blood shed, from Abel, till the last.

Note, God often delayeth his judgments but while more, and greater sins, prepare for heavier plagues.

One reason why we are not presently avenged, and delivered from persecutors, is because more must yet suffer, before they are ripe for signal vengeance. Our souls may be under the altar in heaven, clothed in white, before the day of revenge.

12. And I beheld when he had opened the sixth seal, and lo, there was a great earthquake, and the sun became black as sackcloth of hair, and the moon became as blood. 13. And the stars of heaven fell unto the earth, even as a fig-tree casteth her untimely figs when she is shaken of a mighty wind.

12, 13. The great calamities that were to follow (on the Jews, say some, and on the world, say others) were so dismal, that they were represented to me, as the darkening of the sun, and the moon looking like blood, and the stars falling from heaven; as if heaven and earth were dissolving.

14. And the heaven departed as a scroll when it is rolled together: and every mountain and island were moved out of their place.

14. And it was represented to me, as the dissolution of heaven, and subversion of the earth.

Note, Some think, this is only of the subversion of Judea. Others (because that was done already) that it was the overthrow of the heathen powers by Constantine. Others, that it was the shaking of the empire by the Goths. And others, that it is the last dissolution of the world.

15. And the kings of the earth, and the great men, and the rich men, and the chief captains, and the mighty men, and every bond-man, and every free-man hid themselves in the dens, and in the rocks of the mountains. 16. And said to the mountains and rocks, Fall on us, and hide us from the face of him that sitteth on the throne, and from the wrath of the Lamb: 17. For the great day of his wrath is come: and who shall be able to stand.

15, 16, 17. Note, 1. If this was meant of the ruin of the Jews, it was indeed exceeding dreadful: and dreadful have God's executions since been on heathens, and other enemies of Christ.

Note, 2. Greatness, nor numbers, will save none from misery and terror, when the day of God's revenging justice is come, which they would not before believe. Any sort of hope of deliverance would be then welcome: but all help will fail, and all hopes will be in vain, to them that know not the day of grace.

Proud men are able now to oppress the innocent, to scorn the faithful, and to domineer in the ruins and blood of saints; calumniating them, as the vilest malefactors: but wicked princes, lords, and judges, and bloody soldiers, will then all cry out, The great day of his wrath is come, and who is able to stand?

CHAP. VII.

AND after these things, I saw four angels standing on the four corners of the earth, holding the four winds of the earth, that the wind should not blow on the earth, nor on the sea, nor on any tree.

1. God's decree for the suspending of his dreadful executions (especially on Judea) was declared to me, by the apparition of four angels, standing on the four corners of the earth, who were to hold the four winds from blowing to the hurt of any creature.
Note, 1. The winds are called four, according to popular opinion.
Note, 2. By this, it is unlikely that the four beasts are so numbered, with respect to the four quarters of the earth, signifying the executioners of Providence.

2. And I saw another angel ascending from the east, having the seal of the living God: and he cried with a loud voice to the four angels, to whom it was given to hurt the earth and the sea, 3. Saying, Hurt not the earth, neither the sea, nor the trees, till we have sealed the servants of our God in their foreheads.

2. Note, 1. The east, where the sun riseth, is noted in prophecies, as the way, whence we are to expect our blessings, from Christ, the rising sun: whence came the old ceremony of worshipping, in the church, only towards the east.
2. The seal of God is, his gracious, sealed commission.
3. The loud voice and cry signifieth, God's great care to preserve the faithful.
4. The seal in the forehead is, God's notification of those whom he will preserve. In Ezek. ix. 4. it is as by the letter, Tau. But the text seemeth to mean no more than that God made known, to the destroying angels, every one that was to be preserved.

4. And I heard the number of them which were sealed, and there were sealed an hundred and forty and four thousand, of all the tribes of the children of Israel. 5. Of the tribe of Judah were sealed twelve thousand. Of the tribe of Reuben were sealed twelve thousand. Of the tribe of Gad were sealed twelve thousand. 6. Of the tribe of Aser were sealed twelve thousand. Of the tribe of Nepthalim were sealed twelve thousand. Of the tribe of Manasses were sealed twelve thousand. 7. Of the tribe of Simeon were sealed twelve thousand. Of the tribe of Levi were sealed twelve thousand. Of the tribe of Issachar were sealed twelve thousand. 8. Of the tribe of Zebulon were sealed twelve thousand. Of the tribe of Joseph were sealed twelve thousand. Of the tribe of Benjamin were sealed twelve thousand.

4, 5, &c. All these were to be preserved from the destruction coming.
Note, 1. Not that there were just twelve thousand of each tribe, but that the number was great in itself, though small, as to the number of them that perished. 2. Joseph is put for Ephraim, and Dan is left out; some think, the tribe being almost worn out; or for what other reason, is unknown.

9. After this, I beheld, and lo, a great multitude which no man could number, of all nations, and kindreds, and people, and tongues, stood before the throne, and before the Lamb, clothed with white robes, and palms in their hands:

9. And it was not only the believing Jews that were to be preserved, but the Gentile Christians, in a multitude innumerable, who worship God joyfully in holy assemblies, celebrating honourably the praises of Christ, represented by their spirits magnifying God and the Lamb joyfully in heaven.

10. And cried with a loud voice, saying, Salvation to our God which sitteth, upon the throne, and unto the Lamb.

10. They praised God and their Redeemer, as the author of salvation.
Note, The heretics of those times (as such do now, accused these great multitudes, and separated from them, as unworthy of their communion, while they were unworthy of church-communion themselves.

11. And all the angels stood round about the throne, and about the elders, and the four beasts, and fell before the throne on their faces, and worshipped God. 12. Saying, Amen: blessing, and glory, and wisdom, and thanksgiving, and honour, and power, and might, be unto our God, for ever and ever. Amen.

11, 12. And I saw the multitude of believers (or ministers) represented by all the angels, joining with the four living wights, and with the twenty-four elders, who represented the church of the Christian Jews, celebrating the praises of God and the Lamb; ascribing to him everlasting blessing, glory, &c.

13. And one of the elders answered, saying unto me, What are these which are arrayed in white robes? and whence came they? 14. And I said unto him, Sir, thou knowest, And he said to me, These are they which came out of great tribulation, and have washed their robes, and made them white in the blood of the Lamb.

13, 14. And one of the elders, in order to inform me, asked me whether I knew what those were that stood arrayed in white: And I told him, that I knew not: but desired him, who knew, to tell me. And he told me, that they were such as had suffered great tribulation for Christ, and were now accepted as righteous before him, through the merits of his blood; and were dignified by him.

15. Therefore are they before the throne of God, and serve him day and night in his temple: and he that sitteth on the throne shall dwell among them. 16. They shall hunger no more, neither thirst any more, neither shall the sun light on them, nor any heat.

15, 16. Note, It is not the least difficulty in this book, to know when it speaketh really of what is done in heaven, and when of what is done on earth, and when of both. This text seemeth to speak chiefly of what is really done in heaven. To expound it only of the liberty, that came to the Christians after the destruction of Jerusalem, is improbable, when the ten persecutions succeeded. To expound it of the advancement of the church by Constantine, must make it to speak only of the species of Christians that formerly suffered, and of no individual persons, but those that were then alive; and is hardly believed by them that believe the reported voice from heaven, *Hodie venenum funditur in ecclesiam;* and that know how quickly Papacy and church corruption sprang out of it. And yet, to exclude all inferior church mercies from this vision, seemeth also unsafe.

17. For the Lamb which is in the midst of the throne, shall feed them, and shall lead them unto living fountains of waters: and God shall wipe away all tears from their eyes.

17. The churches on earth shall have some times of quiet assembling, and learning of Christ and his ministers, the pure word of life, and religion shall flourish, and God shall give them some respite and intermission, or ease, from persecution (under Vespasian and Titus.) But this is but a small foretaste of the heavenly glory, wherein these words shall be fulfilled; where indeed, they shall go out of God's temple no more, and shall have all tears wiped away.

CHAP. VIII.

AND when he had opened the seventh seal, there was silence in heaven about the space of half an hour.

1. There was a little space, after the opening of the seventh seal, before I saw or heard the revelation of it.

2. And I saw the seven angels which stood before God, and to them were given seven trumpets.

2. Seven angels were appointed to publish, as by trumpet, the judgments following. Some think that the temple-worship is here described, where the people without prayed in silence, while the priest within officiated, and the trumpets sounded: which the following words favour.

3. And another angel came and stood at the altar, having a golden censer, and there was given unto him much incense, that he should offer it with the prayers of all saints upon the golden altar, which was before the throne.

3. Another angel represented the high-priest, whose office was, to offer incense at the altar, and to offer up prayers for the people: to which use, he had a golden censer, and a golden altar, to shew the honour of the Christian ministry, and worship; which is all accepted, through Christ's intercession.

4. And the smoke of the incense which came with the prayers of the saints, ascended up before God, out of the angel's hand.

4. And God received, as grateful, the prayers of his people as offered by the ministers, and by Christ.

6. And the angel took the censer, and filled it with the fire of the altar, and cast it into the earth: and there were voices, and thunderings, and lightnings, and an earthquake.

5. And upon the acceptance of the saints' prayers, followed the kindling of God's avenging judgments on the earth.

6. And the seven angels, which had the seven trumpets, prepared themselves to sound.

6. Then did the messengers of God's judgments prepare to publish, or sound them forth.

7. The first angel sounded, and there followed hail, and fire mingled with blood, and they were cast upon

the earth: and the third part of trees was burnt up, and all green grass was burnt up.

<small>7. And the judgment published by the first angel, began with destruction on the countries, such as usually accompany wars, which lay waste land and houses.</small>

8. And the second angel sounded, and as it were a great mountain burning with fire was cast into the sea; and a third part of the sea became blood: 9. And the third part of the creatures which were in the sea, and had life, died; and the third part of the ships were destroyed.

<small>8, 9. That no place should escape the next degree of judgment was represented by a mountain of fire, cast into the sea, which turned the third part of the sea into blood, &c. signifying increased wars and bloodshed, by sea and land.

The particular signification expositors are utterly disagreed in. Dr. H. taketh it for the bloodshed by insurrections in Galilee: others, for the Barbarians ruining the Roman empire: others, for heresies in the church: others, for the bishops' strife for superiority.</small>

10. And the third angel sounded, and there fell a great star from heaven, burning as it were a lamp, and it fell upon the third part of the rivers, and upon the fountains of waters. 11. And the name of the star is called Wormwood; and the third part of the waters became wormwood; and many men died of the waters, because they were made bitter.

<small>10, 11. And next, the judgment was, the infecting of the rivers, and waters, with mortal bitterness, by a star from heaven, that was mortally bitter, falling into them. This signifieth the further extensive progress of the punishment.

Some take this for the fall of a great captain of the Jews: and some, for one of their false, seducing prophets: and some, for the fall of the western empire: and some, for Arrius: some for Pelagius: some, for Mahomet: and some, for heretics in general.</small>

12. And the fourth angel sounded, and the third part of the sun was smitten, and the third part of the moon, and the third part of the stars, so as the third part of them was darkened, and the day shone not for a third part of it, and the night likewise.

<small>12. On the sounding of the fourth angel, the progress of the judgment was represented to me, as the darkening of the third part of the sun, moon, and stars: signifying the fall of some great powers, ecclesiastical or civil.

Some expound it of Vespasian's destroying a third part of the cities of Judea: some, of the beginning of the siege of Jerusalem: some, of Totila's sacking of Rome: some, of the corruption of prelacy, before Popery: some, of Arrianism: some, of the general corruption of the church by Popery.

Lira takes the four angels to be the four heretics (as he doth the four beasts to be the four patriarchs.)</small>

13. And I beheld, and heard an angel flying through the midst of heaven, saying with a loud voice, Woe, woe, woe, to the inhabiters of the earth, by reason of the other voices of the trumpet of the three angels which are yet to sound.

<small>13. This punishment extended but to a third part. But I heard an angel flying in the midst of heaven, loudly crying, Woe, woe, woe, for the greater plagues that were yet to come.

Some expound this out of Josephus of one Jesus son of Annanias that, for many years before the siege, went about pronouncing this woe: others, divers other ways.</small>

CHAP. IX.

AND the fifth angel sounded, and I saw a star fall from heaven unto the earth: and to him was given the key of the bottomless pit. 2. And he opened the bottomless pit, and there arose a smoke out of the pit, as the smoke of a great furnace, and the sun and the air were darkened, by reason of the smoke of the pit.

<small>1, 2. Note, By this, some say, is meant that Jewish seducer that headed the turbulent zealots in the siege of Jerusalem: others apply it to Arrius: most Protestants take it for the Pope: some take it for Christ that had the keys of death and hell, descending to let loose these destroyers. And the smoke is by Protestants mostly taken for the obscuring of holy doctrine and manners; but by the first for the confusions in Jerusalem by the zealots (as the murderers were called.)</small>

3. And there came out of the smoke locusts upon the earth; and unto them was given power, as the scorpions of the earth have power. 4. And it was commanded them that they should not hurt the grass

CHAP. IX. REVELATION. 615

of the earth, neither any green thing, neither any tree, but only those men which have not the seal of God in their foreheads.

3, 4. Note, That this was an increase of God's plagues, is clear; and that it was to be by soldiers, that were not to make an utter desolation, but to captivate and punish the enemies of Christianity. But the particular sense is controverted. Some take it for the foresaid rage of the zealots in Jerusalem; some for the beginning of the Roman assaults; some for Constantine's dejection of the heathens, who yet did not kill them, but gave them a disgraced liberty of idolatry; some take it for the first rising of the Saracens and Mahometans; and some take them for devils that are called locusts; some for heretics; and most Protestants for the Papal clergy and friars; and these by [hurting] mean [deceiving.]

5. And to them it was given that they should not kill them, but that they should be tormented five months: and their torment *was* as the torment of a scorpion when he striketh a man. 6. And in those days shall men seek death, and shall not find it, and shall desire to die, and death shall flee from them.

5, 6. The torment of Christ's enemies shall be worse than death, so that they shall wish for death, and not obtain it. Some by this understand the famine in Jerusalem, and the zealots tormenting the inhabitants, to make them confess where their bread or food was. Others otherwise.

7. And the shapes of the locusts *were* like unto horses, prepared unto battle; and on their heads *were* as it were crowns like gold, and their faces *were* as the faces of men, 8. And they had hair as the hair of women, and their teeth were as *the teeth* of lions. 9. And they had breast-plates as it were breast-plates of iron, and the sound of their wings *was* as the sound of chariots of many horses running to battle. 10. And they had tails like unto scorpions, and there were stings in their tails: and their power *was* to hurt men five months. 11. And they had a king over them, *which is* the angel of the bottomless pit, whose name in the Hebrew tongue *is* Abaddon, but in the Greek tongue hath *his* name Apollyon.

7, 8, &c. That this is the description of a ter- rible army of cruel men, seemeth plain, but who they were, and when, is not so plain: whether the aforesaid Jewish zealots, (who got out of the country into the city, and used the inhabitants cruelly:) or whether it was the Roman army, or the Arabian Mahometans (which many had rather think, than that all this obscure vision spake but of things already done, and known to John, and those of his time, if it was in Domitian's days.) And the Abaddon their king, both sorts think was the devil; though some say, it is Christ, and some an angel that had power to let out such destroyers. Five months being the just time of the zealots rage, before Titus came against the city, confirmeth the first sort of expositors in their opinion: but, as I said, most Protestant writers take this king to be the Pope, or the devil as acting him, and the locusts to be the friars and clergy, and all their tormentings and destroyings to be spiritual: but it is hard to think that deceiving should be meant by such tormenting, as made men wish for death: for their excommunications and persecutions cannot be meant, because those are more against good men, than the bad; and though some of their doctrines be uncomfortable, they have more that flatter men in sin.

12. One woe is past, *and* behold, there come two woes more hereafter.

12. Thus one of the three woes reserved to the three last trumpets, is past, and two follow.

13. And the sixth angel sounded, and I heard a voice from the four horns of the golden altar which is before God, 14. Saying to the sixth angel, which had the trumpet, Loose the four angels which are bound in the great river Euphrates.

13, 14. Those that expound all this of the destruction of Jerusalem, think that by Euphrates is meant Rome, and that the four angels there bound, was the Roman legions which Vespasian had stopped, till he saw what would become of the empire, when Galba. Otho, and Vitellius were killed, and he was chosen emperor; and then he went on to the siege: or else that the Syrian legions, having marched as far as Euphrates, were there stopped. But this exposition hath much said against it; especially that these were then things past, and that ver. 20. the men are described as gross idolaters, which the Jews then were not.

Many others expound it of the Arabians and Turks, who dwelt beyond Euphrates, out of the Roman territories, till they invaded and spoiled them.

15. And the four angels were loosed, which were prepared for an hour and a day, and a month, and a year, for to slay the third part of men.

15. Some gather from [an hour, a day, a month,

and a year,] that from the first great invasion and taking of Babylon to the fall of the Turks, it will be exactly in 1696, that is, twelve years hence: which time will expound. The four angels some take for four Mahometan generals, and parts, before they united in one. And by slaying the third part of men, their cruel devastations and successes.

16. And the number of the army of the horsemen were two hundred thousand thousand: and I heard the number of them.

16. The number of the Roman army, say some: but most say the number of the Mahometans was exceeding great, like locusts overspreading all the countries.

17. And thus I saw the horses in the vision, and them that sat on them, having breast-plates of fire, and of jacinth, and brimstone: and the heads of the horses were as the heads of lions, and out of their mouths issued fire, and smoke, and brimstone.

17. They appeared terribly as fitted to destroy: but some expound it of their false doctrine.

18. By these three was the third part of men killed, by the fire, and by the smoke, and by the brimstone, which issued out of their mouths.

18. Multitudes, say some, killed by the Romans; and, say most others, the exceeding great numbers killed by the Mahometans, Saracens, and Turks.

19. For their power is in their mouth, and in their tails: for their tails were like unto serpents, and had heads, and with them they do hurt.

19. They are both fierce and venomous, and every way destructive. Some expound mouth and tail, of the front and the rear of their armies.

20. And the rest of the men which were not killed by these plagues, yet repented not of the works of their hands, that they should not worship devils, and idols of gold, and silver, and brass, and stone, and of wood, which neither can see, nor hear, nor walk: 21. Neither repented they of their murders, nor of their sorceries, nor of their fornication, nor of their thefts.

20, 21. To take this for the Gnostics, and the spiritual idolatry of the Jews, seem very unlikely. The Mahometans, say others, made the destroying of idols their chief profession, and have not only rooted out image-worship from the eastern Christians, but turned since many great kingdoms and empires from heathenism to Mahometanism: but they repented not under those destructions.

CHAP. X.

AND I saw another mighty angel come down from heaven clothed with a cloud, and a rainbow *was* upon his head, and his face *was as* it were the sun, and his feet as pillars of fire.

1. The circumstances describe the glory of this angel, which some take for Christ, and some for a proper angel.

2. And he had in his hand a little book open: and he set *his* right foot upon the sea, and *his* left foot on the earth.

2. The plain sense is, that he shewed the universality of his commissioned power (sea and land comprehending the world below;) and that the book was the decree of God committed to him to execute. But the conjectured sense is manifold: some say it was God's decree to destroy Jerusalem, and that sea and land was Galilee and Judea: and others, that it was God's decree to destroy the Roman heathen power, and deliver his servants: and others, that it was his decree to destroy the Papacy, and reform and deliver the church: and others, that it was his decree to destroy all oppressing powers, and set up Christ's thousand years reign in righteousness: and others, that it was his decree to end the world, and come in judgment.

3. And cried with a loud voice, as when a lion roareth: and when he had cried, seven thunders uttered their voices.

3. His terrible aspect and cry, was to prepare for a progressive increase of the plagues, signified by seven thunders, which are louder than trumpets.

4. And when the seven thunders had uttered their voices, I was about to write: and I heard a voice from heaven, saying unto me, seal up those things which the seven thunders uttered, and write them not.

4. Say some, because the plagues are so grievous, that (on Jerusalem, say some; on the empire, say others; on the Papacy, say others) they shall be known by experience, and not by words. Therefore write them not at all, say some; or not yet, say others.

CHAP. XI. REVELATION. 617

5. And the angel which I saw stand upon the sea, and upon the earth, lifted up his hand to heaven. 6. And sware by him that liveth for ever and ever, who created heaven and the things that therein are, and the earth, and the things that therein are, and the sea, and the things which are therein, that there should be time no longer. 7. But in the days of the voice of the seventh angel, when he shall begin to sound, the mystery of God should be finished, as he hath declared to his servants the prophets.

5, 6, 7. He sware by God, that there should be no longer delay; that is, say some, of the destruction of the Jews, but till Adrian's time; or, as others, of the ruin of the Roman empire; or, as others, of the church's deliverance from Popery and persecution; or, as others, that there shall be no longer duration of this world; but that, at the seventh trumpet, God's decreed judgments shall be accomplished. Or, as Lira, that the Arian heresy should no longer prosper.

8. And the voice which I heard from heaven spake unto me again, and said, Go and take the little book which is open in the hand of the angel which standeth upon the sea, and upon the earth. 9. And I went unto the angel, and said unto him, Give me the little book: and he said unto me, Take it, and eat it up, and it shall make thy belly bitter, but it shall be in thy mouth sweet as honey.

8, 9. The voice bid me take the book, &c. And I asked the angel for it; who bid me eat it, &c. It shall be pleasant to thee, to know what will be as news; but bitter to know such heavy things: or, it will be sweet to thee, to fore-know the church's deliverance; but bitter, to know the dreadful judgments that effect it, (against the Jews, say some; the Roman empire, say others; the Papal church, say others, &c.)

10. And I took the little book out of the angel's hand, and ate it up, and it was in my mouth sweet as honey: and as soon as I had eaten it, my belly was bitter.

10. The mercy revealed in it, was sweet; but the dreadful judgments of bloodshed, bitter.

11. And he said unto me, Thou must prophesy again before many people, and nations, and tongues, and kings.

11. Say some, when Titus hath destroyed Jerusalem, there is more for thee to prophesy of, which many following emperors, and their armies, will do against them, especially Adrian, to finish their destruction. Or, as others, there are yet greater, and more dreadful things, to be told thee, against many nations and kingdoms. Or, as others; the work of prophecy, or preaching the gospel, suppressed by the Pope, and his prelates, shall be revived again, and prosper, before the end.

CHAP. XI.

AND there was given me a reed like unto a rod, and the angel stood, saying, Rise, and measure the temple of God, and the altar, and them that worship therein.

1. Say some, to measure the temple and the altar-places, as reserved from Adrian's building an idol temple, which, say they, he did only in the outer court. Say others, Measure the church, which shall be reduced to a conformity to the word of God, after all its pollutions by popery. Or, measure it, signifieth, that the church will be a small and measureable thing under the papacy, obscured, but not forsaken of God.

2. But the court which is without the temple, leave out, and measure it not; for it is given unto the Gentiles, and the holy city shall they tread under foot forty and two months.

2. Say some, the outer court, and the city was rebuilt by Adrian, called Ælia, or the Gentiles to live in, and a temple built for Jupiter, and so continued three years and a half, as Antiochus profaned it, Dan. vii. 25. Say others, The outer court and the city left to the Gentiles, is that great part of the visible church left under the papacy to such gross idolatry, as that it hath but the name of Christian, as clothing restored gentilism, and is rejected of God. Some take the 42 months literally, for a certain time of three years and a half: and some, for uncertain time. Christ was three years and a half, in his ministerial labour. And this number is five times here recited: therefore likely to be strictly meant. Some old fathers, and some Papists, understand it strictly of the reign of an Antichrist, which they think is yet to come: some of the time of the Papal reign, which they say will be 1060 years beginning between 365, and 455, and ending between 1625 and 1715: in which space Babylon will fall. Others state the time differently.

3. And I will give power unto my two witnesses, and they shall prophesy a thousand two hundred and

threescore days, clothed in sackcloth.

3. Note, There is great diversity of opinions who these witnesses are: And yet most Protestants think that their time is past, or the most of it, and this prophecy fulfilled: And prophecies use to be plain when they are fulfilled. Some new men say that they were the two churches in Jerusalem, of the Jewish and the Greek language, and their two bishops, who preached all that time against the sins of Jews and Gentiles: For they think that the Jews and Greeks, not understanding the same language; had in Jerusalem, Antioch, Rome, Alexandria, and other great cities, two churches and bishops. Others, that the two witnesses are Enoch and Elias, that shall come when Antichrist cometh. Others, that they are the Old and New Testament, which the papacy shall oppose; or, as others, the preachers of the Old and New Testament named two, because but few, but yet enough to promote the reformation. Brightman saith, It is the scriptures, and the assemblies of the faithful. Others, that it is the godly magistracy and ministry, which the papacy will cast down. Others, that God will hereafter send two, with the spirit of Enoch and Elias, in whom all this shall be literally fulfilled: Others, that it is the martyrs that have in several times opposed popery to the death; Called two, in allusion to many old couples of witnesses, Moses and Aaron, Caleb and Joshua, Ezra and Nehemiah, Haggai and Zachary, Zerubbabel and Joshua, (to which, Zach. iv. 11. this text specially relateth,) Moses and Elias on the mount, &c.

[Clothed in sackcloth,] is doing their office in a time of great affliction: And all this, some think, may be applied to divers couples, that God hath used in divers times and parts of his church; As to the Waldenses and Albigenses; to John Hus and Jeremy of Prague; to John Frederic duke of Saxony and Philip landgrave of Hessle, long imprisoned by Charles V. and afterwards delivered; to the Lutherans and the reformed; to king Edward VI. and his uncle protector duke of Somerset, &c. Even as Christ sent out his disciples by two and two; Paul and Barnabas, &c. Lira's conceit, that Silverius and Mennas were the two witnesses against the Eutychians is vain.

4. **These are the two olive-trees, and the two candlesticks standing before the God of the earth.**

4. These are resembled to the two mentioned, Zach. iv. These are as olive branches that empty themselves into the lamps, even the servants of the Lord of the world for his church.

5. **And if any man will hurt them, fire proceedeth out of their mouth, and devoureth their enemies: and if any man will hurt them, he must in this manner be killed.**

5. If any will persecute or silence them, God will revenge their cause; it refers to Elias, that brought down fire from heaven to destroy the captains and their fifties, 2 Kings, i. 10. and to Moses, Numb. xvi. Or, say others, The word in their mouths shall be as fire against all false doctrines and corruptions.

6. **These have power to shut heaven, that it rain not in the days of their prophecy: and have power over waters, to turn them to blood, and to smite the earth with all plagues, as often as they will.**

6. And the power that God gave their ministry and reforming endeavours, and the revenge that God will use against their persecutors, were expressed to me, as resembling Elias, whose prayer stopped the rain for three years and a half, and the plagues which God by Moses inflicted on Egypt: Christ intimating this, Matt. xvii. When Moses the chief law-giver, and Elias the chief prophet, were the two great witnesses of his glory. And it is notable, that godly magistrates, and godly ministers, have usually prospered together, and fallen together, and magistracy and ministry been together corrupted.

7. **And when they shall have finished their testimony, the beast that ascendeth out of the bottomless pit shall make war against them, and shall overcome them, and kill them.** 8. **And *their dead bodies* shall lie in the street of the great city, which spiritually is called Sodom and Egypt, where also our Lord was crucified.**

7, 8. Note, Christ's witnesses (holy magistrates and ministers) shall be mervellously preserved, till they have finished their testimony, and they have done their work. And then they may be destroyed by the servants of the devil, and exposed to common scorn, and perhaps be denied burial, in the places where they preached and were wonderfully blessed, and their enemies punished. And this will seem, to carnal men, to be God's disowning them, and all that they did: But the same sort of men shall be raised again, and revive their work with more success, and again silence the deluded insulting enemies.

These words [where our Lord was crucified] seem to favour their exposition, who apply all this to Jerusalem. But most Protestants take it for the Roman state of Papal corruption. And some, by their carcases say, is meant the dead carcase of the scripture, or religion, or assemblies, which only is left among them. But it seemeth to me to mean persons: And whether the same thing, as this killing and reviling the witnesses, may not be done at Jerusalem, and elsewhere, again and again in several ages, (the church having had its days and night) I yet know not.

9. **And they of the people, and kindreds, and tongues, and nations, shall see their dead bodies, three**

CHAP. XI. REVELATION. 619

days and a half, and shall not suffer their dead bodies to be put in graves.

9. Say some, They shall literally be cast out, inhumanly unburied; say others, They shall be politically slain, deposed, silenced, imprisoned, and cast by as dead and useless. And not only their persecuting enemies, but the deluded rabble and people, shall see their oppression and insult over them, and not suffer them to be restored, or honoured

10. And they that dwell upon the earth shall rejoice over them, and make merry, and shall send gifts one to another, because these two prophets tormented them that dwelt on the earth.

10. The enemies of the church, and the ungodly rabble, shall triumph and rejoice together in their revenge and conquest of these prophets, and that in the revengeful sense of their own suffering by them, whose preaching was a torment to them, who by godly magistrates also had been punished or restrained from their sin.

Note, 1. Oh, how madly do the wicked rejoice for their victory against the men that would have saved them. 2. One of the great causes of the violence of silencers and persecutors is, the remembrance of their own sufferings by godly magistrates and ministers by punishments and reformation.

11. And after three days and an half, the Spirit of life from God entered into them, and they stood upon their feet, and great fear fell upon them which saw them.

11. Either the same men, or men of the same spirit and office, were restored to the same power and works, to the great wonder of good men, and the great consternation of the bad.

12. And they heard a great voice from heaven, saying unto them, Come up hither, And they ascended up to heaven in a cloud, and their enemies beheld them.

12. The voice of Christ, say, some; of the chief rulers, say others: Come up hither, that is, say some, to heaven, as the reward of their former service, as Christ ascended in a cloud, and as Moses was called away and buried by God, and Elias carried up, Moses not seeing what Joshua must see, and Elias being only translated from a wicked generation before Jehu executed God's judgments on them; so magistrates and ministers, that do great things for the church, are usually taken up to heaven before they see the desired issue, which is left to their successors: Not David, but Solomon must build the temple. Or, as others, Come up into a state of greater prosperity and peace, which is as a heaven in comparison of their persecution: Or, as most Protestants, come now into the desir-

ed state of the visible church reformed from popery and impiety. Their advancement convinced some, and terrified others of their adversaries.

13. And the same hour was there a great earthquake, and the tenth part of the city fell, and in the earthquake were slain of men seven thousand; and the remnant were affrighted, and gave glory to the God of heaven:

13. Say some, Adrian rooted out those Jews that did not turn Christians, and set up the image of a swine at the gate, to put them in despair; upon which the rest turned Christians, and glorified God.

Say others, nine parts of Rome were destroyed before, and under the papacy only the tenth part of old Rome was left, and that fell by this earthquake: Say others, the first stirs by preaching, disputing and war about religion, quickly cast down the tenth part of the Roman church, and then many others turned Protestants: Some think it was the fall of old heathen Rome; and some think that the killing of the witnesses (by papal cruelty) is yet to come, and that Popery shall be restored a few years, and then fall for ever. It seems to relate to the case of Elijah and Elisha, after whose time the house of Ahab dreadfully fell by Jehu.

14. The second woe is past, and behold, the third woe cometh quickly.

14. Note, Thus far, some think, that the revelation shewed John nothing but what was done many years before, and visible to all men there, that is, that all was but the destruction of the Jews; and that of these last woes, the first was by the zealots, the second by Titus, (in which, saith Josephus, eleven hundred thousand persons were killed by sword and famine, besides the captives carried away;) The third by Adrian, when the faction of Barchochebas was cast out of Jerusalem, and were pursued, in which, some say, five hundred thousand were killed, some say, eight hundred thousand, and some, twelve hundred thousand.

Others say, that all the woes respected later times.

15. And the seventh angel sounded, and there were great voices in heaven saying, The Kingdoms of this world are become the Kingdoms of our Lord, and of his Christ, and he shall reign for ever and ever.

15. The foresaid new expositors take this for the triumph of the church for the Jews' destruction and the ceasing of their persecution, and the uniting of the Jew and Gentile Christians in one church at Jerusalem, where Adrian gave them that freedom by which they prospered.

Others think, that this verse speaketh of the Christian emperors owning Christianity, and putting down heathenism: Others think it speaks of the great success of the reformation against Popery: Others think it speaks of Christ's thousand years reign: And others think it speaketh of the last judgment. I see not why we may not take it for the flourishing of the gospel in the Catholic church, begun when persecution abated, but most notably promoted by Constantine.

16. And the four and twenty elders which sat before God on their seats, fell upon their faces, and worshipped God, 17. Saying, We give thee thanks, O Lord God Almighty, which art, and wast, and art to come, because thou hast taken to thee thy great power, and hast reigned. 18. And the nations were angry, and thy wrath is come, and the time of the dead, that they should be judged, and that thou shouldest give reward unto thy servants the prophets, and to the saints, and them that fear thy name, small and great, and shouldest destroy them which destroy the earth.

16, 17, 18. The twenty-four bishops of Judea, say some; Rather, the ministers of the Catholic church, represented by four and twenty elders in the vision; or the whole church, say others: And those in heaven, say others. The reign mentioned is variously expounded, as aforesaid; 1. As against the Jews. 2. As against the heathen emperors. 3. As against the pope, by the reformation. 4. As of the fall of Mahometanism, and the Turkish empire. 5. As of the millennium, and the resurrection and judgment that shall be then. 6. As of the last judgment.

19. And the temple of God was opened in heaven, and there was seen in his temple the ark of his testament, and there were lightnings, and voices, and thunderings, and an earthquake, and great hail.

19. The vision of the opened temple in heaven signifieth, the freedom given to the gospel against persecutors and corruptors; and the pure preaching and profession of it, and God's owning his covenant and church, by his eminent blessing: and the lightnings, &c. signified the great manifestation of Christ's power, for his church, in the commotions and changes in the world, and his judgments on their enemies, as followeth. (But in what instances and periods of time, expositors differ, as aforesaid.)

CHAP. XII.

AND there appeared a great wonder in heaven, a woman clothed with the sun, and the moon under her feet, and upon her head a crown of twelve stars.

1. Some Popes, and their flatterers, have said that, by the woman in heaven, is meant, the Pope, and church of Rome in its power; and by the sun is meant, their spiritual power, as key-bearers of heaven; and by the moon is meant, all princes secular power as under the feet of the Papal church, at least, in order to the ends of the spiritual power, by which he may, if they deserve it, excommunicate and depose them.

By others is understood the Christian church, now raised to honour, and flourishing in grace and wisdom, and having worldly prosperity as a lower part of her blessing; or, say others, trampling on wealth, and worldly things, with a holy contempt, and known by this ensign of honour, that the twelve apostles were its founders, under Christ; and that still they hold fast the apostolical doctrine, and depart not from it by human deprivations, or by heretical seduction and corruption. This is a crown of glory to the pure church, being not yet seduced from Christian, apostolic simplicity.

2. And she being with child, cried, travailing in birth, and pained to be delivered.

2. She laboured with earnest desire to propagate Christianity through the world. Some refer this to the Jewish church desiring Christ's nativity; but most, to the labour of ministers to spread the gospel; and some, especially, to the conversion of the Roman empire.

3. And there appeared another wonder in heaven, and behold, a great red dragon, having seven heads, and ten horns, and seven crowns upon his heads.

3. The devil appeared in the shape of a great red dragon (especially Mars, whom the heathen Romans took for their special god.) His seven heads and crowns signify his great power, especially at Rome, the city that had seven hills, and ruled in the earth: And the ten horns are the kingdoms or provinces of the Roman empire.

4. And his tail drew the third part of the stars of heaven, and did cast them to the earth: and the dragon stood before the woman which was ready to be delivered, for to devour her child as soon as it was born.

4. By his tail, say many, is meant, his subtilty; by heretics he corrupted a third part of Christians; which, saith Dr. H. was by Simon Magus, and the Gnostics: Say others, by all the swarm of heresies. (Lira saith, All this is spoken of the war of Cosroe, king of Persia, against the Christians.) Most Protestants say, it is meant of the Roman, persecuting emperors' successes, acted by Satan, who sought to extirpate Christianity.

CHAP. XII.   REVELATION.   621

5. And she brought forth a manchild, who was to rule all nations with a rod of iron: and her child was caught up unto God, and to his throne.

5. This child, say some, was Christ; others say, Constantine; most say, the church, as prosperous, which in Constantine's time, was to be advanced to power, and prevail against heathenism, both by the word, and by the sword: Or that Christ, by the church, was thus to rule: Or, as others, the martyrs, taken up to God, triumphed by suffering, and furthered the glory of the church. Others think it meaneth that, in the days of the honest heathen emperors, Alexander Severus, Philip Arabs, Constantius Chlorus, &c. the church travailed, as in the pains of childbirth; but was to suffer with patience, as in the wilderness, till Decius, Dioclesian, Max. Hercul. Maxentius and Licinius, had done persecuting: And then it was delivered by Constantine, to an advanced, free church state.

6. And the woman fled into the wilderness, where she hath a place prepared of God, that they should feed her there a thousand two hundred and threescore days.

6. Say some, the church throughout the empire, persecuted by Nero for three years and a half, was put to worship God in obscurity, and as in flight: (But Nero's persecution was before John wrote this, if under Domitian.) Others, more probably, refer it to the later Roman persecutions, under which God kept his church till its deliverance. And some understand it of Antichrist's driving the pure church, as into a wilderness.

7. And there was war in heaven, Michael and his angels fought against the dragon, and the dragon fought, and his angels. 8. And prevailed not, neither was their place found any more in heaven.

7, 8. Some expound this of the conflict at Rome, between Simon Magus and Simon Peter (long before John wrote this, if the story be true.) Others more probably say, it represents the church's persecution by the heathen emperors (especially Dioclesian, Maxentius, Licinius, &c.) and their final overthrow by Constantine, by a war in heaven, of which this was the effect. By Michael some mean Christ; Others, rather that arch-angel, mentioned Dan. x. who was guardian prince over Israel, and is now such to the church. And whether such have real war in the air with devils, is doubtful. But the casting out devil-worship, in the empire, is here meant, as the effect.

9. And the great dragon was cast out, that old serpent called the Devil and Satan, which deceiveth the whole world: he was cast out into the earth, and his angels were cast out with him.

9. By the similitude of casting down from heaven to earth, is signified, that Satan and idolaters were cast out of power and honour in the world, as earth is opposed to the church and empire.

10. And I heard a loud voice, saying in heaven, Now is come salvation, and strength, and the kingdom of our God, and the power of his Christ: for the accuser of our brethren is cast down, which accused them before our God day and night.

10. The church triumphant and militant glorifies God for this wonderful change; which shewed his strength for the setting up of his kingdom, and the exercise of Christ's power, and the salvation of men, by conquering the devil, and the heathens.

Note, 1. If Christian kingdoms be so honourable, and called the kingdoms of God, and the power of Christ, and the fall of devils, let them better consider it, that cry them down under the name of national churches, and would have churches to be only some gathered out of the multitude.

2. Quest. Why doth Satan accuse saints, day and night, to God, who never receives his false accusations? Ans. 1. He hath too many true accusations against them. 2. He sheweth his malice, though without success. 3. He accuseth them, by slanderers and false witnesses, to the rulers of the world, and to the people, to keep them in hatred of faith and godliness.

11. And they overcame him by the blood of the Lamb, and by the word of their Testimony, and they loved not their lives unto the death.

11. Not only Christ, but the faithful under him, conquer Satan, and heathens, and all the church's enemies. 1. By the blood of Christ, whose sufferings, trusted to, are the merit of their successes. 2. By the word of God, preached, pleaded, and witnessed by them. 3. By their sufferings and martyrdoms.

12. Therefore, rejoice ye heavens, and ye that dwell in them; woe to the inhabiters of the earth, and of the sea, for the devil is come down unto you, having great wrath, because he knoweth that he hath but a short time.

12. Lira thought that this was Cosroe, king of Persia, who, being conquered by Heraclius, gave the church great cause of joy, but woefully oppressed his own subjects; though, being old, he had not long to do it. Dr. H. saith, It was the church's joy, and the devil's rage, for the overthrow of Simon Magus; and that now he foresaw the fall of his kingdom, he set on foot Nero's persecution. Others, That the empire turning Christians, the devil raged, by Julian, Valens, and such

others, for a little while, both against laity and clergy. Some think, that it is properly those in heaven that rejoice: Others, that it is the church on earth: Others, that it is both. And some say, It is upon the approach of the millennium, after the fall of Antichrist.

Note, 1. To be delivered from Satan, and see his kingdom fall, is matter of great joy. 2. If Satan rage, because he knoweth his time is short, how much should we be quickened to diligence and hope, when we all know that our time on earth is short.

13. And when the dragon saw that he was cast unto the earth, he persecuted the woman which brought forth the man-child.

13. Saith Lira, when Cosroe saw that he was conquered by Heraclius, he persecuted the Christians in his own dominions, whom Heraclius relieved by two armies. Saith Dr. H. When Satan saw that he was conquered in Simon Magus, he stirred up Rome against the Christians. Say others, more probable, when Satan saw that vigilant pastors had defeated his religious frauds by heretics, he turned to the way of violence by persecutors; first heathens, then Arians. Some say, This containeth all the time from anno 310, to 606. And others, That it is his rage against the reformation since, &c.

14. And to the woman were given two wings of a great eagle, that she might fly into the wilderness, into her place; where she is nourished for a time, and times, and half a time, from the face of the serpent.

14. Christians driven from Rome by heathenish persecution, say some, or after, by Papal, say others, fled up and down, into villages, and remote countries, called a wilderness, where God provided for them, till that storm was past: (As the Waldenses, and such others.)

15. And the serpent cast out of his mouth water, as a flood, after the woman: that he might cause her to be carried away of the flood.

15. The flood, saith Lira, was by Cosroe; saith Dr. H. by Nero; and after by Domitian, and others: say others, it was by all the heathen persecutions; say others, by the Goths, and the invading barbarians; say others, by heresies; and say others, by Popery.

16. And the earth helped the woman, and the earth opened her mouth, and swallowed up the flood which the dragon cast out of his mouth.

16. Say some, The persecution was diverted from the Christians, by the insurrections of the infidel Jews, and their suppression: Say others, The Roman wicked emperors were diverted by the Goths, from mischief: Say others, The Arian Goths were conquered, even by bad emperors: Say others, the prevalency of truth made, even carnal bishops, in councils, help the church: Say others, The visible church consisteth of many bad, worldly men, who, for conjunct interest, help the faithful.

17. And the dragon was wrath with the woman, and went to make war with the remnant of her seed, which keep the commandments of God, and have the testimony of Jesus Christ.

17. Some say, this is Domitian and Trajan's persecution; Others, that it was the Arians, when Satan saw he was dispossessed of heathen Rome: Others, that it is his setting up the papacy, as it persecuted particular Christians, for not corrupting religion.

Note, There is no hope of a desirable peace with Satan or diabolists, while such: though Christians must study, as much as in them lieth, to live peaceably with all men; and especially, study love and peace among themselves. The devil will not lay down his war against Christ, till he be cast down and bound; but the members of Christ's body should not war against each other.

The poor Albigenses, &c. were first, by Diocletian, driven into a barren, mountainous country, and after murdered by Popes and Papists.

CHAP. XIII.

AND I stood upon the sand of the sea, and saw a beast rise up out of the sea, having seven heads, and ten horns, and upon his horns ten crowns, and upon his heads the name of blasphemy.

1. Most of the old fathers expounded this of an Antichrist, that should come toward the end of the world. Some Papists take it to be the second Cosroe, that succeeded his father in Persia. Others take the beast to be the state of the heathen religion at Rome; the seven heads signifying either seven emperors, or the seven hills; and the ten horns, and the crowns, the confederate kingdoms; and the name of blasphemy, the titles of Rome, called, A goddess, and the eternal city, with its idolatrous profession. Others take the two beasts here, to be but one under two relations; that is, the Pope, or Papacy: Or, say some, the Roman kingdom under the Pope, and the Papacy itself, as ecclesiastic. Some take the devil to be this beast; some, the Turkish empire; some, the Greek empire: And some take this first beast to be the Roman empire, as Christian. The hardest part of the controversy is between them that say, it is heathen Rome, and those that say, it is Papal Rome: And the reasons which they give against each other, seem stronger than the assertive reasons of either side; of which, many volumes are written. Some say, that the seven heads are seven kings, which went immediately before Antichrist; and that the name of blasphemy is, say some, the

CHAP. XIII.   REVELATION.   623

cities given the Pope (as God, and Universal Head, or Bishop, and Christ's Universal Vicar, that can forgive sin, and bring souls from purgatory, &c.) Or, as others, his idolatry.

2. And the beast which I saw was like unto a leopard, and his feet were as the feet of a bear, and his mouth as the mouth of a lion: and the dragon gave him his power, and his seat, and great authority.

2. The leopard was the type of the Greeks, the bear, of the Persians, and the lion, of the Babylonians: And all are set together, to signify the cruelty of the first beast, and variety of its exercise. This was the heathen idolatry, as exercised by Domitian, &c. say some, to which Satan made the imperial power to contribute its utmost help. Or, as others, it was the Papal idolatry and cruelty, which Satan now propagated by Christian names and pretences, as before he had promoted the like, in the name of heathen gods.

3. And I saw one of his heads, as it were wounded to death, and his deadly wound was healed: and all the world wondered after the beast.

3. To pass by those, that expound this of the son of Cosroe, king of Persia, some take it for the burning of the capital at Rome, the head-temple of idols; either in Vitellius's stirs, when after Vespasian rebuilt it; or in Titus's reign, when, being burnt by lightning, Domitian rebuilt it. But it seemeth unlikely that all this should be spoken of so small a matter as a temple. Others expound it of the sacking and taking of Rome five times in forty-two years, by the Goths and Vandals; and the recovery by Justinian, and Belisarius, and Narses. The most learned Protestants say, the deadly wound of the beast was, the overthrow of the heathen, Roman, religion and power; but what the healing was, is the doubt: Julian's cure was too short to be meant: Most think, that the very erecting of the Papacy, is meant, as restoring devilism, or idolatry, under the Christian name. Other Protestants think, that the many schisms in the Papacy, was the deadly wound: And that it was healed by the councils of Constance and Basil. And others think, that the reformation gave the Pope the wound; and that the revolt to Popery, in France, by Henry IV.; in England, by Queen Mary; in Germany, by the overthrow of the Palsgrave, &c. was the healing of it. To wander after him, is, to follow him in blind devotions.

4. And they worshipped the dragon which gave power unto the beast, and they worshipped the beast, saying, Who is like unto the beast? who is able to make war with him?

4. That is, say some, they worship the devil under the name of heathen gods, for making their empire so great, and repairing the wound of their religion. Say others, they honoured and served the Papacy, and him that erected it, thinking it had been God, when it was the devil: admiring the sanctity and power of the Papacy.

5. And there was given unto him a mouth speaking great things, and blasphemies; and power was given unto him to continue forty and two months.

5. This the ancients expound, of an Antichrist not yet come: And others, of Domitian: And others, of the Pope.

6. And he opened his mouth in blasphemy against God, to blaspheme his name, and his tabernacle, and them that dwell in heaven.

6. Say some, he blasphemed the true God and Christ directly; (that is, Domitian persecuting Christians.) Say others, it is the Papal blasphemy, by transubstantiation, image-worship, arrogating God's prerogatives, persecuting them that obey his word, &c.

7. And it was given unto him to make war with the saints, and to overcome them: and power was given him over all kindreds, and tongues, and nations.

7. Those that take the first beast to be Mahomet himself, with his Arabian, Saracen powers; and the second, to be the Turkish Mahometans; do easily tell when, and how the saints were overcome, and nations subjected to him. But several objections lie against this, and so there do against those that apply it to Domitian: And why it may not more plausibly be applied to some following persecutors, especially Diocletian, I see not yet. But that it is meant of the Papal tyranny, is the more easily believed by many that know the truth of the history, that all the ten heathen persecutions, set together, were a little thing, compared to the Papal bloodshed. Mede truly tells us, that Perion reporteth (and divers second him) that, in France alone, a million of the Albigenses and Waldenses were killed: And that Sanders de Vis. Man. l. 3. dem. 34. confesseth, that infinite Lollards were burnt in Europe: And that Vergerius saith that, within thirty years, an hundred and fifty thousand were consumed by the inquisition, and such means. And the numbers murdered in Bohemia, and other countries; and since then in Low-Countries, France, England, Ireland, &c. render the ten persecutions by heathens, as described by our most aggravating old church historians, to appear but as a morsel to the Papal sacrifices.

8. And all that dwell upon the earth shall worship him, whose names are not written in the book of life of the Lamb slain from the foundation of the world.

8. And his great power and victories shall cause the generality of worldly men, to own, admire, and obey him (whether it be the heathen Rome, or Mahometans, or the Pope;) except those chosen children of wisdom, whose names, from the foundation of the world, were, by God's decree, written in the book of the slain Lamb, or in the catalogue of those who were to be saved by Christ crucified.

9. If any man have an ear, let him hear. 10. He that leadeth into captivity, shall go into captivity: he that killeth with the sword, must be killed with the sword. Here is the patience and the faith of the saints.

9, 10. Let all Christians regardfully mark what I say, that they be not, by the success of persecutors or tyrants, tempted from their patience, constancy, or duty: Though these great conquerors and persecutors are awhile adored for their success and power, in the end they shall be used as they used others, commonly when they have conquered and triumphed, others conquer them, and triumph over them; and when they have killed many, they are usually killed themselves. Few famous conquerors die the common death of all men. Therefore, the holy wisdom of God teacheth his saints, as much as is possible, to avoid war, even defensive, and to overcome by faith and patience, especially in the case of persecution, and of private and particular persons towards injurious rulers; though kingdoms may exercise self-defence, lest they tempt all their neighbours to make them their prey.

11. And I beheld another beast coming up out of the earth, and he had two horns like a lamb, and he spake as a dragon.

11. Many say, that by Another beast, is meant, the former in another respect, and that they are but one. But when the text saith, it is another, with so many notes and acts of difference, such presumption doth not expound the sense, but make it, and may say any other improbable thing. Others that say, the first beast was heathen Rome, and the second, Papal Rome, will as hardly as the former make it probable, that heathen Rome was one of the Pope's heads, if he be the beast: Was the first beast but one of the many heads of the second beast? Or, was the heathen religion but one of heathen Rome's own heads? Or, was the Pope's wounded head in being before him? If the heathen Rome, or its heathenism, was the wounded head of the first beast, then the Pope was not the first beast, for that was not one of his heads, especially at its overthrow by Constantine. Grot. and Dr. H. that say the second beast is Apollonius, or magicians or magic, if they so confine it, speak as improbably. Whoever was the second, his lamb-like horns shew him to be an hypocrite pretending to truth, and his dragon-like speech shew him to be the devil's agent. But the reasons prove both one, being against the plain text, some think rather that the first beast was the idolatrous emperors that so cruelly set up image-worship, in the east and west, and the Pope the second beast that flattered them, and rebelliously excommunicated those that were against them; and his first notable power was obtained by engaging himself in the cause of the image-worshippers, and extolling and flattering them; and withal flattering Pipin, and Ch. Martell, and others, to maintain him in his rebellion, by invading the western empire, and then engaging most succeeding princes in the same cause.

And some think that the Pope is the first beast, and the second are his councils, and cardinals, and clergy, and jesuits and friars, that cry him up, and persuade the world to obey and follow him, according to his universal claim.

And if the difficult objections against all these last, should incline us rather to think that it is the heathen empire that is the first beast, I should (by reviewing the history of fact) think that the second beast was (not Apollonius fabled of by Philostratus and Hierocles, but) the whole gowned and literate tribe; learning and the pompous ostentation of it, being then almost as much of the glory, pride, and strength of Rome, as the military power: and I shall shew, anon, how ordinary it was for the first beast, the imperial military power, to arrogate the name of gods, and to have temples, altars, and sacrifices: and the second beast, poets, orators, comedians, philosophers, historians, as well as augurs, and soothsayers, and magicians, and priests, all flattered and applauded these blasphemous emperors; and the great learning of these men was set up against Christianity, as despised foolishness: as they did with Paul at Athens, so did the learned Romans count Christians babblers, and ignorant barbarians: learning (vain and carnal) was as great a glory to Rome as arms, and it is doubtful whether the imperial power, or the literate opposition and scorn, did more hinder the reception of Christianity. But Christ and the cross at last conquered both, and used both to promote the gospel. Yet this might be said to arise out of the earth; for when it was used for enmity and strife against Christ, it was foolishness with God, and as James saith, chap. iii. was earthly, sensual, and devilish causing confusions, and every evil work.

12. And he exerciseth all the power of the first beast before him, and causeth the earth, and them which dwell therein, to worship the first beast, whose deadly wound was healed.

12. If it be the heathen empire that is spoken of, 1. Then it seemeth most like that the deadly wound was the shame and shaking of the empire, by the deaths of Tiberius, Caligula, Claudius, Nero, Galba, Otho, and Vitellius; every emperor, between Augustus and Vespasian, murdered by others, or themselves; and the suspension of Vespasian at first, (or afterward the shake that heathenism had there by the wisdom and honesty of the Antonines, and after of Alexander Severus, and Philip) yet the first soon repaired by Vespasian, Titus, and Domitian, and all the rest, at last

by Dioclesian (after Decius, Aurelian, &c.) And the learned tribe did live in power, and in their senate, and all their city officers, exercise such splendid pomp and rule, as the emperor did in his palace: and caused the Roman city and empire to worship their victorious blasphemous emperors, and with them to continue the common idolatry.

13. And he doth great wonders, so that he maketh fire come down from heaven on the earth in the sight of men.

13. This Roman learning is used to overcome truth and Christianity, and to make men believe that the sun and moon and stars are gods, and have oracles where they speak, and that it is they that conquer the enemies of Rome; so that their power was in the vision represented to me, as if they brought down fire from heaven.

14. And deceiveth them that dwell on the earth, by the means of those miracles, which he had power to do in the sight of the beast, saying to them that dwell on the earth, that they should make an image to the beast, which had the wound by a sword and did live.

14. Their powerful oratory and learning deceiveth the ignorant multitude, to erect images to their victorious blasphemous heathen emperors, who recovered from the foresaid wound by the military murders: images, and altars, and sacrifices, are to be made the means of worshipping them.

15. And he had power to give life unto the image of the beast, that the image of the beast should both speak and cause that as many as would not worship the image of the beast, should be killed.

15. They so deceived the people as that the oracles seemed to them to speak, and to tell them as from the gods, that they must kill all those that would not worship the image of the emperor, and the gods that he worshipped, and would not be of his religion.

16. And he causeth all, both small and great, rich and poor, free and bond, to receive a mark in their right hand, or in their foreheads: 17. And that no man might buy or sell, save he that had the mark, or the name of the beast, or the number of his name.

16, 17. It was the custom of the Romans, in those times, to mark both servants, and many soldiers, as notes of relation and appropriation, meetly on their arms or hands, by which the person marked, as by a badge, livery, or colour, owned his master or captain: and also to mark their slaves, and punished persons, with a brand of disgrace, in the face or hand: the mark of servants, or soldiers, was sometime his master's escutcheon, or chosen badge, and sometime his name, and sometime the chief letters of his name, which leaving out the rest, stood for the name (as M. for Marcus, L. for Lucius, S. P. Q. R. for *Senatus Populusque Romanus, &c.*) And it sometime fell out that these letters were numeral (as M. D. C. L. I. V. are with us.) Now this text serveth to some to mean that the flattering literate tribe in Rome (orators, senators, poets, priests, auspices, &c.) who were the second beast did, by their laws, orations, poems, comedies, oracles, and deceits, cause the people commonly to come under obligations, thus to enslave themselves to the idolatrous emperors, to own them as petty gods, and offer at their altars and sacrifices, and to worship the idols also which they worshipped, and so to be the owners of, and actors in, their idolatry: and in order hereto to honour them by receiving their badges, or their names, or the chief letters of their names: and it fell out that the chief letters here meant were Numeral and Nominative both, and made up 666.

And if it be (as most Protestants think) Rome-papal, that is the second here meant, then as the first beast is the Papacy, as idolatrous and potent, so the second is likest to be the flattering clergy who are to the Popes much like what the literate Romans aforesaid were to the heathen emperors: I mean his prelates, councils, jesuits, and friars of all sorts; these have pretended to abundance of miracles, to advance the Papacy and its corruptions of religion, insomuch that they make such miracles one of the chief marks of their church, Gregory's dialogues, and such other, led the way: and their monstrous legends feign so many, and so shamefully (of St. Francis, St. Dominic, and multitudes more) as makes men suspect that this tribe are the miracle-working beast; not but that many miracles are true, that are written of Gregory Neocesar; Martin, and others, by Euseb. Socrat. Sulp. Severus, Augustin, &c. which were all for the confirmation of the Christian faith, and not for Popery; and many of the monks, and others, of whom these fictions are written, were holy men, and God did some wonders at their prayers: and it is this which the legenders take occasion from to add their multitudes of falsehoods, and then to persuade men, that all these were miracles wrought for God's attestation to Popery: it being usual for that clergy to persecute the living saints that are not for their wills and ways, and to canonise those, as wonders of sanctity, whose strictness and austerity is joined with subjection to the Papal dominion. Such men's writings as Baronius, Bellarmine, Genebrard, &c. With their many false councils, and Jesuits that compass sea and land to promote the Papal kingdom, do seem much more fully to do the part of the second beast for the Papacy, than the poets, priests, &c. did for the heathen idolatrous empire. And the mark in their right hand or forehead seemeth to be some professing badge, by which they tie themselves to worship the beast and his image, that is, subject themselves, by consent, to the Papal sovereignty and canons, and idolatry, or corrupt imagery and scenical worship: and herein the Papacy so far exceedeth the severity of the said heathens, that they do, by the laws of their church, put strict oaths, upon all the clergy to believe many new articles of faith, and to obey the Pope; yea, and on princes to exterminate all that the Pope will but call heretics: and that those temporal lords shall be excommunicated, deposed, and damned, that will not do it, no man, called by them a heretic, may so much as make a will or have the benefits of the law, no not of his liberty, or life, but be tormented in the inquisitions, or burnt. No minister may preach Christ's gospel, that is not a subject of the Popes; nor any Christian else meet to worship God, no nor read the Bible in a known tongue, but by his licence, and theirs that he empowereth. These things are far more than to forbid buying and selling without the mark of the beast, or his name.

18. Here is wisdom. Let him that hath understanding count the number of the beast, for it is the number of a man, and his number is six hundred threescore and six.

18. Here is work for the sagacity of a sharp-witted man: let such try to find out the beast by the number of his name; for it pleaseth not God more plainly to reveal it. Tv is numeral letters, which denominate a man; and the letters are χέν which in numbering signify DCLVVVI, or 666.

About this name and number the fathers, Papists, and Protestants, are of many minds among themselves. The first general difference is, whether it signify the name of a man properly, or only some other mark that belongeth to him, called his name? And the next whether the name belong to a single person, or to a state, or policy, or party? Of the Protestants many think it is a man's name, but belonging to the Papacy in common: Junius taketh it for the canon law and decretals: Broughton for Adonikam, Ezra ii. 13. Brightman reciteth these, and divers names, found out by divers fancies, Titan, Lampetis, Ninetes, Cacos, Odegos, Alethes, Blaberos, Palas, Baseanos, Ammes, Adicos in Arethas, Ecclesia, Italica, and Romagnus. All which he rejecteth, and fasteneth on that which Irenæus chose of old, which is Lateinos. And he thinks that this number of the name, to be received, was meant of the Greeks, who were brought to submit to the Latin church; and so all the Greeks that so submit, receiving the number, are joined in the guilt and damnation with them that had the mark or the name itself.

This is clear that all they, that only find out a name, or number, which are not imposed, and by the subjects received, speak not at all to the text. It is only the receiving of the mark, name, or number, that is here mentioned: it is the subjects badge. If the racked word Lateinos be used as added to Catholic, and put instead of Roman, it may reach the Papists, whose name and badge now is to be [Roman Catholics, as distinct from all others, that are but mere Christian Catholics.]

But lately most Protestants take the number of the name to be but some characteristical acts or marks: some say, it is the system of Papal corruptions in doctrine and worship; some (as Mr. Potter) make it the number of 25, as the square root of six hundred sixty-six, and he largely tells us how many ways it suiteth Rome. But how is this number of 25 received as a badge by reprobates? Some say, that patriarchal and metropolitan (and such like) idolaters and persecutors are the image of Papacy, and that PERJURY is the mark of the beast, who by false oaths bindeth all to him, and to his prelates; so that whoever will not be perjured, by false and wicked oaths, are not received into his church, nor tolerated by them: and I read not in history that ever any party on earth did so long, and so violently, bind men by wicked oaths, and involve all sorts in heinous perjury, as the Pope and his prelates have long done and do: Abbot Uspergensis lamenteth it in his days that priests and people were commonly involved in perjury, swear, or suffer, is their law; and when interest requireth it, unswearing and forswearing is as violently imposed, and whole countries absolved from their oaths to their sovereigns. PERJURY, PERFIDIOUSNESS, and PERSECUTION, seem to be the mark of the Papal dominion: and (as my old fellow-minister in the same congregation) Mr. Nath. Stephens saith, The name of the beast seemeth most likely to be his assumed power, or pretended authority; to which it is that he maketh all to swear: and the oath or subjection is not to the number, but to the power or persons marked by that number; the number being but the name abbreviated, and the name the notification of the party, or policy, to which men consent.

But Mr. N. Stephens thinks that 666 is the time between the beginning of the Roman monarchy, according to Daniel's computation, as it respected the church, which was in Pompey's time, and the rise of Antichrist, which he thinks was in 666. (Anno Dom.) and so is just 666 years: for he taketh (as many others do) the title of universal bishop given Boniface III. by Phocas, to set up Antichrist first; and the antecedent fall of the Roman empire to be that by the Goths, &c. But I am past doubt, that neither wicked Phocas, nor Boniface themselves, did mean that the universality should extend over all the world, but only over the empire; for what pretence could Phocas have to give power or titles to his subjects, to rule in all princes' dominions on earth? They only meant that he should be before the bishop of Constantinople, the prime bishop in the universal empire; and that Leo challenged before Phocas: but the claim, of governing all the world, came up by degrees long after both; and it was about 700 years before the Popes cast off their subjection to emperors and kings.

On the other side, those that appropriate all this to heathen Rome, are not of one mind. Some take the beast to be the heathen worship as it stood at Rome, and the Roman empire, supporting it, to be represented by seven heads, that is, particular emperors or hills, and the ten horns to be ten confederate kings, and tributary: and that Domitian is specially meant, as a self idolizing blasphemer and persecutor, for three years and a half; and that the magic, auguries, and oracles, are the second beast; and especially Apollonius; that the image is the idol-worship set up in the rest of the empire in imitation of Rome: and all were compelled to bear some mark of their god, or his name, or some numeral letters signifying his name, branded on them; but that it being not revealed then what those letters signify, it cannot be known now, save that it was a discriminating note received by some, and not by others.

But others think, that Vespasian was the beast, and Antichrist, 1. Because some foolish Jews took him (as they had done Herod) at first to be the Messiah. 2. Because he answered to Antiochus Epiph. who before him violated and profaned the temple and worship. 3. Because Christ seemed to lead them to that interpretation, Matt. xxiv. by assimilating the case to that in Daniel. 4. Because he was said to work miracles, to cure a blind man, &c. 5. Because he so destroyed the sacred nation, and enslaved the remainder; which the Christians were far from rejoicing in, being still much inclined to the honour of Jerusalem, and thinking that a glorious throne of Christ was there to be erected, and grieving for them, as Paul did, Rom. x. & xi. 6. And these gather the name from the letters of Teitan, as if Titus had been so called by allusion to Titan. And Hesychius saith that Titan was to be written as of old, Teitân, as containing the number of 666.

Others rather lay the name and mark on all the heathen emperors, as idolaters and persecutors, or enemies at least to Christians. And, 1. They may well prove that it was very ordinary with them to usurp some degree of deity while they lived, or to be deified by the senate, or their successors, when they were dead; and to have altars erected to or for them, and sacrifices offered accordingly. Of Augustus himself there is full evidence, Virgil and Horace deify him, and mention his devoted sacrifices and altars. So doth Valerius Maximus invocate Tiberius, and Propertius calls him God. Claudius is called Divus in an old monument. The self-deifying of Caius Caligula and Domitian, is commonly known: it is no wonder that the great worth of the Antonines, especially M. Aurelius Philosophus, made the Romans deify him when he was dead, and would have done so, for his sake, by his successors of the Antonine race, had not they, by the inhuman villanies of Commodus and Heliogabalus, changed their minds, (though Antonine accepted not this while he lived.) Many emperors presumed to deify their wives when dead: and indeed building temples over their dead bodies, and erecting altars there, was too soon imitated by the zealous Christians over the graves, bones, or suffering-places, of the martyrs. Aurel. Victor saith indeed, that Dioclesian was the first after Domitian (and Caligula) that sufferrd himself publicly to be called LORD, and named and adored as God : (but not the first that was deified by the senate, or flatterers, especially poets.)

And they that used to mark or stigmatize their servants, soldiers, and slaves, he that will read may see in Piguorius de Servis; out of Ambrose de obit. Valentin. Plin. jun. Ep Ausonius ; Petronius Arbiter; Sueton. de Calig. Aetius Amidenus Medic.

And it is not impossible to invent congruous numeral letters that might be the abbreviations of their names: and though John writing in Greek put [χξς.] yet seeing the emperors and Roman subjects were Latins, who can doubt but that the letters, being at once nominative and numeral, were Latin, and not Greek, however Teitan, and Oulpius, and Lateinos, &c. be instanced by many.

For instance [T. FLAV. VESPAS. C. DIV.] is the abbreviation of [Tito Flavio Vespasiano Cæsari Divo.] (The father and son had the same name) the numeral letters are [D. C. L. V. V. V. I.]

[T. FLAV. DOM. C. DIV. VOT.] that is, [Tito Flavio Domitiano Cæsari Divo Votum] the numeral letters of the abbreviation are D. C. L. V. V. V. I.] Galba, Otho, Vitellius, are not worth the naming.

[D. ULP. TRAJANO C. VOT.] that is, [Divo Ulpio Trajano Cæsari. Votum] is, [D. C. L. V. V. I.

[ÆL. ADRIANO C. AUG. VOT.] that is, [Ælio Adriano Cæsari Augusto Votum] is, [D. C. L. V. V. V. V. I.]

[DIV. Æ. LU. VER. ANTON. C.] that is, [Divo Ælio Lucio Varo Antonino Cæsari] D. C. L. V. V. V. I.

So [DIV. AUREL. ANTON. C. VOT.] is, [Divo Aurelio Antonino Cæsari Votum.] D. C. L. V. V. I.

So [DIVO VALER. C. VOT.] is, [Divo Valeriano Cæsari Votum] D. C. L. V. V. V. I.

So [DIV. AUREL. C. VOT.] is, [Divo Aureliano Cæsari Votum] D. C. L. V. V. V. I.

So [VA. DIOCLES. VOT.] that is, [Valerio Dioclesiano Votum] D. C. L. V. V. V. I.

So [DIV. HERCUL. VOT.] that is, [Divo Herculio Votum] C. L. V. V. V. I.

I do but give instances how easy it is to conceive how such nominal marks might be given and received : but that de facto it was just so, or why that number is chosen, who can tell.

CHAP. XIV.

AND I looked, and lo, a Lamb stood on the mount Sion, and with him an hundred forty and four thousand, having his Father's name written in their foreheads.

1. Next the Vision shewed me Christ, as a Lamb, standing on Mount Sion, &c. These hundred forty and four thousand, seem to be only the faithful Christian Jews, that stuck to Christianity, through suffering ; the number being the same, as chap. vii. and the number of twelve, which is the square root of this number, noting a respect to the twelve tribes, as the number of twelve apostles did : therefore the place is called Mount Sion, (their holy place ;) whether it be in heaven, or in the Catholic church, that they are supposed to be. Doubtless, many Christian Jews thought that the New Jerusalem should be int he place where the old was at Christ's coming. The name of God (and of the Lamb, say some copies) in their foreheads, signifieth their open profession of fidelity to the Father and the Son, and God's gracious noting them for his own. And it helps us to expound what the mark of the beast was, even some open signal obliging profession of idol-worship.

2. And I heard a voice from heaven, as the voice of many waters,

and as the voice of a great thunder: and I heard the voice of harpers harping with their harps: 3. And they sung as it were a new song before the throne, and before the four beasts, and the elders, and no man could learn that song, but the hundred and forty and four thousand, which were redeemed from the earth.

2, 3. The voice of many waters signified the multitude of converts that by the gospel were gathered to this church on mount Sion, who praised God with the melody of harps, or joyful psalmody: and it was new psalms of praise for man's redemption, and the grace of Christ which they sung as before God and the cherubims, and the holy church, which none of the Jews were fit to sing, save the foresaid chosen saved number.

4. These are they which are not defiled with women, for they are virgins: these are they which follow the Lamb whithersoever he goeth: these were redeemed from among men, being the first fruits unto God, and to the Lamb. 5. And in their mouth was found no guile: for they are without fault before the throne of God.

4, 5. The vision being of those in heaven, as the precedents of the Christian church at Jerusalem, that should afterward succeed them; they were the first-fruits of the apostles' ministry, described Acts i. and ii. and iii. and iv. who were eminent in purity and love, free from idolatry and fornication, as a people chosen out of the Jewish nation unto Christ; and as they were holy on earth, they are faultless and perfect now in heaven.

6. And I saw another angel fly in the midst of heaven, having the everlasting gospel to preach unto them that dwell on the earth, and to every nation, and kindred, and tongue, and people.

6. Whether the midst of heaven have the mystical senses that divers give, or be only [sent from heaven to earth] I know not: some say, it is called the everlasting gospel, because it was decreed from everlasting; some, because it endureth to everlasting, or tendeth to life everlasting. By the gospel some understand only the glad tidings of the fall of the Roman empire; some, the doctrine of reformation, and the tidings of the fall of Popery; and some, the common doctrine of salvation by Christ, as it was now more freely and universally to be published to the Gentile world.

7. Saying with a loud voice, Fear God, and give glory to him, for the hour of his judgment is come: and worship him that made heaven and earth, and the sea, and the fountains of waters.

7. Away with your idols that are no gods, and turn to and fear the true and living God, who made heaven and earth: for the time is come that he will judge and destroy idolaters. Other expositions I omit.

8. And there followed another angel, saying, Babylon is fallen, is fallen, that great city, because she made all nations drink of the wine of the wrath of her fornication.

8. Another part of my vision was another angel, &c. implying a further revelation to me. Whether it signify also another sort of preachers on earth, and who; as some say, the Albigenses and Waldenses, or Luther, Zuinglius, or Illyricus and his century writers, let them tell that know.

Babylon is here described (and more fully after) to be that great city that drew all nations unto idolatry, whether this were Rome as heathen, or Rome as Papal, or Rome as containing both, see my advertisement.

9. And the third angel followed them, saying with a loud voice, If any man worship the beast and his image, and receive his mark in his forehead, or in his hand, 10. The same shall drink of the wine of the wrath of God, which is poured out, without mixture, into the cup of his indignation, and he shall be tormented with fire and brimstone, in the presence of the holy angels, and in the presence of the Lamb.

9, 10. Those that partake of the sins of idolatrous Babylon (or Rome) shall partake of her plagues; and the judgment that overthroweth her shall extend to all her companions in idolatry, and also the punishment in the life to come; and Christ and his angels will execute and behold it, as just and good.

Some, to save their charity, say that damnation is not denounced to all that only have the name of the beast, or the number, but only to them that receive his mark as his slaves, and worship him and his image. But I think receiving his name, and its number, is included in receiving the mark. But all may be pardoned to the penitent believers.

Whether this angel be Luther, Chemnitius, Whittaker, and such others, I leave to the proof of the affirmers: it is enough to me, that this additional revelation and punishment, is notified to John as by another angel.

Though many think that only temporal punishment is here meant; doubtless the same sin deserveth more.

11. And the smoke of their torment ascendeth up for ever and

ever. And they have no rest day nor night, who worship the beast, and his image, and whosoever receiveth the mark of his name.

11. Though temporal calamity be here included, this seems plainly to mean hell: and the mark of his name, is here made equal to [his mark] ver. 9. O the restless misery that is prepared for the impenitent!

12. Here is the patience of the saints; here are they that keep the commandments of God, and the faith of Jesus.

1℃. This misery of impenitent idolaters and enemies of Christ, will shew the world, how wise and happy the saints were, that by patient suffering did overcome, and kept to the end, the commands of God, and the faith of Jesus. Faith, obedience, and patience, are all necessary to salvation.

13. And I heard a voice from heaven, saying unto me, Write, Blessed are the dead that die in the Lord, from henceforth, yea, saith the Spirit, that they may rest from their labours, and their works do follow them.

13. Though it be always happy to be at rest with Christ, the sufferings of those times will be so great, as will make it seem a reasonable blessedness, to go to that rest, where they shall no more labour or suffer, but receive the fruit of their labours and works performed for Christ on earth. Some make this to be but a promise of after freedom from persecution here: the text proveth a blessedness for separated souls before the resurrection: for by the Greek, [henceforth] signifieth from this time forward. The Socinians therefore abuse the text, that make the blessedness to be but resting in a state of death, till the resurrection. For life, with God's service and acceptance in a time of persecution, is a greater blessing than mere death.

14. And I looked, and behold, a white cloud, and upon the cloud one sat, like unto the Son of man, having on his head a golden crown, and in his hand a sharp sickle. 15. And another angel came out of the temple, crying with a loud voice, to him that sat on the cloud, Thrust in thy sickle and reap, for the time is come for thee to reap, for the harvest of the earth is ripe. 16. And he that sat on the cloud thrust in his sickle on the earth, and the earth was reaped.

14, 15, 16. Some understand this of an angel in the likeness of a man: but most of Christ, or an angel like Christ. The other angel seemeth to signify but another part of the vision, and execution reaping the harvest, is punishing sinners ripe for destruction.

17. And another angel came out of the temple which is in heaven, he also having a sharp sickle. 18. And another angel came out from the altar, which had power over fire, and cried with a loud cry to him that had the sharp sickle, saying, Thrust thy sharp sickle, and gather the clusters of the vine of the earth, for her grapes are fully ripe. 19. And the angel thrust in his sickle into the earth, and gathered the vine of the earth, and cast it into the great wine-press of the wrath of God. 20. And the wine-press was trodden without the city, and blood came out of the wine-press, even unto the horse-bridles, by the space of a thousand and six hundred furlongs.

17—20. Of the difference between the harvest, and the vintage, and the two angels, and their executions, opinions are various. Some make it to be two degrees of our plague, some to be two; some say conjunct, some say distant. Some say, one is the destruction of the Turkish empire, and the other (the vintage) of the Roman Papacy before Christ's coming. Some say, the first is the completing of the elect as converted, and the latter the destroying of Antichrist. Some say, it speaketh of the last judgment, some, of the fall only of heathen Rome, and some, of other executions. It is clear that it speaketh of divers degrees of execution of God's judgments on the idolaters, signified as by divers angels appearance, words and deeds; but whether it meant any beside the Roman heathen idolatry, and their consenting countries sufferings; and whether the sixteen hundred furlongs signify any more than diffused plagues, and whether it was means of Trajan's executions in Syria, &c. as Grotius thought, or of the country about Rome, or any determinate space, and where, and which of the six or seven senses of [power over fire] is right, besides a mere destroying power, are all things which I cannot determine.

Mr. Brightman hath found England to be the thousand six hundred furlongs, and Cranmer to be the angel that had power over fire, because he held his right hand to be burnt, and Thomas Cromwell to be the executing angel: and some that can make themselves believe, that so small a spot of ground as England, is it that this tragedy is acted on, have thought that they found here the killing of the two witnesses (magistracy and ministry, and the two beasts, and the number of their names, in the Greek letters here mentioned,

X (ch) ξ (x) ς (st) and the wounding and the healing, and the mark of the beast PER, as referring to Ch. (church) and St. (state;) and in a word, that almost half the Revelation spake of England. But unless they can prove that the two beasts have their off-spring, who bear their father's image, and are dispersed as Cain's offspring was, so that the same thing is acted over by them, in several lands and ages, which was acted by the first, I shall, rather than this, confine the exposition to that empire and state, that the church suffered under when John wrote.

CHAP. XV.

AND I saw another sign in heaven, great and marvellous, seven angels having the seven last plagues, for in them is filled up the wrath of God.

1. Seven plagues, which are all to be poured out on the idolatrous persecuting empire, as it were by seven angels.

2. And I saw as it were a sea of glass, mingled with fire, and them that had gotten the victory over the beast, and over his image and over his mark, and over the number of his name, stand on the sea of glass, having the harps of God.

2. I saw a sea like that in the temple, signifying purity, and the multitude of worshippers; mingled with fire, signifying the altar-sacrifices, and their zeal, and God's acceptance, and them that by patient suffering had overcome, by keeping themselves undefiled from owning the Roman idolatry, by owning the idol, or his image, or mark, or the numeral letters of his name; and they stood on this sea, having the harps on which they sang the praises of God, as was used in the temple.

3. And they sing the song of Moses the servant of God, and the song of the Lamb, saying, Great and marvellous are thy works, Lord, God Almighty, just and true are thy ways, thou king of saints.

3. And they, being many of them the first Christian Jews, sang Moses' song after the drowning of Pharaoh, the case being like their deliverance from the Roman tyrants, and the song of Christ, suited to the joyful praises of God, for the work of man's redemption and salvation; saying, Great, &c. Thou glorifiest thy power in conquering the greatest, proudest enemies, and delivering thy servants from the great dangers, even by miracles of providence; and thy justice and truth, O most holy lover, and king of saints, are magnified in thy avenging them on their cruel enemies.

4. Who shall not fear thee, O Lord, and glorify thy name? for thou only art holy; for all nations shall come and worship before thee, for thy judgments are made manifest.

4. This demonstration of thy greatness, holiness, and justice, shall move the nations to fear and glorify thee, as the only most holy God, and to fear and worship thee, because of thy judgments.

5. And after that I looked, and behold, the temple of the tabernacle of the testimony in heaven was opened: 6. And the seven angels came out of the temple, having the seven plagues, clothed in pure and white linen, and having their breast girded with golden girdles.

5, 6. The holy place and God's decree seemed to be opened; and seven pure and glorious angels, honourably girded to execute God's will, came forth with the seven last plagues that are to finish the destruction of the idolatrous, potent, persecuting Roman empire.

7. And one of the four beasts gave unto the seven angels seven golden vials full of the wrath of God, who liveth for ever and ever.

7. Those that undertake to tell whom these angels, and this living wight, signified on earth, go farther than I can, who know no more but that the seven plagues were thus represented.

8. And the temple was filled with smoke from the glory of God, and from his power, and no man was able to enter into the temple, till the seven plagues of the seven angels were fulfilled.

8. And the dreadfulness of God's wrath, as a consuming fire, striking even his worshippers with fear, and in the execution disturbing the church's peace, was represented to me by the filling of the temple with smoke, from the glory of God, &c.

CHAP. XVI.

AND I heard a great voice out of the temple, saying to the seven angels, Go your ways, and pour out the vials of the wrath of God upon the earth.

1. I heard a great voice out of the temple, sending these angels to pour out the vials, and execute God's wrath.

2. And the first went and poured out his vial upon the earth: and

there fell a noisome and grievous sore upon the men which had the mark of the beast, and upon them which worshipped his image.

2. Of the great plague in wicked Commodus' reign (that killed, in Rome alone, two thousand a day;) and of the like, in the reign of several persecutors, even till Constantine's reign; and of the bloodshed and fire, and the resemblance of this, to the plagues of Egypt: see Dr. H. on the text, and Grotius before him. Others say, it is the Papists' torment of conscience, when Popery is fallen.

3. And the second angel poured out his vial upon the sea, and it became as the blood of a dead man: and every living soul died in the sea. 4. And the third angel poured out his vial upon the rivers and fountains of waters, and they became blood.

3, 4. That these signify a progress of the same judgment on the idolaters, is clear: but whether by the sea, and the rivers, and fountains, signify things so distinct, as many think; and which, of their many conjectured significations, are right, I cannot say.

5. And I heard the angel of the waters say, Thou art righteous, O Lord, which art, and wast, and shalt be, because thou hast judged thus.

5. The angel that executed God's judgments on the idolatrous nations, performed it with praise and glory to God, for his justice on persecuting idolaters.

Note, The angels in heaven were not ignorant of what God thus did on earth; and as God's mercy hindered not his execution of justice, so their pity kept them not from triumphing over these destroyed sinners, and giving God the glory of their punishment.

6. For they have shed the blood of saints and prophets, and thou hast given them blood to drink, for they are worthy. 7. And I heard another out of the altar say, Even so, Lord God Almighty, true and righteous are thy judgments.

6, 7. Note, 1. God and angels will rejoice in the terrible revenge of the blood of saints. 2. The angel from the altar signifieth, the consent of the souls under the altar, and of the church of holy worshippers on earth, who pray for deliverance. 3. Were it never so certain, that it is idolatrous, heathen Rome that is here meant, it consequently inferreth that, if Papal Rome have equalled, yea, far exceeded them, in shedding the blood of saints, their punishment shall be as great or greater. It is no small aggravation of Papal bloodshed (by massacres, inquisitions, burnings, &c.) that they father all on Christ himself, and do it as Christians; yea, and, in so many ages, make it the necessary defence of their kingdom: and they shall find, that God knoweth a saint when men call him a heretic; and will not be so mocked as to disown Christ's sheep, for such forged marks.

8. And the fourth angel poured out his vial upon the sun, and power was given unto him to scorch men with fire. 9. And men were scorched with great heat, and blasphemed the name of God, which hath power over these plagues: and they repented not, to give him glory.

8, 9. Some take this to signify a great drought, and dearth, that came in the days of Commodus: and after, of Maximinus. Many take the sun here, for Antichrist, that calleth himself so: others, for governors: some, for the king of Spain; some, for the German emperor; or some such Papal luminary: some, for the scripture, as tormenting Papists: some, for Christ, as sending forth his word and judgments. I can go no further than the general sure sense; that a greater plague, that fell on the idolatrous empire, made them lay all the blame on the Christians, and rage the more; but cured not their idolatry, or persecution.

10. And the fifth angel poured out his vial upon the seat of the beast, and his kingdom was full of darkness, and they gnawed their tongues for pain, 11. And blasphemed the God of heaven because of their pains and their sores, and repented not of their deeds.

10, 11. The plain, general sense of all this is, to liken idolatrous, persecuting Rome, and the suffering Christians, to Pharaoh, and the Israelites; and liken God's plagues on Rome, to the Egyptian plagues: And to tell us that, as Pharaoh's heart was hardened, till destruction fell on him and his, so will be the idolatrous Romans.

By the seat of the beast is meant Rome, with the imperial power (or Papal, say many:) and by darkness, the confusions there, and diminutions of their glory: In heathen Rome these were many and great; the soldiers setting up, and pulling down, and killing emperors, till they set the empire to sale: Emperors set up, and warring against each other: few dying a natural death: Valerian taken, captivated, and made his footstool, by Sapores, and fled. To be an emperor was the next way to murder, or some odious disgrace and death, by him that could overcome and kill him.

And Papal Rome was subdued by the barbarians. Other expositors are many.

12. And the sixth angel poured out his vial upon the great river Euphrates, and the water thereof

was dried up, that the way of the kings of the east might be prepared.

12. That this signifieth a further progress towards idolatrous, persecuting Rome's destruction, and the church's deliverance, is clear; but what Euphrates signifieth, and what its drying up, and what, The way of the kings of the east, expositors greatly differ in. Some take Euphrates literally; some, mystically: some, for the Turks; some, for the chief champions of Antichrist; some, for the chief strength and garrison of Babylon; some, for the Pope's riches, and great tributes and revenues; and some, for the river Tibris, in Rome, and so, for Rome itself. And these take the drying of it up to be, the ruin of Maxentius, by Constantine, destroyed in the Tiber: Others think, the drying up, to be the destruction of the Turks: And so they vary in the rest. But some think, that this is but a further assimilation of the case to the Israelites, when the Red sea was dried up for their escape, and to prepare the way for Pharaoh's ruin: and signifieth, that the danger and impediments of the Christians' deliverance were removed, by the overthrow of all the idolater's forces, the ruin of Dioclesian, Maxim. Herculius, Galer. Maxim. Maxentius, Licinius; that so the Christians, by and with Constantine, might triumph. And some think, it is a weakening the Roman power, toward Euphrates, to let in the Persians, and others, to afflict them.

13. And I saw three unclean spirits like frogs come out of the mouth of the dragon, and out of the mouth of the beast, and out of the mouth of the false prophet. 14. For they are the spirits of devils working miracles, which go forth unto the kings of the earth, and of the whole world, to gather them to the battle of that great day of God Almighty.

13, 14. As, when Ahab was to be destroyed, the devil was a lying spirit in the mouth of all his prophets, and bid them, Go and prosper; and Zidkiah made horns, to signify his victory; so I saw, as it were, three devils, like the frogs of Egypt; or three lying spirits, sent by Satan, and encouraged by the idolatrous persecuting emperors, and by his flattering oracles, augurs, orators, &c. to persuade all the foresaid princes to fight against Constantine; especially Maxentius and Licinius; that they might fall, as Ahab and Pharaoh did.

Or, say others, they were Popish missionaries, and priests, and friars, sent out by antichristian civil power, and antichristian ecclesiastical powers, to draw men to Popery and idolatry, that they may be destroyed when God shall judge them. The day of God, some take, as before, for Constantine's victories against idolaters; others, for the day of the Pope's fall; and others, for the last day of judgment.

15. Behold, I come as a thief; Blessed is he that watcheth and keepeth his garments, lest he walk naked, and they see his shame.

15. My coming will be, when men expect me not: Blessed is he that prepareth not for shame and confusion, when his sin and hypocrisy shall, by my judgment, be brought to light, by complying with the higher powers in sin, as thinking that I will be long in coming, to take down sinners, and set up saints.

16. And he gathered them together into a place called in the Hebrew tongue, Armageddon.

16. The devil's prophets provoked them to gather, and fight to their destruction.

Note, Here the dragon is expounded to be devils: And this word [devils] in this book, usually signifieth, those idols (Jupiter, Mars, Apollo, &c.) which the Romans worshipped instead of God: (For Paul tells us, It was devils that they worshipped.) And it being the spirits of these devils, or heathen idols, that are sent out, it seemeth most probable, that it is the war with the heathen idolaters that is here meant. Dr. H. after Grotius, noteth that, in the fight at Rome, Maxentius had a hundred and seventy thousand foot, and eighteen thousand horse, of Romans, Italians. &c. and Constantine had ninety thousand foot, and eight thousand horse, of Germans, Gauls, and Britons: and that the victory was of such consequence, that from that day, the account of years, by indictions, began to commemorate the deliverance of city and church; (which since, is turned into accounting from the birth of Christ.)

But others say, It is the day of the fall of Antichrist: And some say, of the destruction of the Turks. And some say, he that gathered them together, is Christ, or God, by his permitting providence, for their destruction.

17. And the seventh angel poured out his vial into the air, and there came a great voice out of the temple of heaven from the throne, saying, It is done.

17. The angel, that poured his vial into the air, signifieth, the coming down of God's plagues from heaven, on the generality of the enemies. And the voice out of the temple signifieth, that it is done by God's decree, for the vindication of his holy worship, and his church.

[It is done] that is, The last plague on the Roman Pharaoh is now pouring out, and he is to be drowned in the Red sea. God's judgments are accomplished for the extirpation of the heathen Roman empire, and the revenging the blood of the saints, shed by them. As Pharaoh's cruelties increased, before the Israelites were delivered, so Dioclesian made the cruelest slaughters, before the heathen beast was to be destroyed: and then they were ripe, and the time was come. Or, as others, the end of the world.

18. And there were voices, and thunders, and lightnings; and there was a great earthquake, such as was not, since men were upon the earth, so mighty an earthquake, and so great.

CHAP. XVII.   REVELATION.   633

18. The great commotions which went to these great changes, and subversion of the heathen powers, was represented to me as by thunderings, lightnings, and the greatest earthquake. Say some, it is the changes by the Ostrogoths, and such others: Say others, there were literally such dreadful earthquakes before Totilas took Rome: Say others, it is yet to come before Antichrist's fall: And say others, before the day of judgment.

19. And the great city was divided into three parts, and the cities of the nations fell: and great Babylon came in remembrance before God, to give unto her the cup of the wine of the fierceness of his wrath.

19. And Rome was then divided between, heathens, Christians, and worldly men, that were indifferent for religion: Or, say others, heathens, orthodox, and heretics: It is taken from Ezek. v. Others say, that literally the third part was destroyed by Totilas; and say others, by Alaricus; others say, it is three in relation to the three princes, the dragon, the beast, and the false prophet; others, that Antichrist's kingdom was falling by being divided in itself.

20. And every island fled away, and the mountains were not found.

20. As earthquakes shake mountains and islands; so all the dependants of Rome fall with it.

21. And there fell upon men a great hail out of heaven, every stone about the weight of a talent: and men blasphemed God because of the plague of the hail; for the plague thereof was exceeding great.

21. God's executions bruised and broke them, as great hail would do the tender plants, and yet they did but blaspheme God the more. A talent is threescore pound. God's judgments pursued the scattered Roman citizens, say some; the Papists, say others; and all wicked Christians, say others.

CHAP. XVII.

AND there came one of the seven angels which had the seven vials, and talked with me, saying unto me, Come hither, I will shew unto thee the judgment of the great whore, that sitteth upon many waters: 2. With whom the kings of the earth have committed fornication, and the inhabiters of the earth have been made drunk with the wine of her fornication.

1. Some say, 1. I will shew thee what is coming from God, on imperial, heathen, idolatrous Rome, who by power and by learning (by the first and second beast) hath drawn kings and nations with her to idolatry.

Others say, it is Papal Rome, and they prove it, because if they had not been married to God before by the profession of Christianity, they could not have been adulterers. To which the former say, 1. That fornication may be the sin of the unmarried. 2. That by fornication is meant idolatry, and God's right may serve to infer this guilt, though men be not married to him by consent: And that it is incredible that all the heathen world are no idolaters, because they were not professed Christians. By the Whore is meant the same as the Woman, the second two-horned beast; and the false prophet, say many, that is, the church of Rome, with the whole body of the Roman clergy; which others deny.

3. So he carried me away in the Spirit into the wilderness: and I saw a woman sit upon a scarlet-coloured beast, full of names of blasphemy, having seven heads, and ten horns.

3. Into the wilderness, say some, to represent the desolation; say others, because it was a revelation not to be yet openly known in the city; for if the rulers had known of all these terrible predictions against them, they would have raged by persecution against Christians; and therefore all this prophecy was to be obscure, and not communicated so long commonly as other scriptures. Others say, it was to shew that Antichrist's kingdom is barren, without a drop of grace: Others, that solitude is fittest for contemplation: Others, that the wilderness is heathenism brought in by Popery. Others, that as the true church was driven into a wilderness of solitude and suffering, so now shall Papists be. Others, that the Papacy is a wilderness, as an apostatical church succeeding the apostolical church.

Who is the great whore, whether Rome Pagan, Rome Papal, or Rome hereafter fallen to future antichrist, I once for all, refer the reader to my postscript.

4. And the woman was arrayed in purple and scarlet-colour, and decked with gold and precious stones and pearls, having a golden cup in her hand, full of abominations and filthiness of her fornications.

4. Idolatrous Rome was represented to me as a woman richly and splendidly arrayed, by her wealth, and pomp, and power, enticing the world to her idolatry.

5. And upon her forehead was a name written, MYSTERY, BABYLON THE GREAT, THE MOTHER OF HARLOTS, AND ABOMINATIONS OF THE EARTH.

5. The name written was, [Mystery, Babylon, &c.] that is mystical (not literal) Babylon, the great city Rome, the mother of idolatry and wickedness, propagating them by her power and learning, to all the nations of her dominions, and further in the world. As Babylon was the idolatrous, cruel captivator of the ancient Jews, overthrowing their kingdom; so was idolatrous proud Rome, the captivator and persecutor of Jew and Gentile Christians, and the great enemy of the church.

6. And I saw the woman drunken with the blood of the saints, and with the blood of the martyrs of Jesus: and when I saw her, I wondered with great admiration.

6. Idolatry was not her only crime, but the guilt of being as drunk with holy blood. But her pomp and her bloodiness seemed wonderful.

7. And the angel said unto me, Wherefore didst thou marvel: I will tell thee the mystery of the woman, and of the beast that carrieth her, which hath the seven heads and ten horns.

7. Note, Seeing God professeth to open the mystery, who this mother of harlots is, it is safest to add as little, on pretence of fuller exposition, as we can.

8. The beast that thou sawest was, and is not, and shall ascend out of the bottomless pit, and go into perdition, and they that dwell on the earth shall wonder, (whose names were not written in the book of life from the foundation of the world) when they behold the beast that was, and is not, and yet is.

8. Some take this as fitted to the time when the empire should first be Christian: as if it meant, Rome was the beast when it was Pagan, but now is not when it is Christian, but will be again when it was Papal and antichristian. Or, Rome is the idolatrous beast under the Pagan; but is not now under that form; but yet is under the Papal form: Many other expositions I pass by. They that expound all of Pagan Rome, say that the sense is [I shall notify the beast, which is the Roman emperor, by that one who now reigneth, which is Domitian.] He was in the government when his father Vespasian was abroad: And he afterwards ceased, while his father and brother Titus reigned, and then resumed it, raised by Satan to persecute the church; and then is basely killed himself.

Rather thus: [I am now shewing thee the fall and destruction of the beast and whore, and will now notify him to thee accordingly.] The beast or emperor at this fall will be the bloodiest of all persecutors, Diocleaian: Of whom then it may be said, He was emperor, but discouraged by the ill success of his persecution, he, with Maxim. Herculius, laid down the empire, and both betook themselves to a private life: But after the devil would fain have restored them, and they attempted to rise out of their privacy; but did it to their own destruction, being both killed when Constantine prevailed: As were Licinius and Maxentius, who would have done their work. So that when Constantine was destroying the Pagan empire, it was true, that Dioclesian (and Maxim. Herc ul.) was emperor, and now is not, and yet is, that is, in being, though not in power, but will rise to his perdition.

And the idolaters shall be struck with wonder and consternation, when they see so cruel and great a tyrant brought to nought.

9. And here is the mind which hath wisdom: the seven heads are seven mountains, on which the woman sitteth. 10. And there are seven kings, five are fallen, and one is, and the other is not yet come; and when he cometh, he must continue a short space. 11. And the beast that was, and is not, even he is the eighth, and is of the seven, and goeth into perdition.

9, 10, 11. That the seven mountains are those of Rome is very plain: But who were the seven kings I confess I know not. Here is work for a searching head (the mind that hath wisdom.) But it is matter of fact, which when the thing was newly done, the mind that hath wisdom might know: but how can we know it, but by history, without a new revelation? And history herein is lame, and much uncertain, and the work of man, and men are liars; and few Christians were writers till three hundred years after Christ; and the first Christians had many fabulous reporters among them, (as their spurious writings shew.) When John wrote this book, and whether all at once, or at many years distance of the parts, is unknown, (however confident men may talk.) Eusebius trusteth divers fabulous authors, and reports, for want of better, though he be credible of himself. I take the style, and words of the book, to be the best history of the time, which intimateth that part of it, at least, was written before the siege of Jerusalem, which maketh me the easilier believe Epiphanius, that John was first banished into Patmos in the reign of Claudius, and there wrote part of the book, at least. For though some of it might be written of things past, it is hardly credible that most of it should be such.

This verse hath many expositions: many say, it speaketh not of individual kings, but of seven sorts of government, viz. kings, consuls, decemvirs, dictators, tribunes military, and emperors; and the Pope they make to be the seventh and eighth. But so much is said against this, as I cannot answer: As, 1. That it is not mere power, but idolatrous and persecuting power, that the text describeth; and none of these persecuted, save the emperors; nor were they so idolatrous as Athens, and other places. 2. That the mere imperial power as the pillar of idolatry, is plainly made the beast; therefore not the five antecedent. 3. That indeed these five were no supreme power; for that was only in the senate, which had the legislative power till violence ravished them of it; which when it did, the consuls, decemvirs, and tribunes, had but a part: No, nor the emperors long, or oft. These were not several sovereigns, but parts of the supreme, as the Tribuni Plebis were; and some of them very short. And the Pontifices Max. might as well be named as some of them. And who the seventh and eighth head were, is said with so great difficulties, difference and confusion, as would be tiresome to repeat,

The Papists' opinions about a future Antichrist, and theirs that apply all to Mahomet I will not repeat.

They that expound it of particular Cesars also, are opposed by many hard objections. Some of them apply all to the seven emperors, that the Christians were first troubled by, viz. Claudius, Nero, Galba, Otho Vitellius, Vespasian, Titus, and Domitian the eighth: But three or four of these persecuted not Some think that seven, here signifieth, not a determinate number, but many. They seem the same with the seven heads, chap. xiii. And if the ten horns signify not precisely just ten, why shou'd the seven? I, that understand it not, may say, it is as probable as some of these that this be the sense [it being the time of the fall of the beast and whore that I am speaking of] there shall be, at that time, seven Cesars alive at once, of whom Dioclesian, Constantius, Chlorus, Galerius, Maximianus, Severus, and Galerius Maximinus, are fallen at the time when Constantine is destroying idolatry: Constantine is the sixth who is then in being: Licinius is after to be used as one of them, seeming then a friend. The bloody Dioclesian who, with Max. Herculius, laid down the rule, is one of the seven, and together will, by the devil's instigation, attempt again to be the eighth, but to his own perdition. Whether Maxentius pass only for a partial usurper after, or pass for the eighth, rather than Dioclesian, I let pass. Both Licinius and Maxentius continued but a short space.

12. And the ten horns, which thou sawest, are ten kings, which have received no kingdom as yet: but receive power as kings one hour with the beast.

12. Say some, they are twelve heathen kings, that are not full kings, but tributary to Rome. Say others, they are the Gothish and other extraneous kings, that are not in the empire, but are confederates. Some say, it is the tyrants that have headed the devil's kingdom in seven several ages, but this is a vain Popish evasion. That ten kings were dependent on Pagan Rome, is clear; and that ten or more of the barbarians broke the Christian empire: But which is meant is the doubt.

13. These have one mind and shall give their power and strength unto the beast. 14. These shall make war with the Lamb, and the Lamb shall overcome them: for he is the Lord of lords, and King of kings, and they that are with him, are called, and chosen, and faithful.

13, 14. The ten idolatrous dependent kingdoms shall assist and support the Roman Pagan empire with their power and strength: But Christ, who overcometh Rome, will overcome them also; for he is over all kings and kingdoms, and will help the Christian army under Constantine. Or, say others, ten kings shall give their power to the Pope, and make war against Christ, that is, his doctrine and worship, and Christ and the reformers shall overcome them. But these cannot be the same barbarous kingdoms of Goths, &c. forementioned, but mostly others.

15. And he saith unto me, The waters which thou sawest, where the whore sitteth, are peoples, and multitudes, and nations, and tongues.

15. This idolatrous Roman power ruleth over many great and populous nations of the earth: Or, as others, the Papal idolatrous power is upheld by many nations, even all the empire.

16. And the ten horns, which thou sawest upon the beast, These shall hate the whore, and shall make her desolate and naked, and shall eat her flesh, and burn her with fire.

16. The ten nations, that before upheld the Roman idolatry, shall turn against her, and be the instruments of her destruction. The Britons, Gauls, Germans and divers others, first fought with Constantine against the Pagans, and many more of them after turned Christians. Or, say others, The reformation shall be wrought by princes that have forsaken Popery. Whether it speak only of destroying the idolatrous Roman power, or of destroying the houses, or the city itself, is controverted: The latter is not yet performed, nor the first as to the Papacy.

17. For God hath put in their hearts to fulfil his will, and to agree and give their kingdom unto the beast, until the words of God shall be fulfilled.

17. God hath so over-ruled them, and all their hearts, that eventually they shall serve the Pagan empire, say some, or the Papal power, say others, till the time that God will pull them down, as he foretold.

Note, God can so order things, that all his judgments shall be executed by sinners, without causing any one of their sins.

18. And the woman which thou sawest is that great city, which reigneth over the kings of the earth.

16. It is certainly Rome that then reigned. It is certain then that Pagan, imperial Rome, was at that time the beast, on which the whore sat: And certain, that Pagan idolatry was it that then made Rome the whore: But whether (besides this) Christian imperial Rome under Constantine, or under the western emperors after, or imperial Constantinople, or Rome as the Pope's seat (before 606, or after only, or when) be the whore. And whether their very different sort of sin make them two or three whores, or the concord, in general, or similitude, make Pagan and Papal Rome to be the same whore, as meant in this text, these and other are the doubts: But the certain part must not be doubted of.

CHAP. XVIII.

AND after these things I saw another angel come down from heaven, having great power; and the earth was lightened with his glory.

1. The fall of Rome is so great a work, that it was shewn me by an angel of wondrous glory. Those that tell us that this angel was an eminent preacher, and such other particularities of filling the earth with his glory, go further than my knowledge goeth.

2. And he cried mightily with a strong voice, saying, Babylon the great is fallen, is fallen, and is become the habitation of devils, and the hold of every foul spirit, and a cage of every unclean and hateful bird.

2. The language of those times was to call deserted ruined places where no man dwelt, the places haunted by devils and goblins, and satyrs, and owls, and serpents. So that this signifieth, Desolation: And the Jews then thinking that, as Babylon that before captivated them is destroyed, so the very city of Rome would be; the prophecy calleth the destruction of the Pagan empire and idolatry, with all its retinue of literate upholders, by the name and titles of the destruction of the city. For it was not Babylon, as a city, nor qua Roma, as this city, nor as a rich and great city, but as the great idolatrous power which captivated and persecuted the church; therefore it is destroyed, not as a great or rich city, but as Babylon: And so it is desolate. Some think that this is spoken of it, as when Rome was burnt in part by Totilas, and the remnant of Pagans destroyed by Alaricus: That is more than I can prove. But it being the Pagan empire, that captivated the church, that made it Babylon, I think Babylon fell when that fell, though many Pagans did survive.

3. For all nations have drunk of the wine of the wrath of her fornication and the kings of the earth have committed fornication with her, and the merchants of the earth are waxed rich through the abundance of her delicacies.

3. For their power and learning have spread the poison, or drunkenness, of their idolatry to all nations, and the kings of the earth have been encouraged in the guilt; and her wealth and grandeur, have promoted all pride and sensuality in the nations, that have traded with her, or depended on her. Others say, It is the sale of pardons, indulgencies, and ceremonies, and church-preferments, that are her merchandise and delicacies.

4. And I heard another voice from heaven, saying, Come out of her, my people, that ye be not partakers of her sins, and that ye receive not of her plagues. 5. For her sins have reached unto heaven, and God hath remembered her iniquities.

4, 5. That is, Away from idolatrous Pagan Rome, as Lot fled from Sodom; if you love your lives and souls, avoid all partaking in her sins: Eat not things offered to idols, imitate them not, and comply not with them in any act of idolatry, or other sin: For the time of her destruction is at hand, and you may suffer with her if you sin with her, and fly not from her.

Or, Come out from Popery, and partake not of the sin, lest you partake of the plagues. Here, say some Protestants, we answer the question, Where was your church before Luther? And why do you separate from Popery? To the first, say they, our church was in Babylon, where God bore with it, till he called it out; To the second, God commanded us to come out. No doubt we must partake of no men's sins.

6. Reward her even as she rewarded you, and double unto her double according to her works: in the cup which she hath filled fill to her double.

6. God, who is her judge, will have you lay doubly more on her than she laid on you by persecution: And this is no injustice; it being for sin against him, and not only as against you. This giveth the reason of God's execution by Constantine; but alloweth no private men to take arms against government, on pretence of revenging the injuries of the church.

7. How much she hath glorified herself, and lived deliciously, so much torment and sorrow give her. For she saith in her heart, I sit a queen, and am no widow, and shall see no sorrow.

7. The sins of Sodom were pride, fullness, idleness, and unmercifulness: And Pagan Rome, grown proud and sensual by power and wealth shall now suffer debasement and dejection. Or

Rome Papal, that saith, I am the successor of Peter, and the mother of all churches, shall be dejected, and destroyed for her pride and cruelty.

8. Therefore shall her plagues come in one day, death, and mourning, and famine; and she shall be utterly burnt with fire; for strong is the Lord God who judgeth her.

8. The fall of the Pagan empire shall be sudden and terrible, like the burning of a city. Or, say others, the remnant of Pagans shall be burnt out of Christian Rome by Alaricus, &c. Say others, Papal Rome shall be cast down: Say others, burnt. But it is not like if the city were burnt, but some would rebuild it, as we did London.

9. And the kings of the earth, who have committed fornication, and lived deliciously with her, shall bewail her, and lament for her, when they shall see the smoke of her burning: 10. Standing afar off for the fear of her torment, saying, Alas, Alas, that great city Babylon, that mighty city! for in one hour is thy judgment come.

9. The nations, that were her companions in idolatry, shall bewail her great and sudden fall. Obj. Papal Rome falls not suddenly. Ans. We know not what it may do yet: But it is certain Pagan Rome did.

11. And the merchants of the earth shall weep and mourn over her, for no man buyeth her merchandise any more. 12. The merchandise of gold and silver, and precious stones, and of pearls, and fine linen, and purple, and silk, and scarlet, and all thyine wood, and all manner vessels of ivory, and all manner vessels of most precious wood, and of brass, and iron, and marble, 13. And cinnamon, and odours, and ointments, and frankincense, and wine, and oil, and fine flour, and wheat, and beast, and sheep, and horses, and chariots, and slaves, and souls of men.

11, 12, 13. The pride and greatness of Rome, bought up all that many countries could bring in, of all sorts for necessity and delight; and they fed the Pagan idolatry and tyranny: Others apply it to Papal pardons, offices, and preferments. But these were rather bought at Rome, than sold thither. By [souls of men] some understand Pagan Roman slaves, some their murdering idolatry, and some, Papal soul-murderers.

14. And the fruits that thy soul lusted after, are departed from thee, and all things which were dainty and goodly, are departed from thee, and thou shalt find them no more at all. 15. The merchants of these things, which were made rich by her, shall stand afar off for the fear of her torment, weeping and wailing, 16. And saying, Alas, alas, that great city, that was clothed in fine linen, and purple, and scarlet, and decked with gold and precious stones, and pearls! 17. For in one hour so great riches is come to nought.

14, 15, &c. Rome's pride and sensuality found all the countries money for all sorts of commodities, whose market ceaseth by her destruction.

17. And every ship-master, and all the company in ships, and sailors, and as many as trade by sea, stood afar off. 18. And cried, when they saw the smoke of her burning, saying, What city is like unto this great city? 19. And they cast dust on their heads, and cried, weeping and wailing, saying, Alas, alas, that great city, wherein were made rich all that had ships in the sea, by reason of her costliness! for in one hour is she desolate.

17, 18, 19. The fall of the Pagan power and religion, being the political life of the city, is thus represented in vision to John, under the shew of the burning of the city buildings (as our eyes saw London burning three days, 1666, September 2, 3, and 4.) Or, say others, The fall of Rome Papal was thus represented: But others say, that Rome Papal shall be thus really burnt and destroyed.

20. Rejoice over her, thou heathen, and ye holy apostles and prophets, for God hath avenged you on her.

20. It was this same Roman idolatrous power, which murdered the holy apostles and many prophets that are now in heaven: And they shall rejoice in the vindictive justice of God: And so shall the church on earth; not as it is revenge on private enemies, but as it is God's public deliverance of his church, and vindication of his truth, and cause, and glory.

21. And a mighty angel took up a stone like a great millstone, and cast it into the sea, saying, Thus, with violence, shall that great city

Babylon be thrown down, and shall be found no more at all.

21. The Pagan empire was never again restored; for Julian did but begin to attempt it, and was killed, before he could so much as lay any foundation for it. Yea, Rome was never more the seat of the empire, much less of the Pagan empire: For Constantine did but, as it were, take up his quarters there for a short time, and removed the seat to Constantinople: And his successors in the west, had but the lesser part of the empire, and were, sometimes at Rome, and sometimes at Milan, and sometimes at Ravenna, and after in France and Germany.

22. And the voice of harpers, and musicians, and of pipers, and trumpeters, shall be heard no more at all in thee: and no craftsmen, of whatsoever craft he be, shall be found any more in thee: and the sound of a millstone shall be heard no more at all in thee. 23. And the light of a candle shall shine no more at all in thee: and the voice of the bridegroom, and of the bride, shall be heard no more at all in thee: for thy merchants were the great men of the earth: for by thy sorceries were all nations deceived.

22, 23. Thus, as by the emblem of a city totally ruined and deserted, was the fall of Pagan Rome represented to John: And that you may know, that it was not the burning and desertion of the material buildings that is meant, be now tells you that, by the merchants, he meant the nations that consented to, and upheld her idolatry and power.

24. And in her was found the blood of prophets, and of saints, and of all that were slain upon the earth.

24. God dealt thus severely with her, because she had not only been the murderer of apostles and prophets, and the primitive Christians, at Rome and abroad, in all her dominions, in upholding her idols, but (as Jerusalem) had by imitating former persecutors, justified them, and so suffereth for all. The considering of Dan. vii. 11. Jer. li. 63, and xxv. 10. Ezek. xvii. 13. and xxvii. 12, 13. will help to expound all this.

Others say, It is Papal Rome, and how the blood of apostles and prophets was found in her, they tell us from Matt. xxiii. 25. And how the blood of saints will be found in her, is easily proved.

CHAP. XIX.

AND after these things I heard a great voice of much people in heaven, saying, Hallelujah, salvation, and glory, and honour, and power, unto the Lord our God.

1. The saints in heaven, and the Christians on earth, gave praise to God, and glorified him for this great work.

2. For true and righteous are his judgments, for he hath judged the great whore, which did corrupt the earth with her fornication, and hath avenged the blood of his servants at her hand. 3. And again they said, Allelujah: and her smoke rose up for ever and ever.

2, 3. They glorified God for holy and amiable justice, and destroying the mother of idolatry and nest of luxury and cruelty. God will have great glory by destroying the persecutors and wicked, and in delivering his saints, and in the freedom of the gospel.

4. And the four and twenty elders, and the four beasts, fell down, and worshipped God that sat on the throne, saying, Amen, Allelujah.

4. And the consenting praises of the church, especially of Christian Jews, was represented to me under the oft-mentioned similitude of the temple-worship, where the twelve tribes were doubly represented (by twelve oxen, and twelve lions) and four cherubims were about the mercy-seat. Jews and Gentile Christians praise God for the fall of Babylon.

5. And a voice came out of the throne, saying, Praise our God, all ye his servants, and ye that fear him, both small and great.

5. And God himself, and his ministers, called to all his church to join in these his praises.

6. And I heard as it were, the voice of a great multitude, and as the voice of many waters, and as the voice of mighty thunderings, saying, Allelujah: for the Lord God omnipotent reigneth: 7. Let us be glad and rejoice, and give honour to him: for the marriage of the Lamb is come, and his wife hath made herself ready. 8. And to her was granted, that she should be arrayed in fine linen, clean and white: for the fine linen is the righteousness of saints.

6, 7, 8. And the raising of the Catholic church in numbers, and extent, and power, to the visible glory of Christ, was represented to me by the voice as of a great multitude, &c. saying, Praise the Lord, for his kingdom is coming in power,

CHAP. XIX.   REVELATION.   639

and his church shall be promoted by the rulers of the earth, and the kingdoms of the world shall be visibly the kingdoms of the Lord, and of his Christ: And Christ and his church will appear to the world in honour and joy, as marriages used to be celebrated. And the Catholic church shall be clothed with the notes of honour and purity, or righteousness, (or shall publicly worship him in his instituted ordinances.)

9. And he saith unto me, Write, Blessed *are* they which are called unto the marriage supper of the Lamb. And he saith unto me, These are the true sayings of God.

9. Happy are they that shall see the fall of Babylon, and the deliverance and advancement of the Christian church, and shall have their place and part in that public reign of Christ, by his Christian magistrates and pastors, and in the public praises of the flourishing Christ (much more they that shall see his reign in the kingdom of glory.)

10. And I fell at his feet to worship him: and he said unto me, See thou do it not: I am thy fellow-servant, and of thy brethren, that have the testimony of Jesus, to worship God: for the testimony of Jesus, is the spirit of prophecy.

10. I thought that I owed so great honour to such a messenger of so glad tidings, that I fell at his feet to worship him, (not with divine worship, as God, but as his angel;) but he forbade it me, and bid me worship God only, and not angels, by such prostration: (For though we may, by prostration, do worship to a prince or parent, yet to do it to angels that are invisible, will be too like the heathen sort of worship, and encourage those that offer angels unwarrantable worship.) I am a servant of Christ, and a fellow-servant to thee and thy brethren the prophets; and your office of publishing the gospel, and mine in this prophecy, are much like: The spirit of prophecy, by which you are Christ's messengers and witnesses, is that testimony of Jesus, which you and I, as fellow-servants, are in our several capacities employed.

11. And I saw heaven opened, and behold, a white horse, and he that sat upon him, was called faithful and true, and in righteousness he doth judge, and make war.

11. Having spoken in general of the fall of Babylon, he now sheweth how Christ in its overthrow will do execution on those his enemies, till he have rooted them out; and how the beast will struggle before he be quite destroyed, and that not in Rome only.

12. His eyes were as a flame of fire, and on his head were many crowns, and he had a name written, that no man knew, but he himself. 13. And he was clothed with a vesture dipt in blood, and his name is called, The Word of God.

12, 13. His flaming eyes signify his glory and omniscience; and his many crowns, the many kingdoms which he shall subdue and reign over. What his unknown name is, we must not inquire. His bloody vesture signifieth his victory over his enemies, purchased with his church's deliverance by his own blood: And his known name is, The Word of God.

14. And the armies, which were in heaven followed him upon white horses clothed in fine linen, white and clean.

14. And the executioners of his justice on Babylon, &c. were represented to me by an army of heavenly ones following him on white horses, and clothed in white, &c.

15. And out of his mouth goeth a sharp sword, that with it he shall smite the nations: and he shall rule them with a rod of iron; and he treadeth the wine-press of the fierceness and wrath of Almighty God.

15. The word of his mouth, is as a sharp sword to overcome the heathen world, and all his enemies, by converting his chosen, and denouncing his judgments on the incurable, which he will execute, and that presently by the sword of his warriors, by whom he will crush the rebels, and on them he will execute God's vindictive justice.

16. And he hath on his vesture, and on his thigh, a name written, KING OF KINGS, AND LORD OF LORDS.

16. For besides [the Word of God,] he hath another name on his thigh (where the sword is worn), King of Kings, &c. For he will reign, and all kings and lords are under him, and he will subdue his foes.

17. And I saw an angel standing in the sun, and he cried with a loud voice, saying to all the fowls that fly in the midst of heaven, Come and gather yourselves together unto the supper of the great God: 18. That ye may eat the flesh of kings, and the flesh of captains, and the flesh of mighty men, and the flesh of horses, and of them that sit on them, and the flesh of all men, both free and bond, both small and great.

17, 18. It cannot be expected that the whole

idolatrous empire of Babylon be destroyed without war: And he will conquer that is King of kings, and Lord of lords: And commanders and soldiers shall be a 'prey to the fowls; which was fulfilled on Maxentius, Licinius, &c. Others say, it is destruction of the Popish kings. And others, that it signifieth not their death, but the fall of Popery.

19. And I saw the beast, and the kings of the earth, and their armies, gathered together to make war against him that sat on the horse, and against his army. 20. And the beast was taken, and with him the false prophet, that wrought miracles before him, with which he deceived them that had received the mark of the beast, and them that worshipped his image. These both were cast alive into a lake of fire burning with brimstone.

19, 20. The Pagan emperors were conquered, and with them the literate seducers, (senators, orators, poets, philosophers, augurs, aruspices, priests, who by such poetical fable is, as Ovid's Metamorphosis, and by feigned predictions, oracles, and such pretended miracles as Eunapius boasteth of by many of their philosophers, but especially by the power of their abused learning, called by Paul, (the wisdom of the world, which is foolishness with God, and science falsely so called) who deceived the princes and people into a high opinion of their idols, and a contempt of Christianity, as foolishness: The imperial power and the learned seducers were rooted out, and as Sodom, cast into utter destruction, and judged to damnation.

Others say, that the beast here is the Pope, and the false prophet, with him, is himself also, he being the beast as civil ruler, and the prophet as ecclesiastical: But the text plainly maketh them two. Others say, it is the Pope and his clergy, jesuits, friars, &c.

21. And the remnant were slain with the sword of him that sat upon the horse, which sword proceeded out of his mouth: and all the fowls were filled with their flesh.

21. The memory of their conquered emperors and philosophers, senators, poets, &c. is continued in history (as Pilate's in the creed) to their perpetual shame, and so they are said to be cast alive into the lake: But the multitudes of soldiers and people that fought for them, were slain, and cast into oblivion; or some converted by the word, and some confounded. Or, as others, the Papists are some converted, and others for obstinacy condemned.

CHAP. XX.

AND I saw an Angel come down from heaven, having the key of the bottomless pit, and a great chain in his hand. 2. And he laid hold on the dragon, that old serpent, which is the Devil and Satan, and bound him a thousand years. 3. And cast him into the bottomless pit, and shut him up, and set a seal upon him, that he should deceive the nations no more, till the thousand years should be fulfilled: and after that, he must be loosed a little season.

1, 2, 3. And as for the notice of the state of the church, after the extirpation of the Pagan empire and idolatry, it was shewn me under the appearance of an angel coming from heaven with power to restrain the devil, and he laid hold on him, and imprisoned, and surely shut him up, as in a bottomless pit, that he might deceive the nations now turned to Christ, no more for a thousand years (or a long time): But then he will be permitted a little while, to deceive many churches.

Note, Satan ever since, to this day, hath kept about four parts of six of the world in heathenism; so that it must be the world then under the Roman empire that he is bound from deceiving. Whether a thousand years be taken strictly, or for a long time, is uncertain: Some take it to be a promise of his one thousand years restraint after the fall of the Pagan empire; and many for a thousand years after the fall of the Papacy. The former think it is all past; the latter (mostly) think it is all yet to come, but some, that it began in 1560. It is not a promise that Satan shall not in that thousand years, corrupt the Christian church with any great sin, but that he shall not seduce them from Christianity, till after a thousand years. Just at, or about that space of time, Mahometanism, which began farther off, about 606, did invade the eastern churches, and overcome the Christian powers, and set up a false prophet, an enemy to Christ, and bring Christianity into captivity and scorn.

4. And I saw thrones, and they sat upon them: and judgment was given unto them: and I saw the souls of them that were beheaded for the witness of Jesus, and for the word of God, and which had not worshipped the beast, neither his image, neither had received his mark upon their foreheads, or in their hands: and they lived and reigned with Christ a thousand years.

4. And the happy following state of the church, was further represented to me by the appearance of thrones, where men sat in judgment, shewing the dominion of Christians over their enemies. And I thought I saw the souls of the martyrs, whom the Pagans murdered, and not only of

them, but of all sound Christians, who had abstained from all participation in the Pagan idolatry, and they lived and reigned, as superior to their enemies, with Christ, the King of the church, a thousand years.

Note, Here is no talk of the body's resurrection, but the soul's living and reigning with Christ: And it seemeth to mean, that as the souls of the faithful live and reign with Christ in heaven, for duration: so the successors of such shall partake on earth of such a reign, as Christ will exercise in his church: And if yet many corruptions and troubles consist in this imperfect state, with Christ's own reign in the soul, and in the church, why may it not consist with this promised reign of saints in the empire over Pagans? As Christ's reign here is more or less prevalent against public sin, so shall their participation with him be. Both heavenly and earthly reign seem here spoken of: the first, as in reality, though in the vision, but to shew the other.

5. But the rest of the dead lived not again—until the thousand years were finished. This is the first resurrection. 6. Blessed and holy is he that hath part in the first resurrection: on such 'the second death hath no power, but they shall be priests of God, and of Christ, and shall reign with him a thousand years.

5, 6. The rest of the dead, even the subdued Pagans, (or Papists, say others) were kept as in a state of death, out of power, till the dragon revived their power again a thousand years after. Happy are the holy Christians, who shall be partakers in the privileges, blessings, and comforts of this delivered and advanced church: they shall no more fall under the Pagan power (or Papal, say others) nor partake with them of that utter destruction which is as a second death: Even as holy souls, with Christ in heaven, have there the state of a first resurrection before the body rise, and are secured from the condemnation of the wicked.

7. And when the thousand years are expired, Satan shall be loosed out of his prison, 8. And shall go out to deceive the nations, which are in the four quarters of the earth, Gog and Magog, to gather them together to battle: and the number of whom is as the sand of the sea.

7, 8. There are several expositions of this: Some say that, by the thousand years, is meant precisely that time, which fell out either from Constantine's edict 611. till the Turks subdued Greece; or from Alaricus's sacking Rome, till the Turks took Constantinople; and that the fall of the eastern churches, under the infidel power, was the letting loose of Satan: Others say, that a thousand years signifieth only a long undeterminate time, and that it was the church's prosperity, till the Papacy corrupted all, and tyrannised: Others say, it was a thousand years before Antichrist should come: Others, that it will be a thousand years after the fall of the Papacy, in which religion shall flourish under holy princes and pastors: Others, that after the fall of the Papal Antichrist, Christ will visibly return, and set up a holy kingdom, whose chief seat shall be at Jerusalem.

Some say, that it will be a resurrection of bodies, some only political. Some say, that the thousand years began at Christ's birth, or at the apostles' preaching: Others, at the destruction of Jerusalem, and ended about Hildebrand's time. Some (as before said) at Constantine's empire, and ended at Boniface VIII. that killed the Albigenses, &c. Others, that it began at 1560. He that knoweth which of these is the right, let him tell it, for I do not. By Gog and Magog many understand the Turks; others, all sorts of Christ's enemies: Whoever they be, a war they will attempt against the church, and will be overthrown.

9. And they went up on the breadth of the earth, and compassed the camp of the saints about, and the beloved city: and fire came down from God out of heaven, and devoured them.

9. This text seemeth the hardest of all the rest: those that say, the holy city is Constantinople; some of them are put to say, that Gog and Magog's destruction, as by fire, is yet to come: but the text seemeth to speak of it, as done before they could take the city. Others say, it was Tamerlane, (an infidel, and therefore sent, from God against his own inclination:) that raised Bajazet's siege, and carried him about in a cage of iron in scorn, till he wilfully dashed out his own brains; and so Andronicus was delivered. Others refer it to Baldwin's, and other Christians, taking Constantinople, against the Turkish power: but because the Turks afterwards took it, these seem not to agree with the text. Others think it is a war yet to come, say some, at Jerusalem, which shall by Christ be made the holy city, or his chief royal seat; and there will be his thousand years reign on earth. Others take the holy city to mean the reformed churches, which shall again be assaulted by all sorts of enemies, before the day of judgment. And some take the camp of the saints, and the beloved city, to be the seven Asian churches to whom John wrote. Whatever it be, if it be past, I understand not what, or when it was; if it be to come, time must expound it. In general it is sure, that enemies will oft assault the church, and God will defend it.

10. And the devil that deceived them, was cast into the lake of fire and brimstone, where the beast and false prophet, are, and shall be tormented day and night, for ever and ever.

10. When Christ hath delivered his church from

Pagan cruelty, the same dragon, or devil, will seek new instruments to assault it, from age to age, and most notably at the last: but he shall be conquered after all, and be cast out into torment, as the Pagan powers and deceivers were.

11. And I saw a great white throne, and him that sat on it, from whose face the earth and the heaven fled away, and there was found no place for them.

11. Some think that this speaketh not of the day of judgment, but of the calling of the Jews: and some think the meaning is, that when Christ sets up the thousand years refined church, (by a resurrection, and his visible presence, say some; or by a holy government and people, and deliverance from enemies, say others;) both the power of infidels, (Turks and heathens,) which are meant by the earth; and the corrupted church, (both Papal and Greek, &c. meant by heaven) shall all vanish, that the holy city may take place. But most say, it describeth the day of judgment.

12. And I saw the dead, small and great, stand before God: and the books were opened: and another book was opened, which is the book of life: and the dead were judged out of those things which were written in the books, according to their works.

12. When Christ hath overcome his church's enemies, he will judge the world, and the book of their own doings and consciences shall be opened, and also God's book of life, (the scripture, or gospel-law) say some, which is the rule of judgment; or the book of God's decrees, say others, in which all are enrolled that shall be saved. And they shall be judged according to their works, the matter of fact being recorded in their book, and the matter of right in God's law, and the conclusion in his decree: to be judged according to their works, is to be then justified or condemned, as they have sincerely kept Christ's law of grace, by which they shall be tried; or have not kept it, by faith, repentance, and sincere obedience, the condition of salvation.

13. And the sea gave up her dead which were in it: and death and hell delivered up the dead which were in them: and they were judged every man according to their works.

13. All that were any way dead, were judged according to their works, by the law that they were under.

14. And death and hell were cast into the lake of fire. This is the second death. 15. And whosoever was not found written in the book of life, was cast into the lake of fire.

14, 15. And death and hades, that is, mortality, shall to his saints be by Christ for ever abolished, or, as some take it, those wicked men, that death and hell shall deliver up to judgment, shall be cast into hell-fire. This utter abolition (or this damnation) is called the second death. And whosoever hath not right to salvation by the gospel-covenant, or law of grace, and is not by God enrolled among the heirs of life, was cast into the lake of fire.

Mr. Potter, and many others, expound all this confidently, (and the two following chapters) of Christ's judging, and rewarding, and punishing men, in this life: but others, as confidently, of the life to come. Though this makes the text difficult, it maketh no great doctrinal controversy, both being commonly believed.

CHAP. XXI.

AND I saw a new heaven and a new earth: for the first heaven and the first earth were passed away; and there was no more sea.

1. Note, That the corrupt state of the world, and the degenerate church, may be called the old heaven and earth, is granted: and that the church, before the end, may be so reformed and blessed, as that heaven and earth may be said to be now: and also that fire at last shall dissolve the earth, and that heaven, that fell under the curse for man's sin, and there shall be (no annihilation, but) a new heaven and earth, is plain in Peter, &c. But which of these is the sense of this text is doubtful. I incline most to the latter, that it is the new world, that shall follow the conflagration, and judgment. If any ask what the new earth shall be for? he must take up with what God hath told us; Therein shall dwell righteousness, and the creature be delivered from the bondage of corruption, into the glorious liberty of the sons of God, and all things shall be restored. Whether we shall then dwell on earth, or only a new-made generation, is not so clear. But the Jerusalem, now in heaven, consisteth of spirits: and this must come down from heaven, and these spirits must be again, at the resurrection, embodied: and do not new bodies suit with a new earth, as spirits with heaven? Obj. This will be to our loss. Ans. No, God will dwell with man, and be no stranger to us then in heaven: heaven and earth will not be seperated as now. As our bodies will be (no clog to the souls, but) spiritual, incorruptible bodies, so earth will be made suitable to them. It is no diminution to the glory of the sun to shine on bodies, no nor of God to vouchsafe them his influence.

2. And I John, saw the holy city, New Jerusalem, coming down from God out of heaven, prepared as a bride adorned for her husband.

2. Not new created souls, but immortal souls, coming down with Christ, say some; before the day of judgment, say others, after. Many texts seem to place it here, and not in heaven only.

after the resurrection. This is the life of preparation on our part; but souls in heaven are further prepared by Christ.

3. And I heard a great voice out of heaven, saying, Behold the tabernacle of God *is* with men, and he will dwell with them, and they shall be his people, and God himself shall be with them, *and be* their God.

3. Wherever the place be, God's presence in glory, will make it a heaven to us. But if it did speak only of an advancement by holy reformation and peace on earth, it would be so far like to heaven.

4. And God shall wipe away all tears from their eyes; and there shall be no more death, neither sorrow, nor crying, neither shall there be any more pain: for the former things are passed away.

4. If they be in the right, who expound this of a thousand years freedom from persecutions, and all sorrows on earth, in a New Jerusalem, I am sure it will be a more joyful time, when it shall be performed in the proper sense of the words, after the general resurrection. And I see no probability that the promise of [no more death] and the rest that follow should be meant of any earthly state, before that time. The new Jerusalem, and the new heaven and earth, must be at once expected: and that is, when all these things are dissolved by fire, at the judgment of the great day! O desirable blessed day!

5. And he that sat upon the throne, said, Behold, I make all things new. And he said unto me, Write: for these words are true and faithful.

5. It is true that at Constantine's delivering the church, there was as it were a new world. And I am in hope yet, that there may be such a reformation and advancement of piety and unity before the last day, as may be called a new world in a fuller sense: but not up to this description of the new Jerusalem.

6. And he said unto me, It is done. I am Alpha and Omega, the beginning and the end. I will give unto him that is athirst of the fountain of the water of life freely.

6. Say some, [I am he, that hath thus delivered the church from idolaters and persecutors; and now all, that will, shall have the blessed privileges of the church.] Rather, [I have prepared the church for the state of blessedness; and I, that am the principal, efficient and ultimate end of all, will give life everlasting, in the new Jerusalem, to every believing thirsty soul.

7. He that overcometh shall inherit all things: and I will be his God, and he shall be my son.

7. He that overcometh temptations to the end, shall, as my son, inherit full felicity in me, who will be his God.

8. But the fearful, and unbelieving, and the abominable, and murderers, and whoremongers, and sorcerers, and idolaters, and all liars, shall have their part in the lake which burneth with fire and brimstone: which is the second death.

8. But those that, being cowardly, forsake me for fear of suffering, and trust not me, and those that live in filthiness, and cruelty, and unrighteousness, and idolatry, and all false deceivers shall be damned.

9. And there came unto me one of the seven angels, which had the seven vials full of the seven last plagues, and talked with me, saying, Come hither, I will shew thee the bride, the Lamb's wife.

9. By the bride is meant the new Jerusalem, that is, say some, the delivered church in Constantine's time and after: 2. Say others, the reformed church at the fall of Popery. 3. Say others, a prosperous time before the thousand years. 4. Say others, the Jews' conversion in great splendour at Jerusalem. 5. Say others, Christ's visible reign with the martyrs, and others, raised from death a thousand years before the rest. 6. Rather the new heaven and earth after the last judgment, when the flaming sword, and partition-wall shall be taken down, and God dwell with man.

10. And he carried me away in the spirit to a great and high mountain, and shewed me that great city, the holy Jerusalem, descending out of heaven from God,

10. Say some, the church, as here advanced to purity and liberty by the heavenly power: rather the souls, that were with Christ, coming with him to meet those that shall be then alive and changed, advanced to that perfection, in which they shall for ever be glorified with the Lord. Though some glimpse of this may be in happy reformation, concord, and deliverance here before.

11. Having the glory of God: and her light *was* like unto a stone most precious, even like a jasper stone, clear as crystal;

11. Its glory and strength was represented to me, as made of jasper, clear as crystal, God's own glory shining out.

12. And had a wall great and high, *and* had twelve gates, and at

the gates twelve angels, and names written thereon, which are *the names* of the twelve tribes of the children of Israel.

12. John being a Jew, and the Jews the first Christians, who had commonly an expectation of Christ's more special relation to them than to others, and they being the first specimen of the Catholic church, the revelation of the new Jerusalem (and perhaps also of some antecedent happy state) is represented as shaped to the Jews' expectations; and as typified by the old Jerusalem. And its wall is its strength and safety, and separation from others. Its gates are for entrance, and the guardian angels numbered according to the twelve tribes; as were the apostles, who yet founded all the churches.

13. On the east, three gates; on the north, three gates; on the south, three gates; and on the west, three gates.

13. Note, Not that this must be thought the shape of it; but that its glory was represented by such a shape.

14. And the wall of the city had twelve foundations, and in them the names of the twelve apostles of the Lamb.

14. As the church on earth is founded by the doctrine and witness of the twelve apostles, so is the new Jerusalem described as related to them, it being but the church militant perfected and made triumphant.

15. And he that talked with me, had a golden reed to measure the city, and the gates thereof, and the wall thereof. 16. And the city lieth four square, and the length is as large as the breadth. And he measured the city with the reed twelve thousand furlongs. The length and the breadth and the height are equal.

15, 16. By this representation, (like that in Ezekiel) the firmness and perfection, and greatness, of the new Jerusalem, was signified.

17. And he measured the wall thereof, an hundred *and* forty *and* four cubits, according to the measure of a man, that is, of the angel.

17. The angel appearing as a man, his measure is taken as a common human measure.

18. And the building of the wall of it was of jasper: and the city *was* pure gold, like unto clear glass. 19. And the foundations of the wall of the city *were* garnished with all manner of precious stones. The first foundation *was* jasper; the second, a sapphire; the third, a chalcedony; the fourth, an emerald; 20. The fifth, a sardonyx; the sixth, a sardius; the seventh, a chrysolyte; the eighth, a beryl; the ninth, a topaz; the tenth, a chrysoprasus; the eleventh, a jacinth; the twelfth, an amethyst.

18, 19, 20. That the new Jerusalem is represented by these precious stones, as firm, precious, lucid, and glorious, and by the number of twelve, as suited to the twelve apostles, and so in them to the twelve tribes of Israel, as typical of the new Jerusalem, is all that I understand of this: what each precious stone distinctly signifieth, you may read in them that know, (or take on them to know) more.

21. And the twelve gates *were* twelve pearls; every several gate was of one pearl: and the street of the city *was* pure gold, as it were transparent glass.

21. If there shall be any state, on this side eternity, which answereth this glorious representation, how much more will the perfected glorious triumphant church answer it?

22. And I saw no temple therein: for the Lord God Almighty, and the Lamb, are the temple of it.

22. Some expound this of liberty to serve God in every place, as well as in temples, (who yet would destroy them as conventiclers, that do so.) But the text seemeth to mean, that this new Jerusalem is the perfect state, which is above our instituted lower means, God will be our all.

23. And the city had no need of the sun, neither of the moon, to shine in it; for the glory of God did lighten it, and the Lamb *is* the light thereof.

23. Prophetical hyperboles and allegories, may put as high terms as these for a state of mere reformation, and church prosperity: but seeing that it must be a force, and not an exposition, which so restraineth it, without proof, we must believe that it hath a higher accomplishment.

24. And the nations of them which are saved shall walk in the light of it: and the kings of the earth do bring their glory and honour into it.

24. And those, that shall be converted out of all nations, of the Gentiles, shall, as well as Abraham

and the Christian Jews, lay up and find a treasure with Christ in the new Jerusalem.

Note, They that expound this of the thousand years reign of raised martyrs at Jerusalem, and they that expound it of a peculiar Jewish church there, after the Jews' conversion, say, that the nations round about shall not have the same confirmation and glory, as the new Jerusalem, but be liable to trials still. Dr. Hammond, who expoundeth it of the church's prosperity after Constantine's success, giveth these reasons, 1. Because the new Jerusalem descendeth from heaven. Answ. 1. So it may to judgment, and yet return to heaven. 2. Or rather, the new heaven and earth shall be open as one. An immortal glory, in the new earth, after the resurrection, may be the new Jerusalem. 2. He argueth from Gal. iv. 26. as if the Jerusalem above were only the church militant: but that we deny.

25. And the gates of it shall not be shut at all by day: for there shall be no night there. 26. And they shall bring the glory and honour of the nations into it.

25, 26. There shall be no danger of the entrance of enemies or traitors; but all worldly glory and blessings by saints referred to this end, shall there be found in the transcendent perfect state.

27. And there shall in no wise enter into it any thing that defileth, neither *whatsoever* worketh abomination, or *maketh* a lie: but they which are written in the Lamb's book of life.

27. Sure this proveth that it is somewhat better than the thousand years after Constantine, that is here meant; for alas, how much abomination and deceit entered in that time! what hatred, false accusations, worldliness, pride, cruelty, and contention?

2. Note, None but saints cleansed from gross sin, will be found written in the Lamb's book of life. It is a vile slander on the orthodox doctrine of election, that we say, the elect may be saved how wickedly soever they live; when we say, that it is one decree of God that electeth men to be holy, obedient, persevere, and be saved.

CHAP. XXII.

AND he shewed me, a pure river of water of life, clear as crystal, proceeding out of the throne of God and of the Lamb.

1. By this some understand baptism, that bindeth all to purity: some the gospel (not muddied by usurpers' corrupt canons:) and some, the spirit in greater measure: and some, the heavenly influence for illumination and life for ever. All these in their seasons may be expected.

2. In the midst of the street of it, and on either side of the river, *was there* the tree of life, which bare twelve *manner* of fruits, *and* yielded her fruit every month: and the leaves of the tree *were* for the healing of the nations.

2. As in the prosperous church militant, everlasting life is open, and given to all accepters, by the doctrine of the apostles, and continually represented and conferred in the sacraments, and by the word, the Spirit of Christ accompanying his ordinances, the preaching of the word is for the healing of the unbelievers and the unconverted: so, in the new Jerusalem, where the end of all his is attained, the glory is represented by the means that are past, that brought them thither, by which men were sanctified, and the nations healed: the means being eminently (though not formally) in the attained end. But the better the church is on earth, the more it thus resembleth the new Jerusalem.

3. And there shall be no more curse: but the throne of God and of the Lamb shall be in it; and his servants shall serve him; 4. And they shall see his face; and his name *shall be* in their foreheads.

3, 4. Thus it appeareth that the new Jerusalem is a state of immortality (by the tree of life,) and freedom from the curse, or all punishment for sin, and the very throne of God, and Christ shall be visibly in it, and they see God's face: and though somewhat tending to all this be in the church militant, this seemeth a description of the church triumphant.

5. And there shall be no night there; and they need no candle, neither light of the sun; for the Lord God giveth them light: and they shall reign for ever and ever.

5. There shall be no want of knowledge, nor need of ministers, teaching, scripture, or such means. For God will be to them above, and instead of these; and they shall reign for ever. And what more can be hoped for by man? Why should forced expositions darken this?

6. And he said unto me, These sayings *are* faithful and true. And the Lord God of the holy prophets sent his angel to shew unto his servants the things which must shortly be done.

6. As Christ, Matt. xxiv. told them by such devastations as that generation should see, and yet adjoineth the signs of the end of the world; just so doth he, by this revelation, shew John the fall of Pagan Babylon, and the church's deliverance, and yet shortly annex a thousand years after, and then the end of the world: all was to be shortly, but not shortly equally with the first parts. But

It is not to be said, that he almost passed by the things that were shortly to be done, and said almost all of the Papal Rome. The certainty of the revelation is the hope and joy of firm believers.

7. Behold, I come quickly; Blessed *is* he that keepeth the sayings of the prophecy of this book.

7. Think not that I delay my coming, as slack of performing my promise: some of this will be quickly done, and the last ere long. To understand, and believe this prophecy will be comfortable: but to keep the precepts of it, avoid the sins threatened; believe the promise of my victories and coming, and wait in patience, is needful to all.

8. And I John saw these things, and heard *them*. And when I had heard and seen, I fell down to worship before the feet of the angel which shewed me these things.

8. Note, All faulty worship of angels is not idolatry, nor maketh a church idolatrous: it was not divine worship which John gave the angel: if really he wrote most of this book against Popish idolatry, as many think, he would never be twice guilty of worse than their praying to angels and saints themselves, when he condemned: for they worship them not, as gods, though amiss. John thought veneration was the angel's due.

9. Then saith he unto me, See *thou do it* not: for I am thy fellow-servant, and of thy brethren the prophets, and of them which keep the sayings of this book. Worship God.

9. See before, chap. xix. 10. God is jealous of any thing too like idolatry.
Note, Are angels our fellow-servants? Love them then, and be thankful to God for their love and help; and rejoice in this privilege, and think it not unlikely that you should live with them for ever. O what a people should we be then in holiness!

10. And he saith unto me, Seal not the sayings of the prophecy of this book: for the time is at hand.

10. The most of it is to be performed ere long in the ruin of the Pagan persecuting empire.

11. He that is unjust, let him be unjust still: and he which is filthy, let him be filthy still: and he that is righteous, let him be righteous still; and he that is holy, let him be holy still. 12. And behold, I come quickly, and my reward *is* with me, to give every man according as his work shall be.

11, 12. I come quickly to fulfil and execute this prophecy; and then I will take and judge men, as I find them; there shall be no more place for preparation; as it was with the wise and foolish virgins, Matt. xxv. when the midnight cry was, The bridegroom cometh, as I find you, I will use you.

13. I am Alpha and Omega, the beginning and the ending, the first and the last.

14. I am God eternal, the first cause, and ultimate end of all things: able to fulfil my will and word.

14. Blessed *are* they that do his commandments, that they may have right to the tree of life, and may enter in through the gates into the city.

14. Blessed are they that do what Christ requireth to salvation in his law of grace, (or purify their heart and life) that they may, by his free gift, have right to enter into the new Jerusalem, and live with Christ for ever.

15. For without *are* dogs, and sorcerers, and whoremongers, and murderers, and idolaters, and whosoever loveth and *maketh* a lie.

15. For all filthy, cruel, persecuting, idolatrous persons, and liars, and deceitful teachers, and hypocrites, (though called Christians,) are shut out of the holy city, as dogs are turned out of the house.

16. I Jesus have sent mine angel to testify unto you these things in the churches, I am the root and the offspring of David, *and* the bright and morning star.

16. I Jesus have sent my angel to tell these things to John, that he may tell them to the churches of Asia, and by them to others (the matter much concerning those churches then alive.) Take these as my own words, who am the Messiah prophesied of, as the Root and Son of David, and am the light of the world, sent to teach men the way of life.

17. And the Spirit and the bride say, Come. And let him that heareth say, Come. And let him that is athirst, come: and whosoever will, let him take the water of life freely.

17. And seeing church-deliverance now, and the glory of the new Jerusalem at last, are the effects of my coming, as my spirit teacheth men to desire my coming, and my church and chosen do desire it; so let all desire it that would partake of that felicity. For all shall have it by my free gift, who do but believingly desire it. For I will shut out none but final obstinate refusers.

18. For I testify unto every man that heareth the words of the prophecy of this book, If any man shall add unto these things, God shall add unto him the plagues that are written in this book: 19. And if any man shall take away from the words of the book of this prophecy, God shall take away his part out of the book of life, and out of the holy city, and *from* the things which are written in this book.

18, 19. If any wilfully corrupt this prophecy in words or sense, to draw men from believing it, to the belief of their own corrupt additions, God will add to them his plagues, and deprive them of any part of the blessings here foretold, and shut them out of this holy city of God.

Note, It is dangerous then to make bold, cabalistical, fanatic expositions of this book, and to call our own conceits the sense of the Revelation: and it is dangerous groundlessly to expect more prophecies of God's usage of his church; or to add to any of his word, or diminish from it, and father any of our errors on Christ, and on his Spirit, which hath here finished that book, which must be the universal church's rule of life.

20. He which testifieth these things, saith, Surely, I come quickly. Amen. Even so come, Lord Jesus.

20. Jesus, who is the author of this Revelation, surely promiseth that he will come quickly, by degrees to perform all his word, and charged you not to question it through unbelief, or to faint by doubting, as if he did fail by his delay. And let us all with faith, hope, and desire, prepare and earnestly pray for his coming: even so, come Lord Jesus.

21. The grace of our Lord Jesus Christ *be* with you all. Amen.

21. I conclude all with this best request to God for you, and benediction to you, that the grace of our Lord Jesus, which is our preparation for glory, and our earnest, pledge, and foretaste of it, may be with you, to prepare you, and seal you up, as the certain heirs of that blessed state, and save you from all sin, and temptation, and enemies that would deprive you of it. Amen.

MR. BAXTER'S OWN ACCOUNT

OF THE

CAUSE OF HIS IMPRISONMENT:

Left under his own Hand to be printed with this Paraphrase.

READER,

It is like you have heard how I was for this Book, by the instigation of Sir Roger L'Estrange, and some of the Clergy, imprisoned near two years, by Sir Geo. Gefferys, Sir Francis Withins, and the rest of the Judges of the King's-Bench, after their preparatory restraints and attendants under the most reproachful words, as if I had been the most odious person living, and not suffered at all to speak for myself; and had not the King taken off my fine, I had continued in prison till death. Because many desire to know, what all this was for, I have here written the Eight Accusations which (after the great clergy-search of my book) were brought in as seditious. I have uttered never a word, accused, that you may know the worst: what I said of the murderers of Christ, and the hypocrite Pharisees, and their sins, the Judge said I meant it of the Church of England, though I have written for it, and still communicate with it. The accused words are, The Paraphrase: I. On Matt. v. 19. II. On Mark iii. 6. III. On Mark ix. 39. IV. On Mark xi. 31. V. On Mark xii. 38, 39, 40. VI. On Luke x. 2. VII. On John xi. 57. VIII. On Acts xv. 2. *Note,* These were all: though a Reverend Doctor, that knoweth his own name, put into their hands some Accusations out of Rom. xiii. &c. as against the King, to touch my life, but their discretion forbid them to use or name them.

RICHARD BAXTER.

FINIS.